The Preservation of Historic Architecture

The Preservation of Historic Architecture

*The U.S. Government's Official Guidelines
for Preserving Historic Homes*

Department of the Interior

THE LYONS PRESS
Guilford, Connecticut
An imprint of the Globe Pequot Press

Special contents of this edition copyright © 2004 by Morris Book Publishing LLC.

10 9 8 7 6 5 4

The Lyons Press is an imprint of the Globe Pequot Press.

Printed in the United States of America

ISBN 978-1-59228-126-8

The Library of Congress Cataloging-in-Publication Data is available on file.

Contents

The Preservation of
Historic Architecture

1

Assessing Cleaning and Water-Repellent Treatments for Historic Masonry Buildings

Robert C. Mack, FAIA
Anne Grimmer

Inappropriate cleaning and coating treatments are a major cause of damage to historic masonry buildings. While either or both treatments may be appropriate in some cases, they can be very destructive to historic masonry if they are not selected carefully. Historic masonry, as considered here, includes stone, brick, architectural terra cotta, cast stone, concrete and concrete block. It is frequently cleaned because cleaning is equated with improvement. Cleaning may sometimes be followed by the application of a water-repellent coating. However, unless these procedures are carried out under the guidance and supervision of an architectural conservator, they may result in irrevocable damage to the historic resource.

The purpose of this Brief is to provide information on the variety of cleaning methods and materials that are available for use on the *exterior* of historic masonry buildings, and to provide guidance in selecting the most appropriate method or combination of methods. The difference between water-repellent coatings and waterproof coatings is explained, and the purpose of each, the suitability of their application to historic masonry buildings, and the possible consequences of their inappropriate use are discussed.

The Brief is intended to help develop sensitivity to the qualities of historic masonry that makes it so special, and to assist historic building owners and property managers in working cooperatively with architects, architectural conservators and contractors (Fig. 1). Although specifically intended for historic buildings, the information is applicable to all masonry buildings. This publication updates and expands *Preservation Brief 1: The Cleaning and Waterproof Coating of Masonry Buildings*. The Brief is not meant to be a cleaning manual or a guide for preparing specifications. Rather, it provides general information to raise awareness of the many factors involved in selecting cleaning and water-repellent treatments for historic masonry buildings.

Figure 1. Low-to medium-pressure steam (hot-pressurized water washing), is being used to clean the exterior of the U.S. Tariff Commission Building, the first marble building constructed in Washington, D.C., in 1839. This method was selected by an architecural conservator as the "gentlest means possible" to clean the marble. Steam can soften heavy soiling deposits such as those on the cornice and column capitals, and facilitate easy removal. Note how these deposits have been removed from the right side of the cornice which has already been cleaned.

Figure 2. Biological growth as shown on this marble foundation can usually be removed using a low-pressure water wash, possibly with a non-ionic detergent added to it, and scrubbing with a natural or synthetic bristle brush.

Figure 3. This small test area has revealed a red brick patch that does not match the original beige brick. This may explain why the building was painted, and may suggest to the owner that it may be preferable to keep it painted.

Preparing for a Cleaning Project

Reasons for cleaning. First, it is important to determine whether it is appropriate to clean the masonry. The objective of cleaning a historic masonry building must be considered carefully before arriving at a decision to clean. There are several major reasons for cleaning a historic masonry building: **improve the appearance of the building** by removing unattractive dirt or soiling materials, or non-historic paint from the masonry; **retard deterioration** by removing soiling materials that may be damaging the masonry; or **provide a clean surface** to accurately match repointing mortars or patching compounds, or to conduct a condition survey of the masonry.

Identify what is to be removed. The general nature and source of dirt or soiling material on a building must be identified to remove it in the *gentlest means possible* — that is, in the most effective, yet least harmful, manner. Soot and smoke, for example, require a different cleaning agent to remove than oil stains or metallic stains. Other common cleaning problems include biological growth such as mold or mildew, and organic matter such as the tendrils left on masonry after removal of ivy (Fig. 2).

Consider the historic appearance of the building. If the proposed cleaning is to remove paint, it is important in each case to learn whether or not unpainted masonry is historically appropriate. And, it is necessary to consider why the building was painted (Fig. 3). Was it to cover bad repointing or unmatched repairs? Was the building painted to protect soft brick or to conceal deteriorating stone? Or, was painted masonry simply a fashionable

treatment in a particular historic period? Many buildings were painted at the time of construction or shortly thereafter; retention of the paint, therefore, may be more appropriate historically than removing it. And, if the building appears to have been painted for a long time, it is also important to think about whether the paint is part of the character of the historic building and if it has acquired significance over time.

Consider the practicalities of cleaning or paint removal. Some gypsum or sulfate crusts may have become integral with the stone and, if cleaning could result in removing some of the stone surface, it may be preferable not to clean. Even where unpainted masonry is appropriate, the retention of the paint may be more practical than removal in terms of long range preservation of the masonry. In some cases, however, removal of the paint may be desirable. For example, the old paint layers may have built up to such an extent that removal is necessary to ensure a sound surface to which the new paint will adhere.

Study the masonry. Although not always necessary, in some instances it can be beneficial to have the coating or paint type, color, and layering on the masonry researched before attempting its removal. Analysis of the nature of the soiling or of the paint to be removed from the masonry, as well as guidance on the appropriate cleaning method, may be provided by professional consultants, including architectural conservators, conservation scientists and preservation architects. The State Historic Preservation Office (SHPO), local historic district commissions, architectural review boards and preservation-oriented websites may also be able to supply useful information on masonry cleaning techniques.

Understanding the Building Materials

The construction of the building must be considered when developing a cleaning program because inappropriate cleaning can have a deleterious effect on the masonry as well as on other building materials. The masonry material or materials must be correctly identified. It is sometimes difficult to distinguish one type of stone from another; for example, certain sandstones can be easily confused with limestones. Or, what appears to be natural stone may not be stone at all, but cast stone or concrete. Historically, cast stone and architectural terra cotta were frequently used in combination with natural stone, especially for trim elements or on upper stories of a building where, from a distance, these substitute materials looked like real stone (Fig. 4). Other features on historic buildings that appear to be stone, such as decorative cornices, entablatures and window hoods, may not even be masonry, but metal.

Identify prior treatments. Previous treatments of the building and its surroundings should be researched and building maintenance records should be obtained, if available. Sometimes if streaked or spotty areas do not seem to get cleaner following an initial cleaning, closer inspection and analysis may be warranted. The discoloration may turn out not to be dirt but the remnant of a water-repellent coating applied long ago which has darkened the surface of the masonry over time (Fig. 5). Successful removal may require testing several cleaning agents to find something that will dissolve and remove the coating. Complete removal may not always be possible. Repairs may have been stained to match a dirty building, and cleaning may make these differences apparent. De-icing salts used near the building that have dissolved can

Figure 5. Repeated water washing did not remove the staining inside this limestone porte cochere. Upon closer examination, it was determined to be a water-repellent coating that had been applied many years earlier. An alkaline cleaner may be effective in removing it.

migrate into the masonry. Cleaning may draw the salts to the surface, where they will appear as efflorescence (a powdery, white substance), which may require a second treatment to be removed. Allowances for dealing with such unknown factors, any of which can be a potential problem, should be included when investigating cleaning methods and materials. Just as more than one kind of masonry on a historic building may necessitate multiple cleaning approaches, unknown conditions that are encountered may also require additional cleaning treatments.

Choose the appropriate cleaner. The importance of testing cleaning methods and materials cannot be over emphasized. Applying the wrong cleaning agents to historic masonry can have disastrous results. Acidic cleaners can be extremely damaging to acid-sensitive stones, such as marble and limestone, resulting in etching and dissolution of these stones. Other kinds of masonry can also be damaged by incompatible cleaning agents, or even by cleaning agents that are usually compatible. There are also numerous kinds of sandstone, each with a considerably different geological composition. While an acid-based cleaner may be safely used on some sandstones, others are acid-sensitive and can be severely etched or dissolved by an acid cleaner. Some sandstones contain water-soluble minerals and can be eroded by water cleaning. And, even if the stone type is correctly identified, stones, as well as some bricks, may contain unexpected impurities, such as iron particles, that may react negatively with a particular cleaning agent and result in staining. Thorough understanding of the physical and chemical properties of the masonry will help avoid the inadvertent selection of damaging cleaning agents.

Figure 4. The foundation of this brick building is limestone, but the decorative trim above is architectural terra cotta intended to simulate stone.

3

Figure 6. Timed water soaking can be very effective for cleaning limestone and marble as shown here at the Marble Collegiate Church in New York City. In this case, a twelve-hour water soak using a multi-nozzle manifold was followed by a final water rinse. Photo: Diane S. Kaese, Wiss, Janney, Elstner Associates, Inc., N.Y., N.Y.

Other building materials also may be affected by the cleaning process. Some chemicals, for example, may have a corrosive effect on paint or glass. The portions of building elements most vulnerable to deterioration may not be visible, such as embedded ends of iron window bars. Other totally unseen items, such as iron cramps or ties which hold the masonry to the structural frame, also may be subject to corrosion from the use of chemicals or even from plain water. The only way to prevent problems in these cases is to study the building construction in detail and evaluate proposed cleaning methods with this information in mind. However, due to the very likely possibility of encountering unknown factors, any cleaning project involving historic masonry should be viewed as unique to that particular building.

Cleaning Methods and Materials

Masonry cleaning methods generally are divided into three major groups: water, chemical, and abrasive. *Water methods* soften the dirt or soiling material and rinse the deposits from the masonry surface. *Chemical cleaners* react with dirt, soiling material or paint to effect their removal, after which the cleaning effluent is rinsed off the masonry surface with water. *Abrasive methods* include blasting with grit, and the use of grinders and sanding discs, all of which mechanically remove the dirt, soiling material or paint (and, usually, some of the masonry surface). Abrasive cleaning is also often followed with a water rinse. *Laser cleaning*, although not discussed here in detail, is another technique that is used sometimes by conservators to clean small areas of historic masonry. It can be quite effective for cleaning limited areas, but it is expensive and generally not practical for most historic masonry cleaning projects.

Although it may seem contrary to common sense, masonry cleaning projects should be carried out starting at the bottom and proceeding to the top of the building always keeping all surfaces wet below the area being cleaned. The rationale for this approach is based on the principle that dirty water or cleaning effluent dripping from cleaning in progress above will leave streaks on a dirty surface but will not streak a clean surface as long as it is kept wet and rinsed frequently.

Water Cleaning

Water cleaning methods are generally the *gentlest means possible*, and they can be used safely to remove dirt from all types of historic masonry.* There are essentially four kinds of water-based methods: soaking; pressure water washing; water washing supplemented with non-ionic detergent; and steam, or hot-pressurized water cleaning. Once water cleaning has been completed, it is often necessary to follow up with a water rinse to wash off the loosened soiling material from the masonry.

Soaking. Prolonged spraying or misting with water is particularly effective for cleaning limestone and marble. It is also a good method for removing heavy accumulations of soot, sulfate crusts or gypsum crusts that tend to form in protected areas of a building not regularly washed by rain. Water is distributed to lengths of punctured hose or pipe with non-ferrous fittings hung from moveable scaffolding or a swing stage that continuously mists the surface of the masonry with a very fine spray (Fig. 6). A timed on-off spray is another approach to using this cleaning technique. After one area has been cleaned, the apparatus is moved on to another. Soaking is often used in combination with water washing and is also followed by a final water rinse. Soaking is a very slow method — it may take several days or a week—but it is a very gentle method to use on historic masonry.

Water Washing. Washing with low-pressure or medium-pressure water is probably one of the most commonly used methods for removing dirt or other pollutant soiling from historic masonry buildings (Fig. 7). Starting with a very low pressure (100 psi or below), even using a garden hose, and progressing as needed to slightly higher pressure —generally no higher than 300-400 psi—is always the recommended way to begin. Scrubbing with natural bristle or synthetic bristle brushes—never metal which can abrade the surface and leave metal particles that can stain the masonry—can help in cleaning areas of the masonry that are especially dirty.

Water Washing with Detergents. Non-ionic detergents –which are not the same as soaps –are synthetic organic compounds that are especially effective in removing oily soil. (Examples of some of the numerous proprietary non-ionic detergents include Igepal by GAF, Tergitol by Union Carbide and Triton by Rohm & Haas.) Thus, the addition of a non-ionic detergent, or surfactant, to a low- or medium-pressure water wash can be a useful aid in the cleaning

---

*Water cleaning methods may not be appropriate to use on some badly deteriorated masonry because water may exacerbate the deterioration, or on gypsum or alabaster which are very soluble in water.

process. (A non-ionic detergent, unlike most household detergents, does not leave a solid, visible residue on the masonry.) Adding a non-ionic detergent and scrubbing with a natural bristle or synthetic bristle brush can facilitate cleaning textured or intricately carved masonry. This should be followed with a final water rinse.

Steam/Hot-Pressurized Water Cleaning. Steam cleaning is actually low-pressure hot water washing because the steam condenses almost immediately upon leaving the hose. This is a gentle and effective method for cleaning stone and particularly for acid-sensitive stones. Steam can be especially useful in removing built-up soiling deposits and dried-up plant materials, such as ivy disks and tendrils. It can also be an efficient means of cleaning carved stone details and, because it does not generate a lot of liquid water, it can sometimes be appropriate to use for cleaning interior masonry (Figs. 8-9).

Potential hazards of water cleaning. Despite the fact that water-based methods are generally the most gentle, even they can be damaging to historic masonry. Before beginning a water cleaning project, it is important to make sure that all mortar joints are sound and that the building is watertight. Otherwise water can seep through the walls to the interior, resulting in rusting metal anchors and stained and ruined plaster.

Some water supplies may contain traces of iron and copper which may cause masonry to discolor. Adding a chelating or complexing agent to the water, such as EDTA (ethylene diamine tetra-acetic acid), which inactivates other metallic ions, as well as softens minerals and water hardness, will help prevent staining on light-colored masonry.

Any cleaning method involving water should never be done in cold weather or if there is any likelihood of frost or freezing because water within the masonry can freeze, causing spalling and cracking. Since a masonry wall may take over a week to dry after cleaning, no water cleaning should be permitted for several days prior to the first average frost date, or even earlier if local forecasts predict cold weather.

Most essential of all, it is important to be aware that using water at too high a pressure, a practice common to "power washing" and "water blasting", is very abrasive and can easily etch marble and other soft stones, as well as some types of brick (Figs. 10-11). In addition, the distance of the nozzle from the masonry surface and the type of nozzle, as well as gallons per minute (gpm), are also important variables in a water cleaning process that can have a significant impact on the outcome of the project. This is why it is imperative that the cleaning be closely monitored to ensure that the cleaning operators do not raise the pressure or bring the nozzle too close to the masonry in an effort to "speed up" the process. The appearance of grains of stone or sand in the cleaning effluent on the ground is an indication that the water pressure may be too high.

Figure 7. Glazed architectural terra cotta often may be cleaned successfully with a low-pressure water wash and hand scrubbing supplemented, if necessary, with a non-ionic detergent. Photo: National Park Service Files.

Chemical Cleaning

Chemical cleaners, generally in the form of proprietary products, are another material frequently used to clean historic masonry. They can remove dirt, as well as paint and other coatings, metallic and plant stains, and graffiti. Chemical cleaners used to remove dirt and soiling include **acids**, **alkalies** and **organic compounds.** Acidic cleaners, of course, should not be used on masonry that is acid sensitive. Paint removers are **alkaline**, based on **organic solvents** or other chemicals.

Chemical Cleaners to Remove Dirt

Both alkaline and acidic cleaning treatments include the use of water. Both cleaners are also likely to contain surfactants (wetting agents), that facilitate the chemical reaction that removes the dirt. Generally, the masonry is wet first for both types of cleaners, then the chemical cleaner is sprayed on at very low pressure or brushed onto the surface. The cleaner is left to dwell on the masonry for an amount of time recommended by the product manufacturer or, preferably, determined by testing, and rinsed off with a low- or moderate-pressure cold, or sometimes hot, water wash. More than one application of the cleaner may be necessary, and it is always a good practice to test the product manufacturer's recommendations concerning dilution rates and dwell times. Because each cleaning situation is unique, dilution rates and dwell times can vary considerably. The masonry surface may be scrubbed lightly with natural or synthetic bristle brushes prior to rinsing. After rinsing, pH strips should be applied to the surface to ensure that the masonry has been neutralized completely.

Figure 8. (Left) Low-pressure (under 100 psi) steam cleaning (hot-pressurized water washing), is part of the regular maintenance program at the Jefferson Memorial, Washington, D.C. The white marble interior of this open structure is subject to constant soiling by birds, insects and visitors. (Right) This portable steam cleaner enables prompt cleanup when necessary. Photos: National Park Service Files.

Acidic Cleaners. Acid-based cleaning products may be used on **non-acid sensitive** masonry, which generally includes: granite, most sandstones, slate, unglazed brick and unglazed architectural terra cotta, cast stone and concrete (Fig. 12). Most commercial acidic cleaners are composed primarily of hydrofluoric acid, and often include some phosphoric acid to prevent rust-like stains from developing on the masonry after the cleaning. Acid cleaners are applied to the pre-wet masonry which should be kept wet while the acid is allowed to "work", and then removed with a water wash.

Alkaline Cleaners. Alkaline cleaners should be used on **acid-sensitive** masonry, including: limestone, polished and unpolished marble, calcareous sandstone, glazed brick and glazed architectural terra cotta, and polished granite. (Alkaline cleaners may also be used sometimes on masonry materials that are not acid sensitive—after testing, of course

—but they may not be as effective as they are on acid-sensitive masonry.) Alkaline cleaning products consist primarily of two ingredients: a non-ionic detergent or surfactant; and an alkali, such as potassium hydroxide or ammonium hydroxide. Like acidic cleaners, alkaline products are usually applied to pre-wet masonry, allowed to dwell, and then rinsed off with water. (Longer dwell times may be necessary with alkaline cleaners than with acidic cleaners.) Two additional steps are required to remove alkaline cleaners after the initial rinse. First the masonry is given a slightly acidic wash—often with acetic acid—to neutralize it, and then it is rinsed again with water.

Chemical Cleaners to Remove Paint and Other Coatings, Stains and Graffiti

Removing paint and some other coatings, stains and graffiti can best be accomplished with alkaline paint removers, organic solvent paint removers, or other cleaning compounds. The removal of layers of paint from a masonry surface usually involves applying the remover either by brush, roller or spraying, followed by a thorough water wash. As with any chemical cleaning, the manufacturer's recommendations regarding application procedures should always be tested before beginning work.

Alkaline Paint Removers. These are usually of much the same composition as other alkaline cleaners, containing potassium or ammonium hydroxide, or trisodium phosphate. They are used to remove oil, latex and acrylic paints, and are effective for removing multiple layers of paint. Alkaline cleaners may also remove some acrylic, water-repellent coatings. As with other alkaline cleaners, both an acidic neutralizing wash and a final water rinse are generally required following the use of alkaline paint removers.

Organic Solvent Paint Removers. The formulation of organic solvent paint removers varies and may include a combination of solvents, including methylene chloride, methanol, acetone, xylene and toluene.

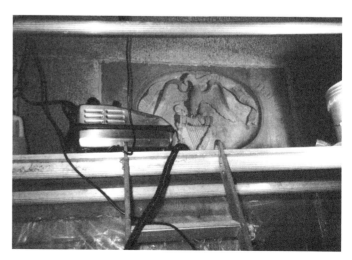

Figure 9. (Left) This small steam cleaner—the size of a vacuum cleaner—offers a very controlled and gentle means of cleaning limited, or hard-to-reach areas or carved stone details. (Right) It is particularly useful for interiors where it is important to keep moisture to a minumum, such as inside the Washington Monument, Washington, D.C., where it was used to clean the commemorative stones. Photos: Audrey T. Tepper.

Figure 10. High-pressure water washing too close to the surface has abraded and, consequently, marred the limestone on this early-20th century building.

Other Paint Removers and Cleaners. Other cleaning compounds that can be used to remove paint and some painted graffiti from historic masonry include paint removers based on N-methyl-2-pyrrolidone (NMP), or on petroleum-based compounds. Removing stains, whether they are industrial (smoke, soot, grease or tar), metallic (iron or copper), or biological (plant and fungal) in origin, depends on carefully matching the type of remover to the type of stain (Fig. 13). Successful removal of stains from historic masonry often requires the application of a number of different removers before the right one is found. The removal of layers of paint from a masonry surface is usually accomplished by applying the remover either by brush, roller or spraying, followed by a thorough water wash (Fig. 14).

Potential hazards of chemical cleaning. Since most chemical cleaning methods involve water, they have many of the potential problems of plain water cleaning. Like water methods, they should not be used in cold weather because of the possibility of freezing. Chemical cleaning should never be undertaken in temperatures below 40 degrees F (4 degrees C), and generally not below 50 degrees F. In addition, many chemical cleaners simply do not work in cold temperatures. Both acidic and alkaline cleaners can be dangerous to cleaning operators and, clearly, there are environmental concerns associated with the use of chemical cleaners.

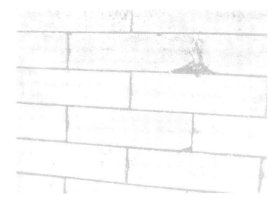

Figure 11. Rinsing with high-pressure water following chemical cleaning has left a horizontal line of abrasion across the bricks on this late-19th century row house.

If not carefully chosen, chemical cleaners can react adversely with many types of masonry. Obviously, acidic cleaners should not be used on acid-sensitive materials; however, it is not always clear exactly what the composition is of any stone or other masonry material. For, this reason, testing the cleaner on an inconspicuous spot on the building is always necessary. While certain acid-based cleaners may be appropriate if used as directed on a particular type of masonry, if left too long or if not adequately rinsed from the masonry they can have a negative effect. For example, hydrofluoric acid can etch masonry leaving a hazy residue (whitish deposits of silica or calcium fluoride salts) on the surface. While this efflorescence may usually be removed by a second cleaning—although it is likely to be expensive and time-consuming—**hydrofluoric acid** can also leave calcium fluoride salts or a colloidal silica deposit on masonry which may be impossible to remove (Fig. 15). Other acids, particularly **hydrochloric (muriatic) acid**, which is very powerful, should not be used on historic masonry, because it can dissolve lime-based mortar, damage brick and some stones, and leave chloride deposits on the masonry.

Figure 12. A mild acidic cleaning agent is being used to clean this heavily soiled brick and granite building. Additional applications of the cleaner and hand-scrubbing, and even poulticing, may be necessary to remove the dark stains on the granite arches below. Photo: Sharon C. Park, FAIA.

Alkaline cleaners can stain sandstones that contain a ferrous compound. Before using an alkaline cleaner on sandstone it is always important to test it, since it may be difficult to know whether a particular sandstone may contain a ferrous compound. Some alkaline cleaners, such as **sodium hydroxide (caustic soda or lye)** and **ammonium bifluoride**, can also damage or leave disfiguring brownish-yellow stains and, in most cases, should not be used on historic masonry. Although alkaline cleaners will not etch a masonry surface as acids can, they are caustic and can burn the surface. In addition, alkaline cleaners can deposit potentially damaging salts in the masonry which can be difficult to rinse thoroughly.

Abrasive and Mechanical Cleaning

Generally, abrasive cleaning methods are not appropriate for use on historic masonry buildings. Abrasive cleaning methods are just that—abrasive. Grit blasters, grinders, and sanding discs all operate by *abrading* the dirt or paint off the surface of the masonry, rather than *reacting* with the dirt and the masonry which is how water and chemical methods work. Since the abrasives do not differentiate between the dirt and the masonry, they can also remove the outer surface of the masonry at the same time, and result in permanently damaging the masonry. Brick, architectural terra cotta, soft stone, detailed carvings, and polished surfaces are especially susceptible to physical and aesthetic damage by abrasive methods. Brick and architectural terra cotta are fired products which have a smooth, glazed surface which can be removed by abrasive blasting or grinding (Figs. 18-19). Abrasively-cleaned masonry is damaged aesthetically as well as physically, and it has a rough surface which tends to hold dirt and the roughness will make future cleaning more difficult. Abrasive cleaning processes can also increase the likelihood of subsurface cracking of the masonry. Abrasion of carved details causes a rounding of sharp corners and other loss of delicate features, while abrasion of polished surfaces removes the polished finish of stone.

Figure 14. Chemical removal of paint from this brick building has revealed that the cornice and window hoods are metal rather than masonry.

Mortar joints, especially those with lime mortar, also can be eroded by abrasive or mechanical cleaning. In some cases, the damage may be visual, such as loss of joint detail or increased joint shadows. As mortar joints constitute a significant portion of the masonry surface (up to 20 per cent in a brick wall), this can result in the loss of a considerable amount of the historic fabric. Erosion of the mortar joints may also permit increased water penetration, which will likely necessitate repointing.

Figure 13. Sometimes it may be preferable to paint over a thick asphaltic coating rather than try to remove it, because it can be difficult to remove completely. However, in this case, many layers of asphaltic coating were removed through multiple applications of a heavy duty chemical cleaner. Each application of the cleaner was left to dwell following the manufacturer's reccommendations, and then rinsed thoroughly. (As much as possible of the asphalt was first removed with wooden scrapers.) Although not all the asphalt was removed, this was determined to be an acceptable level of cleanliness for the project.

Figure 15. The whitish deposits left on the brick by a chemical paint remover may have resulted from inadequate rinsing or from the chemical being left on the surface too long and may be impossible to remove.

Poulticing to Remove Stains and Graffiti

a

b

c

Graffiti and stains, which have penetrated into the masonry, often are best removed by using a poultice. A poultice consists of an absorbent material or clay powder (such as kaolin or fuller's earth, or even shredded paper or paper towels), mixed with a liquid (solvent or other remover) to form a paste which is applied to the stain (Figs. 16-17). As it dries, the paste absorbs the staining material so that it is not redeposited on the masonry surface. Some commercial cleaning products and paint removers are specially formulated as a paste or gel that will cling to a vertical surface and remain moist for a longer period of time in order to prolong the action of the chemical on the stain. Pre-mixed poultices are also available as a paste or in powder form needing only the addition of the appropriate liquid. The masonry must be pre-wet before applying an alkaline cleaning agent, but not when using a solvent. Once the stain has been removed, the masonry must be rinsed thoroughly.

d

Figure 16. (a) The limestone base was heavily stained by runoff from the bronze statue above. (b) A poultice consisting of copper stain remover and ammonia mixed with fuller's earth was applied to the stone base and covered with plastic sheeting to keep it from drying out too quickly. (c) As the poultice dried, it pulled the stain out of the stone. (d) The poultice residue was removed carefully from the stone surface with wooden scrapers and the stone was rinsed with water. Photos: John Dugger.

Figure 17. A poultice is being used to remove salts from the brownstone statuary on the facade of this late-19th century stone church. Photo: National Park Service Files.

Figure 18. The glazed bricks in the center of the pier were covered by a signboard that protected them being damaged by the sandblasting which removed the glaze from the surrounding bricks.

Figure 19. A comparison of undamaged bricks surroundng the electrical conduit with the rest of the brick facade emphasizes the severity of the erosion caused by sandblasting.

Abrasive Blasting. Blasting with abrasive grit or another abrasive material is the most frequently used abrasive method. *Sandblasting* is most commonly associated with abrasive cleaning. Finely ground silica or glass powder, glass beads, ground garnet, powdered walnut and other ground nut shells, grain hulls, aluminum oxide, plastic particles and even tiny pieces of sponge, are just a few of the other materials that have also been used for abrasive cleaning. Although abrasive blasting is not an appropriate method of cleaning historic masonry, it can be safely used to clean some materials. Finely-powdered walnut shells are commonly used for cleaning monumental bronze sculpture, and skilled conservators clean delicate museum objects and finely detailed, carved stone features with very small, micro-abrasive units using aluminum oxide.

A number of current approaches to abrasive blasting rely on materials that are not usually thought of as abrasive, and not as commonly associated with traditional abrasive grit cleaning. Some patented abrasive cleaning processes—one dry, one wet—use finely-ground glass powder intended to "erase" or remove dirt and surface soiling only, but not paint or stains (Fig. 20). Cleaning with baking soda (sodium bicarbonate) is another patented process. Baking soda blasting is being used in some communities as a means of quick graffiti removal. However, it should not be used on historic masonry which it can easily abrade and can permanently "etch" the graffiti into the stone; it can also leave potentially damaging salts in the stone which cannot be removed. Most of these abrasive grits may be used either dry or wet, although dry grit tends to be used more frequently.

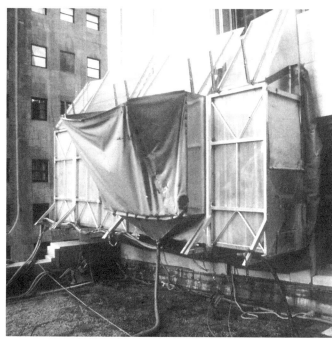

Figure 20. (Left) A comparison of the limestone surface of a 1920s office building before and after "cleaning" with a proprietary abrasive process using fine glass powder clearly shows the effectiveness of this method. But this is an abrasive technique and it has "cleaned" by removing part of the masonry surface with the dirt. Because it is abrasive, it is generally not recommended for large-scale cleaning of historic masonry, although it may be suitable to use in certain, very limited cases under controlled circumstances. (Right) A vacum chamber where the used glass powder is collected for environmentally safe disposal is a unique feature of this particular process. The specially-trained operators in the chamber wear protective clothing, masks and breathing equipment. Photos: Tom Keohan.

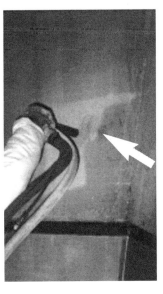

Figure 21. Low-pressure blasting with ice pellets or ice crystals (left) is an abrasive cleaning method that is sometimes recommended for use on interior masonry because it does not involve large amounts of water. However, like other abrasive materials, ice crystals "clean" by removing a portion of the masonry surface with the dirt, and may not remove some stains that have penetrated into the masonry without causing further abrasion (right). Photos: Audrey T. Tepper.

Ice particles, or pelletized dry ice (carbon dioxide or CO_2), are another medium used as an abrasive cleaner (Fig. 21). This is also too abrasive to be used on most historic masonry, but it may have practical application for removing mastics or asphaltic coatings from some substrates.

Some of these processes are promoted as being more environmentally safe and not damaging to historic masonry buildings. However, it must be remembered that they are abrasive and that they "clean" by removing a small portion of the masonry surface, even though it may be only a minuscule portion. The fact that they are essentially abrasive treatments must always be taken into consideration when planning a masonry cleaning project. *In general, abrasive methods should not be used to clean historic masonry buildings.* In some, very limited instances, highly-controlled, gentle abrasive cleaning may be appropriate on selected, hard-to-clean areas of a historic masonry building if carried out under the watchful supervision of a professional conservator. But, abrasive cleaning should never be used on an entire building.

Grinders and Sanding Disks. Grinding the masonry surface with mechanical grinders and sanding disks is another means of abrasive cleaning that should not be used on historic masonry. Like abrasive blasting, grinders and disks do not really clean masonry but instead grind away and abrasively remove and, thus, damage the masonry surface itself rather than remove just the soiling material.

Planning A Cleaning Project

Once the masonry and soiling material or paint have been identified, and the condition of the masonry has been evaluated, planning for the cleaning project can begin.

Testing cleaning methods. In order to determine the *gentlest means possible,* several cleaning methods or materials may have to be tested prior to selecting the best one to use on the building. Testing should always begin with the gentlest and least invasive method proceeding gradually, if necessary, to more complicated methods, or a combination of methods. All too often simple methods, such as low-pressure water wash, are not even considered, yet they frequently are effective, safe, and not expensive. Water of slightly higher pressure or with a non-ionic detergent additive also may be effective. It is worth repeating that these methods should always be tested prior to considering harsher methods; they are safer for the building and the environment, often safer for the applicator, and relatively inexpensive.

The level of cleanliness desired also should be determined prior to selection of a cleaning method. Obviously, the intent of cleaning is to remove most of the dirt, soiling material, stains, paint or other coating. A "brand new" appearance, however, may be inappropriate for an older building, and may require an overly harsh cleaning method to be achieved. When undertaking a cleaning project, it is important to be aware that some stains simply may not be removable. It may be wise, therefore, to agree upon a slightly lower level of cleanliness that will serve as the standard for the cleaning project. The precise amount of residual dirt considered acceptable may depend on the type of masonry, the type of soiling and difficulty of total removal, and local environmental conditions.

Cleaning tests should be carried out in an area of sufficient size to give a true indication of their effectiveness. It is preferable to conduct the test in an inconspicuous location on the building so that it will not be obvious if the test is not successful. A test area may be quite small to begin, sometimes as small as six square inches, and gradually may be increased in size as the most appropriate methods and cleaning agents are determined. Eventually the test area may be expanded to a square yard or more, and it should include several masonry units and mortar joints (Fig. 22). It should be remembered that a single building may have several types of masonry and that even similar materials may have different surface finishes. Each material and different finish should be tested separately. Cleaning tests should be evaluated only after the masonry has dried completely. *The results of the tests may indicate that several methods of cleaning should be used on a single building.*

When feasible, test areas should be allowed to weather for an extended period of time prior to final evaluation. A waiting period of a full year would be ideal in order to expose the test patch to a full range of seasons. If this is not possible, the test patch should weather for at least a month or two. For any building which is considered historically important, the delay is insignificant compared to the potential damage and disfigurement which may result from using an incompletely tested method. *The successfully cleaned test patch should be protected as it will serve as a standard against which the entire cleaning project will be measured.*

Environmental considerations. The potential effect of any method proposed for cleaning historic masonry should be evaluated carefully. Chemical cleaners and paint removers may damage trees, shrubs, grass, and plants. A plan must be provided for environmentally safe removal and disposal of the cleaning materials and the rinsing effluent before beginning the cleaning project. Authorities from the local regulatory agency—usually under the jurisdiction of the federal or state Environmental Protection Agency (EPA) should be consulted prior to beginning a cleaning project, especially if it involves anything more than plain water washing. This advance planning will ensure that the cleaning effluent or run-off, which is the combination of the cleaning agent and the substance removed from the masonry, is handled and disposed of in an environmentally sound and legal manner. Some alkaline and acidic cleaners can be neutralized so that they can be safely discharged into storm sewers. However, most solvent-based cleaners cannot be neutralized and are categorized as pollutants, and must be disposed of by a licensed transport, storage and disposal facility. Thus, it is always advisable to consult with the appropriate agencies before starting to clean to ensure that the project progresses smoothly and is not interrupted by a stop-work order because a required permit was not obtained in advance.

Vinyl guttering or polyethylene-lined troughs placed around the perimeter of the base of the building can serve to catch chemical cleaning waste as it is rinsed off the building. This will reduce the amount of chemicals entering and polluting the soil, and also will keep the cleaning waste contained until it can be removed safely. Some patented cleaning systems have developed special equipment to facilitate the containment and later disposal of cleaning waste.

Concern over the release of volatile organic compounds (VOCs) into the air has resulted in the manufacture of new, more environmentally responsible cleaners and paint removers, while some materials traditionally used in cleaning may no longer be available for these same reasons. Other health and safety concerns have created additional cleaning challenges, such as lead paint removal, which is likely to require special removal and disposal techniques.

Cleaning can also cause damage to non-masonry materials on a building, including glass, metal and wood. Thus, it is usually necessary to cover windows and doors, and other features that may be vulnerable to chemical cleaners. They should be covered with plastic or polyethylene, or a masking agent that is applied as a liquid which dries to form a thin protective film on glass, and is easily peeled off after the cleaning is finished. Wind drift, for example, can also damage other property by carrying cleaning chemicals onto nearby automobiles, resulting in etching of the glass or spotting of the paint finish. Similarly, airborne dust can enter surrounding buildings, and excess water can collect in nearby yards and basements.

Safety considerations. Possible health dangers of each method selected for the cleaning project must be considered before selecting a cleaning method to avoid harm to the

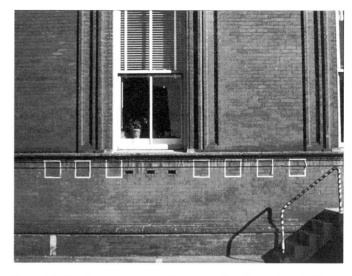

Figure 22. Cleaning test areas may be quite small at first and gradually increase in size as testing determines the "gentlest means possible". Photo: Frances Gale.

cleaning applicators, and the necessary precautions must be taken. The precautions listed in Material Safety Data Sheets (MSDS) that are provided with chemical products should always be followed. Protective clothing, respirators, hearing and face shields, and gloves must be provided to workers to be worn at all times. Acidic and alkaline chemical cleaners in both liquid and vapor forms can also cause serious injury to passers-by (Fig. 23). It may be necessary to schedule cleaning at night or weekends if the building is located in a busy urban area to reduce the potential danger of chemical overspray to pedestrians. Cleaning during non-business hours will allow HVAC systems to be turned off and vents to be covered to prevent dangerous chemical fumes from entering the building which will also ensure the safety of the building's occupants. Abrasive and mechanical methods produce dust which can pose a serious health hazard, particularly if the abrasive or the masonry contains silica.

Water-Repellent Coatings and Waterproof Coatings

To begin with, it is important to understand that waterproof coatings and water-repellent coatings are not the same. Although these terms are frequently interchanged and commonly confused with one another, they are completely different materials. **Water-repellent coatings** —often referred to incorrectly as "sealers", but which do not or should not seal— are intended to keep liquid water from penetrating the surface but to allow water vapor to enter and leave, or pass through, the surface of the masonry (Fig. 24). Water-repellent coatings are generally *transparent*, or clear, although once applied some may darken or discolor certain types of masonry while others may give it a glossy or shiny appearance. **Waterproof coatings** seal the surface from liquid water and from water vapor. They are usually *opaque*, or pigmented, and include bituminous coatings and some elastomeric paints and coatings.

Water-Repellent Coatings

Water-repellent coatings are formulated to be vapor permeable, or "breathable". They do not seal the surface completely to water vapor so it can enter the masonry wall as well as leave the wall. While the first water-repellent coatings to be developed were primarily acrylic or silicone resins in organic solvents, now most water-repellent coatings are water-based and formulated from modified siloxanes, silanes and other alkoxysilanes, or metallic stearates. While some of these products are shipped from the factory ready to use, other waterborne water repellents must be diluted at the job site. Unlike earlier water-repellent coatings which tended to form a "film" on the masonry surface, modern water-repellent coatings actually penetrate into the masonry substrate slightly and, generally, are almost invisible if properly applied to the masonry. They are also more vapor permeable than the old coatings, yet they still reduce the vapor permeability of the masonry. Once inside the wall, water vapor can condense at cold spots producing liquid water which, unlike water vapor, cannot escape through a water-repellent coating. The liquid water within the wall, whether from condensation, leaking gutters, or other sources, can cause considerable damage.

Water-repellent coatings are not consolidants. Although modern water repellents may penetrate slightly beneath the masonry surface, instead of just "sitting" on top of it, they do not perform the same function as a consolidant which is to "consolidate" and replace lost binder to strengthen deteriorating masonry. Even after many years of laboratory study and testing few consolidants have proven very effective. The composition of fired products such as brick and architectural terra cotta, as well as many types of building stone, does not lend itself to consolidation.

Some modern water-repellent coatings which contain a binder intended to replace the natural binders in stone that have been lost through weathering and natural erosion are described in product literature as both a water repellent and a consolidant. The fact that newer water-repellent coatings penetrate beneath the masonry surface instead of just forming a layer on top of the surface may indeed convey at least some consolidating properties to certain stones. However, a water-repellent coating cannot be considered a consolidant. In some instances, a water-repellent or "preservative" coating, if applied to already damaged or spalling stone, may form a surface crust which, if it fails, may exacerbate the deterioration by pulling off even more of the stone (Fig. 25).

Is a Water-Repellent Treatment Necessary?

Water-repellent coatings are frequently applied to historic masonry buildings for the wrong reason. They also are often applied without an understanding of what they are and what they are intended to do. And these coatings can be very difficult, if not impossible, to remove from the masonry if they fail or become discolored. Most importantly, the application of water-repellent coatings to historic masonry is usually unnecessary.

Figure 23. A tarpaulin protects and shields pedestrians from potentially harmful spray while chemical cleaning is underway on the granite exterior of the U.S. Treasury Building, Washington, D.C.

Most historic masonry buildings, unless they are painted, have survived for decades without a water-repellent coating and, thus, probably do not need one now. Water penetration to the interior of a masonry building is seldom due to porous masonry, but results from poor or deferred maintenance. Leaking roofs, clogged or deteriorated gutters and downspouts, missing mortar, or cracks and open joints around door and window openings are almost always the cause of moisture-related problems in a historic masonry building. **If historic masonry buildings are kept watertight and in good repair, water-repellent coatings should not be necessary.**

Rising damp (capillary moisture pulled up from the ground), or condensation can also be a source of excess moisture in masonry buildings. A water-repellent coating will not solve this problem either and, in fact, may be likely to exacerbate it. Furthermore, a water-repellent coating should never be applied to a damp wall. Moisture in the wall would reduce the ability of a coating to adhere to the masonry and to penetrate below the surface. But, if it did adhere, it would hold the moisture inside the masonry because, although a water-repellent coating is permeable to water vapor, liquid water cannot pass through it. In the case of rising damp, a coating may force the moisture to go even higher in the wall because it can slow down evaporation, and thereby retain the moisture in the wall.

Excessive moisture in masonry walls may carry waterborne soluble salts from the masonry units themselves or from the mortar through the walls. If the water is permitted to come to the surface, the salts may appear on the masonry surface as efflorescence (a whitish powder) upon evaporation. However, the salts can be potentially dangerous if they remain in the masonry and crystallize

Figure 24. Although the application of a water-repellent coating was probably not needed on either of these buildings, the coating on the brick building (above), is not visible and has not changed the character of the brick. But the coating on the brick column (below), has a high gloss that is incompatible with the historic character of the masonry.

beneath the surface as subflorescence. Subflorescence eventually may cause the surface of the masonry to spall, particularly if a water-repellent coating has been applied which tends to reduce the flow of moisture out from the subsurface of the masonry. Although many of the newer water-repellent products are more breathable than their predecessors, they can be especially damaging if applied to masonry that contains salts, because they limit the flow of moisture through masonry.

When a Water-Repellent Coating May be Appropriate

There are some instances when a water-repellent coating may be considered appropriate to use on a historic masonry building. Soft, incompletely fired brick from the 18th- and early-19th centuries may have become so porous that paint or some type of coating is needed to protect it from further deterioration or dissolution. When a masonry building has been neglected for a long period of time, necessary repairs may be required in order to make it watertight. If, following a reasonable period of time after the building has been made watertight and has dried out completely, moisture appears actually to be penetrating through the repointed and repaired masonry walls, then the application of a water-repellent coating may be considered *in selected areas only*. This decision should be made in consultation with an architectural conservator. And, if such a treatment is undertaken, it should not be applied to the entire exterior of the building.

Anti-graffiti or barrier coatings are another type of clear coating—although barrier coatings can also be pigmented—that may be applied to exterior masonry, but they are not formulated primarily as water repellents. The purpose of these coatings is to make it harder for graffiti to stick to a masonry surface and, thus, easier to clean. But, like water-repellent coatings, in most cases the application of anti-graffiti coatings is generally not recommended for historic masonry buildings. These coatings are often quite shiny which can greatly alter the appearance of a historic masonry surface, and they are not always effective (Fig. 26). Generally, other ways of discouraging graffiti, such as improved lighting, can be more effective than a coating. However, the application of anti-graffiti coatings may be appropriate in some instances on vulnerable areas of historic masonry buildings which are frequent targets of graffiti that are located in out-of-the-way places where constant surveillance is not possible.

Some water-repellent coatings are recommended by product manufacturers as a means of keeping dirt and pollutants or biological growth from collecting on the surface of masonry buildings and, thus, reducing the need for frequent cleaning. While this at times may be true, in some cases a coating may actually retain dirt more than uncoated masonry. Generally, the application of a water-repellent coating is not recommended on a historic masonry building as a means of preventing biological growth. Some water-repellent coatings may actually encourage biological growth on a masonry wall. Biological growth on masonry buildings has traditionally been kept at bay through regularly-scheduled cleaning as part of a maintenance plan. Simple cleaning of the masonry with low-pressure water using a natural- or synthetic-bristled scrub brush can be very effective if done on a regular basis. Commercial products are also available which can be sprayed on masonry to remove biological growth.

In most instances, a water-repellent coating is not necessary if a building is watertight. The application of a water-repellent coating is not a recommended treatment for historic masonry buildings unless there is a specific

Figure 25. *The clear coating applied to this limestone molding has failed and is taking off some of the stone surface as it peels. Photo: Frances Gale.*

problem which it may help solve. If the problem occurs on only part of the building, it is best to treat only that area rather than an entire building. Extreme exposures such as parapets, for example, or portions of the building subject to driving rain can be treated more effectively and less expensively than the entire building. Water-repellent coatings are not permanent and must be reapplied

Figure 26. *The anti-graffiti or barrier coating on this column is very shiny and would not be appropriate to use on a historic masonry building. The coating has discolored as it has aged and whitish streaks reveal areas of bare concrete where the coating was incompletely applied.*

periodically although, if they are truly invisible, it can be difficult to know when they are no longer providing the intended protection.

Testing a water-repellent coating by applying it in one small area may not be helpful in determining its suitability for the building because a limited test area does not allow an adequate evaluation of such a treatment. Since water may enter and leave through the surrounding untreated areas, there is no way to tell if the coated test area is "breathable." But trying a coating in a small area may help to determine whether the coating is visible on the surface or if it will otherwise change the appearance of the masonry.

Waterproof Coatings

In theory, waterproof coatings usually do not cause problems as long as they exclude all water from the masonry. If water does enter the wall from the ground or from the inside of a building, the coating can intensify the damage because the water will not be able to escape. During cold weather this water in the wall can freeze causing serious mechanical disruption, such as spalling.

In addition, the water eventually will get out by the path of least resistance. If this path is toward the interior, damage to interior finishes can result; if it is toward the exterior, it can lead to damage to the masonry caused by built-up water pressure (Fig. 27).

In most instances, waterproof coatings should not be applied to historic masonry. The possible exception to this might be the application of a waterproof coating to below-grade exterior foundation walls as a last resort to stop water infiltration on interior basement walls. **Generally, however, waterproof coatings, which include** *elastomeric paints,* **should almost never be applied above grade to historic masonry buildings.**

Figure 27. *Instead of correcting the roof drainage problems, an elastomeric coating was applied to the already saturated limestone cornice. An elastomeric coating holds moisture in the masonry because it does not "breathe" and does not allow liquid moisture to escape. If the water pressure builds up sufficiently it can cause the coating to break and pop off as shown in this example, often pulling pieces of the masonry with it. Photo: National Park Service Files.*

Summary

A well-planned cleaning project is an essential step in preserving, rehabilitating or restoring a historic masonry building. Proper cleaning methods and coating treatments, when determined necessary for the preservation of the masonry, can enhance the aesthetic character as well as the structural stability of a historic building. Removing years of accumulated dirt, pollutant crusts, stains, graffiti or paint, if done with appropriate caution, can extend the life and longevity of the historic resource. Cleaning that is carelessly or insensitively prescribed or carried out by inexperienced workers can have the opposite of the intended effect. It may scar the masonry permanently, and may actually result in hastening deterioration by introducing harmful residual chemicals and salts into the masonry or causing surface loss. Using the wrong cleaning method or using the right method incorrectly, applying the wrong kind of coating or applying a coating that is not needed can result in serious damage, both physically and aesthetically, to a historic masonry building. Cleaning a historic masonry building should always be done using the *gentlest means possible* that will clean, but not damage the building. It should always be taken into consideration before applying a water-repellent coating or a waterproof coating to a historic masonry building whether it is really necessary and whether it is in the best interest of preserving the building.

Selected Reading

Architectural Ceramics: Their History, Manufacture and Conservation. A Joint Symposium of English Heritage and the United Kingdom Institute for Conservation, September 22-25, 1994. London: English Heritage, 1996.

Ashurst, Nicola. *Cleaning Historic Buildings. Volume One: Substrates, Soiling & Investigation. Volume Two: Cleaning Materials & Processes.* London: Donhead Publishing Ltd., 1994.

Association for Preservation Technology. *Special Issue: Preservation of Historic Masonry.* Papers from the Symposium on Preservation Treatments for Historic Masonry: Consolidants, Coatings, and Water Repellents, New York, New York, November 11-12, 1994. *APT Bulletin.* Vol. XXVI, No. 4 (1995).

Grimmer, Anne E. *Preservation Brief 6: Dangers of Abrasive Cleaning to Historic Buildings.* Washington, D.C.: Preservation Assistance Division, National Park Service, U.S. Department of the Interior, 1979.

Grimmer, Anne E. *Keeping it Clean: Removing Exterior Dirt, Paint, Stains and Graffiti from Historic Masonry Buildings.* Washington, D.C.: Preservation Assistance Division, National Park Service, U.S. Department of the Interior, 1988.

Park, Sharon C., AIA. *Preservation Brief 39: Holding the Line: Controlling Unwanted Moisture in Historic Buildings.* Washington, D.C.: Heritage Preservation Services, National Park Service, U.S. Department of the Interior, 1996.

Powers, Robert M. *Preservation Tech Note, Masonry No. 3, "Water Soak Cleaning of Limestone".* Washington, D.C.: Preservation Assistance Division, National Park Service, U.S. Department of the Interior, 1992.

Sinvinski, Valerie. "Gentle Blasting." *Old-House Journal.* Vol. XXIV, No. 4 (July-August 1996), pp. 46-49.

Weaver, Martin E. *Conserving Buildings: A Guide to Techniques and Materials.* New York: John Wiley & Sons, Inc., 1993.

Weaver, Martin E. *Preservation Brief 38: Removing Graffiti from Historic Masonry.* Washington, D.C.: Preservation Assistance Division, National Park Service, U.S. Department of the Interior, 1995.

Winkler, E.M. *Stone in Architecture: Properties, Durability.* Third, completely revised and extended edition. Berlin, Germany: Springer-Verlag, 1997.

Acknowledgments

Robert C. Mack, FAIA, is a principal in the firm of MacDonald & Mack Architects, Ltd., an architectural firm that specializes in historic buildings in Minneapolis, Minnesota.
Anne Grimmer is a Senior Architectural Historian in the Technical Preservation Services Branch, Heritage Preservation Services Program, National Park Service, Washington, D.C.

The original version of *Preservation Brief 1: The Cleaning and Waterproof Coating of Masonry Buildings* was written by Robert C. Mack, AIA. It inaugurated the *Preservation Briefs* series when it was published in 1975.

The following historic preservation specialists provided technical review of this publication: Frances Gale, Training Director, National Center for Preservation Technology and Training, National Park Service, Natchitoches, LA; Judith M. Jacob, Architectural Conservator, Building Conservation Branch, Northeast Cultural Resources Center, National Park Service, N.Y., NY; Robert M. Powers, Architectural Conservator, Powers and Company, Inc., Philadelphia, PA; Antonio Aguilar, Kaaren Dodge, JoEllen Hensley, Gary Sachau, John Sandor and Audrey T. Tepper, Technical Preservation Services Branch, Heritage Preservation Services Program, National Park Service, Washington, D.C.; and Kay D. Weeks, Heritage Preservation Services Program, National Park Service, Washington, D.C.

Front Cover: Chemical cleaning of the brick and architectural terra cotta frieze on the 1880s Pension Building, Washington, D.C. (now the National Building Museum), is shown here in progress. Photo: Christina Henry.

Photographs used to illustrate this Brief were taken by Anne Grimmer unless otherwise credited.

November 2000

2

Repointing Mortar Joints in Historic Masonry Buildings

Robert C. Mack, FAIA
John P. Speweik

Figure 1. After removing deteriorated mortar, an experienced mason repoints a portion of this early-20th century limestone building. Photo: Robert C. Mack, FAIA.

Masonry — brick, stone, terra-cotta, and concrete block — is found on nearly every historic building. Structures with all-masonry exteriors come to mind immediately, but most other buildings at least have masonry foundations or chimneys. Although generally considered "permanent," masonry is subject to deterioration, especially at the mortar joints. Repointing, also known simply as "pointing" or—somewhat inaccurately—"tuck pointing"*, is the process of removing deteriorated mortar from the joints of a masonry wall and replacing it with new mortar (Fig. 1). Properly done, repointing restores the visual and physical integrity of the masonry. Improperly done, repointing not only detracts from the appearance of the building, but may also cause physical damage to the masonry units themselves.

The purpose of this Brief is to provide general guidance on appropriate materials and methods for repointing historic masonry buildings and it is intended to benefit building owners, architects, and contractors. The Brief should serve as a guide to prepare specifications for repointing historic masonry buildings. It should also help develop sensitivity to the particular needs of historic masonry, and to assist historic building owners in working cooperatively with architects, architectural conservators and historic preservation consultants, and contractors. Although specifically intended for historic buildings, the guidance is appropriate for other masonry buildings as well. This publication updates *Preservation Briefs 2: Repointing Mortar Joints in Historic Brick Buildings* to include all types of historic unit masonry. The scope of the earlier Brief has also been expanded to acknowledge that the many buildings constructed in the first half of the 20th century are now historic and eligible for listing in the National Register of Historic Places, and that they may have been originally constructed with portland cement mortar.

*Tuckpointing technically describes a primarily decorative application of a raised mortar joint or lime putty joint on top of flush mortar joints.

Historical Background

Mortar consisting primarily of lime and sand has been used as an integral part of masonry structures for thousands of years. Up until about the mid-19th century, lime or quicklime (sometimes called lump lime) was delivered to construction sites, where it had to be slaked, or combined with water. Mixing with water caused it to boil and resulted in a wet lime putty that was left to mature in a pit or wooden box for several weeks, up to a year. Traditional mortar was made from lime putty, or slaked lime, combined with local sand, generally in a ratio of 1 part lime putty to 3 parts sand by volume. Often other ingredients, such as crushed marine shells (another source of lime), brick dust, clay, natural cements, pigments, and even animal hair were also added to mortar, but the basic formulation for lime putty and sand mortar remained unchanged for centuries until the advent of portland cement or its forerunner, Roman cement, a natural, hydraulic cement.

Portland cement was patented in Great Britain in 1824. It was named after the stone from Portland in Dorset which it resembled when hard. This is a fast-curing, hydraulic cement which hardens under water. Portland cement was first manufactured in the United States in 1872, although it was imported before this date. But it was not in common use throughout the country until the early 20th century. Up until the turn of the century portland cement was considered primarily an additive, or "minor ingredient" to help accelerate mortar set time. By the 1930s, however, most masons used a mix of equal parts portland cement and lime putty. Thus, the mortar found in masonry structures built between 1873 and 1930 can range from pure lime and sand mixes to a wide variety of lime, portland cement, and sand combinations.

In the 1930s more new mortar products intended to hasten and simplify masons' work were introduced in the U.S. These included **masonry cement**, a premixed, bagged mortar which is a combination of portland cement and ground limestone, and **hydrated lime**, machine-slaked lime that eliminated the necessity of slaking quicklime into putty at the site.

Identifying the Problem Before Repointing

The decision to repoint is most often related to some obvious sign of deterioration, such as disintegrating mortar, cracks in mortar joints, loose bricks or stones, damp walls, or damaged plasterwork. It is, however, erroneous to assume that repointing alone will solve deficiencies that result from other problems (Fig. 2). The root cause of the deterioration—leaking roofs or gutters, differential settlement of the building, capillary action causing rising damp, or extreme weather exposure—should always be dealt with prior to beginning work. Without appropriate repairs to eliminate the source of the problem, mortar deterioration will continue and any repointing will have been a waste of time and money.

Use of Consultants. Because there are so many possible causes for deterioration in historic buildings, it may be desirable to retain a consultant, such as a historic architect or architectural conservator, to analyze the building. In addition to determining the most appropriate solutions to the problems, a consultant can

Figure 2. Much of the mortar on this building has been leached away by water from a leaking downspout. The downspout must be replaced and any other drainage problems repaired before repointing. Photo: Robert C. Mack, FAIA.

prepare specifications which reflect the particular requirements of each job and can provide oversight of the work in progress. Referrals to preservation consultants frequently can be obtained from State Historic Preservation Offices, the American Institute for Conservation of Historic and Artistic Works (AIC), the Association for Preservation Technology (APT), and local chapters of the American Institute of Architects (AIA).

Finding an Appropriate Mortar Match

Preliminary research is necessary to ensure that the proposed repointing work is both physically and visually appropriate to the building. Analysis of unweathered portions of the historic mortar to which the new mortar will be matched can suggest appropriate mixes for the repointing mortar so that it will not damage the building because it is excessively strong or vapor impermeable. Examination and analysis of the masonry units—brick, stone or terra cotta—and the techniques used in the original construction will assist in maintaining the building's historic appearance (Figs. 3-4). A simple, non-technical, evaluation of the masonry units and mortar can provide information concerning the relative strength and permeability of each–critical factors in selecting the repointing mortar—while a visual analysis of the historic mortar can provide the information necessary for developing the new mortar mix and application techniques.

Although not crucial to a successful repointing project, for projects involving properties of special historic significance, a mortar analysis by a qualified laboratory can be useful by providing information on the original ingredients. However, there are limitations with such an analysis, and replacement mortar specifications should not be based solely on laboratory analysis. Analysis requires interpretation, and there are important factors which affect the condition and performance of the mortar that cannot be established through laboratory analysis. These may include: the original water content, rate of curing, weather conditions during original construction, the method of mixing and placing the mortar, and the cleanliness and condition of the sand. *The most useful information that can come out of laboratory analysis is the identification of sand by*

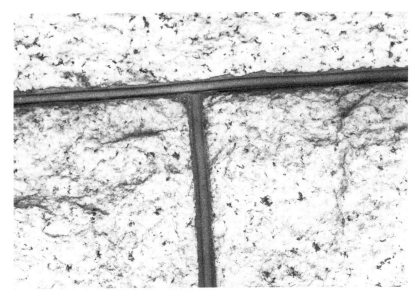

Figure 3. Good-quality repointing closely replicates the original in composition, texture, joint type and profile on this 19th century brick building (left), and on this late-19th century granite on H.H. Richardson's Glessner House in Chicago (right). Photos: Charles E. Fisher: Sharon C. Park, FAIA.

gradation and color. This allows the color and the texture of the mortar to be matched with some accuracy because sand is the largest ingredient by volume.

In creating a repointing mortar that is compatible with the masonry units, the objective is to achieve one that matches the historic mortar as closely as possible, so that the new material can coexist with the old in a sympathetic, supportive and, if necessary, sacrificial capacity. The exact physical and chemical properties of the historic mortar are not of major significance as long as the new mortar conforms to the following criteria:

• The new mortar must match the historic mortar in color, texture and tooling. (If a laboratory analysis is undertaken, it may be possible to match the binder components and their proportions with the historic mortar, if those materials are available.)

• The sand must match the sand in the historic mortar. (The color and texture of the new mortar will usually fall into place if the sand is matched successfully.)

• The new mortar must have **greater vapor permeability** and be **softer** (measured in compressive strength) than the masonry units.

• The new mortar must be **as vapor permeable** and **as soft or softer** (measured in compressive strength) than the historic mortar. (Softness or hardness is not necessarily an indication of permeability; old, hard lime mortars can still retain high permeability.)

Properties of Mortar

Mortars for repointing should be softer or more permeable than the masonry units and no harder or more impermeable than the historic mortar to prevent damage to the masonry units. It is a common error to assume that hardness or high strength is a measure of appropriateness, particularly for lime-based historic mortars. Stresses within a wall caused by expansion, contraction, moisture migration, or settlement must be accommodated in some manner; in a masonry wall these

Figure 4. (left) The poor quality of this repointing–it appears to have been "tooled" with the mason's finger–does not match the delicacy of the original beaded joint on this 19th-century brick wall. (right) It is obvious that the repointing on this "test patch" is not an appropriate replacement mortar joint for this early-19th century stone foundation. Photos: Lee H. Nelson, FAIA.

stresses should be relieved by the mortar rather than by the masonry units. A mortar that is stronger in compressive strength than the masonry units, will not "give," thus causing the stresses to be relieved through the masonry units—resulting in permanent damage to the masonry, such as cracking and spalling, that cannot be repaired easily (Fig. 5). While stresses can also break the bond between the mortar and the masonry units, permitting water to penetrate the resulting hairline cracks, this is easier to correct in the joint through repointing than if the break occurs in the masonry units.

Permeability, or rate of vapor transmission, is also critical. High lime mortars are more permeable than denser cement mortars. Historically, mortar acted as a bedding material–not unlike an expansion joint–rather than a "glue" for the masonry units, and moisture was able to migrate through the mortar joints rather than the masonry units. When moisture evaporates from the masonry it deposits any soluble salts either on the surface as *efflorescence* or below the surface as *subflorescence*. While salts deposited on the surface of masonry units are usually relatively harmless, salt crystallization within a masonry unit creates pressure that can cause parts of the outer surface to spall off or delaminate. If the mortar does not permit moisture or moisture vapor to migrate out of the wall and evaporate, the result will be damage to the masonry units.

Components of Mortar

Sand. Sand is the largest component of mortar and the material that gives mortar its distinctive color, texture and cohesiveness. Sand must be free of impurities, such as salts or clay. The three key characteristics of sand are: particle shape, gradation and void ratios.

Figure 5. The use of hard, portland-cement mortar that is less permeable than the soft bricks has resulted in severe damage to this brick wall. Moisture trapped in the wall was unable to evaporate through the mortar which is intended to be sacrificial, and thus protect the bricks. As a result the moisture remained in the walls until water pressure eventually popped the surface off the bricks. Photo: National Park Service Files.

When viewed under a magnifying glass or low-power microscope, particles of sand generally have either rounded edges, such as found in beach and river sand, or sharp, angular edges, found in crushed or manufactured sand. For repointing mortar, rounded or natural sand is preferred for two reasons. It is usually similar to the sand in the historic mortar and provides a better visual match. It also has better working qualities or plasticity and can thus be forced into the joint more easily, forming a good contact with the remaining historic mortar and the surface of the adjacent masonry units. Although manufactured sand is frequently more readily available, it is usually possible to locate a supply of rounded sand.

The gradation of the sand (particle size distribution) plays a very important role in the durability and cohesive properties of a mortar. Mortar must have a certain percentage of large to small particle sizes in order to deliver the optimum performance. Acceptable guidelines on particle size distribution may be found in ASTM C 144 (American Society for Testing and Materials). However, in actuality, since neither historic nor modern sands are always in compliance with ASTM C 144, matching the same particle appearance and gradation usually requires sieving the sand.

A scoop of sand contains many small voids between the individual grains. A mortar that performs well fills all these small voids with binder (cement/lime combination or mix) in a balanced manner. Well-graded sand generally has a 30 per cent void ratio by volume. Thus, 30 per cent binder by volume generally should be used, unless the historic mortar had a different binder: aggregate ratio. This represents the 1:3 binder to sand ratios often seen in mortar specifications.

For repointing, sand generally should conform to ASTM C 144 to assure proper gradation and freedom from impurities; some variation may be necessary to match the original size and gradation. Sand color and texture also should match the original as closely as possible to provide the proper color match without other additives.

Lime. Mortar formulations prior to the late-19th century used lime as the primary binding material. Lime is derived from heating limestone at high temperatures which burns off the carbon dioxide, and turns the limestone into quicklime. There are three types of limestone—calcium, magnesium, and dolomitic—differentiated by the different levels of magnesium carbonate they contain which impart specific qualities to mortar. Historically, calcium lime was used for mortar rather than the dolomitic lime (calcium magnesium carbonate) most often used today. But it is also important to keep in mind the fact that the historic limes, and other components of mortar, varied a great deal because they were natural, as opposed to modern lime which is manufactured and, therefore, standardized. Because some of the kinds of lime, as well as other components of mortar, that were used historically are no longer readily available, even when a conscious effort is made to replicate a "historic" mix, this may not be achievable due to the differences between modern and historic materials.

Lime, itself, when mixed with water into a paste is very plastic and creamy. It will remain workable and soft indefinitely, if stored in a sealed container. Lime (calcium hydroxide) hardens by carbonation absorbing carbon dioxide primarily from the air, converting itself to calcium carbonate. Once a lime and sand mortar is mixed and placed in a wall, it begins the process of carbonation. If lime mortar is left to dry too rapidly, carbonation of the mortar will be reduced, resulting in poor adhesion and poor durability. In addition, lime mortar is slightly water soluble and thus is able to re-seal any hairline cracks that may develop during the life of the mortar. Lime mortar is soft, porous, and changes little in volume during temperature fluctuations, thus making it a good choice for historic buildings. *Because of these qualities, high calcium lime mortar may be considered for many repointing projects, not just those involving historic buildings.*

For repointing, lime should conform to ASTM C 207, Type S, or Type SA, Hydrated Lime for Masonry Purposes. This machine-slaked lime is designed to assure high plasticity and water retention. The use of quicklime which must be slaked and soaked by hand may have advantages over hydrated lime in some restoration projects if time and money allow.

Lime putty. Lime putty is slaked lime that has a putty or paste-like consistency. It should conform to ASTM C 5. Mortar can be mixed using lime putty according to ASTM C 270 property or proportion specification.

Portland cement. More recent, 20th-century mortar has used portland cement as a primary binding material. A straight portland cement and sand mortar is extremely hard, resists the movement of water, shrinks upon setting, and undergoes relatively large thermal movements. When mixed with water, portland cement forms a harsh, stiff paste that is quite unworkable, becoming hard very quickly. (Unlike lime, portland cement will harden regardless of weather conditions and does not require wetting and drying cycles.) Some portland cement assists the workability and plasticity of the mortar without adversely affecting the finished project; it also provides early strength to the mortar and speeds setting. Thus, it may be appropriate to add some portland cement to an essentially lime-based mortar even when repointing relatively soft 18th or 19th century brick under some circumstances when a slightly harder mortar is required. The more portland cement that is added to a mortar formulation the harder it becomes— and the faster the initial set.

For repointing, portland cement should conform to ASTM C 150. White, non-staining portland cement may provide a better color match for some historic mortars than the more commonly available grey portland cement. But, it should not be assumed, however, that white portland cement is always appropriate for all historic buildings, since the original mortar may have been mixed with grey cement. The cement should not have more than 0.60 per cent alkali to help avoid efflorescence.

Masonry cement. Masonry cement is a preblended mortar mix commonly found at hardware and home repair stores. It is designed to produce mortars with a compressive strength of 750 psi or higher when mixed

MORTAR ANALYSIS

Methods for analyzing mortars can be divided into two broad categories: **wet chemical** and **instrumental**. Many laboratories that analyze historic mortars use a simple **wet-chemical** method called *acid digestion*, whereby a sample of the mortar is crushed and then mixed with a dilute acid. The acid dissolves all the carbonate-containing minerals not only in the binder, but also in the aggregate (such as oyster shells, coral sands, or other carbonate-based materials), as well as any other acid-soluble materials. The sand and fine-grained acid-insoluble material is left behind. There are several variations on the simple acid digestion test. One involves collecting the carbon dioxide gas given off as the carbonate is digested by the acid; based on the gas volume the carbonate content of the mortar can be accurately determined (Jedrzejewska, 1960). Simple acid digestion methods are rapid, inexpensive, and easy to perform, but the information they provide about the original composition of a mortar is limited to the color and texture of the sand. The gas collection method provides more information about the binder than a simple acid digestion test.

Instrumental analysis methods that have been used to evaluate mortars include polarized light or thin-section microscopy, scanning electron microscopy, atomic absorption spectroscopy, X-ray diffraction, and differential thermal analysis. All instrumental methods require not only expensive, specialized equipment, but also highly-trained experienced analysts. However, instrumental methods can provide much more information about a mortar. Thin-section microscopy is probably the most commonly used instrumental method. Examination of thin slices of a mortar in transmitted light is often used to supplement acid digestion methods, particularly to look for carbonate-based aggregate. For example, the new ASTM test method, ASTM C 1324-96 "Test Method for Examination and Analysis of Hardened Mortars" which was designed specifically for the analysis of modern lime-cement and masonry cement mortars, combines a complex series of wet chemical analyses with thin-section microscopy.

The drawback of most mortar analysis methods is that mortar samples of known composition have not been analyzed in order to evaluate the method. Historic mortars were not prepared to narrowly defined specifications from materials of uniform quality; they contain a wide array of locally derived materials combined at the discretion of the mason. While a particular method might be able to accurately determine the original proportions of a lime-cement-sand mortar prepared from modern materials, the usefulness of that method for evaluating historic mortars is questionable unless it has been tested against mortars prepared from materials more commonly used in the past.

Lorraine Schnabel.

Figure 6. Tinted mortar. (left)Black mortar with a beaded joint was used here on this late-19th century hard pressed red brick and, (center) a dark brown tinted mortar with an almost flush joint was used on this early-20th century Roman brick. (right) When constructed at the turn-of-the-century, this building was pointed with a dark gray mortar to blend with the color of the stone, but the light-colored mortar used in spot repointing has destroyed this harmony and adversely impacts the building's historic character. Photos: Anne Grimmer.

with sand and water at the job site. It may contain hydrated lime, but it always contains a large amount of portland cement, as well as ground limestone and other workability agents, including air-entraining agents. Because masonry cements are not required to contain hydrated lime, and generally do not contain lime, they produce high strength mortars that can damage historic masonry. *For this reason, they generally are not recommended for use on historic masonry buildings.*

Lime mortar (pre-blended). Hydrated lime mortars, and pre-blended lime putty mortars with or without a matched sand are commercially available. Custom mortars are also available with color. In most instances, pre-blended lime mortars containing sand may not provide an exact match; however, if the project calls for total repointing, a pre-blended lime mortar may be worth considering as long as the mortar is compatible in strength with the masonry. If the project involves only selected, "spot" repointing, then it may be better to carry out a mortar analysis which can provide a custom pre-blended lime mortar with a matching sand. In either case, if a preblended lime mortar is to be used, it should contain Type S or SA hydrated lime conforming to ASTM C 207.

Water. Water should be potable—clean and free from acids, alkalis, or other dissolved organic materials.

Other Components

Historic components. In addition to the color of the sand, the texture of the mortar is of critical importance in duplicating historic mortar. Most mortars dating from the mid-19th century on—with some exceptions—have a fairly homogeneous texture and color. Some earlier mortars are not as uniformly textured and may contain lumps of partially burned lime or "dirty lime", shell (which often provided a source of lime, particularly in coastal areas), natural cements, pieces of clay, lampblack or other pigments, or even animal hair. The visual characteristics of these mortars can be duplicated through the use of similar materials in the repointing mortar.

Replicating such unique or individual mortars will require writing new specifications for each project. If possible, suggested sources for special materials should be included. For example, crushed oyster shells can be obtained in a variety of sizes from poultry supply dealers.

Pigments. Some historic mortars, particularly in the late 19th century, were tinted to match or contrast with the brick or stone (Fig. 6). Red pigments, sometimes in the form of brick dust, as well as brown, and black pigments were commonly used. Modern pigments are available which can be added to the mortar at the job site, but they should not exceed 10 per cent by weight of the portland cement in the mix, and carbon black should be limited to 2 per cent. Only synthetic mineral oxides, which are alkali-proof and sun-fast, should be used to prevent bleaching and fading.

Modern components. Admixtures are used to create specific characteristics in mortar, and whether they should be used will depend upon the individual project. *Air-entraining agents*, for example, help the mortar to resist freeze-thaw damage in northern climates. *Accelerators* are used to reduce mortar freezing prior to setting while *retarders* help to extend the mortar life in hot climates. Selection of admixtures should be made by the architect or architectural conservator as part of the specifications, not something routinely added by the masons.

Generally, modern chemical additives are unnecessary and may, in fact, have detrimental effects in historic masonry projects. The use of antifreeze compounds is not recommended. They are not very effective with high lime mortars and may introduce salts, which may cause efflorescence later. A better practice is to warm the sand and water, and to protect the completed work from freezing. No definitive study has determined whether air-entraining additives should be used to resist frost action and enhance plasticity, but in areas of extreme exposure requiring high-strength mortars with lower permeability, air-entrainment of 10-16 percent may be desirable (see formula for "severe weather exposure" in **Mortar Type and Mix**). Bonding agents are not a substitute for proper joint preparation, and they should generally be avoided. If the joint is properly prepared, there will be a good bond between the new mortar and the adjacent surfaces. In addition, a bonding agent is difficult to remove if smeared on a masonry surface (Fig. 7).

Mortar Type and Mix

Mortars for repointing projects, especially those involving historic buildings, typically are custom mixed in order to ensure the proper physical and visual qualities. These materials can be combined in varying proportions to create a mortar with the desired performance and durability. The actual specification of a particular mortar type should take into consideration all of the factors affecting the life of the building including: current site conditions, present condition of the masonry, function of the new mortar, degree of weather exposure, and skill of the mason. Thus, no two repointing projects are exactly the same. Modern materials specified for use in repointing mortar should conform to specifications of the American Society for Testing and Materials (ASTM) or comparable federal specifications, and the resulting mortar should conform to ASTM C 270, Mortar for Unit Masonry.

Specifying the proportions for the repointing mortar for a specific job is not as difficult as it might seem. Five mortar types, each with a corresponding recommended mix, have been established by ASTM to distinguish high strength mortar from soft flexible mortars. The ASTM designated them in decreasing order of approximate general strength as Type M (2,500 psi), Type S (1,800 psi), Type N (750 psi), Type O (350 psi) and Type K (75 psi). (The letters identifying the types are from the words MASON WORK using every other letter.) Type K has the highest lime content of the mixes that contain portland cement, although it is seldom used today, except for some historic preservation projects. The designation "L" in the accompanying chart identifies a straight lime and sand mix. Specifying the appropriate ASTM mortar by proportion of ingredients, will ensure the desired physical properties. Unless specified otherwise, measurements or proportions for mortar mixes are always given in the following order: cement-lime-sand. Thus, a Type K mix, for example, would be referred to as 1-3-10, or 1 part cement to 3 parts lime to 10 parts sand. Other requirements to create the desired visual qualities should be included in the specifications.

Figure 8. Due to inadequate joint preparation, the repointing mortar has not adhered properly and is falling out of the joint. Photo: Robert C. Mack, FAIA.

The strength of a mortar can vary. If mixed with higher amounts of portland cement, a harder mortar is obtained. The more lime that is added, the softer and more plastic the mortar becomes, increasing its workability. A mortar strong in compressive strength might be desirable for a hard stone (such as granite) pier holding up a bridge deck, whereas a softer, more permeable lime mortar would be preferable for a historic wall of soft brick. Masonry deterioration caused by salt deposition results when the mortar is less permeable that the masonry unit. A strong mortar is still more permeable than hard dense stone. However, in a wall constructed of soft bricks where the masonry unit itself has a relatively high permeability or vapor transmission rate, a soft, high lime mortar is necessary to retain sufficient permeability.

Budgeting and Scheduling

Repointing is both expensive and time consuming due to the extent of handwork and special materials required. It is preferable to repoint only those areas that require work rather than an entire wall, as is often specified. But, if 25 to 50 per cent or more of a wall needs to be repointed, repointing the entire wall may be more cost effective than spot repointing. Total repointing may also be more sensible when access is difficult, requiring the erection of expensive scaffolding (unless the majority of the mortar is sound and unlikely to require replacement in the foreseeable future). Each project requires judgement based on a variety of factors. Recognizing this at the outset will help to prevent many jobs from becoming prohibitively expensive.

In scheduling, seasonal aspects need to be considered first. Generally speaking, wall temperatures between 40 and 95 degrees F (8 and 38 degrees C) will prevent freezing or excessive evaporation of the water in the mortar. Ideally, repointing should be done in shade, away from strong sunlight in order to slow the drying process, especially during hot weather. If necessary, shade can be provided for large-scale projects with appropriate modifications to scaffolding.

The relationship of repointing to other work proposed on the building must also be recognized. For example, if paint removal or cleaning is anticipated, and if the mortar joints are basically sound and need only selective repointing, it is generally better to postpone repointing

Figure 7. The dark stain on either side of the vertical joint on this sandstone watertable probably resulted from the use of a bonding agent that was not properly cleaned off the masonry after repointing. Photo: Anne Grimmer.

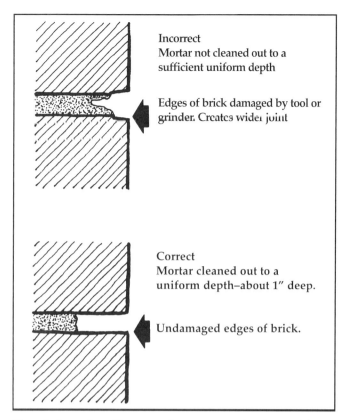

Figure 9. Comparison of incorrect and correct preparation of mortar joints for repointing. Drawing: Robert C. Mack, FAIA, and David W. Look, AIA.

Incorrect
Mortar not cleaned out to a sufficient uniform depth

Edges of brick damaged by tool or grinder. Creates wider joint

Correct
Mortar cleaned out to a uniform depth–about 1" deep.

Undamaged edges of brick.

until after completion of these activities. However, if the mortar has eroded badly, allowing moisture to penetrate deeply into the wall, repointing should be accomplished before cleaning. Related work, such as structural or roof repairs, should be scheduled so that they do not interfere with repointing and so that all work can take maximum advantage of erected scaffolding.

Building managers also must recognize the difficulties that a repointing project can create. The process is time consuming, and scaffolding may need to remain in place for an extended period of time. The joint preparation process can be quite noisy and can generate large quantities of dust which must be controlled, especially at air intakes to protect human health, and also where it might damage operating machinery. Entrances may be blocked from time to time making access difficult for both building tenants and visitors. Clearly, building managers will need to coordinate the repointing work with other events at the site.

Contractor Selection

The ideal way to select a contractor is to ask knowledgeable owners of recently repointed historic buildings for recommendations. Qualified contractors then can provide lists of other repointing projects for inspection. More commonly, however, the contractor for a repointing project is selected through a competitive bidding process over which the client or consultant has only limited control. In this situation it is important to ensure that the specifications stipulate that masons must have a minimum of five years' experience with repointing historic masonry buildings to be eligible to bid on the project. Contracts are awarded to the lowest *responsible*

bidder, and bidders who have performed poorly on other projects usually can be eliminated from consideration on this basis, even if they have the lowest prices.

The contract documents should call for unit prices as well as a base bid. Unit pricing forces the contractor to determine in advance what the cost addition or reduction will be for work which varies from the scope of the base bid. If, for example, the contractor has fifty linear feet less of stone repointing than indicated on the contract documents but thirty linear feet more of brick repointing, it will be easy to determine the final price for the work. Note that each type of work—brick repointing, stone repointing, or similar items—will have its own unit price. The unit price also should reflect quantities; one linear foot of pointing in five different spots will be more expensive than five contiguous linear feet.

Execution of the Work

Test Panels. These panels are prepared by the contractor using the same techniques that will be used on the remainder of the project. Several panel locations—preferably not on the front or other highly visible location of the building—may be necessary to include all types of masonry, joint styles, mortar colors, and other problems likely to be encountered on the job. If cleaning tests, for

Figure 10. Using a hammer and masonry chisel is the least damaging and, thus, generally the preferred method of removing old mortar in preparation for repointing historic masonry. Photo: John P. Speweik.

Figure 11. The damage to the edges and corners of these historic bricks was caused by using a mechanical grinder to rake out the joints. Note the overcutting of the head joint and the damage to the arises (corners) of the bricks. Photo: Lee H. Nelson, FAIA.

Figure 12.. A power grinder, operated correctly by a skilled mason may be used in preparation for repointing to cut wide, horizontal mortar joints, typical of many early-20th century brick structures without causing damage to the brick. Note the use of protective safety equipment. Photo: Robert C. Mack, FAIA.

example, are also to be undertaken, they should be carried out in the same location. Usually a 3 foot by 3 foot area is sufficient for brickwork, while a somewhat larger area may be required for stonework. These panels establish an acceptable standard of work and serve as a benchmark for evaluating and accepting subsequent work on the building.

Joint Preparation. Old mortar should be removed to a minimum depth of 2 to 2-$1/2$ times the width of the joint to ensure an adequate bond and to prevent mortar "popouts" (Fig. 8). For most brick joints, this will require removal of the mortar to a depth of approximately $1/2$ to 1 inch; for stone masonry with wide joints, mortar may need to be removed to a depth of several inches. Any loose or disintegrated mortar beyond this minimum depth also should be removed (Fig. 9).

Although some damage may be inevitable, careful joint preparation can help limit damage to masonry units. The traditional manner of removing old mortar is through the use of hand chisels and mash hammers (Fig. 10). Though labor-intensive, in most instances this method poses the least threat for damage to historic masonry units and produces the best final product.

The most common method of removing mortar, however, is through the use of power saws or grinders. The use of power tools by unskilled masons can be disastrous for historic masonry, particularly soft brick. Using power saws on walls with thin joints, such as most brick walls, almost always will result in damage to the masonry units by breaking the edges and by overcutting on the head, or vertical joints (Fig. 11).

However, small pneumatically-powered chisels generally can be used safely and effectively to remove mortar on historic buildings as long as the masons maintain appropriate control over the equipment.

Under certain circumstances, thin diamond-bladed grinders may be used to cut out *horizontal* joints only on hard portland cement mortar common to most early-20th century masonry buildings (Fig. 12). Usually, automatic tools most successfully remove old mortar without damaging the masonry units when they are used in combination with hand tools in preparation for repointing. Where horizontal joints are uniform and fairly wide, it may be possible to use a power masonry saw to assist the removal of mortar, such as by cutting along the middle of the joint; final mortar removal from the sides of the joints still should be done with a hand chisel and hammer. Caulking cutters with diamond blades can sometimes be used successfully to cut out joints without damaging the masonry. Caulking cutters are slow; they do not rotate, but vibrate at very high speeds, thus minimizing the possibility of damage to masonry units (Fig. 13). Although mechanical tools may be used safely in limited circumstances to cut out horizontal joints in preparation for repointing, they should never be used on vertical joints because of the danger of slipping and cutting into the brick above or below the vertical joint. Using power tools to remove mortar without damaging the surrounding masonry units also necessitates highly skilled masons experienced in working on historic masonry buildings. Contractors

Figure 13. (left) In preparation for repointing, the mortar joints on these granite steps are first cut out mechanically (note the vacuum attached to the cutting tool in foreground to cut down on dust). (right) Final removal of the old mortar is done by hand to avoid damage to the edges of the joints. Mechanical preparation of horizontal joints by an experienced mason may sometimes be acceptable, especially where the joints are quite wide and the masonry is a very hard stone. Photos: Anne Grimmer.

should demonstrate proficiency with power tools before their use is approved.

Using any of these power tools may also be more acceptable on hard stone, such as quartzite or granite, than on terra cotta with its glass-like glaze, or on soft brick or stone. The test panel should determine the acceptability of power tools. If power tools are to be permitted, the contractor should establish a quality control program to account for worker fatigue and similar variables.

Mortar should be removed cleanly from the masonry units, leaving square corners at the back of the cut. Before filling, the joints should be rinsed with a jet of water to remove all loose particles and dust. At the time of filling, the joints should be damp, but with no standing water present. For masonry walls—limestone, sandstone and common brick—that are extremely absorbent, it is recommended that a continual mist of water be applied for a few hours before repointing begins.

Mortar Preparation. Mortar components should be measured and mixed carefully to assure the uniformity of visual and physical characteristics. Dry ingredients are measured by volume and thoroughly mixed before the addition of any water. Sand must be added in a damp, loose condition to avoid over sanding. Repointing mortar is typically pre-hydrated by adding water so it will just hold together, thus allowing it to stand for a period of time before the final water is added. Half the water should be added, followed by mixing for approximately 5 minutes. The remaining water should then be added in small portions until a mortar of the desired consistency is reached. The total volume of water necessary may vary from batch to batch, depending on weather conditions. It is important

to keep the water to a minimum for two reasons: first, a drier mortar is cleaner to work with, and it can be compacted tightly into the joints; second, with no excess water to evaporate, the mortar cures without shrinkage cracks. Mortar should be used within approximately 30 minutes of final mixing, and "retempering," or adding more water, should not be permitted.

Using Lime Putty to Make Mortar. Mortar made with lime putty and sand, sometimes referred to as roughage or course stuff, should be measured by volume, and may require slightly different proportions from those used with hydrated lime (Fig. 14). No additional water is usually needed to achieve a workable consistency because enough water is already contained in the putty. Sand is proportioned first, followed by the lime putty, then mixed for five minutes or until all the sand is thoroughly coated with the lime putty. But mixing, in the familiar sense of turning over with a hoe, sometimes may not be sufficient if the best possible performance is to be obtained from a lime putty mortar. Although the old practice of chopping, beating and ramming the mortar has largely been forgotten, recent field work has confirmed that lime putty and sand rammed and beaten with a wooden mallet or ax handle, interspersed by chopping with a hoe, can significantly improve workability and performance. The intensity of this action increases the overall lime/sand contact and removes any surplus water by compacting the other ingredients. It may also be advantageous for larger projects to use a mortar pan mill for mixing. Mortar pan mills which have a long tradition in Europe produce a superior lime putty mortar not attainable with today's modern paddle and drum type mixers.

For larger repointing projects the lime putty and sand can be mixed together ahead of time and stored indefinitely, on or off site, which eliminates the need for piles of sand on the job site. This mixture, which resembles damp brown sugar, must be protected from the air in sealed containers with a wet piece of burlap over the top or sealed in a large plastic bag to prevent evaporation and premature carbonation. The lime putty and sand mixture can be recombined into a workable plastic state months later with no additional water.

If portland cement is specified in a lime putty and sand mortar—Type O (1:2:9) or Type K (1:3:11)—the portland cement should first be mixed into a slurry paste before adding it to the lime putty and sand. Not only will this ensure that the portland cement is evenly distributed throughout the mixture, but if dry portland cement is added to wet ingredients it tends to "ball up," jeopardizing dispersion. (Usually water must be added to the lime putty and sand anyway once the portland cement is introduced.) Any color pigments should be added at this stage and mixed for a full five minutes. The mortar should be used within 30 minutes to 1 ½ hours and it should not be retempered. Once portland cement has been added the mortar can no longer be stored.

Filling the Joint. Where existing mortar has been removed to a depth of greater than 1 inch, these deeper areas should be filled first, compacting the new mortar in several layers. The back of the entire joint should be filled successively by applying approximately ¼ inch of mortar, packing it well into the back corners. This

Figure 14. Mixing mortar using lime putty: (a) proportioning sand; (b) proportioning lime putty; (c) placing lime putty on top of sand; (d) mixing sand over lime putty; (e) hand mixing mortar; and, (f) sample of mortar after mixing. Photos: John P. Speweik.

application may extend along the wall for several feet. As soon as the mortar has reached thumb-print hardness, another 1/4 inch layer of mortar—approximately the same thickness—may be applied. Several layers will be needed to fill the joint flush with the outer surface of the masonry. It is important to allow each layer time to harden before the next layer is applied; most of the mortar shrinkage occurs during the hardening process and layering thus minimizes overall shrinkage.

When the final layer of mortar is thumb-print hard, the joint should be tooled to match the historic joint (Fig. 15). Proper timing of the tooling is important for uniform color and appearance. If tooled when too soft, the color will be lighter than expected, and hairline cracks may occur; if tooled when too hard, there may be dark streaks called "tool burning," and good closure of the mortar against the masonry units will not be achieved.

If the old bricks or stones have worn, rounded edges, it is best to recess the final mortar slightly from the face of the masonry. This treatment will help avoid a joint which is visually wider than the actual joint; it also will avoid creation of a large, thin featheredge which is easily damaged, thus admitting water (Fig. 16). After tooling, excess mortar can be removed from the edge of the joint by brushing with a natural bristle or nylon brush. Metal bristle brushes should never be used on historic masonry.

Curing Conditions. The preliminary hardening of high-lime content mortars—those mortars that contain more lime by volume than portland cement, i.e., Type O (1:2:9), Type K (1:3:11), and straight lime/sand, Type "L"(0:1:3) —takes place fairly rapidly as water in the mix is lost to the porous surface of the masonry and through evaporation. A high lime mortar (especially Type "L") left to dry out too rapidly can result in chalking, poor adhesion, and poor durability. Periodic wetting of the repointed area after the mortar joints are thumb-print hard and have been finish tooled may significantly accelerate the carbonation process. When feasible, misting using a hand sprayer with a fine nozzle can be simple to do for a day or two after repointing. Local conditions will dictate the frequency of wetting, but initially it may be as often as every hour and gradually reduced to every three or four hours. Walls should be covered with burlap for the first three days after repointing. (Plastic may be used, but it should be tented out and not placed directly against the wall.) This helps keep the walls damp and protects them from direct sunlight. Once carbonation of the lime has begun, it will continue for many years and the lime will gain strength as it reverts back to calcium carbonate within the wall.

Aging the Mortar. Even with the best efforts at matching the existing mortar color, texture, and materials, there will usually be a visible difference between the old and

Figure 15. *The profile of the repointed joints on the left replicate the historic joints around the corner to the right on the front of this stone building in Leesburg, VA. The contractor's pride in the repointing work is evident by the signature in the vertical joint. Photo: Anne Grimmer.*

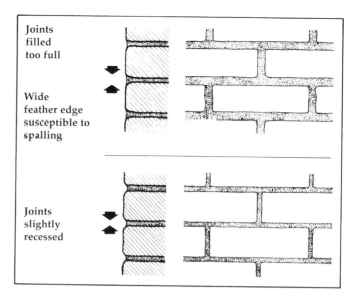

Figure 16. *Comparison of visual effect of full mortar joints vs. slightly recessed joints. Filling joints too full hides the actual joint thickness and changes the character of the original brickwork. Drawing: Robert C. Mack, FAIA.*

new work, partly because the new mortar has been matched to the unweathered portions of the historic mortar. Another reason for a slight mismatch may be that the sand is more exposed in old mortar due to the slight erosion of the lime or cement. Although spot repointing is generally preferable and some color difference should be acceptable, if the difference between old and new mortar is too extreme, it may be advisable in some instances to repoint an entire area of a wall, or an entire feature such as a bay, to minimize the difference between the old and the new mortar. If the mortars have been properly matched, usually the best way to deal with surface color differences is to let the mortars age naturally. Other treatments to overcome these differences, including cleaning the non-repointed areas or staining the new mortar, should be carefully tested prior to implementation.

Staining the new mortar to achieve a better color match is generally not recommended, but it may be appropriate in some instances. Although staining may provide an initial match, the old and new mortars may weather at different rates, leading to visual differences after a few seasons. In addition, the mixtures used to stain the mortar may be harmful to the masonry; for example, they may introduce salts into the masonry which can lead to efflorescence.

Cleaning the Repointed Masonry. If repointing work is carefully executed, there will be little need for cleaning other than to remove the small amount of mortar from the edge of the joint following tooling. This can be done with a stiff natural bristle or nylon brush after the mortar has dried, but before it is initially set (1-2 hours). Mortar that has hardened can usually be removed with a wooden paddle or, if necessary, a chisel.

Further cleaning is best accomplished with plain water and natural bristle or nylon brushes. If chemicals must

be used, they should be selected with extreme caution. Improper cleaning can lead to deterioration of the masonry units, deterioration of the mortar, mortar smear, and efflorescence. New mortar joints are especially susceptible to damage because they do not become fully cured for several months. Chemical cleaners, particularly acids, should never be used on dry masonry. The masonry should always be completely soaked once with water before chemicals are applied. After cleaning, the walls should be flushed again with plain water to remove all traces of the chemicals.

Several precautions should be taken if a freshly repointed masonry wall is to be cleaned. First, the mortar should be fully hardened before cleaning. Thirty days is usually sufficient, depending on weather and exposure; as mentioned previously, the mortar will continue to cure even after it has hardened. Test panels should be prepared to evaluate the effects of different cleaning

Figure 17. *This photograph shows the significant visual change to the character of this historic brick building that has resulted from improper repointing procedures and a noticeably increased thickness of the mortar joints. Photo: Lee H. Nelson, FAIA.*

Mortar Types			
(Measured by volume)			
Designation	Cement	Hydrated Lime or Lime Putty	Sand
M	1	$1/4$	3 - 3 $3/4$
S	1	$1/2$	4 - 4 $1/2$
N	1	1	5 - 6
O	1	2	8 - 9
K	1	3	10 - 12
"L"	0	1	2 $1/4$ - 3

Suggested Mortar Types for Different Exposures			
	Exposure		
Masonry Material	Sheltered	Moderate	Severe
Very Durable: granite, hard-cored brick, etc.	O	N	S
Moderately Durable: limestone, durable stone, molded brick	K	O	N
Minimally Durable: soft hand-made brick	"L"	K	O

methods. Generally, on newly repointed masonry walls, only very low pressure (100 psi) water washing supplemented by stiff natural bristle or nylon brushes should be used, except on glazed or polished surfaces, where only soft cloths should be used.**

New construction "bloom" or efflorescence occasionally appears within the first few months of repointing and usually disappears through the normal process of weathering. If the efflorescence is not removed by natural processes, the safest way to remove it is by dry brushing with stiff natural or nylon bristle brushes followed by wet brushing. Hydrochloric (muriatic) acid, is generally ineffective, and it should not be used to remove efflorescence. It may liberate additional salts, which, in turn, can lead to more efflorescence.

Surface Grouting is sometimes suggested as an alternative to repointing brick buildings, in particular. This process involves the application of a thin coat of cement-based grout to the mortar joints and the mortar/brick interface. To be effective the grout must extend slightly onto the face of the masonry units, thus widening the joint visually. The change in the joint appearance can alter the historic character of the structure to an unacceptable degree. In addition, although masking of the bricks is intended to keep the grout off the remainder of the face of the bricks, some level of residue, called "veiling," will inevitably remain. Surface grouting cannot substitute for the more extensive work of repointing, and it is not a recommended treatment for historic masonry.

**Additional information on masonry cleaning is presented in *Preservation Briefs 1: The Cleaning and Waterproof Coating of Masonry Buildings*, Robert C. Mack, AIA, Washington, D.C.: Technical Preservation Services, National Park Service, U.S. Department of the Interior, 1975; and *Keeping it Clean: Removing Exterior Dirt, Paint, Stains & Graffiti from Historic Masonry Buildings*, Anne E. Grimmer, Washington, D.C.: Technical Preservation Services, National Park Service, U.S. Department of the Interior, 1988.

Summary

For the Owner/Administrator. The owner or administrator of a historic building should remember that repointing is likely to be a lengthy and expensive process. First, there must be adequate time for evaluation of the building and investigation into the cause of problems. Then, there will be time needed for preparation of the contract documents. The work itself is precise, time-consuming and noisy, and scaffolding may cover the face of the building for some time. Therefore, the owner must carefully plan the work to avoid problems. Schedules for both repointing and other activities will thus require careful coordination to avoid unanticipated conflicts. The owner must avoid the tendency to rush the work or cut corners if the historic building is to retain its visual integrity and the job is to be durable.

For the Architect/Consultant. Because the primary role of the consultant is to ensure the life of the building, a knowledge of historic construction techniques and the special problems found in older buildings is essential. The consultant must assist the owner in planning for logistical problems relating to research and construction. It is the consultant's responsibility to determine the *cause* of the mortar deterioration and ensure that it is corrected before the masonry is repointed. The consultant must also be prepared to spend more time in project inspections than is customary in modern construction.

For the Masons. Successful repointing depends on the masons themselves. Experienced masons understand the special requirements for work on historic buildings and the added time and expense they require. The entire masonry crew must be willing and able to perform the work in conformance with the specifications, even when the specifications may not be in conformance with standard practice. At the same time, the masons should not hesitate to question the specifications if it appears that the work specified would damage the building.

Visually Examining the Mortar and the Masonry Units

A simple in-situ comparison will help determine the hardness and condition of the mortar and the masonry units. Begin by scraping the mortar with a screwdriver, and gradually tapping harder with a cold chisel and mason's hammer. Masonry units can be tested in the same way beginning, even more gently, by scraping with a fingernail. This relative analysis which is derived from the 10-point hardness scale used to describe minerals, provides a good starting point for selection of an appropriate mortar. It is described more fully in "The Russack System for Brick & Mortar Description" referenced in **Selected Reading** at the end of this Brief.

Mortar samples should be chosen carefully, and picked from a variety of locations on the building to find unweathered mortar, if possible. Portions of the building may have been repointed in the past while other areas may be subject to conditions causing unusual deterioration. There may be several colors of mortar dating from different construction periods or sand used from different sources during the initial construction. Any of these situations can give false readings to the visual or physical characteristics required for the new mortar. Variations should be noted which may require developing more than one mix.

1) Remove with a chisel and hammer three or four unweathered samples of the mortar to be matched from several locations on the building. (Set the largest sample aside—this will be used later for comparison with the repointing mortar). Removing a full representation of samples will allow selection of a "mean" or average mortar sample.

2) Mash the remaining samples with a wooden mallet, or hammer if necessary, until they are separated into their constituent parts. There should be a good handful of the material.

3) Examine the powdered portion—the lime and/or cement matrix of the mortar. Most particularly, note the color. There is a tendency to think of historic mortars as having white binders, but grey portland cement was available by the last quarter of the 19th century, and traditional limes were also sometimes grey. Thus, in some instances, the natural color of the historic binder may be grey, rather than white. The mortar may also have been tinted to create a colored mortar, and this color should be identified at this point.

4) Carefully blow away the powdery material (the lime and/or cement matrix which bound the mortar together).

5) With a low power (10 power) magnifying glass, examine the remaining sand and other materials such as lumps of lime or shell.

6) Note and record the wide range of color as well as the varying sizes of the individual grains of sand, impurities, or other materials.

Other Factors to Consider

Color. Regardless of the color of the binder or colored additives, the sand is the primary material that gives mortar

Figure 19. Mortar joints of 18th century brick buildings were often as much as 1/2 inch wide, cut flush and struck with a grapevine joint, but for window and door surrounds where a finer quality rubbed brick was used, mortar joints were very thin. Photo: National Park Service Files.

its color. A surprising variety of colors of sand may be found in a single sample of historic mortar, and the different sizes of the grains of sand or other materials, such as incompletely ground lime or cement, play an important role in the texture of the repointing mortar. Therefore, when specifying sand for repointing mortar, it may be necessary to obtain sand from several sources and to combine or screen them in order to approximate the range of sand colors and grain sizes in the historic mortar sample.

Pointing Style. Close examination of the historic masonry wall and the techniques used in the original construction will assist in maintaining the visual qualities of the building (Fig. 18). Pointing styles and the methods of producing them should be examined. It is important to look at both the horizontal and the vertical joints to determine the order in which they were tooled and whether they were the same style. Some late-19th and early-20th century buildings, for example, have horizontal joints that were raked back while the vertical joints were finished flush and stained to match the bricks, thus creating the illusion of horizontal bands. Pointing styles may also differ from one facade to another; front walls often received greater attention to mortar detailing than side and rear walls (Fig. 19). **Tuckpointing** is not true repointing but the

Figure 20. This stone garden wall was tuckpointed to match the tuckpointing on the c. 1920s house on the property. Photo: Anne Grimmer.

Figure 18. A cross-section of mortar joint types. (a) Grapevine joints on a mid-18th century brick building; (b) flush joints on a mid-to-late 19th century brick building; (c) beaded joints on a late-19th century brick building; (d) early-20th century beaded joints on rough-cut limestone where the vertical joints were struck prior to the horizontal joints; (e) raked joints on 1920s wire brick; (f) horizontal joints on a 1934 building designed by Frank Lloyd Wright were raked back from the face of the bricks, and the vertical joints were filled with a red-tinted mortar to emphasize the horizontality of the narrow bricks, and struck flush with the face of the bricks; (g) the joints on this 20th century glazed terra-cotta tile building are raked slightly, emphasizing the glazed block face. Photos: National Park Service Files (a,b,e); Robert C. Mack, FAIA (c,d,f,g).

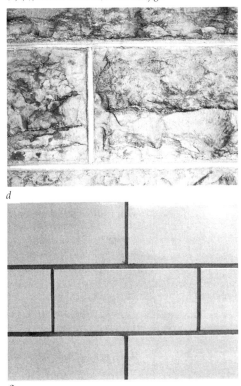

application of a raised joint or lime putty joint on top of flush mortar joints (Fig. 20). **Penciling** is a purely decorative, painted surface treatment over a mortar joint, often in a contrasting color.

Masonry Units. The masonry units should also be examined so that any replacement units will match the historic masonry. Within a wall there may be a wide range of colors, textures, and sizes, particularly with hand-made brick or rough-cut, locally-quarried stone. Replacement units should blend in with the full range of masonry units rather than a single brick or stone.

Matching Color and Texture of the Repointing Mortar

New mortar should match the unweathered interior portions of the historic mortar. The simplest way to check the match is to make a small sample of the proposed mix and allow it to cure at a temperature of approximately 70 degrees F for about a week, or it can be baked in an oven to speed up the curing; this sample is then broken open and the surface is compared with the surface of the largest "saved" sample of historic mortar.

If a proper color match cannot be achieved through the use of natural sand or colored aggregates like crushed marble or brick dust, it may be necessary to use a modern mortar pigment.

During the early stages of the project, it should be determined how closely the new mortar should match the historic mortar. Will "quite close" be sufficient, or is "exactly" expected? The specifications should state this clearly so that the contractor has a reasonable idea how much time and expense will be required to develop an acceptable match.

The same judgment will be necessary in matching replacement terra cotta, stone or brick. If there is a known source for replacements, this should be included in the specifications. If a source cannot be determined prior to the bidding process, the specifications should include an estimated price for the replacement materials with the final price based on the actual cost to the contractor.

Conclusion

A good repointing job is meant to last, at least 30 years, and preferably 50-100 years. Shortcuts and poor craftsmanship result not only in diminishing the historic character of a building, but also in a job that looks bad, and will require future repointing sooner than if the work had been done correctly (Fig. 17). The mortar joint in a historic masonry building has often been called a wall's "first line of defense." Good repointing practices guarantee the long life of the mortar joint, the wall, and the historic structure. Although careful maintenance will help preserve the freshly repointed mortar joints, it is important to remember that mortar joints are intended to be sacrificial and will probably require repointing some time in the future. Nevertheless, if the historic mortar joints proved durable for many years, then careful repointing should have an equally long life, ultimately contributing to the preservation of the entire building.

Selected Reading

Ashurst, John & Nicola. *Practical Building Conservation. Vol. 3: Mortars, Plasters and Renders*. New York: Halsted Press, a Division of John Wiley & Sons, Inc., 1988.

Cliver, E. Blaine. "Tests for the Analysis of Mortar Samples." *Bulletin of the Association for Preservation Technology*. Vol. 6, No. 1 (1974), pp. 68-73.

Coney, William B., AIA. *Masonry Repointing of Twentieth-Century Buildings*. Illinois Preservation Series. Number 10. Springfield, IL: Division of Preservation Services, Illinois Historic Preservation Agency, 1989.

Davidson, J.I. "Masonry Mortar." *Canadian Building Digest*. CBD 163. Ottawa, ONT: Division of Building Research, National Research Council of Canada, 1974.

Ferro, Maximillian L., AIA, RIBA. "The Russack System for Brick and Mortar Description: A Field Method for Assessing Masonry Hardness." *Technology and Conservation*. Vol. 5, No. 2 (Summer 1980), pp. 32-35.

Hooker, Kenneth A. "Field Notes on Repointing." *Aberdeen's Magazine of Masonry Construction*. Vol. 4, No. 8 (August 1991), pp. 326-328.

Jedrzejewska, H. "Old Mortars in Poland: A New Method of Investigation." *Studies in Conservation*. Vol. 5, No. 4 (1960), pp. 132-138.

"Lime's Role in Mortar." *Aberdeen's Magazine of Masonry Construction*. Vol. 9, No. 8 (August 1996), pp. 364-368.

Phillips, Morgan W. "Brief Notes on the Subjects of Analyzing Paints and Mortars and the Recording of Moulding Profiles: The Trouble with Paint and Mortar Analysis." *Bulletin of the Association for Preservation Technology*. Vol. 10, No. 2 (1978), pp. 77-89.

Preparation and Use of Lime Mortars: An Introduction to the Principles of Using Lime Mortars. Scottish Lime Centre for Historic Scotland. Edinburgh: Historic Scotland, 1995.

Schierhorn, Carolyn. "Ensuring Mortar Color Consistency." *Aberdeen's Magazine of Masonry Construction*. Vol. 9, No. 1 (January 1996), pp. 33-35.

"Should Air-Entrained Mortars Be Used?" *Aberdeen's Magazine of Masonry Construction*. Vol. 7, No. 9 (September 1994), pp. 419-422.

Sickels-Taves, Lauren B. "Creep, Shrinkage, and Mortars in Historic Preservation." *Journal of Testing and Evaluation, JTEVA*. Vol. 23, No. 6 (November 1995), pp. 447-452.

Speweik, John P. *The History of Masonry Mortar in America, 1720-1995*. Arlington, VA: National Lime Association, 1995.

Speweik, John P. "Repointing Right: Why Using Modern Mortar Can Damage a Historic House." *Old-House Journal*. Vol. XXV, No. 4 (July-August 1997), pp. 46-51.

Technical Notes on Brick Construction. Brick Institute of America, Reston, VA.
"Moisture Resistance of Brick Masonry: Maintenance." 7F. February 1986.
"Mortars for Brick Masonry." 8 Revised II. November 1989.
"Standard Specification for Portland Cement-Lime Mortar for Brick Masonry." 8A Revised. September 1988.
"Mortar for Brick Masonry-Selection and Controls." 8B Reissued. September 1988. (July/August 1976).
"Guide Specifications for Brick Masonry, Part V Mortar and Grout." 11E Revised. September 1991.
"Bonds and Patterns in Brickwork." 30 Reissued. September 1988.

Useful Addresses

Brick Institute of America
11490 Commerce Park Drive
Reston, VA 22091

National Lime Association
200 N. Glebe Road, Suite 800
Arlington, VA 22203

Portland Cement Association
5420 Old Orchard Road
Skokie, IL 60077

Acknowledgments

Robert C. Mack, FAIA, is a principal in the firm of MacDonald & Mack, Architects, Ltd., an architectural firm that specializes in historic buildings in Minneapolis, Minnesota. **John P. Speweik, CSI,** Toledo, Ohio, is a 5th-generation stonemason, and principal in U.S. Heritage Group, Inc., Chicago, Illinois, which does custom historic mortar matching. **Anne Grimmer,** Senior Architectural Historian, Heritage Preservation Services Program, National Park Service, was responsible for developing and coordinating the revision of this Preservation Brief, incorporating professional comments, and the technical editing.

The authors and the editor wish to thank the following for the professional and technical review they provided: Mark Macpherson and Ron Peterson, Masonry Restoration Contractors, Macpherson-Towne Company, Minneapolis, MN; Lorraine Schnabel, Architectural Conservator, John Milner Associates, Inc., Philadelphia, PA; Lauren B. Sickels-Taves, Ph.D., Architectural Conservator, Biohistory International, Huntington Woods, MI; and the following National Park Service professional staff, including: E. Blaine Cliver, Chief, Historic American Buildings Survey/Historic American Engineering Record; Douglas C. Hicks, Deputy Superintendent, Historic Preservation Training Center, Frederick, MD; Chris McGuigan, Supervisory Exhibits Specialist, Historic Preservation Training Center, Frederick, MD; Charles E. Fisher, Sharon C. Park, FAIA, John Sandor, Technical Preservation Services Branch, Heritage Preservation Services, and Kay D. Weeks, Heritage Preservation Services.

The original version of this brief, *Repointing Mortar Joints in Historic Brick Buildings*, was written by Robert C. Mack in 1976, and was revised and updated in 1980 by Robert C. Mack, de Teel Patterson Tiller, and James S. Askins.

Front Cover: Repointing a historic brick building using a lime-based mortar. Traditional lime mortars have a consistency that enables the mortar to cling to a repointing tool while in a vertical position. Photo: John P. Speweik.

October 1998

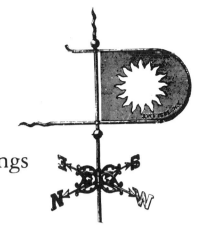

3

Conserving Energy in Historic Buildings

Baird M. Smith, AIA

With the dwindling supply of energy resources and new efficiency demands placed on the existing building stock, many owners of historic buildings and their architects are assessing the ability of these buildings to conserve energy with an eye to improving thermal performance. This brief has been developed to assist those persons attempting energy conservation measures and weatherization improvements such as adding insulation and storm windows or caulking of exterior building joints. In historic buildings, many measures can result in the inappropriate alteration of important architectural features, or, perhaps even worse, cause serious damage to the historic building materials through unwanted chemical reactions or moisture-caused deterioration. This brief recommends measures that will achieve the greatest energy savings with the least alteration to the historic buildings, while using materials that do not cause damage and that represent sound economic investments.

Inherent Energy Saving Characteristics of Historic Buildings

Many historic buildings have energy-saving physical features and devices that contribute to good thermal performance. Studies by the Energy Research and Development Adminis-

Figure 1. This 1891 Courthouse and Post Office in Rochester, New York, has built-in energy conserving features such as, heavy masonry walls, operable windows, an interior skylighted atrium which provides light and ventilation, and roof-top ventilators which keep the building cooler in the summer. Also note the presence of awnings in this old photograph.

tration (see bibliography) show that the buildings with the poorest energy efficiency are actually those built between 1940

Figure 2. Shutters can be used to minimize the problem of summer heat gain by shading the windows. If operable shutters are in place, their use will help reduce the summer cooling load. (Photo: Baird Smith)

and 1975. Older buildings were found to use less energy for heating and cooling and hence probably require fewer weatherization improvements. They use less energy because they were built with a well-developed sense of physical comfort and because they maximized the natural sources of heating, lighting and ventilation. The historic building owner should understand these inherent energy-saving qualities.

The most obvious (and almost universal) inherent energy saving characteristic was the use of *operable windows* to provide natural ventilation and light. In addition, historic commercial and public buildings often include interior light/ventilation courts, roof-top ventilators, clerestories or skylights (see figure 1). These features provide energy efficient fresh air and light, assuring that energy consuming mechanical devices may be needed only to supplement the natural energy sources. Any time the mechanical heating and air conditioning equipment can be turned off and the windows opened, energy will be saved.

1

Figure 3. Southern mansions typify climate conscious design. The wide roof overhangs, exterior porches, shade trees, heavy masonry walls (painted white), and living quarters on the second floor (to catch evening breezes and escape the radiant heat from the earth's surface) all are energy saving characteristics which provide reasonably comfortable living spaces without mechanical air conditioning. (Photo: Marcia Axtmann Smith)

Early builders and architects dealt with the poor thermal properties of windows in two ways. First, the number of windows in a building was kept to only those necessary to provide adequate light and ventilation. This differs from the approach in many modern buildings where the percentage of windows in a wall can be nearly 100%. Historic buildings, where the ratio of glass to wall is often less than 20%, are better energy conservers than most new buildings. Secondly, to minimize the heat gain or loss from windows, historic buildings often include interior or exterior shutters, interior venetian blinds, curtains and drapes, or exterior awnings (see figure 2). Thus, a historic window could remain an energy efficient component of a building.

There are other physical characteristics that enable historic buildings to be energy efficient. For instance, in the warmer climates of the United States, buildings were often built to minimize the heat gain from the summer sun. This was accomplished by introducing exterior balconies, porches, wide roof overhangs, awnings and shade trees. In addition, many of these buildings were designed with the living spaces on the second floor to catch breezes and to escape the radiant heat from the earth's surface. Also, exterior walls were often painted light colors to reflect the hot summer sun, resulting in cooler interior living spaces (see figure 3).

Winter heat loss from buildings in the northern climates was reduced by using heavy masonry walls, minimizing the number and size of windows, and often using dark paint colors for the exterior walls. The heavy masonry walls used so typically in the late 19th century and early 20th century, exhibit characteristics that improve their thermal performance beyond that formerly recognized (see figure 4). It has been determined that walls of large mass and weight (thick brick or stone) have the advantage of *high thermal inertia*, also known as the "M factor." This inertia modifies the thermal resistance (R factor)* of the wall by lengthening the time scale of heat transmission. For instance, a wall with high thermal inertia, subjected to solar radiation for an hour, will absorb the heat at its outside surface, but transfer it to the interior over a period as long as 6 hours. Conversely, a wall having the same R factor, but low thermal inertia, will transfer the heat in perhaps 2 hours. High thermal inertia is the reason many older public and commercial buildings, without modern air conditioning, still feel cool on the inside throughout the summer. The heat from the midday sun does not penetrate the buildings until late afternoon and evening, when it is unoccupied.

---

*R factor is the measure of the ability of insulation to decrease heat flow. The higher the factor, the better the thermal performance of the material.

2

Although these characteristics may not typify all historic buildings, the point is that historic buildings often have thermal properties that need little improvement. One must understand the inherent energy-saving qualities of a building, and assure, by re-opening the windows for instance, that the building functions as it was intended.

To reduce heating and cooling expenditures there are two broad courses of action that may be taken. First, begin **passive measures** to assure that a building and its existing components function as efficiently as possible without the necessity of making alterations or adding new materials. The second course of action is **preservation retrofitting**, which includes altering the building by making appropriate weatherization measures to improve thermal performance. Undertaking the passive measures and the preservation retrofitting recommended here could result in a 50% decrease in energy expenditures in historic buildings.

Passive Measures

The first passive measures to utilize are **operational controls**; that is, controlling *how* and *when* a building is used. These controls incorporate programmatic planning and scheduling efforts by the owner to minimize usage of energy-consuming equipment. A building owner should survey and quantify all aspects of energy usage, by evaluating the monies expended for electricity, gas, and fuel oil for a year, and by surveying how and when each room is used. This will identify ways of conserving energy by initiating operational controls such as:

- lowering the thermostat in the winter, raising it in the summer
- controlling the temperature in those rooms actually used
- reducing the level of illumination and number of lights (maximize natural light)
- using operable windows, shutters, awnings and vents as originally intended to control interior environment (maximize fresh air)
- having mechanical equipment serviced regularly to ensure maximum efficiency
- cleaning radiators and forced air registers to ensure proper operation

Figure 4. Heavy masonry walls in office buildings dramatically reduce the need for summer cooling because the thermal inertia (M factor) of the massive wall increases its thermal resistance (R factor), thus delaying the heat transfer into the building until late afternoon when the office workers have gone home. (Photo: Baird Smith)

Figure 5. Moisture migration through walls and roofing occurs as a matter of course in northern winter climates. Problems occur if there is no vapor barrier because the moisture may saturate the insulation and greatly reduce its thermal performance, as well as creating the potential for deterioration of the adjacent materials.

a. Typical wood frame wall where moist inside air freely migrates to the outside. Moisture may condense in the wall cavity and be absorbed into the adjacent materials and evaporate as the wall is heated by the sun.

b. Typical wall condition with insulation and a vapor barrier facing in (toward the heated side of the wall). The vapor barrier prevents moisture migration, thus keeping the insulation dry.

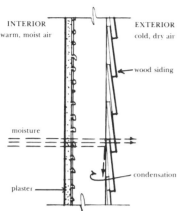

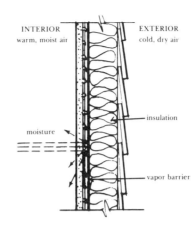

The passive measures outlined above can save as much as 30% of the energy used in a building. They should be the first undertakings to save energy in any existing building and are particularly appropriate for historic buildings because they do not necessitate building alterations or the introduction of new materials that may cause damage. Passive measures make energy sense, common sense, and preservation sense!

Preservation Retrofitting

In addition to passive measures, building owners may undertake certain retrofitting measures that will not jeopardize the historic character of the building and can be accomplished at a reasonable cost. Preservation retrofitting improves the thermal performance of the building, resulting in another 20%–30% reduction in energy.

When considering retrofitting measures, historic building owners should keep in mind that there are no permanent

solutions. One can only meet the standards being applied today with today's materials and techniques. In the future, it is likely that the standards and the technologies will change and a whole new retrofitting plan may be necessary. Thus, owners of historic buildings should limit retrofitting measures to those that achieve reasonable energy savings, at reasonable costs, with the least intrusion or impact on the character of the building. Overzealous retrofitting, which introduces the risk of damage to historic building materials, should not be undertaken.

The preservation retrofitting measures presented here, were developed to address the three most common problems in historic structures caused by some retrofitting actions. The first problem concerns retrofitting actions that necessitated inappropriate building alterations, such as the wholesale removal of historic windows, or the addition of insulating

The Secretary of the Interior's Standards for Historic Preservation Projects

The Standards for Historic Preservation were developed for the Historic Preservation Fund Grants-in-Aid Program and authorized by the National Historic Preservation Act of 1966. The standards are also used for determining whether a rehabilitation project qualifies as a "certified rehabilitation" pursuant to Section 2124 of the Tax Reform Act of 1976. There are eight "General Standards" (listed below), and additional specific standards and guidelines for the various categories of historic preservation projects.

General Standards

(Those shown in bold print are most applicable to preservation retrofitting.)

1. **Every reasonable effort shall be made to provide a compatible use for a property that requires minimal alteration of the building structure, or site and its environment, or to use a property for its originally intended purpose.**
2. **The distinguishing original qualities or character of a building, structure, or site and its environment shall not be destroyed. The removal or alteration of any historic material or distinctive architectural features should be avoided when possible.**
3. **All buildings, structures, and sites shall be recognized as products of their own time. Alterations, which have no**

historical basis and which seek to create an earlier appearance, shall be discouraged.
4. Changes, which may have taken place in the course of time, are evidence of the history and development of a building, structure, or site and its environment. These changes may have acquired significance in their own right, and this significance shall be recognized and respected.
5. **Distinctive stylistic features or examples of skilled craftsmanship, which characterize a building, structure, or site, shall be treated with sensitivity.**
6. **Deteriorated architectural features shall be repaired rather than replaced, wherever possible. In the event replacement is necessary, the new material should match the material being replaced in composition, design, color, texture, and other visual qualities. Repair or replacement of missing architectural features should be based on accurate duplications of features, substantiated by historical, physical, or pictorial evidence rather than on conjectural designs or the availability of different architectural elements from other buildings or structures.**
7. The surface cleaning of structures shall be undertaken with the gentlest means possible. Sandblasting and other cleaning methods that will damage the historic building materials shall not be undertaken.
8. Every reasonable effort shall be made to protect and preserve archeological resources affected by, or adjacent to any acquisition, protection, stabilization, preservation, rehabilitation, restoration, or reconstruction project.

aluminum siding, or installing dropped ceilings in significant interior spaces. To avoid such alterations, refer to the Secretary of the Interior's "Standards for Historic Preservation Projects" which provide the philosophical and practical basis for all preservation retrofitting measures.

The second problem area is to assure that retrofitting measures do not create moisture-related deterioration problems. One must recognize that large quantities of moisture are present on the interior of buildings.

In northern climates, the moisture may be a problem during the winter when it condenses on cold surfaces such as windows. As the moisture passes through the walls and roof it may condense within these materials, creating the potential for deterioration. The problem is avoided if a vapor barrier is added *facing in* (see figure 5).

In southern climates, insulation and vapor barriers are handled quite differently because moisture problems occur in the summer when the moist outside air is migrating to the interior of the building. In these cases, the insulation is installed with the vapor barrier *facing out* (opposite the treatment of northern climates). Expert advice should be sought to avoid moisture-related problems to insulation and building materials in southern climates.

The third problem area involves the avoidance of those materials that are chemically or physically incompatible with existing materials, or that are improperly installed. A serious problem exists with certain cellulose insulations that use ammonium or aluminum sulfate as a fire retardant, rather than boric acid which causes no problems. The sulfates react with moisture in the air forming sulfuric acid which can cause damage to most metals (including plumbing and wiring), building stones, brick and wood. In one instance, a metal building insulated with cellulose of this type collapsed when the sulfuric acid weakened the structural connections! To avoid problems such as these, refer to the recommendations provided here, and consult with local officials, such as a building inspector, the better business bureau, or a consumer protection agency.

Before a building owner or architect can plan retrofitting measures, some of the existing physical conditions of the building should be investigated. The basic building components (attic, roof, walls and basement) should be checked to determine the methods of construction used and the presence of insulation. Check the insulation for full coverage and whether there is a vapor barrier. This inspection will aid in determining the need for additional insulation, what type of insulation to use (batt, blown-in, or poured), and where to install it. In addition, sources of air infiltration should be checked at doors, windows, or where floor and ceiling systems meet the walls. Lastly, it is important to check the condition of the exterior wall materials, such as painted wooden siding or brick, and the condition of the roof, to determine any weather tightness of the building. A building owner must assure that rain and snow are kept out of the building before expending money for weatherization improvements.

Retrofitting Measures

The following listing includes the most common retrofitting measures; some measures are highly recommended for a preservation retrofitting plan, but, as will be explained, others are less beneficial or even harmful to the historic building:

- Air Infiltration
- Attic Insulation
- Storm Windows
- Basement and Crawl Space Insulation
- Duct and Pipe Insulation
- Awnings and Shading Devices
- Doors and Storm Doors
- Vestibules
- Replacement Windows
- Wall Insulation—Wood Frame
- Wall Insulation—Masonry Cavity Walls
- Wall Insulation—Installed on the Inside
- Wall Insulation—Installed on the Outside
- Waterproof Coatings for Masonry

The recommended measures to preservation retrofitting begin with those at the top of the list. The first ones are the simplest, least expensive, and offer the highest potential for saving energy. The remaining measures are not recommended for general use either because of potential technical and preservation problems, or because of the costs outweighing the anticipated energy savings. Specific solutions must be determined based on the facts and circumstances of the particular problem; therefore, advice from professionals experienced in historic preservation, such as, architects, engineers and mechanical contractors should be solicited.

Air Infiltration: Substantial heat loss occurs because cold outside air infiltrates the building through loose windows, doors, and cracks in the outside shell of the building. Adding weatherstripping to doors and windows, and caulking of open cracks and joints will substantially reduce this infiltration. Care should be taken not to reduce infiltration to the point where the building is completely sealed and moisture migration is prevented. Without some infiltration, condensation problems could occur throughout the building. Avoid caulking and weatherstripping materials that, when applied, introduce inappropriate colors or otherwise visually impair the architectural character of the building. Reducing air infiltration should be the first priority of a preservation retrofitting plan. The cost is low, little skill is required, and the benefits are substantial.

Attic Insulation: Heat rising through the attic and roof is a major source of heat loss, and reducing this heat loss should be one of the highest priorities in preservation retrofitting. Adding insulation in accessible attic spaces is very effective in saving energy and is generally accomplished at a reasonable cost, requiring little skill to install. The most common attic insulations include blankets of fiberglass and mineral wool, blown-in cellulose (treated with boric acid only), blowing wool, vermiculite, and blown fiberglass. If the attic is unheated (not used for habitation), then the insulation is placed between the floor joists with the **vapor barrier facing down.** If flooring is present, or if the attic is heated, the insulation is generally placed between the roof rafters with **vapor barrier facing in.** All should be installed according to the manufacturer's recommendations. A weatherization manual entitled, "In the Bank . . . or Up the Chimney" (see the bibliography) provides detailed descriptions about a variety of installation methods used for attic insulation. The manual also recommends the amount of attic insulation used in various parts of the country. If the attic has some insulation, add more (but *without* a vapor barrier) to reach the total depth recommended.

Problems occur if the attic space is not properly ventilated. This lack of ventilation will cause the insulation to become saturated and lose its thermal effectiveness. The attic is adequately ventilated when the net area of ventilation (free area of a louver or vent) equals approximately 1/300 of the attic floor area. With adequate attic ventilation, the addition of attic insulation should be one of the highest priorities of a preservation retrofitting plan.

If the attic floor is inaccessible, or if it is impossible to add insulation along the roof rafters, consider attaching insulation to the ceilings of the rooms immediately below the attic. Some insulations are manufactured specifically for these cases and include a durable surface which becomes the new ceiling. This option should not be considered if it causes irreparable damage to historic or architectural spaces or features; however, in other cases, it could be a recommended measure of a preservation retrofitting plan.

Storm Windows: Windows are a primary source of heat loss because they are both a poor thermal barrier (R factor of only 0.89) and often a source of air infiltration. Adding storm windows greatly improves these poor characteristics. If a building has existing storm windows (either wood or metal framed), they should be retained. Assure they are tight fitting and in good working condition. If they are not in place, it is a recommended measure of a preservation retrofitting plan to add new metal framed windows on the exterior. This will result in a window assembly (historic window plus storm window) with an R factor of 1.79 which outperforms a double paned window assembly (with an air space up to ½") that only has an R factor of 1.72. When installing the storm windows, be careful not to damage the historic window frame. If the metal frames visually impair the appearance of the building, it may be necessary to paint them to match the color of the historic frame (see figure 6).

Triple-track metal storm windows are recommended because they are readily available, in numerous sizes, and at a reasonable cost. If a pre-assembled storm window is not available for a particular window size, and a custom-made storm window is required, the cost can be very high. In this case, compare the cost of manufacture and installation with the expected cost savings resulting from the increased thermal efficiency. Generally, custom-made storm windows, of either wood or metal frames, are not cost effective, and would not be recommended in a preservation retrofitting plan.

Interior storm window installations can be as thermally effective as exterior storm windows; however, there is high potential for damage to the historic window and sill from condensation. With storm windows on the interior, the outer sash (in this case the historic sash) will be cold in the winter, and hence moisture may condense there. This condensation often collects on the flat surface of the sash or window sill causing paint to blister and the wood to begin to deteriorate.

Rigid plastic sheets are used as interior storm windows by attaching them directly to the historic sash. They are not quite as effective as the storm windows described previously because of the possibility of air infiltration around the historic sash. If the rigid plastic sheets are used, assure that they are installed with minimum damage to the historic sash, removed periodically to allow the historic sash to dry, and that the historic frame and sash are completely caulked and weatherstripped.

In most cases, interior storm windows of either metal frames or of plastic sheets are not recommended for preservation retrofitting because of the potential for damage to the historic window. If interior storm windows are in place, the potential for moisture deterioration can be lessened by opening (or removing, depending on the type) the storm windows during the mild months allowing the historic window to dry thoroughly.

Basement and Crawl Space Insulation: Substantial heat is lost through cold basements and crawl spaces. Adding insulation in these locations is an effective preservation retrofitting measure and should be a high priority action. It is complicated, however, because of the excessive moisture that is often present. One must be aware of this and assure that insulation is properly installed for the specific location. For instance, in crawl spaces and certain unheated basements, the insulation is generally placed between the first floor joists (the ceiling of the basement) with the **vapor barrier facing up.** Do not staple the insulation in place, because the staples often rust away. Use special anchors developed for insulation in moist areas such as these.

In heated basements, or where the basement contains the heating plant (furnace), or where there are exposed water and sewer pipes, insulation should be installed against foundation walls. Begin the insulation within the first floor joists, and proceed down the wall to a point at least 3 feet below the

Figure 6. The addition of triple track storm windows, as shown here, greatly improves the thermal performance of existing window assemblies, with a minimal impact on the appearance of the building. (Photo: Baird Smith)

exterior ground level if possible, with the **vapor barrier facing in.** Use either batt or rigid insulation.

Installing insulation in the basement or crawl space should be a high priority of a preservation retrofitting plan, as long as adequate provision is made to ventilate the unheated space, perhaps even by installing an exhaust fan.

Duct and Pipe Insulation: Wrapping insulation around heating and cooling ducts and hot water pipes, is a recommended preservation retrofitting measure. Use insulation which is intended for this use and install it according to manufacturer's recommendations. Note that air conditioning ducts will be cold in the summer, and hence moisture will condense there. Use insulation with the **vapor barrier facing out,** away from the duct. These measures are inexpensive and have little potential for damage to the historic building.

Awnings and Shading Devices: In the past, awnings and trees were used extensively to provide shade to keep buildings cooler in the summer. If awnings or trees are in place, keep them in good condition, and take advantage of their energy-saving contribution. Building owners may consider adding awnings or trees if the summer cooling load is substantial. If awnings are added, assure that they are installed without damaging the building or visually impairing its architectural character (see figure 7). If trees are added, select deciduous trees that provide shade in the summer but, after dropping their leaves, would allow the sun to warm the building in the winter. When planting trees, assure that they are no closer than 10 feet to the building to avoid damage to the foundations. Adding either awnings or shade trees may be expensive, but in hot climates, the benefits can justify the costs.

Doors and Storm Doors: Most historic wooden doors, if they are solid wood or paneled, have fairly good thermal properties and should not be replaced, especially if they are important architectural features. Assure that the frames and doors have proper maintenance, regular painting, and that caulking and weatherstripping is applied as necessary.

A storm door would improve the thermal performance of the historic door; however, recent studies indicate that installing a storm door is not normally cost effective in residential settings. The costs are high compared to the anticipated savings. Therefore, storm doors should only be added to buildings in cold climates, and added in such a way to minimize the visual impact on the building's appearance. The storm door design should be compatible with the architectural character of the building and may be painted to match the colors of the historic door.

Vestibules: Vestibules create a secondary air space at a doorway to reduce air infiltration occurring while the primary door is open. If a vestibule is in place, retain it. If not, adding a vestibule, either on the exterior or interior, should be carefully considered to determine the possible visual impact on the character of the building. The energy savings would be comparatively small compared to construction costs. Adding a vestibule should be considered in very cold climates, or where door use is very high, but in either case, the additional question of visual intrusion must be resolved before it is added. For most cases with historic buildings, adding a vestibule is not recommended.

Replacement Windows: Unfortunately, a common weatherization measure, especially in larger buildings, has been the replacement of historic windows with modern double paned windows. The intention was to improve the thermal performance of the existing windows and to reduce long-term maintenance costs. The evidence is clear that adding exterior storm windows is a viable alternative to replacing the historic windows and it is the recommended approach in preservation retrofitting. However, if the historic windows are severely deteriorated and their repair would be impractical, or economically infeasible, then replacement windows may be warranted. The new windows, of either wood or metal, should closely match the historic windows in size, number of panes, muntin shape, frame, color and reflective qualities of the glass.

Wall Insulation—Wood Frame: The addition of wall insulation in a wood frame building is generally not recommended as a preservation retrofitting measure because the costs are high, and the potential for damage to historic building materials is even higher. Also, wall insulation is not particularly effective for small frame buildings (one story) because the heat loss from the uninsulated walls is a relatively small percentage of the total, and part of that can be attributed to infiltration. If, however, the historic building is two or more stories, and is located in a cold climate, wall insulation may be considered if extreme care (as explained later) is exercised with its installation.

The installation of wall insulation in historic frame buildings can result in serious technical and preservation problems. As discussed before, insulation must be kept dry to function properly, and requires a vapor barrier and some provision for air movement. Introducing insulation in wall cavities, without a vapor barrier and some ventilation can be disastrous. The insulation would become saturated, losing its thermal properties, and in fact, actually increasing the heat loss through the wall. Additionally, the moisture (in vapor form) may condense into water droplets and begin serious deterioration of adjacent building materials such as sills, window frames, framing and bracing. The situation is greatly complicated, because correcting such problems could necessitate the complete (and costly) dismantling of the exterior or interior wall surfaces. It should be clear that adding wall insulation has the potential for causing serious damage to historic building materials.

If adding wall insulation to frame buildings is determined to be absolutely necessary, the first approach should be to consider the careful removal of the exterior siding so that it may later be reinstalled. Then introduce batt insulation with the **vapor barrier facing in** into the now accessible wall cavity. The first step in this approach is an investigation to determine if the siding can be removed without causing serious damage.

Figure 7. The awnings on the Willard Library in Evansville, Indiana, reduce heat gain in the summer and, when they are raised in the winter, radiant heat from the sun provides free supplementary heat. (Photo: Lee H. Nelson)

Figure 8. The white material seen between the wooden wall studs is urea-formaldehyde foam. It is injected into the wall cavity wet, and as it cures, large quantities of moisture are given off creating the potential for serious deterioration of adjacent materials and may cause paint to blister on interior and exterior wall surfaces. Additionally, foam can shrink as much as that shown here (about 7% by volume), thus reducing the predicted insulating performance. Until some of the technical problems are corrected, its use is not recommended in historic structures. (Photo: Baird Smith)

If it is feasible, introducing insulation in this fashion provides the best possible solution to insulating a wall, and provides an excellent opportunity to view most of the structural system for possible hidden structural problems or insect infestations. A building owner should not consider this approach if it would result in substantial damage to or loss of historic wooden siding. Most siding, however, would probably withstand this method if reasonable care is exercised.

The second possible approach for wall insulation involves injecting or blowing insulation into the wall cavity. The common insulations are the loose fill types that can be blown into the cavity, the poured types, or the injected types such as foam. Obviously a vapor barrier cannot be simultaneously blown into the space. However, an equivalent vapor barrier can be created by assuring that the interior wall surfaces are covered with an impermeable paint layer. Two layers of oil base paint or one layer of impermeable latex paint constitute an acceptable vapor barrier. Naturally, for this to work, the paint layer must cover all interior surfaces adjacent to the newly installed wall insulation. Special attention should be given to rooms that are major sources of interior moisture— the laundry room, the bathrooms and the kitchen.

In addition to providing a vapor barrier, make provisions for some air to circulate in the wall cavity to help ventilate the insulation and the wall materials. This can be accomplished in several ways. One method is to install small screened vents (about 2 inches in diameter) at the base of each stud cavity. If this option is taken, the vents should be as inconspicuous as possible. A second venting method can be used where the exterior siding is horizontally lapped. Assure that each piece of siding is separated from the other, allowing some air to pass between them. Successive exterior paint layers often seal the joint between each piece of siding. Break the paint seal (carefully insert a chisel and twist) between the sections of exterior siding to provide the necessary ventilation for the insulation and wall materials.

With provisions for a vapor barrier (interior paint layer) and wall ventilation (exterior vents) satisfied, the appropriate type of wall insulation may then be selected. There are three recommended types to consider: blown cellulose (with boric acid as the fire retardant), vermiculite, or perlite. Cellulose is the preferred wall insulation because of its higher R factor and its capability to flow well into the various spaces within a wall cavity.

There are two insulation types that are not recommended for wall insulation: urea-formaldehyde foams, and cellulose which uses aluminum or ammonium sulfate instead of boric acid as a fire retardant. The cellulose treated with the sulfates reacts with moisture in the air and forms sulfuric acid which corrodes many metals and causes building stones to slowly disintegrate. This insulation is not appropriate for use in historic buildings.

Although urea-formaldehyde foams appear to have potential as retrofit materials (they flow into any wall cavity space and have a high R factor) their use is not recommended for preservation retrofitting until some serious problems are corrected. The major problem is that the injected material carries large quantities of moisture into the wall system. As the foam cures, this moisture must be absorbed into the adjacent materials. This process has caused interior and exterior paint to blister, and caused water to actually puddle at the base of a wall, creating the likelihood of serious deterioration to the historic building materials. There are other problems that affect both historic buildings and other existing buildings. Foams are a two-part chemical installed by franchised contractors. To obtain the exact proportion of the two parts, the foam must be mixed and installed under controlled conditions of temperature and humidity. There are cases where the controls were not followed and the foam either cured improperly, not attaining the desired R factor, or the

foam continued to emit a formaldehyde smell. In addition, the advertised maximum shrinkage after curing (3%) has been tested and found to be twice as high (see figure 8). Until this material is further developed and the risks eliminated, it is clearly not an appropriate material for preservation retrofitting.

Wall Insulation — Masonry Cavity Walls: Some owners of historic buildings with masonry cavity wall construction have attempted to introduce insulation into the cavity. This is not good practice because it ignores the fact that masonry cavity walls normally have acceptable thermal performance, needing no improvement. Additionally, introducing insulation into the cavity will most likely result in condensation problems and alter the intended function of the cavity. The air cavity acts as a vapor barrier in that moist air passing through the inner wythe of masonry meets the cold face of the outer wythe and condenses. Water droplets form and fall to the bottom of the wall cavity where they are channeled to the outside through weep holes. The air cavity also improves the thermal performance of the wall because it slows the transfer of heat or cold between the two wythes, causing the two wall masses to function independently with a thermal cushion between them.

Adding insulation to this cavity alters the vapor barrier and thermal cushion functions of the air space and will likely clog the weep holes, causing the moisture to puddle at the base of the wall. Also, the addition of insulation creates a situation where the moisture dew point (where moisture condenses) moves from the inner face of the outer wythe, into the outer wythe itself. Thus, during a freeze this condensation will freeze, causing spalling and severe deterioration. The evidence is clear that introducing insulation, of any type, into a masonry cavity wall is not recommended in a preservation retrofitting plan.

Wall Insulation—Installed on the Inside: Insulation could be added to a wall whether it be wooden or masonry, by attaching the insulation to furring strips mounted on the interior wall faces. Both rigid insulation, usually 1 or 2 inches thick, and batt insulation, generally 3½ inches thick, can be added in this fashion, with the **vapor barrier facing in.** Extra caution must be exercised if rigid plastic foam insulation is used because it can give off dense smoke and rapidly spreading flame when burned. Therefore, it must be installed with a fireproof covering, usually ½ inch gypsum wallboard. Insulation should not be installed on the inside if it necessitates relocation or destruction of important architectural decoration, such as cornices, chair rails, or window trims, or causes the destruction of historic plaster or other wall finishes. Insulation installed in this fashion would be expensive and could only be a recommended preservation retrofitting measure if it is a large building, located in a cold climate, and if the interior spaces and features have little or no architectural significance.

Wall Insulation—Installed on the Outside: There is a growing use of aluminum or vinyl siding installed directly over historic wooden sidings, supposedly to reduce long-term maintenance and to improve the thermal performance of the wall. From a preservation viewpoint, this is a poor practice for several reasons. New siding covers from view existing or potential deterioration problems or insect infestations. Additionally, installation often results in damage or alteration to existing decorative features such as beaded weatherboarding, window and door trim, corner boards, cornices, or roof trim. The cost of installing the artificial sidings, compared with the modest increase, if any, in the thermal performance of the wall does not add up to an effective energy-saving measure. The use of artificial siding is not recommended in a preservation retrofitting plan.

Good preservation practice would assure regular maintenance of the existing siding through periodic painting and caulking. Where deterioration is present, individual pieces of siding should be removed and replaced with matching new ones. Refer to the earlier sections of this brief for recommended retrofitting measures to improve the thermal performance of wood frame walls.

Waterproof Coatings for Masonry: Some owners of historic buildings use waterproof coatings on masonry believing it would improve the thermal performance of the wall by keeping it dry (dry masonry would have a better R factor than when wet). Application of waterproof coatings is not recommended because the coatings actually trap moisture within the masonry, and can cause spalling and severe deterioration during a freezing cycle.

In cases where exterior brick is painted, consider continued periodic painting and maintenance, since paints are an excellent preservation treatment for brick. When repainting, a building owner might consider choosing a light paint color in warm climates, or a dark color in cold climates, to gain some advantage over the summer heat gain or winter heat loss, whichever the case may be. These colors should match those used historically on the building or should match colors available historically.

Mechanical Equipment

A detailed treatise of recommended or not recommended heating or air conditioning equipment, or of alternative energy sources such as solar energy or wind power, is beyond the scope of this brief. The best advice concerning mechanical equipment in historic buildings is to assure that the existing equipment works as efficiently as possible. If the best professional advice recommends replacement of existing equipment, a building owner should keep the following considerations in mind. First, as technology advances in the coming years, the equipment installed now will be outdated rapidly relative to the life of the historic building. Therefore, it may be best to wait and watch, until new technologies (such as solar energy) become more feasible, efficient, and inexpensive. Secondly, do not install new equipment and ductwork in such a way that its installation, or possible later removal, will cause irreversible damage to significant historic building materials. The concept of complete invisibility, which necessitates hiding piping and ductwork within wall and floor systems, may not always be appropriate for historic buildings because of the damage that often results. Every effort should be made to select a mechanical system that will require the least intrusion into the historic fabric of the building and that can be updated or altered without major intervention into the wall and floor systems. These points should be considered when weighing the decision to replace a less than efficient exiting system with a costly new system, which may cause substantial damage to the historic building materials and in turn may prove inefficient in the future.

SUMMARY

The primary focus of this brief has been to describe ways to achieve the maximum energy savings in historic buildings without jeopardizing the architectural, cultural and historical qualities for which the properties have been recognized. This can be accomplished through undertaking the passive measures and the "recommended" preservation retrofitting. Secondly, this brief has emphasized the benefits of undertaking the retrofitting measures in phases so that the actual energy savings anticipated from each retrofitting measure can be realized. Thus, the "not recommended" retrofitting measures, with potential for damage or alteration of historic building materials, would not have to be undertaken, because the maximum feasible savings would have already been accomplished.

Lastly, and perhaps most important, we must recognize that the technologies of retrofitting and weatherization are relatively new. Unfortunately, most current research and product development is directed toward *new construction*. It is hoped that reports such as this, and the realization that fully 30% of all construction in the United States now involves work on existing buildings, will stimulate the development of new products that can be used with little hesitation in historic buildings. Until that time, owners of historic buildings can undertake the preservation retrofitting measures recommended here and greatly reduce the energy used for heating and cooling, without destroying those historic and architectural qualities that make the building worthy of preservation.

BIBLIOGRAPHY

Recommended Weatherization Manuals and Instruction Booklets

Nielsen, Sally E., ed. *Insulating the Old House.* Portland, Maine: Greater Portland Landmarks, Inc., 1977. Available from Greater Portland Landmarks, Inc., 165 State Street, Portland, Maine.

Making the Most of Your Energy Dollars in Home Heating and Cooling. Washington, D.C.: 1975. National Bureau of Standards, Consumer Information Series 8. Available from the Superintendent of Documents, U.S. Government Printing Office, Washington, D.C. 20402. Stock Number C13.53:8.

In the Bank . . . or Up the Chimney. Washington, D.C.: April 1975. Available from the Superintendent of Documents, U.S. Government Printing Office, Washington, D.C. 20402. Stock Number 023-000-00297-3.

Other Suggested Readings

American Society of Heating, Refrigerating and Air Conditioning Engineers, Inc. *ASHRAE Handbook of Fundamentals.* New York: ASHRAE, 1972.

"Energy Conservation and Historic Preservation," supplement to *11593*, Vol. 2, No. 3. Washington, D.C.: Office of Archeology and Historic Preservation, U.S. Department of the Interior, June 1977.

General Services Administration. *Energy Conservation Guidelines for Existing Office Buildings.* Washington, D.C.: General Services Administration, February 1977.

"The Overselling of Insulation." *Consumer Reports,* February 1978, pp. 67-73.

Petersen, Stephen R. *Retrofitting Existing Housing for Energy Conservation: An Economic Analysis,* Building Science Series 64. Washington, D.C.: U.S. Government Printing Office, December 1974.

Rossiter, Walter J., et al. *Urea-Formaldehyde Based Foam Insulations: An Assessment of Their Properties and Performance.* National Bureau of Standards, Technical Note 946. Washington, D.C.: July 1977.

Smith, Baird M. "National Benefits of Rehabilitating Existing Buildings," supplement to *11593*, Vol 2, No. 5. Washington, D.C.: Office of Archeology and Historic Preservation, U.S. Department of the Interior, October 1977.

Thermal Transmission Corrections for Dynamic Conditions—M Factor. Brick Institute of America, Technical Notes on Brick Construction, 4 B, pp. 1-8. McLean, Virginia: March/April 1977.

The weathervane on the front cover is reproduced from *J. W. Fiske 1893* by permission of Wallace-Homestead Books, Des Moines, Iowa.

The line illustration for this brief was prepared by the author.

4

Roofing for Historic Buildings

Sarah M. Sweetser

Significance of the Roof

A weather-tight roof is basic in the preservation of a structure, regardless of its age, size, or design. In the system that allows a building to work as a shelter, the roof sheds the rain, shades from the sun, and buffers the weather.

During some periods in the history of architecture, the roof imparts much of the architectural character. It defines the style and contributes to the building's aesthetics. The hipped roofs of Georgian architecture, the turrets of Queen Anne, the Mansard roofs, and the graceful slopes of the Shingle Style and Bungalow designs are examples of the use of roofing as a major design feature.

But no matter how decorative the patterning or how compelling the form, the roof is a highly vulnerable element of a shelter that will inevitable fail. A poor roof will permit the accelerated deterioration of historic building materials—masonry, wood, plaster, paint—and will cause general disintegration of the basic structure. Furthermore, there is an urgency involved in repairing a leaky roof since such repair costs will quickly become prohibitive. Although such action is desirable as soon as a failure is discovered, temporary patching methods should be carefully chosen to prevent inadvertent damage to sound or historic roofing materials and related features. Before any repair work is performed, the historic value of the materials used on the roof should be understood. Then a complete internal and external inspection of the roof should be planned to determine all the causes of failure and to identify the alternatives for repair or replacement of the roofing.

Historic Roofing Materials in America

Clay Tile: European settlers used clay tile for roofing as early as the mid-17th century; many pantiles (S-curved tiles), as well as flat roofing tiles, were used in Jamestown, Virginia. In some cities such as New York and Boston, clay was popularly used as a precaution against such fire as those that engulfed London in 1666 and scorched Boston in 1679.

Tiles roofs found in the mid-18th century Moravian settlements in Pennsylvania closely resembled those found in Germany. Typically, the tiles were 14–15″ long, 6–7″ wide with a curved butt. A lug on the back allowed the tiles to hang on the lathing without nails or pegs. The tile surface was usually scored with finger marks to promote drainage. In the Southwest, the tile roofs of the Spanish missionaries (mission tiles) were first manufactured (ca. 1780) at the Mission San Antonio de Padua in California. These semicircular tiles were

Repairs on this pantile roof were made with new tiles held in place with metal hangers. (Main Building, Ellis Island, New York)

made by molding clay over sections of logs, and they were generally 22″ long and tapered in width.

The plain or flat rectangular tiles most commonly used from the 17th through the beginning of the 19th century measured about 10″ by 6″ by ½″, and had two holes at one end for a nail or peg fastener. Sometimes mortar was applied between the courses to secure the tiles in a heavy wind.

In the mid-19th century, tile roofs were often replaced by sheet-metal roofs, which were lighter and easier to install and maintain. However, by the turn of the century, the Romanesque Revival and Mission style buildings created a new demand and popularity for this picturesque roofing material.

Slate: Another practice settlers brought to the New World was slate roofing. Evidence of roofing slates have been found also among the ruins of mid-17th-century Jamestown. But because of the cost and the time required to obtain the material, which was mostly imported from Wales, the use of slate was initially limited. Even in Philadelphia (the second largest city in the English-speaking world at the time of the Revolution) slates were so rare that "The Slate Roof House" distinctly referred to William Penn's home built late in the 1600s. Sources of native slate were known to exist along the eastern seaboard from Maine to Virginia, but difficulties in inland transportation limited its availability to the cities, and contributed to its expense. Welsh slate continued to be imported until the development of canals and railroads in the mid-19th century made American slate more accessible and economical.

Slate was popular for its durability, fireproof qualities, and

The Victorians loved to used different colored slates to create decorative patterns on their roofs, an effect which cannot be easily duplicated by substitute materials. Before any repair work on a roof such as this, the slate sizes, colors, and position of the patterning should be carefully recorded to assure proper replacement. (Ebenezer Maxwell Mansion, Philadelphia, Pennsylvania, photo courtesy of William D. Hershey)

Replacement of particular historic details is important to the individual historic character of a roof, such as the treatment at the eaves of this rounded butt wood shingle roof. Also note that the surface of the roof was carefully sloped to drain water away from the side of the dormer. In the restoration, this function was augmented with the addition of carefully concealed modern metal flashing. (Mount Vernon, Virginia)

Galvanized sheet-metal shingles imitating the appearance of pantiles remained popular from the second half of the 19th century into the 20th century. (Episcopal Church, now the Jerome Historical Society Building, Jerome, Arizona, 1927)

aesthetic potential. Because slate was available in different colors (red, green, purple, and blue-gray), it was an effective material for decorative patterns on many 19th-century roofs (Gothic and Mansard styles). Slate continued to be used well into the 20th century, notably on many Tudor revival style buildings of the 1920s.

Shingles: Wood shingles were popular throughout the country in all periods of building history. The size and shape of the shingles as well as the detailing of the shingle roof differed according to regional craft practices. People within particular regions developed preferences for the local species of wood that most suited their purposes. In New England and the Delaware Valley, white pine was frequently used: in the South, cypress and oak; in the far west, red cedar or redwood. Sometimes a protective coating was applied to increase the durability of the shingle such as a mixture of brick dust and fish oil, or a paint made of red iron oxide and linseed oil.

Commonly in urban areas, wooden roofs were replaced with more fire resistant materials, but in rural areas this was not a major concern. On many Victorian country houses, the practice of wood shingling survived the technological advances of metal roofing in the 19th century, and near the turn of the century enjoyed a full revival in its namesake, the Shingle Style. Colonial revival and the Bungalow styles in the 20th century assured wood shingles a place as one of the most fashionable, domestic roofing materials.

Metal: Metal roofing in America is principally a 19th-century phenomenon. Before then the only metals commonly used were lead and copper. For example, a lead roof covered "Rosewell," one of the grandest mansions in 18th-century Virginia. But more often, lead was used for protective flashing. Lead, as well as copper, covered roof surfaces where wood, tile, or slate shingles were inappropriate because of the roof's pitch or shape.

Copper with standing seams covered some of the more notable early American roofs including that of Christ Church (1727–1744) in Philadelphia. Flat-seamed copper was used on many domes and cupolas. The copper sheets were imported from England until the end of the 18th century when facilities for rolling sheet metal were developed in America.

Sheet iron was first known to have been manufactured here by the Revolutionary War financier, Robert Morris, who had a rolling mill near Trenton, New Jersey. At his mill Morris produced the roof of his own Philadelphia mansion, which he started in 1794. The architect Benjamin H. Latrobe used sheet iron to replace the roof on Princeton's "Nassau Hall," which had been gutted by fire in 1802.

The method for corrugating iron was originally patented in England in 1829. Corrugating stiffened the sheets, and allowed greater span over a lighter framework, as well as reduced installation time and labor. In 1834 the American architect William Strickland proposed corrugated iron to cover his design for the market place in Philadelphia.

Galvanizing with zinc to protect the base metal from rust was developed in France in 1837. By the 1850s the material was used on post offices and customhouses, as well as on train sheds and factories. In 1857 one of the first metal roofs in the

Repeated repair with asphalt, which cracks as it hardens, has created a blistered surface on this sheet-metal roof and built-in gutter, which will retain water. Repairs could be made by carefully heating and scraping the surface clean, repairing the holes in the metal with a flexible mastic compound or a metal patch, and coating the surface with a fibre paint. (Roane County Courthouse, Kingston, Tennessee, photo courtesy of Building Conservation Technology, Inc.)

A Chicago firm's catalog dated 1896 illustrates a method of unrolling, turning the edges, and finishing the standing seam on a metal roof.

Tin shingles, commonly embossed to imitate wood or tile, or with a decorative design, were popular as an inexpensive, textured roofing material. These shingles 8³/₈ inch by 12¹/₂ inch on the exposed surface) were designed with interlocking edges, but they have been repaired by surface nailing, which may cause future leakage. (Ballard House, Yorktown, Virginia, photo by Gordie Whittington, National Park Service)

South was installed on the U.S. Mint in New Orleans. The Mint was thereby "fireproofed" with a 20-gauge galvanized, corrugated iron roof on iron trusses.

Tin-plate iron, commonly called "tin roofing," was used extensively in Canada in the 18th century, but it was not as common in the United States until later. Thomas Jefferson was an early advocate of tin roofing, and he installed a standing-seam tin roof on "Monticello" (ca. 1770–1802). The Arch Street Meetinghouse (1804) in Philadelphia had tin shingles laid in a herringbone pattern on a "piazza" roof.

However, once rolling mills were established in this country, the low cost, light weight, and low maintenance of tin plate made it the most common roofing material. Embossed tin shingles, whose surfaces created interesting patterns, were popular throughout the country in the late 19th century. Tin roofs were kept well-painted, usually red; or, as the architect A. J. Davis suggested, in a color to imitate the green patina of copper.

Terne plate differed from tin plate in that the iron was dipped in an alloy of lead and tin, giving it a duller finish. Historic, as well as modern, documentation often confuses the two, so much that it is difficult to determine how often actual "terne" was used.

Zinc came into use in the 1820s, at the same time tin plate was becoming popular. Although a less expensive substitute for lead, its advantages were controversial, and it was never widely used in this country.

Other Materials: Asphalt shingles and roll roofing were used in the 1890s. Many roofs of asbestos, aluminum, stainless steel, galvinized steel, and lead-coated copper may soon have historic values as well. Awareness of these and other traditions of roofing materials and their detailing will contribute to more sensitive preservation treatments.

Locating the Problem

Failures of Surface Materials

When trouble occurs, it is important to contact a professional, either an architect, a reputable roofing contractor, or a craftsman familiar with the inherent characteristics of the particular historic roofing system involved. These professionals may be able to advise on immediate patching procedures and help plan more permanent repairs. A thorough examination of the roof should start with an appraisal of the existing condition and quality of the roofing material itself. Particular attention should be given to any southern slope because year-round exposure to direct sun may cause it to break down first.

Wood: Some historic roofing materials have limited life expectancies because of normal organic decay and "wear." For example, the flat surfaces of wood shingles erode from exposure to rain and ultraviolet rays. Some species are more hardy than others, and heartwood, for example, is stronger and more durable than sapwood.

Ideally, shingles are split with the grain perpendicular to

the surface. This is because if shingles are sawn across the grain, moisture may enter the grain and cause the wood to deteriorate. Prolonged moisture on or in the wood allows moss or fungi to grow, which will further hold the moisture and cause rot.

Metal: Of the inorganic roofing materials used on historic buildings, the most common are perhaps the sheet metals: lead, copper, zinc, tin plate, terne plate, and galvanized iron. In varying degrees each of these sheet metals are likely to deteriorate from chemical action by pitting or streaking. This can be caused by airborn pollutants; acid rainwater; acids from lichen or moss; alkalis found in lime mortars or portland cement, which might be on adjoining features and washes down on the roof surface; or tannic acids from adjacent wood sheathings or shingles made of red cedar or oak.

Corrosion from "galvanic action" occurs when dissimilar metals, such as copper and iron, are used in direct contact. Corrosion may also occur even though the metals are physically separated; one of the metals will react chemically against the other in the presence of an electrolyte such as rainwater. In roofing, this situation might occur when either a copper roof is decorated with iron cresting, or when steel nails are used in copper sheets. In some instances the corrosion can be prevented by inserting a plastic insulator between the dissimilar materials. Ideally, the fasteners should be a metal sympathetic to those involved.

Iron rusts unless it is well-painted or plated. Historically this problem was avoided by use of tin plating or galvinizing. But this method is durable only as long as the coating remains intact. Once the plating is worn or damaged, the exposed iron will rust. Therefore, any iron-based roofing material needs to be undercoated, and its surface needs to be kept well-painted to prevent corrosion.

One cause of sheet metal deterioration is fatigue. Depending upon the size and the gauge of the metal sheets, wear and metal failure can occur at the joints or at any protrusions in the sheathing as a result from the metal's alternating movement to thermal changes. Lead will tear because of "creep," or the gravitational stress that causes the material to move down the roof slope.

Slate: Perhaps the most durable roofing materials are slate and tile. Seemingly indestructable, both vary in quality. Some slates are hard and tough without being brittle. Soft slates are more subject to erosion and to attack by airborne and rain-

water chemicals, which cause the slates to wear at nail holes, to delaminate, or to break. In winter, slate is very susceptible to breakage by ice, or ice dams.

Tile: Tiles will weather well, but tend to crack or break if hit, as by tree branches, or if they are walked on improperly. Like slates, tiles cannot support much weight. Low quality tiles that have been insufficiently fired during manufacture, will craze and spall under the effects of freeze and thaw cycles on their porous surfaces.

Failures of Support Systems

Once the condition of the roofing material has been determined, the related features and support systems should be examined on the exterior and on the interior of the roof. The gutters and downspouts need periodic cleaning and maintenance since a variety of debris fill them, causing water to back up and seep under roofing units. Water will eventually cause fasteners, sheathing, and roofing structure to deteriorate. During winter, the daily freeze-thaw cycles can cause ice floes to develop under the roof surface. The pressure from these ice floes will dislodge the roofing material, especially slates, shingles, or tiles. Moreover, the buildup of ice dams above the gutters can trap enough moisture to rot the sheathing or the structural members.

Many large public buildings have built-in gutters set within the perimeter of the roof. The downspouts for these gutters may run within the walls of the building, or drainage may be through the roof surface or through a parapet to exterior downspouts. These systems can be effective if properly maintained; however, if the roof slope is inadequate for good runoff, or if the traps are allowed to clog, rainwater will form pools on the roof surface. Interior downspouts can collect debris and thus back up, perhaps leaking water into the surrounding walls. Exterior downspouts may fill with water, which in cold weather may freeze and crack the pipes. Conduits from the built-in gutter to the exterior downspout may also leak water into the surrounding roof structure or walls.

Failure of the flashing system is usually a major cause of roof deterioration. Flashing should be carefully inspected for failure caused by either poor workmanship, thermal stress, or metal deterioration (both of flashing material itself and of the fasteners). With many roofing materials, the replacement of flashing on an existing roof is a major operation, which may require taking up large sections of the roof surface. Therefore, the installation of top quality flashing material on

This detail shows slate delamination caused by a combination of weathering and pollution. In addition, the slates have eroded around the repair nails, incorrectly placed in the exposed surface of the slates. (Lower Pontalba Building, New Orleans, photo courtesy of Building Conservation Technology, Inc.)

Temporary stabilization or "mothballing" with materials such as plywood and building paper can protect the roof of a project until it can be properly repaired or replaced. (Narbonne House, Salem, Massachusetts)

These two views of the same house demonstrate how the use of a substitute material can drastically affect the overall character of a structure. The textural interest of the original tile roof was lost with the use of asphalt shingles. Recent preservation efforts are replacing the tile roof. (Frank House, Kearney, Nebraska, photo courtesy of the Nebraska State Historical Society, Lincoln, Nebraska)

a new or replaced roof should be a primary consideration. *Remember, some roofing and flashing materials are not compatible.*

Roof fasteners and clips should also be made of a material compatible with all other materials used, or coated to prevent rust. For example, the tannic acid in oak will corrode iron nails. Some roofs such as slate and sheet metals may fail if nailed too rigidly.

If the roof structure appears sound and nothing indicates recent movement, the area to be examined most closely is the roof substrate—the sheathing or the battens. The danger spots would be near the roof plates, under any exterior patches, at the intersections of the roof planes, or at vertical surfaces such as dormers. Water penetration, indicating a breach in the roofing surface or flashing, should be readily apparent, usually as a damp spot or stain. Probing with a small pen knife may reveal any rot which may indicate previously undetected damage to the roofing membrane. Insect infestation evident by small exit holes and frass (a sawdust-like debris) should also be noted. Condensation on the underside of the roofing is undesirable and indicates improper ventilation. Moisture will have an adverse effect on any roofing material; a good roof stays dry inside and out.

Repair or Replace

Understanding potential weaknesses of roofing material also requires knowledge of repair difficulties. Individual slates can be replaced normally without major disruption to the rest of the roof, but replacing flashing on a slate roof can require substantial removal of surrounding slates. If it is the substrate or a support material that has deteriorated, many surface materials such as slate or tile can be reused if handled carefully during the repair. Such problems should be evaluated at the outset of any project to determine if the roof can be effectively patched, or if it should be completely replaced.

Will the repairs be effective? Maintenance costs tend to multiply once trouble starts. As the cost of labor escalates, repeated repairs could soon equal the cost of a new roof.

The more durable the surface is initially, the easier it will be to maintain. Some roofing materials such as slate are expensive to install, but if top quality slate and flashing are used, it will last 40–60 years with minimal maintenance. Although the installation cost of the roof will be high, low maintenance needs will make the lifetime cost of the roof less expensive.

Historical Research

In a restoration project, research of documents and physical investigation of the building usually will establish the roof's history. Documentary research should include any original plans or building specifications, early insurance surveys, newspaper descriptions, or the personal papers and files of people who owned or were involved in the history of the building. Old photographs of the building might provide evidence of missing details.

Along with a thorough understanding of any written history of the building, a physical investigation of the roofing and its structure may reveal information about the roof's construction history. Starting with an overall impression of the structure, are there any changes in the roof slope, its configuration, or roofing materials? Perhaps there are obvious patches or changes in patterning of exterior brickwork where a gable roof was changed to a gambrel, or where a whole upper story was added. Perhaps there are obvious stylistic changes in the roof line, dormers, or ornamentation. These observations could help one understand any important alteration, and could help establish the direction of further investigation.

Because most roofs are physically out of the range of careful scrutiny, the "principle of least effort" has probably limited the extent and quality of previous patching or replacing, and usually considerable evidence of an earlier roof surface remains. Sometimes the older roof will be found as an underlayment of the current exposed roof. Original roofing may still be intact in awkward places under later features on a roof. Often if there is any unfinished attic space, remnants of roofing may have been dropped and left when the roof was being built or repaired. If the configuration of the roof has been changed, some of the original material might still be in place under the existing roof. Sometimes whole sections of the roof and roof framing will have been left intact under the higher roof. The profile and/or flashing of the earlier roof may be apparent on the interior of the walls at the level of the alteration. If the sheathing or lathing appears to have survived changes in the roofing surface, they may contain evidence of the roofing systems. These may appear either as dirt marks, which provide "shadows" of a roofing material, or as nails broken or driven down into the wood, rather than pulled out during previous alterations or repairs. Wooden headers in the roof framing may indicate that earlier chimneys or skylights have been removed. Any metal ornamentation that might have existed may be indicated by anchors or unusual markings along the ridge or at other edges of the roof. This primary evidence is essential for a full understanding of the roof's history.

Caution should be taken in dating early "fabric" on the evidence of a single item, as recycling of materials is not a mid-20th-century innovation. Carpenters have been reusing materials, sheathing, and framing members in the interest of economy for centuries. Therefore, any analysis of the materials found, such as nails or sawmarks on the wood, requires an accurate knowledge of the history of local building practices before any final conclusion can be accurately reached. It is helpful to establish a sequence of construction history for the roof and roofing materials; any historic fabric or pertinent evidence in the roof should be photographed, measured, and recorded for future reference.

During the repair work, useful evidence might unexpectedly appear. It is essential that records be kept of any type of work on a historic building, before, during, and after the project. Photographs are generally the easiest and fastest method, and should include overall views and details at the gutters, flashing, dormers, chimneys, valleys, ridges, and eaves. All photographs should be immediately labeled to insure accurate identification at a later date. Any patterning or design on the roofing deserves particular attention. For example, slate roofs are often decorative and have subtle changes in size, color, and texture, such as a gradually decreasing coursing length from the eave to the peak. If not carefully noted before a project begins, there may be problems in replacing the surface. The standard reference for this phase of the work is *Recording Historic Buildings,* compiled by Harley J. McKee for the Historic American Buildings Survey, National Park Service, Washington, D.C., 1970.

Replacing the Historic Roofing Material

Professional advice will be needed to assess the various aspects of replacing a historic roof. With some exceptions, most historic roofing materials are available today. If not, an architect or preservation group who has previously worked with the same type material may be able to recommend suppliers. Special roofing materials, such as tile or embossed metal shingles, can be produced by manufacturers of related products that are commonly used elsewhere, either on the exterior or interior of a structure. With some creative thinking and research, the historic materials usually can be found.

Because of the roof's visibility, the slate detailing around the dormers is important to the character of this structure. Note how the slates swirl from a horizontal pattern on the main roof to a diamond pattern on the dormer roofs and side walls. (18th and Que Streets, NW, Washington, D.C.)

Craft Practices: Determining the craft practices used in the installation of a historic roof is another major concern in roof restoration. Early builders took great pride in their work, and experience has shown that the "rustic" or irregular designs commercially labled "Early American" are a 20th-century invention. For example, historically, wood shingles underwent several distinct operations in their manufacture including splitting by hand, and smoothing the surface with a draw knife. In modern nomenclature, the same item would be a "tapersplit" shingle which has been dressed. Unfortunately, the rustic appearance of today's commercially available "handsplit" and re-sawn shingle bears no resemblance to the hand-made roofing materials used on early American buildings.

Good design and quality materials for the roof surface, fastenings, and flashing minimize roofing failures. This is essential on roofs such as on the National Cathedral where a thorough maintenance inspection and minor repairs cannot be done easily without special scaffolding. However, the success of the roof on any structure depends on frequent cleaning and repair of the gutter system. (Washington, D.C., photo courtesy of John Burns, A.I.A.)

Early craftsmen worked with a great deal of common sense; they understood their materials. For example they knew that wood shingles should be relatively narrow; shingles much wider than about 6″ would split when walked on, or they may curl or crack from varying temperature and moisture. It is important to understand these aspects of craftsmanship, remembering that people wanted their roofs to be weather-tight and to last a long time. The recent use of "mother-goose" shingles on historic structures is a gross underestimation of the early craftsman's skills.

Supervision: Finding a modern craftsman to reproduce historic details may take some effort. It may even involve some special instruction to raise his understanding of certain historic craft practices. At the same time, it may be pointless (and expensive) to follow historic craft practices in any construction that will not be visible on the finished product. But if the roofing details are readily visible, their appearance should be based on architectural evidence or on historic prototypes. For instance, the spacing of the seams on a standing-seam metal roof will affect the building's overall scale and should therefore match the original dimensions of the seams.

Many older roofing practices are no longer performed because of modern improvements. Research and review of specific detailing in the roof with the contractor before beginning the project is highly recommended. For example, one early craft practice was to finish the ridge of a wood shingle roof with a roof "comb"—that is, the top course of one slope of the roof was extended uniformly beyond the peak to shield the ridge, and to provide some weather protection for the raw horizontal edges of the shingles on the other slope. If the "comb" is known to have been the correct detail, it should be used. Though this method leaves the top course vulnerable to the weather, a disguised strip of flashing will strengthen this weak point.

Detail drawings or a sample mock-up will help ensure that the contractor or craftsman understands the scope and special requirements of the project. It should never be assumed that the modern carpenter, slater, sheet metal worker, or roofer will know all the historic details. Supervision is as important as any other stage of the process.

Special problems inherent in the design of an elaborate historic roof can be controlled through the use of good materials and regular maintenance. The shape and detailing are essential elements of the building's historic character, and should not be modified, despite the use of alternative surface materials. (Gamwell House, Bellingham, Washington)

Alternative Materials

The use of the historic roofing material on a structure may be restricted by building codes or by the availability of the materials, in which case an appropriate alternative will have to be found.

Some municipal building codes allow variances for roofing materials in historic districts. In other instances, individual variances may be obtained. Most modern heating and cooking is fueled by gas, electricity, or oil—none of which emit the hot embers that historically have been the cause of roof fires. Where wood burning fireplaces or stoves are used, spark arrestor screens at the top of the chimneys help to prevent flaming material from escaping, thus reducing the number of fires that start at the roof. In most states, insurance rates have been equalized to reflect revised considerations for the risks involved with various roofing materials.

In a rehabilitation project, there may be valid reasons for replacing the roof with a material other than the original. The historic roofing may no longer be available, or the cost of obtaining specially fabricated materials may be prohibitive. But

the decision to use an alternative material should be weighed carefully against the primary concern to keep the historic character of the building. If the roof is flat and is not visible from any elevation of the building, and if there are advantages to substituting a modern built-up composition roof for what might have been a flat metal roof, then it may make better economic and construction sense to use a modern roofing method. But if the roof is readily visible, the alternative material should match as closely as possible the scale, texture, and coloration of the historic roofing material.

Asphalt shingles or ceramic tiles are common substitute materials intended to duplicate the appearance of wood shingles, slates, or tiles. Fire-retardant, treated wood shingles are currently available. The treated wood tends, however, to be brittle, and may require extra care (and expense) to install. In some instances, shingles laid with an interlay of fire-retardent building paper may be an acceptable alternative.

Lead-coated copper, terne-coated steel, and aluminum/zinc-coated steel can successfully replace tin, terne plate, zinc, or lead. Copper-coated steel is a less expensive (and less durable) substitute for sheet copper.

The search for alternative roofing materials is not new. As early as the 18th century, fear of fire cause many wood shingle or board roofs to be replaced by sheet metal or clay tile. Some historic roofs were failures from the start, based on over-ambitious and naive use of materials as they were first developed. Research on a structure may reveal that an inadequately designed or a highly combustible roof was replaced early in its history, and therefore restoration of a later roof material would have a valid precedent. In some cities, the substitution of sheet metal on early row houses occurred as soon as the rolled material became available.

Cost and ease of maintenance may dictate the substitution of a material wholly different in appearance from the original. The practical problems (wind, weather, and roof pitch) should be weighed against the historical consideration of scale, texture, and color. Sometimes the effect of the alternative material will be minimal. But on roofs with a high degree of visibility and patterning or texture, the substitution may seriously alter the architectural character of the building.

Temporary Stabilization

It may be necessary to carry out an immediate and temporary stabilization to prevent further deterioration until research can determine how the roof should be restored or rehabilitated, or until funding can be provided to do a proper job. A simple covering of exterior plywood or roll roofing might provide adequate protection, but any temporary covering should be applied with caution. One should be careful not to overload the roof structure, or to damage or destroy historic evidence or fabric that might be incorporated into a new roof at a later date. In this sense, repairs with caulking or bituminous patching compounds should be recognized as potentially harmful, since they are difficult to remove, and at their best, are very temporary.

Precautions

The architect or contractor should warn the owner of any precautions to be taken against the specific hazards in installing the roofing material. Soldering of sheet metals, for instance, can be a fire hazard, either from the open flame or from overheating and undected smoldering of the wooden substrate materials.

Thought should be given to the design and placement of any modern roof appurtenances such as plumbing stacks, air vents, or TV antennas. Consideration should begin with the placement of modern plumbing on the interior of the building, otherwise a series of vent stacks may pierce the roof membrane at various spots creating maintenance problems as well as aesthetic ones. Air handling units placed in the attic space will require vents which, in turn, require sensitive design. Incorporating these in unused chimneys has been very successful in the past.

Whenever gutters and downspouts are needed that were not on the building historically, the additions should be made as unobtrusively as possible, perhaps by painting them out with a color compatible with the nearby wall or trim.

Maintenance

Although a new roof can be an object of beauty, it will not be protective for long without proper maintenance. At least twice a year, the roof should be inspected against a checklist. All changes should be recorded and reported. Guidelines should be established for any foot traffic that may be required for the maintenance of the roof. Many roofing materials should not be walked on at all. For some—slate, asbestos, and clay tile—a self-supporting ladder might be hung over the ridge of the roof, or planks might be spanned across the roof surface. Such items should be specifically designed and kept in a storage space accessible to the roof. If exterior work ever requires hanging scaffolding, use caution to insure that the anchors do not penetrate, break, or wear the roofing surface, gutters, or flashing.

Any roofing system should be recognized as a membrane that is designed to be self-sustaining, but that can be easily damaged by intrusions such as pedestrian traffic or fallen tree branches. Certain items should be checked at specific times. For example, gutters tend to accumulate leaves and debris during the spring and fall and after heavy rain. Hidden gutter screening both at downspouts and over the full length of the gutter could help keep them clean. The surface material would require checking after a storm as well. Periodic checking of the underside of the roof from the attic after a storm or winter freezing may give early warning of any leaks. Generally, damage from water or ice is less likely on a roof that has good flashing on the outside and is well ventilated and insulated on the inside. Specific instructions for the maintenance of the different roof materials should be available from the architect or contractor.

Summary

The essential ingredients for replacing and maintaining a historic roof are:

• Understanding the historic character of the building and being sympathetic to it.

• Careful examination and recording of the existing roof and any evidence of earlier roofs.

• Consideration of the historic craftsmanship and detailing and implementing them in the renewal wherever visible.

• Supervision of the roofers or maintenance personnel to assure preservation of historic fabric and proper understanding of the scope and detailing of the project.

• Consideration of alternative materials where the original cannot be used.

• Cyclical maintenance program to assure that the staff understands how to take care of the roof and of the particular trouble spots to safeguard.

With these points in mind, it will be possible to preserve the architectural character and maintain the physical integrity of the roofing on a historic building.

This Preservation Brief was written by Sarah M. Sweetser, Architectural Historian, Technical Preservation Services Division. Much of the technical information was based upon an unpublished report prepared under contract for this office by John G. and Diana S. Waite. Some of the historical information was from Charles E. Peterson, FAIA, "American Notes," *Journal of the Society of Architectural Historians.*
The illustrations for this brief not specifically credited are from the files of the Technical Preservation Services Division.

Decorative features such as cupolas require extra maintenance. The flashing is carefully detailed to promote run-off, and the wooden ribbing must be kept well-painted. This roof surface, which was originally tin plate, has been replaced with lead-coated copper for maintenance purposes. (Lyndhurst, Tarrytown, New York, photo courtesy of the National Trust for Historic Preservation)

Additional readings on the subject of roofing are listed below.

Boaz, Joseph N., ed. *Architectural Graphic Standards.* New York: John Wiley and Sons, Inc., 1970. (Modern roofing types and detailing)

Briggs, Martin S. *A Short History of the Building Crafts.* London: Oxford University Press, 1925. (Descriptions of historic roofing materials)

Bulletin of the Association for Preservation Technology. Vol. 2 (nos. 1-2) 1970. (Entirely on roofing)

Holstrom, Ingmar; and Sandstrom, Christina. *Maintenance of Old Buildings: Preservation from the Technical and Antiquarian Standpoint.* Stockholm: National Swedish Building Research, 1972. (Contains a section on roof maintenance problems)

Insall, Donald. *The Care of Old Buildings Today.* London: The Architectural Press, 1972. (Excellent guide to some problems and solutions for historic roofs)

Labine, R.A. Clem. "Repairing Slate Roofs." *The Old House Journal* 3 (no. 12, Dec. 1975): 6-7.

Lefer, Henry. "A Birds-eye View." *Progressive Architecture.* (Mar. 1977), pp. 88-92. (Article on contemporary sheet metal)

National Slate Association. *Slate Roofs.* Reprint of 1926 edition, now available from the Vermont Structural Slate Co., Inc., Fairhaven, VT 05743. (An excellent reference for the many designs and details of slate roofs)

Peterson, Charles E. "Iron in Early American Roofs." *The Smithsonian Journal of History* 3 (no. 3). Edited by Peter C. Welsh. Washington, D.C.: Smithsonian Institution, 1968, pp. 41-76.

Waite, Diana S. *Nineteenth Century Tin Roofing and its Use at Hyde Hall.* Albany: New York State Historic Trust, 1971.

——. "Roofing for Early America." *Building Early America.* Edited by Charles E. Peterson. Radnor, Penn.: Chilton Book Co., 1976.

5

Preservation of Historic Adobe Buildings

Whether built in the 17th century or in the 20th century, adobe buildings share common problems of maintenance and deterioration. This brief discusses the traditional materials and construction of adobe buildings and the causes of adobe deterioration. It also makes recommendations for preserving historic adobe buildings. By its composition, adobe construction is inclined to deteriorate; however, the buildings can be made durable and renewable when properly maintained.

What is Adobe?

The adobe, or sun-dried brick, is one of the oldest and most common building materials known to man. Traditionally, adobe bricks were never kiln fired. Unbaked adobe bricks consisted of sand, sometimes gravel, clay, water, and often straw or grass mixed together by hand, formed in wooden molds, and dried by the sun. Today some commercially available adobe-like bricks are fired. These are similar in size to unbaked bricks, but have a different texture, color, and strength. Similarly some adobe bricks have been stabilized, containing cement, asphalt, and/or bituminous materials, but these also differ from traditional adobe in their appearance and strength.

Traditional adobe construction techniques in North America have not varied widely for over 3½ centuries. Adobe

SAN XAVIER DEL BAC, TUCSON VICINITY, ARIZONA. *Built entirely of adobe construction (1783–1797), this is one of the finest Spanish Colonial churches in the United States, having an elaborate frontispiece of molded, carved, and painted brick imitating stone. (National Park Service)*

building methods employed in the Southwest in the 16th century are still used today. Because adobe bricks are not fired in a kiln as are clay bricks, they do not permanently harden, but remain unstable—they shrink and swell constantly with their changing water content. Their strength also fluctuates with their water content: the higher the water content, the lower the strength.

Adobe will not permanently bond with metal, wood, or stone because it exhibits much greater movement than these other materials, either separating, cracking, or twisting where they interface. Yet, many of these more stable building materials such as fired brick, wood, and lime and cement mortars are nonetheless used in adobe construction. For example, stone may be used for a building's foundation, and wood may be used for its roof or its lintels and doorways. In the adobe building, these materials are generally held in place by their own weight or by the compressive weight of the wall above them. Adobe construction possibilities and variations in design have therefore been somewhat limited by the physical constraints of the material.

Preserving and rehabilitating a deteriorated adobe building is most successful when the techniques and methods used for restoration and repairs are as similar as possible to the techniques used in the original construction.

Adobe Construction Techniques

The Brick: The adobe brick is molded from sand and clay mixed with water to a plastic consistency. Commonly, straw or grass is included as a binder. Although they do not help reinforce the bricks or give them added long-term strength, straw and grass do help the bricks shrink more uniformly while they dry. More important for durability, however, is the inherent clay-to-sand ratio found in native soil. The prepared mud is placed in wooden forms, tamped, and leveled by hand. The bricks are then "turned-out" of the mold to dry on a level surface covered with straw or grass so that the bricks will not stick. After several days of drying, the adobe bricks are ready for air-curing. This consists of standing the bricks on end for a period of 4 weeks or longer.

Mortar: Historically, most adobe walls were composed of adobe bricks laid with mud mortar. Such mortar exhibited the same properties as the bricks: relatively weak and susceptible to the same rate of hygroscopic (moisture absorptive) swelling and shrinking, thermal expansion and contraction, and deterioration. Consequently, no other material has been as successful in bonding adobe bricks. Today, cement and lime mortars are commonly used with stabilized adobe bricks, but cement mortars are incompatible with unstabilized adobe because the two have different thermal expansion and contraction rates. Cement mortars thereby accelerate the deterioration of adobe bricks since the mortars are stronger than the adobe.

Building Foundations: Early adobe building foundations varied because of the difference in local building practices and availability of materials. Many foundations were large and substantially constructed, but others were almost non-existent. Most often, adobe building foundations were constructed of bricks, fieldstones, or cavity walls (double) infilled with rubble stone, tile fragments, or seashells. Adobe buildings were rarely constructed over basements or crawlspaces.

Walls: Since adobe construction was load-bearing with low structural strength, adobe walls tended to be massive, and seldom rose over 2 stories. In fact, the maximum height of adobe mission churches in the Southwest was approximately 35 feet. Often buttresses braced exterior walls for added stability.

In some parts of the Southwest, it was common to place a long wooden timber within the last courses of adobe bricks. This timber provided a long horizontal bearing plate for the roof thereby distributing the weight of the roof along the wall.

Roofs: Early Southwest adobe roofs (17th–mid–19th centuries) tended to be flat with low parapet walls. These roofs consisted of logs which supported wooden poles, and which in turn supported wooden lathing or layers of twigs covered with packed adobe earth. The wood was aspen, mesquite, cedar, or whatever was available. Roughly dressed logs (called "*vigas*") or shaped squared timbers were spaced on close (2–3 feet or less) centers resting either on the horizontal wooden member which topped the adobe wall, or on decorated cantilevered blocks, called "corbels," which were set into the adobe wall. Traditionally, these *vigas* often projected through the wall facades creating the typical adobe

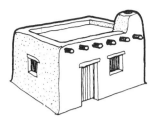

flat roof, small openings

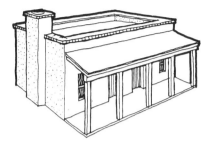

brick coping, wood porch

hip roof, wood trim

Evolution of Roof Forms. *The roofs of early adobe buildings were flat, made with mud, with low parapets. Later, brick copings were placed on top of parapets and chimneys to protect them from erosion, and shed roof porches were added to shelter doors and windows. After the railroad reached the Southwest, hip roofs and wooden trim began to appear as sawn lumber, shingles, tile, and sheet metal became available. (Drawing by Albert N. Hopper)*

Roof Bearing. *A roof bearing timber placed within the adobe walls provides even support for the weight of the roof. (Farm Security Administration Collection, Library of Congress)*

Roof Framing. *Viga logs and savinos are seen in the interior of the adobe building. Often the wooden materials that compose the traditional flat adobe roof create interesting and pleasing patterns on the ceilings of the interior rooms. (Photo by Russell Lee, Farm Security Administration Collection, Library of Congress)*

construction detail copied in the 20th-century revival styles. Wooden poles about 2 inches in diameter (called "*latias*") were then laid across the top of the *vigas*. Handsplit planks (called "*cedros*" if cedar and "*savinos*" if cypress) instead of poles were used when available. In some areas, these were laid in a herringbone pattern. In the west Texas and Tucson areas, *saguaro* (cactus) ribs were used to span between *vigas*. After railroad transportation arrived in most areas, sawn boards and planks, much like roof sheathing, became available and was often used in late-19th- and early-20th-century buildings or for repairs to earlier ones.

Next cedar twigs, plant fibers, or fabric were placed on top of the poles or planks. These served as a lathing on which the 6 or more inches of adobe earth was compacted. If planks were used, twigs were not necessary. A coating of adobe mud was then applied overall. The flat roofs were sloped somewhat toward drains of hollowed logs (called "*canales*," or "*gargolas*"), tile, or sheet metal that projected through the parapet walls.

Gable and hipped roofs became increasingly popular in adobe buildings in the 19th and 20th centuries. "Territorial" styles and preferences for certain materials developed. For example, roof tiles were widely used in southern California. Although the railroad brought in some wooden shingles and some terra-cotta, sheet metal roofing was the prevalent material for roofs in New Mexico.

Floors: Historically, flooring materials were placed directly on the ground with little or no subflooring preparation. Flooring materials in adobe buildings have varied from earth to adobe brick, fired brick, tile, or flagstone (called "*lajas*"), to conventional wooden floors.

Traditional Surface Coatings

Adobe surfaces are notoriously fragile and need frequent maintenance. To protect the exterior and interior surfaces of new adobe walls, surface coatings such as mud plaster, lime plaster, whitewash, and stucco have been used. Such coatings applied to the exterior of adobe construction have retarded surface deterioration by offering a renewable surface to the adobe wall. In the past, these methods have been inexpensive and readily available to the adobe owner as a solution to periodic maintenance and visual improvement. However, recent increases in labor costs and changes in cultural and socio-economic values have caused many adobe building owners to seek more lasting materials as alternatives to these traditional and once-inexpensive surface coatings.

Mud Plaster: Mud plaster has long been used as a surface coating. Like adobe, mud plaster is composed of clay, sand, water, and straw or grass, and therefore exhibits sympathetic properties to those of the original adobe. The mud plaster bonds to the adobe because the two are made of the same materials. Although applying mud plaster requires little skill, it is a time-consuming and laborious process. Once in place, the mud plaster must be smoothed. This is done by hand; sometimes deerskins, sheepskins, and small, slightly rounded stones are used to smooth the plaster to create a "polished" surface. In some areas, pink or ochre pigments are mixed into the final layer and "polished."

Whitewash: Whitewash has been used on earthen buildings since before recorded history. Consisting of ground gypsum rock, water, and clay, whitewash acts as a sealer, which can be either brushed on the adobe wall or applied with large pieces of coarse fabric such as burlap.

Initially, whitewash was considered inexpensive and easy to apply. But its impermanence and the cost of annually renewing it has made it less popular as a surface coating in recent years.

Lime Plaster: Lime plaster, widely used in the 19th century as both an exterior and interior coating, is much harder than mud plaster. It is, however, less flexible and cracks easily. It consists of lime, sand, and water and is applied in heavy coats with trowels or brushes. To make the lime plaster adhere to adobe, walls are often scored diagonally with hatchets, making grooves about 1 1/2 inches deep. The grooves are filled with a mixture of lime mortar and small chips of stone or broken roof tiles. The wall is then covered heavily with the lime plaster.

Cement Stucco: In the United States, cement stucco came into use as an adobe surface coating in the early 20th century for the revival styles of Southwest adobe architecture. Cement stucco consists of cement, sand, and water and it is applied with a trowel in from 1 to 3 coats over a wire mesh nailed to the adobe surface. This material has been very popular because it requires little maintenance when applied over fired or stabilized adobe brick, and because it can be easily painted.

It should be noted however, that the cement stucco does not create a bond with unfired or unstabilized adobe; it relies on the wire mesh and nails to hold it in place. Since nails cannot bond with the adobe, a firm surface cannot be guaranteed. Even when very long nails are used, moisture within the adobe may cause the nails and the wire to rust, thus, losing contact with the adobe.

Other Traditional Surface Coatings: These have included items such as paints (oil base, resin, or emulsion), portland cement washes, coatings of plant extracts, and even coatings of fresh animal blood (mainly for adobe floors). Some of these coatings are inexpensive and easy to apply, provide temporary surface protection, and are still available to the adobe owner.

Adobe Deterioration

When preservation or rehabilitation is contemplated for a historic adobe building, it is generally because the walls or roof of the building have deteriorated in some fashion—walls may be cracked, eroded, pitted, bulging, or the roof may be sagging. In planning the stabilization and repair of an adobe building, it is necessary:

● To determine the nature of the deterioration
● To identify and correct the source of the problem causing the deterioration
● To develop rehabilitation and restoration plans that are sensitive to the integrity of the historic adobe building
● To develop a maintenance program once the rehabilitation or restoration is completed.

General Advice: There are several principles that when followed generally result in a relatively stable and permanent adobe resource.

1. Whenever possible, secure the services or advice of a professional architect or other preservationist proficient in adobe preservation and stabilization. Although this may be more costly than to "do-it-yourself," it will probably be less expensive in the long run. Working with a deteriorated adobe building is a complex and difficult process. Irreversible damage may be done by well-meaning but inexperienced "restorationists." Moreover, professional assistance may be required to interpret local code requirements.

2. Never begin restoration or repairs until the problems that

Deteriorated Adobe Building. *By virtue of its fragile nature, the adobe building must be restored by thorough, systematic, and professional measures that will insure its future survival. (Technical Preservation Services Division)*

Structural Damage and Cracking. *Sagging, bulging, and cracking of walls and roofs are signs of serious problems in the adobe building. It is always advisable to secure professional services in the repair of such problems. (National Park Service)*

have been causing the deterioration of the adobe have been found, analyzed, and solved. For instance, sagging or bulging walls may be the result of a problem called "rising damp" and/or excessive roof loads. Because adobe deterioration is almost always the end product of a combination of problems, it takes a trained professional to analyze the deterioration, identify the source or sources of deterioration, and halt the deterioration before full restoration begins.

3. Repair or replace adobe building materials with the same types of materials used originally and use the same construction techniques. Usually the best and the safest procedure is to use traditional building materials. Repair or replace deteriorated adobe bricks with similar adobe bricks. Repair or replace rotted wooden lintels with similar wooden lintels. The problems created by introducing dissimilar replacement materials may cause problems far exceeding those which deteriorated the adobe in the first place.

Sources of Deterioration

The following are some common signs and sources of adobe deterioration and some common solutions. It should be cautioned again, however, that adobe deterioration is often the end-product of more than one of these problems. The remedying of only one of these will not necessarily arrest deterioration if others are left untreated.

Structural Damage: There are several common structural problems in adobe buildings, and while the results of these problems are easy to see, their causes are not. Many of these problems originate from improper design or construction, insufficient foundations, weak or inadequate materials, or the effects of external forces such as wind, water, snow, or earthquakes. In any case, the services of a soils engineer and/or structural engineer knowledgeable in adobe construction may be necessary to evaluate these problems. Solutions may involve repairing foundations, realigning leaning and bulging walls, buttressing walls, inserting new window and door lintels, and repairing or replacing badly deteriorated roof structures.

There are many tell-tale signs of structural problems in adobe buildings, the most common being cracks in walls, foundations, and roofs. In adobe, cracks are generally quite visible, but their causes may be difficult to diagnose. Some cracking is normal, such as the short hairline cracks that are caused as the adobe shrinks and continues to dry out. More

extensive cracking, however, usually indicates serious structural problems. In any case, cracks, like all structural problems, should be examined by a professional who can make recommendations for their repair.

Water Related Problems: Generally, adobe buildings deteriorate because of moisture, either excessive rainwater or ground water. Successful stabilization, restoration, and the ultimate survival of an adobe building depends upon how effectively a structure sheds water. The importance in keeping an adobe building free from excessive moisture cannot be overestimated. The erosive action of rainwater and the subsequent drying out of adobe roofs, parapet walls, and wall surfaces can cause furrows, cracks, deep fissures, and pitted surfaces to form. Rain saturated adobe loses its cohesive strength and sloughs off forming rounded corners and parapets. If left unattended, rainwater damage can eventually destroy adobe walls and roofs, causing their continued deterioration and ultimate collapse. Standing rainwater that accumulates at foundation level and rain splash may cause "coving" (the hollowing-out of the wall just above grade level).

Ground water (water below ground level) might be present because of a spring, a high water table, improper drainage, seasonal water fluctuations, excessive plant watering, or changes in grade on either side of the wall. Ground water rises through capillary action into the wall and causes the adobe to erode, bulge, and cove. Coving is also caused by spalling during the freeze-thaw cycles. As water rises from the ground into the wall, the bond between the clay particles in the adobe brick breaks down. In addition, dissolved minerals or salts brought up from the soil by the water can be deposited on or near the surface of the wall as the moisture evaporates. If these deposits become heavily concentrated, they too can deteriorate the adobe fabric. As the adobe dries out, shrinkage cracks usually appear; loose sections of adobe bricks and mud plaster may crumble.

A water-tight roof with proper drainage is the best protection against rainfall erosion. Adobe wall and roof surfaces properly maintained with traditional tiles or surface coatings generally resist the destructive effects of rainwater. Roof drains should be in good repair and sufficient to carry rainwater run-off from the roof. In an effort to halt the destructive effects of rainwater, 19th-century builders often capped parapet walls with fired bricks. These bricks were harder and better suited to weather the erosive action of rainwater; however, the addition of a brick cap to an existing parapet wall creates a drastic change in a structure's appearance and fabric. The use of traditional lime mortar with the fired brick is advised because it is more water-tight and compatible with the harder brick.

Rainwater that has accumulated at adobe foundations should be diverted away from the building. This may be done by regrading, by building gravel-filled trenches or brick, tile, or stone drip gutters, or by any technique that will effectively remove the standing rainwater. Regrading is perhaps the best solution because defective gutters and trenches may in effect collect and hold water at the base of the wall or foundation.

In repairing "coving," the damage caused by rain splash, adobe bricks stabilized with soil cement might be considered. On the other hand, concrete patches, cement stucco, and curb-like buttresses against the coving usually have a negative effect because moisture may be attracted and trapped behind the concrete.

Cement stucco and cement patches have the potential for specific kinds of water related adobe deterioration. The thermal expansion coefficient of cement stucco is 3 to 10 times greater than that of adobe resulting in cracking of the stucco. Cracks allow both liquid water and vapor to penetrate the adobe beneath, and the stucco prevents the wall from drying.

As the moisture content of the adobe increases, there is a point at which the adobe will become soft like putty. When the wall becomes totally saturated, the adobe mud will flow as a liquid. This varies with the sand, clay, and silt content of the adobe.

If the adobe becomes so wet that the clay reaches its plastic limit, or if the adobe is exposed to a freeze-thaw action, serious damage can result. Under the weight of the roof, the wet adobe may deform or bulge. Since the deterioration is hidden from view by the cement stucco, damage may go undetected for some time. Traditional adobe construction techniques and materials should therefore, be used to repair or rebuild parts of the walls.

The destructive effects of moisture on adobe buildings may be substantially halted by several remedies.

1. Shrubs, trees, and other foundation plantings may be causing physical damage. Their roots may be growing into the adobe, and/or they may be trapping excessive moisture in their roots and conducting it into walls. Their removal might be considered to halt this process.
2. Level ground immediately adjacent to the walls may be causing poor drainage. Regrading could be considered so that the ground slopes away from the building, eliminating rainwater pools.
3. The installation of footing drains may be considered. Trenches about 2 to 2½ feet wide and several feet deep are dug around the adobe building at the base of the walls or at the foundation if there is any. If the soil is weak, it may be necessary to slope the sides of the trench to prevent cave-in of the trench and subsequent damage to the wall. The walls and bottom of the trench should be lined with a polyethylene vapor barrier to prevent the collected water from saturating the surrounding soil and adobe wall. Clay tile, or plastic pipe, which drain to a sump or to an open gutter, are then laid in the bottom of the trench. The trench is filled with gravel to within 6 inches of grade. The remaining excavation is then filled to grade with porous soil.

A Word of Caution: *Plant removal, regrading, or trenching may be potentially destructive to archeological remains associated with historic adobe building sites. Any disturbance of the ground should, therefore, be undertaken with prudence and careful planning.*

Once any one or all of these solutions has effectively minimized the problems of rising ground water, the coving

and deterioration of the walls can be corrected by patching the area with new adobe mud and by applying traditional surface coatings. It should be remembered, however, that unless the capillary action is stopped effectively, this erosive condition will certainly continue. Most important, surface coatings and patching only repair the effects of ground water and wind erosion, they cannot cure the cause.

Coving. *Salts deposited by rising ground water can evaporate and cause spalling of the adobe bricks at the base of the wall, a serious condition called "coving." Coving can also be caused and/or exacerbated by the erosion of rain splash. (National Park Service)*

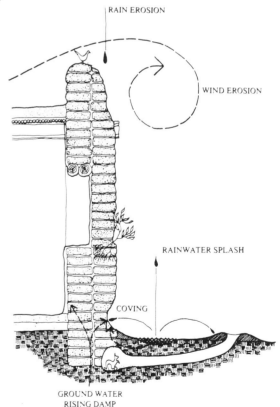

Water, Wind, Animal, Insect, and Vegetation Damage. *Most deterioration of adobe buildings can be directly correlated with the presence of either excessive rainwater, groundwater, or both. Successful adobe stabilization and restoration depends upon keeping the adobe building moisture free, repaired, and well maintained. (Drawing by David W. Look, AIA, based on sketches by Albert N. Hopper)*

Wind Erosion: Wind-blown sand has often been cited as a factor in adobe fabric erosion. Evidence of wind erosion is often difficult to isolate because the results are similar to water erosion; however, furrowing caused by wind is usually more obvious at the upper half of the wall and at the corners, while coving from rainsplash and ground water is usually at the lower third of the wall.

Maintenance is the key to mitigating the destructive effects of wind erosion. Wind damage on adobe walls and roof surfaces should be repaired with new adobe mud. Any traditional surface coating may be applied to protect against any possible future destructive effects. If high wind is a continuing problem, a wind screen or breaker might be built, using fencing or trees. Care should be taken to plant trees far enough away from the structure so that the roots will not destroy the foundation or trap moisture.

Vegetation, Insects, and Vermin: Vegetation and pests are natural phenomena that can accelerate adobe deterioration. Seeds deposited by the wind or by animals may germinate in adobe walls or roofs as they would in any soil. The action of roots may break down adobe bricks or cause moisture retention which will harm the structure. Animals, birds, and insects often live in adobe structures, burrowing and nesting in walls or in foundations. These pests undermine and destroy the structural soundness of the adobe building. The possibility of termite infestation should not be overlooked since termites can travel through adobe walls as they do through natural soil. Wood members (lintels, floors, window and door shutters, and roof members) are all vulnerable to termite attack and destruction.

It is important to rid adobe structures immediately of all plant, animal, and insect pests and to take preventive measures against their return. Seedlings should be removed from the adobe as soon as they are discovered. Large plants should be removed carefully so that their root systems will not dislodge adobe material. Pest control involving the use of chemicals should be examined carefully in order to assess the immediate and longlasting effects of the chemicals on the adobe building. Professional advice in this area is important not only because chemicals may be transported into the walls by capillary action and have a damaging effect on the adobe fabric, but also for reasons of human and environmental safety.

Material Incompatibilities: As adobe buildings are continually swelling and shrinking, it is likely that repair work has already been carried out sometime during the life of the building. Philosophies regarding adobe preservation have changed, and so have restoration and rehabilitation techniques. Techniques acceptable only 10 years ago are no longer considered appropriate. Until recently, adobe bricks have been repointed with portland cement; deteriorated wooden lintels and doors have been replaced with steel ones; and adobe walls have been sprayed with plastic or latex surface coatings. The hygroscopic nature of adobe has rendered these techniques ineffective and, most important, destructive. The high strength of portland cement mortar and stucco has caused the weaker adobe brick to crack and crumble during the differential expansion of these incompatible materials. Steel lintels are much more rigid than adobe. When the building expands, the adobe walls twist because they are more flexible than the steel. Plastic and latex wall coatings have been used to seal the surface, keeping it from expanding with the rest of the brick. Portions of the wall have consequently broken off. In some instances, incompatible materials can be removed from the building without subsequently damaging the structure. Other times, this is not possible. Professional advice is therefore recommended.

Repairing and Maintaining the Historic Adobe Building

Once the adobe deterioration and any resulting structural damage is repaired, the restoration of the adobe building can proceed. Careful attention should be given to replace, repair, and/or reproduce all damaged materials with traditional or original materials.

Patching and Repairing Adobe Brick: In patching and replacing adobe brick, every reasonable effort should be made to find clay with a texture and color similar to the original fabric. When an individual adobe brick has partially disintegrated, it may be patched in place. The deteriorated material may be scraped out and replaced with appropriate adobe mud. Often fragments of the original adobe brick have been ground up, mixed with water, and reused to patch the eroded area. However, some professionals advise against the reuse of material which has spalled off because it frequently contains a high concentration of salts.

If a substantial amount of the brick has been destroyed or spalled, commercially made adobe bricks and half-bricks can be obtained, or they may be made at the site or nearby. Generally these are 3 or 4 inches thick, and ideally they are composed of unstabilized adobe (that is, without any chemical additives). The deteriorated adobe bricks should be scraped out to insert the new bricks. If most of the brick is not deteriorated, then the deteriorated portion may be replaced with a half-brick. It may be necessary to cut back into undeteriorated portions of the brick to achieve a flush fit of the new or half-bricks. Spray (do not soak) the new brick and surrounding area lightly with water to facilitate a better bond. Too much moisture can cause swelling. Always use traditional adobe mud mortar.

When entire bricks or sections of the brick walls have to be replaced, caution should be exercised when buying ready-made bricks. Many are now manufactured using stabilizing agents (portland cement, lime, or emulsified asphalt) in their composition. While the inclusion of these agents in new adobe bricks is a technical advancement in their durability, they will prove incompatible with the fabric of the historic

Cement Mortar Incompatibility. *The stronger and less flexible cement mortar has caused the softer adobe bricks to crumble thus leaving a "honeycomb" of cement mortar joints. (National Park Service)*

adobe building. Concrete blocks and cinderblocks are likewise tempting solutions to extensive adobe brick replacement; but, like commercially stabilized adobe bricks, they are not compatible with older and more unstable adobe bricks. However, concrete blocks have been used for interior partitions successfully.

Patching and Replacing Mortar: In repairing loose and deteriorated adobe mortar, care should also be taken to match the original material, color, and texture. Most important, never replace adobe mud mortar with lime mortar or portland cement mortar. It is a common error to assume that mortar hardness or strength is a measure of its suitability in adobe repair or reconstruction. Mortars composed of portland cement or lime do not have the same thermal expansion rate as adobe brick. With the continual thermal expansion and contraction of adobe bricks, portland cement or lime mortars will cause the bricks—the weaker material—to crack, crumble, and eventually disintegrate.

It is recognized, however, that some late historic adobe buildings have always had portland cement or lime mortars used in their initial construction. The removal and replacement of these mortars with mud mortar is not advised because their removal is usually destructive to the adobe bricks.

In repairing adobe cracks, a procedure similar to repointing masonry joints may be used. It is necessary to rake out the cracks to a depth of 2 or 3 times the width of a mortar joint to obtain a good "key" (mechanical bond) of the mortar to the adobe bricks. The bricks should be sprayed lightly with water to increase the cohesive bond. A trowel or a large grout gun with new adobe mud mortar may then be used to fill the cracks.

Repairing and Replacing Wooden Members: Rotted or termite infested wood members such as *vigas, savinos,* lintels, wall braces, or flooring should be repaired or replaced. Wood should always be replaced with wood. For carved corbels, however, specially formulated low-strength epoxy consolidants and patching compounds may be used to make repairs, thus saving original craftsmanship. Tests, however, should be made prior to repairs to check on desired results since they usually are not reversible. This is an area of building repair that ought not be attempted by the amateur. For further information, see *Epoxies for Wood Repairs in Historic Buildings*, cited in the reading list of this brief.

Patching and Replacing Surface Coatings: Historically, almost every adobe building surface was coated. When these coatings deteriorate, they need to be replaced. Every effort should be made to recoat the surface with the same material that originally coated the surface.

When the coating has been mud plaster, the process requires that the deteriorated mud plaster be scraped off and replaced with like materials and similar techniques, attempting in all cases to match the repair work as closely as possible to the original. It is always better to cover adobe with mud plaster even though the mud plaster must be renewed more frequently.

The process is not so simple where lime plaster and portland cement stuccos are involved. As much of the deteriorated surface coating as possible should be removed without damaging the adobe brick fabric underneath. Never put another coat of lime plaster or portland cement stucco over a deteriorated surface coating. If serious deterioration does exist on the surface, then it is likely that far greater deterioration exists below. Generally this problem is related to water, in which case it is advisable to consult a professional.

If extensive recoatings in lime plaster or portland cement stucco are necessary, the owner of an adobe building might consider furring out the walls with lathing, then plastering over, thus creating a moisture barrier. Always patch with the same material that is being replaced. Although lime plaster and portland cement stucco are less satisfactory as a surface coating, many adobe buildings have always had them as a surface coating. Their complete removal is inadvisable as the process may prove to be more damaging than the natural deterioration.

Roofs: Flat adobe roofs should be restored and maintained with their original form and materials; however, it may not be feasible or prudent to restore or reconstruct a flat adobe roof on a building if the roof has previously been modified to a gable roof with sheet metal, tiles, or wood shingles.

If an existing flat adobe roof is restored with a fresh layer of adobe mud over an existing mud roof, care should be taken to temporarily support the roof during the work because adobe mud is heavier wet than after it has cured. If not supported, the roof may collapse or deflect. If the wooden roof supports are allowed to sag during such work, the wood may take a permanent deflection, resulting in inadequate drainage and/or "ponding" at low points. Ponding is especially damaging to adobe roofs since standing water will eventually soak through the mud and cause the wooden roof members to rot.

On an adobe building, it is not advisable to construct a new roof that is heavier than the roof it is replacing. If the walls below have uncorrected moisture problems, the added weight of a new roof may cause the walls to bulge (a deformation caused while the adobe mud is in a plastic state). If the walls are dry but severely deteriorated, the added weight may cause the walls to crack or crumble (compression failure).

Floors, Windows, Doors, Etc.: Windows, doors, floors, and other original details of the older adobe building should be retained whenever feasible. It is, however, understandable when the demands of modern living make it necessary to change some of these features: thermal windows and doors, easily maintained floors, etc. But every reasonable effort should be made to retain original interior and exterior details.

Maintenance

Cyclical maintenance has always been the key to successful adobe building survival. As soon as rehabilitation or restoration has been completed, some program of continuing maintenance should be initiated. Changes in the building should particularly be noted. The early stages of cracking, sagging, or bulging in adobe walls should be monitored regularly. All water damage should be noted and remedied at its earliest possible stages. Plant, animal, and insect damage should be halted before it becomes substantial. The roof should be inspected periodically. Surface coatings must be inspected frequently and repaired or replaced as the need indicates.

Mechanical systems should be monitored for break-down. For instance, leaking water pipes and condensation can be potentially more damaging to the adobe building than to a brick, stone, or frame structure. Observing adobe buildings for subtle changes and performing maintenance on a regular basis is a policy which cannot be over emphasized. It is the nature of adobe buildings to deteriorate, but cyclical maintenance can substantially deter this process, thus producing a relatively stable historic adobe building.

Summary

In conclusion, to attempt the preservation of an adobe building is almost a contradiction. Adobe is a formed-earth material, a little stronger perhaps than the soil itself, but a material whose nature is to deteriorate. The preservation of historic adobe buildings, then, is a broader and more complex problem than most people realize. The propensity of adobe to deteriorate is a natural, on-going process. While it would be desirable to arrest that process in order to safeguard the building, no satisfactory method has yet been developed. Competent preservation and maintenance of historic adobe buildings in the American Southwest must (1) accept the adobe material and its natural deterioration, (2) understand the building as a system, and (3) understand the forces of nature which seek to return the building to its original state.

BIBLIOGRAPHY

Books:

Baer, Kurt; and Rudinger, Huge. *Architecture of the California Missions*. Los Angeles: University of California Press, 1958.

Boundreau, E. H. *Making the Adobe Brick*. Berkeley, Calif.: Fifth Street Press, 1971.

Bunting, Bainbridge. *Early Architecture in New Mexico*. Albuquerque: University of New Mexico Press, 1976.

— *Of Earth and Timbers Made: New Mexico Architecture*. Albuquerque: University of New Mexico Press, 1974.

Clifton, James R. *Preservation of Historic Adobe Structures: A Status Report*. Washington, D.C.: National Bureau of Standards Technical Note 934, US Government Printing Office, Stock No. 003–003–01740–0, Feb. 1977.

McHenry, Paul Graham, Jr. *Adobe—Build it Yourself*. Tucson, Ariz.: University of Arizona Press, 1973.

Phillips, Morgan W.; and Selwyn, Judith E. *Epoxies for Wood Repairs in Historic Buildings*. Washington, D.C.: Heritage Conservation and Recreation Service, 1978.

Articles, Periodicals, and Bibliographies:

"Adobe, Past and Present." Reprinted from *El Palacio*. Vol. 77, no. 4 (1971).

"An Architectural Guide to Northern New Mexico." *New Mexico Architecture*. Vol. 12, nos. 9 and 10 (Sept.–Oct. 1970).

Adobe News. Los Lunas New Mexico. Published bimonthly.

Barnes, Mark R. "Adobe Bibliography." The Association for Preservation Technology *Bulletin*. Vol. 7, no. 1 (1975).

Eyre, T. A. "The Physical Properties of Adobe Used as a Building Material." *The University of New Mexico Bulletin*. Engineering Series. Vol. 1, no. 3 (1935).

George, Eugene. "Adobe Bibliography." The Association for Preservation Technology *Bulletin*. Vol. 5, no. 4 (1974).

Haapala, K. V. "Stabilizing and Restoring Old Adobe Structures in California." *Newsletter of the National Association of Restoration Specialists*. Murphy, Calif., June 1972.

Hooker, Van Dorn. "To Hand Plaster or Not?" *New Mexico Architecture*. Vol. 19, no. 5 (Sept.–Oct. 1977).

Many individuals have contributed to the direction, the content and the final form of this Preservation Brief. The text and illustration materials were prepared by de Teel Patterson Tiller, Architectural Historian, and David W. Look, AIA, Technical Preservation Services Division. Much of the technical information was based upon an unpublished report prepared under contract for this office by Ralph H. Comey, Robert C. Giebner, and Albert N. Hopper, College of Architecture, University of Arizona, Tucson. Valuable suggestions and comments were made by architects Eugene George, Austin, Texas; John P. Conron, Santa Fe; and David G. Battle, Santa Fe. Other staff members who provided editorial assistance include H. Ward Jandl, and Kay D. Weeks.

Renewing the Surface Coating. *Traditionally, adobe surface coatings that protected the fragile adobe building fabric were renewed every few years. Recently however, high labor costs have made this a relatively expensive process. Women are seen here recoating an adobe wall with mud plaster mixed with straw at Chamisal, New Mexico. (Photo by Russell Lee, Farm Security Administration Collection, Library of Congress)*

6

Dangers of Abrasive Cleaning to Historic Buildings

Anne E. Grimmer

"The surface cleaning of structures shall be undertaken with the gentlest means possible. Sandblasting and other cleaning methods that will damage the historic building materials shall not be undertaken."—The Secretary of the Interior's "Standards for Historic Preservation Projects."

Abrasive cleaning methods are responsible for causing a great deal of damage to historic building materials. To prevent indiscriminate use of these potentially harmful techniques, this brief has been prepared to explain abrasive cleaning methods, how they can be physically and aesthetically destructive to historic building materials, and why they generally are not acceptable preservation treatments for historic structures. There are alternative, less harsh means of cleaning and removing paint and stains from historic buildings. However, careful testing should preceed general cleaning to assure that the method selected will not have an adverse effect on the building materials. A historic building is irreplaceable, and should be cleaned using only the "gentlest means possible" to best preserve it.

What is Abrasive Cleaning?

Abrasive cleaning methods include all techniques that physically abrade the building surface to remove soils, discolorations or coatings. Such techniques involve the use of certain *materials* which impact or abrade the surface under pressure, or abrasive *tools and equipment.* Sand, because it is readily available, is probably the most commonly used type of grit material. However, any of the following materials may be substituted for sand, and all can be classified as abrasive substances: ground slag or volcanic ash, crushed (pulverized) walnut or almond shells, rice husks, ground corncobs, ground coconut shells, crushed eggshells, silica flour, synthetic particles, glass beads and micro-balloons. Even *water* under pressure can be an abrasive substance. Tools and equipment that are abrasive to historic building materials include wire brushes, rotary wheels, power sanding disks and belt sanders.

The use of water in combination with grit may also be classified as an abrasive cleaning method. Depending on the manner in which it is applied, water *may* soften the impact of the grit, but water that is too highly pressurized can be very abrasive. There are basically two different methods which can be referred to as "wet grit," and it is important to differentiate between the two. One technique involves the addition of a stream of water to a regular sandblasting nozzle. This is done primarily to cut down dust, and has very little, if any, effect on reducing the aggressiveness, or cutting action of the grit particles. With the second technique, a very small amount of grit is added to a pressurized water stream. This method may be controlled by regulating the amount of grit fed into the water stream, as well as the pressure of the water.

Why Are Abrasive Cleaning Methods Used?

Usually, an abrasive cleaning method is selected as an expeditious means of quickly removing years of dirt accumulation, unsightly stains, or deteriorating building fabric or finishes, such as stucco or paint. The fact that sandblasting is one of the best known and most readily available building cleaning treatments is probably the major reason for its frequent use.

Many mid-19th century brick buildings were painted immediately or soon after completion to protect poor quality brick or to imitate another material, such as stone. Sometimes brick buildings were painted in an effort to produce what was considered a more harmonious relationship between a building and its natural surroundings. By the 1870s, brick buildings

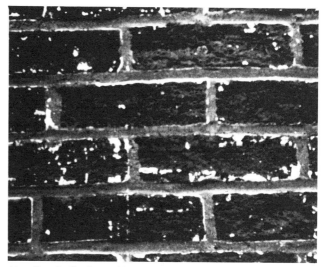

Abrading the Surface without Removing the Paint. *Even though the entire outer surface layer of the brick has been sandblasted off, spots of paint still cling to the masonry. Sandblasting or other similarly abrasive methods are not always a successful means of removing paint.*

Abrasively Cleaned vs. Untouched Brick. *Two brick rowhouses with a common façade provide an excellent point of comparison when only one of the houses has been sandblasted. It is clear that abrasive blasting, by removing the outer surface, has left the brickwork on the left rough and pitted, while that on the right still exhibits an undamaged and relatively smooth surface. Note that the abrasive cleaning has also removed a considerable portion of the mortar from the joints of the brick on the left side, which will require repointing.*

were often left unpainted as mechanization in the brick industry brought a cheaper pressed brick and fashion decreed a sudden preference for dark colors. However, it was still customary to paint brick of poorer quality for the additional protection the paint afforded.

It is a common 20th-century misconception that all historic masonry buildings were initially unpainted. If the intent of a modern restoration is to return a building to its original appearance, removal of the paint not only may be historically inaccurate, but also harmful. Many older buildings were painted or stuccoed at some point to correct recurring maintenance problems caused by faulty construction techniques, to hide alterations, or in an attempt to solve moisture problems. If this is the case, removal of paint or stucco may cause these problems to reoccur.

Another reason for paint removal, particularly in rehabilitation projects, is to give the building a "new image" in response to contemporary design trends and to attract investors or tenants. Thus, it is necessary to consider the purpose of the intended cleaning. While it is clearly important to remove unsightly stains, heavy encrustations of dirt, peeling paint or other surface coatings, it may not be equally desirable to remove paint from a building which originally was painted. Many historic buildings which show only a slight amount of soil or discoloration are much better left as they are. A thin layer of soil is more often protective of the building fabric than it is harmful, and seldom detracts from the building's

architectural and/or historic character. Too thorough cleaning of a historic building may not only sacrifice some of the building's character, but also, misguided cleaning efforts can cause a great deal of damage to historic building fabric. Unless there are stains, graffiti or dirt and pollution deposits which are destroying the building fabric, it is generally preferable to do as little cleaning as possible, or to repaint where necessary. It is important to remember that a historic building does not have to look as if it were newly constructed to be an attractive or successful restoration or rehabilitation project. For a more thorough explanation of the philosophy of cleaning historic buildings see Preservation Briefs: No. 1 "The Cleaning and Waterproof Coating of Masonry Buildings," by Robert C. Mack, AIA.

Problems of Abrasive Cleaning

The crux of the problem is that abrasive cleaning is just that—abrasive. An abrasively cleaned historic structure may be physically as well as aesthetically damaged. Abrasive methods "clean" by eroding dirt or paint, but at the same time they also tend to erode the surface of the building material. In this way, abrasive cleaning is destructive and causes irreversible harm to the historic building fabric. If the fabric is brick, abrasive methods remove the hard, outer protective surface, and therefore make the brick more susceptible to rapid weathering and deterioration. Grit blasting may also increase the water permeability of a brick wall. The impact of the grit particles tends to erode the bond between the mortar and the brick, leaving cracks or enlarging existing cracks where water can enter. Some types of stone develop a protective patina or "quarry crust" parallel to the worked surface (created by the movement of moisture towards the outer edge), which also may be damaged by abrasive cleaning. The rate at which the material subsequently weathers depends on the quality of the inner surface that is exposed.

Abrasive cleaning can destroy, or substantially diminish, decorative detailing on buildings such as a molded brickwork or architectural terra-cotta, ornamental carving on wood or stone, and evidence of historic craft techniques, such as tool marks and other surface textures. In addition, perfectly sound and/or "tooled" mortar joints can be worn away by abrasive techniques. This not only results in the loss of historic craft detailing but also requires repointing, a step involving considerable time, skill and expense, and which might not have been necessary had a gentler method been chosen. Erosion and pitting of the building material by abrasive cleaning creates a greater surface area on which dirt and pollutants collect. In this sense, the building fabric "attracts" more dirt, and will require more frequent cleaning in the future.

In addition to causing physical and aesthetic harm to the historic fabric, there are several adverse environmental effects of dry abrasive cleaning methods. Because of the friction caused by the abrasive medium hitting the building fabric, these techniques usually create a considerable amount of dust, which is unhealthy, particularly to the operators of the abrasive equipment. It further pollutes the environment around the job site, and deposits dust on neighboring buildings, parked vehicles and nearby trees and shrubbery. Some adjacent materials not intended for abrasive treatment such as wood or glass, may also be damaged because the equipment may be difficult to regulate.

Wet grit methods, while eliminating dust, deposit a messy slurry on the ground or other objects surrounding the base of the building. In colder climates where there is the threat of frost, any wet cleaning process applied to historic masonry structures must be done in warm weather, allowing ample time for the wall to dry out thoroughly before cold weather sets in. Water which remains and freezes in cracks and openings of the masonry surface eventually may lead to spalling. High-pressure wet cleaning may force an inordinate amount of water into the walls, affecting interior materials such as plaster or joist ends, as well as metal building components within the walls.

Variable Factors

The greatest problem in developing practical guidelines for cleaning any historic building is the large number of variable and unpredictable factors involved. Because these variables make each cleaning project unique, it is difficult to establish specific standards at this time. This is particularly true of abrasive cleaning methods because their inherent potential for causing damage is multiplied by the following factors:
— the type and condition of the material being cleaned;
— the size and sharpness of the grit particles or the mechanical equipment;
— the pressure with which the abrasive grit or equipment is applied to the building surface;
— the skill and care of the operator; and
— the constancy of the pressure on all surfaces during the cleaning process.

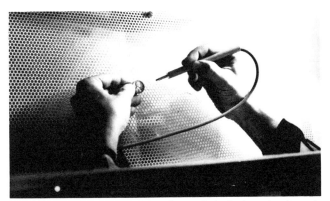

Micro-Abrasive Cleaning. *This small, pencil-sized micro-abrasive unit is used by some museum conservators to clean small objects. This particular micro-abrasive unit is operated within the confines of a box (approximately 2 cubic feet of space), but a similar and slightly larger unit may be used for cleaning larger pieces of sculpture, or areas of architectural detailing on a building. Even a pressure cleaning unit this small is capable of eroding a surface, and must be carefully controlled.*

"Line Drop." *Even though the operator of the sandblasting equipment is standing on a ladder to reach the higher sections of the wall, it is still almost impossible to have total control over the pressure. The pressure of the sand hitting the lower portion of the wall will still be greater than that above, because of the "line drop" in the distance from the pressure source to the nozzle. (Hugh Miller)*

Pressure: The damaging effects of most of the variable factors involved in abrasive cleaning are self evident. However, the matter of pressure requires further explanation. In cleaning specifications, pressure is generally abbreviated as "psi" (pounds per square inch), which technically refers to the "tip" pressure, or the amount of pressure at the nozzle of the blasting apparatus. Sometimes "psig," or pressure at the gauge (which may be many feet away, at the other end of the hose), is used in place of "psi." These terms are often incorrectly used interchangeably.

Despite the apparent care taken by most architects and building cleaning contractors to prepare specifications for pressure cleaning which will not cause harm to the delicate fabric of a historic building, it is very difficult to ensure that the same amount of pressure is applied to all parts of the building. For example, if the operator of the pressure equipment stands on the ground while cleaning a two-story structure, the amount of force reaching the first story will be greater than that hitting the second story, even if the operator stands on scaffolding or in a cherry picker, because of the "line drop" in the distance from the pressure source to the nozzle. Although technically it may be possible to prepare cleaning specifications with tight controls that would eliminate all but a small margin of error, it may not be easy to find professional cleaning firms willing to work under such restrictive conditions. The fact is that many professional building cleaning firms do not really understand the extreme delicacy of historic building fabric, and how it differs from modern construction materials. Consequently, they may accept building cleaning projects for which they have no experience.

The amount of pressure used in any kind of cleaning treatment which involves pressure, whether it is dry or wet grit, chemicals or just plain water, is crucial to the outcome of the cleaning project. Unfortunately, no standards have been established for determining the correct pressure for cleaning each of the many historic building materials which would not cause harm. The considerable discrepancy between the way the building cleaning industry and architectural conservators define "high" and "low" pressure plays a significant role in the difficulty of creating standards.

Nonhistoric/Industrial: A representative of the building cleaning industry might consider "high" pressure *water* cleaning to be anything over 5,000 psi, or even as high as 10,000 to 15,000 psi! Water under this much pressure may be necessary to clean industrial structures or machinery, but would destroy most historic building materials. Industrial *chemical* cleaning commonly utilizes pressures between 1,000 and 2,500 psi.

Spalling Brick. *This soft, early 19th-century brick was sandblasted in the 1960s; consequently, severe spalling has resulted. Some bricks have almost totally disintegrated, and will eventually have to be replaced. (Robert S. Gamble)*

Historic: By contrast, conscientious dry or wet abrasive cleaning of a historic structure would be conducted within the range of 20 to 100 psi at a range of 3 to 12 inches. Cleaning at this low pressure requires the use of a very fine 00 or 0 mesh grit forced through a nozzle with a ¼ inch opening. A similar, even more delicate method being adopted by architectural conservators uses a micro-abrasive grit on small, hard-to-clean areas of carved, cut or molded ornament on a building facade. Originally developed by museum conservators for cleaning sculpture, this technique may employ glass beads, micro-balloons, or another type of micro-abrasive gently powered at approximately 40 psi by a very small, almost pencil-like pressure instrument. Although a slightly larger pressure instrument may be used on historic buildings, this technique still has limited practical applicability on a large scale building cleaning project because of the cost and the relatively few technicians competent to handle the task. In general, architectural conservators have determined that only through very controlled conditions can most historic building material be abrasively cleaned of soil or paint without measurable damage to the surface or profile of the substrate.

Yet some professional cleaning companies which sepcialize in cleaning historic masonry buildings use chemicals and water at a pressure of approximately 1,500 psi, while other cleaning firms recommend lower pressures ranging from 200 to 800 psi for a similar project. An architectural conservator might decide, *after testing*, that some historic structures could be cleaned properly using a moderate pressure (200–600 psi), or even a high pressure (600–1800 psi) water rinse. However,

cleaning historic buildings under such high pressure should be considered an exception rather than the rule, and would require *very careful* testing and supervision to assure that the historic surface materials could withstand the pressure without gouging, pitting or loosening.

These differences in the amount of pressure used by commercial or industrial building cleaners and architectural conservators point to one of the main problems in using abrasive means to clean historic buildings: misunderstanding of the potentially fragile nature of historic building materials. There is no one cleaning formula or pressure suitable for all situations. Decisions regarding the proper cleaning process for historic structures can be made only after careful analysis of the building fabric, and testing.

How Building Materials React to Abrasive Cleaning Methods

Brick and Architectural Terra-Cotta: Abrasive blasting does not affect all building materials to the same degree. Such techniques quite logically cause greater damage to softer and more porous materials, such as brick or architectural terra-cotta. When these materials are cleaned abrasively, the hard, outer layer (closest to the heat of the kiln) is eroded, leaving the soft, inner core exposed and susceptible to accelerated weathering. Glazed architectural terra-cotta and ceramic veneer have a baked-on glaze which is also easily damaged by abrasive cleaning. Glazed architectual terra-cotta was designed for easy maintenance, and generally can be cleaned using detergent and water; but chemicals or steam may be needed to remove more persistent stains. Large areas of brick or architectural terra-cotta which have been painted are best left painted, or repainted if necessary.

Plaster and Stucco: Plaster and stucco are types of masonry finish materials that are softer than brick or terra-cotta; if treated abrasively these materials will simply disintegrate. Indeed, when plaster or stucco is treated abrasively it is usually with the intention of removing the plaster or stucco from whatever base material or substrate it is covering. Obviously, such abrasive techniques should not be applied to clean sound plaster or stuccoed walls, or decorative plaster wall surfaces.

Building Stones: Building stones are cut from the three main categories of natural rock: dense, igneous rock such as granite; sandy, sedimentary rock such as limestone or sandstone; and crystalline, metamorphic rock such as marble. As op-

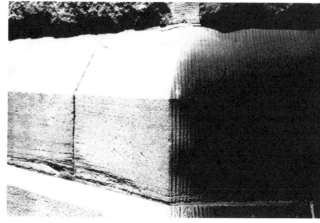

Abrasive Cleaning of Tooled Granite. *Even this carefully controlled "wet grit" blasting has erased vertical tooling marks in the cut granite blocks on the left. Not only has the tooling been destroyed, but the damaged stone surface is now more susceptible to accelerated weathering.*

posed to kiln-dried masonry materials such as brick and architectural terra-cotta, building stones are generally homogeneous in character at the time of a building's construction. However, as the stone is exposed to weathering and environmental pollutants, the surface may become friable, or may develop a protective skin or patina. These outer surfaces are very susceptible to damage by abrasive or improper chemical cleaning.

Building stones are frequently cut into ashlar blocks or "dressed" with tool marks that give the building surface a specific texture and contribute to its historic character as much as ornately carved decorative stonework. Such detailing is easily damaged by abrasive cleaning techniques; the pattern of tooling or cutting is erased, and the crisp lines of moldings or carving are worn or pitted.

Occasionally, it may be possible to clean small areas of rough-cut granite, limestone or sandstone having a heavy dirt encrustation by using the "wet grit" method, whereby a small amount of abrasive material is injected into a controlled, pressurized water stream. However, this technique requires very careful supervision in order to prevent damage to the stone. Polished or honed marble or granite should *never* be treated abrasively, as the abrasion would remove the finish in much the way glass would be etched or "frosted" by such a process. It is generally preferable to underclean, as too strong a cleaning procedure will erode the stone, exposing a new and increased surface area to collect atmospheric moisture and dirt. Removing paint, stains or graffiti from most types of stone may be accomplished by a chemical treatment carefully selected to best handle the removal of the particular type of paint or stain without damaging the stone. (See section on the "Gentlest Means Possible")

Abrasive Cleaning of Wood. *This wooden windowsill, molding and paneling have been sandblasted to remove layers of paint in the rehabilitation of this commercial building. Not only is some paint still embedded in cracks and crevices of the woodwork, but more importantly, grit blasting has actually eroded the summer wood, in effect raising the grain, and resulting in a rough surface.*

Wood: Most types of wood used for buildings are soft, fibrous and porous, and are particularly susceptible to damage by abrasive cleaning. Because the summer wood between the lines of the grain is softer than the grain itself, it will be worn away by abrasive blasting or power tools, leaving an uneven surface with the grain raised and often frayed or "fuzzy." Once this has occurred, it is almost impossible to achieve a smooth surface again except by extensive hand sanding, which is expensive and will quickly negate any costs saved earlier by sandblasting. Such harsh cleaning treatment also obliterates historic tool marks, fine carving and detailing, which precludes its use on any interior or exterior woodwork which has been hand planed, milled or carved.

Metals: Like stone, metals are another group of building materials which vary considerably in hardness and durability. Softer metals which are used architecturally, such as tin, zinc, lead, copper or aluminum, generally should not be cleaned abrasively as the process deforms and destroys the original surface texture and appearance, as well as the acquired patina. Much applied architectural metal work used on historic buildings—tin, zinc, lead and copper—is often quite thin and soft, and therefore susceptible to denting and pitting. Galvanized sheet metal is especially vulnerable, as abrasive treatment would wear away the protective galvanized layer.

In the late 19th and early 20th centuries, these metals were often cut, pressed or otherwise shaped from sheets of metal into a wide variety of practical uses such as roofs, gutters and flashing, and façade ornamentation such as cornices, friezes, dormers, panels, cupolas, oriel windows, etc. The architecture of the 1920s and 1930s made use of metals such as chrome, nickel alloys, aluminum and stainless steel in decorative exterior panels, window frames, and doorways. Harsh abrasive blasting would destroy the original surface finish of most of these metals, and would increase the possiblity of corrosion.

However, conservation specialists are now employing a sensitive technique of glass bead peening to clean some of the harder metals, in particular large bronze outdoor sculpture. Very fine (75–125 micron) glass beads are used at a low pressure of 60 to 80 psi. Because these glass beads are completely spherical, ther are no sharp edges to cut the surface of the metal. After cleaning, these statues undergo a lengthy process of polishing. Coatings are applied which protect the surface from corrosion, but they must be renewed every 3 to 5 years. A similarly delicate cleaning technique employing glass beads has been used in Europe to clean historic masonry structures without causing damage. But at this time the process has not been tested sufficiently in the United States to recommend it as a building conservation measure.

Sometimes a very fine *smooth* sand is used at a low pressure to clean or remove paint and corrosion from copper flashing and other metal building components. Restoration architects recently found that a mixture of crushed walnut shells and copper slag at a pressure of approximately 200 psi was the only way to remove corrosion successfully from a mid-19th century terne-coated iron roof. Metal cleaned in this manner must be painted immediately to prevent rapid recurrence of corrosion. It is thought that these methods "work harden" the surface by compressing the outer layer, and actually may be good for the surface of the metal. But the extremely complex nature and the time required by such processes make it very expensive and impractical for large-scale use at this time.

Cast and wrought iron architectural elements may be gently sandblasted or abrasively cleaned using a wire brush to remove layers of paint, rust and corrosion. Sandblasting was, in fact, developed originally as an efficient maintenance procedure for engineering and industrial structures and heavy machinery—iron and steel bridges, machine tool frames, engine frames, and railroad rolling stock—in order to clean and prepare them for repainting. Because iron is hard, its surface, which is naturally somewhat uneven, will not be noticeably damaged by controlled abrasion. Such treatment will, however, result in a small amount of pitting. But this slight abrasion creates a good surface for paint, since the iron must be repainted immediately to prevent corrosion. Any abrasive cleaning of metal building components will also remove the caulking from joints and around other openings. Such areas must be recaulked quickly to prevent moisture from entering and rusting the metal, or causing deterioration of other building fabric inside the structure.

When is Abrasive Cleaning Permissible?

For the most part, abrasive cleaning is destructive to historic building materials. A limited number of special cases have been explained when it may be appropriate, if supervised by a skilled conservator, to use a delicate abrasive technique on some historic building materials. The type of "wet grit" cleaning which involves a small amount of grit injected into a stream of low pressure water may be used on small areas of stone masonry (i.e., rough cut limestone, sandstone or unpolished granite), where milder cleaning methods have not been totally successful in removing harmful deposits of dirt and pollutants. Such areas may include stone window sills, the tops of cornices or column capitals, or other detailed areas of the façade.

This is still an abrasive technique, and without proper caution in handling, it can be *just as harmful to the building surface as any other abrasive cleaning method.* Thus, the decision to use this type of "wet grit" process should be made only after consultation with an experienced building conservator. Remember that *it is very time consuming and expensive to use any abrasive technique on a historic building in such a manner that it does not cause harm to the often fragile and friable building materials.*

At this time, and only under certain circumstances, abrasive cleaning methods may be used in the rehabilitation of interior spaces of warehouse or industrial buildings for contemporary uses.

Interior spaces of factories or warehouse structures in which the masonry or plaster surfaces do not have significant design, detailing, tooling or finish, and in which wooden architectural features are not finished, molded, beaded or worked by hand, may be cleaned abrasively in order to remove layers of paint and industrial discolorations such as smoke, soot, etc. It is expected after such treatment that brick surfaces will be rough and pitted, and wood will be somewhat frayed or "fuzzy"

Permissible Abrasive Cleaning. *In accordance with the Secretary of the Interior's* Guidelines for Rehabilitation Projects, *it may be acceptable to use abrasive techniques to clean an industrial interior space such as that illustrated here, because the masonry surfaces* do not *have significant design, detailing, tooling or finish, and the wooden architectural features are not finished, molded, beaded or worked by hand.*

with raised wood grain. These nonsignificant surfaces will be damaged and have a roughened texture, but because they are interior elements, they will not be subject to further deterioration caused by weathering.

Historic Interiors that Should Not Be Cleaned Abrasively

Those instances (generally industrial and some commercial properties), when it may be acceptable to use an abrasive treatment on the interior of historic structures have been described. But for the majority of historic buildings, the Secretary of the Interior's *Guidelines for Rehabilitation* do not recommend "changing the texture of exposed wooden architectural features (including structural members) and masonry surfaces through sandblasting or use of other abrasive techniques to remove paint, discolorations and plaster. . . ."

Thus, it is not acceptable to clean abrasively interiors of historic residential and commercial properties which have *finished* interior spaces featuring milled woodwork such as doors, window and door moldings, wainscoting, stair balustrades and mantelpieces. Even the most modest historic *house* interior, although it may not feature elaborate detailing, contains plaster and woodwork that is architecturally significant to the original design and function of the house. Abrasive cleaning of such an interior would be destructive to the historic integrity of the building.

Abrasive cleaning is also impractical. Rough surfaces of abrasively cleaned wooden elements are hard to keep clean. It is also difficult to seal, paint or maintain these surfaces which can be splintery and a problem to the building's occupants. The force of abrasive blasting may cause grit particles to lodge in cracks of wooden elements, which will be a nuisance as the grit is loosened by vibrations and gradually sifts out. Removal of plaster will reduce the thermal and insulating value of the walls. Interior brick is usually softer than exterior brick, and generally of a poorer quality. Removing surface plaster from such brick by abrasive means often exposes gaping mortar joints and mismatched or repaired brickwork which was never intended to show. The resulting bare brick wall may require repointing, often difficult to match. It also may be necessary to apply a transparent surface coating (or sealer) in order to prevent the mortar and brick from "dusting." However, a sealer may not only change the color of the brick, but may also compound any existing moisture problems by restricting the normal evaporation of water vapor from the masonry surface.

"Gentlest Means Possible"

There are alternative means of removing dirt, stains and paint from historic building surfaces that can be recommended as more efficient and less destructive than abrasive techniques. The "gentlest means possible" of removing dirt from a building surface can be achieved by using a low-pressure water wash, scrubbing areas of more persistent grime with a natural bristle (never metal) brush. Steam cleaning can also be used effectively to clean some historic building fabric. Low-pressure water or steam will soften the dirt and cause the deposits to rise to the surface, where they can be washed away.

A third cleaning technique which may be recommended to remove dirt, as well as stains, graffiti or paint, involves the use of commercially available chemical cleaners or paint removers, which, when applied to masonry, loosen or dissolve the dirt or stains. These cleaning agents may be used in combination with water or steam, followed by a clear water wash to remove the residue of dirt and the chemical cleaners from the masonry. A natural bristle brush may also facilitate this type of chemically assisted cleaning, particularly in areas of heavy dirt deposits or stains, and a wooden scraper can be

Do not Abrasively Clean these Interiors. *Most historic residential and some commercial interior spaces contain finished plaster and wooden elements such as this stair balustrade and paneling which contribute to the historic and architectural character of the structure. Such interiors should not be subjected to abrasive techniques for the purpose of removing paint, dirt, discoloration or plaster.*

useful in removing thick encrustations of soot. A limewash or absorbent talc, whiting or clay poultice with a solvent can be used effectively to draw out salts or stains from the surface of the selected areas of a building façade. It is almost impossible to remove paint from masonry surfaces without causing some damage to the masonry, and it is best to leave the surfaces as they are or repaint them if necessary.

Some physicists are experimenting with the use of pulsed laser beams and xenon flash lamps for cleaning historic masonry surfaces. At this time it is a slow, expensive cleaning method, but its initial success indicates that it may have an increasingly important role in the future.

There are many chemical paint removers which, when applied to painted wood, soften and dissolve the paint so that it can be scraped off by hand. Peeling paint can be removed from wood by hand scraping and sanding. Particularly thick layers of paint may be softened with a heat gun or heat plate, providing appropriate precautions are taken, and the paint film scraped off by hand. Too much heat applied to the same spot can burn the wood, and the fumes caused by burning paint are dangerous to inhale, and can be explosive. Furthermore, the hot air from heat guns can start fires in the building cavity. Thus, adequate ventilation is important when using a heat gun or heat plate, as well as when using a chemical stripper. A torch or open flame should never be used.

Preparations for Cleaning: It cannot be overemphasized that all of these cleaning methods must be approached with cau-

tion. When using any of these procedures which involve water or other liquid cleaning agents on masonry, it is imperative that *all* openings be tightly covered, and all cracks or joints be well pointed in order to avoid the danger of water penetrating the building's facade, a circumstance which might result in serious moisture related problems such as efflorescence and/or subflorescence. Any time water is used on masonry as a cleaning agent, either in its pure state or in combination with chemical cleaners, it is very important that the work be done in warm weather when there is no danger of frost for several months. Otherwise water which has penetrated the masonry may freeze, eventually causing the surface of the building to crack and spall, which may create another conservation problem more serious to the health of the building than dirt.

Each kind of masonry has a unique composition and reacts differently with various chemical cleaning substances. Water and/or chemicals may interact with minerals in stone and cause new types of stains to leach out to the surface immediately, or more gradually in a delayed reaction. What may be a safe and effective cleaner for certain stain on one type of stone, may leave unattractive discolorations on another stone, or totally dissolve a third type.

Testing: Cleaning historic building materials, particularly masonry, is a technically complex subject, and thus, should never be done without expert consultation and testing. No cleaning project should be undertaken without first applying the intended cleaning agent to a representative test patch area in an inconspicuous location on the building surface. The test patch or patches should be allowed to weather for a period of time, preferably through a complete seasonal cycle, in order to determine that the cleaned area will not be adversely affected by wet or freezing weather or any by-products of the cleaning process.

Mitigating the Effects of Abrasive Cleaning

There are certain restoration measures which can be adopted to help preserve a historic building exterior which has been damaged by abrasive methods. Wood that has been sandblasted will exhibit a frayed or "fuzzed" surface, or a harder wood will have an exaggerated raised grain. The only way to remove this rough surface or to smooth the grain is by laborious sanding. Sandblasted wood, unless it has been extensively sanded, serves as a dustcatcher, will weather faster, and will present a continuing and ever worsening maintenance problem. Such wood, after sanding, should be painted or given a clear surface coating to protect the wood, and allow for somewhat easier maintenance.

There are few successful preservative treatments that may be applied to grit-blasted exterior masonry. Harder, denser stone may have suffered only a loss of crisp edges or tool marks, or other indications of craft technique. If the stone has a compact and uniform composition, it should continue to weather with little additional deterioration. But some types of sandstone, marble and limestone will weather at an accelerated rate once their protective "quarry crust" or patina has been removed.

Softer types of masonry, particularly brick and architectural terra-cotta, are the most likely to require some remedial treatment if they have been abrasively cleaned. Old brick, being essentially a soft, baked clay product, is greatly susceptible to increased deterioration when its hard, outer skin is removed through abrasive techniques. This problem can be minimized by painting the brick. An alternative is to treat it with a clear sealer or surface coating but this will give the masonry a glossy or shiny look. It is usually preferable to paint the brick rather than to apply a transparent sealer since

Hazards of Sandblasting and Surface Coating. *In order to "protect" this heavily sandblasted brick, a clear surface coating or sealer was applied. Because the air temperature was too cold at the time of application, the sealer failed to dry properly, dripping in places, and giving the brick surface a cloudy appearance.*

sealers reduce the transpiration of moisture, allowing salts to crystallize as subflorescence that eventually spalls the brick. If a brick surface has been so extensively damaged by abrasive cleaning and weathering that spalling has already begun, it may be necessary to cover the walls with stucco, if it will adhere.

Of course, the application of paint, a clear surface coating (sealer), or stucco to deteriorating masonry means that the historical appearance will be sacrificed in an attempt to conserve the historic building materials. However, the original color and texture will have been changed already by the abrasive treatment. At this point it is more important to try to preserve the brick, and there is little choice but to protect it from "dusting" or spalling too rapidly. As a last resort, in the case of severely spalling brick, there may be no option but to replace the brick—a difficult, expensive (particularly if custom-made reproduction brick is used), and lengthy process. As described earlier, sandblasted interior brick work, while not subject to change of weather, may require the application of a transparent surface coating or painting as a maintenance procedure to contain loose mortar and brick dust. (See Preservation Briefs: No. 1 for a more thorough discussion of coatings.)

Metals, other than cast or wrought iron, that have been pitted and dented by harsh abrasive blasting usually cannot be smoothed out. Although fillers may be satisfactory for smoothing a painted surface, exposed metal that has been damaged usually will have to be replaced.

Summary

Sandblasting or other abrasive methods of cleaning or paint removal are by their nature destructive to historic building materials and should not be used on historic buildings except in a few well-monitored instances. There are exceptions when certain types of abrasive cleaning may be permissible, but only if conducted by a trained conservator, and if cleaning is necessary for the preservation of the historic structure.

There is no one formula that will be suitable for cleaning all historic building surfaces. Although there are many commerical cleaning products and methods available, it is impossible to state definitively which of these will be the most effective without causing harm to the building fabric. It is often difficult to identify ingredients or their proportions contained in cleaning products; consequently it is hard to predict how a product will react to the building materials to be cleaned. Similar uncertainties affect the outcome of other cleaning methods as they are applied to historic building materials. Further advances in understanding the complex nature of the many variables of the cleaning techniques may someday provide a better and simpler solution to the problems. But until that time, the process of cleaning historic buildings must be approached with caution through trial and error.

It is important to remember that historic building materials are neither indestructible, nor are they renewable. They must be treated in a responsible manner, which may mean little or no cleaning at all if they are to be preserved for future generations to enjoy. If it is in the best interest of the building to clean it, then it should be done "using the gentlest means possible."

Selected Reading List

Ashurst, John. *Cleaning Stone and Brick.* Technical Pamphlet 4. London: Society for the Protection of Ancient Buildings, 1977.

Asmus, John F. "Light Cleaning: Laser Technology for Surface Preparation in the Arts." *Technology and Conservation,* 3: 3 (Fall 1978), pp. 14–18.

"The Bare-Brick Mistake." *The Old House Journal,* I: 2 (November 1973), p. 2

Brick Institute of America. *Colorless Coatings for Brick Masonry.* Technical Notes on Brick Construction, Number 7E (September/October 1976).

Gilder, Cornelia Brooke. *Property Owner's Guide to the Maintenance and Repair of Stone Buildings.* Technical Series/No. 5. Albany, New York: The Preservation League of New York State, 1977.

Prudon, Theodore H.M. "The Case Against Removing Paint from Brick Masonry." *The Old House Journal,* III: 2 (February 1975), pp. 6–7

———— "Removing Stains from Masonry." *The Old House Journal,* V: 5 (May 1977), pp. 58–59.

Stambolov, T., and J.R.J. Van Asperen de Boer. *The Deterioration and Conservation of Porous Building Materials in Monuments: A Review of the Literature.* Second enlarged edition. Rome: International Centre for Conservation, 1976.

Weiss, Norman R. "Cleaning of Building Exteriors: Problems and Procedures of Dirt Removal." *Technology and Conservation,* 2/76 (Fall 1976), pp. 8–13.

———— *Exterior Cleaning of Historic Masonry Buildings.* Draft. Washington, D.C.: Office of Archeology and Historic Preservation, Heritage Conservation and Recreation Service, U.S. Department of the Interior, 1976.

This Preservation Brief was written by Anne E. Grimmer, Architectural Historian, Technical Preservation Services Division. Valuable suggestions and comments were made by Hugh C. Miller, AIA, Washington, D.C.; Martin E. Weaver, Ottawa, Ontario, Canada; Terry Bryant, Downers Grove, Illinois; Daniel C. Cammer, McLean, Virginia; and the professional staff of Technical Preservation Services Division. Deborah Cooney edited the final manuscript.

The illustrations for this brief not specifically credited are from the files of the Technical Preservation Services Division.

7

The Preservation of Historic Glazed Architectural Terra-Cotta

de Teel Patterson Tiller

Glazed architectural terra-cotta was significant in the development of important architectural idioms in this country—specifically, the "Chicago School," the High Rise and the Historic or Beaux Arts styles. In fact, glazed architectural terra-cotta is one of the most prevalent masonry building materials found in the urban environment today (Fig. 1). Popular between the late 19th century and the 1930s, glazed architectural terra-cotta offered a modular, varied and relatively inexpensive approach to wall and floor construction. It was particularly adaptable to vigorous and rich ornamental detailing. However, with changing vogues in materials and architectural styles and rising production costs, glazed architectural terra-cotta fell into disfavor and disuse by the mid-20th century.

Today, information on the maintenance, rehabilitation and replacement of glazed architectural terra-cotta is limited, as are sources of new glazed architectural terra-cotta. This report, then, will discuss some of the major deterioration problems that commonly occur in historic glazed architectural terra-cotta, methods of determining the extent of that deterioration and recommendations for the maintenance, repair and replacement of the deteriorated historic material.

What is Terra-Cotta?

Generically, the broadest definition of terra-cotta refers to a high grade of weathered or aged clay which, when mixed with sand or with pulverized fired clay, can be molded and fired at high temperatures to a hardness and compactness not obtainable with brick. Simply put, terra-cotta is an enriched molded clay brick or block. The word *terra-cotta* is derived from the Latin word *terra-cocta*—literally, "cooked earth." Terra-cotta clays vary widely in color according to geography and types, ranging from red and brown to white.

Terra-cotta was usually hollow cast in blocks which were open to the back, like boxes, with internal compartment-like stiffeners called webbing (Fig. 2). Webbing substantially strengthened the load-bearing capacity of the hollow terra-cotta block without greatly increasing its weight.

Terra-cotta blocks were often finished with a glaze; that is, a slip glaze (clay wash) or an aqueous solution of metal salts was brushed or sprayed on the air-dried block before firing. Glazing changed the color, imitated different finishes, and produced a relatively impervious surface on the weather face of the final product. The glaze on the terra-cotta unit possessed excellent weathering properties when properly maintained. It had rich color and provided a hard surface that was not easily chipped off. Glazing offered unlimited and fade-resistant colors to the designer. Even today, few building materials can match the glazes on terra-cotta for the range and, most importantly, the durability of colors.

Types of Terra-Cotta

Historically there are four types or categories of terra-cotta which have enjoyed wide use in the history of the American building arts: 1) brownstone, 2) fireproof construction, 3) ceramic veneer, and 4) glazed architectural.

Brownstone terra-cotta is the variety of this masonry material used earliest in American buildings (mid- to late 19th century). The brownstone type is a dark red or brown block either glazed (usually a slip glaze) or unglazed. It was hollow cast and was generally used in conjunction with other masonry in imitation of sandstone, brick or real brownstone. It is often found in the architecture of Richard Upjohn, James Renwick, H. H. Richardson and is associated with the Gothic and Romanesque Revival movements through such ornamental detailing as moldings, finials and capitals.

Fireproof construction terra-cotta was extensively developed as a direct result of the growth of the High Rise building in America. Inexpensive, lightweight and fireproof, these rough-finished hollow building blocks were ideally suited to span the I-beam members in floor, wall and ceiling construction (Fig. 3). Certain varieties are still in production today, although fireproof construction terra-cotta is no longer widely employed in the building industry.

Ceramic veneer was developed during the 1930s and is still used extensively in building construction today. Unlike traditional architectural terra-cotta, ceramic veneer is not hollow cast, but is as its name implies: a veneer of glazed ceramic tile which is ribbed on the back in much the same fashion as bathroom tile. Ceramic veneer is frequently attached to a grid of metal ties which has been anchored to the building.

Glazed architectural terra-cotta was the most complex development of terra-cotta as a masonry building material in this country. The hollow units were hand cast in molds or carved in clay and heavily glazed (often in imitation of stone) and fired. Sometimes called "architectural ceramics," glazed architectural terra-cotta was developed and refined throughout the first third of the 20th century and has been closely associated with the architecture of Cass Gilbert, Louis Sullivan, and Daniel H. Burnham, among others. Significant examples in this country include the Woolworth Building (1913) in New York City and the Wrigley Building (1921) in Chicago.

Late 19th and early 20th century advertising promoted the durable, impervious and adaptable nature of glazed archi-

Figure 1. Terra-Cotta Detailing. *Adaptable to every nuance of color, texture, and modeling, glazed architectural terra-cotta was ideally suited to satisfy the tastes of an eclectic age. Its popularity was, however, short lived; it endured only 30 or 40 years after its introduction as a building material late in the 19th century.* (Larry Payne, Houston, Texas)

tectural terra-cotta. It provided for crisp, vigorous modeling of architectural details as the molds were cast directly from clay prototypes without loss of refinement. Glazed architectural terra-cotta could accommodate subtle nuances of modeling, texture and color. Compared to stone, it was easier to handle, quickly set and more affordable to use. Thought to be fireproof and waterproof, it was readily adaptable to structures of almost any height. The cost of molding the clay, glazing and firing the blocks, when compared to carving

Figure 2. Webbing. *Webbing, or the hollow internal compartment construction of glazed architectural terra-cotta blocks, made them inexpensive to produce, easy to handle and light in construction; these were significant factors in the popularity of the material in the first decades of this century.*

stone, represented a considerable savings, especially when casts were used in a modular fashion—that is, repeated over and over again. Maintenance of the fired and glazed surface was easy; it never needed paint and periodic washings restored its original appearance.

With the passage of time, many of the phenomenal claims of the early proponents of glazed architectural terra-cotta have proven true. There are many examples throughout this country that attest to the durability and permanence of this material. Yet present-day deterioration of other significant glazed architectural terra-cotta resources ultimately belie those claims. Why? Historically, the lack of foresight or understanding about the nature and limitations of the material has, in many instances, allowed serious deterioration problems to occur that are only now becoming apparent.

Characteristics of Glazed Architectural Terra-Cotta as a Building Material

Glazed architectural terra-cotta has many material properties similar to brick or stone. It also has many material properties radically different from those traditional masonry materials. It is those differences which must be considered for a better understanding of some of the material characteristics of glazed architectural terra-cotta when it is used as a building material.

Difficult to identify: Glazed architectural terra-cotta probably comprises one of the largest if not the largest constituent material in some of our urban environments today. However, the infinite varieties of glazing have hidden this fact from the casual observer. One of the attractive features of glazed architectural terra-cotta in its time was that it could be finished (glazed) in exact imitation of stone. In fact, many building owners and architects alike are often surprised to discover that what they presumed to be a granite or limestone building is glazed architectural terra-cotta instead.

Two separate systems: Historically, glazed architectural terra-cotta has been used in association with two specific and very different types of building systems: as part of a traditional *load-bearing* masonry wall in buildings of modest height, and as a *cladding material* in High Rise construction. As cladding, glazed architectural terra-cotta often utilized an extensive metal anchoring system to attach it or to "hang it" onto a wall framing system or superstructure (Fig. 4). In the first instance the anchoring was limited; in the second, the anchoring was often extensive and complex. Likewise, in the first instance, deterioration has generally been limited. However, where glazed architectural terra-cotta was used as clad-

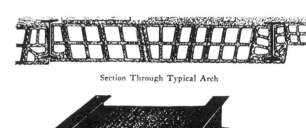

Section Through Typical Arch

Perspective of Typical Arch

Figure 3. Fireproof construction terra-cotta. *Perspective and section through fireproof construction terra-cotta and I-beam detailing in industrial floor construction.* (*Detail,* "Sweets" *Industrial Catalogue of Building Construction, 1906*)

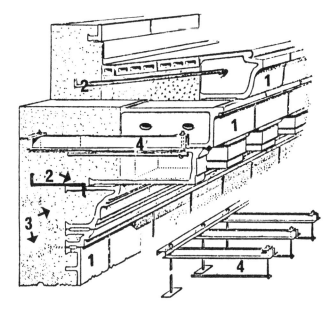

Figure 4. Typical Construction Detail of Glazed Architectural Terra-Cotta Ornament. *Construction detailing was often complex. The terra-cotta units (1) which were laid in mortar were fitted with holes or slots to receive the metal anchors (2) (often called "Z" straps or "light iron") which were often fitted directly to the building frame. Masonry backfill (3)(either brick or poured cement) was laid between the terra-cotta units, with the building frame encasing the metal anchor. Overhanging or protruding elements were further secured by metal dowels or outriggers (4). (Detail, Architectural Terra Cotta, Charles E. White, Jr., 1920)*

ding, particularly in high rise construction, present-day deterioration and failure are often severe.

Complexity of deterioration: Deterioration is, by nature of the design, infinitely complex—particularly when glazed architectural terra-cotta has been used as a cladding material. Deterioration creates a "domino"-like breakdown of the whole system: glazed units, mortar, metal anchors, and masonry backfill. In no other masonry system is material failure potentially so complicated.

Poor original design: The root of deterioration in glazed architectural terra-cotta systems often lies in a misapplication of the material. Historically, glazed architectural terra-cotta was viewed as a highly waterproof system needing neither flashing, weep holes nor drips. This supposition, however, has proved to be untrue, as serious water-related failure was evident early in the life of many glazed architectural terra-cotta clad or detailed buildings.

Common Deterioration Problems

No one case of deterioration in glazed architectural terra-cotta is ever identical to another owing to the infinite number of variations with the material: original manufacture, original installation inconsistencies, number of component parts, ongoing repairs or the various types and sources of deterioration. However, certain general statements may be made on the nature of glazed architectural terra-cotta deterioration.

Material failure can most commonly be attributed to water-related problems. However, less frequent though no less severe causes may include: faulty original craftsmanship, which is often cited but hard to determine; stress-related deterioration; damage caused by later alterations and additions; or inappropriate repairs.

Water-related deterioration: As with most building conservation and rehabilitation problems, water is a principal source of deterioration in glazed architectural terra-cotta. Terra-cotta systems are highly susceptible to such complex water-

related deterioration problems as glaze crazing, glaze spalling and material loss, missing masonry units and deteriorated metal anchoring, among others.

Crazing, or the formation of small random cracks in the glaze, is a common form of water-related deterioration in glazed architectural terra-cotta. When the new terra-cotta unit first comes from the kiln after firing, it has shrunken (dried) to its smallest possible size. With the passage of time, however, it expands as it absorbs moisture from the air, a process which may continue for many years. The glaze then goes into tension because it has a lesser capacity for expansion than the porous tile body; it no longer "fits" the expanding unit onto which it was originally fired. If the strength of the glaze is exceeded, it will crack (craze) (Fig. 5). Crazing is a process not unlike the random hairline cracking on the surface of an old oil painting. Both may occur as a normal process in the aging of the material. Unless the cracks visibly extend into the porous tile body beneath the glaze, crazing should not be regarded as highly serious material failure. It does, however, tend to increase the water absorption capability of the glazed architectural terra-cotta unit.

Figure 5. Crazing. *Water and air-borne moisture entering the glazed architectural terra-cotta causes expansion of the porous clay body which increases its volume. This, in turn, is sufficient to upset the "fit" of the glaze and to make it shatter, commonly called crazing.*

Spalling, the partial loss of the masonry material itself, is, like crazing, caused by water and is usually a result not only of air-borne water but more commonly of water trapped within the masonry system itself. Trapped water is often caused by poor water detailing in the original design, insufficient maintenance, rising damp or a leaking roof. In most cases, trapped water tends to migrate outward through masonry walls where it eventually evaporates. In glazed architectural terra-cotta, the water is impeded in its journey by the relatively impervious glaze on the surface of the unit which acts as a water barrier. The water is stopped at the glaze until it builds up sufficient pressure (particularly in the presence of widely fluctuating temperatures) to pop off sections of the glaze (glaze spalling) or to cause the wholesale destruction of portions of the glazed architectural terra-cotta unit itself (material spalling).

Glaze spalling may appear as small coin-size blisters where the glaze has ruptured and exposed the porous tile body beneath (Fig. 6). This may occur as several spots on the surface or, in more advanced cases of deterioration, it may result in the wholesale disappearance of the glaze. Spalling of the glaze may also be symptomatic of deterioration (rusting) of the internal metal anchoring system which holds the terra-cotta units together and to the larger building structure. The increase in volume of the metal created by rusting creates increased internal pressures in the terra-cotta unit which, in

Figure 6. Glaze Spalling. *Blistering of the glaze, like crazing, is the result of the increase in water in the porous clay body and the subsequent destruction of the glaze as a result of water migration and pressure. Glaze spalling may also be caused by deterioration of metal anchors behind the terra-cotta unit.*

Figure 7. Material Spalling. *Excessive expansion of the porous tile body caused by water and freezing temperatures produces major material spalling, a situation often difficult to repair.*

turn, may spall the glaze, or in more extreme cases, cause material spalling.

Material spalling is a particularly severe situation. Not only is the visual integrity of the detailing impaired, but a large area of the porous underbody, webbing and metal anchoring is exposed to the destructive effects of further water entry and deterioration (Fig. 7). Both glaze and material spalling must be dealt with as soon as possible.

Figure 8. Deterioration of Exposed Detailing. *Exposed or freestanding terra-cotta detailing (parapets, urns, balusters, etc.) have traditionally been subject to the most severe vicissitudes of deterioration as a result of freezing temperatures and water.* (Colorado State Historic Preservation Office)

Missing units is a serious situation which particularly plagues architectural terra-cotta systems. Unlike brick or stone, damaged glazed architectural terra-cotta is exceedingly difficult to replace. New production is extremely limited. Missing units create gaps which increase the structural load on the remaining pieces and also permit water to enter the system. Exposed or freestanding glazed architectural terra-cotta detailing (balusters, urns, parapet walls, etc.) are particularly susceptible to extensive loss of material (Fig. 8). These elements face the most severe vicissitudes of water- and temperature-related deterioration in direct proportion to the extent of their exposure. The replacement of missing units should be a high priority work item in the rehabilitation of glazed architectural terra-cotta.

Deterioration of metal anchoring: Deteriorated anchoring systems are perhaps the most difficult form of glazed architectural terra-cotta deterioration to locate or diagnose. Often, the damage must be severe and irreparable before it is noticed on even the most intense "prima facie" examination. Water which enters the glazed architectural terra-cotta system can rust the anchoring system and substantially weaken or completely disintegrate those elements. Where water has been permitted to enter the system, some deterioration has more than likely taken place. Partial deterioration results in staining and material spalling. Total deterioration and the lack of any anchoring system may result in the loosening of the units themselves, threatening the architectural or structural integrity of the building. Recently, falling glazed architectural terra-cotta units have become a serious safety concern to many building owners and municipal governments (Fig. 9). Early detection of failing anchoring systems is exceedingly difficult.

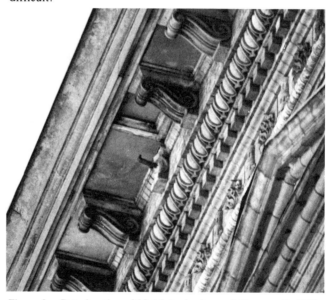

Figure 9. Deterioration of Metal Anchoring and Masonry Backfill. *Trapped water may deteriorate masonry backfill or rust metal anchoring causing overhanging architectural elements to loosen and drop from the building. This is particularly true when unmaintained roof drainage systems fail and soak the masonry system. Note the exposed metal anchoring.*

Deterioration of mortar and other adjacent materials: Deteriorated mortar has always been a key to the survival or failure of any masonry system. This is particularly true with glazed architectural terra-cotta. In recognition of the fragile nature of the system, the need for insuring a relatively dry internal system is important. Sound mortar is the "first line" of defense in terra-cotta systems. It is a maintenance "must." Deteriorated mortar joints are a singularly culpable source of water and, therefore, of deterioration. Mortar deterioration may result from improper original craftsmanship or air-

and water-borne pollution. More often, however, lack of on-going maintenance is mainly responsible. Deteriorated mortar should not be overlooked as a major source of glazed architectural terra-cotta failure.

The deterioration of materials adjoining the glazed architectural terra-cotta (flashing, capping, roofing, caulking around windows and doors) bears significant responsibility in its deterioration. When these adjoining materials fail, largely as a result of lack of maintenance, water-related deterioration results. For instance, it is not uncommon to find wholesale terra-cotta spalling in close proximity to a window or doorway where the caulking has deteriorated.

Stress-related deterioration: Stress-related deterioration of glazed architectural terra-cotta frequently occurs in high rise buildings. The evolution of stress relieving details (flexible joints, shelf angles, etc.) occurred late in the development of American building construction. Consequently, most early continuously clad High Rise buildings (c.1900–1920s) had little or no provisions for normal material and building movement in their original design. The development of large stress-related cracks or wholesale material deterioration is often caused by unaccommodated building-frame shortening under load, thermal expansion and contraction of the façade and moisture expansion of the glazed architectural terra-cotta units themselves (Fig. 10). Cracks running through many units or stories or large areas of material deterioration often indicate stress-related problems. This sort of deterioration, in turn, permits significant water entry into the terra-cotta system.

Figure 10. Structural Cracking. *Structural cracking, whether static (nonmoving) or dynamic (moving or active), should be caulked to prevent water entry into the glazed architectural terra-cotta system. Note the exposed webbing.*

Inappropriate repairs: Inappropriate repairs result because using new terra-cotta for replacement of deteriorated or missing glazed architectural terra-cotta has generally been impractical. Repairs, therefore, have traditionally been made in brick or cementitious build ups of numerous materials such as stucco or fiberglass. Some materials *are appropriate* temporary or permanent replacements, while others are not. (These issues are discussed at a later point in this report.) However, improper anchoring or bonding of the repair work or visual incompatibility of repairs have themselves, with the passage of time, become rehabilitation problems: replacement brick that is pulling free, cement stucco that is cracking and spalling, or a cement or bituminous repairs that are not visually compatible with the original material.

Alteration damage: Alteration damage has occurred as a result of the installation of such building additions as signs, screens, marquees or bird proofing. These installations often necessitated the boring of holes or cutting of the glazed architectural terra-cotta to anchor these additions to the building frame beneath. As the anchoring or caulking deteriorated, or as these elements were removed in subsequent renovation

work, these holes have become significant sources of water-related damage to the glazed architectural terra-cotta system.

Deterioration Inspection and Analysis

Certain deterioration in glazed architectural terra-cotta may be on the building surface and patently obvious to the casual observer—crazing, spalling, deterioration of mortar joints. Other deterioration may be internal or within the masonry system and hard to determine—deterioration of anchoring, deterioration behind the glaze, crumbling of internal webbing. Prima facie, "first inspection," examination may indicate surface deterioration problems while not revealing others. This demonstrates one of the most frustrating aspects of dealing with deteriorated glazed architectural terra-cotta: that there are two systems or levels of deterioration, one which is visible and the other which is not.

Material failure in glazed architectural terra-cotta is necessarily complex. For this reason, it is generally advised that the examination and repair of this material should be the responsibility of an experienced professional. Few restorationists have experience in the inspection, repair and replacement of glazed architectural terra-cotta. This is certainly never the province of the amateur or the most well-intentioned but inexperienced architect or engineer. There are some methods of internal and external inspection and analysis which are relatively simple to the trained professional. Other methods, however, are expensive, time consuming, and only in the experimental stage at this writing. These all generally preclude the use of anyone but an experienced professional.

Preliminary cleaning: Before a terra-cotta building is analyzed for deterioration, it is often advisable, but not always necessary, to clean the surface of the material. This is particularly true when the material has been exposed to the vicissitudes of heavy urban pollution. While most building materials are cleaned for "cosmetic" purposes, the cleaning of glazed architectural terra-cotta for the purpose of inspection and analysis may be advised. Dirt on glazed architectural terra-cotta often hides a multitude of problems. It is only with cleaning that these problems become obvious. Recommended cleaning procedures are covered later in the report.

Methods of inspection:
Prima facie analysis is the unit by unit, first-hand, external inspection of the glazed architectural terra-cotta building surface. Special note of all visible surface deterioration (staining, crazing, spalling, cracking, etc.) should be made on elevation drawings. Binoculars are often used where cost, height, or inaccessibility prevent easy inspection. However, much deterioration may go unnoticed unless scaffolding or window-washing apparatus is used in a true "hands on" inspection of each unit of the façade.

Tapping, a somewhat inexact method of detection of internal deterioration is, nevertheless, the most reliable inspection procedure presently available. Quite simply, tapping is the striking of each unit with a wooden mallet. When struck, an undamaged glazed architectural terra-cotta unit gives a pronounced ring, indicating its sound internal condition. Conversely, deteriorated units (i.e., units which are failing internally) produce a flat, hollow sound. Metal hammers are never to be used, as they may damage the glazed surface of the unit. Extensive experience is the best teacher with this inspection method.

Infrared scanning is only in the experimental stage at this time, but its use seems to hold great promise in locating deteriorated internal material in terra-cotta. All materials emit heat—heat which can be measured in terms of infrared light. While infrared light cannot be seen by the human eye, it can be measured by infrared scanning. Infrared photography, a kind of infrared scanning, has been of particular use in detecting sources of heat loss in buildings in recent years.

Broken or loose internal terra-cotta pieces have a less firm attachment to the surrounding firm or attached pieces and, therefore, have different thermal properties, i.e., temperatures. These temperature differences become evident on the infrared scan and may serve as a fair indication of internal material deterioration in terra-cotta.

Sonic testing has been successfully used for some time to detect internal cracking of concrete members. In the hands of an experienced operator, there are conditions where it can detect internal failure in glazed architectural terra-cotta. Sonic testing registers the internal configuration of materials by penetrating the material with sound waves and reading the patterns that "bounce back" from the originating source of the sound. Readings at variance with those from undeteriorated material might indicate collapsed webbing or pools of water in the interior of the terra-cotta unit.

Metal detection is a nondestructive and generally useful way of locating the position of internal metal anchoring. Metal detectors indicate the presence of metals by electro-magnetic impulses. These impulses are transmitted onto an oscilloscope where they may be seen or they are converted to sound patterns which may be heard by the operator. Original drawings are eminently useful in predicting where internal metal anchoring should be. Metal detectors can confirm that indeed they are still there. Without original drawings, the contractor or architect can still locate the metal anchoring, however. No reading where an anchor would be expected could indicate a missing anchor or one that has seriously deteriorated. The information produced by metal detection is, at best, only rough. However, it is the most viable way of locating the internal metal anchoring without physically removing, thus irreparably damaging, the glazed architectural terra-cotta units themselves.

Laboratory analysis may be carried out on samples of removed original material to find glaze absorption, permeability or glaze adhesion, or to evaluate material for porosity. These tests are useful in determining the present material characteristics of the historic glazed architectural terra-cotta and how they may be expected to perform in the future.

Maintenance, Repair and Replacement

Deterioration in glazed architectural terra-cotta is, by definition, insidious in that the outward signs of decay do not always indicate the more serious problems within. It is, therefore, of paramount importance that the repair and replacement of deteriorated glazed architectural terra-cotta not be undertaken unless the causes of that deterioration have been determined and repaired. As mentioned before, one of the primary agents of deterioration in glazed architectural terra-cotta is water. Therefore, water-related damage can be repaired only when the sources of that water have been eliminated. Repointing, caulking and replacement of missing masonry pieces are also of primary concern. Where detailing to conduct water in the original design has been insufficient, the installation of new flashing or weep holes might be considered.

Where stress-related or structural problems have caused the deterioration of glazed architectural terra-cotta, the services of a structural engineer should be sought to mitigate these problems. This may include the installation of relieving joints, shelf angles or flexible joints. In any case, stress-related and structural deterioration, like water-related deterioration, must be stopped before effective consolidation or replacement efforts may begin.

Cleaning: The successful cleaning of glazed architectural terra-cotta removes excessive soil from the glazed surface without damaging the masonry unit itself. Of the many cleaning materials available, the most widely recommended are water, detergent, and a natural or nylon bristle brush. More

stubborn pollution or fire-related dirt or bird droppings can be cleaned with steam or weak solutions of muriatic or oxalic acid.

A note of caution: Any acids, when used in strong enough solutions, may themselves deteriorate mortar and "liberate" salts within the masonry system, producing a situation called efflorescence. For further information on this situation, refer to: "Preservation Briefs 1: The Cleaning and Waterproof Coating of Masonry Buildings," Heritage Conservation and Recreation Service, Department of the Interior, Washington D.C.

Commercial cleaning solutions may be appropriate but probably are not necessary when water and detergent will suffice. There are, however, certain cleaning techniques for glazed architectural terra-cotta which are definitely *not* recommended and which would damage the surface of the material. These include: all abrasive cleaning measures (especially sandblasting), the use of strong acids (particularly fluoride-based acids), high-pressure water cleaning and the use of metal bristle brushes. All of these techniques will irreparably harm the glaze in one fashion or another and subsequently expose the porous tile body to the damaging effects of water.

It is important to remember that glazed architectural terra-cotta was designed to be cleaned cheaply and easily. This, in fact, was one of its major assets and was much advertised in the selling of the material early in this century.

Waterproofing: The covering of crazed glazing (see Fig. 5) with waterproof coatings is the subject of an on-going controversy today. The question involves whether or not the micro-cracks conduct substantial amounts of water into the porous tile body. Tests indicate that the glaze on new unexposed terra-cotta is itself not completely waterproof. Some testing also indicates that most crazing on historic glazed terra-cotta does not substantially increase the flow of moisture into the porous tile body when compared to new material. Excessive and serious crazing is, however, an exception and the coating of those areas on a limited scale may be wholly appropriate.

In an effort to stem water-related deterioration, architects and building owners often erroneously attribute water-related damage to glaze crazing when the source of the deterioration is, in fact, elsewhere: deteriorated caulking, flashing, etc. The waterproof coating of glazed architectural terra-cotta walls may cause problems on its own. Outward migration of water vapor normally occurs through the mortar joints in these systems. The inadvertent sealing of these joints in the wholesale coating of the wall may exacerbate an already serious situation. Spalling of the glaze, mortar, or porous body will, more than likely, result.

Repointing: Repointing of mortar which is severely deteriorated or improperly or infrequently maintained is one of the most useful preservation activities that can be performed on historic glazed architectural terra-cotta buildings. On-going and cyclical repointing guarantees the long life of this material. Repointing should always be carried out with a mortar which has a compressive strength (measured in p.s.i.) *lower* than the adjacent masonry unit. Hard (Portland cement) or coarsely screened mortars may cause point loading and/or prevent the outward migration of the water through the mortar joints, both of which ultimately damage the terra-cotta unit. Repointing with waterproof caulking compounds or similar waterproof materials should never be undertaken because, like waterproof coatings, they impede the normal outward migration of moisture through the masonry joints. Moisture then may build sufficient pressure behind the waterproof caulk and the glaze on the terra-cotta to cause damage to the unit itself.

Repair of glaze spalling: Glaze spalling is also a highly culpable source of water-related deterioration in glazed architectural terra-cotta. It is important to coat or seal these blistered areas (see Fig. 6) and to prevent further entry of water into the system by this route. All loose or friable material should be removed. This may be done easily by hand; chisels or similar small tools are most effective. The exposed material is then painted over. At this time, no permanently effective reglazing materials are available. However, there are several acrylic-based proprietary products and masonry paints which can be used effectively to protect these exposed areas, thus preventing the entry of water. These materials are effective for 5 to 7 years and can be reapplied. They also can be tinted to approximate closely the original glaze color.

Repair of minor material spalling: Minor material spalling, where visual or cosmetic considerations are negligible, should be treated in a manner similar to glaze spalling damage. That is, areas where small portions of the body and glaze have spalled and which are far removed from close scrutiny (i.e., detailing on entablatures, upper story windows, etc.) are best remedied by painting with a masonry paint or an acrylic-based proprietary product. Units on which material spalling is easily observed (on the street level, door surrounds, etc.), and on which visual integrity is a consideration, may be better replaced. Patching is not appropriate. Stucco-like or cementitious build-ups are difficult to form satisfactorily, safely and compatibly in situ to replace missing pieces of glazed architectural terra-cotta. Cementitious repairs never satisfactorily bond to the original material. The differential expansion coefficients of the two materials (the repair and the original) preclude a safe, effective and long-term attachment.

Repair of major spalling: Glazed architectural terra-cotta units, which have spalled severely thereby losing much of their material and structural integrity in the wall, should be replaced. Partial in situ repair will not be long lasting and may, in fact, cause complicated restoration problems at a later date. Appropriate methods of replacement are discussed at a later point in this report.

Temporary stabilization: Stabilization measures are necessary when deterioration is so severe as to create a situation where pieces of glazed architectural terra-cotta may fall from the building. This is a particular concern with greatly exposed detailing: cornices, balconies, balustrades, urns, columns, buttresses, etc. Restoration work on these pieces is expensive and often must be carried on over a period of time. Unstable terra-cotta pieces are often removed or destroyed in lieu of such measures. This is particularly true in areas of heavy traffic-related vibrations or in earthquake zones. There are, however, less severe measures which may be employed on a temporary basis. Substantial success has been achieved in securing unstable glazed architectural terra-cotta pieces with metal strapping and nylon net (Fig. 11). While these measures should not be seen as permanent preservation solutions, they do offer temporary alternatives to the wanton destruction of significant glazed architectural terra-cotta detailing in the name of public safety and local code compliance.

Repair of addition and structural damage: Holes, sign anchors, slots for channel steel, or structural cracking in the surface of glazed architectural terra-cotta cladding should be permanently sealed with a material that will expand with the normal dynamics of the surrounding material, yet effectively keep water out of the system. Any one of a number of commercially available waterproof caulking compounds would be appropriate for this work. Holes and static (nonmoving) cracks may be caulked with butyl sealants or acrylic latex caulks. For dynamic (moving or active) cracks, the polysulfide caulks are most often used, although others may be safely employed. It is, however, important to remember that these waterproof caulking compounds are not viable repointing materials and should not be used as such.

Figure 11. Temporary Stabilization Measures. *Falling glazed architectural terra-cotta detailing has become a source of concern, particularly in dense urban areas and locations of high seismic activity. Nylon netting and metal strapping, while not seen as permanent preservation measures, do offer a temporary alternative to the removal of these elements.*

Temporary replacement: Temporary replacement measures should be implemented when missing units are scheduled to be replaced but work cannot be undertaken immediately. Lengthy delivery time, prorating of work or seasonal considerations may postpone replacement work. Severe deterioration should at least be ameliorated until work can begin. Temporary repointing, removal and saving of undamaged units to be reset later, or the temporary installation of brick infill to retard further deterioration might be considered.

Removing earlier repairs: Removing earlier repairs may be necessary when the work has either deteriorated or has become visually incompatible. Cementitious stucco, caulkings with black bituminous compounds or brick repair work may become structurally or visually unstable or incompatible and should be removed and properly rehabilitated.

Replacement of glazed architectural terra-cotta: Replacement of severely spalled, damaged, or missing glazed architectural terra-cotta elements is always difficult. Certainly, in-kind replacement is advisable, but it has a number of drawbacks. Stone, fiberglass, and precast concrete are also viable choices, but like in-kind replacement, also have their inherent problems.

Several notes on replacement: When replacing glazed architectural terra-cotta, all of the original deteriorated material should be completely removed. Half bricks or similar cosmetic replacement techniques are not advised.

—When possible and where applicable, replacement units should be anchored in a manner similar to the original. Both structural and visual compatibility are major considerations when choosing replacement materials.

—Removing and reanchoring damaged glazed architectural terra-cotta is an extremely difficult if not impossible task. The complexity of the interlocking system of masonry units, backfill, and metal anchoring system precludes the removal of the glazed architectural terra-cotta unit without destroying it. Reanchoring deteriorated units is likewise impossible. Therefore, if the terra-cotta in question is loose, severely deteriorated, or its structural integrity in serious question, it is best removed and replaced.

In-kind replacement is possible today, but only on a limited basis. Most new glazed architectural terra-cotta is machine made, not hand made as the original. Thus, the porous tile body of the new material tends to be more uniform but less dense and often not as durable. The glaze on the new glazed architectural terra-cotta tends to be thinner than that on the older material and subsequently more brittle. Machine processing has also produced a glaze that is uniform in color as opposed to historic glazes which were slightly mottled and, therefore, richer. Visual compatibility *is* an important consideration when replacing in-kind.

Only a fairly limited inventory of in-kind pieces is presently available for replacement such as plain ashlar blocks and the simpler details such as cappings and sills. When deterioration severely damages the more ornate pieces (urns, cartouche work, balusters, etc.) either expensive hand casting or alternative materials must be sought. There is a tendency today to replace damaged ornamental work with simpler, cheaper and more readily available units. This decision *cannot*, however, be supported, as the removal of this work inevitably diminishes the character and integrity of the building. Another major consideration in choosing in-kind replacement is the question of delivery time, which is often quite lengthy. If new glazed architectural terra-cotta is chosen as a replacement material, the architect or building owner should plan far in advance.

Stone may be a suitable replacement material for damaged glazed architectural terra-cotta. Its durability makes it highly appropriate, although the increase in weight over the original hollow units may be of some concern. The fact that historic glazed architectural terra-cotta was glazed in imitation of stone, however, may make the choice of stone as a replacement material a fortuitous one. Metal anchoring may be accommodated easily in the carving. Cost, however, is the major drawback in stone replacement, particularly where rich detailing must be carved to match the original.

Fiberglass replacement is a viable alternative, particularly when rich and elaborate ornamentation has to be duplicated. Casting from original intact pieces can produce numerous sharp copies of entablatures, moldings, balusters, voussoirs, etc. Anchoring is easily included in casting.

Significant drawbacks in using fiberglass replacement are color compatibility, fire code violations and poor weathering and aging properties. The appropriate coloring of fiberglass is exceedingly difficult in many instances. Painting is often unsatisfactory, as it discolors at a rate different than that of the historic glazed original. While fiberglass casting is lighter than the original units and, therefore, of great interest in the rehabilitation of buildings in areas of high seismic activity, many fire code requirements cannot be met with the use of this material.

Precast concrete units show great promise in replacing glazed architectural terra-cotta at this writing. Precast concrete units can, like fiberglass, replicate nuances of detail in a modular fashion; they can also be cast hollow, use light-weight aggregate and be made to accommodate metal anchoring when necessary. Concrete can be colored or tinted to match the original material with excellent results. It is cost effective and once production is in process, precast concrete can be produced quickly and easily.

Experience shows that it is advisable to use a clear masonry coating on the weather face of the precast concrete units to guarantee the visual compatibility of the new unit, to prevent moisture absorption, to obtain the proper reflectivity in imitation of the original glaze and to prevent weathering of the unit itself. Precast concrete replacement units are presently enjoying great use in replicating historic glazed architectural terra-cotta and show promise for future rehabilitation programs.

Once the replacement material is selected (new glazed architectural terra-cotta, stone, precast concrete, or fiberglass), it must be reanchored into the masonry system. Original metal anchoring came in numerous designs, materials and coatings ranging from bituminous-coated iron to bronze. While most of these anchors are no longer available, they may be easily replicated in large quantities either in the original material when appropriate or out of more durable and available metals such as stainless steel.

Since the masonry backfill is already in place in the historic building, the new replacement unit with anchoring may simply be fitted into the existing backfill by boring a hole or slot for anchor and bedding the anchor and the unit itself in mortar. When replacing historic glazed architectural terra-cotta which originally employed metal anchoring, it is important to replace that anchoring when replacing the unit. Serious problems may result if anchoring is omitted in restoration when it was used originally. It is erroneous to assume that mortar alone will be sufficient to hold these replacement pieces in place.

Summary

Today, many of this country's buildings are constructed of glazed architectural terra-cotta. However, many of these are in a state of serious deterioration and decay. Glazed architectural terra-cotta was, in many ways, the "wonder" material of the American building industry in the late 19th century and during the first decades of the 20th century. New technology and methods of rehabilitation now hold promise for the restoration and rehabilitation of these invaluable and significant resources. Restoration/rehabilitation work on glazed architectural terra-cotta is demanding and will not tolerate half-way measures. Today's preservation work should equal the spirit, attention to detail, pride in workmanship and care which characterized the craftsmanship associated with this widely used, historic masonry material.

Suggested Further Readings

"Recipes for Baked Earth." *Progressive Architecture*, (November, 1977).

McIntyre, W.A. *Investigations into the Durability of Architectural Terra Cotta.* Special Report 12. London: Department of Scientific and Industrial Research, Building Research Station, 1929.

Prudon, Theodore H.M. "Architectural Terra-Cotta: Analyzing the Deterioration Problems and Restoration Approaches." *Technology and Conservation*, Vol. 3 (Fall, 1978). pp. 30–38.

Prudon, Theodore H.M. *Terra Cotta as a Building Material, A Bibliography.* Ottawa, Ontario: Association for Preservation Technology, 1976.

The illustrations for this brief not specifically credited are from the files of the Technical Preservation Services Division.

This Preservation Brief was written by de Teel Patterson Tiller, Architectural Historian, Technical Preservation Services Division. Information for this publication was based in part upon interviews and consultation with Theodore H.M. Prudon, The Ehrenkrantz Group, P.C., New York, New York. Additional comments and information were provided by Si A. Bortz, Illinois Institute of Technology Research Institute, Chicago, Illinois, and Jerry G. Stockbridge, Wiss, Janney, Elstner, and Associates, Northbrook, Illinois.

8

Aluminum and Vinyl Siding on Historic Buildings

The Appropriateness of Substitute Materials for Resurfacing Historic Wood Frame Buildings.

John H. Myers, revised by Gary L. Hume

> Standard 6 of the Secretary of the Interior's "Standards for Rehabilitation" states that "deteriorated architectural features shall be repaired rather than replaced, wherever possible. In the event replacement is necessary, the new material should match the material being replaced in composition, design, color, texture, and other visual qualities." Therefore, the Secretary's Standards and their accompanying Guidelines *never recommend* resurfacing frame buildings with any new material that does not duplicate the historic material because of the strong potential of altering the character of the historic building.

A historic building is a product of the cultural heritage of its region, the technology of its period, the skill of its builders, and the materials used for its construction. To assist owners, developers and managers of historic property in planning and completing rehabilitation project work that will meet the Secretary's "Standards for Rehabilitation"(36 CFR 67), the following planning process has been developed by the National Park Service and is applicable to all historic buildings. This planning process is a sequential approach to the preservation of historic wood frame buildings. It begins with the premise that historic materials should be retained wherever possible. When retention, including retention with some repair, is not possible, then *replacement of the irreparable historic material can be considered.* The purpose of this approach is to determine the appropriate level of treatment for the preservation of historic wood frame buildings. The planning process has the following four steps:

1. Identify and preserve those materials and features that are important in defining the *building's historic character.* This may include features such as wood siding, brackets, cornices, window architraves, doorway pediments, and their finishes and colors.

2. Undertake routine maintenance on historic materials and features. Routine maintenance generally involves the least amount of work needed to preserve the materials and features of the building. For example, maintenance of a frame building would include caulking and painting; or, where paint is extensively cracking and peeling, its removal and the re-application of a protective paint coating.

3. Repair historic materials and features. For a historic material such as wood siding, repair would generally involve patching and piecing-in with new material according to recognized preservation methods.

Photo: Lee H. Nelson

Photo: Hugh C. Miller

Photo: John H. Myers

Historic wood sidings exhibit rich and varied surface textures. They range from hand-split clapboards of short lengths with feather-edged ends, to pit or mill sawn boards which can be beveled, rabbeted, milled, or beaded.

Photo: Laurie Robin Hammel

When a building is in need of maintenance, such as the house on the right which needs painting, some owners consider installing aluminum or vinyl siding. The result, like the house on the left, can be a complete loss of architectural character due to the covering of details (cornice), the removal of features (window trim), and a change of scale due to inappropriate siding dimensions.

4. Replace severely damaged or deteriorated historic materials and features in kind. Replacing sound or repairable historic material is never recommended; however, if the historic material cannot be repaired because of the extent of deterioration or damage, then it will be necessary to *replace* an entire character-defining feature such as the building's siding. The preferred treatment is always replacement in kind, that is, with the same material. Because this approach is not always feasible, provision is made under the recommended treatment options in the Guidelines that accompany the Secretary of the Interior's Standards to consider the use of a compatible substitute material. A substitute material should only be considered, however, if the form, detailing, and overall appearance of the substitute material conveys the visual appearance of the historic material, and the application of the substitute material does not damage, destroy or obscure historic features.

In many cases, the replacement of wood siding on a historic building is proposed because little attention has been given to the retention of historic materials. Instead, the decision to use a substitute material is made because: (1) it is assumed that aluminum or vinyl siding will be a maintenance-free material; and (2) there is the desire to give a building a "remodeled" or "renovated" appearance. A decision to replace historic material must, however, be carefully considered for its impact on the historic resource—even when the model planning process has been followed and the appropriate treatment is replacement.

Therefore, this brief focuses on the visual and physical consequences of using a substitute material such as aluminum or vinyl siding for new siding installations on a wood frame historic building. These concerns include the potential of *damaging* or *destroying* historic material and features; the potential of *obscuring* historic material and features; and, most important, the potential of *diminishing the historic character* of the building.

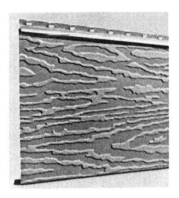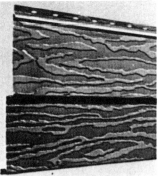

Photo: Technical Preservation Services

Aluminum and vinyl siding are available in a variety of widths and colors, but the optional wood graining is not characteristic of real wood siding.

The Historic Character of Buildings and Districts

The character or "identity" of a historic building is established by its form, size, scale and decorative features. It is also influenced by the choice of materials for the walls—by the dimension, detailing, color, and other surface characteristics. This is particularly true for wood frame buildings which are the typical objects of aluminum or vinyl siding applications. Since wood has always been present in abundance in America, it has been a dominant building material in most parts of the country. Early craftsmen used wood for almost every aspect of building construction: for structural members such as posts, beams and rafters, and for cladding materials and decorative details, such as trim, shakes, and siding.

The variety of tools used, coupled with regional differences in design and craftsmanship, has resulted in a richness and diversity of wood sidings in America. For example, narrow boards with beveled, lapped joints called "clapboards" were used on New England frame dwellings. The size and shape of the "clapboards" were determined by the process of hand splitting or "riving" bolts of wood.

The width, the short lengths, the beveled lapping, the "feathered" horizontal joints, and the surface nailing of the clapboards created a distinctive surface pattern that is recognizable as an important part of the historic character of these structures.

The sawn and hand-planed clapboards used throughout the Mid-Atlantic and Southern states in the eighteenth and early nineteenth centuries, by contrast, have a wide exposure—generally between six and eight inches. The exposure of the siding, frequently coupled with a beaded edge, created a very different play of light and shadow on the wall surface, thus resulting in a different character. The "German" or "Novelty siding"—a milled siding that is thin above and thicker below with a concave bevel—was used throughout many parts of the United States in the late nineteenth and early twentieth century but with regional variations in material, profile, and dimensions. One variation of this type of milled siding was called "California siding" and was milled with a rabbetted or shiplap edge to insure a tight installation of the weatherboards. Shingles were also commonly used as an exterior cladding material, and in buildings such as the Bungalow style houses, were often an important character-defining feature of the exterior. Shingles were often applied in decorative patterns by varying the lap, thus creating alternating rows of narrow exposures and wide exposures. Shingles were also cut in geometric patterns such as diamond shapes and applied in patterns. This treatment was commonly used in the gable end of shingled houses. Siding and wood shingles were often used in combination with materials such as cobblestone and brick in Bungalow style buildings to create a distinctive interplay of surfaces and materials.

The primary concern, therefore, in considering replacement siding on a historic building, is the potential loss of those features such as the beaded edge, "drop" profile, and the patterns of application. Replacing historic wood siding with new wood, or aluminum or vinyl siding could severely diminish the unique aspects of historic materials

Photo: Nancy J. Long

Two originally similar houses. When aluminum was installed on the house on the right, the barge boards, scrollwork, columns, and railings were removed. The distinctive shingled gable and attic vent were covered, further compromising the building's architectural integrity.

75

Photo: John H. Myers

This brick rowhouse was covered with vertical and horizontal aluminum siding. Such treatment is inappropriate for historic masonry buildings.

and craftsmanship. The inappropriate use of substitute siding is especially dramatic where sufficient care is not taken by the owner or applicator and the width of the clapboards is altered, shadow reveals are reduced, and molding or trim is changed or removed at the corners, at cornices or around windows and doors. Because substitute siding is usually added on *top* of existing siding, details around windows and doors may appear set back from the siding rather than slightly projecting; and if the relationship of molding or trim to the wall is changed, it can result in the covering or removal of these historic features. New substitute siding with embossed wood graining—intended to simulate the texture of wood—is also visually inappropriate. Exaggerated graining would have been undesirable on real wood siding and is generally found only after sandblasting, a destructive and totally unacceptable treatment for wood.

While this discussion focuses primarily on the historic character of individual wood frame buildings, of equal importance is the context of buildings that comprise a historic district or neighborhood. Changes to the character-defining features of a building, such as distinctive clapboarding and other wall surfaces and decorative trim, always have an impact on more than *just* that building; they also alter the historic visual relationship between the buildings in the district. If character-defining weather-

boards, clapboards or shingles are replaced on a number of buildings in a historic district, the historic character of the entire district may be seriously damaged. Because of the potential impact some substitute materials have on the character of a neighborhood or district, many communities regulate their use through zoning ordinances and design review boards. These ordinances and review boards usually require review and approval of proposed alterations to a historic building that could potentially impact the historic character of the building or the district, including the application of substitute materials, such as aluminum or vinyl siding.

Preservation of a building or district and its historic character is based on the assumption that the retention of historic materials and features and their craftsmanship are of primary importance. Therefore, the underlying issue in any discussion of replacement materials is whether or not the integrity of historic materials and craftsmanship has been lost. Structures are historic because the materials and craftsmanship reflected in their construction are tangible and irreplaceable evidence of our cultural heritage. To the degree that substitute materials destroy and/or conceal the historic fabric, they will always subtract from the basic integrity of historically and architecturally significant buildings.

The Products and Their Installation

The use of aluminum and vinyl siding really involves two separate industries. The siding materials themselves, including a variety of inside and outside corner pieces, trim and molding pieces and panning for window and door frames, are produced by a comparatively small number of manufacturers. The product information, advertising, and any manufacturer's warranties on the product itself are handled by this part of the industry. The installation of aluminum or vinyl siding is generally carried out by independent contractors or applicators, who are frequently called "home improvement" contractors, and they are not affiliated with the manufacturers. The manufacturer's warranties normally do not cover the installation, or any damage or defect resulting from the installation process.

Since the manufacturer has little control over the quality of the installation, both the quality of the work and the sensitivity of the application are variable. This variation in quality has traditionally been a problem in the industry and one which the industry and its professional associations have attempted to correct through publishing and disseminating information on the proper application of vinyl and aluminum siding.

Although it is sometimes argued that an artificial siding application is reversible since it can be removed, there is frequently irreversible damage to historic building materials if decorative features or trim are permitted to be cut down or destroyed, or removed by applicators and discarded. The installation process requires that the existing surface be flat and free of "obstructions" so that the new siding will be smooth and even in appearance. To achieve the requisite flat surface, furring strips are usually placed over the wall surface (vertical furring strips for horizontal aluminum or vinyl siding and vice-versa for vertical siding). The potential danger in this type of surface preparation is that the furring strips may change the relationship between the plane of the wall and the projecting elements such as windows, door trim, the cornice, or any other projecting trim or molding. Projecting details may also cause a problem. To retain them, additional cutting and fitting will usually be required. Further, additional or special molding pieces, or "accessories" as they are called by the industry, such as channels, inserts and drip caps, will be needed to fit the siding around the architectural features. This custom fitting of the siding will be more labor-intensive, adding to the cost of the siding installation.

The existing wall fabric is further damaged by the nailing necessary to apply siding. Either by nailing directly to the building fabric or by nailing the furring strips to the old siding, the installation of aluminum or vinyl siding will leave numerous holes in wood siding, molding, trim, window and door frames. When applied to brick or other masonry units, the nail penetrations attaching the furring strips and siding can cause irreversible cracking or spalling of the masonry. Although this reference to damaging masonry is included as a point of fact, the application of aluminum or vinyl siding is highly inappropriate to historic masonry buildings.

The Use of Aluminum or Vinyl Siding on Historic Buildings

The maintenance and periodic painting of wood frame structures is a time-consuming effort and often a substantial expense for the homeowner. It is therefore understandable that a product which promises relief from periodic painting and gives the building a new exterior cladding would have considerable appeal. For these reasons, aluminum and vinyl siding have been used extensively in upgrading and rehabilitating the nation's stock of wood frame residential buildings. For historic residential buildings, aluminum or vinyl siding may be an acceptable alternative *only* if (1) the existing siding is so deteriorated or damaged that it cannot be repaired; (2) the substitute material can be installed without irreversibly damaging or obscuring the architectural features and trim of the building; and (3) the substitute material can match the historic material in size, profile and finish so that there is no change in the character of the historic building. In cases where a non-historic artificial siding has been applied to a building, the removal of such a siding, and the application of aluminum or vinyl siding would, in most cases, be an acceptable alternative, as long as the above-mentioned first two conditions are met.

There are, however, also certain disadvantages in the use of a substitute material such as aluminum or vinyl siding, and these factors should be carefully considered before a decision is made to use such a material rather than the preferred replacement with new wood siding duplicating the old.

Applying Siding without Dealing with Existing Problems

Since aluminum and vinyl sidings are typically marketed as home improvement items, they are frequently applied to buildings in need of maintenance and repair. This can result in concealing problems which are the early warning signs of deterioration. Minor uncorrected problems can progress to the point where expensive, major repairs to the structure become necessary.

If there is a hidden source of water entry within the wall or leakage from the roof, the installation of any new siding will not solve problems of deterioration and rotting that are occurring within the wall. If deferred maintenance has allowed water to enter the wall through deteriorated gutters and downspouts, for example, the cosmetic surface application of siding will not arrest these problems. In fact, if the gutters and downspouts are not repaired, such problems may become exaggerated because water may be channeled behind the siding. In addition to drastically reducing the efficiency of most types of wall insulation, such excessive moisture levels within the wall can contribute to problems with interior finishes such as paints or wallpaper, causing peeling, blistering or staining of the finishes.

It cannot be overemphasized that a cosmetic treatment to hide difficulties such as peeling paint, stains or other indications of deterioration is not a sound preservation practice; it is no substitute for proper care and maintenance. Aluminum and vinyl siding are not directly at fault in these situations since property owners should determine the nature and source of their problems, then make appropriate repairs. The difficulty arises when owners perceive the siding as the total solution to their required maintenance and forgo other remedial action.

Durability and Cost

The questions of durability and relative costs of aluminum or vinyl siding compared to the maintenance cost of historic materials are complex. It is important to consider these questions carefully because both types of siding are marketed as long lasting, low maintenance materials. Assuming that the substitute sidings are not damaged, and that they will weather and age normally, there will be inevitable changes in color and gloss as time passes. A normal application of aluminum or vinyl siding is likely to cost from two to three times as much as a good paint job on wood siding. A sensitive application, retaining existing trim, will cost more. Therefore, to break even on expense, the new siding should last as long as two or three paintings before requiring maintenance. On wood two coats of good quality paint on a properly prepared surface can last from 8 to 10 years, according to the U.S. Department of Agriculture. If a conservative life of seven years is assumed for paint on wood, then aluminum and vinyl siding should last 15 to 21 years before requiring additional maintenance, to break even with the maintenance cost for painting wood siding. Once painted, the aluminum and vinyl siding will require repainting with the same frequency as wood.

While aluminum siding can dent upon impact and the impact resistance of vinyl siding decreases in low temperatures and, therefore, is susceptible to cracking from sharp impact, these materials are generally not more vulnerable than wood siding and shingles. All siding materials are subject to damage from storm, fire, and vandalism; however, there is a major difference in the repairability of wood siding versus substitute materials such as aluminum and vinyl. Although they can all be repaired, it is much easier to repair wood siding and the repair, after painting, is generally imperceptible. In addition, a major problem in the repairability of aluminum and vinyl siding, as mentioned above, is matching color since the factory finishes change with time. Matching the paint for wood siding has a greater likelihood of success.

Energy

Because of high fuel costs, there is a concern for energy conservation in historic materials as well as in substitute materials. Because aluminum and vinyl siding can be produced with an insulating backing, these products are sometimes marketed as improving the thermal envelope of a historic building. The aluminum and vinyl material themselves are not good insulators, and the thickness of any insulating backing would, of necessity, be too small to add to the energy efficiency of a historic building. What energy savings did accrue as a result of a siding application would probably be as much the result of the creation of an air space between the old and new siding as the addition of insulating material. If the historic wood siding were removed in the course of installing the aluminum or vinyl siding (even with an insulating backing), the net result would likely be a loss in overall thermal efficiency for the exterior sheathing.

Preservation Briefs Number 3, "Conserving Energy in Historic Buildings," notes that the primary sources of energy loss in small frame buildings are the doors, windows and roof. It is, therefore, more cost-effective to apply storm windows, weatherstripping and attic insulation than to treat the sidewalls of these structures. There are numerous publications on energy retrofitting which explain techniques of determining cost-effectiveness based on utility costs, R-factors or materials and initial cost of the treatment. Persons interested in this approach may wish to read "Retrofitting Existing Houses for Energy Conservation: An Economic Analysis" published by the National Bureau of Standards, or the U.S. Department of Housing and Urban Development booklet "In the Bank or Up the Chimney." One such study in Providence, Rhode Island, determined that for a two-story house, twenty-five feet square, the payback period for twenty-three storm windows, two storm doors and six inches of attic insulation (R-20) was 4.4 years while the payback period of aluminum siding with an R-factor of 2.5 was 29.96 years. Most of the information which is available supports the position that aluminum or vinyl siding will not have a reasonable payback on an energy-saving basis alone.

Summary

The intent of this brief has been to delineate issues that should be considered when contemplating the use of aluminum or vinyl sidings on historic buildings and assessing under what circumstances substitute materials such as artificial siding may be used without damaging the integrity of the historic building or adversely changing its historic character. Many property owners are faced with decisions weighing the historic value of their building and its maintenance cost against the possible benefit of aluminum and vinyl siding materials. To assist in making these decisions, "The Secretary of the Interior's Standards for Rehabilitation and Guidelines for Rehabilitating Historic Buildings"

have been published and are available from National Park Service Regional Offices and State Historic Preservation Offices. Further, since rehabilitation projects for income-producing historic buildings often seek tax benefits under the 1981 Economic Recovery Tax Act, as amended, it is essential that all work, such as the replacement of exterior siding, be carried out in conformance with the Standards and be consistent with the building's historic character to insure that the tax benefits are not denied.

As stated earlier, the application of aluminum and vinyl siding is frequently considered as an alternative to the maintenance of the original historic material. The implication is that the new material is an economical and long-lasting alternative and therefore somehow superior to the historic material. In reality, historic building materials such as wood, brick and stone, when properly maintained, are generally durable and serviceable materials. Their widespread existence on tens of thousands of old buildings after many decades in serviceable condition is proof that they are the original economic and long-lasting alternatives. All materials, including aluminum and vinyl siding can fall into disrepair if abused or neglected; however, the maintenance, repair and retention of historic materials are always the most architecturally appropriate and usually the most economically sound measures when the objective is to preserve the unique qualities of historic buildings.

The appropriate preservation decision on the use of a substitute material in the rehabilitation of a historic building must always center on two principal concerns: the possible damage or destruction of historic building materials; and, the possible negative impact on the historic character of the building and the historic district or setting in which the building is located. Because applications of substitute materials such as aluminum and vinyl siding can either destroy or conceal historic building material and features and, in consequence, result in the loss of a building's historic character, they are not recommended by the National Park Service. Such destruction or concealment of historic materials and features confuses the public perception of that which is truly historic and that which is imitative.

Reading List

"Condensation Problems in Your House: Prevention and Solution." Information Bulletin No. 373. Washington, D.C.: U.S. Department of Agriculture, 1974.

Kiefer, Matthew J. *"Vinyl and Aluminum Siding: Pro and Con."* Report to the Ashmont Hill Study Committee. Boston, Massachusetts: The Boston Landmarks Commission, 1977.

"Landmark and Historic District Commission." Vol. 4. No. 5. Washington, D.C.: National Trust for Historic Preservation. October 1978.

"Moisture Conditions in Walls and Ceilings of a Simulated Older Home in Winter." Madison, Wisconsin: Forest Products Laboratory-USDA, 1977.

"Performance Criteria for Exterior Wall Systems." Washington, D.C.: National Bureau of Standards, 1974.

"Rehab Right." Oakland, California: City of Oakland Planning Department, 1978.

Skoda, Leopold F. *"Performance of Residential Siding Materials."* Washington, D.C.: National Bureau of Standards, 1972.

Wood Handbook: Wood as an Engineering Material. Washington, D.C.: Forest Products Laboratory. U.S. Department of Agriculture, 1974.

This Preservation Brief was written by John H. Myers, Historical Architect, formerly with Technical Preservation Services, and was published first in 1979. The Brief was substantially revised in 1984 by Gary L. Hume, Deputy Division Chief, Preservation Assistance Division. H. Ward Jandl, Chief, Technical Preservation Services Branch, and the following Branch staff members are to be thanked for reviewing the manuscript and making suggestions that were incorporated into the final text: Emogene A. Bevitt, Kay Davidson Weeks, and Susan Dynes.

This publication has been prepared pursuant to the Economic Recovery Tax Act of 1981 which directs the Secretary of the Interior to certify rehabilitations of historic buildings that are consistent with their historic character; the advice and guidance provided in this Brief will assist property owners in complying with the requirements of this law.

Preservation Briefs 8 has been developed under the technical editorship of Lee H. Nelson, AIA, Chief, Preservation Assistance Division, National Park Service, U.S. Department of the Interior, Washington, D.C. 20240. Comments on the usefulness of this information are welcomed and can be sent to Mr. Nelson at the above address.

9
The Repair of
Historic Wooden Windows

John H. Myers —————————————————————————————

The windows on many historic buildings are an important aspect of the architectural character of those buildings. Their design, craftsmanship, or other qualities may make them worthy of preservation. This is self-evident for ornamental windows, but it can be equally true for warehouses or factories where the windows may be the most dominant visual element of an otherwise plain building (see figure 1). Evaluating the significance of these windows and planning for their repair or replacement can be a complex process involving both objective and subjective considerations. The *Secretary of the Interior's Standards for Rehabilitation,* and the accompanying guidelines, call for respecting the significance of original materials and features, repairing and retaining them wherever possible, and when necessary, replacing them in kind. This **Brief** is based on the issues of significance and repair which are implicit in the standards, but the primary emphasis is on the technical issues of planning for the repair of windows including evaluation of their physical condition, techniques of repair, and design considerations when replacement is necessary.

Figure 1. *Windows are frequently important visual focal points, especially on simple facades such as this mill building. Replacement of the multipane windows here with larger panes could dramatically change the appearance of the building. The areas of missing windows convey the impression of such a change. Photo: John T. Lowe*

Much of the technical section presents repair techniques as an instructional guide for the do-it-yourselfer. The information will be useful, however, for the architect, contractor, or developer on large-scale projects. It presents a methodology for approaching the evaluation and repair of existing windows, and considerations for replacement, from which the professional can develop alternatives and specify appropriate materials and procedures.

Architectural or Historical Significance

Evaluating the architectural or historical significance of windows is the first step in planning for window treatments, and a general understanding of the function and history of windows is vital to making a proper evaluation. As a part of this evaluation, one must consider four basic window functions: admitting light to the interior spaces, providing fresh air and ventilation to the interior, providing a visual link to the outside world, and enhancing the appearance of a building. No single factor can be disregarded when planning window treatments; for example, attempting to conserve energy by closing up or reducing the size of window openings may result in the use of *more* energy by increasing electric lighting loads and decreasing passive solar heat gains.

Historically, the first windows in early American houses were casement windows; that is, they were hinged at the side and opened outward. In the beginning of the eighteenth century single- and double-hung windows were introduced. Subsequently many styles of these vertical sliding sash windows have come to be associated with specific building periods or architectural styles, and this is an important consideration in determining the significance of windows, especially on a local or regional basis. Site-specific, regionally oriented architectural comparisons should be made to determine the significance of windows in question. Although such comparisons may focus on specific window types and their details, the ultimate determination of significance should be made within the context of the whole building, wherein the windows are one architectural element (see figure 2).

After all of the factors have been evaluated, *windows should be considered significant to a building if they:* 1) are original, 2) reflect the original design intent for the building, 3) reflect period or regional styles or building practices, 4) reflect changes to the building resulting from major periods or events, or 5) are examples of exceptional craftsmanship or design. Once this evaluation of significance has been completed, it is possible to pro-

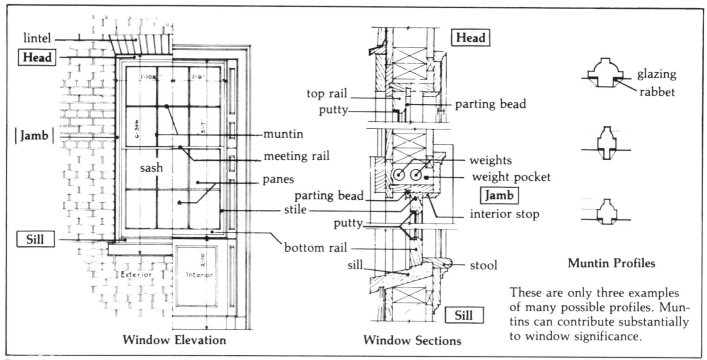

Figure 2. *These drawings of window details identify major components, terminology, and installation details for a wooden double-hung window.*

ceed with planning appropriate treatments, beginning with an investigation of the physical condition of the windows.

Physical Evaluation

The key to successful planning for window treatments is a careful evaluation of existing physical conditions on a unit-by-unit basis. A graphic or photographic system may be devised to record existing conditions and illustrate the scope of any necessary repairs. Another effective tool is a window schedule which lists all of the parts of each window unit. Spaces by each part allow notes on existing conditions and repair instructions. When such a schedule is completed, it indicates the precise tasks to be performed in the repair of each unit and becomes a part of the specifications. In any evaluation, one should note at a minimum, 1) window location, 2) condition of the paint, 3) condition of the frame and sill, 4) condition of the sash (rails, stiles and muntins), 5) glazing problems, 6) hardware, and 7) the overall condition of the window (excellent, fair, poor, and so forth).

Many factors such as poor design, moisture, vandalism, insect attack, and lack of maintenance can contribute to window deterioration, but moisture is the primary contributing factor in wooden window decay. All window units should be inspected to see if water is entering around the edges of the frame and, if so, the joints or seams should be caulked to eliminate this danger. The glazing putty should be checked for cracked, loose, or missing sections which allow water to saturate the wood, especially at the joints. The back putty on the interior side of the pane should also be inspected, because it creates a seal which prevents condensation from running down into the joinery. The sill should be examined to insure that it slopes downward away from the building and allows water to drain off. In addition, it may be advisable to cut a dripline along the underside of the sill. This almost invisible treatment will insure proper water run-off, particu-

larly if the bottom of the sill is flat. Any conditions, including poor original design, which permit water to come in contact with the wood or to puddle on the sill must be corrected as they contribute to deterioration of the window.

One clue to the location of areas of excessive moisture is the condition of the paint; therefore, each window should be examined for areas of paint failure. Since excessive moisture is detrimental to the paint bond, areas of paint blistering, cracking, flaking, and peeling usually identify points of water penetration, moisture saturation, and potential deterioration. Failure of the paint should not, however, be mistakenly interpreted as a sign that the wood is in poor condition and hence, irreparable. Wood is frequently in sound physical condition beneath unsightly paint. After noting areas of paint failure, the next step is to inspect the condition of the wood, particularly at the points identified during the paint examination.

Each window should be examined for operational soundness beginning with the lower portions of the frame and sash. Exterior rainwater and interior condensation can flow downward along the window, entering and collecting at points where the flow is blocked. The sill, joints between the sill and jamb, corners of the bottom rails and muntin joints are typical points where water collects and deterioration begins (see figure 3). The operation of the window (continuous opening and closing over the years and seasonal temperature changes) weakens the joints, causing movement and slight separation. This process makes the joints more vulnerable to water which is readily absorbed into the end-grain of the wood. If severe deterioration exists in these areas, it will usually be apparent on visual inspection, but other less severely deteriorated areas of the wood may be tested by two traditional methods using a small ice pick.

An ice pick or an awl may be used to test wood for soundness. The technique is simply to jab the pick into a wetted wood surface at an angle and pry up a small sec-

Figure 3. *Deterioration of poorly maintained windows usually begins on horizontal surfaces and at joints where water can collect and saturate the wood. The problem areas are clearly indicated by paint failure due to moisture. Photo: Baird M. Smith, AIA*

tion of the wood. Sound wood will separate in long fibrous splinters, but decayed wood will lift up in short irregular pieces due to the breakdown of fiber strength.

Another method of testing for soundness consists of pushing a sharp object into the wood, perpendicular to the surface. If deterioration has begun from the hidden side of a member and the core is badly decayed, the visible surface may appear to be sound wood. Pressure on the probe can force it through an apparently sound skin to penetrate deeply into decayed wood. This technique is especially useful for checking sills where visual access to the underside is restricted.

Following the inspection and analysis of the results, the scope of the necessary repairs will be evident and a plan for the rehabilitation can be formulated. Generally the actions necessary to return a window to "like new" condition will fall into three broad categories: 1) routine maintenance procedures, 2) structural stabilization, and 3) parts replacement. These categories will be discussed in the following sections and will be referred to respectively as Repair Class I, Repair Class II, and Repair Class III. Each successive repair class represents an increasing level of difficulty, expense, and work time. Note that most of the points mentioned in Repair Class I are routine maintenance items and should be provided in a regular maintenance program for any building. The neglect of these routine items can contribute to many common window problems.

Before undertaking any of the repairs mentioned in the following sections all sources of moisture penetration should be identified and eliminated, and all existing decay fungi destroyed in order to arrest the deterioration process. Many commercially available fungicides and wood preservatives are toxic, so it is extremely important to follow the manufacturer's recommendations for application, and store all chemical materials away from children and animals. After fungicidal and preservative treatment the windows may be stabilized, retained, and restored with every expectation for a long service life.

Repair Class I: Routine Maintenance

Repairs to wooden windows are usually labor intensive and relatively uncomplicated. On small scale projects this allows the do-it-yourselfer to save money by repairing all or part of the windows. On larger projects it presents the opportunity for time and money which might otherwise be spent on the removal and replacement of existing windows, to be spent on repairs, subsequently saving all or part of the material cost of new window units. Regardless of the actual costs, or who performs the work, the evaluation process described earlier will provide the knowledge from which to specify an appropriate work program, establish the work element priorities, and identify the level of skill needed by the labor force.

The routine maintenance required to upgrade a window to "like new" condition normally includes the following steps: 1) some degree of interior and exterior paint removal, 2) removal and repair of sash (including reglazing where necessary), 3) repairs to the frame, 4) weatherstripping and reinstallation of the sash, and 5) repainting. These operations are illustrated for a typical double-hung wooden window (see figures 4a-f), but they may be adapted to other window types and styles as applicable.

Historic windows have usually acquired many layers of paint over time. Removal of excess layers or peeling and flaking paint will facilitate operation of the window and restore the clarity of the original detailing. Some degree of paint removal is also necessary as a first step in the proper surface preparation for subsequent refinishing (if paint color analysis is desired, it should be conducted prior to the onset of the paint removal). There are several safe and effective techniques for removing paint from wood, depending on the amount of paint to be removed. Several techniques such as scraping, chemical stripping, and the use of a hot air gun are discussed in "Preservation Briefs: 10 Paint Removal from Historic Woodwork" (see Additional Reading section at end).

Paint removal should begin on the interior frames, being careful to remove the paint from the interior stop and the parting bead, particularly along the seam where these stops meet the jamb. This can be accomplished by running a utility knife along the length of the seam, breaking the paint bond. It will then be much easier to remove the stop, the parting bead and the sash. The interior stop may be initially loosened from the sash side to avoid visible scarring of the wood and then gradually pried loose using a pair of putty knives, working up and down the stop in small increments (see figure 4b). With the stop removed, the lower or interior sash may be withdrawn. The sash cords should be detached from the sides of the sash and their ends may be pinned with a nail or tied in a knot to prevent them from falling into the weight pocket.

Removal of the upper sash on double-hung units is similar but the parting bead which holds it in place is set into a groove in the center of the stile and is thinner and more delicate than the interior stop. After removing any paint along the seam, the parting bead should be carefully pried out and worked free in the same manner as the interior stop. The upper sash can be removed in the same manner as the lower one and both sash taken to a convenient work area (in order to remove the sash the interior stop and parting bead need only be removed from one side of the window). Window openings can be covered with polyethylene sheets or plywood sheathing while the sash are out for repair.

The sash can be stripped of paint using appropriate techniques, but if any heat treatment is used (see figure 4c), the glass should be removed or protected from the sudden temperature change which can cause breakage. An

Figure 4a. *The following series of photographs of the repair of a historic double-hung window use a unit which is structurally sound but has many layers of paint, some cracked and missing putty, slight separation at the joints, broken sash cords, and one cracked pane. Photo: John H. Myers*

Figure 4b. *After removing paint from the seam between the interior stop and the jamb, the stop can be pried out and gradually worked loose using a pair of putty knives as shown. To avoid visible scarring of the wood, the sash can be raised and the stop pried loose initially from the outer side. Photo: John H. Myers*

Figure 4c. *Sash can be removed and repaired in a convenient work area. Paint is being removed from this sash with a hot air gun while an asbestos sheet protects the glass from sudden temperature change. Photo: John H. Myers*

Figure 4d. *Reglazing or replacement of the putty requires that the existing putty be removed manually, the glazing points be extracted, the glass removed, and the back putty scraped out. To reglaze, a bed of putty is laid around the perimeter of the rabbet, the pane is pressed into place, glazing points are inserted to hold the pane (shown), and a final seal of putty is beveled around the edge of the glass. Photo: John H. Myers*

Figure 4e. *A common repair is the replacement of broken sash cords with new cords (shown) or with chains. The weight pocket is often accessible through a removable plate in the jamb, or by removing the interior trim. Photo: John H. Myers*

Figure 4f. *Following the relatively simple repairs, the window is weathertight, like new in appearance, and serviceable for many years to come. Both the historic material and the detailing and craftsmanship of this original window have been preserved. Photo: John H. Myers*

overlay of aluminum foil on gypsum board or asbestos can protect the glass from such rapid temperature change. It is important to protect the glass because it may be historic and often adds character to the window. Deteriorated putty should be removed manually, taking care not to damage the wood along the rabbet. If the glass is to be removed, the glazing points which hold the glass in place can be extracted and the panes numbered and removed for cleaning and reuse in the same openings. With the glass panes out, the remaining putty can be removed and the sash can be sanded, patched, and primed with a preservative primer. Hardened putty in the rabbets may be softened by heating with a soldering iron at the point of removal. Putty remaining on the glass may be softened by soaking the panes in linseed oil, and then removed with less risk of breaking the glass. Before reinstalling the glass, a bead of glazing compound or linseed oil putty should be laid around the rabbet to cushion and seal the glass. Glazing compound should only be used on wood which has been brushed with linseed oil and primed with an oil based primer or paint. The pane is then pressed into place and the glazing points are pushed into the wood around the perimeter of the pane (see figure 4d). The final glazing compound or putty is applied and beveled to complete the seal. The sash can be refinished as desired on the inside and painted on the outside as soon as a "skin" has formed on the putty, usually in 2 or 3 days. Exterior paint should cover the beveled glazing compound or putty and lap over onto the glass slightly to complete a weathertight seal. After the proper curing times have elapsed for paint and putty, the sash will be ready for reinstallation.

While the sash are out of the frame, the condition of the wood in the jamb and sill can be evaluated. Repair and refinishing of the frame may proceed concurrently with repairs to the sash, taking advantage of the curing times for the paints and putty used on the sash. One of the most common work items is the replacement of the sash cords with new rope cords or with chains (see figure 4e). The weight pocket is frequently accessible through a door on the face of the frame near the sill, but if no door exists, the trim on the interior face may be removed for access. Sash weights may be increased for easier window operation by elderly or handicapped persons. Additional repairs to the frame and sash may include consolidation or replacement of deteriorated wood. Techniques for these repairs are discussed in the following sections.

The operations just discussed summarize the efforts necessary to restore a window with minor deterioration to "like new" condition (see figure 4f). The techniques can be applied by an unskilled person with minimal training and experience. To demonstrate the practicality of this approach, and photograph it, a Technical Preservation Services staff member repaired a wooden double-hung, two over two window which had been in service over ninety years. The wood was structurally sound but the window had one broken pane, many layers of paint, broken sash cords and inadequate, worn-out weatherstripping. The staff member found that the frame could be stripped of paint and the sash removed quite easily. Paint, putty and glass removal required about one hour for each sash, and the reglazing of both sash was accomplished in about one hour. Weatherstripping of the sash and frame, replacement of the sash cords and reinstallation of the sash, parting bead, and stop required an hour and a half. These times refer only to individual operations; the entire proc-

ess took several days due to the drying and curing times for putty, primer, and paint, however, work on other window units could have been in progress during these lag times.

Repair Class II: Stabilization

The preceding description of a window repair job focused on a unit which was operationally sound. Many windows will show some additional degree of physical deterioration, especially in the vulnerable areas mentioned earlier, but even badly damaged windows can be repaired using simple processes. Partially decayed wood can be waterproofed, patched, built-up, or consolidated and then painted to achieve a sound condition, good appearance, and greatly extended life. Three techniques for repairing partially decayed or weathered wood are discussed in this section, and all three can be accomplished using products available at most hardware stores.

One established technique for repairing wood which is split, checked or shows signs of rot, is to: 1) dry the wood, 2) treat decayed areas with a fungicide, 3) waterproof with two or three applications of boiled linseed oil (applications every 24 hours), 4) fill cracks and holes with putty, and 5) after a "skin" forms on the putty, paint the surface. Care should be taken with the use of fungicide which is toxic. Follow the manufacturers' directions and use only on areas which will be painted. When using any technique of building up or patching a flat surface, the finished surface should be sloped slightly to carry water away from the window and not allow it to puddle. Caulking of the joints between the sill and the jamb will help reduce further water penetration.

When sills or other members exhibit surface weathering they may also be built-up using wood putties or homemade mixtures such as sawdust and resorcinol glue, or whiting and varnish. These mixtures can be built up in successive layers, then sanded, primed, and painted. The same caution about proper slope for flat surfaces applies to this technique.

Wood may also be strengthened and stabilized by consolidation, using semi-rigid epoxies which saturate the porous decayed wood and then harden. The surface of the consolidated wood can then be filled with a semi-rigid epoxy patching compound, sanded and painted (see figure 5). Epoxy patching compounds can be used to build up

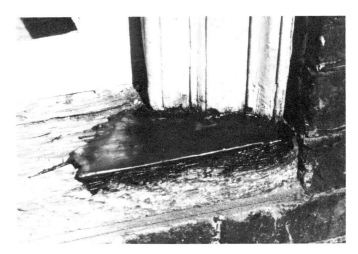

Figure 5. *This illustrates a two-part epoxy patching compound used to fill the surface of a weathered sill and rebuild the missing edge. When the epoxy cures, it can be sanded smooth and painted to achieve a durable and waterproof repair. Photo: John H. Myers*

missing sections or decayed ends of members. Profiles can be duplicated using hand molds, which are created by pressing a ball of patching compound over a sound section of the profile which has been rubbed with butcher's wax. This can be a very efficient technique where there are many typical repairs to be done. Technical Preservation Services has published *Epoxies for Wood Repairs in Historic Buildings* (see Additional Reading section at end), which discusses the theory and techniques of epoxy repairs. The process has been widely used and proven in marine applications; and proprietary products are available at hardware and marine supply stores. Although epoxy materials may be comparatively expensive, they hold the promise of being among the most durable and long lasting materials available for wood repair.

Any of the three techniques discussed can stabilize and restore the appearance of the window unit. There are times, however, when the degree of deterioration is so advanced that stabilization is impractical, and the only way to retain some of the original fabric is to replace damaged parts.

Repair Class III: Splices and Parts Replacement

When parts of the frame or sash are so badly deteriorated that they cannot be stabilized there are methods which permit the retention of some of the existing or original fabric. These methods involve replacing the deteriorated parts with new matching pieces, or splicing new wood into existing members. The techniques require more skill and are more expensive than any of the previously discussed alternatives. It is necessary to remove the sash and/or the affected parts of the frame and have a carpenter or woodworking mill reproduce the damaged or missing parts. Most millwork firms can duplicate parts, such as muntins, bottom rails, or sills, which can then be incorporated into the existing window, but it may be necessary to shop around because there are several factors controlling the practicality of this approach. Some woodworking mills do not like to repair old sash because nails or other foreign objects in the sash can damage expensive knives (which cost far more than their profits on small repair jobs); others do not have cutting knives to duplicate muntin profiles. Some firms prefer to concentrate on larger jobs with more profit potential, and some may not have a craftsman who can duplicate the parts. A little searching should locate a firm which will do the job, and at a reasonable price. If such a firm does not exist locally, there are firms which undertake this kind of repair and ship nationwide. It is possible, however, for the advanced do-it-yourselfer or craftsman with a table saw to duplicate moulding profiles using techniques discussed by Gordie Whittington in "Simplified Methods for Reproducing Wood Mouldings," *Bulletin* of the Association for Preservation Technology, Vol. III, No. 4, 1971, or illustrated more recently in *The Old House*, Time-Life Books, Alexandria, Virginia, 1979.

The repairs discussed in this section involve window frames which may be in very deteriorated condition, possibly requiring removal; therefore, caution is in order. The actual construction of wooden window frames and sash is not complicated. Pegged mortise and tenon units can be disassembled easily, *if* the units are out of the building. The installation or connection of some frames to the surrounding structure, especially masonry walls, can complicate the work immeasurably, and may even require dismantling of the wall. It may be useful, therefore, to take the following approach to frame repair: 1) conduct regular maintenance of sound frames to achieve the longest life possible, 2) make necessary repairs in place wherever possible, using stabilization and splicing techniques, and 3) if removal is necessary, thoroughly investigate the structural detailing and seek appropriate professional consultation.

Another alternative may be considered if parts replacement is required, and that is sash replacement. If extensive replacement of parts is necessary and the job becomes prohibitively expensive it may be more practical to purchase new sash which can be installed into the existing frames. Such sash are available as exact custom reproductions, reasonable facsimiles (custom windows with similar profiles), and contemporary wooden sash which are similar in appearance. There are companies which still manufacture high quality wooden sash which would duplicate most historic sash. A few calls to local building suppliers may provide a source of appropriate replacement sash, but if not, check with local historical associations, the state historic preservation office, or preservation related magazines and supply catalogs for information.

If a rehabilitation project has a large number of windows such as a commercial building or an industrial complex, there may be less of a problem arriving at a solution. Once the evaluation of the windows is completed and the scope of the work is known, there may be a potential economy of scale. Woodworking mills may be interested in the work from a large project; new sash in volume may be considerably less expensive per unit; crews can be assembled and trained on site to perform all of the window repairs; and a few extensive repairs can be absorbed (without undue burden) into the total budget for a large number of sound windows. While it may be expensive for the average historic home owner to pay seventy dollars or more for a mill to grind a custom knife to duplicate four or five bad muntins, that cost becomes negligible on large commercial projects which may have several hundred windows.

Most windows should not require the extensive repairs discussed in this section. The ones which do are usually in buildings which have been abandoned for long periods or have totally lacked maintenance for years. It is necessary to thoroughly investigate the alternatives for windows which do require extensive repairs to arrive at a solution which retains historic significance and is also economically feasible. Even for projects requiring repairs identified in this section, if the percentage of parts replacement per window is low, or the number of windows requiring repair is small, repair can still be a cost effective solution.

Weatherization

A window which is repaired should be made as energy efficient as possible by the use of appropriate weatherstripping to reduce air infiltration. A wide variety of products are available to assist in this task. Felt may be fastened to the top, bottom, and meeting rails, but may have the disadvantage of absorbing and holding moisture, particularly at the bottom rail. Rolled vinyl strips may also be tacked into place in appropriate locations to reduce infiltration. Metal strips or new plastic spring strips may be used on the rails and, if space permits, in the channels between the sash and jamb. Weatherstripping is a historic treatment, but old weatherstripping (felt) is not likely to perform very satisfactorily. Appropriate contemporary weatherstripping should be considered an integral part of the repair process for windows. The use of sash locks installed on the meeting rail will insure that the sash are kept tightly closed so that the weatherstripping will function more effectively to reduce infiltration. Although such locks will not always be historically accurate, they will usually be viewed as an acceptable contemporary modification in the interest of improved thermal performance.

Many styles of storm windows are available to improve the thermal performance of existing windows. The use of exterior storm windows should be investigated whenever feasible because they are thermally efficient, cost-effective, reversible, and allow the retention of original windows (see "Preservation Briefs: 3"). Storm window frames may be made of wood, aluminum, vinyl, or plastic; however, the use of unfinished aluminum storms should be avoided. The visual impact of storms may be minimized by selecting colors which match existing trim color. Arched top storms are available for windows with special shapes. Although interior storm windows appear to offer an attractive option for achieving double glazing with minimal visual impact, the potential for damaging condensation problems must be addressed. Moisture which becomes trapped between the layers of glazing can condense on the colder, outer prime window, potentially leading to deterioration. The correct approach to using interior storms is to create a seal on the interior storm while allowing some ventilation around the prime window. In actual practice, the creation of such a durable, airtight seal is difficult.

Window Replacement

Although the retention of original or existing windows is always desirable and this **Brief** is intended to encourage that goal, there is a point when the condition of a window may clearly indicate replacement. The decision process for selecting replacement windows should *not* begin with a survey of contemporary window products which are available as replacements, but should begin with a look at the windows which are being replaced. Attempt to understand the contribution of the window(s) to the appearance of the facade including: 1) the pattern of the openings and their size; 2) proportions of the frame and sash; 3) configuration of window panes; 4) muntin profiles; 5) type of wood; 6) paint color; 7) characteristics of the glass; and 8) associated details such as arched tops, hoods, or other decorative elements. Develop an understanding of how the window reflects the period, style, or regional characteristics of the building, or represents technological development.

Armed with an awareness of the significance of the existing window, begin to search for a replacement which retains as much of the character of the historic window as possible. There are many sources of suitable new windows. Continue looking until an acceptable replacement can be found. Check building supply firms, local woodworking mills, carpenters, preservation oriented magazines, or catalogs or suppliers of old building materials, for product information. Local historical associations and state historic preservation offices may be good sources of information on products which have been used successfully in preservation projects.

Consider energy efficiency as one of the factors for replacements, but do not let it dominate the issue. Energy conservation is no excuse for the wholesale destruction of historic windows which can be made thermally efficient by historically and aesthetically acceptable means. In fact, a historic wooden window with a high quality storm window added should thermally outperform a new double-glazed metal window which does not have thermal breaks (insulation between the inner and outer frames intended to break the path of heat flow). This occurs because the wood has far better insulating value than the metal, and in addition many historic windows have high ratios of wood to glass, thus reducing the area of highest heat transfer. One measure of heat transfer is the U-value, the number of Btu's per hour transferred through a square foot of material. When comparing thermal performance, the lower the U-value the better the performance. According to *ASHRAE 1977 Fundamentals,* the U-values for single glazed wooden windows range from 0.88 to 0.99. The addition of a storm window should reduce these figures to a range of 0.44 to 0.49. A non-thermal break, double-glazed metal window has a U-value of about 0.6.

Conclusion

Technical Preservation Services recommends the retention and repair of original windows whenever possible. We believe that the repair and weatherization of existing wooden windows is more practical than most people realize, and that many windows are unfortunately replaced because of a lack of awareness of techniques for evaluation, repair, and weatherization. Wooden windows which are repaired and properly maintained will have greatly extended service lives while contributing to the historic character of the building. Thus, an important element of a building's significance will have been preserved for the future.

Additional Reading

ASHRAE Handbook-1977 Fundamentals. New York: American Society of Heating, Refrigerating and Air-conditioning Engineers, 1978 (chapter 26).

Ferro, Maximillian. *Preservation: Present Pathway to Fall River's Future.* Fall River, Massachusetts: City of Fall River, 1979 (chapter 7).

"Fixing Double-Hung Windows." *Old House Journal* (no. 12, 1979): 135.

Look, David W. "Preservation Briefs: 10 Paint Removal from Historic Woodwork." Washington, DC: Technical Preservation Services, U.S. Department of the Interior, forthcoming.

Morrison, Hugh. *Early American Architecture.* New York: Oxford University Press, 1952.

Phillips, Morgan, and Selwyn, Judith. *Epoxies for Wood Repairs in Historic Buildings.* Washington, DC: Technical Preservation Services, U.S. Department of the Interior (Government Printing Office, Stock No. 024-016-00095-1), 1978.

Rehab Right. Oakland, California: City of Oakland Planning Department, 1978 (pp. 78-83).

"Sealing Leaky Windows." *Old House Journal* (no. 1, 1973): 5.

Smith, Baird M. "Preservation Briefs: 3 Conserving Energy in Historic Buildings." Washington, DC: Technical Preservation Services, U.S. Department of the Interior, 1978.

1981

10

Exterior Paint Problems on Historic Woodwork

Kay D. Weeks and David W. Look, AIA

A cautionary approach to paint removal is included in the guidelines to "The Secretary of the Interior Standards for Historic Preservation Projects." Removing paints down to bare wood surfaces using harsh methods can permanently damage those surfaces; therefore such methods are not recommended. Also, total removal obliterates evidence of the historical paints and their sequence and architectural context.

This Brief expands on that advice for the architect, building manager, contractor, or homeowner by identifying and describing common types of paint surface conditions and failures, then recommending appropriate treatments for preparing exterior wood surfaces for repainting[1] to assure the best adhesion and greatest durability of the new paint. Although the Brief focuses on responsible methods of "paint removal," several paint surface conditions will be described which do not require any paint removal, and still others which can be successfully handled by limited paint removal. In all cases, the information is intended to address the concerns related to *exterior wood*. It will also be generally assumed that, because houses built before 1950 involve one or more layers of lead-base paint,[2] the majority of conditions warranting paint removal will mean dealing with this toxic substance along with the dangers of the paint removal tools and chemical strippers themselves.

Purposes of Exterior Paint

Paint[3] applied to exterior wood must withstand yearly extremes of both temperature and humidity. While never expected to be more than a temporary physical shield—requiring re-application every 5-8 years—its importance should not be minimized. Because one of the main causes of wood deterioration is moisture penetration, a primary purpose for painting wood is to exclude such moisture, thereby slowing deterioration not only of a building's exterior siding and decorative features but, ultimately, its underlying structural members. Another important purpose for painting wood is, of course, to define and accent architectural features and to improve appearance.

Treating Paint Problems in Historic Buildings

Exterior paint is constantly deteriorating through the processes of weathering, but in a program of regular maintenance—assuming all other building systems are functioning properly—surfaces can be cleaned, lightly scraped, and hand sanded in preparation for a new finish coat. Unfortunately, these are ideal conditions. More often, complex maintenance problems are inherited by owners of historic buildings, including areas of paint that have failed[4] beyond the point of mere cleaning, scraping, and hand sanding (although much so-called "paint failure" is attributable to interior or exterior moisture problems or surface preparation and application mistakes with previous coats).

Although paint problems are by no means unique to historic buildings, treating multiple layers of hardened, brittle paint on complex, ornamental—and possibly fragile—exterior wood surfaces necessarily requires an extremely cautious approach (see figure 1). In the case of recent construction, this level of concern is not needed because the wood is generally less detailed and, in addition, retention of the sequence of paint layers as a partial record of the building's history is not an issue.

When historic buildings are involved, however, a special set of problems arises—varying in complexity depending upon their age, architectural style, historical importance, and physical soundness of the wood—which must be carefully evaluated so that decisions can be made that are sensitive to the longevity of the resource.

Justification for Paint Removal

At the outset of this Brief, it must be emphasized that removing paint from historic buildings—with the exception of cleaning, light scraping, and hand sanding as part of routine maintenance—should be avoided unless absolutely essential. *Once conditions warranting removal have*

---

[1] General paint type recommendations will be made, but paint color recommendations are beyond the scope of this Brief.

[2] Douglas R. Shier and William Hall, *Analysis of Housing Data Collected in a Lead-Based Paint Survey in Pittsburgh, Pennsylvania, Part 1*, National Bureau of Standards, Inter-Report 77-1250, May 1977.

[3] Any pigmented liquid, liquefiable, or mastic composition designed for application to a substrate in a thin layer which is converted to an opaque solid film after application. *Paint and Coatings Dictionary*, 1978. Federation of Societies for Coatings and Technology.

[4] For purposes of the Brief, this includes any area of painted exterior woodwork displaying signs of peeling, cracking, or alligatoring to bare wood. See descriptions of these and other paint surface conditions as well as recommended treatments on pp. 5-10.

Fig. 1 *Excessive paint build-up on architectural details such as this ornamental bracket does not in itself justify total paint removal. If paint is cracked and peeling down to bare wood, however, it should be removed using the gentlest means possible. Photo: David W. Look, AIA.*

Fig. 2 *A traditionally painted bay window has been stripped to bare wood, then varnished. In addition to being historically inaccurate, the varnish will break down faster as a result of the sun's ultraviolet rays than would primer and finish coats of paint. Photo: David W. Look, AIA.*

been identified, the general approach should be to remove paint to the next sound layer using the gentlest means possible, then to repaint (see figure 2). Practically speaking as well, paint can adhere just as effectively to existing paint as to bare wood, providing the previous coats of paint are also adhering uniformly and tightly to the wood and the surface is properly prepared for repainting—cleaned of dirt and chalk and dulled by sanding. But, if painted exterior wood surfaces display continuous patterns of deep cracks or if they are extensively blistering and peeling so that bare wood is visible, then the old paint should be completely removed before repainting. The only other justification for removing all previous layers of paint is if doors, shutters, or windows have literally been "painted shut," or if new wood is being pieced-in adjacent to old painted wood and a smooth transition is desired (see figure 3).

Paint Removal Precautions

Because paint removal is a difficult and painstaking process, a number of costly, regrettable experiences have occurred—and continue to occur—for both the historic building and the building owner. Historic buildings have been set on fire with blow torches; wood irreversibly scarred by sandblasting or by harsh mechanical devices such as rotary sanders and rotary wire strippers; and layers of historic paint inadvertently and unnecessarily removed. In addition, property owners, using techniques that substitute speed for safety, have been injured by toxic lead vapors or dust from the paint they were trying to

Fig. 3 *If damage to parts of a wooden element is severe, new sections of wood will need to be pieced-in. When such piecing is required, paint on the adjacent woodwork should be removed so that the old and new woods will make a smooth profile when joined. After repainting, the repair should be virtually impossible to detect. Photo: Morgan W. Phillips.*

remove or by misuse of the paint removers themselves.

Owners of historic properties considering paint removal should also be aware of the amount of time and labor involved. While removing damaged layers of paint from a door or porch railing might be readily accomplished within a reasonable period of time by one or two people, removing paint from larger areas of a building can, without professional assistance, easily become unmanageable and produce less than satisfactory results. The amount of work involved in any paint removal project must therefore be analyzed on a case-by-case basis. Hiring qualified professionals will often be a cost-effective decision due to the expense of materials, the special equipment required, and the amount of time involved. Further, paint removal companies experienced in dealing with the inherent health and safety dangers of paint removal should have purchased such protective devices as are needed to mitigate any dangers and should also be aware of State or local environmental and/or health regulations for hazardous waste disposal.

All in all, paint removal is a messy, expensive, and potentially dangerous aspect of rehabilitating or restoring historic buildings and should not be undertaken without careful thought concerning first, its necessity, and second, which of the available recommended methods is the safest and most appropriate for the job at hand.

Repainting Historic Buildings for Cosmetic Reasons

If existing exterior paint on wood siding, eaves, window sills, sash, and shutters, doors, and decorative features shows no evidence of paint deterioration such as chalking, blistering, peeling, or cracking, then there is no *physical reason* to repaint, much less remove paint! Nor is color fading, of itself, sufficient justification to repaint a historic building.

The decision to repaint may not be based altogether on paint failure. Where there is a new owner, or even where ownership has remained constant through the years, taste in colors often changes. Therefore, if repainting is primarily to alter a building's primary and accent colors, a technical factor of paint accumulation should be taken into consideration. When paint builds up to a thickness of approximately 1/16" (approximately 16-30 layers), one or more extra coats of paint may be enough to trigger cracking and peeling in limited or even widespread areas of the building's surface. This results because excessively thick paint is less able to withstand the shrinkage or pull of an additional coat as it dries and is also less able to tolerate thermal stresses. Thick paint invariably fails at the weakest point of adhesion—the oldest layers next to the wood. Cracking and peeling follow. Therefore, if there are no signs of paint failure, it may be somewhat risky to add still another layer of unneeded paint simply for color's sake (extreme changes in color may also require more than one coat to provide proper hiding power and full color). When paint appears to be nearing the critical thickness, a change of accent colors (that is, just to limited portions of the trim) might be an acceptable compromise without chancing cracking and peeling of paint on wooden siding.

If the decision to repaint is nonetheless made, the "new" color or colors should, at a minimum, be appropriate to the style and setting of the building. On the other hand, where the intent is to restore or accurately reproduce the colors originally used or those from a significant period in the building's evolution, they should be based on the results of a paint analysis.[5]

Identification of Exterior Paint Surface Conditions/Recommended Treatments

It is assumed that a preliminary check will already have been made to determine, first, that the painted exterior surfaces are indeed wood—and not stucco, metal, or other wood substitutes—and second, that the wood has not decayed so that repainting would be superfluous. For example, if any area of bare wood such as window sills has been exposed for a long period of time to standing water, wood rot is a strong possibility (see figure 4). Repair or replacement of deteriorated wood should take place before repainting. After these two basic issues have been resolved, the surface condition identification process may commence.

The historic building will undoubtedly exhibit a variety of exterior paint surface conditions. For example, paint on the wooden siding and doors may be adhering firmly; paint on the eaves peeling; and paint on the porch balusters and window sills cracking and alligatoring. The accurate identification of each paint problem is therefore the first step in planning an appropriate overall solution.

Paint surface conditions can be grouped according to their relative severity: CLASS I conditions include minor blemishes or dirt collection and generally require *no* paint removal; CLASS II conditions include failure of the top layer or layers of paint and generally require *limited* paint removal; and CLASS III conditions include substantial or multiple-layer failure and generally require *total* paint removal. It is precisely because conditions will vary at different points on the building that a careful inspection is critical. Each item of painted exterior woodwork (i.e., siding, doors, windows, eaves, shutters, and decorative elements) should be examined early in the planning phase and surface conditions noted.

CLASS I Exterior Surface Conditions Generally Requiring No Paint Removal

• **Dirt, Soot, Pollution, Cobwebs, Insect Cocoons, etc.**

Cause of Condition

Environmental "grime" or organic matter that tends to cling to painted exterior surfaces and, in particular, protected surfaces such as eaves, do not constitute a paint problem unless painted over rather than removed prior to repainting. If not removed, the surface deposits can be a barrier to proper adhesion and cause peeling.

Recommended Treatment

Most surface matter can be loosened by a strong, direct stream of water from the nozzle of a garden hose. Stubborn dirt and soot will need to be scrubbed off using 1/2 cup of household detergent in a gallon of water with a medium soft bristle brush. The cleaned surface should then be rinsed thoroughly, and permitted to dry before further inspection to determine if repainting is necessary. Quite often, cleaning provides a satisfactory enough result to postpone repainting.

---

[5] See the Reading List for paint research and documentation information. See also *The Secretary of the Interior's Standards for Historic Preservation Projects with Guidelines for Applying the Standards* for recommended approaches on paints and finishes within various types of project work treatments.

• Mildew

Cause of Condition

Mildew is caused by fungi feeding on nutrients contained in the paint film or on dirt adhering to any surface. Because moisture is the single most important factor in its growth, mildew tends to thrive in areas where dampness and lack of sunshine are problems such as window sills, under eaves, around gutters and downspouts, on the north side of buildings, or in shaded areas near shrubbery. It may sometimes be difficult to distinguish mildew from dirt, but there is a simple test to differentiate: if a drop of household bleach is placed on the suspected surface, mildew will immediately turn white whereas dirt will continue to look like dirt.

Recommended Treatment

Because mildew can only exist in shady, warm, moist areas, attention should be given to altering the environment that is conducive to fungal growth. The area in question may be shaded by trees which need to be pruned back to allow sunlight to strike the building; or may lack rain gutters or proper drainage at the base of the building. If the shady or moist conditions can be altered, the mildew is less likely to reappear. A recommend solution for removing mildew consists of one cup non-ammoniated detergent, one quart household bleach, and one gallon water. When the surface is scrubbed with this solution using a medium soft brush, the mildew should disappear; however, for particularly stubborn spots, an additional quart of bleach may be added. After the area is mildew-free, it should then be rinsed with a direct stream of water from the nozzle of a garden hose, and permitted to dry thoroughly. When repainting, specially formulated "mildew-resistant" primer and finish coats should be used.

• Excessive Chalking

Cause of Condition

Chalking—or powdering of the paint surface—is caused by the gradual disintegration of the resin in the paint film. (The amount of chalking is determined both by the formulation of the paint and the amount of ultraviolet light to which the paint is exposed.) In moderation, chalking is the ideal way for a paint to "age," because the chalk, when rinsed by rainwater, carries discoloration and dirt away with it and thus provides an ideal surface for repainting. In excess, however, it is not desirable because the chalk can wash down onto a surface of a different color beneath the painted area and cause streaking as well as rapid disintegration of the paint film itself. Also, if a paint contains too much pigment for the amount of binder (as the old white lead carbonate/oil paints often did), excessive chalking can result.

Recommended Treatment

The chalk should be cleaned off with a solution of ½ cup household detergent to one gallon water, using a medium soft bristle brush. After scrubbing to remove the chalk, the surface should be rinsed with a direct stream of water from the nozzle of a garden hose, allowed to dry thoroughly, (but not long enough for the chalking process to recur) and repainted, using a non-chalking paint.

• Staining

Cause of Condition

Staining of paint coatings usually results from excess

Fig. 4 *Paint films wear unevenly depending on exposure and location. Exterior locations which are susceptible to accelerated deterioration are horizontal surfaces such as window sills. These and similar areas will require repainting more often than less vulnerable surfaces. In the case of this window sill where paint has peeled off and adjacent areas have cracked and alligatored, the paint should be totally removed. Prior to repainting, any weathered wood should be rejuvenated using a solution of 3 cups exterior varnish, 1 oz. paraffin wax, and mineral spirits/ paint thinner/or turpentine to make 1 gallon. Liberal brush application should be made. This formula was tested over a 20-year period by the U.S. Department of Agriculture's Forest Products Laboratory and proved to be just as effective as water-repellent preservatives containing pentachlorophenol. After the surface has thoroughly dried (2-3 days of warm weather), the treated surface can be painted. A high quality oil-base primer followed by two top coats of a semi-gloss oil-enamel or latex-enamel paint is recommended. Photo: Baird M. Smith, AIA.*

moisture reacting with materials within the wood substrate. There are two common types of staining, neither of which requires paint removal. The most prevalent type of stain is due to the oxidation or rusting of iron nails or metal (iron, steel, or copper) anchorage devices. A second type of stain is caused by a chemical reaction between moisture and natural extractives in certain woods (red cedar or redwood) which results in a surface deposit of colored matter. This is most apt to occur in new replacement wood within the first 10-15 years.

Recommended Treatment

In both cases, the source of the stain should first be located and the moisture problem corrected.

When stains are caused by rusting of the heads of nails used to attach shingles or siding to an exterior wall or by rusting or oxidizing iron, steel, or copper anchorage devices adjacent to a painted surface, the metal objects themselves should be hand sanded and coated with a rust-inhibitive primer followed by two finish coats. (Exposed nail heads should ideally be countersunk, spot primed, and the holes filled with a high quality wood filler except where exposure of the nail head was part of the original construction system or the wood is too fragile to withstand the countersinking procedure.)

Discoloration due to color extractives in replacement wood can usually be cleaned with a solution of equal parts denatured alcohol and water. After the affected area has been rinsed and permitted to dry, a "stain-blocking primer" especially developed for preventing this type of stain should be applied (two primer coats are recommended for severe cases of bleeding prior to the finish coat). Each primer coat should be allowed to dry at least 48 hours.

CLASS II Exterior Surface Conditions Generally Requiring Limited Paint Removal

• Crazing

Cause of Condition

Crazing—fine, jagged interconnected breaks in the top layer of paint—results when paint that is several layers thick becomes excessively hard and brittle with age and is consequently no longer able to expand and contract with the wood in response to changes in temperature and humidity (see figure 5). As the wood swells, the bond between paint layers is broken and hairline cracks appear. Although somewhat more difficult to detect as opposed to other more obvious paint problems, it is well worth the time to scrutinize all surfaces for crazing. If not corrected, exterior moisture will enter the crazed surface, resulting in further swelling of the wood and, eventually, deep cracking and alligatoring, a Class III condition which requires total paint removal.

Recommended Treatment

Crazing can be treated by hand or mechanically sanding the surface, then repainting. Although the hairline cracks may tend to show through the new paint, the surface will be protected against exterior moisture penetration.

Fig. 5 *Crazing—or surface cracking—is an exterior surface condition which can be successfully treated by sanding and painting. Photo: Courtesy, National Decorating Products Association.*

• Intercoat Peeling

Cause of Condition

Intercoat peeling can be the result of improper surface preparation prior to the last repainting. This most often occurs in protected areas such as eaves and covered porches because these surfaces do not receive a regular rinsing from rainfall, and salts from air-borne pollutants thus accumulate on the surface. If not cleaned off, the new paint coat will not adhere properly and that layer will peel.

Another common cause of intercoat peeling is incompatibility between paint types (see figure 6). For example, if oil paint is applied over latex paint, peeling of the top

coat can sometimes result since, upon aging, the oil paint becomes harder and less elastic than the latex paint. If latex paint is applied over old, chalking oil paint, peeling can also occur because the latex paint is unable to penetrate the chalky surface and adhere.

Recommended Treatment

First, where salts or impurities have caused the peeling, the affected area should be washed down thoroughly after scraping, then wiped dry. Finally, the surface should be hand or mechanically sanded, then repainted.

Where peeling was the result of using incompatible paints, the peeling top coat should be scraped and hand or mechanically sanded. Application of a high quality oil type exterior primer will provide a surface over which either an oil or a latex topcoat can be successfully used.

Fig. 6 *This is an example of intercoat peeling. A latex top coat was applied directly over old oil paint and, as a result, the latex paint was unable to adhere. If latex is being used over oil, an oil-base primer should be applied first. Although much of the peeling latex paint can be scraped off, in this case, the best solution may be to chemically dip strip the entire shutter to remove all of the paint down to bare wood, rinse thoroughly, then repaint. Photo: Mary L. Oehrlein, AIA.*

• Solvent Blistering

Cause of Condition

Solvent blistering, the result of a less common application error, is not caused by moisture, but by the action of ambient heat on paint solvent or thinners in the paint film. If solvent-rich paint is applied in direct sunlight, the top surface can dry too quickly and, as a result, solvents become trapped beneath the dried paint film. When the solvent vaporizes, it forces its way through the paint film, resulting in surface blisters. This problem occurs more often with dark colored paints because darker colors absorb more heat than lighter ones. To distinguish between solvent blistering and blistering caused by moisture, a blister should be cut open. If another layer of paint is visible, then solvent blistering is likely the problem whereas if bare wood is revealed, moisture is probably to blame. Solvent blisters are generally small.

Recommended Treatment

Solvent-blistered areas can be scraped, hand or mechanically sanded to the next sound layer, then repainted. In order to prevent blistering of painted surfaces, paint should not be applied in direct sunlight.

• Wrinkling

Cause of Condition

Another error in application that can easily be avoided is wrinkling (see figure 7). This occurs when the top layer of paint dries before the layer underneath. The top layer of paint actually moves as the paint underneath (a primer, for example) is drying. Specific causes of wrinkling include: (1) applying paint too thick; (2) applying a second coat before the first one dries; (3) inadequate brushing out; and (4) painting in temperatures higher than recommended by the manufacturer.

Recommended Treatment

The wrinkled layer can be removed by scraping followed by hand or mechanical sanding to provide as even a surface as possible, then repainted following manufacturer's application instructions.

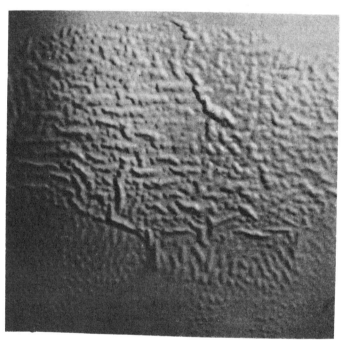

Fig. 7 *Wrinkled layers can generally be removed by scraping and sanding as opposed to total paint removal. Following manufacturers' application instructions is the best way to avoid this surface condition. Photo: Courtesy, National Decorating Products Association.*

CLASS III Exterior Surface Conditions Generally Requiring Total Paint Removal

If surface conditions are such that the majority of paint will have to be removed prior to repainting, it is suggested that a small sample of intact paint be left in an inconspicuous area either by covering the area with a metal plate, or by marking the area and identifying it in some way. (When repainting does take place, the sample should not be painted over). This will enable future investigators to have a record of the building's paint history.

• Peeling

Cause of Condition

Peeling to bare wood is most often caused by excess interior or exterior moisture that collects behind the paint film, thus impairing adhesion (see figure 8). Generally beginning as blisters, cracking and peeling occur as moisture causes the wood to swell, breaking the adhesion of the bottom layer.

Recommended Treatment

There is no sense in repainting before dealing with the moisture problems because new paint will simply fail. Therefore, the first step in treating peeling is to locate and remove the source or sources of the moisture, not only because moisture will jeopardize the protective coating of paint but because, if left unattended, it can ultimately cause permanent damage to the wood. Excess interior moisture should be removed from the building through installation of exhaust fans and vents. Exterior moisture should be eliminated by correcting the following conditions prior to repainting: faulty flashing; leaking gutters; defective roof shingles; cracks and holes in siding and trim; deteriorated caulking in joints and seams; and shrubbery growing too close to painted wood. After the moisture problems have been solved, the wood must be permitted to dry out thoroughly. The damaged paint can then be scraped off with a putty knife, hand or mechanically sanded, primed, and repainted.

Fig. 8 *Peeling to bare wood—one of the most common types of paint failure—is usually caused by an interior or exterior moisture problem. Photo: Anne E. Grimmer.*

• Cracking/Alligatoring

Cause of Condition

Cracking and alligatoring are advanced stages of crazing (see figure 9). Once the bond between layers has been broken due to intercoat paint failure, exterior moisture is able to penetrate the surface cracks, causing the wood to swell and deeper cracking to take place. This process continues until cracking, which forms parallel to grain, extends to bare wood. Ultimately, the cracking becomes an overall pattern of horizontal and vertical breaks in the paint layers that looks like reptile skin; hence, "alligatoring." In advanced stages of cracking and alligatoring, the surfaces will also flake badly.

Recommended Treatment

If cracking and alligatoring are present only in the top layers they can probably be scraped, hand or mechanically sanded to the next sound layer, then repainted. However, if cracking and/or alligatoring have progressed to bare wood and the paint has begun to flake, it will need to be totally removed. Methods include scraping or paint removal with the electric heat plate, electric heat gun, or chemical strippers, depending on the particular area involved. Bare wood should be primed within 48 hours, then repainted.

Fig. 9 *Cracking, alligatoring, and flaking are evidence of long-term neglect of painted surfaces. The remaining paint on the clapboard shown here can be removed with an electric heat plate and wide-bladed scraper. In addition, unsound wood should be replaced and moisture problems corrected before primer and top coats of paint are applied. Photo: David W. Look, AIA.*

Selecting the Appropriate/Safest Method to Remove Paint

After having presented the "hierarchy" of exterior paint surface conditions—from a mild condition such as mildewing which simply requires cleaning prior to repainting to serious conditions such as peeling and alligatoring which require total paint removal—one important thought bears repeating: if a paint problem has been identified that warrants either limited or total paint removal, the gentlest method possible for the particular wooden element of the historic building should be selected from the many available methods.

The treatments recommended—based upon field testing as well as onsite monitoring of Department of Interior grant-in-aid and certification of rehabilitation projects—are therefore those which take three over-riding issues into consideration (1) the continued protection and preservation of the historic exterior woodwork; (2) the retention of the sequence of historic paint layers; and (3) the health and safety of those individuals performing the paint removal. By applying these criteria, it will be seen that no paint removal method is without its drawbacks and all recommendations are qualified in varying degrees.

Methods for Removing Paint

After a particular exterior paint surface condition has been identified, the next step in planning for repainting—if paint removal is required—is selecting an appropriate method for such removal.

The method or methods selected should be suitable for the specific paint problem as well as the particular wooden element of the building. Methods for paint removal can be divided into three categories (frequently, however, a combination of the three methods is used).

Each method is defined below, then discussed further and specific recommendations made:

Abrasive—"Abrading" the painted surface by manual and/or mechanical means such as scraping and sanding. Generally used for surface preparation and limited paint removal.

Thermal—Softening and raising the paint layers by applying heat followed by scraping and sanding. Generally used for total paint removal.

Chemical—Softening of the paint layers with chemical strippers followed by scraping and sanding. Generally used for total paint removal.

• Abrasive Methods (Manual)

If conditions have been identified that require limited paint removal such as crazing, intercoat peeling, solvent blistering, and wrinkling, scraping and hand sanding should be the first methods employed before using mechanical means. Even in the case of more serious conditions such as peeling—where the damaged paint is weak and already sufficiently loosened from the wood surface—scraping and hand sanding may be all that is needed prior to repainting.

Recommended Abrasive Methods (Manual)

Putty Knife/Paint Scraper: Scraping is usually accomplished with either a putty knife or a paint scraper, or both. Putty knives range in width from one to six inches and have a beveled edge. A putty knife is used in a pushing motion going under the paint and working from an area of loose paint toward the edge where the paint is still firmly adhered and, in effect, "beveling" the remaining layers so that as smooth a transition as possible is made between damaged and undamaged areas (see figure 10).

Paint scrapers are commonly available in $1\frac{5}{16}$, $2\frac{1}{2}$, and $3\frac{1}{2}$ inch widths and have replaceable blades. In addition, profiled scrapers can be made specifically for use on moldings. As opposed to the putty knife, the paint scraper is used in a pulling motion and works by raking the damaged areas of paint away.

The obvious goal in using the putty knife or the paint scraper is to selectively remove the affected layer or layers of paint; however, both of these tools, particularly the paint scraper with its hooked edge, must be used with care to properly prepare the surface and to avoid gouging the wood.

Sandpaper/Sanding Block/Sanding sponge: After manually removing the damaged layer or layers by scraping, the uneven surface (due to the almost inevitable removal of varying numbers of paint layers in a given area) will need to be smoothed or "feathered out" prior to repainting. As stated before, hand sanding, as opposed to harsher mechanical sanding, is recommended if the area is relatively limited. A coarse grit, open-coat flint sandpaper—the least expensive kind—is useful for this purpose because, as the sandpaper clogs with paint it must be discarded and this process repeated until all layers adhere uniformly.

Blocks made of wood or hard rubber and covered with sandpaper are useful for handsanding flat surfaces. Sanding sponges—rectangular sponges with an abrasive aggregate on their surfaces—are also available for detail work that requires reaching into grooves because the sponge easily conforms to curves and irregular surfaces. All sanding should be done with the grain.

Summary of Abrasive Methods (Manual)

Recommended: Putty knife, paint scraper, sandpaper, sanding block, sanding sponge.
Applicable areas of building: All areas.
For use on: Class I, Class II, and Class III conditions.
Health/Safety factors: Take precautions against lead dust, eye damage; dispose of lead paint residue properly.

Fig. 10 *An excellent example of inadequate scraping before repainting, the problems here are far more than cosmetic. This improperly prepared surface will permit moisture to get behind the paint film which, in turn, will result in chipping and peeling. Photo: Baird M. Smith, AIA.*

• **Abrasive Methods (Mechanical)**

If hand sanding for purposes of surface preparation has not been productive or if the affected area is too large to consider hand sanding by itself, mechanical abrasive methods, i.e., power-operated tools may need to be employed; however, it should be noted that the majority of tools available for paint removal can cause damage to fragile wood and must be used with great care.

Recommended Abrasive Methods (Mechanical)

Orbital sander: Designed as a finishing or smoothing tool—not for the removal of multiple layers of paint—the oribital sander is thus recommended when limited paint removal is required prior to repainting. Because it sands in a small diameter circular motion (some models can also be switched to a back-and-forth vibrating action), this tool is particularly effective for "feathering" areas where paint has first been scraped (see figure 11). The abrasive surface varies from about 3×7 inches to 4×9 inches and sandpaper is attached either by clamps or sliding clips. A medium grit, open-coat aluminum oxide sandpaper should be used; fine sandpaper clogs up so quickly that it is ineffective for smoothing paint.

Belt sander: A second type of power tool—the belt sander—can also be used for removing limited layers of paint but,

in this case, the abrasive surface is a continuous belt of sandpaper that travels at high speeds and consequently offers much less control than the orbital sander. Because of the potential for more damage to the paint or the wood, use of the belt sander (also with a medium grit sandpaper) should be limited to flat surfaces and only skilled operators should be permitted to operate it within a historic preservation project.

Fig. 11 *The orbital sander can be used for limited paint removal, i.e., for smoothing flat surfaces after the majority of deteriorated paint has already been scraped off. Photo: Charles E. Fisher, III.*

Not Recommended

Rotary Drill Attachments: Rotary drill attachments such as the rotary sanding disc and the rotary wire stripper should be avoided. The disc sander—usually a disc of sandpaper about 5 inches in diameter secured to a rubber based attachment which is in turn connected to an electric drill or other motorized housing—can easily leave visible circular depressions in the wood which are difficult to hide, even with repainting. The rotary wire stripper—clusters of metals wires similarly attached to an electric drill-type unit—can actually shred a wooden surface and is thus to be used exclusively for removing corrosion and paint from metals.

Waterblasting: Waterblasting above 600 p.s.i. to remove paint is not recommended because it can force water into the woodwork rather than cleaning loose paint and grime from the surface; at worst, high pressure waterblasting causes the water to penetrate exterior sheathing and damages interior finishes. A detergent solution, a medium soft bristle brush, and a garden hose for purposes of rinsing, is the gentlest method involving water and is recommended when cleaning exterior surfaces prior to repainting.

Sandblasting: Finally—and undoubtedly most vehemently "not recommended"—sandblasting painted exterior woodwork will indeed remove paint, but at the same time can scar wooden elements beyond recognition. As with rotary wire strippers, sandblasting erodes the soft porous fibers (spring wood) faster than the hard, dense fibers (summer wood), leaving a pitted surface with ridges and valleys. Sandblasting will also erode projecting areas of carvings and moldings before it removes paint from concave areas (see figure 12). Hence, this abrasive method is potentially the most damaging of all possibilities, even if a contractor promises that blast pressure can be controlled so that the paint is removed without harming the historic exterior woodwork. (For Additional Information, See Presevation Briefs 6, "Dangers of Abrasive Cleaning to Historic Buildings".)

Fig. 12 *Sandblasting has permanently damaged this ornamental bracket. Even paint will not be able to hide the deep erosion of the wood. Photo: David W. Look, AIA.*

Summary of Abrasive Methods (Mechanical)

Recommended: Orbital sander, belt sander (skilled operator only).
Applicable areas of building: Flat surfaces, i.e., siding, eaves, doors, window sills.
For use on: Class II and Class III conditions.
Health/Safety factors: Take precautions against lead dust and eye damage; dispose of lead paint residue properly.
Not Recommended: Rotary drill attachments, high pressure waterblasting, sandblasting.

• Thermal Methods

Where exterior surface conditions have been identified that warrant total paint removal such as peeling, cracking, or alligatoring, two thermal devices—the electric heat plate and the electric heat gun—have proven to be quite successful for use on different wooden elements of the historic building. One thermal method—the blow torch—is not recommended because it can scorch the wood or even burn the building down!

Recommended Thermal Methods

Electric heat plate: The electric heat plate (see figure 13) operates between 500 and 800 degrees Fahrenheit (not hot enough to vaporize lead paint), using about 15 amps of power. The plate is held close to the painted exterior surface until the layers of paint begin to soften and blister, then moved to an adjacent location on the wood while the softened paint is scraped off with a putty knife (it should be noted that the heat plate is most successful when the paint is very thick!). With practice, the operator can successfully move the heat plate evenly across a flat surface such as wooden siding or a window sill or door in a continuous motion, thus lessening the risk of scorching the wood in an attempt to reheat the edge of the paint sufficiently for effective removal. Since the electric heat plate's coil is "red hot," extreme caution should be taken to avoid igniting clothing or burning the skin. If an extension cord is used, it should be a heavy-duty cord (with 3-prong grounded plugs). A heat plate could overload a circuit or, even worse, cause an electrical fire; therefore, it is recommended that this implement be used with a single circuit and that a fire extinguisher always be kept close at hand.

Fig. 13 *The electric heat plate (with paint scraper) is particularly useful for removing paint down to bare wood on flat surfaces such as doors, window frames, and siding. After scraping, some light sanding will probably be necessary to smooth the surface prior to application of primer and top coats. Photo: David W. Look, AIA.*

Electric heat gun: The electric heat gun (electric hot-air gun) looks like a hand-held hairdryer with a heavy-duty metal case (see figure 14). It has an electrical resistance coil that typically heats between 500 and 750 degrees Fahrenheit and, again, uses about 15 amps of power which requires a heavy-duty extension cord. There are some heat guns that operate at higher temperatures but they should not be purchased for removing old paint because of the danger of lead paint vapors. The temperature is controlled by a vent on the side of the heat gun. When the vent is closed, the heat increases. A fan forces a stream of hot air against the painted woodwork, causing a blister to form. At that point, the softened paint can be peeled back with a putty knife. It can be used to best advantage when a paneled door was originally varnished, then painted a number of times. In this case, the paint will come off quite easily, often leaving an almost pristine varnished surface behind. Like the heat plate, the heat gun works best on a heavy paint build-up. (It is, however, not very successful on only one or two layers of paint or on surfaces that have only been varnished. The varnish simply becomes sticky and the wood scorches.)

Although the heat gun is heavier and more tiring to use than the heat plate, it is particularly effective for removing paint from detail work because the nozzle can be directed at curved and intricate surfaces. Its use is thus more limited than the heat plate, and most successfully used in conjunction *with* the heat plate. For example, it takes about two to three hours to strip a paneled door with a heat gun, but if used in combination with a heat plate for the large, flat area, the time can usually be cut in half. Although a heat gun seldom scorches wood, it can cause fires (like the blow torch) if aimed at the dusty cavity between the exterior sheathing and siding and interior lath and plaster. A fire may smolder for hours before flames break through to the surface. Therefore, this thermal device is best suited for use on solid decorative elements, such as molding, balusters, fretwork, or "gingerbread."

Fig. 14 *The nozzle on the electric heat gun permits hot air to be aimed into cavities on solid decorative elements such as this applied column. After the paint has been sufficiently softened, it can be removed with a profiled scraper. Photo: Charles E. Fisher, III.*

Not Recommended

Blow Torch: Blow torches, such as hand-held propane or butane torches, were widely used in the past for paint removal because other thermal devices were not available. With this technique, the flame is directed toward the paint until it begins to bubble and loosen from the surface. Then the paint is scraped off with a putty knife. Although this is a relatively fast process, at temperatures between 3200 and 3800 degrees Fahrenheit the open flame is not only capable of burning a careless operator and causing severe damage to eyes or skin, it can easily scorch or ignite the wood. The other fire hazard is more insidious. Most frame buildings have an air space between the exterior sheathing and siding and interior lath and plaster. This cavity usually has an accumulation of dust which is also easily ignited by the open flame of a blow torch. Finally, lead-base paints will vaporize at high temperatures, releasing toxic fumes that can be unknowingly inhaled. Therefore, because both the heat plate and the heat gun are generally safer to use—that is, the risks are much more controllable—the blow torch should definitely be avoided!

Summary of Thermal Methods

Recommended: Electric heat plate, electric heat gun.
Applicable areas of building: Electric heat plate—flat surfaces such as siding, eaves, sash, sills, doors. Electric heat gun—solid decorative molding, balusters, fretwork, or "gingerbread."
For use on: Class III conditions.
Health/Safety factors: Take precautions against eye damage and fire. Dispose of lead paint residue properly.
Not Recommended: Blow torch.

• Chemical Methods

With the availability of effective thermal methods for total paint removal, the need for chemical methods—in the context of preparing historic exterior woodwork for repainting—becomes quite limited. Solvent-base or caustic strippers may, however, play a supplemental role in a number of situations, including:

• Removing paint residue from intricate decorative features, or in cracks or hard to reach areas if a heat gun has not been completely effective;
• Removing paint on window muntins because heat devices can easily break the glass;
• Removing varnish on exterior doors after all layers of paint have been removed by a heat plate/heat gun if the original varnish finish is being restored;
• Removing paint from detachable wooden elements such as exterior shutters, balusters, columns, and doors by dip-stripping when other methods are too laborious.

Recommended Chemical Methods (Use With Extreme Caution)

Because all chemical paint removers can involve potential health and safety hazards, no wholehearted recommendations can be made from that standpoint. Commonly known as "paint removers" or "strippers," both solvent-base or caustic products are commercially available that, when poured, brushed, or sprayed on painted exterior woodwork are capable of softening several layers of paint at a time so that the resulting "sludge"—which should be remembered is nothing less than the sequence of historic paint layers—can be removed with a putty knife. Detachable wood elements such as exterior shutters can also be "dip-stripped."

Solvent-base Strippers: The formulas tend to vary, but generally consist of combinations of organic solvents such as methylene chloride, isopropanol, toluol, xylol, and methanol; thickeners such as methyl cellulose; and various additives such as paraffin wax used to prevent the volatile solvents from evaporating before they have time to soak through multiple layers of paint. Thus, while some solvent-base strippers are quite thin and therefore unsuitable for use on vertical surfaces, others, called "semi-paste" strippers, are formulated for use on vertical surfaces or the underside of horizontal surfaces.

However, whether liquid or semi-paste, there are two important points to stress when using any solvent-base stripper: First, the vapors from the organic chemicals can be highly toxic if inhaled; skin contact is equally dangerous because the solvents can be absorbed; second, many solvent-base strippers are flammable. Even though application out-of-doors may somewhat mitigate health and safety hazards, a respirator with special filters for organic solvents is recommended and, of course, solvent-base strippers should never be used around open flames, lighted cigarettes, or with steel wool around electrical outlets.

Although appearing to be the simplest for exterior use, a particular type of solvent-base stripper needs to be mentioned here because it can actually cause the most problems. Known as "water-rinsable," such products have a high proportion of methylene chloride together with emulsifiers. Although the dissolved paint can be rinsed off with water with a minimum of scraping, this ultimately creates more of a problem in cleaning up and properly disposing of the sludge. In addition, these strippers can leave a gummy residue on the wood that requires removal with solvents. Finally, water-rinsable strippers tend to raise the grain of the wood more than regular strippers.

On balance, then, the regular strippers would seem to work just as well for exterior purposes and are perhaps even better from the standpoint of proper lead sludge disposal because they must be hand scraped as opposed to rinsed off (a coffee-can with a wire stretched across the top is one effective way to collect the sludge; when the putty knife is run across the wire, the sludge simply falls into the can. Then, when the can is filled, the wire is removed, the can capped, and the lead paint sludge disposed of according to local health regulations).

Caustic Strippers: Until the advent of solvent-base strippers, caustic strippers were used exclusively when a chemical method was deemed appropriate for total paint removal prior to repainting or refinishing. Now, it is more difficult to find commercially prepared caustic solutions in hardware and paint stores for home-owner use with the exception of lye (caustic soda) because solvent-base strippers packaged in small quantities tend to dominate the market.

Most commercial dip stripping companies, however, continue to use variations of the caustic bath process because it is still the cheapest method available for removing paint. Generally, dip stripping should be left to professional companies because caustic solutions can dissolve skin and permanently damage eyes as well as present serious disposal problems in large quantities.

If exterior shutters or other detachable elements are be-

ing sent out[6] for stripping in a caustic solution, it is wise to see samples of the company's finished work. While some companies do a first-rate job, others can leave a residue of paint in carvings and grooves. Wooden elements may also be soaked too long so that the wood grain is raised and roughened, requiring extensive hand sanding later. In addition, assurances should be given by these companies that caustic paint removers will be neutralized with a mild acid solution or at least thoroughly rinsed with water after dipping (a caustic residue makes the wood feel slippery). If this is not done, the lye residue will cause new paint to fail.

Summary of Chemical Methods

Recommended, with extreme caution: Solvent-base strippers, caustic strippers.

Applicable areas of buildings: decorative features, window muntins, doors, exterior shutters, columns, balusters, and railings.

For use on: Class III Conditions.

Health/Safety factors: Take precautions against inhaling toxic vapors; fire; eye damage; and chemical poisoning from skin contact. Dispose of lead residue properly

General Paint Type Recommendations

Based on the assumption that the exterior wood has been painted with oil paint many times in the past and the existing top coat is therefore also an oil paint,* it is recommended that for CLASS I and CLASS II paint surface conditions, a top coat of high quality oil paint be applied when repainting. The reason for recommending oil rather than latex paints is that a coat of latex paint applied directly over old oil paint is more apt to fail. The considerations are twofold. First, because oil paints continue to harden with age, the old surface is sensitive to the added stress of shrinkage which occurs as a new coat of paint dries. Oil paints shrink less upon drying than latex paints and thus do not have as great a tendency to pull the old paint loose. Second, when exterior oil paints age, the binder releases pigment particles, causing a chalky surface. Although for best results, the chalk (or dirt, etc.) should *always* be cleaned off prior to repainting, a coat of new oil paint is more able to penetrate a chalky residue and adhere than is latex paint. Therefore, unless it is possible to thoroughly clean a heavy chalked surface, oil paints—on balance—give better adhesion.

If however, a latex top coat is going to be applied over several layers of old oil paint, an oil primer should be applied first (the oil primer creates a flat, porous surface to which the latex can adhere). After the primer has thoroughly dried, a latex top coat may be applied. In the long run, changing paint types is more time consuming and expensive. An application of a new oil-type top coat on the old oil paint is, thus, the preferred course of action.

---

6 Marking the original location of the shutter by number (either by stamping numbers into the end grain with metal numeral dies or cutting numbers into the end with a pen knife) will minimize difficulties when rehanging them.

* If the top coat is latex paint (when viewed by the naked eye or, preferably, with a magnifying glass, it looks like a series of tiny craters) it may either be repainted with new latex paint or with oil paint. Normal surface preparation should precede any repainting.

If **CLASS III** conditions have necessitated total paint removal, there are two options, both of which assure protection of the exterior wood: (1) an oil primer may be applied followed by an oil-type top coat, preferably by the same manufacturer; or (2) an oil primer may be applied followed by a latex top coat, again using the same brand of paint. It should also be noted that primers were never intended to withstand the effects of weathering; therefore, the top coat should be applied as soon as possible after the primer has dried.

Conclusion

The recommendations outlined in this Brief are cautious because at present there is no completely safe and effective method of removing old paint from exterior woodwork. This has necessarily eliminated descriptions of several methods still in a developmental or experimental stage, which can therefore neither be recommended nor precluded from future recommendation. With the ever-increasing number of buildings being rehabilitated, however, paint removal technology should be stimulated and, in consequence, existing methods refined and new methods developed which will respect both the historic wood and the health and safety of the operator.

Reading List

Batcheler, Penelope Hartshorne, "Paint Color Research and Restoration." *Technical Leaflet 15.* Nashville: American Association for State and Local History (undated).

"Danger: Restoration May Be Hazardous to Your Health." *The Old House Journal.* Vol. 4, No. 5 (May 1976), pp. 9-11.

Gola, Edward F. "Avoiding Mistakes in Exterior Painting." *The Old House Journal.* Vol. 4, No. 6 (June 1976), pp. 1, 4-5.

"How to Assure a Satisfactory Paint Job." *Scientific Section: Circular 784.* Washington, DC: National Paint, Varnish and Lacquer Association (undated).

Labine, Clem. "Selecting the Best Exterior Paint." *The Old House Journal.* Vol. 4, No. 7 (July 1976), pp. 1, 10-11.

Morton, W. Brown III and Hume, Gary L. *The Secretary of the Interior's Standards for Historic Preservation Projects with Guidelines for Applying the Standards.* Washington, DC: Department of Interior, 1979.

Paint Problem Solver. St. Louis: National Decorating Products Association, 1980.

"Special Issue: Exterior Painting." *The Old House Journal.* Vol. 4, No. 4 (April 1981), pp. 71-94.

Thorsen, John W. "Hazardous Waste: What is it? How to Handle it." *Professional Decorating & Coating Action.* Vol. 43, No. 4 (September 1981), pp. 4-5.

Special thanks go to Baird M. Smith, AIA (formerly Chief, Preservation Technology Branch, TPS) for providing general direction in the development of the manuscript. In addition, the following individuals are to be thanked for their contributions as technical experts in the field: Royal T. Brown, National Paint and Coatings Association, Washington, D.C.; Dr. Judith E. Selwyn, Preservation Technology Associates, Boston, Massachusetts; and Dennis R. Vacca, Pratt & Lambert Co., Carlstadt, New Jersey. Finally, thanks go to several National Park Service staff members whose valuable comments were incorporated into the text and who contributed to the production of the brief: James A. Caufield, Anne E. Grimmer, Jean E. Travers, David G. Battle, Sharon C. Park, AIA, Charles E. Fisher III, Sara K. Blumenthal, and Martha A. Gutrick.

11

Rehabilitating Historic Storefronts

H. Ward Jandl

This woodcut of the Joy Building, built in 1808 in Boston, shows early storefronts with shutters; note the profusion of signs covering the facade, advertising the services of the tenants.

The storefront is the most important architectural feature of many historic commercial buildings. It also plays a crucial role in a store's advertising and merchandising strategy to draw customers and increase business. Not surprisingly, then, the storefront has become the feature most commonly altered in a historic commercial building. In the process, these alterations may have completely changed or destroyed a building's distinguishing architectural features that make up its historic character.

As more and more people come to recognize and appreciate the architectural heritage of America's downtowns, however, a growing interest can be seen in preserving the historic character of commercial buildings. The sensitive rehabilitation of storefronts can result not only in increased business for the owner but can also provide evidence that downtown revitalization efforts are succeeding (see figure 1).

Once a decision is made to rehabilitate a historic commercial building, a series of complex decisions faces the owner, among them:

- if the original storefront has survived largely intact but is in a deteriorated condition, what repairs should be undertaken?

- if the storefront has been modernized at a later date, should the later alterations be kept or the building restored to its original appearance or an entirely new design chosen?

- if the building's original retail use is to be changed to office or residential, can the commercial appearance of the building be retained while accommodating the new use?

This Preservation Brief is intended to assist owners, architects, and planning officials in answering such questions about how to evaluate and preserve the character of historic storefronts. In so doing, it not only addresses the

THE SIX HUNDRED BLOCK MAIN STREET

Figure 1. *Inappropriate storefront alterations over the years—metal cladding, oversized signs and canopies—have detracted from the character of this historic district in Van Buren, Arkansas. A carefully considered rehabilitation plan for Main Street, including the removal of poorly designed signs, false fronts and the selection of an appropriate exterior paint color palette, serves to enhance the visual environment and preserves the district's sense of time and place. Photo above: Bob Dunn; Drawing, David Fitts*

basic design issues associated with storefront rehabilitation, but recommends preservation treatments as well. Finally, although the Brief focuses on storefront rehabilitation, it is important to review this specific work in the broader context of preserving and maintaining the overall structure. Money spent on storefront rehabilitation may be completely wasted if repair and maintenance problems on the rest of the building are neglected.

Historical Overview

Commercial establishments of the 18th and early 19th centuries were frequently located on the ground floor of buildings and, with their residentially scaled windows and doors, were often indistinguishable from surrounding houses. In some cases, however, large bay or oriel windows comprised of small panes of glass set the shops apart from their neighbors. Awnings of wood and canvas and signs over the sidewalk were other design features seen on some early commercial buildings. The ground floors of large commercial establishments, especially in the first decades of the 19th century, were distinguished by regularly spaced, heavy piers of stone or brick, infilled with paneled doors or small paned window sash. Entrances were an integral component of the facade, typically not given any particular prominence although sometimes wider than other openings.

The ready availability of architectural cast iron after the 1840's helped transform storefront design as architects and builders began to experiment using iron columns and lintels at the ground floor level. Simultaneous advances in the glass industry permitted manufacturing of large panes of glass at a reasonable cost. The combination of these two technical achievements led to the storefront as we know it today—large expanses of glass framed by thin structural elements. The advertisement of the merchant and his products in the building facade and display windows quickly became critical factors in the competitive commercial atmosphere of downtowns. In the grouping of these wide-windowed facades along major commercial streets, the image of America's cities and towns radically changed.

The first cast iron fronts were simple post-and-lintel construction with little decoration. As iron craftsmen became more adept and as more ornate architectural styles became popular, cast iron fronts were given Italianate, Venetian Gothic, and French Second Empire details. Cast iron storefronts could be selected directly from catalogs, which began to appear in the early 1850's. Standardized sills, columns, and lintels could be arranged to create fronts of all sizes, styles and configurations. In the 1870's sheet metal storefronts became popular; they were also sold in standardized sizes and configurations through manufacturers' catalogs (see figure 2).

The typical 19th century storefront consisted of single or double doors flanked by display windows (see figure 3). The entrance was frequently recessed, not only to protect the customer from inclement weather but to increase the amount of space in which to display merchandise. In some cases an additional side door provided access to the upper floors. Thin structural members of cast iron or wood, rather than masonry piers, usually framed the storefront. The windows themselves were raised off the ground by wood, cast iron or pressed metal panels or bulkheads; frequently, a transom or series of transoms (consisting of single or multiple panes of glass) were

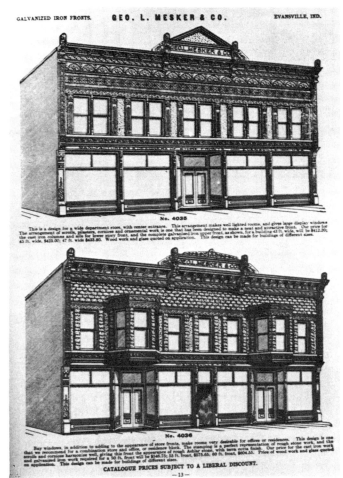

Figure 2. *These 19th century galvanized iron storefronts could be purchased from George L. Mesker & Co. in Evansville, Indiana.*

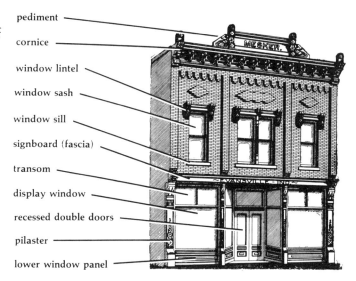

Figure 3. *Become familiar with the architectural features typical of historic commercial buildings. A close look at a storefront's construction materials, features and relationship to the upper stories will help in determining how much of the original facade remains.*

This particular storefront is No. 4016 in the George L. Mesker and Company catalog of 1905. One of Mesker's most popular designs, it featured cast-iron sills, columns and lintels, galvanized iron lintel and main cornice, window caps and pediment.

placed above each window and door. The signboard above the storefront (the fascia covering the structural beam) became a prominent part of the building. Canvas awnings, or in some cases tin or wooden canopies, often shaded storefronts of the late 19th century. Iron fronts were frequently put onto existing buildings as a way of giving them an up-to-date appearance. Except for expanding the display window area to the maximum extent possible and the increasing use of canvas awnings, few major technical innovations in storefront design can be detected from the 1850's through 1900.

The first decades of the 20th century saw the growing use of decorative transom lights (often using small prismatic glass panes) above display windows; in some cases, these transoms could be opened to permit air circulation into the store. Electric incandescent lights enabled storeowners to call attention to their entrance and display windows and permitted nighttime shopping. In the 1920's and 1930's a variety of new materials were introduced into the storefront, including aluminum and stainless steel framing elements, pigmented structural glass (in a wide variety of colors), tinted and mirrored glass, glass block and neon. A bewildering number of proprietary products also appeared during this period, many of which went into storefronts including Aklo, Vitrolux, Vitrolite, and Extrudalite. Highly colored and heavily patterned marble was a popular material for the more expensive storefronts of this period. Many experiments were made with recessed entries, floating display islands, and curved glass. The utilization of neon lighting further transformed store signs into elaborate flashing and blinking creations. During this period design elements were simplified and streamlined; transom and signboard were often combined. Signs utilized typefaces for the period, including such stylized lettering as "Broadway," "Fino" and "Monogram." Larger buildings of this period, such as department stores, sometimes had fixed metal canopies, with lighting and signs as an integral component of the fascia (see figure 4).

Because commercial architecture responds to a variety of factors—environmental, cultural, and economic, distinct regional variations in storefronts can be noted. Fixed metal canopies supported by guy wires, for example, were common in late 19th and early 20th century storefronts in southern states where it was advantageous to have shaded entrances all year long. Such a detail was less common in the northeast where moveable canvas awnings predominated. These awnings could be lowered in summer to keep buildings cooler and raised in winter when sunlight helps to heat the building.

Evaluating the Storefront

The important key to a successful rehabilitation of a historic commercial building is planning and selecting treatments that are sensitive to the architectural character of the storefront. As a first step, it is therefore essential to identify and evaluate the existing storefront's construction materials; architectural features; and the relationship of those features to the upper stores (see figure 5). This evaluation will permit a better understanding of the storefront's role in, and significance to, the overall design of the building. A second and equally important step in planning the rehabilitation work is a careful examination of the storefront's physical conditions to determine the ex-

tent and nature of rehabilitation work needed (see figure 6). In most cases, this examination is best undertaken by a qualified professional.

Figure 4. *This storefront in New York City designed by Raymond Loewy typifies the streamlined look of the 1930's. Added to an earlier buiding, the front utilizes glass, stainless steel and neon to make a modern statement. This is a good example of a later storefront which has acquired significance and should be retained in any rehabilitation.*

Figure 5. *In some cases, as in the storefront on the extreme left, it is a simple matter to determine original appearance by looking at neighboring storefronts. Removal of the board and batten fasciaboard, pent roof, and "colonial" style door, all of which could be undertaken at minimal cost, would restore the original proportions and lines of the building. Photo: Day Johnston*

Guidelines for Rehabilitating Existing Historic Storefronts

1. Become familiar with the style of your building and the role of the storefront in the overall design. Don't "early up" a front. Avoid stock "lumberyard colonial" detailing such as coach lanterns, mansard overhangings, wood shakes, nonoperable shutters, and small paned windows except where they existed historically.

2. Preserve the storefront's character even though there is a new use on the interior. If less exposed window area is desirable, consider the use of interior blinds and insulating curtains rather than altering the existing historic fabric.

3. Avoid use of materials that were unavailable when the storefront was constructed; this includes vinyl and aluminum siding, anodized aluminum, mirrored or tinted glass, artificial stone, and brick veneer.

4. Choose paint colors based on the building's historical appearance. In general do not coat surfaces that have never been painted. For 19th century storefronts, contrasting colors may be appropriate, but avoid too many different colors on a single facade.

Figure 6. *Storefronts of the 1940's, 50's, and 60's were frequently installed by attaching studs or a metal grid over an early front and applying new covering materials. If the existing storefront is a relatively recent addition with little or no architectural merit, begin by removing the covering materials in several places as was done here. If this preliminary investigation reveals evidence of an earlier front, such as this cast-iron column, carefully remove the later materials to assess the overall condition of the historic storefront. The black mastic visible on the lower masonry panels was used for installing pigmented structural glass. Some attachment methods for modern facings, such as mastic or metal lath, may have seriously damaged the original fabric of the buiding, and this must be taken into account in the rehabilitation process. Photo: Bob Dunn*

The following questions should be taken into consideration in this two-part evaluation:

Construction Materials, Features, and Design Relationships

Storefront's Construction Materials: What are the construction materials? Wood? Metal? Brick or other masonry? A combination?

Storefront's Architectural Features: What are the various architectural features comprising the storefront and how are they arranged in relationship to each other?

- Supporting Columns/Piers:
    What do the columns or piers supporting the storefront look like? Are they heavy or light in appearance? Are they flush with the windows or do they protrude? Are they all structural elements or are some columns decorative?
- Display Windows and Transoms:
    Are the display windows and transoms single panes of glass or are they subdivided? Are they flush with the

facade or are they recessed? What is the proportion of area between the display windows and transom? Are there window openings in the base panels to allow natural light into the basement?
- Entrances:
    Are the entrances centered? Are they recessed? Is one entrance more prominent than the others? How is the primary retail entrance differentiated from other entrances? Is there evidence that new entrances have been added or have some been relocated? Are the doors original or are they later replacements?
- Decorative Elements:
    Are there any surviving decorative elements such as molded cornices, column capitals, fascia boards, brackets, signs, awnings or canopies? Is there a belt-course, cornice, or fascia board between the first and second floor? Are some elements older than others indicating changes over time?

Storefront's Relationship to Upper Stories: Is there a difference in materials between the storefront and upper stories? Were the storefront and floors above it created as an overall design or were they very different and unrelated to each other?

It is also worthwhile to study the neighboring commercial buildings and their distinctive characteristics to look for similarities (canopies, lighting, signs) as well as differences. This can help determine whether the storefront in question is significant and unique in its own right and/or whether it is significant as part of an overall commercial streetscape.

Physical Condition

Mild Deterioration: Do the surface materials need repair? Is paint flaking? Are metal components rusting? Do joints need recaulking where materials meet glass windows? Mild deterioration generally requires only maintenance level treatments.

Moderate Deterioration: Can rotted or rusted or broken sections of material be replaced with new material to match the old? Can solid material (such as Carrara glass) from a non-conspicuous location be used on the historic facade to repair damaged elements? Do stone or brick components need repointing? Is the storefront watertight with good flashing connections? Are there leaky gutters or air conditioner units which drip condensation on the storefront? Is caulking needed? Moderate deterioration generally requires patching or splicing of the existing elements with new pieces to match the deteriorated element.

Severe Deterioration: Have existing facing materials deteriorated beyond repair through vandalism, settlement, or water penetration? Is there a loss of structural integrity? Is the material rusted through, rotted, buckling, completely missing? Are structural lintels sagging? Are support columns settled or out of alignment? Severe deterioration generally requires replacement of deteriorated elements as part of the overall rehabilitaton.

In evaluating whether the existing storefront is worthy of preservation, recognize that good design can exist in any period; a storefront added in 1930 *may* have greater architectural merit than what is replaced (see figure 4). In commercial historic districts, it is often the diversity of styles and detailing that contribute to the character; removing a storefront dating from 1910 simply because other buildings in the district have been restored to their 1860's appearance may not be the best preservation approach. If the storefront design is a good example of its period and if it has gained significance over time, it should be retained as part of the historical evolution of the building (this architectural distinctiveness could also be an economic asset as it may attract attention to the building).

Deciding a Course of Action

The evaluation of the storefront's architectural features and physical condition will help determine the best course of action in the actual rehabilitation work. The following recommendations, adapted from the Secretary of the Interior's "Standards for Rehabilitation" and the accompanying interpretive guidelines, are designed to ensure that the historic commercial character of the building is retained in the rehabilitation process.

If the original or significant storefront exists, repair and retain the historic features using recommended treatments (see following sections on rehabilitating metal, wood and masonry storefronts as well as the guidelines for rehabilitating existing historic storefronts found on page 3).

If the original or significant storefront no longer exists or is too deteriorated to save, undertake a contemporary design which is compatible with the rest of the building in scale, design, materials, color and texture; or undertake an accurate restoration based on historical research and physical evidence (see section on "Replacement Storefronts"). Where an original or significant storefront no longer exists and *no* evidence exists to document its early appearance, it is generally preferable to undertake a contemporary design that retains the commercial "flavor" of the building. The new storefront design should not draw attention away from the historic building with its detailing but rather should respect the existing historic character of the overall building. A new design that copies traditional details or features from neighboring buildings or other structures of the period may give the building a historical appearance which blends in with its neighbors but which never, in fact, existed. For this reason, use of conjectural designs, even if based on similar buildings elsewhere in the neighborhood or the availability of different architectural elements from other buildings or structures, is generally not recommended.

Rehabilitating Metal Storefronts

Rehabilitating metal storefronts can be a complex and time-consuming task. Before steps are taken to analyze or treat deteriorated storefronts, it is necessary to know which metal is involved, because each has unique properties and distinct preservation treatments. Storefronts were fabricated using a variety of metals, including cast iron, bronze, copper, tin, galvanized sheet iron, cast zinc, and stainless steel. Determining metallic composition can be a difficult process especially if components are encrusted with paint. Original architect's specifications (sometimes available from permit offices, town halls, or records of the original owner) can be important clues in this regard and should be checked if at all possible.

Iron—a magnetic, gray-white malleable metal, readily susceptible to oxidation. Cast iron, most commonly found in storefronts, is shaped by molds and can withstand great compressive loads. Rolled sheet iron, sometimes galvanized with zinc, also was used in storefront construction. Stainless steel began to appear in storefronts after 1930.

Zinc—a medium-hard, bluish-white metal, widely used as a protective coating for iron and steel. It is softer than iron and is nonmagnetic.

Copper—a nonmagnetic, corrosion-resistant, malleable metal, initially reddish-brown but when exposed to the atmosphere turns brown to black to green.

Bronze and brass—nonmagnetic, abrasive-resistant alloys combining copper with varying amounts of zinc, lead, or tin. These copper alloys, more commonly found in office buildings or large department stores, range in color from lemon yellow to golden brown to green depending on their composition and are well suited for casting (see figure 7).

Aluminum—a lightweight, nonmagnetic metal commonly found on storefronts dating from the 1920's and 30's. Its brightness and resistance to corrosion has made it a popular storefront material in the 20th century.

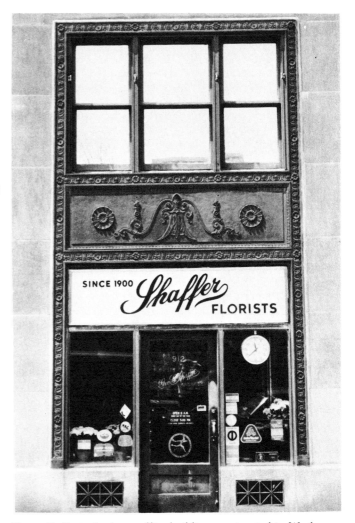

Figure 7. *Part of a large office building constructed in Washington, D.C. in 1928, this finely detailed bronze storefront is typical of many constructed during this period. It should be noted that the original grilles, spandrel panel and window above are all intact. Photo: David W. Look, AIA*

Repair and Replacement of Metal

Simply because single components of a storefront need repair or replacement should not be justification for replacing an entire storefront. Deteriorated metal architectural elements can be repaired by a variety of means, although the nature of the repair will depend on the extent of the deterioration, the type of metal and its location, and the overall cost of such repairs. Patches can be used to mend, cover or fill a deteriorated area. Such patches should be a close match to the original material to prevent galvanic corrosion. Splicing—replacement of a small section with new material—should be undertaken on structural members only when temporary bracing has been constructed to carry the load. Reinforcing—or bracing the damaged element with additional new metal material—can relieve fatigue or overloading in some situations.

If metal components have deteriorated to a point where they have actually failed (or are missing), replacement is the only reasonable course of action. If the components are significant to the overall design of the storefront, they should be carefully removed and substituted with components that match the original in material, size and detailing (see figure 8).

Figure 8. *When the Grand Opera House in Wilmington, Delaware, was rehabilitated, missing cast-iron columns were cast of aluminum to match the original; in this particular case, because these columns do not carry great loads, aluminum proved to be successful substitute. Photo: John G. Waite*

Before going to the expense of reproducing the original, it may be useful to check salvage yards for compatible components. Missing parts of cast iron storefronts can be replaced by new cast iron members that are reproductions of the original. New wooden patterns, however, usually need to be made if the members are large. This procedure tends to be expensive (it is usually impossible to use existing iron components as patterns to cast large elements because cast iron shrinks 1/5 inch per foot as it cools). In some situations, less expensive substitute materials such as aluminum, wood, plastics, and fiberglass, painted to match the metal, can be used without compromising the architectural character of the resource.

Cleaning and Painting

Cast iron storefronts are usually encrusted with layers of paint which need to be removed to restore crispness to the details. Where paint build-up and rust are not severe

problems, handscraping and wire-brushing are viable cleaning methods. While it is necessary to remove all rust before repainting, it is not necessary to remove all paint. For situations involving extensive paint build-up and corrosion, mechanical methods such as low-pressure gentle dry grit blasting (80-100 psi) can be effective and economical, providing a good surface for paint. Masonry and wood surfaces adjacent to the cleaning area, however, should be protected to avoid inadvertent damage from the blasting. It will be necessary to recaulk and putty the heads of screws and bolts after grit blasting to prevent moisture from entering the joints. Cleaned areas should be painted immediately after cleaning with a rust-inhibiting primer to prevent new corrosion. Before any cleaning is undertaken, local codes should be checked to ensure compliance with environmental safety requirements.

Storefronts utilizing softer metals (lead, tin), sheet metals (sheet copper), and plated metals (tin and terneplate) should not be cleaned mechanically (grit blasting) because their plating or finish can be easily abraded and damaged. It is usually preferable to clean these softer metals with a chemical (acid pickling or phosphate dipping) method. Once the surface of the metal has been cleaned of all corrosion, grease, and dirt, a rust-inhibiting primer coat should be applied. Finish coats especially formulated for metals, consisting of lacquers, varnishes, enamels or special coatings, can be applied once the primer has dried. Primer and finish coats should be selected for chemical compatibility with the particular metal in question.

Bronze storefronts, common to large commercial office buildings and major department stores of the 20th century, can be cleaned by a variety of methods; since all cleaning removes some surface metal and patina, it should be undertaken only with good reason (such as the need to remove encrusted salts, bird droppings or dirt). Excessive cleaning can remove the texture and finish of the metal. Since this patina can protect the bronze from further corrosion, it should be retained if possible. If it is desirable to remove the patina to restore the original surface of the bronze, several cleaning methods can be used: chemical compounds including rottenstone and oil, whiting and ammonia, or precipitated chalk and ammonia, can be rubbed onto bronze surfaces with a soft, clean cloth with little or no damage. A number of commercial cleaning companies successfully use a combination of 5% oxalic acid solution together with *finely* ground India pumice powder. Fine glass-bead blasting (or peening) and crushed walnut shell blasting also can be acceptable mechanical methods if carried out in controlled circumstances under low (80-100 psi) pressure. Care should be taken to protect any adjacent wood or masonry from the blasting.

The proper cleaning of metal storefronts should not be considered a "do-it-yourself" project. The nature and condition of the material should be assessed by a competent professional, and the work accomplished by a company specializing in such work.

Rehabilitating Wooden Storefronts

The key to the successful rehabilitation of wooden storefronts is a careful evaluation of existing physical conditions. Moisture, vandalism, insect attack, and lack of maintenance can all contribute to the deterioration of wooden storefronts. Paint failure should not be mistakenly interpreted as a sign that the wood is in poor condition and therefore irreparable. Wood is frequently in sound physical condition beneath unsightly paint. An ice pick or awl may be used to test wood for soundness—decayed wood that is jabbed will lift up in short irregular pieces; sound wood will separate in long fibrous splinters.

Repair and Replacement of Wood

Storefronts showing signs of physical deterioration can often be repaired using simple methods. Partially decayed wood can be patched, built up, chemically treated or consolidated and then painted to achieve a sound condition, good appearance, and greatly extended life.

To repair wood showing signs of rot, it is advisable to dry the wood; carefully apply a fungicide such as pentachlorophenol (a highly toxic substance) to all decayed areas; then treat with 2 or 3 applications of boiled linseed oil (24 hours between applications). Afterward, fill cracks and holes with putty; caulk the joints between the various wooden members; and finally prime and paint the surface.

Partially decayed wood may also be strengthened and stabilized by consolidation, using semi-rigid epoxies which saturate porous decayed wood and then harden. The consolidated wood can then be filled with a semi-rigid epoxy patching compound, sanded and painted. More information on epoxies can be found in the publication "Epoxies for Wood Repairs in Historic Buildings," cited in the bibliography.

Where components of wood storefronts are so badly deteriorated that they cannot be stabilized, it is possible to replace the deteriorated parts with new pieces (see figure 9). These techniques all require skill and some expense, but are recommended in cases where decorative elements, such as brackets or pilasters, are involved. In some cases, missing edges can be filled and rebuilt using wood putty or epoxy compounds. When the epoxy cures, it can be sanded smooth and painted to achieve a durable and waterproof repair.

Figure 9. *Rather than replace an entire wooden storefront when there is only localized deterioration, a new wooden component can be pieced-in, as seen here in this column base. The new wood will need to be given primer and top coats of a high quality exterior paint—either an oil-base or latex system. Also wood that is flaking and peeling should be scraped and hand-sanded prior to repainting. Photo: H. Ward Jandl*

Repainting of Wood

Wooden storefronts were historically painted to deter the harmful effects of weathering (moisture, ultraviolet rays from the sun, wind, etc.) as well as to define and accent architectural features. Repainting exterior woodwork is thus an inexpensive way to provide continued protection from weathering and to give a fresh appearance to the storefront.

Before repainting, however, a careful inspection of all painted wood surfaces needs to be conducted in order to determine the extent of surface preparation necessary, that is, whether the existing layers of paint have deteriorated to the point that they will need to be partially or totally removed prior to applying the new paint.

As a general rule, removing paint from historic exterior woodwork should be avoided unless absolutely essential. Once conditions warranting removal have been identified, however, paint can be removed to the next sound layer using the gentlest method possible, then the woodwork repainted. For example, such conditions as mildewing, excessive chalking, or staining (from the oxidization of rusting nails or metal anchorage devices) generally require only thorough surface cleaning prior to repainting. Intercoat peeling, solvent blistering, and wrinkling require removal of the affected layer using mild abrasive methods such as hand scraping and sanding. In all of these cases of limited paint deterioration, after proper surface preparation the exterior woodwork may be given one or more coats of a high quality exterior oil finish paint.

On the other hand, if painted wood surfaces display continuous patterns of deep cracks or if they are extensively blistering and peeling so that bare wood is visible, the old paint should be completely removed before repainting. (It should be emphasized that because peeling to bare wood—the most common type of paint problem—is most often caused by excess interior or exterior moisture that collects behind the paint film, the first step in treating peeling is to locate and remove the source or sources of moisture. If this is not done, the new paint will simply peel off.)

There are several acceptable methods for total paint removal, depending on the particular wooden element involved. They include such thermal devices as an electric heat plate with scraper for flat surfaces such as siding, window sills, and doors or an electric hot-air gun with profiled scraper for solid decorative elements such as gingerbread or molding. Chemical methods play a more limited, supplemental role in removing paint from historic exterior woodwork; for example, caustic or solvent-base strippers may be used to remove paint from window muntins because thermal devices can easily break the glass. Detachable wooden elements such as exterior shutters, balusters and columns, can probably best be stripped by means of immersion in commercial dip tanks because other methods are too laborious. Care must be taken in rinsing all chemical residue off the wood prior to painting or the new paint will not adhere.

Finally, if the exterior woodwork has been stripped to bare wood, priming should take place within 48 hours (unless the wood is wet, in which case it should be permitted to dry before painting). Application of a high quality oil type exterior primer will provide a surface over which either an oil or latex top coat can be successfully used.

Rehabilitating Masonry Storefronts

Some storefronts are constructed of brick or stone, and like their metal and wooden counterparts, also may have been subjected to physical damage or alterations over time. Although mortar may have disintegrated, inappropriate surface coatings applied, and openings reduced or blocked up, careful rehabilitation will help restore the visual and physical integrity of the masonry storefront

Repair and Replacement of Masonry

If obvious signs of deterioration—disintegrating mortar, spalling bricks or stone—are present, the causes (ground moisture, leaky downspouts, etc.) should be identified and corrected. Some repointing may be necessary on the masonry surface, but should be limited to areas in which so much mortar is missing that water accumulates in the mortar joints, causing further deterioration. New mortar should duplicate the composition, color, texture, and hardness, as well as the joint size and profile of the original. Badly spalling bricks may have to be replaced. Deteriorated stone may be replaced in kind, or with a matching substitute material; in some cases where not visually prominent, it may be covered with stucco, possibly scored to resemble blocks of stone.

Cleaning Masonry

Inappropriate cleaning techniques can be a major source of damage to historic masonry buildings. Historic masonry should be cleaned only when necessary to halt deterioration or to remove graffiti and stains, and always with the gentlest means possible, such as water and a mild detergent using natural bristle brushes, and/or a non-harmful chemical solution, both followed by a low-pressure water rinse.

It is important to remember that many mid-19th century brick buildings were painted immediately or soon after construction to protect poor quality brick or to imitate stone. Some historic masonry buildings not originally painted were painted at a later date to hide alterations or repairs, or to solve recurring maintenance or moisture problems. Thus, whether for reasons of historical tradition or practicality, it may be preferable to retain existing paint. If it is readily apparent that paint is not historic and is a later, perhaps unsightly or inappropriate treatment, removal may be attempted, but only if this can be carried out without damaging the historic masonry. Generally, paint removal from historic masonry may be accomplished successfully only with the use of specially formulated chemical paint removers. No abrasive techniques, such as wet or dry sandblasting should be considered. If non-historic paint cannot be removed without using abrasive methods, it is best to leave the masonry painted, although repainting in a compatible color may help visually.

Removing unsightly mastic from masonry presents a similarly serious problem. Its removal by mechanical means may result in abrading the masonry, and chemical and heat methods may prove ineffective, although solvents like acetone will aid in softening the hardened mastic. If the mastic has become brittle, a flat chisel may be used to pop it off; but this technique, if not undertaken with care, may result in damaging the masonry. And even if total removal is possible, the mastic may have permanently stained the masonry. Replacement of these masonry sec-

tions marred by mastic application may be one option in limited situations; individual pieces of stone or bricks that have been damaged by inappropriate alterations may be cut out and replaced with new pieces that duplicate the original. However, since an exact match will be nearly impossible to achieve, it may be necessary to paint the repaired masonry in order to create a harmonious facade. Replacement of a large area with new materials may not be acceptable as it may give the building a new, non historic appearance inappropriate to the building style and period.

Designing Replacement Storefronts

Where an architecturally or historically significant storefront no longer exists or is too deteriorated to save, a new front should be designed which is compatible with the size, scale, color, material, and character of the building. Such a design should be undertaken based on a thorough understanding of the building's architecture and, where appropriate, the surrounding streetscape (see figure 10). For example, just because upper floor windows are arched is not sufficient justification for designing arched openings for the new storefront. The new design should "read" as a storefront; filling in the space with brick or similar solid material is inappropriate for historic buildings. Similarly the creation of an arcade or other new design element, which alters the architectural and historic character of the building and its relationship with the street, should be avoided. The guidelines on page 8 can assist in developing replacement storefront designs that respect the historic character of the building yet meet current economic and code requirements.

Guidelines for Designing Replacement Storefronts

1. *Scale:* Respect the scale and proportion of the existing building in the new storefront design.

2. *Materials:* Select construction materials that are appropriate to the storefronts; wood, cast iron, and glass are usually more appropriate replacement materials than masonry which tends to give a massive appearance.

3. *Cornice:* Respect the horizontal separation between the storefront and the upper stories. A cornice or fascia board traditionally helped contain the store's sign.

4. *Frame:* Maintain the historic planar relationship of the storefront to the facade of the building and the streetscape (if appropriate). Most storefront frames are generally composed of horizontal and vertical elements.

5. *Entrances:* Differentiate the primary retail entrance from the secondary access to upper floors. In order to meet current code requirements, out-swinging doors generally must be recessed. Entrances should be placed where there were entrances historically, especially when echoed by architectural detailing (a pediment or projecting bay) on the upper stories.

6. *Windows:* The storefront generally should be as transparent as possible. Use of glass in doors, transoms, and display areas allows for visibility into and out of the store.

7. *Secondary Design Elements:* Keep the treatment of secondary design elements such as graphics and awnings as simple as possible in order to avoid visual clutter to the building and its streetscape.

Figure 10. *(A) This existing storefront, added in the 1950's to a late 19th century brick building, extends beyond the plane of the facade; faced with anodized aluminum and permastone, it does not contribute to the architectural and historic character of the building. (B) This replacement design uses "lumberyard colonial" detailing, such as barn-type doors, shutters, small paned windows, and a wood shake pent roof. The design, detailing, and choice of materials are clearly inappropriate to this commercial building. (C) This replacement design retains the 1950's projecting canopy but symmetrical placement of the doors relates well to the second floor windows above; this contemporary design is compatible with the scale and character of the building. (D) This replacement design accurately restores the original appearance of the building; based on historical research and physical evidence, it too is an acceptable preservation approach. Drawings: Sharon C. Park, AIA*

A restoration program requires thorough documentation of the historic development of the building prior to initiating work. If a restoration of the original storefront is contemplated, old photographs and prints, as well as physical evidence, should be used in determining the form and details of the original. Because storefronts are particularly susceptible to alteration in response to changing marketing techniques, it is worthwhile to find visual documentation from a variety of periods to have a clear understanding of the evolution of the storefront. Removal of later additions that contribute to the character of the building should not be undertaken.

Other Considerations

Pigmented Structural Glass

The rehabilitation of pigmented structural glass storefronts, common in the 1930's, is a delicate and often frustrating task, due to the fragility and scarcity of the material. Typically the glass was installed against masonry walls with asphaltic mastic and a system of metal shelf angles bolted to the walls on three-foot centers. Joints between the panels were filled with cork tape or an elastic joint cement to cushion movement and prevent moisture infiltration.

The decision to repair or replace damaged glass panels should be made on a case-by-case basis. In some instances, the damage may be so minor or the likelihood of finding replacement glass so small, that repairing, reanchoring and/or stabilizing the damaged glass panel may be the only prudent choice. If the panel is totally destroyed or missing, it may be possible to replace with glass salvaged from a demolition; or a substitute material, such as "spandrel glass," which approximates the appearance of the original. Although pigmented structural glass is no longer readily available, occasionally long-established glass "jobbers" will have a limited supply to repair historic storefronts.

Awnings

Where based on historic precedent, consider the use of canvas awnings on historic storefronts (see figure 11).

Awnings can help shelter passersby, reduce glare, and conserve energy by controlling the amount of sunlight hitting the store window, although buildings with northern exposures will seldom functionally require them. Today's canvas awnings have an average life expectancy of between 4 and 7 years. In many cases awnings can disguise, in an inexpensive manner, later inappropriate alterations and can provide both additional color and a strong store identification. Fixed aluminum awnings and awnings simulating mansard roofs and umbrellas are generally inappropriate for older commercial buildings. If awnings are added, choose those that are made from soft canvas or vinyl materials rather than wood or metal; be certain that they are installed without damaging the building or visually impairing distinctive architectural features and can be operable for maximum energy conservation effect.

Figure 11. *Try to locate old photographs or prints to determine what alterations have been made to the storefront and when they were undertaken. Awnings were common elements of storefronts at the turn of the century. They can be equally useful today.*

Signs

Signs were an important aspect of 19th and early 20th century storefronts and today play an important role in defining the character of a business district. In examining historic streetscape photographs, one is struck by the number of signs—in windows, over doors, painted on exterior walls, and hanging over (and sometimes across) the street. While this confusion was part of the character of 19th century cities and towns, today's approach toward signs in historic districts tends to be much more conservative. Removal of some signs can have a dramatic effect in improving the visual appearance of a building; these include modern backlit fluorescent signs, large applied signs with distinctive corporate logos, and those signs attached to a building in such a way as to obscure significant architectural detailing. For this reason, their removal is encouraged in the process of rehabilitation. If new signs are designed, they should be of a size and style compatible with the historic building and should not cover or obscure significant architectural detailing or features. For many 19th century buildings, it was common to mount signs on the lintel above the first story. Another common approach, especially at the turn of the century, was to paint signs directly on the inside of the display windows. Frequently this was done in gold leaf. New hanging signs may be appropriate for historic commercial buildings, if they are of a scale and design compatible with the historic buildings. Retention of signs and advertising painted on historic walls, if of historic or artistic interest (especially where they provide evidence of early or original occupants), is encouraged.

Paint Color

Paint analysis can reveal the storefront's historic paint colors and may be worth undertaking if a careful restoration is desired. If not, the paint color should be, at a minimum, appropriate to the style and setting of the building. This also means that if the building is in a historic district, the color selection should complement the building in question as well as other buildings in the block. In general, color schemes for wall and major decorative trim or details should be kept simple; in most cases the color or colors chosen for a storefront should be used on other painted exterior detailing (windows, shutter, cornice, etc.) to unify upper and lower portions of the facade.

Windows

Glass windows are generally the most prominent features in historic storefronts, and care should be taken to ensure that they are properly maintained. For smaller paned windows with wooden frames, deteriorated putty should be removed manually, taking care not to damage wood along the rabbet. To reglaze, a bead of linseed oil-based putty should be laid around the perimeter of the rabbet; the glass pane pressed into place; glazing points inserted to hold the pane; and a final seal of putty beveled around the edge of the glass. For metal framed windows, glazing compound and special glazing clips are used to secure the glass; a final seal of glazing compound then is often applied. If the glass needs replacing, the new glass should match the original in size, color and reflective qualities. Mirrored or tinted glass are generally inappropriate replacements for historic storefronts. The replacement of cracked or missing glass in large windows should be undertaken by professional glaziers.

Code Requirements

Alterations to a storefront called for by public safety, handicapped access, and fire codes can be difficult design problems in historic buildings. Negotiations can be undertaken with appropriate officials to ensure that all applicable codes are being met while maintaining the historic character of the original construction materials and features. If, for instance, doors opening inward must be changed, rather than replace them with new doors, it may be possible to reverse the hinges and stops so that they will swing outward.

Summary

A key to the successful rehabilitation of historic commercial buildings is the sensitive treatment of the first floor itself (see figure 12). Wherever possible, significant storefronts (be they original or later alterations), including windows, sash, doors, transoms, signs and decorative features, should be repaired in order to retain the historic character of the building. Where original or early storefronts no longer exist or are too deteriorated to save, the commercial character of the building should nonetheless be preserved—either through an accurate restoration based on historic research and physical evidence or a contemporary design which is compatible with the scale, design, materials, color and texture of the historic building. The sensitive rehabilitation of historic storefronts will not only enhance the architectural character of the overall building but will contribute to rejuvenating neighborhoods or business districts as well.

Figure 12. *This photograph of three late 19th century commercial buildings clearly shows the impact of preserving and rehabilitating storefronts. The one on the right has been totally obscured by a "modern" front added in the 1950's. Although inappropriate alterations have taken place on the left storefront, it is still possible to determine the original configuration of the doors and display windows. The storefront in the middle has remained intact. Although in need of some minor maintenance work, the appeal of the original design and materials is immediately apparent.*

Additional Reading

Bryan, John M. and the Triad Architectural Associates. *Abbeville, South Carolina: Using Grant-in-Aid Funds for Rehabilitation Planning and Project Work in the Commercial Town Square.* Washington, D.C.: Technical Preservation Services Division, U.S. Department of the Interior, 1980.

Gayle, Margot and Edmund V. Gillon, Jr. *Cast Iron Architecture in New York.* New York: Dover Publications, Inc., 1971.

Gayle, Margot and David W. Look and John G. Waite. *Metals in America's Historic Buildings: Uses and Preservation Treatments.* Washington, D.C.: Technical Preservation Services Division, U.S. Department of the Interior, 1980.

Gelbloom, Mara. "Old Storefronts." *The Old-House Journal* VI, No. 3 (March 1978), pp. 25-34.

Grimmer, Anne E. "Dangers of Abrasive Cleaning to Historic Buildings." (Preservation Briefs 6), Washington, D.C.: Technical Preservation Services Division, U.S. Department of the Interior, 1979.

Guthrie, Susan. *Main Street Historic District, Van Buren, Arkansas: Using Grant-in-Aid Funds for Storefront Rehabilitation.* Washington, D.C.: Technical Preservation Services Division, U.S. Department of the Interior, 1980.

Hartmann, Robert R. "Design for the Business District, Part I." Racine, Wisconsin: Racine Urban Aesthetics, Inc., 1979.

Hensley, Tom. "The Preservation of Historic Pigmented Structural Glass (Vitrolite and Carrara Glass)." Denver: Rocky Mountain Regional Office, National Park Service, 1981.

Marsh, Ellen. "An Introduction to Storefront Rehabilitation." *Conserve Neighborhoods,* No. 7 (Summer 1979).

Mintz, Norman. "A Practical Guide to Storefront Rehabilitation." Technical Series No. 2.: Albany, N.Y.: Preservation League of New York State, 1977.

Myers, John H. *The Repair of Historic Wooden Windows.* (Preservation Briefs 9). Washington, D.C.: Technical Preservation Services Division, U.S. Department of the Interior, 1980.

Park, Sharon C. *Storefront Rehabilitation: A 19th Century Commercial Building.* Washington, D.C.: Technical Preservation Services Division, U.S. Department of the Interior, 1980.

Phillips, Morgan W. and Dr. Judith E. Selwyn. "Epoxies for Wood Repairs in Historic Buildings." Washington, D.C.: Technical Preservation Services Division, U.S. Department of the Interior, 1978.

Rifkind, Carole. *Main Street: The Face of Urban America.* New York: Harper and Row, 1977.

The Secretary of the Interior's Standards for Rehabilitation and Guidelines for Rehabilitating Historic Buildings. Washington, D.C.: Technical Preservation Services Division, U.S. Department of the Interior, 1980.

Weeks, Kay D. and David W. Look. "Exterior Paint Problems on Historic Woodwork." (Preservation Briefs 10). Washington, D.C.: Technical Preservation Services, U.S. Department of the Interior, 1982.

Special thanks go to Kay D. Weeks and Sharon C. Park, AIA, for providing technical and editorial direction in the development of this Preservation Brief. The following individuals are also to be thanked for reviewing the manuscript and making suggestions: Norman Mintz, New York, N.Y.; Judith Kitchen, Columbus, Ohio; Jim Vaseff, Atlanta, Georgia,; and Tom Moriarity, Washington, D.C. Finally thanks go to Technical Preservation Service Branch staff members, especially Martha A. Gutrick, Michael J. Auer and Anne E. Grimmer, whose valuable comments were incorporated into the final text and who contributed to the publication of the brief.

This publication has been prepared pursuant to the Economic Recovery Tax Act of 1981 which directs the Secretary of the Interior to certify rehabilitations of historic buildings that are consistent with their historic character; the advice and guidance provided in this brief will assist property owners in complying with the requirements of this law.

Preservation Briefs 11 has been developed under the technical editorship of Lee H. Nelson, AIA, Chief, Preservation Assistance Division, National Park Service, U.S. Department of the Interior, Washington, D.C. 20240. Comments on the usefulness of this information are welcomed and can be sent to Mr. Nelson at the above address.

12

The Preservation of Historic Pigmented Structural Glass

(Vitrolite and Carrara Glass)

The dramatic growth and popularization of the early 20th century Art Deco, Streamline, and Moderne architectural styles were fueled, in part, by technological advances in the building materials industry. New products, such as stainless steel and plastics, enlarged the realm of architectural design. The more traditional materials, on the other hand, quickly developed fresh, innovative forms and uses. For example, the architectural glass industry became especially creative, introducing a series of new glass products known as structural glass. Used predominately for wall surfacing, these now familiar products included glass building blocks, reinforced plate glass, and pigmented structural glass. Pigmented structural glass, popularly known under such trade names as Carrara Glass, Sani Onyx (or Rox), and Vitrolite, revolutionized the business and rapidly became a favorite building material of the period's architects and designers.

The versatility of pigmented structural glass contributed to its popularity. Not only could the material be applied to both the exterior and interior, the glass could be sculptured, cut, laminated, curved, colored, textured, and illuminated. Often applied directly over existing architecture to remodel older buildings—as well as in new construction—a veneer of pigmented structural glass had the ability to define a building's architectural character as new and up-to-date. Pigmented structural glass also complemented the period's silvery metal accents and affinity for slick, shiny surfaces. A successful application of a structural glass veneer often resulted in a streamlined look characteristic of the Art Moderne architectural style.

As tastes changed and production costs rose, however, pigmented structural glass fell into disfavor and disuse by mid-20th century. With today's rekindled interest in the Art Deco, Art Moderne, and Streamline styles the preservation and replacement of pigmented structural glass have now become an integral part of many rehabilitation projects, particularly in relation to commercial storefronts. This brief, then, was developed in order to address some of the major deterioration problems associated with pigmented structural glass and to recommend methods for maintaining, repairing, and—if necessary—replacing damaged or missing pieces of pigmented structural glass.

Early Manufacture and Use of Pigmented Structural Glass

Although pigmented structural glass enjoyed widespread popularity from the beginning of the Great Depression to the outbreak of World War II, its origins can be traced to the turn of the century. In 1900, the Marietta Manufacturing Company claimed to be the first producer of pigmented structural glass, rolling the first sheet of a "substitute for marble," Sani Onyx. Penn-American Plate Glass Company quickly joined its ranks, manufacturing white and black Carrara Glass around 1906. Penn-American Plate Glass no doubt selected the name "Carrara" for the white glass's close resemblance to the white marble of the Carrara quarries of Italy. Shortly thereafter, Libby-Owens-Ford Glass began production of their own version called Vitrolite.

Initially, Sani Onyx was produced for such utilitarian purposes as refrigerator linings. Manufacturers perceived the glass as a practical, easily cleaned, and sanitary product. Its uses, however, expanded rapidly. By the second decade of the 20th century, consumers viewed pigmented structural glass as an inexpensive substitute for marble counter tops, table tops, wainscoting, and restroom partitions. The first large-scale interior architectural application of pigmented structural glass was in the Woolworth Building (1912–1913) when Architect Cass Gilbert sheathed the restrooms with Carrara Glass. Later in the decade, the decorative possibilities of the glass received even more attention.

As the century progressed, architects began to substitute pigmented structural glass for traditional building materials in new construction. Large expanses of architectural detailing such as sleek door surrounds, polished interior lobbies, and striking commercial storefronts became expected and familiar features within new, expanding downtown business districts in the 1920s and 1930s (see fig. 1).

In addition, designers quickly found pigmented structural glass to be an increasingly popular modernizing material for older and out-of-date buildings. As a result, storefronts became a favorite subject for "modernization." New Deal programs, including low-rate insured Federal

Fig. 1. *The Club Moderne, Anaconda, Montana, reflects the exceptional historic detailing associated with pigmented structural glass—polished-mirror finish, rounded corners, and horizontal polychrome bands. Photo: Jet Lowe, Historic American Engineering Record.*

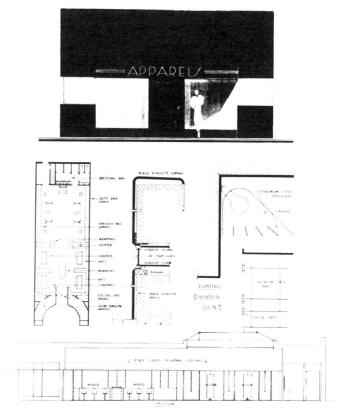

Fig. 2. *The extensive use of rich, black Vitrolite in this design impressed the judges of the 1935 "Modernize Main Street" competition, and the architects were awarded first prize. Courtesy, The Architectural Record.*

Housing Administration loans in combination with a "Modernize Main Street" competition sponsored by the *Architectural Record* and Libby-Owens-Ford Glass, stimulated the remodeling fervor. By 1940, pigmented structural glass veneers had become synonymous with the "modern look." The numerous pigmented structural glass storefronts surviving today are testimony to the popularity of these remodelings.

The winners of the 1935 "Modernize Main Street" competition illustrated what many considered good contemporary design. The judges of the competition, including Albert Kahn, William Lescaze, and John Root, awarded architects who incorporated "simplicity," "economy," "unbroken horizontal lines," "expressed function," and "pure colors contrasting light and shadow" in their designs. Simplicity of design often translated into curvilinear recessed entries which protected consumers from inclement weather—eliminating cumbersome canvas or metal awnings—and providing additional display window space (see fig. 2). The first and second stories of many 19th century storefronts had disappeared by 1940, hidden behind simple, yet striking, modern pigmented structural glass veneers.

Although the glass was originally produced only in white, the range of colors from which architects could choose soon included black, beige, and ivory. By the 1930s, more exotic colors such as tropic green, forest green, robin blue, suntan, and jade were offered by the principal manufacturers in addition to the stock colors of gray, yellow, and tan. Agate or marbleized treatments in fanciful imitation of the "real" materials were also available. The back surface was occasionally silvered to give a rich mirror finish (see fig. 3). Most of these colors and finishes were available in standard thicknesses from 11/32 inch to 1-1/4 inches. The glass's smooth exterior was obtained either by fire polishing during the normal glass fabrication process or by mechanical polishing when a high mirror finish was desired. In both cases, the smooth, slick, reflective surface made the material intensely

popular with architects or designers who sought the "modern look."

Although focusing on exterior applications, architects also utilized pigmented structural glass for interior spaces (see fig. 4), replacing the porous and more expensive marble and offering a highly polished, uniform visual appearance in keeping with design trends of the 1920s and 1930s. Other uses of the material included small, high-style installations in hotels, office lobbies, bars, and lounges (see figs. 5 and 6).

Fig. 3. *The Russell Stover Candies, Nashville, Tennessee, shows the company's historic use of deep, mirrored violet pigmented structural glass storefronts. Photo: Douglas A. Yorke, Jr., AIA.*

Fig. 4. *White pigmented structural glass was used in this remodeling of the U.S. Custom House, Denver, Colorado. Photo: Gregory D. Kendrick.*

Historic Material and Installation Specifications

Early 20th century advertisers often promoted pigmented structural glass as a new panacea of the building materials industry. Their claims were not without substance. Unlike masonry units such as terra cotta, pigmented structural glass would not warp, swell, or craze. Nor was the glass highly susceptible to staining, fading, or burning. Like most glass products, it was impervious to moisture and could be easily maintained and usually cleaned with a damp cloth. Adaptable to a wide range of uses, the glass could be colored and textured to attain brilliant visual qualities. Perhaps most important, when compared to marble, the glass was easier to handle, less expensive to use, and simpler to install.

The key to proper preservation and repair of both interior and exterior pigmented structural glass is a thorough understanding of the original material specifications and detailed installation techniques. Fortunately, these specifications and techniques remain virtually unchanged from their first early 20th century application (see fig. 7).

Exterior Installation

Essentially, the glass veneer was applied to a dry, smooth, and solid masonry or plaster-on-masonry substrate using an asphaltic masonry adhesive. Manufacturers recommended against affixing the glass directly to wood, either lath or paneling. Glass thicknesses of 11/32 inch or 7/16 inch were most common for commercial storefronts.

Shelf angles—18-gauge brass or stainless steel, 3 inch square with a 1/2 inch leg fastened directly to the masonry substrate—were used to provide additional support. Inserted along the bottom edge of the panels, they supported every second course of glass and were thus spaced not more than 3 feet apart. Horizontally, the angles were spaced approximately one every 18 inches with at least two used for any piece.

Actual installation involved applying daubs (2 inches to 3

inches in diameter) of hot asphalt-based mastic adhesive to the glass and then attaching the glass directly to the substrate. Manufacturers of the mastic recommended coverage of about 50 percent of the glass panels. A full 3 inch width of mastic coverage was recommended around detail edges or any holes in the panels. The mastic was applied in a molten state after being melted in an electric "hot cup." (Hot cups are still manufactured for this specific purpose and are made to hold enough mastic for a single daub.)

The next step in the installation procedure was to push the glass panel onto the masonry substrate. Every horizontal seam and abutment was separated by a 1/16 inch thick adhesive cork tape recessed from the front surface by 1/8 inch. Vertical edges were kept apart at a uniform 1/32 inch. In either case, the joint opening was then buttered with a joint cement which was colored to match the surrounding glass.

Proper detailing at the edges of the veneer could prolong the life of the pigmented structural glass. For example, to prevent possible chipping and cracking of the glass where it met the sidewalk, a cushion of neoprene or leather was provided and the exposed surface then caulked (see fig. 8). The side edges of the glass were detailed in a variety of methods or the glass simply terminated at the desired location with the ends ground smooth (see fig. 9). In either case, the edge was secured to the substrate with a mastic and the joints or void filled with joint cement or caulking compound. Where the edge of the glass abutted another material, such as the brickwork of a neighboring storefront, the glass was held back 1/8 inch to 1/4 inch from the adjacent material. The gap was usually filled with pliable caulk to permit expansion and to prevent moisture migration (see figs. 10 and 11).

Interior Installation

Construction methods and materials were quite similar for interior and exterior uses of pigmented structural glass. Most interior veneers were the same thickness and approximate dimension of those used for exteriors. Minor differences did, however, exist. For example, joints between the pieces of glass could be reduced to little more

Fig. 5. *Gentlemen's Lounge, Hermitage Hotel, Nashville, Tennessee, presents a dynamic visual arrangement of horizontal black and green pigmented structural glass panels. Photo: Douglas A. Yorke, Jr., AIA.*

Fig. 6. *Owners of the Hadley Dean Glass Company Warehouse, St. Louis, Missouri, preserved the unusual polychrome pigmented structural glass interior lobby. Photo: Paul Marshall.*

than hairline cracks for interior applications due to the limited thermal expansion of the substrate. On the other hand, the use of glass as an indoor ceiling material created unusual installation requirements.

Ceiling slabs 11/32 inch in thickness were attached to 1 inch *x* 4 inch wood furring strips with mastic (a full 4 inch width coverage was recommended around the edge of the panels). Brass wood screws and small rosettes, protected with felt exterior covers, provided additional support (see fig. 12).

As a nonveneer material, pigmented structural glass was generally used for counter and table tops and restroom partitions. Counter tops presented little or no unusual installation problems. Partitions, however, often involved formidable installation challenges; for example, enormous glass panels, weighing up to 16.25 pounds per square foot and measuring 1 inch to 1-1/4 inches in thickness were used. The desired thickness was obtained by cementing two 7/16 inch slabs together with mastic. To accommodate this heavy yet fragile load, a reinforced support and connection system was developed which utilized metal sleeves, iron anchors, and steel straps bolted directly into the glass panels.

Reasons for Damage

Although deterioration of pigmented structural glass itself is rare or unheard of, failure of the mechanical support system which bonds the glass modules to the wall is almost always the cause of failure, cracking, slipping, or loss. Therefore, damage is usually attributable to one or a

combination of the following:

- Deterioration of the Joint Cement
- Hardening and Failure of the Mastic Adhesive
- Impact Due to Accident/Vandalism

Deterioration of the Joint Cement

Historically, the cement joint between glass panels was intended to provide an integrated, watertight surface. Unfortunately, the traditional joint cement did not possess a long lifespan. Cracked or open joints have been the consequence, usually resulting from improper original application of the cement or from the normal thermal expansion and contraction cycle associated with

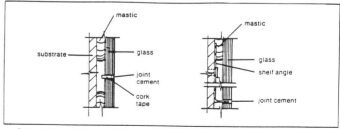

Basic exterior construction details (*Dwgs: D. Beals for Building Conservation Technology*)

Fig. 7. *In the installation process, hot asphaltic mastic was applied to the ribbed or textured back of each glass panel. The panel was then pressed against a masonry wall and supported by metal shelf angles which were usually bolted to the masonry substrate on 3-foot centers. The joints between the panels were filled with cork tape or joint cement. The end result was a modular veneer of clean, uniform glass panels. Courtesy,* **Bulletin for the Association for Preservation Technology**, *13 (1981).*

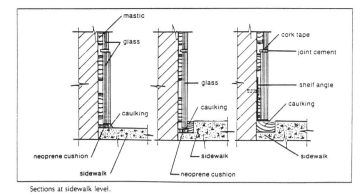

Sections at sidewalk level.

Fig. 8. *Courtesy, Bulletin for the Association for Preservation Technology, 13 (1981).*

weathering. Cracked or open cement joints then accelerated deterioration of the masonry substrate and/or the mastic adhesive bond by allowing water to penetrate the internal system. Water entering the system weakened the bond between the mastic and the masonry substrate or rusted the anchoring shelves. This caused the individual glass panels to gradually slip away from their original positions and fall.

Hardening and Failure of Mastic Adhesive

Failure due to long-term hardening of the original mastic adhesive has accounted for a substantial loss of pigmented structural glass panels. The petroleum-based mastics normally possessed a 30 to 40 year lifespan. Once flexibility of the adhesive is lost, the glass panels become vulnerable to slippage and eventual destruction (see fig. 13).

Impact Due to Accident/Vandalism

Glass breakage through impact is virtually impossible to prevent. The material is, by its nature, vulnerable to loss through vandalism or accident (see fig. 14).

Maintenance and Repair of Pigmented Structural Glass

The maintenance of a dry masonry substrate, mastic, and metal anchors is essential to the longevity of a pigmented structural glass veneer. Thus, repointing cracked or open joints—particularly at ground level where glass abuts concrete—and caulking of slightly cracked glass panels is an ongoing concern. Where drainage to conduct water away from the wall is faulty or insufficient, the problem should be immediately corrected. For example, roof flashing, downspouts, and gutters should be repaired or new systems installed.

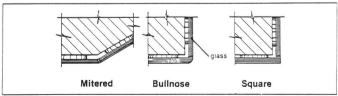

Exterior corners.

Fig. 9. *Courtesy, Bulletin for the Association for Preservation Technology, 13 (1981).*

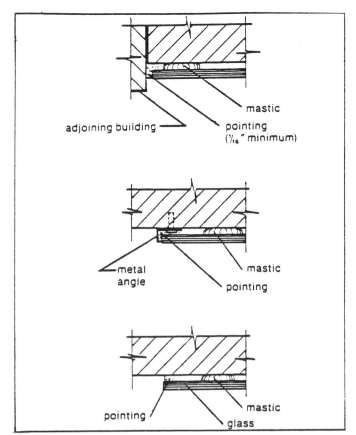

Termination details.

Fig. 10. *Courtesy, Bulletin for the Association for Preservation Technology, 13 (1981).*

Repair of Cement Joints

Cracked or open cement joints, particularly in exterior applications, can present a serious preservation problem because they permit water to penetrate the internal system of a pigmented structural glass veneer. Rusting metal anchors or deteriorating mastic adhesive may be the result. Although the traditional joint cements are easily colored and may be neatly applied, they are no longer recommended for the repair of pigmented structural glass because their longevity is limited. Present-day silicone compounds, on the other hand, offer flexibility, relative impermeability to moisture, ease of installation, and a long lifespan. The proper color match can be obtained by mixing the compound with tinted polyester resins.

Patching Glass Cracks

Any glass panel that can be repaired should not be replaced. Thus, the decision to repair or replace damaged historic pigmented structural glass panels always needs to be made on a case-by-case basis. In many instances, the damage may be so minor or the likelihood of finding suitable replacement glass panels so small that repairing, reanchoring, and/or stabilizing the damaged glass is the only prudent choice.

A slightly chipped or cracked pigmented structural glass panel left unrepaired will inevitably become a source of water infiltration. Careful patching of those cracks with an appropriately colored, flexible caulk will deter moisture penetration while still allowing expansion and contraction with temperature fluctuations. Although patching is by no

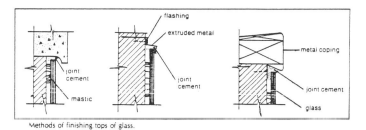

Methods of finishing tops of glass.

Fig. 11. *Courtesy,* **Bulletin for the Association for Preservation Technology,** *13 (1981).*

means a permanent solution, it will help to protect the material from further damage due to the effects of weather (see fig. 15).

Removal of Pigmented Structural Glass Panels

Removal of existing glass panels from a wall in order to reapply mastic adhesive that is failing or to replace broken panels (see also paragraphs on "Replacement of Damaged/Missing Glass Panels") is an exacting operation because the mastic used to attach the glass panels to the wall may have become hard and extremely difficult to separate from the ribbed backing of the glass. Fortunately, commercial solvents may be purchased which are capable of softening the hardened mastic, such as methyl ethyl ketone, methyl isobutyl ketone, and acetone. These solvents may be introduced into the cavity behind the glass with a crook-necked polyethylene laboratory squeeze bottle or a large syringe without a needle. (Solvents should be stored in fire-safe metal containers until used and should also be handled with extreme care so that they do not come into contact with the skin.) Such methods make it easy to direct the solvent into the narrow separation between the glass panel and the wall with a minimum of waste and effort. After the mastic has softened, two people using a taut piano wire sawing down from the top can safely and efficiently separate the glass from the wall.

If time is a concern, a fast, simple removal method is to carefully pry the panels off with a broad flat tool such as a nail puller. A small piece of wood placed between the flat tool and glass will minimize splintering of the edges. Stubborn pieces can be removed by squirting the mastic with a solvent (as described above), then letting it set

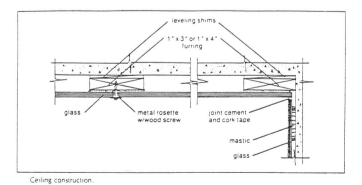

Ceiling construction.

Fig. 12. *Courtesy,* **Bulletin for the Association for Preservation Technology,** *13 (1981).*

Fig. 13. *The pigmented structural glass panel has separated and fallen, exposing the substrate and hardened, brittle daubs of mastic. Photo: Douglas A. Yorke, Jr., AIA.*

several minutes. This procedure softens the mastic, making it more pliable. The piano wire/sawing method may be useful in removing the topmost glass panels of a continuous face where no edges occur. The wire can be effectively worked into the joints and will cut through the mastic. With care, a high percentage of the glass panels can be salvaged using this method (see fig. 16).

Another method of removing glass panels that has proven to be effective if the solvent-and-wire method cannot be used, involves directing steam at the face of the panel in order to soften the mastic. Although this method can be time-consuming, averaging up to 10 minutes per panel, the glass can be successfully removed. Remaining

Fig. 14. *The vast majority of damaged pigmented structural glass panels are found at ground level, the result of vandalism or improper caulking between the glass panel and the concrete sidewalk. Photo: Thomas Keohan.*

Fig. 15. *Owners of this small barber shop, Denver, Colorado, have successfully preserved the historic character of their pigmented structural glass storefront by patching the cracked panels with a dark caulking compound. Photo: Gregory D. Kendrick.*

mastic may then be removed by directing additional steam on the panel, soaking the panels in hot water to further soften the mastic—or applying appropriate chemical solvents—and scraping off the softened mastic.

Reinstallation of Glass Panels

Due to an accumulation of soot behind the glass, the surface of the masonry substrate usually needs to be cleaned before panels or a wall of pigmented structural glass are reinstalled. After removal of the glass panels has been completed, the substrate should be cleaned using a mild detergent and water, then allowing sufficient time for it to dry. The old glass must also be thoroughly cleaned of soot, grease, or old mastic that would impair bonding of the new adhesive. A mild solution of water and household ammonia will generally clean the surface adequately. The glass may then be reinstalled following a system established during removal.

In reinstalling the glass panels (or new panels to replace any historic glass that has been broken), it is recommended that the mastic adhesive used throughout the 1930s and 1940s be used, because it is still the best bonding material. Although modern silicone compounds offer workability, adhesion, and flexibility, they tend to be expensive when used in the necessary quantity. On the other hand, butyl adhesives do not provide sufficient adhesion on non-porous materials such as pigmented structural glass. Polysulfide-based, synthetic rubber sealants do not have the short set-up time of the traditional hot-melt asphalt mastic and thus present installation difficulties. Finally, epoxies do not appear to have the plasticity essential for longevity of a glass veneer.

Replacement of Damaged/Missing Glass Panels

Production of pigmented structural glass in the United States ceased several years ago, and only in rare cases have inventories been discovered. Yet, checking all the obvious and not so obvious sources for replacement may prove to be rewarding. Occasionally, long established "jobbers" will have a limited supply of pigmented structural glass. It is not uncommon for glass contractors to buy entire stocks of glass when companies or supply houses go out of business and to use this original material to make repairs on historic buildings.

Locating a source for new glass similar to the historic pigmented structural glass is as much of a problem as finding the original glass. Until about 10 years ago, glass companies near Bavaria in Western Germany were producing a pigmented structural glass called "Detopak." At present, these factories appear to be the only suppliers in the world. The glass is made in small batches, and the color can vary due to the lack of modern mechanization in the pigmenting process. For this reason, American importers generally only deal in white and black glass.

If a satisfactory replacement panel cannot be located, one alternative is to remove a piece of glass from an inconspicuous part of the building and position it on the more prominent facade. Modern spandrel glass, a new substitute material described below, may be considered as a replacement for the less visible area.

Substitute Material for Damaged/Missing Glass Panels

If replacement glass cannot be found to replace broken or missing panels, a compatible substitute material may be considered if it conveys the same visual appearance as the historic material, i.e., color, size, and reflectivity. Two of the historic producers of pigmented structural glass now manufacture a similar product known generically as

Fig. 16. *A worker carefully removes a large glass panel by placing a small piece of wood between a flat prying bar and the glass, then exerting steady pressure. The majority of panels were removed without damage using this procedure. Photo: Thomas Keohan.*

"spandrel glass" and marketed under the trade names of Spandrelite and Vitrolux. This heavy plate glass has a ceramic frit or colored ceramic surface fired to the back of the glass. Stock colors are available in a range of grays, browns, bronzes, and black. Custom colors are also available.

A second option simulates the appearance of pigmented structural glass by spraying paint, carefully tinted to match the historic glass, onto the back of plate glass. However, the paint may fade over a long period of time and thus require periodic reapplication.

Sheet plastics may also be used and are available in a range of colors, sizes, and thicknesses. These materials are more suitable for interior applications, however, where the negative effects of ultra-violet light are lessened.

Conclusion

The preservation of pigmented structural glass remains more a materials issue than a detailing problem. The glass panels were and are extremely susceptible to breakage due to accident or vandalism. In addition, many of the historic installation materials such as the mastic adhesive and joint cement did not possess a long lifespan. Periodic maintenance, inspection, careful repair, and selective replacement—in like kind—are essential for the longevity of any historic pigmented structural glass veneer.

Even though the architectural glass industry has continued to expand its production of different types of glazing, the imaginative innovations of Carrara Glass, Sani Oxyx, and Vitrolite in the early part of this century have not been surpassed. New technology, combined with human artistry, produced exteriors and interiors alive with color and dimension. Glittering movie palaces, sparkling restaurants, and streamlined storefronts as well as the more mundane kitchens, restrooms, and laboratories exemplified the extensive variety and potential of pigmented structural glass. Carrara Glass, Sani Onyx, and Vitrolite were integrally linked to the architecture and interior design of the 1930s and 1940s and helped to define what was "modern." Thus, every effort should be made to preserve this significant historic material in both the innovative buildings of the Art Deco, Streamline, and Moderne styles as well as the "modernization" of earlier structures.

This Preservation Brief is partially adapted from an article entitled "Material Conservation for the Twentieth Century: The Case for Structural Glass," written by Douglas A. Yorke, Jr., AIA, which appeared in the *Bulletin for the Association for Preservation Technology*, 13 (1981), and from an unpublished manuscript by Thomas L. Hensley of the National Park Service. Preservation Brief 12 was edited by Gregory D. Kendrick, Historian, under the technical editorship of de Teel

Patterson Tiller, both of the Rocky Mountain Regional Office, National Park Service. We wish to thank Mr. Yorke for permission to use his article and photographic material. Finally, we want to acknowledge Thomas G. Keohan, Field Representative, Mountains/Plains Regional Office, National Trust for Historic Preservation for donating photographs and assistance to this project.

Additional Reading

Gay, Charles Merick and Parker, Harry. *Materials and Methods of Architectural Construction.* New York: John Wiley and Sons, Inc., 1931.

Glass, Paints, Varnishes and Brushes: Their History, Manufacture and Use. New York: Pittsburgh Plate Glass Company, 1923.

Hornbostel, Caleb. *Construction Materials.* New York: John Wiley and Sons, Inc., 1978.

Kidder, Frank E. and Parker, Harry. *The Architect's and Builder's Handbook,* 15th ed., New York: John Wiley and Sons Inc., 1913.

McGrath, Raymond and Frost, A.C. *Glass in Architecture and Decoration.* London: The Architectural Press, 1937.

"Modernize Main Street." *Architectural Record* 78 (October 1935): 209–266.

Ramsey, Charles George and Sleeper, Harold Reeves. *Architectural Graphic Standards,* 3rd ed., New York: John Wiley and Sons, Inc., 1941.

Richey, H. G. *Richey's Reference Handbook for Builders, Architects and Construction Engineers.* New York: Simmons-Boardman Publishing Corporation, 1951.

The Secretary of the Interior's Standards for Rehabilitation and Guidelines for Rehabilitating Historic Buildings (Revised 1983). Washington, D.C.: Technical Preservation Services Division, U.S. Department of the Interior.

Standard Building Code. Birmingham, Alabama: Southern Building Code Congress International, Inc., 1979.

Sweet's Architectural Catalogue, 22nd annual ed., New York: F.W. Dodge Corporation, Sweet's Catalogue Service, 1927–1928; Section B, pp. 1406–1409, (Vitrolite product literature).

Sweet's Indexed Catalogue of Building Construction. New York: Architectural Record Company, 1906.

Time Saver Standards, 1st ed., New York: Architectural Record, 1946.

Yorke, Douglas A. Jr., AIA. "Materials Conservation for the Twentieth Century: The Case for Structural Glass." *APT* 13 (1981): 19–30.

13

The Repair and Thermal Upgrading of Historic Steel Windows

Sharon C. Park, AIA

The Secretary of the Interior's "Standards for Rehabilitation" require that where historic windows are individually significant features, or where they contribute to the character of significant facades, their distinguishing visual qualities must not be destroyed. Further, the rehabilitation guidelines recommend against changing the historic appearance of windows through the use of inappropriate designs, materials, finishes, or colors which radically change the sash, depth of reveal, and muntin configuration; the reflectivity and color of the glazing; or the appearance of the frame.

Windows are among the most vulnerable features of historic buildings undergoing rehabilitation. This is especially the case with rolled steel windows, which are often mistakenly not deemed worthy of preservation in the conversion of old buildings to new uses. The ease with which they can be replaced and the mistaken assumption that they cannot be made energy efficient except at great expense are factors that typically lead to the decision to remove them. In many cases, however, repair and retrofit of the historic windows are more economical than whole-sale replacement, and all too often, replacement units are unlike the originals in design and appearance. If the windows are important in establishing the historic character of the building (see fig. 1), insensitively designed replacement windows may diminish—or destroy—the building's historic character.

This *Brief* identifies various types of historic steel windows that dominated the metal window market from 1890-1950. It then gives criteria for evaluating deterioration and for determining appropriate treatment, ranging from routine maintenance and weatherization to extensive repairs, so that replacement may be avoided where possible.[1] This information applies to do-it-yourself jobs and to large rehabilitations where the volume of work warrants the removal of all window units for complete overhaul by professional contractors.

This *Brief* is not intended to promote the repair of ferrous metal windows in every case, but rather to insure that preservation is always the first consideration in a rehabilitation project. Some windows are not important elements in defining a building's historic character; others are highly significant, but so deteriorated that repair is infeasible. In such cases, the *Brief* offers guidance in evaluating appropriate replacement windows.

Fig. 1 Often highly distinctive in design and craftsmanship, rolled steel windows play an important role in defining the architectural character of many later nineteenth and early twentieth century buildings. Art Deco, Art Moderne, the International Style, and Post World War II Modernism depended on the slim profiles and streamlined appearance of metal windows for much of their impact. Photo: William G. Johnson.

---

[1]The technical information given in this brief is intended for most ferrous (or magnetic) metals, particularly rolled steel. While stainless steel is a ferrous metal, the cleaning and repair techniques outlined here must not be used on it as the finish will be damaged. For information on cleaning stainless steel and non-ferrous metals, such as bronze, Monel, or aluminum, refer to *Metals in America's Historic Buildings* (see bibliography).

HISTORICAL DEVELOPMENT

Although metal windows were available as early as 1860 from catalogues published by architectural supply firms, they did not become popular until after 1890. Two factors combined to account for the shift from wooden to metal windows about that time. Technology borrowed from the rolling industry permitted the mass production of rolled steel windows. This technology made metal windows cost competitive with conventional wooden windows. In addition, a series of devastating urban fires in Boston, Baltimore, Philadelphia, and San Francisco led to the enactment of strict fire codes for industrial and multistory commercial and office buildings.

As in the process of making rails for railroads, rolled steel windows were made by passing hot bars of steel through progressively smaller, shaped rollers until the appropriate angled configuration was achieved (see fig. 2). The rolled steel sections, generally 1/8" thick and 1" - 1 1/2" wide, were used for all the components of the windows: sash, frame, and subframe (see fig. 3). With the addition of wire glass, a fire-resistant window resulted. These rolled steel windows are almost exclusively found in masonry or concrete buildings.

A byproduct of the fire-resistant window was the strong metal frame that permitted the installation of larger windows and windows in series. The ability to have expansive amounts of glass and increased ventilation dramatically changed the designs of late 19th and early 20th century industrial and commercial buildings.

The newly available, reasonably priced steel windows soon became popular for more than just their fire-resistant qualities. They were standardized, extremely durable, and easily transported. These qualities led to the use of steel windows in every type of construction, from simple industrial and institutional buildings to luxury commercial and apartment buildings. Casement, double-hung, pivot, projecting, austral, and continuous windows differed in operating and ventilating capacities. Figure 4 outlines the kinds and properties of metal windows available then and now. In addition, the thin profiles of metal windows contributed to the streamlined appearance of the Art Deco, Art Moderne, and International Styles, among others.

The extensive use of rolled steel metal windows continued until after World War II when cheaper, non-corroding aluminum windows became increasingly popular. While aluminum windows dominate the market today, steel windows are still fabricated. Should replacement of original windows become necessary, replacement windows may be available from the manufacturers of some of the earliest steel windows. Before an informed decision can be made whether to repair or replace metal windows, however, the significance of the windows must be determined and their physical condition assessed.

Cover illustration: from *Hope's Metal Windows and Casements: 1818-1926*, currently Hope's Architectural Products, Inc. Used with permission.

122

ROLLING SECTION FROM BAR

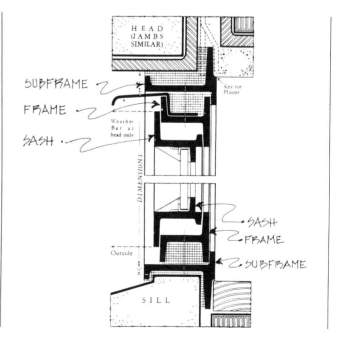

Fig. 2. The process of rolling a steel bar into an angled section is illustrated above. The shape and size of the rolled section will vary slightly depending on the overall strength needed for the window opening and the location of the section in the assembly: subframe, frame, or sash. The 1/8" thickness of the metal section is generally standard. Drawing: A Metal Window Dictionary. Used with permission.

Fig. 3 A typical section through the top and bottom of a metal window shows the three component parts of the window assembly: subframe, frame, and sash. Drawings: Catalogue No. 15, January 1931; International Casement Co., Inc., presently Hope's Architectural Products, Inc., Jamestown, NY. Used with permission.

EVALUATION

Historic and Architectural Considerations

An assessment of the significance of the windows should begin with a consideration of their function in relation to the building's historic use and its historic character. Windows that help define the building's historic character should be preserved even if the building is being converted to a new use. For example, projecting steel windows used to introduce light and an effect of spaciousness to a warehouse or industrial plant can be retained in the conversion of such a building to offices or residences.

Other elements in assessing the relative importance of the historic windows include the design of the windows and their relationship to the scale, proportion, detailing and architectural style of the building. While it may be easy to determine the aesthetic value of highly ornamented windows, or to recognize the importance of streamlined windows as an element of a style, less elaborate windows can also provide strong visual interest by their small panes or projecting planes when open, particularly in simple, unadorned industrial buildings (see fig. 5).

One test of the importance of windows to a building is to ask if the overall appearance of the building would be changed noticeably if the windows were to be removed or radically altered. If so, the windows are important in defining the building's historic character, and should be repaired if their physical condition permits.

Physical Evaluation

Steel window repair should begin with a careful evaluation of the physical condition of each unit. Either drawings or photographs, liberally annotated, may be used to record the location of each window, the type of operability, the condition of all three parts—sash, frame and subframe—and the repairs essential to its continued use.

Specifically, the evaluation should include: presence and degree of corrosion; condition of paint; deterioration of the metal sections, including bowing, misalignment of the sash, or bent sections; condition of the glass and glazing compound; presence and condition of all hardware, screws, bolts, and hinges; and condition of the masonry or concrete surrounds, including need for caulking or resetting of improperly sloped sills.

Corrosion, principally rusting in the case of steel windows, is the controlling factor in window repair; therefore, the evaluator should first test for its presence. Corrosion can be light, medium, or heavy, depending on how much the rust has penetrated the metal sections. If the rusting is merely a surface accumulation or flaking, then the corrosion is light. If the rusting has penetrated the metal (indicated by a bubbling texture), but has not caused any structural damage, then the corrosion is medium. If the rust has penetrated deep into the metal, the corrosion is heavy. Heavy corrosion generally results in some form of structural damage,through delamination,

to the metal section, which must then be patched or spliced. A sharp probe or tool, such as an ice pick, can be used to determine the extent of corrosion in the metal. If the probe can penetrate the surface of the metal and brittle strands can be dug out, then a high degree of corrosive deterioration is present.

In addition to corrosion, the condition of the paint, the presence of bowing or misalignment of metal sections, the amount of glass needing replacement, and the condition of the masonry or concrete surrounds must be assessed in the evaluation process. These are key factors in determining whether or not the windows can be repaired in place. The more complete the inventory of existing conditions, the easier it will be to determine whether repair is feasible or whether replacement is warranted.

Rehabilitation Work Plan

Following inspection and analysis, a plan for the rehabilitation can be formulated. The actions necessary to return windows to an efficient and effective working condition will fall into one or more of the following categories: routine maintenance, repair, and weatherization. The routine maintenance and weatherization measures described here are generally within the range of do-it-yourselfers. Other repairs, both moderate and major, require a professional contractor. Major repairs normally require the removal of the window units to a workshop, but even in the case of moderate repairs, the number of windows involved might warrant the removal of all the deteriorated units to a workshop in order to realize a more economical repair price. Replacement of windows should be considered only as a last resort.

Since moisture is the primary cause of corrosion in steel windows, it is essential that excess moisture be eliminated and that the building be made as weathertight as possible before any other work is undertaken. Moisture can accumulate from cracks in the masonry, from spalling mortar, from leaking gutters, from air conditioning condensation runoff, and from poorly ventilated interior spaces.

Finally, before beginning any work, it is important to be aware of health and safety risks involved. Steel windows have historically been coated with lead paint. The removal of such paint by abrasive methods will produce toxic dust. Therefore, safety goggles, a toxic dust respirator, and protective clothing should be worn. Similar protective measures should be taken when acid compounds are used. Local codes may govern the methods of removing lead paints and proper disposal of toxic residue.

ROUTINE MAINTENANCE

A preliminary step in the routine maintenance of steel windows is to remove surface dirt and grease in order to ascertain the degree of deterioration, if any. Such minor cleaning can be accomplished using a brush or vacuum followed by wiping with a cloth dampened with mineral spirits or denatured alcohol.

Double-hung industrial windows duplicated the look of traditional wooden windows. Metal double-hung windows were early examples of a building product adapted to meet stringent new fire code requirements for manufacturing and high-rise buildings in urban areas. Soon supplanted in industrial buildings by less expensive pivot windows, double-hung metal windows regained popularity in the 1940s for use in speculative suburban housing.

Austral windows were also a product of the 1920s. They combined the appearance of the double-hung window with the increased ventilation and ease of operation of the projected window. (When fully opened, they provided 70% ventilation as compared to 50% ventilation for double-hung windows.) Austral windows were often used in schools, libraries and other public buildings.

Pivot windows were an early type of industrial window that combined inexpensive first cost and low maintenance. Pivot windows became standard for warehouses and power plants where the lack of screens was not a problem. The window shown here is a horizontal pivot. Windows that turned about a vertical axis were also manufactured (often of iron). Such vertical pivots are rare today.

Casement windows adapted the English tradition of using wrought iron casements with leaded cames for residential use. Rolled steel casements (either single, as shown, or paired) were popular in the 1920s for cottage style residences and Gothic style campus architecture. More streamlined casements were popular in the 1930s for institutional and small industrial buildings.

Projecting windows, sometimes called awning or hopper windows, were perfected in the 1920s for industrial and institutional buildings. They were often used in "combination" windows, in which upper panels opened out and lower panels opened in. Since each movable panel projected to one side of the frame only, unlike pivot windows, for example, screens could be introduced.

Continuous windows were almost exclusively used for industrial buildings requiring high overhead lighting. Long runs of clerestory windows operated by mechanical tension rod gears were typical. Long banks of continuous windows were possible because the frames for such windows were often structural elements of the building.

Fig. 4 Typical rolled steel windows available from 1890 to the present. The various operating and ventilating capacities in combination with the aesthetics of the window style were important considerations in the selection of one window type over another. Drawings: Sharon C. Park, AIA.

If it is determined that the windows are in basically sound condition, the following steps can be taken: 1) removal of light rust, flaking and excessive paint; 2) priming of exposed metal with a rust-inhibiting primer; 3) replacement of cracked or broken glass and glazing compound; 4) replacement of missing screws or fasteners; 5) cleaning and lubrication of hinges; 6) repainting of all steel sections with two coats of finish paint compatible with the primer; and 7) caulking the masonry surrounds with a high quality elastomeric caulk.

Recommended methods for removing light rust include manual and mechanical abrasion or the application of chemicals. Burning off rust with an oxy-acetylene or propane torch, or an inert gas welding gun, should never be attempted because the heat can distort the metal. In addition, such intense heat (often as high as 3800° F) vaporizes the lead in old paint, resulting in highly toxic fumes. Furthermore, such heat will likely result in broken glass. Rust can best be removed using a wire brush, an aluminum oxide sandpaper, or a variety of power tools

Fig. 5 Windows often provide a strong visual element to relatively simple or unadorned industrial or commercial buildings. This design element should be taken into consideration when evaluating the significance of the windows. Photo: Michael Auer.

adapted for abrasive cleaning such as an electric drill with a wire brush or a rotary whip attachment. Adjacent sills and window jambs may need protective shielding.

Rust can also be removed from ferrous metals by using a number of commercially prepared anti-corrosive acid compounds. Effective on light and medium corrosion, these compounds can be purchased either as liquids or gels. Several bases are available, including phosphoric acid, ammonium citrate, oxalic acid and hydrochloric acid. Hydrochloric acid is generally not recommended; it can leave chloride deposits, which cause future corrosion. Phosphoric acid-based compounds do not leave such deposits, and are therefore safer for steel windows. However, any chemical residue should be wiped off with damp cloths, then dried immediately. Industrial blow-dryers work well for thorough drying. The use of running water to remove chemical residue is never recommended because the water may spread the chemicals to adjacent surfaces, and drying of these surfaces may be more difficult. Acid cleaning compounds will stain masonry; therefore plastic sheets should be taped to the edge of the metal sections to protect the masonry surrounds. The same measure should be followed to protect the glazing from etching because of acid contact.

Measures that remove rust will ordinarily remove flaking paint as well. Remaining loose or flaking paint can be removed with a chemical paint remover or with a pneumatic needle scaler or gun, which comes with a series of chisel blades and has proven effective in removing flaking paint from metal windows. Well-bonded paint may serve to protect the metal further from corrosion, and need not be removed unless paint build-up prevents the window from closing tightly. The edges should be feathered by sanding to give a good surface for repainting.

Next, any *bare* metal should be wiped with a cleaning solvent such as denatured alcohol, and dried immediately in preparation for the application of an anti-corrosive primer. Since corrosion can recur very soon after metal has been exposed to the air, the metal should be primed immediately after cleaning. Spot priming may be required periodically as other repairs are undertaken. Anti-corrosive primers generally consist of oil-alkyd based paints rich in zinc or zinc chromate.[2] Red lead is no longer available because of its toxicity. All metal primers, however, are toxic to some degree and should be handled carefully. Two coats of primer are recommended. Manufacturer's recommendations should be followed concerning application of primers.

REPAIR

Repair in Place

The maintenance procedures described above will be insufficient when corrosion is extensive, or when metal window sections are misaligned. Medium to heavy corrosion that has not done any structural damage to the metal sections can be removed either by using the chemical cleaning process described under "Routine Maintenance" or by sandblasting. Since sandblasting can damage the masonry surrounds and crack or cloud the glass, metal or plywood shields should be used to protect these materials. The sandblasting pressure should be low, 80-100 pounds per square inch, and the grit size should be in the range of #10-#45. Glass peening beads (glass pellets) have also been successfully used in cleaning steel sections. While sand-blasting equipment comes with various nozzle sizes, pencil-point blasters are most useful because they give the operator more effective control over the direction of the spray. The small aperture of the pencil-point blaster is also useful in removing dried putty from the metal sections that hold the glass. As with any cleaning technique, once the bare metal is exposed to air, it should be primed as soon as possible. This includes the inside rabbeted section of sash where glazing putty has been removed. To reduce the dust, some local codes allow only wet blasting. In this case, the metal must be dried immediately, generally with a blow-drier (a step that the owner should consider when calculating the time and expense involved). Either form of sandblasting metal covered with lead paints produces toxic dust. Proper precautionary measures should be taken against toxic dust and silica particles.

Bent or bowed metal sections may be the result of damage to the window through an impact or corrosive expansion. If the distortion is not too great, it is possible to realign the metal sections without removing the window to a metal fabricator's shop. The glazing is generally removed and pressure is applied to the bent or bowed section. In the case of a muntin, a protective 2 x 4 wooden bracing can be placed behind the bent portion and a wire cable with a winch can apply progressively more pressure over several days until the section is realigned. The 2 x 4 bracing is necessary to distribute the pressure evenly over the damaged section. Sometimes a section, such as the bottom of the frame, will bow out as a result of pressure exerted by corrosion and it is often necessary to cut the metal section to relieve this pressure prior to pressing the section back into shape and making a welded repair.

Once the metal sections have been cleaned of all corrosion and straightened, small holes and uneven areas resulting from rusting should be filled with a patching material and sanded smooth to eliminate pockets where water can accumulate. A patching material of steel fibers and an epoxy binder may be the easiest to apply. This steel-based epoxy is available for industrial steel repair; it can also be found in auto body patching compounds or in plumber's epoxy. As with any product, it is important to follow the manufacturer's instructions for proper use and best results. The traditional patching technique—melting steel welding rods to fill holes in the metal sections—may be difficult to apply in some situations; moreover, the window glass must be removed during the repair process, or it will crack from the expansion of the heated metal sections. After these repairs, glass replacement, hinge lubrication, painting, and other cosmetic repairs can be undertaken as necessary.

[2]Refer to Table IV. Types of Paint Used for Painting Metal in *Metals in America's Historic Buildings,* p. 139. (See bibliography).

To complete the checklist for routine maintenance, cracked glass, deteriorated glazing compound, missing screws, and broken fasteners will have to be replaced; hinges cleaned and lubricated; the metal windows painted, and the masonry surrounds caulked. If the glazing must be replaced, all clips, glazing beads, and other fasteners that hold the glass to the sash should be retained, if possible, although replacements for these parts are still being fabricated. When bedding glass, use only glazing compound formulated for metal windows. To clean the hinges (generally brass or bronze), a cleaning solvent and fine bronze wool should be used. The hinges should then be lubricated with a non-greasy lubricant specially formulated for metals and with an anti-corrosive agent. These lubricants are available in a spray form and should be used periodically on frequently opened windows.

Final painting of the windows with a paint compatible with the anti-corrosive primer should proceed on a dry day. (Paint and primer from the same manufacturer should be used.) Two coats of finish paint are recommended if the sections have been cleaned to bare metal. The paint should overlap the glass slightly to insure weathertightness at that connection. Once the paint dries thoroughly, a flexible exterior caulk can be applied to eliminate air and moisture infiltration where the window and the surrounding masonry meet.

Caulking is generally undertaken after the windows have received at least one coat of finish paint. The perimeter of the masonry surround should be caulked with a flexible elastomeric compound that will adhere well to both metal and masonry. The caulking used should be a type intended for exterior application, have a high tolerance for material movement, be resistant to ultraviolet light, and have a minimum durability of 10 years. Three effective compounds (taking price and other factors into consideration) are polyurethane, vinyl acrylic, and butyl rubber. In selecting a caulking material for a window retrofit, it is important to remember that the caulking compound may be covering other materials in a substrate. In this case, some compounds, such as silicone, may not adhere well. Almost all modern caulking compounds can be painted after curing completely. Many come in a range of colors, which eliminates the need to paint. If colored caulking is used, the windows should have been given two coats of finish paint prior to caulking.

Repair in Workshop

Damage to windows may be so severe that the window sash and sometimes the frame must be removed for cleaning and extensive rust removal, straightening of bent sections, welding or splicing in of new sections, and reglazing. These major and expensive repairs are reserved for highly significant windows that cannot be replaced; the procedures involved should be carried out only by skilled workmen. (see fig. 6a—6f.)

As part of the orderly removal of windows, each window should be numbered and the parts labelled. The operable metal sash should be dismantled by removing the hinges; the fixed sash and, if necessary, the frame can then be unbolted or unscrewed. (The subframe is usually left in place. Built into the masonry surrounds, it can only be cut out with a torch.) Hardware and hinges should be labelled and stored together.

The two major choices for removing flaking paint and corrosion from severely deteriorated windows are dipping in a chemical bath or sandblasting. Both treatments require removal of the glass. If the windows are to be dipped, a phosphoric acid solution is preferred, as mentioned earlier. While the dip tank method is good for fairly evenly distributed rust, deep set rust may remain after dipping. For that reason, sandblasting is more effective for heavy and uneven corrosion. Both methods leave the metal sections clean of residual paint. As already noted, after cleaning has exposed the metal to the air, it should be primed immediately after drying with an anti-corrosive primer to prevent rust from recurring.

Sections that are seriously bent or bowed must be straightened with heat and applied pressure in a workshop. Structurally weakened sections must be cut out, generally with an oxy-acetylene torch, and replaced with sections welded in place and the welds ground smooth. Finding replacement metal sections, however, may be difficult. While most rolling mills are producing modern sections suitable for total replacement, it may be difficult to find an exact profile match for a splicing repair. The best source of rolled metal sections is from salvaged windows, preferably from the same building. If no salvaged windows are available, two options remain. Either an ornamental metal fabricator can weld flat plates into a built-up section, or a steel plant can mill bar steel into the desired profile.

While the sash and frame are removed for repair, the subframe and masonry surrounds should be inspected. This is also the time to reset sills or to remove corrosion from the subframe, taking care to protect the masonry surrounds from damage.

Missing or broken hardware and hinges should be replaced on all windows that will be operable. Salvaged windows, again, are the best source of replacement parts. If matching parts cannot be found, it may be possible to adapt ready-made items. Such a substitution may require filling existing holes with steel epoxy or with plug welds and tapping in new screw holes. However, if the hardware is a highly significant element of the historic window, it may be worth having reproductions made.

Following are illustrations of the repair and thermal upgrading of the rolled steel windows in a National Historic Landmark (fig. 6). Many of the techniques described above were used during this extensive rehabilitation. The complete range of repair techniques is then summarized in the chart titled *Steps for Cleaning and Repairing Historic Steel Windows* (see fig. 7).

Fig. 6 a. View of the flanking wing of the State Capitol where the rolled steel casement windows are being removed for repair.

Fig. 6 b. View from the exterior showing the deteriorated condition of the lower corner of a window prior to repair. While the sash was in relatively good condition, the frame behind was rusted to the point of inhibiting operation.

Fig. 6 c. View of the rusted frame which was unscrewed from the subframe and removed from the window opening and taken to a workshop for sandblasting. In some cases, severely deteriorated sections of the frame were replaced with new sections of milled bar steel.

Fig. 6 d. View looking down towards the sill. The subframes appeared very rusted, but were in good condition once debris was vacuumed and surface rust was removed, in place, with chemical compounds. Where necessary, epoxy and steel filler was used to patch depressions in order to make the subframe serviceable again.

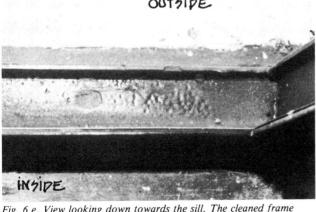

Fig. 6 e. View looking down towards the sill. The cleaned frame was reset in the window opening. The frame was screwed to the refurbished subframe at the jamb and the head only. The screw holes at the sill, which had been the cause of much of the earlier rusting, were infilled. Vinyl weatherstripping was added to the frame.

Fig. 6 f. View from the outside of the completely refurbished window. In addition to the steel repair and the installation of vinyl weatherstripping, the exterior was caulked with polyurethane and the single glass was replaced with individual lights of thermal glass. The repaired and upgraded windows have comparable energy efficiency ratings to new replacement units while retaining the historic steel sash, frames and subframes.

Fig. 6. The repair and thermal upgrading of the historic steel windows at the State Capitol, Lincoln, Nebraska. This early twentieth century building, designed by Bertram Goodhue, is a National Historic Landmark. Photos: All photos in this series were provided by the State Building Division.

STEPS FOR CLEANING AND REPAIRING HISTORIC STEEL WINDOWS

Work Item	Recommended Techniques	Tools, Products and Procedures	Notes
	*(Must be done in a workshop)		
1. Removing dirt and grease from metal	General maintenance and chemical cleaning	Vacuum and bristle brushes to remove dust and dirt; solvents (denatured alcohol, mineral spirits), and clean cloths to remove grease.	Solvents can cause eye and skin irritation. Operator should wear protective gear and work in ventilated area. Solvents should not contact masonry. Do not flush with water.
2. Removing Rust/ Corrosion			
Light	Manual and mechanical abrasion	Wire brushes, steel wool, rotary attachments to electric drill, sanding blocks and disks.	Handsanding will probably be necessary for corners. Safety goggles and masks should be worn.
	Chemical cleaning	Anti-corrosive jellies and liquids (phosphoric acid preferred); clean damp cloths.	Protect glass and metal with plastic sheets attached with tape. Do not flush with water. Work in ventilated area.
Medium	Sandblasting/abrasive cleaning	Low pressure (80-100 psi) and small grit (#10-#45); glass peening beads. Pencil blaster gives good control.	Removes both paint and rust. Codes should be checked for environmental compliance. Prime exposed metal promptly. Shield glass and masonry. Operator should wear safety gear.
Heavy	*Chemical dip tank	Metal sections dipped into chemical tank (phosphoric acid preferred) from several hours to 24 hours.	Glass and hardware should be removed. Protect operator. Deepset rust may remain, but paint will be removed.
	*Sandblasting/ abrasive cleaning	Low pressure (80-100 psi) and small grit (#10-#45).	Excellent for heavy rust. Remove or protect glass. Prime exposed metal promptly. Check codes for environmental compliance. Operator should wear safety gear.
3. Removing flaking paint.	Chemical method	Chemical paint strippers suitable for ferrous metals. Clean cloths.	Protect glass and masonry. Do not flush with water. Have good ventilation and protection for operator.
	Mechanical abrasion	Pneumatic needle gun chisels, sanding disks.	Protect operator; have good ventilation. Well-bonded paint need not be removed if window closes properly.
4. Aligning bent, bowed metal sections	Applied pressure	Wooden frame as a brace for cables and winch mechanism.	Remove glass in affected area. Realignment may take several days.
	*Heat and pressure	Remove to a workshop. Apply heat and pressure to bend back.	Care should be taken that heat does not deform slender sections.

Work Item	Recommended Techniques	Tools, Products and Procedures	Notes
	*(Must be done in a workshop)		
5. Patching depressions	Epoxy and steel filler	Epoxy fillers with high content of steel fibers; plumber's epoxy or autobody patching compound.	Epoxy patches generally are easy to apply, and can be sanded smooth. Patches should be primed.
	Welded patches	Weld in patches using steel rods and oxy-acetylene torch or arc welder.	Prime welded sections after grinding connections smooth.
6. Splicing in new metal sections	*Cut out decayed sections and weld in new or salvaged sections	Torch to cut out bad sections back to 45° joint. Weld in new pieces and grind smooth.	Prime welded sections after grinding connection smooth.
7. Priming metal sections	Brush or spray application	At least one coat of anti-corrosive primer on bare metal. Zinc-rich primers are generally recommended.	Metal should be primed as soon as it is exposed. If cleaned metal will be repaired another day, spot prime to protect exposed metal.
8. Replacing missing screws and bolts	Routine maintenance	Pliers to pull out or shear off rusted heads. Replace screws and bolts with similar ones, readily available.	If new holes have to be tapped into the metal sections, the rusted holes should be cleaned, filled and primed prior to redrilling.
9. Cleaning, lubricating or replacing hinges and other hardware	Routine maintenance, solvent cleaning	Most hinges and closure hardware are bronze. Use solvents (mineral spirits), bronze wool and clean cloths. Spray with non-greasy lubricant containing anti-corrosive agent.	Replacement hinges and fasteners may not match the original exactly. If new holes are necessary, old ones should be filled.
10. Replacing glass and glazing compound	Standard method for application	Pliers and chisels to remove old glass, scrape putty out of glazing rabbet, save all clips and beads for reuse. Use only glazing compound formulated for metal windows.	Heavy gloves and other protective gear needed for the operator. All parts saved should be cleaned prior to reinstallation.
11. Caulking masonry surrounds	Standard method for application	Good quality (10 year or better) elastomeric caulking compound suitable for metal.	The gap between the metal frame and the masonry opening should be caulked; keep weepholes in metal for condensation run-off clear of caulk.
12. Repainting metal windows	Spray or brush	At least 2 coats of paint compatible with the anti-corrosive primer. Paint should lap the glass about 1/8″ to form a seal over the glazing compound.	The final coats of paint and the primer should be from the same manufacturer to ensure compatibility. If spraying is used, the glass and masonry should be protected.

Fig. 7. STEPS FOR CLEANING AND REPAIRING HISTORIC STEEL WINDOWS. Compiled by Sharon C. Park, AIA.

WEATHERIZATION

Historic metal windows are generally not energy efficient; this has often led to their wholesale replacement. Metal windows can, however, be made more energy efficient in several ways, varying in complexity and cost. Caulking around the masonry openings and adding weatherstripping, for example, can be do-it-yourself projects and are important first steps in reducing air infiltration around the windows. They usually have a rapid payback period. Other treatments include applying fixed layers of glazing over the historic windows, adding operable storm windows, or installing thermal glass in place of the existing glass. In combination with caulking and weatherstripping, these treatments can produce energy ratings rivaling those achieved by new units.[3]

Weatherstripping

The first step in any weatherization program, caulking, has been discussed above under "Routine Maintenance." The second step is the installation of weatherstripping where the operable portion of the sash, often called the ventilator, and the fixed frame come together to reduce perimeter air infiltration (see fig. 8). Four types of weatherstripping appropriate for metal windows are spring-metal, vinyl strips, compressible foam tapes, and sealant beads. The spring-metal, with an integral friction fit mounting clip, is recommended for steel windows in good condition. The clip eliminates the need for an applied glue; the thinness of the material insures a tight closure. The weatherstripping is clipped to the inside channel of the rolled metal section of the fixed frame. To insure against galvanic corrosion between the weatherstripping (often bronze or brass), and the steel window, the window must be painted prior to the installation of the weatherstripping. This weatherstripping is usually applied to the entire perimeter of the window opening, but in some cases, such as casement windows, it may be best to avoid weatherstripping the hinge side. The natural wedging action of the weatherstripping on the three sides of the window often creates an adequate seal.

Vinyl weatherstripping can also be applied to metal windows. Folded into a "V" configuration, the material forms a barrier against the wind. Vinyl weatherstripping is usually glued to the frame, although some brands have an adhesive backing. As the vinyl material and the applied glue are relatively thick, this form of weatherstripping may not be appropriate for all situations.

Compressible foam tape weatherstripping is often best for large windows where there is a slight bending or distortion of the sash. In some very tall windows having closure hardware at the sash mid-point, the thin sections

of the metal window will bow away from the frame near the top. If the gap is not more than 1/4", foam weatherstripping can normally fill the space. If the gap exceeds this, the window may need to be realigned to close more tightly. The foam weatherstripping comes either with an adhesive or plain back; the latter variety requires application with glue. Compressible foam requires more frequent replacement than either spring-metal or vinyl weatherstripping.

A fourth type of successful weatherstripping involves the use of a caulking or sealant bead and a polyethylene bond breaker tape. After the window frame has been thoroughly cleaned with solvent, permitted to dry, and primed, a neat bead of low modulus (firm setting) caulk, such as silicone, is applied. A bond breaker tape is then applied to the operable sash covering the metal section where contact will occur. The window is then closed until the sealant has set (2-7 days, depending on temperature and humidity). When the window is opened, the bead will have taken the shape of the air infiltration gap and the bond breaker tape can be removed. This weatherstripping method appears to be successful for all types of metal windows with varying degrees of air infiltration.

Since the several types of weatherstripping are appropriate for different circumstances, it may be necessary to use more than one type on any given building. Successful weatherstripping depends upon using the thinnest material adequate to fill the space through which air enters. Weatherstripping that is too thick can spring the hinges, thereby resulting in more gaps.

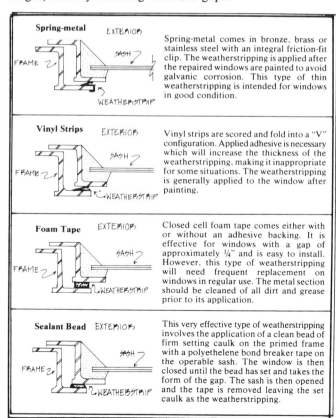

Fig. 8 APPROPRIATE TYPES OF WEATHERSTRIPPING FOR METAL WINDOWS. Weatherstripping is an important part of upgrading the thermal efficiency of historic steel windows. The chart above shows the jamb section of the window with the weatherstripping in place. Drawings: Sharon C. Park, AIA.

---

[3]One measure of energy efficiency is the U-value (the number of BTUs per hour transferred through a square foot of material). The lower the U-value, the better the performance. According to *ASHRAE HANDBOOK-1977 Fundamentals*, the U-value of historic rolled steel sash with single glazing is 1.3. Adding storm windows to the existing units or reglazing with 5/8" insulating glass produces a U-value of .69. These methods of weatherizing historic steel windows compare favorably with rolled steel replacement alternatives: with factory installed 1" insulating glass (.67 U-value); with added thermal-break construction and factory finish coatings (.62 U-value).

Thermal Glazing

The third weatherization treatment is to install an additional layer of glazing to improve the thermal efficiency of the existing window. The decision to pursue this treatment should proceed from careful analysis. Each of the most common techniques for adding a layer of glazing will effect approximately the same energy savings (approximately double the original insulating value of the windows); therefore, cost and aesthetic considerations usually determine the choice of method. Methods of adding a layer of glazing to improve thermal efficiency include adding a new layer of transparent material to the window; adding a separate storm window; and replacing the single layer of glass in the window with thermal glass.

The least expensive of these options is to install a clear material (usually rigid sheets of acrylic or glass) over the original window. The choice between acrylic and glass is generally based on cost, ability of the window to support the material, and long-term maintenance outlook. If the material is placed over the entire window and secured to the frame, the sash will be inoperable. If the continued use of the window is important (for ventilation or for fire exits), separate panels should be affixed to the sash without obstructing operability (see fig. 9). Glass or acrylic panels set in frames can be attached using magnetized gaskets, interlocking material strips, screws or adhesives. Acrylic panels can be screwed directly to the metal windows, but the holes in the acrylic panels should allow for the expansion and contraction of this material. A compressible gasket between the prime sash and the storm panel can be very effective in establishing a thermal cavity between glazing layers. To avoid condensation, 1/8'' cuts in a top corner and diagonally opposite bottom corner of the gasket will provide a vapor bleed, through which moisture can evaporate. (Such cuts, however, reduce thermal performance slightly.) If condensation does occur, however, the panels should be easily removable in order to wipe away moisture before it causes corrosion.

The second method of adding a layer of glazing is to have independent storm windows fabricated. (Pivot and austral windows, however, which project on either side of the window frame when open, cannot easily be fitted with storm windows and remain operational.) The storm window should be compatible with the original sash configuration. For example, in paired casement windows, either specially fabricated storm casement windows or sliding units in which the vertical meeting rail of the slider reflects the configuration of the original window should be installed. The decision to place storm windows on the inside or outside of the window depends on whether the historic window opens in or out, and on the visual impact the addition of storm windows will have on the building. Exterior storm windows, however, can serve another purpose besides saving energy: they add a layer of protection against air pollutants and vandals, although they will partially obscure the prime window. For highly ornamental windows this protection can determine the choice of exterior rather then interior storm windows.

The third method of installing an added layer of glazing is to replace the original single glazing with thermal glass. Except in rare instances in which the original glass is of special interest (as with stained or figured glass), the glass can be replaced if the hinges can tolerate the weight of the additional glass. The rolled metal sections for steel windows are generally from 1'' - 1 1/2'' thick. Sash of this thickness can normally tolerate thermal glass, which ranges from 3/8'' - 5/8''. (Metal glazing beads, readily available, are used to reinforce the muntins, which hold the glass.) This treatment leaves the window fully operational while preserving the historic appearance. It is, however, the most expensive of the treatments discussed here. (See fig. 6f).

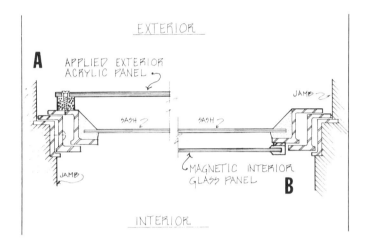

Fig. 9 Two examples of adding a second layer of glazing in order to improve the thermal performance of historic steel windows. Scheme A (showing jamb detail) is of a ¼'' acrylic panel with a closed cell foam gasket attached with self-tapping stainless steel screws directly to the exterior of the outwardly opening sash. Scheme B (showing jamb detail) is of a glass panel in a magnetized frame affixed directly to the interior of the historic steel sash. The choice of using glass or acrylic mounted on the inside or outside will depend on the ability of the window to tolerate additional weight, the location and size of the window, the cost, and the long-term maintenance outlook. Drawing: Sharon C. Park, AIA.

WINDOW REPLACEMENT

Repair of historic windows is always preferred within a rehabilitation project. Replacement should be considered only as a last resort. However, when the extent of deterioration or the unavailability of replacement sections renders repair impossible, replacement of the entire window may be justified. In the case of significant windows, replacement in kind is essential in order to maintain the historic character of the building. However, for less significant windows, replacement with compatible new windows may be acceptable. In selecting compatible replacement windows, the material, configuration, color, operability, number and size of panes, profile and proportion of metal sections, and reflective quality of the original glass should be duplicated as closely as possible.

A number of metal window manufacturing companies produce rolled steel windows. While stock modern window designs do not share the multi-pane configuration of historic windows, most of these manufacturers can reproduce the historic configuration if requested, and the cost is not excessive for large orders (see figs. 10a and 10b). Some manufacturers still carry the standard pre-World War II multi-light windows using the traditional 12" x 18" or 14" x 20" glass sizes in industrial, commercial, security, and residential configurations. In addition, many of the modern steel windows have integral weatherstripping, thermal break construction, durable vinyl coatings, insulating glass, and other desirable features.

Fig. 10 a. A six-story concrete manufacturing building prior to the replacement of the steel pivot windows. Photo: Charles Parrott.

Fig. 10 b. Close-up view of the new replacement steel windows which matched the multi-lighted originals exactly. Photo: Charles Parrott.

Windows manufactured from other materials generally cannot match the thin profiles of the rolled steel sections. Aluminum, for example, is three times weaker than steel and must be extruded into a box-like configuration that does not reflect the thin historic profiles of most steel windows. Wooden and vinyl replacement windows generally are not fabricated in the industrial style, nor can they reproduce the thin profiles of the rolled steel sections, and consequently are generally not acceptable replacements.

For product information on replacement windows, the owner, architect, or contractor should consult manufacturers' catalogues, building trade journals, or the Steel Window Institute, 1230 Keith Building, Cleveland, Ohio 44115.

SUMMARY

The National Park Service recommends the retention of significant historic metal windows whenever possible. Such windows, which can be a character-defining feature of a historic building, are too often replaced with inappropriate units that impair rather than complement the overall historic appearance. The repair and thermal upgrading of historic steel windows is more practicable than most people realize. Repaired and properly maintained metal windows have greatly extended service lives. They can be made energy efficient while maintaining their contribution to the historic character of the building.

BIBLIOGRAPHY

ASHRAE Handbook - 1977 Fundamentals. New York: American Society of Heating, Refrigerating and Airconditioning Engineers, 1978.

Crittal, W. F. *A Metal Window Dictionary.* London:Curwen Press, 1926. Reprinted by B.T. Batsford, Ltd., 1953.

Gayle, Margot; David W. Look, AIA; John G. Waite.*Metals in America's Historic Buildings: Uses and Preservation Treatments.* Technical Preservation Services, U.S. Department of the Interior. Washington,D.C.: U.S.Government Printing Office, 1980.

Gillet, William. "Steel Windows." *Windows and Glass in the Exterior of Buildings.* National Academy of Sciences Publication 478. Washington, D.C.: 1957,75-78.

Sarton, R. H. "Selecting and Specifying an Appropriate Type of Steel Window." *Metalcraft.* Vol 6, No. 1 (January, 1931): 43-48, 64-65.

Sweet's Architectural Catalogue. 13th Edition, New York, Sweets Catalogue Service, Inc., 1918.

The author gratefully acknowledges the invaluable assistance of co-worker Michael Auer in preparing this brief for publication. This publication is an extension of research initiated by Frederec E. Kleyle. Special thanks are given to Hope's Architectural Products, Inc., Jamestown, NY, for their generous contribution of historic metal window catalogues which were an invaluable source of information. The following individuals are also to be thanked for reviewing the manuscript and making suggestions: Hugh Miller, Chief, Park Historic Architecture Division, National Park Service; Barclay L. Rogers, Museum Services, National Park Service; Susan M. Young, Steel Window Institute, and Danny Schlichenmaier, State Building Division, Lincoln, Nebraska. Finally, thanks go to Technical Preservation Services Branch staff and to cultural resources staff of the National Park Service Regional Offices, whose valuable comments were incorporated into the final text and who contributed to the publication of this brief.

This publication has been prepared pursuant to the Economic Recovery Tax Act of 1981, which directs the Secretary of the Interior to certify rehabilitations of historic buildings that are consistent with their historic character; the guidance provided in this brief will assist property owners in complying with the requirements of this law.

14

New Exterior Additions to Historic Buildings: Preservation Concerns

Kay D. Weeks

Because a new exterior addition to a historic building can damage or destroy significant materials and can change the building's character, an addition should be considered only after it has been determined that the new use cannot be met by altering nonsignificant, or secondary, interior spaces. If the new use cannot be met in this way, then an attached addition may be an acceptable alternative if carefully planned. A new addition should be constructed in a manner that preserves significant materials and features and preserves the historic character. Finally, an addition should be differentiated from the historic building so that the new work is not confused with what is genuinely part of the past.

Change is as inevitable in buildings and neighborhoods as it is in individuals and families. Never static, buildings and neighborhoods grow, diminish, and continue to evolve as each era's technological advances bring conveniences such as heating, street paving, electricity, and air conditioning; as the effects of violent weather, uncontrolled fire, or slow unchecked deterioration destroy vulnerable material; as businesses expand, change hands, become obsolete; as building codes are established to enhance life safety and health; or as additional family living space is alternately needed and abandonded.

Preservationists generally agree that the history of a building, together with its site and setting, includes not only the period of original construction but frequently later alterations and additions. While each change to a building or neighborhood is undeniably part of its history—much like events in human life—not every change is equally important. For example, when a later, clearly nonsignificant addition is removed to reveal the original form, materials, and craftsmanship, there is little complaint about a loss to history.

When the subject of *new* exterior additions is introduced, however, areas of agreement usually tend to diminish. This is understandable because the subject raises some serious questions. Can a historic building be enlarged for a new use without destroying what is historically significant? And just what *is* significant about each particular historic building that should be preserved? Finally, what new construction is appropriate to the old building?

The vast amount of literature on the subject of change to America's built environment reflects widespread interest as well as divergence of opinion. New additions have been discussed by historians within a social and political, framework; by architectural historians in terms of construction technology and style; and by urban planners as successful or unsuccessful contextual design. Within the historic preservation programs of the National Park Service, however, the focus has been and will continue to be the protection of those resources identified as worthy of listing in the National Register of Historic Places.

National Register Listing—Acknowledging Change While Protecting Historical Significance

Entire districts or neighborhoods may be listed in the National Register of Historic Places for their significance to a certain period of American history (e.g., activities in a commercial district between 1870 and 1910). This "framing" of historic districts has led to a concern that listing in the National Register may discourage any physical change beyond a certain historical period—particularly in the form of attached exterior additions. This is not the case. National Register listing does *not* mean that an entire building or district is frozen in time and that no change can be made without compromising the historical significance. It also does not mean that each portion of a historic building is equally significant and must be retained intact and without change. Admittedly, whether an attached new addition is small or large, there will always be *some* loss of material and *some* change in the form of the historic building. There will also generally be some change in the relationship between the buildings and its site, neighborhood or district. Some change is thus anticipated within each rehabilitation of a building for a contemporary use.

Scope of National Park Service Interest in New Exterior Additions

The National Park Service interest in new additions is simply this—a new addition to a historic building has the potential to damage and destroy significant historic material and features and to change its historic character. A new addition also has the potential to change how one perceives what is genuinely historic and thus to diminish those qualities that make the building eligible for listing in the National Register of Historic Places. Once these basic preservation issues have been addressed, all other aspects of designing and constructing a new addition to extend the useful life of the historic building rest with the creative skills of the architect.

The intent of this Brief, then, is to provide guidance to owners and developers planning additions to their historic buildings. A project involving a new addition to a historic building is considered acceptable within the framework of the National Park Service's standards if it:

1. Preserves significant historic materials and features; and
2. Preserves the historic character; and
3. Protects the historical significance by making a visual distinction between old and new.

Paralleling these key points, the Brief is organized into three sections. Case study examples are provided to point out acceptable and unacceptable preservation approaches where new use requirements were met through construction of an exterior addition. These examples are included to suggest ways that change to historic buildings can be sensitively accomplished, not to provide indepth project analyses, endorse or critique particular architectural design, or offer cost and construction data.

1. Preserving Significant Historic Materials and Features

Connecting a new exterior addition always involves some degree of material loss to an external wall of a historic building and, although this is to be expected, it can be minimized. On the other hand, damage or destruction of *significant* materials and craftsmanship such as pressed brick, decorative marble, cast stone, terra-cotta, or architectural metal should be avoided, when possible.

Generally speaking, preservation of historic buildings is enhanced by avoiding all but minor changes to primary or "public" elevations. Historically, features that distinguish one building or a row of buildings and can be seen from the streets or sidewalks are most likely to be the significant ones. This can include window patterns, window hoods, or shutters; porticoes, entrances, and doorways; roof shapes, cornices, and decorative moldings; or commercial storefronts with their special detailing, signs, and glazing. Beyond a single building, entire blocks of urban or residential structures are often closely related architecturally by their materials, detailing, form, and alignment. Because significant materials and features should be *preserved*, not damaged or hidden, the first place to consider constructing a new addition is where such material loss will be minimized. This will frequently be on a secondary side or rear elevation. For both economic and social reasons, secondary elevations were often constructed of "common" material and were less architecturally ornate or detailed.

In constructing the new addition, one way to minimize overall material loss is simply to reduce the size of the new addition in relationship to the historic building. If a new addition will abut the historic building along one elevation or wrap around a side and rear elevation, the integration of historic and new interiors may result in a high degree of loss—exterior walls as well as significant interior spaces and features. Another way to minimize loss is to limit the size and number of openings between old and new. A particularly successful method to reduce damage is to link the new addition to the historic block by means of a hyphen or connector. In this way, only the connecting passageway penetrates a historic side wall; the new addition can be visually and functionally related

while historic materials remain essentially intact and historic exteriors remain uncovered.

Although a general recommendation is to construct a new addition on a secondary elevation, there are several exceptions. First, there may simply be no secondary elevation—some important freestanding buildings have significant materials and features on all sides, making any aboveground addition too destructive to be considered. Second, a structure or group of structures together with their setting (for example, in a National Historic Park) may be of such significance in American history that any new addition would not only damage materials and alter the buildings' relationship to each other and the setting, but seriously diminish the public's ability to appreciate a historic event or place. Finally, there are other cases where an existing side or rear elevation was historically intended to be highly visible, is of special cultural importance to the neighborhood, or possesses associative historical value. Then, too, a secondary elevation should be treated as if it were a primary elevation and a new addition should be avoided.

Photo: Maxwell Mackenzie

Photo: Gary L. Hume

Historic residential structure with new office addition. This approach preserves significant historic materials and features.

Built in 1903 as the private residence of a wealthy mine owner, the 3½ story building utilizes a variety of materials, including granite, limestone, marble, and cast iron. Of special interest is the projecting conservatory on a prominent side elevation. The Walsh-McLean House in Washington, D.C., has been used as the Indonesian Embassy since 1954. When additional administrative space was required for the embassy in 1981, loss of significant exterior materials was minimized by utilizing a narrow hyphen connector that cuts through a side wall behind the distinctive conservatory. Finally, the modestly scaled addition is well set back on the adjoining site, thus preserving the historic character of this individually-listed property.

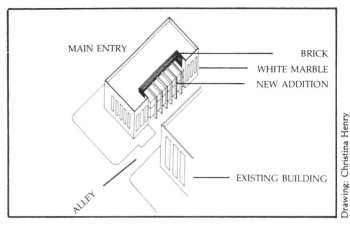

Historic bank structure with new drive-in bank addition. This approach preserves significant materials and features.

The bank building in Winona, Minnesota, (Purcell, Feick, and Elmslie, 1911-1912) is a noteworthy example of Prairie School architecture. Of particular significance is the ornamental work in terra-cotta and stained glass. In 1969-70 a brick addition was joined to the historic structure on the unoramented north and east party walls. This responsible approach successfully met additional square footage requirements for bank operations while retaining the historic banking room with its stained glass panels and skylighted space.

Historic library with new reading room addition. This approach preserves significant historic materials and features.

When Washington, D.C.'s Folger Shakespeare Library (Paul P. Cret, 1929) required additional space for a new reading room in 1983, significant exterior materials and interior spaces were respected. This expansion was successfully accomplished by filling-in a nonsignificant, common brick, U-shaped service area on the building's rear elevation, thus permitting almost total savings of the historic decorative marble on significant front and side facades. The new reading room addition was sensitively joined to the historic library by a limited number of doorways, further enhancing overall preservation of historic materials.

Historic city market with flanking new retail additions. This approach preserves significant historic materials and features.

An aerial view shows the two-level connectors (circled) between Indianapolis' 1886 City Market and the new retail business wings. Historic openings on both levels at the rear of the building have been utilized for entrance and egress to the new additions, requiring minimal intrusion in the historic fabric of the side walls. A detail photograph shows how the glass and metal connectors parallel the form of the historic round-headed window openings. Finally, because the new additions are essentially detached from the original market building, the external form and the interior plan, with its significant cast-iron roofing system, have been retained and preserved.

DEMOLISHED

Photo: A. Pierce Bounds

Photo: Lee H. Nelson, FAIA

Historic cast-iron storefront re-installed as facade on modern department store. This approach results in the destruction of significant materials and features.

Where there is need for a substantially larger building, the most destructive approach is to demolish everything but the facade of the historic building. In the example above, the 3-story-cast-iron front was originally the facade of a large, 19th century department store. In the 1970s, when the rest of the building was demolished, the metal facade was dismantled, then re-assembled on a new site where it has become the ornamental entrance to a modern department store.

Photo: Michael J. Auer

Historic theater and office building with new office addition. This approach results in the destruction of significant materials and features.

Materials and features comprise the life history of a building from its initial construction to its present configuration; their destruction thus represents an equivalent and unfortunate loss to history. Chase's Theater and Riggs Building were constructed in Washington, D.C. in 1911-1912 as one architectural unit. Originally 11 bays wide, it featured elaborate granite, terra-cotta and marble ornamentation (see "before" above). As part of a plan to increase office space in a prime downtown location, 6 side bays and the significant theater space of the historic structure were demolished to make way for a major new addition (see "after" below).

2. Preserving the Historic Character

The second, equally important, consideration is whether or not the new addition will preserve the resource's historic character. The historic character of each building may differ, but a methodology of establishing it remains the same. Knowing the uses and functions a building has served over time will assist in making what is essentially a physical evaluation. But while written and pictorial documentation can provide a framework for establishing the building's history, *the historic character, to a large extent, is embodied in the physical aspects of the historic building itself—its shape, its materials, its features, its craftsmanship, its window arrangements, its colors, its setting, and its interiors.* It is only after the historic character has been correctly identified that reasonable decisions about the extent—or limitations—of change can be made.

To meet National Park Service preservation standards, a new addition must be "compatible with the size, scale, color, material, and character" of the building to which it is attached or its particular neighborhood or district. A new addition will always change the size or actual bulk of the historic building. But an addition that bears no relationship to the proportions and massing of the historic building—in other words, one that overpowers the historic form and changes the scale will usually compromise the historic character as well. The appropriate size for a new addition varies from building to building; it could never be stated in a tidy square or cubic footage ratio, but the historic building's existing proportions, site, and setting can help set some general parameters for enlargement. To some extent, there is a predictable relationship between the size of the historic resource and the degree of change a new addition will impose.

For example, in the case of relatively low buildings (small-scale residential or commercial structures) it is difficult, if not impossible, to minimize the impact of adding an entire new floor even if the new addition is set back from the plane of the facade. Alteration of the historic proportions and profile will likely change the building's character. On the other hand, a rooftop addition to an eight story building in a historic district of other tall buildings might not affect the historic character simply because the new work would not be visible from major streets. A number of methods have been used to help predict the effect of a proposed rooftop addition on the historic building and district, including pedestrian sight lines, three-dimensional schematics and computer-assisted design (CAD). Sometimes a rough full-size mock up of a section or bay of the proposed addition can be constructed using temporary material; the mock-up can then be photographed and evaluated from critical vantage points.

In the case of freestanding residential structures, the preservation considerations are generally twofold. First, a large addition built out on a highly visible elevation can radically alter the historic form or obscure features such as a decorative cornice or window ornamentation. Second, an addition that fills in a planned void on a highly visible elevation (such as a "U" shaped plan or feature such as a porch) may also alter the historic form and, as a result, change the historic character.

Some historic structures such as government buildings, metropolitan museums, or libraries may be so massive in size that a large-scale addition may not compromise the historic character. Yet similar expansion of smaller buildings would be dramatically out of scale. In summary, where any new addition is proposed, correctly assessing the *relationship* between actual size and relative scale will be a key to preserving the character of the historic building.

Constructing the new addition on a secondary side or rear elevation—in addition to material preservation—will also address preservation of the historic character. Primarily, such placement will help to preserve the building's historic form and relationship to its site and setting. Historic landscape features, including distinctive grade variations, need to be respected; and any new landscape features such as plants and trees kept at a scale and density that would not interfere with appreciation of the historic resource itself.

In highly developed urban areas, locating a new addition on a less visible side or rear elevation may be impossible simply because there is no available space. In this instance, there may be alternative ways to help preserve the historic character. If a new addition is being connected to the adjacent historic building on a primary elevation, the addition may be set back from the front wall plane so the outer edges defining the historic form are still apparent. In still other cases, some variation in material, detailing, and color may provide the degree of differentiation necessary to avoid changing the essential proportions and character of the historic building.

Historic townhouse with compatible new stairtower addition. This approach preserves the historic character.

Creating two separate means of egress from the upper floors may be a fire code requirement in certain types of rehabilitation projects. This may involve a second stair within the historic building or an exterior fire stair. To meet preservation concerns, an exterior fire stair should always be subordinate to the historic structure in size and scale, and preferably, placed on a secondary side or rear elevation. Finally, as in any other type of addition, the material and color should be compatible with the historic character of the building. Because this modest brick stairtower has been placed on a rear elevation as a subsidiary unit, the form, features and detailing of the historic building have been preserved.

Historic university building with incompatible new stairtower addition. This approach changes the historic character.

In contrast, this stairtower has been constructed on a highly visible side elevation and, together with its width and height, has obscured the historic form and roofline. The materials and color of the addition further enhance its prominence.

Photo: Rodney Gary

Photo: Rodney Gary

Historic residential structure with new drive-in bank addition. This approach preserves the historic character.

Built in 1847 and individually listed in the National Register in 1973, the Stephen Upson House in Athens, Georgia, is a two-story, five-bay structure featuring a distinctive columned portico. Of particular importance in its successful conversion from residential to commercial use in 1984 was the sensitive utilization of a sloping, tree-shaded historic site consisting of over 6 acres. A low-scale office and drive-in bank addition have been attached by a small glass connector at the rear of the historic building. A drawing, below, shows how the three-unit addition has been stepped down the hill, each unit set further back from the historic structure as it extends horizontally. As a result, the new addition is only partially visible from the historic "approach;" it can, however, be seen at full size from a new service road on the rear elevation (see photos, above).

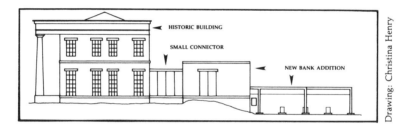

Drawing: Christina Henry

Photo: Joseph Borysthen Tcacz.

Historic bank with compatible new bank addition. This approach preserves the historic character.

The overall size of an 1893 bank in Salem, Massachusetts, was nearly doubled in 1974 when a new addition was constructed on an adjacent lot, yet the addition is compatible with the historic character. A deep set-back and similarity in scale permit the historic form to be appreciated; the addition is also compatible in materials and color. Finally, the pattern of arched and rectangular openings of the historic building is suggested in the new work.

Photo: Harry Weese & Associates

Photo: Baird M. Smith, AIA

Historic library with new addition for "uncommon" and rare books. This approach preserves the historic character.

Designed by architect Henry Ives Cobbs and completed in 1892, the Newberry Library in downtown Chicago extends the length of a city block and features a series of elongated, arch-headed windows. In 1981, when additional space was required with light and humidity control for storage of the rare book collection, a 10-story, windowless brick addition was linked to the historic block on side and rear elevations. Although constituting major expansion, the new wing still reads as a subsidiary unit to the substantially larger historic library complex. Its simple rectangular shape and lack of ornamentation stand in contrast with the highly articulated historic library complex; the rhythm of the historic windows is suggested in the windowless addition through a series of recessed square and arched bands. This is one example of a solution that is considered compatible with the historic character.

Historic residential buildings with incompatible three-story rooftop addition. This approach changes the historic character.

The historic character of one building or an entire row of buildings may be radically altered by even one highly visible, inappropriately scaled rooftop addition. This is partly because the proportions or dimensions of a historic building play such a major role in determining its identity. Major expansion at the roofline alters the proportions and profile of the building—a change that is particularly noticeable when seen in outline against the sky. A modest clerestory addition (extending across townhouses to the right) is almost overlooked because the focal point of the row is a three-story, pyramidally-shaped glass and metal addition whose mass, size, and scale overpowers the block's residential character.

Photo: David Kroll

Photo: David Kroll

Historic commercial building with compatible new, one-story rooftop addition. This approach preserves the historic character.

This rooftop addition—sharing a similarity to the example above in its use of glass and metal and an angular shape—has been set back from both the front and side roof edges against a party wall, thus preserving the character of the historic building as well as the district. Although the addition appears to be very small from a street perspective, in actuality it is spacious enough to be used as a business conference room and employee lounge.

Historic commercial building with compatible new 2-story rooftop addition. This approach preserves the historic character.

Small-scale residential or commercial buildings are extremely difficult to expand at the roofline. An additional story will usually result in a radical change to the historic building's proportions and profile, even when the addition is set back from the roof edge. In this particular case, however, the prominence of the resource's parapet and corner tower together with the deep setback made it possible to successfully add two new stories to a small-scale historic building.

Private residence with incompatible new office addition. This approach changes the historic character.

Successfully introducing a new addition into a residential neighborhood depends in large measure on the degree of visibility from the streets and sidewalks. In a neighborhood where lots were historically small, but deep, and houses were constructed close together, adding a new room to a secondary elevation may often be undertaken without changing the historic character. The historic character of this late 19th/early 20th century wood-frame residential structure was compromised when a masonry wrap-around addition was constructed on highly visible elevations within the district. Historic features were also destroyed in making changes necessary for office use.

Historic office building with incompatible new 4-story rooftop addition. This approach changes the historic character.

In this example, the historic character of a similarly-scaled commercial building has been radically changed by the addition of four stories that intentionally repeat the distinctive historic parapet feature at each level. The net effect is to have created a new four-story building atop a four-story historic building.

Historic commercial structure with incompatible new greenhouse addition. This approach changes the historic character.

Glass—particularly in conjunction with inappropriate location, scale, and form—can be an exceedingly troublesome material. In theory, glass would seem to be the perfect material for a new addition because the historic building's materials and features can be "read" through the transparent material. But glass is never fully invisible during the day because of its reflective nature; at night, the bright light in a glass addition may become a somewhat disturbing aspect that competes with the historic building. This large greenhouse restaurant addition, constructed on a highly visible side elevation within the district, is also flush with the historic facade. Inappropriate scale and high visibility coupled with the amount of glass used in this particular addition have radically altered the character of a modest freestanding structure and its setting.

3. Protecting the Historical Significance— Making a Visual Distinction Between Old and New

The following statement of approach could be applied equally to the preservation of districts, sites, buildings, structures, and objects of National Register significance: "A conservator works within a conservation ethic so that the integrity of the object as an historic entity is maintained. The concern is not just with the original state of the object, but the way in which it has been changed and used over the centuries. Where a new intervention must be made to save the object, either to stabilize it or to consolidate it, it is generally accepted that those interventions must be *clear, obvious, and reversible*. It is this same attitude to change that is relevant to conservation policies and attitudes to historic towns . . ."[1]

Rather than establishing a clear and obvious difference between old and new, it might seem more in keeping with the historic character simply to repeat the historic form, material, features, and detailing in a new addition. But when the new work is indistinguishable from the old in appearance, then the "real" National Register property may no longer be perceived and appreciated by the public. Thus, the third consideration in planning a new addition is to be sure that it will protect those visual qualities that made the building eligible for listing in the National Register of Historic Places.

A question often asked is what if the historic character is *not* compromised by an addition that appears to have been built in the same period? A small porch or a wing that copied the historic materials and detailing placed on a *rear* elevation might not alter the public perception of the historic form and massing. Therefore, it is conceivable that a modest addition could be replicative without changing the resource's historic character; generally, however, this approach is not recommended because using the same wall plane, roof line, cornice height, materials, siding lap, and window type in an addition can easily make the new work appear to be part of the historic building. If this happens on a visible elevation, it becomes unclear as to which features are historic and which are new, thus confusing the authenticity of the historic resource itself.

The National Park Service policy on new additions, adopted in 1967, is an outgrowth and continuation of a general philosophical approach to change first expressed by John Ruskin in England in the 1850s, formalized by William Morris in the founding of the Society for the Protection of Ancient Buildings in 1877, expanded by the Society in 1924 and, finally, reiterated in the 1964 Venice Charter—a document that continues to be followed by 64 national committees of the International Council on Monuments and Sites (ICOMOS). The 1967 *Administrative Policies for Historical Areas of the National Park System* thus states, " . . . a modern addition should be readily distinguishable from the older work; however, the new work should be harmonious with the old in scale, proportion, materials, and color. Such additions should be as inconspicuous as possible from the public view." Similarly, the Secretary of the Interior's 1977 "Standards for Rehabilitation" call for the new work to be "compatible with the size, scale, color, material, and character of the property, neighborhood, or environment."

Photos: Noré V. Winter

Historic bank with new bank addition. This approach protects the historical significance of the resource by making a visual distinction between what is old and what is new.

Constructed in the early 1890s in Durango, Colorado, the split-faced ashlar bank structure is characterized by its flat roof, rounded form at the main entrance, a series of large arched window and door openings, and heavily textured surfaces. When additional office space was needed in 1978 to serve a commercially revitalized historic district, the new work was respectful of the historic structure through its proportional similarities, and alignment of openings and cornice. While echoing the historic bank's arched and rectangular shapes, the addition features a contrasting, smooth-faced brick that—together with the variation in window size, recessed detailing, and exaggerated verticality of the pilasters—places the new work in a clearly contemporary idiom and also permits the historic building to predominate.

---

[1] Roy Worskett, RIBA, MRTIP, "Improvement of Urban Design in Europe and the United States: New Buildings in Old Settings." Background Report (prepared July, 1984) for Seminar at Strasbourg, France, October, 1984.

Protecting the Historical Significance—Making a Visual Distinction Between Old and New

Photo: Carleton Knight, III

Photo: Kay D. Weeks

Historic library with new library wing. This approach protects the historical significance of the resource by making a visual distinction between what is old and what is new.

Charles Follen McKim's Boston Public Library, a 3 story, granite-faced, rectangular structure built between 1888-1895, was significantly expanded in 1973 by Phillip Johnson's new library addition on highly visible side and rear elevations. While the new addition is closely related to the historic block in its basic proportions, Johnson's bold use of material and detailing—juxtaposed to McKim's delicately patterned facade—provide clear differentiation between old and new and result in an addition that is unequivocally a product of its own time.

Private residence with new addition. This approach does not protect the historical significance of the resource because it fails to make a visual distinction between what is old and what is new.

The most distinctive portion of this c. 1900 wood-frame residence—the decorative gable and three-part window—was repeated in a new addition to the left. As a result of copying the form, features and detailing of the new addition on the front elevation, the historic building and the new addition are virtually indistinguishable.

Photos: Jerry Liebman

Historic post office with new commercial entrance addition. This approach protects the historical significance of the resource by making a visual distinction between what is old and what is new.

An 1810 granite and wood structure in Chester, Connecticut has been used over its long history as a post office, a school, and most recently, for two businesses—one downstairs and one upstairs. In 1985, as part of the conversion of the second floor into a graphic arts studio, an extensively deteriorated straight-run wooden stair was replaced by this small new entrance and stairtower addition. Because of the addition's deep set-back and restrained size, the form, features, and detailing of the historic structure continue to dominate both site and streetscape; moreover, the new work has a separate identity and could not be mistaken as part of the historic building.

NEW ROOFTOP ADDITION

Drawing: National Register files

Historic city hall with new rooftop office addition. This approach does not protect the historical significance of the resource because it fails to make a visual distinction between what is old and what is new.

The drawing shows a proposed penthouse addition to a former municipal building. Originally a flat-roofed structure with a modestly detailed cornice, the proposed new addition has changed the proportions and profile, creating a verticality and degree of ornamentation that never existed historically. These changes have effectively *re-defined* the historic character. With its highly replicative ornamentation, the addition has become an integral component of the historic design. The result is that a passerby would probably not be able to tell that the rooftop addition is new and not part of the original construction.

NEW EXTERIOR ADDITIONS TO HISTORIC BUILDINGS

Preserve Significant Historic Materials and Features

Avoid constructing an addition on a primary or other character-defining elevation to ensure preservation of significant materials and features.

Minimize loss of historic material comprising external walls and internal partitions and floor plans.

Preserve the Historic Character

Make the size, scale, massing, and proportions of the new addition compatible with the historic building to ensure that the historic form is not expanded or changed to an unacceptable degree.

Place the new addition on an inconspicuous side or rear elevation so that the new work does not result in a radical change to the form and character of the historic building.

Consider setting an infill addition or connector back from the historic building's wall plane so that the form of the historic building–or buildings– can be distinguished from the new work.

Set an additional story well back from the roof edge to ensure that the historic building's proportions and profile are not radically changed.

Protect the Historic Significance–Make a Visual Distinction Between Old and New

Plan the new addition in a manner that provides some differentiation in material, color, and detailing so that the new work does not appear to be part of the historic building. The character of the historic resource should be identifiable after the addition is constructed.

Conclusion

A major goal of our technical assistance program is a heightened awareness of significant materials and the historic character *prior* to construction of a new exterior addition so that essential change may be effected within a responsible preservation context. In summary, then, these are the three important preservation questions to ask when planning a new exterior addition to a historic resource:

1. **Does the proposed addition preserve significant historic materials and features?**

2. **Does the proposed addition preserve the historic character?**

3. **Does the proposed addition protect the historical significance by making a visual distinction between old and new?**

If the answer is YES to all three questions, then the new addition will protect significant historic materials and the historic character and, in doing so, will have satisfactorily addressed those concerns generally held to be fundamental to historic preservation.

Additional Reading

Architecture: The AIA Journal, "Old and New," November, 1983.

Brolin, Brent C. *Architecture in Context: Fitting New Buildings with Old.* New York: Van Nostrand Reinhold, 1980.

Good Neighbors: Building Next to History. State Historical Society of Colorado, 1980.

International Council on Monuments and Sites (ICOMOS), *International Charter for the Conservation and Restoration of Monuments and Sites, (Venice Charter),* 1966.

National Trust for Historic Preservation. *Old and New Architecture: Design Relationship.* Washington, D.C.: Preservation Press, 1980.

Rehab Right: How to Rehabilitate Your Oakland House Without Sacrificing Architectural Assets. City of Oakland Planning Department, Oakland, California, 1978.

Ruskin, John. *The Seven Lamps of Architecture.* London: George Allen and Unwin, Ltd., 1925.

Schmertz, Mildred F., and Architectural Record Editors. *New Life for Old Buildings.* New York, Architectural Record Books, McGraw-Hill, 1980.

The Secretary of the Interior's Standards for Rehabilitation and Guidelines for Rehabilitating Historic Buildings. Washington, D.C.: Preservation Assistance Division, National Park Service U.S. Department of the Interior, rev. 1983.

The following historic buildings with new additions are listed in the order in which they appeared in sections 1., 2., and 3. Those approaches to constructing new additions that met all three preservation concerns addressed in Preservation Briefs 14 are in boldface; the date of the new addition is given together with the name of the project architect(s):

1. **Preserves** Significant Historic Materials and Features

Walsh-McLean House (Indonesian Embassy), Washington, D.C. New addition, 1981, The Architects Collaborative (TAC).

Merchant's National Bank, Winona, Minnesota. New addition, 1969-1970, Dykins and Handford.

City Market, Indianapolis, Indiana. New addition, 1977, James Associates.

Folger Shakespeare Library, Washington, D.C. New addition, 1983, Hartman-Cox.

Chase's Theater and Riggs Building, Washington, D.C.

Historic cast-iron facade on new department store (ZCMI Building), Salt Lake City, Utah.

2. Preserves the Historic Character

Montgomery Street residence, Federal Hill, Baltimore, Maryland. New addition, 1983, James R. Grieves Associates, Inc.

Brown University stairtower addition, Providence, Rhode Island.

Stephen Upson House, Athens, Georgia. New addition, 1978-1979, The Group Five Architects and Designers.

Salem 5¢ Savings Bank, Salem, Massachusetts. New addition, 1974, Padjen Architects.

Historic residential buildings with rooftop addition, Boston, Massachusetts.

Nutz & Grosskopf Building, Indianapolis, Indiana. New addition, 1984, Robert V. Donelson, AIA.

Newberry Library, Chicago, Illinois. New addition, 1981, Harry Weese & Associates.

Historic commercial building with new rooftop addition, Denver, Colorado.

Historic commercial building, with rooftop addition, Washington, D.C.

Private residence with medical office addition, Providence, Rhode Island.

Historic commercial building with new greenhouse addition, Newport, Rhode Island.

3. Protects the Historical Significance by Making a Visual Distinction Between Old and New

Burns National Bank, Durango, Colorado. New addition, 1978, John Pomeroy, Architect.

Boston Public Library, Boston, Massachusetts. New addition, 1973, Johnson/Burgee Architects.

Historic post office with new entrance/stairtower addition, Chester, Connecticut. New addition, 1985, Thomas A. Norton, AIA.

Private residence, Chevy Chase, Maryland

Historic city hall with proposed new rooftop addition, New Orleans, Louisiana.

First, special thanks go to Ernest A. Connally, Gary L. Hume, and W. Brown Morton, III for their efforts in establishing and refining our preservation and rehabilitation standards over the past 20 years. (The "Secretary of the Interior's Standards for Historic Preservation Projects" constitute the policy framework of this, and every technical publication developed in the Preservation Assistance Division.) H. Ward Jandl, Chief, Technical Preservation Services Branch, is credited with overall supervision of the project. Next, appreciation is extended to the Branch professional staff, the NPS cultural programs regional offices, the Park Historic Architecture Division, and the National Conference of State Historic Preservation Officers for their thoughtful comments. Finally, the following specialists in the field are thanked for their time in reviewing and commenting on the manuscript: Bruce Judd, AIA, Noré V. Winter, John Cullinane, AIA, Ellen Beasley, Vicki Jo Sandstead, Judith Kitchen, Andrea Nadel, Martha L. Werenfels, Diane Pierce, Colden Florance, FAIA, and H. Grant Dehart, AIA. The photograph of Chicago's Newberry Library with the Harry Weese & Associates' 1981 addition was graciously lent to us by David F. Dibner, FAIA, and Amy Dibner-Dunlap, co-authors of *Buildings Additions Design,* McGraw-Hill, 1985. The front page "logo" by Noré Winter is a detail of historic Burns National Bank, Durango, Colorado, with John Pomeroy's 1978 addition.

15

Preservation of Historic Concrete: Problems and General Approaches

William B. Coney, A.I.A.

The Secretary of the Interior's ''Standards for Rehabilitation'' require that deteriorated architectural features shall be repaired rather than replaced. When the severity of deterioration requires removal of historic material, its replacement should match the material being replaced in composition, design, color, texture, and other visual qualities.

''Concrete'' is a name applied to any of a number of compositions consisting of sand, gravel, crushed stone, or other coarse material, bound together with various kinds of cementitious materials, such as lime or cements. When water is added, the mix undergoes a chemical reaction and hardens. An extraordinarily versatile building material, concrete is used for the utilitarian, the ornamental, and the monumental. While early proponents of modern concrete considered it to be permanent, it is, like all materials, subject to deterioration. This Brief surveys the principal problems posed by concrete deterioration, their likely causes, and approaches to their remedies. In almost every instance, remedial work should only be undertaken by qualified professionals. Faulty concrete repair can worsen structural problems and lead to further damage or safety hazards. Concrete repairs are not the province of do-it-yourselfers. Consequently, the corrective measures discussed here are included for general information purposes only; they do not provide ''how to'' advice.

HISTORICAL OVERVIEW

The Romans found that the mixture of lime putty with pozzolana, a fine volcanic ash, would harden under water. The result was possibly the first hydraulic cement. It became a major feature of Roman building practice, and was used in many buildings and engineering projects such as bridges and aqueducts. Concrete technology was kept alive during the Middle Ages in Spain and Africa, with the Spanish introducing a form of concrete to the New World in the first decades of the 16th century. It was used by both the Spanish and English in coastal areas stretching from

Florida to South Carolina. Called ''tapia,'' or ''tabby,'' the substance was a creamy white, monolithic masonry material composed of lime, sand, and an aggregate of shells, gravel, or stone mixed with water. This mass of material was placed between wooden forms, tamped, and allowed to dry, the building arising in layers, about one foot at a time.

Despite its early use, concrete was slow in achieving widespread acceptance as a building material in the United States. In 1853, the second edition of Orson S. Fowler's *A Home for All* publicized the advantages of ''gravel wall'' construction to a wide audience, and poured gravel wall buildings appeared across the United States (see fig. 1). Seguin, Texas, 35 miles east

Fig. 1. Milton House, Milton, Wisconsin (1844). An early example of gravel wall construction with 12- to 15-inch thick monolithic concrete walls coated on the exterior with stucco. Photo: William B. Coney.

of San Antonio, came to be called "The Mother of Concrete Cities" for some 90 concrete buildings made from local "lime water" and gravel (see fig. 2). Impressed by the economic advantages of poured gravel wall or "lime-grout" construction, the Quartermaster General's Office of the War Department embarked on a campaign to improve the quality of building for frontier military posts. As a result, lime-grout structures were built at several western posts, such as the buildings that were constructed with 12- or 18-inch-thick walls at Fort Laramie, Wyoming between 1872 and 1885. By the 1880s sufficient experience had been gained with unreinforced concrete to permit construction of much larger buildings. The Ponce de Leon Hotel in St. Augustine, Florida, is a notable example from this period (see fig. 3).

Reinforced concrete in the United States dates from 1860, when S.T. Fowler obtained a patent for a reinforced concrete wall. In the early 1870s William E. Ward built his own house in Port Chester, New York, using concrete reinforced with iron rods for all structural elements. Despite these developments, such construction remained a novelty until after 1880, when in-

novations introduced by Ernest L. Ransome made reinforced concrete more practicable. The invention of the horizontal rotary kiln allowed production of a cheaper, more uniform and reliable cement, and led to the greatly increased acceptance of concrete after 1900.

During the early 20th century Ransome in Beverly, Massachusetts, Albert Kahn in Detroit, and Richard E. Schmidt in Chicago promoted concrete for utilitarian buildings with their "factory style," featuring an exposed concrete skeleton filled with expanses of glass. Thomas Edison's cast-in-place reinforced concrete homes in Union Township, New Jersey, proclaimed a similarly functional emphasis in residential construction (see fig. 4). From the 1920s onward, concrete began to be used with spectacular design results: in James J. Earley and Louis Bourgeois' exuberant, graceful Baha'i Temple in Wilmette, Illinois (see cover); and in Frank Lloyd Wright's masterpiece "Fallingwater" near Mill Run, Pennsylvania (see fig. 5). Eero Saarinen's soaring Terminal Building at Dulles International Airport outside Washington, D.C., exemplifies the masterful use of concrete achieved in the Modern era.

Fig. 2. *Sebastopol House, Seguin, Texas (1856). This Greek Revival dwelling is one of the few remaining poured-in-place concrete structures in this Texas town noted for its construction of over 90 concrete buildings in the mid-nineteenth century. The high parapets surrounding the flat roof were lined and served as a water reservoir to cool the house. Photo: Texas Historical Commission.*

Fig. 4. *Thomas A. Edison's Cast-in-Place Houses, Union Township, New Jersey (1909). This construction photo shows the formwork for the cast-in-place reinforced concrete houses built as low-cost housing using a standard 25- by 30-foot module. Photo: Edison National Historical Site.*

Fig. 3. *Ponce de Leon Hotel, St. Augustine, Florida (1885-87). An example of unreinforced concrete used on a grand scale, this Spanish Colonial Revival hotel was designed by Carrere and Hastings and commissioned by railroad magnate Henry Flagler. The building now serves as the main campus hall for Flagler College. Photo: Flagler College.*

Fig. 5. *"Fallingwater," near Mill Run, Pennsylvania (1936-37). This dramatic reinforced concrete residence by Frank Lloyd Wright is anchored into bedrock on the hillside and cantilevered over the stream. The great tensile strength of reinforced concrete made this type of construction possible. Photo: Paul Mayen.*

CAUSES OF CONCRETE DETERIORATION

Deterioration in concrete can be caused by environmental factors, inferior materials, poor workmanship, inherent structural design defects, and inadequate maintenance (see figs. 6, 7, and 8).

Environmental factors are a principal source of concrete deterioration. Concrete absorbs moisture readily, and this is particularly troublesome in regions of recurrent freeze-thaw cycles. Freezing water produces expansive pressure in the cement paste or in nondurable aggregates. Carbon dioxide, another atmospheric component, can cause the concrete to deteriorate by reacting with the cement paste at the surface.

Materials and workmanship in the construction of early concrete buildings are potential sources of problems. For example, aggregates used in early concrete, such as cinders from burned coal and certain crushed brick, absorb water and produce a weak and porous concrete. Alkali-aggregate reactions within the concrete can result in cracking and white surface staining. Ag-

Fig. 7. *Battery Commander's Station, Ft. Washington, Maryland (1904). This reinforced concrete tower with a cantilevered balcony is showing serious deterioration. Water has penetrated the slab, causing freeze-thaw spalling around the posts and corrosion of the reinforcing bars. This internal corrosion is causing expansion inside the slab and creating major horizontal cracks in the concrete. Under the balcony can be seen the network of hardened white calcified deposits, which have exuded through cracks in the concrete as a result of alkali-aggregate reaction. Photo: Lee H. Nelson, FAIA.*

Fig. 8. *Meridian Hill, Washington, D.C. (1934). This reinforced concrete pier has lost much of its projecting molding partly from accidental impact and partly from spalling induced by freeze-thaw action. Evidence of moisture leaching out from the interior through cracks is seen as white deposits on the surface of this exposed aggregate concrete. Photo: Lee H. Nelson, FAIA.*

Fig. 6. *Battery Fortifications, Ft. Washington, Maryland (1891-97). This unreinforced concrete fortification exhibits several kinds of deterioration: the diagonal structural crack due to uneven settlement, the long horizontal crack at the cold joint, the spalling of the concrete surface coating, and vegetative growth. Photo: Sharon C. Park, AIA.*

gregates were not always properly graded by size to ensure an even distribution of elements from small to large. The use of aggregates with similarly sized particles normally produced a poorly consolidated and therefore weaker concrete.

Early builders sometimes inadvertently compromised concrete by using seawater or beach sand in the mix or by using calcium chloride or a similar salt as an additive to make the concrete more "fireproof." A common practice, until recently, was to add salt to strengthen concrete or to lower the freezing point during cold-weather construction. These practices cause problems over the long term.

In addition, early concrete was not vibrated when poured into forms as it is today. More often it was tamped or rodded to consolidate it, and on floor slabs it was often rolled with increasingly heavier rollers filled with water. These practices tended to leave voids (areas of no concrete) at congested areas, such as at reinforcing bars at column heads and other critical structural locations. Areas of connecting voids seen when concrete forms are removed are known as "honeycombs" and can reduce the protective cover over the reinforcing bars.

Other problems caused by poor workmanship are not unknown today. If the first layer of concrete is allowed to harden before the next one is poured next to or on top of it, joints can form at the interface of the layers. In some cases, these "cold joints" visibly detract from the architecture, but are otherwise harmless. In other cases, "cold joints" can permit water to infiltrate, and subsequent free-thaw action can cause the joints to move. Dirt packed in the joints allows weeds to grow, further opening paths for water to enter. Inadequate curing can also lead to problems. If moisture leaves newly poured concrete too rapidly because of low humidity, excessive exposure to sun or wind, or use of too porous a substrate, the concrete will develop shrinkage cracks and will not reach its full potential strength.

Structural Design Defects in historic concrete structures can be an important cause of deterioration. For example, the amount of protective concrete cover around reinforcing bars was often insufficient. Another design problem in early concrete buildings is related to the absence of standards for expansion-contraction joints to prevent stresses caused by thermal movements, which may result in cracking.

Improper Maintenance of historic buildings can cause long-term deterioration of concrete. Water is a principal source of damage to historic concrete (as to almost every other material) and prolonged exposure to it can cause serious problems. Unrepaired roof and plumbing leaks, leaks through exterior cladding, and unchecked absorption of water from damp earth are potential sources of building problems. Deferred repair of cracks allowing water penetration and freeze-thaw attacks can even cause a structure to collapse. In some cases the application of waterproof surface coatings can aggravate moisture-related problems by trapping water vapor within the underlying material.

MAJOR SIGNS OF CONCRETE DETERIORATION

Cracking occurs over time in virtually all concrete. Cracks vary in depth, width, direction, pattern, location, and cause. Cracks can be either active or dormant (inactive). Active cracks widen, deepen, or migrate through the concrete. Dormant cracks remain unchanged. Some dormant cracks, such as those caused by shrinkage during the curing process, pose no danger, but if left unrepaired, they can provide convenient channels for moisture penetration, which normally causes further damage.

Structural cracks can result from temporary or continued overloads, uneven foundation settling, or original design inadequacies. Structural cracks are active if the overload is continued or if settlement is ongoing; they are dormant if the temporary overloads have been removed, or if differential settlement has stabilized. Thermally-induced cracks result from stresses produced by temperature changes. They frequently occur at the ends or corners of older concrete structures built without expansion joints capable of relieving such stresses. Random surface cracks (also called "map" cracks due to their resemblance to the lines on a road map) that deepen over time and exude a white gel that hardens on the surface are caused by an adverse reaction between the alkalis in a cement and some aggregates.

Since superficial repairs that do not eliminate underlying causes will only tend to aggravate problems, professional consultation is recommended in almost every instance where noticable cracking occurs.

Spalling is the loss of surface material in patches of varying size. It occurs when reinforcing bars corrode, thus creating high stresses within the concrete. As a result, chunks of concrete pop off from the surface. Similar damage can occur when water absorbed by porous aggregates freezes. Vapor-proof paints or sealants, which trap moisture beneath the surface of the impermeable barrier, also can cause spalling. Spalling may also result from the improper consolidation of concrete during construction. In this case, water-rich cement paste rises to the surface (a condition known as laitance). The surface weakness encourages scaling, which is spalling in thin layers.

Deflection is the bending or sagging of concrete beams, columns, joists, or slabs, and can seriously affect both the strength and structural soundness of concrete. It can be produced by overloading, by corrosion, by inadequate construction techniques (use of low-strength concrete or undersized reinforcing bars, for example), or by concrete creep (long-term shrinkage). Corrosion may cause deflection by weakening and ultimately destroying the bond between the rebar and the concrete, and finally by destroying the reinforcing bars themselves. Deflection of this type is preceded by significant cracking at the bottom of the beams or at column supports. Deflection in a structure without widespread cracking, spalling, or corrosion is frequently due to concrete creep.

Stains can be produced by alkali-aggregate reaction, which forms a white gel exuding through cracks and hardening as a white stain on the surface. Efflorescence is a white, powdery stain produced by the leaching of lime from Portland cement, or by the pre-World War II practice of adding lime to whiten the concrete. Discoloration can also result from metals inserted into the concrete, or from corrosion products dripping onto the surface.

Erosion is the weathering of the concrete surface by wind, rain, snow, and salt air or spray. Erosion can also be caused by the mechanical action of water channeled over concrete, by the lack of drip grooves in beltcourses and sills, and by inadequate drainage.

Corrosion, the rusting of reinforcing bars in concrete, can be a most serious problem. Normally, embedded reinforcing bars are protected against corrosion by being buried within the mass of the concrete and by the high alkalinity of the concrete itself. This protection, however, can be destroyed in two ways. First, by carbonation, which occurs when carbon dioxide in the air reacts chemically with cement paste at the surface and reduces the alkalinity of the concrete. Second, chloride ions from salts combine with moisture to produce an electrolyte that effectively corrodes the reinforcing bars. Chlorides may come from seawater additives in the original mix, or from prolonged contact with salt spray or de-icing salts. Regardless of the cause, corrosion of reinforcing bars produces rust, which occupies significantly more space than the original metal, and causes expansive forces within the concrete. Cracking and spalling are frequent results. In addition, the load-carrying capacity of the structure can be diminished by the loss of concrete, by the loss of bond between reinforcing bars and concrete, and by the decrease in thickness of the reinforcing bars themselves. Rust stains on the surface of the concrete are an indication that internal corrosion is taking place.

PLANNING FOR CONCRETE PRESERVATION

Whatever the causes of deterioration, careful analysis, supplemented by testing, is vital to the success of any historic concrete repair project. Undertaken by experienced engineers or architects, the basic steps in a program of testing and analysis are document review, field survey, testing, and analysis.

Document Review. While plans and specifications for older concrete buildings are rarely extant, they can be an invaluable aid, and every attempt should be made to find them. They may provide information on the intended composition of the concrete mix, or on the type and location of reinforcing bars. Old photographs, records of previous repairs, documents for buildings of the same basic construction or age, and news reports may also document original construction or changes over time.

Field Survey. A thorough visual examination can assist in locating and recording the type, extent, and severity of stress, deterioration, and damage.

Testing. Two types of testing, on-site and laboratory, can supplement the field condition survey as necessary. On-site, nondestructive testing may include use of a calibrated metal detector or sonic tests to locate the position, depth, and direction of reinforcing bars (see fig. 9). Voids can frequently be detected by "sounding" with a metal hammer. Chains about 30 inches long attached to a 2-foot-long crossbar, dragged over the slabs while listening for hollow reverberations, can locate areas of slabs that have delaminated. In order to find areas of walls that allow moisture to penetrate to the building interior, areas may be tested from the outside by spraying water at the walls and then inspecting the interior for water. If leaks are not readily apparent, sophisticated equipment is available to measure the water permeability of concrete walls.

If more detailed examinations are required, nondestructive instruments are available that can assist in determining the presence of voids or internal cracks, the location and size of rebars, and the strength of the concrete. Laboratory testing can be invaluable in determining the composition and characteristics of historic concrete and in formulating a compatible design mix

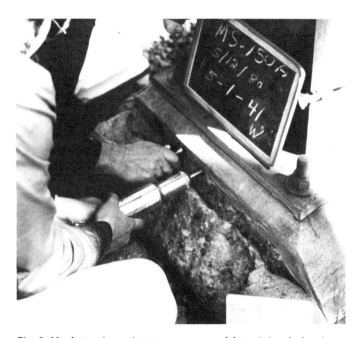

Fig. 9. *Nondestructive sonic tests are one way of determining the location and soundness of internal reinforcing bars and the hardness of the concrete. There are a variety of other nondestructive tests provided by professional consultants that will help in the evaluation of the structural integrity of concrete prior to major repair work. Photo: Feld, Kaminetzky and Cohen and American Concrete Institute.*

for repair materials (see fig. 10). These tests, however, are expensive. A well-equipped concrete laboratory can analyze concrete samples for strength, alkalinity, carbonation, porosity, alkali-aggregate reaction, presence of chlorides, and past composition.

Fig. 10. Testing of actual samples of concrete in the lab may be necessary to determine the strength and condition of the concrete. In this sample, the surface, which is lighter than the sound concrete core, shows that carbonation has taken place. Carbonation reduces the alkalinity in concrete and may hasten corrosion of reinforcing bars close to the surface. Photo: Stella L. Marusin.

Analysis. Analysis is probably the most important step in the process of evaluation. As survey and test results are revised in conjunction with available documentation, the analysis should focus on determining the nature and causes of the concrete problems, on assessing both the short-term and long-term effects of the deterioration, and on formulating proper remedial measures.

CONCRETE REPAIR

Repairs should be undertaken only after the planning measures outlined above have been followed. Repair of historic concrete may consist of either patching the historic material or filling in with new material worked to match the historic material. If replacement is necessary, duplication of historic materials and detailing should be as exact as possible to assure a repair that is functionally and aesthetically acceptable (see fig. 11). The correction and elimination of concrete problems can be difficult, time-consuming, and costly. Yet the temptation to resort to temporary solutions should be avoided, since their failure can expose a building to further and more serious deterioration, and in some cases can mask underlying structural problems that could lead to serious safety hazards (see fig. 12).

Principal concrete repair treatments are discussed below. While they are presented separately here, in practice, preservation projects typically incorporate multiple treatments (see figs. 13a-i).

Fig. 11. Meridian Hill, Washington, D.C. (1934). It is important to match the visual qualities, such as color and texture, when repairs or replacement sections are undertaken. In this case, the new replacement step, located second from the left, matches the original pebble-finish surface of the adjacent historic steps. Photo: Sharon C. Park, AIA.

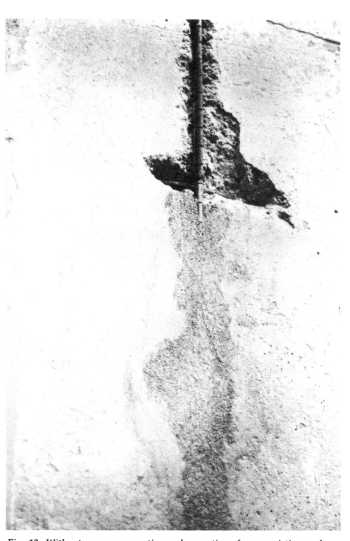

Fig. 12. Without proper preparation and correction of a pre-existing problem, repairs will fail. Insufficient concrete at the surface caused this patch around a reinforcing bar to fail within a year. In this case, a structural engineer should have assessed the need for this rod so close to the surface. Redundant rods are often cut out prior to patching. Photo: Alonzo White.

Fig. 13a. Buckling concrete under a painted surface indicates underlying deterioration. It is often difficult to assess the amount of deterioration until the area has been cleaned and examined closely.

Fig. 13c. Narrow cracks often need to be widened to receive concrete patches. Here a pneumatic chisel is being used.

Fig. 13e. A spalled area of concrete has been cleaned back to a sound surface, and is being coated with a bonding agent to increase adherence of the new concrete patch.

Fig. 13g. A soft brush is used to smooth the patch and to blend it with the adjacent historic concrete.

Fig. 13a-i. Virginia Heating Plant, Arlington, Virginia (1941). This reinforced concrete building exhibits several serious problems, including cracking, spalling, and corrosion of reinforcing bars. As a result of careful planning and close supervision, successful repairs have been carried out. Photos: Alonzo White and Sharon C. Park, AIA.

Fig. 13b. Upon removal of the deteriorated surface, a pocket of poorly mixed concrete (mostly sand and gravel) was easily chiseled out. The reinforcing rods were in good condition.

Fig. 13d. Deteriorated or redundant reinforcing bars are removed after evaluation by a structural engineer. An acetylene torch is being used to cut out the bars.

Fig. 13f. Workmen are applying patching concrete and using a trowel to form ridges to match the appearance of the historic concrete ridges that were originally created by the form boards.

Fig. 13h. This active crack at a window sill and in the foundation wall has been filled with a flexible sealant. This area was subsequently painted with a masonry paint compatible with the sealant.

Fig. 13i. Upon completion of all repairs, the building was painted. The finished repair of the deterioration seen in 13a and b is shown in this photograph. The patch matches the texture and detailing of the historic concrete.

Repair of Cracking. Hairline, nonstructural cracks that show no sign of worsening normally need not be repaired. Cracks larger than hairline cracks, but less than approximately one-sixteenth of an inch, can be repaired with a mix of cement and water. If the crack is wider than one-sixteenth of an inch, fine sand should be added to the mix to allow for greater compactibility, and to reduce shrinkage during drying. Field trials will determine whether the crack should be routed (widened and deepened) minimally before patching to allow sufficient penetration of the patching material. To ensure a long-term repair, the patching materials should be carefully selected to be compatible with the existing concrete as well as with subsequent surface treatments such as paint or stucco.

When it is desirable to reestablish the structural integrity of a concrete structure involving dormant cracks, epoxy injection repair should be considered. An epoxy injection repair is made by sealing the crack on both sides of a wall or a structural member with an epoxy mortar, leaving small holes, or ''ports'' to receive the epoxy resin. After the surface mortar has hardened, epoxy is pumped into the ports. Once the epoxy in the crack has hardened, the surface mortar can be ground off, but the repair may be visually noticeable. (It is possible to inject epoxy without leaving noticeable patches, but the procedure is much more complex.)

Other cracks are active, changing their width and length. Active structural cracks will move as loads are added or removed. Thermal cracks will move as temperatures fluctuate. Thus, expansion-contraction joints may have to be introduced before repair is undertaken. Active cracks should be filled with sealants that will adhere to the sides of the cracks and will compress or expand during crack movement. The design, detailing, and execution of sealant-filled cracks require considerable attention, or else they will detract from the appearance of the historic building.

Random (map) cracks throughout a structure are difficult to correct, and may be unrepairable. Repair, if undertaken, requires removing the cracked concrete. A compatible concrete patch to replace the removed concrete is then installed. For some buildings without significant historic finishes, an effective and economical repair material is probably a sprayed concrete coating, troweled or brushed smooth. Because the original concrete will ultimately contaminate new concrete, buildings with map cracks will present continuing maintenance problems.

Repair of Spalling. Repair of spalling entails removing the loose, deteriorated concrete and installing a compatible patch that dovetails into the existing sound concrete. In order to prevent future crack development after the spall has been patched and to ensure that the patch matches the historic concrete, great attention must be paid to the treatment of rebars, the preparation of the existing concrete substrate, the selection of compatible patch material, the development of good contact between patch and substrate, and the curing of the patch.

Once the deteriorated concrete in a spalled area has been removed, rust on the exposed rebars must be removed by wire brush or sandblasting. An epoxy coating applied immediately over the cleaned rebars will diminish the possiblity of further corrosion. As a general rule, if the rebars are so corroded that a structural engineer determines they should be replaced, new supplemental reinforcing bars will normally be required, assuming that the rebar is important to the strength of the concrete. If not, it is possible to cut away the rebar.

Proper preparation of the substrate will ensure a good bond between the patch and the existing concrete. If a large, clean break or other smooth surface is to be patched, the contact area should be roughened with a hammer and chisel. In all cases, the substrate should be kept moist with wet rags, sponges, or running water for at least an hour before placement of the patch. Bonding between the patch and substrate can be encouraged by scrubbing the substrate with cement paste, or by applying a liquid bonding agent to the surface of the substrate. Admixtures such as epoxy resins, latexes, and acrylics in the patch may also be used to increase bonding, but this may cause problems with color matching if the surfaces are to be left unpainted.

Compatible matching of patch material to the existing concrete is critical for both appearance and durability. In general, repair material should match the composition of the original material (as revealed by laboratory analysis) as closely as possible so that the properties of the two materials, such as coefficient of thermal expansion and strength, are compatible. Matching the color and texture of the existing concrete requires special care. Several test batches of patching material should be mixed by adding carefully selected mineral pigments that vary slightly in color. After the samples have cured, they can be compared to the historic concrete and the closest match selected.

Contact between the patch and the existing concrete can be enhanced through the use of anchors, preferably stainless-steel hooked pins, placed in holes drilled into the structure and secured in place with epoxy. Good compaction of the patch material will encourage the contact. Compaction is difficult when the patch is ''laid-up'' with a trowel without the use of forms; however, by building up thin layers of concrete, each layer can be worked with a trowel to achieve compaction. Board forms will be necessary for large patches. In cases where the existing concrete has a significant finish, care must be taken to pin the form to the existing concrete without marring the surface. The patch in the form can be consolidated by rodding or vibration.

Because formed concrete surfaces normally develop a sheen that does not match the surface texture of most historic concrete, the forms must be removed before the patch has fully set. The surface of the patch must then be finished to match the historic concrete. A brush or wet sponge is particularly useful in achieving matching textures. It may be difficult to match historic concrete surfaces that were textured, as a result of exposed aggregate for example, but it is important that these visual qualities be matched. Once the forms are removed, holes from the bolts must also be patched and finished to match adjacent surfaces.

Regardless of size, a patch containing cement binder (especially Portland cement) will tend to shrink during drying. Adequate curing of the patch may be achieved by keeping it wet for several days with damp burlap bags. It should be noted that although greater amounts of sand will reduce overall shrinkage, patches with a high sand content normally will not bond well to the substrate.

Repair of Deflection. Deflection can indicate significant structural problems and often requires the strengthening or replacement of structural members. Because deflection can lead to structural failure and serious safety hazards, its repair should be left to engineering professionals.

Repair of Erosion. Repair of eroded concrete will normally require replacing lost surface material with a compatible patching material (as outlined above) and then applying an appropriate finish to match the historic appearance. The elimination of water coursing over concrete surfaces should be accomplished to prevent further erosion. If necessary, drip grooves at the underside of overhanging edges of sills, beltcourses, cornices, and projecting slabs should be installed.

SUMMARY

Many early concrete buildings in the United States are threatened by deterioration. Effective protection and maintenance are the keys to the durability of concrete. Even when historic concrete structures are deteriorated, however, many can be saved through preservation projects involving sensitive repair (see figs. 14a-c), or replacement of deteriorated concrete with carefully selected matching material (see figs. 15a-c). Successful restoration of many historic concrete structures in America demonstrates that techniques and materials now available can extend the life of such structures for an indefinite period, thus preserving significant cultural resources.

Fig. 14a. Spalled concrete was most noticeable at locations of concentrated rebars. Deteriorated concrete, the 1960s stucco finish, and corrosion were removed by grit-blasting. Photo: Robert Bell.

Fig. 14b. Board screeds were attached to the building to recreate the sharp edges of the original detail. Photo: Robert Bell.

Fig. 14c. Once the repair work was complete, the entire building was sprayed with a concrete mixture consisting of pea-gravel, cement, and sand, which was then hand-troweled. Finally, the building was lightly grit-blasted to remove the cement paste and reproduce the exposed agregate finish. Photo: Harry J. Hunderman.

Fig. 14a-c. Unity Temple, Oak Park, Illinois (1906). Architect Frank Lloyd Wright used cast-in-place concrete with an exposed aggregate finish. However, reinforcing bars placed too close to the surface resulted in corrosion, cracking, and spalling. A superficial repair in the 1960s coated the surface with a concrete mix and Portland cement paint which produced a stucco-like finish and accelerated deterioration. Repair work was undertaken in 1971.

Fig. 15a. The spindle-type railings were deteriorated beyond repair. The concrete was cracked or broken and the center reinforcing rods were exposed and badly rusted.

Fig. 15b. Deteriorated spindles were removed. The original 1914 molds were still available and used in casting new concrete spindles, but had they not been available, new molds could have been made to match the originals.

Fig.15c. The new concrete spindles have been installed. This sensitive renovation reused the historic concrete cap railing and stone piers, as they were still in sound condition.

Fig. 15a-c. Columbia River Highway, Oregon. This historic highway overlooking the Columbia River Gorge was constructed from 1913 to 1922 and contains a number of significant concrete bridges. These photos illustrate the sensitive replacement of the concrete spindle-type balusters on the Young Creek (Shepperd's Dell) Bridge of 1914. Photos: James Norman, Oregon Department of Transportation.

BIBLIOGRAPHY

Concrete Repair and Restoration. ACI Compilation No. 5. Detroit: American Concrete Institute, 1980. Reprint of *Concrete International: Design & Construction.* Vol. 2, No. 9 (September 1980).

Condit, Carl W. *American Building: Materials and Techniques from the First Colonial Settlements to the Present.* Chicago: University of Chicago Press, 1968.

Hime, W.G. "Multitechnique Approach Solves Construction Materials Failure Problems." *American Chemical Society.* Vol. 46, No. 14 (1974).

Huxtable, Ada Louise. "Concrete Technology in U.S.A." *Progressive Architecture.* (October 1960).

Onderdonk, Francis S. *The Ferro-Concrete Style.* New York: Architectural Book Publishing Company, Inc., 1928.

Perenchio, W.F., and Marusin, S.L. "Short-Term Chloride Penetration into Relatively Impermeable Concretes." *Concrete International.* Vol. 5, No. 4 (April 1983), pp. 34-41.

Pfiefer, D.W., Perenchio, W.F., and Marusin, S.L. "Research on Sealers, Coatings and Specialty Concretes for Barrier Films and Layers on Concrete Structures." *Proceedings of the RILEM Seminar on the Durability of Concrete Structures Under Normal Outdoor Exposure,* Hanover, Federal Republic of Germany, March 26-29, 1984.

Pfiefer, D.W. "Steel Corrosion Damage on Vertical Concrete, Parts I & II." *Concrete Construction.* (February 1981).

Prudon, Theodore. "Confronting Concrete Realities." *Progressive Architecture.* (November 1981), pp. 131-137.

Ropke, John C. *Concrete Problems, Causes & Cures.* New York: McGraw-Hill, 1982.

Sabnis, Gajanan, ed. *Rehabilitation, Renovation and Preservation of Concrete and Masonry Structures.* ACI-SP-85. Detroit: American Concrete Institute, 1985.

This Preservation Brief was prepared under contract with the National Park Service by William B. Coney, Senior Architect for Wiss, Janney, Elstner Associates, Inc. in Northbrook, Illinois. The author would like to thank others who aided in the research and writing of the Brief: William F. Perenchio, Thomas L. Rewerts, Rexford L. Selbe, John Fraczek, and Bruce S. Kaskell, all of Wiss, Janney, Elstner Associates, Inc. Architects Gordon D. Orr, Jr., and Robert A. Bell provided information on the restoration of Milton House and Unity Temple, respectively. Barbara M. Posadas, Department of History, Northern Illinois University, lent her considerable editorial skill to the entire Brief. Tony C. Liu, James R. Clifton, and Michael J. Paul of the American Concrete Institute Committee 364, reviewed and commented on the manuscript, along with Lee H. Nelson, H. Ward Jandl, Kay D. Weeks, Sharon C. Park, and Michael J. Auer of the National Park Service.

Cover: Baha'i Temple, Wilmette, Illinois (1933). Photo: William B. Coney.

GPO 854-963

16

The Use of Substitute Materials on Historic Building Exteriors

Sharon C. Park, AIA

The Secretary of the Interior's *Standards for Rehabilitation* require that "deteriorated architectural features be repaired rather than replaced, wherever possible. In the event that replacement is necessary, the new material should match the material being replaced in composition, design, color, texture, and other visual properties." Substitute materials should be used only on a limited basis and only when they will match the appearance and general properties of the historic material and will not damage the historic resource.

Introduction

When deteriorated, damaged, or lost features of a historic building need repair or replacement, it is almost always best to use historic materials. In limited circumstances substitute materials that imitate historic materials may be used if the appearance and properties of the historic materials can be matched closely and no damage to the remaining historic fabric will result.

Great care must be taken if substitute materials are used on the exteriors of historic buildings. Ultra-violet light, moisture penetration behind joints, and stresses caused by changing temperatures can greatly impair the performance of substitute materials over time. Only after consideration of all options, in consultation with qualified professionals, experienced fabricators and contractors, and development of carefully written specifications should this work be undertaken.

The practice of using substitute materials in architecture is not new, yet it continues to pose practical problems and to raise philosophical questions. On the practical level the inappropriate choice or improper installation of substitute materials can cause a radical change in a building's appearance and can cause extensive physical damage over time. On the more philosophical level, the wholesale use of substitute materials can raise questions concerning the integrity of historic buildings largely comprised of new materials. In both cases the integrity of the historic resource can be destroyed.

Some preservationists advocate that substitute materials should be avoided in all but the most limited cases. The fact is, however, that substitute materials are being used more frequently than ever in preservation projects, and in many cases with positive results. They can be cost-effective, can permit the accurate visual duplication of historic materials, and last a reasonable time. Growing evidence indicates that with proper planning, careful specifications and supervision, substitute materials can be used successfully in the process of restoring the visual appearance of historic resources.

This Brief provides general guidance on the use of substitute materials on the exteriors of historic buildings. While substitute materials are frequently used on interiors, these applications are not subject to weathering and moisture penetration, and will not be discussed in this Brief. Given the general nature of this publication, specifications for substitute materials are not provided. The guidance provided should not be used in place of consultations with qualified professionals. This Brief includes a discussion of when to use substitute materials, cautions regarding their expected performance, and descriptions of several substitute materials, their advantages and disadvantages. This review of materials is by no means comprehensive, and attitudes and findings will change as technology develops.

Historical Use of Substitute Materials

The tradition of using cheaper and more common materials in imitation of more expensive and less available materials is a long one. George Washington, for example, used wood painted with sand-impregnated paint at Mount Vernon to imitate cut ashlar stone. This technique along with scoring stucco into block patterns was fairly common in colonial America to imitate stone (see illus. 1, 2).

Molded or cast masonry substitutes, such as dry-tamp cast stone and poured concrete, became popular in place of quarried stone during the 19th century. These masonry units were fabricated locally, avoiding

Illus. 1. An early 18th-century technique for imitating carved or quarried stone was the use of sand-impregnated paint applied to wood. The facade stones and quoins are of wood. The Lindens (1754), Washington, D.C. Photo: Sharon C. Park, AIA.

Illus. 2. Stucco has for many centuries represented a number of building materials. Seen here is the ground floor of a Beaux Arts mansion, circa 1900, which represents a finely laid stone foundation wall executed in scored stucco. Photo: Sharon C. Park, AIA.

Illus. 3. Casting concrete to represent quarried stone was a popular late 19th-century technique seen in this circa 1910 mail-order house. While most components were delivered by rail, the foundations and exterior masonry were completed by local craftsmen. Photo: Sharon C. Park, AIA.

Illus. 4. The 19th-century also produced a variety of metal products used in imitation of other materials. In this case, the entire exterior of the Long Island Safety Deposit Company is cast-iron representing stone. Photo: Becket Logan, Friends of Cast Iron Architecture.

expensive quarrying and shipping costs, and were versatile in representing either ornately carved blocks, plain wall stones or rough cut textured surfaces. The end result depended on the type of patterned or textured mold used and was particularly popular in conjunction with mail order houses (see illus. 3). Later, panels of cementitious perma-stone or formstone and less expensive asphalt and sheet metal panels were used to imitate brick or stone.

Metal (cast, stamped, or brake-formed) was used for storefronts, canopies, railings, and other features, such as galvanized metal cornices substituting for wood or stone, stamped metal panels for Spanish clay roofing tiles, and cast-iron column capitals and even entire building fronts in imitation of building stone (see illus. no. 4).

Terra cotta, a molded fired clay product, was itself a substitute material and was very popular in the late 19th and early 20th centuries. It simulated the ap-

pearance of intricately carved stonework, which was expensive and time-consuming to produce. Terra cotta could be glazed to imitate a variety of natural stones, from brownstones to limestones, or could be colored for a polychrome effect.

Nineteenth century technology made a variety of materials readily available that not only were able to imitate more expensive materials but were also cheaper to fabricate and easier to use. Throughout the century, imitative materials continued to evolve. For example, ornamental window hoods were originally made of wood or carved stone. In an effort to find a cheaper substitute for carved stone and to speed fabrication time, cast stone, an early form of concrete, or cast-iron hoods often replaced stone. Toward the end of the century, even less expensive sheet metal hoods, imitating stone, also came into widespread use. All of these materials, stone, cast stone, cast-iron, and various pressed metals were in

a

b

c

d

Illus. 5. The four historic examples of various window hoods shown are: (a) stone; (b) cast stone; (c) cast-iron; and (d) sheet metal. The criteria for selecting substitute materials today (availability, quality, delivery dates, cost) are not much different from the past. Photo: Sharon C. Park, AIA.

When to Consider Using Substitute Materials in Preservation Projects

Because the overzealous use of substitute materials can greatly impair the historic character of a historic structure, all preservation options should be explored thoroughly before substitute materials are used. It is important to remember that the purpose of repairing damaged features and of replacing lost and irreparably damaged ones is both to match visually what was there and to cause no further deterioration. For these reasons it is not appropriate to cover up historic materials with synthetic materials that will alter the appearance, proportions and details of a historic building and that will conceal future deterioration (see illus. 6).

Some materials have been used successfully for the repair of damaged features such as epoxies for wood infilling, cementitious patching for sandstone repairs, or plastic stone for masonry repairs. Repairs are preferable to replacement whether or not the repairs are in kind or with a synthetic substitute material (see illus. 7).

In general, four circumstances warrant the consideration of substitute materials: 1) the unavailability of historic materials; 2) the unavailability of skilled craftsmen; 3) inherent flaws in the original materials; and 4) code-required changes (which in many cases can be extremely destructive of historic resources).

Cost may or may not be a determining factor in considering the use of substitute materials. Depending on the area of the country, the amount of material needed, and the projected life of less durable substitute materials, it may be cheaper in the long run to use the original material, even though it may be harder to find. Due to many early failures of substitute materials, some preservationist are looking abroad to find materials (especially stone) that match the historic materials in an effort to restore historic

production at the same time and were selected on the basis of the availability of materials and local craftsmanship, as well as durability and cost (see illus. 5). The criteria for selection today are not much different.

Many of the materials used historically to imitate other materials are still available. These are often referred to as the traditional materials: wood, cast stone, concrete, terra cotta and cast metals. In the last few decades, however, and partly as a result of the historic preservation movement, new families of synthetic materials, such as fiberglass, acrylic polymers, and epoxy resins, have been developed and are being used as substitute materials in construction. In some respects these newer products (often referred to as high tech materials) show great promise; in others, they are less satisfactory, since they are often difficult to integrate physically with the porous historic materials and may be too new to have established solid performance records.

Illus. 6. Substitute materials should never be considered as a cosmetic cover-up for they can cause great physical damage and can alter the appearance of historic buildings. For example, a fiberglass coating was used at Ranchos de Taos, NM, in place of the historic adobe coating which had deteriorated. The waterproof coating sealed moisture in the walls and caused the spalling shown. It was subsequently removed and the walls were properly repaired with adobe. Photo: Lee H. Nelson, FAIA.

Illus. 7. Whenever possible, historic materials should be repaired rather than replaced. Epoxy, a synthetic resin, has been used to repair the wood window frame and sill at the Auditors Building (1878) Washington, DC. The cured resin is white in this photo and will be primed and painted. Photo: Lee H. Nelson, FAIA.

Illus. 9. Simple solutions should not be overlooked when materials are no longer available. In the case of the Morse-Libby Mansion (1859), Portland, ME, the deteriorated brownstone porch beam was replaced with a carved wooden beam painted with sand impregnated paint. Photo: Stephen Sewall.

Illus. 8. Even when materials are not locally available, it may be possible and cost effective to find sources elsewhere. For example, the local sandstone was no longer available for the restoration of the New York Shakespeare Festival Public Theater. The deteriorated sandstone window hoods, were replaced with stone from Germany that closely matched the color and texture of the historic sandstone. Photo: John G. Waite.

Illus. 10. The use of substitute materials is not necessarily cheaper or easier than using the original materials. The complex process of fabricating the polyester bronze reproduction pieces of the gilded wood molding for the clockcase at Independence Hall required talented artisans and substantial mold-making time. From left to right is the final molded polyester bronze detail; the plaster casting mold; the positive and negative interim neoprene rubber molds; and the expertly carved wooden master. Photo: Courtesy of Independence National Historical Park.

buildings accurately and to avoid many of the uncertainties that come with the use of substitute materials.

1. The unavailability of the historic material. The most common reason for considering substitute materials is the difficulty in finding a good match for the historic material (particularly a problem for masonry materials where the color and texture are derived from the material itself). This may be due to the actual unavailability of the material or to protracted delivery dates. For example, the local quarry that supplied the sandstone for a building may no longer be in operation. All efforts should be made to locate another quarry that could supply a satisfactory match (see illus. 8). If this approach fails, substitute materials such as dry-tamp cast stone or textured precast concrete may be a suitable substitute if care is taken to ensure that the detail, color and texture of the original stone are matched. In some cases, it may be possible to use a sand-impregnated paint on wood

as a replacement section, achieved using readily available traditional materials, conventional tools and work skills. (see illus. 9). Simple solutions should not be overlooked.

2. The unavailability of historic craft techniques and lack of skilled artisans. These two reasons complicate any preservation or rehabilitation project. This is particularly true for intricate ornamental work, such as carved wood, carved stone, wrought iron, cast iron, or molded terra cotta. However, a number of stone and wood cutters now employ sophisticated carving machines, some even computerized. It is also possible to cast substitute replacement pieces using

Illus. 11. *The unavailability of historic craft techniques is another reason to consider substitute materials. The original first floor cast iron front of the Grand Opera House, Wilmington, DE, was missing; the expeditious reproduction in cast aluminum was possible because artisans working in this medium were available. Photo: John G. Waite.*

Illus. 12. *Substitute materials may be considered when the original materials have not performed well. For example, early sheet metals used for roofing, such as tinplate, were reasonably durable, but the modern equivalent, terne-coated steel, is subject to corrosion once the thin tin plating is damaged. Terne-coated stainless steel or lead-coated copper (shown here) are now used as substitutes. Photo: John G. Waite.*

aluminum, cast stone, fiberglass, polymer concretes, glass fiber reinforced concretes and terra cotta. Mold making and casting takes skill and craftsmen who can undertake this work are available. (see illus. 10, 11). Efforts should always be made, prior to replacement, to seek out artisans who might be able to repair ornamental elements and thereby save the historic features in place.

3. Poor original building materials. Some historic building materials were of inherently poor quality or their modern counterparts are inferior. In addition, some materials were naturally incompatible with other materials on the building, causing staining or galvanic corrosion. Examples of poor quality materials were the very soft sandstones which eroded quickly. An example of poor quality modern replacement material is the tin coated steel roofing which is much less durable than the historic tin or terne iron which is no longer available. In some cases, more durable natural stones or precast concrete might be available as substitutes for the soft stones and modern terne-coated stainless steel or lead-coated copper might produce a more durable yet visually compatible replacement roofing (see illus. 12).

4. Code-related changes. Sometimes referred to as life and safety codes, building codes often require changes to historic buildings. Many cities in earthquake zones, for example, have laws requiring that overhanging masonry parapets and cornices, or freestanding urns or finials be securely reanchored to new structural frames or be removed completely. In some cases, it may be acceptable to replace these heavy historic elements with light replicas (see illus. 13). In other cases, the extent of historic fabric removed may be so great as to diminish the integrity of the resource. This could affect the significance of the structure and jeopardize National Register status. In addition, removal of repairable historic materials could result in loss of Federal tax credits for rehabilitation. Department of the Interior regulations make

Illus. 13. *Code-related changes are of concern in historic preservation projects because the integrity of the historic resource may be irretrievably affected. In the case of the Old San Francisco Mint, the fiberglass cornice was used to bring the building into seismic conformance. The original cornice was deteriorated, and the replacement (1982) was limited to the projecting pediment. The historic stone fascia was retained as were the stone columns. The limited replacement of deteriorated material did not jeopardize the integrity of the building. Photo: Walter M. Sontheimer.*

clear that the Secretary of the Interior's Standards for Rehabilitation take precedence over other regulations and codes in determining whether a project is consistent with the historic character of the building undergoing rehabilitation.

Two secondary reasons for considering the use of substitute materials are their lighter weight and for some materials, a reduced need of maintenance. These reasons can become important if there is a need to keep dead loads to a minimum or if the feature being replaced is relatively inaccessible for routine maintenance.

Cautions and Concerns

In dealing with exterior features and materials, it must be remembered that moisture penetration, ultra-violet degradation, and differing thermal expansion and contraction rates of dissimilar materials make any repair or replacement problematic. To ensure that a repair or replacement will perform well over time, it is critical to understand fully the properties of both the original and the substitute materials, to install replacement materials correctly, to assess their impact on adjacent historic materials, and to have reasonable expectations of future performance.

Many high tech materials are too new to have been tested thoroughly. The differences in vapor permeability between some synthetic materials and the historic materials have in some cases caused unexpected further deterioration. It is therefore difficult to recommend substitute materials if the historic materials are still available. As previously mentioned, consideration should always be given first to using traditional materials and methods of repair or replacement before accepting unproven techniques, materials or applications.

Substitute materials must meet three basic criteria before being considered: they must be compatible with the historic materials in appearance; their physical properties must be similar to those of the historic materials, or be installed in a manner that tolerates differences; and they must meet certain basic performance expectations over an extended period of time.

Matching the Appearance of the Historic Materials

In order to provide an appearance that is compatible with the historic material, the new material should match the details and craftsmanship of the original as well as the color, surface texture, surface reflectivity and finish of the original material (see illus. 14). The closer an element is to the viewer, the more closely the material and craftsmanship must match the original.

Matching the color and surface texture of the historic material with a substitute material is normally difficult. To enhance the chances of a good match, it is advisable to clean a portion of the building where new materials are to be used. If pigments are to be added to the substitute material, a specialist should determine the formulation of the mix, the natural aggregates and the types of pigments to be used. As all exposed material is subject to ultra-violet degradation, if possible, samples of the new materials made during the early planning phases should be tested or allowed to weather over several seasons to test for color stability.

Fabricators should supply a sufficient number of samples to permit on-site comparison of color, texture, detailing, and other critical qualities (see illus. 15, 16). In situations where there are subtle variations in color and texture within the original materials, the

Illus. 14. The visual qualities of the historic feature must be matched when using substitute materials. In this illustration, the lighter weight mineral fiber cement shingles used to replace the deteriorated historic slate roof were detailed to match the color, size, shape and pattern of the original roofing and the historic snow birds were reattached. Photo: Sharon C. Park, AIA.

Illus. 15. Poor quality workmanship can be avoided. In this example, the crudely cast concrete entrance pier (shown) did not match the visual qualities of the remaining historic sandstone (not shown). The aggregate is too large and exposed; the casting is not crisp; the banded tooling edges are not articulated; and the color is too pale. Photo: Sharon C. Park, AIA.

Illus. 16. The good quality substitute materials shown here do match the historic sandstone in color, texture, tooling and surface details. Dry-tamp cast stone was used to match the red sandstone that was no longer available. The reconstructed first floor incorporated both historic and substitute materials. Sufficient molds were made to avoid the problem of detecting the substitutes by their uniformity. Photo: Sharon C. Park, AIA.

Illus. 17. Care must be taken to ensure that the replacement materials will work within a predesigned system. At the Norris Museum, Yellowstone National Park, the 12-inch diameter log rafters, part of an intricate truss system, had rotted at the inner core from the exposed ends back to a depth of 48 inches. The exterior wooden shells remained intact. Fiberglass rods (left photo) and specially formulated structural epoxy were used to fill the cleaned out cores and a cast epoxy wafer end with all the detail of the original wood graining was laminated onto the log end (right photo). This treatment preserved the original feature with a combination of repair and replacement using substitute materials as part of a well thought out system. Photos: Courtesy of Harrison Goodall.

substitute materials should be similarly varied so that they are not conspicuous by their uniformity.

Substitute materials, notably the masonry ones, may be more water-absorbent than the historic material. If this is visually distracting, it may be appropriate to apply a protective vapor-permeable coating on the substitute material. However, these clear coatings tend to alter the reflectivity of the material, must be reapplied periodically, and may trap salts and moisture, which can in turn produce spalling. For these reasons, they are *not* recommended for use on historic materials.

Illus. 18. Substitute materials must be properly installed to allow for expansion, contraction, and structural security. The new balustrade (a polymer concrete modified with glass fibers) at Carnegie Hall, New York City, was installed with steel structural supports to allow window-washing equipment to be suspended securely. In addition, the formulation of this predominantly epoxy material allowed for the natural expansion and contraction within the predesigned joints. Photo: Courtesy of MJM Studios.

Matching the Physical Properties

While substitute materials can closely match the appearance of historic ones, their physical properties may differ greatly. The chemical composition of the material (i.e., presence of acids, alkalines, salts, or metals) should be evaluated to ensure that the replacement materials will be compatible with the historic resource. Special care must therefore be taken to integrate and to anchor the new materials properly (see illus. 17). The thermal expansion and contraction coefficients of each adjacent material must be within tolerable limits. The function of joints must be understood and detailed either to eliminate moisture penetration or to allow vapor permeability. Materials that will cause galvanic corrosion or other chemical reactions must be isolated from one another.

To ensure proper attachment, surface preparation is critical. Deteriorated underlying material must be cleaned out. Non-corrosive anchoring devices or fasteners that are designed to carry the new material and to withstand wind, snow and other destructive elements should be used (see illus. 18). Properly chosen fasteners allow attached materials to expand and contract at their own rates. Caulking, flexible sealants or expansion joints between the historic material and the substitute material can absorb slight differences of movement. Since physical failures often result from poor anchorage or improper installation techniques, a structural engineer should be a member of any team undertaking major repairs.

Some of the new high tech materials such as epoxies and polymers are much stronger than historic materials and generally impermeable to moisture. These differences can cause serious problems unless the new materials are modified to match the expansion and contraction properties of adjacent historic materials more closely, or unless the new materials are isolated from the historic ones altogether. When stronger or vapor impermeable new materials are used alongside historic ones, stresses from trapped moisture or differing expansion and contraction rates generally hasten deterioration of the weaker historic material. For this reason, a conservative approach to repair or replacement is recommended, one that uses more pliant materials rather than high-strength ones (see illus. 19). Since it is almost impossible for substitute materials to match the properties of historic materials perfectly, the new system incorporating new and historic materials should be designed so that if material failures occur, they occur within the new material rather than the historic material.

Performance Expectations

While a substitute material may appear to be acceptable at the time of installation, both its appearance and its performance may deteriorate rapidly. Some materials are so new that industry standards are not available, thus making it difficult to specify quality control in fabrication, or to predict maintenance requirements and long term performance. Where possible, projects involving substitute materials in similar circumstances should be examined. Material specifications outlining stability of color and texture; compressive or tensile strengths if appropriate; the acceptable range of thermal coefficients, and the durability of coatings and finishes should be included in the contract documents. Without these written documents, the owner may be left with little recourse if failure occurs (see illus. 20, 21).

The tight controls necessary to ensure long-term performance extend beyond having written performance standards and selecting materials that have a successful track record. It is important to select qualified fabricators and installers who know what they are doing and who can follow up if repairs are necessary. Installers and contractors unfamiliar with specific substitute materials and how they function in your local environmental conditions should be avoided.

The surfaces of substitute materials may need special care once installed. For example, chemical residues or mold release agents should be removed completely prior to installation, since they attract pollutants and cause the replacement materials to appear dirtier than the adjacent historic materials. Furthermore, substitute materials may require more frequent cleaning, special cleaning products and protection from impact by hanging window-cleaning scaffolding. Finally, it is critical that the substitute materials be identified as part of the historical record of the building so that proper care and maintenance of all the building materials continue to ensure the life of the historic resource.

Illus. 19. When the physical properties are not matched, particularly thermal expansion and contraction properties, great damage can occur. In this case, an extremely rigid epoxy replacement unit was installed in a historic masonry wall. Because the epoxy was not modified with fillers, it did not expand or contract systematically with the natural stones in the wall surrounding it. Pressure built up resulting in a vertical crack at the center of the unit, and spalled edges to every historic stone that was adjacent to the rigid unit. Photo: Walter M. Sontheimer.

Illus. 20. Long-term performance can be affected by where the substitute material is located. In this case, fiberglass was used as part of a storefront at street level. Due to the brittle nature of the material and the frequency of impact likely to occur at this location, an unsightly chip has resulted. Photo: Sharon C. Park, AIA.

Illus. 21. *Change of color over time is one of the greatest problems of synthetic substitute materials used outdoors. Ultra-violet light can cause materials to change color over time; some will lighten and others will darken. In this photograph, the synthetic patching material to the sandstone banding to the left of the window has aged to a darker color. Photos: Sharon C. Park, AIA.*

Illus. 22. *A fiber reinforced polymer (fiberglass) cornice and precast concrete elements replaced deteriorated features on the 19th-century exterior. Photo: Sharon C. Park, AIA.*

Choosing an Appropriate Substitute Material

Once all reasonable options for repair or replacement in kind have been exhausted, the choice among a wide variety of substitute materials currently on the market must be made (see illus. 22). The charts at the end of this Brief describe a number of such materials, many of them in the family of modified concretes which are gaining greater use. The charts do not include wood, stamped metal, mineral fiber cement shingles and some other traditional imitative materials, since their properties and performance are better known. Nor do the charts include vinyls or molded urethanes which are sometimes used as cosmetic claddings or as substitutes for wooden millwork. Because millwork is still readily available, it should be replaced in kind.

The charts describe the properties and uses of several materials finding greater use in historic preservation projects, and outline advantages and disadvantages of each. It should not be read as an endorsement of any of these materials, but serves as a reminder that numerous materials must be studied carefully before selecting the appropriate treatment. Included are three predominantly masonry materials (cast stone, precast concrete, and glass fiber reinforced concrete); two predominantly resinous materials (epoxy and glass fiber reinforced polymers also known as fiberglass), and cast aluminum which has been used as a substitute for various metals and woods.

Summary

Substitute materials—those products used to imitate historic materials—should be used only after all other options for repair and replacement in kind have been ruled out. Because there are so many unknowns regarding the long-term performance of substitute materials, their use should not be considered without a thorough investigation into the proposed materials, the fabricator, the installer, the availability of specifications, and the use of that material in a similar situation in a similar environment.

Substitute materials are normally used when the historic materials or craftsmanship are no longer available, if the original materials are of a poor quality or are causing damage to adjacent materials, or if there are specific code requirements that preclude the use of historic materials. Use of these materials should be limited, since replacement of historic materials on a large scale may jeopardize the integrity of a historic resource. Every means of repairing deteriorating historic materials or replacing them with identical materials should be examined *before* turning to substitute materials.

The importance of matching the appearance and physical properties of historic materials and, thus, of finding a successful long-term solution cannot be overstated. The successful solutions illustrated in this Brief were from historic preservation projects involving professional teams of architects, engineers, fabricators, and other specialists. Cost was not necessarily a factor, and all agreed that whenever possible, the historic materials should be used. When substitute materials were selected, the solutions were often expensive and were reached only after careful consideration of all options, and with the assistance of expert professionals.

FOLLOWING ARE DESCRIPTIONS OF VARIOUS SUBSTITUTE MATERIALS

Cast Aluminum

Material: Cast aluminum is a molten aluminum alloy cast in permanent (metal) molds or one-time sand molds which must be adjusted for shrinkage during the curing process. Color is from paint applied to primed aluminum or from a factory finished coating. Small sections can be bolted together to achieve intricate or sculptural details. Unit castings are also available for items such as column plinth blocks.

Application: Cast aluminum can be a substitute for cast-iron or other decorative elements. This would include grillwork, roof crestings, cornices, ornamental spandrels, storefront elements, columns, capitals, and column bases and plinth blocks. If not self-supporting, elements are generally screwed or bolted to a structural frame. As a result of galvanic corrosion problems with dissimilar metals, joint details are very important.

Close-up detail showing the crisp casting in aluminum of this 19th-century replica column and capital for a storefront. Photo: Sharon C. Park, AIA.

Advantages:
- light weight (1/2 of cast-iron)
- corrosion-resistant, non-combustible
- intricate castings possible
- easily assembled, good delivery time
- can be prepared for a variety of colors
- long life, durable, less brittle than cast iron

Disadvantages:
- lower structural strength than cast-iron
- difficult to prevent galvanic corrosion with other metals
- greater expansion and contraction than cast-iron; requires gaskets or caulked joints
- difficult to keep paint on aluminum

Checklist:
- Can existing be repaired or replaced in-kind?
- How is cast aluminum to be attached?
- Have full-size details been developed for each piece to be cast?
- How are expansion joints detailed?
- Will there be a galvanic corrosion problem?
- Have factory finishes been protected during installation?
- Are fabricators/installers experienced?

The new cast aluminum storefront replaced the lost 19th-century cast-iron original. Photo: Sharon C. Park, AIA.

PROs and CONs of VARIOUS SUBSTITUTE MATERIALS

Cast Stone *(dry-tamped)*:

Material: Cast stone is an almost-dry cement, lime and aggregate mixture which is dry-tamped into a mold to produce a dense stone-like unit. Confusion arises in the building industry as many refer to high quality precast concrete as cast stone. In fact, while it is a form of precast concrete, the dry-tamp fabrication method produces an outer surface ressembling a stone surface. The inner core can be either dry-tamped or poured full of concrete. Reinforcing bars and anchorage devices can be installed during fabrication.

Application: Cast stone is often the most visually similar material as a replacement for unveined deteriorated stone, such as brownstone or sandstone, or terra cotta in imitation of stone. It is used both for surface wall stones and for ornamental features such as window and door surrounds, voussoirs, brackets and hoods. Rubber-like molds can be taken of good stones on site or made up at the factory from shop drawings.

Dry-tamped cast stone can reproduce the sandy texture of some natural stones. Photo: Sharon C. Park, AIA.

Advantages:
- replicates stone texture with good molds (which can come from extant stone) and fabrication
- expansion/contraction similar to stone
- minimal shrinkage of material
- anchors and reinforcing bars can be built in
- material is fire-rated
- range of color available
- vapor permeable

Disadvantages:
- heavy units may require additional anchorage
- color can fade in sunlight
- may be more absorbent than natural stone
- replacement stones are obvious if too few models and molds are made

Checklist:
- Are the original or similar materials available?
- How are units to be installed and anchored?
- Have performance standards been developed to ensure color stability?
- Have large samples been delivered to site for color, finish and absorption testing?
- Has mortar been matched to adjacent historic mortar to achieve a good color/tooling match?
- Are fabricators/installers experienced?

Glass Fiber Reinforced Concretes (GFRC)

Material: Glass fiber reinforced concretes are lightweight concrete compounds modified with additives and reinforced with glass fibers. They are generally fabricated as thin shelled panels and applied to a separate structural frame or anchorage system. The GFRC is most commonly sprayed into forms although it can be poured. The glass must be alkaline resistant to avoid deteriorating effects caused by the cement mix. The color is derived from the natural aggregates and if necessary a small percentage of added pigments.

Application: Glass fiber reinforced concretes are used in place of features originally made of stone, terra cotta, metal or wood, such as cornices, projecting window and door trims, brackets, finials, or wall murals. As a molded product it can be produced in long sections of repetitive designs or as sculptural elements. Because of its low shrinkage, it can be produced from molds taken directly from the building. It is installed with a separate non-corrosive anchorage system. As a predominantly cementitious material, it is vapor permeable.

This glass fiber reinforced concrete sculptural wall panel will replace the seriously damaged resin and plaster original. A finely textured surface was achieved by spraying the GFRC mix into molds that were created from the historic panel and resculpted based on historic photographs. Photo: Courtesy of MJM Studios.

Advantages:
- lightweight, easily installed
- good molding ability, crisp detail possible
- weather resistant
- can be left uncoated or else painted
- little shrinkage during fabrication
- molds made directly from historic features
- cements generally breathable
- material is fire-rated

Disadvantages:
- non-loadbearing use only
- generally requires separate anchorage system
- large panels must be reinforced
- color additives may fade with sunlight
- joints must be properly detailed
- may have different absorption rate than adjacent historic material

Checklist:
- Are the original materials and craftsmanship still available?
- Have samples been inspected on the site to ensure detail/texture match?
- Has anchorage system been properly designed?
- Have performance standards been developed?
- Are fabricators/installers experienced?

Precast Concrete

Material: Precast concrete is a wet mix of cement and aggregate poured into molds to create masonry units. Molds can be made from existing good surfaces on the building. Color is generally integral to the mix as a natural coloration of the sand or aggregate, or as a small percentage of pigment. To avoid unsightly air bubbles that result from the natural curing process, great care must be taken in the initial and long-term vibration of the mix. Because of its weight it is generally used to reproduce individual units of masonry and not thin shell panels.

Application: Precast concrete is generally used in place of masonry materials such as stone or terra cotta. It is used both for flat wall surfaces and for textured or ornamental elements. This includes wall stones, window and door surrounds, stair treads, paving pieces, parapets, urns, balusters and other decorative elements. It differs from cast stone in that the surface is more dependent on the textured mold than the hand tamping method of fabrication.

*Textured molds can produce a variety of high quality carved, quarried, and tooled surfaces in concrete.
Photo: Sharon C. Park, AIA.*

Advantages:
- easily fabricated, takes shape well
- rubber molds can be made from building stones
- minimal shrinkage of material
- can be load bearing or anchorage can be cast in
- expansion/contraction similar to stone
- material is fire-rated
- range of color and aggregate available
- vapor permeable

Disadvantages:
- may be more moisture absorbent than stone although coatings may be applied
- color fades in sunlight
- heavy units may require additional anchorage
- small air bubbles may disfigure units
- replacement stones are conspicuous if too few models and molds are made

Checklist:
- Is the historic material still available?
- What are the structural/anchorage requirements?
- Have samples been matched for color/texture/absorption?
- Have shop drawings been made for each shape?
- Are there performance standards?
- Has mortar been matched to adjacent historic mortar to achieve good color/tooling match?
- Are fabricators/installers experienced?

Fiber Reinforced Polymers—
Known as Fiberglass

Material: Fiberglass is the most well known of the FRP products generally produced as a thin rigid laminate shell formed by pouring a polyester or epoxy resin gel-coat into a mold. When tack-free, layers of chopped glass or glass fabric are added along with additional resins. Reinforcing rods and struts can be added if necessary; the gel coat can be pigmented or painted.

Application: Fiberglass, a non load-bearing material attached to a separate structural frame, is frequently used as a replacement where a lightweight element is needed or an inaccessible location makes frequent maintenance of historic materials difficult. Its good molding ability and versatility to represent stone, wood, metal and terra cotta make it an alternative to ornate or carved building elements such as column capitals, bases, spandrel panels, beltcourses, balustrades, window hoods or parapets. Its ability to reproduce bright colors is a great advantage.

A fiberglass cornice for the reconstruction of an 18th-century wooden clockcase is being lifted in pre-fabricated sections. The level of detail is intricate and of high quality. Photo: Courtesy of Independence National Historical Park.

Advantages:
- lightweight, long spans available with a separate structural frame
- high ratio of strength to weight
- good molding ability
- integral color with exposed high quality pigmented gel-coat or takes paint well
- easily installed, can be cut, patched, sanded
- non-corrosive, rot-resistant

Disadvantages:
- requires separate anchorage system
- combustible (fire retardants can be added); fragile to impact.
- high co-efficient of expansion and contraction requires frequently placed expansion joints
- ultra-violet sensitive unless surface is coated or pigments are in gel-coat
- vapor impermeability may require ventilation detail

Checklist:
- Can original materials be saved/used?
- Have expansion joints been designed to avoid unsightly appearance?
- Are there standards for color stability/durability?
- Have shop drawings been made for each piece?
- Have samples been matched for color and texture?
- Are fabricators/installers experienced?
- Do codes restrict use of FRP?

Epoxies *(Epoxy Concretes, Polymer Concretes)*:

Material: Epoxy is a resinous two-part thermo-setting material used as a consolidant, an adhesive, a patching compound, and as a molding resin. It can repair damaged material or recreate lost features. The resins which are poured into molds are usually mixed with fillers such as sand, or glass spheres, to lighten the mix and modify their expansion/contraction properties. When mixed with aggregates, such as sand or stone chips, they are often called epoxy concrete or polymer concrete, which is a misnomer as there are no cementitious materials contained within the mix. Epoxies are vapor impermeable, which makes detailing of the new elements extremely important so as to avoid trapping moisture behind the replacement material. It can be used with wood, stone, terra cotta, and various metals.

Application: Epoxy is one of the most versatile of the new materials. It can be used to bind together broken fragments of terra cotta; to build up or infill missing sections of ornamental metal; or to cast missing elements of wooden ornaments. Small cast elements can be attached to existing materials or entire new features can be cast. The resins are poured into molds and due to the rapid setting of the material and the need to avoid cracking, the molded units are generally small or hollow inside. Multiple molds can be combined for larger elements. With special rods, the epoxies can be structurally reinforced. Examples of epoxy replacement pieces include: finials, sculptural details, small column capitals, and medallions.

This replica column capital was made using epoxy resins poured into a mold taken from the building. The historic wooden column shaft was repaired during the restoration. Photo: Courtesy Dell Corporation.

Advantages:
- can be used for repair/replacement
- lightweight, easily installed
- good casting ability; molds can be taken from building
- material can be sanded and carved.
- color and ultra-violet screening can be added; takes paint well
- durable, rot and fungus resistant

Disadvantages:
- materials are flammable and generate heat as they cure and may be toxic when burned
- toxic materials require special protection for operator and adequate ventilation while curing
- material may be subject to ultra-violet deterioration unless coated or filters added
- rigidity of material often must be modified with fillers to match expansion coefficients
- vapor impermeable

Checklist:
- Are historic materials available for molds, or for splicing-in as a repair option?
- Has the epoxy resin been formulated within the expansion/contraction coefficients of adjacent materials?
- Have samples been matched for color/finish?
- Are fabricators/installers experienced?
- Is there a sound sub-strate of material to avoid deterioration behind new material?
- Are there performance standards?

Columns were repaired and a capital was replaced in epoxy on this 19th-century 2-story porch. Photo: Dell Corporation

Further Reading: Substitute Materials

Berryman, Nancy D.; Susan M. Tindal, *Terra Cotta; Preservation of an Historic Material.* Chicago: Landmarks Preservation Council of Illinois, 1984.

Brookes, A.J., *Cladding of Buildings.* New York: Longman Inc., 1983.

Fisher, Thomas, "The Sincerest Form of Flattery," *Progressive Architecture* (Nov. 1985).

Gayle Margot; David W. Look, AIA; John G. Waite, *Metals in America's Historic Buildings: Uses and Preservation Treatments.* Washington, D.C.: Preservation Assistance Division, National Park Service, U.S. Department of the Interior, 1980.

Historic Building Facades. New York: New York Landmarks Conservancy, 1986.

Hornbostel, Caleb, *Construction Materials: Types, Uses and Applications,* New York: John Wiley and Sons, Inc., 1978.

Lynch, Michael F; William J. Higgins, *The Maintenance and Repair of Architectural Sandstone,* New York Landmarks Conservancy, 1982.

National Park Service, Rocky Mountain Regional Office, *Preservation Briefs 12: The Preservation of Historic Pigmented Structural Glass.* Washington, D.C.: Preservation Assistance Division, National Park Service, U.S. Department of the Interior, 1984.

Phillips, Morgan and Judith Selwyn, *Epoxies for Wood Repairs in Historic Buildings.* Washington, D.C.: Preservation Assistance Division, National Park Service, U.S. Department of the Interior, 1978.

Phillips, Morgan W., *The Morse-Libby Mansion: A Report on Restoration Work.* Washington, D.C.: Preservation Assistance Division, National Park Service, U.S. Department of the Interior, 1977.

Tiller, deTeel Patterson, *Preservation Briefs 7: The Preservation of Historic Glazed Architectural Terra-Cotta.* Washington, D.C.: Preservation Assistance Division, National Park Service, U.S. Department of the Interior, 1979.

Acknowledgements

The author gratefully acknowledges the invaluable assistance of co-worker Michael Auer in editing this manuscript. The following individuals are to be thanked for their technical assistance: Mary Oehrlein A.I.A., Washington, D.C.; John G. Waite, Albany, NY: Hyman Myers, R.A., Philadelphia, PA; Thomas Fisher, Stamford, CT; Harrison Goodall, Kinnelon, NJ. In addition, the staff of Preservation Assistance Division, the cultural resources staff of the National Park Service Regional Offices, and Stan Graves, on behalf of the National Conference of State Historic Preservation Officers, provided useful comments that were incorporated into the manuscript.

This publication has been prepared pursuant to Section 101(h) of the National Historic Preservation Act, as amended, which directs the Secretary of the Interior to develop and make available information concerning historic properties. The guidance provided in this Brief will also assist property owners in complying with the requirements of the Internal Revenue Code of 1986.

Preservation Briefs: 16 has been developed under the technical editorship of Lee H. Nelson, FAIA, Chief, Preservation Assistance Division, National Park Service, U.S. Department of the Interior, P.O. Box 37127, Washington, D.C. 20013-7127. Comments on the usefulness of this information are welcome and can be sent to Mr. Nelson at the above address.

Cover photograph: Independence Hall, Philadelphia, PA; the 1972 installation of a combination wood and fiberglass clockcase duplicating the lost 18th century original. Photo: Courtesy of Independence National Historical Park.

17

Architectural Character: Identifying the Visual Aspects of Historic Buildings as an Aid to Preserving Their Character

Lee H. Nelson, FAIA

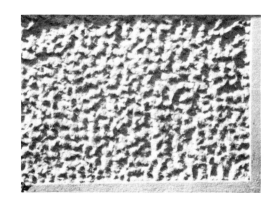

The Secretary of the Interior's "Standards for Historic Preservation Projects" embody two important goals: 1) the preservation of historic materials and, 2) the preservation of a building's distinguishing character. Every old building is unique, with its own identity and its own distinctive character. Character refers to all those visual aspects and physical features that comprise the appearance of every historic building. Character-defining elements include the overall shape of the building, its materials, craftsmanship, decorative details, interior spaces and features, as well as the various aspects of its site and environment.

The purpose of this Brief is to help the owner or the architect identify those features or elements that give the building its *visual character* and that should be taken into account in order to preserve them to the maximum extent possible.

There are different ways of understanding old buildings. They can be seen as examples of specific building types, which are usually related to a building's function, such as schools, courthouses or churches. Buildings can be studied as examples of using specific materials such as concrete, wood, steel, or limestone. They can also be considered as examples of an historical period, which is often related to a specific architectural style, such as Gothic Revival farmhouses, one-story bungalows, or Art Deco apartment buildings.

There are many other facets of an historic building besides its functional type, its materials or construction or style that contribute to its historic qualities or significance. Some of these qualities are feelings conveyed by the sense of time and place or in buildings associated with events or people. A complete understanding of any property may require documentary research about its style, construction, function, its furnishings or contents; knowledge about the original builder, owners, and later occupants; and knowledge about the evolutionary history of the building. Even though buildings may be of historic, rather than architectural significance, it is their tangible elements that embody its significance for association with specific events or persons and it is those *tangible elements* both on the exterior and interior that should be preserved.

Therefore, the approach taken in this Brief is limited to identifying those visual and tangible aspects of the historic building. While this may aid in the planning process for carrying out any ongoing or new use or restoration of the building, this approach is not a substitute for developing an understanding about the significance of an historic building and the district in which it is located.

If the various materials, features and spaces that give a building its visual character are not recognized and preserved, then essential aspects of its character may be damaged in the process of change.

A building's character can be irreversibly damaged or changed in many ways, for example, by inappropriate repointing of the brickwork, by removal of a distinctive side porch, by changes to the window sash, by changes to the setting around the building, by changes to the major room arrangements, by the introduction of an atrium, by painting previously unpainted woodwork, etc.

A Three-Step Process to Identify A Building's Visual Character

This Brief outlines a three-step approach that can be used by anyone to identify those materials, features and spaces that contribute to the visual character of a building. This approach involves first examining the building from afar to understand its overall setting and architectural context; then moving up very close to appreciate its materials and the craftsmanship and surface finishes evident in these materials; and then going into and through the building to perceive those spaces, rooms and details that comprise its interior visual character.

Step 1: Identify the Overall Visual Aspects

Identifying the overall visual character of a building is nothing more than looking at its distinguishing physical aspects without focusing on its details. The major contributors to a building's overall character are embodied in the general aspects of its *setting;* the *shape* of the building; its *roof* and roof features, such as chimneys or cupolas; the various *projections* on the building, such as porches or bay windows; the *recesses* or voids in a building, such as open galleries, arcades, or recessed balconies; the *openings* for windows and doorways; and finally the various exterior *materials* that contribute to the building's character. Step one involves looking at the building from a distance to understand the character of its site and setting, and it involves walking around the building where that is possible. Some buildings will have one or more sides that are more important than the others because they are more highly visible. This does not mean that the rear of the building is of no value whatever but it simply means that it is less important to the overall character. On the other hand, the rear may have an interesting back porch or offer a private garden space or some other aspect that may contribute to the visual character. Such a general approach to looking at the building and site will provide a better understanding of its overall character without having to resort to an infinitely long checklist of its possible features and details. Regardless of whether a building is complicated or relatively plain, it is these broad categories that contribute to an understanding of the overall character rather than the specifics of architectural features such as moldings and their profiles.

Step 2: Identify the Visual Character at Close Range

Step two involves looking at the building at close range or arm's length, where it is possible to see all the surface qualities of the materials, such as their *color* and *texture,* or surface evidence of craftsmanship or age. In some instances, the visual character is the result of the juxtaposition of materials that are contrastingly different in their color and texture. The surface qualities of the materials may be important because they impart the very sense of craftsmanship and age that distinguishes historic buildings from other buildings. Furthermore, many of these close up qualities can be easily damaged or obscured by work that affects those surfaces. Examples of this could include painting previously unpainted masonry, rotary disk sanding of smooth wood siding to remove paint, abrasive cleaning of tooled stonework, or repointing reddish mortar joints with gray portland cement.

There is an almost infinite variety of surface materials, textures and finishes that are part of a building's character which are fragile and easily lost.

Step 3: Identify the Visual Character of the Interior Spaces, Features and Finishes

Perceiving the character of interior spaces can be somewhat more difficult than dealing with the exterior.

In part, this is because so much of the exterior can be seen at one time and it is possible to grasp its essential character rather quickly. To understand the interior character, it is necessary to move through the spaces one at a time. While it is not difficult to perceive the character of one individual room, it becomes more difficult to deal with spaces that are interconnected and interrelated. Sometimes, as in office buildings, it is the vestibules or lobbies or corridors that are important to the interior character of the building. With other groups of buildings the visual qualities of the interior are related to the plan of the building, as in a church with its axial plan creating a narrow tunnel-like space which obviously has a different character than an open space like a sports pavilion. Thus the shape of the space may be an essential part of its character. With some buildings it is possible to perceive that there is a visual linkage in a sequence of spaces, as in a hotel, from the lobby to the grand staircase to the ballroom. Closing off the openings between those spaces would change the character from visually linked spaces to a series of closed spaces. For example, in a house that has a front and back parlor linked with an open archway, the two rooms are perceived together, and this visual relationship is part of the character of the building. To close off the open archway would change the character of such a residence.

The importance of interior features and finishes to the character of the building should not be overlooked. In relatively simple rooms, the primary visual aspects may be in features such as fireplace mantels, lighting fixtures or wooden floors. In some rooms, the absolute plainness is the character-defining aspect of the interior. So-called secondary spaces also may be important in their own way, from the standpoint of history or because of the family activities that occurred in those rooms. Such secondary spaces, while perhaps historically significant, are not usually perceived as important to the *visual* character of the building. Thus we do not take them into account in the visual understanding of the building.

Conclusion

Using this three-step approach, it is possible to conduct a walk through and identify all those elements and features that help define the visual character of the building. In most cases, there are a number of aspects about the exterior and interior that are important to the character of an historic building. The visual emphasis of this brief will make it possible to ascertain those things that should be preserved because their loss or alteration would diminish or destroy aspects of the historic character whether on the outside, or on the inside of the building.

For sale by the Superintendent of Documents, U.S. Government Printing Office
Washington, D.C. 20402

Overall Visual Character: Shape

The shape of a building can be an important aspect of its overall visual character. The building illustrated here, for example, has a distinctive horizontal box-like shape with the middle portion of the box projecting up an extra story. This building has other visual aspects that help define its overall character, including the pattern of vertical bands of windows, the decorative horizontal bands which separate the base of the building from the upper floors, the dark brown color of the brick, the large arched entranceway, and the castle-like tower behind the building.

Overall Visual Character: Shape

It should not be assumed that only large or unusual buildings have a shape that is distinctive or identifiable. The front wall of this modest commercial building has a simple three-part shape that is the controlling aspect of its overall visual character. It consists of a large center bay with a two story opening that combines the storefront and the windows above. The upward projecting parapet and the decorative stonework also relate to and emphasize its shape. The flanking narrow bays enframe the side windows and the small iron balconies, and the main entrance doorway into the store. Any changes to the center portion of this three-part shape, could drastically affect the visual character of this building. Photo by Emogene A. Bevitt

Overall Visual Character: Openings

Window and door openings can be important to the overall visual character of historic buildings. This view shows only part of a much larger building, but the windows clearly help define its character, partly because of their shape and rhythm: the upper floor windows are grouped in a 4,3,4,1,4 rhythm, and the lower floor windows are arranged in a regular 1,1,1,... rhythm. The individual windows are tall, narrow and arched, and they are accented by the different colored arched heads, which are connected where there are multiple windows so that the color contrast is a part of its character. If additional windows were inserted in the gap of the upper floors, the character would be much changed, as it would if the window heads were painted to match the color of the brick walls. Photo by Susan I. Dynes

Overall Visual Character: Openings

The opening illustrated here dominates the visual character of this building because of its size, shape, location, materials, and craftsmanship. Because of its relation to the generous staircase, this opening places a strong emphasis on the principal entry to the building. Enclosing this arcade-like entry with glass, for example, would materially and visually change the character of the building. Photo by Lee H. Nelson.

Overall Visual Character: Roof and Related Features

This building has a number of character-defining aspects which include the windows and the decorative stonework, but certainly the roof and its related features are visually important to its overall visual character. The roof is not only highly visible, it has elaborate stone dormers, and it also has decorative metalwork and slatework. The red and black slates of differing sizes and shapes are laid in patterns that extend around the roof of this large and freestanding building. Any changes to this patterned slatework, or to the other roofing details would damage the visual character of the building. Photo by Laurie R. Hammel

Overall Visual Character: Projections

A projecting porch or balcony can be very important to the overall visual character of almost any building and to the district in which it is located. Despite the size of this building (3 1/2 stories), and its distinctive roofline profile, and despite the importance of the very large window openings, the lacy wrap-around iron balcony is singularly important to the visual character of this building. It would seriously affect the character to remove the balcony, to enclose it, or to replace it with a balcony lacking the same degree of detail of the original material. Photo by Baird M. Smith

Overall Visual Character: Roof and Related Features

On this building, the most important visual aspects of its character are the roof and its related features such as the dormers and chimneys. The roof is important to the visual character because its steepness makes it highly visible, and its prominence is reinforced by the patterned tinwork, the six dormers and the two chimneys. Changes to the roof or its features, such as removal or alterations to the dormers, for example, would certainly change the character of this building. This does not discount the importance of its other aspects, such as the porch, the windows, the brickwork, or its setting; but the roof is clearly crucial to understanding the overall visual character of this building as seen from a distance. Photo by Lee H. Nelson

Overall Visual Character: Projections

Since these are row houses, any evaluation of their visual exterior character is necessarily limited to the front and rear walls; and while there are a number of things competing for attention in the front, it is the half round projecting bays with their conical roofs that contribute most prominently to the visual character. Their removal would be a devastating loss to the overall character, but even if preserved, the character could be easily damaged by changes to their color (as seen in the left bay which has been painted a dark color), or changes to their windows, or changes to their tile roofs. Though these houses have other fine features that contribute to the visual character and are worthy of preservation, these half-round bays demonstrate the importance of projecting features on an already rich and complex facade. Because of the repetitive nature of these projecting bays on adjacent row houses, along with the buildings' size, scale, openings, and materials, they also contribute to the overall visual character of the streetscape in the historic district. Any evaluation of the visual character of such a building should take into account the context of this building within the district. Photo by Lee H. Nelson

Overall Visual Character: Projections

Many buildings have projecting features such as porches, bay windows, or overhanging roofs, that help define their overall visual character. This projecting porch because of its size and shape, and because it copies the pitch and material of the main roof, is an important contributor to the visual character of this simple farmhouse. The removal or alteration of this porch would drastically alter the character of this building. If the porch were enclosed with wood or glass, or if gingerbread brackets were added to the porch columns, if the tin roof was replaced with asphalt, or if the porch railing was opened to admit a center stairway, the overall visual character could be seriously damaged. Although this projecting porch is an important feature, almost any other change to this house, such as changes to the window pattern, or changes to the main roof, or changes to the setting, would also change its visual character. Photo by Hugh C. Miller

Overall Visual Character: Trim

If one were to analyze the overall shape or form of this building, it would be seen that it is a gable-roofed house with dormers and a wrap-around porch. It is similar to many other houses of the period. It is the wooden trim on the eaves and around the porch that gives this building its own identify and its special visual character. Although such wooden trim is vulnerable to the elements, and must be kept painted to prevent deterioration; the loss of this trim would seriously damage the overall visual character of this building, and its loss would obliterate much of the close-up visual character so dependent upon craftsmanship for the moldings, carvings, and the see-through jigsaw work. Photo by Hugh C. Miller

Overall Visual Character: Setting

In the process of identifying the overall visual character, the aspect of setting should not be overlooked. Obviously, the setting of urban row houses differs from that of a mansion with a designed landscape. However, there are many instances where the relationship between the building and its place on the streetscape, or its place in the rural environment, in other words its setting, may be an important contributor to its overall character.

In this instance, the corner tower and the arched entryway are important contributors to the visual character of the building itself, but there is also a relationship between the building and the two converging streets that is also an important aspect of this historic building. The curb, sidewalk, fence, and the yard interrelate with each other to establish a setting that is essential to the overall visual character of the historic property. Removing these elements or replacing them with a driveway or parking court would destroy an important visual aspect. Photo by Lee H. Nelson

Overall Visual Character: Setting

Among the various visual aspects relating to the setting of an historic property are such site features as gardens, walks, fences, etc. This can include their design and materials. There is a dramatic difference in the visual character between these two fence constructions—one utilizing found materials with no particular regard to their uniformity of size or placement, and the other being a product of the machine age utilizing cast iron components assembled into a pattern of precision and regularity. If the corral fence were to be repaired or replaced with lumberyard materials its character would be dramatically compromised. The rhythm and regularity of the cast iron fence is so important to its visual character that its character could be altered by accidental damage or vandalism, if some of the fence top spikes were broken off thus interrupting the rhythm or pattern. Photos by Lee H. Nelson

Overall Visual Character: Setting

Even architecturally modest buildings frequently will have a setting that contributes to their overall character. In this very urban district, set-backs are the exception, so that the small front yard is something of a luxury, and it is important to the overall character because of its design and materials, which include the iron fence along the sidewalk, the curved walk leading to the porch, and the various plantings. In a district where parking spaces are in great demand, such front yards are sometimes converted to off-street parking, but in this instance, that would essentially destroy its setting and would drastically change the visual character of this historic property. Photo by Lee H. Nelson

Arm's Length Visual Character: Materials

At arm's length, the visual character is most often determined by the surface qualities of the materials and craftsmanship; and while these aspects are often inextricably related, the original choice of materials often plays the dominant role in establishing the close-range character because of the color, texture, or shape of the materials.

In this instance, the variety and arrangement of the materials is important in defining the visual character, starting with the large pieces of broken stone which form the projecting base for the building walls, then changing to a wall of roughly rectangular stones which vary in size, color, and texture, all with accentuated, projecting beads of mortar, then there is a rather precise and narrow band of cut and dressed stones with minimal mortar joints, and finally, the main building walls are composed of bricks, rather uniform in color, with fairly generous mortar joints. It is the juxtaposition and variety of these materials (and of course, the craftsmanship) that is very important to the visual character. Changing the raised mortar joints, for example, would drastically alter the character at arm's length. Photo by Lee H. Nelson

Arm's Length Visual Character: Craft Details

There are many instances where craft details dominate the arm's length visual character. As seen here, the craft details are especially noticeable because the stones are all of a uniform color, and they are all squared off, but their surfaces were worked with differing tools and techniques to create a great variety of textures, resulting in a tour-de-force of craft details. This texture is very important at close range. It was a deliberately contrived surface that is an important contributor to the visual character of this building. Photo by Lee H. Nelson

Arm's Length Visual Character: Craft Details

The arm's length visual character of this building is a combination of the materials and the craft details. Most of the exterior walls of this building consist of early 20th century Roman brick, precisely made, unusually long bricks, in varying shades of yellow-brown, with a noticeable surface spotting of dark iron pyrites. While this brick is an important contributor to the visual character, the related craft details are perhaps more important, and they consist of: unusually precise coursing of the bricks, almost as though they were laid up using a surveyor's level; a row of recessed bricks every ninth course, creating a shadow pattern on the wall; deeply recessed mortar joints, creating a secondary pattern of shadows; and a toothed effect where the bricks overlap each other at the corner of the building. The cumulative effect of this artisanry is important to the arm's length visual character, and it is evident that it would be difficult to match if it were damaged, and the effect could be easily damaged through insensitive treatments such as painting the brickwork or by careless repointing. Photo by Lee H. Nelson

177

Arm's Length Visual Character: Craft Details

On some buildings, there are subtle aspects of visual character that cannot be perceived from a distance. This is especially true of certain craft details that can be seen only at close range. On this building, it is easily understood that the narrow, unpainted, and weathered clapboards are an important aspect of its overall visual character; but at close range there are a number of subtle but very important craft details that contribute to the handmade quality of this building, and which clearly differentiate it from a building with machine sawn clapboards. The clapboards seen here were split by hand and the bottom edges were not dressed, so that the boards vary in width and thickness, and thus they give a very uneven shadow pattern. Because they were split from oak that is unpainted, there are occasional wavy rays in the wood that stand against the grain. Also noticeable is the fact that the boards are of relatively short lengths, and that they have feather-edged ends that overlap each other, a detail that is very different from butted joints. The occasional large nail heads and the differential silver-gray weathering add to the random quality of the clapboards. All of these qualities contribute to the arm's length visual character. Photo by Lee H. Nelson

Arm's Length Visual Character: Craft Details

While hand-split clapboards are distinctive visual elements in their own way, machine-sawn and painted wood siding is equally important to the overall visual character in most other instances. At arm's length, however, the machine sawn siding may not be so distinctive; but there might be other details that add visual character to the wooden building, such as the details of wooden trim and louvered shutters around the windows (as seen here), or similar surface textures on other buildings, such as the saw marks on wall shingles, the joints in leaded glass, decorative tinwork on a rain conductor box, the rough surface of pebble-dash stuccowork, or the pebbly surface of exposed aggregate concrete. Such surfaces can only be seen at arm's length and they add to the visual character of a historic building. Photo by Hugh C. Miller

Interior Visual Character: Individually Important Spaces

In assessing the interior visual character of any historic building, it is necessary to ask whether there are spaces that are important to the character of this particular building, whether the building is architecturally rich or modest, or even if it is a simple or utilitarian structure.

The character of the individually important space which is illustrated here is a combination of its size, the twin curving staircases, the massive columns and curving vaulted ceilings, in addition to the quality of the materials in the floor and in the stairs. If the ceiling were to be lowered to provide space for heating ducts, or if the stairways were to be enclosed for code reasons, the shape and character of this space would be damaged, even if there was no permanent physical damage. Such changes can easily destroy the visual character of an individually important interior space. Thus, it is important that the visual aspects of a building's interior character be recognized before planning any changes or alterations. Photo by National Portrait Gallery

Interior Visual Character: Related Spaces

Many buildings have interior spaces that are visually or physically related so that, as you move through them, they are perceived not as separate spaces, but as a sequence of related spaces that are important in defining the interior character of the building. The example which is illustrated here consists of three spaces that are visually linked to each other.

The first of these spaces is the vestibule which is of a generous size and unusual in its own right, but more important, it visually relates to the second space which is the main stairhall.

The hallway is the circulation artery for the building, and leads both horizontally and vertically to other rooms and spaces, but especially to the open and inviting stairway.

The stairway is the third part of this sequence of related spaces, and it provides continuing access to the upper floors.

These related spaces are very important in defining the interior character of this building. Almost any change to these spaces, such as installing doors between the vestibule and the hallway, or enclosing the stair would seriously impact their character and the way that character is perceived. Top photo by Mel Chamowitz, others by John Tennant

Interior Visual Character: Interior Features

Interior features are three-dimensional building elements or architectural details that are an integral part of the building as opposed to furniture. Interior features are often important in defining the character of an individual room or space. In some instances, an interior feature, like a large and ornamental open stairway may dominate the visual character of an entire building. In other instances, a modest iron stairway (like the one illustrated here) may be an important interior feature, and its preservation would be crucial to preserving the interior character of the building. Such features can also include the obvious things like fireplace mantles, plaster ceiling medallions, or panelling, but they also extend to features like hardware, lighting fixtures, bank tellers cages, decorative elevator doors, etc. Photo by David W. Look

Interior Visual Character: Interior Features

Modern heating or cooling devices usually add little to the interior character of a building; but historically, radiators, for instance, may have contributed to the interior character by virtue of their size or shape, or because of their specially designed bases, piping, and decorative grillage or enclosures. Sometimes they were painted with several colors to highlight their integral, cast-in details. In more recent times, it has been common to overpaint and conceal such distinctive aspects of earlier heating and plumbing devices, so that we seldom have the opportunity to realize how important they can be in defining the character of interior rooms and spaces. For that reason, it is important to identify their character-defining potential, and consider their preservation, retention, or restoration. Photo by David W. Look

Interior Visual Character: Surface Materials and Finishes

When identifying the visual character of historic interior spaces one should not overlook the importance of those materials and finishes that comprise the surfaces of walls, floors and ceilings. The surfaces may have evidence of either hand-craft or machine-made products that are important contributors to the visual character, including patterned or inlaid designs in the wood flooring, decorative painting practices such as stenciling, imitation marble or wood grain, wallpapering, tinwork, tile floors, etc.

The example illustrated here involves a combination of real marble at the base of the column, imitation marble patterns on the plaster surface of the column (a practice called scagliola), and a tile floor surface that uses small mosaic tiles arranged to form geometric designs in several different colors. While such decorative materials and finishes may be important in defining the interior visual character of this particular building, it should be remembered that in much more modest buildings, the plainness of surface materials and finishes may be an essential aspect of their historic character. Photo by Lee H. Nelson

Fragility of A Building's Visual Character

Some aspects of a building's visual character are fragile and are easily lost. This is true of brickwork, for example, which can be irreversibly damaged with inappropriate cleaning techniques or by insensitive repointing practices. At least two factors are important contributors to the visual character of brickwork, namely the brick itself and the craftsmanship. Between these, there are many more aspects worth noting, such as color range of bricks, size and shape variations, texture, bonding patterns, together with the many variable qualities of the mortar joints, such as color, width of joint and tooling. These qualities could be easily damaged by painting the brick, by raking out the joint with power tools, or repointing with a joint that is too wide. As seen here during the process of repointing, the visual character of this front wall is being dramatically changed from a wall where the bricks predominate, to a wall that is visually dominated by the mortar joints. Photo by Lee H. Nelson

The Architectural Character Checklist/Questionnaire

Lee H. Nelson, FAIA
National Park Service

This checklist can be taken to the building and used to identify those aspects that give the building and setting its essential visual qualities and character. This checklist consists of a series of questions that are designed to help in identifying those things that contribute to a building's character. The use of this checklist involves the three-step process of looking for: 1) the overall visual aspects, 2) the visual character at close range, and 3) the visual character of interior spaces, features and finishes.

Because this is a process to identify *architectural character*, it does not address those intangible qualities that give a property or building or its contents its historic significance, instead this checklist is organized on the assumption that historic significance is embodied in those *tangible* aspects that include the building's setting, its form and fabric.

Step One

1. Shape

What is there about the form or shape of the building that gives the building its identity? Is the shape distinctive in relation to the neighboring buildings? Is it simply a low, squat box, or is it a tall, narrow building with a corner tower? Is the shape highly consistent with its neighbors? Is the shape so complicated because of wings, or ells, or differences in height, that its complexity is important to its character? Conversely, is the shape so simple or plain that adding a feature like a porch would change that character? Does the shape convey its historic function as in smoke stacks or silos?

Notes on the Shape or Form of the Building:

_____

_____

2. Roof and Roof Features

Does the roof shape or its steep (or shallow) slope contribute to the building's character? Does the fact that the roof is highly visible (or not visible at all) contribute to the architectural identity of the building? Are certain roof features important to the profile of the building against the sky or its background, such as cupolas, multiple chimneys, dormers, cresting, or weathervanes? Are the roofing materials or their colors or their patterns (such as patterned slates) more noticeable than the shape or slope of the roof?

Notes on the Roof and Roof Features:

_____

_____

3. Openings

Is there a rhythm or pattern to the arrangement of windows or other openings in the walls; like the rhythm of windows in a factory building, or a three-part window in the front bay of a house; or is there a noticeable relationship between the width of the window openings and the wall space between the window openings? Are there distinctive openings, like a large arched entranceway, or decorative window lintels that accentuate the importance of the window openings, or unusually shaped windows, or patterned window sash, like small panes of glass in the windows or doors, that are important to the character? Is the plainness of the window openings such that adding shutters or gingerbread trim would radically change its character? Is there a hierarchy of facades that make the front windows more important than the side windows? What about those walls where the absence of windows establishes its own character?

Notes on the Openings:

_____

_____

4. Projections

Are there parts of the building that are character-defining because they project from the walls of the building like porches, cornices, bay windows, or balconies? Are there turrets, or widely overhanging eaves, projecting pediments or chimneys?

Notes on the Projections:

_____

_____

5. Trim and Secondary Features

Does the trim around the windows or doors contribute to the character of the building? Is there other trim on the walls or around the projections that, because of its decoration or color or patterning contributes to the character of the building? Are there secondary features such as shutters, decorative gables, railings, or exterior wall panels?

Notes on the Trim and Secondary Features:

_____

_____

6. Materials

Do the materials or combination of materials contribute to the overall character of the building as seen from a distance because of their color or patterning, such as broken faced stone, scalloped wall shingling, rounded rock foundation walls, boards and battens, or textured stucco?

Notes on the Materials:

_____

_____

7. Setting

What are the aspects of the setting that are important to the visual character? For example, is the alignment of buildings along a city street and their relationship to the sidewalk the essential aspect of its setting? Or, conversely, is the essential character dependent upon the tree plantings and out buildings which surround the farmhouse? Is the front yard important to the setting of the modest house? Is the specific site important to the setting such as being on a hilltop, along a river, or, is the building placed on the site in such a way to enhance its setting? Is there a special relationship to the adjoining streets and other buildings? Is there a view? Is there fencing, planting, terracing, walkways or any other landscape aspects that contribute to the setting?

Notes on the Setting:

_____

_____

Step Two

8. Materials at Close Range

Are there one or more materials that have an inherent texture that contributes to the close range character, such as stucco, exposed aggregate concrete, or brick textured with vertical grooves? Or materials with inherent colors such as smooth orange-colored brick with dark spots of iron pyrites, or prominently veined stone, or green serpentine stone? Are there combinations of materials, used in juxtaposition, such as several different kinds of stone, combinations of stone and brick, dressed stones for window lintels used in conjunction with rough stones for the wall? Has the choice of materials or the combinations of materials contributed to the character?

Notes on the Materials at Close Range:

_____

_____

9. Craft Details

Is there high quality brickwork with narrow mortar joints? Is there hand-tooled or patterned stonework? Do the walls exhibit carefully struck vertical mortar joints and recessed horizontal joints? Is the wall shinglework laid up in patterns or does it retain evidence of the circular saw marks or can the grain of the wood be seen through the semi-transparent stain? Are there hand split or hand-dressed clapboards, or machine smooth beveled siding, or wood rusticated to look like stone, or Art Deco zigzag designs executed in stucco?

   Almost any evidence of craft details, whether handmade or machinemade, will contribute to the character of a building because it is a manifestation of the materials, of the times in which the work was done, and of the tools and processes that were used. It further reflects the effects of time, of maintenance (and/or neglect) that the building has received over the years. All of these aspects are a part of the surface qualities that are seen only at close range.

Notes on the Craft Details:

_____

_____

Step Three

10. Individual Spaces

Are there individual rooms or spaces that are important to this building because of their size, height, proportion, configuration, or function, like the center hallway in a house, or the bank lobby, or the school auditorium, or the ballroom in a hotel, or a courtroom in a county courthouse?

Notes on the Individual Spaces:

_____

_____

11. Related Spaces and Sequences of Spaces

Are there adjoining rooms that are visually and physically related with large doorways or open archways so that they are perceived as related rooms as opposed to separate rooms? Is there an important sequence of spaces that are related to each other, such as the sequence from the entry way to the lobby to the stairway and to the upper balcony as in a theatre; or the sequence in a residence from the entry vestibule to the hallway to the front parlor, and on through the sliding doors to the back parlor; or the sequence in an office building from the entry vestibule to the lobby to the bank of elevators?

Notes on the Related Spaces and Sequences of Spaces:

_____

_____

12. Interior Features

Are there interior features that help define the character of the building, such as fireplace mantels, stairways and balustrades, arched openings, interior shutters, inglenooks, cornices, ceiling medallions, light fixtures, balconies, doors, windows, hardware, wainscotting, panelling, trim, church pews, courtroom bars, teller cages, waiting room benches?

Notes on the Interior Features:

_____

_____

13. Surface Finishes and Materials

Are there surface finishes and materials that can affect the design, the color or the texture of the interior? Are there materials and finishes or craft practices that contribute to the interior character, such as wooden parquet floors, checkerboard marble floors, pressed metal ceilings, fine hardwoods, grained doors or marblized surfaces, or polychrome painted surfaces, or stencilling, or wallpaper that is important to the historic character? Are there surface finishes and materials that, because of their plainness, are imparting the essential character of the interior such as hard or bright, shiny wall surfaces of plaster or glass or metal?

Notes on the Surface Finishes and Materials:

_____

_____

14. Exposed Structure

Are there spaces where the exposed structural elements define the interior character such as the exposed posts, beams, and trusses in a church or train shed or factory? Are there rooms with decorative ceiling beams (non-structural) in bungalows, or exposed vigas in adobe buildings?

Notes on the Exposed Structure:

_____

This concludes the three-step process of identifying the visual aspects of historic buildings and is intended as an aid in preserving their character and other distinguishing qualities. It is not intended as a means of understanding the significance of historical properties or districts, nor of the events or people associated with them. That can only be done through other kinds of research and investigation.

This Preservation Brief was originally developed as a slide talk/methodology in 1982 to discuss the use of the Secretary of the Interior's Standards for Rehabilitation in relation to preserving historic character; and it was amplified and modified in succeeding years to help guide preservation decisionmaking, initially for maintenance personnel in the National Park Service. A number of people contributed to the evolution of the ideas presented here. Special thanks go to Emogene Bevitt and Gary Hume, primarily for the many and frequent discussions relating to this approach in its evolutionary stages; to Mark Fram, Ontario Heritage Foundation, Toronto, for suggesting several additions to the Checklist; and more recently, to my co-workers, both in Washington and in our regional offices, especially Ward Jandl, Sara Blumenthal, Charles Fisher, Sharon Park, AIA, Jean Travers, Camille Martone, Susan Dynes, Michael Auer, Anne Grimmer, Kay Weeks, Betsy Chittenden, Patrick Andrus, Carol Shull, Hugh Miller, FAIA, Jerry Rogers, Paul Alley, David Look, AIA, Margaret Pepin-Donat, Bonnie Halda, Keith Everett, Thomas Keohan, the Preservation Services Division, Mid-Atlantic Region, and several reviewers in state preservation offices, especially Ann Haaker, Illinois; and Stan Graves, AIA, Texas; for providing very critical and constructive review of the manuscript.

This publication has been prepared pursuant to the National Historic Preservation Act of 1966, as amended. Comments on the usefulness of this information are welcomed and can be sent to Mr. Nelson, Preservation Assistance Division, National Park Service, U.S. Department of the Interior, P.O. Box 37127, Washington, D.C. 20013-7127.

18

Rehabilitating Interiors in Historic Buildings
Identifying and Preserving Character-defining Elements

H. Ward Jandl

A floor plan, the arrangement of spaces, and features and applied finishes may be individually or collectively important in defining the historic character of the building and the purpose for which it was constructed. Thus, their identification, retention, protection, and repair should be given prime consideration in every preservation project. Caution should be exercised in developing plans that would radically change character-defining spaces or that would obscure, damage or destroy interior features or finishes.

While the exterior of a building may be its most prominent visible aspect, or its "public face," its interior can be even more important in conveying the building's history and development over time. Rehabilitation within the context of the Secretary of the Interior's Standards for Rehabilitation calls for the preservation of exterior *and* interior portions or features of the building that are significant to its historic, architectural and cultural values.

Interior components worthy of preservation may include the building's **plan** (sequence of spaces and circulation patterns), the building's **spaces** (rooms and volumes), individual architectural **features**, and the various **finishes** and **materials** that make up the walls, floors, and ceilings. A theater auditorium or sequences of rooms such as double parlors or a lobby leading to a stairway that ascends to a mezzanine may comprise a building's most important spaces. Individual rooms may contain notable features such as plaster cornices, millwork, parquet wood floors, and hardware. Paints, wall coverings, and finishing techniques such as graining, may provide color, texture, and patterns which add to a building's unique character.

Virtually all rehabilitations of historic buildings involve some degree of interior alteration, even if the buildings are to be used for their original purpose. Interior rehabilitation proposals may range from preservation of existing features and spaces to total reconfigurations. In some cases, depending on the building, restoration may be warranted to preserve historic character adequately; in other cases, extensive alterations may be perfectly acceptable.

This Preservation Brief has been developed to assist building owners and architects in identifying and evaluating those elements of a building's interior that

contribute to its historic character and in planning for the preservation of those elements in the process of *rehabilitation*. The guidance applies to all building types and styles, from 18th century churches to 20th century office buildings. The Brief does not attempt to provide specific advice on preservation techniques and treatments, given the vast range of buildings, but rather suggests general preservation approaches to guide construction work.

Identifying and Evaluating the Importance of Interior Elements Prior to Rehabilitation

Before determining what uses might be appropriate and before drawing up plans, a thorough professional assessment should be undertaken to identify those tangible architectural components that, prior to rehabilitation, convey the building's sense of time and place—that is , its "historic character." Such an assessment, accomplished by walking through and taking account of each element that makes up the interior, can help ensure that a truly compatible use for the building, one that requires minimal alteration to the building, is selected.

Researching The Building's History

A review of the building's history will reveal why and when the building achieved significance or how it contributes to the significance of the district. This information helps to evaluate whether a particular rehabilitation treatment will be appropriate to the building and whether it will preserve those tangible components of the building that convey its significance for association with specific events or persons along with its architectural importance. In this regard, National Register files may prove useful in explaining why and for what period of time the

183

building is significant. In some cases research may show that later alterations are significant to the building; in other cases, the alterations may be without historical or architectural merit, and may be removed in the rehabilitation.

Identifying Interior Elements

Interiors of buildings can be seen as a series of primary and secondary spaces. The goal of the assessment is to identify which elements contribute to the building's character and which do not. Sometimes it will be the sequence and flow of spaces, and not just the individual rooms themselves, that contribute to the building's character. This is particularly evident in buildings that have strong central axes or those that are consciously asymmetrical in design. In other cases, it may be the size or shape of the space that is distinctive. The importance of some interiors may not be readily apparent based on a visual inspection; sometimes rooms that do not appear to be architecturally distinguished are associated with important persons and events that occurred within the building.

Primary spaces, are found in all buildings, both monumental and modest. Examples may include foyers, corridors, elevator lobbies, assembly rooms, stairhalls, and parlors. Often they are the places in the building that the public uses and sees; sometimes they are the most architecturally detailed spaces in the building, carefully proportioned and finished with costly materials. They may be functionally and architecturally related to the building's external appearance. In a simpler building, a primary space may be distinguishable only by its location, size, proportions, or use. Primary spaces are always important to the character of the building and should be preserved.

Secondary spaces are generally more utilitarian in appearance and size than primary spaces. They may include areas and rooms that service the building, such as bathrooms, and kitchens. Examples of secondary spaces in a commercial or office structure may include storerooms, service corridors, and in some cases, the offices themselves. Secondary spaces tend to be of less importance to the building and may accept greater change in the course of work without compromising the building's historic character.

Spaces are often designed to interrelate both visually and functionally. The **sequence of spaces**, such as vestibule-hall-parlor or foyer-lobby-stair-auditorium or stairhall-corridor-classroom, can define and express the building's historic function and unique character. Important sequences of spaces should be identified and retained in the rehabilitation project.

Floor plans may also be distinctive and characteristic of a style of architecture or a region. Examples include Greek Revival and shotgun houses. Floor plans may also reflect social, educational, and medical theories of the period. Many 19th century psychiatric institutions, for example, had plans based on the ideas of Thomas Kirkbride, a Philadelphia doctor who authored a book on asylum design.

In addition to evaluating the relative importance of the various spaces, the assessment should identify architectural **features** and **finishes** that are part of the

Figure 1. This architect-designed interior reflects early 20th century American taste: the checkerboard tile floor, wood wainscot, coffered ceiling, and open staircase are richly detailed and crafted by hand. Not only are the individual architectural features worthy of preservation, but the planned sequence of spaces—entry hall, stairs, stair landings, and loggia—imparts a grandeur that is characteristic of high style residences of this period. This interior is of Greystone, Los Angeles, California. Photography for HABS by Jack E. Boucher

Figure 2. The interiors of mills and industrial buildings frequently are open, unadorned spaces with exposed structural elements. While the new uses to which this space could be put are many—retail, residential, or office—the generous floor-to-ceiling height and exposed truss system are important character-defining features and should be retained in the process of rehabilitation.

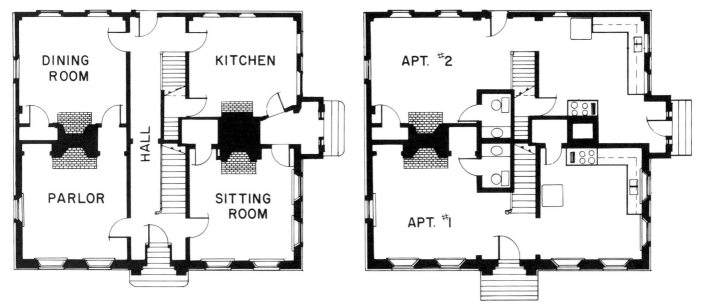

Figure 3. The floor plan at left is characteristic of many 19th century Greek Revival houses, with large rooms flanking a central hall. In the process of rehabilitation, the plan (at right) was drastically altered to accommodate two duplex apartments. The open stair was replaced with one that is enclosed, two fireplaces were eliminated, and Greek Revival trim around windows and doors was removed. The symmetry of the rooms themselves was destroyed with the insertion of bathrooms and kitchens. Few vestiges of the 19th century interior survived the rehabilitation. Drawing by Neal A. Vogel

Figure 4. Many institutional buildings possess distinctive spaces or floor plans that are important in conveying the significance of the property. Finding new compatible uses for these buildings and preserving the buildings' historic character can be a difficult, if not impossible, task. One such case is Mechanics Hall in Worcester, Massachusetts, constructed between 1855 and 1857. This grand hall, which occupies the entire third floor of the building, could not be subdivided without destroying the integrity of the space.

Figure 5. The interior of a simply detailed worker's house of the 19th century may be as important historically as the richly ornamented interior seen in figure 1. Although the interior of this house has not been properly maintained, the wide baseboards, flat window trim, and four-panel door are characteristic of workers' housing during this period and deserve retention during rehabilitation.

interior's history and character. Marble or wood wainscoting in corridors, elevator cabs, crown molding, baseboards, mantels, ceiling medallions, window and door trim, tile and parquet floors, and staircases are among those features that can be found in historic buildings. Architectural finishes of note may include grained woodwork, marbleized columns, and plastered walls. Those features that are characteristic of the building's style and period of construction should, again, be retained in the rehabilitation.

Features and finishes, even if machine-made and *not* exhibiting particularly fine craftsmanship, may be character-defining; these would include pressed metal ceilings and millwork around windows and doors. The interior of a plain, simple detailed worker's house of the 19th century may be as important historically as a richly ornamented, high-style townhouse of the same period. Both resources, if equally intact, convey important information about the early inhabitants and deserve the same careful attention to detail in the preservation process.

The location and condition of the building's existing heating, plumbing, and electrical systems also need to be noted in the assessment. The visible features of historic systems—radiators, grilles, light fixtures, switchplates, bathtubs, etc.—can contribute to the overall character of the building, even if the systems themselves need upgrading.

Assessing Alterations and Deterioration

In assesesessing a building's interior, it is important to ascertain the extent of alteration and deterioration that may have taken place over the years; these factors help determine what degree of change is appropriate in the project. Close examination of existing fabric and original floorplans, where available, can reveal which alterations have been **additive**, such as new partitions inserted for functional or structural reasons and historic features covered up rather than destroyed. It can also reveal which have been **subtractive**, such as key walls removed and architectural features destroyed. If an interior has been modified by additive changes and if these changes have not acquired significance, it may be relatively easy to remove the alterations and return the interior to its historic appearance. If an interior has been greatly altered through subtractive changes, there may be more latitude in making further alterations in the process of rehabilitation because the integrity of the interior has been compromised. At the same time, if the interior had been exceptionally significant, and solid documentation on its historic condition is available, reconstruction of the missing features may be the preferred option.

It is always a recommended practice to photograph interior spaces and features thoroughly prior to rehabilitation. Measured floor plans showing the existing conditions are extremely useful. This documentation is invaluable in drawing up rehabilitation plans and specifications and in assessing the impact of changes to the property for historic preservation certification purposes.

Drawing Up Plans and Executing Work

If the historic building is to be rehabilitated, it is critical that the new use not require substantial alteration of distinctive spaces or removal of character-defining architectural features or finishes. If an interior loses the physical vestiges of its past as well as its historic function, the sense of time and place associated both with the building and the district in which it is located is lost.

The recommended approaches that follow address common problems associated with the rehabilitation of historic interiors and have been adapted from the Secretary of the Interior's Standards for Rehabilitation and Guidelines for Rehabilitating Historic Buildings. Adherence to these suggestions can help ensure that character-defining interior elements are preserved in the process of rehabilitation. The checklist covers a range of situations and is not intended to be all-inclusive. Readers are strongly encouraged to review the full set of guidelines before undertaking *any* rehabilitation project.

Figure 6. This corridor, located in the historic Monadnock Building in Chicago, has glazed walls, oak trim, and marble wainscotting, and is typical of those found in late 19th and early 20th century office buildings. Despite the simplicity of the features, a careful attention to detail can be noted in the patterned tile floor, bronze mail chute, and door hardware. The retention of corridors like this one should be a priority in rehabilitation projects involving commercial buildings.

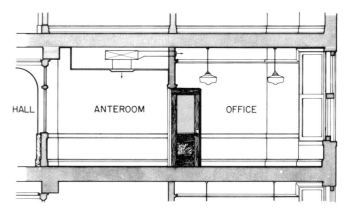

Figure 7. When the Monadnock Building was rehabilitated, architects retained the basic floor plan on the upper floors consisting of a double-loaded corridor with offices opening onto it. The original floor-to-ceiling height in the corridors and outside offices—the most important spaces—was maintained by installing needed air conditioning ductwork in the less important anterooms. In this way, the most significant interior spaces were preserved intact. Drawing by Neal A. Vogel

Recommended Approaches for Rehabilitating Historic Interiors

1. Retain and preserve floor plans and interior spaces that are important in defining the overall historic character of the building. This includes the size, configuration, proportion, and relationship of rooms and corridors; the relationship of features to spaces; and the spaces themselves such as lobbies, reception halls, entrance halls, double parlors, theaters, auditoriums, and important industrial or commercial use spaces. Put service functions required by the building's new use, such as bathrooms, mechanical equipment, and office machines, in secondary spaces.

2. Avoid subdividing spaces that are characteristic of a building type or style or that are directly associated with specific persons or patterns of events. Space may be subdivided both vertically through the insertion of new partitions or horizontally through insertion of new floors or mezzanines. The insertion of new additional floors should be considered only when they will not damage or destroy the structural system or obscure, damage, or destroy character-defining spaces, features, or finishes. If rooms have already been subdivided through an earlier insensitive renovation, consider removing the partitions and restoring the room to its original proportions and size.

3. Avoid making new cuts in floors and ceilings where such cuts would change character-defining spaces and the historic configuration of such spaces. Inserting of a new atrium or a lightwell is appropriate only in very limited situations where the existing interiors are not historically or architecturally distinguished.

4. Avoid installing dropped ceilings below ornamental ceilings or in rooms where high ceilings are part of the building's character. In addition to obscuring or destroying significant details, such treatments will also change the space's proportions. If dropped ceilings are installed in buildings that lack character-defining spaces, such as mills and factories, they should be well set back from the windows so they are not visible from the exterior.

5. Retain and preserve interior features and finishes that are important in defining the overall historic character of the building. This might include columns, doors, cornices, baseboards, fireplaces and mantels, paneling, light fixtures, elevator cabs, hardware, and flooring; and wallpaper, plaster, paint, and finishes such as stenciling, marbleizing, and graining; and other decorative materials that accent interior features and provide color, texture, and patterning to walls, floors, and ceilings.

6. Retain stairs in their historic configuration and location. If a second means of egress is required, consider constructing new stairs in secondary spaces. (For guidance on designing compatible new additions, see Preservation Brief 14, "New Exterior Additions to Historic Buildings.") The application of fire-retardant coatings, such as intumescent paints; the installation of fire suppression systems, such as sprinklers; and the construction of glass enclosures can in many cases permit retention of stairs and other character-defining features.

7. Retain and preserve visible features of early mechanical systems that are important in defining the overall historic character of the building, such as radiators, vents, fans, grilles, plumbing fixtures, switchplates, and lights. If new heating, air conditioning, lighting and plumbing systems are installed, they should be done in a way that does not destroy character-defining spaces, features and finishes. Ducts, pipes, and wiring should be installed as inconspicuously as possible: in secondary spaces, in the attic or basement if possible, or in closets.

8. Avoid "furring out" perimeter walls for insulation purposes. This requires unnecessary removal of window trim and can change a room's proportions. Consider alternative means of improving thermal performance, such as installing insulation in attics and basements and adding storm windows.

9. Avoid removing paint and plaster from traditionally finished surfaces, to expose masonry and wood. Conversely, avoid painting previously unpainted millwork. Repairing deteriorated plasterwork is encouraged. If the plaster is too deteriorated to save, and the walls and ceilings are not highly ornamented, gypsum board may be an acceptable replacement material. The use of paint colors appropriate to the period of the building's construction is encouraged.

10. Avoid using destructive methods—propane and butane torches or sandblasting—to remove paint or other coatings from historic features. Avoid harsh cleaning agents that can change the appearance of wood. (For more information regarding appropriate cleaning methods, consult Preservation Brief 6, "Dangers of Abrasive Cleaning to Historic Buildings.")

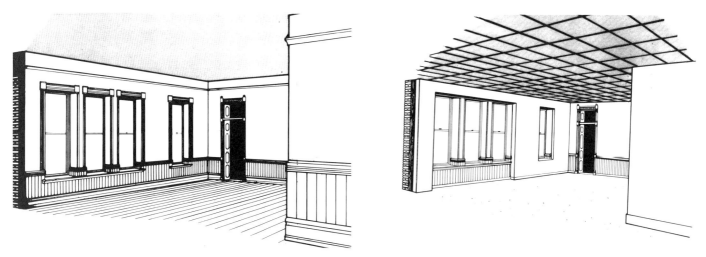

Figure 8. Furring out exterior walls to add insulation and suspending new ceilings to hide ductwork and wiring can change a room's proportions and can cause interior features to appear fragmented. In this case, a school was converted into apartments, and individual classrooms became living rooms, bedrooms, and kitchens. On the left is an illustration of a classroom prior to rehabilitation; note the generous floor-to-ceiling height, wood wainscotting, molded baseboard, picture molding, and Eastlake Style door and window trim. After rehabilitation, on the right, only fragments of the historic detailing survive: the ceiling has been dropped below the picture molding, the remaining wainscotting appears to be randomly placed, and some of the window trim has been obscured. Together with the subdivision of the classrooms, these rehabilitation treatments prevent a clear understanding of the original classroom's design and space. If thermal performance must be improved, alternatives to furring out walls and suspending new ceilings, such as installing insulation in attics and basements, should be considered. Drawings by Neal A. Vogel

Figure 9. The tangible reminders of early mechanical systems can be worth saving. In this example, in the Old Post Office in Washington, D.C., radiators encircle Corinthian columns in a decorative manner. Note, too, the period light fixtures. These features were retained when the building was rehabilitated as retail and office space. Photo: Historic American Buildings Survey

Figure 10. In this case plaster has been removed from perimeter walls, leaving brick exposed. In removing finishes from historic masonry walls, not only is there a loss of historic finish, but raw, unfinished walls are exposed, giving the interior an appearance it never had. Here, the exposed brick is of poor quality and the mortar joints are wide and badly struck. Plaster should have been retained and repaired, as necessary.

Figure 11. These dramatic ''before'' and ''after'' photographs show a severely deteriorated space restored to its original elegance: plaster has been repaired and painted, the scagliola columns have been restored to match marble using traditional craft techniques, and missing decorative metalwork has been re-installed in front of the windows. Although some reorganization of the space took place, notably the relocation of the front desk, the overall historic character of the space has been preserved. These views are of the lobby in the Willard Hotel, Washington, D.C. Credit: Commercial Photographers (left); Carol M. Highsmith (right)

Meeting Building, Life Safety and Fire Codes

Buildings undergoing rehabilitation must comply with existing building, life safety and fire codes. The application of codes to specific projects varies from building to building, and town to town. Code requirements may make some reuse proposals impractical; in other cases, only minor changes may be needed to bring the project into compliance. In some situations, it may be possible to obtain a code variance to preserve distinctive interior features. (It should be noted that the Secretary's Standards for Rehabilitation take precedence over other regulations and codes in determining whether a rehabilitation project qualifies for Federal tax benefits.) A thorough understanding of the applicable regulations and close coordination with code officials, building inspectors, and fire marshals can prevent the alteration of significant historic interiors.

Sources of Assistance

Rehabilitation and restoration work should be undertaken by professionals who have an established reputation in the field.

Given the wide range of interior work items, from ornamental plaster repair to marble cleaning and the application of graining, it is possible that a number of specialists and subcontractors will need to be brought in to bring the project to completion. State Historic Preservation Officers and local preservation organizations may be a useful source of information in this regard. Good sources of information on appropriate preservation techniques for specific interior features and finishes include the *Bulletin* of the Association for Preservation Technology and *The Old-House Journal*; other useful publications are listed in the bibliography.

Protecting Interior Elements During Rehabilitation

Architectural features and finishes to be preserved in the process of rehabilitation should be clearly marked on plans *and at the site*. This step, along with careful supervision of the interior demolition work and protection against arson and vandalism, can prevent the unintended destruction of architectural elements that contribute to the building's historic character.

Protective coverings should be installed around architectural features and finishes to avoid damage in the course of construction work and to protect workers. Staircases and floors, in particular, are subjected to dirt and heavy wear, and the risk exists of incurring costly or irreparable damage. In most cases, the best, and least costly, preservation approach is to design and construct a protective system that enables stairs and floors to be used yet protects them from damage. Other architectural features such as mantels, doors, wainscotting, and decorative finishes may be protected by using heavy canvas or plastic sheets.

Summary

In many cases, the interior of a historic building is as important as its exterior. The careful identification and evaluation of interior architectural elements, after undertaking research on the building's history and use, is critically important *before* changes to the building are contemplated. Only *after* this evaluation should new uses be decided and plans be drawn up. The best rehabilitation is one that preserves and protects those rooms, sequences of spaces, features and finishes that define and shape the overall historic character of the building.

This Preservation Brief is based on a discussion paper prepared by the author for a National Park Service regional workshop held in March, 1987, and on a paper written by Gary Hume, "Interior Spaces in Historic Buildings," October, 1987. Appreciation is extended to the staff of Technical Preservation Services Branch and to the staff of NPS regional offices who reviewed the manuscript and provided many useful suggestions. Special thanks are given to Neal A. Vogel, a summer intern with the NPS, for many of the illustrations in this Brief.

This publication has been prepared pursuant to the National Historic Preservation Act of 1966, as amended. Preservation Briefs 18 was developed under the editorship of Lee H. Nelson, FAIA, Chief, Preservation Assistance Division, National Park Service, U.S. Department of the Interior, P.O. Box 37127, Washington, D.C. 20013-7127. Comments on the usefulness of this information are welcomed and may be sent to Mr. Nelson at the above address.

Selected Reading List

There are few books written exclusively on preserving historic interiors, and most of these tend to focus on residential interiors. Articles on the subject appear regularly in *The Old-House Journal*, the *Bulletin of the Association for Preservation Technology*, and *Historic Preservation Magazine*.

Ferro, Maximilian L., and Melissa L. Cook. *Electric Wiring and Lighting in Historic American Buildings.* New Bedford, Massachusetts: AFC/A Nortek Company, 1984.

Fisher, Charles E. *Temporary Protection of Historic Stairways During Rehabilitation Work.* Preservation Tech Note. Washington, D.C.: Preservation Assistance Division, National Park Service, U.S. Department of the Interior, 1985.

Jennings, Jan, and Herbert Gottfried. *American Vernacular Interior Architecture 1870-1940.* New York: Van Nostrand Reinhold Company, 1988.

Johnson, Ed. *Old House Woodwork Restoration: How to Restore Doors, Windows, Walls, Stairs and Decorative Trim to Their Original Beauty.* Englewood Cliffs, New Jersey: Prentice-Hall, Inc., 1983.

Labine, Clem, and Carolyn Flaherty (editors). *The Old-House Journal Compendium.* Woodstock, New York: The Overlook Press, 1980.

The Secretary of the Interior's Standards for Rehabilitation and Guidelines for Rehabilitating Historic Buildings. Washington, D.C.: Preservation Assistance Division, National Park Service, U.S. Department of the Interior, rev. 1983.

U.S. Department of Housing and Urban Development. *Rehabilitation Guidelines*, volumes 1-11. Washington, D.C.: U.S. Department of Housing and Urban Development, 1980-84.

Winkler, Gail Caskey, and Roger W. Moss. *Victorian Interior Decoration: American Interiors 1830-1900.* New York: Henry Holt and Company, 1986.

October 1988

Cover: Detail of carving on interior shutter. Hammond-Harwood House, Annapolis, Maryland.

19

The Repair and Replacement of Historic Wooden Shingle Roofs

Sharon C. Park, AIA

U.S. Department of the Interior, National Park Service
Preservation Assistance Division, Technical Preservation Services

The Secretary of the Interior's "Standards for Rehabilitation" call for the repair or replacement of missing architectural features "based on accurate duplication of features, substantiated by historic, physical, or pictorial evidence rather than on conjectural designs." On a wooden shingle roof, it is important not only to match the size, shape, texture, and configuration of historic shingles, but also to match the craftsmanship and details that characterize the historic roof. Proper installation and maintenance will extend the life of the new roof.

Introduction

Wooden shingle roofs are important elements of many historic buildings. The special visual qualities imparted by both the *historic shingles* and the *installation patterns* should be preserved when a wooden shingle roof is replaced. This requires an understanding of the size, shape, and detailing of the historic shingle and the method of fabrication and installation. These combined to create roofs expressive of particular architectural styles, which were often influenced by regional craft practices. The use of wooden shingles from the early settlement days to the present illustrates an extraordinary range of styles (see illus. 1, 2, 3, 4).

Wooden shingle roofs need periodic replacement. They can last from 15 to over 60 years, but the shingles should be replaced before there is deterioration of other wooden components of the building. Appropriate replacement shingles are available, but careful research, design, specifications, and the selection of a skilled roofer are necessary to assure a job that will both preserve the appearance of the historic building and extend the useful life of the replacement roof.

Unfortunately, the wrong shingles are often selected or are installed in a manner incompatible with the appearance of the historic roof. There are a number of reasons why the wrong shingles are selected for replacement roofs. They include the failure to identify the appearance of the original shingles; unfamiliarity with available products; an inadequate budget; or a *confusion in terminology*. In any discussion about historic roofing materials and practices, it is important to understand the historic definitions of terms like "shingles," as well as the modern definitions or use of those terms by craftsmen and the industry. Historically, from the first buildings in America, these wooden roofing products were called *shingles,* regardless of whether they were the earliest handsplit or the later machine-sawn type. The term *shake* is a relatively recent one, and today is used by the industry to distinguish the sawn products from the split products, but through most of our building history there has been no such distinction.

Considering the confusion among architects and others regarding these terms as they relate to the appearance of early roofs, it should be stated that there is a considerable body of documentary information about historic roofing practices and materials in this country, and that many actual specimens of historic shingles from various periods and places have been collected and preserved so that their historic appearances are well established. Essentially, the rustic looking shake that we see used so much today has little in common with the shingles that were used on most of our early buildings in America.

Throughout this **Brief,** the term *shingle* will be used to refer to historic wooden roofs in general, whether split or sawn, and the term *shake* will be used only when it refers to a commercially available product. The variety and complexity of terminology used for currently available products will be seen in the accompanying chart entitled "Shingles and Shakes."

This **Brief** discusses what to look for in historic wooden shingle roofs and when to replace them. It discusses ways to select or modify modern products to duplicate the appearance of a historic roof, offers guidance on proper installation, and provides information on coatings and maintenance procedures to help preserve the new roof.*

(***Preservation Brief 4: Roofing for Historic Buildings** discusses research methods, analysis of deterioration, and the general significance of historic roofs.)

Wooden Shingle Roofs in America

Because trees were plentiful from the earliest settlement days, the use of wood for all aspects of construction is not surprising. Wooden shingles were lightweight, made with simple tools, and easily installed. Wooden shingle roofs were prevalent in the Colonies, while in Europe at the same time, thatch, slate and tile were the prevalent roofing materials. Distinctive roofing patterns exist in various regions of the country that were settled by the English, Dutch, Germans, and Scandinavians. These patterns and features include the size, shape and exposure length of shingles, special treatments such as swept valleys, combed ridges, and decorative butt end or long side-lapped beveled handsplit shingles. Such features impart a special character to each building, and prior to any restoration or rehabilitation project the physical and photographic evidence should be carefully researched in order to document the historic building as much as possible. Care should be taken not to assume that aged or deteriorated shingles in photographs represent the historic appearance.

Shingle Fabrication. Historically wooden shingles were usually thin (3/8″–3/4″), relatively narrow (3″–8″), of varying length (14″–36″), and almost always smooth. The traditional method for making wooden shingles in the 17th and 18th centuries was to handsplit them from log sections known as bolts (see illus. 5A). These bolts were quartered or split into wedges. A mallet and froe (or ax) were used to split or rive out thin planks of wood along the grain. If a tapered shingle was desired, the bolt was flipped after each successive strike with the froe and mallet. The wood species varied according to available local woods, but only the heartwood, or inner section, of the log was usually used. The softer sapwood generally was not used because it deteriorated quickly. Because handsplit shingles were somewhat irregular along the split surface, it was necessary

1. *The Rolfe-Warren House, a tidewater Virginia property, was restored to its 18th-century appearance in 1933. The handsplit and dressed wooden shingles are typical of the tidewater area with special features such as curved butts, projecting ridge comb and closed swept valleys at the dormer roof connections. Circa 1970 Photo: Association for the Preservation of Virginia Antiquities.*

2. *Handsplit and dressed shingles were also used on less elaborate buildings as seen in the restoration of the circa 1840 kitchen at the Winedale Inn, Texas. The uneven surfaces of the handsplit shingles were generally dressed or smoothed with a draw-knife to keep the rainwater from collecting in the wood grain and to ensure that the shingles lay flat on the sub-roof. Photo: Thomas Taylor.*

3. *Readily available and inexpensive sawn shingles were used not only for roofs, but also for gables and wall surfaces. The circa 1891 Chambers House, Eugene, Oregon used straight sawn butts for the majority of the roof and hexagonal butts for the lower portion of the corner tower. Decorative shingles in the gable ends and an attractive wooden roof cresting feature were also used. Photo: Lane County Historical Society.*

4. *With the popularity of the revival of historic styles in the late 19th and early 20th centuries, a new technique was developed to imitate English thatch roofs. For the Tudor Revival thatch cottages, steaming and curving of sawn shingles provided an undulating pattern to this picturesque roof shape. Photo: Courtesy of C.H. Roofing.*

to dress or plane the shingles on a shavinghorse with a draw-knife or draw-shave (see illus. 5B) to make them fit evenly on the roof. This reworking was necessary to provide a tight-fitting roof over typically open shingle lath or sheathing boards. Dressing, or smoothing of shingles, was almost universal, no matter what wood was used or in what part of the country the building was located, except in those cases where a temporary or very utilitarian roof was needed.

Shingle fabrication was revolutionized in the early 19th century by steam-powered saw mills (see illus. 6). Shingle mills made possible the production of uniform shingles in mass quantities. The sawn shingle of uniform taper and smooth surface eliminated the need to hand dress. The supply of wooden shingles was therefore no longer limited by local factors. These changes coincided with (and in turn increased) the popularity of architectural styles such as Carpenter Gothic and Queen Anne that used shingles to great effect.

Handsplit shingles continued to be used in many places well after the introduction of machine sawn shingles. There were, of course, other popular roofing materials, and some regions rich in slate had fewer examples of wooden shingle roofs. Some western

5. Custom Handsplit shingles are still made the traditional way with a mallet and froe or ax. For these cypress shingles, a "bolt" section of log (photo A) the length of the shingle has been sawn and is ready to be split into wedge-shaped segments. Handsplit shingles are fabricated with the ax or froe cutting the wood along the grain and separating, or riving, the shingle away from the remaining wedge. The rough surfaces are dressed on a shavinghorse using a draw-knife as shown above (photo B). Note the long wooden shingles covering the work shed in photo A. Photos: Al Honeycutt, North Carolina Division of Archives and History.

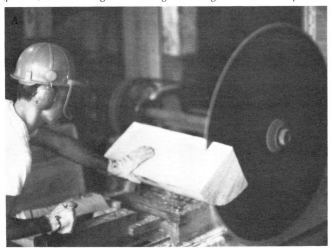

6. Modern machine-made shingles are sawn. Shown are: (photo A) Eastern White Pine quarter split shingle block on equalizer saw being trimmed to parallel the ends; and (photo B) the restored 19th-century shingle mill saw cutting tapered flitches or shingles. The thickness and taper can be precisely controlled. Photo: Steve Ruscio, The Shingle Mill.

"boom" towns used sheet metal because it was light and easily shipped. Slate, terneplate, and clay tile were used on ornate buildings and in cities that limited the use of flammable wooden shingles. Wooden shingles, however, were never abandoned. Even in the 20th century, architectural styles such as the Colonial Revival and Tudor Revival, used wooden shingles.

Modern wooden shingles, both sawn and split, continue to be made, but it is important to understand how these new products differ from the historic ones and to know how they can be modified for use on historic buildings. Modern commercially available shakes are generally thicker than the historic handsplit counterpart and are usually left "undressed" with a rough, corrugated surface. The rough surface shake, furthermore, is often promoted as suitable for historic preservation projects because of its rustic appearance. It is an erroneous assumption that the more irregular the shingle, the more authentic or "historic" it will appear.

Historic Detailing and Installation Techniques. While the size, shape and finish of the shingle determine the roof's texture and scale, the installation patterns and details give the roof its unique character. Many details reflect the craft practices of the builders and the architectural style prevalent at the time of construction. Other details had specific purposes for reducing moisture penetration to the structure. In addition to the most visible aspects of a shingle roof, the details at the rake boards, eaves, ridges, hips, dormers, cupolas, gables, and chimneys should not be overlooked.

The way the shingles were laid was often based on functional and practical needs. Because a roof is the most vulnerable element of a building, many of the roofing details that have become distinctive features were first developed simply to keep water out. Roof combs on the windward side of a roof protect the ridge line. Wedges, or cant strips, at dormer cheeks roll the water away from the vertical wall. Swept valleys and fanned hips keep the grain of the wood in the shingle parallel to the angle of the building joint to aid water

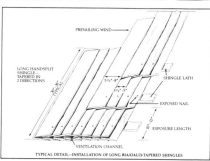

8. The long biaxially tapered handsplit shingles on the Ephrata Cloisters in Pennsylvania were overlapped both vertically and horizontally. The insert sketch shows channels under the shingles that provided ventilation and drainage of any trapped moisture. The aged appearance of these handsplit and dressed shingles belies their original smoothness. Replacement shingles should match the original, not the aged appearance. Photo: National Park Service; Sketch: Reed Engle.

7. The reshingling of the circa 1856 Stovewood House in Decorah, Iowa, revealed the original open sheathing boards and pole rafters. Sawn cedar shingles were used as a replacement for the historic cedar shingles seen still in place at the ridge. A new starter course is being laid at the eaves. Photo: Norwegian-American Museum, Decorah, Iowa.

9. This 1927 view of the reshingling of the French Castle at Old Fort Niagara, N.Y., shows the wooden sleepers being laid (see arrow) over solid sheathing in order to raise the shingles up slightly to allow under-shingle ventilation. Note that the horizontal strips are not continuous to allow airflow and trapped moisture to drain away. This cedar roof has lasted for over 60 years in a harsh moist environment. Photo: Old Fort Niagara, Assoc. Inc.

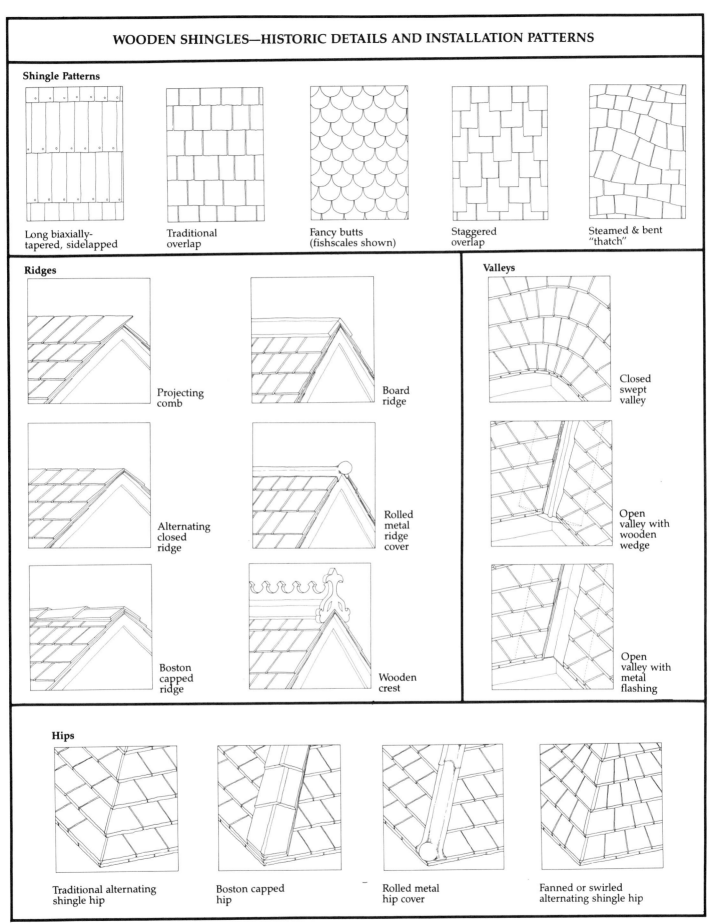

WOODEN SHINGLES—HISTORIC DETAILS AND INSTALLATION PATTERNS

Shingle Patterns

Long biaxially-tapered, sidelapped

Traditional overlap

Fancy butts (fishscales shown)

Staggered overlap

Steamed & bent "thatch"

Ridges

Projecting comb

Board ridge

Alternating closed ridge

Rolled metal ridge cover

Boston capped ridge

Wooden crest

Valleys

Closed swept valley

Open valley with wooden wedge

Open valley with metal flashing

Hips

Traditional alternating shingle hip

Boston capped hip

Rolled metal hip cover

Fanned or swirled alternating shingle hip

10. *The Historic Details and Installation Patterns Chart illustrates a number of special features found on wooden roofs. Documented examples of these features, different for every building and often reflecting regional variations, should be accurately reproduced when a replacement roof is installed. Chart: Sharon C. Park; delineation by Kaye Ellen Simonson.*

run-off. The slight projection of the shingles at the eaves directs the water run-off either into a gutter or off the roof away from the exterior wall. These details varied from region to region and from style to style. They can be duplicated even with the added protection of modern flashing.

In order to have a weathertight roof, it was important to have adequate coverage, proper spacing of shingles, and straight grain shingles. Many roofs were laid on open shingle lath or open sheathing boards (see illus. 7). Roofers typically laid three layers of shingles with approximately 1/3 of each shingle exposed to the weather. Spaces between shingles (1/8"–1/2" depending on wood type) allowed the shingles to expand when wet. It was important to stagger each overlapping shingle by a minimum of 1-1/2" to avoid a direct path for moisture to penetrate a joint. Doubling or tripling the starter course at the eave gave added protection to this exposed surface. In order for the roof to lay as flat as possible, the thickness, taper and surface of the shingles was relatively uniform; any unevenness on handsplit shingles had already been smoothed away with a drawknife. To keep shingles from curling or cupping, the shingle width was generally limited to less than 10".

Not all shingles were laid in evenly spaced, overlapping, horizontal rows. In various regions of the country, there were distinct installation patterns; for example, the biaxially-tapered long shingles occasionally found in areas settled by the Germans (see illus. 8). These long shingles were overlapped on the side as well as on top. This formed a ventilation channel under the shingles that aided drying. Because ventilation of the shingles can prolong their life, roofers paid attention to these details (see illus. 9).

Early roofers believed that applied coatings would protect the wood and prolong the life of the roof. In many cases they did; but in many cases, the shingles were left to weather naturally and they, too, had a long life. Eighteenth-century coatings included a pine pitch coating not unlike turpentine, and boiled linseed oil or fish oil mixed with oxides, red lead, brick dust, or other minerals to produce colors such as yellow, Venetian red, Spanish brown, and slate grey. In the 19th century, in addition to the earlier colors, shingles were stained or painted to complement the building colors: Indian red, chocolate brown, or brown-green. During the Greek Revival and later in the 20th century with other revival styles, green was also used. Untreated shingles age to a silver-grey or soft brown depending on the wood species.

The craft traditions of the builders often played an important role in the final appearance of the building. The Historic Details and Installation Patterns Chart (see illus. 10) identifies many of the features found on historic wooden roofs. These elements, different on each building, should be preserved in a re-roofing project.

Replacing Deteriorated Roofs: Matching the Historic Appearance

Historic wooden roofs using straight edgegrain heartwood shingles have been known to last over sixty years. Fifteen to thirty years, however, is a more realistic lifespan for most premium modern wooden shingle roofs. Contributing factors to deterioration include the

11. The replacement sawn red cedar shingles matched the deteriorated shingles exactly for this barn re-roofing. The old shingles, seen to the far left, were removed as the new shingles were installed. Even the horizontal coursing matched because the exposure length for both old and new shingles was the same. Photo: Williamsport Preservation Training Center.

thinness of the shingle, the durability of the wood species used, the exposure to the sun, the slope of the roof, the presence of lichens or moss growing on the shingle, poor ventilation levels under the shingle or in the roof, the presence of overhanging tree limbs, pollutants in the air, the original installation method, and the history of the roof maintenance. Erosion of the softer wood within the growth rings is caused by rainwater, wind, grit, fungus and the breakdown of cells by ultraviolet rays in sunlight. If the shingles cannot adequately dry between rains, if moss and lichens are allowed to grow, or if debris is not removed from the roof, moisture will be held in the wood and accelerate deterioration. Moisture trapped under the shingle, condensation, or poorly ventilated attics will also accelerate deterioration.

In addition to the eventual deterioration of wooden shingles, impact from falling branches and workmen walking on the roof can cause localized damage. If, however, over 20% of the shingles on any one surface appear eroded, cracked, cupped or split, or if there is evidence of pervasive moisture damage in the attic, replacement should be considered. If only a few shingles are missing or damaged, selective replacement may be possible. For limited replacement, the old shingle is removed and a new shingle can be inserted and held in place with a thin metal tab, or "babbie." This reduces disturbance to the sound shingles above. In instances where a few shingles have been cracked or the joint of overlapping shingles is aligned and thus forms a passage for water penetration, a metal flashing piece slipped under the shingle can stop moisture temporarily. If moisture is getting into the attic, repairs must be made quickly to prevent deterioration of the roof structural framing members.

When damage is extensive, replacement of the shingles will be necessary, but the historic sheathing or shingle lath under the shingles may be in satisfactory condition. Often, the historic sheathing or shingle laths, by their size, placement, location of early nail holes, and water stain marks, can give important infor-

12. *Inappropriately selected and installed wooden shingles can drastically alter the historic character of a building. This tavern historically was roofed with handsplit and dressed shingles of a relatively smooth appearance. In this case, a commercially available shake was used to effect a "rustic" appearance. Photo: National Park Service.*

mation regarding the early shingles used. Before specifying a replacement roof, it is important to *establish the original shingle material, configuration, detailing and installation* (see illus. 11). If the historic shingles are still in place, it is best to remove several to determine the size, shape, exposure length, and special features from the unweathered portions. If there are already replacement shingles on the roof, it may be necessary to verify through photographic or other research whether the shingles currently on the roof were an accurate replacement of the historic shingles.

The following information is needed in order to develop accurate specifications for a replacement shingle:

Original wood type (White Oak, Cypress, Eastern White Pine, Western, Red Cedar, etc.)
Size of shingle (length, width, butt thickness, taper)
Exposure length and nailing pattern (amount of exposure, placement and type of nails)
Type of fabrication (sawn, handsplit, dressed, beveled, etc.)
Distinctive details (hips, ridges, valleys, dormers, etc.)
Decorative elements (trimmed butts, variety of pattern, applied color coatings, exposed nails)
Type of substrate (open shingle lath or sheathing, closed sheathing, insulated attics, sleepers, etc.)

Replacement roofs must comply with local codes which may require, for example, the use of shingles treated with chemicals or pressure-impregnated salts to retard fire. These requirements can usually be met without long-term visual effects on the appearance of the replacement roof.

The accurate duplication of a wooden shingle roof will help ensure the preservation of the building's architectural integrity. Unfortunately, the choice of an inappropriate shingle or poor installation can severely detract from the building's historic appearance (see illus. 12). There are a number of commercially available wooden roofing products as well as custom roofers who can supply specially-made shingles for historic preservation projects (see Shingle and Shake Chart, illus. 13). Unless restoration or reconstruction is being

undertaken, shingles that match the visual appearance of the historic roof without replicating every aspect of the original shingles will normally suffice. For example, if the historic wood species is no longer readily available, Western Red Cedar or Eastern White Pine may be acceptable. Or, if the shingles are located high on a roof, sawn shingles or commercially available shakes with the rustic faces factory-sawn off may adequately reproduce the appearance of an historic handsplit and dressed shingle.

There will always be certain features, however, that are so critical to the building's character that they should be accurately reproduced. Following is guidance on matching the most important visual elements.

Highest Priority in Replacement Shingles:
• best quality wood with a similar surface texture
• matching size and shape: thickness, width, length
• matching installation pattern: exposure length, overlap, hips, ridges, valleys, etc.
• matching decorative features: fancy butts, color, exposed nails

Areas of Acceptable Differences:
• species of wood
• method of fabrication of shingle, if visual appearance matches
• use of fire-retardants, or preservative treatments, if visual impact is minimal
• use of modern flashing, if sensitively installed
• use of small sleepers for ventilation, if the visual impact is minimal and rake boards are sensitively treated
• method of nailing, if the visual pattern matches

Treatments and Materials to Avoid:
• highly textured wood surfaces and irregular butt ends, unless documented
• standardized details (prefab hips, ridges, panels, etc.) unless documented
• too wide shingles or those with flat grain (which may curl), unless documented

What is Currently Available

Types of Wood: Western Red Cedar, Eastern White Pine, and White Oak are most readily available today. For custom orders, cypress, red oak, and a number of other historically used woods may still be available. Some experiments using non-traditional woods (such as yellow pine and hemlock) treated with preservative chemicals are being tested for the new construction market, but are generally too thick, curl too easily, or have too pronounced a grain for use on historic buildings.

Method of manufacture: Commercially available modern shingles and shakes are for the most part machine-made. While commercially available shakes are promoted by the industry as handsplit, most are split by machine (this reduces the high cost of hand labor). True handsplit shingles, made the traditional way with a froe and mallet, are substantially more expensive, but are more authentic in appearance than the rough, highly textured machine-split shakes. An experienced shingler can control the thickness of the handsplit shingle and keep the shingle surface grain relatively

AVAILABLE WOODEN SHINGLES AND SHAKES FOR RE-ROOFING

TYPE		SIZE	DESCRIPTION	NOTES
Custom split & dressed		Made to match historic shingles	Handsplit the traditional way with froe & mallet. Tapered. Surfaces dressed for smoothness	Appropriate if: • Worked to match uniformly dressed original shingles
Tapersplit*		Typically: L = 15″, 18″, 24″ W = 4″–14″ Butts vary 1/2″–3/4″	Commercially available. Handsplit the traditional way with froe & mallet. Tapered. Bundles contain varying widths & butt thicknesses. Surfaces may be irregular along grain.	Appropriate if: • irregular surfaces are dressed • butt thicknesses ordered uniform • wide shingles are split

Straightsplit		Typically:
		L = 15″, 18″, 24″
		W = 4″–14″
		Butts vary
		  mediums = 3/8–3/4″
		  heavies = 3/4–1 1/4″
			Commercially available. Hand or machine split without taper. Bundles contain varying butt thicknesses; often very wide shingles. Surface may be irregular along the grain. Thick shingles not historic.	Not appropriate for most preservation projects
				• Limited use of thin, even straightsplits on some cabins, barns, etc.

Handsplit* resawn		Typically:
		L = 15″, 18″, 24″
		W = 4″–14″
		Butts vary
		  mediums = 3/8–3/4″
		  heavies = 3/4–1 1/4″
			Commercially available. Machine split and sawn on the backs to taper. Split faces often irregular, even corrugated in appearance. Butt thickness vary and may be too wide.	Not appropriate for preservation projects

Tapersawn*		Typically: L = 15″, 18″, 24″ W = 4″–14″ Butts vary 1/2″–3/4″	Commercially available. Made from split products with sawn surfaces. Tapered. Butt thicknesses vary and shingles may be too wide. Saw marks may be pronounced.	Appropriate if: • butt thicknesses ordered uniform • wide shingles are split • pronounced saw marks sanded

Sawn- straight butt		Typically:
		L = 16″ –.40 (<3/8″)
		  18″ –.45
		  24″ –.50 (1/2″)
		W = Varies by order
			Custom or commercially available. Tapered. Sawn by circular saw.	Appropriate to reproduce historic sawn shingles

Sawn- fancy butt		Typically:
		L = 16″ –.40 (<3/8″)
		  18″ –.45
		  24″ –.50 (1/2″)
		W = Varies by order
			Custom or commercially available. Tapered. Sawn by circular saw. A variety of fancy butts available	Appropriate to reproduce historic fancy butts

Steam-bent		Varies by order to match, "Thatch" roofs	Custom or commercially available. Tapered. Thin sawn shingles are steamed and bent into rounded forms.	Appropriate to reproduce "thatch" shingles

13. *This chart identifies a variety of shingles and shakes used for reroofing buildings. The * identifies product names used by the Red Cedar Shingle and Handsplit Shake Bureau, although shingles and shakes of the types described are available in other woods. Manufacturers define "Shakes" as split products while "shingles" refer to sawn products. Shingle, however, is the historic term used to describe wooden roofing products, regardless of how they were made. Whether shingles or shakes are specified for re-roofing, they should match the size and appearance of the historic shingles. Chart: Sharon C. Park; delineation by Kaye Ellen Simonson.*

even. To have an even roof installation, it is important to have handsplit shingles of uniform taper and to have less than 1/8th variation across the surface of the shingle. For that reason, it is important to dress the shingles or to specify uniform butt thickness, taper, and surfaces. Commercially available shakes are shipped with a range of butt sizes within a bundle (e.g., 1/2", 5/8", 3/4" as a mix) unless otherwise specified. Commercially available shakes with the irregular surfaces sawn off are also available. In many cases, except for the residual circular saw marks, these products appear not unlike a dressed handsplit shingle.

Sawn shingles are still made much the same way as they were historically—using a circular saw. The circular saw marks are usually evident on the surface of most sawn shingles. There are a number of grooved, striated, or steamed shingles of the type used in the 20th century to effect a rustic or thatched appearance. Custom sawn shingles with fancy butts or of a specified thickness are still available through mill shops. In fact, shingles can be fabricated to the weathered thickness in order to be integrated into an existing historic roof. If sawn shingles are being used as a substitute for dressed handsplit shingles, it may be desirable to belt sand the surface of the sawn shingles to reduce the prominence of the circular saw marks.

As seen from the Shingle and Shake chart, few of the commercially available shakes can be used without some modification or careful specification. Some, such as heavy shakes with a corrugated face, should be avoided altogether. While length, width, and butt configuration can be specified, it is more difficult to ensure that the thickness and the texture will be correct. For that reason, whatever shingle or shake is desired, it is important to view samples, preferably an entire bundle, before specifying or ordering. If shingles are to be trimmed at the site for special conditions, such as fanned hips or swept valleys, additional shingles should be ordered.

Coatings and Treatments: Shingles are treated to obtain a fire-retardant rating; to add a fungicide preservative (generally toxic); to revitalize the wood with a penetrating stain (oil as well as water-based); and to give color.

While shingles can be left untreated, local codes may require that only fire-retardant shingles be used. In those circumstances, there are several methods of obtaining rated shingles (generally class "B" or "C"). The most effective and longest-lasting treatment is to have treated salts pressure-impregnated into the wood cells after the shingles have been cut. Another method (which must be periodically renewed) is to apply chemicals to the surface of the shingles. If treated shingles need trimming at the site, it is important to check with the manufacturer to ensure that the fire-retardant qualities will not be lost. Pressure-impregnated shingles, however, may usually be trimmed without loss of fire-retardant properties.

The life of a shingle roof can be drastically shortened if moss, lichens, fungi or bacterial spores grow on the wood. Fungicides (such as chromated copper arsenate, CCA) have been found to be effective in inhibiting such fungal growth, but most are toxic. Red cedar has a natural fungicide in the wood cells and unless the shingles are used in unusually warm, moist environments, or where certain strains of spores are found, an applied fungicide is usually not needed. For most woods, the Forest Products Laboratory of the U.S. Department of Agriculture has found that fungicides do extend the life of the shingles by inhibiting growth on or in the wood. There are a variety available. Care should be taken in applying these chemicals and meeting local code requirements for proper handling.

Penetrating stains and water repellent sealers are sometimes recommended to revitalize wood shingles subject to damage by ultraviolet rays. Some treatments are oil-borne, some are water-borne, and some are combined with a fungicide or a water repellent. If any of these treatments is to be used, they should be identified as part of the specifications. Manufacturers should be consulted regarding the toxicity or other potential complications arising from the use of a product or of several in combination. It is also important not to coat the shingles with vapor-impermeable solutions that will trap moisture within the shingle and cause rotting from beneath.

Specifications for the Replacement Roof

Specifications and roofing details should be developed for each project. Standard specifications may be used as a basic format, but they should be modified to reflect the conditions of each job. Custom shingles can still be ordered that accurately replicate a historic roof, and if the roof is simple, an experienced shingler could install it without complicated instructions. Most rehabilitation projects will involve competitive bidding, and each contractor should be given very specific information as to what type of shingles are required and what the installation details should be. For that reason, both written specifications and detailed drawings should be part of the construction documents.

For particularly complex jobs, it may be appropriate to indicate that only roofing contractors with experience in historic preservation projects be considered (see illus. 14). By pre-qualifying the bidders, there is greater assurance that a proper job will be done. For smaller jobs, it is always recommended that the owner or architect find a roofing contractor who has recently completed a similar project and that the roofers are similarly experienced.

Specifications identify exactly what is to be received from the supplier, including the wooden shingles, nails, flashing, and applied coatings. The specifications also include instructions on removing the old roofing (sometimes two or more earlier roofs), and on preparing the surface for the new shingles, such as repairing damage to the lath or sheathing boards. If there are to be modifications to a standard product, such as cutting beveled butts, planing off residual surface circular saw marks, or controlling the mixture of acceptable widths (3"–8"), these too should be specified. Every instruction for modifying the shingles themselves should be written into the specifications or they may be overlooked.

The specifications and drawn details should describe special features important to the roof. Swept valleys, combed ridges, or wedged dormer cheek run-offs should each be detailed not only with the patterning of the shingles, but also with the placement of flashing or other unseen reinforcements. There are some modern products that appear to be useful. For example, paper-

Replacement Roofing for Appomattox Manor: City Point Unit of Petersburg National Battlefield, Hopewell, Virginia

A. The later non-historic shingles were removed from Appomattox Manor (circa 1840 with later additions) and roofing paper was installed for temporary protection during the re-shingling.

B. These weathered historic 19th-century handsplit and dressed shingles were found in place under a later altered roof. Note the straight butt eave shingles under the curved butts of the historic dormer shingles.

D. The fanned hips (seen here), swept valleys, and projecting ridge combs were installed as part of the re-roofing project. Special features, when documented, should be reproduced when re-shingling historic roofs.

Excerpts from Specifications:

Type of wood to be used: Western Red Cedar.
Grade of wood and manufacturing process: Number One, Tapersplit Shakes, 100% clear, 100% edgegrain, 100% heartwood, no excessive grain sweeps, curvatures not to exceed 1/2" from level plain in length of shake; off grade (7% tolerance) material must *not* be used.
Size of the shingle: 18" long, 5/8" butt tapered to 1/4" head, 3"–4" wide, sawn curved butts, 5 1/2" exposure
Surface finish and any applied coatings: relatively smooth natural grain, no more than 1/8" variation in surface texture, butt thickness to be uniform throughout bundles. Site dipped with fire-rated chemicals tinted with red iron oxide for opaque color.
Type of nails and flashing: double hot dipped galvanized nails sized to penetrate sheathing totally; metal flashing to be 20 oz. lead-coated copper, or terne-coated stainless steel; additional flashing reinforcement to be aluminum foil type with fiber backing to use at hips, ridges, eaves, and valleys.
Type of sheathing: uninsulated attic, any deteriorated 3/4" sheathing boards, spaced 1/2"–3/4", to be replaced in kind.

C. The replacement shingles (see specifications above), matched the historic shingles and were of such high quality that little hand dressing was needed at the site. The building paper, a temporary protection, was removed as the shingles were installed on the sheathing boards.

E. In order to achieve a "Class B" fire-rating, the shingles were dipped in fire-retardant chemicals and allowed to dry prior to installation. Iron oxide was added to this chemical dip to stain the shingles to match the historic red color. These coatings will need periodic reapplication.

14. Original 19th-century handsplit and dressed wooden shingles 18" long, 3"–4" wide, and 5/8" thick were found in place on the Appomattox Manor at Hopewell, Virginia. The butts were curved and evidence of a red stain remained. The specifications and details were researched so that the appearance of the historic shingles and installation patterns could be matched in the re-shingling project. Photos: John Ingle.

coated and reinforced metal-laminated flashing is easy to use and, in combination with other flashing, gives added protection over eaves and other vulnerable areas; adhesives give a stronger attachment at projecting roofing combs that could blow away in heavy wind storms. Clear or light-colored sealants may be less obvious than dark mastic often used in conjunction with flashing or repairs. These modern treatments should not be overlooked if they can prolong the life of the roof without changing its appearance.

Roofing Practices to Avoid

Certain common roofing practices for modern installations should be avoided in re-roofing a historic building unless specifically approved in advance by the architect. These practices interfere with the proper drying of the shingles or result in a sloppy installation that will accelerate deterioration (see illus. 15). They include improper coverage and spacing of shingles, use of staples to hold shingles, inadequate ventilation, particularly for heavily insulated attics, use of heavy building felts as an underlayment, improper application of surface coatings causing stress in the wood surfaces, and use of inferior flashing that will fail while the shingles are still in good condition.

Avoid skimpy shingle coverage and heavy building papers. It has become a common modern practice to lay impregnated roofing felts under new wooden shingle roofs. The practice is especially prevalent in roofs that do not achieve a full triple layering of shingles. Historically, approximately one third of each single was exposed, thus making a three-ply or three-layered roof. This assured adequate coverage. Due to the expense of wooden shingles today, some roofers expose more of the shingle if the pitch of the roof allows, and compensate for less than three layers of shingles by using building felts interwoven at the top of each row of shingles. This absorptive material can hold moisture on the underside of the shingles and accelerate deterioration. If a shingle roof has proper coverage and proper flashing, such felts are unnecessary as a general rule.

15. *These commercially available roofing products with rustic split faces are not appropriate for historic preservation projects. In addition to the inaccurate appearance, the irregular surfaces and often wide spaces between shingles will allow wind-driven moisture to penetrate up and under them. The excessively wide boards will tend to cup, curl and crack. Moss, lichens and debris will have a tendency to collect on these irregular surfaces, further deteriorating the roofing. Photo: Sharon C. Park.*

However, the selective use of such felts or other reinforcements at ridges, hips and valleys does appear to be beneficial.

Beware of heavily insulated attic rafters. Historically, the longest lasting shingle roofs were generally the ones with the best roof ventilation. Roofs with shingling set directly on solid sheathing and where there is insulation packed tightly between the wooden rafters without adequate ventilation run the risk of condensation-related moisture damage to wooden roofing components. This is particularly true for air-conditioned structures. For that reason, if insulation must be used, it is best to provide ventilation channels between the rafters and the roof decking, to avoid heavy felt building papers, to consider the use of vapor barriers, and perhaps to raise the shingles slightly by using "sleepers" over the roof deck. This practice was popular in the 1920s in what the industry called a "Hollywood" installation, and examples of roofs lasting 60 years are partly due to this under-shingle ventilation (refer to illus. 9).

Avoid staples and inferior flashing. The common practice of using pneumatic staple guns to affix shingles can result in shooting staples through the shingles, in crushing the wood fibers, or in cracking the shingle. Instead, corrosion-resistant nails, generally with barked or deformed shanks long enough to extend about 3/4" into the roof decking, should be specified. Many good roofers have found that the pneumatic nail guns, fitted with the proper nails and set at the correct pressure with the nails just at the shingle surface, have worked well and reduced the stress on shingles from missed hammer blows. If red cedar is used, copper nails should not be specified because a chemical reaction between the wood and the copper will reduce the life of the roof. Hot-dipped, zinc-coated, aluminum, or stainless steel nails should be used. In addition, copper flashing and gutters generally should not be used with red cedar shingles as staining will occur, although there are some historic examples where very heavy gauge copper was used which outlasted the roof shingles. Heavier weight flashing (20 oz.) holds up better than lighter flashing, which may deteriorate faster than the shingles. Some metals may react with salts or chemicals used to treat the shingles. This should be kept in mind when writing specifications. Terne-coated stainless steel and lead-coated copper are generally the top of the line if copper is not appropriate.

Avoid patching deteriorated roof lath or sheathing with plywood or composite materials. Full size lumber may have to be custom-ordered to match the size and configuration of the original sheathing in order to provide an even surface for the new shingles. It is best to avoid plywood or other modern composition boards that may deteriorate or delaminate in the future if there is undetected moisture or leakage. If large quantities of shingle lath or sheathing must be removed and replaced, the work should be done in sections to avoid possible shifting or collapse of the roof structure.

Avoid spray painting raw shingles on a roof after installation. Rapidly drying solvent in the paint will tend to warp the exposed surface of the shingles. Instead, it is best to dip new shingles prior to installation to keep all of the wood fibers in the same tension. Once the entire shingle has been treated, however, later coats can be limited to the exposed surface.

Maintenance

The purpose of regular or routine maintenance is to extend the life of the roof. The roof must be kept clean and inspected for damage both to the shingles and to the flashing, sheathing, and gutters. If the roof is to be walked on, rubber soled shoes should be worn. If there is a simple ridge, a ladder can be hooked over the roof ridge to support and distribute the weight of the inspector.

Keeping the roof free of debris is important. This may involve only sweeping off pine needles, leaves and branches as needed. It may involve trimming over-hanging branches. Other aspects of maintenance, such as removal of moss and lichen build-up, are more diffi-cult. While they may impart a certain charm to roofs, these moisture-trapping organisms will rot the shingles and shorten the life of the roof. Buildups may need scraping and the residue removed with diluted bleach-ing solutions (chlorine), although caution should be used for surrounding materials and plants. Some roof-ers recommend power washing the roofs periodically to remove the dead wood cells and accumulated debris. While this makes the roof look relatively new, it can put a lot of water under shingles, and the high pres-sure may crack or otherwise damage them. The added water may also leach out applied coatings.

If the roof has been treated with a fungicide, stain, or revitalizing oil, it will need to be re-coated every few years (usually every 4–5). The manufacturer should be consulted as to the effective life of the coating. With the expense associated with installation of wood shingles, it is best to extend the life of the roof as long as possi-ble. One practical method is to order enough shingles in the beginning to use for periodic repairs.

Periodic maintenance inspections of the roof may reveal loose or damaged shingles that can be selectively replaced before serious moisture damage occurs (see illus. 16). Keeping the wooden shingles in good condi-tion and repairing the roof, flashing and guttering, as needed, can add years of life to the roof.

16. Routine maintenance is necessary to extend the life of the roof. On this roof, the shingles have not seriously eroded, but the presence of lichens and moss is becoming evident and there are a few cracked and missing shingles. The moss spores should be removed, missing shingles replaced, and small pieces of metal flashing slipped under cracked shingles to keep moisture from penetrating. Photo: Williamsport Preservation Training Center.

Cover Photo: 1907 view of a young couple's first home in a cedar stump with a shingled roof. Photo: Historical Society of Seattle and King County, Washington.

Conclusion

A combination of careful research to determine the historic appearance of the roof, good specifications, and installation details designed to match the historic roof, and long-term maintenance, will make it possible to have not only a historically authentic roof, but a cost-effective one. It is important that professionals be part of the team from the beginning. A preservation architect should specify materials and construction techniques that will best preserve the roof's historic appearance. The shingle supplier must ensure that the best product is delivered and must stand behind the guarantee if the shipment is not correct. The roofer must be knowledgeable about traditional craft prac-tices. Once the new shingle roof is in place, it must be properly maintained to give years of service.

Acknowledgements

The author gratefully acknowledges the invaluable assistance of co-worker Michael Auer in preparing this brief for publication. In addition, the following individuals are to be thanked for their contri-bution to this manuscript: Reed Engle, Historical Architect, NPS; John Ingle, Historical Architect, NPS; Martin Obando, Eastern Dis-trict Manager, Red Cedar Shingle & Handsplit Shake Bureau; and Peter Sandbeck, North Carolina Division of Archives and History. Appreciation is extended to: the staff of Technical Preservation Serv-ices Branch and NPS regional offices; Michael Lynch of the Office of Parks, Recreation and Historic Preservation in Albany, New York; and to Penelope H. Batcheler and William Brookover, Historical Archi-tects, Independence National Historic Park, for their review of this manuscript and constructive comments. Special thanks are given to Kaye Ellen Simonson for the illustrations in the charts.

This publication has been prepared pursuant to the National His-toric Preservation Act of 1966, as amended. Preservation Brief 19 was developed under the technical editorship of Lee H. Nelson, FAIA, Chief, Preservation Assistance Division, National Park Service, U.S. Department of the Interior, P.O. Box 37127, Washington, D.C. 20013-7127. Comments on the usefulness of this information are welcomed and may be sent to Mr. Nelson at the above address.

Further Reading

Bucher, Robert C. "The Long Shingle." *Pennsylvania Folklife*, Vol. XVIII, No. 4, Summer 1969.

Cox, Richard E. "Wooden Shingles from the Fortress of Louisbourg." *Bulletin of the Association for Preservation Technology*, Vol. II, Nos. 1–2 1970 p.p. 65.

Engle, Reed. "Restoring a Roofing." *CRM Bulletin*, a publication of the National Park Service, Vol. 8, No. 6 Dec. 1985.

Kidder, F.E. *Building Construction and Superintendence*, Part II. New York: William T. Comstock, 1902.

LeVan, Susan. "Fire-Retardant Treatments for Wood Shingles." *Techline*, Madison, Wisconsin: U.S.D.A. Forest Service, 1988.

Niemiec, S.S. and T.D. Brown. *"Care and Maintenance of Wood Shingle and Shake Roofs."* Oregon State University Extension Service, Septem-ber 1988. Publication #EC 1271.

The Old House Journal, Vol. XI, No. 3, April 1983. Special Roof Issue.

Peterson, Charles E. (editor). *Building Early America*. Radnor, Pennsyl-vania: Chilton Book Co. 1976.

Stevens, John. "Shingles." *Bulletin of the Association for Preservation Technology*, Vol. II, Nos. 1–2 1970, pp. 74.

Sweetser, Sarah M. *Preservation Briefs 4: Roofing for Historic Buildings.* Washington, D.C.: Technical Preservation Services Division, National Park Service, U.S. Department of the Interior, 1978.

Tollesten, Kristin. "Shingles and Shingled Roofs." *No Future Without the Past*. Rome, Italy: ICOMOS, 1981. pp. 347–360.

20

The Preservation of Historic Barns

Michael J. Auer

From the days when Thomas Jefferson envisioned the new republic as a nation dependent on citizen-farmers for its stability and its freedom, the family farm has been a vital image in the American consciousness. As the main structures of farms, barns evoke a sense of tradition and security, of closeness to the land and community with the people who built them. Even today the rural barn raising presents a forceful image of community spirit. Just as many farmers built their barns before they built their houses, so too many farm families look to their old barns as links with their past. Old barns, furthermore, are often community landmarks and make the past present. Such buildings embody ethnic traditions and local customs; they reflect changing farming practices and advances in building technology. In the imagination they represent a whole way of life (Fig. 1).

Unfortunately, historic barns are threatened by many factors. On farmland near cities, barns are often seen only in decay, as land is removed from active agricultural use. In some regions, barns are dismantled for lumber, their beams sold for reuse in living rooms. Barn raisings have given way to barn razings. Further threats to historic barns and other farm structures are posed by changes in farm technology, involving much larger machines and production facilities, and changes in the overall farm economy, including increasing farm size and declining rural populations.[1]

Yet historic barns can be refitted for continued use in agriculture, often at great savings over the cost of new buildings. This Brief encourages the preservation of historic barns and other agricultural structures by encouraging their maintenance and use *as* agricultural buildings, and by advancing their sensitive rehabilitation for new uses when their historic use is no longer feasible.

Fig. 1. Arch roof, native limestone walls two feet thick at the base, porthole window, dormers, silos, rooftop ventilators, weathervanes, windmill, fences, fields, and family pride in the builder are all components of the historic character of this Iowa barn. Photo: John Walter, Successful Farming.

Historic Barn Types

Dutch Barns

The first great barns built in this country were those of the Dutch settlers of the Hudson, Mohawk, and Schoharie valleys in New York State and scattered sections of New Jersey.[2] On the exterior, the most notable feature of the Dutch barn is the broad gable roof, which in early examples (now extremely rare), extended very low to the ground. On the narrow end the Dutch barn features center doors for wagons and a door to the stock aisles on one or both of the side ends. A pent roof (or pentice) over the center doors gave some slight protection from the elements. The siding is typically horizontal, the detailing simple. Few openings other than doors and traditional holes for martins puncture the external walls.[3] The appearance is of massiveness and simplicity, with the result that Dutch barns seem larger than they actually are.

To many observers the heavy interior structural system is the most distinctive aspect of the Dutch barn. Mortised, tenoned and pegged beams are arranged in "H"-shaped units that recall church interiors, with columned aisles alongside a central space (here used for threshing). This interior arrangement, more than any other characteristic, links the Dutch barn with its Old World forebears. The ends of cross beams projecting through the columns are often rounded to form "tongues," a distinctive feature found only in the Dutch barn.

Relatively few Dutch barns survive. Most of these date from the late 18th century. Fewer yet survive in good condition, and almost none unaltered. Yet the remaining examples of this barn type still impress with the functional simplicity of their design and the evident pride the builders took in their work.

Built in the late 1700s, this New York Dutch barn survives in excellent condition. Gable roof, center wagon doors with pent roof, stock door at the corner and horizontal clapboarding are all typical features of the Dutch barn. Three holes for martins, traditional features of Dutch barns, can be seen near the top of the facade (they have been plugged and are lighter than the surrounding clapboards). Photo: Clarke Blair.

Bank Barns

The bank barn gets its name from a simple but clever construction technique: the barn is built into the side of a hill, thus permitting two levels to be entered from the ground. The lower level housed animals, the upper

The gently sloping roadbed in this photograph shows the "bank" from which bank barns get their name. Massive timbers stretching across the full width of the barn create the overhang that also characterizes these barns. In barns with brick end walls, patterns were sometimes created by leaving spaces between bricks. The device furnishes ventilation as well as decoration. Photo: Jack E. Boucher, HABS.

levels served as threshing floor and storage. The hillside entrance gave easy access to wagons bearing wheat or hay. (Fodder could also be dropped through openings in the floor to the stabling floor below.) The general form of the bank barn remained the same whether it was built into a hillside or not. Where a hill was lacking, a "bank" was often created by building up an earthen ramp to the second level.

Bank barns were ordinarily constructed with their long side, or axis, parallel to the hill, and on the south side of it. This placement gave animals a sunny spot in which to gather during the winter. To take further advantage of the protection its location afforded, the second floor was extended, or cantilevered, over the first. The overhang sheltered animals from inclement weather. The extended forebay thus created is one of the most characteristic features of these barns. In some bank barns, the projecting beams were not large enough to bear the entire weight of the barn above. In these cases, columns or posts were added beneath the overhang for structural support.

In the earliest examples of bank barns narrow-end side walls are frequently stone or brick, with openings for ventilation. (Since "curing" green hay can generate enough heat to start a fire through spontaneous combustion, adequate ventilation in barns is vital.)

Crib Barns

This late-nineteenth century crib barn is located in eastern Tennessee, in what is now the Great Smoky Mountains National Park. The central driveway between the cribs allowed a team and wagon to drive through after unloading. The materials and details are typical of the region. They include, on the exterior: hand-hewn saddle notched logs on the lower, crib portion; board framing on the upper, loft area; wood shingle roof. The interior features wood hinges on the crib doors and earth floor. Photo: Robert Madden.

Crib barns form another barn type significant in American agriculture. Found throughout the South and Southeast, crib barns are especially numerous in the Appalachian and Ozark Mountain States of North Carolina, Virginia, Kentucky, Tennessee and Arkansas. Composed simply of one, two, four or sometimes six cribs that served as storage for fodder or pens for cattle or pigs, crib barns may or may not have a hayloft above. Crib barns were typically built of unchinked logs, although they were sometimes covered with vertical wood siding. Unaltered examples of early crib barns normally have roofs of undressed wood shingles. In time, shingle roofs were usually replaced with tin or asphalt. The rustic appearance of crib barns is one of their most striking features.

The cribs sometimes face a covered gallery or aisle running across the front. In another arrangement, the cribs are separated by a central driveway running through the building. This latter arrangement defines the *double crib barn*.

In double crib barns the second story hayloft is sometimes cantilevered over the ground floor, resulting in a barn of striking appearance.

Round Barns

George Washington owned a round barn. And in 1826 the Shaker community at Hancock, Massachusetts, built a round barn that attracted considerable publicity.[4] Despite these early examples, however, round barns were not built in numbers until the 1880s, when agricultural colleges and experiment stations taught progressive farming methods based on models of industrial efficiency. From this time until well into the 1920s, round barns appeared on farms throughout the country, flourishing especially in the Midwest.[5]

Round barns were promoted for a number of reasons. The circular form has a greater volume-to-surface ratio than the rectangular or square form. For any given size, therefore, a circular building will use fewer materials than other shapes, thus saving on material costs. Such barns also offer greater structural stability than rectangular barns. And because they can be built with self-supporting roofs, their interiors can remain free of structural supporting elements, thereby providing vast storage capabilities. The circular interior layout was also seen as more efficient, since the farmer could work in a continuous direction.

In general, multi-sided barns—frequently of 12 or 16 sides—are earlier than "true round" barns. Earlier examples also tend to be wood sided, while later ones tend to be brick or glazed tile. Interior layouts also underwent an evolution. Early round barns placed cattle stanchions on the first floor, with the full volume of the floor above used for hay storage. In later barns, the central space rose from the ground floor through the entire building. Cattle stanchions arranged around a circular manger occupied the lower level; the circular wagon drive on the level above permitted hay to be unloaded into the central mow as the wagon drove around the perimeter. In the last stage of round barn development, a center silo was added when silos became regular features on the farm (in the last decades of the nineteenth century). In some cases, the silo projected through the roof.

The claims for the efficiency of the round barn were overstated, and it never became the standard barn, as its proponents had hoped. Nevertheless, a great number were built, and many remain today the most distinctive farm structures in the communities in which they stand.

Circular barns are found throughout the country, but are especially numerous in the Midwest. This 1911 Illinois round barn is 60 feet in diameter. The cupola atop the hipped roof is 60 feet above ground. Its 10 single and 5 double stalls on the ground floor were fed from a loft. The square windows spaced at regular intervals around the perimeter add a note of simple contrast to the overall circular motif. Photo: Keith A. Sculle, Illinois Historic Preservation Agency.

Prairie Barns

A peak roof projecting above a hayloft opening is one of the most familiar images associated with barns. The feature belongs to the prairie barn, also known as the Western barn. The larger herds associated with agriculture in the West and Southwest required great storage space for hay and feed. Accordingly, prairie barns are on average much larger than the other barns discussed in this brief.[6] Long, sweeping roofs, sometimes coming near the ground, mark the prairie barn; the extended roof created great storage space. (Late in the nineteenth century, the adoption of the gambrel roof enlarged the storage capacity of the haymow even more.)

Affinities of this barn type with the Dutch barn are striking: the long, low roof lines, the door in the gable end, and the internal arrangement of stalls in aisles on either side of the central space are all in the tradition of the Dutch barn.

The long, sweeping roof is a characteristic of the Prairie or Western barn. The projecting peak over the hayloft is another. This Iowa barn was built about 1910. Photo: Mary Humstone.

Others

The barn types discussed here are only some of the barns that have figured in the history of American agriculture. As with Dutch barns, some reflect the traditions of the people who built them: Finnish log barns in Idaho, Czech and German-Russian house barns in South Dakota, and "three-bay" English barns in the northeast. Some, like the New England connected barn, stem from regional or local building traditions. Others reflect the availability of local building materials: lava rock (basalt) in south-central Idaho, logs in the southeast, adobe in California and the southwest. Others are best characterized by the specialized uses to which they were put: dairy barns in the upper midwest, tobacco barns in the east and southeast, hop-drying barns in the northwest, and rice barns in South Carolina. Other historic barns were built to patterns developed and popularized by land-grant universities, or sold by Sears, Roebuck and Company and other mail-order firms. And others fit no category at all: these barns attest to the owner's tastes, wealth, or unorthodox ideas about agriculture. All of these barns are also part of the heritage of historic barns found throughout the country.

In the early 20th century barn patterns were developed by agricultural schools and prefabricated units were sold by mail-order firms. This Maryland barn was bought about 1920 from a Sears catalogue. Photo: Robert J. Hughes

Panels on this 1900 Kentucky tobacco barn open to aid in the curing process. Photo: Christine Amos, Kentucky Heritage Council.

The two ventilating towers are the character-defining aspect of this Oregon hop-drying barn. Photo: Allan Nelson.

Preservation of Historic Barns

Understanding Barns and Their History

Historic barns are preserved for a number of reasons. Some are so well built that they remain useful even after a hundred years or more. Many others are intimately connected with the families who built them and the surrounding communities. Others reflect developments in agricultural science or regional building types.

Before restoring a historic barn or rehabilitating it for a new use, an owner should study the building thoroughly. This process involves finding out when the barn was built, who built it, and why. It means understanding how the building was changed through the years. It means assessing the condition of the barn, and understanding its components. This process has as its end an appreciation of the building's historic character, that is, the sense of time and place associated with it. It is this physical presence of the past that gives historic buildings their significance.

To assess the historic character of a barn, an owner should study old photographs, family records, deeds, insurance papers, and other documents that might reveal the building's appearance and history. Neighbors and former owners are often important sources of information. Local libraries, historical societies and preservation organizations are additional sources of help.

As part of this overall evaluation, the following elements should be assessed for their contributions to the property. They are the principal tangible aspects of a barn's historic character, and should be respected in any work done on it.

Setting. Setting is one of the primary factors contributing to the historic character of a barn (see Fig. 2). Farmers built barns in order to help them work the land; barns belong on farms, where they can be seen in relation to the surrounding fields and other structures in the farm complex. A barn crowded by suburbs is not a barn in the same sense as is a barn clustered with other farm buildings, or standing alone against a backdrop of cornfields. Hence, the preservation of barns should not be divorced from the preservation of the setting: farms and farmland, ranches and range, orchards, ponds, fields, streams and country roads.

Other important elements of setting include fences, stone walls, roads, paths, barnyards, corrals, and ancillary structures such as windmills and silos. (Silos, indeed, have become so closely associated with barns as nearly to have lost their "separate" identities.) These features help place the building in the larger agricultural context, relating it to its purpose in the overall rural setting.

Form. The shape of barns, as with other buildings, is of great importance in conveying their character. (For round barns, the shape *is* the defining feature of the type.) Often the form of a barn is visible from a distance. Often, too, more than one side can be seen at the same time, and from several different approaches. As a general rule, the rear and sides of a barn are not as differentiated from the front, or as subordinated to it, as in other buildings.

The roof is among the most important elements of building form. Barns are no exception. The gable roof on Dutch and Prairie barns, the cone-shaped, dome-shaped, eight- or twelve-sided roof of round barns, and the gambrel roof of the "typical" barn are among the most prominent features on these buildings. A barn roof can often be seen from a distance, and for this reason must be considered a major feature.

Materials. Among the major impressions given by well-maintained historic barns are those of strength, solidity and permanence (see Fig. 3). These impressions largely result from the durability and ruggedness of the materials used in them. Weathered wood siding, irregularly shaped stones, or roughhewn logs on the exterior; dressed beams, posts scarred by years of use, and plank flooring on the interior all contribute to the special character of barns.

Fig. 2. Mountains, fields, fences, sheds, trees: The setting of this enormous Montana barn is an important element of its character. The barn was built in 1887–1889 after disastrous livestock losses in the winter of 1886–1887. It could hold 500 cattle and store a quarter-million cubic feet of hay. Photo: John N. DeHaas, Jr., Montana Historical Society.

Fig. 3. The stone walls of this Delaware barn are its most notable feature. Built about 1810, the barn is a bank barn. Photo: Valerie Cesna, Delaware Bureau of Archeology and Historic Preservation.

Openings. Unlike historic residential, industrial and commercial buildings, barns generally have few openings for windows and doors. Yet the openings found in barns are important both to their functioning and to their appearance. Typically, large wagon doorways and openings to the hayloft are among the most striking features on barns. Not as prominent as these large openings, but important from a functional perspective, are the ventilator slits found on many barns. With important exceptions (dairy barns, for example), windows are few, and are normally small. The relative absence of openings for windows and doors adds to the overall impression of massiveness and solidity conveyed by many historic barns, and is one of the reasons why they often appear to be larger than they are.

Interior Spaces. The impression received upon stepping into many historic barns is that of *space* (see Fig. 4). Not infrequently, the entire building appears as a single large space. To enter these buildings is sometimes to experience the entire expanse of the building at once. Even when haylofts and animal stalls "consume" part of the building, they often do not keep the full expanse of the interior from being seen. In large barns, this can be an imposing sight. More commonly, the barn is a combination of confined spaces on the lower floor and a large open space above; in this case, the contrast between the confined and open spaces is also striking. The openness of the interior, furthermore, often contrasts with the "blankness" typical of many barn exteriors, with their relatively few openings.

Fig. 4. Nowhere is the sense of space associated with barn interiors more evident than in a round barn. The storage capacity of this 1930 barn is immense. Just visible midway up the wall is a circular track and pulley system used to move hay from the wagon entrance on the lower level and to distribute it around the loft. When needed, hay was dropped to the stalls below through an opening in the loft floor. Photo: Keith A. Sculle, Illinois Historic Preservation Agency.

Structural Framework. The exposed structural framework is a major component of the character of most historic barns (see Fig. 5). Typically, barns were built for strictly utilitarian purposes. Accordingly, barn builders made no effort to conceal the structural system. Yet for that very reason, barns achieve an authenticity that accounts for much of their appeal.

Fig. 5. The exposed structural framework of this large 1890 Illinois barn is impressive. In a recent rehabilitation a portion of the haymow floor (see arrow) was raised to provide clearance for large machinery. Photo: Dale Humphrey, Galesburg Register Mail.

In some barns, the load-bearing members are of enormous dimensions, and the complex system of beams, braces, posts, rafters and other elements of the revealed framework create an imposing sight. Yet even in small barns, the structural system can be an important feature, helping to determine the historic character of the building.

Decorative Features. Historic barns, like modern ones, are structures built for *use*. Nevertheless, decorative elements are not lacking on barns. Foremost among these is color (red being most common). Dutch barns traditionally sported distinctively shaped martin holes in the upper reaches of the building. Traditional hex signs on Pennsylvania barns are so well known as to have entered the mainstream of popular culture and taken on a life of their own (see Fig. 6). Decorative paint schemes, including contrasting colors to "pick out" cross members of the external framework, are common (these most frequently take the form of diamonds or "X's" on the main doors). Sign painters often took advantage of the size and visibility of barns in an age before billboards. "Mail Pouch Tobacco" signs were nearly as numerous in the first quarter of the 20th century as patent medicine ads were in the last quarter of the 19th. Another decorative motif on historic barns is the arrangement of spacings between bricks to form decorative patterns (as well as to ventilate the barn).

Fig. 6. Hex signs are among the wide range of decorative elements found on American barns. Photo: Lee H. Nelson.

In addition to these elements, arched window hoods, patterned slate roofs, fanciful cupolas, weathervanes, lightning rods and ornamented metal ventilator hoods can be found on historic barns. Finally, individual farmers and barn builders sometimes added personal touches, as when they carved or painted their names on anchor beams, or painted their names and the date over the entrance.

The elements discussed here are major components of historic barns. Yet no list can convey the full historic character of an individual building. It is very important, therefore, to study each structure carefully before undertaking any project to restore it or to adapt it to new uses.

Maintenance

If a building is to be kept in good repair, periodic maintenance is essential. Barns should be routinely inspected for signs of damage and decay, and problems corrected as soon as possible. Water is the single greatest cause of building materials deterioration. The repair of roof leaks is therefore of foremost importance. Broken or missing panes of glass in windows or cupolas are also sources of moisture penetration, and should be replaced, as should broken ventilation louvers. Gutters and downspouts should be cleaned once or twice a year. Proper drainage and grading should be ensured, particularly in low spots around the foundation where water can collect.

Moisture is one major threat to historic buildings. Insects, especially termites, carpenter ants and powder post beetles, are another. Regular examinations for infestations are essential.

Additional periodic maintenance measures include repair or replacement of loose or missing clapboards,

and inspections of foundations for cracks and settlements. Vegetation growing on the barn should be removed, and shrubs or trees near it should be cleared if they obstruct access, or, more serious, if roots and other growths threaten the foundation. Soil and manure build-ups against the foundation should be removed. Such build-ups hold water and snow against wooden elements, and promote rot. They also promote insect infestations. Door hardware should be checked for proper fitting and lubricated yearly. Lightning rods should be kept in proper working order, or added, if missing.

Repair

Many historic barns require more serious repairs than those normally classed as "routine maintenance" (see Fig. 7). Damaged or deteriorated features should be repaired rather than replaced wherever possible. If replacement is necessary, the new material should match the historic material in design, color, texture, and other visual qualities and, where possible, material. The design of replacements for missing features (for example, cupolas and dormers) should be based on historic, physical, or pictorial evidence.

Many barn owners have substantial experience in the care of farm structures. Where expertise is lacking, it will be necessary to consult structural engineers, masons, carpenters, and architects, as appropriate. In addition, for many repairs, a knowledge of historic building techniques may be necessary.

Structural Repairs. Ensuring the structural soundness of a historic barn is vital both to its continued usefulness and to the safety of its occupants. The following signs of structural settlements may require the services of a structural engineer to evaluate: major cracks in masonry walls, visible bowing, leaning and misalignment of walls, sagging windows and doors, separation of cladding from structural frames, trusses pulling away from seating points at support walls, sagging joists and rafters, and noticeable dips in the roof between rafters. To correct these problems, masonry foundations may have to be reset or partially rebuilt. Sills and plates may need to be repaired or replaced. Walls may have to be straightened and tied into the structural system more securely. Individual structural members may need bracing or splicing.

Roofing. Moisture can damage historic materials severely, and, in extreme cases, jeopardize the structural integrity of a building. Every effort must be made to secure a weathertight roof. This may require merely patching a few missing shingles on a roof that is otherwise sound. In more severe cases, it may require repairing or replacing failing rafters and damaged sheathing. Such extreme intervention, however, is not usual. More typical is the need to furnish "a new roof," that is, to replace the wooden shingles, asphalt shingles, slate shingles or metal covering the roof. Replacing one type of roofing with another can produce a drastic change in the appearance of historic buildings. Great care should be taken, therefore, to assess the

Fig. 7. Now part of Antietam National Battlefield, this bank barn (built in the 1820s and enlarged in 1898 and 1914) looks out over fields and hills where Union and Confederate armies fought on the bloodiest day in American history. Owned by the National Park Service, the barn underwent major repairs: (a) the foundation was regraded for better drainage; (b) the deteriorated metal roof was removed; (c) removal of the metal roof disclosed the rotten wall plate and roof rafters; (d) these elements were replaced, and collars to hold a new gutter system were added; (e) new downspouts and drain pipes were installed to carry water off the roof and away from the foundation; (f) damaged structural members were strengthened with new sections; (g) new roof and other work finished, the barn remains a working farm structure. Photos: (a–f), Courtesy, Williamsport Preservation Training Center, NPS; (g), Jack E. Boucher, HABS.

contribution of the roof to the appearance and character of the barn before replacing one type of roofing material with another. While some substitute materials (such as synthetic slate shingles) can be considered, the highest priority should be to replace in-kind, and to match the visual qualities of the historic roof. Gutters and downspouts should be replaced if damaged or missing. Finally, dormers, cupolas, metal ventilators and other rooftop "ornaments" provide needed ventilation, and should be repaired if necessary.

Exterior. In addition to the roof and the foundation, other exterior elements may need repair, including siding, brick and stonework, dormers and cupolas, windows and doors. Shutters may be falling off, doors may need to be rehung, and missing louvers replaced. The exterior may need repainting. (Unpainted brick or stone barns, however, should never be painted.) In the case of masonry barns, repointing may be necessary. If so, mortar that is compatible in appearance and composition with the historic mortar must be used. Using mortar high in portland cement can damage historic brick or stone. Masonry cleaning should be undertaken only when necessary to halt deterioration or to remove heavy dirt, and using the gentlest means possible. Sandblasting and other physical or chemical treatments that damage historic materials should not be used. Likewise, power washing under high pressure can also damage building material.

Interior. Typical interior repairs may include removing and replacing rotten floorboards, and repair or replacement of partitions, storage bins, gutters and stalls. Concrete floors may be cracked and in need of repair. Wiring and plumbing may need major overhaul.

Rehabilitation

Some barns have served the same uses for generations, and need only periodic repairs and routine maintenance. Others have become obsolete and need extensive updating for modern farming methods. (To house livestock, for example, a barn may need new feeding, watering, waste removal, electrical, plumbing and ventilation systems.) Similarly, barns that can no longer be used for agriculture at all normally require changes to adapt them for commercial, office, or residential use. In such cases barns need more extensive work than the maintenance and repair treatments outlined above. However, when rehabilitiating a historic barn for a new farming operation or a new use entirely, care must be taken to preserve its historic character while making needed changes (see Figs. 8, 9 and 10).

A successful rehabilitation project is best guaranteed when a work plan is drawn up by someone familiar with the evaluation of historic structures, and when it is carried out by contractors and workmen experienced with the building type and committed to the goal of retaining the historic character of the property. Help in formulating rehabilitation plans and in locating experienced professionals is normally available from the State Historic Preservation Office and local preservation groups.

The following approaches should be observed when carrying out rehabilitation projects on historic barns:

1. Preserve the historic setting of the barn as much as possible. Modern farming practices do not require the great number of outbuildings, lots, fences, hedges,

Fig. 8. Built in the Gothic Revival style in the 1890s, this four-story Indiana barn had fallen into disuse, and was deteriorating. In the process of returning it to use, the owner installed a new roof that matches the wooden shingles found beneath the deteriorating asphalt shingle roof; removed the modern asbestos shingle siding; repaired the windows, and reconstructed the cupola (including its lightning rod and weathervane). (Before and after views are of opposite sides of barn.) Photos: Before, Courtesy, Gary Post-Tribune; *After, Courtesy,* Kankakee Valley News.

walls and other elements typical of historic farms. Yet such features, together with fields, woods, ponds, and other aspects of the farm setting can be important to the character of historic barns. The functional relationship between the barn and silo is particularly significant and should also be maintained.

2. Repair and repaint historic siding rather than cover barns with artificial siding. Siding applied over the entire surface of a building can give it an entirely different appearance, obscure craft details, and mask ongoing deterioration of historic materials underneath. The resurfacing of historic farm buildings with any new material that does not duplicate the historic material is never a recommended treatment.

Fig. 9. This enormous Ohio barn (285 feet by 125) was built between 1909 and 1912. It was one of 102 structures on "America's Finest Farm." (Other buildings included the world's largest greenhouse and the world's largest barn—nearly 800 feet long). The barn seen here was rehabilitated for use as headquarters for an international agricultural firm. Although the use has changed, comparison of the interior photographs shows that the barn has retained its historic character. (After view, interior, is taken from a cross axis; distortion is from fish-eye lens.) Photos: Exterior and interior, after: Ron Kuntz, UPI; Interior, before: Courtesy, Barberton (Ohio) Historical Society.

Fig. 10. This 1910 Vermont round barn is 80 feet in diameter. Disused and decaying, the building was converted to a community center, with artists' studios and spaces for weddings, parties and conferences. The barn underwent extensive structural repair and other work. Careful selection of new use permitted the building to be rehabilitated while retaining its principal spaces and features—and its historic character—intact. Photos: Jay White.

3. Repair rather than replace historic windows whenever possible, and avoid "blocking them down" or covering them up. Avoid the insertion of numerous new window openings. They can give a building a domestic appearance, radically altering a barn's character. However, if additional light is needed, add new windows carefully, respecting the size and scale of existing window openings.

4. Avoid changing the size of door openings whenever possible. Increasing the height of door openings to accommodate new farm machinery can dramatically alter the historic character of a barn. If larger doors are needed, minimize the visual change. Use new track-hung doors rather than oversized rolled steel doors, which give an industrial appearance incompatible with most historic barns. If the barn has wood siding, the new doors should match it. If historic doors are no longer needed, fix them shut instead of removing them and filling in the openings.

5. Consider a new exterior addition only if it is essential to the continued use of a historic barn. A new addition can damage or destroy historic features and materials and alter the overall form of the historic building. If an addition is required, it should be built in a way that minimizes damage to external walls and internal plan. It should also be compatible with the historic barn, but sufficiently differentiated from it so that the new work is not confused with what is genuinely part of the past.

6. Retain interior spaces and features as much as possible. The internal volume of a barn is often a major character-defining feature, and the insertion of new floors, partitions, and structures within the barn can drastically impair the overall character of the space. Similarly, interior features should also be retained to the extent possible.

7. Retain as much of the historic internal structural system as possible. Even in cases where it is impractical to keep all of the exposed structural system, it may be possible to keep sufficiently extensive portions of it to convey a strong sense of the interior character. Wholesale replacement of the historic structural system with a different system should be avoided.

Housing: A Special Concern

The conversion of barns to housing is not new, but has become increasingly popular in recent years. Yet the changes involved in converting most barns to housing are so great that such conversions rarely preserve the historic character of the resource. Ordinarily, numerous windows are inserted, walls are heavily insulated and refinished, the interior volume is greatly reduced, chimneys and other fixtures normally lacking in barns are added, and site changes, such as close-in parking and residential landscaping are made, giving the building a greatly altered site. Many other barns are "converted" to houses by dismantling them, discarding the exterior, and reusing the internal structural system in a new building. The beams are saved, but the barn is lost.

In cases where the conversion from barns to houses has been successful, the positive outcome results in large measure from the careful choice of the barn: A modest-sized barn with a sufficient number of existing residential-scale windows, in which nearly the whole internal volume can be used as is, without building numerous new partitions or extending a new floor across the open space (haylofts in such cases serving as loft-space for "second story" bedrooms).

Summary

Historic barns form a vital part of our Nation's heritage. Not every historic barn can be saved from encroaching development, or easily brought back into productive use. Yet thousands of such structures can be repaired or rehabilitated for continued agricultural use or for new functions without destroying the very qualities that make them worth saving. By carefully examining the historic significance of each structure, owners of historic barns can draw up plans that preserve and reuse these historic structures while maintaining their historic character.

Selected Reading

Arthur, Eric and Dudley Witney. *The Barn: A Vanishing Landmark in North America.* Greenwich, CT: New York Graphic Society Ltd., 1972.

Fitchen, John. *The New World Dutch Barn: A Study of Its Characteristics, Its Structural System, and Its Probable Erectional Procedures.* Syracuse, NY: Syracuse University Press, 1968.

Halsted, Byron D., ed. *Barns, Sheds and Outbuildings.* New York: O. Judd Co., 1881. Rpt.: Brattleboro, VT: Stephen Greene Press, 1977.

Humstone, Mary. *Barn Again! A Guide to Rehabilitation of Older Farm Buildings.* Des Moines, IA: Meredith Corporation and the National Trust for Historic Preservation, 1988.

Klamkin, Charles. *Barns: Their History, Preservation and Restoration.* New York: Hawthorn, 1973.

Schuler, Stanley. *American Barns: In a Class by Themselves*, Exton, PA: Schiffer Publishing Ltd., 1984.

Schultz, LeRoy G., comp. *Barns, Stables and Outbuildings: A World Bibliography in English, 1700–1983.* Jefferson, NC, and London: McFarland & Co., 1986.

Stokes, Samuel N., et al. *Saving America's Countryside: A Guide to Rural Conservation.* Baltimore and London: Johns Hopkins University Press, 1989.

Cover photograph: Prairie barn with monitor roof, North Dakota. Photo: Mary Humstone.

NOTES

[1] Noré V. Winter, "Design on the Farm: A Rural Preservation Forum," Unpublished proceedings from a Conference sponsored by the National Trust for Historic Preservation, Denver, Colorado, January 13–14, 1986.

[2] Descriptions of the primary barn types featured in this section are heavily indebted to Eric Arthur and Dudley Witney, *The Barn: A Vanishing Landmark in North America.* Greenwich, CT: New York Graphic Society, Ltd., 1972.

[3] John Fitchen, *The New World Dutch Barn: A Study of Its Characteristics, Its Structural System, and Its Probable Erectional Procedures.* Syracuse, NY: Syracuse University Press, 1968, p. 136.

[4] Washington's "round" barn, actually a 16-sided barn, is shown in Lowell J. Soike, *Without Right Angles: The Round Barns of Iowa.* Des Moines: Iowa State Historical Department, 1983. Round, octagonal and other polygonal barns are normally all classed as "round barns." When it is necessary to be more precise, the term "true round" is used to distinguish round barns from hexagonal, octagonal, or other polygonal barns. The Shaker Round Barn is a true round barn. Gutted by fire in 1864, the barn was rebuilt shortly thereafter. See Polly Matherly and John D. McDermott, Hancock Shaker Village National Historic Landmark study, History Division, National Park Service, Washington, D.C.

[5] In addition to the sources mentioned above, the following studies were important sources for this section: Mark L. Peckham, "Central Plan Dairy Barns of New York Thematic Resources," Albany: New York State Division for Historic Preservation, 1984; and James E. Jacobsen and Cheryl Peterson, "Iowa Round Barns: The Sixty Year Experiment Thematic Resources," Des Moines: Iowa State Historical Department, 1986. These thematic studies document barns listed in the National Register of Historic Places.

[6] Charles Klamkin, *Barns: Their History, Preservation, and Restoration.* New York: Hawthorn, 1973, p. 57.

Acknowledgements

The author gratefully acknowledges the invaluable assistance of Mary Humstone, National Trust for Historic Preservation, Mountains/Plains Regional Office, and Sharon C. Park, Kay D. Weeks, and Robert Powers of the National Park Service. Significant contributions were also made by Stan Graves, Texas Historical Commission, on behalf of the National Conference of State Historic Preservation Officers; Shirley Dunn, Dutch Barn Preservation Society, Rensselaer, NY; Janis King, Knoxville, IL; Marilyn Fedelchak, National Trust for Historic Preservation; Fred Swader, U.S. Department of Agriculture, and Linda McClelland, National Register of Historic Places. In addition, useful comments and technical assistance were provided by the staff of the Technical Preservation Services Branch, directed by H. Ward Jandl, by the cultural resources staff of National Park Service Regional Offices, by Jack Boucher, Catherine Lavoie and Ellen Minnich of the Historic American Buildings Survey, and by Alicia Weber of the Park Historic Architecture Division.

This publication has been prepared pursuant to the National Historic Preservation Act, as amended, which directs the Secretary of the Interior to develop and make available information concerning historic properties. Preservation Brief 20 has been developed under the direction of Lee H. Nelson, FAIA, Chief, Preservation Assistance Division, National Park Service, P.O. Box 37127, Washington, D.C. 20013-7127.

21

Repairing Historic Flat Plaster— Walls and Ceilings

Marylee MacDonald

U.S. Department of the Interior   National Park Service
Preservation Assistance Division   Technical Preservation Services

Plaster in a historic building is like a family album. The handwriting of the artisans, the taste of the original occupants, and the evolving styles of decoration are embodied in the fabric of the building. From modest farmhouses to great buildings, regardless of the ethnic origins of the occupants, plaster has traditionally been used to finish interior walls.

A versatile material, plaster could be applied over brick, stone, half-timber, or frame construction. It provided a durable surface that was easy to clean and that could be applied to flat or curved walls and ceilings.

Plaster could be treated in any number of ways: it could receive stenciling, decorative painting, wallpaper, or whitewash. This variety and the adaptability of the material to nearly any building size, shape, or configuration meant that plaster was the wall surface chosen for nearly all buildings until the 1930s or 40s (Fig. 1).

Historic plaster may first appear so fraught with problems that its total removal seems the only alternative. But there are practical and historical reasons for saving it. First, three-coat plaster is unmatched in strength

Fig. 1. Left: Schifferstadt, Frederick, Maryland, 1756. Right: First Christian Church, Eugene, Oregon, 1911. Although these two structures are separated in history by over 150 years and differences in size, ethnic origin, geography, construction techniques, and architectural character, their builders both used plaster as the interior surface coating for flat and curved walls. Photo left: Kay Weeks. Photo right: Kaye Ellen Simonson.

and durability. It resists fire and reduces sound transmission. Next, replacing plaster is expensive. A building owner needs to think carefully about the condition of the plaster that remains; plaster is often not as badly damaged as it first appears. Of more concern to preservationists, however, original lime and gypsum plaster is part of the building's historic fabric—its smooth-troweled or textured surfaces and subtle contours evoke the presence of America's earlier craftsmen. Plaster can also serve as a plain surface for irreplaceable decorative finishes. For both reasons, plaster walls and ceilings contribute to the historic character of the interior and should be left in place and repaired if at all possible (Fig. 2).

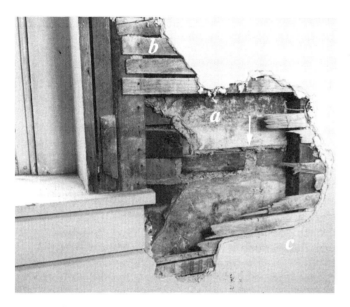

Fig. 2. A hole in the wall of a 1760s Custom House in Chestertown, Maryland illustrates the evolution of the room. (a) The original plaster was applied directly to an exterior masonry wall and the chairrail (missing here, see arrow) was in place before the wet plaster was applied to the wall. Sometime later when the interior was modified, the masonry was furred out. Machine-sawn wood lath (b) was nailed to the furring strips and (c) new three-coat plaster was applied. Photo: Maryland Historical Trust.

The approaches described in this Brief stress repairs using *wet* plaster, and traditional materials and techniques that will best assist the preservation of historic plaster walls and ceilings—and their appearance. Dry wall repairs are not included here, but have been written about extensively in other contexts. Finally, this Brief describes a replacement option when historic plaster cannot be repaired. Thus, a veneer plaster system is discussed rather than dry wall. Veneer systems include a coat or coats of *wet* plaster—although thinly applied—which can, to a greater extent, simulate traditional hand-troweled or textured finish coats. This system is generally better suited to historic preservation projects than dry wall.

To repair plaster, a building owner must often enlist the help of a plasterer. Plastering is a skilled craft, requiring years of training and special tools (Fig. 3). While minor repairs can be undertaken by building owners, most repairs will require the assistance of a plasterer.

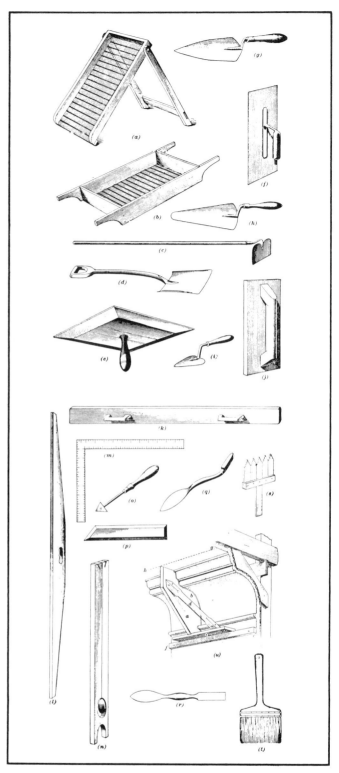

Fig. 3. Many of these traditional plastering tools are still used today: (a) screen to separate coarse sand from fine sand; (b) lime screen to remove unslaked particles of lime; (c) hoe; (d) shovel; (e) hawk to hold small amounts of plaster; (f) angle float to apply finishes to inside angles; (g), (h), (i) assorted trowels to apply basecoats and finish coat; (j) padded float to level off humps and fill in hollows caused by other tools; (k) a two-handled float or "darby" to float larger surfaces; (l) a simple straight edge; (m) a square to test the trueness of angles; (n) plumb to check verticality of plastered surfaces; (o), (p), (q), (r) jointing and mitering tools to pick out angles in decorative moldings; (s) comb made of sharpened lath pieces to scratch the basecoat of plaster; (t) brush to dampen plaster surfaces while they are worked smooth; (u) template made of wood and metal to cut a required outline for a fancy mold.

Historical Background

Plasterers in North America have relied on two materials to create their handiwork—lime and gypsum. Until the end of the 19th century, plasterers used lime plaster. Lime plaster was made from four ingredients: lime, aggregate, fiber, and water. The lime came from ground-and-heated limestone or oyster shells; the aggregate from sand; and the fiber from cattle or hog hair. Manufacturing changes at the end of the 19th century made it possible to use gypsum as a plastering material. Gypsum and lime plasters were used in combination for the base and finish coats during the early part of the 20th century; gypsum was eventually favored because it set more rapidly and, initially, had a harder finish.

Not only did the basic plastering material change, but the method of application changed also. In early America, the windows, doors, and all other trim were installed before the plaster was applied to the wall (Fig. 4). Generally the woodwork was prime-painted before plastering. Obtaining a plumb, level wall, while working against built-up mouldings, must have been difficult. But sometime in the first half of the 19th century, builders began installing wooden plaster "grounds" around windows and doors and at the base of the wall. Installing these grounds so that they were level and plumb made the job much easier because the plasterer could work from a level, plumb, straight surface. Woodwork was then nailed to the "grounds" after the walls were plastered (Fig. 5). Evidence of plaster behind trim is often an aid to dating historic houses, or to discerning their physical evolution.

Fig. 4. *The builders of this mid-18th century house installed the baseboard moulding first, then applied a mud and horse hair plaster (called paling) to the masonry wall. Lime was used for the finish plaster. Also shown are the hacking marks which prepared the wall for a subsequent layer of plaster. Photo: Kay Weeks.*

Fig. 5 (a). *The photo above shows the use of wooden plaster "grounds" nailed to the wall studs of the mid-19th century Lockwood House in Harpers Ferry, West Virginia. This allowed the plasterer to work flush with the surface of the grounds. Afterwards, the carpenter could nail the finish woodwork to the ground, effectively hiding the joint between the plaster and the ground. The trim was painted after its installation, leaving a paint outline on the plaster. Fig. 5 (b). The photo below shows door trim and mouldings in place after the plastering was complete. Photos: Kaye Ellen Simonson.*

Lime Plaster

When building a house, plasterers traditionally mixed bags of quick lime with water to "hydrate" or "slake" the lime. As the lime absorbed the water, heat was given off. When the heat diminished, and the lime and water were thoroughly mixed, the lime putty that resulted was used to make plaster.

When lime putty, sand, water, and animal hair were mixed, the mixture provided the plasterer with "coarse stuff." This mixture was applied in one or two layers to build up the wall thickness. But the best plaster was done with three coats. The first two coats made up the coarse stuff; they were the *scratch* coat and the *brown* coat. The finish plaster, called "setting stuff" contained a much higher proportion of lime putty, little aggregate, and no fiber, and gave the wall a smooth white surface finish.

Compared to the 3/8-inch-thick layers of the scratch and brown coats, the finish coat was a mere 1/8-inch thick. Additives were used for various finish qualities.

For example, fine white sand was mixed in for a "float finish." This finish was popular in the early 1900s. (If the plasterer raked the sand with a broom, the plaster wall would retain swirl marks or stipples.) Or marble dust was added to create a hard-finish white coat which could be smoothed and polished with a steel trowel. Finally, a little plaster of Paris, or "gauged stuff," was often added to the finish plaster to accelerate the setting time.

Although lime plaster was used in this country until the early 1900s, it had certain disadvantages. A plastered wall could take more than a year to dry; this delayed painting or papering. In addition, bagged quick lime had to be carefully protected from contact with air, or it became inert because it reacted with ambient moisture and carbon dioxide. Around 1900, gypsum began to be used as a plastering material.

Gypsum Plaster

Gypsum begins to cure as soon as it is mixed with water. It sets in minutes and completely dries in two to three weeks. Historically, gypsum made a more rigid plaster and did not require a fibrous binder. However, it is difficult to tell the difference between lime and gypsum plaster once the plaster has cured.

Despite these desirable working characteristics, gypsum plaster was more vulnerable to water damage than lime. Lime plasters had often been applied directly to masonry walls (without lathing), forming a suction bond. They could survive occasional wind-driven moisture or water wicking up from the ground. Gypsum plaster needed protection from water. Furring strips had to be used against masonry walls to create a dead air space. This prevented moisture transfer.

In rehabilitation and restoration projects, one should rely on the plasterer's judgment about whether to use lime or gypsum plaster. In general, gypsum plaster is the material plasterers use today. Different types of aggregate may be specified by the architect such as clean river sand, perlite, pumice, or vermiculite; however, if historic finishes and textures are being replicated, sand should be used as the base-coat aggregate. Today, if fiber is required in a base coat, a special gypsum is available which includes wood fibers. Lime putty, mixed with about 35 percent gypsum (gauging plaster) to help it harden, is still used as the finish coat.

Lath

Lath provided a means of holding the plaster in place. Wooden lath was nailed at right angles directly to the structural members of the buildings (the joists and studs), or it was fastened to non-structural spaced strips known as furring strips. Three types of lath can be found on historic buildings (Fig. 6).

Wood Lath. Wood lath is usually made up of narrow, thin strips of wood with spaces in between. The plasterer applies a slight pressure to push the wet plaster through the spaces. The plaster slumps down on the inside of the wall, forming plaster "keys." These keys hold the plaster in place.

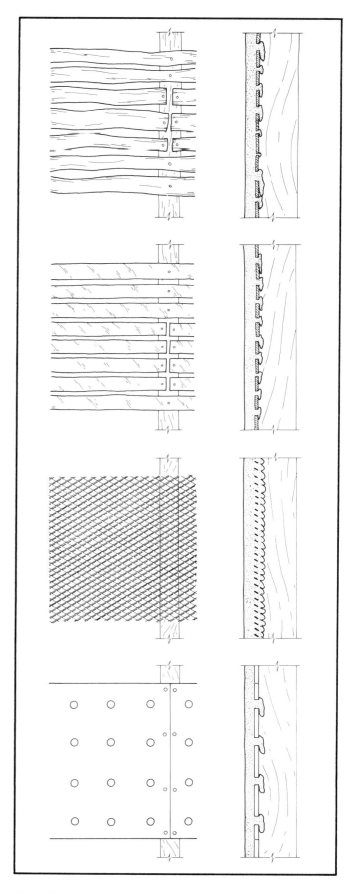

Fig. 6. Top to bottom: Hand-riven lath, machine-sawn wood lath, expanded metal (diamond mesh) lath, and perforated gypsum board lath. Profile views of their keying characteristics are shown to the right. For plaster repairs or replastering, galvanized metal lath is the most reliable in terms of longevity, stability, and proper keying. Drawing: Kaye Ellen Simonson.

Metal Lath. Metal lath, patented in England in 1797, began to be used in parts of the United States toward the end of the 19th century. The steel making up the metal lath contained many more spaces than wood lath had contained. These spaces increased the number of keys; metal lath was better able to hold plaster than wood lath had been.

Rock Lath. A third lath system commonly used was rock lath (also called plaster board or gypsum-board lath). In use as early as 1900, rock lath was made up of compressed gypsum covered by a paper facing. Some rock lath was textured or perforated to provide a key for wet plaster. A special paper with gypsum crystals in it provides the key for rock lath used today; when wet plaster is applied to the surface, a crystalline bond is achieved.

Rock lath was the most economical of the three lathing systems. Lathers or carpenters could prepare a room more quickly. By the late 1930s, rock lath was used almost exclusively in residential plastering.

Common Plaster Problems

When plaster dries, it is a relatively rigid material which should last almost indefinitely. However, there are conditions that cause plaster to crack, effloresce, separate, or become detached from its lath framework (Fig. 7). These include:

- Structural Problems
- Poor Workmanship
- Improper Curing
- Moisture

Structural Problems

Overloading. Stresses within a wall, or acting on the house as a whole, can create stress cracks. Appearing as diagonal lines in a wall, stress cracks usually start at a door or window frame, but they can appear anywhere in the wall, with seemingly random starting points.

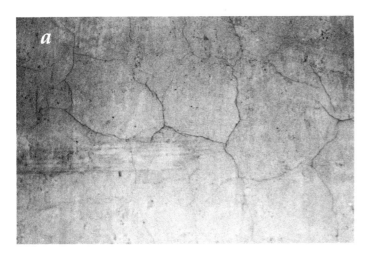

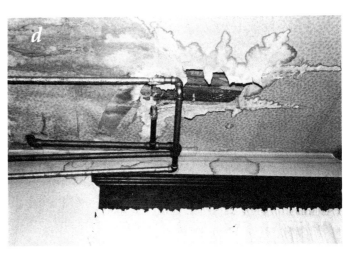

Fig. 7 (a) to (d). A series of photographs taken in different rooms of an early 20th century house in West Virginia reveal a variety of plaster wall surface problems, most of which can easily be remedied through sensitive repair: Hairline cracks (a) in an otherwise sound wall can be filled with joint compound or patching plaster. The wall can also be canvassed or wallpapered. Stress cracks (b) in plaster over a kitchen door frame can be repaired using fiberglass mesh tape and joint compound. Settlement cracks (c) in a bedroom can be similarly repaired. The dark crack at the juncture between walls, however, may be a structural crack and should be investigated for its underlying cause. Moisture damage (d) from leaking plumbing on the second floor has damaged both wallpaper and plaster in the dining room. After fixing the leaking pipes, the wall covering and rotted plaster will need to be replaced and any holes repaired. Photos: Kay Weeks.

Builders of now-historic houses had no codes to help them size the structural members of buildings. The weight of the roof, the second and third stories, the furniture, and the occupants could impose a heavy burden on beams, joists, and studs. Even when houses were built properly, later remodeling efforts may have cut in a doorway or window without adding a structural beam or "header" across the top of the opening. Occasionally, load-bearing members were simply too small to carry the loads above them. Deflection or wood "creep" (deflection that occurs over time) can create cracks in plaster.

Overloading and structural movement (especially when combined with rotting lath, rusted nails, or poor quality plaster) can cause plaster to detach from the lath. The plaster loses its key. When the mechanical bond with the lath is broken, plaster becomes loose or bowed. If repairs are not made, especially to ceilings, gravity will simply cause chunks of plaster to fall to the floor.

Settlement/Vibration. Cracks in walls can also result when houses settle. Houses built on clay soils are especially vulnerable. Many types of clay (such as montmorillonite) are highly expansive. In the dry season, water evaporates from the clay particles, causing them to contract. During the rainy season, the clay swells. Thus, a building can be riding on an unstable footing. Diagonal cracks running in opposite directions suggest that house settling and soil conditions may be at fault. Similar symptoms occur when there is a nearby source of vibration—blasting, a train line, busy highway, or repeated sonic booms.

Lath movement. Horizontal cracks are often caused by lath movement. Because it absorbs moisture from the air, wood lath expands and contracts as humidity rises and falls. This can cause cracks to appear year after year. Cracks can also appear between rock lath panels. A nail holding the edge of a piece of lath may rust or loosen, or structural movement in the wood framing behind the lath may cause a seam to open. Heavy loads in a storage area above a rock-lath ceiling can also cause ceiling cracks.

Errors in initial building construction such as improper bracing, poor corner construction, faulty framing of doors and windows, and undersized beams and floor joists eventually "telegraph" through to the plaster surface.

Poor Workmanship

In addition to problems caused by movement or weakness in the structural framework, plaster durability can be affected by poor materials or workmanship.

Poorly proportioned mix. The proper proportioning and mixing of materials are vital to the quality of the plaster job. A bad mix can cause problems that appear years later in a plaster wall. Until recently, proportions of aggregate and lime were mixed on the job. A plasterer may have skimped on the amount of cementing material (lime or gypsum) because sand was the cheaper material. Oversanding can cause the plaster to weaken or crumble (Fig. 8). Plaster made from a poorly proportioned mix may be more difficult to repair.

Fig. 8. Too much aggregate (sand) and not enough cementing material (lime or gypsum) in the base coat has made this plaster surface weak and crumbly. Besides losing its key with the lath, the layers are disintegrating. It will most likely need to be totally removed and replaced with all new plaster. Photo: Marylee MacDonald.

Incompatible basecoats and finish coats. Use of perlite as an aggregate also presented problems. Perlite is a lightweight aggregate used in the base coat instead of sand. It performs well in cold weather and has a slightly better insulating value. But if a smooth lime finish coat was applied over perlited base coats on wood or rock lath, cracks would appear in the finish coat and the entire job would have to be re-done. To prevent this, a plasterer had to add fine silica sand or finely crushed perlite to the finish coat to compensate for the dramatically differing shrinkage rates between the base coat and the finish coat.

Improper plaster application. The finish coat is subject to "chip cracking" if it was applied over an excessively dry base coat, or was insufficiently troweled, or if too little gauging plaster was used. Chip cracking looks very much like an alligatored paint surface. Another common problem is called map cracking—fine, irregular cracks that occur when the finish coat has been applied to an oversanded base coat or a very thin base coat.

Too much retardant. Retarding agents are added to slow down the rate at which plaster sets, and thus inhibit hardening. They have traditionally included ammonia, glue, gelatin, starch, molasses, or vegetable oil. If the plasterer has used too much retardant, however, a gypsum plaster will not set within a normal 20 to 30 minute time period. As a result, the surface becomes soft and powdery.

Inadequate plaster thickness. Plaster is applied in three coats over wood lath and metal lath—the scratch, brown, and finish coats. In three-coat work, the scratch coat and brown coat were sometimes applied on successive days to make up the required wall thickness. Using rock lath allowed the plasterer to apply one base coat and the finish coat—a two-coat job.

If a plasterer skimped on materials, the wall may not have sufficient plaster thickness to withstand the normal stresses within a building. The minimum total thickness for plaster on gypsum board (rock lath) is 1/2 inch. On metal lath the minimum thickness is 5/8 inch; and for wood lath it is about 3/4 to 7/8 inch. This minimum plaster thickness may affect the thickness of trim projecting from the wall's plane.

Improper Curing

Proper temperature and air circulation during curing are key factors in a durable plaster job. The ideal temperature for plaster to cure is between 55–70 degrees Fahrenheit. However, historic houses were sometimes plastered before window sashes were put in. There was no way to control temperature and humidity.

Dryouts, freezing, and sweat-outs. When temperatures were too hot, the plaster would return to its original condition before it was mixed with water, that is, calcined gypsum. A plasterer would have to spray the wall with alum water to re-set the plaster. If freezing occurred before the plaster had set, the job would simply have to be re-done. If the windows were shut so that air could not circulate, the plaster was subject to sweat-out or rot. Since there is no cure for rotted plaster, the affected area had to be removed and replastered.

Moisture

Plaster applied to a masonry wall is vulnerable to water damage if the wall is constantly wet. When salts from the masonry substrate come in contact with water, they migrate to the surface of the plaster, appearing as dry bubbles or efflorescence. The source of the moisture must be eliminated before replastering the damaged area.

Sources of Water Damage. Moisture problems occur for several reasons. Interior plumbing leaks in older houses are common. Roofs may leak, causing ceiling damage. Gutters and downspouts may also leak, pouring rain water next to the building foundation. In brick buildings, dampness at the foundation level can wick up into the above-grade walls. Another common source of moisture is splash-back. When there is a paved area next to a masonry building, rainwater splashing up from the paving can dampen masonry walls. In both cases water travels through the masonry and damages interior plaster. Coatings applied to the

interior are not effective over the long run. The moisture problem must be stopped on the outside of the wall.

Repairing Historic Plaster

Many of the problems described above may not be easy to remedy. If major structural problems are found to be the source of the plaster problem, the structural problem should be corrected. Some repairs can be made by removing only small sections of plaster to gain access. Minor structural problems that will not endanger the building can generally be ignored. Cosmetic damages from minor building movement, holes, or bowed areas can be repaired without the need for wholesale demolition. However, it may be necessary to remove deteriorated plaster caused by rising damp in order for masonry walls to dry out. Repairs made to a wet base will fail again.

Canvassing Uneven Wall Surfaces

Uneven wall surfaces, caused by previous patching or by partial wallpaper removal, are common in old houses. As long as the plaster is generally sound, cosmetically unattractive plaster walls can be "wallpapered" with strips of a canvas or fabric-like material. Historically, canvassing covered imperfections in the plaster and provided a stable base for decorative painting or wallpaper.

Filling Cracks

Hairline cracks in wall and ceiling plaster are not a serious cause for concern as long as the underlying plaster is in good condition. They may be filled easily with a patching material (see **Patching Materials,** page 13). For cracks that re-open with seasonal humidity change, a slightly different method is used. First the crack is widened slightly with a sharp, pointed tool such as a crack widener or a triangular can opener. Then the crack is filled. For more persistent cracks, it may be necessary to bridge the crack with tape. In this instance, a fiberglass mesh tape is pressed into the patching material. After the first application of a quick-setting joint compound dries, a second coat is used to cover the tape, feathering it at the edges. A third coat is applied to even out the surface, followed by light sanding. The area is cleaned off with a damp sponge, then dried to remove any leftover plaster residue or dust.

When cracks are larger and due to structural movement, repairs need to be made to the structural system *before* repairing the plaster. Then, the plaster on each side of the crack should be removed to a width of about 6 inches down to the lath. The debris is cleaned out, and metal lath applied to the cleared area, leaving the existing wood lath in place. The metal lath usually prevents further cracking. The crack is patched with an appropriate plaster in three layers (i.e., basecoats and finish coat). If a crack seems to be expanding, a structural engineer should be consulted.

Replacing Delaminated Areas of the Finish Coat

Sometimes the finish coat of plaster comes loose from the base coat (Fig. 9). In making this type of repair, the plasterer paints a liquid plaster-bonding agent onto the areas of base-coat plaster that will be replastered with a new lime finish coat. A homeowner wishing to repair small areas of delaminated finish coat can use the methods described in **Patching Materials**.

Fig. 9. The smooth-troweled lime finish coat has delaminated from the brown coat underneath. This is another repair that can be undertaken without further loss of the historic plaster. Photo: Marylee MacDonald.

Patching Holes in Walls

For small holes (less than 4 inches in diameter) that involve loss of the brown and finish coats, the repair is made in two applications. First, a layer of basecoat plaster is troweled in place and scraped back below the level of the existing plaster. When the base coat has set but not dried, more plaster is applied to create a smooth, level surface. One-coat patching is not generally recommended by plasterers because it tends to produce concave surfaces that show up when the work is painted. Of course, if the lath only had one coat of plaster originally, then a one-coat patch is appropriate (Fig. 10).

For larger holes where all three coats of plaster are damaged or missing down to the wood lath, plasterers generally proceed along these lines. First, all the old plaster is cleaned out and any loose lath is re-nailed. Next, a water mist is sprayed on the old lath to keep it from twisting when the new, wet plaster is applied, or better still, a bonding agent is used. To provide more reliable keying and to strengthen the patch, expanded metal lath (diamond mesh) should be attached to the wood lath with tie wires or nailed over the wood lath with lath nails (Fig. 11). The plaster is then applied in three layers over the metal lath, lapping each new layer of plaster over the old plaster so that old and new are evenly joined. This stepping is recommended to produce a strong, invisible patch (Fig. 12). Also, if a patch is made in a plaster wall that is slightly wavy, the contour of the patch should be made to conform to the irregularities of the existing work. A flat patch will stand out from the rest of the wall.

Fig. 10 (a) and (b). In this New Hampshire residence dating from the 1790s, the original plaster was a single coat of lime, sand, and horsehair applied over split lath. A one-coat repair, in this case, is appropriate. To the left: a flat sheet of galvanized expanded metal lath is placed over the patch area and an outline marked with a large soft lumber crayon. The metal lath is then cut to fit the hole and nailed to the lath. To the right: the edges of the original plaster and wood lath beneath have been thoroughly soaked with water. A steel trowel is used to apply the plaster in large, rough strokes. Finally, it will be scraped and smoothed off. Because only one coat of plaster is used, without a finish coat, a clean butt-joint is made with the original plaster. Photos: John Leeke.

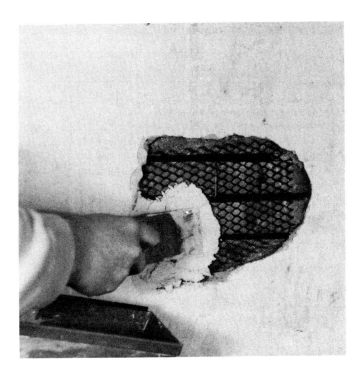

Fig. 11. Repairs are being made to the historic plaster in an early 20th century residence in Tennessee. A fairly sizeable hole in three-coat plaster extends to the wood lath. Expanded metal lath has been cut to fit the hole, then attached to the wood lath with a tie-wire. Two ready-mix gypsum base coats are in the process of being applied. After they set, the finish coat will be smooth-troweled gauged lime to match the existing wall. Photo: Walter Jowers.

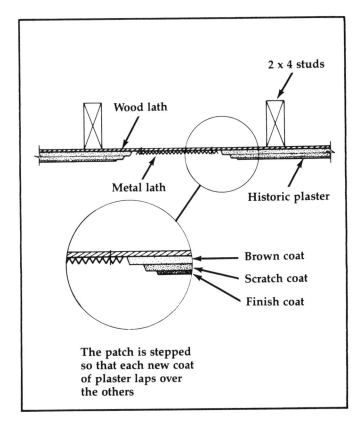

Fig. 12. This explains how a hole in historic plaster is repaired over the existing wood lath. First, metal lath is secured over the wood lath with a tie wire, then the new plaster is applied in three layers, "stepped" so that each new coat overlaps the old plaster to create a good adhesive bond. Drawing: Kaye Ellen Simonson.

Patching Holes in Ceilings

Hairline cracks and holes may be unsightly, but when portions of the ceiling come loose, a more serious problem exists (Fig. 13). The keys holding the plaster to the ceiling have probably broken. First, the plaster around the loose plaster should be examined. Keys may have deteriorated because of a localized moisture problem, poor quality plaster, or structural overloading; yet, the surrounding system may be intact. If the areas surrounding the loose area are in reasonably good condition, the loose plaster can be reattached to the lath using flat-head wood screws and plaster washers (Fig. 14). To patch a hole in the ceiling plaster, metal lath is fastened over the wood lath; then the hole is filled with successive layers of plaster, as described above.

Fig. 13. This beaded ceiling in one of the bedrooms of the 1847 Lockwood House, Harpers Ferry, West Virginia, is missing portions of plaster due to broken keys. This is attributable, in part, to deterioration of the wood lath. Photo: Kaye Ellen Simonson.

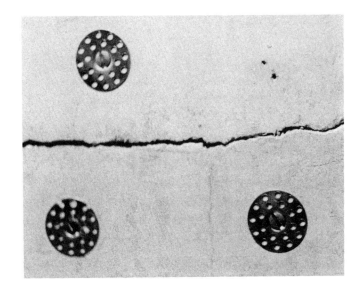

Fig. 14. In a late 18th century house in Massachusetts, flat-head wood screws and plaster washers were used to reattach loose ceiling plaster to the wood lath. After the crack is covered with fiberglass mesh tape, both the taped crack and the plaster washers will be skim-coated with a patching material. Photo: John Obed Curtis.

223

Establishing New Plaster Keys

If the back of the ceiling lath is accessible (usually from the attic or after removing floor boards), small areas of bowed-out plaster can be pushed back against the lath. A padded piece of plywood and braces are used to secure the loose plaster. After dampening the old lath and coating the damaged area with a bonding agent, a fairly liquid plaster mix (with a glue size retardant added) is applied to the backs of the lath, and worked into the voids between the faces of the lath and the back of the plaster. While this first layer is still damp, plaster-soaked strips of jute scrim are laid across the backs of the lath and pressed firmly into the first layer as reinforcement. The original lath must be secure, otherwise the weight of the patching plaster may loosen it.

Loose, damaged plaster can also be re-keyed when the goal is to conserve decorative surfaces or wallpaper. Large areas of ceilings and walls can be saved. This method requires the assistance of a skilled conservator—it is not a repair technique used by most plasterers. The conservator injects an acrylic adhesive mixture through holes drilled in the face of the plaster (or through the lath from behind, when accessible). The loose plaster is held firm with plywood bracing until the adhesive bonding mixture sets. When complete, gaps between the plaster and lath are filled, and the loose plaster is secure (Fig. 15).

Fig. 15. When ceiling repairs are made with wet plaster or with an injected adhesive mixture, the old loose plaster must be supported with a plywood brace until re-keying is complete. Photo: John Leeke.

Replastering Over the Old Ceiling

If a historic ceiling is too cracked to patch or is sagging (but not damaged from moisture), plasterers routinely keep the old ceiling and simply relath and replaster over it. This repair technique can be used if lowering the ceiling slightly does not affect other ornamental features. The existing ceiling is covered with 1x3-inch wood furring strips, one to each joist, and fastened completely through the old lath and plaster using a screw gun. Expanded metal lath or gypsum board lath is nailed over the furring strips. Finally, two or three coats are applied according to traditional methods. Replastering over the old ceiling saves time, creates much less dust than demolition, and gives added fire protection.

When Damaged Plaster Cannot be Repaired—Replacement Options

Partial or complete removal may be necessary if plaster is badly damaged, particularly if the damage was caused by long-term moisture problems. Workers undertaking demolition should wear OSHA-approved masks because the plaster dust that flies into the air may contain decades of coal soot. Lead, from lead-based paint, is another danger. Long-sleeved clothing and head-and-eye protection should be worn. Asbestos, used in the mid-twentieth century as an insulating and fireproofing additive, may also be present and OSHA-recommended precautions should be taken. If plaster in adjacent rooms is still in good condition, walls should not be pounded—a small trowel or pry bar is worked behind the plaster carefully in order to pry loose pieces off the wall.

When the damaged plaster has been removed, the owner must decide whether to replaster over the existing lath or use a different system. This decision should be based in part on the thickness of the original plaster and the condition of the original lath. Economy and time are also valid considerations. It is important to ensure that the wood trim around the windows and doors will have the same "reveal" as before. (The "reveal" is the projection of the wood trim from the surface of the plastered wall). A lath and plaster system that will give this required depth should be selected.

Replastering—Alternative Lath Systems for New Plaster

Replastering old wood lath. When plasterers work with old lath, each lath strip is re-nailed and the chunks of old plaster are cleaned out. Because the old lath is dry, it must be thoroughly soaked before applying the base coats of plaster, or it will warp and buckle; furthermore, because the water is drawn out, the plaster will fail to set properly. As noted earlier, if new metal lath is installed *over* old wood lath as the base for new plaster, many of these problems can be avoided and the historic lath can be retained (Fig. 16). The ceiling should still be sprayed unless a vapor barrier is placed behind the metal lath.

Replastering over new metal lath. An alternative to re-using the old wood lath is to install a different lathing system. Galvanized metal lath is the most expensive, but also the most reliable in terms of longevity, stability, and proper keying. When lathing over open joists, the plasterer should cover the joists with kraft paper or a polyethylene vapor barrier. Three coats of wet plaster are applied consecutively to form a solid, monolithic unit with the lath. The scratch coat keys into the metal lath; the second, or brown, coat bonds to the scratch coat and builds the thickness; the third, or finish coat, consists of lime putty and gauging plaster.

Replastering over new rock lath. It is also possible to use rock lath as a plaster base. Plasterers may need to remove the existing wood lath to maintain the woodwork's reveal. Rock lath is a 16x36-inch, 1/2-inch thick, gypsum-core panel covered with absorbent paper with gypsum crystals in the paper. The crystals in the paper bond the wet plaster and anchor it securely. This type of lath requires two coats of new plaster—the brown coat and the finish coat. The gypsum lath itself takes the place of the first, or scratch, coat of plaster.

Painting New Plaster

The key to a successful paint job is proper drying of the plaster. Historically, lime plasters were allowed to cure for at least a year before the walls were painted or papered. With modern ventilation, plaster cures in a shorter time; however, fresh gypsum plaster with a lime finish coat should still be perfectly dry before paint is applied—or the paint may peel. (Plasterers traditionally used the "match test" on new plaster. If a match would light by striking it on the new plaster surface, the plaster was considered dry.) Today it is best to allow new plaster to cure two to three weeks. A good alkaline-resistant primer, specifically formulated for new plaster, should then be used. A compatible latex or oil-based paint can be used for the final coat.

A Modern Replacement System

Veneer Plaster. Using one of the traditional lath and plaster systems provides the highest quality plaster job. However, in some cases, budget and time considerations may lead the owner to consider a less expensive replacement alternative. Designed to reduce the cost of materials, a more recent lath and plaster system is less expensive than a two-or-three coat plaster job, but only slightly more expensive than drywall. This plaster system is called veneer plaster.

Fig. 16. In the restoration of a ca. 1830s house in Maine, split-board lath has been covered with expanded metal lath in preparation for new coats of plaster. This method permits the early lath to be saved while the metal lath, with its superior keying, serves as reinforcement. Photo: National Park Service files.

The system uses gypsum-core panels that are the same size as drywall (4x8 feet), and specially made for veneer plaster. They can be installed over furring channels to masonry walls or over old wood lath walls and ceilings. Known most commonly as "blueboard," the panels are covered with a special paper compatible with veneer plaster. Joints between the 4-foot wide sheets are taped with fiberglass mesh, which is bedded in the veneer plaster. After the tape is bedded, a thin, 1/16-inch coat of high-strength veneer plaster is applied to the entire wall surface. A second veneer layer can be used as the "finish" coat, or the veneer plaster can be covered with a gauged lime finish-coat—the same coat that covers ordinary plaster (Fig. 17).

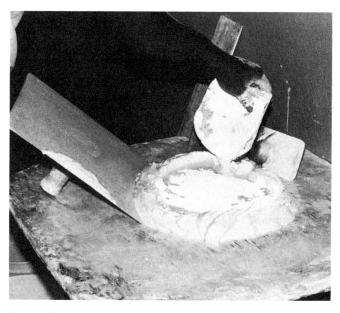

Fig. 17. This contemporary plasterer is mixing a lime finish coat in much the same way as America's earlier artisans. The ring consists of lime putty; the white powder inside is gauging plaster. After the mixture is blended, a steel trowel will be used to apply it. It should be noted that a traditional lime finish coat can be applied over a veneer plaster base coat to approximate the look of historic plaster walls and ceilings. Photo: Marylee MacDonald.

Although extremely thin, a two-coat veneer plaster system has a 1,500 psi rating and is thus able to withstand structural movements in a building or surface abrasion. With either a veneer finish or a gauged lime-putty finish coat, the room will be ready for painting almost immediately. When complete, the troweled or textured wall surface looks more like traditional plaster than drywall.

The thin profile of the veneer system has an added benefit, especially for owners of uninsulated masonry buildings. Insulation can be installed between the pieces of furring channel used to attach blueboard to masonry walls. This can be done without having to furr out the window and door jambs. The insulation plus the veneer system will result in the same thickness as the original plaster. Occupants in the rooms will be more comfortable because they will not be losing heat to cold wall surfaces.

Summary

The National Park Service recommends retaining historic plaster if at all possible. Plaster is a significant part of the "fabric" of the building. Much of the building's history is documented in the layers of paint and paper found covering old plaster. For buildings with decorative painting, conservation of historic flat plaster is even more important. Consultation with the National Park Service, with State Historic Preservation Officers, local preservation organizations, historic preservation consultants, or with the Association for Preservation Technology is recommended. Where plaster cannot be repaired or conserved using one of the approaches outlined in this Brief, documentation of the layers of wallpaper and paint should be undertaken before removing the historic plaster. This information may be needed to complete a restoration plan.

Patching Materials

Plasterers generally use ready-mix base-coat plaster for patching, especially where large holes need to be filled. The ready-mix plaster contains gypsum and aggregate in proper proportions. The plasterer only needs to add water.

Another mix plasterers use to patch cracks or small holes, or for finish-coat repair, is a "high gauge" lime putty (50 percent lime; 50 percent gauging plaster). This material will produce a white, smooth patch. It is especially suitable for surface repairs.

Although property owners cannot duplicate the years of accumulated knowledge and craft skills of a professional plasterer, there are materials that can be used for do-it-yourself repairs. For example, fine cracks can be filled with an all-purpose drywall joint compound. For bridging larger cracks using fiberglass tape, a homeowner can use a "quick-setting" joint compound. This compound has a fast drying time—60, 90, or 120 minutes. Quick-setting joint compound dries because of a chemical reaction, not because of water evaporation. It shrinks less than all-purpose joint compound and has much the same workability as ready-mix base-coat plaster. However, because quick-set joint compounds are hard to sand, they should only be used to bed tape or to fill large holes. All-purpose joint compound should be used as the final coat prior to sanding.

Homeowners may also want to try using a ready-mix perlited base-coat plaster for scratch and brown coat repair. The plaster can be hand-mixed in small quantities, but bagged ready-mix should be protected from ambient moisture. A "mill-mixed pre-gauged" lime finish coat plaster can also be used by homeowners. A base coat utilizing perlite or other lightweight aggregates should only be used for making small repairs (less than 4 ft. patches). For large-scale repairs and entire room re-plastering, see the precautions in Table 1 for using perlite.

Homeowners may see a material sold as "patching plaster" or "plaster of Paris" in hardware stores. This dry powder cannot be used by itself for plaster repairs. It must be combined with lime to create a successful patching mixture.

When using a lime finish coat for any repair, wait longer to paint, or use an alkaline-resistant primer.

TABLE 1
REPLASTERING
Selected Plaster Bases/Compatible Basecoats and Finish Coats

Traditional Plaster Bases	Compatible Basecoats	Compatible Finish Coats
OLD WOOD LATH	gypsum/sand plaster	lime putty/gauging plaster
	gypsum/perlite plaster [2]	lime putty/gauging plaster
METAL LATH	gypsum/sand plaster (high strength)	lime putty/gauging plaster
	gypsum/perlite plaster [2]	lime putty/gauging plaster
GYPSUM (ROCK) LATH PANELS	gypsum/sand plaster	lime putty/gauging plaster
	gypsum/perlite plaster [2]	lime putty/gauging plaster
UNGLAZED BRICK/CLAY TILE	gypsum/perlite plaster [2] (masonry type)	lime putty/gauging plaster
Modern Plaster Base	Compatible Basecoat	Compatible Finish Coat
GYPSUM CORE VENEER PANELS (BLUE BOARD)	veneer plaster	veneer plaster or lime putty/gauging plaster

---

[1] On traditional bases (wood, metal, and rock lath), the thickness of base coat plaster is one of the most important elements of a good plaster job. Grounds should be set to obtain the following minimum plaster thicknesses: (1) Over rock lath—1/2" (2) Over brick, clay tile, or other masonry—5/8" (3) Over metal lath, measured from face of lath—5/8" (4) Over wood lath—7/8". In no case should the total plaster thickness be less than 1/2". The allowance for the finish coat is approximately 1/16" which requires the base coat to be 7/16" for 1/2" grounds. This is a *minimum* base coat thickness on rock lath. The standard for other masonry units and metal lath is 5/8" thick, including the finish. Certain types of construction or fire ratings may require an increase in plaster thickness (and/or an increase in the gypsum to aggregate ration) but never a thinner application of plaster than recommended above. Job experience indicates that thin applications of plaster often evidence cracking where normal applications to standard grounds do not. This condition is a direct result of the inability of thin section areas to resist external forces as adequately as thicker, normal applications of plaster.

[2] Perlite is a lightweight aggregate often used in gypsum plaster in place of sand. It performs well in cold weather and has a slightly better insulating value than sand. In a construction with metal lath, perlite aggregate is not recommended in the basecoat except under a sand or "float" finish. When gypsum/perlite basecoats are used over any other base (i.e., wood, rock lath, brick) and the finish coat is to be a "white" finish coat (smooth-troweled gauged lime putty) it is necessary to add fine silica sand or perlite fines to the finish coat. This measure prevents cracking of the "white" finish coat due to differential shrinkage.

Plaster Terms

Scratch coat. The first base coat put on wood or metal lath. The wet plaster is "scratched" with a scarifier or comb to provide a rough surface so the next layer of base coat will stick to it.

Brown coat. The brown coat is the second application of wet, base-coat plaster with wood lath or metal systems. With gypsum board lath (rock lath, plasterboard), it is the only base coat needed.

Finish coat. Pure lime, mixed with about 35 percent gauging plaster to help it harden, is used for the very thin surface finish of the plaster wall. Fine sand can be added for a sanded finish coat.

Casing Bead. Early casing bead was made of wood. In the 19th century, metal casing beads were sometimes used around fireplace projections, and door and window openings. Like a wood ground, they indicate the proper thickness for the plaster.

Corner Bead. Wire mesh with a rigid metal spline used on outside corners. Installing the corner bead plumb is important.

Cornerite. Wire mesh used on inside corners of adjoining walls and ceilings. It keeps corners from cracking.

Ground. Plasterers use metal or wood strips around the edges of doors and windows and at the bottom of walls. These grounds help keep the plaster the same thickness and provide a stopping edge for the plaster. Early plaster work, however, did not use grounds. On early buildings, the woodwork was installed and primed before plastering began. Some time in the early 19th century, a transition occurred, and plasterers applied their wall finish before woodwork was installed.

Gypsum. Once mined from large gypsum quarries near Paris (thus the name plaster of Paris), gypsum in its natural form is calcium sulfate. When calcined (or heated), one-and-a-half water molecules are driven off, leaving a hemi-hydrate of calcium sulfate. When mixed with water, it becomes calcium sulfate again. While gypsum was used in base-coat plaster from the 1890s on, it has always been used in finish coat and decorative plaster. For finish coats, gauging plaster was added to lime putty; it causes the lime to harden. Gypsum is also the ingredient in moulding plaster, a finer plaster used to create decorative mouldings in ornamental plasterwork.

Lime. Found in limestone formations or shell mounds, naturally occurring lime is calcium carbonate. When heated, it becomes calcium oxide. After water has been added, it becomes calcium hydroxide. This calcium hydroxide reacts with carbon dioxide in the air to recreate the original calcium carbonate.

Screed. Screeds are strips of plaster run vertically or horizontally on walls or ceilings. They are used to plumb and straighten uneven walls and level ceilings. Metal screeds are used to separate different types of plaster finishes or to separate lime and cement plasters.

Reading List

Ashurst, John and Ashurst, Nicola. *Practical Building Conservation, English Heritage Technical Handbook, Volume 3. Mortars, Plasters and Renders.* New York: Halsted Press, 1988.

Gypsum Construction Handbook. Chicago: United States Gypsum Company, 1986.

Hodgson, Frederick Thomas. *Plaster and Plastering: Mortars and Cements, How to Make and How to Use.* New York: The Industrial Publication Company, 1901.

Jowers, Walter. "Plaster Patching, Part II." Restoration Primer. *New England Builder,* November, 1987, pp. 41–43.

Leeke, John. "Problems with Plaster, Part One." *Landmarks Observer,* Vol. 12. March/April, 1985., pp. 10, 14. Also "Problems with Plaster, Part Two." Vol. 12., May/June, 1985, p. 12.

——————. "Saving Irreplaceable Plaster." *Old House Journal.* Vol. XV, No. 6, November/December, 1987, pp. 51–55.

McKee, Harley J., FAIA. *Introduction to Early American Masonry—Stone, Brick, Mortar, and Plaster.* New York: National Trust for Historic Preservation and Columbia University, 1973.

Phillips, Morgan. "Adhesives for the Reattachment of Loose Plaster," *A.P.T. Bulletin,* Vol. XII, No. 2, 1980, pp. 37–63.

Poore, Patricia. "The Basics of Plaster Repair." *Old House Journal,* Vol. 16, No. 2, March/April, 1988, pp. 29–35.

Shivers, Natalie. *Walls and Molding: How to Care for Old and Historic Wood and Plaster.* Washington, D.C.: National Trust for Historic Preservation, 1989.

Stagg, W. D. and B. Pegg. *Plastering: A Craftsman's Encyclopedia.* Woodstock, New York: Beekman Publishers, 1976.

Van den Branden, F. and Thomas L. Hartsell. *Plastering Skills.* Homewood, Illinois: American Technical Publishers, Inc., 1984.

Weaver, Martin. "Nuts and Bolts: Properly Plastered." *Canadian Heritage.* Aug./Sept., 1981, pp. 34–36. Also "Nuts and Bolts: Fixing Plaster." Oct., 1981, pp. 33–35.

Acknowledgements

Preservation Brief 21 was based on an article in *Old House Restoration* on repairing historic plaster published by the University of Illinois at Urbana-Champaign, 1984. Kay D. Weeks, Preservation Assistance Division, Technical Preservation Services Branch, expanded the article and made substantial contributions to its development as a Brief. Special thanks go to the technical experts in the field who reviewed and comment upon the draft manuscript: Andrew Ladygo (Society for the Preservation of New England Antiquities), David Flaharty, Gilbert Wolf (National Plastering Industries), Michael Kempster, and Walter Jowers. Insightful comments were offered by the Technical Preservation Services Branch which is directed by H. Ward Jandl. Finally, staff member Karen Kummer, Small Homes Council-Building Research Council, University of Illinois, provided invaluable production assistance.

The publication has been prepared pursuant to the National Historic Preservation Act of 1966, as amended. Preservation Briefs 21 was developed under the technical editorship of Lee H. Nelson, FAIA, Chief, Preservation Assistance Division, National Park Service, Department of the Interior, P.O. Box 37127, Washington, D.C. 20013–7127. Comments on the usefulness of this information are welcomed and may be sent to Mr. Nelson at the above address.

22

The Preservation and Repair of Historic Stucco

Anne Grimmer

The term "stucco" is used here to describe a type of exterior plaster applied as a two-or-three part coating directly onto masonry, or applied over wood or metal lath to a log or wood frame structure. Stucco is found in many forms on historic structures throughout the United States. It is so common, in fact, that it frequently goes unnoticed, and is often disguised or used to imitate another material. Historic stucco is also sometimes incorrectly viewed as a sacrificial coating, and consequently removed to reveal stone, brick or logs that historically were never intended to be exposed. Age and lack of maintenance hasten the deterioration of many historic stucco buildings. Like most historic building materials, stucco is at the mercy of the elements, and even though it is a protective coating, it is particularly susceptible to water damage.

Stucco is a material of deceptive simplicity: in most cases its repair should not be undertaken by a property

owner unfamiliar with the art of plastering. Successful stucco repair requires the skill and experience of a professional plasterer. Therefore, this Brief has been prepared to provide background information on the nature and components of traditional stucco, as well as offer guidance on proper maintenance and repairs. The Brief will outline the requirements for stucco repair, and, when necessary, replacement. Although several stucco mixes representative of different periods are provided here for reference, this Brief does not include specifications for carrying out repair projects. Each project is unique, with its own set of problems that require individual solutions.

Historical Background

Stucco has been used since ancient times. Still widely used throughout the world, it is one of the most common of traditional building materials (Fig. 1). Up until

Fig. 1. These two houses in a residential section of Winchester, Virginia, illustrate the continuing popularity of stucco (a) from this early 19th century, Federal style house on the left, (b) to the English Cotswold style cottage that was built across the street in the 1930's. Photos: Anne Grimmer.

229

the late 1800's, stucco, like mortar, was primarily lime-based, but the popularization of portland cement changed the composition of stucco, as well as mortar, to a harder material. Historically, the term "plaster" has often been interchangeable with "stucco"; the term is still favored by many, particularly when referring to the traditional lime-based coating. By the nineteenth century "stucco," although originally denoting fine interior ornamental plasterwork, had gained wide acceptance in the United States to describe exterior plastering. "Render" and "rendering" are also terms used to describe stucco, especially in Great Britain. Other historic treatments and coatings related to stucco in that they consist at least in part of a similarly plastic or malleable material include: parging and pargeting, wattle and daub, "cob" or chalk mud, pisé de terre, rammed earth, briqueté entre poteaux or bousillage, half-timbering, and adobe. All of these are regional variations on traditional mixtures of mud, clay, lime, chalk, cement, gravel or straw. Many are still used today.

The Stucco Tradition in the United States

Stucco is primarily used on residential buildings and relatively small-scale commercial structures. Some of the earliest stucco buildings in the United States include examples of the Federal, Greek and Gothic Revival styles of the eighteenth and the nineteenth centuries that emulated European architectural fashions. Benjamin Henry Latrobe, appointed by Thomas Jefferson as Surveyor of Public Buildings of the United States in 1803, was responsible for the design of a number of important stucco buildings, including St. John's Church (1816), in Washington, D.C. (Fig. 2). Nearly half a century later Andrew Jackson Downing also advocated the use of stucco in his influential book *The Architecture of Country Houses*, published in 1850. In Downing's opinion, stucco was superior in many respects to plain brick or stone because it was cheaper, warmer and dryer, and could be "agreeably" tinted. As a result of his advice, stuccoed Italianate style urban and suburban villas proliferated in many parts of the country during the third quarter of the nineteenth century.

Revival Styles Promote Use of Stucco

The introduction of the many revival styles of architecture around the turn of the twentieth century, combined with the improvement and increased availability of portland cement resulted in a "craze" for stucco as a building material in the United States. Beginning about 1890 and gaining momentum into the 1930's and 1940's, stucco was associated with certain historic architectural styles, including: Prairie; Art Deco, and Art Moderne; Spanish Colonial, Mission, Pueblo, Mediterranean, English Cotswold Cottage, and Tudor Revival styles; as well as the ubiquitous bungalow and "four-square" house (Fig. 3). The fad for Spanish Colonial Revival, and other variations on this theme, was especially important in furthering stucco as a building material in the United States during this period, since stucco clearly looked like adobe (Fig. 4).

Fig. 2. St. John's Church, Washington, D.C., constructed of brick and stuccoed immediately upon completion in 1816, reflects the influence of European, and specifically English, architectural styles. Photo: Russell Jones, HABS Collection.

Fig. 3. The William Gray and Edna S. Purcell House, Minneapolis, Minnesota, was designed in 1913 by the architects Purcell and Elmslie in the Prairie style. Stuccoed in a salmon-pink, sand (float) finish, it is unusual in that it featured a 3-color geometric frieze stencilled below the eaves of the 2nd story. The Minneapolis Institute of Art has removed the cream-colored paint added at a later date, and restored the original color and texture of the stucco. Photo: Courtesy MacDonald and Mack Partnership.

Although stucco buildings were especially prevalent in California, the Southwest and Florida, ostensibly because of their Spanish heritage, this period also spawned stucco-coated, revival-style buildings all over the United States and Canada. The popularity of stucco as a cheap, and readily available material meant that by the 1920's, it was used for an increasing variety of building types. Resort hotels, apartment buildings, private mansions and movie theaters, railroad stations, and even gas stations and tourist courts took advantage of the "romance" of period styles, and adopted the stucco construction that had become synonymous with these styles (Fig. 5).

A Practical Building Material

Stucco has traditionally been popular for a variety of reasons. It was an inexpensive material that could simulate finely dressed stonework, especially when "scored" or "lined" in the European tradition. A stucco coating over a less finished and less costly substrate such as rubblestone, fieldstone, brick, log or wood frame, gave the building the appearance of being a more expensive and important structure. As a weather-repellent coating, stucco protected the building from wind and rain penetration, and also offered a certain amount of fire protection. While stucco was usually applied during construction as part of the building design, particularly over rubblestone or fieldstone, in some instances it was added later to protect the structure, or when a rise in the owner's social status demanded a comparable rise in his standard of living.

Composition of Historic Stucco

Before the mid-to-late nineteenth century, stucco consisted primarily of hydrated or slaked lime, water and sand, with straw or animal hair included as a binder. Natural cements were frequently used in stucco mixes after their discovery in the United States during the 1820's. Portland cement was first manufactured in the United States in 1871, and it gradually replaced natural cement. After about 1900, most stucco was composed primarily of portland cement, mixed with some lime. With the addition of portland cement, stucco became even more versatile and durable. No longer used just as a coating for a substantial material like masonry or log, stucco could now be applied over wood or metal lath attached to a light wood frame. With this increased strength, stucco ceased to be just a veneer and became a more integral part of the building structure.

Fig. 4. The elaborate Spanish Colonial Revival style of this building designed by Bertram Goodhue for the 1915 Panama California Exposition held in San Diego's Balboa Park emphasizes the sculptural possibilities of stucco. Photo: C.W. Snell, National Historic Landmark Files.

Fig. 5. During the 19th and 20th centuries stucco has been a popular material not only for residential, but also for commercial buildings in the Spanish style. Two such examples are (a) the 1851 Ernest Hemingway House, Key West, Florida, built of stuccoed limestone in a Spanish Caribbean style; and (b) the Santa Fe Depot (Union Station), San Diego, California, designed by the architects Bakewell and Brown in 1914 in a Spanish Colonial Revival style, and constructed of stucco over brick and hollow tile. Photos: (a) J.F. Brooks, HABS Collection, (b) Marvin Rand, HABS Collection.

Today, gypsum, which is hydrated calcium sulfate or sulfate of lime, has to a great extent replaced lime. Gypsum is preferred because it hardens faster and has less shrinkage than lime. Lime is generally used only in the finish coat in contemporary stucco work.

The composition of stucco depended on local custom and available materials. Stucco often contained substantial amounts of mud or clay, marble or brick dust, or even sawdust, and an array of additives ranging from animal blood or urine, to eggs, keratin or gluesize (animal hooves and horns), varnish, wheat paste, sugar, salt, sodium silicate, alum, tallow, linseed oil, beeswax, and wine, beer, or rye whiskey. Waxes, fats and oils were included to introduce water-repellent properties, sugary materials reduced the amount of water needed and slowed down the setting time, and alcohol acted as an air entrainer. All of these additives contributed to the strength and durability of the stucco.

The appearance of much stucco was determined by the color of the sand—or sometimes burnt clay, used in the mix, but often stucco was also tinted with natural pigments, or the surface whitewashed or colorwashed after stuccoing was completed. Brick dust could provide color, and other coloring materials that were not affected by lime, mostly mineral pigments, could be added to the mix for the final finish coat. Stucco was

also marbled or marbleized—stained to look like stone by diluting oil of vitriol (sulfuric acid) with water, and mixing this with a yellow ochre, or another color (Fig. 6). As the twentieth century progressed, manufactured or synthetic pigments were added at the factory to some prepared stucco mixes.

Methods of Application

Stucco is applied directly, without lath, to masonry substrates such as brick, stone, concrete or hollow tile (Fig. 7). But on wood structures, stucco, like its interior counterpart plaster, must be applied over lath in order to obtain an adequate key to hold the stucco. Thus, when applied over a log structure, stucco is laid on horizontal wood lath that has been nailed on vertical wood furring strips attached to the logs (Fig. 8). If it is applied over a wood frame structure, stucco may be applied to wood or metal lath nailed directly to the wood frame; it may also be placed on lath that has been attached to furring strips. The furring strips are themselves laid over building paper covering the wood sheathing (Fig. 9). Wood lath was gradually superseded by expanded metal lath introduced in the late-nineteenth and early-twentieth century. When stuccoing over a stone or brick substrate, it was customary to cut back or rake out the mortar joints if they were not already recessed by natural weathering or

Fig. 6. Arlington House, Arlington, Virginia, was built between 1802–1818 of brick covered with stucco. It was designed by George Hadfield for George Washington Parke Custis, grandson of Martha Washington, and was later the home of Robert E. Lee. This photograph taken on June 28, 1864, by Captain Andrew J. Russell, a U.S. Signal Corps photographer, shows the stucco after it had been marbleized during the 1850's. Yellow ochre and burnt umber pigments were combined to imitate Sienna marble, and the stucco, with the exception of the roughcast foundation, was scored to heighten the illusion of stone. Photo: National Archives, Arlington House Collection, National Park Service.

Fig. 7. Patches of stucco have fallen off this derelict 19th century structure exposing the rough-cut local stone substrate. The missing wood entablature on the side and the rough wood lintel now exposed above a second-floor window, offer clues that the building was stuccoed originally. Photo: National Park Service Files.

Fig. 8. Removal of deteriorated stucco in preparation for stucco repair on this late-18th century log house in Middleway, West Virginia, reveals that the stucco was applied to hand-riven wood lath nailed over vertical wood strips attached to the logs. Photo: Anne Grimmer.

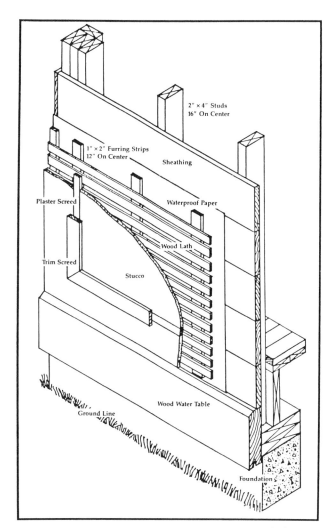

Fig. 9. This cutaway drawing shows the method of attachment for stucco commonly used on wood frame or balloon frame structures from the late-19th to the 20th century. Drawing: Brian Conway, "Illinois Preservation Series Number 2: Stucco."

erosion, and sometimes the bricks themselves were gouged to provide a key for the stucco. This helped provide the necessary bond for the stucco to remain attached to the masonry, much like the key provided by wood or metal lath on frame buildings.

Like interior wall plaster, stucco has traditionally been applied as a multiple-layer process, sometimes consisting of two coats, but more commonly as three. Whether applied directly to a masonry substrate or onto wood or metal lath, this consists of a first "scratch" or "pricking-up" coat, followed by a second scratch coat, sometimes referred to as a "floating" or "brown" coat, followed finally by the "finishing" coat. Up until the late-nineteenth century, the first and the second coats were of much the same composition, generally consisting of lime, or natural cement, sand, perhaps clay, and one or more of the additives previously mentioned. Straw or animal hair was usually added to the first coat as a binder. The third, or finishing coat, consisted primarily of a very fine mesh grade of lime and sand, and sometimes pigment. As already noted, after the 1820's, natural cement was also a common ingredient in stucco until it was replaced by portland cement.

A

B

C

D

Fig. 10. (a) Tudor Place, Washington, D.C. (1805–1816), was designed by Dr. William Thornton. Like its contemporary, Arlington House, it is stuccoed and scored, with a roughcast base, but here the stucco is a monochromatic sandstone color tinted by sand and mineral pigments (b). Although the original stucco was replaced in the early-20th century with a portland cement-based stucco, the family, who retained ownership until 1984 when the house was opened to the public, left explicit instructions for future stucco repairs. The mix recommended for repairing hairline cracks (c), consists of sharp sand, cement and lime, burnt umber, burnt sienna, and a small amount of raw sienna. Preparation of numerous test samples, the size of "a thick griddle cake," will be necessary to match the stucco color, and when the exact color has been achieved, the mixture is to be diluted to the "consistency of cream," brushed on the wall and rubbed into the cracks with a rubber sponge or float. Note the dark color visible under the eaves intended to replicate the stronger color of the original limewashed stucco (d). Photos: Anne Grimmer.

Both masonry and wood lath must be kept wet or damp to ensure a good bond with the stucco. Wetting these materials helps to prevent them from pulling moisture out of the stucco too rapidly, which results in cracking, loss of bond, and generally poor quality stuccowork.

Traditional Stucco Finishes

Until the early-twentieth century when a variety of novelty finishes or textures were introduced, the last coat of stucco was commonly given a smooth, troweled finish, and then scored or lined in imitation of ashlar. The illusion of masonry joints was sometimes enhanced by a thin line of white lime putty, graphite, or some other pigment. Some nineteenth century buildings feature a water table or raised foundation of rough-cast stucco that differentiates it from the stucco surface above, which is smooth and scored (Fig. 10). Other novelty or textured finishes associated with the "period" or revival styles of the early-twentieth century include: the English cottage finish, adobe and Spanish, pebble-dashed or dry-dash surface, fan and sponge texture, reticulated and vermiculated, roughcast (or wet dash), and sgraffito (Fig. 11).

Repairing Deteriorated Stucco

Regular Maintenance

Although A. J. Downing alluded to stuccoed houses in Pennsylvania that had survived for over a century in relatively good condition, historic stucco is inherently not a particularly permanent or long-lasting building material. Regular maintenance is required to keep it in good condition. Unfortunately, many older or historic buildings are not always accorded this kind of care.

Because building owners knew stucco to be a protective, but also somewhat fragile coating, they employed a variety of means to prolong its usefulness. The most common treatment was to whitewash stucco, often annually. The lime in the whitewash offered protection and stability and helped to harden the stucco. Most importantly, it filled hairline cracks before they could develop into larger cracks and let in moisture. To improve water repellency, stucco buildings were also sometimes coated with paraffin, another type of wax, or other stucco-like coatings, such as oil mastics.

Assessing Damage

Most stucco deterioration is the result of water infiltration into the building structure, either through the roof, around chimneys, window and door openings, or excessive ground water or moisture penetrating through, or splashing up from the foundation. Potential causes of deterioration include: ground settlement, lintel and door frame settlement, inadequate or leaking gutters and downspouts, intrusive vegetation, moisture migration within walls due to interior condensation and humidity, vapor drive problems caused by furnace, bathroom and kitchen vents, and rising damp resulting from excessive ground water and poor drainage around the foundation. Water infiltration will cause wood lath to rot, and metal lath and nails to rust, which eventu-

Fig. 11. The Hotel Washington, Washington, D.C. (1916–1917), is notable for its decorative **sgraffito** surfaces. Stucco panels under the cornice and around the windows feature classical designs created by artists who incised the patterns in the outer layer of red-colored stucco while still soft, thereby exposing a stucco undercoat of a contrasting color. Photo: Kaye Ellen Simonson.

ally will cause stucco to lose its bond and pull away from its substrate.

After the cause of deterioration has been identified, any necessary repairs to the building should be made first before repairing the stucco. Such work is likely to include repairs designed to keep excessive water away from the stucco, such as roof, gutter, downspout and flashing repairs, improving drainage, and redirecting rainwater runoff and splash-back away from the building. Horizontal areas such as the tops of parapet walls or chimneys are particularly vulnerable to water infiltration, and may require modifications to their original design, such as the addition of flashing to correct the problem.

Previous repairs inexpertly carried out may have caused additional deterioration, particularly if executed in portland cement, which tends to be very rigid, and therefore incompatible with early, mostly soft lime-based stucco that is more "flexible." Incompatible repairs, external vibration caused by traffic or construction, or building settlement can also result in cracks which permit the entrance of water and cause the stucco to fail (Fig. 12).

Before beginning any stucco repair, an assessment of the stucco should be undertaken to determine the extent of the damage, and how much must be replaced or repaired. Testing should be carried out systematically on all elevations of the building to determine the overall condition of the stucco. Some areas in need of repair will be clearly evidenced by missing sections of stucco or stucco layers. Bulging or cracked areas are obvious places to begin. Unsound, punky or soft areas that have lost their key will echo with a hollow sound when tapped gently with a wooden or acrylic hammer or mallet.

Identifying the Stucco Type

Analysis of the historic stucco will provide useful information on its primary ingredients and their proportions, and will help to ensure that the new replacement stucco will duplicate the old in strength, composition, color and texture as closely as possible. However, unless authentic, period restoration is required, it may not be worthwhile, nor in many instances possible, to attempt to duplicate *all* of the ingredients (particularly some of the additives), in creating the new stucco mor-

tar. Some items are no longer available, and others, notably sand and lime—the major components of traditional stucco—have changed radically over time. For example, most sand used in contemporary masonry work is manufactured sand, because river sand, which was used historically, is difficult to obtain today in many parts of the country. The physical and visual qualities of manufactured sand versus river sand, are quite different, and this affects the way stucco works, as well as the way it looks. The same is true of lime, which is frequently replaced by gypsum in modern stucco mixes. And even if identification of all the items in the historic stucco mix were possible, the analysis would still not reveal how the original stucco was mixed and applied.

There are, however, simple tests that can be carried out on a small piece of stucco to determine its basic make-up. A dilute solution of hydrochloric (muriatic) acid will dissolve lime-based stucco, but not portland cement. Although the use of portland cement became common after 1900, there are no precise cut-off dates, as stuccoing practices varied among individual plasterers, and from region to region. Some plasterers began using portland cement in the 1880's, but others may have continued to favor lime stucco well into the early-twentieth century. While it is safe to assume that a late-eighteenth or early-nineteenth century stucco is lime-based, late-nineteenth or early-twentieth century

Fig. 12. (a) Water intrusion caused by rusting metal, or (b) plant growth left unattended will gradually enlarge these cracks, resulting in spalling, and eventually requiring extensive repair of the stucco. Photos: National Park Service Files.

Fig. 13. (a) In preparation for repainting, hairline cracks on this Mediterranean style stucco apartment building were filled with a commercial caulking compound; (b) dirt is attracted and adheres to the texture of the caulked areas, and a year after painting, these inappropriate repairs are highly obvious. Photos: Anne Grimmer.

stucco may be based on either lime or portland cement. Another important factor to take into consideration is that an early lime-stucco building is likely to have been repaired many times over the ensuing years, and it is probable that at least some of these patches consist of portland cement.

Planning the Repair

Once the extent of damage has been determined, a number of repair options may be considered. Small hairline cracks usually are not serious and may be sealed with a thin slurry coat consisting of the finish coat ingredients, or even with a coat of paint or white-wash. Commercially available caulking compounds are not suitable materials for patching hairline cracks. Because their consistency and texture is unlike that of stucco, they tend to weather differently, and attract more dirt; as a result, repairs made with caulking compounds may be highly visible, and unsightly (Fig. 13). Larger cracks will have to be cut out in preparation for more extensive repair. Most stucco repairs will require the skill and expertise of a professional plasterer (Fig. 14).

In the interest of saving or preserving as much as possible of the historic stucco, patching rather than whole-sale replacement is preferable. When repairing heavily textured surfaces, it is not usually necessary to replace an entire wall section, as the textured finish, if well-executed, tends to conceal patches, and helps them to blend in with the existing stucco. However, because of the nature of smooth-finished stucco, patching a number of small areas scattered over one elevation may not be a successful repair approach unless the stucco has been previously painted, or is to be painted following the repair work. On unpainted stucco such patches are hard to conceal, because they may not match exactly or blend in with the rest of the historic stucco surface. For

Fig. 14. This poorly executed patch is not the work of a professional plasterer. While it may serve to keep out water, it does not match the original surface, and is not an appropriate repair for historic stucco. Photo: Betsy Chittenden.

this reason it is recommended, if possible, that stucco repair be carried out in a contained or well-defined area, or if the stucco is scored, the repair patch should be "squared-off" in such a way as to follow existing scoring. In some cases, especially in a highly visible location, it may be preferable to restucco an entire wall section or feature. In this way, any differences between the patched area and the historic surface will not be so readily apparent.

Repair of historic stucco generally follows most of the same principles used in plaster repair. First, all deteriorated, severely cracked and loose stucco should be removed down to the lath (assuming that the lath is securely attached to the substrate), or down to the masonry if the stucco is directly applied to a masonry substrate. A clean surface is necessary to obtain a good

237

bond between the stucco and substrate. The areas to be patched should be cleaned of all debris with a bristle brush, and all plant growth, dirt, loose paint, oil or grease should be removed (Fig. 15). If necessary, brick or stone mortar joints should then be raked out to a depth of approximately 5/8" to ensure a good bond between the substrate and the new stucco.

To obtain a neat repair, the area to be patched should be squared-off with a butt joint, using a cold chisel, a hatchet, a diamond blade saw, or a masonry bit. Sometimes it may be preferable to leave the area to be patched in an irregular shape which may result in a less conspicuous patch. Proper preparation of the area to be patched requires very sharp tools, and extreme caution on the part of the plasterer not to break keys of surrounding good stucco by "over-sounding" when removing deteriorated stucco. To ensure a firm bond, the new patch must not overlap the old stucco. If the stucco has lost its bond or key from wood lath, or the lath has deteriorated or come loose from the substrate, a decision must be made whether to try to reattach the old lath, to replace deteriorated lath with new wood lath, or to leave the historic wood lath in place and supplement it with modern expanded metal lath. Unless authenticity is important, it is generally preferable (and easier) to nail new metal lath over the old wood lath to support the patch. Metal lath that is no longer

securely fastened to the substrate may be removed and replaced in kind, or left in place, and supplemented with new wire lath.

When repairing lime-based stucco applied directly to masonry, the new stucco should be applied in the same manner, directly onto the stone or brick. The stucco will bond onto the masonry itself without the addition of lath because of the irregularities in the masonry or those of its mortar joints, or because its surface has been scratched, scored or otherwise roughened to provide an additional key. Cutting out the old stucco at a diagonal angle may also help secure the bond between the new and the old stucco. For the most part it is not advisable to insert metal lath when restuccoing historic masonry in sound condition, as it can hasten deterioration of the repair work. Not only will attaching the lath damage the masonry, but the slightest moisture penetration can cause metal lath to rust. This will cause metal to expand, eventually resulting in spalling of the stucco, and possibly the masonry substrate too.

If the area to be patched is properly cleaned and prepared, a bonding agent is usually not necessary. However, a bonding agent may be useful when repairing hairline cracks, or when dealing with substrates that do not offer a good bonding surface. These may include dense stone or brick, previously painted or stuccoed

Fig. 15. (a) After reattaching any loose wood lath to the furring strips underneath, the area to be patched has been cleaned, the lath thoroughly wetted, and (b) the first coat of stucco has been applied and scratched to provide a key to hold the second layer of stucco. Photos: Betsy Chittenden.

masonry, or spalling brick substrates. A good mechanical bond is always preferable to reliance on bonding agents. Bonding agents should not be used on a wall that is likely to remain damp or where large amounts of salts are present. Many bonding agents do not survive well under such conditions, and their use could jeopardize the longevity of the stucco repair.

A stucco mix compatible with the historic stucco should be selected after analyzing the existing stucco. It can be adapted from a standard traditional mix of the period, or based on one of the mixes included here. Stucco consisting mostly of portland cement generally will not be physically compatible with the softer, more flexible lime-rich historic stuccos used throughout the eighteenth and much of the nineteenth centuries. The differing expansion and contraction rates of lime stucco and portland cement stucco will normally cause the stucco to crack. Choosing a stucco mix that is durable and compatible with the historic stucco on the building is likely to involve considerable trial and error, and probably will require a number of test samples, and even more if it is necessary to match the color. It is best to let the stucco test samples weather as long as possible—ideally one year, or at least through a change of seasons, in order to study the durability of the mix and its compatibility with the existing stucco, as well as the weathering of the tint if the building will not be painted and color match is an important factor. If the test samples are not executed on the building, they should be placed next to the stucco remaining on the building to compare the color, texture and composition of the samples with the original. The number and thickness of stucco coats used in the repair should also match the original.

After thoroughly dampening the masonry or wood lath, the first, scratch coat should be applied to the masonry substrate, or wood or metal lath, in a thickness that corresponds to the original if extant, or generally about 1/4" to 3/8". The scratch coat should be scratched or cross-hatched with a comb to provide a key to hold the second coat. It usually takes 24–72 hours, and longer in cold weather, for each coat to dry before the next coat can be applied. The second coat should be about the same thickness as the first, and the total thickness of the first two coats should generally not exceed about 5/8". This second or leveling coat should be roughened using a wood float with a nail protruding to provide a key for the final or finish coat. The finish coat, about 1/4" thick, is applied after the previous coat has initially set. If this is not feasible, the base coat should be thoroughly dampened when the finish coat is applied later. The finish coat should be worked to match the texture of the original stucco (Fig. 16).

Colors and Tints for Historic Stucco Repair

The color of most early stucco was supplied by the aggregate included in the mix—usually the sand. Sometimes natural pigments were added to the mix, and eighteenth and nineteenth-century scored stucco was often marbleized or painted in imitation of marble or granite. Stucco was also frequently coated with whitewash or a colorwash. This tradition later evolved

into the use of paint, its popularity depending on the vagaries of fashion as much as a means of concealing repairs. Because most of the early colors were derived from nature, the resultant stucco tints tended to be mostly earth-toned. This was true until the advent of brightly colored stucco in the early decades of the twentieth century. This was the so-called "Jazz Plaster" developed by O.A. Malone, the "man who put color into California," and who founded the California Stucco Products Corporation in 1927. California Stucco was revolutionary for its time as the first stucco/plaster to contain colored pigment in its pre-packaged factory mix.

When patching or repairing a historic stucco surface known to have been tinted, it may be possible to determine through visual or microscopic analysis whether the source of the coloring is sand, cement or pigment. Although some pigments or aggregates used traditionally may no longer be available, a sufficiently close color-match can generally be approximated using sand, natural or mineral pigments, or a combination of these. Obtaining such a match will require testing and comparing the color of dried test samples with the original. Successfully combining pigments in the dry stucco mix prepared for the finish coat requires considerable skill. The amount of pigment must be carefully measured for each batch of stucco. Overworking the mix can make the pigment separate from the lime. Changing the amount of water added to the mix, or using water to apply the tinted finish coat, will also affect the color of the stucco when it dries.

Generally, the color obtained by hand-mixing these ingredients will provide a sufficiently close match to cover an entire wall or an area distinct enough from the rest of the structure that the color differences will not be obvious. However, it may not work for small patches conspicuously located on a primary elevation, where color differences will be especially noticeable. In these instances, it may be necessary to conceal the repairs by painting the entire patched elevation, or even the whole building.

Many stucco buildings have been painted over the years and will require repainting after the stucco repairs have been made. Limewash or cement-based paint, latex paint, or oil-based paint are appropriate coatings for stucco buildings. The most important factor to consider when repainting a previously painted or coated surface is that the new paint be compatible with any coating already on the surface. In preparation for repainting, all loose or peeling paint or other coating material not firmly adhered to the stucco must be removed by hand-scraping or natural bristle brushes. The surface should then be cleaned.

Cement-based paints, most of which today contain some portland cement and are really a type of limewash, have traditionally been used on stucco buildings. The ingredients were easily obtainable. Furthermore, the lime in such paints actually bonded or joined with the stucco and provided a very durable coating. In many regions, whitewash was applied annually during spring cleaning. Modern, commercially available premixed masonry and mineral-based paints may also be used on historic stucco buildings.

Fig. A

Fig. B

Fig. C

Fig. D

Fig. 16. (a) *In preparation for stucco repair, this plasterer is mixing the dry materials in a mortar box with a mortar hoe (note the 2 holes in the blade), pulling it through the box using short choppy strokes. After the dry materials are thoroughly combined, water is added and mixed with them using the same choppy, but gradually lengthening stokes, making sure that the hoe cuts completely through the mix to the bottom of the box. (b) The deteriorated stucco has been cut away, and new metal lath has been nailed to the clapboarding in the area to be patched. (Although originally clapboarded when built in the 19th century, the house was stuccoed around the turn-of-the-century on metal lath nailed over the clapboard.) (c) The first, scratch coat and the second coat have been applied here, and await the spatterdash or rough-cast finish of the final coat (d) which was accomplished by the plasterer using a whisk broom to throw the stucco mortar against the wall surface. This well-executed patch is barely discernable, and lacks only a coat of paint to make it blend completely with the rest of the painted wall surface. Photos: Anne Grimmer.*

If the structure must be painted for the first time to conceal repairs, almost any of these coatings may be acceptable depending on the situation. Latex paint, for example, may be applied to slightly damp walls or where there is an excess of moisture, but latex paint will not stick to chalky or powdery areas. Oil-based, or alkyd paints must be applied only to dry walls; new stucco must cure up to a year before it can be painted with oil-based paint.

Contemporary Stucco Products

There are many contemporary stucco products on the market today. Many of them are not compatible, either physically or visually, with historic stucco buildings. Such products should be considered for use only after consulting with a historic masonry specialist. However, some of these prepackaged tinted stucco coatings may be suitable for use on stucco buildings dating from the late-nineteenth or early-twentieth century, as long as the color and texture are appropriate for the period and style of the building. While some masonry contractors may, as a matter of course, suggest that a water-repellent coating be applied after repairing old stucco, in most cases this should not be necessary, since color-washes and paints serve the same purpose, and stucco itself is a protective coating.

Cleaning Historic Stucco Surfaces

Historic stucco buildings often exhibit multiple layers of paint or limewash. Although some stucco surfaces may be cleaned by water washing, the relative success of this procedure depends on two factors: the surface texture of the stucco, and the type of dirt to be removed. If simply removing airborne dirt, **smooth unpainted stucco,** and **heavily-textured painted stucco** may sometimes be cleaned using a low-pressure water wash, supplemented by scrubbing with soft natural bristle brushes, and possibly non-ionic detergents. Organic plant material, such as algae and mold, and metallic stains may be removed from stucco using poultices and appropriate solvents. Although these same methods may be employed to clean **unpainted roughcast, pebble-dash, or any stucco surface featuring exposed aggregate,** due to the surface irregularities, it may be difficult to remove dirt, without also removing portions of the decorative textured surface. Difficulty in cleaning these surfaces may explain why so many of these textured surfaces have been painted.

When Total Replacement is Necessary

Complete replacement of the historic stucco with new stucco of either a traditional or modern mix will probably be necessary only in cases of extreme deterioration—that is, a loss of bond on over 40–50 per cent of the stucco surface. Another reason for total removal might be that the physical and visual integrity of the historic stucco has been so compromised by prior incompatible and ill-conceived repairs that patching would not be successful.

When stucco no longer exists on a building there is more flexibility in choosing a suitable mix for the replacement. Since compatibility of old and new stucco will not be an issue, the most important factors to consider are durability, color, texture and finish. Depending on the construction and substrate of the building, in some instances it may be acceptable to use a relatively strong cement-based stucco mortar. This is certainly true for many late-nineteenth and early-twentieth century buildings, and may even be appropriate to use on some stone substrates even if the original mortar would have been weaker, as long as the historic visual qualities noted above have been replicated. Generally, the best principle to follow for a masonry building is that the stucco mix, whether for repair or replacement of historic stucco, should be somewhat weaker than the masonry to which it is to be applied in order not to damage the substrate.

General Guidance for Historic Stucco Repair

A skilled professional plasterer will be familiar with the properties of materials involved in stucco repair and will be able to avoid some of the pitfalls that would hinder someone less experienced. General suggestions for successful stucco repair parallel those involving restoration and repair of historic mortar or plaster. In addition, the following principles are important to remember:

• Mix only as much stucco as can be used in one and one-half to two hours. This will depend on the weather (mortar will harden faster under hot and dry, or sunny conditions); and experience is likely to be the best guidance. Any remaining mortar should be discarded; it should not be retempered.

• Stucco mortar should not be over-mixed. (Hand mix for 10–15 minutes after adding water, or machine mix for 3–4 minutes after all ingredients are in mixer.) Over-mixing can cause crazing and discoloration, especially in tinted mortars. Over-mixing will also tend to make the mortar set too fast, which will result in cracking and poor bonding or keying to the lath or masonry substrate.

• Wood lath or a masonry substrate, but not metal lath, must be thoroughly wetted before applying stucco patches so that it does not draw moisture out of the stucco too rapidly. To a certain extent, bonding agents also serve this same purpose. Wetting the substrate helps retard drying.

• To prevent cracking, it is imperative that stucco not dry too fast. Therefore, the area to be stuccoed should be shaded, or even covered if possible, particularly in hot weather. It is also a good idea in hot weather to keep the newly stuccoed area damp, at approximately 90 per cent humidity, for a period of 48 to 72 hours.

• Stucco repairs, like most other exterior masonry work, should not be undertaken in cold weather (below 40 degrees fahrenheit, and preferably warmer), or if there is danger of frost.

Historic Stucco Textures

Most of the oldest stucco in the U.S. dating prior to the late-nineteenth century, will generally have a **smooth, troweled finish** (sometimes called a **sand** or **float finish**), possibly scored to resemble ashlar masonry units. Scoring may be incised to simulate masonry joints, the scored lines may be emphasized by black or white penciling, or the lines may simply be drawn or painted on the surface of the stucco. In some regions, at least as early as the first decades of the nineteenth century, it was not uncommon to use a **roughcast finish** on the foundation or base of an otherwise **smooth-surfaced** building (Fig. a). **Roughcast** was also used as an overall stucco finish for some outbuildings, and other less important types of structures.

A wide variety of decorative surface textures may be found on revival style stucco buildings, particularly residential architecture. These styles evolved in the late-nineteenth century and peaked in popularity in the early decades of the twentieth century. Frank Lloyd Wright favored a **smooth finish** stucco, which was imitated on much of the Prairie style architecture inspired by his work. Some of the more picturesque surface textures include: **English Cottage** or **English Cotswold finish**; **sponge finish** (Fig. b); **fan texture**; **adobe finish** (Fig. c), and **Spanish** or **Italian finish.** Many of these finishes and countless other regional and personalized variations on them are still in use.

The most common early-twentieth century stucco finishes are often found on bungalow-style houses, and include: **spatter** or **spatterdash** (sometimes called **roughcast, harling,** or **wetdash**), and **pebbledash** or **drydash.** The **spatterdash** finish is applied by throwing the stucco mortar against the wall using a whisk broom or a stiff fiber brush, and it requires considerable skill on the part of the plasterer to achieve a consistently rough wall surface. The mortar used to obtain this texture is usually composed simply of a regular sand, lime, and cement mortar, although it may sometimes contain small pebbles or crushed stone aggregate, which replaces one-half the normal sand content. The **pebbledash** or **drydash finish** is accomplished manually by the plasterer throwing or "dashing" dry pebbles (about 1/8" to 1/4" in size), onto a coat of stucco freshly applied by another plasterer. The pebbles must be thrown at the wall with a scoop with sufficient force and skill that they will stick to the stuccoed wall. A more even or uniform surface can be achieved by patting the stones down with a wooden float. This finish may also be created using a texturing machine (Figs. d–f illustrate 3 versions of this finish. Photos: National Park Service Files).

Fig. A

Fig. B

Fig. C

Fig. D

Fig. E

Fig. F

Summary

Stucco on historic buildings is especially vulnerable not only to the wear of time and exposure to the elements, but also at the hands of well-intentioned "restorers," who may want to remove stucco from eighteenth and nineteenth century structures, to expose what they believe to be the original or more "historic" brick, stone or log underneath. Historic stucco is a character-defining feature and should be considered an important historic building material, significant in its own right. While many eighteenth and nineteenth century buildings were stuccoed at the time of construction, others were stuccoed later for reasons of fashion or practicality. As such, it is likely that this stucco has acquired significance over time, as part of the history and evolution of a building. Thus, even later, non-historic stucco should be retained in most instances; and similar logic dictates that new stucco should not be applied to a historic building that was not stuccoed previously. When repairing historic stucco, the new stucco should duplicate the old as closely as possible in strength, composition, color and texture.

Mixes for Repair of Historic Stucco

Historic stucco mixes varied a great deal regionally, depending as they did on the availability of local materials. There are probably almost as many mixes that can be used for repair of historic stucco as there are historic stucco buildings. For this reason it is recommended that at least a rudimentary analysis of the existing historic stucco be carried out in order to determine its general proportions and primary ingredients. However, if this is not possible, or if test results are inconclusive, the following mixes are provided as reference. Many of the publications listed under "Selected Reading" include a variety of stucco mixes and should also be consulted for additional guidance.

Materials Specifications should conform to those contained in *Preservation Briefs 2: Repointing Mortar Joints in Historic Brick Buildings*, and are as follows:

- Lime should conform to ASTM C–207, Type S, Hydrated Lime for Masonry Purposes.
- Sand should conform to ASTM C–144 to assure proper gradation and freedom from impurities. Sand, or other type of aggregate, should match the original as closely as possible.
- Cement should conform to ASTM C–150, Type II (white, non-staining), portland cement.
- Water should be fresh, clean and potable.
- If hair or fiber is used, it should be goat or cattle hair, or pure manilla fiber of good quality, 1/2" to 2" in length, clean, and free of dust, dirt, oil, grease or other impurities.
- Rules to remember: More lime will make the mixture more plastic, but stucco mortar with a very large proportion of lime to sand is more likely to crack because of greater shrinkage; it is also weaker and slower to set. More sand or aggregate, will minimize shrinkage, but make the mixture harder to trowel smooth, and will weaken the mortar.

Soft Lime Stucco (suitable for application to buildings dating from 1700–1850)

A.J. Downing's Recipe for Soft Lime Stucco
1   part lime
2   parts sand
(A.J. Downing, "The Architecture of Country Houses," 1850)

Vieux Carre Masonry Maintenance Guidelines
Base Coats (2):
1   part by volume hydrated lime
3   parts by volume aggregate [sand]—size to match original
6   pounds/cubic yards hair or fiber
Water to form a workable mix.
Finish Coat:
1   part by volume hydrated lime
3   parts aggregate [sand]—size to match original
Water to form a workable mix.
Note: No portland cement is recommended in this mix, but if it is needed to increase the workability of the mix and to decrease the setting time, the amount of portland cement added should never exceed 1 part to 12 parts lime and sand.
("Vieux Carre Masonry Maintenance Guidelines," June, 1980.)

"Materials for Soft Brick Mortar and for Soft Stucco"
5   gallons hydrated lime
10   gallons sand
1   quart white, non-staining portland cement (1 cup only for pointing)
Water to form a workable mix.
(Koch and Wilson, Architects, New Orleans, Louisiana, February, 1980)

Mix for Repair of Traditional Natural Cement or Hydraulic Lime Stucco
1   part by volume hydrated lime
2   parts by volume white portland cement
3   parts by volume fine mason's sand
If hydraulic lime is available, it may be used instead of lime-cement blends.
("Conservation Techniques for the Repair of Historical Ornamental Exterior Stucco, January, 1990)

Early-twentieth century Portland Cement Stucco

1   part portland cement
2 1/2   parts sand
Hydrated lime = to not more than 15% of the cement's volume
Water to form a workable mix.
The same basic mix was used for all coats, but the finish coat generally contained more lime than the undercoats. ("Illinois Preservation Series No. 2: Stucco," January, 1980)

American Portland Cement Stucco Specifications
(c. 1929)
Base Coats:
5   pounds, dry, hydrated lime
1   bag portland cement (94 lbs.)
Not less than 3 cubic feet (3 bags) sand (passed through a #8 screen)
Water to make a workable mix.
Finish Coat:
Use WHITE portland cement in the mix in the same proportions as above.
To color the stucco add not more than 10 pounds pigment for each bag of cement contained in the mix.

Selected Reading

Ashurst, John, and Nicola Ashurst. *Practical Building Conservation, English Heritage Technical Handbook, Volume 3. Mortars, Plasters and Renders.* New York: Halsted Press, 1988.

Conway, Brian D. *Illinois Preservation Series Number 2: Stucco.* Springfield, IL: Illinois Department of Conservation, Division of Historic Sites, 1980.

Grimmer, Anne E. *Keeping it Clean: Removing Exterior Dirt, Paint, Stains and Graffiti from Historic Masonry Buildings.* Washington, D.C.: National Park Service, U.S. Department of the Interior, 1988.

Hodgson, Frederick T. *Plaster and Plastering. Mortars and Cements, How to Make, and How to Use . . . with An Illustrated Glossary of Terms.* New York: The Industrial Publication Company, 1901.

Johnson, LeRoy, Jr. (editor). *Handbook of Maintenance Techniques for Building Conservation in the Strand Historic District, Galveston, Texas.* (Revised edition originally published in 1980 as *Preservation Maintenance Handbook,* prepared by Michael Emrick, AIA, for the Galveston Historical Foundation.) Austin, TX: Texas Historical Commission, 1984.

Jowers, Walter. "Bungalow Building Materials: How to Repair Stucco." *The Old-House Journal.* Vol. XIII, No. 4 (May 1985), pp. 80–83.

MacDonald, Marylee. *Preservation Briefs 21: Repairing Historic Flat Plaster-Walls and Ceilings.* Washington, D.C.: National Park Service, U.S. Department of the Interior, 1989.

Mack, Robert C., AIA, de Teel Patterson Tiller, and James S. Askins. *Preservation Briefs 2: Repointing Mortar Joints in Historic Brick Buildings.* Washington, D.C.: National Park Service, U.S. Department of the Interior, 1980.

McKee, Harley J., FAIA. *Introduction to Early American Masonry—Stone, Brick, Mortar and Plaster.* Washington, D.C.: National Trust for Historic Preservation and Columbia University, 1973.

Matero, Frank G., Mary Hardy, Antonio Rava and Joel Snodgrass. *Conservation Techniques for the Repair of Historical Ornamental Exterior Stucco.* (With a Case Study for the Repair of the Cabildo Pedimental Sculpture). Report prepared for the Division of Historic Preservation, Office of Cultural Development, Louisiana Department of Culture, Recreation and Development by The Center for Preservation Research, Columbia University, New York. January 1990.

Portland Cement Plaster (Stucco) Manual. Skokie, IL: Portland Cement Association, 1980.

Van Den Branden, F., and Thomas L. Hartsell. *Plastering Skills.* Second edition. Homewood, IL: American Technical Publishers, Inc., 1984.

Vieux Carre Masonry Maintenance Guidelines. Revised from the initial report prepared by Mary L. Oehlein in 1977. New Orleans, LA: Vieux Carre Commission, 1980.

Whitewash & Coldwater Paints. Bulletin No. 304–G. Washington, D.C.: National Lime Association, 1955.

Worsham, Gibson. "Exterior Plaster Restoration at the Lord Morton House, Lexington, Kentucky." *Association for Preservation Technology Bulletin.* Vol. XIII, No. 4 (1981), pp. 27–33.

Acknowledgements

The author gratefully acknowledges the technical expertise contributed to the preparation of this publication by Gilbert Wolf, National Plastering Industries; Walter Jowers; Brian Conway, Michigan Bureau of History; and master plasterer, Lawrence Ring, Sr. In addition, invaluable comments were provided by Michael Auer, Charles Fisher, Lauren Meier, Sharon Park, and Kay Weeks, professional staff of the Technical Preservation Services Branch, National Park Service; professional staff of the Cultural Resources program, Mid-Atlantic Regional Office, National Park Service; and S. Elizabeth Sasser of the Williamsport Preservation Training Center, National Park Service.

This publication has been prepared pursuant to the National Historic Preservation Act of 1966, as amended, which directs the Secretary of the Interior to develop and make available information concerning historic properties. Comments on the usefulness of this publication may be directed to H. Ward Jandl, Chief, Technical Preservation Services Branch, Preservation Assistance Division, National Park Service, P.O. Box 37127, Washington, D.C. 20013-7127.

Cover Photograph: St. James Church, Goose Creek, Berkeley County, South Carolina (1713–1719), is constructed of brick covered with stucco. Although much restored, it is notable for its ornamental stucco detailing, including rusticated quoins, cherub head "keystones" above the windows, flaming hearts, and a pelican in piety—symbol of the sacrament, in the pediment over the front door. Photo: Gary Hume.

23

Preserving Historic Ornamental Plaster

David Flaharty

From the time America struggled for a new identity as a constitutional republic—and well into the 20th century—its architecture and its decorative detailing remained firmly rooted in the European classicism of Palladio, Wren, and Mansart.

Together with skilled masons and carpenters, ornamental plasterers saw their inherited trade flourish from the mid-18th century until the Depression years of the 1930s. During this two hundred year period, as the Georgian and Federal styles yielded to the revivals—Greek, Rococo, Gothic, Renaissance, and Spanish—decorative plaster reflected each style, resulting in the wide variety of ornamentation that survives. The traditional methods of producing and installing interior decorative plaster were brought from Europe to this country intact and its practice remains virtually unchanged to this day.

Fig. 1. Ornamental plaster studios employed the following personnel: Draftsmen to interpret architectural details in shop drawings; sculptors who modelled in clay; modelmakers who assembled sculpted, plain-run and pre-cast elements into an ornamental unit; moldmakers who made rigid or flexible negative tooling; casters who made production units; finishers (often the caster's wives) who cleaned the casts; and laborers who assisted skilled personnel in operating efficiently. This studio was in Philadelphia, c. 1915. Photo: Courtesy, M. Earle Felber.

Styles of Decorative Plaster in America, 18th–20th Centuries

a

b

c

d

e

(a) **Kenmore, Fredericksburg, Virginia. c. 1752.** Georgian in style with ornamental ceilings based on Batty Langley's 1739 English style book, the plasterwork was executed by a Frenchman in the mid-1770s. This house was built by Col. Fielding Lewis and has the most elaborate ornamentation of any in the period. *Photo: Historic American Buildings Survey Collection.*

(b) **Old West Church, Boston, Massachusetts. c. 1806.** Designed by Asher Benjamin, this church in the Federal-Adamesque style became the prototype for many other New England churches through publication of plans in Benjamin's **American Builder's Companion.** *Photo: Courtesy, Stanley P. Mixon (copy).*

(c) **Lyndhurst, Tarrytown, New York, c. 1838.** This Gothic Revival villa on the Hudson River was built for financier Jay Gould by Alexander Jackson Davis. A versatile architect, Davis was simultaneously at work on Greek Revival buildings in New York City. Both styles called for elaborate ornamental plasterwork. *Photo: Jack E. Boucher, Historic American Buildings Survey.*

(d) **Gaineswood, Demopolis, Alabama, c. 1842–60.** These Greek Revival columns were drawn from Minard Lafever's **The Beauties of Modern Architecture** of 1835. This bold new style began in New York City and quickly spread south and west. *Photo: Historic American Buildings Survey Collection.*

(e) **Ohio Theater, Columbus Ohio, c. 1928.** An example of the "Golden Age" of movie palaces, Thomas Lamb's "Spanish" style interior is a typical example of the plasterwork executed just prior to the Depression years. Ornament was site cast, often on the stage, while the orchestra was scaffolded for installation. *Photo: National Park Service files.*

Like flat walls and ceilings, historic *ornamental* plaster is made of gypsum and lime which are stable and durable materials. An extremely versatile material, plaster can be modelled, cast, incised, colored, stamped, or stencilled. However, as an integral part of the building system it is subject to the typical problems of water intrusion, structural movement, vibration and insensitive alterations, both incrementally and from adaptive use projects. This Preservation Brief has been prepared to assist property owners, architects, contractors, and Federal agency managers in identifying the causes of ornamental plaster failure, specifying repair and replacement techniques and engaging qualified professionals to do the work. The scope of this Brief is limited to the repair and restoration of **existing ornamental plaster;** certain forms of decorative plaster such as scagliola, composition ornament, and artificial Caen Stone are not addressed, nor is the design and installation of ornamental plasterwork in new construction. Finally, guidance on using substitute materials to match the historic appearance of ornamental plaster-work—a legitimate option within the *Secretary of Interior's Standards for Historic Preservation Projects*—is not discussed here, but will be the subject of another Brief on interiors.

The Ornamental Plaster Trade

Shop Personnel. As builders and architects were hired by an increasingly affluent clientele, ornamental plaster shops developed from the single artisan operations of the 18th century into the complex establishments of the early 20th century. American plaster studios employed immigrant and, later, native craftsmen (see Fig. 1). Plasterers' guilds were in existence in Philadelphia in the 1790s. In 1864, a plasterers' union was organized in the United States with members from the British Isles whose work there had been limited to palaces and churches. English and European craftsmen came to America where the demand for their skills had increased by the decade, offering them the unparalleled opportunity to open their own shops. Over the years, plaster elements became so popular in decorating interior spaces that a major industry was established. By the 1880s, catalogs were available from which property owners could select ornamentation for their splendid new buildings (see Fig. 2).

Methods of Production. Historically, ornamental plasterwork has been produced in two ways: it would be *run in place* (or on a bench) at the site; or *cast in molds* in a workshop. Plain plaster molding without surface ornamentation was usually created directly on the wall, or run on a flat surface such as a plasterer's workbench and attached to the wall after it set. Ornament such as coffering for ceilings, centers for light fixtures (medallions), brackets, dentils, or columns were cast in hide glue (gelatin) or plaster molds in an offsite shop, often in more than one piece, then assembled and installed in the building.

Decorative Plaster Forms—Cornices, Medallions, Coffers. Three decorative plaster forms in particular— the cornice, the ceiling medallion, and the coffered ceiling—historically comprised much of the ornamental

Fig. 2. *This parlor medallion and pendant drops shown in a mid-19th century row house in Annapolis, Maryland were originally ordered from a catalog. A local plasterer ran the plain cornice and band ribbon, the curved corners of which were bench run, set with a plaster adhesive and pointed at the joints. Photo: M. E. Warren.*

plasterers' business. These forms appear individually or in combination from the 18th to 20th century, irrespective of stylistic changes.

For example, an elaborate parlor cornice consisted of plain moldings made of gypsum and lime run atop temporary lattice strips around the room. Tooling for plain-run moldings called for a sheet metal template of the molding profile mounted on a wooden "horse" (see Figs. 3 and 4). Mitering was accomplished using a plaster and lime putty gauge (mix) tooled with miter rods at the joints (see Fig. 5). Decorative "enrichments" such as leaves, egg and dart moldings, and bead and reel units were cast in the shop and applied to the plain runs using plaster as an adhesive (see Fig. 6). Painting, glazing, and even gilding followed. Large houses often had plain- run cornices on the upper floors which were not used for entertaining; modest houses also boasted cornice work without cast enrichment.

Among the most dramatic of ornamental plaster forms is the parlor **ceiling medallion.** Vernacular houses often used plain-run concentric circles from which lighting fixtures descended, usually hung from a wrought iron hook embedded in the central ceiling joist. More

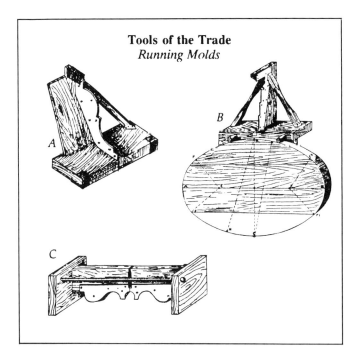

Tools of the Trade
Running Molds

Fig. 3. *A running mold consists of a sheet metal profile blade nailed to a stock and slipper. A triangular brace also acts as a handle. Such a mold produces a clean plain plaster molding if it travels in the same place each pass as a gypsum and lime putty gauge is troweled ahead of the moving blade. (A) is a typical mold for a cornice; (B) produces a diminished run as the hinges close together; and (C) is a pin mold that is used to surround elliptical forms such as arches. In addition, running molds may revolve around pivot points, trammels, and mandrels.*

Fig. 4. *Running a Cornice. The historic method of producing a cornice is unchanged today. A running mold or template is pushed along a lattice strip nailed to the wall. Base coat plaster is gypsum and sand; finishing plaster is added with small tools and stuffed wearing rubber gloves because lime burns the skin. As many as 20 passes are required to complete a smooth run; this particular cornice was formed in two stages, top and bottom, because it was so large. Cornices this size also have to be blocked and lathed to minimize the amount of applied material. Photo: Old-House Journal.*

Fig. 5. *Mitering a Plain-Run Cornice. Mitering requires great dexterity using the miter rod. In this case, a return at a chimney breast is tooled using an infill of gypsum and lime. Internal and external miters are required with the internal being the most difficult. Another method is to run a length of cornice (using the same blade) on a bench and set it in place, later to point the joints. Photo: Old-House Journal.*

Fig. 6. *Enriching a Plain-Run Cornice. After a cornice is run and mitered, cast enrichments are stuck in recessed sinkages planned to receive the casts. Ornamental models are made to engage with one another, resulting in unbroken lines or courses. A shop-cast ornament is soaked in water until saturated and pressed into its sinkage using wet plaster as an adhesive. Once the casts have been installed, they are carefully pointed at the joints and at the miters so that they appear as a continuous, repetitive design. Photo: Old-House Journal.*

elaborate medallions were composed of shop-cast pieces, such as acanthus foliage often alternating with anthemia or other decorative designs. Medallions usually related stylistically to the cornice ornament found in the room and could be created with or without a plain-run surround (see Fig. 7). Of particular importance to the art of ornamental plaster was the mid-19th century double parlor plan. Architects often specified matching medallions of robust proportions and ornamentation. Later, in 20th century American Colonial Revival architecture, architects called for Federal style ceiling medallions. Some of the more successful were graceful one-piece units, utilizing classical motifs such as garlands and swags, and in their simplicity, reminiscent of Adamesque designs of the 1760s.

a

b

Fig. 7. Running and Enriching a Ceiling Medallion. The method of running and enriching a ceiling medallion remains the same today. (a) First, a plain-run surround is spun from a pivot point centered in the ceiling field. (b) Ornament layout is determined using plane geometric principles; segmented locations are deeply scratched to provide a rough surface for adequate bonding using plaster as an adhesive. Historically, cast enrichments could be bought from local suppliers and set individually, allowing architects to compose medallions to suit room dimensions and period motifs. Photos: Peter Sanders.

Fig. 8. Casting a Coffering Unit. Ceiling coffers are made the same way today except, historically, a hide glue mold was poured over an ornamental model whereas today urethane molding rubber is used. Now, as then, the plaster casts are made with steel channel irons embedded on the back of each panel. The coffers are hung from carrying irons fixed to the ceiling above by means of twisting wires to level each coffer to its neighbor. Afterward, the panels are fastened together and the joints pointed with plaster. Photo: David Flaharty.

Fig. 9. The elaborate coffered ceiling was designed for the Willard Hotel in Washington, D.C. (1902–04) by Henry Janeway Hardenbergh. The coffered ceiling was restored as part of a rehabilitation project in the 1980s. Photo: Carol M. Highsmith.

Yet another significant decorative form is the **coffered ceiling.** Coffering units were cast in the shop or onsite, then installed with hanging wires to form the ceiling (see Fig 8). Ceiling design varied from period to period as to depth, panel shape, and ornamental complexity. Not always flat, coffering is seen inside domes, within barrel vaults and groin ceilings, along overhead ribs and soffits. Rosettes are usually centered in the panels and often enrich the intersections of elaborate stiles bordering the panels. Flat ceiling coffers are generally

identical in reflected plan; on domed or barrel ceilings, coffers differ from course to course so as to appear identical from various sight lines. The finish treatment of a coffered ceiling frequently exhibits the height of the painter's craft. Foremost examples of ceiling coffering include the United States Capitol, and Washington D. C.'s Union Station. As a popular decorative form with inherent acoustical benefits, the coffered ceiling is seen across the United States in many large public spaces such as theaters, courthouses, railroad stations, and hotels (see Fig. 9).

Unfortunately, these supposedly enduring decorative forms created by ornamental plaster tradesmen are subjected to the ravages of both nature and man and, consequently, seldom remain as originally designed. Minor changes of taste are perhaps the least injurious to plasterwork. Considerably greater damage and deterioration are caused by radical changes in building use and poor maintenance practices. Fortunately, in most cases, the form, detailing, and finish of historic ornamental plaster can be recaptured through careful repair and restoration.

Causes of Ornamental Plaster Damage

Ornamental Plaster Substrate. For flat plaster walls and ceilings, as well as decorative forms, the system to attach interior plaster to walls and ceilings primarily consisted of 1/4" x 1-1/4" wooden lathing strips nailed 3/8" apart against studs and joists. First a *scratch coat* consisting of sand, lime, and cattle hair was troweled on the lath and pressed through the slots so as to slump over and form "keys." Next, a *brown coat* was applied to establish flat and plumb surfaces. The earliest plasterwork consisted of two coats of lime and sand plaster; later in the 19th century, a third or *finish coat* was applied that consisted of both lime *and gypsum.* Decorative units were generally attached to the substrate using plaster as an adhesive.

Signs of Failure. Failure of the substrate is more typical than failure of the plaster ornament itself. Among the reasons for deterioration, **structural movement** (see Fig. 10) and **water intrusion** (see Fig. 11) are the most deleterious. Buildings move and settle, causing deflection and delamination which result in stress cracking. These cracks often begin at the corners of windows and doors and extend upward at acute angles (see Fig. 12). Roof or plumbing leaks make finishes discolor and peel and cause efflorescence, especially on plain-run or enriched cornices. Unheated buildings with water intrusion are subject to **freeze-thaw cycles** which ultimately result in base coat and ornamental plaster failure (see Fig. 13).

Fig. 11. The cornice of an Iowa courthouse has been severely damaged from a roof leak. In order to repair the ornamental plaster, a thixotropic rubber impression will be taken (with the paint build-up undisturbed). The efflorescence will be removed and fresh plaster casts installed so that egg and dart, dentil and leaf molding are perfectly aligned. Photo: National Park Service files.

Fig. 12. Settlement caused stress cracking through both flat wall and ornamental plaster. Repairs to the cornice molding involve chamfering the stress cracks to a "V groove" and patching with a mixture of gypsum and lime. The cornice can be countersunk-screwed to its substrate to prevent further movement. Screw heads are then plastered over. The crack running through the painting will need to be filled carefully, and the painting restored by a trained conservator. Photo: Jack E. Boucher, Historic American Buildings Survey.

Fig. 10. Structural settling has caused this ceiling to deflect. Prior to restoring the damaged plaster and final repainting, a structural engineer experienced in historic preservation will be engaged to shore-up the ceiling from below and reattach the sagging ceiling plaster with the joists above (see also Fig. 17 under Immediate Action.) Photo: National Park Service files.

Fig. 13. *Water intrusion and freeze/thaw cycles caused extensive efflorescence and ornamental plaster failure. The plaster needed almost total replacement within the rehabilitation project. Photo: Commercial Photographics.*

Fig. 14. *A mitered portion of this impost capital abacus has fallen, revealing the plaster adhesive material. Repairs are made by obtaining a section through the abacus, making a bench-run length, cutting, fitting, and readhering the missing piece. Finally, the joints are pointed. Photo: Lee H. Nelson, FAIA.*

In addition, keying and adhesive properties may be further jeopardized by **weak original mixes** (see Fig. 14) that were improperly applied. Substrate failure typically results from **faulty lathing or rusty lath nails,** causing ceilings to fall. In the 20th century, **vibration** from heavy vehicular traffic, nearby blasting, and even repeated sonic booms may contribute to damaging ornamental plaster. **Inadequate support** in an original design may also be to blame when particularly heavy units have simply broken off over time (Fig. 15). Finally, new mechanical systems, suspended ceilings and partition walls insensitively installed in adaptive use projects, show little regard for the inspired decorations of earlier periods (see Fig. 16).

Repairing and Replacing. Plaster failure is a matter of degree. For example, top coat failure can be repaired by

Fig. 15. *U. S. Treasury Cash Room, Washington, D.C. c. 1830. Designed by Robert Mills in the Greek Revival style, the unreinforced shell flutes most likely broke as a result of their weight. As part of an overall restoration of the room, the broken parts were molded on site, recast, then re-attached using wooden strips to pin them in place. Photo: Laurie R. Hammel.*

Fig. 16. *The Auditorium Building, Chicago, Illinois, 1889, by Louis Sullivan. Earlier insensitive alterations were removed prior to restoration of the room. In the photo, a partition wall has already been removed; the electrical conduit and a ventilation grille followed. Plaster patching and painting were the final steps of restoration work. Photo: National Park Service files.*

applying a new finish coat over a sound early substrate. Also, if cracking or loss of all three coats has occurred and is not combined with major structural failure, it can be repaired much like flat wall plaster. For ornamental plaster, however, repair beyond patching is often equivalent to targeted replacement of entire lengths or portions of run-in-place and cast ornamentation. Pieces that are deteriorated or damaged beyond plain patching must be **removed and replaced with new pieces** that exactly match the existing historic plaster. For this reason, partial restoration is often a more accurate term than repair. But whichever term is used, it is not recommended that repair of ornamental plaster be undertaken at any level by property owners; it is a craft requiring years of training and experience. A qualified professional should always be called in to make an inventory of ornamental plaster enrichments and to identify those details which are repairable onsite and which should be removed for repair or remanufacture in the shop.

Immediate Action

Once the cause and extent of damage have been determined, treatments such as shoring, stabilization, and limited demolition can begin, preparatory to repairing or restoring historic ornamental plaster.

First, roof or plumbing leaks must be repaired to eliminate the problem of water intrusion. General structural repairs should be undertaken to arrest building movement, which weakens the base coat plasters to which the ornamental enrichments are attached. Ornamental plaster deflection should be corrected by shoring from below followed by re-anchoring (see Fig. 17).

Testing for poor adhesion of base coat to lath or ornament to base coat, should be conducted to reduce further loss of enrichment. Adaptive use intrusions should be carefully removed to protect the existing decorative plasterwork.

Code-required fire suppression systems should be evaluated at this time. Modern building codes may require heat/smoke/flame detectors and automatic sprinkler systems of various types and applications. Fire suppression systems as well as all mechanical systems (HVAC, plumbing and electrical) systems should be designed so that they accomplish their purpose with minimal impact on the decorative plaster. Plumbing for an automatic sprinkler system, for example, can be run above new and existing coffering so that the sprinkler heads barely protrude from the rosette centers in the coffered design. Access should be provided for future system maintenance or repair.

A 20th Century Shop Tour—Personnel, Materials, and Processes

Before discussing how decorative forms such as cornices, medallions, and ceiling coffers are repaired onsite and in the shop by ornamental plasterers, the "shop tour" explains traditional casting processes used in conjunction with updated materials. A shop tour can be exciting, but confusing to the layman without some explanation of modeling, molding, and casting activities. For a prospective client, a visit to the plaster studio or site can be of value in choosing a qualified plastering contractor.

Shop and Personnel. Generally, a highly functional shop should look well organized—that is, not in disarray with remnants of past projects lying about to impede current production. Old molds may be in abundance, but hanging from the wall or otherwise "on file." Machinery (saws and drill presses) and hand tools should appear well maintained. In short, one might evaluate such a studio as one does an auto mechanic's shop: does it inspire confidence? This is the time to look around and ask questions. What is the shop's past project work experience? Is the firm mostly involved in new construction work or total reconstruction? More important than the way the shop looks, is the personnel sufficiently experienced in making **repairs** to historic decorative plaster? What about training and apprenticeships? How did the staff learn the trade? The more that is known about the total operation the better.

Fig. 17 (a) Where this ceiling was suffering from structural failure, the first step was to shore it up from below. (b) Toggle bolts were used to reattach the plaster molding to the ceiling joists. The ceiling was then patched with gypsum and lime, prior to restoring the significant paint finishes. Photos: National Park Service files.

Molding Rubber. Familiarity with contemporary molding rubbers is desirable. There are several formulations currently on the market. In the past, flexible molds were made with hide glue melted in a double boiler and poured over plaster originals which had been prepared with an appropriate parting agent. Of the newer rubbers, latex (painted on the model coat by coat) is time consuming and has little dimensional accuracy; polysulfide distorts under pressure; and silicone is needlessly expensive. Urethane rubber, with a 30-durometer hardness, is the current choice. Urethanes are manufactured as pourable liquids and as thixotropic pastes so that they can be used on vertical or overhead surfaces. The paste is especially useful for onsite impressions of existing ornament; the liquid is best used in the shop much as hide glue or gelatin was historically. Urethane rubber has the ability to reproduce detail as fine as a fingerprint and does not degrade during most ornamental plaster projects. No flexible molding material lasts forever, so spare casts should be maintained for future remolding.

Molding Plaster. Molding plaster will also be in evidence; it is the product most similar to that used historically. This plaster is finely ground to accept the detail of the rubber molds, not so hard as to prohibit tooling, and combines readily with finish lime. High-strength plaster is available in varying densities, some with added components for specific purposes. Most shops maintain these varieties, but use molding plaster for typical work.

Sheet Metal Templates. The contractor's familiarity with sheet metal is critical. Accurate template blades are required to reproduce both straight and curved sections of moldings (see Fig. 3, above). The blades must be carefully cut, filed, and sanded in order to form exact reproductive units. A tour of a sizeable shop will include observation of running techniques and the results of this activity should be much in evidence. Regardless of size, these runs should be smooth and true when made by qualified craftsmen.

Models. Models, whether of capitals, cornices, medallions or cartouches, are made as whole units or in parts depending on project demands. Completeness, accurate dimensions, and attention to historic styles are essential ingredients of successful models. Each part of a model has a name, i.e., dentil, guilloche, rinceau or bolection molding, modillion, egg and dart, and the designers and restorers of these ornaments should know their names. Failure to identify these parts correctly should be of concern to a prospective client.

Molds. Molds are "negative forms" produced from completed models. Simple flood molds require a separator or barrier coat over the original and a surrounding fence to prevent the liquid rubber from leaking out. Larger or more complicated molds are made in pieces or with a layer of rubber supported by a plaster shell or mother mold attached to a wooden or metal frame. Following completion of a successful mold, the original model is discarded because it is now possible for it to be accurately reproduced.

Casting the Molds. Casting operations should appear clean and efficient. A skillful caster's output can be voluminous and often looks effortless as it is being produced. Raw materials are close at hand, molds are rarely without curing plaster in them, production is stored so as not to warp while it is still wet and each cycle, from mixing to pouring, setting, and demolding is accomplished so as not to waste time or break plaster casts. A good caster generally obviates the need for a finishing department.

Two other aspects should be noted. Shipping facilities are critical to move the product to the restoration site safely. Drawing and design space should be separate from the production floor. In summary, the modern ornamental plaster shop inevitably looks quite different from that pictured earlier in this Preservation Brief (see Fig. 1, above), but, with the exception of contemporary tools and materials, the operations are the same. The following sections discuss how repairs are made by today's plaster tradesmen.

Repairing Historic Ornamental Plaster

Cornice. A plain run or ornamented plaster cornice which has undergone damage or severe deterioration can often be repaired. Footage which is beyond repair should be identified and be carefully demolished to expose the underlying structure beneath to which the molding was secured. To replace the missing lengths, the first step is to obtain a cross-section, or profile, through the cornice from finish ceiling to finish wall lines. This is best accomplished using one of these methods:

1. A section through the cornice may be determined by sawing through the molding, inserting a sheet metal blank in the slot and tracing the profile directly on the template. This is considerably more accurate than the profile gauge, but will require re-pointing the saw kerf; alternatively, the cut may be made on one of the deteriorated pieces, provided it was removed as an intact unit.

2. The section may be obtained by making a thixotropic rubber impression of the molding, casting the result in fresh plaster and sawing through the cast to transfer the cross-section to a sheet metal template.

With the section determined, it is drawn onto 22-gauge galvanized sheet metal, cut with tin snips and carefully filed to the line. The template is checked periodically against the original profile to assure a perfect match. With the template blade finally complete, it is nailed to stock and slipper (see Fig. 3, above), ready for running the replacement footage.

Short lengths of new cornice are best run on a bench using gypsum and lime; the reproduction molding should be somewhat longer than the required length (see Fig 18). The new footage is cut and fit in place to match the existing cornice, then securely countersunk-screwed to studs, joists and/or blocking. The resulting joints are pointed with flat mitering rods, flush with adjacent members (see Fig. 5, above).

Fig. 18. Repairing a Cornice. (a) In the restoration of the Henry Hirshfeld House, a 19th century residence in Austin, Texas, removal of a tin ceiling revealed a damaged plain-run cornice. Photo: John Volz, AIA. (b) A section through the molding was taken, a template blade cut, horsed-up, and run on a bench using gypsum and lime. Photo: Charles E. Fisher. (c) The new cornice was then cut, fitted, and applied to new blocking between wall and ceiling. The external miter and returns were pointed using the miter rod. After the ceiling restoration was complete, other finishes, such as wallpaper, were applied. Photo: Candace Volz.

Longer lengths of cornice may be run in place, much as they were historically. Care should be taken that the position of the running mold engages with the existing work at either end of the run. Yet another method is to bench run the cornice to five or six feet, make a rubber mold of the model, and pre-cast the replacement parts either at the site or in the shop.

If the damaged cornice is ornamented, samples of the enrichment should be removed, making sure that whole original units are obtained. This is a difficult process, since these units were stuck into plain-run recesses called "sinkages" using plaster as an adhesive. In order to insert a flat chisel behind the ornament to break the bond, some units may have to be sacrificed. Sacrifice should be minimal. The excised enrichment should then be removed to the shop for rubber molding and casting either with or without the paint buildup, depending on the demands of the project. Whereas molding with several layers of paint make it hard to discern new casts from originals, paint-stripped molding reveals the remarkable talents of the period modelmakers. As noted, contemporary rubber materi-

als have "fingerprint detail" capability. Modern casts are then applied to the new or original runs, again using plaster as an adhesive.

Ceiling Medallion. Ceiling medallions are often in greater jeopardy than cornices because the joist-lath-basecoat support system is susceptible to deflection and the force of gravity. The problems of ceiling failure are more frequent in the centers of parlors because circular-run and shop-cast ornament is often quite heavy and was not historically attached with any additional mechanical fasteners such as bolts and screws.

If the lath or keys have failed, plaster ceiling ornament may be saved, in whole or in part, by removing floor boards above, then drilling and injecting each lath with an elastic acrylic or epoxy material to reattach plaster to lath, and lath to the joists. This is a recently developed procedure which should only be undertaken by experienced professionals. The consolidation and reattachment process has been used successfully in period structures with dramatic results when important plaster and painted surfaces would otherwise have been lost.

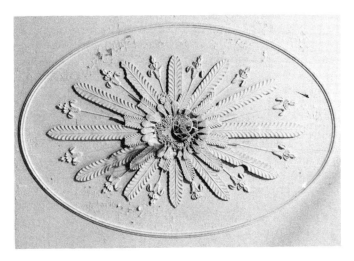

Fig. 19. Ceiling medallions may need repair or replacement. The ornamental plasterer takes impressions of the existing plaster, then casts new plaster elements. Adhesive plaster is used to reattach the new pieces. Left: Damaged elliptical medallion from Rockland, Fairmount Park, Philadelphia, Pennsylvania. Photo: David Flaharty. Right: Fragments of a medallion from the Bennett House, Charleston, South Carolina. The fragments serve as documentation for the replacement medallion. Photo: Peter Sanders.

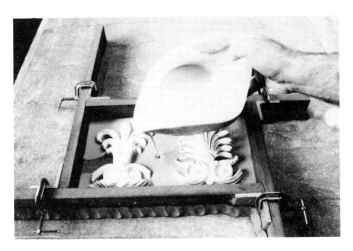

Fig. 20. Repairing a Medallion. Left: The plaster models shown are first lathered with a parting agent (liquid soap). To make a flood mold, urethane rubber is poured between wood fences clamped together and dammed with clay. Right: Casting plaster is then spooned into the two-part urethane mold. The mold showing six ornaments in the process of being cast is called a "gang mold." The others are simply single molds. Photos: David Flaharty.

Historic lighting fixtures often hung from elaborate ceiling medallions. When these fixtures were later converted to gas and electrical service, the central ornamental plaster canopies were sometimes damaged by insensitive tradesmen. More recent adaptive use projects may have caused additional damage.

Damaged ceiling medallions (see Fig. 19a) can be repaired by carefully removing representative plaster ornamentation, molding and recasting in the shop (see Fig. 20) and replacing the new enrichments so that they align perfectly with the original pattern. Polyvinyl acetate bonding agents are applied to the background and ornament so that the adhesive plaster grips tightly. Alternatively, a severely damaged medallion (see 19b) can be replaced using the fragments as physical documentation to cast a visually accurate replacement.

Sections of plain-run circular molding may also be repaired by determining a section through the run and the radius from molding to pivot point. As with cornices, the run should be made on a bench to a length greater than required, then cut and fit in place. Circular run sections are installed using plaster adhesives on bonded surfaces or modern construction adhesives after referring to manufacturers' instructions as to whether the adhesive is recommended for use on wet or dry materials. Coarse-threaded, galvanized screws are often countersunk to aid the bond; if possible, the screws should be inserted at points that will ultimately be covered with cast enrichments.

Ceiling medallions frequently appear in matching double parlors. It is not unusual for one ceiling to fail while its mate remains undamaged. The flat plastered ceiling over the location of the missing medallion often has a "ghost," confirming that a ceiling medallion once ornamented the parlor. The missing medallion may be remanufactured by securing a section, dimensions, and samples of cast enrichments from the surviving ornament and accurately following the original procedure (see Fig. 7, above). The ceiling on which the new work is to be set should be examined for its soundness and, if necessary, relathed (with self-furring metal lath) and plastered. The pivot point for a circular run is screwed into a wooden block, force-fit into the center electrical box, and removed after the run is completed.

After 1850, particularly in the South, ceiling medallions were often designed with cast ornament only; no plain-run surround was used. Repair of such medallions proceeds as described above but without bordering molding.

An important point needs to be made about **adding** ceiling medallions (or any other kind of ornamental plaster element) when there is a lack of historical evidence. If there is no ghost mark or other documentation, indicating a medallion once existed, then the room should remain *unornamented* as it was historically. Adding conjectural ornamentation of any type or material (i.e., shop-cast or glass fiber reinforced plaster or polystyrene foam substitutes) can create a false sense of historical development contrary to the preservation principles stated in *The Secretary of the Interior's Standards for Historic Preservation Projects.* However, if there is clear indication that a ceiling medallion once existed, but there is inadequate documentation for its replacement, a medallion compatible with the room's historic character may be considered. Professional advice should be sought.

Coffered Ceiling. Like cornices and medallions, coffered ceilings suffer from poor maintenance practices and structural problems; however, these individually cast ceiling units are particularly vulnerable when a building is being rehabilitated and great care is not taken in executing the work. In the most serious of cases, portions of a roof can collapse, dropping heavy debris through the hanging coffering panels, and demolishing large portions of the ornamentation (see Fig. 21).

But even this level of damage can usually be remedied by restoration professionals. Immediate action calls for shoring the areas adjacent to the damage, and inspecting the hanging apparatus for unforeseen detachment

Fig. 21. The Yiddish Arts Theater, New York City, c. 1920s. The concrete roof of this building collapsed, damaging portions of the existing Moorish style coffered ceiling. The square coffer unit was easily identifiable and was removed to a casting shop for reproduction. Photo: David Flaharty.

and deflection. New channel iron is used to stabilize the existing coffers and ties reinforced, as necessary. An intact coffering unit is then identified and carefully removed to a casting shop for molding and casting (see Fig. 22). When re-hung, the units are painted to match the historic coffering (see Fig. 23).

Coffered ceilings appear with plain run or enriched cornices. In most cases it is recommended that the cornice be repaired first in order to achieve straight and level moldings. Then the damaged coffers should be replaced with the matching new coffers and the joints between pointed. Access from above is critical.

Finding and Evaluating a Contractor

When ornamental plaster damage or deterioration has been identified, the historic property owner, architect,

Fig. 22. Repairing a Coffered Ceiling. As part of the theater rehabilitation, the coffered ceiling panels are being reproduced in urethane rubber molds and reinforced with open weave burlap and wood fiber. Steel channel irons can be seen, attached to the backs of the casts. Later, these irons are used to hang the panels from a superstructure at the site. Photo: David Flaharty.

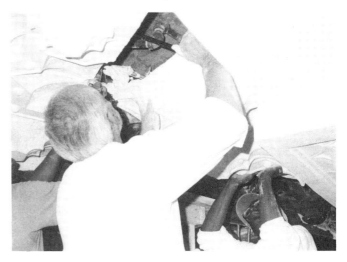

Fig. 23. A pre-cast coffer is lifted into place to abut adjacent panels. Tie wire will be fastened to the channel irons and the superstructure above, twisted to level, and finally wadded with wood fiber soaked in plaster to prevent the wire from stretching. Photo: David Flaharty.

or developer should secure the services of a reputable restoration contractor before proceeding further. It is clear as more and more projects are undertaken, that there is a wide disparity of skills within the trade today. This is partly due to the introduction of gypsum board as a substitute for traditional plastering. As gypsum board became popular after World War II, plasterers saw the demand for their skills decline. Plastering techniques were forgotten because they were often not passed down within shops and families. However, ornamental plaster studios have seen a resurgence in demand for their services in the last decade, particularly as more historic buildings are rehabilitated (see Fig. 24).

Locating an experienced contractor who is suitable for your **particular project** is the goal. First, many professional preservation organizations can provide references for suitable restoration contractors. Local plasterers' unions should also be able to identify contractors with experience in ornamental plaster restoration projects. Architects with preservation and restoration project experience may recommend contractors they feel have done a good job for them in the past. Museums with period rooms have engaged craftsmen to assemble the backgrounds for display of antique furniture and decorative arts. Finally, historical societies, either national, state, or municipally organized, may have funded projects which repaired and restored ornamental plaster.

Once several contractors have been identified, their specific abilities need to be evaluated. Prospective contractors should be invited to visit the job site to see and define the scope of work; written proposals, including prices, from all bidders, are essential for comparison. References should be provided and investigated. An outside consultant may be engaged or an informal adviser designated to aid in evaluating the experience and proposals of the bidders. To get a total picture, a completed project should ideally be visited by the prospective client with the contractor present to answer questions which often arise.

Finally, although this may not always be achievable, the bidder's studio may be visited, preferably on a normal working day (see **A 20th Century Shop Tour,** above.) Alternatively, the bidder may be visited while working onsite. Some ornamental plasterers simply do not have shops. They prefer to cast onsite, adhering the casts while the plaster is wet, and coordinating the job closely with the architect, who inspects each unit as it is cast and before it is installed.

Conclusion

Decorative plasterwork is usually a component of the historic character of interiors and, consequently, *The Secretary of the Interior's Standards for Historic Preservation Projects* call for its protection, maintenance, and repair. Where decorative plasterwork has deteriorated beyond repair, it should be replaced to match the old. Based on physical documentation, both repair and replacement can be accomplished using traditional molding plaster

Fig. 24. *This plaster studio is well organized, with ample work space. Note the plaster casts hanging neatly on the wall. Photo: Berry and Homer, Philadelphia.*

and casting procedures, together with the best of the modern molding materials available. Once a "lost art" after the Depression years, the skills of today's ornamental plasterers are increasingly in demand as part of historic preservation project teams. The ingenious and inspired decorative work created by our earlier architects and artisans can now be assured an extended life.

Bibliography

Bankart, George. *The Art of the Plasterer.* London: B. T. Batsford, 1908.

Dalton, Byron William. *Practical Plastering and Cement Finishing and Related Subjects.* Chicago, Illinois: Byron William Dalton, 1949.

Flaharty, David. "Ornamental Plaster Restoration." *Fine Homebuilding.* No. 57, December, 1989/January 1990, pp. 38–42.

Garrison, John Mark. "Decorative Plaster: Running Cornices." *The Old-House Journal.* Vol. XII., No. 101, December, 1984, pp. 214–219.

_____. "Casting Decorative Plaster." *The Old-House Journal.* Vol. XIII, No. 9, November, 1985, pp. 186–189.

Gypsum Construction Handbook. Chicago, Illinois: United States Gypsum Co., 1986.

Harris, Cyril M., editor. *Illustrated Dictionary of Historic Architecture.* New York: Dover Publications, 1983.

Millar, William. *Plastering, Plain and Decorative.* London: B. T. Batsford, 1897.

Phillips, Morgan. "Adhesives for the Reattachment of Loose Plaster," *Association for Preservation Technology Bulletin,* Vol. XII, No. 2, 1980, pp. 37–63.

Van den Branden, F. and Hartsell, Thomas L. *Plastering Skills.* Homewood, Illinois: American Technical Publishers, Inc., 1984.

Acknowledgements

Thanks go to the technical experts in the field who reviewed and commented upon the draft manuscript: M. Earle Felber, Andrew Ladygo (Jefferson Poplar Forest), Lee H. Nelson, FAIA, Gilbert Wolf (National Plastering Industries), and Stephen Zychal (Ornamental Plastering, Inc.). Insightful comments were offered Gary L. Hume, Acting Chief, Preservation Assistance Division, Karen Kummer, Small Homes Council-Building Research Council, University of Illinois, NPS cultural resources program regional offices, and the staff of Technical Preservation Services Branch, H. Ward Jandl, Chief. *Old-House Journal and Fine Homebuilding* were most generous to grant permission to use photographs from their publications. **Kay D. Weeks is credited with coordinating this cooperative publication project and general editorship.**

24

Heating, Ventilating, and Cooling Historic Buildings: Problems and Recommended Approaches

Sharon C. Park, AIA

The need for modern mechanical systems is one of the most common reasons to undertake work on historic buildings. Such work includes upgrading older mechanical systems, improving the energy efficiency of existing buildings, installing new heating, ventilation or air conditioning (HVAC) systems, or—particularly for museums—installing a climate control system with humidification and dehumidification capabilities. Decisions to install new HVAC or climate control systems often result from concern for occupant health and comfort, the desire to make older buildings marketable, or the need to provide specialized environments for operating computers, storing artifacts, or displaying museum collections. Unfortunately, occupant comfort and concerns for the objects within the building are sometimes given greater consideration than the building itself. In too many cases, applying modern standards of interior climate comfort to historic buildings has proven detrimental to historic materials and decorative finishes.

This Preservation Brief underscores the importance of careful planning in order to balance the preservation objectives with interior climate needs of the building. It is not intended as a technical guide to calculate tonnage or to size piping or ductwork. Rather, this Brief identifies some of the problems associated with installing mechanical systems in historic buildings and recommends approaches to minimizing the physical and visual damage associated with installing and maintaining these new or upgraded systems.

Historic buildings are not easily adapted to house modern precision mechanical systems. Careful planning must be provided early on to ensure that decisions made during the design and installation phases of a new system are appropriate. Since new mechanical and other related systems, such as electrical and fire suppression, can use up to 10% of a building's square footage and 30%–40% of an overall rehabilitation budget, decisions must be made in a systematic and coordinated manner. The installation of inappropriate

mechanical systems may result in any or all of the following:

- large sections of historic materials are removed to install or house new systems.
- historic structural systems are weakened by carrying the weight of, and sustaining vibrations from, large equipment.
- moisture introduced into the building as part of a new system migrates into historic materials and causes damage, including biodegradation, freeze/thaw action, and surface staining.
- exterior cladding or interior finishes are stripped to install new vapor barriers and insulation.
- historic finishes, features, and spaces are altered by dropped ceilings and boxed chases or by poorly located grilles, registers, and equipment.
- systems that are too large or too small are installed before there is a clearly planned use or a new tenant.

For historic properties it is critical to understand what spaces, features, and finishes are historic in the building, what should be retained, and what the *realistic* heating, ventilating, and cooling needs are for the building, its occupants, and its contents. A systematic approach, involving preservation planning, preservation design, and a follow-up program of monitoring and maintenance, can ensure that new systems are successfully added—or existing systems are suitably upgraded—while preserving the historic integrity of the building.

No set formula exists for determining what type of mechanical system is best for a specific building. Each building and its needs must be evaluated separately. Some buildings will be so significant that every effort must be made to protect the historic materials and systems in place with minimal intrusion from new systems. Some buildings will have museum collections that need special climate control. In such cases, curatorial needs must be considered—but not to the ultimate detriment of the historic building resource. Other buildings will be rehabilitated for commercial use. For them, a variety of systems might be acceptable, as long as significant spaces, features, and finishes are retained.

Most mechanical systems require upgrading or replacement within 15–30 years due to wear and tear or the availability of improved technology. Therefore, historic buildings should not be greatly altered or otherwise sacrificed in an effort to meet short-term systems objectives.

History of Mechanical Systems

The history of mechanical systems in buildings involves a study of inventions and ingenuity as building owners, architects, and engineers devised ways to improve the interior climate of their buildings. Following are highlights in the evolution of heating, ventilating, and cooling systems in historic buildings.

Eighteenth Century. Early heating and ventilation in America relied upon common sense methods of *managing the environment* (see figure 1). Builders purposely sited houses to capture winter sun and prevailing summer cross breezes; they chose materials that could help protect the inhabitants from the elements, and took precautions against precipitation and damaging drainage patterns. The location and sizes of windows, doors, porches, and the floor plan itself often evolved to maximize ventilation. Heating was primarily from fireplaces or stoves and, therefore, was at the source of delivery. In 1744, Benjamin Franklin designed his "Pennsylvania stove" with a fresh air intake in order to maximize the heat radiated into the room and to minimize annoying smoke.

Thermal insulation was rudimentary—often wattle and daub, brick and wood nogging. The comfort level for occupants was low, but the relatively small difference between internal and external temperatures and relative humidity allowed building materials to expand and contract with the seasons.

Regional styles and architectural features reflected regional climates. In warm, dry and sunny climates, thick adobe walls offered shelter from the sun and kept the inside temperatures cool. Verandas, courtyards, porches, and high ceilings also reduced the impact of the sun. Hot and humid climates called for elevated living floors, louvered grilles and shutters, balconies, and interior courtyards to help circulate air.

Nineteenth Century. The industrial revolution provided the technological means for *controlling the environment* for the first time (see figure 2). The dual developments of steam energy from coal and industrial mass production made possible early central heating systems with distribution of heated air or steam using metal ducts or pipes. Improvements were made to early wrought iron boilers and by late century, steam and low pressure hot water radiator systems were in common use, both in offices and residences. Some large institutional buildings heated air in furnaces and distributed it throughout the building in brick flues with a network of metal pipes delivering heated air to individual rooms. Residential designs of the period often used gravity hot air systems utilizing decorative floor and ceiling grilles.

Ventilation became more scientific and the introduc-

1. *Eighteenth century and later vernacular architecture depended on the siting of the building, deciduous trees, cross ventilation, and the placement of windows and chimneys to maximize winter heating and natural summer cooling. Regional details, as seen in this Virginia house, include external chimneys and a separate summer kitchen to reduce fire risk and isolate heat in the summer. Photo: NPS Files.*

2. *Nineteenth century buildings continued to use architectural features such as porches, cupolas, and awnings to make the buildings more comfortable in summer, but heating was greatly improved by hot water or steam radiators. Photo: NPS Files*

tion of fresh air into buildings became an important component of heating and cooling. Improved forced air ventilation became possible in mid-century with the introduction of power-driven fans. Architectural features such as porches, awnings, window and door transoms, large open-work iron roof trusses, roof monitors, cupolas, skylights and clerestory windows helped to dissipate heat and provide healthy ventilation.

Cavity wall construction, popular in masonry structures, improved the insulating qualities of a building and also provided a natural cavity for the dissipation of moisture produced on the interior of the building. In some buildings, cinder chips and broken masonry filler between structural iron beams and jack arch floor vaults provided thermal insulation as well as fireproofing. Mineral wool and cork were new sources of lightweight insulation and were forerunners of contemporary batt and blanket insulation.

The technology of the age, however, was not sufficient to produce "tight" buildings. There was still only a moderate difference between internal and external temperatures. This was due, in part, to the limitations of early insulation, the almost exclusive use of single glazed windows, and the absence of air-tight construction. The presence of ventilating fans and the reliance on architectural features, such as operable windows, cupolas and transoms, allowed sufficient air movement to keep buildings well ventilated. Building materials could behave in a fairly traditional way, expanding and contracting with the seasons.

Twentieth Century. The twentieth century saw intensive development of new technologies and the notion of fully *integrating mechanical systems* (see figure 3). Oil and gas furnaces developed in the nineteenth century were improved and made more efficient, with electricity becoming the critical source of power for building systems in the latter half of the century. Forced air heating systems with ducts and registers became popular for all types of buildings and allowed architects to experiment with architectural forms free from mechanical encumbrances. In the 1920s large-scale theaters and auditoriums introduced central air conditioning, and by mid-century forced air systems which combined heating and air conditioning in the same ductwork set a new standard for comfort and convenience. The combination and coordination of a variety of systems came together in the post-World War II highrise buildings; complex heating and air conditioning plants, electric elevators, mechanical towers, ventilation fans, and full service electric lighting were integrated into the building's design.

The insulating qualities of building materials improved. Synthetic materials, such as spun fiberglass batt insulation, were fully developed by mid-century. Prototypes of insulated thermal glazing and integral storm window systems were promoted in construction journals. Caulking to seal out perimeter air around window and door openings became a standard construction detail.

The last quarter of the twentieth century has seen making HVAC systems more energy efficient and better integrated. The use of vapor barriers to control moisture migration, thermally efficient windows, caulking

and gaskets, compressed thin wall insulation, has become standard practice. New integrated systems now combine interior climate control with fire suppression, lighting, air filtration, temperature and humidity control, and security detection. Computers regulate the performance of these integrated systems based on the time of day, day of the week, occupancy, and outside ambient temperature.

3. *The circa 1928 Fox Theater in Detroit, designed by C. Howard Crane, was one of the earliest twentieth century buildings to provide air conditioning to its patrons. The early water-cooled system was recently restored. Commercial and highrise buildings of the twentieth century were able, mostly through electrical power, to provide sophisticated systems that integrated many building services. Photo: William Kessler and Associates, Architects.*

Climate Control and Preservation

Although twentieth century mechanical systems technology has had a tremendous impact on making historic buildings comfortable, the introduction of these new systems in older buildings is not without problems. The attempt to meet and maintain modern climate control standards *may in fact be damaging to historic resources*. Modern systems are often over-designed to compensate for inherent inefficiencies of some historic buildings materials and plan layouts. Energy retrofit measures, such as installing exterior wall insulation and vapor barriers or the sealing of operable window and vents, ultimately affect the performance and can reduce the life of aging historic materials.

In general, the greater the differential between the interior and exterior temperature and humidity levels, the greater the potential for damage. As natural vapor pressure moves moisture from a warm area to a colder, dryer area, condensation will occur on or in building materials in the colder area (see figure 4). Too little humidity in winter, for example, can dry and crack historic wooden or painted surfaces. Too much humidity in winter causes moisture to collect on cold surfaces, such as windows, or to migrate into walls. As a result, this condensation deteriorates wooden or metal windows and causes rotting of walls and wooden structural elements, dampening insulation and holding moisture against exterior surfaces. Moisture migration through walls can cause the corrosion of metal anchors, angles, nails or wire lath, can blister and peel exterior paint, or can leave efflorescence and salt deposits on exterior masonry. In cold climates, freeze-thaw damage can result from excessive moisture in external walls.

To avoid these types of damage to a historic building, it is important to understand how building components work together as a system. Methods for controlling interior temperature and humidity and improving ventilation must be considered in any new or upgraded HVAC or climate control system. While certain energy retrofit measures will have a positive effect on the overall building, installing effective vapor barriers in historic walls is difficult and often results in destruction of significant historic materials (see figure 5).

5. The installation of vapor retarders in walls of historic buildings in an effort to contain interior moisture can cause serious damage to historic finishes as shown here. In this example, all the wall plaster and lath have been stripped in preparation for a vapor barrier prior to replastering. Controlling interior temperature and relative humidity can be more effective than adding insulation and vapor barriers to historic perimeter walls. Photo: Ernest A. Conrad, P.E.

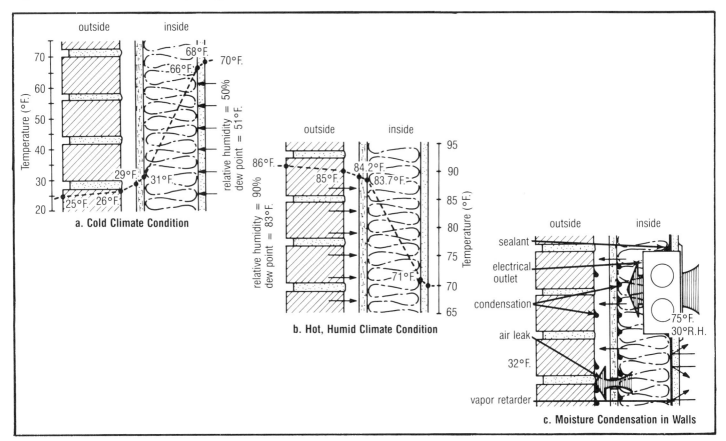

4. Mechanical heating and cooling systems change the interior climate of a building. Moisture in the air will dissipate from the warmer area of a building to the colder area and can cause serious deterioration of historic materials. Condensation can form if the dew point occurs within the building wall, particularly one that has been insulated (see a and b). Even when vapor retarders are installed (c), any non-continuous areas will provide spaces for moisture to pass. Wall Section Drawings: NPS files

Planning the New System

Climate control systems are generally classified according to the medium used to condition the temperature: air, water, or a combination of both (see overview on page 6). The complexity of choices facing a building owner or manager means that a *systematic approach* is critical in determining the most suitable system for a building, its contents, and its occupants. No matter which system is installed, a change in the interior climate will result. This physical change will in turn affect how the building materials perform. New registers, grilles, cabinets, or other accessories associated with the new mechanical system will also visually change the interior (and sometimes the exterior) appearance of the building. Regardless of the type or extent of a mechanical system, the owner of a historic building should know *before* a system is installed what it will look like and what problems can be anticipated during the life of that system. The potential harm to a building and costs to an owner of selecting the wrong mechanical system are very great.

The use of a building and its contents will largely determine the best type of mechanical system. The historic building materials and construction technology as well as the size and availability of secondary spaces within the historic structure will affect the choice of a system. It may be necessary to investigate a combination of systems. In each case, the needs of the user, the needs of the building, and the needs of a collection or equipment must be considered. It may not be necessary to have a comprehensive climate control system if climate-sensitive objects can be accommodated in special areas or climate-controlled display cases. It may not be necessary to have central air conditioning in a mild climate if natural ventilation systems can be improved through the use of operable windows, awnings, exhaust fans, and other "low-tech" means. Modern standards for climate control developed for new construction may not be achievable or desirable for historic buildings. *In each case, the lowest level of intervention needed to successfully accomplish the job should be selected.*

Before a system is chosen, the following planning steps are recommended:

1. **Determine the use of the building.** The proposed use of the building (museum, commercial, residential, retail) will influence the type of system that should be installed. The number of people and functions to be housed in a building will establish the level of comfort and service that must be provided. Avoid uses that require major modifications to significant architectural spaces. What is the intensity of use of the building: intermittent or constant use, special events or seasonal events? Will the use of the building require major new services such as restaurants, laundries, kitchens, locker rooms, or other areas that generate moisture that may exacerbate climate control within the historic space? In the context of historic preservation, uses that require radical reconfigurations of historic spaces are inappropriate for the building.

2. **Assemble a qualified team.** This team ideally should consist of a preservation architect, mechanical engineer, electrical engineer, structural engineer, and preservation consultants, each knowledgeable in codes and local requirements. If a special use (church, mu-

seum, art studio) or a collection is involved, a specialist familiar with the mechanical requirements of that building type or collection should also be hired.

Team members should be familiar with the needs of historic buildings and be able to balance complex factors: the preservation of the historic architecture (aesthetics and conservation), requirements imposed by mechanical systems (quantified heating and cooling loads), building codes (health and safety), tenant requirements (quality of comfort, ease of operation), access (maintenance and future replacement), and the overall cost to the owner.

3. **Undertake a condition assessment of the existing building and its systems.** What are the existing construction materials and mechanical systems? What condition are they in and are they reusable (see figure 6)? Where are existing chillers, boilers, air handlers, or cooling towers located? Look at the condition of all other services that may benefit from being integrated into a new system, such as electrical and fire suppression systems. Where can energy efficiency be improved to help downsize any new equipment added, and which of the historic features, e.g. shutters, awnings, skylights, can be reused (see figure 7)? Evaluate air infiltration through the exterior envelope; monitor the interior for temperature and humidity levels with hygrothermographs for at least a year. Identify building, site, or equipment deficiencies or the presence of asbestos that must be corrected prior to the installation or upgrading of mechanical systems.

6. *A condition assessment during the planning stage would identify this round radiator in a small oval-shaped vestibule as a significant element of the historic heating system. In upgrading the mechanical system, the radiator should be retained. Photo: Michael C. Henry, P.E., AIA.*

Overview of HVAC Systems

WATER SYSTEMS: Hydronic radiators, Fan coil, or radiant pipes

Water systems are generally called *hydronic* and use a network of pipes to deliver water to hot water radiators, radiant pipes set in floors or fan coil cabinets which can give both heating and cooling. Boilers produce hot water or steam; chillers produce chilled water for use with fan coil units. Thermostats control the temperature by zone for radiators and radiant floors. Fan coil units have individual controls. Radiant floors provide quiet, even heat, but are not common.

Advantages: Piped systems are generally easier to install in historic buildings because the pipes are smaller than ductwork.
Disadvantages: There is the risk, however, of hidden leaks in the wall or burst pipes in winter if boilers fail. Fan coil condensate pans can overflow if not properly maintained. Fan coils may be noisy.

Hydronic Radiators: Radiators or baseboard radiators are looped together and are usually set under windows or along perimeter walls. New boilers and circulating pumps can upgrade older systems. Most piping was cast iron although copper systems can be used if separately zoned. Modern cast iron baseboards and copper fin-tubes are available. Historic radiators can be reconditioned.

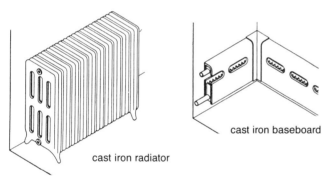

cast iron baseboard

cast iron radiator

Fan Coil Units: Fan coil systems use terminal cabinets in each room serviced by 2, 3, or 4 pipes approximately 1-1/2″ each in diameter. A fan blows air over the coils which are serviced by hot or chilled water. Each fan coil cabinet can be individually controlled. Four-pipe fan coils can provide both heating and cooling all year long. Most piping is steel. Non-cabinet units may be concealed in closets or custom cabinetry, such as benches, can be built.

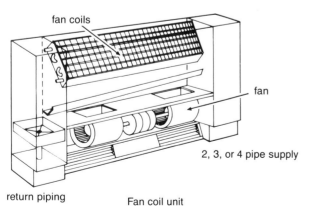

fan coils

fan

2, 3, or 4 pipe supply

return piping   Fan coil unit

CENTRAL AIR SYSTEMS

The basic heating, ventilation and air conditioning (HVAC) system is all-air, single zone fan driven designed for low, medium or high pressure distribution. The system is composed of compressor drives, chillers, condensers, and furnace depending on whether the air is heated, chilled or both. Condensers, generally air cooled, are located outside. The ducts are sheet metal or flexible plastic and can be insulated. Fresh air can be circulated. Registers can be designed for ceilings, floors and walls. The system is controlled by thermostats; one per zone.

Advantages: Ducted systems offer a high level of control of interior temperature, humidity, and filtration. Zoned units can be relatively small and well concealed.
Disadvantages: The damage from installing a ducted system without adequate space can be serious for a historic building. Systems need constant balancing and can be noisy.

Basic HVAC: Most residential or small commercial systems will consist of a basic furnace with a cooling coil set in the unit and a refrigerant compressor or condenser located outside the building. Heating and cooling ductwork is usually shared. If sophisticated humidification and dehumidification is added to the basic HVAC system, a full climate control system results. This can often double the size of the equipment.

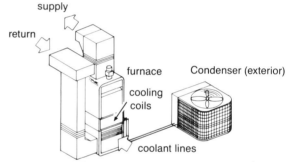

supply

return

furnace   Condenser (exterior)

cooling coils

coolant lines

Heating furnace with cooling coil

Basic Heat Pump/Air System: The heat pump is a basic HVAC system as described above except for the method of generating hot and cold air. The system operates on the basic refrigeration cycle where latent heat is extracted from the ambient air and is used to evaporate refrigerant vapor under pressure. Functions of the condenser and evaporator switch when heating is needed. Heat pumps, somewhat less efficient in cold climates, can be fitted with electric resistance coil.

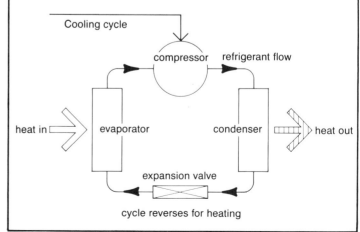

Cooling cycle

compressor   refrigerant flow

heat in   evaporator   condenser   heat out

expansion valve

cycle reverses for heating

COMBINED AIR AND WATER SYSTEMS

These systems are popular for restoration work because they combine the ease of installation for the piped system with the performance and control of the ducted system. Smaller air handling units, not unlike fan coils, may be located throughout a building with service from a central boiler and chiller. In many cases the water is delivered from a central plant which services a complex of buildings.

This system overcomes the disadvantages of a central ducted system where there is not adequate horizontal or vertical runs for the ductwork. The equipment, being smaller, may also be quieter and cause less vibration. If only one air handler is being utilized for the building, it is possible to house all the equipment in a vault outside the building and send only conditioned air into the structure.

Advantages: flexibility for installation using greater piping runs with shorter ducted runs; Air handlers can fit into small spaces.
Disadvantages: piping areas may have undetected leaks; air handlers may be noisy.

Water-serviced Air Handlers:

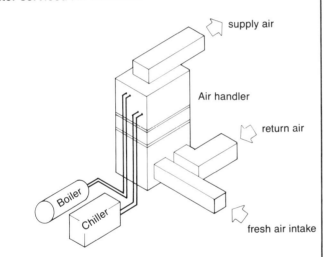

Typical Systems Layout:

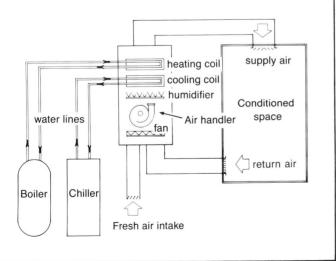

OTHER SYSTEM COMPONENTS

Non-systems components should not be overlooked if they can make a building more comfortable without causing damage to the historic resource or its collection.

Advantages: components may provide acceptable levels of comfort without the need for an entire system.
Disadvantages: Spot heating, cooling and fluxuations in humidity may harm sensitive collections or furnishings. If an integrated system is desirable, components may provide only a temporary solution.

Portable Air Conditioning:

Most individual air conditioners are set in windows or through exterior walls which can be visually as well as physically damaging to historic buildings. Newer portable air conditioners are available which sit in a room and exhaust directly to the exterior through a small slot created by a raised window sash.

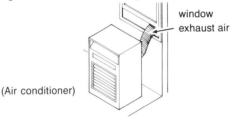

Fans: Fans should be considered in most properties to improve ventilation. Fans can be located in attics, at the top of stairs, or in individual rooms. In moderate climates, fans may eliminate the need to install central air systems.

Dehumidifiers: For houses without central air handling systems, a dehumidifier can resolve problems in humid climates. Seasonal use of dehumidifiers can remove moisture from damp basements and reduce fungal growth.

Heaters: Portable radiant heaters, such as those with water and glycol, may provide temporary heat in buildings used infrequently or during systems breakdowns. Care should be taken not to create a fire hazard with improperly wired units.

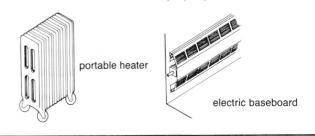

Compiled by Sharon C. Park. Sketches adapted from *Architectural Graphic Standards* with permission from John Wiley and Sons.

4. **Prioritize architecturally significant spaces, finishes, and features to be preserved.** Significant architectural spaces, finishes and features should be identified and evaluated at the outset to ensure their preservation. This includes significant existing mechanical systems or elements such as hot water radiators, decorative grilles, elaborate switchplates, and non-mechanical architectural features such as cupolas, transoms, or porches. Identify non-significant spaces where mechanical equipment can be placed and secondary spaces where equipment and distribution runs on both a horizontal and vertical basis can be located. Appropriate secondary spaces for housing equipment might include attics, basements, penthouses, mezzanines, false ceiling or floor cavities, vertical chases, stair towers, closets, or exterior below-grade vaults (see figure 8).

5. **Become familiar with local building and fire codes.** Owners or their representatives should meet early and often with local officials. Legal requirements should be checked; for example, can existing ductwork be reused or modified with dampers? Is asbestos abatement required? What are the energy, fire, and safety codes and standards in place, and how can they be met while maintaining the historic character of the building? How are fire separation walls and rated mechanical systems to be handled between multiple tenants? Is there a requirement for fresh air intake for stair towers that will affect the exterior appearance of the building? Many of the health, energy, and safety code requirements will influence decisions made for mechanical equipment for climate control. It is importance to know what they are before the design phase begins.

6. **Evaluate options for the type and size of systems.** A matrix or feasibility studies should be developed to balance the benefits and drawbacks of various systems. Factors to consider include heating and/or cooling, fuel type, distribution system, control devices, generating equipment and accessories such as filtration, and humidification. What are the initial installation costs, projected fuel costs, long-term maintenance, and life-cycle

costs of these components and systems? Are parts of an existing system being reused and upgraded? The benefits of added ventilation should not be overlooked (see figure 9). What are the trade-offs between one large central system and multiple smaller systems? Should there be a forced air ducted system, a 2-pipe fan coil system, or a combined water and air system? What space is available for the equipment and distribution system? Assess the fire-risk levels of various fuels. Understand the advantages and disadvantages of the various types of mechanical systems available. *Then evaluate each of these systems in light of the preservation objectives established during the design phase of planning.*

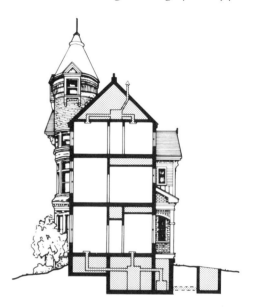

8. *In considering options for new systems, existing spaces should be evaluated for their ability to house new equipment. This sketch shows several areas where new mechanical equipment could be located to avoid damaging significant spaces. Sketch: NPS files*

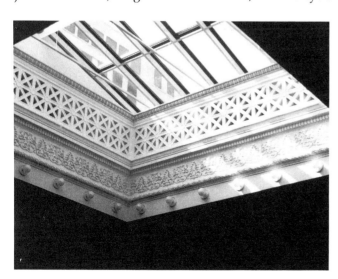

7. *Operable skylights and grilles that can be adapted for return air should be identified as part of the planning phase for new or upgraded mechanical systems. Photo: Dianne Pierce, NPS files.*

9. *Improving ventilation through traditional means should not be overlooked in planning new or upgraded HVAC systems. In mild climates, good exhaust fans can often eliminate the need for air conditioning or can reduce equipment size by reducing cooling loads. Photo: Ernest A. Conrad, P.E.*

266

Designing the new system

In designing a system, it is important to anticipate how it will be installed, how damage to historic materials can be minimized, and how visible the new mechanical system will be within the restored or rehabilitated spaces (see figure 10 a–f). Mechanical equipment space needs are often overwhelming; in some cases, it may be advantageous to look for locations outside of the building, including ground vaults, to house some of the equipment but only if it there is no adverse impact to the historic landscape or adjacent archeological resources. Various means for reducing the heating and cooling loads (and thereby the size of the equipment) should be investigated. This might mean reducing slightly the comfort levels of the interior, increasing the number of climate control zones, or improving the energy efficiency of the building.

The following activities are suggested during the design phase of the new system:

1. Establish specific criteria for the new or upgraded mechanical system. New systems should be *installed with a minimum of damage* to the resource and should be visually *compatible with the architecture* of the building. They should be installed in a way that is *easy to service,* maintain, and upgrade in the future. There should be *safety and back-up monitors in place* if buildings have collections, computer rooms, storage vaults or special conditions that need monitoring. The new *systems should work within the structural limits* of the historic building. They should produce *no undue vibration, no undue noise, no dust or mold,* and *no excess moisture* that could damage the historic building materials. If any equipment is to be located outside of the building, there should be *no impact to the historic appearance of building or site,* and there should be *no impact on archeological resources.*

2. Prioritize the requirements for the new climate control system. The use of the building will determine the level of interior comfort and climate control. Sometimes, various temperature zones may safely be created within a historic building. This zoned approach may be appropriate for buildings with specialized collections storage, for buildings with mixed uses, or for large buildings with different external exposures, occupancy patterns, and delivery schedules for controlled air. Special archives, storage vaults or computer rooms may need a completely different climate control from the rest of the building. Determine temperature and humidity levels for occupants and collections and ventilation requirements between differing zones. Establish if the system is to run 24 hours a day or only during operating or business hours. Determine what controls are optimum (manual, computer, preset automatic, or other). The size and location of the equipment to handle these different situations will ultimately affect the design of the overall system as well.

3. Minimize the impact of the new HVAC on the existing architecture. Design criteria for the new system should be based on the type of architecture of the historic resource. Consideration should be given as to whether or not the delivery system is visible or hidden. Utilitarian and industrial spaces may be capable of accepting a more visible and functional system. More formal, ornate spaces which may be part of an interpretive program may require a less visible or disguised system. A ducted system should be installed without ripping into or boxing out large sections of floors, walls, or ceilings. A wet pipe system should be installed so that hidden leaks will not damage important decorative finishes. In each case, not only the type of system (air, water, combination), but its distribution (duct, pipe) and delivery appearance (grilles, cabinets, or registers) must be evaluated. It may be necessary to use a combination of different systems in order to preserve the historic building. Existing chases should be reused whenever possible.

4. Balance quantitative requirements and preservation objectives. The ideal system may not be achievable for each historic resource due to cost, space limitations, code requirements, or other factors beyond the owner's control. However, significant historic spaces, finishes, and features can be preserved in almost every case, even given these limitations. For example, if some ceiling areas must be slightly lowered to accommodate ductwork or piping, these should be in secondary areas away from decorative ceilings or tall windows. If modern fan coil terminal units are to be visible in historic spaces, consideration should be given to custom designing the cabinets or to using smaller units in more locations to diminish their impact. If grilles and registers are to be located in significant spaces, they should be designed to work within the geometry or placement of decorative elements. All new elements, such as ducts, registers, pipe-runs, and mechanical equipment should be installed in a reversible manner to be removed in the future without further damage to the building (see fig 11).

Systems Performance and Maintenance

Once the system is installed, it will require routine maintenance and balancing to ensure that the proper performance levels are achieved. In some cases, extremely sophisticated, computerized systems have been developed to control interior climates, but these still need monitoring by trained staff. If collection exhibits and archival storage are important to the resource, the climate control system will require constant monitoring and tuning. Back-up systems are also needed to prevent damage when the main system is not working. The owner, manager, or chief of maintenance should be aware of all aspects of the new climate control system and have a plan of action before it is installed.

Regular training sessions on operating, monitoring, and maintaining the new system should be held for both curatorial and building maintenance staff. If there are curatorial reasons to maintain constant temperature or humidity levels, only individuals thoroughly trained in how the HVAC systems operates should be able to adjust thermostats. Ill-informed and haphazard attempts to adjust comfort levels, or to save energy over weekends and holidays, can cause great damage.

10. *The following photographs illustrate recent preservation projects where careful planning and design retained the historic character of the resources.*

before

after

a. Before and after of a circa 1900 school entrance. The radiators have been replaced with a two-pipe fan coil system built into bench seats. The ceiling was preserved and no exposed elements were required to add air conditioning. Piping runs are under the benches and there was no damage to the masonry walls. Photos: Notter Finegold + Alexander Inc. and Lautman Photography, Washington.

historic

after

d. Auditors Buildings, Washington, D.C. This upper floor workspace had been modified over the years with dropped ceilings and partitions. In the recent restoration, the open plan workspace was restored, the false ceiling was removed, and the fireproof construction was exposed. A variable air volume (VAV) system using round double shell exposed ductwork is in keeping with the industrial character of the architectural space. Photo: Kenneth Wyner Photography, courtesy of Notter Finegold + Alexander Inc. Before view provided by Notter Finegold + Alexander/Mariani.

c. Conference room, Auditors Building, Washington, D.C. The historic steam radiators were retained for heating. The cast iron ceiling register was retained as a decorative element, but made inoperable to meet fire codes. Photo: Kenneth Wyner Photography courtesy of Notter Finegold + Alexander Inc.

b. Central air conditioning was installed in the corridors of this circa 1900 school building by adding an air handler over the entrance from a vestibule. The custom-designed slot registers provide linear diffusers without detracting from the architecture of the space. Photo: Lautman Photography courtesy of Notter Finegold + Alexander Inc.

e. Town Hall, Andover, MA. The upstairs auditorium was restored and new mechanical systems were installed. Perimeter baseboard radiation provides heat and air handlers, located in the attic space provide air conditioning. The cast iron ceiling grille was adapted for return air and the supply registers were installed in a symmetrical and regular manner to minimize impact on the historic ceiling. Photo: David Hewitt/Anne Garrison for Ann Beha Associates.

f. Homewood, Baltimore, MD. This elegant circa 1806 residence is now a house museum. The registers for the forced air ducted system seen behind the table legs, are grained to blend with the historic baseboards. The HVAC system uses a water/air system where chilled water and steam heat are converted to conditioned air. Photo: Courtesy Homewood Museum, Johns Hopkins University.

HVAC Do's and Don'ts

DO's:

- Use shutters, operable windows, porches, curtains, awnings, shade trees and other historically appropriate non-mechanical features of historic buildings to reduce the heating and cooling loads. Consider adding sensitively designed storm windows to existing historic windows.

- Retain or upgrade existing mechanical systems whenever possible: for example, reuse radiator systems with new boilers, upgrade ventilation within the building, install proper thermostats or humidistats.

- Improve energy efficiency of existing buildings by installing insulation in attics and basements. Add insulation and vapor barriers to exterior walls *only* when it can be done without further damage to the resource.

- In major spaces, retain decorative elements of the historic system whenever possible. This includes switchplates, grilles and radiators. Be creative in adapting these features to work within the new or upgraded system.

- Use space in existing chases, closets or shafts for new distribution systems.

- Design climate control systems that are compatible with the architecture of the building: hidden system for formal spaces, more exposed systems possible in industrial or secondary spaces. In formal areas, avoid standard commercial registers and use custom slot registers or other less intrusive grilles.

- Size the system to work within the physical constraints of the building. Use multi-zoned smaller units in conjunction with existing vertical shafts, such as stacked closets, or consider locating equipment in vaults underground, if possible.

- Provide adequate ventilation to the mechanical rooms as well as to the entire building. Selectively install air intake grilles in less visible basement, attic, or rear areas.

- Maintain appropriate temperature and humidity levels to meet requirements without accelerating the deterioration of the historic building materials. Set up regular monitoring schedules.

- Design the system for maintenance access and for future systems replacement.

- For highly significant buildings, install safety monitors and backup features, such as double pans, moisture detectors, lined chases, and battery packs to avoid or detect leaks and other damage from system failures.

- Have a regular maintenance program to extend equipment life and to ensure proper performance

- Train staff to monitor the operation of equipment and to act knowledgeably in emergencies or breakdowns.

- Have an emergency plan for both the building and any curatorial collections in case of serious malfunctions or breakdowns.

DON'TS:

- Don't install a new system if you don't need it.

- Don't switch to a new type of system (e.g. forced air) unless there is sufficient space for the new system or an appropriate place to put it.

- Don't over-design a new system. Don't add air conditioning or climate control if they are not absolutely necessary.

- Don't cut exterior historic building walls to add through-wall heating and air conditioning units. These are visually disfiguring, they destroy historic fabric, and condensation runoff from such units can further damage historic materials.

- Don't damage historic finishes, mask historic features, or alter historic spaces when installing new systems.

- Don't drop ceilings or bulkheads across window openings.

- Don't remove repairable historic windows or replace them with inappropriately designed thermal windows.

- Don't seal operable windows, unless part of a museum where air pollutants and dust are being controlled.

- Don't place condensers, solar panels, chimney stacks, vents or other equipment on visible portions of roofs or at significant locations on the site.

- Don't overload the building structure with the weight of new equipment, particularly in the attic.

- Don't place stress on historic building materials through the vibrations of the new equipment.

- Don't allow condensation on windows or within walls to rot or spall adjacent historic building materials.

270

Maintenance staff should learn how to operate, monitor, and maintain the mechanical equipment. They must know where the maintenance manuals are kept. Routine maintenance schedules must be developed for changing and cleaning filters, vents, and condensate pans to control fungus, mold, and other organisms that are dangerous to health. Such growths can harm both inhabitants and equipment. (In piped systems, for example, molds in condensate pans can block drainage lines and cause an overflow to leak onto finished surfaces). Maintenance staff should also be able to monitor the appropriate gauges, dials, and thermographs. Staff must be trained to intervene in emergencies, to know where the master controls are, and whom to call in an emergency. As new personnel are hired, they will also require maintenance training.

In addition to regular cyclical maintenance, thorough inspections should be undertaken from time to time to evaluate the continued performance of the climate control system. As the system ages, parts are likely to fail, and signs of trouble may appear. Inadequately ventilated areas may smell musty. Wall surfaces may show staining, wet patches, bubbling or other signs of moisture damage. Routine tests for air quality, humidity, and temperature should indicate if the system is performing properly. If there is damage as a result of the new system, it should be repaired immediately and then closely monitored to ensure complete repair.

Equipment must be accessible for maintenance and should be visible for easy inspection. Moreover, since mechanical systems last only 15–30 years, the system itself must be "reversible." That is, the system must be installed in such a way that later removal will not damage the building. In addition to servicing, the back-up monitors that signal malfunctioning equipment must be routinely checked, adjusted, and maintained. Checklists should be developed to ensure that all aspects of routine maintenance are completed and that data is reported to the building manager.

Conclusion

The successful integration of new systems in historic buildings can be challenging. Meeting modern HVAC requirements for human comfort or installing controlled climates for museum collections or for the operation of complex computer equipment can result in both visual and physical damage to historic resources. Owners of historic buildings must be aware that the final result will involve balancing multiple needs; no perfect heating, ventilating, and air conditioning system exists. In undertaking changes to historic buildings, it is best to have the advice and input of trained professionals who can:

assess the condition of the historic building,
evaluate the significant elements that should be preserved or reused,
prioritize the preservation objectives,
understand the impact of new interior climate conditions on historic materials,
integrate preservation with mechanical and code requirements,
maximize the advantages of various new or upgraded mechanical systems,
understand the visual and physical impact of various installations,
identify maintenance and monitoring requirements for new or upgraded systems, and
plan for the future removal or replacement of the system.

Too often the presumed climate needs of the occupants or collections can be detrimental to the long-term preservation of the building. With a careful balance between the preservation needs of the building and the interior temperature and humidity needs of the occupants, a successful project can result.

11. During the restoration of this 1806 National Historic Landmark (photo a), a new climate control system was installed. The architects removed all the earlier mechanical equipment from the house and installed new equipment in a 30' × 40' concrete vault located underground 150 feet from the house itself (photo b). Only conditioned air is blown into the house reusing much of the circa 1930s ductwork. Photos: Thomas C. Jester.

Bibliography

Banham, Reyner. *The Architecture of the Well-Tempered Environment.* London: The Architectural Press, 1969.

Burns, John A., AIA. *Energy Conserving Features Inherent in Older Homes.* Washington: U.S. Department of Housing and Urban Development and U.S. Department of the Interior, 1982.

Cowan, Henry J. *Science and Building; Structural and Environmental Design in the Nineteenth and Twentieth Centuries.* New York: John Wiley & Sons, 1978.

Ferguson, Eugene S. "An Historical Sketch of Central Heating: 1800–1860," in *Building Early America* (Charles Peterson, editor) Philadelphia: Chilton Book Co., 1976.

Fitch, James Marston. *American Building; The Environmental Forces That Shape It.* Boston: Houghton Mifflin Co., 1972.

Giedion, Siegfried. *Mechanization Takes Command; a Contribution to Anonymous History.* New York: Oxford University Press, 1948.

Merritt, Frederick S. *Building Engineering and Systems Design.* New York: Van Nostrand Reinhold Co, 1979.

Smith, Baird M. *Preservation Briefs 3: Conserving Energy in Historic Buildings.* Washington, DC: U.S. Department of the Interior, 1978.

Turberg, Edward. *A History of American Building Technology.* Durham: Durham Technical Institute, 1981.

Acknowledgements

The author gratefully acknowledges the invaluable assistance of Michael C. Henry, P.E., AIA, in the development and technical editing of this Preservation Brief. Technical review was also provided by Ernest A. Conrad, P.E. Thanks is also given to staff members of the National Park Service Cultural Resources Programs, including Tom Keohan and Catherine Colby, Rocky Mountain Region; Michael Crowe, Western Region; Mark Chavez, Midwest Region; Randall J. Biallas, AIA, Chief, Park Historic Architecture Division, and George A. Thorsen, Historical Architect, Denver Service Center. Special thanks is also given to Michael J. Auer of Technical Preservation Services for his editorial assistance in preparing this paper and Tim Buehner for his assistance with the illustrations.

This publication has been prepared pursuant to the National Historic Preservation Act of 1966, as amended, which directs the Secretary of the Interior to develop and make available information concerning historic properties. Preservation Brief 24 was developed under the editorship of H. Ward Jandl, Chief, Technical Preservation Services. Comments on the usefulness of this publication may be directed to Chief, Technical Preservation Services Branch, Preservation Assistance Division, National Park Service, P.O. Box 37127, Washington, D.C. 20013–7127.

cover photo: This historic coal boiler continues in use after its conversion to an oil-fired boiler. Photo: NPS files

25

The Preservation of Historic Signs

Michael J. Auer

"Signs" refers to a great number of verbal, symbolic or figural markers. Posters, billboards, graffiti and traffic signals, corporate logos, flags, decals and bumper stickers, insignia on baseball caps and tee shirts: all of these are "signs." Buildings themselves can be signs, as structures shaped like hot dogs, coffee pots or Chippendale highboys attest. The signs encountered each day are seemingly countless, for language itself is largely symbolic. This Brief, however, will limit its discussion of "signs" to lettered or symbolic messages affixed to historic buildings or associated with them.

Signs are everywhere. And everywhere they play an important role in human activity. They identify. They direct and decorate. They promote, inform, and advertise. Signs are essentially social. They name a human activity, and often identify who is doing it. Signs allow the owner to communicate with the reader, and the people inside a building to communicate with those outside of it.

Signs speak of the people who run the businesses, shops, and firms. Signs are signatures. They reflect the owner's tastes and personality. They often reflect the ethnic makeup of a neighborhood and its character, as well as the social and business activities carried out there. By giving concrete details about daily life in a former era, historic signs allow the past to speak to the present in ways that buildings by themselves do not (Figs. 1 and 2). And multiple surviving historic signs on the same building can indicate several periods in its history or use. In this respect, signs are like archeological layers that reveal different periods of human occupancy and use.

Historic signs give continuity to public spaces, becoming part of the community memory. They sometimes become landmarks in themselves, almost without regard for the building to which they are attached, or the property on which they stand. Furthermore, in an age of uniform franchise signs and generic plastic "box" signs, historic signs often attract by their individuality: by a clever detail, a daring use of color and motion, or a reference to particular people, shops, or events.

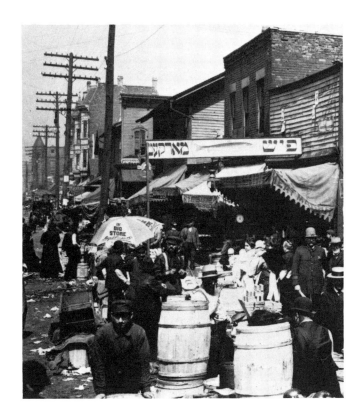

1. Detail from a busy Chicago street market, about 1905. The sign over the sidewalk depicts a fish. It also gives the Hebrew letters for the English words "Fish Market." The sign offers information about the people who patronized the store that is not available from looking at the buildings. They were European Jews who were beginning to learn English. Chicago Historical Society, negative number ICHi–19155.

Yet historic signs pose problems for those who would save them. Buildings change uses. Businesses undergo change in ownership. New ownership or use normally brings change in signs. Signs are typically part of a business owner's sales strategy, and may be changed to reflect evolving business practices or to project a new image.

2. *N. Main Street, Rockford, Illinois, 1929. Signs give a wealth of information about a particular time and place. Photo: Lake County (IL) Museum, Curt Teich Postcard Archives.*

Signs also change to reflect trends in architecture and technology: witness the Art Deco and Depression Modern lettering popular in the 1920s and 1930s, and the use of neon in the 1940s and 1950s.

The cultural significance of signs combined with their often transitory nature makes the preservation of historic signs fraught with questions, problems, and paradoxes. If the common practice in every period has been to change signs with regularity, when and how should historic signs be kept? If the business is changing hands, how can historic signs be reused? The subject is an important one, and offers opportunities to save elements that convey the texture of daily life from the past.

This Brief will attempt to answer some of the preservation questions raised by historic signs. It will discuss historic sign practices, and show examples of how historic signs have been preserved even when the business has changed hands or the building itself has been converted to a new use.

Historic Sign Types and Practices
Pre-Nineteenth Century

American sign practices originated largely in Europe. The earliest commercial signs included *symbols* of the merchant's goods or tradesman's craft. Emblems were mounted on poles, suspended from buildings, or painted on hanging wooden boards. Such symbolic signs were necessary in a society where few could read, although verbal signs were not entirely unknown. A sheep signified a tailor, a tankard a tavern. The red and white striped pole signifying the barbershop, and the three gold balls outside the pawnshop are two such emblems that can occasionally be seen

today (Fig. 3). (The barber's sign survives from an era when barbers were also surgeons; the emblem suggests bloody bandages associated with the craft. The pawnbroker's sign is a sign of a sign: it derives from the coat of arms of the Medici banking family.)

a

b

3. *(a) Once commonplace, the three balls symbolizing the pawnbroker are now rare. These date from the 1920s (the supports are much more recent, as is the storefront to which they are attached). (b) Objects associated with a business continue to be used as signs. Photos: Thomas C. Jester.*

Flat signs with lettering mounted flush against the building gradually replaced hanging, symbolic signs. The suspended signs posed safety hazards, and creaked when they swayed in the wind: "The creaking signs not only kept the citizens awake at night, but they knocked them off their horses, and occasionally fell on them too." The result, in England, was a law in 1762 banning large projecting signs. In 1797 all projecting signs were forbidden, although some establishments, notably "public houses," retained the hanging sign tradition."[1]

By the end of the eighteenth century, the hanging sign had declined in popularity. Flat or flush-mounted signs, on the other hand, had become standard. Like symbolic signs, however, the tradition of projecting signs has survived into the present.

Nineteenth Century Signs and Sign Practices

Surviving nineteenth-century photographs depict a great variety of signs. The list of signs discussed here is by no means exhaustive.

Fascia signs, placed on the fascia or horizontal band between the storefront and the second floor, were among the most common. The fascia is often called the "signboard," and as the word implies, provided a perfect place for a sign—then as now. The narrowness of the fascia imposed strict limits on the sign maker, however, and such signs usually gave little more than the name of the business and perhaps a street number.

Similar to fascia signs were signs between the levels of windows across the upper facade. Such signs were mounted on horizontal boards or painted on the build-

ing. Signs of this type tended to use several "lines" of text, the name of business and short description, for example. The message, reading from top to bottom, sometimes covered several stories of the building. Other *painted signs* presented figures, products, or scenes. Such signs were typically more vertical than horizontal in emphasis. Whether such painted signs featured text or images, they became major features of the building, as their makers intended them to be. The building itself often became a backdrop for the sign.

Signs in the form of *plaques, shields, and ovals* were used on many nineteenth-century buildings (Fig 4). Such signs had the advantage of being easily replaced as tenants came and went. They also easily incorporated images as well as lettering.

4. *This circa 1866 view of a San Francisco building shows the range of signs used in the nineteenth century: Symbolic signs (the spectacles over the entrance); fascia signs; plaques, often in the shape of shields and normally used by insurance companies, in part to symbolize the protective function of insurance; posters, wall signs, window signs, hanging signs, and rooftop signs. Photo: Library of Congress.*

Hanging or projecting signs, both lettered and symbolic, were also common in the nineteenth century, although less so than previously. Projecting signs were often paired with another at a 45° angle for increased visibility. Occasionally a sign would stretch out from the building across the sidewalk, supported by a post at the street.

Goldleaf signs, and signs painted or etched on glass in windows, doors and transoms were quite common.

Porcelain enamel signs were also very popular in the latter half of the nineteenth century and into the mid-twentieth century. Signs carved from stone or wood also appeared frequently, especially on institutional buildings. Painted shutters and even window shades provided additional advertising space.

Posters found their way into display windows when they weren't pasted onto the building. *Sidewalk signs* or "sandwich boards" offered another chance to catch the eye of any passerby not watching the graphics overhead.

Nineteenth-century tenants looking for additional advertising space found it in unexpected places. They used the *entrance steps* to mount signs in a variety of ways: Handrails, risers, skirts, and balusters sported signs that gave businesses on upper levels a chance to attract notice.

Awnings offered other opportunities for keeping a name before the public. The fringe or skirt of the awning, as well as the panel at the side were the usual places for a name or street number. *Flags*, particularly hung from the upper floors, and *banners*, sometimes stretching across the sidewalk, also appeared on buildings.

Rooftop signs appeared with greater frequency in the second half of the nineteenth century than previously. Earlier rooftop signs tended to be relatively simple—often merely larger versions of the horizontal signs typically found on lower levels. Late in the century the signs became more ornate as well as more numerous. These later rooftop signs were typically found on hotels, theaters, banks and other large buildings.

The sign types described here were not used in isolation. Window and awning signs attracted sidewalk pedestrians and people in the street. Upper level signs reached viewers at greater distances. If signs were numerous, however, they were nonetheless usually small in scale.

As the century wore on, signs increased in size and scale. Wall signs several stories high were not uncommon in the second half of the century (Fig 5). This development reflects changes in urban life as the century headed to its close. Cities were experiencing rapid population growth. Buildings became bigger and taller. Elevated trains and electric trolleys increased the pace of city life. And when it comes to signs, speed alters scale. The faster people travel, the bigger a sign has to be before they can see it.

Twentieth Century Signs and Sign Practices

The advent of the twentieth century approximately coincided with the coming of electricity, which gave signs light and, later, movement. Illuminated signs were not unknown before electricity. An advertisement printed about 1700 mentioned a nighttime sign lit by candles, and in 1840 the legendary showman P.T. Barnum built a huge sign illuminated by gas.[2] But electricity was safer and cheaper than candles, kerosene and gas. Its widespread use gave signs a prominence they retain today: illuminated signs dominate the streets at night.

Electricity permitted signs to be illuminated by light shining onto them, but the real revolution occurred when lightbulbs were used to *form* the images and words on signs (Fig 6). Lightbulbs flashing on and off

5. *Painted figures and lines of text cover this building in New York City, about 1890. The woman is distributing handbills. The painted workman on the ladder is putting up a poster. Altogether the signs are striking examples of the signmaker's art in the late nineteenth century. Photo: Courtesy of the New-York Historical Society, New York City.*

made new demands on the attention of passersby. Lightbulbs blinking in sequence could also simulate movement. Add this property to the mix, and a dramatic transformation of American streets resulted.

Moving signs were not unknown prior to the advent of electricity, for wind-driven signs had made their appearance in the nineteenth century. But electricity gave signs an unparalleled range of motion. This movement added yet another element to the life of the street.

Neon is another great twentieth-century contribution to the signmaker's art. "Neon," coined from the Greek word for "new," is a "new gas." It has the useful property of glowing when an electric charge passes through it. (Argon, krypton, xenon and helium share this property. Only neon and argon, however, are typically used in commercial signs.) Encased in glass tubes shaped into letters or symbols, neon offered signmakers an opportunity to mold light into an infinite variety of shapes, colors, and images. Combined with an electric timer, the neon tubing could present images moving in succession.

Neon first appeared in signs in the 1920s, and reached its height of popularity in the 1940s. The first documented neon commercial sign in the United States was at a Packard Motor Car dealership in Los Angeles in 1923.[3] After a period of decline, it underwent a renaissance, beginning in the 1970s. Artists experimented with neon as a conscious art-form, and several notable architects further helped in its revival.[4] Renewed interest in this colorful medium also sparked interest in preserving historic neon signs.

Along with such developments as the coming of electricity and then neon, stylistic movements influenced twentieth-century signs. In particular, Art Deco and Streamlined Moderne affected not just buildings, but their signs as well.

7. In the 1930s and 1940s, signs built into storefronts became popular. This example is from Guthrie, Oklahoma. Photo: H. Ward Jandl.

6. This view of Cleveland taken about 1910 shows how electricity transformed American cities. These dramatic and highly visible signs no doubt provided excellent advertising for "A & W Electric Signs." Its signs—at the bottom of the photograph—also proclaim the company to be the "exclusive agents" for a maker of "electric on enamel signs." Photo: Library of Congress.

Architects working in these styles often integrated signs and buildings into a unified design. This was particularly true of storefronts built using pigmented structural glass, commonly known as "Carrara glass," and porcelain enamel on steel panels. These materials allowed words and images to be etched into the glass or enamel, or to be constructed in different colors and patterns as part of an overall design for the building. Such storefronts were popular from the 1920s into the 1940s (Fig. 7).

As the century advanced, new styles took hold. The late 1950s brought signs with fins, star bursts, and other images reflecting a new fascination with outer space (Fig. 8).

In the decades after World War II signs were also transformed by a group of materials now known generically as "plastic." Plastic had several advantages over wood, metal and other traditional sign materials. As the name indicates, "plastic" can take almost any shape. It can also take almost any color. Plastic is translucent. Lit from behind, it appears to glow. It is relatively durable. Above all, it is inexpensive, and can be mass produced. Plastic quickly became the dominant sign material.

8. In the late 1950s and early 1960s, the country turned its attention to outer space. Wings, fins, and satellite shapes appeared, as in this example in Long Beach, California. Photo: Peter Phillips.

Another profound influence on signs in this period stemmed from business trends rather than from technological breakthroughs or design movements: the rise of chain stores and franchises. National firms replaced many local businesses. Standard corporate signs went up; local trademarks came down. The rise of mass culture, of which the national chain is but one expression, has meant the rise of standardization, and the elimination of regional differences and local character.

The decline of gold-leafing and other traditional sign techniques contributed to these trends. Mass-produced signs have replaced local signs that differed from owner to owner and from signmaker to signmaker. The result is not just sameness, but impersonality as well: It is becoming rarer, for example, to find owners' names on signs. Whether the trend toward sameness can successfully be resisted is yet to be seen. (Some crafts, such as gold-leafing and porcelain enameling, for example, have experienced a revival of sorts.) But the preservation of historic signs is one way to ensure that at least some of these expressions of local history continue to enliven our streets.

Sign Regulation

Historic commercial areas have customarily been a riot of signs. Yet if clutter has ample precedent, so do efforts to control it. Early attempts to regulate signs in this country include those of professional associations of advertisers, such as the International Bill Posters Organization of North America, founded in St. Louis in 1872.[5]

However, early efforts by municipalities to enact sign regulations met with disfavor in the courts, which traditionally opposed any regulatory effort based on aesthetic concerns. Early successes in the legal arena, such as the 1911 case, *St. Louis Gunning Advertising Company v. City of St. Louis*, were realized when proponents of sign controls argued that signs and billboards endangered public health and safety.

Yet gradually courts found merit in the regulation of private property for aesthetic reasons. In 1954 the U.S. Supreme Court handed down the landmark decision, *Berman v. Parker*, in which the court declared: "It is within the power of the legislature to determine that the community should be beautiful as well as healthy, spacious as well as clean, well balanced as well as carefully patrolled."[6]

With the blessing of the courts, communities across the nation have enacted sign controls to reduce "urban blight." And where historic buildings are concerned, the growth of local review commissions has added to the momentum for controls in historic districts.

Typically, sign controls regulate the number, size and type of signs. In some cases, moving or projecting signs are prohibited. Often such ordinances also regulate sign placement—owners are told to line up their signs with others on the block, for example. Materials, likewise, are prescribed: wood is encouraged, plastic discouraged or forbidden altogether. Sign controls often specify lighting sources: indirect illumination (light shining onto the sign) is often required instead of neon tubing, bare lightbulbs, or "backlighting," used in most plastic signs. Some ordinances forbid lighting completely. (Neon, especially, is still held in disfavor in some areas.) Finally, ordinances sometimes require signs to be "compatible" in color and other design qualities with the facade of the building and the overall appearance of the street.

Existing signs frequently do not meet requirements set forth in sign controls. They are too big, for example, or project too far from the building. Typically, sign ordinances permit such "nonconforming" existing

signs to remain, but only for a specified period, after which they must be removed. If they need repair before then, or if the business changes owners, they must likewise be removed.

Sign controls offer communities the chance to reduce visual blight. They can also assist in producing both a new visibility and a new viability for historic commercial districts. Yet sign ordinances are not without problems. Sign controls satisfy contemporary ideas of "good taste." But "bad taste" has ample historic precedent. And in any case, tastes change. What is tasteful today may be dated tomorrow. Sign controls can impose a uniformity that falsifies history. Most historic districts contain buildings constructed over a long period of time, by different owners for different purposes; the buildings reflect different architectural styles and personal tastes. By requiring a standard sign "image" in such matters as size, material, typeface and other qualities, sign controls can mute the diversity of historic districts. Such controls can also sacrifice signs of some age and distinction that have not yet come back into fashion.[7] Neon serves as an instructive example in this regard: once "in," then "out," then "in" again. Unfortunately, a great number of notable signs were lost because sign controls were drafted in many communities when neon was "out." Increasingly, however, communities are enacting ordinances that recognize older and historic signs and permit them to be kept. The National Park Service encourages this trend.

Sign as Icon

Signs often become so important to a community that they are valued long after their role as commercial markers has ceased. They become landmarks, loved because they have been visible at certain street corners—or from many vantage points across the city—for a long time (Fig. 9). Such signs are valued for their familiarity, their beauty, their humor, their size, or even their grotesqueness. In these cases, signs transcend their conventional role as vehicles of information, as identifiers of something else. When signs reach this stage, they accumulate rich layers of meaning. They no longer merely advertise, but are valued in and of themselves. They become icons.

9. *Signs are often popular neighborhood landmarks. This is one in Butte, Montana. Photo: Jet Lowe, HAER.*

Preserving Historic Signs

Historic signs can contribute to the character of buildings and districts. They can also be valued in themselves, quite apart from the buildings to which they may be attached. However, any program to preserve historic signs must recognize the challenges they present. These challenges are not for the most part technical. Sign preservation is more likely to involve aesthetic concerns and to generate community debate. Added to these concerns are several community goals that often appear to conflict: retaining diverse elements from the past, encouraging artistic expression in new signs, zoning for aesthetic concerns, and reconciling business requirements with preservation.

Preserving historic signs is not always easy. But the intrinsic merit of many signs, as well as their contribution to the overall character of a place, make the effort worthwhile. Observing the guidelines given below can help preserve both business and history.

Retaining Historic Signs

Retain historic signs whenever possible, particularly when they are:
- associated with historic figures, events or places (Fig. 10).
- significant as evidence of the history of the product, business or service advertised (Fig. 11).
- significant as reflecting the history of the building or the development of the historic district. A sign may be the only indicator of a building's historic use (Fig. 12).
- characteristic of a specific historic period, such as gold leaf on glass, neon, or stainless steel lettering.
- integral to the building's design or physical fabric, as when a sign is part of a storefront made of Carrara glass or enamel panels, or when the name of the historic firm or the date are rendered in stone, metal

a

b

10. *This fading sign was painted in Baltimore in 1931 or 1932. It survives from the campaign to enact the 21st Amendment to the United States Constitution, which repealed Prohibition. Such fading brick wall signs are known as "ghost signs." Photo: Thomas C. Jester.*

11. *(a) Signs for Bull Durham Tobacco once covered walls all over the country. (b) Similarly, Simple Simon and the Pie Man appeared on Howard Johnson signs nationwide. This one has been moved to a shop for repair. Photos: (a) Jack Boucher, HABS; (b) Len Davidson.*

or tile (Fig. 13). In such cases, removal can harm the integrity of a historic property's design, or cause significant damage to its materials.

- outstanding examples of the signmaker's art, whether because of their excellent craftsmanship, use of materials, or design (Fig. 14).
- local landmarks, that is, signs recognized as popular focal points in a community (Fig. 15).

- elements important in defining the character of a district, such as marquees in a theater district.

Maintaining and Repairing Historic Signs

Maintenance of historic signs is essential for their long-term preservation. Sign maintenance involves periodic inspections for evidence of damage and deterioration

12. The sign on this historic building gives important information about its past. Photo: Thomas C. Jester.

14. This Ogden, Utah, sign is a superb example of neon. Photo: deTeel Patterson Tiller.

13. Historic signs were often built into a property—and often under foot. Photo: Richard Wagner, National Trust for Historic Preservation.

15. The sign for the Busy Bee Cafe is well-known throughout Dubuque, Iowa. Photo: National Park Service, Rocky Mountain Regional Office.

Lightbulbs may need replacement. Screws and bolts may be weakened, or missing altogether. Dirt and other debris may be accumulating, introduced by birds or insects, and should be cleaned out. Water may be collecting in or on sign cabinets, threatening electrical connections. The source of water penetration should be identified and sealed. Most of these minor repairs are routine maintenance measures, and do not call for special expertise. All repairs, however, require caution. For example, electricity should be turned off when working around electric signs.

More extensive repairs should be undertaken by professionals. The sign industry is a large and active one. Sign designers, fabricators and skilled craftsmen are located throughout the country. Once in danger of being lost altogether, gold leaf on glass and porcelain enamel are undergoing revivals, and the art of bending neon tubes is now widely practiced. Finding help from qualified sources should not be difficult. Before contracting for work on historic signs, however, owners should check references, and view other projects completed by the same company.

Major repairs may require removal of the sign to a workshop. Since signs are sometimes damaged while the building is undergoing repair, work on the building should be scheduled while the sign is in the shop. (If the sign remains in place while work on the building is in progress, the sign should be protected.)

Repair techniques for specific sign materials are discussed below (see "Repairing Historic Sign Materials" on page 10). The overall goal in repairs such as supplying missing letters, replacing broken neon tubing, or splicing in new members for deteriorated sections is to restore a sign that is otherwise whole. **Recognize, however, that the apparent age of historic signs is one of their major features; do not "over restore" signs so that all evidence of their age is lost, even though the appearance and form may be recaptured.**

Reusing Historic Signs

If a building or business has changed hands, historic signs associated with former enterprises in the building should be reused if possible by:
- keeping the historic sign—unaltered. This is often possible even when the new business is of a different nature from the old. Preferably, the old sign can be left in its historic location; sometimes, however, it may be necessary to move the sign elsewhere on the building to accommodate a new one. Conversely, it may be necessary to relocate new signs to avoid hiding or overwhelming historic ones, or to redesign proposed new signs so that the old ones may remain. (The legitimate advertising needs of current tenants, however, must be recognized.)

  Keeping the old sign is often a good marketing strategy. It can exploit the recognition value of the old name and play upon the public's fondness for the old sign. The advertising value of an old sign can be immense. This is especially true when the sign is a community landmark.
- relocating the sign to the interior, such as in the lobby or above the bar in a restaurant. This option is less preferable than keeping the sign outside the

building, but it does preserve the sign, and leaves open the possibility of putting it back in its historic location.
- modifying the sign for use with the new business. This may not be possible without destroying essential features, but in some cases it can be done by changing details only (Fig. 16). In other respects, the sign may be perfectly serviceable as is.

If none of these options is possible, the sign could be donated to a local museum, preservation organization or other group.

16. (a) The Jayhawk Hotel in Topeka, Kansas, was built in 1926; (b) Its prominent and popular rooftop signs were deteriorating when the hotel closed; (c) The new owners converted the building to offices, but were able to keep the historic signs by changing "HOTEL" to "TOWER." The new, repaired, signs reuse three of the historic letters: T, O, and E. Photos: (a and b) Kiene and Bradley; Courtesy, Kansas State Historical Society; (c) Kansas State Historical Society.

Repairing Historic Sign Materials

Porcelain Enamel. Porcelain enamel is among the most durable of materials used in signs.[8] Made of glass bonded onto metal (usually steel) at high temperatures, it keeps both its high gloss and its colors for decades. Since the surface of the sign is essentially glass, porcelain enamel is virtually maintenance free; dirt can be washed off with soap and water and other glass cleaners.

Porcelain enamel signs can be damaged by direct blows from stones and other sharp objects. If both the enamel surface and the undercoat are scratched, the metal surface can rust at the impact site. Because the bond between glass and metal is so strong, however, the rust does not "travel" behind the glass, and the rust is normally confined to localized areas. The sign edges can also rust if they were never enamelled. To treat the problem, clean the rust off carefully, and touch-up the area with cold enamel (a type of epoxy used mostly in jewelry), or with enamel paints.

Dents in porcelain enamel signs should be left alone. Attempting to hammer them out risks further damage.

Goldleaf or gilding. Goldleaf or gilding is both elegant and durable. These properties made it among the most popular sign materials in the nineteenth and early twentieth centuries. Surface-gilded signs (for example, gilded raised letters or symbols found on the exterior) typically last about 40 years. Damage to these signs occurs from weather and abrasion. Damage to gilded signs on glass normally occurs when the protective coating applied over the gilding is removed by harsh cleaning chemicals or scratched by scrub brushes. The sign can then flake upon subsequent cleanings.

Historic gilded signs can be repaired, typically by regilding damaged areas. An oil size is painted on the surface. The gold leaf is applied when the surface has become sufficiently "tacky." Similarly, historic "reverse on glass" goldleaf signs can be repaired—by experts. A sample of the flaking sign is first taken to determine its composition. Reverse on glass signs use goldleaf ranging from 12 to 23 karats. The gold is alloyed with copper and silver in varying amounts for differences in color. (Surface gilding—on raised letters, picture frames and statehouse domes—uses 23 karat gold. Pure gold, 24 karat, is too soft to use in such applications.) The damaged portions of the sign are then regilded in the same manner as they were done historically: the inside surface of the glass is coated with a gelatin; gold leaves about three inches square are then spread over the area. The new letter or design is then drawn in reverse on the new leaf, and coated with a backing paint (normally a chrome yellow). With the new design thus sealed, the rest of the leaf is removed. The

(continued next page)

17. *Glen Echo Park near Washington, D.C., is an early 20th century amusement park. (It is the home of the first bumper car ride in the world.) Its neon signs needed repair: (a) tubes were broken and the surrounding "metal cans" needed work also; (b) and (c) removal of the back of "Candy Corner" sign revealed debris from insects and birds; (d) preparing the "metal cans" from the "Pop Corn" sign for remounting; (e) and (f) neon fabricators installing the new tubing in the repaired and remounted cans; (g) repairs finished, the relit signs enliven the park once again. Photos: (a–c) Stan Fowler; (d–f) Larry Kanter; (g) Rebecca Hammel.*

sign is then sealed with a clear, water-resistant varnish.

Gilded signs, both surface and reverse on glass, can be cleaned gently with soap and water, using a soft cloth. Additionally, for glass signs, the varnish backing should be replaced every seven years at the latest.

Neon. Neon signs can last 50 years, although 20–25 years is more typical. When a neon sign fails, it is not because the gas has "failed," but because the system surrounding it has broken down. The glass tubes have been broken, for example, thus letting the gas escape, or the electrodes or transformers have failed. If the tube is broken, a new one must be made by a highly skilled "glass bender." After the hot glass tube has been shaped, it must undergo "purification" before being refilled with gas. The glass and the metal electrode at the end of the tube are heated in turns. As these elements become hot, surface impurities burn off into the tube. The resulting vapor is then removed through "evacuation"—the process of creating a vacuum. Only then is the

"neon" gas (neon or mercury-argon) added. Neon gives red light, mercury-argon produces blue. Other colors are produced by using colored glass and any of dozens of phosphor coatings inside the tube. Green, for example, can be produced by using mercury-argon in yellow glass. Since color is so important in neon signs, it is vital to determine the original color or colors. A neon studio can accomplish this using a number of specialized techniques.

A failing transformer can cause the neon sign to flicker intensely, and may have to be replaced. Flickering neon can also indicate a problem with the gas pressure inside the tube. The gas may be at too high or too low a pressure. If so, the gas must be repumped.

Repairs to neon signs also include repairs to the surrounding components of the sign. The "metal cans" that often serve as backdrops to the tubing may need cleaning or, in case of rust, scraping and repainting.

As with gilded signs, repair of neons signs is not a matter for amateurs (Fig. 17).

New Signs and Historic Buildings

Preserving old signs is one thing. Making new ones is another. Closely related to the preservation of historic signs on historic buildings is the subject of new signs for historic buildings. Determining what new signs are appropriate for historic buildings, however, involves a major paradox: Historic sign practices were not always "sympathetic" to buildings. They were often unsympathetic to the building, or frankly contemptuous of it. Repeating some historic practices, therefore, would definitely not be recommended.

Yet many efforts to control signage lead to bland sameness. For this reason the National Park Service discourages the adoption of local guidelines that are too restrictive, and that effectively dictate uniform signs within commercial districts. Instead, it encourages communities to promote diversity in signs—their sizes, types, colors, lighting, lettering and other qualities. It also encourages business owners to choose signs that reflect their own tastes, values, and personalities. At the same time, tenant sign practices can be stricter than sign ordinances. The National Park Service therefore encourages businesses to fit their sign programs to the building.

The following points should be considered when designing and constructing new signs for historic buildings:
- signs should be viewed as part of an overall graphics system for the building. They do not have to do all the "work" by themselves. The building's form, name and outstanding features, both decorative and functional, also support the advertising function of a sign. Signs should work with the building, rather than against it.
- new signs should respect the size, scale and design of the historic building. Often features or details of the building will suggest a motif for new signs.
- sign placement is important: new signs should not obscure significant features of the historic building. (Signs above a storefront should fit within the his-

toric signboard, for example.)
- new signs should also respect neighboring buildings. They should not shadow or overpower adjacent structures.
- sign materials should be compatible with those of the historic building. Materials characteristic of the building's period and style, used in contemporary designs, can form effective new signs.
- new signs should be attached to the building carefully, both to prevent damage to historic fabric, and to ensure the safety of pedestrians. Fittings should penetrate mortar joints rather than brick, for example, and signloads should be properly calculated and distributed.

Conclusion

Historic signs once allowed buyers and sellers to communicate quickly, using images that were the medium of daily life. Surviving historic signs have not lost their ability to speak. But their message has changed. By communicating names, addresses, prices, products, images and other fragments of daily life, they also bring the past to life (Fig. 18).

18. Sign painters pausing from their work, 1932. Photo: Courtesy, Cumquat Publishing Co. and Tettaton Sign Co., St. Louis, Missouri.

> *With halting steps I paced the streets, and passed the sign of "The Crossed Harpoons"—but it looked too expensive and jolly there. . . . Moving on, I at last came to a dim sort of light not far from the docks, and heard a forlorn creaking in the air; and looking up, saw a swinging sign over the door with a white painting upon it, faintly representing a tall straight jet of misty spray, and these words underneath—"The Spouter-Inn:—Peter Coffin."*
>
> The creaking wooden sign in *Moby Dick* identifies public lodging. But it also does a great deal more than that. It projects an image. It sets a mood and defines a place. The ability to convey commercial *and* symbolic messages is a property of all signs, not just those in novels.
>
> Every sign hanging outside a door, standing on a roof, extending over a storefront, or marching across a wall transmits messages from the sign maker to the sign reader. Mixed in with names, addresses, business hours and products are images, personalities, values and beliefs.

Selected Reading List

DiLamme, Philip. *American Streamline: A Handbook of Neon Advertising Design.* Cincinnati: ST Publications, 1988.

Evans, Bill and Andrew Lawson. *Shopfronts.* New York: Van Nostrand Reinhold Co., 1981.

The Gilder's Manual. Washington, D.C.: The Society of Gilders, 1991. (Reprint of *The Gilder's Manual; A Practical Guide to Gilding in All its Branches.* New York: Excelsior Publishing House, 1876.)

Liebs, Chester. *Main Street to Miracle Mile: American Roadside Architecture.* Boston: Little, Brown and Company/ New York Graphics Society, 1985.

National Main Street Center. *Main Street Guidelines: Signs for Main Street.* Washington, D.C.: National Trust for Historic Preservation, 1987.

Phillips, Peter H. "Sign Controls for Historic Signs," PAS Memo. Chicago: American Planning Association, November 1988.

Smith, Kent. *Gold Leaf Techniques.* Cincinnati: ST Publications, 1989.

Stage, William. *Ghost Signs: Brick Wall Signs in America.* Cincinnati: ST Publications, 1989.

Stern, Rudi. *Let There Be Neon.* New York: Harry N. Abrams, Inc., 1979. (Rev. 1988).

Cover photograph: Terra cotta wheel with Studebaker banner, 1926, Lakewood, Ohio. Photo: Frank Wrenick.

NOTES

[1] Bill Evans and Andrew Lawson, *Shopfronts.* New York: Van Nostrand Reinhold Co., 1981, p. 109, 114.

[2] Charles L.H. Wagner, *The Story of Signs: An Outline History of the Sign Arts from Earliest Recorded Times to the Present "Atomic Age".* Boston: Arthur MacGibbon, 1954, p. 37.

[3] Rudi Stern, *Let There Be Neon.* New York: Harry N. Abrams, Inc. 1979, p. 19.

[4] See Robert Venturi, Denise Scott Brown, and Steven Izenour, *Learning from Las Vegas.* Rev. ed. Cambridge, MA: MIT Press, 1977.

[5] George H. Kramer, "Preserving Historic Signs in the Commercial Landscape: The Impact of Regulation." (Unpublished Masters Thesis: University of Oregon, 1989), p. 15. This section on sign regulation is heavily indebted to this work. See especially Chapter 2, History of Sign Regulation and Chapter 3, Mechanics of Sign Regulation, pp. 7–60.

[6] *Berman v. Parker* involved the condemnation of an older building for an urban renewal project. The decision "ironically would prove to be a major spur to a new wave of local preservation laws. . . ." Christopher J. Duerksen, ed. *A Handbook on Historic Preservation Law.* Washington, D.C.: The Conservation Foundation and The National Center for Preservation Law, 1983, p. 7.

[7] A balanced approach to sign controls is offered by Peter H. Phillips, "Sign Controls for Historic Signs," *PAS Memo,* November 1988. (Published by American Planning Association, Washington, D.C.).

[8] See John Tymoski, "Porcelain Enamel: The Sign Industry's Most Durable Material," *Signs of the Times,* December 1990, pp. 66–71. For goldleaf, see October 1984 and November 1990 special issues of *Signs of the Times.* An excellent short "course" in neon evaluation is offered in "Neon: The Good, the Bad, and the Ugly," by Paul R. Davis, *Identity,* Spring 1991, pp. 56–59.

Acknowledgements

The author gratefully acknowledges the invaluable assistance of Beth Savage, National Register of Historic Places. The author is also indebted to Rebecca Shiffer of The Society for Commercial Archeology, and to other colleagues in the cultural resources programs of the National Park Service, sign artists in private practice, and professionals and preservationists in a number of organizations. These include staff of the Technical Preservation Services Branch, directed by H. Ward Jandl, especially Kay Weeks, Anne Grimmer, Sharon C. Park, and Thomas C. Jester; staff of the National Park Service Regional Offices, especially Michael Crowe, Thomas Keohan, Catherine Colby and Christopher Jones; deTeel Patterson Tiller and Stephen Morris, Interagency Resources Division; Caroline Bedinger, Historic American Engineering Record; Catherine Lavoie and Sara Leach, Historic American Buildings Survey, and Stan Fowler of Glen Echo Park. Significant contributions were also made by Peter Phillips, Yuma County Planning Department; Pratt Cassity of the National Alliance of Preservation Commissions; Betsy Jackson, Doug Loescher and Kennedy Smith of the National Trust for Historic Preservation; Richard Longstreth, George Washington University; Richard Wagner, David H. Gleason Associates, Inc.; Michael Jackson, Illinois Historic Preservation Agency; Vance Kelley, Kansas State Historical Society; William Pencek, Maryland Historical Trust; Chere Jiusto, Montana Historical Society, and Gerron Hite and Stan Graves, Texas State Historical Commission (the latter on behalf of the National Conference of State Historic Preservation Officers). The following artists and professionals active in the sign industry offered publications, photographs, technical material, and advice: Lynn Baxter and Tod Swormstedt, ST Publications; Kent Smith, Kent Smith Signs; Craig Kraft, Kraft Studios; Larry Kanter, Neon Projects; Len Davidson, Davidson Neon Design; Thomas Ellis, The Enamelist Society; Timothy Pugh, the Porcelain Enamel Institute; William Adair, Goldleaf Studios.

This publication has been prepared pursuant to the National Historic Preservation Act of 1966, as amended, which directs the Secretary of the Interior to develop and make available information concerning historic properties. Preservation Brief 25 was developed under the editorship of H. Ward Jandl, Chief, Technical Preservation Services. Comments on the usefulness of this publication may be directed to Chief, Technical Preservation Services Branch, Preservation Assistance Division, National Park Service, P.O. Box 37127, Washington, D.C. 20013–7127.

26

The Preservation and Repair of Historic Log Buildings

Bruce D. Bomberger

The intent of this Brief is to present a concise history and description of the diversity of American log buildings and to provide basic guidance regarding their preservation and maintenance. A log building is defined as a building whose structural walls are composed of horizontally laid or vertically positioned logs. While this Brief will focus upon horizontally-laid, corner-notched log construction, and, in particular, houses as a building type, the basic approach to preservation presented here, as well as many of the physical treatments, can be applied to virtually any kind of log structure.

Log buildings, because of their distinct material, physical structure, and sometimes their architectural design, can

develop their own unique deterioration problems. The information presented here is intended to convey the range of appropriate preservation techniques available. It does not, however, detail how to perform these treatments; this work should be left to professionals experienced in the preservation of historic log buildings.

Despite the publication since the 1930s of a number of books and articles on the history of log construction in America, some misconceptions persist about log buildings. Log cabins were not the first type of shelter built by all American colonists. The term "log cabin" today is often loosely applied to any type of log house, regardless of its form and the historic context of its set-

Fig. 1. Log construction was practical in the rough frontier and climate of Alaska, where it was used for a variety of structures such as the Sourdough Lodge (c. 1903) near Gakona. Built to serve the trail leading to the Klondike gold discoveries, this 1-story, L-shaped roadhouse is primarily of horizontal log construction with vertical logs in the front gable. Photo: National Park Service Files.

a   *b*   *c*

Fig. 2. Logs, both round and hewn, continued to be a basic construction material throughout much of the 19th century, here illustrated by (a) these c. 1831 industrial workers' houses for forgemen at the Mt. Etna Iron Furnace in Pennsylvania, and (b) the Larsson-Ostlund House built by Swedish immigrants in New Sweden, Maine, during the 1870s. (c) Corner detail of the Larsson-Ostlund House with the original clapboarding removed during restoration shows close-fitting log joints in the Scandinavian style that did not require chinking. Photos: (a) Jet Lowe, HAER Collection, (b-c) Maine Historic Preservation Commission.

ting. "Log cabin" or "log house" often conjures up associations with colonial American history and rough frontier life (Fig. 1). While unaltered colonial era buildings in general are rare, historic log buildings as a group are neither as old nor as rare as generally believed. One and two-story log houses were built in towns and settlements across the country until about the middle of the 19th century, and in many areas, particularly in the West, as well as the Midwest and southern mountain regions, log continued to be a basic building material despite the introduction of wooden balloon frame construction (Fig. 2). By the early 20th century, the popularity of "rustic" architecture had revived log construction throughout the country, and in many areas where it had not been used for decades.

A distinction should be drawn between the traditional meanings of "log cabin" and "log house." "Log cabin" generally denotes a simple one, or one-and-one-half story structure, somewhat impermanent, and less finished or less architecturally sophisticated. A "log cabin" was usually constructed with *round* rather than hewn, or hand-worked, logs, and it was the first generation homestead erected quickly for frontier shelter. "Log house" historically denotes a more permanent, *hewn*-log dwelling, either one or two stories, of more complex design, often built as a second generation replacement. Many of the earliest 18th and early 19th century log houses were traditionally clad, sooner or later, with wood siding or stucco.

Historical Background

No other architectural form has so captured the imagination of the American people than the log cabin. Political supporters of 1840 presidential candidate William Henry Harrison appropriated the log cabin as a campaign symbol. The log cabin was birthplace and home for young Abe Lincoln, as well as other national figures, and assumed by many 19th century historians to be the very first type of house constructed by English colonists. In 1893 Frederick Jackson Turner in his influential paper, *The Significance of the Frontier in American History* suggested that European colonists had adopted this means of shelter from the Indians.

More recent 20th century scholarship has demonstrated that horizontal log buildings were not the first form of shelter erected by all colonists in America. Nor was log construction technology invented here, but brought by Northern and Central European colonists. Finnish and Swedish settlers are credited with first introducing horizontal log building in the colony of New Sweden (now Pennsylvania) on the upper shores of Delaware Bay in 1638, who later passed on their tradition of log construction to the Welsh settlers in Pennsylvania.

During the 17th and 18th centuries, new waves of Eastern and Central Europeans, including Swiss and Germans, came to America bringing their knowledge of log construction. Even the Scotch-Irish, who did not possess a log building tradition of their own, adapted the form of the stone houses of their native country to log construction, and contributed to spreading it across the frontier. In the Mississippi Valley, Colonial French fur traders and settlers had introduced vertical log construction in the 17th century.

Through the late 18th and early 19th centuries, frontier settlers erected log cabins as they cleared land, winding their way south in and along the Appalachian valleys through the back country areas of Maryland, Virginia, the Carolinas and Georgia. They moved westward across the Appalachian Mountain barrier into the Ohio and Mississippi River valleys transporting their indispensable logcraft with them, into Kentucky and Tennessee, and as far to the southwest as eastern Texas. Log buildings are known to have been con-

Fig. 3. This mid-19th century double-pen corncrib on the Jamison Farm in Rowan County, North Carolina, is an example of a type of log building that did not require chinking. Photo: Denise Whitley.

structed as temporary shelters by soldiers during the Revolutionary War, and across the country, Americans used logs not only to build houses, but also commercial structures, schools, churches, gristmills, barns, corncribs and a variety of outbuildings (Fig. 3).

Around the mid-19th century, successive generations of fur traders, metal prospectors, and settlers that included farmers and ranchers began to construct log buildings in the Rocky Mountains, the Northwest, California, and Alaska (Fig. 4). In California and Alaska, Americans encountered log buildings that had been erected by Russian traders and colonists in the late 18th and early 19th centuries. Scandinavian and Finnish immigrants who settled in the Upper Midwest later in the 19th century also brought their own log building techniques with them. And, many log structures in the Southwest, particularly in New Mexico, show Hispanic influences of its early settlers.

While many parts of the country never stopped building with logs, wooden balloon frame construction had made it obsolete in some of the more populous parts of the country by about the mid-19th century. However, later in the century, log construction was employed in new ways. In the 1870s, wealthy Americans initiated the Great Camp Movement for rustic vacation retreats in the Adirondack Mountains of upstate New York. Developers such as William Durant, who used natural materials, including wood shingles, stone, and log—often with its bark retained to emphasize the Rustic style—designed comfortable summer houses and lodges that blended with the natural setting (Fig. 5). Durant and other creators of the Rustic style drew upon Swiss chalets, traditional Japanese design, and other sources for simple compositions harmonious with nature.

The Adirondack or Rustic style was balanced in the West with construction of the Old Faithful Inn at Yellowstone National Park in Wyoming, designed by Robert C. Reamer, and begun in 1903 (Fig. 6). This popular resort was tremendously influential in its use of locally-available natural materials, especially log, and gave impetus to Rustic as a true national style. From the turn of the century through the 1920s, Gustav

Fig. 5. The main lodge of Echo Camp on Raquette Lake in New York State was built in 1883 by the governor of Connecticut. It typifies the Adirondack style in the use of exposed round logs with crowns, and porches and balconies constructed with bowed logs and round log columns. Photo: Courtesy The Adirondack Museum.

a   b

Fig. 6. (a) Old Faithful Inn, Yellowstone National Park, Wyoming, shown here in 1912, brought the Rustic style to the West in 1903 in an original design, and a scale befitting its setting. (b) Although only the first story is of horizontal log construction, the use of logs is striking in the trestle work and cribbed piers around the entrance. Photo: (a) Courtesy National Park Service, (b) Laura Soulliere Harrison.

Fig. 4. Beginning around the mid-19th century, entire western boomtowns were hastily constructed of frame and log, such as the buildings in Bannack, Montana, the site of the State's first gold discovery. Photo: National Park Service Files.

Fig. 7. The Civilian Conservation Corps built many recreational log structures across the country in the 1930s and 40s, including this rustic log gateway to Camp Morton, Lycoming County, Pennsylvania. Photo: Courtesy Lycoming County Historical Society and Museum.

Stickley and other leaders of the Craftsman Movement promoted exposed log construction. During the 1930s and 40s, the Civilian Conservation Corps (CCC) used log construction extensively in many of the country's Federal and State parks to build cabins, lean-tos, visitor centers, and maintenance and support buildings that are still in service (Fig. 7).

Traditional Log Construction

Plan and Form

When settlers took the craft of log construction with them onto the frontier, they successfully adapted it to regional materials, climates and terrains. One of the most notable characteristics of the earliest 18th and 19th century log houses is the plan and form. The plan can sometimes provide clues to the ethnic origin or route of migration of the original inhabitant or builder. *But in the absence of corroborating documentary evidence, it is important not to infer too much about the ethnic craft traditions of a particular log house.*

Historians have identified a number of traditional house plans and forms as prototypes (Fig. 8). They were often repeated with simple variations. The basic unit of each of these types is the one room enclosure formed by four log walls joined at their corners, called a single "pen" or "crib." The single pen was improved upon by installing interior partitions or by adding another log pen. Some variations of historic log house plans include: the typically mid-Atlantic "continental" plan, consisting of a single-pen of three rooms organized around a central hearth; the "saddlebag" or double-pen plan, composed of two contiguous log pens; and the "dogtrot" plan, formed by two pens separated by an open passage space (sometimes enclosed later), all covered by a continuous roof. The continental plan originated in central and eastern Europe and is attributed to 18th century German immigrants to Pennsylvania. Non-log interior partition walls form the multi-room plan within the exterior log walls. The saddlebag plan consists of two adjoining log pens that share a central chimney. A saddlebag is often the evolution of a single pen with an end chimney, expanded by adding a second pen onto the chimney endwall. The saddlebag was built in a number of different regions across the country. The dogtrot plan may be seen with variation in many parts of the country, although it is sometimes, perhaps erroneously, considered the most typically southern, because its covered passageway provided both air circulation and shelter from the heat. All these plan types were typically built in the form of one or one-and-one-half story settlement cabins.

A somewhat different form evolved in the West around the middle of the 19th century which became especially distinctive of the Rocky Mountain cabin. While the entrance doorway to most earlier log houses was generally placed beneath the eaves, as a means of adapting to the greater snowfall in the Rockies, here the entrance was placed in the gable end, and sometimes protected from roof slides by a porch supported by two corner posts created by an extension of the roof beyond the gable wall (Fig. 9).

From the late 18th through the mid-19th centuries, Americans also built many substantial two-story log

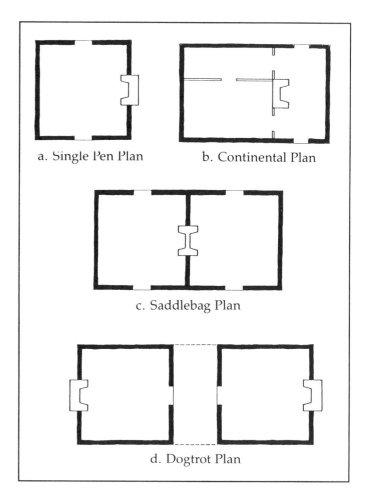

a. Single Pen Plan   b. Continental Plan

c. Saddlebag Plan

d. Dogtrot Plan

Fig. 8. These log house plans represent some of the basic housing forms constructed during the 18th and 19th centuries, and include: (a) single pen, (b) continental, (c) saddlebag, and (d) dogtrot. Drawing: James Caufield.

Fig. 9. This historic log building on the Walker Ranch in Boulder, Colorado is an example of the Rocky Mountain cabin form which is typified by the entrance door being located in the gable end. Photo: Bernard Weisgerber.

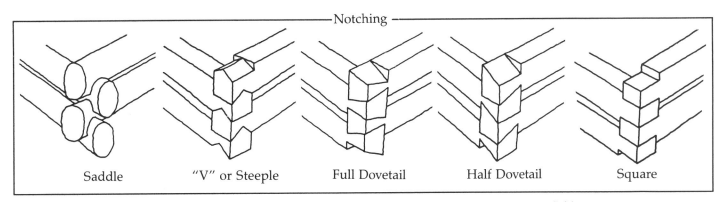

Notching

Saddle "V" or Steeple Full Dovetail Half Dovetail Square

Fig. 10. Five examples of the more common historical methods of corner notching. Drawing: James Caufield.

houses in towns throughout the eastern half of the country. In rural areas two-story log houses were sometimes built to replace earlier, first-generation settlement cabins, but just as often the early hewn-log house was retained and enlarged. A second story was added by removing the roof and gables, constructing a second floor, laying additional courses of logs, and building a new roof, or reassembling the old one. Each generation of owners might expand an early log core building by adding on new log pens, or masonry or wood frame extensions. The addition of a rear ell, or infill construction to link a formerly free-standing outbuilding, such as a kitchen to the log main house was particularly common. Such a layering of alterations is part of the evolution of many log buildings.

Corner Notching and Other Fastening Techniques

Corner notching is another of the characteristic features of log construction. Most notching methods provide structural integrity, by locking the log ends in place, and give the pen rigidity and stability. Like the floor plan, the type of corner notching can sometimes be a clue to the ethnic craft origin of a log building, but it is important not to draw conclusions based only on notching details. Numerous corner notching techniques have been identified throughout the country (Fig. 10). They range from the simple "saddle" notching, which demands minimal time and hewing skill, to the very common "V" notching or "steeple" notching, to "full dovetail" notching, one of the tightest but most time-consuming to accomplish, "half-dovetail" notching which is probably one of the most common, and "square" notching secured with pegs or spikes.

The notching method on some of the earliest eastern cabins and most 19th century western cabins, particularly saddle notching, left an extended log end or "crown." Crowns are especially pronounced or exaggerated in Rustic style structures, and sometimes they are cut shorter as the wall rises, creating a buttress effect at the corners of the building.

Another method of securing log ends consists of fastening logs that are laid without notching ("false notching") with tenons into vertical corner posts, or using spikes or pegs to attach them to vertical corner planks. Vertically positioned logs were secured at their top and bottom ends, usually into roof and sill plate timbers.

Selecting Logs and Assembling the Building

Although wood selection was most likely to be determined by availability, chestnut, white oak, cedar, and fir were preferred because these trees could provide

a

b

c

Fig. 11. Log-hewing tools and techniques: (a) scoring the log with a single-bladed felling axe, or "pole axe" in preparation for removing a uniform thickness of wood; (b) removal to depth of scoring; (c) finish hewing with a broad axe. Photos: Courtesy Bernard Weisgerber.

long, straight, rot-resistant logs. Pine, which also provided long straight logs, was also used in areas where it was plentiful. Woods were often mixed, utilizing harder, heavier rot-resistant wood such as white oak for the foundation "sill log", and lighter, more-easily hewn wood such as yellow poplar for the upper log courses.

One of the principal advantages of log construction was the economy of tools required to complete a structure (Fig. 11). A felling axe was the traditional tool for bringing down the tree and cutting the logs to length. For many frontier and western structures the round logs were debarked or used in their original form with the bark left on, or one or more sides of the logs were hewn flat with a broadaxe, or more finely finished with an adze as smooth thick planks. Notching was done with an axe, hatchet or saw; openings for doors and windows were usually cut after the logs were set into place, and door and window frames, particularly jambs, were put in place during construction to help hold the logs in place. Roof framing members and floor joists were either hewn from logs or of milled lumber. A log cabin could be raised and largely completed with as few as two to four different tools, including a felling axe, a broad axe, and a hand saw or crosscut saw.

The upper gable walls were completed with logs if the roof was constructed with purlins, which is more typical of Scandinavian or Finnish construction, and western and 20th century Rustic styles. However, vertical or horizontal weatherboard sheathing was commonly used throughout the country to cover wood-framed gables.

Chinking and Daubing

The horizontal spaces or joints between logs are usually filled with a combination of materials that together is known as "chinking" and "daubing." Chinking and daubing completed the exterior walls of the log pen by sealing them against driving wind and snow, helping them to shed rain, and blocking the entry of vermin. In addition, chinking and daubing could compensate for a minimal amount of hewing and save time if immediate shelter was needed. Not all types of log buildings were chinked. Corncribs, and sometimes portions of barns where ventilation was needed were not chinked. While more typical of Swedish or Finnish techniques, and not as common in American log construction, tight-fitting plank-hewn or scribed-fit round logs have little or no need for chinking and daubing.

A variety of materials were used for chinking and daubing, including whatever was most conveniently at hand. Generally though, it is a three-part system applied in several steps. The chinking consists of two parts: first, a dry, bulky, rigid blocking, such as wood slabs or stones is inserted into the joint, followed by a soft packing filler such as oakum, moss, clay, or dried animal dung (Fig. 12). Daubing, which completes the system, is the outer wet-troweled finish layer of varying composition, but often consisting of a mixture of clay and lime or other locally available materials. Instead of daubing, carefully fitted quarter poles or narrow wood strips were sometimes nailed lengthwise across the log joints.

Chinking, especially the daubing, is the least durable part of a log building. It is susceptible to cracking as a

Fig. 12. The log joints have been cleaned out in preparation for new daubing exposing carefully laid stone chinking in this building in Virginia. Photo: Bernard Weisgerber.

result of freeze-thaw action, structural settlement, drying of the logs, and a thermal expansion-contraction rate that differs from that of the logs. Seasonal deterioration of chinking necessitates continual inspection and regular patching or replacement.

Exterior Wall Treatments

Although the exterior logs of cabins in the West, and 20th century Rustic buildings are generally not covered, many 18th and 19th century log houses east of the Mississippi, with the exception of some of the simpler cabins and houses in remote or poorer areas, were covered with exterior cladding. The exterior of the log walls was covered for both aesthetic and practical reasons either as soon as the building was completed or sometime later.

In some instances, the exterior (and interior) of the logs was whitewashed. This served to discourage insects, and sealed hairline cracks in the daubing and fissures between the daubing and logs. Although the solubility of whitewash allows it to heal some of its own hairline cracks with the wash of rain, like daubing it has to be periodically reapplied. Usually, a more permanent covering such as wood siding or stucco was applied to the walls, which provided better insulation and protection, and reduced the maintenance of the log walls.

Sometimes log houses were sided or stuccoed later in an attempt to express a newly-achieved financial or social status. Many log houses were immediately sided and trimmed upon completion to disguise their simple construction beneath Georgian, Federal and later architectural styles. Frequently a log house was covered, or recovered, when a new addition was erected in order to harmonize the whole, especially if the original core and its addition were constructed of different materials such as log and wood frame (Fig. 13).

Vertical wood furring strips were generally nailed to the logs prior to applying weatherboarding or stucco (Fig. 14). This ensured that the walls would be plumb, and provided a base on which to attach the clapboards, or on which to nail the wood lath for stucco.

Fig. 13. Historic wood clapboard siding originally applied to conceal the fact that this house was built in two sections of different materials has been inappropriately removed from the 1793 log portion. Photo: National Park Service Files.

Fig. 14. Removal of the historic wood siding from the 1804 Zachariah Price DeWitt House in Butler County, Ohio, reveals that the clapboards were attached to vertical wood furring strips nailed to the logs. Photo: National Park Service Files.

Foundations

Log building foundations varied considerably in quality, material, and configuration. In many cases, the foundation consisted of a continuous course of flat stones (with or without mortar), several piers consisting of rubblestone, single stones, brick, short vertical log pilings, or horizontal log "sleepers" set on grade. The two "sill logs," were laid directly upon one of these types of foundations.

Climate and intended permanence of the structure were the primary factors affecting foundation construction. The earliest log cabins, and temporary log dwellings in general, were the most likely to be constructed on log pilings or log sleepers set directly on grade. Where a more permanent log dwelling was intended, or where a warm, humid climate accelerated wood decay, such as in the South, it was sometimes more common to use stone piers which allowed air to circulate beneath the sill logs. Full cellars were not generally

included in the original construction of most of the earliest log houses, but root cellars were often dug later.

Roofs

Log buildings were roofed with a variety of different framing systems and covering materials. Like log house plans and corner notching styles, the types of roof framing systems used were often variations on particular ethnic and regional carpentry traditions. In most cases wood shingles were the first roof covering used on the earliest 18th and 19th century log houses. As wood shingle roofs deteriorated, many were replaced with standing seam metal roofs, many of which continue to provide good service today. Later pioneer log buildings west of the Mississippi were likely to be roofed with metal or roll roofing, or even with sod. Other log buildings have been re-roofed in the 20th century with asphalt shingles. For some rustic log buildings in the West and Great Camps in the Adirondacks, asphalt shingles are the original historic roofing material.

Chimneys

Ethnic tradition and regional adaptation also influenced chimney construction and placement. Chimneys in log houses were usually built of stone or brick, a combination of the two, or even clay-lined, notched logs or smaller sticks (Fig. 15). Later log buildings were frequently constructed with only metal stacks to accommodate wood stoves. The chimneys of log buildings erected in cold climates tended to be located entirely inside the house to maximize heat retention. In the South, where winters were less severe the chimney stack was more typically constructed outside the log walls. With the advent of more efficient heating systems, interior chimneys were frequently demolished or relocated and rebuilt to maximize interior space.

Fig. 15. The mid-19th century O'Quinn House, Moore County, North Carolina, provides a rare surviving example of a clay-lined log chimney. Although the logs of the house are saddle-notched, the chimney logs are "V" notched. The roof was extended out over the chimney to protect the daubing from the weather, and the chimney stack would have originally projected through a hole in the roof. Photo: Michael Southern.

Fig. 16. This photograph of the interior of a 1793 log house in Maryland reveals much about historic log building construction and interior finish treatments. To the left of the plank door plaster has been removed exposing the stone chinking and daubing; remnants of vertical furring strips attached to the logs show evidence of traditional horizontal lath, while the hole broken through the plaster wall on the right shows the use of diagonal lath. The open door reveals a very steep, enclosed stairway typical of many early log houses. Although plaster has been removed from the ceiling, the wall to the right of the door shows the original plaster finish and fine woodwork including beaded chair rail, floor and door molding. Photo: National Park Service Files.

Interior Finishes

Logs on the interiors of many of the simpler cabins and Rustic style structures were often given a flattened surface or left exposed. But, in the more finished log houses of the 18th and 19th century, they were more commonly covered for most of the same reasons that the exterior of the logs was covered—improved insulation, ease of maintenance, aesthetics, and keeping out vermin. Covering the interior log walls with planks, lath and plaster, boards pasted with newspaper, fabric such as muslin, or wallpaper increased their resistance to air infiltration and their insulation value. Finished walls could be cleaned and painted more easily, and plastered walls and ceilings obscured the rough log construction and prepared interior surfaces for decorative wood trim in the current styles (Fig. 16).

Historical Evaluation and Damage Assessment

Before undertaking preservation work on a historic log building, its history and design should be investigated, and physical condition evaluated. It is always advisable to hire a historical architect or qualified professional experienced in preservation work to supervise the project. In addition, State Historic Preservation Offices, regional offices of the National Park Service, and local historical commissions may also provide technical and procedural advice.

The historical investigation should be carried out in conjunction with a visual inspection of the log building. Physical assessment needs to be systematic and thorough. It should include taking notes, photographs or video recording, and making drawings of existing conditions, including overall and detail views. This will serve as a record of the appearance and condition which can be referred to once work is under way. A physical assessment should also identify causes of deterioration, not just symptoms or manifestations and, in some instances, may need to include a structural investigation.

Foundation Inspection

The foundation of a log building should always be inspected before beginning work because, as in any building, foundation-related problems can transfer structural defects to other components of the building. Settling of the foundation is a typical condition of log buildings. If settlement is not severe and is no longer active, it is not necessarily a problem. If, however, settlement is active or uneven, if it is shifting structural weight to unintended bearing points away from the intended main bearing points of the corner notches and sill log, serious wall deflections may have resulted. Causes of settlement may include foundation or chimney stones or sill logs that have sunk into the ground, decay of log pilings, log sleepers, or of the sill logs themselves.

Log Inspection

Foundation problems usually result in damage to the sill logs and spandrels, which are often the most susceptible to deterioration. Sill logs, along with the corner notching, tend to bear most of the weight of the building, and are closest to vegetation and the ground, which harbors wood-destroying moisture and insects. If the sill log has come into contact with the ground, deterioration is probably underway or likely to begin (Fig. 17). It is also important to check the drainage around the building. The building assessment should note the condition of each log and attempt to identify the sources of problems that appear to exist.

Sill log inspection should not necessitate destruction of historic exterior cladding if it exists. Inspection can usually be made in areas where cladding is missing,

Fig. 17. Contact of this building's sill log with the ground has led to its decay, infestation by wood-destroying insects, and resulting building settlement. Photo: Anne Grimmer.

loose, or deteriorated. Sill log, as well as upper log, deterioration may also be revealed by loose or peeling areas of the cladding. If pieces of cladding must be removed for log inspection, they should be labeled and saved for reinstallation, or as samples for replacement work. Historic cladding generally need not be disturbed unless there are obvious signs of settling or other indications of deterioration.

Other areas of the log walls which are particularly susceptible to deterioration include window and door sills, corner notches, and crowns, and any other areas regularly saturated by rain run-off or backsplash. The characteristic design feature of Adirondack or Rustic style log buildings of leaving log ends or crowns to extend beyond the notched corners of the building positions the crowns beyond the drip-line of the roof edge. This makes them vulnerable to saturation from roof run-off, and a likely spot for deterioration. Saddle notching in which the cut was made out of the top surface of the log and which cups upward, and flat notching, may also be especially susceptible to collecting run-off moisture.

Detection of decay requires thorough inspection. Probing for rot should be done carefully since repair techniques can sometimes save even badly deteriorated logs. Soft areas should be probed with a small knife blade or icepick to determine the depth of decay. Logs should be gently tapped at regular intervals up and down their lengths with the tool handle to detect hollow-sounding areas of possible interior decay. Long cracks which run with the wood grain, called "checks," are not signs of rot, but are characteristic features of the seasoning of the logs. However, a check can admit moisture and fungal decay into a log, especially if it is located on the log's upper surface. Checks should also be probed with a tool blade to determine whether decay is underway inside the log.

Sill log ground contact and relative moisture content also provide ideal conditions for certain types of insect infestation. Wood building members, such as sill logs or weatherboarding, less than eight inches from the ground, should be noted as a potential problem for monitoring or correction. Sighting of insects, or their damage, or telltale signs of their activity, such as mud tunnels, exit holes, or "frass," a sawdust-like powder, should be recorded. Insect infestation is best treated by a professionally licensed exterminator, as the chemicals used to kill wood-destroying insects and deter re-infestation are generally toxic.

Roof Inspection

Along with the foundation, the roof is the other most vital component of any building. The roof system consists of, from top to bottom, the covering, usually some form of shingles or metal sheeting and flashing; board sheathing or roof lath strips; the framing structure, such as rafters or purlins; the top log, sometimes referred to as the "roof plate" or "rafter plate;" and, sometimes, but not always, gutters and downspouts.

The roof and gutters should be inspected and checked for leaks both from the exterior, as well as inside if possible. Inspection may reveal evidence of an earlier roof type, or covering, and sometimes remnants of more than one historic covering material. The roof may be the result of a later alteration, or raised when a second

Fig. 18. Exposed roofing members of Rustic style buildings such as this structure at Yellowstone National Park are highly susceptible to deterioration. Photo: Laura Soulliere Harrison.

story was added, or repaired as the result of storm or fire damage. Often, roof framing may be composed of reused material recycled from earlier buildings. Inspection of the roof framing should note its configuration and condition. Typical problems to look for are framing members that have been dislodged from their sockets in the roof plate, or that are cracked, ridge damage, sagging rafters, broken ties and braces, and decay of exterior exposed rafter or purlin ends, especially common on Rustic style buildings (Fig. 18).

Other Features

The rest of the building should also be inspected as part of the overall assessment, including siding, window sash and frames, door frames and leafs, chimneys, porches, and interior walls, trim, and finishes. Any of these features may exhibit deterioration problems, inherent to the material or to a construction detail, or may show the effects of problems transmitted from elsewhere, such as a deformed or mis-shapen window frame resulting from a failed sill log. The inspection should note alterations and repairs made over time, and identify those modifications which have acquired significance and should be preserved. Nothing should be removed or altered before it has been examined and its historical significance noted.

Preservation Treatments

Since excessive moisture promotes and hastens both fungal and insect attack, it should be dealt with immediately. Not only must the roof and gutters be repaired —if none exist, gutters should probably be added—but the foundation grade should be sloped to ensure drainage away from the building. If the distance from the ground to the sill log or exterior sheathing is less than eight inches, the ground should be graded to achieve this minimum distance. Excess vegetation and debris such as firewood, dead leaves, or rubbish should be cleared from the foundation perimeter, and climbing vines whose leaves retain moisture and tendrils erode daubing, should be killed and removed. Moisture problems due to faulty interior plumbing should also be remedied. Solving or reducing moisture problems may in itself end or halt the progress of rot and wood-destroying insects.

Log Repair

Stabilizing and repairing a log that has been only partially damaged by decay or insects is always preferable to replacing it. Retaining the log, rather than substituting a new one, preserves more of the building's integrity, including historic tool marks and the wood species which may no longer be obtainable in original dimensions. Log repair can generally be done with the log in place at less cost, in less time, and with less damage to building fabric, than by removing, and installing a new hewn and notched replacement log. Log repair is accomplished by two basic methods: traditional methods of splicing-in new or old wood, or through the use of epoxies. These treatments are sometimes combined, and may also be used in conjunction with reinforcing members. *Historic log repair, whether it involves patching techniques or the use of epoxies, should always be performed only by an experienced craftsperson or architectural conservator.*

Wood Splicing

Wood splicing can involve several types of techniques. Also referred to as "piecing-in" or "Dutchman" repair, it involves treating a localized area of deterioration by cutting out the decayed area of the log, and carefully carving and installing a matching, seasoned wood replacement plug or splice. The wood species, if available, and the direction and pattern of the grain should match that of adjacent original wood. The location and depth of decay should determine the splicing technique to be used. In a case where decay runs deep within a log, a full-depth segment containing the affected area can be cut out, severing the log completely, and a new segment of log spliced in, using angled "scarf" joints or square-cut "half-lap" joints (Fig. 19). The splice is secured to the severed log by angling lag screws or bolts through the upper and lower surfaces that will be concealed by daubing.

Splicing can also be performed using epoxy as an adhesive. A log with shallow decay on its outer face can be cut back to sound depth, and a half-log face spliced on, adhered with epoxy, screws or bolts. A technique for the repair of badly deteriorated log crowns involves cutting them back to sound wood, and into the notching joint if necessary, and installing new crowns cut to match. Fiberglass or aluminum reinforcement rods are inserted into holes drilled into the new crowns, and into corresponding holes drilled in the ends of the original cut-off logs. Epoxy is used as an adhesive to attach and hold the new crowns in place. Long lag screws can be angled up through the underside of the crown into the log above to provide additional support for the repair.

Epoxy Consolidation and Repair

In some instances, epoxies may be used by themselves to consolidate and fill the voids left by deteriorated wood. Epoxies are versatile in performance, relatively easy to use by experts, and, after curing, may be shaped with wood-working tools. Their use requires that sufficient sound wood survives for the epoxy to adhere. But they can be used to stabilize rotted wood, return full or greater than original strength to decayed structure-bearing members, and to reconstitute the shape of decayed log ends. Epoxies resist decay and

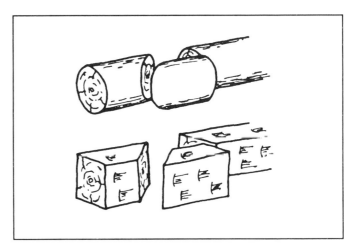

Fig. 19. *Log splicing with scarf joints. Drawing: Harrison Goodall.*

a

b

Fig. 20. *(a) These deteriorated log crowns were (b) repaired with new crowns which were attached to the historic logs with reinforcing bars and epoxy. Epoxy repair of log crowns is most successful when the repaired crowns are protected from excess moisture by a roof overhang. Photos: Harrison Goodall.*

insects, and while epoxy itself is resistant to moisture, epoxy tends to cause adjacent wood to retain moisture rather than dry out, and if not used in the right location, can actually further a continuing cycle of wood decay. Hence, epoxy repairs are most successful in areas where they are protected from moisture. Epoxies, of which there are a variety of commercially-available products on the market, are prepared in essentially two forms: a liquid consolidant and a flexible putty filler. Each consists of a resin and a hardener which must be mixed prior to use.

The technique of treating, for an example, a decayed log crown with epoxies is begun by removing loose decayed wood, and drying the area if necessary (Fig. 20). The rot-affected cavity and surface of the log end is then saturated with liquid epoxy by repeated brushing, or by soaking it in a plastic bag filled with epoxy that is attached to the log. The porous condition of the rot-damaged wood will draw up the epoxy like a lamp wick. Once the liquid epoxy has saturated the log end and cured, the log end has been consolidated, and is ready for the application of an epoxy putty filler. The filler resin and hardener must also be mixed; pigments must be mixed with the filler epoxy to color the patch, and more importantly to protect it from ultraviolet sunlight. The filler can be applied with a putty knife, pressing it into the irregularities of the cavity. The cured patch can be worked like wood and painted with an opaque stain or a dull finish paint to help it blend with surrounding wood, although epoxy repairs can be difficult to disguise on natural, unpainted wood.

Epoxies can be used to consolidate and repair other areas of a log, including rotted internal areas which have not yet progressed to damage the log's outer surface. Saturation of small internal areas can be accomplished by drilling several random holes into the log through an area that will be concealed by daubing, and then pouring in liquid epoxy. If a pure resin is used, it should be a casting resin to minimize shrinkage, and it is best to fill voids with a resin that contains aggregates such as sand, or micro-balloons. Epoxy is frequently used by architectural conservators to strengthen deteriorated structural members. The damaged log can be strengthened by removing the deteriorated wood, and filling the void by imbedding a reinforcing bar in epoxy filler, making sure the void is properly sealed to contain the epoxy before using it (Fig. 21). Sometimes larger decayed internal areas of a log can be more easily accessed and repaired from the interior of a structure. This may be a useful technique if it can be accomplished without causing undue damage to the interior finishes in the log building. However, despite its many advantages, epoxy may not be an appropriate treatment for all log repairs, and it should not be used in an attempt to conceal checking, or extensive log surface patching that is exposed to view, or logs that are substantially decayed or collapsed.

Log Replacement

Repairing or replacing only a segment of a log is not always possible. Replacement of an entire log may be the only solution if it has been substantially lost to decay and collapsed under the weight of logs above it. Log replacement, which should be carried out only by experienced craftspersons, is begun by temporarily

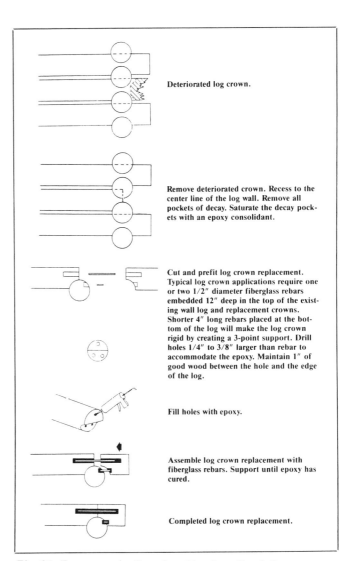

Deteriorated log crown.

Remove deteriorated crown. Recess to the center line of the log wall. Remove all pockets of decay. Saturate the decay pockets with an epoxy consolidant.

Cut and prefit log crown replacement. Typical log crown applications require one or two 1/2" diameter fiberglass rebars embedded 12" deep in the top of the existing wall log and replacement crowns. Shorter 4" long rebars placed at the bottom of the log will make the log crown rigid by creating a 3-point support. Drill holes 1/4" to 3/8" larger than rebar to accommodate the epoxy. Maintain 1" of good wood between the hole and the edge of the log.

Fill holes with epoxy.

Assemble log crown replacement with fiberglass rebars. Support until epoxy has cured.

Completed log crown replacement.

Fig. 21. Epoxy repair. Drawing: Harrison Goodall.

supporting the logs above, and then jacking them up just enough to insert the new log. Potential danger to the structure may include creating inadequate temporary bearing points, and crushing chinking and interior finishes which may have settled slowly into non-original positions that cannot withstand jacking.

To begin the process of log replacement, the entire length of the log must be inspected from the exterior and the interior of the structure to determine whether it supports any structural members or features, and how their load can be taken up by bracing during jacking and removal. On the exterior, sheathing such as weatherboard, and adjacent chinking, must be removed along the length of the log to perform this inspection. Likewise, on the interior, abutting partition walls and plaster may also need to be removed around the log to determine what, if any, features are supported by or tied into the log to be removed.

A replacement log should be obtained to match the wood species of the original being removed. If it is a hewn log, then the replacement must be hewn to replicate the dimensions and tool marks of the original (Fig. 22). If the same wood species cannot be obtained in the original dimensions, a substitute species may have to be used, and may even be preferable in some instances

Fig. 22. The lighter-colored replacement log in this barn matches the dimensions and hewing marks of the original logs, and will darken in time to blend visually with the other logs. Photo: Bernard Weisgerber.

if a more durable wood can be found than the original wood species. It should, however, be chosen to match the visual characteristics of the original species as closely as possible.

Wood Preservatives

In most instances, the use of chemical wood preservatives is not generally recommended on historic log buildings. Preservatives tend to change the color or appearance of the logs. In addition, many are toxic, they tend to leach out of the wood over time, and like paint, must be periodically reapplied. Many of the late 19th and early 20th century Rustic structures were constructed of logs with the bark left on which may provide protection, while others have been painted. However, some log buildings, and especially log houses that have been inappropriately stripped of historic cladding in an earlier restoration, and now show signs of weathering, such as deep checking, may be exceptions to this guidance. A preservative treatment may be worth considering in these cases. Boiled linseed oil may sometimes be appropriate to use on selected exposures of a building that are particularly vulnerable to weathering, although linseed oil does tend to darken over time. Borate solutions, which do not alter the color or appearance of wood, may be another of the few effective, non-hazardous preservatives available. However, borate solutions do not penetrate dry wood well, and thus the wood must be green or wet. Because borate solutions are water-soluble, after treating, the wood must be coated with a water-repellent coating. In some instances, it may be appropriate to reapply varnish where it was used as the original finish treatment. Pressure-treating, while effective for new wood, is not applicable to in-place log treatment, and is generally not effective for large timbers and logs because it does not penetrate deeply enough.

Foundation Repair

The foundation should have good drainage, be stable, adequately support the building as well as any future floorloads, and keep the sill log sufficiently clear of the ground and moisture to deter decay and insect infestation. Log buildings with cellars are less likely to suffer

problems than those built upon the ground or with crawl spaces, as long as the cellar is kept dry and ventilated. Because the foundations of many log buildings were neither dug nor laid below the frostline, they generally tend to be susceptible to freeze-thaw ground heaving and settlement. Also, as previously noted, some foundations consisted of wooden sleepers or pilings in direct contact with the ground. If a foundation problem is minor, such as the need for repointing or resetting a few stones, work should address only those areas. Loose stones should be reset in their original locations if possible. A clearly inadequate foundation that has virtually disappeared into the ground, or where large areas of masonry have buckled or sunk, resulting in excessively uneven or active settlement, will need to be rebuilt using modern construction methods but to match the historic appearance.

Chinking Repair

Repair of chinking, whether it is finished on the exterior with wooden strips or with daubing, should not be done until all log repair or replacement, structural jacking and shoring is completed, and all replacement logs have seasoned. Historically, patching and replacing daubing on a routine basis was a seasonal chore. This was because environmental factors—building settlement, seasonal expansion and contraction of logs, and moisture infiltration followed by freeze-thaw action—cracks and loosens daubing. If the exterior log walls are exposed, and the chinking or daubing requires repair, as much of the remaining inner blocking filler and daubing should be retained as possible. A daubing formula and tooled finish that matches the historic daubing, if known, should be used, or based on one of the mixes listed here. For the most part, modern commercially-available chinking products are not suitable for use on historic log buildings, although an exception might be on the interior of a log building where it will be covered by plaster or wood, and will not be visible. These products tend to have a sandy appearance that may be compatible with some historic daubing, but the color, and other visual and physical characteristics are generally incompatible with historic log surfaces.

Sections of wood chinking which are gone or cannot be made weathertight should be replaced with same-sized species saplings or quarter poles cut to fit. Generally, unless bark was used originally, it should be removed before nailing the new wood chinking replacements tightly into place.

Analysis of daubing can be done in much the same way as mortar analysis. If that is not feasible, by crushing a loose piece of daubing its constituent parts can be exposed, which may typically include lime, sand, clay, and, as binders, straw or animal hair. The color imparted by the sand or pigmented constituents should be noted, and any areas of original daubing should be recorded with color film for later reference. Daubing that is loose or is not adhered to the logs must first be cleaned out by hand. Blocking filler should be left intact, refitting only loose pieces. (Sometimes it may be difficult to obtain a good bond in which case it may be necessary to clean out the joint entirely.) If needed, soft filler should be added, such as jute or bits of fiberglass batt, pressed firmly into voids with a stick or blunt tool. Concealed reinforcement may sometimes be used, depending upon the authenticity of the restoration. This can include galvanized nails partially inserted only on the upper side of the log to allow for the daubing to move with the upper log and keep the top joint sealed, or galvanized wire mesh secured with galvanized nails (Fig. 23). Like repointing masonry, daubing should not be done in full sun, excessive heat or when freezing temperatures are expected. The daubing materials should be dry-mixed, the chinking rechecked as being tight and secure, and the mix wetted and stirred to a stiff, paste-like consistency. The mix dries quickly, so no more daubing should be prepared at a time than can be applied in about 30 minutes. A test patch of new daubing, either on the building, or in a mock-up elsewhere, will help test the suitability of the formula's color and texture match.

Before applying the daubing, the chinking area, including filler and log surfaces to be covered, should be sprayed with water to prevent the dry filler from too rapidly drawing off the daubing moisture which will result in hairline cracking. A trowel, ground to the width of the daubing, is used to press the daubing into the chinking space, and to smooth the filled areas. Wide or deep chinking spaces or joints may have to be daubed in layers, to prevent sagging and separation from the logs, by applying one or two scratch coats before finishing the surface.

Daubing Mixes			
	parts (volume)	**material**	
Mix A.	1/4	cement	
	1	lime	
	4	sand	
	1/8	dry color	
		hog bristles or excelsior	

(Donald A. Hutslar, "Log Cabin Restoration: Guidelines for the Historical Society," American Association for State and local History, Technical Leaflet No. 74, "History News," Vol. 29, No. 5 (May 1974.)

Mix B.	6	sand
	4	lime
	1	cement

Mix C.	1	portland cement
	4–8	lime
	7–10	sand

Mix B and C are reprinted from "Log Structures: Preservation and Problem-Solving," by Harrison Goodall and Renee Friedman, Nashville, TN: American Association for State and Local History, 1980.

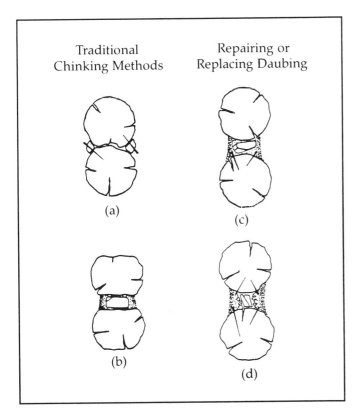

Traditional Chinking Methods

Repairing or Replacing Daubing

(a)

(b)

(c)

(d)

Fig. 23. Illustrated are various methods of chinking and daubing: (a) wood strips, or thin saplings nailed in place; and (b) 3-part system consisting of an inner blocking filler of stones or wood slabs, together with soft filler, such as clay, stuffed around the blocking, composes the chinking, and wet-applied daubing. Concealed aids that may improve the adherence of new daubing include (c) galvanized nails, or (d) galvanized mesh lath. Drawing: James Caufield.

Portland cement was a part of the original daubing used in many late 19th and early 20th century log buildings, and is therefore appropriate to include in repairing buildings of this period. Although a small amount of portland cement may be added to a lime, clay and sand mix for workability, there should not be more than 1 part portland cement to 2 parts of lime in daubing mixes intended for most historic log buildings. Portland cement tends to shrink and develop hairline cracks, and retain moisture, all of which can be potentially damaging to the logs.

Interior Treatments

There is no single appropriate way to finish or restore the interior of a historic log house. Each building and its history is unique. The temptation should be resisted to impart an unfinished frontier character by removing plaster to expose interior log walls or joists in the ceiling. Instead, interior treatments should be based on existing evidence, and guided by old photographs, written documentation, and interviews with previous owners. Interior features and finishes that might exist in some 18th and 19th century log houses include wood paneled walls, wood moldings, stairs, and fireplace mantels; where they have survived, these features should be retained. Many of the more rustic log buildings built later in the 19th or early 20th century intentionally featured exposed interior log walls, sometimes with the logs peeled and varnished. If interior plaster is severely damaged or has previously been removed, and evidence such as lath ghosting on the logs exists, walls should be replastered or recovered with gypsum board or dry wall to match the historic appearance.

Preserving Log Buildings in Their Historic Settings

Log buildings are too often viewed as portable resources. Like other historic buildings, moved or relocated log structures can suffer a loss of integrity of materials and of setting (Fig. 24). Historic buildings listed in the National Register of Historic Places may be subject to loss of that status if moved. Despite the popularity of dismantling and relocating log buildings, they should be moved only as a last resort, if that is the only way to save them from demolition. If they must be moved, it is preferable that they be moved intact—that is, in one piece rather than disassembled. Disassembling and moving a log building can result in considerable loss of the historic building materials. While the logs and roof framing members can be numbered for reassembly, dismantling a log building can result in loss of such features as foundation and chimney, chinking and daubing, exterior cladding, and interior finishes. Furthermore, log buildings can rarely be put back together as easily as they were taken apart.

b

Fig. 24. Some towns still retain a high number of early log houses. (a) Middleway, West Virginia, is a small village dominated by 18th and 19th century log houses, and, with the exception of outbuildings, all are clad in original wood siding or stucco. Removal of one of the houses from this streetscape would not only result in a loss of integrity to the building, but also to the historic district. (b) The original wood clapboard of two of these c. 1830 log houses in Stouchsburg, Pennsylvania, has been covered with asphalt siding, and later porches added. Rehabilitation plans might appropriately include retention of the porches as having acquired significance over time, and removal of the asphalt siding. Uneven spacing between the two upper left windows of the house on the left, and the center chimney are indications that the house was built in two stages. Photos: (a) Anne Grimmer, (b) Pennsylvania Historical and Museum Commission.

a

Fig. 25. (a) Prior to rehabilitation, the exterior of this late 18th century log house was sided with wood clapboard, which had been covered over by a later artificial siding, while the upper gallery of the second floor porch was stuccoed. (b) During the rehabilitation both the historic wood siding and stucco were removed to expose the logs, the gables were sided with wood shingles, and what would have originally been milled wood columns supporting the porch were replaced with rough, unmilled log posts. Collectively, these treatments diminished the building's architectural integrity, and gave it an appearance it never had. (c) The depth that the window frames extend out beyond the log surface allowing space for siding is an indication that cladding was part of the building's original construction. Photos: National Park Service Files.

Summary

Historic log buildings regardless of whether they are of horizontal or vertical construction, or whether they are 18th century log houses or early 20th century Rustic style cabins, are unique. Their conservation essentially centers on the preservation and repair of the logs, and appropriate repairs to chinking and daubing, which like repointing of masonry, is necessary to ensure that most log buildings are weathertight. Log building preservation may be accomplished with a variety of techniques including splicing and piecing-in, the use of epoxy, or a combination of patching and epoxy, and often, selected replacement. But, like any historic building, a log structure is a system that functions through the maintenance of the totality of its parts.

The exterior of many of the earliest late 18th and 19th century log buildings, and particularly those east of the Mississippi, were commonly covered at the time of construction or later with some type of cladding, either horizontal or vertical wood siding, stucco, or sometimes a combination. If extant, this historic cladding, which may be hidden under a later, non-historic artificial siding such as aluminum, vinyl, or asbestos, should be preserved and repaired, or replaced if evidence indicates that it existed, as a significant character-defining feature of the building (Fig. 25).

Selected Reading

Briscoe, Frank. "Wood-Destroying Insects." *The Old-House Journal*. Vol. XIX, No. 2 (March/April 1991), pp. 34–39.

Caron, Peter. "Jacking Techniques for Log Buildings." *Association for Preservation Technology Bulletin*. Special Issue: *Alberta Culture*. Vol. XX, No. 4 (1988), pp. 42–54.

Cotton, J. Randall. "Log Houses in America." *The Old-House Journal*. Vol. XVIII, No. 1 (January/February 1990), pp. 37–44.

Elbert, Duane E., and Keith A. Sculle. *Log Buildings in Illinois: Their Interpretation and Preservation*. Illinois Preservation Series: Number 3. Springfield, IL: Illinois Department of Conservation, Division of Historic Sites, 1982.

Goodall, Harrison. "Log Crown Repair and Selective Replacement Using Epoxy and Fiberglass Reinforcing Rebars: Lamar Barn, Yellowstone National Park, Wyoming." *Preservation Tech Notes*, Exterior Woodwork Number 3. Washington, D.C.: Preservation Assistance Division, National Park Service, U.S. Department of the Interior, 1989.

_____, and Renee Friedman. *Log Structures: Preservation and Problem-Solving*. Nashville, TN: American Association for State and Local History, 1980.

Hutslar, Donald A. *The Architecture of Migration: Log Construction in the Ohio Country, 1750–1850*. Athens, OH: Ohio University Press, 1986.

_____. *Log Cabin Restoration: Guidelines for the Historical Society*. American Association for State and Local History Technical Leaflet 74. *History News*. Vol. 29, No. 5, May 1974.

Jordan, Terry G. *American Log Buildings: An Old World Heritage*. Chapel Hill, NC: The University of North Carolina Press, 1985.

Kaiser, Harvey H. *Great Camps of the Adirondacks*. Boston: David R. Godine Publisher, Inc., 1986.

Merrill, William. "Wood Deterioration: Causes, Detection and Prevention." American Association for State and Local History Technical Leaflet 77. *History News*. Vol. 29, No. 8, August, 1974.

Rowell, R.M., J.M. Black, L.R. Gjovik, and W.C. Feist. *Protecting Log Cabins from Decay*. U.S.D.A. Forest Service Products Laboratory, General Technical Report, FPL–11. Madison, WI: Forest Products Laboratory, Forest Service, U.S. Department of Agriculture, 1977.

St. George, R.A. *Protecting Log Cabins, Rustic Work and Unseasoned Wood from Injurious Insects in the Eastern United States*. Farmer's Bulletin No. 2104, United States Department of Agriculture. Washington, D.C.: Government Printing Office, 1962 (Rev. 1970).

Tweed, William C., Laura E. Soulliere, and Henry G. Law. *National Park Service Rustic Architecture: 1916–1942*. San Francisco, CA: Division of Cultural Resource Management, Western Regional Office, National Park Service, February 1977.

Wilson, Mary. *Log Cabin Studies*. Cultural Resources Report No. 9. Ogden, UT: United States Department of Agriculture, Forest Service, 1984.

Acknowledgements

The author, a Preservation Specialist at the Pennsylvania Historical and Museum Commission, wishes to thank those experts who reviewed and commented upon the draft manuscript: James Caufield; J. Randall Cotton; Harrison Goodall; Donald A. Hutslar; Terry G. Jordan; Bernard Weisgerber; Rodd Wheaton; and National Park Service professional staff. **Anne E. Grimmer is credited with directing this cooperative publication project and general editorship.**

This publication has been prepared pursuant to the National Historic Preservation Act of 1966, as amended, which directs the Secretary of the Interior to develop and make available information concerning historic properties. Comments on the usefulness of this publication may be directed to H. Ward Jandl, Chief, Technical Preservation Services Branch, Preservation Assistance Division, National Park Service, P.O. Box 37127, Washington, D.C. 20013-7127.

Cover Photograph (logo): The log cabin was used on this 1840 campaign medal to symbolize frontier life and democratic egalitarianism, a platform that successfully elected William Henry Harrison to the presidency. Photo: The State Museum of Pennsylvania, Pennsylvania Historical and Museum Commission.

27

The Maintenance and Repair of Architectural Cast Iron

John G. Waite, AIA

Historical Overview by Margot Gayle

In Cooperation with the
New York Landmarks Conservancy

The preservation of cast-iron architectural elements, including entire facades, has gained increasing attention in recent years as commercial districts are recognized for their historic significance and revitalized. This Brief provides general guidance on approaches to the preservation and restoration of historic cast iron.

Cast iron played a preeminent role in the industrial development of our country during the 19th century. Cast-iron machinery filled America's factories and made possible the growth of railroad transportation. Cast iron was used extensively in our cities for water systems and street lighting. As an architectural metal, it made possible bold new advances in architectural designs and building technology, while providing a richness in ornamentation (Fig. 1).

This age-old metal, an iron alloy with a high carbon content, had been too costly to make in large quantities until the mid-18th century, when new furnace technology in England made it more economical for use in construction. Known for its great strength in compression, cast iron in the form of slender, non-flammable pillars, was introduced in the 1790s in English cotton mills, where fires were endemic. In the United States, similar thin columns were first employed in the 1820s in theaters and churches to support balconies.

By the mid-1820s, one-story iron storefronts were being advertised in New York City. Daniel Badger, the Boston foundryman who later moved to New York, asserted that in 1842 he fabricated and installed the first rolling iron shutters for iron storefronts, which provided protection against theft and external fire. In the years ahead, and into the 1920s, the practical cast-iron storefront would become a favorite in towns and cities from coast to coast. Not only did it help support the load of the upper floors, but it provided large show windows for the display of wares and allowed natural light to flood the interiors of the shops. Most importantly, cast-iron storefronts were inexpensive to assemble, requiring little on-site labor.

A tireless advocate for the use of cast iron in buildings was an inventive New Yorker, the self-taught architect/engineer James Bogardus. From 1840 on, Bogardus extolled its virtues of strength, structural stability, durability, relative lightness, ability to be cast in almost any shape and, above all, the fire-resistant qualities so sought after in an age of serious urban conflagrations. He also stressed that the foundry casting processes, by which cast iron was made into building elements, were thoroughly compatible with the new concepts of prefabrication, mass production, and use of identical interchangeable parts.

Fig. 1. The Haughwout Building in New York City is an excellent example of the quality and character of mass-produced cast-iron architecture. Once wood patterns were made, any number of elements could be cast, as was done with each of these repetitive bays. Photo: New York City Landmarks Preservation Commission.

In 1849 Bogardus created something uniquely American when he erected the first structure with self-supporting, multi-storied exterior walls of iron. Known as the Edgar Laing Stores, this corner row of small four-story warehouses that looked like one building was constructed in lower Manhattan in only two months. Its rear, side, and interior bearing walls were of brick; the floor framing consisted of timber joists and girders. One of the cast-iron walls was load-bearing, supporting the wood floor joists. The innovation was its two street facades of self-supporting cast iron, consisting of multiples of only a few pieces—Doric-style engaged columns, panels, sills, and plates, along with some applied ornaments (cover photo and Fig. 2). Each component of the facades had been cast individually in a sand mold in a foundry, machined smooth, tested for fit, and finally trundled on horse-drawn drays to the building site. There they were hoisted into position, then bolted together and fastened to the conventional structure of timber and brick with iron spikes and straps (Fig. 3).

The second iron-front building erected was a quantum leap beyond the Laing Stores in size and complexity. Begun in April 1850 by Bogardus, with architect Robert Hatfield, the five-story Sun newspaper building in Baltimore was both cast-iron-fronted and cast-iron-framed. In Philadelphia, several ironfronts were begun in 1850: The Inquirer Building, the Brock Stores, and the Penn Mutual Building (all three have been demolished). The St. Charles Hotel of 1851 at 60 N. Third Street is the oldest ironfront in America. Framing with cast-iron columns and wrought-iron beams and trusses was visible on a vast scale in the New York Crystal Palace of 1853.

In the second half of the 19th century, the United States was in an era of tremendous economic and territorial growth. The use of iron in commercial and public buildings spread rapidly, and hundreds of iron-fronted buildings were erected in cities across the country from 1849 to beyond the turn of the century. Outstanding examples of ironfronts exist in Baltimore, Galveston, Louisville, Milwaukee, New Orleans, Philadelphia, Richmond, Rochester (N.Y.), and especially New York City where the SoHo Cast Iron Historic District alone has 139 iron-fronted buildings (Fig. 1). Regrettably, a large proportion of ironfronts nationwide have been demolished in downtown redevelopment projects, especially since World War II.

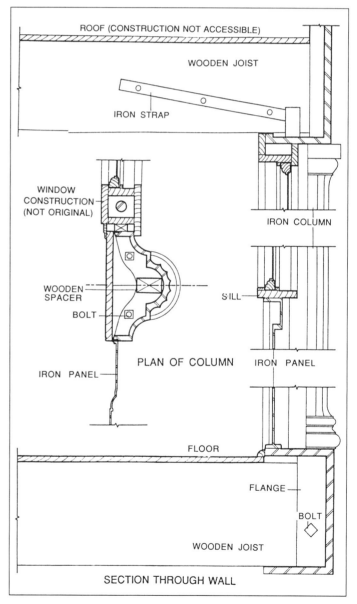

Fig. 2. The Edgar Laing Stores Block in New York City was designed by James Bogardus. It was the first building constructed with facades of self-supporting cast iron. This corner view shows the Doric-style engaged columns, panels, and spandrel beams; the loss of most of the original ornamental castings give it an austere look. As part of an urban renewal project, the facades were carefully disassembled in 1971 for later re-erection in another location—only to have its iron parts stolen for scrap. Photo: Jack E. Boucher, HABS Collection.

Fig. 3. Section drawing through the wall of Edgar Laing Stores showing how the cast-iron facade components were anchored to the wood floor and roof framing members. Drawing: John G. Waite, HABS Collection.

Fig. 4. The 1904 grand stairway of the former Frear's department store in Troy, N.Y. was constructed of cast iron, as was the frame of the skylight above. Some ornamental wrought iron was also employed. This use of iron was typical in major commercial buildings constructed throughout the United States. Courtesy: Rensselaer County Historical Society.

Fig. 5. The Slatter Family Tomb in Mobile, Alabama, consisting of a cast-iron mausoleum and fence, exhibits the wide range of uses of the material in the 19th century. Photo: Jack E. Boucher, HABS Collection.

In addition to these exterior uses, many public buildings display magnificent exposed interior ironwork, at once ornamental and structural (Fig. 4). Remarkable examples have survived across the country, including the Peabody Library in Baltimore; the Old Executive Office Building in Washington, D.C.; the Bradbury Building in Los Angeles; the former Louisiana State Capitol; the former City Hall in Richmond; Tweed Courthouse in New York; and the state capitols of California, Georgia, Michigan, Tennessee, and Texas. And it is iron, of course, that forms the great dome of the United States Capitol, completed during the Civil War. Ornamental cast iron was a popular material in the landscape as well, appearing as fences, fountains with statuary, lampposts, furniture, urns, gazebos, gates, and enclosures for cemetery plots (Fig. 5). With such widespread demand, many American foundries that had been casting machine parts, bank safes, iron pipe, or cookstoves added architectural iron departments (Fig. 6). These called for patternmakers with sophisticated design capabilities, as well as knowledge of metal shrinkage and other technical aspects of casting. Major companies included the Hayward Bartlett Co. in Baltimore; James L. Jackson, Cornell Brothers, J. L. Mott, and Daniel D. Badger's Architectural Iron Works in Manhattan; Hecla Ironworks in Brooklyn; Wood & Perot of Philadelphia; Leeds & Co., the

Shakspeare (sic) Foundry, and Miltenberger in New Orleans; Winslow Brothers in Chicago; and James McKinney in Albany, N.Y.

Cast iron was the metal of choice throughout the second half of the 19th century. Not only was it a fire-resistant material in a period of major urban fires, but also large facades could be produced with cast iron at less cost than comparable stone fronts, and iron buildings could be erected with speed and efficiency. The largest standing example of framing with cast-iron columns and wrought-iron beams is Chicago's sixteen-story Manhattan Building, the world's tallest skyscraper when built in 1890 by William LeBaron Jenney. By this time, however, steel was becoming available nationally, and was structurally more versatile and cost-competitive. Its increased use is one reason why building with cast iron diminished around the turn of the century after having been so eagerly adopted only fifty years before. Nonetheless, cast iron continued to be used in substantial quantities for many other structural and ornamental purposes well into the 20th century: storefronts; marquees; bays and large window frames for steel-framed, masonry-clad buildings; and street and landscape furnishings, including subway kiosks.

The 19th century left us with a rich heritage of new building methods, especially construction on an altogether new scale that was made possible by the use of metals. Of these, cast iron was the pioneer, although its period of intensive use lasted but a half century. Now the surviving legacy of cast-iron architecture, much of which continues to be threatened, merits renewed appreciation and appropriate preservation and restoration treatments.

What is Cast Iron?

Cast iron is an alloy with a high carbon content (at least 1.7% and usually 3.0 to 3.7%) that makes it more resistant to corrosion than either wrought iron or steel. In addition to carbon, cast iron contains varying amounts of silicon, sulfur, manganese, and phosphorus.

While molten, cast iron is easily poured into molds, making it possible to create nearly unlimited decorative and structural forms. Unlike wrought iron and steel, cast iron is too hard and brittle to be shaped by hammering, rolling, or pressing. However, because it is more rigid and more resistant to buckling than other forms of iron, it can withstand great compression loads. Cast iron is relatively weak in tension, however, and fails under tensile loading with little prior warning.

The characteristics of various types of cast iron are determined by their composition and the techniques used in melting, casting, and heat treatment. Metallurgical constituents of cast iron that affect its brittleness, toughness, and strength include ferrite, cementite, pearlite, and graphite carbon. Cast iron with flakes of carbon is called gray cast iron. The "gray fracture" associated with cast iron was probably named for the gray, grainy appearance of its broken edge caused by the presence of flakes of free graphite, which account for the brittleness of cast iron. This brittleness is the important distinguishing characteristic between cast iron and mild steel.

Compared with cast iron, wrought iron is relatively soft, malleable, tough, fatigue-resistant, and readily worked by forging, bending, and drawing. It is almost pure iron, with less than 1% (usually 0.02 to 0.03%) carbon. Slag varies between 1% and 4% of its content and exists in a purely physical association, that is, it is not alloyed. This gives wrought iron its characteristic laminated (layered) or fibrous structure.

Wrought iron can be distinguished from cast iron in several ways. Wrought-iron elements generally are simpler in form and less uniform in appearance than cast-iron elements, and contain evidence of rolling or hand working. Cast iron often contains mold lines, flashing, casting flaws, and air holes. Cast-iron elements are very uniform in appearance and are frequently used repetitively. Cast-iron elements are often bolted or screwed together, whereas wrought-iron pieces are either riveted or forge-molded (heat welded) together.

Mild steel is now used to fabricate new hand-worked metal work and to repair old wrought-iron elements. Mild steel is an alloy of iron and is not more than 2% carbon, which is strong but easily worked in block or ingot form. Mild steel is not as resistant to corrosion as either wrought iron or cast iron.

Maintenance and Repair

Many of the maintenance and repair techniques described in the Brief, particularly those relating to cleaning and painting, are potentially dangerous and should be carried out only by experienced and qualified workmen using protective equipment suitable to the task. In all but the most simple repairs, it is best to involve a preservation architect or building conservator to assess the condition of the iron and prepare contract documents for its treatment.

As with any preservation project, the work must be preceded by a review of local building codes and environmental protection regulations to determine whether any conflicts exist with the proposed treatments. If there are conflicts, particularly with cleaning techniques or painting materials, then waivers or variances need to be negotiated, or alternative treatments or materials adopted.

Deterioration

Common problems encountered today with cast-iron construction include badly rusted or missing elements, impact damage, structural failures, broken joints, damage to connections, and loss of anchorage in masonry (Figs. 7, 8).

Oxidation, or rusting, occurs rapidly when cast iron is exposed to moisture and air. The minimum relative humidity necessary to promote rusting is 65%, but this

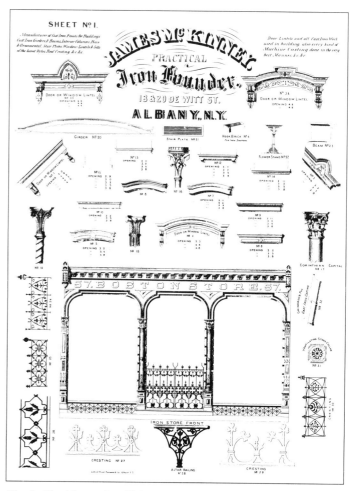

Fig. 6. Sheet from a late 19th century manufacturer's trade catalog illustrates some of the products available from foundries, such as storefronts, girders and beams, columns, stairs, window lintels and sills, and roof crestings. Courtesy: Albany Institute of History and Art.

Fig. 7. Despite an impact that shattered the main castings, this fence post remains upright, demonstrating the great strength of cast iron. Originally, the post was held together by a long bolt that extended from the finial to the base. Photo: John G. Waite.

figure can be lower in the presence of corrosive agents, such as sea water, salt air, acids, acid precipitation, soils, and some sulfur compounds present in the atmosphere, which act as catalysts in the oxidation process. Rusting is accelerated in situations where architectural details provide pockets or crevices to trap and hold liquid corrosive agents. Furthermore, once a rust film forms, its porous surface acts as a reservoir for liquids, which in turn causes further corrosion. If this process is not arrested, it will continue until the iron is entirely consumed by corrosion, leaving nothing but rust.

Galvanic corrosion is an electrochemical action that results when two dissimilar metals react together in the presence of an electrolyte, such as water containing salts or hydrogen ions (Fig. 9). The severity of the galvanic corrosion is based

Fig. 8. Structural cracks, gaps at joints between components, and a large opening where part of the console bracket is missing are the problems evident in this cast-iron assembly. Photo: Ford, Powell & Carson.

on the difference in potential between the two metals, their relative surface areas, and time. If the more noble metal (higher position in electrochemical series) is much larger in area than the baser, or less noble, metal, the deterioration of the baser metal will be more rapid and severe. If the more noble metal is much smaller in area than the baser metal, the deterioration of the baser metal will be much less significant. Cast iron will be attacked and corroded when it is adjacent to more noble metals such as lead or copper.

Fig. 9. Galvanic corrosion occurred where a patch of copper was installed alongside the cast-iron cap at the base of a fountain. The use of terne-coated stainless flashings with appropriate caulking would have been a more suitable repair. Photo: John G. Waite.

Graphitization of cast iron, a less common problem, occurs in the presence of acid precipitation or seawater. As the iron corrodes, the porous graphite (soft carbon) corrosion residue is impregnated with insoluble corrosion products. As a result, the cast-iron element retains its appearance and shape but is weaker structurally. Graphitization occurs where cast iron is left unpainted for long periods or where caulked joints have failed and acidic rainwater has corroded pieces from the backside. Testing and identification of graphitization is accomplished by scraping through the surface with a knife to reveal the crumbling of the iron beneath. Where extensive graphitization occurs, usually the only solution is replacement of the damaged element.

Castings may also be fractured or flawed as a result of imperfections in the original manufacturing process, such as air holes, cracks, and cinders, or cold shuts (caused by the "freezing" of the surface of the molten iron during casting because of improper or interrupted pouring). Brittleness is another problem occasionally found in old cast-iron elements. It may be a result of excessive phosphorus in the iron, or of chilling during the casting process.

Condition Assessment

Before establishing the appropriate treatment for cast-iron elements in a building or structure, an evaluation should be made of the property's historical and architectural significance and alterations, along with its present condition. If the work involves more than routine maintenance, a qualified professional should be engaged to develop a historic structure report which sets forth the historical development of the property, documents its existing condition, identifies problems of repair, and provides a detailed listing of recommended work items with priorities. Through this process the significance and condition of the cast iron can be evaluated and appropriate treatments proposed. For fences, or for single components of a building such as a facade, a similar but less extensive analytical procedure should be followed.

The nature and extent of the problems with the cast-iron elements must be well understood before proceeding with work. If the problems are minor, such as surface corrosion, flaking paint, and failed caulking, the property owner may be able to undertake the repairs by working directly with a knowledgeable contractor. If there are major problems or extensive damage to the cast iron, it is best to secure the services of an architect or conservator who specializes in the conservation of historic buildings. Depending on the scope of work, contract documents can range from outline specifications to complete working drawings with annotated photographs and specifications

To thoroughly assess the condition of the ironwork, a close physical inspection must be undertaken of every section of the iron construction including bolts, fasteners, and brackets (Fig. 10). Typically, scaffolding or a mechanical lift is employed for close inspection of a cast-iron facade or other large structures. Removal of select areas of paint may be the only means to determine the exact condition of connections, metal fasteners, and intersections or crevices that might trap water.

Fig. 11. Major cracks in the piers of this cast-iron storefront in Galveston, Texas resulted from the transfer of load onto the iron from internal brick piers eroded by rising damp. This crack was inappropriately filled with concrete, which trapped moisture and accelerated internal corrosion, pushing the iron further apart. Photo: Ford, Powell & Carson.

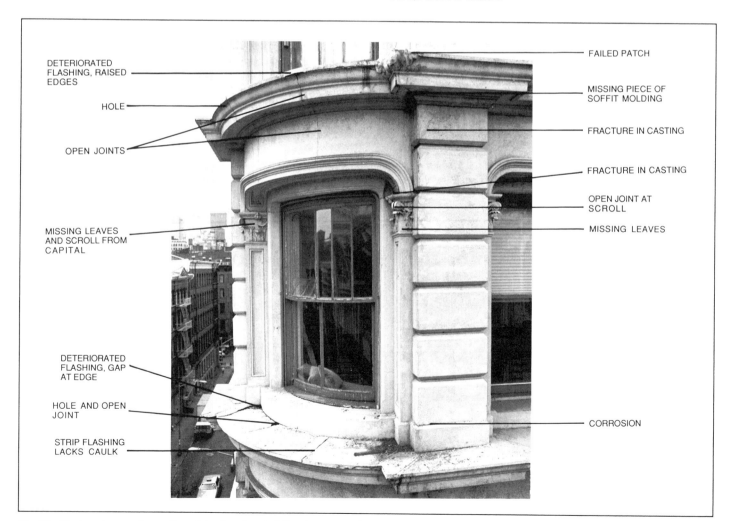

Fig. 10. During close-up inspection of the Gunther Building in New York City, photographs of each bay were taken to use in a survey of existing conditions. Photo: Willcox Dunn.

An investigation of load-bearing elements, such as columns and beams, will establish whether these components are performing as they were originally designed, or the stress patterns have been redistributed. Areas that are abnormally stressed must be examined to ascertain whether they have suffered damage or have been displaced (Fig. 11). Damage to a primary structural member is obviously critical to identify and evaluate; attention should not be given only to decorative features.

The condition of the building, structure, or object; diagnosis of its problems; and recommendations for its repair should be recorded by drawings, photographs, and written descriptions, to aid those who will be responsible for its conservation in the future.

Whether minor or major work is required, the retention and repair of historic ironwork is the recommended preservation approach over replacement. All repairs and restoration work should be reversible, when possible, so that modifications or treatments that may turn out to be harmful to the long-term preservation of the iron can be corrected with the least amount of damage to the historic ironwork.

Cleaning and Paint Removal

When there is extensive failure of the protective coating and/or when heavy corrosion exists, the rust and most or all of the paint must be removed to prepare the surfaces for new protective coatings. The techniques available range from physical processes, such as wire brushing and grit blasting, to flame cleaning and chemical methods. The selection of an appropriate technique depends upon how much paint failure and corrosion has occurred, the fineness of the surface detailing, and the type of new protective coating to be applied. Local environmental regulations may restrict the options for cleaning and paint removal methods, as well as the disposal of materials.

Many of these techniques are *potentially dangerous* and should be carried out only by experienced and qualified workers using proper eye protection, protective clothing, and other workplace safety conditions. Before selecting a process, test panels should be prepared on the iron to be cleaned to determine the relative effectiveness of various techniques. The cleaning process will most likely expose additional coating defects, cracks, and corrosion that have not been obvious before (Fig. 12).

There are a number of techniques that can be used to remove paint and corrosion from cast iron:

Hand scraping, chipping, and wire brushing are the most common and least expensive methods of removing paint and light rust from cast iron (Fig. 13a, b). However, they do not remove all corrosion or paint as effectively as other methods. Experienced craftsmen should carry out the work to reduce the likelihood that surfaces may be scored or fragile detail damaged.

Low-pressure grit blasting (commonly called abrasive cleaning or sandblasting) is often the most effective approach to removing excessive paint build-up or substantial corrosion. Grit blasting is fast, thorough, and economical, and it allows the iron to be cleaned in place. The aggregate can be iron slag or sand; copper slag should not be used on iron because of the potential for electrolytic

Fig. 12. Paint stripping exposed a large defect under a faulty patch at a joint of this wide cast-iron watertable. The damage can be repaired mechanically by splicing in a cast-iron replacement piece. Photo: Peter Jensen, Kapell and Kostow Architects.

reactions. Some sharpness in the aggregate is beneficial in that it gives the metal surface a "tooth" that will result in better paint adhesion. The use of a very sharp or hard aggregate and/or excessively high pressure (over 100 pounds per square inch) is unnecessary and should be avoided. Adjacent materials, such as brick, stone, wood, and glass, must be protected to prevent damage. Some local building codes and environmental authorities prohibit or limit dry sandblasting because of the problem of airborne dust.

Wet sandblasting is more problematic than dry sandblasting for cleaning cast iron because the water will cause instantaneous surface rusting and will penetrate deep into open joints. Therefore, it is generally not considered an effective technique. Wet sandblasting reduces the amount of airborne dust when removing a heavy paint build-up, but disposal of effluent containing lead or other toxic substances is restricted by environmental regulations in most areas.

Flame cleaning of rust from metal with a special multi-flame head oxyacetylene torch requires specially skilled operators, and is expensive and potentially dangerous. However, it can be very effective on lightly to moderately corroded iron. Wire brushing is usually neccessary to finish the surface after flame cleaning.

Chemical rust removal, by acid pickling, is an effective method of removing rust from iron elements that can be easily removed and taken to a shop for submerging in vats of dilute phosphoric or sulfuric acid. This method does not damage the surface of iron, providing that the iron is neutralized to pH level 7 after cleaning. Other chemical rust removal agents include ammonium citrate, oxalic acid, or hydrochloric acid-based products.

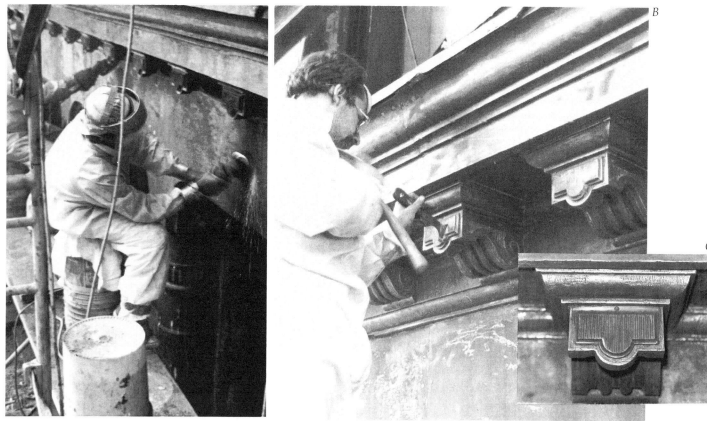

B

C

Fig. 13. Surface preparation may involve several different techniques. Where chemical paint stripping is involved, careful planning of the sequence of work and inspection by an architect or conservator to ensure strict compliance with the contract documents is important to minimize the risk of problems. After the chemical paste and paint was scraped off, the remaining paint and chemical residue were removed with a wire brush (a) and scrapers selected or cut to fit the shape of the iron surfaces (b). The surface was then wiped with solvent to create a completely clean surface prior to repainting(c). Photos: Raymond M. Pepi, Building Conservation Associates.

Chemical paint removal using alkaline compounds, such as methylene chloride or potassium hydroxide, can be an effective alternative to abrasive blasting for removal of heavy paint build-up (Fig. 13). These agents are often available as slow-acting gels or pastes. Because they can cause burns, protective clothing and eye protection must be worn. Chemicals applied to a non-watertight facade can seep through crevices and holes, resulting in damage to the building's interior finishes and corrosion to the backside of the iron components. If not thoroughly neutralized, residual traces of cleaning compounds on the surface of the iron can cause paint failures in the future (Fig. 14). For these reasons, field application of alkaline paint removers and acidic cleaners is not generally recommended.

Following any of these methods of cleaning and paint removal, the newly cleaned iron should be painted immediately with a corrosion-inhibiting primer before new rust begins to form. This time period may vary from minutes to hours depending on environmental conditions. If priming is delayed, any surface rust that has developed should be removed with a clean wire brush just before priming, because the rust prevents good bonding between the primer and the cast iron surface and prevents the primer from completely filling the pores of the metal.

Painting and Coating Systems

The most common and effective way to preserve architectural cast iron is to maintain a protective coating of paint on the metal. Paint can also be decorative, where historically appropriate .

Before removing paint from historic architectural cast iron, a microscopic analysis of samples of the historic paint sequencing is recommended. Called paint seriation analysis, this process must be carried out by an experienced architectural conservator. The analysis will identify the historic paint colors, and other conditions, such as whether the paint was matte or gloss, whether sand was added to the paint for texture, and whether the building was polychromed or marbleized. Traditionally many cast-iron elements were painted to resemble other materials, such as limestone or sandstone. Occasionally, features were faux-painted so that the iron appeared to be veined marble.

Thorough surface preparation is necessary for the adhesion of new protective coatings. All loose, flaking, and deteriorated paint must be removed from the iron, as well as dirt and mud, water-soluble salts, oil, and grease. Old paint that is tightly adhered may be left on the surface of the iron if it is compatible with the proposed coatings. The retention of old paint also preserves the historic paint sequence of the building and avoids the hazards of removal and disposal of old lead paint.

It is advisable to consult manufacturer's specifications or technical representatives to ensure compatibility between the surface conditions, primer and finish coats, and application methods.

For the paint to adhere properly, the metal surfaces must be absolutely dry before painting. Unless the paint selected is specifically designed for exceptional conditions, painting should not take place when the temperature is expected to fall below 50 degrees Fahrenheit within 24 hours or when the relative humidity is above 80 per cent; paint should not be applied when there is fog, mist, or rain in the air. Poorly prepared surfaces will cause the failure of even the best paints, while even moderately priced paints can be effective if applied over well-prepared surfaces.

Selection of Paints and Coatings

The types of paints available for protecting iron have changed dramatically in recent years due to federal, state, and local regulations that prohibit or restrict the manufacture and use of products containing toxic substances such as lead and zinc chromate, as well as volatile organic compounds and substances (VOC or VOS). Availability of paint types varies from state to state, and manufacturers continue to change product formulations to comply with new regulations.

Fig. 14. Major problems can result if work is undertaken without proper sequencing and precautions. On this building, a strong alkaline paint remover was used, and apparently was not adequately rinsed or neutralized. Over a period of months, the newly applied paint began to peel and streaks of rust appeared on the iron. Photo: Kim Lovejoy.

Traditionally, red lead has been used as an anti-corrosive pigment for priming iron. Red lead has a strong affinity for linseed oil and forms lead soaps, which become a tough and elastic film impervious to water that is highly effective as a protective coating for iron. At least two slow-drying linseed oil-based finish coats have traditionally been used over a red lead primer, and this combination is effective on old or partially-deteriorated surfaces. Today, in most areas, the use of paints containing lead is prohibited, except for some commercial and industrial purposes.

Today, alkyd paints are very widely used and have largely replaced lead-containing linseed-oil paints. They dry faster than oil paint, with a thinner film, but they do not protect the metal as long. Alkyd rust-inhibitive primers contain

pigments such as iron oxide, zinc oxide, and zinc phosphate. These primers are suitable for previously painted surfaces cleaned by hand tools. At least two coats of primer should be applied, followed by alkyd enamel finish coats.

Latex and other water-based paints are not recommended for use as primers on cast iron because they cause immediate oxidation if applied on bare metal. Vinyl acrylic latex or acrylic latex paints may be used as finish coats over alkyd rust-inhibitive primers, but if the primer coats are imperfectly applied or are damaged, the latex paint will cause oxidation of the iron. Therefore, alkyd finish coats are recommended.

High-performance coatings, such as zinc-rich primers containing zinc dust, and modern epoxy coatings, can be used on cast iron to provide longer-lasting protection. These coatings typically require highly clean surfaces and special application conditions which can be difficult to achieve in the field on large buildings (Fig. 13c). These coatings are used most effectively on elements which have been removed to a shop, or newly cast iron.

One particularly effective system has been first to coat commercially blast-cleaned iron with a zinc-rich primer, followed by an epoxy base coat, and two urethane finish coats. Some epoxy coatings can be used as primers on clean metal or applied to previously-painted surfaces in sound condition. Epoxies are particularly susceptible to degradation under ultraviolet radiation and must be protected by finish coats which are more resistant. There have been problems with epoxy paints which have been shop-applied to iron where the coatings have been nicked prior to installation. Field touching-up of epoxy paints is very difficult, if not impossible. This is a concern since iron exposed by imperfections in the base coat will be more likely to rust and more frequent maintenance will be required.

A key factor to take into account in selection of coatings is the variety of conditions on existing and new materials on a particular building or structure. One primer may be needed for surfaces with existing paint; another for newly cast, chemically stripped, or blast-cleaned cast iron; and a third for flashings or substitute materials; all three followed by compatible finish coats.

Application Methods

Brushing is the traditional and most effective technique for applying paint to cast iron. It provides good contact between the paint and the iron, as well as the effective filling of pits, cracks, and other blemishes in the metal. The use of spray guns to apply paint is economical, but does not always produce adequate and uniform coverage. For best results, airless sprayers should be used by skilled operators. To fully cover fine detailing and reach recesses, spraying of the primer coat, used in conjunction with brushing, may be effective.

Rollers should never be used for primer coat applications on metal, and are effective for subsequent coats only on large, flat areas. The appearance of spray-applied and roller-applied finish coats is not historically appropriate and should be avoided on areas such as storefronts which are viewed close at hand.

Caulking, Patching, and Mechanical Repairs

Most architectural cast iron is made of many small castings assembled by bolts or screws (Fig. 16a). Joints between pieces were caulked to prevent water from seeping in and causing rusting from the inside out. Historically, the seams were often caulked with white lead paste and sometimes backed with cotton or hemp rope; even the bolt and screw heads were caulked to protect them from the elements and to hide them from view. Although old caulking is sometimes found in good condition, it is typically crumbled from weathering, cracked from the structural settlement, or destroyed by mechanical cleaning. It is essential to replace deteriorated caulking to prevent water penetration. For good adhesion and performance, an architectural-grade polyurethane sealant or traditional white lead paste is preferred.

Water that penetrates the hollow parts of a cast-iron architectural element causes rust that may streak down over other architectural elements. The water may freeze, causing the ice to crack the cast iron. Cracks reduce the strength of the total cast-iron assembly and provide another point of entry for water. Thus, it is important that cracks be made weathertight by using caulks or fillers, depending on the width of the crack.

Filler compounds containing iron particles in an epoxy resin binder can be used to patch superficial, non-structural cracks and small defects in cast iron. The thermal expansion rate of epoxy resin alone is different from that of iron, requiring the addition of iron particles to ensure compatibility and to control shrinkage. Although the repaired piece of metal does not have the same strength as a homogeneous piece of iron, epoxy-repaired members do have some strength. Polyester-based putties, such as those used on auto bodies, are also acceptable fillers for small holes.

In rare instances, major cracks can be repaired by brazing or welding with special nickel-alloy welding rods. Brazing or welding of cast iron is very difficult to carry out in the field and should be undertaken only by very experienced welders.

In some cases, mechanical repairs can be made to cast iron using iron bars and screws or bolts. In extreme cases,

deteriorated cast iron can be cut out and new cast iron spliced in place by welding or brazing. However, it is frequently less expensive to replace a deteriorated cast-iron section with a new casting rather than to splice or reinforce it. Cast-iron structural elements that have failed must either be reinforced with iron and steel or replaced entirely.

A wobbly cast-iron balustrade or railing can often be fixed by tightening all bolts and screws. Screws with stripped threads and seriously rusted bolts must be replaced. To compensate for corroded metal around the bolt or screw holes, new stainless steel bolts or screws with a larger diameter need to be used. In extreme cases, new holes may need to be tapped.

The internal voids of balusters, newel posts, statuary, and other elements should not be filled with concrete; it is an inappropriate treatment that causes further problems (Fig. 15). As the concrete cures, it shrinks, leaving a space between the concrete and cast iron. Water penetrating this space does not evaporate quickly, thus promoting further rusting. The corrosion of the iron is further accelerated by the alkaline nature of concrete. Where cast-iron elements have been previously filled with concrete, they need to be taken apart, the concrete and rust removed, and the interior surfaces primed and painted before the elements are reassembled.

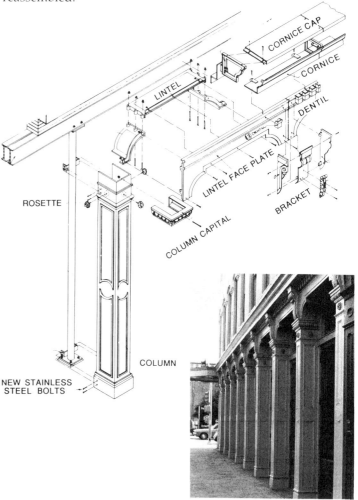

Fig. 15. In an effort to repair this stair railing, concrete was poured around the wood spacer inside the railing casting. Water penetrated the railing and reacted with the concrete to accelerate the corrosion of the iron. Photo: John G. Waite.

Fig. 16. Architectural cast iron is made of many small components bolted and screwed together. (a) This exploded view of a storefront illustrates the variety of elements, including brackets, fasteners, and holes for bolts. (b) The storefront was replicated in cast iron because of the extensive damage and structural failure, a detail of which is shown in Fig. 11. Drawing and photo: Historical Arts & Casting, Inc.

Duplication and Replacement

The replacement of cast-iron components is often the only practical solution when such features are missing, severely corroded, or damaged beyond repair, or where repairs would be only marginally useful in extending the functional life of an iron element (Fig. 16).

Sometimes it is possible to replace small, decorative, non-structural elements using intact sections of the original as a casting pattern. For large sections, new patterns of wood or plastic made slightly larger in size than the original will need to be made in order to compensate for the shrinkage of the iron during casting (cast iron shrinks approximately 1/8 inch per foot as it cools from a liquid into a solid). Occasionally, a matching replacement can be obtained from the existing catalogs of iron foundries. Small elements can be custom cast in iron at small local foundries, often at a cost comparable to substitute materials. Large elements and complex patterns will usually require the skills and facilities of a larger firm that specializes in replication.

The Casting Process

Architectural elements were traditionally cast in sand molds. The quality of the special sands used by foundries is extremely important; unlike most sands they must be moist. Foundries have their own formulas for sand and its admixtures, such as clay, which makes the sand cohesive even when the mold is turned upside down.

A two-part mold (with a top and a bottom, or cope and drag) is used for making a casting with relief on both sides, whereas an open-top mold produces a flat surface on one side (Fig. 17a). For hollow elements, a third pattern and mold are required for the void. Many hollow castings are made of two or more parts that are later bolted, screwed, or welded together, because of the difficulty of supporting an interior core between the top and bottom sand molds during the casting process.

The molding sand is compacted into flasks, or forms, around the pattern. The cope is then lifted off and the pattern is removed, leaving the imprint of the pattern in the small mold. Molten iron, heated to a temperature of approximately 2700 degrees Fahrenheit, is poured into the mold and then allowed to cool (Fig. 17b). The molds are then stripped from the casting; the tunnels to the mold (sprues) and risers that allowed release of air are cut off; and ragged edges (called "burrs") on the casting are ground smooth.

The castings are shop-primed to prevent rust, and laid out and preassembled at the foundry to ensure proper alignment and fit. When parts do not fit, the pieces are machined to remove irregularities caused by burrs, or are rejected and recast until all of the cast elements fit together properly. Most larger pieces then are taken apart before shipping to the job site, while some small ornamental parts may be left assembled.

Fig. 17. (a) A two-part mold, consisting of a cope (top) and drag (bottom) for a newel post. Photo: Architectural Iron Company, Inc.
(b) Molten iron being poured into a mold containing sand at a foundry. The iron casting process has changed little in the past two centuries.
Photo: Karen Huebner.

Fig. 18. This cast-iron storefront cornice was corroded beyond the point of repair, and could not be removed easily for replacement. Terne-coated stainless steel, the most durable metal for flashing cast iron, was applied to the cornice and fitted as closely as possible to the historic profile. Although painting is not necessary to protect terne-coated stainless steel, the cornice should be painted to be consistent with the historic character of the building. A primer which is compatible with the terne coating should be used. Photo: Dean Koga, Robert E. Meadows, P.C., Architects.

Dismantling and Assembly of Architectural Components

It is sometimes necessary to dismantle all or part of a cast-iron structure during restoration, if repairs cannot be successfully carried out in place. Dismantling should be done only under the direction of a preservation architect or architectural conservator who is experienced with historic cast iron. Extreme care must be taken since cast iron is very brittle, especially in cold weather.

Dismantling should follow the reverse order of construction and re-erection should occur, as much as possible, in the exact order of original assembly. Each piece should be numbered and keyed to record drawings. When work must be carried out in cold weather, care needs to be taken to avoid fracturing the iron elements by uneven heating of the members.

Both new castings and reused pieces should be painted with a shop-applied prime coat on all surfaces. All of the components should be laid out and preassembled to make sure that the alignment and fit are proper. Many of the original bolts, nuts, and screws may have to be replaced with similar fasteners of stainless steel.

After assembly at the site, joints that were historically caulked should be filled with an architectural-grade polyurethane sealant or the traditional white lead paste. White lead has the advantage of longevity, although its use is restricted in many areas.

Flashings

In some instances, it may be necessary to design and install flashings to protect areas vulnerable to water penetration. Flashings need to be designed and fabricated carefully so that they are effective, as well as unobtrusive in appearance. The most durable material for flashing iron is terne-coated stainless steel (Fig. 18). Other compatible materials are terne-coated steel and galvanized steel; however, these require more frequent maintenance and are less durable. Copper and lead-coated copper are not recommended for use as flashings in contact with cast iron because of galvanic corrosion problems. Galvanic problems can also occur with the use of aluminum if certain types of electrolytes are present.

Substitute Materials

In recent years, a number of metallic and non-metallic materials have been used as substitutes for cast iron, although they were not used historically with cast iron. The most common have been cast aluminum, epoxies, reinforced polyester (fiberglass), and glass fiber-reinforced concrete (GFRC). Factors to consider in using substitute materials are addressed in **Preservation Briefs 16**, which emphasizes that "every means of repairing deteriorating historic materials or replacing them with identical materials should be examined before turning to substitute materials."

Cast aluminum has been used recently as a substitute for cast iron, particularly for ornately-detailed decorative elements. Aluminum is lighter in weight, more resistant to corrosion, and less brittle than cast iron. However, because it is dissimilar from iron, its placement in contact with or near cast iron may result in galvanic corrosion, and thus should be avoided. Special care must be taken in the application of paint coatings, particularly in the field. It is often difficult to achieve a durable coating after the original finish has failed. Because aluminum is weaker than iron, careful analysis is required whenever aluminum is being considered as a replacement material for structural cast-iron elements.

Epoxies are two-part, thermo-setting, resinous materials which can be molded into virtually any form. When molded, the epoxy is usually mixed with fillers such as sand, glass balloons, or stone chips. Since it is not a metal, galvanic corrosion does not occur. When mixed with sand or stone, it is often termed epoxy concrete or polymer concrete, a misnomer because no cementitious materials are included. Epoxies are particularly effective for replicating small, ornamental sections of cast iron. Since it is not a metal, galvanic corrosion does not occur. Epoxy elements must have a protective coating to shield them from ultraviolet degradation. They are also flammable and cannot be used as substitutes for structural cast-iron elements.

Reinforced polyester, commonly known as *fiberglass*, is often used as a lightweight substitute for historic materials, including cast iron, wood, and stone. In its most common form, fiberglass is a thin, rigid, laminate shell formed by pouring a polyester resin into a mold and then adding fiberglass for reinforcement. Like epoxies, fiberglass is non-

Fig. 20. The location of the feature must be taken into account if a substitute replacement material is being considered. This lightweight fiberglass column at street level sustained damage from impact within a few years of installation. The great strength of cast iron makes it ideal for storefronts and elements that must withstand heavy use. Photo: Building Conservation Associates.

Fig. 19. (a) Fiberglass columns and aluminum capitals were installed to replicate the ornamental features on the east facade of the New Market Theater in Portland, Oregon, that had been destroyed by previous occupants. Like cast iron, crisp ornamental details can be achieved with cast aluminum. Although aluminum may be in contact with fiberglass, galvanic corrosion may result when aluminum is in direct contact with cast iron. Photo: William J. Hawkins, III · (b) The west facade of the theatre retains its original cast iron features. Photo: George McMath.

corrosive, but is susceptible to ultraviolet degradation. Because of its rather flimsy nature, it cannot be used as a substitute for structural elements, cannot be assembled like cast iron and usually requires a separate anchorage system. It is unsuitable for locations where it is susceptible to damage by impact (Fig. 20), and is also flammable.

Glass fiber-reinforced concrete, known as *GFRC*, is similar to fiberglass except that a lightweight concrete is substituted for the resin. GFRC elements are generally fabricated as thin shell panels by spraying concrete into forms. Usually a separate framing and anchorage system is required. GFRC elements are lightweight, inexpensive, and weather resistant. Because GFRC has a low shrinkage co-efficient, molds can be made directly from historic elements.

However, GFRC is very different physically and chemically from iron. If used adjacent to iron, it causes corrosion of the iron and will have a different moisture absorption rate. Also, it is not possible to achieve the crisp detail that is characteristic of cast iron.

Maintenance

A successful maintenance program is the key to the long-term preservation of architectural cast iron. Regular inspections and accurate record-keeping are essential. Biannual inspections, occurring ideally in the spring and fall, include the identification of major problems, such as missing elements and fractures, as well as minor items such as failed caulking, damaged paint, and surface dirt.

Records should be kept in the form of a permanent maintenance log which describes routine maintenance tasks and records the date a problem is first noted, when it was corrected, and the treatment method. Painting records are important for selecting compatible paints for touch-up and subsequent repainting. The location of the work and the type, manufacturer, and color of the paint should be noted in the log. The same information also should be assembled and recorded for caulking.

Superficial dirt can be washed off well-painted and caulked cast iron with low-pressure water. Non-ionic detergents may be used for the removal of heavy or tenacious dirt or stains, after testing to determine that they have no adverse effects on the painted surfaces. Thick grease deposits and residue can be removed by hand scraping. Water and detergents or non-caustic degreasing agents can be used to clean off the residue. Before repainting, oil and grease must be removed so that new coatings will adhere properly.

The primary purpose of the maintenance program is to control corrosion. As soon as rusting is noted, it should be carefully removed and the protective coating of the iron renewed in the affected area. Replacement of deteriorated caulking, and repair or replacement of failed flashings are also important preventive maintenance measures.

Summary

The successful conservation of cast-iron architectural elements and objects is dependent upon an accurate diagnosis of their condition and the problems affecting them, as well as the selection of appropriate repair, cleaning, and painting procedures. Frequently, it is necessary to undertake major repairs to individual elements and assemblies; in some cases badly damaged or missing components must be replicated. The long-term preservation of architectural cast iron is dependent upon both the undertaking of timely, appropriate repairs and the commitment to a regular schedule of maintenance.

Detail of polychromed cast-iron facade at 23 Petaluma Boulevard, Petaluma, Calif. (1886; O'Connell and Lewis, Architectural Iron Work, San Francisco). Photo: Don Meacham.

Reading List

Ashurst, John, and Nicola Ashurst with Geoff Wallis and Dennis Toner. *Practical Building Conservation: English Heritage Technical Handbook: Volume 4 Metals.* Aldershot, Hants: Gower Technical Press, 1988.

Badger, Daniel D., with a new introduction by Margot Gayle. *Badger's Illustrated Catalogue of Cast-Iron Architecture.* New York: Dover Publications, Inc., 1981; reprint of 1865 edition published by Baker & Godwin, Printers, New York.

Gayle, Margot, and Edmund V. Gillon, Jr. *Cast-Iron Architecture in New York: A Photographic Survey.* New York: Dover Publications Inc., 1974.

Gayle, Margot, David W. Look, AIA, and John G. Waite. *Metals in America's Historic Buildings: Part I. A Historical Survey of Metals; Part II. Deterioration and Methods of Preserving Metals.* Washington, D.C.: Preservation Assistance Division, National Park Service, U.S. Department of the Interior, 1980.

Hawkins, William John III. *The Grand Era of Cast Iron Architecture in Portland.* Portland, Oregon: Binford & Mort, 1976.

Howell, J. Scott. *"Architectural Cast Iron: Design and Restoration,"* The *Journal of the Association for Preservation Technology.* Vol XIX, Number 3 (1987), pp. 51-55.

Park, Sharon C., AIA. *Preservation Briefs 16: The Use of Substitute Materials on Historic Building Exteriors.* Washington D. C.: Preservation Assistance Division, National Park Service, U. S. Department of the Interior, 1988.

Robertson, E. Graeme, and Joan Robertson. *Cast Iron Decoration: A World Survey.* New York: Watson-Guptill Publications, 1977.

Southworth, Susan and Michael. *Ornamental Ironwork: An Illustrated Guide to Its Design, History, and Use in American Architecture.* Boston: David R. Godine, 1978.

Waite, Diana S. *Ornamental Ironwork: Two Centuries of Craftsmanship in Albany and Troy, New York.* Albany, NY: Mount Ida Press, 1990.

Acknowledgements

This Preservation Brief was developed by the New York Landmarks Conservancy's Technical Preservation Services Center under a cooperative agreement with the National Park Service's Preservation Assistance Division, and with partial funding from the New York State Council on the Arts. The following individuals are to be thanked for their technical assistance: Robert Baird, Historical Arts & Casting; Willcox Dunn, Architect and Cast Iron Consultant; William Foulks, Mesick Cohen Waite Architects; Elizabeth Frosch, New York City Landmarks Preservation Commission; William Hawkins, III, FAIA, McMath Hawkins Dortignacq; J. Scott Howell, Robinson Iron Company; David Look, AIA, National Park Service; Donald Quick, Architectural Iron Company; Maurice Schickler, Facade Consultants International; Joel Schwartz, Schwartz and Schwartz Metalworks; and Diana Waite, Mount Ida Press. Kim Lovejoy was project coordinator and editor for the Conservancy; Charles Fisher was project coordinator and editor for the National Park Service.

This publication has been prepared pursuant to the National Historic Preservation Act amendments of 1980, which direct the Secretary of the Interior to develop and make available information concerning historic properties. Comments on the usefulness of this information and information on how to obtain copies may be directed either to the Chief, Preservation Assistance Division, National Park Service, U.S. Department of the Interior, P.O. Box 37127, Washington, D.C. 20013-7127, or to the Director, Technical Preservation Services Center, New York Landmarks Conservancy, 141 Fifth Avenue, New York, NY 10010.

28

Painting Historic Interiors

Sara B. Chase

The paint Americans used in the past is undeniably part of a technological and commercial record. But beyond that, the colors we have chosen and continue to select for our interior living and working spaces—bright and exuberant, purposefully somber, or a combination of hues—reflect our nation's cultural influences and our individual and collective spirit (see Figures 1, 2). Paint color is a simple, direct expression of the time, and of taste, values, and mood. To consider paint only as a protective coating is to misunderstand its meaning as an important aspect of America's heritage.

This Brief is about historic interior paints and choosing new paints for historic interiors if repainting is necessary or desirable. It addresses a variety of materials and features: plaster walls and ceilings; wooden doors, molding, and trim; and metal items such as radiators and railings. It provides background information about some of the types of paint which were used in the past, discusses the more common causes and effects of interior paint failure, and explains the principal factors guiding decisions about repainting, including what level of paint investigation may be appropriate. Careful thought should be given to each interior paint project, depending on the history of the building and its painted surfaces. Treatments may range from protecting extant decorative surfaces, to ordering custom-made paint that replicates the original paint color, to using today's paint straight off the shelf and out of the can.

Finally, stripping old paints or applying new oil/alkyd paints poses serious health and safety concerns; the State Historic Preservation Officer should be contacted for current legal and technical information on removal, disposal, and health and safety precautions.

Constituents of Historic Paint: Pigment, Binder, and Vehicle

Paint is a dispersion of small solid particles, usually crystalline, in a liquid

Figure 1. Researching the interior paint history is the key to a successful preservation or restoration project. The decorative detailing can be appreciated in this Puerto Rico theater primarily because of appropriate paint color and paint placement. Photo: Max Toro.

A

B

Figure 2. Paints—plain and colored—have been used throughout our history to define and accent interior spaces. Three examples serve to illustrate a variety of geographical and cultural influences, building types and uses, and interior designs from the 18th to the 20th century. (a) San Jose de Gracia Church, Las Trampas, New Mexico (1760). Photo: Kirk Gittings. (b) Frank Lloyd Wright Home and Studio, Oak Park, Ilinois (1889-98). Photo: Philip Turner for HABS. (c) U. S. Customs House, Trading Floor (1908), New York City. Photo: National Park Service files.

C

Early tinting pigments for house paints consisted of the earth pigments—ochres, siennas, umbers made from iron-oxide-containing clay—and a few synthesized colorants such as Prussian blue, or mercuric sulfide (crimson). From the early 1800s on more pigments were developed and used to offer a wider and brighter variety of hues.

Binder. The most common binder in interior paints was, and still is, oil. Chalk was sometimes added to water-based paints to help bind the pigment particles together. Other common binders included hide glue and gelatin.

Vehicle. The fluid component was termed the vehicle, or medium, because it carried the pigment. Historically, vehicles included turpentine in oil paints and water in water-based paints, but other vehicles were sometimes used, such as milk in casein paints.

Oil-Based and Water-Based Paints

The two major types of paint are termed oil-based and water-based. For *oil-based paints,* linseed oil was frequently chosen because it is a drying oil. When thinned with an organic solvent such as turpentine for easier spreading, its drying speed was enhanced. To make the drying even faster, drying agents such as cobalt compounds were frequently added. Because the addition of driers was most successfully done in hot or boiling oil, boiled linseed oil was preferable. The drying rate of linseed oil paints was relatively rapid at first, for several days immediately after application, and paint soon felt dry to the touch; it is important to remember, however, that linseed oil paint continues to dry—or more precisely, to cross-link—over decades and thus continues to a point of brittleness as the paint ages. Strong and durable with a surface sheen, oil-based paints were mainly used for wood trim and metal.

Whitewashes and distemper paints differed from oil paints in appearance primarily because the vehicle was water. *Water-based paints* were always flat, having no gloss of their own. Because the paint film dried to the touch as soon as

medium. Applied to a surface, this liquid has the special quality of becoming a solid, protective film when it dries. Paint also enhances the appearance of surfaces. A late Victorian writer observed that the coming of a painter to a house was cause for celebration. Indeed, these statements not only indicate the chemical and physical complexity of paint, but also its emotional impact.

Pigment. Pigment made the paint opaque, thus preventing deterioration of the substrate caused by ultra-violet light, and added color, thus making the paint attractive. White lead, a whitish corrosion product of lead, was most often used to provide opacity. The white pigment in a colored paint is often called the "hiding" pigment. In addition to preventing the sun's damaging rays from hitting the surface of the substrate, the white lead also helped prevent the growth of mold and mildew. Not until early in the 20th century was a successful substitute, titanium dioxide (TiO_2), patented, and even then, it did not come into prevalent use by itself until the mid-20th century (earlier in the century, titanium oxide and white lead were often mixed). Zinc oxide was used briefly as a hiding pigment after 1850 (see Figure 3).

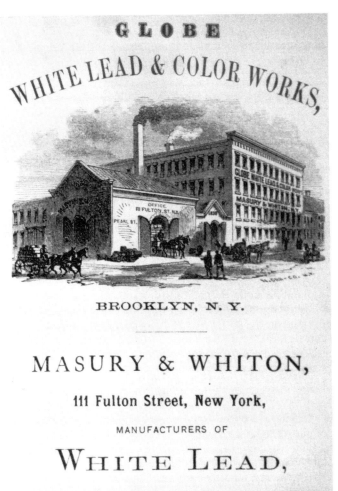

GLOBE
WHITE LEAD & COLOR WORKS,

BROOKLYN, N. Y.

MASURY & WHITON,

111 Fulton Street, New York,

MANUFACTURERS OF

WHITE LEAD,

FRENCH AND AMERICAN ZINC,

AND

Painters' Colors.

Figure 3. There were numerous companies producing white lead in the United States by mid-19th century. Shown is one manufacturer's trade flyer. Of note, production figures for white lead showed a marked increase after 1850, but a steady decline after 1880. This was, in part, due to a change of taste and style at the end of the 19th century—stains and clear finishes were preferred over opaque paints for interior decorative treatments.

the water evaporated, driers were not needed. Water-base paints were fairly strong, with the pigments well bound as in hide glue distempers, but they did not hold up to abrasion. Wood trim, therefore, was rarely painted with these types of paint historically, though interior plaster surfaces were frequently coated with whitewash and calcimine. Distemper paints were commonly used for decorative work.

Recent Changes to Paint Constituents. Until the mid-20th century, almost all paints used in America could be divided according to the type of binder each had. Chemists sought to improve paints, especially when the two world wars made traditional paint components scarce and expensive. Modern paints are far more complex chemically and physically than early paints. More ingredients have been added to the simple three-part system of pigment, binder, and vehicle. Fillers or extenders such as clay and chalk were put in to make oil paints flow better and to make them

Types of Historic Paints

Historic paints were often made with what was available, rather than adhering to strict formulas. Recipes for successful formulas can be found in historic documents, such as newspapers, illustrating the combinations of ingredients which could be used to produce a paint.

Oil-based paints: Linseed oil, a volatile thinner such as turpentine; a hiding pigment (usually white lead) and coloring pigments.

Enamels: natural resin varnish was added to oil-based paint to provide a hard, more glossy surface.

Glaze: a translucent layer applied to protect the paint and to impart a more uniform gloss surface. Usually made from linseed oil with natural resin varnish added. Some glazes have small quantities of tinting pigments such as verdigris or Prussian blue; some had no pigments added.

Water-based paints: Water, pigment, and a binder, such as hide glue, other natural glues, or gums. Usually used on interior plaster surfaces.

Whitewash: often used on interior plaster surfaces in utilitarian spaces and, at times, used on interior beams; consisted of water, slaked lime, salt, and a variety of other materials. Occasionally a pigment (usually an ochre or other earth pigment) was added to provide tint or color.

Distemper: used for interior applications, were made from water, glues (one or more different natural glues, gelatine, and gums) with whiting as the basic white pigment to which other tinting pigments were added.

Calcimine, or kalsomine: often used on interior surfaces and is another common name for distemper.

Tempera: paint prepared with pigment, egg yolk or white and water; used almost exclusively for decorative treatments.

Gouache: a water-based paint made of whiting, pigment, water, and gum arabic as the binder; used almost exclusively for decorative treatments.

Milk-based paint:

Casein: also called milk paint, was made with hydrated (slaked) lime, pigment, and milk. Most often oil was added, making a strong emulsion paint. Various recipes call for a large variety of additives to increase durability. Casein paints were also used for exterior surfaces.

cheaper as well. Mildewcides and fungicides were prevalent and popular until their environmental hazards were seen to outweigh their benefits. New formulations which retard the growth of the mildew and fungi are being used. As noted, lead was eliminated after 1950. Most recently, volatile organic solvents in oil paint and thinners have been categorized as environmentally hazardous.

A major difference in modern paints is the change in binder from the use of natural boiled linseed oil to an alkyd oil which is generally derived from soybean or safflower oil. Use of synthetic resins, such as acrylics and epoxies, has become prevalent in paint manufacture in the last 30 years or so. Acrylic resin emulsions in latex paints, with water thinners, have also become common.

Pre-1875 Paints

Production and Appearance. How were paints made prior to the widespread use of factory-made paint after 1875? How did they look? The answers to these questions are provided more to underscore the differences between early paints and today's paints than for practical purposes. Duplicating the composition and appearance of historic paints, including the unevenness of color, the irregularity of surface texture, the depth provided by a glaze topcoat, and the directional lines of application, can be extremely challenging to a contemporary painter who is using modern materials.

The pigments used in early paints were coarsely and unevenly ground, and they were dispersed in the paint medium by hand; thus, there is a subtle unevenness of color across the surface of many pre-1875 paints (see Figure 4). The dry pigments had to be ground in oil to form a paste and the paste had to be successively thinned with more oil and turpentine before the paint was ready for application. The thickness of the oil medium produced the shiny surface desired in the 18th century. In combination with the cylindrical (or round) shaped brushes with wood handles and boar bristles, it also produced a paint film with a surface texture of brush strokes.

Figure 4. The Boston Stone (1737), a surviving relic of early paint production, was used for pigment grinding in the shop of Thomas Child of Boston, a London-trained painter and stainer. The early paint-grinding tool is the logo of the National Paint and Coatings Association. Photo: Courtesy, SPNEA.

Geographical Variation. The early churches and missions built by the French in Canada and the Spanish in the southwestern United States often had painted decoration on whitewashed plaster walls, done with early water-based paints. By the mid-17th century oil paint was applied to wood trim in many New England houses, and whitewash was applied to walls. These two types of paint, one capable of highly decorative effects such as imitating marble or expensive wood and the other cheap to make and relatively easy to apply, brightened and enhanced American interiors. In cities such as Boston, Philadelphia, New York, and later, Washington, painters and stainers who were trained guildsmen from England practiced their craft and instructed apprentices. The painter's palette of colors included black and white and grays, buffs and tans, ochre yellows and iron oxide reds, and greens (from copper compounds) as well as Prussian blue. That such painting

was valued and that a glossy appearance on wood was important are substantiated by evidence of clear and tinted glazes which may be found by microscopic examination.

Brush Marks. Early paints did not dry out to a flat level surface. Leveling, in fact, was a property of paint that was much sought after later, but until well into the 19th century, oil paints and whitewashes showed the signs of brush marks. Application therefore was a matter of stroking the brush in the right direction for the best appearance. The rule of thumb was to draw the brush in its final stokes in the direction of the grain of the wood. Raised-field paneling, then, required that the painter first cover the surface with paint and afterward draw the brush carefully along the vertical areas from bottom to top and along the top and bottom bevels of the panel horizontally from one side to the other.

In the 19th and early 20th centuries, for very fine finishes, several coats were applied with each coat being rubbed down with rotten stone or pumice after drying. A four to five coat application was typical; however nine coats were not uncommon at the end of the century for finishes in some of the grand mansions. Generally, they were given a final glaze finish. Though expensive, this type of finish would last for decades and give a rich, smooth appearance.

Color. Color matching is complicated by the fact that all early paints were made by hand. Each batch of paint, made by painters using books of paint "recipes" or using their own experience and instincts, might well have slight variations in color—a little darker or lighter, a little bluer and so on. The earliest known book of paint formulations by an American painter is the 1812 guide by Hezekiah Reynolds. It gives instructions for the relative quantities of tinting pigments to be added to a base, but even with proportions held constant, the amount of mixing, or dispersion, varied from workman to workman and resulted in color variations.

Knowing all of the facts about early paints can aid in microscopic paint study. For example, finding very finely and evenly ground pigments, equally dispersed throughout the ground or vehicle, is an immediate clue that the paint was not made by hand but, rather, in a factory.

By the first decades of the 19th century more synthetic pigments were available—chrome yellow, chrome green, and shades of red. Discoveries of light, bright, clear colors in the plaster and mosaic decoration of dwellings at Pompeii caught the fancy of many Americans and came together with the technology of paint to make for a new palette of choice, with more delicacy than many of the somewhat greyed-down colors of the 18th century. Of course, the blues which could be produced with Prussian blue in the 18th and 19th centuries were originally often strong in hue. That pigment—as were a number of others—is fugitive, that is, it faded fairly quickly and thus softened in appearance. It should be remembered that high style houses from the mid-17th to late 19th centuries often had wallpaper rather than paint on the walls of the important rooms and hallways.

Glossy/Flat. Another paint innovation of the early 19th century was the use of flatter oil paints achieved by adding more turpentine to the oil, which thus both thinned and flatted them. By the 1830s the velvety look of flat paint was popular. Wherever decorative plaster was present, as it frequently was during the height of the Federal period, distemper paints were the coating of choice. Being both thin and readily removable with hot water, they permitted the delicate plaster moldings and elaborate floral or botanical elements to be protected and tinted but not obscured by the buildup of many paint layers. (The use of water-based paints on ceilings continued through the Victorian years for the same reasons.)

Unfortunately, flat paints attract dirt, which is less likely to adhere to high gloss surfaces, and are thus harder to wash. Victorians tended to use high gloss clear (or tinted) finishes such as varnish or shellac on much of their wood trim and to use flat or oil paints on walls and ceilings.

Decorative Painting. In interiors, paint could be used creatively and imaginatively, most often to decorate rather than to protect. Decorative forms included stencilling, graining and marbleizing, and *trompe l'oeil* (see Figures 5, 6).

Figure 5. Owners of historic properties often find evidence of decorative painting on interior walls; however, the task of actually preserving or restoring decorative work, such as the complex stencilling pictured here, should only be undertaken by professionals who have specialized training and field experience. Photo: Courtesy, Alexis Elza.

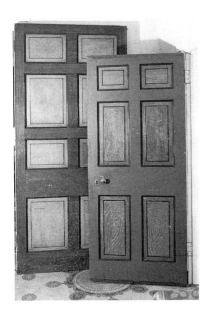

Figure 6. Historic doors may have graining patterns or clear finishes under one or several coats of plain paint, such as these restored 18th and early 19th century doors. Graining may appear even on more vernacular doors of the pre-1850 vintage. Photo: Jack E. Boucher for HABS.

Stencilling. Stencilled designs on walls were often used in the first half of the 19th century in place of wallpaper. Old Sturbridge Village, in Massachusetts, has paintings showing the interiors of a (c. 1815-1820) farmhouse which has both stencilled walls—imitating wallpaper—and painted floors or oiled and painted floor cloths, imitating fine carpets. By 1850 and for the next 60 years thereafter, stencilled and freehand-painted decoration for walls and ceilings became a high as well as a humble art. Owen Jones' ***Grammar of Ornament,*** published in 1859, provided the source for painted decoration from Portland to Peoria, Savannah to San Francisco.

Graining and marbleizing. If floors, walls, and ceilings were decorated by paint in a variety of styles, the wood and stone trim of rooms was not omitted. The use of *faux bois,* that is, painting a plain or common wood such as pine to look like mahogany or some finer wood, or *faux marbre,* painting a wood or plaster surface to look like marble—realistically or fantastically—was common in larger homes of the 18th century. By the early 19th century, both stylized graining and marbleizing adorned the simple rural or small town houses as well. Often baseboards and stair risers were marbleized as were fireplace surrounds. Plain slate was painted to look like fine Italian marble. In many simple buildings, and, later, in the Victorian period, many prominent buildings such as town halls and churches, the wood trim was given a realistic graining to resemble quarter sawn oak, walnut, or a host of other exotic woods.

Trompe L'oeil. Churches, courthouses, and state capitols frequently received yet another remarkable use of paint: *trompe l'oeil* decoration. Applied by skilled artists and artisans, painted designs—most often using distemper paints or oils—could replicate three-dimensional architectural detailing such as ornate molded plaster moldings, medallions, panels, and more.

Factory-Made Paints after 1875

An enormous growth of the paint industry began in the 1860s, stimulated by the invention of a suitable marketing container—the paint can. The first factory-made paints in cans consisted of more finely ground pigments in an oil base; after purchase, additional oil was added to the contents of the can to make up the paint. Such paints saved the time of hand-grinding pigments, and were discussed at length by John Masury in his numerous books. After 1875, factory-made paints were available at a reasonable cost and, as a result, greater numbers of people painted and decorated more of their buildings, and more frequently. The new commercial market created by ready-mixed paint became the cornerstone of our modern paint industry (see Figure 7).

20th Century Paints

By the early decades of the 20th century, popular taste turned away from exuberant colors and decoration. Until the late 1920s both the Colonial Revival and Arts and Crafts styles tended toward more subdued colors and, in the case of Colonial Revival, a more limited palette. The use of *faux* finishes, however, continued. Residential architecture often featured stencilling, such as painted borders above wainscoting or at ceiling and wall edges to imitate decorative wallpaper. Institutional buildings in both cities

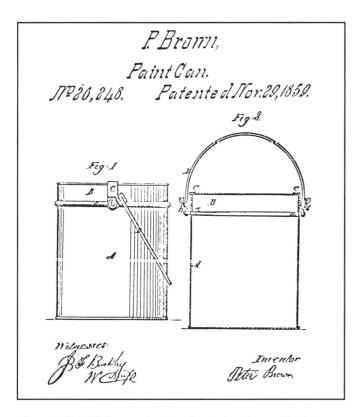

Figure 7. This 1857 patent drawing of a paint can invented by Peter Brown shows a remarkable similarity in design to today's containers. An airtight, carryable container allowed the sale of small amounts of paint. It helped revolutionize the paint industry for typical consumers in the late 19th century because paint was now essentially available to anyone who wanted it.

Figure 8. The lobby foyer of the Paramount Theater in Sacramento, California (1931) features painted plaster columns and cornices which have been finished in gold and silver leaf. The theater, a National Historic Landmark, is noted for its Art Deco style. Photo: Gabriel Moulin Studios.

and small towns used wood graining on metal-clad doors, door and window frames, and staircases, and had stencilled ceilings as well. Many high style public buildings of the 1920s had painted ceilings which imitated the Spanish and Italian late medieval and Renaissance styles.

Although stenciling, gilding, and *faux* finishes can be found, they did not express the modern style of the time. On the other hand, glaze treatments were often used in the early 20th century to "antique" walls and trim that had been painted with neutral colors, especially in Spanish Colonial Revival and Mission architecture. The glazes were applied by ragging, sponging, and other techniques which gave an interesting and uneven surface appearance. Colored plasters were sometimes used, and air brushing employed to give a craftsmanlike appearance to walls, trim, and ceilings. During the same period, Williamsburg paint colors were produced and sold to people who wanted their houses to have a "historic Georgian look." Churches, country clubs, and many private buildings adopted the Williamsburg style from the late 20s onward.

Often decorated with simple molded plaster designs of the Art Deco and Art Moderne styles, interiors of the 1930s and 1940s were frequently accented with metal flake paints in a full range of metallic colors, from copper to bronze (see Figure 8). And enamels, deep but subdued hues, became popular. Paint technology had progressed and varying degrees of gloss were also available, including the mid-range enamels, variously called satin, semi-gloss, or eggshell. In contrast to Victorian paint treatments, this period was characterized by simplicity. To some extent, the

Bauhaus aesthetic influenced taste in the 1950s; interior paints were frequently chosen from a palette limited to a few "earth" colors and a "nearly neutral" palette of off-whites and pale greys.

While the trend in colors and decorative treatments was defined by its simplicity, paint chemists were developing paints of increasing complexity. Experimentation had started early in the 20th century and accelerated greatly after World War II. Of greatest significance was the manufacture of the latex paints for consumer use. Synthetic resin emulsions carried in water offered advantages over the traditional oil paints, and even over the oil/alkyd paints: they did not yellow; they permitted water clean-up until dried; and they emitted no toxic or hazardous fumes from solvent evaporation.

Paint Investigation

Understanding each project's historic preservation goal and knowing what level of information needs to be collected to achieve that goal is an important responsibility of the purchaser of the service. Before someone is hired, the owner or manager needs to decide if a thorough investigation of painted surfaces is actually needed, and *how* to use the results when one is done.

Specialists with both training and field experience conduct paint investigations. These experts use sophisticated instruments and procedures such as field sampling, cross-section analysis, and fluorescent and chemical staining to learn about the components and behaviors of historic paints (see Figure 9). In addition, they utilize written documentation, verbal research, and visual information about past painting in the building in conjunction with findings in the field (Figure 10).

Paint investigation can make several contributions to a project. A complete analysis of the paint layers on surfaces within a structure can tell a great deal about the sequence of alterations that have occurred within a building, as well

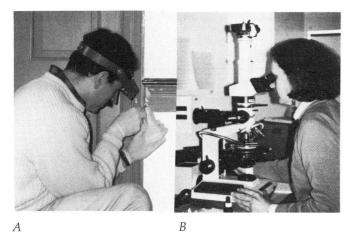

A   B

Figure 9. Conservators are shown in the two-part process of conducting a complete paint investigation: (a) Paint samples are carefully collected onsite. (b) In the laboratory, an ultra violet light microscope is used to identify pigment and binding media. Paint samples are photographed with the camera mounted on top of the microscope. (right). Photo left: Courtesy, Matthew J. Mosca; Photo right: Courtesy, Andrea M. Gilmore.

Figure 10. Written, oral, and pictorial documentation—such as this historical rendering—are combined with essential field research to provide the framework for sound historic preservation decisions. Photo: Courtesy, SPNEA.

as potentially providing ranges of dates for some of these changes. By establishing a full sequence of paint layers (termed a *chromochronology*), together with other research, alterations of various building spaces and features can be associated with specific paint layers. It is by establishing this association that the correct layer is identified; when the correct layer has been identified, the color may be matched.

In addition to its archeological value, paint analysis can determine the types and colors of paint on a given surface (identification of thin glazes, decorative paint schemes, binders and pigments). Beyond color identification, then,

paint analysis is also recommended to diagnose causes of paint failure. Knowing a paint binder can often explain causes as well as guide appropriate preservation or conservation treatments.

Owners and managers should identify all of these needs before deciding on the extent of analysis. For example, a complete paint investigation is usually recommended as part of an historic structure report. For buildings with little documentation, additions and alterations can often be identified, and possibly dated, through analysis. Often the use of such seemingly expensive techniques can save money in the long run when determining the history of building change.

It is possible to do some analysis on site; this is a much simpler process that can be undertaken for less cost than the complex laboratory procedures described above. However, the usefulness of onsite analysis is limited and the results will not be as precise as results from samples that are analyzed in a laboratory with a good microscope. Any short-cut approaches to paint analysis that do not follow scientific procedures are generally not worth the expense. In summary, if preservation and restoration treatments are being undertaken, a complete investigation is recommended; for a rehabilitation project, onsite analysis and color matching may provide an adequate palette.

Choosing a Treatment

Most projects involve re-painting. It is the historic appearance of the interior and the visual impression that will be created by new paint treatments that must be considered before choosing a particular course of action. The type and colors of paint obviously depend on the type of building and the use and interpretation of its interior spaces (see Figure 11). A consistent approach is best.

Preservation. When the treatment goal is preservation, a building's existing historic features and finishes are maintained and repaired, saving as much of the historic paint as possible. Sometimes, cleaning and washing of

Figure 11. A dark layer can be seen beneath the flaking lighter paint on these raised field panels. Depending on the project work goal and the period of the building's history being interpreted, any one of the paint layers could be duplicated in repainting. National Park Service files.

painted surfaces is all that is needed. Or a coating may be applied to protect important examples of history or art (see Figure 12). If repainting is required, the new paint is matched to existing paint colors using the safer, modern formulations. Re-creating earlier surface colors and treatments is not an objective.

Figure 12. When discovered, important examples of history such as this pencilled Civil War graffiti should be preserved. A conservator can easily clean the area, then apply a protective coating. The history this hand-written message possesses is well worth the sacrifice of surface uniformity, even if it interrupts a freshly painted surface. Photo: Kaye Simonson.

Rehabilitation. In a typical rehabilitation, more latitude exists in choosing both the kind of new paint as well as color because the goal is the efficient re-use of interior spaces. Decisions about new paint often weigh factors such as economy and durability—use of a high quality standard paint from a local or national company and application by a qualified contractor. Color choices may be based on paint research reports prepared for interior rooms of comparable date and style. More often, though, current color values and taste are taken into account. Again, the safer paint formulations are used (see Figure 13).

Figure 13. Part of a historic freight depot, this is not a high-style room and its painted surfaces are obviously in poor condition from long-term neglect. Interior spaces that are being converted for a new use in rehabilitation projects can benefit from being repainted in historic period colors rather than a neutral off-white. Photo: National Park Service files.

Interiors of institutional buildings, such as university buildings, city halls, libraries, and churches often contain rich decorative detailing (Figure 14). During rehabilitation, careful choices should be made to retain or restore selected portions of the decorative work as well as match some of the earlier colors to evoke the historic sense of time and place. At the least, it is important to use period-typical paint color and paint placement.

Figure 14. Holes left by insertion of toggle bolts used in the structural strengthening of this ceiling can be seen in the decorative plaster work. Without great expense, a skilled painter can now clean and touch up the damaged areas. This type of targeted repair work can benefit both public and private buildings. Photo: National Park Service files.

Restoration. In a restoration project, the goal is to depict the property as it appeared during its period of greatest significance. This may or may not be the time of its original construction. For example, if a building dated from 1900 but historians deemed its significance to be the 1920s, the appropriate paint color match would be the 1920s layer, not the original 1900 layer.

Based on historical research, onsite collection of paint samples, and laboratory analysis, surface colors and treatments can be re-created to reflect the property at a particular period of time. It should be noted that scholarly findings may yield a color scheme that is not suited to the taste of the contemporary owner, but is nonetheless historically accurate. In restoration, personal taste in color is not at issue; the evidence should be strictly followed.

In the restoration process, colors are custom-matched by professionals to give an accurate representation. If an artist or artisan can be found, the historically replicated paint may be applied using techniques appropriate to the period of the restoration (see Figure 15). Although custom paint manufacture is seldom undertaken, color and glazing are capable of being customized. In some projects, paint may be custom-made using linseed oil and, if building code variances allow it, white lead. For example, the repainting of a number of rooms at Mount Vernon demonstrates that it is possible to replicate historic paints and applications in all aspects; however, as noted, replication of historic paint formulation is not practical for the majority of projects.

Identifying Deteriorated and Damaged Paint Surfaces

Because painted surfaces are subject to abrasion, soiling, water damage, sunlight, and application of incompatible paints they generally need to be repainted or at least reglazed appropriately from time to time.

Abrasion. From the baseboards up to a level of about six feet off the floor, wood trim is constantly subjected to wear

Figure 15. The decorative work on the walls and ceilings of the Senate Chamber, Providence, Rhode Island, City Hall (1875) is a rich combination of paint and gilding on ornate plaster features. It was carefully restored in 1975. Photo: Kate Gilliat. © Providence Preservation Society.

Figure 17. A Federal period fireplace needs careful preparation for repainting. While the soot must obviously be cleaned off, it is important to leave as much of the historic paint intact as possible. Photo: National Park Service files.

from being touched and inadvertently kicked, and from having furniture pushed against it (see Figure 16). Chair rails were in fact intended to take the wear of having chairs pushed back against them instead of against the more delicate plaster wall or expensive wallpaper. Doors in particular, sometimes beautifully grained, receive extensive handling. Baseboards get scraped by various cleaning devices, and the lower rails of windows, as well as window seats, take abuse. The paint in all of these areas tends to become abraded. Two things are important to bear in mind about areas of abraded paint. Samples taken to determine original paint colors and layer sequences will not be accurate except at undamaged edges. Also, dirt and oil or grease need to be removed before applying any new paint because new paint will not adhere to dirty, greasy surfaces.

Dirt. Soiling is another problem of interior paint (see Figure 17). Fireplaces smoked; early coal-fired furnaces put out oily black soot; gas lights and candles left dark smudges. Sometimes the dirt got deposited on plaster walls or ceilings in a way that makes the pattern of the lath behind the plaster quite clear. Another source of dirt was polluted outside air,

from factories or other industries, infiltrating houses and other nearby buildings. Until smokestacks became very high, most air pollution was caused by nearby sources.

In paint investigation, dirt on the surface of paint layers, as seen under the microscope, can be very useful in suggesting the length of time a given paint layer remained exposed, and in distinguishing a finish layer from a prime or undercoat layer. This kind of soiling can happen on any painted surface in a room, but may be slightly heavier in the recesses of moldings and on upward-facing horizontal edges. Using dirt as a sole measure, however, may be misleading if the surfaces have been cleaned. The fracture or bonding between paint layers is often used by professionals as a better means of indicating time differences between layers as well as indicating those layers that are part of a single decoration or painting.

Water. Water, the usual source of deterioration for many kinds of material, is also a prime cause of interior paint failure (see Figure 18). As a liquid, it can come from roof leaks, from faulty plumbing or steam heating systems, or from fire-suppression systems that have misfired. As a vapor, it may come from such human activities as breathing, showering, or cooking. Plaster walls sealed with unpigmented hide-glue are notably susceptible to water damage because it forms a water-soluble layer between the plaster and the paint. This can cause the paint to lose

Figure 16. This residential door shows how scuffed and abraded interior painted surfaces can become over time, particularly if the feature is in a high-use area. In the preservation project, the door was simply cleaned and repainted the same color. Photo: Robert M. Smith, Jr.

Figure 18. The major crack along this cornice indicates that there has been long-term moisture problem in this room. Restoring the plaster work and repainting should be done only after the water problem is solved. Photo: Jack E. Boucher for HABS.

adhesion when even small amounts of moisture come into contact with the water-soluble sealer.

Age/Sunlight. Finally, in historic interiors, especially where there is heavy paint build-up, paint can weaken and fail due to chemical or mechanical reasons. For example, the older linseed oil is, the more brittle it is (see Figure 19). It also darkens when it is covered and gets no ultra-violet exposure. In rooms where there is more sunlight on one area than on others, the oil or even oil/alkyd paint will get discernibly darker in the less exposed areas in as short a time as six months. Painted over, the oil medium in older paints gets quite yellow-brown, thus changing the color of the paint. Prussian blue is one of the tinting pigments that is particularly vulnerable to fading.

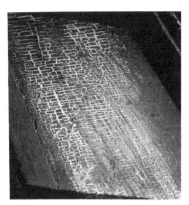

Figure 19. Sunlight typically causes paint deterioration on windows and window sills. This alligatored surface can make paint research difficult, as later paints may have "run in" under earlier ones. This surface should be stripped of all degraded paint prior to repainting. Photo: Richard Graber.

Incompatible Paints. Understanding some basic differences in the strength of various paints helps to explain certain paint problems. Paints that dry to a stronger film are incompatible with those which are weaker. Acrylic latex paints are stronger than oil/alkyd paints. Oil or oil/alkyd paint is stronger than water-based paint such as calcimine. When a stronger paint is applied over a weaker paint, it will tend to pull off any weaker paint which may have begun to lose its bond with its substrate. Thus, on many ceilings of older buildings where oil/alkyd paints have been applied over old calcimine, large strips of paint may be peeling.

Oil or varnish glazes over older paints become brittle with age, and can make removal of later paints rather easy. Sometimes it is possible to take advantage of this characteristic to reveal an earlier decorative treatment such as graining or marbleizing. Getting under the edge of the glaze with a scalpel blade can make the removal of later paints relatively simple, and relatively harmless to the fancier paint treatment. Sometimes, paints separate from each other simply due to poor surface preparation in the past or the hardening of the earlier surface paint. Use of alkaline paint strippers can cause paint to lose adhesion. When insufficiently neutralized, they leave salts in wood which cause oil or oil/alkyd paints to fail to adhere to the surface. If dirt or oily residues are not cleaned from the surfaces to be painted, new paint will not remain well adhered.

Surface Preparation

First, it is important to note that the earlier, linseed oil-based paints were penetrating type paints, forming a bond by absorption into the substrate. Often these thin oil coatings were slightly tinted with an iron-oxide pigment so coverage could be seen; the next coating applied would

adhere to this first oil layer. Modern paints, on the other hand, are primarily bonding paints with little ability to penetrate a substrate. For this reason, surface preparation is extremely important for today's paints.

Before preparing the interior for repainting, all moisture penetration from failing roofs or gutters or from faulty plumbing or interior heating elements should be identified and corrected. A paint job is only as good as the preparation that goes before it. The surface to be painted, old or new, wood, plaster, masonry, or metal must be made sound and capable of taking the paint to be applied.

Scraping and Sanding. The first step in preparing interior wood and plaster surfaces which are coherent and sound is to remove any loose paint (see **Paint Hazards** sidebar). Careful hand scraping is always advisable for historic surfaces. Use of mechanical sanders usually leaves traces of the sander's edges, visible through the new paint film. Hand sanding is also necessary to feather the edges of the firmly adhering layers down to the bare areas so that shadow lines are avoided. Preparing previously painted interior masonry for new paint is basically similar to preparing plaster. Metals elements, such as radiators, valences, or firebacks are somewhat different (see Figure 20). In order to get a sound paint job on metal items, the work is primarily that of sanding to remove any rust before repainting. If the existing paint is well adhered over the entire metal surface, then it may be necessary only to sand lightly to roughen the existing paint, thus providing some "tooth" for the primer and new paint layer. On wood, garnet sanding papers work well. Aluminum oxide and silicon carbide sandpapers are effective on other surfaces as well as wood; emery papers should be used on metals.

Paint Removal. When should surfaces be completely stripped? Obviously, new paint is wasted when applied on

Figure 20. Historic metal components, such as this decorative cast-iron radiator, should be preserved during interior work. Following surface preparation, repainting with rust-inhibiting primer and finish coats is recommended. Photo: Jack E. Boucher for HABS.

old paint which is loose, that is, extensively damaged and deteriorated. Sometimes paint on an architectural feature needs to be removed if it obscures delicate detailing (see Figure 21). For the most part, however, if the surface is intact—and the presence of lead paint has been shown to present no health dangers to building occupants—the existing paint can be overpainted.

Well-adhered, intact paint layers (in at least one area of each room) should be covered with a sturdy protective tape, then painted over with the new paint and left in place to inform future research. The next owner may be interested in the building's past history, and methods of gleaning information from old paints grow more sophisticated all the time.

Heat/Scraping. Propane torches should never be used because they can damage historic wood features. Also, charred areas of wood will not hold the new paint. Use of a heat gun or heat plate may be relatively fast, but has both health and safety drawbacks. Heat oxidizes lead paint, causing poisonous fumes. And old walls may contain fine debris which acts like tinder and smolders when heated, bursting into flame hours after the stripping. (Heat methods are best limited to those interior elements that can be safely removed from the building for stripping and re-installed). Finally, scraping to remove heat-loosened paint may gouge and scar the wood or plaster substrate if not done carefully. Rotary wire brushes cut into wood and should be avoided altogether.

Chemical stripping. Removing paint from wood and plaster features can be done with either caustic strippers (potassium or sodium hydroxide) or solvent strippers (organic compounds such as methylene chloride, methanol, or toluol). Caustic strippers are fairly fast acting, but can weaken wood fibers if left on too long, causing them to raise and separate. They also leave alkaline residues which must be neutralized by an acidic wash (usually white vinegar which contains 4% acetic acid). It is difficult to make the neutralizing 100% effective and, when it is not, chemical reactions between the alkaline residues and the new paint may cause the paint to lose adhesion.

Figure 21. *Stripping paint may sometimes be necessary to reveal the delicate detail of an elaborate piece of interior decoration such as this wood column capital. If total paint removal is deemed appropriate, all paint information should be carefully recorded. Photo: National Park Service files.*

Methylene chloride and other organic compounds are as effective as caustic strippers, but their fumes may be both flammable and toxic. While they may leave wood and plaster surfaces free from harmful residue, the newly cleaned surface must be washed down with mineral spirits or denatured alcohol before priming in order to remove additives, such as wax, that were put in the stripper to retard its drying. All hazard warnings on the labels of chemical strippers should be heeded.

Detergent or vinegar and water. Water-based paints can usually be scrubbed off with hot water with a detergent added. Calcimine and whitewash are difficult to remove; because of the lime or whiting content (calcium carbonate), however, they can be broken down with acids. While strong acids may work quickly, they are very dangerous. Acetic acid in its most common form, vinegar, (4% acetic acid) is often used instead. In areas where any calcimine remains and is evident as chalk, the area can be coated with white shellac, which provides a stable surface for the new paint.

Air pressure. Air pressure of 200-500 psi is effective for flat surfaces if there is a weak substrate surface bond. A flat nozzle is inserted between the paint layer and substrate, and the air pressure simply lifts the loose paint up for easy removal. When used carefully, this method is fast and causes little damage.

Patching and Repair. Once the substrate and its surface are sound and clean, free from crumbling, loose material or dust, the next step is to undercut and fill any cracks in plaster surfaces. Plaster which has lost its key and is sagging should be re-attached or replaced. Friable plaster and punky wood need to be consolidated. Wood surfaces should be made as smooth as they were historically so that the paint film will cover a relatively uniform surface. Rotted wood must be removed and new wood carefully spliced in. Finally, gypsum plaster finishes can be painted as soon as the water has evaporated; a lime putty coat or traditional finish plaster can be primed almost immediately after drying as well, using alkali-resistant primers such as acrylic latex.

Priming. The importance of a primer can hardly be overstated. It is the intermediary material between the immediate substrate, which may be an old paint layer or may be bare wood, plaster, or metal (rarely stone, as around a fireplace opening), and the fresh paint itself. The primer must be capable of being absorbed to some extent by the material underneath while being compatible and cohesive with the paint to be applied on top. Most paint manufacturers will provide explicit instructions about which primers are most compatible with their paints. Those instructions should be followed.

The question of a primer for latex paint continues to be debated. Traditionalists recommend that the primer between an old oil paint and a new latex paint be an oil primer, but the improvements to latex paint in recent years have led many experts to the conclusion that today's top grade latex primers are best for latex finish paints. If a latex primer is selected, the label on the can should specify clearly that it is one which can bond to an older oil or oil/alkyd paint.

The most important general rule to remember is that softer or weaker paints should always go over harder and stronger paints. For instance, because latex is stronger than oil, an oil or oil/alkyd paint can go over a well adhered latex, but the reverse will run the risk of failure. Using primer and finish paints by a single company is a good way to guarantee compatibility.

Choosing Modern Paint Types/Finish Coats

Most frequently today, the project goal is preservation or rehabilitation. Because of the impracticality of replicating historic paints, restoration is least often undertaken. Given current laws restricting the use of toxic ingredients, such as lead, solvents, and thinners, contemporary substitute paints using safer ingredients need to be used. Many paint companies make latex paints in colors that are close to historic colors as well as appropriate gloss levels, but contain no white lead and no hazardous volatile organic compounds.

Work on historic properties generally requires the services of a qualified paint contractor who has had at least five years of experience and who can list comparable jobs that a potential client can see. Then, too, getting a sample or a mock-up of any special work may be advisable before the job starts. While less experienced workers may be acceptable for preparing and priming, it is wise to have the most experienced painters on the finish work.

Oil-based/alkyd paints. Today's version of oil paint has a binder that usually contains some linseed oil (read the paint-can label), but also has one of the improved synthesized oils, frequently soy-based, known as alkyds. They dry hard, have flexibility, and discolor far less than linseed oil. They can also be manufactured to dry with a high sheen, and can take enough tinting pigment to create even the very deep Victorian period colors. However, they all contain volatile organic compounds, and thus are forbidden by law in some parts of the United States. They are also less simple and more dangerous to use, as cleaning up involves mineral spirits.

Acrylic water-borne paints (latex). Latex paints are synthetic resins carried in water. Before the paint dries or cross-links, it can be cleaned up with water. Early in the history of latex paints, some contained styrene/butadiene resins. Now nearly all top-grade latex paints contain acrylic resins, which are superior. Also, until fairly recently, the latex paints, while offering great strength, quick drying, and water clean-up, had some disadvantages for jobs which needed to have an historic look. Today, there are latex product lines with better gloss characteristics and more historic colors from which to choose. In addition, latex paints often have excellent color retention with very little fading. Still, it is always a good idea to buy a quart and "test paint" the color chosen for the job on site before making a total commitment.

Calcimine/whitewash. Modern water-based paints such as calcimine can be purchased today and have much the same appearance as the early ones. The same is true of modern whitewash, although today's whitewashes do not leave the same ropy surface texture as the early ones.

Glazes. Glazes were often part of historic paint treatments. Traditionally oil and turpentine, sometimes with a scant amount of pigment, today's glazes can be formulated with a water base and are relatively simple to apply by brush. An experienced decorative painter should be consulted before

---

Types of Modern Paint

Oil-based/alkyd: Non-volatile oils and resins, with thinners. (Alkyds are synthetic, gelatinous resins compounded from acids and alcohol.) Accept almost any type of coloring/hiding pigments. For use on interior wood and metal.

Acrylic water-borne paints (latex): Suspension of acrylic or polyvinyl resins in water, with other resins, plus hiding and coloring pigments and extenders. Dries by evaporation. Commercially produced acrylic or latex enamels are also available in a complete range of gloss levels which are produced with the addition of various acrylic polymers. Use on interior plaster especially.

Enamels: Modern alkyd paints are adjusted with the addition of synthetic varnishes to produce a complete range of gloss levels.

Metal finishes: Paints marketed for use on metals, can either be alkyd, latex, or epoxy based, or combinations. The primers used for metals are formulated with rust-inhibiting ingredients.

Special finishes: finishes such as urethane and epoxy-based paints, marketed for very high gloss surface treatments.

---

deciding whether to use a glaze coat rather than a high-gloss enamel. The glaze is capable of providing protection as well as a more accurate historic appearance that includes a greater depth to the finish.

Epoxies/Urethane. These were not available until relatively recently and thus are not appropriate for replication of traditional finishes.

Applying Interior Paints

Because flat wall surfaces generally dominate an interior painting job, some flexibility in applicators is suggested below:

Brushes. Natural bristle brushes now have competition from synthetic brushes made of nylon or polyester which work well for applying either oil/alkyd or latex paints. Being harder than natural bristles, they tend to last longer. Since brushes come in a wide and very specific variety of types suited to different types of work, it is important to have a painter who will use the appropriate brush for the paint selected and for each portion of the job. One strong advantage of brushing paint on is that the paint is forced onto the surface and into all of its imperfections. Thus a good brushed-on paint job may last longer if the substrate is sound and the primer and finish coats are compatible and of top quality.

Rollers. There is no harm in using a roller, or even an airless sprayer, to apply a prime coat to a large flat area. Since all contemporary commercial paints dry with a smooth surface anyway, use of a roller or sprayer is acceptable for priming, and even for a first finish coat. However, to get paint well pushed into articulated surfaces and to add some texture to larger flat surfaces, a brush is best.

CAUTION: Before Painting/Know Paint Hazards and Take Action

Before undertaking any project involving paint removal, applicable State and Federal laws on lead paint abatement and disposal must be taken into account and carefully followed. State and Federal requirements may affect options available to owners on both paint removal and repainting. These laws, as well as any requirements prohibiting volatile organic compounds (VOCs), should be requested from the State Historic Preservation Officer in each State.

Below is a summary of the health hazards that owners, managers, and workers need to be aware of before removing paint and repainting:

Lead and other heavy metal compounds. In virtually all paints made before 1950, the white or "hiding" pigment was a lead compound, or more rarely, zinc oxide. Work to remove lead paint such as scraping and dry sanding releases the lead—a highly damaging heavy metal—in dust. Lead dust then enters the human system through pores of the skin and through the lungs. The use of heat for stripping also creates toxic lead fumes which can be inhaled.

To mitigate the hazards of lead paint ingestion, inhalation, or contact, it is extremely important to prevent the dust from circulating by masking room openings and removing all curtains, carpeting, and upholstered furniture. Drop cloths and masking containing lead dust should be carefully enclosed in tight plastic bags before removal. Workers and others in the room should wear High Efficiency Particulate Air (HEPA) filters for lead dust (fume filters if heat stripping is being used), change clothing just outside the room leaving the work clothes inside, and avoid any contact between bare skin (hands) and the paint being removed. Workers should also not eat, drink, or smoke where lead dust is present. Finally, anyone involved in lead paint removal should undergo periodic blood testing. After work, ordinary vacuuming is not enough to remove lead dust; special HEPA vacuums are essential. The surfaces of the room must also be given a final wash with a solution of trisodium phosphate and water, changing the washing solution often and rinsing well.

In addition to lead, early oil paints also had cobalt or other heavy metal compounds in them to accelerate drying. A small amount of mercury is also included in some latex paints to help prevent mildew and mold formation.

Volatile organic compounds (VOCs). Organic paint strippers, such as methylene chloride, and oil/alkyd paints have VOCs as their solvent base. Inhaling these fumes can lead to respiratory and other illnesses, and to cancer. Especially in closed spaces (but in the outdoor environment as well) these compounds pollute the air and can damage health.

Finally, decorative paint work in an historic interior—whether simple or high-style—is well worth preserving or restoring, and when such fancy work is being undertaken, traditional tools should always be used (see Figure 22). To simplify by using short-cut methods or rejecting painted decoration is indeed to dismiss or skew history as well as to lose the enjoyment of a true historic finish.

Figure 22. Traditional water-based paint and artists' brushes are being used to reproduce historic finishes within a restoration project. Photo: Courtesy, Alexis Elza.

Summary

First, it is most important to understand the range of approaches and treatments and to make choices with as much knowledge of the original and subsequent historic paints as possible, using the Secretary of the Interior's Standards for Historic Preservation Projects as a framework.

A paint's patina of age expresses decades or centuries of endurance in the face of changing climate and conditions. Documenting the sequence of interior paint layers and protecting this information for future investigation should be an integral part of any historic preservation project.

Except for the rare, scholarly restorations of historic interiors, most repainting jobs done today will employ modern paint formulations. Modern paints can recreate the appearance of historic colors, gloss and texture in varying degrees, but eliminate earlier toxic components such as white lead and volatile organic compounds.

Additional Reading

Clark, Victor S. *History of Manufacturers in the United States*, Vols. I-III. New York: McGraw-Hill, 1929.

Gettens, Rutherford J. and George L. Stout. *Painting Materials: A Short Encyclopedia.* New York: Dover Publications, 1966.

MacDonald, Marylee. *Preservation Briefs 21: Repairing Historic Flat Plaster—Walls and Ceilings.* Washington, D.C.: National Park Service, U.S. Department of the Interior, 1989.

Masury, John W. *A Popular Treatise on the Art of House-Painting: Plain and Decorative.* New York: D. Appleton & Co.,. 1868.

Weeks, Kay D. and David W. Look, AIA. *Preservation Briefs 10: Exterior Paint Problems on Historic Woodwork.* Washington, D.C.: National Park Service, U.S. Department of the Interior, 1982.

Winkler, Gail Caskey and Roger W. Moss. *Victorian Interior Decoration: American Interiors 1830-1900.* New York: Henry Holt and Company, 1986.

Organizations

National Paint and Coatings Association
1500 Rhode Island Ave. N.W.
Washington, D.C. 20005

Painting and Decorating Contractors of America
3913 Old Lee Highway, Suite 33B
Fairfax, VA 22030

Federation of Societies for Coatings Technology
492 Norristown Rd.
Blue Bell, PA 19422-2350

Photo: Matthew J. Mosca

Acknowledgements

Thanks go to the technical experts in the field who reviewed the draft manuscript and made substantive contributions: Andrea M. Gilmore (Director, Architectural Services, Society for the Preservation of New England Antiquities), Andy Ladygo (Jefferson's Poplar Forest), and Matthew J. Mosca, Historic Paint Research. Insightful comments were also offered by E. Blaine Cliver, Chief, Preservation Assistance Division. In addition, Technical Preservation Services Branch staff members (H. Ward Jandl, Chief) and the NPS Regions provided valuable suggestions on both content and organization.

This publication has been prepared pursuant to the National Historic Preservation Act of 1966, as amended, which directs the Secretary of the Interior to develop and make available information concerning historic properties. Comments on the usefulness of this publication may be directed to: Chief, Preservation Assistance Division, National Park Service, P.O. Box 37127, Washington, D.C. 20013-7127.
Kay D. Weeks served as project director and editor of the cooperative publication project.
June, 1992.

29

The Repair, Replacement, and Maintenance of Historic Slate Roofs

Jeffrey S. Levine

Introduction

Slate is one of the most aesthetically pleasing and durable of all roofing materials. It is indicative at once of the awesome powers of nature which have formed it and the expertise and skill of the craftsman in hand-shaping and laying it on the roof. Installed properly, slate roofs require relatively little maintenance and will last 60 to 125 years or longer depending on the type of slate employed, roof configuration, and the geographical location of the property. Some slates have been known to last over 200 years. Found on virtually every class of structure, slate roofs are perhaps most often associated with institutional, ecclesiastical, and government buildings, where longevity is an especially important consideration in material choices. In the slate quarrying regions of the country, where supply is abundant, slate was often used on farm and agricultural buildings as well.

Because the pattern, detailing, and craftsmanship of slate roofs are important design elements of historic buildings, they should be repaired rather than replaced whenever possible. The purpose of this Preservation Brief is to assist property owners, architects, preservationists, and building managers in understanding the causes of slate roof failures and undertaking the repair and replacement of slate roofs. Details contributing to the character of historic slate roofs are described and guidance is offered on maintenance and the degree of intervention required at various levels of deterioration.

The relatively large percentage of historic buildings roofed with slate during the late nineteenth and early twentieth centuries means that many slate roofs, and the 60 to 125 year life span of the slates most commonly used, may be nearing the end of their serviceable lives at the end of the twentieth century. Too often, these roofs are being improperly repaired or replaced with alternative roofing materials, to the detriment of the historic integrity and appearance of the structure. Increased knowledge of the characteristics of slate and its detailing and installation on the roof can lead to more sensitive interventions in which

original material is preserved and the building's historic character maintained. Every effort should be made to replace deteriorated slate roofs with new slate and to develop an effective maintenance and repair program for slate roofs that can be retained.

History of Slate Use in the United States

Although slate quarrying was not common in the United States until the latter half of the nineteenth century, slate roofing is known to have been used prior to the Revolution. Archeological excavations at Jamestown, Virginia, have unearthed roofing slate in strata dating from 1625-1650 and 1640-1670. Slate roofs were introduced in Boston as early as 1654 and Philadelphia in 1699. Seventeenth century building ordinances of New York and Boston recommended the use of slate or tile roofs to ensure fireproof construction.

In the early years of the Colonies, nearly all roofing slate was imported from North Wales. It was not until 1785 that the first commercial slate quarry was opened in the United States, by William Docher in Peach Bottom Township, Pennsylvania. Production was limited to that which could be consumed in local markets until the middle of the nineteenth century. Knowledge of the nation's abundant stone resources was given commercial impetus at this time by several forces, including a rapidly growing population that demanded housing, advances in quarrying technology, and extension of the railroad system to previously inaccessible markets. Two additional factors helped push the slate industry to maturity: the immigration of Welsh slate workers to the United States and the introduction of architectural pattern and style books (Figure 1). Slate production increased dramatically in the years following the Civil War as quarries were opened in Vermont, New York, Virginia, and Lehigh and Northampton Counties, Pennsylvania. By 1876, roofing slate imports had all but dried up and the United States became a net exporter of the commodity.

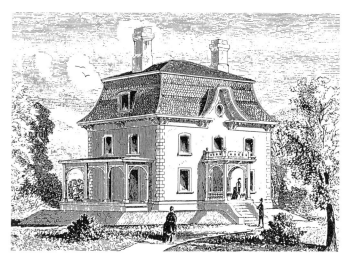

Figure 1. Architectural pattern books of the mid-nineteenth century awakened Americans to the availability and quality of slate for roofing purposes by incorporating slate roofs in their designs. Design XX, ''A French Roof House,'' in A. J. Downing's Victorian Cottage Residences *is shown.*

The U.S. roofing slate industry reached its highest point in both quantity and value of output in the period from 1897 to 1914. In 1899, there were over 200 slate quarries operating in 13 states, Pennsylvania historically being the largest producer of all. The decline of the U.S. roofing slate industry began c.1915 and resulted from several factors, including a decline in skilled labor for both the fabrication and installation of slate and competition from substitute materials, such as asphalt shingles, which could be mass produced, transported and installed at a lower cost than slate. Only recently, with the increasing popularity of historic preservation and the recognition of the superiority of slate over other roofing materials, has slate usage begun to increase.

The Character and Detailing of Historic Slate Roofs

During some periods of architectural history, roof design has gone far beyond the merely functional and contributed much to the character of buildings. Roofs, by their compelling forms, have defined styles and, by their decorative patterns and colors, have imparted both dignity and beauty to buildings. The architectural styles prevalent during the latter half of the nineteenth and early twentieth centuries placed strong emphasis on prominent roof lines and greatly influenced the demand for slate. Slate, laid in multi-colored decorative patterns, was particularly well suited to the Mansard roofs of the Second Empire style, the steeply pitch roofs of the Gothic Revival and High Victorian Gothic styles, and the many prominent roof planes and turrets associated with the Queen Anne style. The Tudor style imitated the quaint appearance of some English slates which, because of their granular cleavage, are thick and irregular. These slates were often laid in a graduated pattern, with the largest slates at the eaves and the courses diminishing in size up the roof slope, or a textural pattern (Figure 2). Collegiate Gothic style buildings, found on many university campuses, were often roofed with slate laid in a graduated pattern.

The configuration, massing, and style of historic slate roofs are important design elements that should be preserved. In addition, several types of historic detailing

were often employed to add visual interest to the roof, essentially elevating the roof to the level of an ornamental architectural element. When repairing or replacing a slate roof, original details affecting its visual character should be retained.

Before repairing or replacing an existing slate roof, it is important to document the existing conditions and detailing of the roof using written, visual, and physical evidence so that original features can be identified and preserved. Documentation should continue through the repair or replacement process as significant details, long obscured, are often rediscovered while carrying out these activities. Local histories, building records, old receipts and ledgers, historic photographs, sketches, and paintings, shadow lines and nail hole patterns on the roof deck, and bits of historic material left over from previous interventions (often found in eave cavities) are all useful sources of information which can be of help in piecing together the original appearance of the roof. Size, shape, color, texture, exposure, and coursing are among the most important characteristics of the original slates which should be documented and matched when repairing or replacing an historic slate roof.

Historically, three types of slate roofing—standard, textural, and graduated—were available according to the architectural effect desired. Standard grade slate roofs were most common. These are characterized by their uniform appearance, being composed of slates approximately 3/16" (0.5cm) thick, of consistent length and width, and having a smooth cleavage surface. Thirty different standard sizes were available, ranging from 10" (25cm) × 6" to 24" × 14" (15cm × 61cm × 35cm). The slates were laid to break joints and typically had square ends and uniform color and exposure. Patterned and polychromatic roofs were created by laying standard slates of different colors and shapes on the roof in such a way as to create sunbursts, flowers, sawtooth and geometric designs, and even initials and dates (Figure 3). On utilitarian structures, such as barns and sheds, large gaps were sometimes left between each slate within a given course to reduce material and installation costs and provide added ventilation for the interior (Figure 4).

Figure 2. The quaint character of this Tudor style residence is derived, in part, from its textural roof.

Figure 3. A sawtooth geometric design composed of red, green, and black slates makes this roof the most visually important feature of the building.

Textural slate roofs incorporate slates of different thicknesses, uneven tails, and a rougher texture than standard slates. Textural slate roofs are perhaps most often associated with Tudor style buildings where slates of different colors are used to enhance the effect.

Graduated slate roofs were frequently installed on large institutional and ecclesiastical structures (Figure 5). The slates were graduated according to thickness, size, and exposure, the thickest and largest slates being laid at the eaves and the thinnest and smallest at the ridge. Pleasing architectural effects were achieved by blending sizes and colors.

Detailing at the hips, ridges and valleys provided added opportunity to ornament a slate roof. Hips and ridges can be fashioned out of slate according to various traditional schemes whereby the slates are cut and overlapped to produce a watertight joint of the desired artistic effect. Traditional slate ridge details are the saddle ridge, strip saddle ridge, and comb ridge, and for hips, the saddle hip, mitered hip, Boston hip, and fantail hip (Figure 6). A more linear effect was achieved by covering the ridges and hips with flashing called "cresting" or "ridge roll" formed out of sheet metal, terra cotta, or even slate (Figure 7). Snow guards, snow boards, and various types of gutter and rake treatments also contributed to the character of historic slate roofs (Figure 8).

Two types of valleys were traditionally employed, the open valley and the closed valley. The open valley is lined with metal over which slates lap only at the sides. Closed valleys are covered with slate and have either a continuous metal lining or metal flashing built in with each course. Open valleys are easier to install and maintain, and are generally more watertight than closed valleys. Round valleys are a type of closed valley with a concave rather than V-shaped section (Figure 9). Given the broader sweep of the round valley, it was not uncommon for roofers to interweave asphalt saturated felts rather than copper sheet in the coursing in order to cut costs.

Figure 4. Widely spaced open slating was often used on utilitarian structures where ventilation was desirable. It provided an interesting texture and visual pattern to often plain structures.

Figure 5. This graduated slate roof is composed of large, thick slates at the eave which are reduced in size and thickness as the slating progresses to the ridge.

Although principally associated with graduated and textural slate roofs, round valleys were infrequently employed due to the difficulty and expense of their installation.

Common types of sheathing used include wood boards, wood battens, and, for fireproof construction on institutional and government buildings, concrete or steel (Figure 10). Solid wood sheathing was typically constructed of tongue and groove, square edged, or shiplapped pine boards of 1″ (2.5 cm) or 1 1/4″ (3 cm) nominal thickness. Boards from 6″ (15 cm) to 8″ (20 cm) wide and tongue and groove boards were generally preferred as they were less likely to warp and curl.

Wood battens, or open wood sheathing, consisted of wood strips, measuring from 2″ (5 cm) to 3″ (7.5 cm) in width, nailed to the roof rafters. Spacing of the battens depended on the length of the slate and equaled the exposure. Slates were nailed to the batten that transected its mid-section. The upper end of the slate rested at least 1/2″ (1.25 cm) on the batten next above. Open wood sheathing was employed primarily on utilitarian, farm, and agricultural structures in the North and on residential buildings in the South where the insulating value of solid wood sheathing was not a strict requirement. To help keep out dust and wind driven rain on residential buildings, mortar was often placed along the top and bottom edge of each batten, a practice sometimes referred to as torching.

Various Roofing Details

Figure 6. Hips are formed at the external angle of two roofing slopes. In (a), the hips at both the roof and the dormer are covered with metal. Note also the open valley and the built-in gutter. In (b), the dormer hip slates have been laid in a fantail pattern to help shed water. Note also the metal ridge cap.

Figure 7. Ridge caps and cresting can be elaborate. Ridges are formed at the long horizontal juncture of two roofing slopes and capping protects this joint from moisture. In (a), a terra cotta capping with a decorative profile complements the finial over the various roof peaks. In (b), the mansard roof has a decorative iron cresting at the break between the lower and the upper roof slopes.

Figure 8. Eave details include snow guards, snow boards, gutter treatments. Snow guards are generally used in areas where ice and snow accumulate to avoid dangerous slides from the roof. In (a) the snow guards are set in two staggered rows above a pole gutter. In (b), the copper wire snow guards are set more frequently up a very steep gable.

Figure 9. Valleys are formed at the internal angle of two roofing slopes. Flashing is often placed under the slate to increase moisture protect at this vulnerable joint. Shown in (a) is a closed valley where the slates are held tight to the valley line. (b) illustrates of a round valley where the transition between the two slopes is a continuous curve. It requires careful workmanship and an experienced roofer.

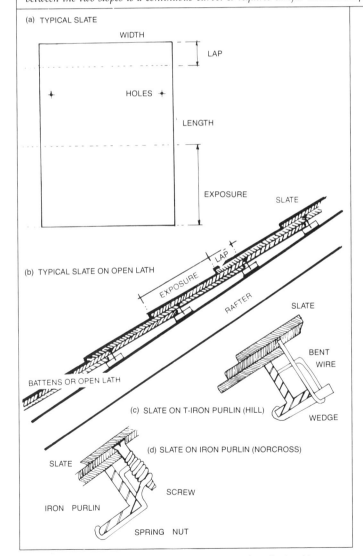

Figure 10. (a) shows a typical slate; exposure may be calculated by subtracting the headlap from the total length of the slate and dividing by two. Slates were typically nailed either to closed wooden decking or to open laths (b). In the late 19th century, with the concern for fireproof construction, special fasteners were developed to secure slate to steel purlins (c) 1881 patent to James G. Hill; (d) 1889 patent to Orlando W. Norcross).

Steel angles substituted for the wood battens in fireproof construction. The slates were secured using wire wrapped around the steel angle, where it was twisted-off tight. Alternately, any of a variety of special fasteners patented over the years could have been used to attach the slate to the steel angle (Figure 10). On roofs with concrete decks, slates were typically nailed to wood nailing strips embedded in the concrete.

Beginning in the late nineteenth century, asphalt saturated roofing felt was installed atop solid wood sheathing. The felt provided a temporary, watertight roof until the slate could be installed atop it. Felt also served to cushion the slates, exclude wind driven rain and dust, and ease slight unevenness between the sheathing boards.

Slate was typically laid in horizontal courses starting at the eaves with a standard headlap of 3″ (7.5 cm) (Figure 10). Headlap was generally reduced to 2″ (5 cm) on Mansard roofs and on particularly steep slopes with more than 20″ (50 cm) of rise per 12″ (30 cm) of run. Conversely, headlap was increased to 4″ (10 cm) or more on low pitched roofs with a rise of 8″ (20 cm) or less per 12″ (30 cm) of horizontal run. The minimum roof slope necessary for a slate roof was 4″ (10 cm) of rise per 12″ (30 cm) of run.

Where Does Slate Come From?

Slate is a fine grained, crystalline rock derived from sediments of clay and fine silt which were deposited on ancient sea bottoms. Superimposed materials gradually consolidated the sedimentary particles into bedded deposits of shale. Mountain building forces subsequently folded, crumpled, and compressed the shale. At the same time, intense heat and pressure changed the original clays into new minerals such as mica, chlorite, and quartz. By such mechanical and chemical processes bedded clays were transformed, or metamorphosed, into slate, whole

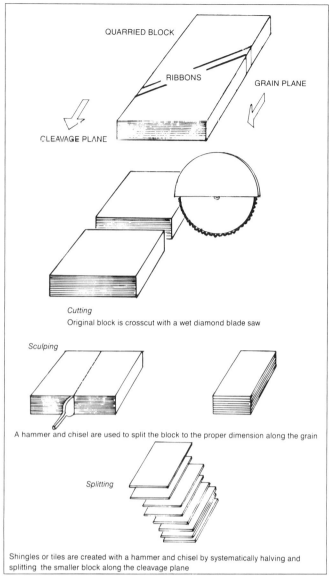

Figure 11. Slate roofing tiles or shingles are still manufactured using traditional methods brought to this country by Welsh immigrants in the nineteenth century. Shown above are the first 3 steps of cutting, sculping and splitting. Once the rough slate tile is made it is trimmed and punched for holes.

geologic ages being consumed in the process. Slates vary in composition, structure, and durability because the degree to which their determinant minerals have been altered is neither uniform nor consistent.

The adaptation of slate for roofing purposes is inextricably linked to its genesis. The manufacturing processes of nature have endowed slate with certain commercially amenable properties which have had a profound influence on the methods by which slate is quarried and fabricated (Figure 11), as well as its suitability for use as a roofing tile.

Slate roofing tiles are still manufactured by hand using traditional methods in a five step process: cutting, sculping, splitting, trimming, and hole punching. In the manufacturing process, large, irregular blocks taken from the quarry are first cut with a saw across the grain in sections slightly longer than the length of the finished roofing slate. The blocks are next sculped, or split along the grain of the slate, to widths slightly larger than the widths of finished slates. Sculping is generally accomplished with a mallet and a broad-faced chisel,

although some types of slate must be cut along their grain. In the splitting area, the slightly oversized blocks are split along their cleavage planes to the desired shingle thickness. The splitter's tools consist of a wooden mallet and two splitting chisels used for prying the block into halves and repeating this process until the desired thinness is reached (Figure 12). The last two steps involve trimming the tile to the desired size and then punching two nail holes toward the top of the slate using a formula based on the size and exposure of the slate.

Minerals, the building blocks of rocks, through their characteristic crystalline structures define the physical properties of the rocks which they compose. Slate consists of minerals that are stable and resistant to weathering and is, therefore, generally of high strength, low porosity, and low absorption. The low porosity and low absorption of slate mitigate the deleterious action of frost on the stone and make it well adapted for roofing purposes. The two most important structural properties of slate are cleavage and grain.

The metamorphic processes of geologic change necessary to produce slate are dependent upon movements in the earth's crust and the heat and pressure generated thereby. For this reason, slate is found only in certain mountainous regions. The most economically important slate deposits in this country lie in the Mid-Atlantic and Northeastern states transversed by or bordering on the Appalachian Mountain chain. Variations in local chemistry and conditions under which the slate was formed have

Figure 12. In the splitting area, the slightly oversized blocks are split along their cleavage planes. The splitter's tools consist of a wooden mallet and splitting chisels. The process of halving the split portions is repeated until a tile or shingle of appropriate thinness is obtained.

Figure 13. Paper thin lamination can be seen flaking off of this weathered, 120 year piece of Pennsylvania Hard-Vein slate.

produced a wide range of colors and qualities and ultimately determine the character of the slate found in these areas.

Slate is available in a variety of colors. The most common are grey, blue-grey, black, various shades of green, deep purple, brick red, and mottled varieties. The presence of carbonaceous matter, derived from the decay of marine organisms on ancient sea floors, gives rise to the black colored slates. Compounds of iron generate the red, purple, and green colored slates.

Generally, the slates of Maine, Virginia, and the Peach Bottom district of York County, Pennsylvania are deep blue-black in color. Those of Virginia have a distinctive lustrous appearance as well due to their high mica content. The slates of Lehigh and Northampton Counties, Pennsylvania, are grayish-black in color. Green, red, purple, and mottled slates derive from the New York-Vermont district. The slate producing region of New York, which centers around Granville and Middle Granville, is particularly important because it contains one of the few commercial deposits of red slate in the world.

Slates are also classified as fading or unfading according to their color stability. Fading slates change to new shades or may streak within a short time after exposure to the atmosphere due to the presence of fine-grained disseminated pyrite. For example, the "weathering green" or "sea-green" slates of New York and Vermont are grayish green when freshly quarried. Upon exposure, from 20% to 60% of the slates typically weather to soft tones of orange-brown, buff, and gray while the others retain their original shade. Slates designated as unfading maintain their original colors for many years.

Color permanence generally provides no indication of the durability of slate. Rather, time has shown that the Vermont and New York slates will last about 125 years; Buckingham Virginia slates 175 years or more; and Pennsylvania Soft-Vein slates in excess of 60 years; Pennsylvania Hard-Vein slates and Peach Bottom slates, neither of which is still quarried, had life spans of roughly 100 and at least 200 years respectively. The life spans provided should be used only as a general guide in determining whether or not an existing slate roof is nearing the end of its serviceable life.

Ribbons are visible as bands on the cleavage face of slate and represent geologic periods during which greater amounts of carbonaceous matter, calcite, or coarse quartz particles were present in the sediment from which the slate was formed. Ribbons typically weather more and were most common in Pennsylvania slate quarries. As they were not as durable as clear slates, ribbon slate is no longer manufactured for roofing purposes. Mottled grey slates from Vermont are the closest match for Pennsylvania ribbon slate available today.

In recent years, slates from China, Africa, Spain and other countries have begun to be imported into the United States, primarily for distribution on the West Coast. The use of imported slates should probably be limited to new construction since their colors and textures often do not match those of U.S. slate.

Deterioration of Slate and Slate Roofs

The durability of a slate roof depends primarily on four factors: the physical and mineralogical properties of the slate; the way in which it is fabricated; installation techniques employed; and, regular and timely maintenance. The first three of these factors are examined below. The maintenance and repair of slate roofs are discussed in later sections of this Brief.

The natural weathering of roofing slate manifests itself as a slow process of chipping and scaling along the cleavage planes (Figure 13). Paper thin laminations flake off the surface of the slate and the slate becomes soft and spongy as the inner layers begin to come apart, or delaminate. The nature of the sound given off by a slate when tapped with one's knuckles or slating hammer is a fair indication of its condition. High-grade slate, when poised upon the fingertips and struck, will emit a clear, solid sound. Severely weathered slates are much less sonorous, and give off a dull thud when tapped.

The weathering of slate is chiefly due to mineral impurities (primarily calcite and iron sulfides) in the slate which, in concert with alternating wet/dry and hot/cold cycles, react to form gypsum (Figure 14). Because gypsum

Figure 14. The white blotches on these Pennsylvania Soft-Vein slates indicate areas where gypsum is leaching out onto the surface of the slates.

Figure 15. View of the underside of slates laid on open sheathing shows that delamination and flaking is just as bad or worse on the underside of slates as on the exposed surface. This is why most slates cannot be flipped over for reuse.

molecules take up about twice as much volume as calcite molecules, internal stresses result from the reaction, causing the slate to delaminate. This type of deterioration is as prominent on the underside of the roof as on the exposed surface due to the leaching and subsequent concentration of gypsum in this area (Figure 15). Consequently, deteriorated roofing slates typically cannot be flipped over and re-used.

The chemical and physical changes which accompany slate weathering cause an increase in absorption and a decrease in both strength and toughness. The tendency of old, weathered slates to absorb and hold moisture can lead to rot in underlying areas of wood sheathing. Such rot can go undetected for long periods of time since, often, there is no accompanying leak. Due to their loss of strength, weathered slates are more prone to breakage, loss of corners, and cracking.

Slates with low calcite content tend to weather slowly. Dense slates, with low porosity, likewise decay slower than slates with equal calcite, but with a greater porosity. The pitch of a roof can also affect its longevity. The steeper the pitch, the longer the slate can be expected to last as water will run off faster and will be less likely to be drawn under the slates by capillary action or driven under by wind forces. Spires and the steep slopes of Mansard roofs often retain their original slate long after other portions of the roof have been replaced. Areas of a roof subject to concentrated water flows and ice damming, such as along eaves and valleys, also tend to deteriorate more rapidly than other areas of the roof.

Mechanical agents, such as thermal expansion and contraction and the action of frost, are subordinate in the weathering of slate, coming into play only after the slate has been materially altered from its original state by the chemical transformation of calcite to gypsum. The more rapid deterioration of slates found on roof slopes with the most severe exposure to the sun, wind, and rain (typically, but not always, a southern exposure) may be attributable to the combined result of the deleterious effects of impurities in the slate and mechanical agents. Atmospheric acids produce only negligible deterioration in roofing slate.

It is difficult to assess the procedures by which a piece of slate has been fabricated without visiting the quarry and

observing the process first hand. The location and size of nail holes, grain orientation, the condition of corners, and the number of broken pieces are all things which may be observed in a shipment of slate to judge the quality of its fabrication. Nail holes should be clean and with a shallow countersink on the face of the slate for the nail head; grain oriented along the length of the slate; and, corners left whole. An allowance for 10% breakage in shipment is typically provided for by the quarry.

Installation problems often involve the improper nailing and lapping of slates. The nailing of slates differs from that of other roofing materials. Slate nails should not be driven tight as is the case with asphalt and wood shingles. Rather, they should be set such that the slate is permitted to hang freely on the nail shank. Nails driven too far will crack the slate and those left projecting will puncture the overlying slate (Figure 16). Nail heads left exposed accelerate roof deterioration by providing a point for water entry. Non-ferrous slater's nails, such as solid copper or stainless steel, should always be used since plain steel and galvanized nails will usually rust out long before the slate itself begins to deteriorate. The rusting of nineteenth century cut nails is a common cause of slate loss on historic roofs.

When joints are improperly broken (i.e., when slates lap the joints in the course below by less than 3″ [7.5 cm]), it is possible for water to pass between the joints, through the nail holes and ultimately to the underlying felt, where it will cause deterioration and leaks to develop. Insufficient headlap can also result in leaks as water entering the joints between slates may have a greater tendency to be wind blown beyond the heads of the slates in the course below.

Occasionally, individual slates are damaged. This may be caused by falling tree limbs, ice dams in gutters, valleys, and chimney crickets, the weight of a workman walking on the roof, or a naturally occurring fault in the slate unit. Whatever the form of damage, if it is caught soon enough, the roof can usually be repaired or selectively replaced and deterioration mitigated.

The ability to lay slate properly so as to produce a water-tight and aesthetically pleasing roof requires training, much practice, and the right tools (Figure 17). The

Figure 16. Detail view of a slate which has been punctured by the head of a nail used to secure the slate in the course below. Likely, the nail was not hammered in far enough when originally installed.

Figure 17. Slater's Tools. The cutter (a) is used to trim slate edges; the slate hammer (b) is used for hammering nails, trimming, cutting and punching holes in slates, and pulling roofing nails; the steak (c) is a T-shaped piece of iron upon which the slater places the edge of a slate to be trimmed; and the ripper (d) is slid under the slates to pull out the nails.

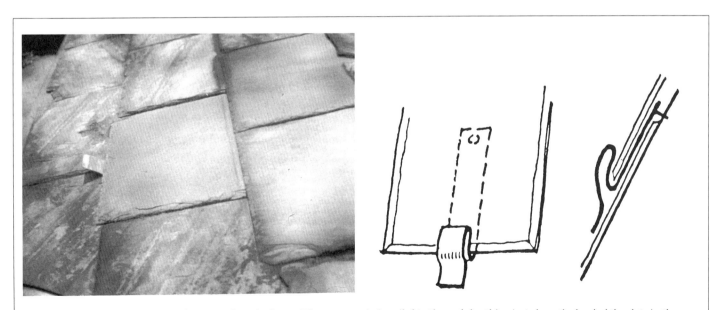

Figure 18. A method of securing replacement slates is shown. The copper strip is nailed to the roof sheathing just above the head of the slate in the course below. The replacement slate is then inserted and the copper tab folded over its tail. This type of repair is not recommended for northern climates where snow and ice can cause the copper tab to fold over, allowing the replacement slate to slide out of position as occurred here on the left.

(a) A ripper is used to remove the nails from the deteriorated slate.

(b) A replacement slate is slid into place.

(c) A new slate is secured in place with a copper nail.

(d) A copper bib is formed to protect the newly created nail hole.

(e) The bib is cut along its edges and bent into a concave shape to create a friction fit.

(f) The slate hammer is used to push the bib in place over the nail head.

Figure 19. Above is a repair sequence for replacing a damaged slate.

The installation and repair of slate roofs should be entrusted only to experienced slaters.

Repairing Slate Roofs

Broken, cracked, and missing slates should be repaired promptly by an experienced slater in order to prevent water damage to interior finishes, accelerated deterioration of the roof and roof sheathing, and possible structural degradation to framing members (Figures 18 and 19).

The damaged slate is first removed by cutting or pulling out its nails with a ripper. If steel cut nails, rather than copper nails, were used in laying the roof, adjacent slates may be inadvertently damaged or displaced in the ripping process, and these, too, will have to be repaired. If the slate does not slide out by itself, the pointed end of the slate hammer can be punched into the slate and the slate dragged out. A new slate, or salvaged slate, which should match the size, shape, texture, and weathered color of the old slate, is then slid into place and held in position by one nail inserted through the vertical joint between the slates in the course above and approximately one inch below the tail of the slate two courses above. To prevent water penetration through the newly created nail hole, a piece of copper with a friction fit, measuring roughly 3" (7.5 cm) in width and 8" (20 cm) in length, is slid lengthwise under the joint between the two slates located directly above the new slate and over the nail. Alternate methods for securing the replacement slate include the use of metal hooks, clips, and straps that are bent over the tail end of the slate. The application of roofing mastic or sealants to damaged slates should *not* be considered a viable repair alternative because these materials, though effective at first, will eventually harden and crack, thereby allowing water to enter (Figure 20). Mastic also makes future repairs more difficult to execute, is unsightly, and, when applied to metal flashings, accelerates their corrosion.

When two or more broken slates lie adjacent to each other in the same course, or when replacing leaky valley flashings, it is best to form pyramids (i.e., to remove a diminishing number of slates from higher courses) to keep the number of bibs required to a minimum. When re-installing the slates, only the top slate in each pyramid will need a bib. Slates along the sides of the pyramid will receive two nails, one above the other, along the upper part of its exposed edge.

When many slates must be removed to effect a repair, the sheathing should be checked for rotted areas and projecting nails. Plywood is generally not a good replacement material for deteriorated wood sheathing due to the relative difficulty of driving a nail through it (the bounce produced can loosen adjacent slates). Instead, new wood boards of similar width and thickness to those being replaced should be used. Because the nominal thickness of today's dimension lumber is slightly thinner than that produced in the past, it may be necessary to shim the new wood boards so that they lie flush with the top surface of adjacent existing sheathing boards. Pressure treated lumber is not recommended due to its tendency to shrink. This can cause the slates to crack and become displaced.

To permit proper re-laying of the slate, the new roof sheathing must be of smooth and solid construction. At least two nails should be placed through the new boards at every rafter and joints between the ends of the boards should occur over rafters. Insufficient nailing will cause the boards to be springy, making nailing of the slates difficult and causing adjacent slates to loosen in the process. Unevenness in the sheathing will show in the finished roof surface and may cause premature cracking of the slate. Roof sheathing in valleys and along hips, ridges, and eaves may be covered with waterproof membrane underlayment rather than roofing felt for added protection against leakage.

In emergency situations, such as when severe hurricanes or tornadoes blow numerous slates off the roof, a temporary roof covering should be installed immediately after the storm to prevent further water damage to the interior of the building and to permit the drying out process to begin. Heavy gauge plastic and vinyl tarpaulins are often used for this purpose, though they are difficult to secure in place and can be blown off in high winds. Roll roofing, carefully stitched in to areas of the remaining roof, is a somewhat more functional solution that will allow sufficient time to document the existing roof conditions, plan repairs, and order materials (Figure 21).

Slate roof repair is viable for localized problems and damaged roofs with reasonably long serviceable lives remaining. If 20% or more of the slates on a roof or roof slope are broken, cracked, missing, or sliding out of position, it is usually less expensive to replace the roof than to execute individual repairs. This is especially true of older roofs nearing the end of their serviceable lives

Figure 20. This roof has been poorly repaired numerous times in the past. The installation of mastic to seal out moisture has only exacerbated the problem. A timely repair and good maintenance could have extended the life of this roof.

Figure 21. As a result of hurricanes and other disasters, it may be necessary to temporarily stabilize a roof until materials can be obtained and a qualified roofing contractor hired. Heavy roofing felt was stitched into this slate roof to stop moisture penetration until matching slate was obtained for repair. Significant slate roofs should not be stripped off and replaced with asphalt shingles. Photograph courtesy of the National Park Service.

because even the most experienced slater will likely damage additional slates while attempting repairs. Depending on the age of the slate, its expected serviceable life, and the cause(s) of deterioration, it may or may not be cost effective to salvage slates. Where deteriorated nails or flashings are the cause of the roof failure, salvage of at least some slates should be possible for use in repairs. When salvaging slates, each must be sounded to discover cracks and faults and the degree to which it has weathered. It is usually wise to salvage slates when only a portion of the roof is to be replaced. In this way, the salvaged slates may be used for future repairs to the remaining sections of the roof.

The Replacement of Deteriorated Roofs

Historic slate roofs should be repaired rather than replaced whenever possible. Before replacing a slate roof, check for isolated damage, corroded and worn flashings, leaky gutters, poor ventilation in the attic, and other possible sources of moisture. All too often slate roofs are mistakenly replaced when, in fact, they could have been effectively repaired. Deciding whether an historic slate roof should be repaired or replaced can be difficult and each roof must be judged separately (see guidance in shaded box on page 16).

If repair is not possible and a new slate roof must be installed, it is important to remember that more than just the replacement of the slate is involved (Figure 22). The old slate should be removed to prevent overloading of the roof timbers. Stripping should be done in sections, with felt installed, to avoid exposing the entire sub-roof to the weather. In the process, rotted wood sheathing should be replaced and the roof timbers checked for signs of stress, including deflection, cracking, and twisting. If such conditions are found, a structural engineer experienced in working with older buildings should be consulted. Other repairs, such as chimney repointing, which may require access to the roof should be completed before the new roof is put on.

Drawings and specifications for a new slate roof should be prepared by a restoration architect, especially if the project is going to be competitively bid or if the roof is particularly complex. Standard specifications, like those published in 1926 by the National Slate Association may be used as a basis for developing specifications appropriate for a particular project. The specifications and drawings should contain all the information necessary to replicate the original appearance of the roof as closely as possible. Certain changes may have to be accepted, however, since several types of slate once prominent in this country, such as ribbon slate, are no longer quarried. It is wise to

(a) Historic documentation was necessary to determine the historic configuration.

(b) Scaffolding was installed early to document existing conditions to determine extent of work.

(c) Slate was removed in sections to avoid stress on timber framing.

(d) Deteriorated sheathing was replaced and rafter tails were reinforced.

(e) Roofing felt was installed over decking; a rubberized membrane was used selectively at the eaves and under some flashing.

(f) Lead coated copper flashing was installed throughout. Seen is the offset between the portico roof and the main roof in progress.

Figure 22. Installing a new roof involves more than just slate. Above is a sequence of views of the roof replacement at Arlington House. Photographs courtesy of the National Park Service. (Sequence continued on page 14.)

(g) Masonry chimneys were repaired and metal crickets were fabricated at the chimneys.

(h) This installation pattern allows the slates to be laid in courses leaving a temporary path of travel to avoid stepping on installed slates.

(i) Although the gutters and snow boards were the last elements installed, their support brackets were installed as the slates were laid.

anticipate the replacement of older roofs so that proper planning can be undertaken and financial resources set aside, thereby, reducing the likelihood of rash last minute decisions.

Roofing slate is sold by the square in the United States. One square is enough to cover 100 square feet (13.3 square meters) of plain roof surface when laid with a standard headlap of 3″ (7.5cm). When ordering slate, considerable lead time should be allowed as delivery may take anywhere from 4 to 12 weeks and even as long as 1 year for special orders. Orders for random widths of a particular slate can generally be filled more quickly than orders for fixed widths. Once on site, slates should be stored on edge, under cover on pallets.

A roof and its associated flashings, gutters, and downspouts function as a system to shed water. Material choices should be made with this in mind. For example, use a single type of metal for all flashings and the rainwater conductor system to avoid galvanic action. Choose materials with life spans comparable to that of the slate, such as non-ferrous nails. Use heavier gauge flashings or sacrificial flashings in areas that are difficult to access or subject to concentrated water flows.

Flashings are the weakest point in any roof. Given the permanence of slate, it is poor economy to use anything but the most durable of metals and the best workmanship for installing flashings. Copper is one of the best flashing materials, and along with terne, is most often associated with historic slate roofs. Copper is extremely durable, easily worked and soldered, and requires little maintenance. Sixteen-ounce copper sheet is the minimum weight recommended for flashings. Lighter weights will not endure the erosive action of dust and grit carried over the roof by rain water. Heavier weight, 20 oz. (565 grams) or 24 oz. (680 grams), copper should be used in gutters, valleys, and areas with limited accessibility. Lead coated copper has properties similar to copper and is even more durable due to its additional lead coating. Lead coated copper is often used in restoration work.

Terne is a less desirable flashing material since it must be painted periodically. Terne coated stainless steel (TCS) is a modern-day substitute for terne. Although more difficult to work than terne, TCS will not corrode if left unpainted; a great advantage, especially in areas that are difficult to access.

Once a metal is chosen, it is important to use it throughout for all flashings, gutters, downspouts, and metal roofs. Mixing of dissimilar metals can lead to rapid corrosion of the more electronegative metal by galvanic action. Where flashings turn up a vertical surface, they should be covered with a cap flashing. Slates which overlap metal flashings should be nailed in such a manner as to avoid puncturing the metal. This may be accomplished by punching a second hole about 2″ (5cm) above the existing hole on the side of the slate not overlapping the metal flashing. It is important that holes be punched from the back side of the slate. In this way, a shallow countersink is created on the face of the slate in which the head of the nail may sit.

◄ *Continuation of the roof repair sequence of Arlington House from page 13.*

Figure 23. Slate roofs should not be walked on if at all possible. For large projects, lifts can be used to inspect roofs periodically to assess maintenance needs. Photograph courtesy of the National Park Service.

The use of artificial, mineral fiber slate is not recommended for restoration work since its rigid appearance is that of a man-made material and not one of nature. Artificial slates may also have a tendency to fade over time. And, although artificial slate costs less than natural slate, the total initial cost of an artificial slate roof is only marginally less than a natural slate roof. This is because all the other costs associated with replacing a slate roof, such as the cost of labor, flashings, and tearing-off the old roof, are equal in both cases. Over the long term, natural slate tends to be a better investment because several artificial slate roofs will have to be installed during the life span of one natural slate roof.

Clear roof expanses can be covered by an experienced slater and one helper at the rate of about two to three squares per day. More complex roofs and the presence of chimneys, dormers, and valleys can bring this rate down to below one square per day. One square per day is a good average rate to use in figuring how long a job will take to complete. This takes into account the installation of flashings and gutters and the set-up and break-down of scaffolding. Tear-off of the existing roof will require additional time.

Maintenance

Given the relatively high initial cost of installing a new slate roof, it pays to inspect its overall condition annually and after severe storms. For safety reasons, it is recommended that building owners and maintenance personnel carry out roof surveys from the ground using binoculars or from a cherry picker (Figure 23). Cracked, broken, misaligned, and missing slates and the degree to which delamination has occurred should be noted, along with failed flashings (pin holes, open seams, loose and misaligned elements, etc.) and broken or clogged downspouts. A roof plan or sketch and a camera can aid in recording problems and discussing them with contractors. In the attic, wood rafters and sheathing should be checked for water stains and rot. Critical areas are typically near the roof plate and at the intersection of roof planes, such as at valleys and hips. Regular maintenance should include cleaning gutters at least twice during the fall and once in early spring, and replacing damaged slates promptly. Every five to seven years

inspections should be conducted by professionals experienced in working with slate and steep slopes. Good record keeping, in the form of a log book and the systematic filing of all bills and samples, can help in piecing together a roof's repair history and is an important part of maintenance.

As part of regular maintenance, an attempt should be made to keep foot traffic off the roof. If maintenance personnel, chimney sweeps, painters, or others must walk on the roof, it is recommended that ladders be hooked over the ridge and that the workmen walk on the ladders to better distribute their weight. If slates are to be walked on, it is best to wear soft soled shoes and to step on the lower-middle of the exposed portion of the slate unit.

Conclusion

Slate roofs are a critical design feature of many historic buildings that cannot be duplicated using substitute materials (Figure 24). Slate roofs can, and should be, maintained and repaired to effectively extend their serviceable lives. When replacement is necessary, details contributing to the appearance of the roof should be retained. High quality slate is still available from reputable quarries and, while a significant investment, can be a cost effective solution over the long term.

Further Reading

Copper And Brass Research Association. *Copper Flashings.* 2nd ed. New York: Copper And Brass Research Association, 1925.

Dale, T. Nelson, and others. *Slate In The United States,* Bulletin 586. Washington, D.C.: U.S. Department of the Interior, United States Geological Survey, 1914.

Heim, David. "Roofing With Slate." *Fine Homebuilding,* No. 20 (April/May 1984): 38–43.

Levine, Jeffrey S. "Slate Roofs For Historic Religious Buildings." *Inspired.* Philadelphia: Philadelphia Historic Preservation Corporation, 1987.

"Slate Quarrying and Shingle Manufacture." *Fine Homebuilding,* No.71 (Jan. 1992): 64–68.

McKee, Harley J. "Slate Roofing." *APT Bulletin,* Vol. 2, Nos. 1–2 (1970): 77–84.

National Slate Association. *Slate Roofs.* 1925. Reprint. Fair Haven, Vermont: Vermont Structural Slate Co., Inc., 1977.

Pierpont, Robert N. "Slate Roofing." *APT Bulletin,* Vol. 19, No. 2 (1987): 10–23.

Sweetser, Sarah M. "Roofing for Historic Buildings." *Preservation Briefs,* No. 4. Washington, D.C.: U.S. Department of the Interior, Technical Preservation Services Division, 1975.

Repair/Replacement Guideline

The following guideline is provided to assist in the repair/replace decision making process:

1. Consider the age and condition of the roof versus its expected serviceable life given the type of slate employed.

2. Calculate the number of damaged and missing slates. Is the number less than about 20%? Is the roof generally in good condition? If so, the roof should be evaluated for repair rather than replacement. Also, keep in mind that the older a roof becomes, the more maintenance it will likely require.

3. Determine if there are active leaks and what their source may be. Do not assume the slates are leaking. Gutters, valleys and flashings are more likely candidates. "False leaks" can be caused by moisture condensation in the attic due to improper ventilation.

4. Check the roof rafters and sheathing for moisture stains. Poke an awl into the wood to determine if it is rotted. Remember that very old, delaminating slates will hold moisture and cause adjacent wood members to deteriorate even if there are no apparent leaks.

5. Are many slates sliding out of position? If so, it may be that ferrous metal fasteners were used and that these are corroding, while the slates are still in good condition. Salvage the slates and re-lay them on the roof. If the slates have worn around the nails holes, it may be necessary to punch new holes before re-laying them.

6. Consider the condition of the roof's flashings. Because slate is so durable, metal flashings often wear out before the slate does. Examine the flashings carefully. Even the smallest pinhole can permit large quantities of water to enter the building.

7. Is the deterioration of the slate uniform? Often this is not the case. It may be that only one slope needs replacement and the other slopes can be repaired. In this way, the cost of replacement can be spread over many years.

8. Press down hard on the slates with your hand. Sound slates will be unaffected by the pressure. Deteriorated slates will feel brittle and will crack. Tap on slates that have fallen out or been removed. A full, deep sound indicates a slate in good condition, while a dull thud suggests a slate in poor condition.

9. Are new slates readily available? Even if replacement is determined to be necessary, the existing roof may have to be repaired to allow time for documentation and the ordering of appropriate replacement slates.

Figure 24. Although slate replacement roofs are expensive, the superiority of materials and craftsmanship will give years of continued service. If amortized over the life of the roof, the replacement cost can be very reasonable. Photograph courtesy of the National Park Service.

Note: measurements in this publication are given in both U.S. Customary System and International (Metric) System for comparative purposes. Metric conversions are in some cases approximate and should not be relied upon in preparing technical specifications.

Acknowledgements

The author, **Jeffrey S. Levine,** is an Architectural Conservator with John Milner Associates, Inc., and gratefully acknowledges the technical review of this publication by the following: Russel Watsky, Watsky Associates; Kenton Lerch, The Structural Slate Company; Matt Millen, Millen Roofing Co.; Alex Echeguren, Echeguren Slate Company; Bill Markcrow, Vermont Structural Slate Company; and Dick Naslund, Department of Geological Sciences, State University of New York at Binghamton. In addition, invaluable comments were provided by Sharon Park, Doug Hicks and Michael J. Auer, National Park Service; Suzanna Barucco, Martin Jay Rosenblum, R.A. & Associates; and Fred Walters, John Milner Associates, Inc. All photographs are by the author unless otherwise noted.

Sharon C. Park, AIA, Senior Historical Architect, Preservation Assistance Division, National Park Service, is credited with directing the development of this publication and with its technical editorship. This publication has been prepared pursuant to the National Preservation Act of 1966, as amended, which directs the Secretary of the Interior to develop and make available information concerning historic properties. Comments on the usefulness of this publication may be directed to H. Ward Jandl, Chief, Technical Preservation Services Branch, Preservation Assistance Division, National Park Service, P.O. Box 37127, Washington, D.C. 20013-7127. Drawings for this publication were prepared by Karin Murr Link.

Cover Photograph: A portion of an advertisement for Slatington-Bangor Slate Syndicate (Slatington, PA) which appeared in the July 1910 issue of Building Age *(Vol.32 No.7).*

30

The Preservation and Repair of Historic Clay Tile Roofs

Anne E. Grimmer and Paul K. Williams

Clay tiles are one of the most distinctive and decorative historic roofing materials because of their great variety of shapes, colors, profiles, patterns, and textures. Traditionally, clay tiles were formed by hand, and later by machine extrusion of natural clay, textured or glazed with color, and fired in high-temperature kilns. The unique visual qualities of a clay tile roof often make it a prominent

feature in defining the overall character of a historic building (Fig. 1). The significance and inherently fragile nature of historic tile roofs dictate that special care and precaution be taken to preserve and repair them.

Clay tile has one of the longest life expectancies among historic roofing materials—generally about 100 years,

SOUTH ELEVATION
SCALE: 3/16" = 1'-0"

Figure 1. Clay tiles used as roof covering and as vertical cladding on the third story and gable ends are important in defining the historic character of the Alfred W. McCune Mansion in Salt Lake City. Designed by the architect S.C. Dallas, and completed in 1901, this brick and brownstone structure is a tiled variation of the Shingle style. Drawing: Clay Fraser, HABS Collection.

and often several hundred. Yet, a regularly scheduled maintenance program is necessary to prolong the life of any roofing system. A complete internal and external inspection of the roof structure and the roof covering is recommended to determine condition, potential causes of failure, or source of leaks, and will help in developing a program for the preservation and repair of the tile roof. Before initiating any repair work on historic clay tile roofs, it is important to identify those qualities important in contributing to the historic significance and character of the building.

This Brief will review the history of clay roofing tiles and will include a description of the many types and shapes of historic tiles, as well as their different methods of attachment. It will conclude with general guidance for the historic property owner or building manager on how to plan and carry out a project involving the repair and selected replacement of historic clay roofing tiles. Repair of historic clay tile roofs is not a job for amateurs; it should be undertaken only by professional roofers experienced in working with clay tile roofs.

Historical Background

The origin of clay roofing tile can be traced independently to two different parts of the world: China, during the Neolithic Age, beginning around 10,000 B.C.; and the Middle East, a short time later. From these regions, the use of clay tile spread throughout Asia and Europe. Not only the ancient Egyptians and Babylonians, but also the Greeks and Romans roofed their buildings with clay tiles, and adaptations of their practice continue in Europe to the present. European settlers brought this roofing tradition to America where it was established in many places by the 17th century.

Archeologists have recovered specimens of clay roofing tiles from the 1585 settlement of Roanoke Island in North Carolina. Clay tile was also used in the early English settlements in Jamestown, Virginia, and nearby St. Mary's in Maryland. Clay roofing tiles were also used in the Spanish settlement of St. Augustine in Florida, and by both the French and Spanish in New Orleans.

Fig. 2. Sunnyside, Washington Irving's house in Tarrytown, New York, dates to about 1656. Although extensively remodeled during the years 1836-1849, the stepped gables and tiled roof still reflect the heritage of its original Dutch builders. Photo: Jack E. Boucher, HABS Collection.

Dutch settlers on the east coast first imported clay tiles from Holland. By 1650, they had established their own full-scale production of clay tiles in the upper Hudson River Valley, shipping tiles south to New Amsterdam (Fig. 2). Several tile manufacturing operations were in business around the time of the American Revolution, offering both colored and glazed tile and unglazed natural terra-cotta tile in the New York City area, and in neighboring New Jersey. A 1774 New York newspaper advertised the availability of locally produced, glazed and unglazed pantiles for sale that were guaranteed to "stand any weather." On the west coast clay tile was first manufactured in wooden molds in 1780 at Mission San Antonio de Padua in California by Indian neophytes under the direction of Spanish missionaries (Fig. 3).

By far the most significant factor in popularizing clay roofing tiles during the Colonial period in America was the concern with fire. Devastating fires in London, 1666, and Boston in 1679, prompted the establishment of building and fire codes in New York and Boston. These fire codes, which remained in effect for almost two centuries, encouraged the use of tile for roofs, especially

Fig. 3. Clay tiles were first produced on the west coast in 1780 at Mission San Antonio de Padua in Monterey County, California. The present church shown here dates from 1810. Photo: Gene Falk.

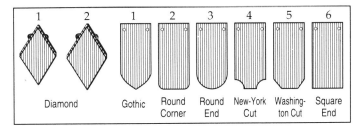

Fig. 4. Many mid- and late-19th century buildings had roofs with uniquely shaped tiles such as fishscale, or another one of the tile shapes that Charles Thomas Davis described as "the six forms of roofing tiles in most common use in this country," and illustrated in his 1884 book *A Practical Treatise on the Manufacture of Bricks, Tiles, Terra-Cotta, Etc.*

Figure 5. (a) Clay tile was a popular roofing material during the Romanesque Revival period, not only for residential structures including these rowhouses in the Dupont Circle Historic District in Washington, D.C., and designed and built by Thomas F. Schneider between 1889-1892, but also for large-scale public buildings such as (b) the Old Federal Courts Building (1894-1901) in St. Paul, Minnesota, designed by Willoughby J. Edbrooke. Photo: (a) Anne Grimmer, and (b) Winsor/Faricy Architects.

in urban areas, because of its fireproof qualities. Clay roofing tile was also preferred because of its durability, ease of maintenance, and lack of thermal conductivity.

Although more efficient production methods had lowered the cost of clay tile, its use began to decline in much of the northeastern United States during the second quarter of the 19th century. In most areas outside city-designated fire districts, wood shingles were used widely; they were more affordable and much lighter, and required less heavy and less expensive roof framing. In addition, new fire-resistant materials were becoming available that could be used for roofing, including slate, and metals such as copper, iron, tinplate, zinc, and galvanized iron. Many of the metal roofing materials could be installed at a fraction of the cost and weight of clay tile. Even the appearance of clay tile was no longer fashionable, and by the 1830s clay roofing tiles had slipped temporarily out of popularity in many parts of the country.

Revival Styles Renew Interest in Clay Roofing Tiles

By the mid-19th century, the introduction of the Italianate Villa style of architecture in the United States prompted a new interest in clay tiles for roofing. This had the effect of revitalizing the clay tile manufacturing industry, and by the 1870s, new factories were in business, including large operations in Akron, Ohio, and Baltimore, Maryland. Clay tiles were promoted by the Centennial Exhibition in Philadelphia in 1876, which featured several prominent buildings with tile roofs, including a pavilion for the state of New Jersey roofed with clay tiles of local manufacture. Tile-making machines were first patented in the 1870s, and although much roofing tile continued to be made by hand, by the 1880s more and more factories were beginning to use machines (Fig. 4). The development of the Romanesque Revival style of architecture in the 1890s further strengthened the role of clay roofing tiles as an American building material (Fig. 5).

Alternative substitutes for clay tiles were also needed to meet this new demand. By about 1855, sheet metal roofs designed to replicate the patterns of clay tile were being produced. Usually painted a natural terra cotta color to emulate real clay tile, these sheet metal roofs became popular because they were cheaper and lighter, and easier to install than clay tile roofs.

Clay roofing tiles fell out of fashion again for a short time at the end of the 19th century, but once more gained acceptance in the 20th century, due primarily to the popularity of the Romantic Revival architectural styles,

including Mission, Spanish, Mediterranean, Georgian and Renaissance Revival in which clay tile roofs featured prominently. With the availability of machines capable of extruding clay in a variety of forms in large quantities, clay tiles became more readily available across the nation. More regional manufacturing plants were established in areas with large natural deposits of clay, including Alfred, New York; New Lexington, Ohio; Lincoln, California; and Atlanta, Georgia; as well as Indiana, Illinois and Kansas.

The popularity of clay tile roofing, and look-alike substitute roofing materials, continues in the 20th century, especially in areas of the South and West—most notably Florida and California—where Mediterranean and Spanish-influenced styles of architecture still predominate (Fig. 6).

Fig. 6. Like many other house of this period in Florida, the roof of the Chester C. Bolton House in Palm Beach features tiles imported from Cuba. These tiles, with their richly varied earth colors, were often laid in thick cement mortar that was intended to give a "rustic" appearance. The residence, which includes the main house (1918-1919) designed by James A. Garfield, and an addition built in 1929 designed by Prentice Sanger, has been described as an English manor house with Spanish details. Photo: Jack E. Boucher, HABS Collection.

Early Tiles

During the 17th and 18th centuries the most common type of clay roofing tiles used in America were flat and rectangular. They measured approximately 10″ × 6″ × 1/2″ (25cm × 15cm × 1.25cm), and had two nail or peg holes at one end through which they were anchored to the roofing laths. Sometimes a strip of mortar was placed between the overlapping rows of tile to prevent the tiles from lifting in high winds. In addition to flat tiles, interlocking S-shaped pantiles were also used in the 18th century. These were formed by molding clay over tapered sections of logs, and were generally quite large. Alternately termed pan, crooked, or Flemish tiles, and measuring approximately 14 1/2″ × 9 1/2″ (37cm × 24cm), these interlocking tiles were hung on roofing lath by means of a ridge or lug located on the upper part of the underside of each tile. Both plain (flat) tile and pantile (S-shaped or curved) roofs were capped at the ridge with semicircular ridge tiles. Clay roofing tiles on buildings in mid-18th century Moravian settlements in Pennsylvania closely resembled those used in Germany at the time. These tiles were about 14″–15″ long × 6″–7″ wide (36cm–38cm × 15cm–18cm) with a curved butt, and with vertical grooves to help drainage. They were also designed with a lug or nib on the back so that the tiles could hang on lath without nails or pegs.

The accurate dating of early roofing tiles is difficult and often impossible. Fragments of tile found at archeological sites may indicate the existence of clay tile roofs, but the same type of tile was also sometimes used for other purposes such as paving, and in bake ovens. To further complicate dating, since clay tile frequently outlasted many of the earliest, less permanent structures, it was often reused on later buildings.

Clay Tile Substitutes

In addition to sheet metal "tile" roofs introduced in the middle of the 19th century, concrete roofing tile was developed as another substitute for clay tile in the latter part of the 19th century (Fig. 7). It became quite popular by the beginning of the 20th century. Concrete tile is composed of a dense mixture of portland cement blended with aggregates, including sand, and pigment, and extruded from high-pressure machines. Although it tends to lack the color permanence and the subtle color variations inherent in natural clay tile, concrete tile continues to be a popular roofing material today because it reproduces the general look of clay tile, if not always the exact profile or proportions of historic clay tile, at a somewhat lower cost and weight. Another modern, slightly cheaper and lighter substitute for clay tile more recently developed consists of a mixture of mineral fiber and cement with pigments added to supply color. While these aggregate tiles also replicate the shape and appearance of clay roofing tiles, they have many of the same dissimilarities to clay tiles that are found in concrete tiles. Thus, like concrete tiles, they are seldom appropriate substitutes for clay tiles.

Fig. 7. (a) Metal ''tile'' roofs of galvanized steel closely resemble the clay tiles they mimic. Often painted to look like terra cotta, their identity can sometimes be revealed by peeling paint or dented ''tiles.'' (b-c) Concrete roofing tiles are generally thicker than clay tiles, and tend to fade and lose their color. Photos: (a-b) Anne Grimmer, (c) National Park Service Files.

Traditional Tile Shapes and Colors

There are two types of clay roofing tiles: interlocking and overlapping. *Interlocking* tiles are designed in pairs so that an extrusion or "lip" on one of the tiles "hooks" over the other tile thereby "locking" or securing the two together; they are also usually nailed to the roof structure. *Overlapping* tiles, which can also function in pairs, generally do not have any sort of "lip" and must be nailed in place. There is a wide range of shapes of historic clay roofing tiles, and many, sometimes with slight variations, are still produced today. There are many variations, and the country of origin of some of them may be revealed in their names, but there are essentially only two kinds of shapes: pantiles and flat tiles. Both pantiles and flat tiles may be either interlocking or overlapping (Figs. 8-9).

Pantiles. The shape most commonly associated with historic clay roofing tiles is probably that of convex or rounded tiles, often grouped together generically as "pan tiles" or "pantiles." These include Spanish tiles—sometimes called "S" tiles, or the similarly shaped Mission tiles, also known as Barrel or Barrel Mission tiles, straight or tapered, as well as Roman tiles, and their Greek variation.

Flat Tiles. Flat, shingle tiles are another type of historic clay roofing tiles. Flat tiles can be completely plain and flat, and, like roofing slates, overlap one another, attached with nails to the roof sheathing. Or they may interlock at the top and on one side. Although the "interlock" holds them together, most interlocking shingle tiles also have one or more holes, usually near the top, for nailing to the roof sheathing. Flat tiles are mostly variations of English or Shingle tiles, and include English Shingle, Closed Shingle, Flat, Shingle or Slab Shingle, as well as French tiles which have a slightly higher and more contoured profile.

Any of the standard tile shapes may be known by a different name in another region of the country, or in different parts of the world. For example, what are known as Spanish or "S" tiles in the United States, may be called Single Roman tiles in England. Sometimes Spanish and Mission tiles are equated despite the fact that the former are usually 1-piece interlocking tiles and the latter are single ½ cylinders that overlap. Since missions and the Mission style are associated with the Americas, Mission tiles in the United States are more commonly referred to as Spanish tiles in England and Europe. In a similar vein, Spanish or "S" tiles, or Barrel tiles, might seem to be more typical of some tiles used in France than what are marketed as French tiles by American manufacturers.

Today some tile manufacturers have given their own trademark name to historic tile shapes. Other companies market uniquely shaped "S" tiles that are more in the shape of a true, but rather low profile "s" without the customary flat portion of traditional American "S" tiles.

Field and Specialty Tile. The tiles that cover the majority of the flat surface of the roof are called *field* tile. Some roof shapes, particularly conical towers or turrets, require tiles of graduated sizes, and some shapes or patterns of field tile also require specially shaped finish tiles to complete the roof covering package. Other uniquely-shaped tiles were made to fit odd-shaped spaces and places including dormers and valleys, roof hips, rakes, ridges and corners. There are also finish tiles that fulfill certain needs, such as eave closures or clay plugs called "birdstops." These are intended to keep out snow and rain, and birds from nesting in the voids under the bottom row of curved tiles. Different patterns and designs can also be created by combining, or mixing and matching flat tiles with dimensional tiles.

Tile Colors. A terra cotta red is the color most commonly associated with historic clay roofing tiles. The reddish color comes from clay with a large percentage of iron oxide, and there are many variations of this natural color to be found in tiles ranging from deep reddish browns to softer and paler oranges and pinks. Lighter buff and beige colors, as well as black, also appear on traditional tile-

Traditional Clay Roofing Tile Shapes and Methods of Attachment

Pantiles

Type	Average Size	Description
Spanish or **"S"** Interlocking	13 1/4" long × 9 3/4" wide Exposure: 10 1/4"	Spanish or "S" tiles are 1-piece interlocking tiles with both a convex and a flat, or almost flat, horizontal surface. A raised lip that projects from the edge of the flat portion is designed to interlock with the edge of the convex, barrel end of the adjacent tile. Spanish tiles are usually laid directly on the wood sheathing, or on roofing felt, and fastened by two nails through holes at the top of the tiles, or sometimes mortared in place. Spanish tiles give a roof surface a fairly low and undulating profile.
Tapered or Straight Mission, Barrel, or Barrel Mission Overlapping	14"–18" up to 22"–24" long Each half cylinder about 3" high × about 8" in diameter Exposure: 11"–15"	Tapered or Straight Mission, Barrel, Barrel Mission, or Pan and Cover tile roofs are created with both a concave and a convex ½ cylinder-shaped tile. The concave (pan) tiles are laid first in vertical rows, and nailed directly to the roof sheathing. The convex (cover) tiles are laid to overlap and cover the vertical spaces, or joints, that separate the vertical rows of the concave tiles. The convex tiles may be fastened to the roof sheathing with very long nails, hooks or hangers, or more commonly laid over, and nailed to vertical wood battens underneath. Mission tile roofs have a higher profile than Spanish or Roman tile roofs.
Roman, Pan and Roll, or **Pan and Cover** Interlocking and Overlapping	12 3/4" long Width from center of 1 cover tile to center of next including width of 1 flat tile is 12" Exposure: 10"	Roman, or Pan and Roll, roofs consist of a two-part tile system which includes a convex barrel cover tile with a rather low profile placed over a flat tile laid directly on the roof sheathing. Like Mission tiles, the convex tiles may be nailed either to battens laid vertically on the roof or directly onto the roof sheathing. Both the convex cover tile and the flat tile may also have nibs at the top by which they interlock with tiles laid in rows above them. Roman tiles may also be cemented in place. A Roman tile roof appears as a series of fairly wide or broad, flat "valleys" alternating with rather low ridges or hills, much like a Spanish tile roof but with wider "flat" sections.
Greek Interlocking and Overlapping	Same size and dimensions as Roman tiles	Greek tiles are essentially a variation of Roman tiles, but the convex tiles that cover the vertical joints between the rows of "pan" tiles are shaped like a gable end or inverted "V". Greek tiles are attached to the roof in the same manner as Roman tiles.

Flat Tiles

Type	Average Size	Description
English Shingle or **Closed Shingle** Interlocking	English Shingle: 13 1/4" long × 8 3/4" wide Exposure: 10 1/8" long × 7 3/4" wide Closed Shingle: 11" long × 8 3/4" wide Exposure: 8" × 8"	English or Shingle tiles are generally plain and smooth-surfaced, but some are intended to imitate slate or wood shingles and are textured accordingly. The underside of these tiles can be either flat and smooth, or may have a corrugated appearance with 4-5 toothlike projections; all are attached with nails.
English Flat or **Slab Shingle** Overlapping	12" × 15" long × 6" × 7" wide, or 12" long × 9"–10" wide Exposure varies according to size of the tile, but is generally slightly less than ½ length of the tile	
French Interlocking	16 1/4" long × 9" wide Exposure: 9"	French tiles feature two deep vertical grooves on the surface that facilitate drainage, and create interesting light and shadow contrasts. A vertical lug projects from the top of these tiles that interlocks with the bottom of the tile laid over it. French tiles also have two nail holes at the top for nailing, and are often given a dab of cement for added security.

Fig. 8. Traditional Clay Roofing Tile Shapes and Methods of Attachment. Drawing: Karin Murr Link.

Clay Roofing Tile Installation Patterns

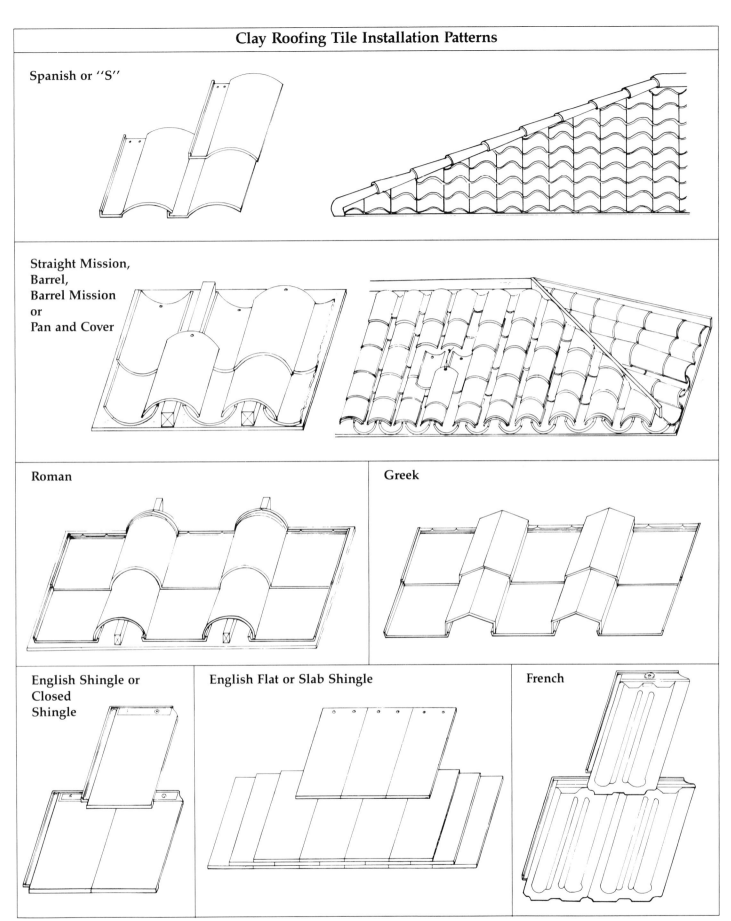

Spanish or "S"

Straight Mission,
Barrel,
Barrel Mission
or
Pan and Cover

Roman

Greek

English Shingle or
Closed
Shingle

English Flat or Slab Shingle

French

Fig. 9. Clay Roofing Tile Installation Patterns. Drawing: Karin Murr Link.

roofed buildings. Buff-colored tiles were made from nearly pure fire clay, and pouring manganese dissolved in water over the tile before firing resulted in smoke brown or black glazed tiles. Toward the end of the 19th century the popularity of colored glazes for roofing tiles increased, and their use and the range of colors continues to expand today. Most historic glazed roofing tiles are in fairly natural hues that range from reds and browns and buffs, to blacks and purples, blues (often created with smalt, or powdered blue glass), and a wide variety of greens (usually created with copper slag). There could be a considerable range in the colors of tiles that were baked over a wood fire because the temperature within the kiln was so uneven; tiles closest to the fire cooked all the way through and turned a darker red, while tiles farthest from the flames were likely to be smoke-stained, and lighter orange in color.

How Tiles are Attached

The method used to attach clay roofing tiles varies according to the shape, size and style of the particular tile. For the most part, traditional and modern methods of installing clay roofing tiles are very similar, except that modern practice always includes the use of wood sheathing and roofing felt. But most of the earliest clay roofing tiles were laid without benefit of wood sheathing and hung directly on roofing laths and battens that were nailed to the roof rafters; this practice continued up into the mid-19th century in some regions. While this method of attachment allowed for plenty of ventilation, and made it easy to find leaks and make repairs, it also meant that the overall watertightness of the roof depended entirely on the tiles themselves.

Gradually, the practice evolved of nailing roofing tiles directly onto continuous wood sheathing, or hanging them from "nibs" on horizontal lath that was attached to roof rafters or sheathing. Some kinds of tile, especially the later Mission or Barrel tiles were laid over vertical strips or battens nailed to the sheathing, or the tiles were fastened to wood purlins with copper wire.

Partly because they do not always fit together very closely, some tile shapes, including Spanish, Barrel or Mission as well as other types of interlocking tiles, are not themselves completely water-repellent when used on very low-pitched roofs. These have always required some form of sub-roofing, or an additional waterproof underlayer, such as felting, a bituminous or a cementitious coating. In some traditional English applications, a treatment called "torching," involved using a simple kind of mortar most commonly consisting of straw, mud, and moss. The tapered Mission tiles of the old Spanish missions in California were also laid in a bed of mud mortar mixed with grass or straw which was their only means of attachment to the very low-pitched reed or twig sheathing (latia) that supported the tiles (Fig. 10).

More recent and contemporary roofing practices require that the tiles be laid on solid 1" (2.5cm) wood sheathing felted with coated base sheets of at least 30 lbs., or built-up membranes or single-ply roof membranes. This substantially increases the watertightness of the roof by adding a second layer of waterproofing. Horizontal and vertical chalk lines are drawn to serve as a guide in laying

Fig. 10. The underside of this roof on the restored barracks at Santa Cruz Mission reveals the twig sheathing or latia to which the clay tiles were traditionally attached with mud mortar. Photo: Gil Sánchez, FAIA.

the tile and to indicate its patterning. Most tiles are designed with one or two holes so they can be attached by copper nails or hangers, and/or with projecting nibs, to interlock or hang on battens or lath attached to the base sheathing.

Before laying the tiles, the copper or lead gutters, flashings and valleys must be installed, preferably using at least #26 gauge (20-24 ounce) corrosion-resistant metal extending a minimum of 12" (30.5cm) under the tile from the edge, or in accordance with the manufacturer's specifications. The long life and expected durability of clay tiles require that, as with the roofing nails, only the best quality metal be selected for the flashing and guttering.

"Field tile" is usually ordered by the number of "squares"— that is, a flat section 10' x 10' (25cm × 25cm)—needed to cover a roof section. The tile company or roofing contractor should calculate the number of tiles needed according to the type of roof, and based on architect's drawings to ensure accuracy. This should include specialty ridge and eave tiles, decorative trim, partial "squares", approximately 10-20 per cent allowance for breakage, and extra tiles to store for repairing incidental damage later on. Once at the site, the tile is evenly distributed in piles on the roof, within easy reach for the roofers.

The tiles are laid beginning with the first course at the lower edge of the roof at the eaves. The method by which roofing tiles are laid and attached varies, depending on the type and design of the tiles and roof shape, as well as on regional practice and local weather conditions. A raised fascia, a cant strip, a double or triple layer of tiles, or special "birdstop" tiles for under the eaves, may be used to raise the first row of tiles to the requisite height and angle necessary for the best functioning of the roof (Fig. 11). The tile is positioned to overhang the previously installed gutter system by at least 1 1/2" (4cm) to ensure that rainwater discharges into the central portion of the gutter. Once this first course is carefully fitted and examined from the ground level for straightness and color nuances, and adjusted accordingly, successive courses are lapped over the ones below as the roofer works diagonally up the roof toward the ridge. Positioning and laying tiles in a 10'× 10' (25cm × 25cm) square may take on the average of 16½ man hours.

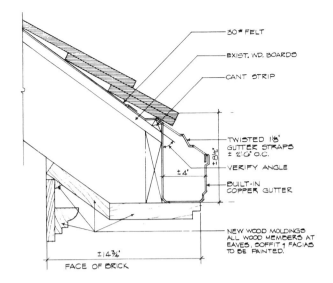

Fig. 11. *Both a cant strip and a double layer of tiles are used here to raise the first row of tiles to ensure proper roof drainage. This drawing was prepared for the restoration of the 1911-1912 Jamaica Pond Boathouse, Jamaica Plain, Massachusetts, which is part of the original Boston Park system designed by Frederick Law Olmsted in the late-19th century. Drawing: Richard White, Architect/Planner.*

Flat Tiles

Most flat clay tiles have one or two holes located at the top, or on a "nib" or "lug" that projects vertically either from the face or the underside of the tiles, for nailing the tile to the sheathing, battens, or furring strips beneath. As successive rows of tile are installed these holes will be covered by the next course of tiles above. Traditionally, clay tiles on the oldest tile roofs were hung on roofing laths with oak wooden pegs. As these wood pegs rotted, they were commonly replaced with nails. Today, copper nails, 13/4" (4.5cm) slaters' nails, are preferred for attaching the tiles because they are the longest lasting, although other corrosion-resistant nails can also be used. Less durable nails reduce the longevity of a clay tile roof which depends on the fastening agents and the other roofing components, as much as on the tiles themselves. Clay roofing tiles, like roofing slates, are intended to hang on the nails, and nailheads should always be left to protrude slightly above the surface of the tile. Nails should not be driven too deeply into the furring strips because too much pressure on the tile can cause it to break during freeze/thaw cycles, or when someone walks on the roof.

Plain flat tiles, like roofing slates, are attached to the roof sheathing only with nails. They are laid in a pattern overlapping one another in order to provide the degree of impermeability necessary for the roof covering. Because plain flat tiles overlap in most cases almost as much of one half of the tile, this type of tile roof covering results in a considerably heavier roof than does an interlocking tile roof which does not require that the tiles overlap to such an extent. Interlocking flat tiles form a single layer, and an unbroken roof covering. Although most interlocking tiles on all but the steepest roofs can technically be expected to remain in place because they hang on protruding nibs from the roofing laths or battens, in contemporary roofing practices they are often likely to be nailed for added security. In most cases it is usually a good idea to nail at least every other tile (Fig. 12).

Pantiles

With Mission or Barrel tiles, where one half-cylinder overlaps another inverted half-cylinder to form a cover and pan (cap and trough) arrangement, the fastening is more complicated. While the pantiles that rest directly on the sheathing are simply nailed in place, there are two ways of attaching the cover tiles that rest on the pantiles. They can be secured by a copper wire nailed to the sheathing or tied to vertical copper strips running behind the tiles (Fig. 13). Another method requires the installation of vertical battens or nailing strips on the roof to which the cover tiles are nailed, or the use of tile nails or hooks, which are hooked to the pantile below and secured with twisted copper wire.

Sometimes cement mortar, or another underlayer such as grass, moss or straw, or hair-reinforced mortar was added under the tiles. Before the use of felting this was a particularly common practice on some of the plain flat tile or Spanish tile roofs with low rises that were themselves not especially waterproof. Mortar also helped to keep driving rain from getting under the pantiles, and it is still customary in contemporary roofing to add a dab of cement mortar to help secure them (Fig. 14).

Ridge or Hip Tiles

At the roof ridge or hip, clay tile is usually attached to a raised stringer with nails and a small amount of mortar, elastic cement or mastic. The joint is sealed with a flexible flashing such as copper or lead. Ridge tiles are often somewhat larger and more decorative than the field tile utilized on the broad sections of the roof.

Roof Pitch and Weather are Factors in Tile Attachment

The means by which clay tile is attached to the sheathing is also partly determined by the roof pitch. *Generally the fastening requirements increase with an increase of roof pitch.* For low-pitched rises of 4"–6" (10cm–15cm) in a 12" (30.5cm) run the weight of the tiles is usually sufficient to hold them in place on the lath by the ridge or "lug" on the underside of the tile, with only the perimeter tiles requiring metal clips to secure them to the sheathing. But the tiles on even these low-pitched roofs are usually nailed for added security, and additional fastening measures are necessary on roofs with a higher pitch, or in areas subject to high winds or earthquakes. For steeper pitched roofs, such as towers, 7"–11" (18cm–28cm), or 12"–15" (30.5cm–38cm) in a 12" (30.5cm) run the tiles are nailed and a band of perimeter tiles three to four tiles thick is secured with clips. For roof rises over 16" (41cm) in a 12" (30.5cm) run, and in areas prone to earthquakes or hurricanes, every tile may be secured with both a nail and a copper or non-corrosive metal clip, and often also with a dab of roofing mastic or mortar.

The installation of clay roofing tiles in areas with significant amounts of snowfall—over 24" (61cm) per year—also varies somewhat from the normal guidelines. Larger battens may be necessary, as well as additional clipping or tying of the tile to securely attach it to the sheathing. The roof structure itself may also need added bracing, as well as the insertion of small snow clips or snow birds that protrude above the surface of the tile to prevent snow and ice from sliding off the roof and damaging the tile.

Figure 12. When constructed in Frankfort, Kentucky, in 1900, the Colonial Revival-style Berry Hill Mansion, and its 1912 Music Room addition were both roofed with ''Imperial'' tiles manufactured by Ludowici-Celadon (a). In 1992 the entire roof was replaced because of deterioration and surface spalling of many of the tiles (b). It was not possible to reproduce the original tiles due to budget limitations, thus Ludowici-Celadon's stock ''Classic Interlocking'' Shingle tiles were selected as replacements which could provide a close, if not exact, match. After tearing off and removing the old tiles, 30 lb. roofing felt was laid over the existing wood sheathing, new lead gutters and valleys were installed, and 90 lb. roll roofing was laid, on which the new tiles were laid. Although most of the field tiles were simply attached by 2 nails to the substrate (c), many of the tiles that had to be cut to fit hips, valleys and dormers were left with only one hole, and had to be wired and then nailed in place (d-e). The exact color and glaze of the original tiles also could not be duplicated because the coloring material is no longer available; however, the new hipped roof terminus for the Music Room roof was custom-made and the replacement field tiles are very similar to the originals (f). The original ridge tiles were designed to ''nest'' and fit perfectly over the field tiles beneath them whereas the new ridge tiles simply overlap one another, but this is barely perceptible when viewed from the ground. Photos: Edwin C. Krebs, AIA.

Figure 13 (a-b). These custom-made tapered mission tiles are being attached to the roof using a special system. This consists of twisted 10-gauge brass or copper wires that run up the roof slope through a new treated roof ridge, and down the other side of the roof. These twisted wires are placed about 12" (30.5cm) apart, and diamond shapes are twisted into them every 6" (15cm). The vertical wires are secured with 10-gauge copper or brass anchors approximately every 4' (1.22m) on center depending on the roof slope. Although these tiles would have originally been laid in mud mortar, this method of attachment is particularly successful in seismic areas. The random placement of the tiles accurately replicates the pattern traditionally used on the early missions. Photos: Gil Sánchez, FAIA.

Preservation and Repair

Identifying Common Problems and Failures

While clay roofing tiles themselves are most likely to deteriorate because of frost damage, a clay tile roof system most commonly fails due to the breakdown of the fastening system. As the wooden pegs that fastened the early tiles to hand-riven battens rotted, they were often replaced with iron nails which are themselves easily corroded by tannic acid from oak battens or sheathing. The deterioration of metal flashing, valleys, and gutters can also lead to the failure of a clay tile roof.

Another area of potential failure of a historic clay tile roof is the support system. Clay tiles are heavy and it is important that the roof structure be sound. If gutters and downspouts are allowed to fill with debris, water can back up and seep under roofing tiles, causing the eventual deterioration of roofing battens, the sheathing and fastening system, or even the roof's structural members (Fig. 15). During freezing weather, ice can build up under tiles and cause breakage during the freeze/thaw cycle. Thus, as with any type of roof, water and improperly maintained rainwater removal and drainage systems are also chief causes for the failure of historic clay tile roofs.

Clay tiles may be either handcrafted or machine-made; in general, roofs installed before the end of the 19th century consist of hand-formed tiles, with machine-made tiles becoming more dominant as technology improved during the 20th century. Clay tile itself, whether made by hand or made by machine, can vary in quality from tile to tile. Efflorescence of soluble salts on the surface may indicate that a tile has excessive porosity which results from underburning during its manufacture. Poor quality porous tiles are particularly susceptible to breaking and exterior surface spalling during freeze-thaw cycles. By letting in moisture, porous tiles can permit the roof battens and roof structure to rot. The problem may be compounded by

waterproof building paper or building felt laid underneath which can, in some instances, prevent adequate ventilation.

Clay roofing tiles can also be damaged by roofers walking carelessly on an unprotected roof while making repairs, or by overhanging tree branches, falling tree limbs, or heavy hail. Broken tiles may no longer provide a continuous waterproof surface, thereby allowing water to penetrate the roofing structure, and may eventually result in its deterioration if the broken tiles are not replaced in a timely manner.

Although modern, machine-made clay tiles are more uniform in appearance than their hand-made counterparts, they also have the potential for failure. Occasionally, entire batches of mass-produced tile can be defective.

Fig. 14. The Spanish or "S" tiles used to re-roof the Mission Revival style Holy Cross Episcopal Church in Sanford, Florida, have corrugated projections or "teeth" on the underside of the flat portion of each tile which adhere to the cement mortar holding them to the roof sheathing. Photo: Walter S. Marder, AIA.

Figure 15. (a) A regular cleaning schedule would have eliminated the plant growth and leaf build-up in this gutter, which, if not removed, will result in serious damage to roof sheathing and structure (b). Photos: (a) Paul K. Williams, and (b) Walter S. Marder. AIA.

Regular Inspection and Maintenance

Broken or missing tiles, or leaks on the interior of the building, are obvious clues that a historic clay tile roof needs repair. Even though it may be clear that the roof is leaking, finding the source of the leak may not be so easy. It may require thorough investigation in the attic, as well as going up on the roof and removing tiles selectively in the approximate area of the roof leak. The source of the leak may not actually be located where it appears to be. Water may come in one place and travel along a roofing member some distance from the actual leak before revealing itself by a water stain, plaster damage, or rotted wooden structural members.

Temporary Protection during Repair

In some instances temporary protection and stabilization may be necessary to prevent further damage or deterioration of a historic clay tile roof. Plywood sheets, plastic, roll roofing, or roofing felt can provide short-term protection until repair or replacement materials can be purchased. Another option may be to erect a temporary scaffold that is encased or covered with clear or semi-transparent polyethylene sheeting over the entire roof. This will not only protect the exposed roofing members during repair or until repairs can be made, but also lets in enough natural light to enable the re-roofing work to take place while sheltering workmen from cold or wet weather.

General Repair Guidance

Once the source and cause of a leak has been identified, appropriate repairs must be made to structural roofing members, wood sheathing, felt or roofing paper if it is part of the roofing membrane, or possibly to vertical roof battens to which the tiles may be attached. If the problem appears limited to gutters and flashing in disrepair, repair or replacement will probably require temporary removal of some of the adjacent tiles to gain access to them. If the roofing tiles are extremely fragile and cannot be walked on even with adequate protection (see below), it may also be necessary to remove several rows or a larger area of tiles and store them for later reinstallation in order to create a "path" to reach the area of repair without damaging existing tiles. Even if most of the tiles themselves appear to be intact but no longer securely attached to the roof substrate due to deterioration of the fastening system or roofing members, all the tiles should be labeled and removed for storage. Regardless of whether the repair project involves removal of only a few damaged tiles, or if all the tiles must be removed and relaid, historic clay roofing tiles are inherently fragile and should be pulled up carefully with the use of a slate ripper. The tiles can be reattached one-by-one with new corrosion-resistant copper nails, copper straps or tabs, "tingles", or another means after the necessary repairs have been made to the roof.

Replacing Individual Tiles

The most difficult aspect of replacing a single broken clay roof tile is doing so without breaking neighboring tiles. While flat shingle tiles can generally be walked on by a careful roofer without likelihood of much damage, high profile pantiles are very fragile and easily broken. By using sheets of plywood, planks, or burlap bags filled with sand to distribute weight, the professional roofer can move about the roof to fix broken tiles or flashing without causing additional damage. Another method involves hooking a ladder on the ridge to support and evenly distribute the weight of the roofer.

A broken tile should be carefully removed with a slate ripper or hacksaw blade inserted under the tile to cut the nail or nails holding it in place. If successive layers of tile are already in place covering the nailholes, it will not be possible to attach the replacement tile with nails through the holes, so an alternative method of attachment will be necessary. By nailing a tab of double thickness copper stripping on the sheathing below the tile, the new replacement tile can be slipped into position and secured in place by bending the copper strip up with a double thickness of the copper over the tile. A slate hook or "tingle" can be used in the same way. This fastening system functions in place of nails (Fig. 16).

When replacing hard-to-match historic tile, and if matching clay tile cannot be obtained, it may be possible to relocate some of the original tiles to the more prominent locations on the roof where the tile is damaged, and insert the new replacement tile in secondary or rear locations, or other areas where it will not show, such as behind chimney stacks, parapets, and dormer windows. Even though replacement tile may initially match the original historic tile when first installed, it is likely to weather or age to a somewhat different color or hue which will become more obvious with time. Thus, care should be taken to insert new replacement tile in as inconspicuous a location as possible. New, machine-made clay tile or concrete tiles should generally not be used to patch roofs of old, hand-made tile because of obvious differences in appearance.

Sources for Replacement Tiles

When restoring or repairing a clay tile roof it is always recommended that as many of the original tiles be retained and reused as possible. Sometimes, particularly when working with "pan and cover" type tile roofs, while many of the "cover" tiles may be broken and require replacement, it may be possible to reuse all or most of the "pan" tiles which are less susceptible to damage than the "cover" tiles. But, in most cases, unless matching replacements can be obtained, if more than about 30 per cent of the roofing tiles are lost, broken, or irreparably damaged, it may be necessary to replace all of the historic tiles with new matching tiles. When counting the number or percentage of missing or broken tiles that need to be replaced, it is important to order extra tiles to allow for breakage and damage during shipping and on the job site. The size of the tiles must be noted, whether they are all the same size, the same size but laid with different amounts of exposure to compensate for changes in perspective, or of graduated sizes according to horizontal rows—typical, for example, on conical or tower roofs (Fig. 17).

Many late-19th and early-20th century tiles are marked on the back with the name of the company that made them, along with the size and the name of that particular tile shape. Some companies that were in business in the United States at the turn of the century are still producing many of the traditional tile shapes, and may be able to supply the necessary replacements. But it is important to be aware that in some cases, although the name of a particular tile pattern may have remained the same, the actual shape, size, thickness and profile may have changed slightly so that the new tile does not match the historic tile closely enough to permit it to serve as a compatible replacement for missing or broken tiles. While such tiles may be acceptable to use on a secondary or less prominent elevation, or to use when an entire tile roof needs replacement, they would not be suitable to use on an area of the roof that is highly visible.

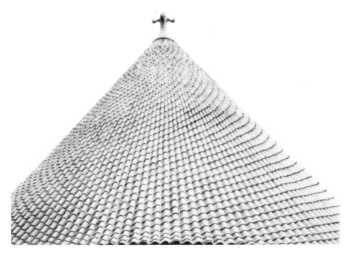

Fig. 17. The rhythm and pattern of these tiles which is so important in defining the character of this roof was created by laying the tiles with different amounts of exposure and using graduated tiles that decrease in size as they reach the top of the cone. Photo: National Park Service Files.

Even if the particular tile is no longer manufactured by a company, the original molds may still exist which can be used to make new tiles to match the historic tiles if the quantity needed is sufficiently large to warrant a custom order. Other companies stock and sell salvaged tile, and keep a variety of old tiles available which can be identified and matched by the number and company imprint on the back of the tiles. Still other companies specialize entirely in custom-made reproduction of historic clay tiles for a specific preservation project.

Modern clay tiles are even more varied than historic tiles. Many shapes and styles are offered in a wide variety of colors and glazes. Several manufacturers produce special color-blended tiles, as well as tiles of different hues that are intended to be carefully mixed when installed. *Yet, it is important to remember that many of these modern tiles may not be appropriate for use on historic clay tile roofs.* The place of manufacture must also be taken into consideration. For instance, tiles made for use in a hot, dry climate may not be able to withstand wet weather, drastic temperature changes or freeze-thaw cycles. Some of the tile shapes, and many of the colors—especially those that are very bright and highly glazed—are completely contemporary in design, and do not represent traditional American styles, and thus, are not suitable for use on historic buildings.

Repairing a Failed Fastening System

Clay roofing tiles, as noted before, frequently outlast their fastening systems. Wood pegs rot, nails rust, and even copper nails that are not adequately driven in can pull out of the roof's structural members. Although it is unusual that all of the clay tiles on a roof need to be replaced unless matching replacements cannot be obtained, it is not uncommon for old tile roofs to be stripped of all their tiles in order to re-lay the tiles with new fastenings and battens. When the fastening system has failed, all the roof tiles must be removed and reattached with new corrosion-resistant fasteners. If possible, all the tiles should be numbered and a diagram should be drawn showing the location of each tile to aid in replicating the original pattern and color variations when the tiles are relaid. Ideally, each tile should be numbered to ensure that it is reinstalled in its original location. But this may not always

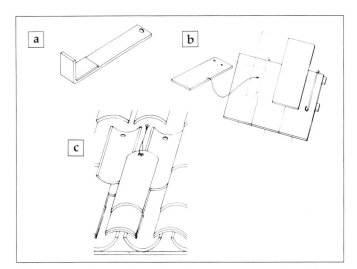

Figure 16. Attachments for repair and replacement of clay tiles include: (a) copper tab, (b) stainless steel or other non-corrosive metal clip, slate hook or "tingle," and (c) nailing and wire nailing. Drawing: Karin Murr Link.

Clay Tile Roofs of Alfred, New York

Taking advantage of high quality local shale ideal for making terra cotta and clay tiles, the Celadon Terra Cotta Company was established in Alfred, New York, in 1889. As a result, an unusually large percentage of historic buildings in this small town are roofed with clay tiles. This includes commercial and residential structures as well as other types of structures not commonly roofed with tile, such as barns and outbuildings. Even early-19th century houses were re-roofed—sometimes incongruously—with clay tiles. Today, the town roofs display an amazing variety of styles and patterns of tiles, many of which may have been factory seconds or experimental designs. In operation for only 20 years when it was destroyed by fire, the company continued manufacturing roofing tiles in New Lexington, Ohio, under the name Ludowici-Celadon. Photos: Terry Palmiter, Courtesy Alfred Historical Society.

be feasible or practical, and it may be enough simply to group the tiles as they are removed by type and size or function—such as field tiles, custom tiles for hips, dormers and ridges, and specially cut pieces. This will help facilitate reinstallation of the tiles. If all of the tiles have to be removed, it is probably a good idea to consider installing a layer of modern roofing felt over the wood sheathing. This will add another layer of waterproofing, while providing temporary protection during re-roofing.

Even if the tiles were originally attached with wooden pegs, it is generally recommended that they be rehung with corrosion-resistant, preferably heavy copper, or aluminum alloy nails or hooks. Today there are numerous non-traditional fastening systems for clay tile roofs, and many of them are patented. Roofing contractors and architects may have individual preferences, and some systems may be better suited than others to fit a particular roof shape or to meet a specific climatic or seismic requirement. Original battens or other roof members that may have deteriorated should be replaced to match the original using pressure-treated wood. Additional support may be necessary, particularly if the original roof was inadequate or poorly designed.

Replacing Flashing

Deteriorated flashing, gutters and downspouts should generally be replaced in kind to match the historic material. Copper or lead-coated copper, if appropriate to the building, or terne-coated stainless steel, is often preferred for use on historic clay tile roofs because of their durability and long lasting qualities. However, copper staining from downspouts can sometimes be a problem on light-colored masonry walls which should be taken into consideration when planning replacements to rainwater removal systems. Clay tile roofs usually have an open valley system where the tiles are separated by metal flashing at intersections of roof sections with different angles. This makes the insertion of new flashing quite easy, as only a few surrounding tiles must be removed in the process. New copper flashing that is too "bright" can be made to blend in and "mellowed" by brush-coating it with boiled linseed oil or proprietary solutions.

Inappropriate Repairs

The most important repair to avoid is replacing broken or missing roof tiles on a historic building with materials other than matching natural clay tiles. Concrete, metal or plastic tiles are generally not appropriate substitutes for clay roofing tiles. They lack the natural color variations of clay tile, and they do not have the same texture, shape, thickness or surface irregularities.

Although much concrete tile and composition tile is produced to resemble the general shape, if not the exact profile, of clay roofing tiles, concrete tile is generally too thick and also lacks the range of colors inherent in natural clay tile. Concrete tile is not a compatible substitute material to repair or replace individual historic clay tiles.

Patching a historic clay tile roof with roofing tar, caulk, asphalt, pieces of metal, or non-matching clay tiles is also inappropriate. Such treatments are visually incompatible. They also have the potential for causing physical damage. Water can collect behind these patches, thus accelerating deterioration of roof sheathing and fastening systems, and

during the expansion and contraction of a freeze-thaw cycle ice build-up at patches can break surrounding tiles.

Summary

Clay roofing tile itself, when correctly installed, requires little or no maintenance. Often, it is the fastening system used to secure the tiles to the sheathing that fails and needs to be replaced rather than the tiles themselves. In fact, because clay tiles frequently outlasted the building structure, it was not unusual for them to be reused on another building. When the fastening system has deteriorated, or the roofing support structure has failed, clay tiles can be removed relatively easily, necessary repairs can be made, and the historic tiles can be re-laid with new corrosion-resistant nails or hooks. Broken or damaged tiles should be replaced promptly to prevent further damage to neighboring tiles or to the roof structure itself.

As with any kind of historic roofing material, regular maintenance, such as cleaning gutters and downspouts, can add to the life of a tile roof. Additional preventive measures may include placing wire mesh over downspout openings or over the entire gutter to prevent debris from collecting and water from backing up. Periodic inspection of the underside of the roof from the attic after a heavy rain or ice storm for water stains may reveal leaks in their early stages which can be eliminated before they escalate into larger, more serious repair problems.

If replacement tile is required for the project, it should match the original tile as closely as possible, since a historic clay tile roof is likely to be one of the building's most significant features. Natural clay tiles have the inherent color variations, texture and color that is so important in defining the character of a historic tile roof. Thus, only traditionally shaped, clay tiles are appropriate for repairing a historic clay tile roof.

Selected Reading

Azevedo, J. "Tile Roofing." *Fine Homebuilding.* No. 60 (April/May 1990), pp. 36–41.

Belle, John, John Ray Hoke, Jr., and Stephen A. Kliment, editors. *Traditional Details for Building Restoration, Renovation, and Rehabilitation.* From the 1932–1951 Editions of [Ramsey/Sleeper] Architectural Graphic Standards." New York: John Wiley & Sons, Inc. 1991.

Davis, Charles Thomas. *A Practical Treatise on The Manufacture of Brick, Tiles, Terra Cotta, Etc.* Philadelphia: Henry Carey Baird & Co., 1884.

Fidler, John. "Tile, Slate and Stone Roofs." *Traditional Homes Technical Information Leaflet.* Number 1. 1991.

Labine, Clem. "How to Repair an Old Roof." *The Old-House Journal.* Vol. XI, No. 3 (April 1983), pp. 64–69

Labine, Clem , and Judith Siegel Lief. "The Rise of the Ornamental Roof," and "Traditional Building's SourceList of Traditional Roofing & Specialties." *Traditional Building.* Vol. 5, No. 3 (May/June/1992), pp. 35–46.

Melville, Ian A., and Ian A. Gordon. *The Repair and Maintenance of Houses.* London: The Estates Gazette Limited, 1973.

Poore, Patricia. "Tile Roofs." *The Old-House Journal.* Vol XV, No. 5 (September/October 1987), pp. 22–29.

"Special Roof Issue." *The Old-House Journal.* Vol XI, No. 3 (April 1983).

Sweetser, Sarah M. *Preservation Briefs 4: Roofing for Historic Buildings.* Washington, D.C.: National Park Service, U.S. Department of the Interior, 1978.

Vogel, Neal A. *Roofing Houses of Worship: Roofing Guidance for Church and Temple Administrators.* Information Series No. 59. Chicago: National Trust for Historic Preservation and Inspired Partnerships, 1992.

White, Richard. *Olmsted Park System, Jamaica Plain Boathouse, Jamaica Plain, Massachusetts: Planning for Preservation of the Boathouse Roof.* Preservation Case Studies. Washington, D.C.: Heritage Conservation and Recreation Service, U.S. Department of the Interior, 1979.

Selected Sources of Clay Roofing Tiles

Boston Valley Terra Cotta
6860 South Abbott Road
Orchard Park, NY 14127
Custom-made architectural terra cotta and clay roofing tiles

C.C.N. Clay Roof Tiles (Canteras Cerro Negro S.A.)
8280 College Parkway, Suite 204
Ft. Myers, FL 33919
Distributors of C.C.N. clay roofing tiles from Argentina

Earth/Forms of Alfred
5704 East Valley Road
Alfred Station, NY 14803
Made-to-order reproduction clay roofing tiles

Gladding, McBean & Co.
P.O. Box 97
Lincoln, CA 95648
Manufacturer since 1875 of terra cotta and clay roofing tiles, and custom reproductions

Hans Sumpf Company, Inc.
40101 Avenue 10
Madera, CA 93638
Made-to-order Mission-style clay roofing tiles

International Roofing Products, Inc.
4929 Wilshire Blvd., Suite 750
Los Angeles, CA 90010
New clay roofing tiles, some suitable for historic buildings

London Tile Co.
65 Walnut Street
New London, OH 44851
Made-to-order reproduction clay roofing tiles

Ludowici-Celadon, Inc.
4757 Tile Plant Road
New Lexington, OH 43764
Manufacturer since 1880s of clay roofing tiles, and custom reproductions

M.C.A. (Maruhachi Ceramics of America, Inc.)
1985 Sampson Avenue
Corona, CA 91719
New clay roofing tiles, some suitable for historic buildings

The Northern Roof Tile Sales Company
P.O. Box 275
Millgrove, Ontario LOR 1VO, Canada
Traditional clay roofing tiles imported from England and South America

Raleigh, Inc.
6506 Business U.S. Route 20
PO Box 448
Belvidere, IL 61008-0448
Inventory of new and salvage clay roofing tiles

Supradur Manufacturing Corp.
P.O. Box 908
Rye, NY 10580
Imports Spanish ("S") clay roofing tiles from France

TileSearch
P.O. Box 580
Roanoke, TX 76262
Computerized network for new and salvage clay roofing tiles

United States Tile Company
P.O. Box 1509
909 West Railroad Street
Corona, CA 91718
New clay roofing tiles, some suitable for historic buildings

Note: Measurements in this publication are given in both the U.S. Customary System and International (Metric) System for comparative purposes. Metric conversions are, in some cases, approximate and should not be relied upon for preparing technical specifications.

Acknowledgements

Anne Grimmer is a senior Architectural Historian with the Preservation Assistance Division of the National Park Service; **Paul K. Williams** is a Cultural Resource Manager with the Air Force. Both authors wish to thank the following individuals for the technical assistance they provided in the preparation of this publication: Edna Kimbro, Architectural Conservator, Watsonville, CA; Edwin S. Krebs, AIA, K. Norman Berry Associates, Louisville, KY; Melvin Mann, TileSearch, Roanoke, TX; Walter S. Marder, AIA, Division of Historical Resources, Tallahassee, FL; Gil Sánchez, FAIA, Gilbert Arnold Sánchez, Incorporated, Santa Cruz, CA; Terry Palmiter and Sandra Scofield, Alfred, NY; and National Park Service professional staff members. In addition, the authors wish to thank Karin Murr Link, who produced the drawings which illustrate this Brief.

This publication has been prepared pursuant to the National Historic Preservation Act of 1966, as amended, which directs the Secretary of the Interior to develop and make available information concerning historic properties. Comments on the usefulness of this publication may be directed to H. Ward Jandl, Chief, Technical Preservation Services Branch, National Park Service, P.O. Box 37127, Washington, D.C. 20013-7127.

Cover photograph: Restoration of the 1820s Indian barracks at Mission Santa Cruz in California included custom-made tapered barrel clay roof tiles based on archeological data found at the site. Photo: Ron Starr Photography.

31

Mothballing Historic Buildings

Sharon C. Park, AIA

When all means of finding a productive use for a historic building have been exhausted or when funds are not currently available to put a deteriorating structure into a useable condition, it may be necessary to close up the building temporarily to protect it from the weather as well as to secure it from vandalism. This process, known as mothballing, can be a necessary and effective means of protecting the building while planning the property's future, or raising money for a preservation, rehabilitation or restoration project. If a vacant property has been declared unsafe by building officials, stabilization and mothballing may be the only way to protect it from demolition.

This Preservation Brief focuses on the steps needed to "de-activate" a property for an extended period of time. The project team will usually consist of an architect, historian, preservation specialist, sometimes a structural engineer, and a contractor. Mothballing should not be done without careful planning to ensure that needed physical repairs are made prior to securing the building. The steps discussed in this Brief can protect buildings for periods of up to ten years; long-term success will also depend on continued, although somewhat limited, monitoring and maintenance. For all but the simplest projects, hiring a team of preservation specialists is recommended to assess the specific needs of the structure and to develop an effective mothballing program.

A vacant historic building cannot survive indefinitely in a boarded-up condition, and so even marginal interim uses where there is regular activity and monitoring, such as a caretaker residence or non-flammable storage, are generally preferable to mothballing. In a few limited cases when the vacant building is in good condition and in a location where it can be watched and checked regularly, closing and locking the door, setting heat levels at just above freezing, and securing the windows may provide sufficient protection for a period of a few years. But if long-term mothballing is the only remaining option, it must be done properly (see fig. 1 & 2). This will require stabilization of the exterior, properly designed security protection, generally some form of interior ventilation - either through mechanical or natural air exchange systems - and continued maintenance and surveillance monitoring.

Comprehensive mothballing programs are generally expensive and may cost 10% or more of a modest rehabilitation budget. However, the money spent on well-planned protective measures will seem small when amortized over the life of the resource. Regardless of the location and condition of the property or the funding available, the following 9 steps are involved in properly mothballing a building:

Figure 1. Proper mothballing treatment: This building has been successfully mothballed for 10 years because the roof and walls were repaired and structurally stabilized, ventilation louvers were added, and the property is maintained. Photo: Charles E. Fisher, NPS.

Figure 2. Improper treatment: Boarding up without adequate ventilation, lack of maintenance, and neglect of this property have accelerated deterioration. Photo; NPS file.

Documentation

1. Document the architectural and historical significance of the building.

2. Prepare a condition assessment of the building.

Stabilization

3. Structurally stabilize the building, based on a professional condition assessment.

4. Exterminate or control pests, including termites and rodents.

5. Protect the exterior from moisture penetration.

Mothballing

6. Secure the building and its component features to reduce vandalism or break-ins.

7. Provide adequate ventilation to the interior.

8. Secure or modify utilities and mechanical systems.

9. Develop and implement a maintenance and monitoring plan for protection.

These steps will be discussed in sequence below. Documentation and stabilization are critical components of the process and should not be skipped over. Mothballing measures should not result in permanent damage, and so each treatment should be weighed in terms of its reversibility and its overall benefit.

Documentation

Documenting the historical significance and physical condition of the property will provide information necessary for setting priorities and allocating funds. The project team should be cautious when first entering the structure if it has been vacant or is deteriorated. It may be advisable to shore temporarily areas appearing

to be structurally unsound until the condition of the structure can be fully assessed (see fig. 3). If pigeon or bat droppings, friable asbestos or other health hazards are present, precautions must be taken to wear the appropriate safety equipment when first inspecting the building. Consideration should be given to hiring a firm specializing in hazardous waste removal if these highly toxic elements are found in the building.

Documenting and recording the building. Documenting a building's history is important because evidence of its true age and architectural significance may not be readily evident. The owner should check with the State Historic Preservation Office or local preservation commission for assistance in researching the building. If the building has never been researched for listing in the National Register of Historic Places or other historic registers, then, at a minimum, the following should be determined:

• The overall historical significance of the property and dates of construction;

• the chronology of alterations or additions and their approximate dates; and,

• types of building materials, construction techniques, and any unusual detailing or regional variations of craftsmanship.

Old photographs can be helpful in identifying early or original features that might be hidden under modern materials. On a walk-through, the architect, historian, or preservation specialist should identify the architecturally significant elements of the building, both inside and out (see fig.4).

Figure 3. Buildings seriously damaged by storms or deterioration may need to be braced before architectural evaluations can be made. Jethro Coffin House. Photo: John Milner Architects.

Figure 4. Documenting the building's history, preparing schematic plans, and assessing the condition of the building will provide necessary information on which to set priorities for stabilization and repair prior to securing the building. Photo: Frederick Lindstrom, HABS.

By understanding the history of the resource, significant elements, even though deteriorated, may be spared the trash pile. For that reason alone, any materials removed from the building or site as part of the stabilization effort should be carefully scrutinized and, if appearing historic, should be photographed, tagged with a number, inventoried, and safely stored, preferably in the building, for later retrieval (see fig. 5).

A site plan and schematic building floor plans can be used to note important information for use when the building is eventually preserved, restored, or rehabilitated. Each room should be given a number and notations added to the plans regarding the removal of important features to storage or recording physical treatments undertaken as part of the stabilization or repair.

Because a mothballing project may extend over a long period of time, with many different people involved, clear records should be kept and a building file established. Copies of all important data, plans, photographs, and lists of consultants or contractors who have worked on the property should be added to the file as the job progresses.

Figure 5. Loose or detached elements should be identified, tagged and stored, preferably on site. Photo: NPS files.

Recording all actions taken on the building will be helpful in the future.

The project coordinator should keep the building file updated and give duplicate copies to the owner. A list of emergency numbers, including the number of the key holder, should be kept at the entrance to the building or on a security gate, in a transparent vinyl sleeve.

Preparing a condition assessment of the building. A condition assessment can provide the owner with an accurate overview of the current condition of the property. If the building is deteriorated or if there are significant interior architectural elements that will need special protection during the mothballing years, undertaking a condition assessment is highly recommended, but it need not be exhaustive.

A modified condition assessment, prepared by an architect or preservation specialist, and in some case a structural engineer, will help set priorities for repairs necessary to stabilize the property for both the short and long-term. It will evaluate the age and condition of the following major elements: foundations; structural systems; exterior materials; roofs and gutters; exterior porches and steps; interior finishes; staircases; plumbing, electrical, mechanical systems; special features such as chimneys; and site drainage.

To record existing conditions of the building and site, it will be necessary to clean debris from the building and to remove unwanted or overgrown vegetation to expose foundations. The interior should be emptied of its furnishing (unless provisions are made for mothballing these as well), all debris removed, and the interior swept with a broom. Building materials too deteriorated to repair, or which have come detached, such as moldings, balusters, and decorative plaster, and which can be used to guide later preservation work, should be tagged, labeled and saved.

Photographs or a videotape of the exterior and all interior spaces of the resource will provide an invaluable record of "as is" conditions. If a videotape is made, oral commentary can be provided on the significance of each space and architectural feature. If 35mm photographic prints or slides are made, they should be numbered, dated, and appropriately identified. Photographs should be cross-referenced with the room numbers on the schematic plans. A systematic method for photographing should be developed; for example, photograph each wall in a room and then take a corner shot to get floor and ceiling portions in the picture. Photograph any unusual details as well as examples of each window and door type.

For historic buildings, the great advantage of a condition assessment is that architectural features, both on the exterior as well as the interior, can be rated on a scale of their importance to the integrity and significance of the building. Those features of the highest priority should receive preference when repairs or protection measures are outlined as part of the mothballing process. Potential problems with protecting these features should be identified so that appropriate interim solutions can be selected. For example, if a building has always been heated and if murals, decorative plaster walls, or examples of patterned wall paper are identified as highly significant, then special care should be taken to regulate the interior climate and to monitor it adequately during the

363

mothballing years. This might require retaining electrical service to provide minimal heat in winter, fan exhaust in summer, and humidity controls for the interior.

Stabilization

Stabilization as part of a mothballing project involves correcting deficiencies to slow down the deterioration of the building while it is vacant. Weakened structural members that might fail altogether in the forthcoming years must be braced or reinforced; insects and other pests removed and discouraged from returning; and the building protected from moisture damage both by weatherizing the exterior envelope and by handling water run-off on the site. Even if a modified use or caretaker services can eventually be found for the building, the following steps should be addressed.

Structurally stabilizing the building. While bracing may have been required to make the building temporarily safe for inspection, the condition assessment may reveal areas of hidden structural damage. Roofs, foundations, walls, interior framing, porches and dormers all have structural components that may need added reinforcement. Structural stabilization by a qualified contractor should be done under the direction of a structural engineer or a preservation specialist to ensure that the added weight of the reinforcement can be sustained by the building and that the new members do not harm historic finishes (see fig. 6). Any major vertical post added during the stabilization should be properly supported and, if necessary, taken to the ground and underpinned.

Figure 6. Interior bracing which will last the duration of the mothballing will protect weakened structural members. Jethro Coffin House. Photo: John Milner Architects.

If the building is in a northern climate, then the roof framing must be able to hold substantial snow loads. Bracing the roof at the ridge and mid-points should be considered if sagging is apparent. Likewise, interior framing around stair openings or under long ceiling spans should be investigated. Underpinning or bracing structural piers weakened by poor drainage patterns may be a good precaution as well. Damage caused by insects, moisture, or from other causes should be repaired or reinforced and, if possible, the source of the damage removed. If features such as porches and dormers are so severely deteriorated

that they must be removed, they should be documented, photographed, and portions salvaged for storage prior to removal.

If the building is in a southern or humid climate and termites or other insects are a particular problem, the foundation and floor framing should be inspected to ensure that there are no major structural weaknesses. This can usually be done by observation from the crawl space or basement. For those structures where this is not possible, it may be advisable to lift selective floor boards to expose the floor framing. If there is evidence of pest damage, particularly termites, active colonies should be treated and the structural members reinforced or replaced, if necessary.

Controlling pests. Pests can be numerous and include squirrels, raccoons, bats, mice, rats, snakes, termites, moths, beetles, ants, bees and wasps, pigeons, and other birds. Termites, beetles, and carpenter ants destroy wood. Mice, too, gnaw wood as well as plaster, insulation, and electrical wires. Pigeon and bat droppings not only damage wood finishes but create a serious and sometimes deadly health hazard.

If the property is infested with animals or insects, it is important to get them out and to seal off their access to the building. If necessary, exterminate and remove any nests or hatching colonies. Chimney flues may be closed off with exterior grade plywood caps, properly ventilated, or protected with framed wire screens. Existing vents, grills, and louvers in attics and crawl spaces should be screened with bug mesh or heavy duty wire, depending on the type of pest being controlled. It may be advantageous to have damp or infected wood treated with insecticides (as permitted by each state) or preservatives, such as borate, to slow the rate of deterioration during the time that the building is not in use.

Securing the exterior envelope from moisture penetration. It is important to protect the exterior envelope from moisture penetration before securing the building. Leaks from deteriorated or damaged roofing, from around windows and doors, or through deteriorated materials, as well as ground moisture from improper site run-off or rising damp at foundations, can cause long-term damage to interior finishes and structural systems. Any serious deficiencies on the exterior, identified in the condition assessment, should be addressed.

To the greatest extent possible, these weatherization efforts should not harm historic materials. The project budget may not allow deteriorated features to be fully repaired or replaced in-kind. Non-historic or modern materials may be used to cover historic surfaces temporarily, but these treatments should not destroy valuable evidence necessary for future preservation work. Temporary modifications should be as visually compatible as possible with the historic building.

Roofs are often the most vulnerable elements on the building exterior and yet in some ways they are the easiest element to stabilize for the long term, if done correctly. "Quick fix" solutions, such as tar patches on slate roofs, should be avoided as they will generally fail within a year or so and may accelerate damage by trapping moisture. They are difficult to undo later when more permanent repairs are undertaken. Use of a tarpaulin over a leaking roof should be thought of only as a very temporary

Figure 7. Non-historic materials are appropriate for mothballing projects when they are used to protect historic evidence remaining for future preservation. This lightweight aluminum channel frame and roofing covers the historic wooden shingle roof. Galvanized mesh panels secure the window openings from intrusion by raccoons and other unwanted guests. Photo: Williamsport Preservation Training Center, NPS.

Figure 8. Appropriate mortar mixes should be used when masonry repairs are undertaken. In this case, a soft lime based mortar is used as an infill between the brick and wooden elements. When full repairs are made during the restoration phase, this soft mortar can easily be removed and missing bricks replaced.

emergency repair because it is often blown off by the wind in a subsequent storm.

If the existing historic roof needs moderate repairs to make it last an additional ten years, then these repairs should be undertaken as a first priority. Replacing cracked or missing shingles and tiles, securing loose flashing, and reanchoring gutters and downspouts can often be done by a local roofing contractor. If the roof is in poor condition, but the historic materials and configuration are important, a new temporary roof, such as a lightweight aluminum channel system over the existing, might be considered (see fig. 7). If the roofing is so deteriorated that it must be replaced and a lightweight aluminum system is not affordable, various inexpensive options might be considered. These include covering the existing deteriorated roof with galvanized corrugated metal roofing panels, or 90 lb. rolled roofing, or a rubberized membrane (refer back to cover photo). These alternatives should leave as much of the historic sheathing and roofing in place as evidence for later preservation treatments.

For masonry repairs, appropriate preservation approaches are essential. For example, if repointing deteriorated brick chimneys or walls is necessary to prevent serious moisture penetration while the building is mothballed, the mortar should match the historic mortar in composition, color, and tooling. The use of hard portland cement mortars or vapor-impermeable waterproof coatings are not appropriate solutions as they can cause extensive damage and are not reversible treatments (see fig. 8).

For wood siding that is deteriorated, repairs necessary to keep out moisture should be made; repainting is generally warranted. Cracks around windows and doors can be beneficial in providing ventilation to the interior and so should only be caulked if needed to keep out bugs and moisture. For very deteriorated wall surfaces on wooden frame structures, it may be necessary to sheathe in plywood panels, but care should be taken to minimize installation damage by planning the location of the nailing or screw

patterns or by installing panels over a frame of battens (see fig. 9). Generally, however, it is better to repair deteriorated features than to cover them over.

Foundation damage may occur if water does not drain away from the building. Run-off from gutters and downspouts should be directed far away from the foundation wall by using long flexible extender pipes equal in length to twice the depth of the basement or crawl space. If underground drains are susceptible to clogging, it is recommended that the downspouts be disconnected from the drain boot and attached to flexible piping. If gutters and downspouts are in bad condition, replace them with inexpensive aluminum units.

Figure 9. Severely deteriorated wooden siding on a farm building has been covered over with painted plywood panels as a temporary measure to eliminate moisture penetration to the interior. Foundation vents and loose floor boards allow air to circulate inside.

If there are no significant landscape or exposed archeological elements around the foundation, consideration should be given to regrading the site if there is a documented drainage problem (see fig. 10). If building up the grade, use a fiber mesh membrane to separate the new soil from the old and slope the new soil 6 to 8 feet (200 cm-266 cm) away from the foundation making sure not to cover up the dampcourse layer or come into contact with skirting boards. To keep vegetation under control, put down a layer of 6 mil black polyethylene sheeting or fiber mesh matting covered with a 2"-4" (5-10 cm.) of washed gravel. If the building suffers a serious rising damp problem, it may be advisable to eliminate the plastic sheeting to avoid trapping ground moisture against foundations.

Figure 10. Regrading around the Booker Tenement at Colonial Williamsburg has protected the masonry foundation wall from excessive damp. This building has been successfully mothballed for over 10 years. Note the attic and basement vents, the temporary stairs, and the informative sign interpreting the history of this building.

Mothballing

The actual mothballing effort involves controlling the long-term deterioration of the building while it is unoccupied as well as finding methods to protect it from sudden loss by fire or vandalism. This requires securing the building from unwanted entry, providing adequate ventilation to the interior, and shutting down or modifying existing utilities. Once the building is de-activated or secured, the long-term success will depend on periodic maintenance and surveillance monitoring.

Securing the building from vandals, break-ins, and natural disasters. Securing the building from sudden loss is a critical aspect of mothballing. Because historic buildings are irreplaceable, it is vital that vulnerable entry points are sealed. If the building is located where fire and security service is available then it is highly recommended that some form of monitoring or alarm devices be used.

To protect decorative features, such as mantels, lighting fixtures, copper downspouts, iron roof cresting, or stained glass windows from theft or vandalism, it may be advisable to temporarily remove them to a more secure location if they cannot be adequately protected within the structure.

Mothballed buildings are usually boarded up, particularly on the first floor and basement, to protect fragile glass windows from breaking and to reinforce entry points (see fig. 11). Infill materials for closing door and window openings include plywood, corrugated panels, metal grates, chain fencing, metal grills, and cinder or cement blocks (see fig. 12). The method of installation should not result in the destruction of the opening and all associated sash, doors, and frames should be protected or stored for future reuse.

Figure 11. Urban buildings often need additional protection from unwanted entry and graffiti. This commercial building uses painted plywood panels to cover expansive glass storefronts and chain link fencing is applied on top of the panels. The upper windows on the street sides have been covered and painted to resemble 19th century sash. Photo: Thomas Jester, NPS.

Generally exterior doors are reinforced and provided with strong locks, but if weak historic doors would be damaged or disfigured by adding reinforcement or new locks, they may be removed temporarily and replaced with secure modern doors (see fig. 13). Alternatively, security gates in a new metal frame can be installed within existing door openings, much like a storm door, leaving the historic door in place. If plywood panels are installed over door openings, they should be screwed in place, as opposed to nailed, to avoid crowbar damage each time the panel is removed. This also reduces pounding vibrations from hammers and eliminates new nail holes each time the panel is replaced.

For windows, the most common security feature is the closure of the openings; this may be achieved with wooden or pre-formed panels or, as needed, with metal sheets or concrete blocks. Plywood panels, properly installed to protect wooden frames and properly ventilated, are the preferred treatment from a preservation standpoint.

There are a number of ways to set insert plywood panels into windows openings to avoid damage to frame and sash (see fig. 14). One common method is to bring the upper and lower sash of a double hung unit to the mid-point of the opening and then to install pre-cut plywood panels using long carriage bolts anchored into horizontal wooden bracing, or strong backs, on the inside face of the window. Another means is to build new wooden blocking frames set into deeply recessed openings, for example in an industrial mill or warehouse, and then to affix the plywood panel to the blocking frame. If sash must be removed prior to installing panels, they should be labeled and stored safely within the building.

Plywood panels are usually 1/2"-3/4" (1.25-1.875 cm.) thick and made of exterior grade stock, such as CDX, or

marine grade plywood. They should be painted to protect them from delamination and to provide a neater appearance. These panels may be painted to resemble operable windows or treated decoratively (see fig. 15). With extra attention to detail, the plywood panels can be

Figure 12. First floor openings have been filled with cinderblocks and doors, window sash and frames have been removed for safe keeping. Note the security light over the windows and the use of a security metal door with heavy duty locks. Photo: H. Ward Jandl, NPS.

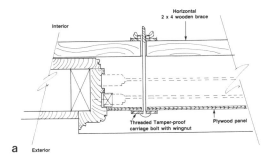

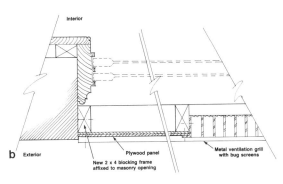

Figure 14. A: Plan detail showing plywood security panel anchored with carriage bolts through to the inside horizontal bracing, or strong backs. B: Plan detail showing section of plywood window panel attached to a new pressure treated wood frame set within the masonry opening. Ventilation should be included whenever possible or necessary.

Figure 13. If historic doors would be damaged by adding extra locks, they should be removed and stored and new security doors added. At this lighthouse, the historic door has been replaced with a new door (seen both inside and outside) with an inset vent and new deadbolt locks. The heavy historic hinges have not been damaged. Photo: Williamsport Preservation Training Center, NPS.

Figure 15. Painting trompe l'oeil scenes on plywood panels is a neighborhood friendly device. In addition, the small sign at the bottom left corner gives information for contacting the organization responsible for the care of the mothballed building. Photo: Lee H. Nelson, FAIA.

trimmed out with muntin strips to give a shadow line simulating multi-lite windows. This level of detail is a good indication that the building is protected and valued by the owner and the community.

If the building has shutters, simply close the shutters and secure them from the interior (see fig. 16). If the building had shutters historically, but they are missing, it may be appropriate to install new shutters, even in a modern material, and secure them in the closed position. Louvered shutters will help with interior ventilation if the sash are propped open behind the shutters.

Figure 16. Historic louvered shutters make excellent security closures with passive ventilation.

There is some benefit from keeping windows unboarded if security is not a problem. The building will appear to be occupied, and the natural air leakage around the windows will assist in ventilating the interior. The presence of natural light will also help when periodic inspections are made. Rigid polycarbonate clear storm glazing panels may be placed on the window exterior to protect against glass breakage. Because the sun's ultraviolet rays can cause fading of floor finishes and wall surfaces, filtering pull shades or inexpensive curtains may be options for reducing this type of deterioration for significant interiors. Some acrylic sheeting comes with built-in ultraviolet filters.

Securing the building from catastrophic destruction from fire, lightning, or arson will require additional security devices. Lightning rods properly grounded should be a first consideration if the building is in an area susceptible to lightning storms. A high security fence should also be installed if the property cannot be monitored closely. These interventions do not require a power source for operation. Since many buildings will not maintain electrical power, there are some devices available using battery packs, such as intrusion alarms, security lighting, and smoke detectors which through audible horn alarms can alert nearby neighbors. These battery packs must be replaced every 3 months to 2 years, depending on type and usage. In combination with a cellular phone, they can also provide some level of direct communication with police and fire departments.

If at all possible, new temporary electric service should be provided to the building (see fig. 17). Generally a telephone

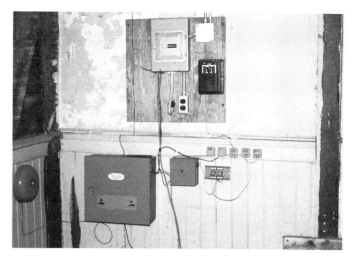

Figure 17. Security systems are very important for mothballed buildings if they are located where fire and security services are available. A temporary electric service with battery back-up has been installed in this building. Intrusion alarms and ionization smoke/fire detectors are wired directly to the nearby security service.

line is needed as well. A hard wired security system for intrusion and a combination rate-of-rise and smoke detector can send an immediate signal for help directly to the fire department and security service. Depending on whether or not heat will be maintained in the building, the security system should be designed accordingly. Some systems cannot work below 32°F (0°C). Exterior lighting set on a timer, photo electric sensor, or a motion/infra-red detection device provides additional security.

Providing adequate ventilation to the interior. Once the exterior has been made weathertight and secure, it is essential to provide adequate air exchange throughout the building. Without adequate air exchange, humidity may rise to unsafe levels, and mold, rot, and insect infestation are likely to thrive (see fig. 18). The needs of each historic resource must be individually evaluated because there are so many variables that affect the performance of each interior space once the building has been secured. A

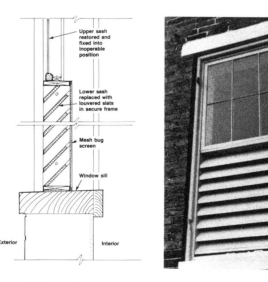

Figure 18. Heavy duty wooden slated louvers were custom fabricated to replace the deteriorated lower sash. The upper sash were rebuilt to retain the historic appearance and to allow light into this vacant historic building. Refer back to Fig. 1 for a view of the building. Photo: Charles E. Fisher, NPS. Drawing by Thomas Vitanza.

mechanical engineer or a specialist in interior climates should be consulted, particularly for buildings with intact and significant interiors. In some circumstances, providing heat during the winter, even at a minimal 45° F (7°C), and utilizing forced-fan ventilation in summer will be recommended and will require retaining electrical service. For masonry buildings it is often helpful to keep the interior temperature above the spring dew point to avoid damaging condensation. In most buildings it is the need for summer ventilation that outweighs the winter requirements.

Many old buildings are inherently leaky due to loose-fitting windows and floorboards and the lack of insulation. The level of air exchange needed for each building, however, will vary according to geographic location, the building's construction, and its general size and configuration.

There are four critical climate zones when looking at the type and amount of interior ventilation needed for a closed up building: hot and dry (southwestern states); cold and damp (Pacific northwest and northeastern states); temperate and humid (Mid-Atlantic states, coastal areas); and hot and humid (southern states and the tropics). (See fig. 19 for a chart outlining guidance on ventilation.)

Once closed up, a building interior will still be affected by the temperature and humidity of the exterior. Without proper ventilation, moisture from condensation may occur and cause damage by wetting plaster, peeling paint,

staining woodwork, warping floors, and in some cases even causing freeze thaw damage to plaster. If moist conditions persist in a property, structural damage can result from rot or returning insects attracted to moist conditions. Poorly mothballed masonry buildings, particularly in damp and humid zones have been so damaged on the interior with just one year of unventilated closure that none of the interior finishes were salvageable when the buildings were rehabilitated.

The absolute minimum air exchange for most mothballed buildings consists of one to four air exchanges every hour; one or two air exchanges per hour in winter and often twice that amount in summer. Even this minimal exchange may foster mold and mildew in damp climates, and so monitoring the property during the stabilization period and after the building has been secured will provide useful information on the effectiveness of the ventilation solution.

There is no exact science for how much ventilation should be provided for each building. There are, however, some general rules of thumb. Buildings, such as adobe structures, located in hot and arid climates may need no additional ventilation if they have been well weatherized and no moisture is penetrating the interior. Also frame buildings with natural cracks and fissures for air infiltration may have a natural air exchange rate of 3 or 4 per hour, and so in arid as well as temperate climates may need no additional ventilation once secured. The most difficult

VENTILATION GUIDANCE CHART

CLIMATE	AIR EXCHANGES		VENTILATION				
Temperature and Humidity	Winter air exchange per hour	Summer air exchange per hour	Frame Buildings passive louvering % of openings louvered		Masonry Buildings passive louvering % of openings louvered		Masonry Buildings fan combination one fan + % louvered
			winter	summer	winter	summer	summer
hot and dry Southwestern areas	less than 1	less than 1	N/A	N/A	N/A	N/A	N/A
cold and damp Northeastern & Pacific northwestern areas	1	2-3	5%	10%	10%	30%	20%
temperate/humid Mid-Atlantic & coastal areas	2	3-4	10%	20%	20%	40%	30%
hot and humid Southern states & tropical areas	3	4 or more	20%	30%	40% or more	80%	40% or more

Figure 19. This is a general guide for the amount of louvering which might be expected for a medium size residential structure with an average amount of windows, attic, and crawl space ventilation. There is currently research being done on effective air exchanges, but each project should be evaluated individually. It will be noticed from the chart that summer louvering requirements can be reduced with the use of an exhaust fan. Masonry buildings need more ventilation than frame buidings. Chart prepared by Sharon C. Park, AIA and Ernest A. Conrad, PE.

buildings to adequately ventilate without resorting to extensive louvering and/or mechanical exhaust fan systems are masonry buildings in humid climates. Even with basement and attic vent grills, a masonry building many not have more than one air exchange an hour. This is generally unacceptable for summer conditions. For these buildings, almost every window opening will need to be fitted out with some type of passive, louvered ventilation.

Depending on the size, plan configuration, and ceiling heights of a building, it is often necessary to have louvered opening equivalent to 5%-10% of the square footage of each floor. For example, in a humid climate, a typical 20'x30' (6.1m x 9.1m) brick residence with 600 sq. ft.(55.5 sq.m) of floor space and a typical number of windows, may need 30-60 sq. ft.(2.75sq.m-5.5 sq. m) of louvered openings per floor. With each window measuring 3'x5'(.9m x 1.5 m) or 15 sq. ft. (1.3 sq.m), the equivalent of 2 to 4 windows per floor may need full window louvers.

Small pre-formed louvers set into a plywood panel or small slit-type registers at the base of inset panels generally cannot provide enough ventilation in most moist climates to offset condensation, but this approach is certainly better than no louvers at all. Louvers should be located to give cross ventilation, interior doors should be fixed ajar at least 4" (10cm) to allow air to circulate, and hatches to the attic should be left open.

Monitoring devices which can record internal temperature and humidity levels can be invaluable in determining if the internal climate is remaining stable. These units can be powered by portable battery packs or can be wired into electric service with data downloaded into laptop computers periodically (see fig. 20). This can also give long-term information throughout the mothballing years. If it is determined that there are inadequate air exchanges to keep interior moisture levels under control, additional passive ventilation can be increased, or, if there is electric service, mechanical exhaust fans can be installed. One fan in a small to medium sized building can reduce the amount of louvering substantially.

If electric fans are used, study the environmental conditions of each property and determine if the fans should be controlled by thermostats or automatic timers. Humidistats, designed for enclosed climate control systems, generally are difficult to adapt for open mothballing conditions. How the system will draw in or exhaust air is also important. It may be determined that it is best to bring dry air in from the attic or upper levels and force it out through lower basement windows (see fig. 21). If the basement is damp, it may be best to zone it from the rest of the building and exhaust its air separately. Additionally, less humid day air is preferred over damper night air, and this can be controlled with a timer switch mounted to the fan.

The type of ventilation should not undermine the security of the building. The most secure installations use custom-made grills well anchored to the window frame, often set in plywood security panels. Some vents are formed using heavy millwork louvers set into existing window openings (refer back to fig.18). For buildings where security is not a primary issue, where the interior is modest, and where there has been no heat for a long time, it may be possible to use lightweight galvanized metal grills in the window openings (refer back to fig.7). A cost effective grill can be made from the expanded metal mesh lath used by plasterers and installed so that the mesh fins shed rainwater to the exterior.

Securing mechanical systems and utilities. At the outset, it is important to determine which utilities and services, such as electrical or telephone lines, are kept and which are cut off. As long as these services will not constitute a fire

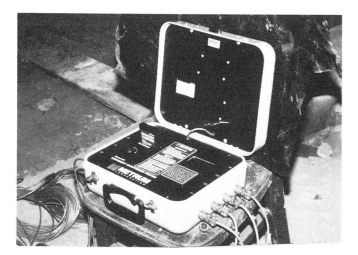

Figure 20. Portable monitors used to record temperature and humidity conditions in historic buildings during mothballing can help identify ventilation needs. This data can be downloaded directly into a lap top computer on site. These monitors are especially helpful over the long term for buildings with significant historic interiors or which are remaining furnished. If interiors are remaining damp or humid, additional ventilation should be added or the source of moisture controlled.

Figure 21. This electric thermostat/humidistat mounted in the attic vent controls a modified ducted air/fan system. The unit uses temporary exposed sheet metal ducts to pull air through the building and exhaust it out of the basement. For over ten years this fan system in combination with 18" x 18" preformed louvers in selective windows has kept the interior dry and with good air exchanges.

hazard, it is advisable to retain those which will help protect the property. Since the electrical needs will be limited in a vacant building, it is best to install a new temporary electric line and panel (100 amp) so that all the wiring is new and exposed. This will be much safer for the building, and allows easy access for reading the meter (see fig. 22).

Most heating systems are shut down in long term mothballing. For furnaces fueled by oil, there are two choices for dealing with the tank. Either it must be filled to the top with oil to eliminate condensation or it should be drained. If it remains empty for more than a year, it will likely rust and not be reusable. Most tanks are drained if a newer type of system is envisioned when the building is put back into service. Gas systems with open flames should be turned off unless there is regular maintenance and frequent surveillance of the property. Gas lines are shut off by the utility company.

If a hot water radiator system is retained for low levels of heat, it generally must be modified to be a self-contained system and the water supply is capped at the meter. This recirculating system protects the property from extensive damage from burst pipes. Water is replaced with a water/glycol mix and the reserve tank must also be filled with this mixture. This keeps the modified system from freezing, if there is a power failure. If water service is cut off, pipes should be drained. Sewerage systems will require special care as sewer gas is explosive. Either the traps must be filled with glycol or the sewer line should be capped off at the building line.

Developing a maintenance and monitoring plan. While every effort may have been made to stabilize the property and to slow the deterioration of materials, natural disasters, storms, undetected leaks, and unwanted intrusion can still occur. A regular schedule for surveillance, maintenance, and monitoring should be established: (See fig. 23 for maintenance chart).

Figure 22. All systems except temporary electric have been shut off at this residence which has been mothballed over 20 years. An electric meter and 100 amp panel box have been set on a plywood panel at the front of the building. It is used for interior lighting and various alarm systems. The building, however, is showing signs of moisture problems with efflourescent stains on the masonry indicating the need for gutter maintenance and additional ventilation for the interior. The vegetation on the walls, although picturesque, traps moisture and is damaging to the masonry. Photo: H. Ward Jandl, NPS.

MAINTENANCE CHART

periodic
- ❑ regular drive by surveillance
- ❑ check attic during storms if possible

monthly walk arounds
- ❑ check entrances
- ❑ check window panes for breakage
- ❑ mowing as required
- ❑ check for graffiti or vandalism

enter every 3 months to air out
- ❑ check for musty air
- ❑ check for moisture damage
- ❑ check battery packs and monitoring equipment
- ❑ check light bulbs
- ❑ check for evidence of pest intrusion

every 6 months; spring and fall
- ❑ site clean-up; pruning and trimming
- ❑ gutter and downspout check
- ❑ check crawlspace for pests
- ❑ clean out storm drains

every 12 months
- ❑ maintenance contract inspections for equipment/utilities
- ❑ check roof for loose or missing shingles
- ❑ termite and pest inspection/treatment
- ❑ exterior materials spot repair and touch up painting
- ❑ remove bird droppings or other stains from exterior
- ❑ check and update building file

Figure 23. Maintenance Chart. Many of the tasks on the maintenance chart can be done by volunteer help or service contracts. Regular visits to the site will help detect intrusion, storm damage, or poor water drainage.

The fire and police departments should be notified that the property will be vacant. A walk-through visit to familiarize these officials with the building's location, construction materials, and overall plan may be invaluable if they are called on in the future.

The optimum schedule for surveillance visits to the property will depend on the location of the property and the number of people who can assist with these activities. The more frequent the visits to check the property, the sooner that water leaks or break-ins will be noticed. Also, the more frequently the building is entered, the better the air exchange. By keeping the site clear and the building in good repair, the community will know that the building has not been abandoned (see fig. 24). The involvement of neighbors and community groups in caring for the property can ensure its protection from a variety of catastrophic circumstances.

The owner may utilize volunteers and service companies to undertake the work outlined in the maintenance chart.

Service companies on a maintenance contract can provide yard, maintenance, and inspection services, and their reports or itemized bills reflecting work undertaken should be added to update the building file.

Figure 24. Once mothballed, a property must still be monitored and maintained. The openings in this historic barn has been modified with a combination of wood louvers and metal mesh panels which require little maintenance. The grounds are regularly mowed, even inside the chain link security fence. Photo: Williamsport Preservation Training Center, NPS.

Components of a Mothballing Project

Document: Brearley House, New Jersey; 2½ story center hall plan house contains a high degree of integrity of circa 1761 materials and significant early 19th century additions. Deterioration was attributable to leaking roof, unstable masonry at gables and chimneys, deteriorating attic windows, poor site drainage, and partially detached gutters. Mothballing efforts are required for approximately 7-10 years.

Stabilize: Remove bat droppings from attic using great caution. Secure historic chimneys and gable ends with plywood panels. Do not take historic chimneys down. Reroof with asphalt shingles and reattach or add new gutters and downspouts. Add extenders to downspouts. Add bug screens to any ventilation areas. Add soil around foundation and slope to gain positive drain; do not excavate as this will disturb archeological evidence.

Mothball: Install security fence around the property. Secure doors and windows with plywood panels (½" exterior grade). Install preformed metal grills in basement and attic openings. Add surface mounted wiring for ionization smoke and fire detection with direct wire to police and fire departments. Shut off heat and drain pipes. Add window exhaust fan set on a thermostatic control. Provide for periodic monitoring and maintenance of the property.

Figure 25. Above is a summary of the tasks that were necessary in order to protect this significant property while restoration funds are raised. Photographs: Michael Mills; Ford Farewell Mills Gatsch Architects.

a. A view showing the exterior of the house in its mothballed condition.

b. Plywood panels stabilize the chimneys. Note the gable vents.

c. The exhaust fan has tamper-proof housing.

MOTHBALLING CHECKLIST

Mothballing Checklist In reviewing mothballing plans, the following checklist may help to ensure that work items are not inadvertently omitted.	Yes	No	Date of action or comment.
Moisture • Is the roof watertight? • Do the gutters retain their proper pitch and are they clean? • Are downspout joints intact? • Are drains unobstructed? • Are windows and doors and their frames in good condition? • Are masonry walls in good condition to seal out moisture? • Is wood siding in good condition? • Is site properly graded for water run-off? • Is vegetation cleared from around the building foundation to avoid trapping moisture?			
Pests • Have nests/pests been removed from the building's interior and eaves? • Are adequate screens in place to guard against pests? • Has the building been inspected and treated for termites, carpenter ants, and rodents? • If toxic droppings from bats and pigeons are present, has a special company been brought in for its disposal?			
Housekeeping • Have the following been removed from the interior: trash, hazardous materials such as inflammable liquids, poisons, and paints and canned goods that could freeze and burst? • Is the interior broom-clean? • Have furnishings been removed to a safe location? • If furnishings are remaining in the building, are they properly protected from dust, pests, ultraviolet light, and other potentially harmful problems? • Have significant architectural elements that have become detached from the building been labeled and stored in a safe place? • Is there a building file?			
Security • Have fire and police departments been notified that the building will be mothballed? • Are smoke and fire detectors in working order? • Are the exterior doors and windows securely fastened? • Are plans in place to monitor the building on a regular basis? • Are the keys to the building in a secure but accessible location? • Are the grounds being kept from becoming overgrown?			
Utilities • Have utility companies disconnected/shut off or fully inspected water, gas, and electric lines? • If the building will not remain heated, have water pipes been drained and glycol added? • If the electricity is to be left on, is the wiring in safe condition?			
Ventilation • Have steps been taken to ensure proper ventilation of the building? • Have interior doors been left open for ventilation purposes? • Has the secured building been checked within the last 3 months for interior dampness or excessive humidity?			

Figure 26.. MOTHBALL CHECKLIST. This checklist will give the building owner or manager a handy reference guide to items that should be addressed when mothballing a historic building. Prepared by H. Ward Jandl, NPS.

Conclusion

Providing temporary protection and stabilization for vacant historic buildings can arrest deterioration and buy the owner valuable time to raise money for preservation or to find a compatible use for the property. A well planned mothballing project involves documenting the history and condition of the building, stabilizing the structure to slow down its deterioration, and finally mothballing the structure to secure it (See fig. 25). The three highest priorities for the building while it is mothballed are 1) to protect the building from sudden loss, 2) to weatherize and maintain the property to stop moisture penetration, and 3) to control the humidity levels inside once the building has been secured. See Mothballing Checklist Figure 26.

While issues regarding mothballing may seem simple, the variables and intricacies of possible solutions make the decision-making process very important. Each building must be individually evaluated prior to mothballing. In addition, a variety of professional services as well as volunteer assistance are needed for careful planning and repair, sensitively designed protection measures, follow-up security surveillance, and cyclical maintenance (see fig. 27).

In planning for the future of the building, complete and systematic records must be kept and generous funds allocated for mothballing. This will ensure that the historic property will be in stable condition for its eventual preservation, rehabilitation, or restoration.

Figure 27. This residential building blends into its neighborhood even though all the windows have been covered over and the front steps are missing. The grounds are maintained and the special attention to decoratively painting the window panels shows that the property is being well cared for until it can be rehabilitated. Photo: Ohio Historical Society.

Acknowledgements

This publication has been prepared pursuant to the National Historic Preservation Act of 1966, as amended, which directs the Secretary of the Interior to develop and make available information concerning historic properties. Comments on the usefulness of this publication may be directed to H. Ward Jandl, Deputy Chief, Preservation Assistance Division, National Park Service, P.O. Box 37127, Washington, D.C. 20013-7127.

The author, Sharon C. Park, Senior Historical Architect, Preservation Assistance Division, National Park Service, would like to acknowledge the assistance of the following individuals in the preparation and review of this publication. H. Ward Jandl served as the technical editor and assisted with producing this Preservation Brief. In addition the following persons have provided invaluable information and illustrations: Ernest A. Conrad, PE; Doug Hicks, NPS Williamsport Preservation Training Center; Thomas C. Taylor, Colonial Williamsburg; Karen Gordon, Seattle Urban Conservation Office; Kevin B. Stoops, Seattle Department of Parks and Recreation; Michael Mills, AIA; Christine Henry, architect, Mary Beth Hirsch, Ohio Historical Society. Thanks also to Preservation Assistance Division staff members Michael J. Auer, Anne E. Grimmer, Kay D. Weeks, Timothy A. Buehner, and Jean Travers, and to the numerous staff members of the NPS Regional offices who submitted comments.

All photographs and drawings are by the author unless otherwise noted.

Cover photograph: Mothballing of this historic house involved a new membrane roof covering over the historic roof and slatted window covers for security and ventilation. Photo: Williamsport Preservation Training Center, NPS.

Further Reading

Cotton, J. Randall. "Mothballing Buildings." *The Old House Journal.* July/August, 1993.

Fisher, Charles E. and Thomas A. Vitanza. "Temporary Window Vents in Unoccupied Historic Buildings." Preservation Tech Note (Windows, No. 10). Washington, DC: National Park Service, 1985.

Frazier Associates. "Mothballing Historic Buildings." Preserving Prince William, 2. County of Prince William, VA, 1990.

Michell, Eleanor. *Emergency Repairs for Historic Buildings.* London: Butterworth Architecture, 1988.

"Mothballing Vacant Buildings," *An Anti-Arson Kit for Preservation and Neighborhood Action.* Washington, DC: Federal Emergency Management Agency, 1982.

Nelson, Lee H. *Preservation Briefs 17. Architectural character- Identifying the Visual Aspects of Historic Buildings as an Aid to Preserving Their Character.* Washington, DC: Government Printing Office, 1988.

Solon, Thomas E. "Security Panels for the Foster-Armstrong House." *Association for Preservation Technology Bulletin.* Vol XVI no. 3 & 4, 1984. (note the design of the panels, but be aware that additional louvering may be needed on other projects).

32

Making Historic Properties Accessible

Thomas C. Jester and Sharon C. Park, AIA

Historically, most buildings and landscapes were not designed to be readily accessible for people with disabilities. In recent years, however, emphasis has been placed on preserving historically significant properties, and on making these properties—and the activities within them—more accessible to people with disabilities. With the passage of the Americans with Disabilities Act in 1990, access to properties open to the public is now a civil right.

This Preservation Brief introduces the complex issue of providing accessibility at historic properties, and underscores the need to balance accessibility and historic preservation. It provides guidance on making historic properties accessible while preserving their historic character; the Brief also provides examples to show that independent physical accessibility at historic properties can be achieved with careful planning, consultation, and sensitive design. While the Brief focuses primarily on making buildings and their sites accessible, it also includes a section on historic landscapes. The Brief will assist historic property owners, design professionals, and administrators in evaluating their historic properties so that the highest level of accessibility can be provided while minimizing changes to historic materials and features. Because many projects encompassing accessibility work are complex, it is advisable to consult with experts in the fields of historic preservation and accessibility before proceeding with permanent physical changes to historic properties.

Modifications to historic properties to increase accessibility may be as simple as a small, inexpensive ramp to overcome one entrance step, or may involve changes to exterior and interior features. The Brief does not provide a detailed explanation of local or State accessibility laws as they vary from jurisdiction to jurisdiction. A concise explanation of several federal accessibility laws is included on page 13.

Planning Accessibility Modifications

Historic properties are distinguished by features, materials, spaces, and spatial relationships that contribute to their historic character. Often these elements, such as steep terrain, monumental steps, narrow or heavy doors,

decorative ornamental hardware, and narrow pathways and corridors, pose barriers to persons with disabilities, particularly to wheelchair users (See Figure 1).

A three-step approach is recommended to identify and implement accessibility modifications that will protect the integrity and historic character of historic properties:

1) Review the historical significance of the property and identify character-defining features;

2) Assess the property's existing and required level of accessibility; and

3) Evaluate accessibility options within a preservation context.

1) Review the Historical Significance of the Property

If the property has been designated as historic (properties that are listed in, or eligible for listing in the National Register of Historic Places, or designated under State or local law), the property's nomination file should be reviewed to learn about its significance. Local preservation commissions and State Historic Preservation Offices can usually provide

Figure 1. It is important to identify the materials, features, and spaces that should be preserved when planning accessibility modifications. These may include stairs, railings, doors, and door surrounds. Photo: National Park Service files.

copies of the nomination file and are also resources for additional information and assistance. Review of the written documentation should always be supplemented with a physical investigation to identify which character-defining features and spaces must be protected whenever any changes are anticipated. If the level of documentation for a property's significance is limited, it may be necessary to have a preservation professional identify specific historic features, materials, and spaces that should be protected.

For most historic properties, the construction materials, the form and style of the property, the principal elevations, the major architectural or landscape features, and the principal public spaces constitute some of the elements that should be preserved. Every effort should be made to minimize damage to the materials and features that convey a property's historical significance when making modifications for accessibility. Very small or highly significant properties that have never been altered may be extremely difficult to modify.

Secondary spaces and finishes and features that may be less important to the historic character should also be identified; these may generally be altered without jeopardizing the historical significance of a property. Non-significant spaces, secondary pathways, later additions, previously altered areas, utilitarian spaces, and service areas can usually be modified without threatening or destroying a property's historical significance.

2) Assess the Property's Existing and Required Level of Accessibility

A building survey or assessment will provide a thorough evaluation of a property's accessibility. Most surveys identify accessibility barriers in the following areas: building and site entrances; surface textures, widths and slopes of walkways; parking; grade changes; size, weight and configuration of doorways; interior corridors and path of travel restrictions; elevators; and public toilets and amenities (See Figure 2). Simple audits can be completed by property owners using readily available checklists (See Further Reading). Accessibility specialists can be hired to assess barriers in more complex properties, especially those with multiple buildings, steep terrain, or interpretive programs. Persons with disabilities can be particularly helpful in assessing specific barriers.

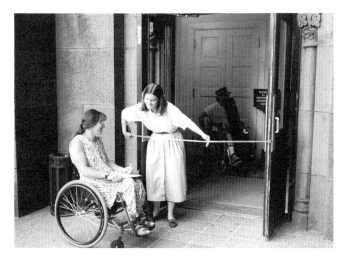

Figure 2. Surveys of historic properties can identify accessibility barriers. Persons with disabilities and accessibility consultants should participate whenever possible. Photo: Thomas Jester.

All applicable accessibility requirements—local codes, State codes and federal laws— should be reviewed carefully before undertaking any accessibility modification. Since many States and localities have their own accessibility regulations and codes (each with their own requirements for dimensions and technical requirements), owners should use the most stringent accessibility requirements when implementing modifications. The Americans with Disability Act Accessibility Guidelines (ADAAG) is the document that should be consulted when complying with the Americans with Disabilities Act (ADA) requirements.

3) Identify and Evaluate Accessibility Options within a Preservation Context

Once a property's significant materials and features have been identified, and existing and required levels of accessibility have been established, solutions can be developed (See Figure 3). Solutions should provide the greatest amount of accessibility without threatening or destroying those materials and features that make a property significant. Modifications may usually be phased over time as funds are available, and interim solutions can be considered until more permanent solutions are implemented. A team comprised of persons with disabilities, accessibility and historic preservation professionals, and building inspectors should be consulted as accessibility solutions are developed.

Modifications to improve accessibility should generally be based on the following priorities:

1) Making the main or a prominent public entrance and primary public spaces accessible, including a path to the entrance;

2) Providing access to goods, services, and programs;

3) Providing accessible restroom facilities; and,

4) Creating access to amenities and secondary spaces.

All proposed changes should be evaluated for conformance with the Secretary of the Interior's "Standards for the Treatment of Historic Properties," which were created for property owners to guide preservation work. These Standards stress the importance of retaining and protecting the materials and features that convey a property's historical significance. Thus, when new features are incorporated for accessibility, historic materials and features should be retained whenever possible. Accessibility modifications should be in scale with the historic property, visually compatible, and, whenever possible, reversible. Reversible means that if the new feature were removed at a later date, the essential form and integrity of the property would be unimpaired. The design of new features should also be differentiated from the design of the historic property so that the evolution of the property is evident. See Making Historic Buildings Accessible on page 9.

In general, when historic properties are altered, they should be made as accessible as possible. However, if an owner or a project team believes that certain modifications would threaten or destroy the significance of the property, the State Historic Preservation Officer should be consulted to determine whether or not any special accessibility provisions may be used. Special accessibility provisions for historic properties will vary depending on the applicable accessibility requirements.

A.

B.

C.

Figure 3. Before implementing accessibility modifications, owners should consider the potential effect on their historic property. At the Derby House in Salem, Massachusetts, several solutions to make the entrance accessible were considered, including regrading (a); a lift (b); and a ramp (c). The solution, an entrance on a secondary elevation, preserves the building's architectural significance and is convenient to designated parking. Drawings: National Park Service Files..

In some cases, programmatic access may be the only option for extremely small or unaltered historic properties, such as a two-story house museum with no internal elevator. Programmatic access for historic properties refers to alternative methods of providing services, information, and experiences when physical access cannot be provided. It

may mean offering an audio-visual program showing an inaccessible upper floor of a historic house museum, providing interpretive panels from a vista at an inaccessible terraced garden, or creating a tactile model of a historic monument for people with visual impairments.

Accessibility Solutions

The goal in selecting appropriate solutions for specific historic properties is to provide a high level of accessibility without compromising significant features or the overall character of the property. The following sections describe accessibility solutions and offer guidance on specific historic property components, namely the building site, entrances, interiors, landscapes, amenities, and new additions. Several solutions are discussed in each section, referencing dimensions and technical requirements from the ADA's accessibility guidelines, ADAAG. State and local requirements, however, may differ from the ADA requirements. Before making any modification owners should be aware of all applicable accessibility requirements.

The Building Site

An accessible route from a parking lot, sidewalk, and public street to the entrance of a historic building or facility is essential. An accessible route, to the maximum extent possible, should be the circulation route used by the general public. Critical elements of accessible routes are their widths, slopes, cross slopes, and surface texture. Each of these route elements must be appropriately designed so that the route can be used by everyone, including people with disabilities. The distance between the arrival and destination points should also be as short as possible. Sites containing designed landscapes should be carefully evaluated before making accessibility modifications. Historic landscapes are described in greater detail on pages 10 and 11.

Providing Convenient Parking. If parking is provided, it should be as convenient as possible for people with disabilities. Specially designated parking can often be created to improve accessibility (See Figure 4). Modifications to parking configurations and pathways should not alter significant landscape features.

Creating an Accessible Route. The route or path through a site to a historic building's entrance should be wide enough, generally at least 3 feet (91 cm), to accommodate visitors

Figure 4. Parking designated for people with disabilities is provided near an accessible entrance to the Springfield Library in Springfield, Massachusetts. Photo: William Smith.

377

with disabilities and must be appropriately graded with a stable, firm, and slip-resistant surface. Existing paths should be modified to meet these requirements whenever possible as long as doing so would not threaten or destroy significant materials and features.

Existing surfaces can often be stabilized by providing a new base and resetting the paving materials, or by modifying the path surface. In some situations it may be appropriate to create a new path through an inaccessible area. At large properties, it may be possible to regrade a slope to less than 1:20 (5%), or to introduce one or more carefully planned ramps. Clear directional signs should mark the path from arrival to destination.

Entrances

Whenever possible, access to historic buildings should be through a primary public entrance. In historic buildings, if this cannot be achieved without permanent damage to character-defining features, at least one entrance used by the public should be made accessible. If the accessible entrance is not the primary public entrance, directional signs should direct visitors to the accessible entrance (See Figure 5). A rear or service entrance should be avoided as the only mean of entering a building.

Figure 5. A universal access symbol clearly marks the Arts and Industries Building in Washington, D.C., and a push plate (right) engages the automatic door-opener. Photo: Thomas Jester.

Creating an accessible entrance usually involves overcoming a change in elevation. Steps, landings, doors, and thresholds, all part of the entrance, often pose barriers for persons with disabilities. To preserve the integrity of these features, a number of solutions are available to increase accessibility. Typical solutions include regrading, incorporating ramps, installing wheelchair lifts, creating new entrances, and modifying doors, hardware, and thresholds.

Regrading an Entrance. In some cases, when the entrance steps and landscape features are not highly significant, it may be possible to regrade to provide a smooth entrance into a building. If the existing steps are historic masonry, they should be buried, whenever possible, and not removed (See Figure 6).

Incorporating Ramps. Permanent ramps are perhaps the most common means to make an entrance accessible. As a new feature, ramps should be carefully designed and appropriately located to preserve a property's historic character (See Figure 7). Ramps should be located at public

Figure 6. Entrances can be regraded to make a building accessible as long as no significant landscape features will be destroyed and as long as the building's historic character is preserved. The Houghton Chapel (a) in Wellesley, Massachusetts, was made accessible by regrading over the historic steps (b). Photos: Carol R. Johnson & Associates.

Figure 7. This ramp is convenient for visitors with disabilities and preserves the building's historic character. The design is also compatible in scale with the building. Photo: William Smith.

entrances used by everyone whenever possible, preferably where there is minimal change in grade. Ramps should also be located to minimize the loss of historic features at the connection points—porch railings, steps, and windows—and should preserve the overall historic setting and character of the property. Larger buildings may have below grade areas that can accommodate a ramp down to an entrance (See Figure 8). Below grade entrances can be considered if the ramp leads to a publicly used interior, such as an auditorium, or if the building is serviced by a public elevator. Ramps can often be incorporated behind

Figure 8. A new below-grade ramp provides access to Lake MacDonald Lodge in Glacier National Park. Photo: Thomas Jester

historic features, such as cheek-walls or railings, to minimize the visual effect (See Figure 9).

The steepest allowable slope for a ramp is usually 1:12 (8%), but gentler slopes should be used whenever possible to accommodate people with limited strength. Greater changes in elevation require larger and longer ramps to meet accessibility scoping provisions and may require an intermediate landing. Most codes allow a slightly steeper ramp for historic buildings to overcome one step.

Ramps can be faced with a variety of materials, including wood, brick, and stone. Often the type and quality of the materials determines how compatible a ramp design will be with a historic property (See Figure 10). Unpainted pressure-treated wood should not be used to construct ramps because it usually appears temporary and is not visually compatible with most historic properties. Railings

Figure 9. This ramp was created by infilling the window-well and slightly modifying the historic railing. The ramp preserves this building's historic character. Photo: Thomas Jester.

Figure 10. This brick ramp provides access to St. Anne's Episcopal Church in Annapolis, Maryland. Its design is compatible with the historic building. Photo: Charity V. Davidson.

should be simple in design, distinguishable from other historic features, and should extend one foot beyond the sloped area (See Figure 11).

Ramp landings must be large enough for wheelchair users, usually at least 5 feet by 5 feet (152.5 cm by 152.5 cm), and the top landing must be at the level of the door threshold. It may be possible to reset steps by creating a ramp to accommodate minor level changes and to meet the threshold without significantly altering a property's historic character. If a building's existing landing is not wide or deep enough to accommodate a ramp, it may be

Figure 11. Simple, contemporary railings that extend beyond the ramp slope make this ramp compatible with the industrial character of this building. Photo: Thomas Jester.

necessary to modify the entry to create a wider landing. Long ramps, such as switchbacks, require intermediate landings, and all ramps should be detailed with an appropriate edge and railing for wheelchair users and visually impaired individuals.

Temporary or portable ramps are usually constructed of light-weight materials and, thus, are rarely safe or visually compatible with historic properties. Moreover, portable ramps are often stored until needed and, therefore, do not meet accessibility requirements for independent access. Temporary and portable ramps, however, may be an acceptable interim solution to improve accessibility until a permanent solution can be implemented (See Figure 12).

Figure 12. The Smithsonian Institution installed a temporary ramp on its visitor's center to allow adequate time to design an appropriate permanent ramp. Photo: Thomas Jester.

Installing Wheelchair Lifts. Platforms lifts and inclined stair lifts, both of which accommodate only one person, can be used to overcome changes of elevation ranging from three to 10 feet (.9 m-3 m) in height. However, many States have restrictions on the use of wheelchair lifts, so all applicable codes should be reviewed carefully before installing one. Inclined stair lifts, which carry a wheelchair on a platform up a flight of stairs, may be employed selectively. They tend to be visually intrusive, although they are relatively reversible. Platform lifts can be used when there is inadequate space for a ramp. However, such lifts should be installed in unobtrusive locations and under cover to minimize maintenance if at all possible (See Figure 13). A similar, but more expensive platform lift has a retracting railing that lowers into the ground, minimizing the visual effect to historic properties (See Figure 14). Mechanical lifts have drawbacks at historic properties with high public visitation because their capacity is limited, they sometimes cannot be operated independently, and they require frequent maintenance.

Considering a New Entrance. When it is not possible to modify an existing entrance, it may be possible to develop a new entrance by creating an entirely new opening in an appropriate location, or by using a secondary window for an opening. This solution should only be considered after exhausting all possibilities for modifying existing entrances (See Figure 15).

Retrofitting Doors. Historic doors generally should not be replaced, nor should door frames on the primary elevation be widened, as this may alter an important feature of a historic design. However, if a building's historic doors have been removed, there may be greater latitude in designing a compatible new entrance. Most accessibility standards require at least a 32" (82 cm) clear opening with manageable door opening pressures. The most desirable preservation solution to improve accessibility is retaining historic doors and upgrading the door pressure with one of several devices. Automatic door openers

Figure 13. Platform lifts like the one used on this building require minimal space and can be removed without damaging historic materials. Shielded with lattice work, this lift is also protected by the roof eaves. Approach path should be stable, firm, and slip resistant. Photo: Sharon Park.

Readily Achievable Accessibility Modifications

Many accessibility solutions can be implemented easily and inexpensively without destroying the significance of historic properties. While it may not be possible to undertake all of the modifications listed below, each change will improve accessibility.

Sites and Entrances

• Creating a designated parking space.

• Installing ramps.

• Making curb cuts.

Interiors

• Repositioning shelves.

• Rearranging tables, displays, and furniture.

• Repositioning telephones.

• Adding raised markings on elevator control buttons.

• Installing flashing alarm lights.

• Installing offset hinges to widen doorways.

• Installing or adding accessible door hardware.

• Adding an accessible water fountain, or providing a paper cup dispenser at an inaccessible water fountain.

Restrooms

• Installing grab bars in toilet stalls.

• Rearranging toilet partitions to increase maneuvering space.

• Insulating lavatory pipes under sinks to prevent burns.

• Installing a higher toilet seat.

• Installing a full-length bathroom mirror.

• Repositioning the paper towel dispenser.

Figure 14. At the Lieutenant Governor's Mansion in Frankfort, Kentucky, a retracting lift (b) was installed to minimize the visual effect on this historic building when not in use (a). Photos: Aging Technology Incorporated.

Figure 15. A new entrance to the elevator lobby replaces a window at Faneuil Hall in Boston, Massachusetts. The new entrance is appropriately differentiated from the historic design. Photo: Paul Holtz.

(operated by push buttons, mats, or electronic eyes) and power-assisted door openers can eliminate or reduce door pressures that are accessibility barriers, and make single or double-leaf doors fully operational (See Figure 16).

Adapting Door Hardware. If a door opening is within an inch or two of meeting the 32" (81 cm) clear opening requirement, it may be possible to replace the standard hinges with off-set hinges to increase the size of the door opening as much as 1 1/2" (3.8 cm). Historic hardware can be retained in place, or adapted with the addition of an automatic opener, of which there are several types. Door hardware can also be retrofitted to reduce door pressures. For example, friction hinges can be retrofitted with ball-bearing inserts, and door closers can be rethreaded to reduce the door pressure.

Altering Door Thresholds. A door threshold that exceeds the allowable height, generally 1/2" (1.3 cm), can be altered or removed with one that meets applicable accessibility

Figure 16. During the rehabilitation of the Rookery in Chicago, the original entrance was modified to create an accessible entrance. Two revolving doors were replaced with a new one flanked by new doors, one of which is operated with a push-plate door opener. Photo: Thomas Jester.

requirements. If the threshold is deemed to be significant, a bevel can be added on each side to reduce its height (See Figure 17). Another solution is to replace the threshold with one that meets applicable accessibility requirements and is visually compatible with the historic entrance.

Moving Through Historic Interiors

Persons with disabilities should have independent access to all public areas and facilities inside historic buildings. The extent to which a historic interior can be modified depends on the significance of its materials, plan, spaces, features, and finishes. Primary spaces are often more difficult to modify without changing their character. Secondary spaces may generally be changed without compromising a building's historic character. Signs should clearly mark the route to accessible restrooms, telephones, and other accessible areas.

Installing Ramps and Wheelchair Lifts. If space permits, ramps and wheelchair lifts can also be used to increase accessibility inside buildings (See Figures 18 & 19). However, some States and localities restrict interior uses of wheelchair lifts for life-safety reasons. Care should be taken to install these new features where they can be readily accessed. Ramps and wheelchair lifts are described in detail on pages 4–6.

Upgrading Elevators. Elevators are an efficient means of providing accessibility between floors. Some buildings have existing historic elevators that are not adequately accessible for persons with disabilities because of their size, location, or detailing, but they may also contribute to the historical significance of a building. Significant historic elevators can usually be upgraded to improve accessibility. Control panels can be modified with a "wand" on a cord to make the control panel accessible, and timing devices can usually be adjusted.

Retrofitting Door Knobs. Historic door knobs and other hardware may be difficult to grip and turn. In recent years, lever-handles have been developed to replace door knobs. Other lever-handle devices can be added to existing hardware. If it is not possible or appropriate to retrofit existing door knobs, doors can be left open during operating hours (unless doing so would violate life safety codes), and power-assisted door openers can be installed. It may only be necessary to retrofit specific doorknobs to create an accessible path of travel and accessible restrooms.

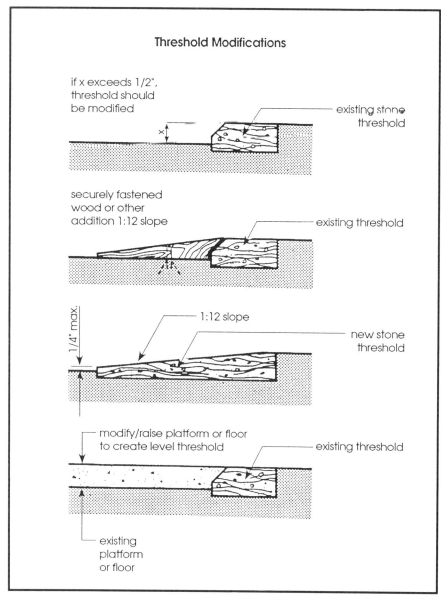

Threshold Modifications

if x exceeds 1/2",
threshold should
be modified

existing stone
threshold

securely fastened
wood or other
addition 1:12 slope

existing threshold

1:12 slope

new stone
threshold

1/4" max.

modify/raise platform or floor
to create level threshold

existing threshold

existing
platform
or floor

Figure 17. Thresholds that exceed allowable heights can be modified several ways to increase accessibility. Source: Uniform Federal Accessibility Standard (UFAS) Retrofit Manual.

be retained in the process of making modifications. For example, larger restrooms can sometimes be reconfigured by relocating or combining partitions to create an accessible toilet stall. Other changes to consider are adding grab bars around toilets, covering hot water pipes under sinks with insulation to prevent burns, and providing a sink, mirror, and paper dispenser at a height suitable for wheelchair users. A unisex restroom may be created if it is technically infeasible to create two fully accessible restrooms, or if doing so would threaten or destroy the significance of the building. It is important to remember that restroom fixtures, such as sinks, urinals, and partitions, may be historic, and therefore, should be preserved whenever possible.

Modifying Other Amenities. Other amenities inside historic buildings may require modification. Seating in a theater, for example, can be made accessible by removing some seats in several areas (See Figure 21). New seating that is accessible can also be added at the end of existing rows, either with or without a level floor surface. Readily removable seats may be installed in wheelchair spaces when the spaces are not required to accommodate wheelchair users. Historic water fountains can be retained and new, two-tiered fountains installed if space permits. If public telephones are provided, it may be necessary to install at least a Text Telephone (TT), also known as a Telecommunication Device for the Deaf (TDD) (See Figure 22). Historic service counters commonly found in banks, theaters, and hotels generally should not be altered. It is preferable to add an accessible counter on the end of a historic counter if feasible. Modified or new counters should not exceed 36" (91.5 cm) in height.

Modifying Interior Stairs. Stairs are the primary barriers for many people with disabilities. However, there are some ways to modify stairs to assist people who are able to navigate them. It may be appropriate to add hand railings if none exist. Railings should be 1 1/4" (3.8 cm) in diameter and return to the wall so straps and bags do not catch. Color-contrasting, slip-resistant strips will help people with visual impairments. Finally, beveled or closed risers are recommended unless the stairs are highly significant, because open risers catch feet (See Figure 20).

Building Amenities

Some amenities in historic buildings, such as restrooms, seating, telephones, drinking fountains, counters, may contribute to a building's historic character. They will often require modification to improve their use by persons with disabilities. In many cases, supplementing existing amenities, rather than changing or removing them, will increase access and minimize changes to historic features and materials.

Upgrading Restrooms. Restrooms may have historic fixtures such as sinks, urinals, or marble partitions that can

Figure 18. Symmetrical ramps at the Mayflower Hotel in Washington, D.C., provide access to the hotel's lower level. The design for the ramps respects the historic character of this landmark building. Photo: Thomas Jester.

MAKING A HISTORIC BUILDING ACCESSIBLE

The Orange County Courthouse (a), located in Santa Ana, California, was rehabilitated in the late 1980s as a county museum. As part of the rehabilitation, the architect sensitively integrated numerous modifications to increase accessibility. To preserve the building's primary elevation, a new public entrance was created on the rear elevation where parking spaces are located. A ramp (b) leads to the accessible entrance that can be opened with a push-plate automatic door-opener (c). Modifications to interior features also increased accessibility. To create an accessible path of travel, offset hinges (d) were installed on doors that were narrower than 32 inches (81.3 cm). Other doors were rethreaded to reduce the door pressure. Beveling the 1" high thresholds (e) reduced their height to approximately 1/4 inch (.64 cm). The project architect also converted a storeroom into an accessible restroom (f). The original stairway, which has open grillwork, was made more accessible by applying slip-resistant pressure tape to the marble steps (g). And the original elevator was upgraded with raised markings, alarm lights, and voice floor indicators. Photos: Milford Wayne Donaldson, FAIA.

MAKING HISTORIC LANDSCAPES ACCESSIBLE

To successfully incorporate access into historic landscapes, the planning process is similar to that of other historic properties. Careful research and inventory should be undertaken to determine which materials and features convey the landscape's historical significance. As part of this evaluation, those features that are character-defining (topographical variation, vegetation, circulation, structures, furnishings, objects) should be identified. Historic finishes, details, and materials that also contribute to a landscape's significance should also be documented and evaluated prior to determining an approach to landscape accessibility. For example, aspects of the pedestrian circulation system that need to be understood include walk width, aggregate size, pavement pattern, texture, relief, and joint details. The context of the walk should be understood including its edges and surrounding area. Modifications to surface textures or widths of pathways can often be made with minimal effect on significant landscape features (a) and (b).

Additionally, areas of secondary importance such as altered paths should be identified -- especially those where the accessibility modifications will not destroy a landscape's significance. By identifying those features that are contributing or non-contributing, a sympathetic circulation experience can then be developed.

After assessing a landscape's integrity, accessibility solutions can be considered. Full access throughout a historic landscape may not always be possible. Generally, it is easier to provide accessibility to larger, more open sites where there is a greater variety of public experiences. However, when a landscape is uniformly steep, it may only be possible to make discrete portions of a historic landscape accessible, and viewers may only be able to experience the landscape from selected vantage points along a prescribed pedestrian or vehicular access route. When defining such a route, the interpretive value of the user experience should be considered; in other words, does the route provide physical or visual access to those areas that are critical to understand the meaning of the landscape?

The following accessibility solutions address three common landscape situations: 1) structures with low integrity landscapes; 2) structures and landscapes of equal significance; and, 3) landscapes of primary significance with inaccessible terrain.

1. The Hunnewell Visitors Center at the Arnold Arboretum in Jamaica Plain, Massachusetts, was constructed in 1892. Its immediate setting has changed considerably over time (c). Since the existing landscape immediately surrounding this structure has little remaining integrity, the new accessibility solution has the latitude to integrate a broad program including site orientation, circulation, interpretation, and maintenance.

   The new design, which has few ornamental plants, references the original planting design principles, with a strong emphasis on form, color, and texture. In contrast with the earlier designs, the new plantings were set away from the facade of this historic building,

(a.) To improve accessibility in Boston's Emerald Necklace Parks, standard asphalt paving was replaced in selected areas with an imbedded aggregate surface that is more in keeping with the landscape's historic appearance. Photo: Charles Birnbaum.

(b.) Only slight widening of this garden path was required to make the historic tennis court and an overlook view of the "Friendly Garden" accessible at Ranchos Los Alamitos, a historic estate with designed gardens in Long Beach, California.

(c.) Hunnewell Visitor's Center before rehabilitation, revealing the altered landscapes. Photo: Jennifer Jones, Carol R. Johnson and associates.

(d.) Hunnewell Visitors Center's entrance following rehabilitation, integrating an accessible path (left), platform, and new steps. Photo: Charles Birnbaum.

allowing the visitor to enjoy its architectural detail. A new walk winds up the gentle earthen berm and is vegetated with plantings that enhance the interpretive experience from the point of orientation (d). The new curvilinear walks also provide a connection to the larger arboretum landscape for everyone.

2. The Eugene O'Neill National Historic Site overlooks the San Ramon Valley, twenty-seven miles east of San Francisco, California. The thirteen-acre site includes a walled courtyard garden on the southeast side of the Tao House, which served as the O'Neill residence from 1937-44 (e). Within this courtyard are character-defining walks that are too narrow by today's accessibility standards, yet are a character-defining element of the historic design. To preserve the garden's integrity, the scale and the characteristics of the original circulation were maintained by creating a wheelchair route which, in part, utilizes reinforced turf. This route allows visitors with disabilities to experience the main courtyard as well.

3. Morningside Park in New York City, New York, designed by Frederick Olmstead, Sr., and Calvert Vaux in 1879, is sited on generally steep, rocky terrain (f). Respecting these dramatic grade changes, which are only accessible by extensive flights of stone stairs, physical access cannot be provided without destroying the park's integrity. In order to provide some accessibility, scenic overlooks were created that provide broad visual access to the park.

(e.) This view shows the new reinforced turf path at the Eugene O'Neill National Historic Site that preserved the narrow Historic Path. Photo: Patricia M. O'Donnell.

(f.) Steep terrain at Morningside Park in New York City cannot be made accessible without threating or destroying this landscape's integrity. Photo: Quennell Rothschild Associates.

Figure 19. Inclined lifts can sometimes overcome interior changes of elevation where space is limited. This lift in Boston's Faneuil Hall created access to the floor and stage level of the State Room. Photo: Paul Holtz.

Considering a New Addition as an Accessibility Solution

Many new additions are constructed specifically to incorporate modern amenities such as elevators, restrooms, fire stairs, and new mechanical equipment. These new additions often create opportunities to incorporate access for people with disabilities. It may be possible, for example, to create an accessible entrance, path to public levels via a ramp, lift, or elevator (See Figure 23). However, a new addition has the potential to change a historic property's appearance and destroy significant building and landscape features. Thus, all new additions should be compatible with the size, scale, and proportions of historic features and materials that characterize a property (See Figure 24).

New additions should be carefully located to minimize connection points with the historic building, such that if the addition were to be removed in the future, the essential form and integrity of the building would remain intact. On the other hand, new additions should also be conveniently located near parking that is connected to an accessible route for people with disabilities. As new additions are incorporated, care should be taken to protect significant landscape features and archeological resources. Finally, the design for any new addition should be differentiated from the historic design so that the property's evolution over time is clear. New additions frequently make it possible to increase accessibility, while simultaneously reducing the level of change to historic features, materials, and spaces.

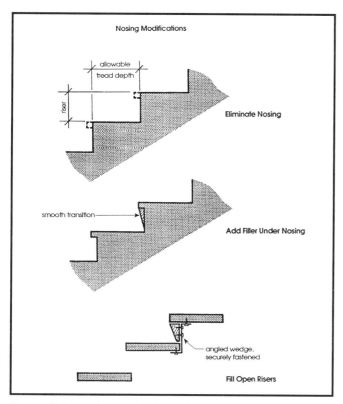

Figure 20. *In certain situations it may be appropriate to modify stair nosings for persons with mobility impairments. Whenever possible, stairs should be modified by adding new materials rather than removing historic materials. Source: UFAS Retrofit Manual.*

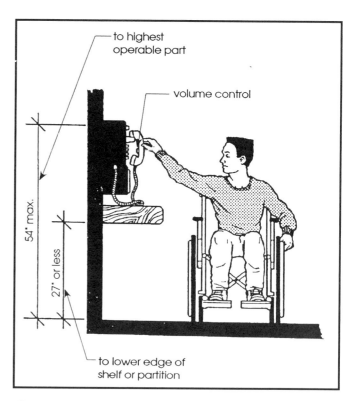

Figure 22. *Amenities such as telephones should be at height that wheelchair users can reach. Changes to many amenities can be adapted with minimal effect on historic materials, features, and spaces. Source: UFAS Retrofit Manual.*

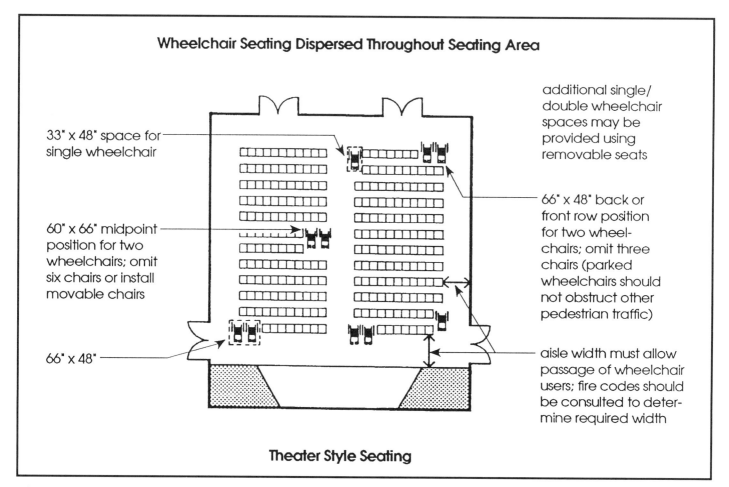

Figure 21. *Seating in historic theaters and auditoriums can be changed to accommodate wheelchair users. Accessible seating areas should be connected to an accessible route from the building entrance. Source: UFAS Retrofit Manual.*

Federal Accessibility Laws

Today, few building owners are exempt from providing accessibility for people with disabilities. Before making any accessibility modification, it is imperative to determine which laws and codes are applicable. In addition to local and State accessibility codes, the following federal accessibility laws are currently in effect:

Architectural Barriers Act (1968)

The Architectural Barriers Act stipulates that all buildings designed, constructed, and altered by the Federal Government, or with federal assistance, must be accessible. Changes made to federal buildings must meet the Uniform Federal Accessibility Standards (UFAS). Special provisions are included in UFAS for historic buildings that would be threatened or destroyed by meeting full accessibility requirements.

Rehabilitation Act (1973)

The Rehabilitation Act requires recipients of federal financial assistance to make their programs and activities accessible to everyone. Recipients are allowed to make their properties accessible by altering their building, by moving programs and activities to accessible spaces, or by making other accommodations.

Americans with Disabilities Act (1990)

Historic properties are not exempt from the Americans with Disabilities Act (ADA) requirements. To the greatest extent possible, historic buildings must be as accessible as non-historic buildings. However, it may not be possible for some historic properties to meet the general accessibility requirements.

Under Title II of the ADA, State and local governments must remove accessibility barriers either by shifting services and programs to accessible buildings, or by making alterations to existing buildings. For instance, a licensing office may be moved from a second floor to an accessible first floor space, or if this is not feasible, a mail service might be provided. However, State and local government facilities that have historic preservation as their main purpose—State-owned historic museums, historic State capitols that offer tours—must give priority to physical accessibility.

Under Title III of the ADA, owners of "public accommodations" (theaters, restaurants, retail shops, private museums) must make "readily achievable" changes; that is, changes that can be easily accomplished without much expense. This might mean installing a ramp, creating accessible parking, adding grab bars in bathrooms, or modifying door hardware. The requirement to remove barriers when it is "readily achievable" is an ongoing responsibility. When alterations, including restoration and rehabilitation work, are made, specific accessibility requirements are triggered.

Recognizing the national interest in preserving historic properties, Congress established alternative requirements for properties that cannot be made accessible without "threatening or destroying" their significance. A consultation process is outlined in the ADA's Accessibility Guidelines for owners of historic properties who believe that making specific accessibility modifications would "threaten or destroy" the significance of their property. In these situations, after consulting with persons with disabilities and disability organizations, building owners should contact the State Historic Preservation Officer (SHPO) to determine if the special accessibility provisions for historic properties may be used. Further, if it is determined in consultation with the SHPO that compliance with the minimum requirements would also "threaten or destroy" the significance of the property, alternative methods of access, such as home delivery and audio-visual programs, may be used.

Figure 23. New additions to historic buildings can be designed to increase accessibility. A new addition links two adjacent buildings used for the Albany, New York, Visitor's Center, and incorporates an accessible entrance, restrooms, and signage. Photo: Clare Adams.

Figure 24. Creating an accessible entrance with a new elevator tower requires a compatible design. This elevator addition blends in with the historic building's materials and provides access to all public levels. Photo: Sharon Park.

387

Conclusion

Historic properties are irreplaceable and require special care to ensure their preservation for future generations. With the passage of the Americans with Disabilities Act, access to historic properties open to the public is a now civil right, and owners of historic properties must evaluate existing buildings and determine how they can be made more accessible. It is a challenge to evaluate properties thoroughly, to identify the applicable accessibility requirements, to explore alternatives and to implement solutions that provide independent access and are consistent with accepted historic preservation standards. Solutions for accessibility should not destroy a property's significant materials, features and spaces, but should increase accessibility as much as possible. Most historic buildings are not exempt from providing accessibility, and with careful planning, historic properties can be made more accessible, so that all citizens can enjoy our Nation's diverse heritage.

Photo: Massachusetts Historical Commission.

Additional Reading

Ballantyne, Duncan S. and Harold Russell Associates, Inc. *Accommodation of Disabled Visitors at Historic Sites in the National Park System.* Washington, D.C.: Park Historic Architecture Division, National Park Service, U.S. Department of the Interior, 1983.

Goldman, Nancy, Ed. *Readily Achievable Checklist: A Survey for Accessibility.* Boston: Adaptive Environments Center, 1993.

Hayward, Judith L. and Thomas C. Jester, compilers. *Accessibility and Historic Preservation Resource Guide.* Windsor, Vermont: Historic Windsor, Inc., 1992, revised 1993.

Jester, Thomas C. *Preserving the Past and Making it Accessible for People with Disabilities.* Washington, D.C.: Preservation Assistance Division, National Park Service, U.S. Department of the Interior, 1992.

Parrott, Charles. *Access to Historic Buildings for the Disabled.* Washington, D.C.: U.S. Department of the Interior, 1980.

Secretary of the Interior's Standards for the Treatment of Historic Properties. Washington, D.C.: Preservation Assistance Division, National Park Service, U.S. Department of the Interior, 1993.

Smith, William D. and Tara Goodwin Frier. *Access to History: A Guide to Providing Access to Historic Buildings for People with Disabilities.* Boston: Massachusetts Historical Commission, 1989.

Standards for Accessible Design: ADA Accessibility Guidelines (ADAAG). Washington, D.C.: U.S. Department of Justice, 1991.

Acknowledgements

Thomas C. Jester is an Architectural Historian with the Preservation Assistance Division of the National Park Service. Sharon C. Park, AIA, is the Senior Historical Architect with the Preservation Assistance Division, National Park Service.

The authors wish to thank Charles A. Birnbaum, ASLA, Historical Landscape Architect with the Preservation Assistance Division, National Park Service, for contributing the section on historic landscapes. The authors gratefully acknowledge the invaluable comments made by the following individuals who reviewed the draft manuscript: William Smith, Massachusetts Historical Commission; Kay Weeks, H. Ward Jandl, Michael Auer, and Charles A. Birnbaum, Preservation Assistance Division, National Park Service; Clare Adams, New York Department of Parks, Recreation and Historic Preservation; Lauren Bowlin, Maryland Historical Trust; Tom Mayes, National Trust for Historic Preservation; Elizabeth Igleheart, Maine Historic Preservation

Commission; Milford Wayne Donaldson, FAIA; Paul Beatty, U.S. Architectural and Transportation Barriers Compliance Board; Mid-Atlantic Regional Office, National Park Service; Western Regional Office, National Park Service.

This publication has been prepared pursuant to the National Historic Preservation Act of 1966, as amended, which directs the Secretary of the Interior to develop and make available information concerning historic properties. Comments about this publication should be directed to H. Ward Jandl, Deputy Chief, Preservation Assistance Division, National Park Service, P.O. Box 37127, Washington, D.C. 20013-7127.

33

The Preservation and Repair of Historic Stained and Leaded Glass

Neal A. Vogel and Rolf Achilles

"Stained glass" can mean colored, painted or enameled glass, or glass tinted with true glass "stains." In this Brief the term refers to both colored and painted glass. "Leaded glass" refers generically to all glass assemblies held in place by lead, copper, or zinc cames. Because the construction, protection, and repair techniques of leaded glass units are similar, whether the glass itself is colored or clear, "stained glass" and "leaded glass" are used interchangeably throughout the text.

Glass is a highly versatile medium. In its molten state, it can be spun, blown, rolled, cast in any shape, and given any color. Once cooled, it can be polished, beveled, chipped, etched, engraved, or painted. Of all the decorative effects possible with glass, however, none is more impressive than "stained glass." Since the days of ancient Rome, stained glass in windows and other building elements has shaped and colored light in infinite ways.

Stained and leaded glass can be found throughout America in a dazzling variety of colors, patterns, and textures (Fig. 1). It appears in windows, doors, ceilings, fanlights, sidelights, light fixtures, and other glazed features found in historic buildings (Fig. 2). It appears in all building types and architectural styles—embellishing the light in a great cathedral, or adding a touch of decoration to the smallest row house or bungalow. A number of notable churches, large mansions, civic buildings, and other prominent buildings boast windows or ceilings by LaFarge, Tiffany, Connick, or one of many other, lesser-known, American masters, but stained or leaded glass also appears as a prominent feature in great numbers of modest houses built between the Civil War and the Great Depression.

This Brief gives a short history of stained and leaded glass in America. It also surveys basic preservation and documentation issues facing owners of buildings with leaded glass. It addresses common causes of deterioration and presents repair, restoration, and protection options. It does not offer detailed advice on specific work treatments. Glass is one of the most durable, yet fragile building materials. While stained glass windows can last for centuries, as the great cathedrals of Europe attest, they can be instantly destroyed by vandals or by careless workmen. Extreme care must therefore be exercised, even in the most minor work. For this reason, virtually all repair or restoration work undertaken on stained and leaded glass must be done by professionals, whether the feature is a magnificent stained glass window or a clear, leaded glass storefront transom. Before undertaking any repair work, building owners or project managers should screen studios carefully, check references, inspect other projects, and require duplicate documentation of any work so that full records can be maintained. Consultants should be employed on major projects.

Figure 1. The door and transom of the Edward Hazlett House, Wheeling, West Virginia (1891-1892), suggest the richness of 19th century leaded glass. Photo: Jack E. Boucher, HABS.

Historical Background

Glassblowers were among the founders of Jamestown in 1607, and early glass manufacturing was also attempted in 17th-century Boston and Philadelphia. Dutch colonists in the New Netherlands enjoyed painted oval or circular medallions that bore the family's coat of arms or illustrated Dutch proverbs. German colonists in the mid-Atlantic region also began early glass ventures. Despite the availability of good natural ingredients, each of these early American glassmakers eventually failed due to production and managerial difficulties. As a result, colonists imported most of their glass from England throughout the 17th and 18th centuries.[1]

Social values as well as high costs also restricted the use of stained and other ornamental glass. This was particularly true with regard to churches. The Puritans, who settled New England, rejected the religious imagery of the Church of England, and built simple, unadorned churches with clear glass windows. Consequently, not much glass remains from the colonial and early national periods. Less than 1% of the Nation's stained and leaded glass predates 1700. Considering the enormous loss of 17th-, 18th-, and early 19th-century buildings, *any* window glass surviving

Figure 3. The entrance to the Morris-Jumel Mansion, New York City, is one of the earliest surviving installations of leaded glass in the country. It features a leaded fanlight and sidelights of large clear roundels and small bulls-eyes of red and orange flashed glass from ca. 1810 . Photo: The American Institute of Architects Library and Archives, Washington, D.C.

from these periods is very significant (Fig. 3). Every effort should be made to document and preserve it.

Despite many failed starts, the War of 1812, and British competition, American glass production increased steadily throughout the 19th century. Stained glass was available on a very limited basis in America during the first quarter of the 19th century, but American stained glass did not really emerge in its own right until the 1840s.[2] The windows at St. Ann and the Holy Trinity Episcopal Church in Brooklyn, New York, made by John and William Jay Bolton between 1843 and 1848, are perhaps the most significant early American stained glass installation (Fig. 4). Other important early stained glass commissions were the glass ceilings produced by the J. & G. H. Gibson Company of Philadelphia for the House and Senate chambers of the United States Capitol in 1859.

America's glass industry boomed during the second half of the 19th century. (And although stained and leaded glass is found nationwide, the manufacturing was based in the Northeast and Midwest, where good natural ingredients for glass, and coal reserves for the kilns were available. Moreover, nearly all of the nationally renowned studios were based in major metropolitan areas of the central and northeastern states—near the manufacturers that supplied their raw materials.) In response to this growth, the industry formed self-regulating associations that established guidelines for business and production. In 1879 the Window Glass Association of America was established, and in 1903 The National Ornamental Glass Manufacturers' Association, precursor of the Stained Glass Association in America, was formed.

The 60 years from about 1870 to 1930 were the high point for stained glass in the U.S. In the early years, American stylistic demands reflected those current in Europe,

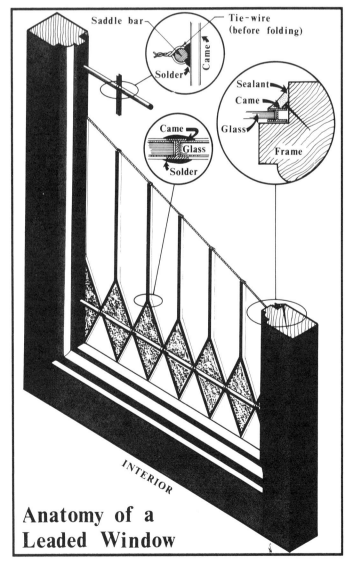

Anatomy of a Leaded Window

Figure 2. Components of a leaded glass window. Drawing: Neal A. Vogel.

Figure 4. The windows at St. Ann and the Holy Trinity Episcopal Church, Brooklyn, New York, were made between 1843-1849 by John and William Jay Bolton. Photo: Leland A. Cook.

including various historic revivals, and aesthetic and geometric patterns. American patterns prevailed thereafter; they tended to be more vivid, brash, and bold (Fig. 5).

After the 1893 Columbia World's Exposition, the Art Nouveau Style became the rage for windows. Sinuous nymphs, leggy maidens, whiplashed curves, lilies, and brambles became standard subjects until World War I. Among the leading proponents of the Art Nouveau Style were glassmakers John LaFarge and Louis Comfort Tiffany. Both men experimented independently throughout the 1870s to develop opalescent glass, which LaFarge was first to incorporate into his windows. Tiffany became the better-known, due in part to his prolific output. He attracted world-class artists and innovative glassmakers to his studio, which produced over 25,000 windows. Today, "Tiffany" remains a household name. His favorite and most popular scenes were naturalistic images of flowers, colorful peacocks and cockatiels, and landscapes at sunrise and sunset (Fig. 6). LaFarge, while appreciated in his own day, gradually slid into relative obscurity, from which he has emerged in recent decades. Tiffany and LaFarge are the greatest names in American stained glass.

In dramatic contrast to the American Art Nouveau style was the Neo-Gothic movement that became so popular for church and university architecture across the country.

Figure 5. Stained glass is an exterior feature as well as an interior one. As part of any preservation project, stained glass should be photographed from the outside as well as the inside. The frame of this Aesthetic Movement window (circa 1880) needs repair. Photo: Neal A. Vogel.

widely accepted and proliferated during the early 20th century.

By 1900, stained and leaded glass was being mass-produced and was available to almost everyone. Leading home journals touted leaded glass windows for domestic use, and a nationwide building boom created an unprecedented demand for stained and leaded art glass windows, door panels, and transoms. Mail order catalogs from sash and blind companies appeared, some offering over 100 low-cost, mass produced designs (although the same catalogs assured buyers that their leaded glass was "made to order") (Fig. 9).

The fading popularity of the ornate Victorian styles, combined with inferior materials used for mass production, and America's entry into World War I (which reduced the availability of lead), essentially eliminated the production of quality leaded glass.[3] The last mail order catalogs featuring stained glass were published in the mid-1920s, and tastes changed to the point that the 1926 *House Beautiful Building Annual* declared: "the crude stained glass windows in many of the Mansard-roof mansions of the 'eighties [1880s] prove how dreadful glass can be when wrongly used." The great age of stained glass was over. However, leaded glass panels have survived in uncounted numbers throughout the country, and are now once again appreciated as major features of historic buildings.

Figure 6. A 1907 window typical of those produced by Tiffany Studios. Characteristics include the use of opalescent glass, intricate leading, copper foil, extensive etching, plating (i.e., several layers of glass), and a scene with perspective that simulates a painting. Hyde Park Union Church, Chicago. Photo: Diana Kincaid.

Charles J. Connick was a leading designer of medieval-style windows characteristic of the style (Fig. 7).

Advocates of the Prairie Style, of whom Frank Lloyd Wright is the best known, rejected Tiffany's naturalistic scenes *and* Connick's Gothic imitations. (Fig. 8). Wright's rectilinear organic abstractions developed simultaneously with the similar aesthetic of the various European Secessionists. The creation of this style was aided by the development of zinc and copper cames in 1893. These cames—much stiffer than lead—made it possible to carry out the linear designs of Prairie School windows with fewer support bars to interfere with the design. At first, these windows had only an elitist following, but they were soon

Dating and Documenting Historic Leaded Glass

Before deciding on any treatment for historic leaded glass, every effort should be made to understand—and to record—its history and composition. Documentation is strongly encouraged for significant windows and other elements. Assigning an accurate date, maker, and style to a stained glass window often requires extensive research and professional help. A documentation and recording project, however, is worth the effort and expense, as insurance against accidents, vandalism, fire and other disasters. The better the information available, the better the restoration can be. The following sources offer some guidelines for dating leaded windows.

Building Context. The history of the building can provide ready clues to the history of its leaded windows, doors, and

Figure 7. Charles J. Connick was another American master of stained glass. He worked in a modernized Neo-Gothic style. This window is from 1921. Photo: Diana Kincaid.

address, 1892-1902), *Tiffany Studios New York or Louis C. Tiffany* (post 1902). Tiffany Studios, like others, did not always sign pieces and the absence of an inscription cannot be used to rule out a particular studio or artist. Windows may feature dated plaques commemorating a donor. However, these do not always indicate the date of the window, since windows were often installed before a donor was found. Nevertheless, these features help establish a reasonable date range.

Composition and Other Stylistic Elements. These elements are more subjective, and call for a fairly broad knowledge of architecture and art history. Do the windows fit the general style of the building? The style of the window may point to a general stylistic period (e.g., Arts & Crafts, Art Nouveau, Prairie School). The imagery or iconography of the windows may also reveal their overall historical context and establish a general time period (Fig. 10).

Framing and Surround. Framing elements and the window surround can reveal information central to dating the window. Do moldings match other interior trim? Has the opening been altered? Is the window set in an iron frame (post-1850s), a steel frame (generally post-World War I), a cast stone frame (seen as early as the 1880s, but popular

other elements. The construction date, and dates of major additions and alterations, should be ascertained. Later building campaigns may have been a time for reglazing. This is especially the case with churches and temples. They were often built with openings glazed with clear leaded glass. Stained glass was added later as finances allowed. Conversely, the windows may be earlier than the building. They may have been removed from one structure and installed in another. Bills, inventories, and other written documents often give clues to the date and composition of leaded glass. Religious congregations, fraternal lodges, and other organizations may have written histories that can aid a researcher.

Inscriptions and Signatures.
Many studios and artists affixed signature plates to their work— often at the lower right hand corner. In the case of Tiffany windows, the signature evolved through several distinct phases, and helps date the piece within a few years: *Tiffany Glass Company* (1886-1892), *Tiffany Glass & Decorating Company* (with

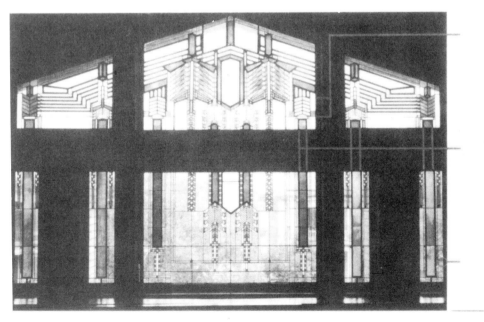

Figure 8. The master bedroom window at Frank Lloyd Wright's Dana House in Springfield, Illinois (1903), reflects the architect's philosophy of providing ornamentation without interfering with the view. Details show profiles of zinc cames. Photo: Leland A. Cook; Courtesy, Chicago Metallic Corporation.

LEADED WHITE AND CLEAR GLASS.

Figure 9. A typical mail-order catalog page of art glass windows available in 1903 from the E. L. Roberts Company, Chicago.

Figure 10. This image illustrates Thomas J. "Stonewall" Jackson and J.E.B. Stuart at the Second Battle of Manassas. The window comprises three of nine panels entitled "The Rise and Fall of the Confederacy" at Rhodes Hall in Atlanta. These windows were executed by Von Gerichten Art Glass Company of Columbus, Ohio, 1905 (installed). A.G. Rhodes reportedly returned one scene to the studio to be redone because the Yankees weren't running fast enough. Photo: Tommy Jones; Courtesy, Georgia Trust for Historic Preservation.

after 1900), or a terra cotta frame (generally after 1900)?

Reinforcement and Leading Details. Does the window or other element have round bars or flat bars? Flat bars began to appear about 1890; round bars, used since the Middle Ages, remained in use until the 1920s, when flat bars supplanted them. Cames can also give dating clues. Zinc cames, for example, developed by a midwestern company in association with Frank Lloyd Wright, first appeared in 1893. In general, however, dating a window by the came alone is difficult. Over one hundred varieties of lead came were available in the early 20th century. Moreover, came was sometimes produced to look old. Henderson's Antique Leading from the 1920s was made "to resemble the old hand wrought lead" and also carried "easy-fix" clip-on Georgian-style ornaments.

Glass. The glass itself can help in dating a window. Opalescent glass, for instance, was patented by John LaFarge in 1880. Tiffany patented two variations on LaFarge's technique in the same year. (Opalescent glass is translucent, with variegated colors resulting from internally refracted light. It features milky colored streaks.) Pre-1880 glass is usually smooth translucent colored glass (painted or not); glass with bold, deep colors is typical of the 1880s and 1890s, along with jewels, drapery glass and rippled glass. But such flamboyance faded out with the rest of Victoriana

by about 1905. However, stained glass styles of the late 19th century continued to appear in ecclesiastical buildings after they passed from general fashion. Leaded beveled plate glass was popular in residential architecture after 1890, and was used profusely until the 1920s.

The level of documentation warranted depends upon the significance of the window, but it is very important to document repair and restoration projects before, during, and after project work. Photographs will normally suffice for most windows (see "Photographing Stained Glass Windows" on page 7). For highly significant windows (generally, those which were not mass produced), rubbings as well as written documentation are recommended. The leading patterns in such windows are complex, particularly in plated windows (which have several layers). Rubbings are therefore encouraged for each layer; they are invaluable if a disaster strikes and reconstruction is required. Annotated rubbings of the leadwork should be done with a wax stone on acid-free vellum.

To document windows properly, inscriptions should be recorded word for word, including misspellings, peculiarities in type style, and other details. Names and inscriptions in or on windows can indicate ethnic heritage, particularly in churches or civic structures where windows often reflect styles and themes from the congregation's or community's origins. Lastly, any conjectural information should be clearly noted as such.

Photographing Stained Glass Windows

Windows should be photographed with daylight color slide film and black & white film in both transmitted and reflected light. Significant windows should be recorded with a positive color film, such as Kodachrome, with a low ISO, since it is more stable, and images should be printed on Resin-Coated paper. Black & white images should be printed on fiber-based paper to be considered archival. Photographing stained glass from the interior is not difficult if a few basic pieces of equipment are used and if a few simple rules are observed. A strong tripod, shutter cable release, light meter, and camera with through-the-lens metering will make the job easier. The key is to photograph windows in even, moderate daylight with the interior dimmed (lights off and, if necessary, with the other windows covered). Although some stained glass is dazzling in sunlight, the camera lens and film react differently from the human eye, which can quickly equalize the high contrast of light and dark glass. Film cannot discriminate this intense contrast, and the result can be a washed-out exposure or "hot spots." A light meter should be used to average out variations within the window, with special consideration for the focal point or most important feature of the window, such as a face. Since there is no precise formula for obtaining a balanced exposure, shots should be bracketed. When photographing on sunny days, shoot away from the sun; shoot eastern windows in the afternoon, western windows in the morning, southern windows at either time, and northern windows at midday. The glass should also be photographed from the inside with reflected light from a flash (positioned away from the camera to provide a raking light and to avoid reflected "hot spots"). Although photographing with a flash will neutralize the transmitted light and black out the glass, interior photography is valuable because it reveals the location and condition of the cames, braces, tie-wires, and other elements. Shoot the windows as centered and straight on as possible to minimize distortion and to keep the window frames from blocking details. Windows should also be photographed from the outside if there is no protective glazing to interfere with the view. This is particularly important with opalescent glass, which was often meant to be read from the exterior as well. As a final note, to photograph glass consistently well, it is essential to limit the variables (by using the same film, camera, and lenses), and to record the camera settings, to compare with the developed pictures and to adjust accordingly next time.

Deterioration of Stained and Leaded Glass

Three elements of leaded glass units are prone to damage and deterioration: the glass itself; the decorative elements (mostly applied paint); and the structural system supporting the glass.

Glass Deterioration

Glass is virtually immune to natural deterioration. Most American glass is quite stable—due to changes in glass composition made in the mid-19th century, particularly the increased silica content and the use of soda lime instead of potash as a source of alkali. Rarely, however, glass impurities or poor processing can cause problems, such as minor *discoloration* or tiny internal fractures (particularly in opalescent glass). And all glass can be darkened by dirt; this can often be removed (see "Cleaning" on page 9). However, while glass does not normally deteriorate, it is susceptible to *scratching* or *etching* by abrasion or chemicals, and to *breakage*.

The greatest cause of breakage or fracture is physical impact. Leaded glass in doors, sidelights, and low windows is particularly susceptible to breakage from accidents or vandalism. When set in operable doors or windows, leaded glass can crack or weaken from excessive force, vibration, and eventually even from normal use. Cracks can also result from improperly set nails or points that hold the window in the frame, or more rarely, by structural movement within the building. Leaded glass that is improperly annealed can crack on its own from internal stress. (Annealing is the process by which the heated glass is slowly cooled; the process is akin to tempering metal.) Glass can also disintegrate from chemical instability or the intense heat of a fire. Finally, windows assembled with long, narrow, angular pieces of glass are inherently prone to cracking. Often the cause of the cracks can be determined by the path they travel: cracks from impact typically radiate straight from the source. Stress cracks caused by heat or improper annealing will travel an irregular path and change direction sharply.

Deterioration of Painted Glass

Painted glass, typically associated with pictorial scenes and figures found in church windows, often presents serious preservation challenges. If fired improperly, or if poor quality mixtures were used, painted glass is especially vulnerable to weathering and condensation. Some studios were notorious for poorly fired paints (particularly those working with opalescent glass), while others had outstanding reputations for durable painted glass. Paints can be applied cold on the glass or fused in a kiln. Since they are produced from ground glass, enamels do not "fade," as often suggested, but rather flake off in particles. Several steps in the painting process can produce fragile paint that is susceptible to flaking. If applied too thick, the paint may not fuse properly to the glass, leaving small bubbles on the surface. This condition, sometimes called "frying," can also result from poor paint mixtures or retouching. Paint failure is more commonly caused by under firing (i.e., baking the glass either at too low a temperature or for too little time). Unfortunately, in American stained glass, the enamels used to simulate flesh tones were typically generated from several layers that were fired at too low a temperature. This means the most difficult features to replicate—faces, hands and feet—are often the first to flake away (Fig. 11).

Structural Deterioration

The greatest and the most common threat to leaded glass is deterioration of the skeletal structure that holds the glass. The structure consists of frame members, and lead or zinc (and occasionally brass or copper) came that secures individual pieces of glass. Frame members include wood sash and muntins that decay, steel t-bars and "saddle bars" that corrode, and terra cotta or stone tracery that can fracture and spall (Fig. 12). When frames fail, leaded glass sags and cracks due to insufficient bracing; it may even fall out from wind pressure or vibration.

Wood sash are nearly always used for residential windows and are common in many institutional windows as well. Left

Figure 12. These stained glass angels appear concerned over the cracked terra cotta frames of the rose window they grace. Photo: Neal A. Vogel.

unprotected, wood and glazing compounds decay over time from moisture and exposure to sunlight—with or without protective storm glazing—allowing glass to fall out.

Steel frames and saddle bars (braces) corrode when not maintained, which accelerates the deterioration of the glazing compound and loosens the glass. Moreover, operable steel ventilators and windows are designed to tight tolerances. Neglect can lead to problems. Eventually, they either fail to close snugly, or corrode completely shut. The leaded glass is then frequently reinstalled in aluminum window units, which require wider sections for equal strength and typically trim an inch or more off the glass border. Instead of relocating glass in aluminum frames, historic steel frames should be repaired. Often the corrosion is superficial; frames in this condition need prepping, painting with a good zinc-enriched paint, and realignment in the frame.

Masonry frames typically last a long time with few problems, but removing leaded glass panels set in hardened putty or mortar can be nearly impossible; as a last resort, glass borders may have to be sacrificed to remove the window.

Occasionally, leaded glass was designed or fabricated with inadequate bracing; this results in bulging or bowing panels; leaded panels should generally not exceed 14 linear feet (4.25 m) around the perimeter without support. More often, the placement of bracing is adequate, but the tie-wires that attach the leaded panels to the primary frame may be broken or disconnected at the solder joints.

Lead and zinc cames are the two most common assembly materials used in stained and other "leaded" glass. The strength and durability of the leaded panel assembly depends upon the type of came, the quality of the craftsmanship, and the glazing concept or design, as well as on the metallic composition of the cames, their cross-section strength, how well they are joined and soldered, and the leading pattern within each panel. Came is prone to natural deterioration from weathering and from thermal expansion and contraction, which causes metal fatigue.

The inherent strength of the assembly system is also related to the cross-section, profile and internal construction of the came (Fig. 13). Came can have a flat, rounded, or "colonial" profile, and aside from a few specialty and perimeter cames (U-channel), is based on a variation of the letter "H"and ranges from ⅛ " (3.2mm) wide to 1½" (38mm) wide. The cross-section strength of came varies depending on the thickness of the heart and flanges. Occasionally, came with reinforced (double) hearts or a steel core was used for rigidity. Such came added strength at the expense of flexibility and was typically used for rectilinear designs, or for strategically placed reinforcement within a curvilinear design.

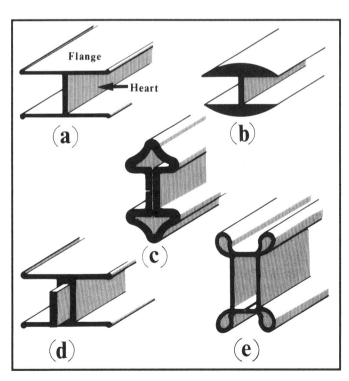

Figure 13. A wide variety of came has been used for ornamental glass in America: (a) flat lead came; (b) round lead came; (c) "Colonial" zinc came; (d) double-heart lead came with a steel core; (e) "Prairie School" zinc came. Drawing: Neal A. Vogel.

Came Types and Properties

Lead Came: Lead is a soft malleable metal (it can be scratched with a fingernail). It naturally produces a protective dark bluish-gray patina. In the mid-19th century, improved smelting processes enabled manufacturers to extract valuable metal impurities from lead, thereby producing 100% pure lead came. The industry reasoned that 100% pure lead came was superior to the less pure variety. Although pure lead came is very workable and contributes to intricate designs, time has proven it to be less durable than medieval came, which contained trace elements of tin, copper, silver, and antimony. Unfortunately, the misconception that pure lead had greater longevity continued throughout the glory years of leaded glass use in America. Most glass conservators use a 100-year rule of thumb for the life expectancy of 19th century came—less for came produced during war times. The demand for lead ammunition and the resulting scarcity of lead required studios to stretch the available lead to its limits, thus resulting in weaker cames. In the 1970s "restoration lead" (ASTM B29-84) was developed based on metallurgic analyses of medieval cames, some of which have lasted for centuries. Restoration lead should always be used when releading historic windows.

Zinc Came: Zinc came is more vulnerable to atmospheric corrosion (particularly from sulfuric acids) than lead, but has proven to be durable in America because it weighs 40% less than lead and its coefficient of expansion is 7% lower. Thus, it is somewhat less susceptible to fatigue from expansion and contraction. Moreover, it is ten times harder than lead, and has three times the tensile strength. Zinc came is strong enough to be self-supporting and requires little bracing to interrupt the window's design. While zinc came is perfect for the geometric designs of Prairie School windows, it is usually too stiff to employ in very curvilinear designs. Zinc can also take several finishes, including a copper or black finish. (As a result, zinc can be mistaken for copper or brass.)

Other Came: Other metals, primarily solid brass and copper, were also occasionally employed as came. They are generally found only in windows between ca. 1890 and ca. 1920.

How the cames are joined in a leaded panel is crucial to their long-term performance. Poor craftsmanship leads to a weak assembly and premature failure, while panels fabricated with interlocking (weaving) cames and lapped leads add strength. Soldered joints often reveal the skill level of the artisan who assembled the window, and can give evidence of past repairs. Solder joints should be neat and contact the heart of the came—wherein lies its greatest strength. Came joints should be examined closely; large globs of solder commonly conceal cames that do not meet. (Lead cames typically crack or break along the outside edge of the solder joint; stronger zinc cames frequently break the solder itself where it bridges junctures.) Weak joints contribute to a loose glass housing, and if glass rattles in the cames when the window is gently tapped, it is an indicator that repair or restoration is needed.

Leading patterns designed with inadequate support also contribute to structural failure. Panels with a series of adjacent parallel lines tend to hinge or "accordion," while lines radiating in concentric circles tend to telescope into a bulge. Stronger leading techniques, support bars, or specialty cames are sometimes required to correct poor original design. Minor sagging and bulging is to be expected in an old window and may not require immediate action. However, when bulges exceed 1½" (38mm) out of plane, they cross into a precarious realm; at that point, glass pieces can crack from severe sagging and pressure. If the bulged area moves when pressed gently, or if surrounding glass is breaking, it is time to address the problem before serious failure results.

Cleaning, Repair, Restoration, and Protection

The level of cleaning, repair, or restoration depends on the condition, quality, and significance of the glass, and, as always, the available budget. Hastily undertaken, overly aggressive, or poorly executed repairs can cause more damage than does prolonged deterioration. Repairs should, therefore, only be undertaken after carefully evaluating the condition of the glass—and only by professionals. Minor cracks, sagging, and oxidation are part of the character of historic leaded glass, and require no treatment. More extensive cracks, major bulges (generally, more than 1½" [38mm]), and other signs of advancing deterioration call for intervention, but caution must always be exercised. And each window must be evaluated separately. In some cases, windows have bulged up to 4" (102mm) out of plane without harming the pieces of glass or risking collapse.

Cleaning

Perhaps the greatest virtue of stained glass is that its appearance is constantly transformed by the ever-changing light. But dirt, soot, and grime can build up on both sides of the glass from pollution, smoke, and oxidation. In churches the traditional burning of incense or candles can eventually deposit carbon layers. These deposits can substantially reduce the transmitted light and make an originally bright window muted and lifeless. Simply cleaning glass will remove harmful deposits, and restore much of its original beauty, while providing the opportunity to inspect its condition closely (Fig. 14). The type of cleaner to use depends on the glass. Water alone should be tried first (soft water is preferable); deionized water should be used for especially significant glass and museum quality restorations. If water alone is insufficient,

Figure 14. The instructor removes one of six etched plates from a ca. 1905 Tiffany window in order to clean the interspaces and provide a rare educational opportunity at a restoration workshop. Cypress Lawn Memorial Park, Colma, California. Photo: Neal A. Vogel.

the next step is to use a non-ionic detergent. Occasionally, windows are covered with a yellowed layer of shellac, lacquer, varnish, or very stubborn grime which requires alcohol, or solvents to remove. Most *unpainted* art glass can be treated with acetone, ethanol, isopropyl alcohol or mineral spirits to remove these coatings if gentler methods have failed. All chemical residue must then be removed with a non-ionic detergent, and the glass rinsed with water (All workers should take normal protective measures when working with toxic chemicals.)

Painted glass must never be cleaned before the stability of the paint is confirmed, and only then with great caution. If the paint is sound, it can be cleaned with soft sponges and cloth. If the paint was improperly fired or simply applied cold, paint can flake off during cleaning and special measures are required such as delicate cleaning with cotton swabs. Occasionally, paint is so fragile the owner must simply accept the windows in their current state rather than risk losing the original surface.

Acidic, caustic, or abrasive cleaners should **never** be used. They can damage glass. Most common household glass cleaners contain ammonia and should not be used either; ammonia can react with the putty or metallic cames.

Repair

As with all elements in older and historic buildings, maintenance of leaded glass units is necessary to prevent more serious problems. It is essential to keep the frame maintained regardless of the material. Often, this simply entails regular painting and caulking, and periodic replacement of the glazing compound. Wood frames should be kept painted and caulked; new sections should be spliced into deteriorated ones, and epoxy repairs should be made where necessary. Masonry frames must be kept well pointed and caulked to prevent moisture from corroding the steel armature and anchors within.

Windows that leak, are draughty, or rattle in the wind (or when gently tapped) indicate that the waterproofing cement ("waterproofing") and sealants have deteriorated and maintenance or restoration is needed. Waterproofing is a compound rubbed over the window—preferably while flat on a table—and pressed under the came flange to form a watertight bond between the leading and the glass. Traditionally, waterproofing was made of linseed oil and whiting, and a coloring agent. (Hardening agents should not be included in the mixture; solvent-based driers should be used sparingly.) The waterproofing allows leaded glass in a vertical position (i.e., in windows) to be used as a weatherproof barrier. It does not provided adequate protection for leaded glass in a horizontal or arched position; leaded glass ceilings and domes must always be protected by a secondary skylight or diffusing skylight.

Sealants (e.g., putties, caulks, and silicones) are used to seal the leaded panel against the sash, and to seal any open joints around the window frame. Sealants have improved dramatically since the development of silicones from World War II technology. Silicones are not without problems, however. Some release acetic acid as they cure. Acetic acid can harm lead, and should never be used on leaded glass. Instead, "neutral cure" silicones should be used. Developed in the early 1970s, "neutral cure" silicones have an expected lifespan of 50 years. These high-tech construction sealants are not sold in consumer supply stores. The appropriate type of sealant depends on the materials to be bonded and on the desired appearance and longevity. When windows are to be restored, the contractor should explain what types of waterproofing and sealants are to be used, and how long they are expected to last. On large projects, a letter from the product manufacturer should be obtained that approves and warranties the proposed application of their product.

Leaded panels will generally outlast several generations of waterproofing. When the waterproofing has failed, the window should be removed from the opening and water-proofed on a bench. Leaded glass cannot be adequately waterproofed in place. Removing the windows will provide an opportunity to perform maintenance on the window surround and to secure the reinforcement. This is far less expensive than totally releading the window, which is typically required if maintenance is deferred. When waterproofing or sealants break down, many building owners attempt to resolve the problem by installing protective glazing, when the window only needs maintenance. Protective glazing is not an alternative to maintenance; in fact, it impedes maintenance if not installed properly and can accelerate the deterioration of the stained glass (see "Protective Glazing and Screens" on page 12).

A very common—but extremely harmful—practice in the American stained glass industry is performing major window repairs in place. The practice is routine among churches where the cost of restoring large windows can be prohibitive. However, undertaking major repairs in place provides only a quick fix. A window cannot be properly repaired or restored in place if it is bulging or sagging far out of plane, if over 5% to 10% of the glass is broken, or if solder joints are failing. Unscrupulous glazers can introduce a great deal of stress into the glass by forcibly flattening the window in place and tacking on additional bracing. At a comfortable distance the window may look fine, but upon close inspection the stress cracks in the glass and broken solder joints become obvious. Windows subjected to this treatment will deteriorate rapidly, and complete, much more costly restoration will likely be necessary within a few years (while a proper repair can easily last two generations or more).

Major repairs to windows are sometimes part of a larger preservation project. In such cases, the risk of damaging the windows can be very great if their removal and reinstallation have not been carefully planned. When major building repairs are also to take place, the windows should be removed first to prevent damage during other work. Windows should be reinstalled as the next-to-last step in the larger project (followed by the painters or others working on the finishes surrounding the stained glass).

And glass should be protected whenever other work is undertaken on buildings—whether or not the windows are also to be repaired. External scaffolding, for example, erected for repointing or roofing projects may offer vandals and thieves easy access to windows and, through them, to building interiors. Finally, stained and leaded glass should always be well protected whenever chemical cleaners are used on the exterior of the building; some products, such as hydrofluoric-acid cleaners, will cause irreversible damage.

Repairs to Glass

Minor repairs, such as replacing a few isolated pieces of broken glass, can be performed in place as a reasonable stop-gap measure. This work, typically called a "drop-in," "stop-in," or "open-lead" repair, entails cutting the came flange around the broken piece of glass at the solder joints, folding it back to repair or replace the old glass, and resoldering the joints. Repairing a zinc came window is not as easy. Zinc cames are too stiff to open up easily, so they must be cut open with a small hack saw and dismantled until the broken area is reached. The glass is then repaired or replaced and the window is reassembled. New cames can be patinated to harmonize with the originals—but only with difficulty. Repatination should never be attempted in place, since it is impossible to clean off harmful residues trapped under the came.

Original glass should always be retained, even though it may be damaged. Replacement glass that exactly or closely matches the original piece can be very difficult to find, and costly to make. An endless variety of glass colors and textures were produced, and given the delicate chemistry of glassmaking, even samples from the same run can be noticeably different. The traditional secrecy that shrouds the glassmaking trade to this very day, as well as environmental bans of historically popular ingredients such as lead and cobalt for deep blues and greens, further hinders accurate reproductions. Therefore, *it is nearly always better to use an imperfect original piece of glass than to replace it.* If the paint is failing on a prominent feature of a window, a coverplate of thin, clear glass can be painted and placed over the original. (The coverplates must be attached mechanically, rather than laminated, so that they can be removed later if necessary.) A reverse image of the fading feature should be painted on the backside of the coverplate in order to get the two painted images as close together as possible. With repetitive designs, stencils can be created to produce multiple duplicates (Fig. 15).

Sometimes replacement is the only option. Fortunately, custom glass houses still exist, including the company that originally supplied much of the glass for Tiffany commissions. Stained and leaded glass has also experienced a resurgence in popularity, and American glassmakers have revived many types of historic glass.

When missing, shattered, and poorly matched glass from later repairs must be replaced, the new pieces should be scribed on the edge (under the came) with the date to prevent any confusion with original glass in the future.

Glass cracks will enlarge over time as the contacting edges grind against each other whenever the window is subject to vibration, thermal expansion and contraction, and other forces such as building movement. Therefore, it is important to repair cracks across important features as soon as they are detected, and while a clean break remains. Years ago, cracks were typically repaired with a "Dutchman" or "false lead" by simply splicing in a cover lead flange over a crack. Although this conceals the crack, it creates an even larger visual intrusion and provides no bond to the glass. Today there are three primary options for repairing broken glass: copper foil (Fig. 16), epoxy edge-gluing (Fig. 17), and silicone edge-gluing. These techniques differ in strength, reversibility, and visual effect, and the appropriate repair must be selected on a case-by-case basis by a restoration specialist.

Copper Foiling: Copper foil has the longest history and, unless the glass is unstable, is generally the best option

Figure 15. New stencils are used to produce matching replacement glass for repetitive stenciled patterns in a ca. 1870 window. Photo: Neal A. Vogel.

Figure 16. This stenciled roundel is being repaired by the copper foil technique. The glass cracked because it was not properly annealed. Once it cracks, it relieves the internal stress and stabilizes. Photo: Neal A. Vogel.

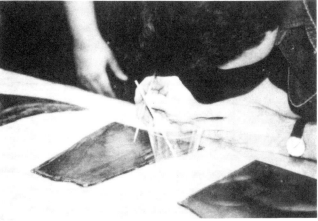

Figure 17. A valuable piece of flashed glass is carefully edge-glued with epoxy and a steady hand. Photo: Neal A. Vogel.

when a piece of glass has only one or two cracks. Copper foil is a thin tape which is applied along each side of the break, trimmed to a minimal width on the faces, and soldered. A copper wire can be soldered on where additional strength is required. However, copper foil repairs should not be used on unstable glass, since heat is required that can cause further damage. Copper foil produces a strong repair, is totally reversible and has a negligible aesthetic impact (a ¹⁄₁₆" [1.6mm] wide line).

Epoxy Edge-Gluing: This technique produces a nearly invisible line and is often used on painted glass, particularly focal points of a window such as a face, or a portion of sky intended to be one continuous piece. Epoxy can even be tinted to match the glass. It is also used for infusing shattered glass or microscopic cracks caused by intense heat from a fire. Epoxy produces a very strong repair, but will deteriorate in sunlight and requires secondary glazing to protect it from UV degradation. Epoxy is the least reversible of the three techniques, and usually the most expensive.

Silicone Edge-Gluing: This repair method has the lowest strength and should be used when a flexible joint is desirable—if, for instance, the window will be under continuous stress. Silicone repairs are easily reversible, and can be removed with a razor blade—when they are done correctly, that is. Silicone edge-gluing is not the same as smearing silicone all over the glass. This unfortunate practice, seen throughout the country, is useless as a repair technique, and usually causes more damage than if the glass were left alone. Silicone is almost clear, but it refracts light differently from glass and is, thus, easily detectable. Silicone is not affected by temperature, humidity or UV light. Silicone repairs are typically the least expensive repair option.

Repairs to Structural Support Systems

Windows may have detached from the saddle bars and begun to sag, bulge, and bow extensively. This point varies from window to window. Generally, however, a window sagging or bulging more than 1½" (38mm) out of plane has reached the point where it should be removed from the opening to be flattened out. Under these conditions, it is essential to note if the support system or leading pattern has failed so it may be corrected before the window is reinstalled. The window must be allowed to flatten over a few weeks in a horizontal position. This will minimize stress on the solder joints and glass. A moderate weight and controlled heat will help coax the window back into its original plane. The process requires patience. Once the window has flattened, the original support system should be reattached and additional support added as necessary. It is crucial to consider the original design so the new support bars do not intrude on important window features. Sometimes small thin braces or "fins" can be manipulated to follow existing lead lines exactly. These give support, but are almost invisible. Flattening windows also provides a good opportunity to apply new waterproofing to help prevent further deterioration. Today, synthetic compounds are used.

Windows should only be removed when they need to be flattened, waterproofed, reinforced or releaded. Allow plenty of time for careful, thorough work. Large projects can take several months, especially if complete releading is necessary. Owners, consulting professionals, and construction managers must therefore ensure that vacant openings will be weathertight for an extended period—whether the opening is covered by plywood, acrylics, or polymer film.

Rebuilding or releading a window is an expensive and involved process. The releading process requires that a window be "unbuilt" before it can be "rebuilt." The glass pieces must be removed from the cames, the old cement must be cleaned from each piece of glass, and all the pieces must be rejoined precisely. At every step the process involves the risk of damaging the glass. Furthermore, exceptional studios had unique leading techniques, and thus the cames should not be replaced casually. Total releading should only be undertaken when necessary to avoid or slow the loss of historic fabric (Fig. 18). (It is essential to request a copy of all window rubbings if the windows are to be completely releaded.)

Figure 18. A craftsman releads a window. The full hood offers protection from lead fumes. Photo: Neal A. Vogel.

Lead and zinc came, however, is intended to be a sacrificial element of a glass unit assembly, as mortar is to brick and paint is to wood; came will break down long before glass and must be replaced; came lasts 75 to 200 years depending on the window's quality, design and environment. A common preservation conflict arises in releading historic windows constructed of flat came: whether to retain historical accuracy by using new flat came, or to use came with a rounded profile for greater strength and durability. The decision must be carefully weighed depending on the significance of the window, the contribution of the came profile to the overall design, and the severity of the deterioration caused by a weak flat came. In most windows, the came profile is essentially lost in transmitted light, but occasionally shadow lines are important and should be reproduced (Fig. 8). Furthermore, it is important to correct technical problems that arise from flimsy original came. Occasionally, a slightly heftier came may be the best solution to resolve weak panels that have not proven the test of time. Under these circumstances, the thicker lead came (even if only ¹⁄₆₄" [0.4mm]) will cause a leaded panel to swell slightly, and the frame, perimeter leads, or glass may have to be trimmed slightly to fit the opening. (Trimming the glass should be the last resort.) This would not be an appropriate solution in a museum-quality restoration or for a highly significant window.

Protective Glazing and Screens

The use of protective glazing (also known as secondary or storm glazing) is highly controversial. Potential benefits of protective glazing are that it can shield windows from wind pressure; increase energy savings; protect against environmental pollutants and UV light; provide vandalism and security protection, and reduce window maintenance. Potential drawbacks are that it can promote condensation; cause heat to build up in the air space and thereby increase the window's expansion/contraction; eliminate natural ventilation; reduce access for maintenance; offer only minimal energy payback for intermittently heated buildings (such as churches and temples), and mar the appearance. Protective glazing can also be presented as a cheaper alternative to full-scale restoration. And all too often protective glazing is installed as a routine matter when there is little threat of damage from vandalism or other causes. Protective glazing, especially when improperly installed, may hasten deterioration of stained glass windows.

Various types of metal grills or screens are also used. They add security and vandalism protection but often impair the appearance of the window (inside and out) by creating new shadows or diffusing transmitted light.

As a general rule, protective layers should not be added. In most cases the potential drawbacks outweigh the potential benefits.

Under some circumstances, however, protective glazing or screens may be necessary. (This applies to windows. Domes and ceilings present a special case. See "Domes and Ceilings" on page 14). A real vandalism or security threat warrants protective glazing, such as when the windows can be reached easily or are in an isolated location (Fig. 19). Protective glazing is also warranted when employed historically on a particular window as original plating (Tiffany Studios, for example, often used plate glass to keep dirt and moisture out of their multi-plated windows). Unusual circumstances (such as when the windows are painted on the outside) may also dictate the use of protective glazing. Finally, protective glazing is warranted when a UV filter is needed to prevent epoxy glass repairs from breaking down.

A variety of protective glazing materials are available. They include polycarbonates, acrylics, laminated glass,

plate glass, and tempered glass. The plastic products are very strong, lightweight, and relatively easy to install, but tend to scratch, haze, and yellow over time, despite UV inhibitors. They also have a high coefficient of expansion and contraction, so the frames must be designed to accommodate change induced by temperature fluctuations. Poor installations in restrictive frames cause distorted reflections from bowing panels. Protective panels of glass are heavier and more difficult to install, making them more expensive than plastic. However, glass will not bow, scratch, or haze and is usually the best option in aesthetic terms; laminated glass provides additional impact resistance.

A common error in installing protective glazing is to create a new window configuration (Fig. 20). Insensitive installations that disregard the original tracery destroy the window's aesthetics—and the building's. When protective glazing is added, it should be ventilated. If a window is not ventilated, heat and condensation may build up in the air space between the ornamental glass and the protective glazing. The surface temperature of unvented glass has been measured up to twice the outdoor ambient temperature. This differential affects the expansion and contraction of the support system, particularly lead cames, thereby accelerating metal fatigue. Protective glazing may also cause condensation on the historic window, depending on the window's orientation, indoor/outdoor humidity, and whether or not the building is air conditioned.

When absolutely necessary, protective glazing should be installed in an independent frame between ⅝" (16mm) and 1" (25mm) from the leaded glass. This allows the protective panel to be removed for periodic maintenance of both the historic window and the new feature. The conditions of the air space between the two elements should be monitored on a regular basis; the glass should not feel hot, and condensation should never collect on the window.

No ideal formulas have been developed for venting the air space between the ornamental glass and the protective glazing, but it is typically vented to the outside (unless the building is air conditioned most of the year). Generally, a gap of several inches is left at the top and bottom when glass is used, or holes are drilled in the protective glazing at the top and bottom when polycarbonates and acrylics are used. Small screens or vents should be added to keep out birds and insects. Finally, it is important to realize that some original plating of glass softened or tinted the transmitted light intentionally, as designed by the original window maker; in this case any new or replacement plating should simulate this effect to respect the artisan's intentions (Fig. 19).

Figure 19. Stained glass in mausoleums requires protective glazing since vandalism is frequent in cemeteries. This plate glass intentionally softened the light transmitted through the window. This feature should be reproduced in the replacement glazing. It may be possible to repair the plate glass and install another, stronger (clear) layer on the outside. Photo: Neal A. Vogel.

Domes and Ceilings

Stained glass domes and ceilings were very popular throughout the Victorian and Classical Revival periods. They are often principal interior features of churches, hotels, restaurants, railway stations, and civic buildings (a). The loss or unsympathetic alteration of leaded glass ceilings and domes is a widespread problem. Poorly planned rehabilitation projects sometimes cause the removal or alteration of overhead leaded glass in order to comply with fire codes or to achieve perceived energy savings; occasionally, they are even concealed above suspended ceilings.

Moreover, stained glass in the horizontal position readily collects dust and dirt over the years and is relatively inaccessible for cleaning. It is also more likely to "creep" or slump when the reinforcement is inadequate. Most importantly, leaded glass cannot be sufficiently weatherproofed in a horizontal (or arched) position. It must always be protected by skylights or "diffusers"—rooftop features that diffuse the natural daylight into the attic or light shaft, and protect the leaded glass ceiling or dome from the elements (b).

Due to the inferior quality of glazing sealants of the late 19th and early 20th centuries, and to deferred maintenance, glass ceilings have frequently been removed or covered with roofing materials. Artificial lighting is then required to backlight the ceiling or dome, which robs the stained glass of its life—the vibrant effects created by ever-changing natural light. All types of artificial lighting can be found from floodlamps to fluorescent tubes. Outside sensors are even used to modulate the light level in an attempt to simulate changes in daylight. However, daylight is impossible to emulate. Moreover, it's free. Artificial lighting

(b). Before repairs began on the vaulted glass ceiling below, a new diffusing skylight was installed to correct recurring leaks. Catacombs (ca. 1920), Cypress Lawn Memorial Park, Colma, California. Photo: Neal A. Vogel.

requires maintenance, introduces an additional fire hazard in the attic, increases the building's electrical load, and is supplied only at a cost.

Stained glass ceilings and domes that have been sealed off from natural light should be investigated for restoration. Once natural light is restored and the stained glass is cleaned, the lighting effect on an interior can be extraordinary. Improved skylight designs and major advances in glazing sealants since World War II (particularly silicones) encourage the restoration of skylights without the fear of inheriting a maintenance nightmare.

(a). Stained glass ceilings and domes are often principal interior features of churches, hotels, restaurants, railway stations, and civic buildings. This one illuminates the Carnegie Free Library in Union, South Carolina. Photo: Jack E. Boucher, HABS.

Figure 20. (a) The aluminum frame grid used for protective glazing totally disregards the original tracery of this Neo-Gothic church. The grid mars the appearance of the window inside and out. It also impairs the overall historic character of the building. (b) Protective glazing in this instance preserves both the appearance of the window and its contribution to the building. The latter building is the Cathedral Basilica of the Assumption (St. Mary's Cathedral), Covington, Kentucky (1895-1910). The window, 67' x 24' (20.4m x 7.3m), is among the largest stained glass windows in the United States. Photos: Neal A. Vogel.

Conclusion

Most of the Nation's stained glass and leaded glass has recently passed, or is quickly approaching, its 100th anniversary—yet much of this glass has not been cleaned or repaired since the day it was installed. With proper care, these important historic features can easily last another hundred years.

Notes

[1]George S. and Helen McKearin, *American Glass*. New York: Crown Pulishers, 1948; Reprinted, New York: Bonanza Books, 1989, pp. 75-131.

[2]Charles E. Peterson, *Building Early America: Contributions toward the History of a Great Industry*. The Carpenters Company of the City and County of Philadelphia. Radnor, PA: Chilton Book Co., 1976, p. 158.

[3]H. Weber Wilson, *Great Glass in American Architecture: Decorative Windows and Doors Before 1920*. New York: E.P. Dutton, 1986, p. 10.

Selected Reading List

The Census of Stained Glass Windows in America. *The Conservation and Restoration of Stained Glass: An Owner's Guide.* Raleigh, NC: Stained Glass Associates, 1988.

Duthie, Arthur Louis. *Decorative Glass Processes: Cutting, Etching, Staining, and Other Traditional Techniques.* New York: The Corning Museum of Glass and Dover Publications, 1982.

Fisher, Charles E., III, ed. *The Window Handbook: Successful Strategies for Rehabilitating Windows in Historic Buildings.* Washington, D.C.: National Park Service and Georgia Institute of Technology. 1986. Rev. 1990.

Frelinghuysen, Alice Cooney. "A New Renaissance: Stained Glass in the Aesthetic Period," *In Pursuit of Beauty: Americans and the Aesthetic Movement.* New York: The Metropolitan Museum of Art, 1986.

Heinz, Thomas A. "Use & Repair of Zinc Cames in Art-Glass Windows." *Old House Journal*, (September/October 1989), pp. 35-38.

Koch, Robert. *Tiffany: Rebel in Glass*. New York: Crown Publishers, Inc., 1964.

Lee, Lawrence, George Seddon and Francis Stephans. *Stained Glass*. New York: Crown Publishers, 1976.

Lloyd, John Gilbert. *Stained Glass in America*. Jenkintown, PA: Foundation Books, 1963.

Rigan, Otto B. *Photographing Stained Glass*. Oregon: Mercury Press, 1983.

Stained Glass Association of America. *SGAA Reference & Technical Manual*, Second Edition Lee's Summit, MO: The Stained Glass Association of America, 1992.

Wilson, H. Weber. *Great Glass in American Architecture: Decorative Windows and Doors Before 1920*. New York: E. P. Dutton, 1986.

Wilson, H. Weber. *Your Residential Stained Glass: A Practical Guide to Repair & Maintenance*. Chambersburg, PA: Architectural Ecology, 1979.

The Window Workbook for Historic Buildings. Washington, DC: Historic Preservation Education Foundation, 1986.

The rose window at St. John Cantius, Chicago (1906-1908), undergoing restoration (interior view). Photo: Neal A. Vogel.

Cover Photograph: St. Michael's Church, Chicago. Window dates from 1902. Photo: Rolf Achilles.

Acknowledgements

Neal A. Vogel is the Technical Services Coordinator for Inspired Partnerships in Chicago, Illinois. **Rolf Achilles,** an Art Historian, serves on the Technical Advisory Committee for Inspired Partnerships. **Michael J. Auer,** Preservation Assistance Division, National Park Service, served as technical editor. Additional assistance was provided by Anne Grimmer, National Park Service.

The authors would like to thank the following individuals, studios and manufacturers who graciously shared information and provided opportunities to review studio, glass processing, and on-site works in progress: Botti Studios of Architectural Arts, Evanston, IL; Bovard Studio, Fairfield, IA; Chicago Metallic Corporation, Chicago, IL; Chicago Art Glass and Jewels, Inc., Plymouth, WI; Conrad Schmitt Studios, Inc., New Berlin, WI; Cummings Studio, North Adams, MA; Cypress Lawn Memorial Park, Colma, CA; Georgia Trust for Historic Preservation, Atlanta, GA; Hollander Glass, Stanton, CA; Jon Lee Art Glass Company, Winono, MN; Shenandoah Studios of Stained Glass, Inc., Front Royal,

VA; Vermont Statehouse, Montpelier, VT. **Special thanks to Arthur J. Femenella, Association of Restoration Specialists, Inc., Hoboken, NJ; Richard L. Hoover, Stained Glass Association of America, Lee's Summit, MO; and H. Weber Wilson, Olitz-Wilson Antiques, Newport, RI, for providing editorial assistance.**

This publication has been prepared pursuant to the National Preservation Act of 1966, as amended, which directs the Secretary of the Interior to develop and make available information concerning historic properties. The text of this publication is not copyrighted, and can be reproduced without penalty. Normal procedures for credit to the authors and the National Park Service are appreciated. Comments on this publication may be directed to H. Ward Jandl, Deputy Chief, Preservation Assistance Division, National Park Service, P.O. Box 37127, Washington, D.C. 20013-7127.

ISSN: 0885-7016

34

Applied Decoration for Historic Interiors
Preserving Composition Ornament

Jonathan Thornton and William Adair, FAAR

Anyone who has ever walked through historic houses and large public buildings, visited an art gallery, picked up a picture frame in an antique shop, or even ridden on an old carrousel has been close to *composition ornament*, but has probably not known what it was or how it was made. This is not surprising, since composition or "compo" was conceived as a substitute for more laboriously produced ornamental plaster and carved wood and stone, so was intended to fool the eye of the viewer (see Fig. 1). The confusion has been heightened over time by makers who claimed to be the sole possessors of secret recipes and by the variety of names and misnomers associated with the material, including *plaster, French stucco,* and *Swedish putty,* to name a few.

Many natural or man-made materials can be made soft or "plastic" by the application of heat and are called "thermoplastics." Composition is a thermoplastic material used to create sculptural relief. It is soft and pliable when pressed into molds; becomes firm and flexible as it cools; and is hard and rigid when fully dry. Typically formulated with chalk, resins, glue, and linseed oil, this combination of materials gives compo its familiar light-to-dark brown color. It is the only one of the so-called thermoplastic materials to be used extensively in architectural decoration because of its low cost.

Generally adhered to wood, historic composition ornament is most often found decorating flat surfaces such as interior cornice and chair rail moldings, door and window surrounds, mantelpieces, wainscot paneling, and staircases—indeed, anywhere that building designers and owners wanted to delight and impress the visitor, but stay within a budget. While composition was cheaper than carved ornament, it was still meticulously hand made and applied; thus, it was more often used in "high style" interiors. But the types of structures historically decorated with composition ornament were more democratic, encompassing residential, commercial, and institutional buildings, and even including specialty applications such as the social saloon of a steamship (see Fig. 2).

Figure 1. An American mantelpiece in the Adam style dating from the early 19th century illustrates composition ornament's reputation as a first-rate imitator of wood. Only the allegorical design, flower baskets, floral swags or festoons, flanking fleur-de-lis ornamentation and pilaster capitals are compo; the panels and simple moldings are carved wood. Photo: Courtesy, Philadelphia Museum of Art: Given by Mrs. Thurston Mason in memory of her sister, Miss Anna P. Stevenson.

Figure 2. Composition ornament has been used in America for over two hundred years in a variety of applications: (a) a floral festoon and basket in the Adam style for an 1803 mantelpiece; (b) the social saloon of an 1866 steamship, S.S. China; (c) scenery panels on a 1916 Allan Herschell carrousel; (d) ceiling decoration in a 1920s hotel; (e) the coffered ceiling of the National Archives library, 1938; (f) a modern reproduction of a Stanford White-designed frame; and (g) 1990s compo ornamentation for a re-modeled residence. (a) Courtesy, Gold Leaf Studios, Inc.; (b) Philip L. Molten; (c) Elizabeth Brick; (d) Courtesy, J.P. Weaver Co.; (e) Courtesy, National Archives; (f) 06.218: Self Portrait of Thomas Wilmer Dewing (1851-1938). American, 1906. Oil on wood panel: 50.8 x 36.8 cm. Courtesy, Freer Gallery of Art, Smithsonian Institution, Washington, D.C.; (g) Courtesy, J.P. Weaver Co.

With proper understanding of the material, historic composition ornament may be successfully cleaned, repaired, or replaced in sections. Unfortunately, because composition is often misidentified as plaster, stucco, or carved wood, the use of inappropriate methods for removing paint is a major cause of its loss (see Fig. 3). The purpose of this Brief is to to assist historic property owners, managers, architects, craftsmen, and preservationists in identifying existing composition ornament, determining the extent of repair and replacement needed and, finally, selecting the most sensitive, non-destructive method of treating it.

Figure 3. When this historic composition window surround was mistakenly identified as plaster, then treated with a caustic paint stripper, a section of it was destroyed. Photo: Byran Blundell.

De-Mystifying the Mix

While various types of moldable composition date to the Italian Renaissance, architectural use of composition did not begin to flourish until the last quarter of the 18th century. During this period, many composition ornament makers in Europe and America supplied the public with complex sculptural decoration. Also, the overly complicated and often intentionally mysterious earlier recipes were now reported to be comprised of a few basic ingredients: animal glue, oil (usually linseed), a hard resin (pine rosin or pitch was cheapest), and a bulking or filling material, generally powdered chalk or whiting (see also Sidebar, *Compo: The Basic Ingredients*).

Compo mixes have been the subject of a good deal of variation and there has never been a set recipe, but the ornament manufacturers of the later 18th and early 19th centuries understood in general terms what their material was and what it could do (see Fig. 4). The advantages of the material were described by a prominent American maker, Robert Wellford, in his advertising broadside of 1801:

"A cheap substitute for wood carving has long been desirable for some situations,

particularly enriched mouldings, etc., and various were the attempts to answer the purpose, the last and most successful is usually termed Composition Ornaments. It is a cement of solid and tenacious materials, which when properly incorporated and pressed into moulds, receives a fine relievo; in drying it becomes hard as stone, strong, and durable, so as to answer most effectually the general purpose of Wood Carving, and not so liable to chip. This discovery was rudely conducted for some time, owing to Carvers declining every connection with it, till, from its low price, it encroached so much upon their employment, that several embarked in this work, and by their superior talents, greatly improved it."

In brief, compo is perhaps best understood as an early thermoplastic that allowed the rapid reproduction of complicated detail for popular use.

Making Composition Ornament: A Process Unchanged

Since the craft has essentially remained the same over time, a description of its historic manufacture is also applicable today (see Fig. 5).

In one container, chunks of amber colored pine rosin or the cheaper black pitch were heated in linseed oil until they melted together and combined completely. In another container (often a double-boiler), previously soaked chunks of animal glue derived from skins and hides were cooked and blended into a uniformly thick solution. The two liquid components were then stirred together. This "batter" was made into a pliable "dough" in a way familiar to any baker. It was poured into a cratered pile of whiting and first mixed with a spatula until it was thick enough to be kneaded by hand. Vigorous folding and kneading in of more whiting was done until the composition had a consistency like modeling clay and was completely uniform.

To mold a decoration, the compo was first warmed in a steamer, and the mold prepared with a thin coating of oil and a dusting with talcum powder. A piece was then kneaded and folded to produce a smooth and wrinkle-free surface on one side. The good side was placed down over the rigid mold, and pressed in loosely with the fingers,

Figure 4. Compo ornament could be applied to simple and complex surfaces, including cornices, friezes, architraves, pilasters, and chimney pieces and to looking glass and picture frames. Manufacturers' ads such as these were commonplace in 19th century America, particularly in eastern cities. Left: Zane, Chapman, & Co. Right: Horton & Waller. Photo left: Courtesy, Jonathan Thornton. Photo right: Courtesy, Gold Leaf Studios, Inc.

a.

b.

c.

d.

e.

f.

g.

Figure 5. The steps of making composition ornament: (a) pouring compo "batter" into a pile of whiting on a warm granite slab; (b) an almost finished ball of composition; (c) warming compo in a steamer; (d) kneading compo; (e) pressing or squeezing compo into a mold using a screw press; (f) slicing ornament from a pressing board; and (g) a compo design made up from several "squeezes." Note its familiar brown color prior to painting, staining, or gilding. Photos: (a)(b) Jonathan Thornton; (c)(d) William Adair; (e) Jonathan Thornton; (f)(g) Lenna Tyler Kast.

leaving excess above the surface of the mold. A damp board was placed over this and the "sandwich" placed in a screw press and squeezed so as to force the compo into the finest detail. It was then removed from the press and turned over so that the mold could be lifted straight up, leaving the compo stuck to the board. Upon cooling to room temperature, the compo gelled, becoming tough and rubbery (the gelling property is due to the glue component which is chemically identical to edible gelatin). At this stage, it was sliced off the board with a thin-bladed knife. The remaining mass of composition still adhered to the board could also be sliced off and reused.

Composition ornament was often fixed to an already prepared wooden substrate at the factory while it was still fresh and flexible, but could be dried and shipped to the final user, who would make it flexible again by steaming on a cloth stretched over a container of boiling water. Instructions for doing this, as well as suitable brads for "fixing," were supplied by some manufacturers. Because of the glue component, steaming the backs of ornaments would make them soft and sticky enough to self-bond without additional glue. Soft ornaments were softened nailed through or pressed down on top of previously driven headless brads (also called sprigs). Strings and wires were often included in the mass during pressing to serve as internal armatures and reinforcements. These measures preserved the integrity of the ornaments even if they cracked.

Originally meant to copy other materials such as wood, plaster, and stone, composition had its own unique properties and advantages that were soon exploited in both technical and artistic terms. It has distinct characteristics in each of its three states: pliable, rubbery, and hard. When warm and pliable, it can be modeled by a skilled worker and it is capable of receiving the finest detail when squeezed into a mold. After it has chilled to room temperature and is gelled, it is rubbery, flexible, and tough. The detail is essentially set and cannot be easily damaged as the ornaments are manipulated (see Fig. 6).

Figure 6. This finished length of compo molding is stuck to its pressing board. The newly made piece will be sliced off the board, then applied. Photo: Jonathan Thornton.

Gelled composition ornaments can be easily bent over curved surfaces without cracking, and unlike a rigid cast material such as plaster, they can be stretched or compressed somewhat to fit a design without damaging the detail. An egg and dart motif, for example, could be made to come out evenly at the corners without making a partial egg or dart. The sculptural vocabulary from the maker's mold collection could be re-arranged at will into larger decorative schemes. In fact, any smaller component of a decoration from a single mold could be sliced free and inserted into any location.

Composition could be carved to heighten detail, correct defects, or undercut ornaments—that were, of necessity, straight-sided—so that they would release from the rigid molds. This could be done in the gelled state or, with more difficulty, after it had finally hardened to stone-like solidity.

Finally, when completely hard, it could be given a polished marble shine with nothing but a damp cloth. It could be stained, coated with any sort of paint, varnish, or oil gilded without any further preparation (see Fig. 7).

Molds and the Creation of Patterns

A technical discussion of composition is not complete without an examination of the molds used to create the ornament. These were the ornament maker's largest investment in time and expense, and were the key to the craft (see Fig. 8).

Figure 7. The coffered ceiling of the 1938 National Archives library in Washington, D.C. features egg-and-dart composition molding finished with a dark brown stain. While compo design is more often light and delicate, here, it has a bold, massive quality. Photo: Bryan Blundell.

Figure 8. Several historic and reproduction compo molds are shown to underscore the variety of materials used to make them: 1. applewood mold 2. pearwood mold 3. boxwood mold encased in beech 4. boxwood mold 5. sulfur mold encased in maple 6. pewter mold encased in pine and oak 7. positive pattern for pitch mold carved in pearwood 8. pitch mold encased in oak 9. composition mold encased in maple 10. epoxy and polyester molds reinforced with glass fabric. Photos: Jonathan Thornton.

Composition molds were always made of rigid materials that would withstand the considerable pressure used in pressing the ornaments. All of these materials and methods have been used in sculptural crafts since the Renaissance. The comparative listing that follows helps explain their advantages and disadvantages.

Wood was carved in reverse to create a negative matrix. This was highly skilled work often performed by a specialist carver, and required a large initial investment in time, but wooden molds would essentially last indefinitely if properly maintained. A further design advantage of reverse carving is that fine incised lines will show up as fine raised lines in the final ornament. (Fine raised lines are notoriously difficult to carve or model in relief.) Molds carved from dense and close-grained fruit woods such as apple and pear seem to have been common in the 18th century. In the 19th century, the most intricate molds were carved in boxwood, often encased or framed by larger and cheaper pieces of timber for ease of handling and to prevent splitting.

Metal alloys such as brass, bronze, and pewter made excellent molds capable of yielding the highest level of detail and were virtually indestructible in use. They were expensive due to the intrinsic value of the metal and because their production involved a variety of complex and skilled steps performed by modelers, pattern makers, and founders. Few historic metal molds have survived, possibly as a result of wartime scrap drives.

Sulfur melts into a clear fluid at about 115° C and could be poured over a positive clay model or another compo ornament. A sulfur mold resembles hard plastic, but is more fragile. Even when framed in wood and reinforced with iron fillings, as was common practice, it was especially vulnerable to breakage. A figural design, such as a frieze of *The Three Graces*, was much easier to model in relief than to carve in reverse, and sulfur was one of the few materials that could be used to make a hard mold from a clay model.

Composition itself could be squeezed over a hard relief pattern (such as another manufacturer's ornament) to make a mold. Composition shrinks as it hardens and so the mold was always smaller than the original. It is also fairly brittle when hard and, like sulfur molds, would tend to crack in the press. Composition "squeeze molds" were ideal for pirating another maker's patterns!

Pitch molds became popular during the late 19th and early 20th centuries. A warm and soft mixture composed primarily of pine pitch was poured into a recess in a wood block or frame. It was then turned over and squeezed down onto an oiled wooden pattern. Pitch molds might crack with age or in the press, but as long as the carved pattern was retained, they could be easily re-made.

Historical Survey

Early History and Renaissance. Press-molded decoration has been used with various soft plastic materials for centuries. For example, it is known that medieval sculptors press-molded organic mixtures to decorate painted sculptures. But because mixtures based on organic binders such as glue, oil, resins, and waxes are prone to various sorts of degradation, actual survivors are rare.

The direct ancestors of the composition craft are most likely found in the Italian Renaissance; however, composition mixtures were not extensively used for architectural decoration during this period, probably due to building traditions as well as relative expense. It is worth nothing that this was an age of experimentation with materials and rediscovery of Greek and Roman designs. Press molded mixtures called pastiglias were used to decorate wooden boxes and picture frames as early as the 14th century (see Fig. 9). Moldable compositions were discussed by various Renaissance writers. The recipes are extremely varied and include, among their more common and understandable ingredients, gypsum, lead carbonate, wood and marble dust, eggs, pigments, sheep's wool, and various oils and resins.

The 18th Century. The first flowering of architectural composition in America took place at the end of the 18th century when ornaments were both imported from England and produced by makers in every major eastern city. All of the conditions were right: molding technologies were well established (architectural *papier mâché*, which, like composition, was produced in molds, had gained widespread acceptance during the middle decades of the century). The raw materials were produced or imported in volume, so the cost of the composition ingredients came down as the cost and availability of highly skilled labor went up. Economic and social conditions favored

Figure 9. A 16th century pastiglia box from Italy features battle scenes from ancient Rome. Pastiglia was a forerunner of composition as we know it today, and one of a family of press-molded and applied interior ornamentation materials. Photo: Pastiglia Casket. White lead pastiglia decoration on gilt alder, 1.29.9 cm. Italy, Venice, 1st half of 16th c.© The Cleveland Museum of Art, John L. Severance Fund, 81.8.

centralized "manufactories" in the production of various arts and crafts.

Design trends also fed into a favorable reception for composition. A more faithful reinterpretation of Greek and Roman design eventually termed "Neoclassical" had taken hold in Europe, championed in England by the architect, Robert Adam, after his return from study in Italy in 1758 (see Fig. 10). Although Adam played no direct role in the "invention" of composition ornament, as has sometimes been said, he patronized English craftsmen who were making it and was generally receptive to new and innovative materials. One early maker, sometimes cited as the "inventor" of composition by his contemporaries, was John Jaques. His name appears in London advertising by 1785, but he was probably in business before then (see Fig. 11).

Figure 10. Shown is an elegant Robert Adam composition overdoor design in Kedleston Hall, Derbyshire, England. Adam had an enormous influence on 18th century Neoclassical design in England and America. Photo: Jonathan Thornton.

As a result of Adam's influence, designers of applied ornament in both Europe and America began to take advantage of a molding process that was ideally suited to producing the detailed, but repetitive, motifs of classical decoration—acanthus leaf, egg and dart, festoons, swags, and paterae—as well as classical themes depicting Greek and Roman gods and goddesses (see Fig. 12). And as the Neoclassical style became more popular, composition ornament makers increased in number.

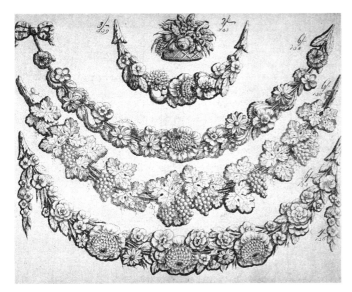

Figure 11. This page of festoon designs is from a Jaques catalog published in England and imported to America in the first decades of the 19th century. Note the similarity of these designs to those shown on the mantelpiece in Fig. 1. Photo: Courtesy, The Winterthur Library: Printed Book and Periodical Collection.

Figure 12. The Nightingale-Brown House, in Providence, Rhode Island, was built in 1792. Original composition ornament can be seen in the flat area above the door molding; matching ornament was used in the room over the mantel. Photo: Courtesy, Irving Haynes and Associates.

The 19th Century. During the early decades of the nineteenth century, Neoclassical—encompassed in America by the terms Federal, Empire, and Greek Revival—was in the ascendancy. Composition makers continued to increase and also to find new uses for their material. Composition picture and mirror frames became common and some makers advertised the suitability of composition ornaments for casting iron firebacks and stoves. Composition ornament was explicitly advertised for exterior use as well, although very little has survived. The interiors of houses and public buildings in every prosperous American city were decorated with composition (see Fig. 13).

When the classically derived Federal and Empire styles gave way to the various revival styles—Rococo, Gothic, Renaissance, and Italianate—composition makers simply made new molds to accommodate them. (Although Rococo and Renaissance styles were not common for architecture in America, they *were* common for furnishings and interior decoration and, in consequence, for composition ornament.)

Along with a proliferation of styles in the mid-to-late decades of the century, there was a parallel growth in the number of moldable and castable materials that shared

Figure 13. Top: Since rooms with fireplaces were centers of social activity in early American houses, mantelpieces often received special decorative attention. This early 19th century mantelpiece in a Philadelphia residence features a panel depicting A Country Dance flanked by floral swags and sculptural busts of Milton and Shakespeare. Bottom: Several American and English makers produced versions of a frieze entitled, The Triumph of Mars. This one, ca. 1800-1810, is in a modest "single" house on John Street in Charleston, South Carolina. Note how several layers of paint are obscuring the detail. Photo top: Gold Leaf Studios, Inc. Photo bottom: Jonathan Thornton.

some features of the composition craft, such as *carton pierre*, *gutta percha*, *fibrous plaster*, *shellac compositions* and, eventually, *celluloid* and *hard rubber*. Composition continued to be the preferred material for detailed decoration on wood where the size of the ornament did not make its cost prohibitive. The publication of practical books by and for craftsmen, beginning in the 19th century, disseminated recipes and procedures to a broad audience and de-mystified the craft. Period composition ornaments called "imitation wood carvings" were widely advertised in manufacturers' catalogs (see Fig. 14). Balls of prepared compo became available from some art supply shops in large cities for use by small volume craftsmen.

During the later years of the century, the Arts and Crafts Movement—as preached by William Morris and his associates and followers—became increasingly important in design and philosophy. Morris stressed honesty to the material in design, exalted spirituality of hand work and rejected manufacturing, mass production and the distinction between "high" art and craft. These trends were

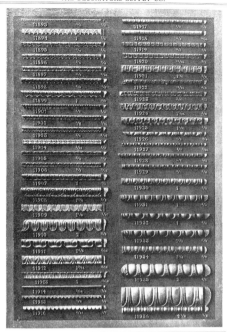

styles, so did the composition trade. Many old firms went out of business and their molds were dispersed or destroyed. The few that remained concentrated on restoration projects or were sustained by diversification into other materials. By the 1950s and 60s, composition as a material and craft had been all but forgotten.

An upsurge in hand craft production that started in the late 60s and has continued to the present—as well as increasing interest in historic preservation—has led to the renewed study of old methods and materials, including composition. The few manufacturers that remain have seen a large increase in their business, and an increasing number of people recognize composition as a unique ornamental material and want to conserve, restore, or create it (see Fig. 18).

Figure 14. Shown are two pages from a current manufacturer's catalog, Ornaments for Woodwork-Furniture featuring festoons and clusters, fabric swags, and egg-and-dart molding. The Decorators Supply Corporation in Chicago, Illinois, was established in 1893, and is in business today. Photos: Courtesy, Decorators Supply Corporation.

Compo Deterioration and Damage

To some degree, the longevity of historic composition ornament is related to the ratio of ingredients in the original mix and to the skill of the craftsman in applying it. But it is far more dependent upon interior climatic conditions and the long-term effects of heat and dampness on both the compo and the wood substrate.

Figure 15. Naturalistically carved lily pattern molds reflect the early 20th century Arts and Crafts movement in the United States. Photo: Jonathan Thornton.

to affect both technology and design in the 20th century. Composition ornament would have been anathema to Morris and his elite clients; most composition production during the last years of the century is best described as Victorian Eclectic.

The 20th Century. The Arts and Crafts and related styles, such as the more decorative Art Nouveau, were well rooted in America by the beginning of the century (see Fig. 15). Pitch molds made from relief-carved patterns had become common in America. The carving tool marks could be accentuated in these patterns in keeping with current vogue. Open-grained woods, such as mahogany, were often chosen so that the finished composition ornaments would have a wood-like grain that showed through stains and varnishes (see Fig. 16). A uniquely 20th century application of composition ornament was in the lavishly decorated movie palaces of the Depression era (see Fig. 17).

As interest in architectural embellishments declined, particularly as a result of the austere post-World War II

Figure 16. The Austin Morey residence, in the Indian Village Historic District of Detroit, Michigan, was designed by architect Louis Kamper, and built between 1902 and 1903. Part of Kamper's design included this grand oak staircase that was decorated with composition ornament. Note the "ghost marks" of missing composition in the close-up. Photo: Robert J. Rucinski.

Figure 17. The Ohio Theater in Columbus, Ohio, was lavishly decorated with gilded plaster and composition ornament. Walls, ceilings, mirror frames, furniture, and carpets—predominately red and gold—were designed by noted theater architect Thomas W. Lamb in 1928. Photo: Rapid Photography Inc.

Figure 18. Shown is the contemporary studio of the J.P. Weaver Company, currently located in Glendale, California. The company has manufactured and sold architectural composition ornament continuously since 1917. Note the long work table and well organized mold storage units behind. Photo: Lenna Tyler Kast.

Variables in mixing and application. Dried compo is inherently hard and somewhat brittle; its increasing brittleness over time is primarily due to the oxidation and hardening of the linseed oil component. The drying oil, in turn, contributes to age cracking. Thus, during initial manufacture, if the oil content was low and the dry filler content (chalk) high, shrinking and cracking over time is less likely to occur. Originally, the compo was probably attached using small, headless brads (1/4") that penetrated the hardening compo as well as the wood substrate. They were used to keep the compo from shifting or warping after it was set in place. If an insufficient number of brads was used by the craftsman during the application process, the compo simply falls off as cracks develop.

Interior environmental conditions. Compo was conceived as a durable substitute for hand-carved wood or marble and decorative plaster; its potential for structural failure is generally due to substrate failure rather than to the compo mix itself. Theoretically, composition will move with atmospheric changes due to the moisture-sensitive glue component. Its breakdown typically occurs when the wood base expands and contracts at different rates than the compo during extreme temperature and humidity fluctuations. Especially when it is close to a source of heat, such as directly over a fireplace, compo develops fissures or shrinkage cracks. Contemporary heating systems in old buildings also contribute to the drying and cracking syndrome.

Planning for Treatment

Simple stabilization and repairs to existing ornamentation can most likely proceed based solely on an analysis of existing conditions (see paragraphs on *Surface Cracking* and *Delamination*, below).

Historical research. For more complex work, a building owner, curator, or conservator should research the history of the building to find out when it was originally designed and constructed; who lived in it at various times; how the building was used; and which features were original and which were added later or removed (see Fig. 19). Some of this information may be found in the National Register of Historic Places.

Questions about the building's interior spaces and their decorative detailing also need to be asked, particularly when portions of the ornamentation will be replaced. Have the interior spaces evolved with successive occupancies or uses? In addition to compo, were other decorative materials used and are there differences in patterns that help date the work? For example, plaster and compo may have been used in the same room, but applied at different times. Receipts from workmen's bills may often be used to establish the dates of decorative detailing.

The historical research dealing with the original construction of the building and its use over time should, in turn, be linked to the scope of work that will take place. Stabilization, conservation, and repair are maximized within the treatment, Preservation. Generally speaking, restoring decorative ornament to a specific earlier period is not recommended unless its historical significance outweighs the potential loss of extant ornament that

Figure 19. A drawing from the 1930s shows original ornament on the wall above a Palladian window in the 1760s Miles-Brewton House, Charleston, South Carolina. When the ornament was subsequently removed and lost, this scale drawing was used as documentation to fabricate matching ornament. Photo: Jonathan Thornton.

characterizes other historical periods. But if a significant interior is missing original features and physical and documentary evidence are conclusive, replication may be appropriate in order to interpret a particular time.

Existing conditions analysis. After historical research is conducted, but before starting work, an analysis of the surface and substrate should be undertaken. These are some of the issues a conservator considers. First, if a surface is painted, the ornamentation material needs to be identified. Is it wood, plaster, composition ornament, or some other type of applied ornamental material? Usually, some of the ornamentation is chipped or broken. Close examination of the exposed material is the first step. If it is white through the entire thickness of the ornament, then it could be plaster or stucco; if it is a darker brown material, it is more likely to be composition.

After having identified the presence of composition ornament, its overall condition can be evaluated. Layers of paint may obscure fine detailing as well as deterioration problems. Degrees of damage and deterioration should be recorded. These are typical questions that need to be answered. Is the surface merely "crazed", requiring no action or limited repair, or are the cracks severe enough to require replacement? Are pieces missing? Are the attachment brads rusted or missing? The condition of the substrate is also important. Is the wood surface intact, or is it in need of repair? After answering key questions, the conservator will make random tests to differentiate original compo from later repairs, some of which may well have been done with plaster, rather than compo (see Fig. 20).

Deciding how to proceed depends upon the overall interpretive goals of treatment. For example, is the interior being restored to an earlier time? In this case, later repairs may be removed and the original appearance replicated. Or is the interior being preserved with limited replacement of lost or damaged historic materials? Not all conditions are foreseeable in conservation work and contingencies must be incorporated into the treatment plan to be considered realistic. As the project progresses, the conservator generally determines the work that needs to be done, and the order in which it should be undertaken.

Treating the Problem with Care

The scope of work is generally based on several factors, including the historical significance of the building's interior, the degree of damage or deterioration of the compo, and the overall interpretive goals of project work. Several examples of repair and replacement follow in order

Figure 20. The Octagon House, in Washington, D.C., was constructed between 1801-1802. During recent project work, it was discovered that early repairs to the composition ornament in this doorway had been made with plaster. The plaster repairs were removed during restoration of the doorway to its original appearance. Photo: Lonnie J. Hovey, AIA.

Compo: The Basic Ingredients (*clockwise from front center*)

Chalk: Chalk is whiting in solid form. It is a type of white, soft limestone.

Glue: Before the invention of synthetic adhesives, glue meant animal or hide glue. This was made by boiling animal skins to extract a protein—collagen—in water, then condensing and drying the collagen until it was in solid form. A variety of types and grades were, and are still, available. Two are shown here.

Linseed oil: This is a yellowish drying oil obtained from flaxseed that is used in paint, varnish, printing ink, and linoleum; it is a key ingredient in composition ornament.

Resin: Resins are organic materials present in wood and exuded from various trees and shrubs. In unrefined form, they often consist of a mixture of solid natural polymers, oils, and volatile aromatic substances.

to suggest a typical scope of work within preservation and restoration projects. Treatments are listed in hierarchical order, from the least intervention to the greatest.

Paint removal. Interior ornament is usually painted many times over during its lifetime and, as a result, the sharp surface detail of the original pattern is obscured. Before attempting to remove paint, it is always advisable to obtain professional advice on the ornamental material to be cleaned as well as the nature of the coatings that are covering it. And whatever the project work goal, at least one sample of intact, well-adhered paint layers on a feature should be preserved for future historical research.

Based on the purpose of treatment, these are some of the questions a conservator routinely asks. How many layers of paint are there? Is it important to trace one layer to a particular occupancy of the building? If so, the stratigraphy (or layering scheme) will be determined prior to paint removal. After the correct layer is identified, the color can be matched. Or, is the building being rehabilitated? If this is the case, period-typical paint colors may be appropriate.

For purposes of this Brief and the guidance paragraphs that follow, it is assumed that all layers of paint are being removed in order to reveal the fine detailing of the composition ornament (see Fig. 21).

Figure 21. *The same theme on two early mantelpieces, A Country Dance, dramatically illustrates the visual difference between cleaned and uncleaned composition ornament. When old paint layers are removed, the exquisite detailing is revealed. Left: George Read II House, 1801-1803, New Castle, Delaware; Right: First Harrison Gray Otis House, 1796, Boston, Massachusetts. Photo left: Gold Leaf Studios, Inc. Photo right: David Bohl. Courtesy, Society for the Preservation of New England Antiquities.*

The next step is to consider various methods of removing paint from the ornament without damaging it, or without being exposed to dangerous substances in the strippers or in the old paint itself! It should be noted from the standpoint of health and safety that most Federal and Empire period compo was meant to imitate marble; thus, the highly toxic white-lead paint was by far the most common original coating.

Caustic strippers based on lye should be avoided for two reasons. First, they will damage and dissolve compo both because they "chew up" the protein structure of the glue and, second, because they are water-based and compo remains soluble in water (see also Fig. 3). If a stripper will damage the protein of your hands, it will do the same to compo!

A conservator will more often use organic solvents, such as methylene chloride, in conjunction with small implements such as a dental tool or toothbrush. (A small area is always tested first to establish the safety and effectiveness of any technique. Improper use of stripping tools can damage intricate surfaces beyond repair.) A solvent is applied according to manufacturer's recommendations, permitted to soak into and soften the paint, then re-applied as necessary, as the conservator gently removes paint from the intricate carved surfaces (see Fig. 22).

It should be emphasized that any amount of exposure to toxic chemicals without proper precautions can cause severe health problems. A hooded, air-fed, personal unit is desirable when using methylene chloride-based strippers if fume hoods or paint spray booths that exhaust effectively to the outside are not available. Organic vapor masks may not

be as effective in protecting against methylene chloride exposure because the filters quickly become exhausted; however, a vapor mask with properly rated organic solvent cartridges can provide an acceptable level of safety when cartridges are regularly changed (see Fig. 23).

Some conservators have had excellent results heat-stripping excess paint layers using *heat guns* and dental tools. This is highly skilled work and its success depends upon the composition ornament being much older than the paint layers that lie on top, but has the capability of working as well or better than chemical methods in the hands of an expert. Precautions must be taken against lead fumes where removal of lead paint is involved.

Cleaning mixtures based on *enzymes* are also used by conservators. This is an effective method because enzyme mixtures can be formulated for very specific purposes (i.e., to dissolve only oil-based paints from protein-glue based compo). They dissolve paint without affecting the wood substrate. But, on the other hand, work can be very slow and the expense would only seem justified on small and rare or important museum objects. Enzymatic cleaners are

Figure 22. *Careful dry scraping of a chimney piece to remove paint residue signaled the successful conclusion of a conservation project at the Octagon House, in Washington, D.C. Photo: Lonnie J. Hovey, AIA.*

Figure 23. *Methylene chloride fumes can be deadly, so protecting the worker is imperative. Left: a hooded, air-fed unit. Right: a vapor mask with organic solvent cartridges. Photo left: William Adair. Photo right: Lonnie J. Hovey, AIA.*

dependent on a high level of skill, technical knowledge and professional training, but they are earning a solid place in the repertoire of professional conservators.

Increased concern about the environment may well render the toxic methylene chloride strippers obsolete in the near future. Manufacturers have already produced "safer" strippers based on *dimethyl esters,* and further research will probably yield other alternatives to chlorinated solvents. Slower acting solvent-type strippers may well be safer to the underlying composition ornament, but additional research and use are needed before making definitive statements.

In summary, most damage to compo occurs during the removal of layers of paint; this is a critical process and should not be attempted without consulting a conservator and should not be undertaken by painting contractors unless they are highly skilled and have had extensive experience in this very delicate procedure.

Proper disposal of residual chemicals and debris must be undertaken to avoid contaminating the environment with solvents and lead, and such disposal is, in fact, now required by federal, state, and local ordinances. The company responsible for removing chemical waste should be licensed to dispose of it, otherwise the property owner may be held accountable if disposal laws are violated.

Refinishing compo ornament usually follows stripping. According to historic evidence uncovered and depending on the existing and desired appearance of the room, compo can be stained, painted, gilded, marbleized, or glazed. Paint types may include distemper, alkyd oil, or latex. A thin coating is recommended so the intricate surface detail is not clogged.

Surface cracking. Surface cracking indicates age and, thus, the history of the ornamentation itself (see Fig. 24). It does not necessarily mean that cracks have to be fixed. But if cracking interferes with the overall design pattern, then the conservator may elect to fill the cracks with suitable fill material. For example, "light weight" spackles bulked with microballoons are excellent because they are soft and compressible and will accommodate changes in the size of cracks due to moisture fluctuation. After stabilization, the surface is finished to match the existing area.

Delamination. Delamination or separation of the compo from the wood substrate is the simplest repair problem to remedy. The conservator begins by testing cracked areas with slight finger pressure to determine which parts of the design need consolidation. Compo sections that have separated from the substrate, but are otherwise intact, can be glued back in place using emulsion type adhesives such as "white" glues or a clear, solvent-release adhesive (see Fig. 25). For vertical surfaces, the glue is painted onto the back of the delaminated compo as well as the wood base and, when slightly tacky, re-attached, and held with clamps until dry.

Figure 24. Treatment would be optional for the age cracking that has occurred in the egg-like portions of this composition ornament. Photo: William Adair.

Figure 25. (a) Adhesive is being applied to this 19th century composition ornament that has de-laminated from its wood substrate; and (b) The compo fragment is held in place until the quick-setting adhesive takes hold. Photos: Jonathan Thornton .

Professional conservators often formulate their own adhesives based on stable synthetic polymers (plastics) dissolved in solvent that will be more reversible, should the need arise, and also offer better long-term stability than many commercial adhesives.

Repairs to broken or damaged compo. When some original compo has been lost, additional work is required to make a repair. One particularly easy and inexpensive method of repairing broken ornamentation is to use non-hardening clay ("plastilina") or polymer-based modeling materials as an impression material to make a mold. After a mold is made from existing ornament, missing or deteriorated portions of the historic design can be duplicated with a durable gypsum plaster (see Fig. 26). Especially in cases where economic considerations dictate procedure, use of this substitute material may be helpful because it is cheaper. Alternatively, an existing studio mold may sometimes be used to make small replacement pieces in a repair project (see Fig. 27).

In another scenario, a repetitive design on a mantelpiece may be damaged or portions missing. Especially if the compo design is complex and several portions of ornament need to be replaced, rigid polymer molds with traditional compo are recommended for the repair work. The mold is created using a section of the original ornament as a model. After replacement pieces are fabricated, they are attached using brads, or finish nails (see Fig. 28). The pointed end of the nail is clipped blunt with snips to avoid possible splitting of the wood substrate. The nail is first hammered into the surface, then countersunk, and the resulting hole filled with gesso putty or additional compo.

Finally, a ready-made replacement piece can be ordered from the catalog of a compo manufacturer, but it is unlikely to be a perfect match to an extant historic decoration

Replacement of missing compo ornamentation. Once-attractive compo may become damaged to such a degree that the remaining fragments are removed by an owner and the entire surface painted over. Thus, if there is some existing composition ornament in a room, such as an overdoor or chair railing, the conservator would most likely look for evidence of other ornament that is now missing.

For example, a mantel may appear as a flat, unornamented surface to the untrained eye, but after many layers of paint are removed by the conservator, shadow images are revealed (see Fig. 29). These images or "ghost marks" are left by the hide glue component of the original mix. Although the glue is water soluble, it will not be completely removed by an organic stripper such as methylene chloride. (But if earlier inappropriate paint removal methods were used, such as water-based strippers, caustic strippers, or mechanical sanding, ghost marks from the glue would be destroyed.)

When the paint stripper dries, a ghost mark left by composition ornament appears slightly darker than the surrounding area where no compo had been attached. In addition, small, square-headed, 1/4" brads used to reinforce the original compo may be embedded in the wood.

In summary, detailed physical evidence, as well as written and pictorial documentation, can provide a valid framework for replacement at a particular site. With careful detective work, missing historic ornamentation may be successfully identified and replaced with matching ornament (see Fig. 30; see also Fig. 19).

Restoration of a "period" interior. When ornamentation is extensively deteriorated and missing, owners often want to re-create the historic appearance through restoration. Physical evidence and other documentation may be used as a basis for the restoration; it should be remembered, however, that as the amount of surviving material diminishes, the greater the chance for inaccuracy when attempting to depict the historic appearance. Choosing restoration as a treatment thus requires exacting documentation prior to work and meticulous attention to detail in the work itself.

Conclusion

Despite its popularity and widespread use as a decorative material, the history of composition ornament has yet to be thoroughly studied. Individual craftsmen have acquired fragmentary knowledge about some designs and historic methods; historians and students of interior decorative design have accumulated knowledge about patterns, artisans, and methods of manufacture and distribution; and curators of historic collections that include compo are knowledgeable about the objects under their care. The combined knowledge of these individuals, together with examples and images of compo ornament from a variety of sources, needs to be synthesized to address the complex issues involving compo repair and preservation. The future of the study of composition ornament, as well as many other facets of architectural, decorative, and fine art history, lies in this sort of cooperative effort.

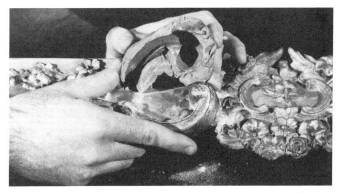

a.

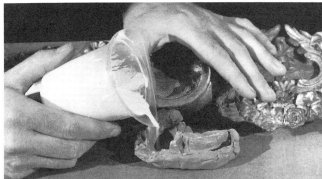

b.

c.

Figure 26. When a small amount of ornamentation needs to be replaced, (a) plastilina clay is recommended as an impression material. Next (b), a plaster-like, liquid material is used to cast the replacement piece. Finally, (c) the new piece is smoothed and fixed in place. Photos: Roland White.

Figure 27. When a compo frieze depicting The Triumph of Mars was found to be damaged, improperly restored, and its intricate design clogged with paint, the first step was to replace a missing wheel on the chariot. Because molds depicting classical themes are part of many professional studio collections, it was possible to fabricate a new wheel from the rubber mold shown here. Photo: William Adair.

Figure 28. A conservator is replacing broken pieces of compo ornamentation on a mantel during restoration of the Nightingale-Brown House in Providence, Rhode Island. Photo: Courtesy, Irving Haynes and Associates.

a.

Whether applied interior ornamentation such as composition ornament is being repaired or restored, treatment should always be preceded by careful documentation and planning.

Figure 30. Based on documentary and physical evidence, missing composition ornament was accurately re-created for the Miles-Brewton House, Charleston, South Carolina. First (a) the conservator used molds to fabricate ornament in small pieces and lengths; and (b) the new ornament was attached to thin birch plywood backing with glue and brads to create larger sections. These sections were then fastened to the original paneling with stainless steel screws. Photos: Jonathan Thornton.

b.

Figure 29. The ghost marks of compo past—floral swags or festoons—are in clear evidence on a mantelpiece in the back bedroom of the George Read II House, New Castle, Delaware. This physical evidence will be used to assure their accurate re-creation in a restoration project. Photo: Courtesy, Gold Leaf Studios, Inc.

Composition and Other Applied Interior Ornamentation

As explained below, compo is a polymer-based material; however, several related materials used to create sculptural relief were sometimes referred to as "compositions" because they combined various ingredients to achieve new and hybrid properties. These related decorative materials can be polymer-based, plaster-based, paper-based, or wood-based. The following terms and definitions are important to know because they provide a background for identifying compo and other applied interior ornamentation *prior* to treatment.

Polymer-based Materials

Polymers are organic, i.e., carbon-based materials comprised of repeated units linked together into long chain-like molecules. Most polymers are soft and pliable (plastic) or can be made so by the application of heat (thermoplastic). In addition to compo and modern synthetic plastics, defined below, polymers include animal glue, horn, natural resins such as shellac, latex rubber, and rosin.

Compo. This thermoplastic mixture based on natural polymers—typically glue, linseed oil, and resin bulked with chalk—has been used extensively to create sculptural relief.

Modern Synthetic Plastics. Starting with cellulose nitrates such as celluloid (1840s), a vast array of man-made polymers has been created. Plastics received their popular name because, like composition, they are generally shaped while soft and pliable, but, due to cost, composition is the only polymer material to be used extensively in architectural decoration until quite recently.

Plaster and Plaster-based Materials

Plaster: This term describes two distinct calcium-based mixes. First, *lime plaster* is made by heating calcium carbonate to produce calcium oxide and slaking it with water to produce calcium hydroxide (lime putty). This material, mixed with fillers and aggregates and applied to surfaces gradually reconverts to calcium carbonate over a period of years. Second, *gypsum plaster* ("Plaster of Paris") is made by heating hydrated calcium sulfate to remove part of the chemically bound water. When water is added, it reconverts to fully hydrated calcium sulfate, setting and hardening in the process. Wet plaster was "run" in cornices; or made in piece-molds and flexible gelatin molds, then applied to interior surfaces.

Stucco: In its earliest use in Europe and America, stucco was a lime putty-based mix for fine interior ornamental plasterwork; historically, "stucco" referred to ornamental (particularly sculptural) plaster work. In the United States by the 19th century, however, stucco was primarily used to describe exterior plastering, usually done with Portland cement-based mixtures.

Fibrous Plaster: This is the term for molded architectural plasterwork which is heavily reinforced with coarse weave cloth as it is built up in the molds.

Fibrous plaster is lightweight, strong, and somewhat flexible and was used to manufacture large architectural units such as balcony fronts, columns, and pilasters.

Pate Coulante (flowing paste). This is a mixture mentioned in one 19th century text that consisted of gypsum plaster, whiting, glue, alum, and sometimes paper pulp. If encountered in an historic interior, it is likely to be indistinguishable from plaster.

Paper-Based Materials

Papier-mâché: This material became popular for interior decoration during the mid-18th century in England and its colonies. *Papier-mâché* was made from soaked rag paper layered into molds with small quantities of glue or starch paste as additional binders. It was usually covered with whiting and glue (gesso) and sometimes gilded. *Papier-mâché* is always hollow and can be distinguished from compo or plaster by gentle tapping.

Anaglypta: This is a trade name for a wallpaper embossed with relief decoration.

Carton-Pierre: This material was based on fully pulped paper fiber extended and hardened with substantial amounts of glue, whiting, and gypsum plaster, and sometimes alum and flour. Carton-pierre was pressed into molds as a plastic mass and allowed to harden. It is mid-way between plaster and papier-mache in weight and density.

Fibrous Slab: This was the name given to layered papier-mache panels heavily impregnated with linseed oil by inventor, C.F. Bielefeld, in the mid-19th century. The composite of paper fiber and hardened linseed oil made a thermoplastic panel that could be shaped and embossed by heating and pressing.

Lincrusta: This material, composed of fiber and dried linseed oil and press molded onto paper backing, was introduced by the linoleum manufacturer, F. Walton, in 1877 and is still made. Typical use is in continuous low-relief friezes at the top of a room.

Wood and Wood-Fiber Based Materials

Wood: Natural wood can also be press molded to a limited extent after it is made plastic by either steam or ammonia. *Pressed wood* architectural elements have been extensively marketed, but would be difficult to mistake for the deeper and sharper relief of most of the other materials described above.

Wood-fiber: Also called saw dust, this cheap and readily available product has been used as a bulking agent in moldable mixtures since before the Renaissance. Numerous recipes consisting of wood fiber and various binders were published in 19th century formulas, and some of these proprietary mixtures or *patent woods* were used to produce small architectural decorations and moldings. Modern particle boards are non-sculptural variations of the material.

Further Reading

Adair, William. "An Investigation of Composition Ornamentation." *The Interiors Handbook for Historic Buildings II.* Washington, D.C.: Historic Preservation Education Foundation, 1993, Chapter 4, pp. 1-7.

Adair, William. *The Frame in America*, 1700-1900: *A Survey of Fabrication, Techniques and Styles.* Washington, D.C.: The American Institute of Architects Foundation, 1983.

Budden, Sophie (ed.). *Gilding and Surface Decoration.* London: United Kingdom Institute for Conservation, 1991. See: Judith Wetherall, "History and Techniques of Composition," pp. 26-29; Jonathan Thornton, "Minding the Gap: Filling Losses in Gilded and Decorated Surfaces," pp. 12-17.

Cotton, J. Randall. "Composition Ornament." *Old-House Journal.* Vol. XXI, No. 1 (January/February 1993), pp. 28-33.

Green, Malcolm. "Conservation and Restoration of Gilded Antiques." The Conservator, 3. United Kingdom for Conservation, 1979.

Hasluck, Paul N. (ed.). *Cassell's Cyclopedia of Mechanics*, 8 vols. London: Cassell and Co., 1904, Chapter 4, p. 164.

_____. *Mounting and Framing Pictures.* London: Cassell and Co., 1899.

Kunou, C.A. *Manual of Gilding and Compo Work.* Los Angeles, California: The Bruce Publishing Co., 1928. Request reprint information from the International Institute for Frame Study, 2126 "O" Street, NW, Washington, D.C. 20037.

Loeffler, R.F. *Step by Step Compo and Mold Making.* Oroville, California: Loeffler-Valac Industries, 1992.

Millar, William. *Plastering Plain & Decorative: A Practical Treatise on the Art & Craft of Plastering and Modelling.* London: B. T. Batsford. New York: John Lane, 1899.

Scott-Mitchell, Frederick. *Practical Gilding.* London: The Trade Papers Publishing Company, 1905.

The Gilder's Manual. New York: Excelsior Publishing House, 1876. Reprinted by the Society of Gilders, Washington, D.C., 1990.

The Secretary of the Interior Standards for the Treatment of Historic Properties. Washington, D.C.: U.S. Department of the Interior, National Park Service, Preservation Assistance Division. Washington, D.C., 1992.

Thornton, Jonathan. "Compo: The History and Technology of 'Plastic' Compositions." *Preprints* of papers presented at the 13th annual meeting, Washington, D.C. American Institute for Conservation, 1985.

Organizations

For information on conservators, contact the following organizations:

Association for Preservation Technology
904 Princess Anne St.
Fredericksburg, VA 22404

National Institute for the Conservation
of Cultural Property
3299 K St., NW, Ste. 403
Washington, D.C. 20007

American Institute for the Conservation
of Historic & Artistic Works
1400 16th St.
Washington, D.C. 20036

Cover photograph: The process of making composition ornament has changed little over the years. In the J.P. Weaver Company, located in Glendale, California, freshly made compo is being kneaded prior to pressing it in a mold.

Acknowledgements

Kay Weeks, project director for this cooperatively produced Brief, is an art historian who serves as technical writer-editor in the Preservation Assistance Division. **Jonathan Thornton** authored the introduction and historical overview portion of the Brief and **William Adair, FAAR**, the planning and treatment portion. The editor and authors wish to extend their gratitude to those people who reviewed and commented on the Preservation Brief in draft form and those who provided illustrative materials. First, National Park Service staff reviewers included H. Ward Jandl, Blaine Cliver, Anne Grimmer, Chuck Fisher, Tim Buehner, Emogene Bevitt, Tom Jester, Michael Auer, and Paul Alley. Specialists in the field included Andrew Ladygo, David Flaharty, Phil Gottfredson, Mark Reinberger, and Lenna Tyler Kast. Photographs were generously donated for the Brief by Philip L. Molten, Elizabeth Brick, Robert J. Rucinski, Lenna Tyler Kast, Bryan Blundell, Thomas Brunk, Lonnie J. Hovey, AIA, Roland White, Irving

Haynes & Associates, the Philadelphia Museum of Art, the Freer Gallery of Art, Winterthur Library, Decorators Supply Corporation, and Rapid Photography, Inc.

This publication has been prepared pursuant to the National Historic Preservation Act of 1966, as amended, which directs the Secretary of the Interior to develop and make available information concerning historic properties. Comments on the usefulness of this publication may be directed to H. Ward Jandl, Deputy Chief, Preservation Assistance Division, National Park Service, P.O. Box 37127, Washington, D.C. 20013-7127.

ISSN: 0885-7017

35

Understanding Old Buildings:
The Process of Architectural Investigation

Travis C. McDonald, Jr.

If you have ever felt a sense of excitement and mystery going inside an old building—whether occupied or vacant—it is probably because its materials and features resonate with the spirit of past people and events. Yet excitement about the unknown is heightened when a historic structure is examined architecturally, and its evolution over time emerges with increasing clarity to reveal the lives of its occupants. Architectural investigation is the critical first step in planning an appropriate treatment—understanding how a building has changed over time and assessing levels of deterioration.

Whether as a home owner making sympathetic repairs, a craftsman or contractor replacing damaged or missing features, or a conservator reconstituting wood or restoring decorative finishes, some type of investigative skill was used to recognize and solve an architectural question or explain a difficult aspect of the work itself.

To date, very little has been written for the layman on the subject of architectural investigation. This Preservation Brief thus addresses the often complex investigative process in broad, easy-to-understand terminology. The logical sequence of planning, investigation and analysis presented in this Brief is applicable to all buildings, geographic locations, periods, and construction types. It is neither a "how to" nor an exhaustive study on techniques or methodologies; rather, it serves to underscore the need for meticulous planning prior to work on our irreplaceable cultural resources.

Determining the Purpose of Investigation

Both the purpose and scope of investigation need to be determined before formulating a particular approach. For example, investigation strictly for research purposes could produce information for an architectural survey or for an historic designation application at the local, state or national level.

Within the framework of *The Secretary of the Interior's Standards for the Treatment of Historic Properties*, investigation is crucial for "identifying, retaining, and preserving the form and detailing of those architectural materials and features that are important in defining the historic character" of a property, whether for repair or replacement. A rehabilitation project, for instance, might require an investigation to determine the historic configuration of interior spaces prior to partitioning a room to meet a compatible new use. Investigation for preservation work can entail more detailed information about an entire building, such as determining the physical sequence of construction to aid in interpretation. Investigation for a restoration project must be even more comprehensive in order to re-capture the exact form, features, finishes, and detailing of every component of the building.

Whether investigation will be undertaken by professionals—architects, conservators, historians—or by interested homeowners, the process is essentially comprised of a preliminary four-step procedure: historical research, documentation, inventory, and stabilization.

Historical Research. Primary historical research of an old building generally encompasses written, visual and oral resources that can provide valuable site-specific information. Written resources usually include letters, legal transactions, account books, insurance policies, institutional papers, and diaries. Visual resources consist of drawings, maps, plats, paintings and photographs. Oral resources are people's remembrances of the past. Secondary resources, comprised of research or history already compiled and written about a subject, are also important for providing a broad contextual setting for a project.

Historical research should be conducted well in advance of physical investigation. This allows time for important written, visual, and oral information to be located, transcribed, organized, studied and used for planning the actual work.

A thorough scholarly study of a building's history provides a responsible framework for the physical investigation; in fact, the importance of the link between written historical research and structural investigation cannot be overestimated. For example, the historical research of a building through deed records may merely determine the sequence of owners. This, in turn, aids the investigation of the building by establishing a chronology and identifying the changes each occupant made to the building. A letter

Figure 2. Early photographs discovered during historical research can be enhanced through photo-micrography to accurately recreate missing elements and details during restoration. The enlargements helped clarify questions about the porch column detail and the type of shutter hardware. photo: E. C. Stanton House, courtesy Seneca Falls Historical Society, New York; insets: NPS North Atlantic Cultural Resource Center, Building Conservation Branch.

may indicate that an occupant painted the building in a certain year; the courthouse files contain the occupant's name and paint analysis of the building will yield the actual color. Two-dimensional documentary research and three-dimensional physical investigation go hand-in-hand in analyzing historic structures. The quality and success of any restoration project is founded upon the initial research.

Documentation. A building should be documented prior to any inventory, stabilization or investigative work in order to record crucial material evidence. A simple, comprehensive method is to take 35 mm photographs of every wall elevation (interior and exterior), as well as general views, and typical and unusual details. The systematic numbering of rooms, windows and doors on the floor plan will help organize this task and also be useful for labelling the photographs. Video coverage with annotated sound may supplement still photographs. Additional methods of documentation include written descriptions, sketches, and measured drawings.

Significant structures, such as individually listed National Register properties or National Historic Landmarks, benefit from professional photographic documentation and accurate measured drawings. Professionals frequently use *The Secretary of the Interior's Standards and Guidelines for Architectural and Engineering Documentation: HABS/HAER Standards.* It should be remembered that the documents created during investigation might play an unforeseen role in future treatment and interpretation.

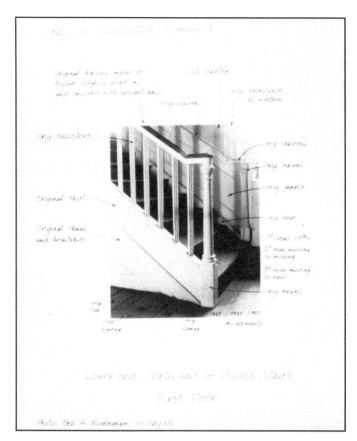

Figure 3. Dating, labeling, and providing annotated photographs is a simple, yet effective, way to document today's preservation efforts for future work and research. A useful document can be created by mounting a photograph upon archival paper and writing the annotations by hand. photo: NPS Preservation Assistance Division Files.

Documentation is particularly valuable when a feature will be removed or altered.

Inventory. The historic building and its components should be carefully inventoried prior to taking any action; premature clean-up of a structure or site can be a mistake. A careful look at all spaces in and around a building may reveal loose architectural artifacts, fragile evidence or clues to historic landscape features. This thorough observation includes materials and features which have fallen off due to deterioration, fragments removed and stored in basements, attics or outbuildings, and even materials which have seemingly been discarded.

In the beginning, anything that seems even remotely meaningful should be saved. A common mistake is to presume to know the value of artifacts or features at the beginning of a project. Even if the period of significance or interpretation is known from the beginning, evidence from all periods should be protected. Documentation for future study or use includes labelling and, if possible, photographing prior to storage in a secure place.

Stabilization. In many cases, emergency stabilization is necessary to ensure that a structure does not continue to deteriorate prior to a final treatment or to ensure the safety of current occupants, investigators, or visitors. Although severe cases might call for structural remedies, in more common situations, preliminary stabilization would be undertaken on a maintenance level. Such work could involve installing a temporary roof covering to keep water out; diverting water away from foundation walls; removing plants that hold water too close to the walls; or securing a

Figure 4. An inventory of animal nests found within hidden spaces of a structure may yield unexpected evidence, such as information about food, decorative arts, and cultural or social traditions of every day life. Typical items of paper, fabric and wood are important artifacts which are generally not found during archeology digs in the ground. photo: Tom Graves, Jr., courtesy Jefferson's Poplar Forest.

Figure 5. Investigation frequently identifies urgent needs of stabilization. Priority must be given to issues of safety and structural integrity. Supplemental support, such as temporary shoring, may be required to prevent collapse and should be reviewed by a structural engineer.

structure against intruding insects, animals and vandals.

An old building may require temporary remedial work on exterior surfaces such as reversible caulking or an impermanent, distinguishable mortar. Or if paint analysis is contemplated in the future, deteriorated paint can be protected without heavy scraping by applying a recognizable "memory" layer over all the historic layers. Stabilization adds to the cost of any project, but human safety and the protection of historical evidence are well worth the extra money.

Investigators and Investigative Skills

General and Specialized Skills. The essential skill needed for any level of investigation is the ability to observe closely and to analyze. These qualities are ideally combined with a hands-on familiarity of historic buildings—and an open mind! Next, whether acquired in a university or in a practical setting, an investigator should have a good general knowledge of history, building design history and, most important, understand both construction and finish technologies.

But it is not enough to know architectural style and building technology from a national viewpoint; the investigator needs to understand regional and local differences as well. While investigative skills are transferable between regions and chronological periods, investigators must be familiar with the peculiarities of any given building type and geographical area.

Architectural survey and comparative fieldwork provides a crucial database for studying regional variations in historic buildings. For example, construction practices can reflect shared experiences of widely diverse backgrounds and traditions within a small geographical area. Contemporary construction practice in an urban area might vary dramatically from that of rural areas in the same region. Neighbors or builders within the same geographical area

Figure 6. An investigator must have the skill and ability to closely observe and analyze the materials with a broad understanding of historic construction practices and technologies. Through the collection of samples and analysis of materials, investigative questions are either answered, refined, or formulated.

Showing the Evolution of an 18th Century Farmhouse

Most structures evolve over time. Houses, perhaps more than other building types, are often subjected to a full range of change that reflects a wide variety of solutions for creating new living space or eliminating outmoded spaces. Architectural changes to historic houses can be studied through the close physical examination of construction and decorative details. Tracing the history of alterations over time is tantamount to "excavating" the structure, somewhat like an archeological investigation. By peeling back its layers of occupation and assembling plan changes, a sequence of consecutive solutions or transformations can be developed that reveals people's ongoing desires for new and improved living conditions.

The example of a Sussex County, Delaware, house--from ca. 1790 to the early 1900s--illustrates how complicated the pattern of change over time can become in outlining an individual house history. The Hunter Farm House was built in the 18th century as a double-cell, double-pile, half-passage plan (a). Two bays across the front and two stories tall, the house possessed back-to-back corner fireplaces with fully paneled fireplace walls in the front and back rooms. A stair in the rear passage provided access to the second floor. A one-story, two-room shed that was attached to the gable wall farthest from the fireplace was accessed by a low door leading from the front room.

During the course of its history, the house was altered at least three times. The five-part illustration shows the house's transformation from an open plan to a Georgian plan and the subsequent addition and re-arrangement of service rooms for cooking and storage. The first remodelling occurred in the early nineteenth century when the lean-to shed was removed, and a two-story, single-pile, two-bay house was moved up and attached to the northwest gable of the existing building (b). (The newly attached building had originally been furnished with opposing doors and windows on the front and back facades, a fireplace on the southeast gable, and double windows on the opposite end.) When the second building was joined to the first, the fireplace in the newer building was relocated to the opposite gable; the front door in the older house moved to a more central position; and a center-hall plan created with a roughly symmetrical front elevation (c). A subsequent alteration later in the nineteenth century included the addition of a one-story rear service ell (d). Finally, in the early 1900s, the one-story service wing was increased. During this last remodeling, the large kitchen hearth was demolished and replaced with a stove and new brick flue (e).

Sidebar: Bernard L. Herman and Gabrielle M. Lanier, University of Delaware. Drawings by: Center for Historic Architecture and Engineering, University of Delaware.

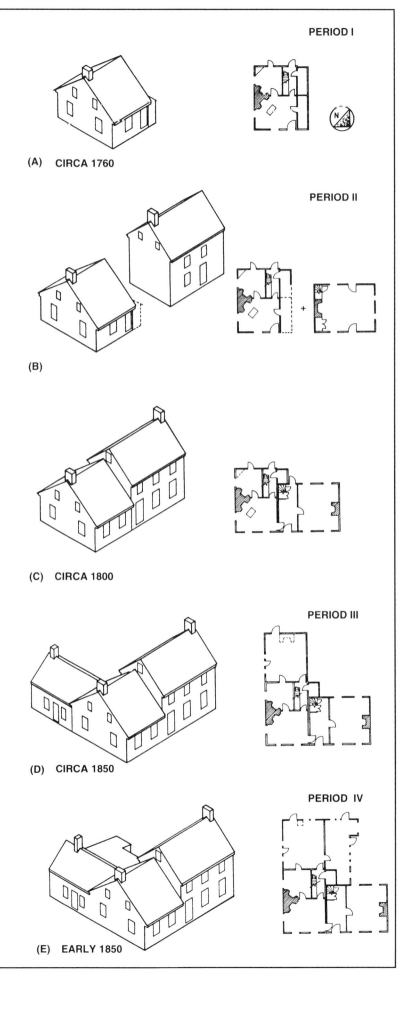

PERIOD I

(A)   CIRCA 1760

PERIOD II

(B)

(C)   CIRCA 1800

PERIOD III

(D)   CIRCA 1850

PERIOD IV

(E)   EARLY 1850

often practice different techniques of constructing similar types of structures contemporaneously. Reliable dating clues for a certain brick bond used in one state might be unreliable for the same period in a different state. Regional variation holds true for building materials as well as construction.

Finally, even beyond regional and local variation, an investigator needs to understand that each building has its own unique history of construction and change over time. Form, features, materials and detailing often varied according to the tastes and finances of both builder and supplier; construction quality and design were also inconsistent, as they are today.

Specialists on a Team. Because architectural investigation requires a wide range of knowledge and many different skills, various people are likely to interact on the same project. While homeowners frequently execute small-scale projects, more complex projects might be directed by a craftsman, an architect or a conservator. For large-scale projects, a team approach may need to be adopted, consisting of professionals interacting with additional consultants. Consulting specialists may include architectural historians, architectural conservators, craftsmen, historic finish analysts, historians, archeologists, architects, curators, and many others. The scope and needs of a specific project dictate the skills of key players.

Architectural investigation often includes the related fields of landscape and archeological investigation. Landscape survey or analysis by horticulturists and landscape architects identify pre-existing features or plantings or those designed as separate or complementary parts of the site. Both above and below-ground archeology contribute information about missing or altered buildings, construction techniques, evidence of lifestyle and material culture, and about the evolution of the historic landscape itself.

Architectural Evidence: Studying the Fabric of the Historic Building:

Original Construction and Later Changes. Research prior to investigation may have indicated the architect, builder or a building's date of construction. In the absence of such information, architectural histories and field guides to architectural style can help identify a structure's age through its form and style.

Any preliminary date, however, has to be corroborated with other physical or documentary facts. Dates given for stylistic periods are general and tend to be somewhat arbitrary, with numerous local variations. Overall form and style can also be misleading due to subsequent additions and alterations. When the basic form seems in conflict with the details, it may indicate a transition between styles or that a style was simply upgraded through new work.

The architectural investigation usually determines original construction details, the chronology of later alterations, and the physical condition of a structure. Most structures over fifty years old have been altered, even if only by natural forces. People living in a house or using a building for any length of time leave some physical record of their time there, however subtle.

A longer period of occupancy generally counts for greater physical change. Buildings acquire a "historic character" as changes are made over time.

Changes to architectural form over time are generally attributable to material durability, improvement in convenience systems, and aesthetics. First, the durability of building materials is affected by weathering, temperature and humidity, by disasters such as storms, floods or fire, or by air pollution from automobiles and industry. Second, changes in architectural form have always been made for convenience' sake—fueled by technological innovations— as people embrace better lighting, plumbing, heating, sanitation, and communication. People alter living spaces to meet changing family needs. Finally, people make changes to architectural form, features, and detailing to conform to current taste and style.

Conducting the Architectural Investigation

Architectural investigation can range from a simple one hour walk-through to a month long or even multi-year project—and varies from looking at surfaces to professional sub-surface examination and laboratory work.

All projects should begin with the simplest, non-destructive processes and proceed as necessary. The sequence of investigation starts with reconnaissance and progresses to surface examination and mapping, sub-surface non-destructive testing, and various degrees of sub-surface destructive testing.

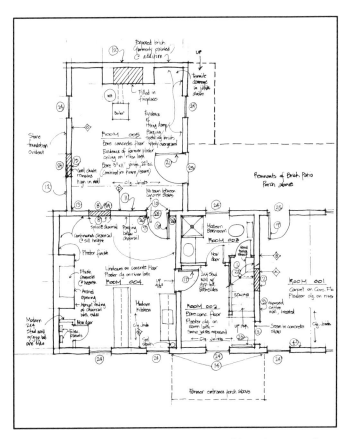

Figure 8. During the initial visit, the architectural investigator may be able to resolve many questions about the building's condition and chronology while recording their observations through field notes and annotated sketches. Drawing by Marianne Graham, courtesy Jefferson's Poplar Forest Restoration Field School.

Looking More Closely at Historic Building Materials and Features

Although brick or wood frame buildings are the most common in this country, similar sets of characteristics and questions can be established for examining log, adobe, steel, or any other material.

Figure A. Careful examination of the masonry reveals different periods of construction and repair through the composition and detailing of bricks and mortar. Depending upon location, open vertical joints may indicate the location of nailing blocks for decorative trim or weeps for drainage. These open joints at the building's cornice show evidence of an earlier wooden entablature extending down two courses below the present trim. The paint ghosts below the lowest blocks confirms the entablature's existence and provides clues to its size and finish.

Masonry. Studying historic brickwork can provide important information about methods of production and construction. For example, the color, size, shape and texture of brick reveals whether it was hand molded and traditionally fired in a clamp with hardwoods, or whether it was machine molded and fired in a kiln using modern fuels. Similarly, the principal component part of masonry mortar, the lime or cement, reveals whether it was produced in a traditional or modern manner. Certain questions need to be asked during investigation. Is the mortar made with a natural or a Portland cement? If a natural cement, did it come from an oyster shell or a limestone source? Is it hydrated or hydraulic? As a construction unit, brick and mortar further reveal something about the time, place and human variables of construction, such as the type of bond, special brick shapes, decorative uses of glazed or rubbed brick, coatings and finishes, and different joints, striking and tooling. Does the bond conform with neighboring or regional buildings of the same period? Does the pattern of "make up" bricks in a Flemish Bond indicate the number of different bricklayers? What is the method of attaching wood trim to the masonry? The same types of questions related to production and construction characteristics can be applied to all types of masonry work, including stone, concrete, terra cotta, adobe and coquina construction. A complete survey undertaken during "surface mapping" can outline the materials and construction practices for the

various periods of a structure, distinguishing the original work as well as the additions, alterations, and replacements.

Figure B. Without damaging or altering historic fabric, X-ray images of wood connections provide internal views of construction materials and techniques. These x-ray images show nails being used to form the connections of a door opening in a wood stud wall covered with plaster and cut wooden lath. A single technician can operate the portable equipment and develop the film on site for immediate analysis. photos: NPS North Atlantic Cultural Resource Center, Building Conservation Branch.

Wood. Buildings constructed with wood have a very different set of characteristics, requiring a different line of questioning. Is the wooden structural system log, timber frame, or balloon frame construction? Evidence seen on the wood surface indicates whether production was by ax, adze, pit saw, mill saw (sash or circular), or band saw. What are the varying dimensions of the lumber used? Finished parts can be sawn, gouged, carved, or planed (by hand or by machine). Were they fastened by notching, mortise and tenon, pegs, or nailing? If nails were used, were they wrought by hand, machine cut with wrought heads, entirely machine cut, or machine wire nails? For much of the nineteenth century the manufacture of nails underwent a series of changes and improvements that are dateable, allowing nails to be used as a tool in establishing periods of construction and alteration. Regardless of region or era, the method of framing, joining and finishing a wooden structure will divulge something about the original construction, its alterations, and the practices of its builders. Finally, does some of the wood appear to be re-used or re-cycled? Re-used and reproduction materials used in early restoration projects have confused many investigators. When no identification record was kept, it can be a problem distinguishing between materials original to the house and later replacement materials.

Figure C. In many cases, new materials or coverings are placed directly over existing exterior features, preserving the original materials underneath. Here, the removal of a modern shingle roof and its underlayment revealed an historic standing seam metal roof. photo: courtesy, Phillips and Opperman, P.A.

Roofs. Exterior features are especially prone to alteration due to weathering and lack of maintenance. Even in the best preserved structures, the exterior often consists of replaced or repaired roofing parts. Roof coverings typically last no more than fifty years. Are several generation of roof coverings still in place? Can the layers be identified? If earlier coverings were removed, the sheathing boards frequently provide clues to the type of covering as well as missing roof features. Dormers, cupolas, finials, cresting, weathervanes, gutters, lightning rods, skylights, balustrades, parapets and platforms come and go as taste, function and maintenance dictate. The roof pitch itself can be a clue to stylistic dating and is unlikely to change unless the entire roof has been rebuilt. Chimneys might hold clues to original roof pitch, flashings, and roof feature attachments. Is it possible to look down a chimney and count the number of flues? This practice has occasionally turned up a missing fireplace. In many parts of the country, nineteenth-century roof coverings evolved from wooden shingles or slate shingles, to metal shingles, to sheet metal, and still later in the twentieth century, to asphaltic or asbestos shingles. Clay tiles can be found covering roofs in seventeenth and eighteenth-century settlements of the east coast as well as western and southwestern Spanish settlements from the same period. Beyond the mid-nineteenth century, and into the twentieth, the range and choice of roof coverings greatly expanded.

Floors. In addition to production and construction clues, floors reveal other information about the interior, such as circulation patterns, furniture placement, the use of carpets, floor cloths, and applied floor finishes. Is there a pattern of tack holes? Tacks or tack holes often indicate the position and even the type of a floor covering. A thorough understanding of the seasonal uses of floor coverings and the technological history of their manufacture provide the background for identifying this type of evidence.

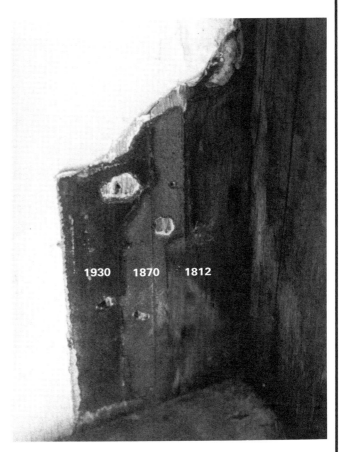

Figure D. Building styles change over time as moldings and trims are added and removed. The ghosts of the previous woodwork are often left behind and preserved under the new trim. This photograph shows distinct profiles of architectural trim from three successive periods. photo: courtesy, Valentine Museum, Richmond, Virginia.

Walls. Walls and their associated trim, both outside and inside, hold many clues to the building's construction and changes made over time. The overall style of moldings, trim and finishes, and their hierarchical relationship, can help explain original construction as well as room usage and social interaction between rooms. Holes, scars, patches, nails, nail holes, screws and other hardware indicate former attachments. Are there "ghosts," or shadow outlines of missing features, or trim attachments such as bases, chair rails, door and window casings, entablatures, cornices, mantels and shelves? Ghosts can be formed by paint, plaster, stucco, wear, weathering or dirt. Interior walls from the eighteenth and early nineteenth-century were traditionally plastered after grounds or finished trim was in place, leaving an absence of plaster on the wall behind them. Evidence of attachments on window casings can also be helpful in understanding certain interior changes. Other clues to look for include the installation of re-used material brought into a house or moved about within a house; worker's or occupant's graffiti, especially on the back of trim; and hidden finishes or wallpaper stuck in crevices or underneath pieces of trim. Stylistic upgrading often resulted in the re-use of outdated trim for blocking or shims. Unexpected discoveries are particularly rewarding. Investigators frequently tell stories about clues that were uncovered from architectural fragments carried off by rats and later found, or left by workers in attics, between walls and under floors.

1812 house disclosed the following information during an investigation: first period bell system, identification of a servant's hall, hidden fireplace, displacement of the service stairs, identification of a servants' quarters, an 1850s furnace system, 1850s gas and plumbing systems, relocation of the kitchen in 1870, early use of 1890s concrete floor slabs and finally, twentieth century utility systems. While the earliest era had been established as the interpretation period, evidence from all periods was documented in order to understand and interpret how the house evolved or changed over time.

Figure E. Discarded items are routinely stored within attics, then forgotten, only to be discovered during a later investigation. Seemingly worthless clutter and debris may help answer many questions. A thorough inventory should be performed before evaluating any object's usefulness.

Figure F. Outdated fixtures and systems are frequently abandoned in place when more modern units are installed. Examining and documenting their existence can provide a technological reference to the history and use of many rooms or structures. photo: NPS Preservation Assistance Division Files.

Attics and Basements. Attics and basements have been known as collection points for out-of-date, out-of-style and cast-off pieces such as mechanical systems, furnishings, family records and architectural fragments. These and other out-of-the-way places of a structure provide an excellent opportunity for non-destructive investigation. Not only are these areas where structural and framing members might be exposed to view, they are also areas which may have escaped the frequent alteration campaigns that occur in the more lived-in parts of a building. If a building has been raised or lowered in height, evidence of change would be found in the attic as well as on the exterior. Evidence of additions might also be detected in both the attic and the basement. Attics frequently provide a "top-side" view at the ceiling below, revealing its material, manner of production and method of attachment. A "bottom-side" view of the roof sheathing or roof covering can be seen from the attic as well.

Basements generally relate more to human service functions in earlier buildings and to mechanical services in more recent eras. For example, a cellar of an urban

Mechanical, Electrical, Plumbing and Other Systems. Systems of utility and convenience bear close scrutiny during investigation. All historic buildings inhabited and used by people reveal some association, at the very minimum, with the necessities of lighting, climate control, water, food preparation, and waste removal. Later installations in a building may include communication, hygiene, food storage, security, and lightning protection systems. Other systems, such as transportation, are related to more specific functions of commercial or public structures. Although research into the social uses of rooms and their furnishings has borne many new studies, parallel research into how people actually carried out the most mundane tasks of everyday life has been fairly neglected. Utility and convenience systems are most prone to alteration and upgrading and, at the same time, less apt to be preserved, documented or re-used. Understanding the history or use of a building, and the history of systems technology can help predict the physical evidence that might be found, and what it will look like after it *is* found.

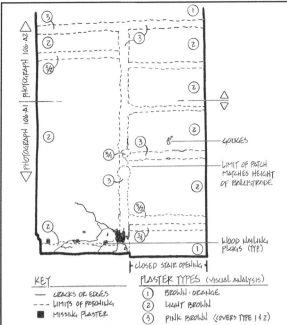

KEY
— CRACKS OR EDGES
--- LIMITS OF PATCHING
■ MISSING PLASTER

PLASTER TYPES (VISUAL ANALYSIS)
① BROWN·ORANGE
② LIGHT BROWN
③ PINK·BROWN (COVERS TYPE 1 & 2)

Figure 9. Raking light is used to show irregularities on flat surfaces. Patches, repairs, and alterations can then be mapped by the shadows or ghosts they cast. In this case, the pattern of patched plaster suggested the removal shelves and a balustrade handrail from the wall. Historical research and plaster analysis confirmed the findings and the sequence of change.

Reconnaissance. An initial reconnaissance trip through a structure—or visual overview—provides the most limited type of investigation. But experienced investigators accustomed to observation and analysis can resolve many questions in a two-to-four hour preliminary site visit. They may be able to determine the consistency of the building's original form and details as well as major changes made over time.

Surface Mapping. The first step in a thorough, systematic investigation is the examination of all surfaces. Surface investigation is sometimes called "surface mapping" since it entails a minute look at all the exterior and interior surfaces. The fourfold purpose of surface mapping is to observe every visible detail of design and construction; develop questions related to evidence and possible alterations; note structural or environmental problems; and help develop plans for any further investigation. Following investigation, a set of documentary drawings and photographs is prepared which record or "map" the evidence.

While relying upon senses of sight and touch, the most useful tool for examining surfaces is a high-powered, portable light used for illuminating dark spaces as well as for enhancing surface subtleties. Raking light at an angle on a flat surface is one of the most effective means of seeing evidence of attachments, repairs or alterations.

Non-Destructive Testing. The next level of investigation consists of probing beneath surfaces using non-destructive methods. Questions derived from the surface mapping examination and analysis will help determine which areas to probe. Investigators have perfected a number of tools and techniques which provide minimal damage to historic fabric. These include x-rays to penetrate surfaces in order to see nail types and joining details; boroscopes, fiber optics and small auto mechanic or dentists' mirrors to look inside of tight spaces; and ultra violet or infra-red lights to observe differences in materials and finishes. The most advanced

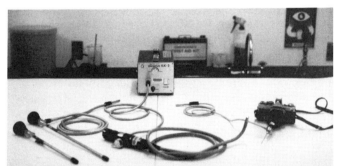

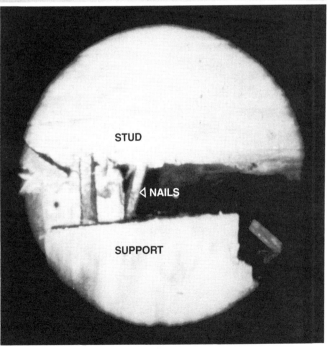

STUD

◁ NAILS

SUPPORT

Figure 10. Top: A boroscope is a fiber-optic tube which can provide views into the framing connections of a wall through an existing crack or hole. Bottom: Once the image is oriented, the investigator can see an open joint between the wood stud and its nailed lateral support. photos: NPS North Atlantic Cultural Resource Center, Building Conservation Branch.

technology combines the boroscope with video cameras using fiber optic illumination. In addition to the more common use of infra-red photography, similar non-destructive techniques used in archeological investigations include remote sensing and ground-penetrating radar.

Small material samples of wood, plaster, mortar, or paint can also be taken for laboratory analysis at this stage of investigation. For instance, a surface examination of a plaster wall using a raking light may show clear evidence of patching which corresponds to a shelf design. Were the shelves original or a later addition? A small sample of plaster from the patched area is analyzed in the laboratory and matches plaster already dated to a third period of construction. A probe further reveals an absence of first period plaster on the wall underneath. The investigator might conclude from this evidence that the shelves were an original feature and that the plaster fill dates their removal and patching to a third period of construction.

Destructive Testing. Most investigations require nothing more than historical research, surface examination and non-destructive testing. In very rare instances the investigation may require a sub-surface examination and the removal of fabric. Destructive testing should be carried out by a professional only after historical research and surface mapping have been fully accomplished and *only after* non-destructive testing has failed to produce the necessary information. Owners should be aware that the work is a form of demolition in which the physical record may be destroyed. Sub-surface examination begins with the most accessible spaces, such as retrofitted service and mechanical chases; loose or previously altered trim, ceilings or floor boards; and pieces of trim or hardware which can be easily removed and replaced.

Non-destructive testing techniques do not damage historic fabric. If non-destructive techniques are not sufficient to resolve important questions, small "windows" can be opened in surface fabric at predetermined locations to see beneath the surface. This type of subsurface testing and removal is sometimes called "architectural archeology" because of its similarity to the more well-known process of trenching in archeology. The analogy is apt because both forms of archeology use a method of destructive investigation.

Photographs, video and drawings should record the before, during and after evidence when the removal of historic fabric is necessary. The selection and sequence of material to be removed requires careful study so that original extant fabric remains *in situ* if possible. If removed, original fabric should be carefully put back or labelled and stored. At least one documentary patch of each historic finish should be retained *in situ* for future research. Treatment and interpretation, no matter how accurate, are usually not final; treatment tends to be cyclical, like history, and documentation must be left for future generations, both on the wall and in the files.

Laboratory Analysis. Laboratory analysis plays a scientific role in the more intuitive process of architectural investigation. One of the most commonly known laboratory procedures used in architectural investigation is that of historic paint analysis. The chronology and stratigraphy of applied layers can establish appropriate colors, finishes, designs or wall coverings. When conducted simultaneously with architectural investigation, the stratigraphy of finishes, like that of stratigraphic soils in archeology, helps determine the sequence of construction or alterations in a building. Preliminary findings from *in situ* examinations of painted finishes on walls or trim are common, but more accurate results come from extensive

Figure 11. The physical evidence of cracks and patches seen during surface mapping suggested an abandoned fireplace. Right: Exploratory testing was used to verify its location. Left: Museum restoration required more detailed probing to discover the original detailing. Plaster and brick were carefully documented and removed to determine the fireplace's type, size, and decoration. The rectangular slots held wooden nailing blocks supporting the mantel and surround. A indicates the inside edge of the surround; B points to the ghost from an iron fireback and C shows the original floor level of the hearth.

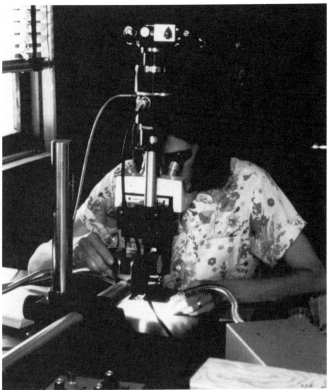

Figure 12. During a thorough investigation, the mortar sample is viewed under a microscope using various lighting to find the presence of coatings or additives. It is then ground and washed in an acid bath to separate and free the sand and fibers. After further cleaning, these fines are stored and used for comparison in matching or dating repairs and alterations. photos: NPS North Atlantic Cultural Resource Center, Building Conservation Branch.

sampling and microscopic laboratory work using chemical analysis and standardized color notations. Consultants without the proper knowledge have been known to cause far more harm than good.

Mortar and plaster analysis often provide a basis for dating construction with minimal intervention. Relatively small samples of the lime-based materials can be chemically separated into their component parts of sands and fines, which are then visually compared to equivalent parts of known or dated samples. A more thorough scientific approach may be used to accurately profile and compare samples of other materials through elemental analysis. Two similar methods in common use are Neutron Activation and Energy Dispersive Spectroscopy (EDS). Neutron Activation identifies the sample's trace elements by monitoring their response to neutron bombardment. EDS measures the response to electron bombardment through

the use of an electron microscope. In both tests, the gathered information is plotted and matched with the reactions of known elements. The results provide a quantitative and qualitative profile of the sample's elemental components for use in further comparisons.

Dendrochronology presents a minimally destructive process for dating wooden members. Also called tree ring dating, this process relies on the comparative wet and dry growth seasons of trees as seen in their rings via a core sample. This technique has two limitations: a very extensive data base must be compiled for climatic conditions over a long span of years and matched with corresponding tree ring samples; and the core samples can only be taken from timber which still has a bark edge. Simple identification of wood species during an investigation can be determined from small samples sent to a forest products laboratory.

After Architectural Investigation: Weighing the Evidence

Evidence, questions, and hypotheses must be continually evaluated during investigation. Like a detective constructing a case, an investigator must sort out information to get at "the facts." Yet, are the "facts" conclusive at any time?

Observations made during the surface mapping may identify random features. These features begin to form patterns; then, sets of patterns, perhaps representing alterations from multiple eras, begin to appear. If the right questions are not asked, the evidence can remain hidden. Hypotheses are formed, questioned, tested, re-formed and either rejected or substantiated. This process is repeated as more "facts" are uncovered and questions asked. Eventually the evidence seems conclusive. These conclusions, in turn, may lead to re-examination, more historical research, and the advice of specialized consultants. At some point, treatment generally follows based on the collective, educated conclusions of an entire professional team.

Keeping a Responsible Record for Future Investigators

The evidence collected during investigation, and any conclusions which can be drawn from it, should be documented in a written report. The complexity of a project dictates the complexity of the resulting record. It may be wise to maintain a report in an expandable format if long or extensive work is expected—additional evidence will undoubtedly need to be incorporated that alters previous conclusions. Reports tend to range from annotated photographs in loose-leaf binders to full-length bound "books."

Putting findings and conclusions in an accessible form helps those who are planning treatment. For example, a rehabilitation project may require documentation to satisfy grant funding or tax credit program requirements; preservation and restoration projects always need careful documentation to guide the work. After work, the investigation report and notes on the treatment itself are made into a permanent file record. Whether or not work is being planned, the architectural investigation report will always be of value to future researchers or owners of the building.

The most common professional document is called an *Historic Structure Report*. This invaluable tool for preservation typically contains historical as well as physical information. Sections include a history of the building, an architectural description of the original structure and changes made over time, the results of all investigations, a record of current conditions or problems, of past repairs and treatments, and recommendations for current and future action. They are seldom definitive; thus, research is a continuing process.

Conclusion

Architectural investigation plays a critical role in making responsible decisions about treating and interpreting historic buildings. A successful project to research, inventory, document, and ultimately treat and interpret a building is directly linked to the knowledge and skills of architectural investigators and other historic preservation specialists. The expressed goal of historic preservation is to protect and preserve materials and features that convey the significant history of a place. Careful architectural investigation—together with historical research—provides a firm foundation for this goal.

Bibliography

Bullock, Orin M. Jr., *The Restoration Manual*. Norwalk, CT.: Silvermine Publishers, 1966.

Burns, John A., editor. *Recording Historic Structures*, Washington, D.C.: The AIA Press, 1989.

Howard, Hugh. *How Old Is This House?*. New York: Noonday Press, 1989.

Howe, Barbara J., Dolores A. Fleming, Emory L. Kemp, and Ruth Ann Overbeck. *Houses and Homes: Exploring Their History*. Nashville, TN.: American Association for State and Local History, 1987.

Judd, Henry A., *Before Restoration Begins*. Nashville, TN.: American Association for State and Local History, 1973.

Kitchen, Judith L., *Caring For Your Old House*. Washington, D.C.: The Preservation Press, 1991.

Seale, William, *Recreating the Historic House Interior*. Nashville, TN.: American Association for State and Local History, 1979.

Secretary of the Interior's Standards for the Treatment of Historic Properties. Washington, D.C.: Preservation Assistance Division, National Park Service, U.S. Department of the Interior, 1992.

Secretary of the Interior's Standards and Guidelines for Architectural and Engineering Documentation: HABS/HAER Standards. Washington, D.C.: HABS/HAER, National Park Service, U.S. Department of the Interior, 1990.

Cover Photo:

An historical architect analyzes and records his investigative findings while on site. photo: courtesy Valentine Museum.

Acknowledgements

Travis C. McDonald, Jr. is an architectural historian who serves as the Restoration Coordinator at Thomas Jefferson's Poplar Forest near Lynchburg, Virginia. He respectively dedicates this work to three masters of architectural investigation: Henry A. Judd, former Chief Historical Architect of the National Park Service; Lee H. Nelson, former Chief, Preservation Assistance Division NPS; and Paul E. Buchanan, former Director of Architectural Research at the Colonial Williamsburg Foundation. The author gratefully acknowledges the following professionals for their help in reviewing this manuscript: Edward A. Chappell, Colonial Williamsburg; E. Blaine Cliver, Preservation Assistance Division NPS; Stanley O. Graves, National Conference of State Historic Preservation Officers; Bernard L. Herman, University of Delaware; H. Ward Jandl, Preservation Assistance Division NPS; Hugh C. Miller, Virginia State Historic Preservation Office; Orlando Ridout V, Maryland Historical Trust; William Seale; and

professional staff members of the National Park Service. Timothy A. Buehner served as project coordinator and Kay D. Weeks as project editor.

All photographs are by the Author unless otherwise noted.

This publication has been prepared pursuant to the National Historic Preservation Act of 1966, as amended, which directs the Secretary of the Interior to develop and make available information concerning historic properties. Comments on the usefulness of this publication may be directed to: Preservation Assistance Division, National Park Service, P.O. Box 37127, Washington, D.C. 20013-7127.

36

Protecting Cultural Landscapes:
Planning, Treatment and Management of Historic Landscapes

Charles A. Birnbaum, ASLA

Cultural landscapes can range from thousands of acres of rural tracts of land to a small homestead with a front yard of less than one acre. Like historic buildings and districts, these special places reveal aspects of our country's origins and development through their form and features and the ways they were used. Cultural landscapes also reveal much about our evolving relationship with the natural world.

A *cultural landscape* is defined as "a geographic area, including both cultural and natural resources and the wildlife or domestic animals therein, associated with a historic event, activity, or person or exhibiting other cultural or aesthetic values." There are four general types of cultural landscapes, not mutually exclusive: *historic sites, historic designed landscapes,* *historic vernacular landscapes, and ethnographic landscapes.* These are defined on the Table on page 2.[1]

Historic landscapes include residential gardens and community parks, scenic highways, rural communities, institutional grounds, cemeteries, battlefields and zoological gardens. They are composed of a number of character-defining features which individually or collectively contribute to the landscape's physical appearance as they have evolved over time. In addition to vegetation and topography, cultural landscapes may include water features such as ponds, streams, and fountains; circulation features such as roads, paths, steps, and walls; buildings; and furnishings, including fences, benches, lights and sculptural objects.

Figure 1: The New York Peace Monument atop Lookout Mountain in the 8,100 acre Chickamauga and Chattanooga National Military Park, Chattanooga, Tennessee, commemorates the reconciliation of the Civil War between the North and South. The strategic high point provides panoramic views to the City of Chattanooga and the Moccasin Bend. Today, it is recognized for its cultural and natural resource value. The memorial, which was added in 1910 is part of this landscape's historic continuum. (courtesy Sam Abell and National Geographic).

DEFINITIONS

Historic Designed Landscape - a landscape that was consciously designed or laid out by a landscape architect, master gardener, architect, or horticulturist according to design principles, or an amateur gardener working in a recognized style or tradition. The landscape may be associated with a significant person(s), trend, or event in landscape architecture; or illustrate an important development in the theory and practice of landscape architecture. Aesthetic values play a significant role in designed landscapes. Examples include parks, campuses, and estates.

Historic Vernacular Landscape - a landscape that evolved through use by the people whose activities or occupancy shaped that landscape. Through social or cultural attitudes of an individual, family or a community, the landscape reflects the physical, biological, and cultural character of those everyday lives. Function plays a significant role in vernacular landscapes. They can be a single property such as a farm or a collection of properties such as a district of historic farms along a river valley. Examples include rural villages, industrial complexes, and agricultural landscapes.

Historic Site - a landscape significant for its association with a historic event, activity, or person. Examples include battlefields and president's house properties.

Ethnographic Landscape - a landscape containing a variety of natural and cultural resources that associated people define as heritage resources. Examples are contemporary settlements, religious sacred sites and massive geological structures. Small plant communities, animals, subsistence and ceremonial grounds are often components.

Figures 2-4: Character-defining landscape features (top to bottom): "Boot Fence" near D. H. Lawrence Ranch, Questa, New Mexico, 1991 (courtesy Cheryl Wagner); paving detail at Ernest Hemingway House National Historic Site, Key West, Florida, 1994 (courtesy author); and, tree planting detail for Jefferson Memorial Park, St. Louis, Missouri (courtesy Office of Dan Kiley)

Most historic properties have a cultural landscape component that is integral to the significance of the resource. Imagine a residential district without sidewalks, lawns and trees or a plantation with buildings but no adjacent lands. A historic property consists of all its cultural resources — landscapes, buildings, archeological sites and collections. In some cultural landscapes, there may be a total absence of buildings.

This Preservation Brief provides preservation professionals, cultural resource managers, and historic property owners a step-by-step process for preserving historic designed and vernacular landscapes, two types of cultural landscapes. While this process is ideally applied to an entire landscape, it can address a single feature such as a perennial garden, family burial plot, or a sentinel oak in an open meadow. This Brief provides a framework and guidance for undertaking projects to ensure a successful balance between historic preservation and change.

Developing a Strategy and Seeking Assistance

Nearly all designed and vernacular landscapes evolve from, or are often dependent on, natural resources. It is these interconnected systems of land, air and water,

vegetation and wildlife which have dynamic qualities that differentiate cultural landscapes from other cultural resources, such as historic structures. Thus, their documentation, treatment, and ongoing management require a comprehensive, multi-disciplinary approach.

Today, those involved in preservation planning and management for cultural landscapes represent a broad array of academic backgrounds, training, and related project experience. Professionals may have expertise in landscape architecture, history, landscape archeology, forestry, agriculture, horticulture, pomology, pollen analysis, planning, architecture, engineering (civil, structural, mechanical, traffic), cultural geography, wildlife, ecology, ethnography, interpretation, material and object conservation, landscape maintenance and management. Historians and historic preservation professionals can bring expertise in the history of the landscape, architecture, art, industry, agriculture, society and other subjects. Landscape preservation teams, including on-site management teams and independent consultants, are often directed by a landscape architect with specific expertise in landscape preservation. It is highly recommended that disciplines relevant to the landscapes' inherent features be represented as well.

Additional guidance may be obtained from State Historic Preservation Offices, local preservation commissions, the National Park Service, local and state park agencies, national and state chapters of the American Society of Landscape Architects, the Alliance for Historic Landscape Preservation, the National Association of Olmsted Parks, and the Catalog of Landscape Records in the United States at Wave Hill among others.[2]

A range of issues may need to be addressed when considering how a particular cultural landscape should be treated. This may include the in-kind replacement of declining vegetation, reproduction of furnishings, rehabilitation of structures, accessibility provisions for people with disabilities, or the treatment of industrial properties that are rehabilitated for new uses.

Preservation Planning for Cultural Landscapes

Careful planning prior to undertaking work can help prevent irrevocable damage to a cultural landscape. Professional techniques for identifying, documenting, evaluating and preserving cultural landscapes have advanced during the past 25 years and are continually being refined. Preservation planning generally involves the following steps: historical research; inventory and documentation of existing conditions; site analysis and evaluation of integrity and significance; development of a cultural landscape preservation approach and treatment plan; development of a cultural landscape management plan and management philosophy; the development of a strategy for ongoing maintenance; and preparation of a record of treatment and future research recommendations.

The steps in this process are not independent of each other, nor are they always sequential. In fact, information gathered in one step may lead to a re-examination or refinement of previous steps. For example, field inventory and historical research are likely to occur simultaneously, and may reveal unnoticed cultural resources that should be protected.

The treatment and management of cultural landscape should also be considered in concert with the management of an entire historic property. As a result, many other studies may be relevant. They include management plans, interpretive plans, exhibit design, historic structures reports, and other.

CULTURAL LANDSCAPE REPORTS

A Cultural Landscape Report (CLR) is the primary report that documents the history, significance and treatment of a cultural landscape. A CLR evaluates the history and integrity of the landscape including any changes to its geographical context, features, materials, and use.

CLR's are often prepared when a change (e.g. a new visitor's center or parking area to a landscape) is proposed. In such instances, a CLR can be a useful tool to protect the landscape's character-defining features from undue wear, alteration or loss. A CLR can provide managers, curators and others with information needed to make management decisions.

A CLR will often yield new information about a landscape's historic significance and integrity, even for those already listed on the National Register. Where appropriate, National Register files should be amended to reflect the new findings.

These steps can result in several products including a Cultural Landscape Report (also known as a Historic Landscape Report), statements for management, interpretive guide, maintenance guide and maintenance records.

Historical Research

Research is essential before undertaking any treatment. Findings will help identify a landscape's historic period(s) of ownership, occupancy and development, and bring greater understanding of the associations and characteristics that make the landscape or history significant. Research findings provide a foundation to make educated decisions for work, and can also facilitate ongoing maintenance and management operations, interpretation and eventual compliance requirements.

A variety of primary and secondary sources may be consulted. Primary archival sources can include historic plans, surveys, plats, tax maps, atlases, U. S. Geological Survey maps, soil profiles, aerial photographs, photographs, stereoscopic views, glass lantern slides, postcards, engravings, paintings, newspapers, journals, construction drawings, specifications, plant lists, nursery catalogs, household records, account books and personal correspondence. Secondary sources include monographs, published histories, theses, National Register forms, survey data, local preservation plans, state contexts and scholarly articles. (See Figures 5–7, page 4.)

Contemporary documentary resources should also be consulted. This may include recent studies, plans, surveys, aerial and infrared photographs, Soil Conservation Service soil maps, inventories, investigations and interviews. Oral histories of residents, managers, and maintenance personnel with a long tenure or historical association can be valuable sources of information about changes to a landscape over many years. (Figures 8–9, page 4) For properties listed in the National Register, nomination forms should be consulted.

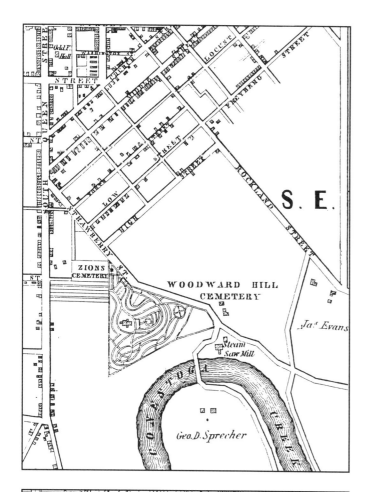

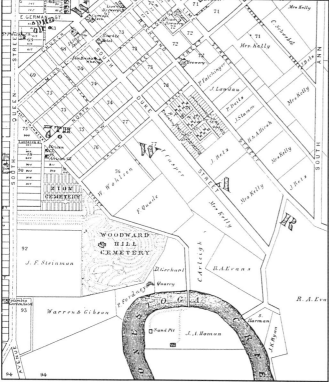

Figures 5-7: Atlases and aerial photographs were useful for understanding the evolution of burial grounds in Lancaster County, Pennsylvania. Comparing the plans from the 1864 and 1875 atlases (courtesy Lancaster County Historical Society) with a 1980 aerial photograph (courtesy Lancaster County Planning Commission) revealed the growth and development of Woodward Hill Cemetery and its geographic context for over a century.

Figures 8, 9: Mary Smith Nelson spent her childhood at the Zane Grey family compound in Lackawaxen, Pennsylvania. Recently, her recollections of nearly eighty years ago helped landscape architects to document the evolution of this cultural landscape. These oral memoirs have since been confirmed by archeological and archival findings. (courtesy National Park Service, Zane Grey House Archives and LANDSCAPES)

Figure 10: Traditional land uses are often the key to long term preservation. Therefore, a knowledge of prior landscape management practices is essential as part of the research phase. Land use patterns were often the result of traditional activities such as agriculture, fishing or mining. In Hanalei, Hawaii for example, taro fields are important because they reflect the continuity of use of the land over time. (courtesy Land and Community Associates)

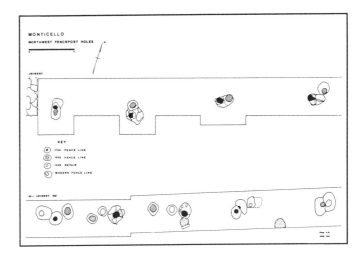

Figure 11: Landscape archeology is an important research tool that can provide location, dating and detail verification for landscape features. At Monticello, the estate of Thomas Jefferson in Charlottesville, Virginia, archeological research has employed both excavational and non-invasive methods. This has included aerial photography, soil resistivity, transect and stratified sampling and photogrammetric recording. As illustrated in the plan above, fence post spacing and alignment can be confirmed with a transect trenching technique.[3] (courtesy Thomas Jefferson Memorial Foundation)

Preparing Period Plans

In the case of designed landscapes, even though a historic design plan exists, it does not necessarily mean that it was realized fully, or even in part. Based on a review of the archival resources outlined above, and the extant landscape today, an *as-built period plan* may be delineated. For all successive tenures of ownership, occupancy and landscape change, *period plans* should be generated (see Figure 13, page 6). Period plans can document to the greatest extent possible the historic appearance during a particular period of ownership, occupancy, or development. Period plans should be based on primary archival sources and should avoid conjecture. Features that are based on secondary or less accurate sources should be graphically differentiated. Ideally, all referenced archival sources should be annotated and footnoted directly on *period plans*.

Where historical data is missing, period plans should reflect any gaps in the CLR narrative text and these limitations considered in future treatment decisions (See Treatments for Cultural Landscapes on page 13.)

Inventorying and Documenting Existing Conditions

Both physical evidence in the landscape and historic documentation guide the historic preservation plan and treatments. To document existing conditions, intensive field investigation and reconnaissance should be conducted at the same time that documentary research is being gathered. Information should be exchanged among preservation professionals, historians, technicians, local residents, managers and visitors.

To assist in the survey process, National Register Bulletins have been published by the National Park Service to aid in identifying, nominating and evaluating designed and rural historic landscapes. Additionally, Bulletins are available for specific landscape types such as battlefields, mining sites, and cemeteries.[6]

Although there are several ways to inventory and document a landscape, the goal is to create a baseline from a detailed record of the landscape and its features as they exist at the present (considering seasonal variations).[7] Each landscape inventory should address issues of boundary delineation, documentation methodologies and techniques, the limitations of the inventory, and the scope of inventory efforts. These are most often influenced by the timetable, budget, project scope, and the purpose of the inventory and, depending on the physical qualities of the property, its scale, detail, and the interrelationship between natural and cultural resources. For example, inventory objectives to develop a treatment plan may differ considerably compared to those needed to develop an ongoing maintenance plan. Once the criteria for a landscape inventory are developed and tested, the methodology should be explained.

Preparing Existing Condition Plans

Inventory and documentation may be recorded in plans, sections, photographs, aerial photographs, axonometric perspectives, narratives, video—or any combination of techniques. Existing conditions should generally be documented to scale, drawn by hand or generated by computer. The scale of the drawings is often determined by the size and complexity of the landscape. Some landscapes may require documentation at more than one scale. For example, a large estate may be documented at a small scale to depict its spatial and visual relationships, while the discrete area around an estate mansion may require a larger scale to illustrate individual plant materials, pavement patterns and other details. The same may apply to an entire rural historic district and a fenced vegetable garden contained within. (See Figures 14-15, page 8).

When landscapes are documented in photographs, *registration points* can be set to indicate the precise location and orientation of features. Registration points should correspond to significant forms, features and spatial relationships within the landscape and its surrounds (see

HISTORIC LANDSCAPE FEATURES	DEGREE OF DOCUMENTATION					
	SITE EVIDENCE	MANNING PLAN	HISTORIC PHOTOS	LETTERS 1914-1946	1955-1993 RECORDS	SECONDARY SOURCES
NATURAL SYSTEMS/TOPOGRAPHY	▲	▲	▲	▲	▲	?
Bedrock (Quarry)	●	●	●	●	●	
Land Contour	●	●	●	●	●	
Rockwork	●	●	●	●	●	
WATER FEATURES	▲	▲	▲	▲	▲	?
Alignment—Cascade	●		●	●	●	
Alignment—Pools & Streams	●	●	●	●	●	
Materials—Cascade	●		●	●	●	
Materials—Pools & Streams	●		●	●	●	
CIRCULATION	▲	▲	▲	▲	▲	?
Alignment—Upland Area	●	●	●	●	●	
Alignment—Perimeter Paths	●	●	●	●	●	
Alignment—Internal Paths		●	●	●	●	
Materials—Upland Area		●	●	●	●	
Materials—Perimeter Paths	●	●	●	●	●	
Materials—Internal Paths		●	●	●	●	
SPATIAL RELATIONSHIPS	▲	▲	▲	▲	▲	?
Garden Site (Quarry)	●	●	●	●		
Viewshed (Cuyahoga Valley)	●		●	●		
Vista over Garden from Terrace			●	●		
Views within Garden		●	●	●	●	
Views within Upland		●	●	●		
Views from Croquet Lawn		●	●			
VEGETATION	▲	▲	▲	▲	▲	?
Native Forest Trees	●	●	●	●	●	
Ornamental Shrubs in Garden	●		●	●	●	
Groundcovers in Garden	●		●	●	●	
Herbaceous Plants in Garden			●	●	●	
SITE FURNISHINGS	▲	▲	▲	▲	▲	?
Lanterns	●		●	●	●	
Seats	●		●	●		
STRUCTURES	▲	▲	▲	▲	▲	?
Torii Gate	●		●		●	
Cistern	●	●		●	●	
Stone Wall Concealing Cistern	●			●	●	
Lagon Bridges			●	●	●	
Umbrella House			●	●		
Trellis/Lattice			●	●		

Figure 12: This chart measures available documentation for character-defining features in the Japanese Garden at Stan Hywet Hall, Akron, Ohio designed by Warren Manning. Areas with little or no historic documentation are noted, thus identifying areas where future treatment options may be restricted. As illustrated, restoration or reconstruction are viable alternatives based on the rich research findings. (courtesy Stan Hywet Hall Foundation, Inc. and Doell and Doell)

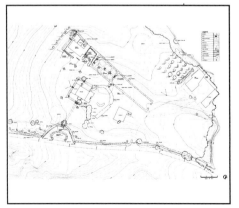
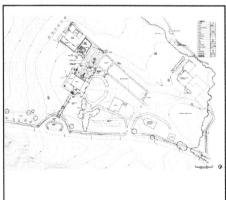
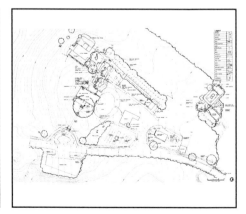

Figure 13: Period plans show the evolution of Aspet, the home of Augustus St. Gaudens, Cornish, New Hampshire. Plans were developed at two scales: first for the entire estate's development, and second for the core area around the house, studio and gardens. For both, plans were generated for five time periods: 1885-1903, 1903-1907, 1907-1926, 1926-1965 and 1965-1992. Illustrated above are the 1885-1903, 1907-1926, and the 1926-1965 plans for the core area. (courtesy National Park Service, North Atlantic Region and Pressley Associates)

READING THE LANDSCAPE

A noted geographer stated, "The attempt to derive meaning from landscapes possesses overwhelming virtue. It keeps us constantly alert to the world around us, demanding that we pay attention not just to some of the things around us but to all of them—the whole visible world in all of its rich, glorious, messy, confusing, ugly, and beautiful complexity."[4]

Landscapes can be read on many levels—landscape as nature, habitat, artifact, system, problem, wealth, ideology, history, place and aesthetic.[5] When developing a strategy to document a cultural landscape, it is important to attempt to read the landscape in its context of place and time. (See Figures 16-17, page 8)

Reading the landscape, like engaging in archival research, requires a knowledge of the resource and subject area as well as a willingness to be skeptical. As with archival research, it may involve serendipitous discoveries. Evidence gained from reading the landscape may confirm or contradict other findings and may encourage the observer and the historian to revisit both primary and secondary sources with a fresh outlook. Landscape investigation may also stimulate other forms of research and survey, such as oral histories or archeological investigations, to supplement what appeared on-site.

There are many ways to read a landscape—whatever approach is taken should provide a broad overview. This may be achieved by combining on-the-ground observations with a bird's-eye perspective. To begin this process, aerial photographs should be reviewed to gain an orientation to the landscape and its setting. Aerial photographs come in different sizes and scales, and can thus portray different levels of detail in the landscape. Aerial photographs taken at a high altitude, for example, may help to reveal remnant field patterns or traces of an abandoned circulation system; or, portions of axial relationships that were part of the original design, since obscured by encroaching woodland areas. Low altitude aerial photographs can point out individual features such as the arrangement of shrub and herbaceous borders, and the exact locations of furnishings, lighting, and fence

alignments. This knowledge can prove beneficial before an on-site visit.

Aerial photographs provide clues that can help orient the viewer to the landscape. The next step may be to view the landscape from a high point such as a knoll or an upper floor window. Such a vantage point may provide an excellent transition before physically entering the cultural landscape.

On ground, evidence should then be studied, including character-defining features, visual and spatial relationships. By reviewing supporting materials from historic research, individual features can be understood in a systematic fashion that show the continuum that exists on the ground today. By classifying these features and relationships, the landscape can be understood as an artifact, possessing evidence of evolving natural systems and human interventions over time.

For example, the on-site investigation of an abandoned turn-of-the-century farm complex reveals the remnant of a native oak and pine forest which was cut and burned in the mid-nineteenth century. This previous use is confirmed by a small stand of mature oaks and the presence of these plants in the emerging secondary woodland growth that is overtaking this farm complex in decline. A ring count of the trees can establish a more accurate age. By *reading* other character-defining features—such as the traces of old roads, remnant hedgerows, ornamental trees along boundary roads, foundation plantings, the terracing of grades and remnant fences —the visual, spatial and contextual relationships of the property as it existed a century ago may be understood and its present condition and integrity evaluated.

The findings of on-site reconnaissance, such as materials uncovered during archival research, may be considered primary data. These findings make it possible to inventory and evaluate the landscape's features in the context of the property's current condition. Character-defining features are located in situ, in relationship to each other and the greater cultural and geographic contexts.

Figure 22, page 11 for an example.) The points may also correspond to historic views to illustrate the change in the landscape to date. These locations may also be used as a management tool to document the landscape's evolution, and to ensure that its character-defining features are preserved over time through informed maintenance operations and later treatment and management decisions.

All features that contribute to the landscape's historic character should be recorded. These include the physical features described on page 1 (e.g. topography, circulation), and the visual and spatial relationships that are character-defining. The identification of existing plants, should be specific, including genus, species, common name, age (if known) and size. The woody, and if appropriate, herbaceous plant material should be accurately located on the existing conditions map. To ensure full representation of successional herbaceous plants, care should be taken to document the landscape in different seasons, if possible.

Treating living plant materials as a curatorial collection has also been undertaken at some cultural landscapes. This process, either done manually or by computer, can track the condition and maintenance operations on individual plants. Some sites, such as the Frederick Law Olmsted National Historic Site, in Brookline, Massachusetts have developed a field investigation numbering system to track all woody plants. (See Table, page 9) Due to concern for the preservation of genetic diversity and the need to replace significant plant materials, a number of properties are beginning to propagate historically important rare plants that are no longer commercially available, unique, or possess significant historic associations. Such herbarium collections become a part of a site's natural history collection.

Once the research and the documentation of existing conditions have been completed, a foundation is in place to analyze the landscape's continuity and change, determine its significance, assess its integrity, and place it within the historic context of similar landscapes.

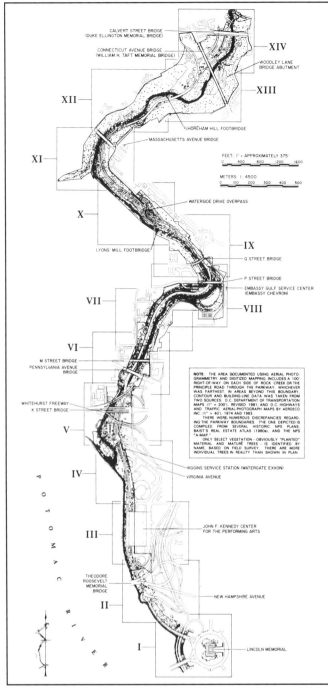

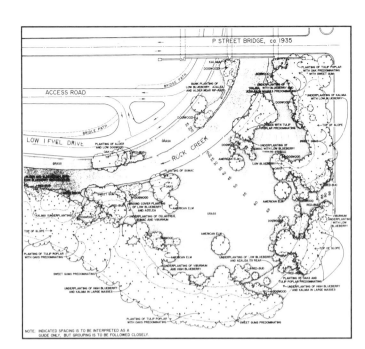

Figures 14 and 15: Existing conditions plans for large corridor landscapes can employ a variety of documentation methodologies. For the 2 -1/2 mile Rock Creek and Potomac Parkway, Washington, D.C., the Historic American Buildings Survey (HABS) used aerial photo-grammetric photographs as the basis for digitized mapping and delineated drawings. Overall documentation was done at a scale of 1" = 40' with a 100' either side geographic context. Contours were shown at 2' intervals, tree canopy with trunk placement for specimen species, bridges (also drawn in detail), roads, and the creek itself. In all, there are 36 drawings measuring 34" x 44" for the project. These two sample drawings include the index to plans (above) and an area of existing conditions documentation (opposite top). (courtesy Historic American Buildings Survey)

Figures 16 and 17: Landscapes cannot be inventoried in a vacuum. Therefore, an understanding of its geographic context or setting should be part of inventory process. At Rancho Los Alamitos, Long Beach, California (middle and bottom opposite), a comparison between the 1936 aerial view with a present day aerial photograph illustrates the encroachments and adjacent developments that will affect the future treatment of visual and spatial relationships. (courtesy Rancho Los Alamitos Foundation)

HISTORIC PLANT INVENTORY

Within cultural landscapes, plants may have historical or botanical significance. A plant may have been associated with a historic figure or event or be part of a notable landscape design. A plant may be an uncommon cultivar, exceptional in size, age, rare and commercially/unavailable. If such plants are lost, there would be a loss of historic integrity and biological diversity of the cultural landscape.To ensure that significant plants are preserved, an inventory of historic plants is being conducted at the North Atlantic Region of the National Park Service.[8] Historical landscape architects work with landscape managers and historians to gather oral and documented history on the plant's origin and potential significance. Each plant is then examined in the field by an expert horticulturist who records its name, condition, age, size, distribution, and, any notable botanic characteristics.

Plants that are difficult to identify or are of potential historical significance are further examined in the laboratory by a plant taxonomist who compares leaf, fruit, and flower characteristics with herbarium specimens for named species, cultivars and varieties. For plants species with many cultivars, such as apples, roses, and grapes, specimens may be sent to specialists for identification.

If a plant cannot be identified, is dying or in decline, and unavailable from commercial nurseries, it may be propagated. Propagation ensures that when rare and significant plants decline, they can be replaced with genetically-identical plants. Cuttings are propagated and grown to replacement size in a North Atlantic Region Historic Plant Nursery.

1. The Arnold Arboretum's preservation technician, lilac specialist, and horticulturist compare lilacs from the Vanderbilt Mansion National Historic Site in Hyde Park, New York with lilac specimens in the Arboretum's living collection. (courtesy Olmsted Center)

3. The Arnold Arboretum's horticulturist, landscape historian, and preservation technician examine shrubs at the Longfellow National Historic Site in Cambridge, MA. (courtesy Olmsted Center)

2. The Arnold Arboretum's horticulturist and preservation technician examine an enormous black locust tree at the Home of F.D. Roosevelt National Historic Site in Hyde Park, NY. (courtesy Olmsted Center)

Site Analysis: Evaluating Integrity and Significance

By analyzing the landscape, its change over time can be understood. This may be accomplished by overlaying the various period plans with the existing conditions plan. Based on these findings, individual features may be attributed to the particular period when they were introduced, and the various periods when they were present.

It is during this step that the *historic significance* of the landscape component of a historic property and its integrity are determined. Historic significance is the recognized importance a property displays when it has been evaluated, including when it has been found to meet National Register Criteria.[9] A landscape may have several areas of historical significance. An understanding of the landscape as a continuum through history is critical in assessing its cultural and historic value. In order for the landscape to have integrity, these character-defining features or qualities that contribute to its significance must be present.

While National Register nominations document the significance and integrity of historic properties, in general, they may not acknowledge the significance of the landscape's design or historic land uses, and may not contain an inventory of landscape features or characteristics. Additional research is often necessary to provide the detailed information about a landscape's evolution and significance useful in making decision for the treatment and maintenance of a historic landscape. Existing National Register forms may be amended to recognize additional areas of significance and to include more complete descriptions of historic properties that have significant land areas and landscape features.

Integrity is a property's historic identity evidenced by the survival of physical characteristics from the property's historic or prehistoric period. The seven qualities of integrity are location, setting, feeling, association, design, workmanship and materials.[10] When evaluating these qualities, care should be taken to consider change itself. For example, when a second-generation woodland overtakes an open pasture in a battlefield landscape, or a woodland edge encloses a scenic vista. For situations such as these, the reversibility and/or compatibility of those features should be considered, both individually, and in the context of the overall landscape. Together, evaluations of significance and integrity, when combined with historic research, documentation of existing conditions, and analysis findings, influence later treatment and interpretation decisions. (See Figure 21-23)

Developing a Historic Preservation Approach and Treatment Plan

Treatment may be defined as work carried out to achieve a historic preservation goal—it cannot be considered in a vacuum. There are many practical and philosophical factors that may influence the selection of a treatment for a landscape. These include the relative historic value of the property, the level of historic documentation, existing physical conditions, its historic significance and integrity, historic and proposed use (e.g. educational, interpretive, passive, active public, institutional or private), long- and short-term objectives, operational and code requirements (e.g. accessibility, fire, security) and costs for anticipated capital improvement, staffing and maintenance. The value of any significant archeological and natural resources

Figure 18: At Lawnfield, the home of President James A. Garfield near Cleveland, Ohio, the Sugar Maple that shadowed the porch during Garfield's 1880 "Front Porch Campaign" is in decline. Cuttings were taken from the historically significant tree by the Holden Arboretum and the National Park Service for eventual in-kind replacement. (courtesy NPS, Midwest Region)

Figure 19: The landscape of Lyndhurst, Tarrytown, New York is significant in American culture and meets Criterion C of the National Register because it embodies the distinctive character of a type and period in American landscape architecture, known as early Picturesque; it possesses high artistic value; and it is the work of a recognized master gardener, Ferdinand Mangold. (courtesy National Trust for Historic Preservation)

Figure 20: Cultural landscapes often contain plant communities such as orchards or meadows—both of which may or may not require a management intervention. When analyzing a landscape, it is important to recognize the present-day biodiversity of these resources—for example at the Fruita Rural Historic District in Capitol Reef National Park in Utah, the landscape contains 2,500 fruit trees associated with settlement and agriculture on the Colorado Plateau (courtesy D. White).

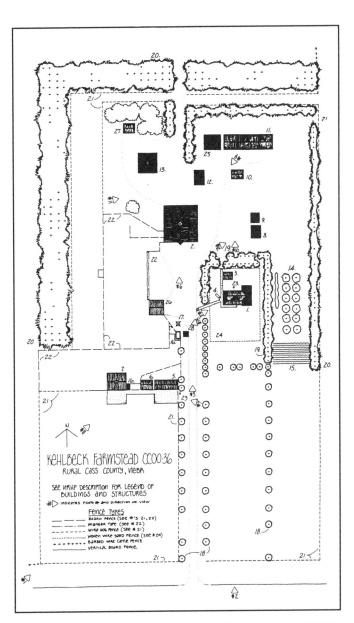

Figure 21: Integrity can involve both continuity and change. This can be evidenced by a detailed review of materials. Although the surface material has changed on some roads through the Port Oneida (near Empire, Michigan) community, the character-defining alignment, width and rows of Sugar Maple trees remain intact. (courtesy NPS, Midwest Region).

Figures 22 and 23: The plan for the Kehlbeck Farmstead, located in Cass County in Southeastern Nebraska, illustrates a well-planned, and aesthetically arranged general farm complex of the twentieth century. The farmstead is composed of 23 contributing and 5 non-contributing resources. Integrity was judged uniformly high because many character-defining resources were present and the visual and spatial relationships intact. Note the varied graphic techniques used to document a variety of fence types, and, the key to photographs illustrating the various landscape features and spatial relationships. The photograph above, labeled #3 on the farmstead, is looking north along the farm lane allee. (courtesy National Register Files)

443

LANDSCAPE INTERPRETATION

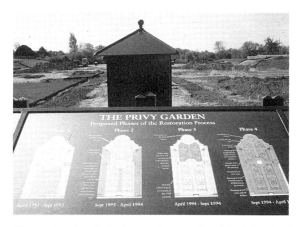

Figures A and B: Archeology and restoration of the Privy Garden at Hampton Court Palace gardens, England. The project is being interpreted to the public in the garden, an indoor exhibition and a multimedia show. The outdoor interpretive display, (above left) includes period plans, aerial photographs and historic images that detail the history of the garden and current work, 1994. (courtesy the author)

Landscape interpretation is the process of providing the visitor with tools to experience the landscape as it existed during its period of significance, or as it evolved to its present state. These tools may vary widely, from a focus on existing features to the addition of interpretive elements. These could include exhibits, self-guided brochures, or a new representation of a lost feature. The nature of the cultural landscape, especially its level of significance, integrity, and the type of visitation anticipated may frame the interpretive approach. Landscape interpretation may be closely linked to the integrity and condition of the landscape, and therefore, its ability to convey the historic character and character-defining features of the past. If a landscape has high integrity, the interpretive approach may be to direct visitors to surviving historic features without introducing obtrusive interpretive devices such as free-standing signs. For landscapes with a diminished integrity, where limited or no fabric remains, the interpretive emphasis may be on using extant features and visual aids (e.g. markers, photographs, etc.) to help visitors visualize the resource as it existed in the past. The primary goal in these situations is to educate the visitor about the landscape's historic themes, associations and lost character-defining features or broader historical, social and physical landscape contexts.

should also be considered in the decision-making process. Therefore, a cultural landscape's preservation plan and the treatment selected will consider a broad array of dynamic and interrelated considerations. It will often take the form of a plan with detailed guidelines or specifications.

Adopting such a plan, in concert with a preservation maintenance plan (page 18-19), acknowledges a cultural landscape's ever-changing existence and the interrelationship of treatment and ongoing maintenance. Performance standards, scheduling and record keeping of maintenance activities on a day-to-day or month-to-month basis, may then be planned for. Treatment, management, and maintenance proposals can be developed by a broad range of professionals and with expertise in such fields as landscape preservation, horticulture, ecology, and landscape maintenance.

The selection of a primary treatment for the landscape, utilizing the Secretary of the Interior's Standards for the Treatment of Historic Properties, establishes an overall historic preservation approach, as well as a philosophical framework from which to operate. Selecting a treatment is based on many factors. They include management and interpretation objectives for the property as a whole, the period(s) of significance, integrity, and condition of individual landscape features.

For all treatments, the landscape's existing conditions and its ability to convey historic significance should be carefully considered. For example, the life work, design philosophy and extant legacy of an individual designer should all be understood for a designed landscape such as an estate, prior to treatment selection. For a vernacular landscape, such as a battlefield containing a largely intact mid-nineteenth century family farm, the uniqueness of that agrarian complex within a local, regional, state, and national context should be considered in selecting a treatment.

The overall historic preservation approach and treatment approach can ensure the proper retention, care, and repair of landscapes and their inherent features.[11] In short, the Standards act as a preservation and management tool for cultural landscapes. The four potential treatments are described in the box opposite.

Landscape treatments can range from simple, inexpensive preservation actions, to complex major restoration or reconstruction projects. The progressive framework is inverse in proportion to the retention of historic features and materials. Generally, preservation involves the least change, and is the most respectful of historic materials. It maintains the form and material of the existing landscape. Rehabilitation usually accommodates contemporary

Figure 24: On some occasions, especially larger landscapes, it is possible to have a primary treatment, with discrete, or secondary areas of another treatment. This is most common for an individual feature in a larger landscape. At the Eugene and Carlotta O'Neill Historic Site, Danville, California the primary treatment selected for the courtyard was restoration. When accommodating universal accessibility requirements, the introduction of a grass paver walk was installed which warranted the removal of a few historic shrubs. This discrete project would be considered a rehabilitation treatment. (courtesy Patricia M. O'Donnell)

TREATMENTS FOR CULTURAL LANDSCAPES

Prior to undertaking work on a landscape, a treatment plan or similar document should be developed. The four primary treatments identified in the Secretary of the Interior's Standards for the Treatment of Historic Properties[12], are :

Preservation is defined as the act or process of applying measures necessary to sustain the existing form, integrity, and materials of an historic property. Work, including preliminary measures to protect and stabilize the property, generally focuses upon the ongoing maintenance and repair of historic materials and features rather than extensive replacement and new construction. New additions are not within the scope of this treatment; however, the limited and sensitive upgrading of mechanical, electrical and plumbing systems and other code-required work to make properties functional is appropriate within a preservation project.

Rehabilitation is defined as the act or process of making possible a compatible use for a property through repair, alterations, and additions while preserving those portions or features which convey its historical or cultural values.

Restoration is defined as the act or process of accurately depicting the form, features, and character of a property as it appeared at a particular period of time by means of the removal of features from other periods in its history and reconstruction of missing features from the restoration period. The limited and sensitive upgrading of mechanical, electrical and plumbing systems and other code-required work to make properties functional is appropriate within a restoration project.

Reconstruction is defined as the act or process of depicting, by means of new construction, the form, features, and detailing of a non-surviving site, landscape, building, structure, or object for the purpose of replicating its appearance at a specific period of time and in its historic location.

Figures 25 and 26: When the American Elm (Ulmus americana) was plagued with Dutch Elm Disease many historic properties relied on the Japanese Zelkova (Zelkova serrata) as a substitute plant. As illustrated, the overall form and scale of these trees is really quite different, and would therefore not be an appropriate substitute plant material under a restoration or reconstruction treatment.

alterations or additions without altering significant historic features or materials, with successful projects involving minor to major change. Restoration or reconstruction attempts to recapture the appearance of a property, or an individual feature at a particular point in time, as confirmed by detailed historic documentation. These last two treatments most often require the greatest degree of intervention and thus, the highest level of documentation.

In all cases, treatment should be executed at the appropriate level reflecting the condition of the landscape, with repair work identifiable upon close inspection and/or indicated in supplemental interpretative information. When repairing or replacing a feature, every effort should be made to achieve visual and physical compatibility. Historic materials should be matched in design, scale, color and texture.

A landscape with a high level of integrity and authenticity may suggest preservation as the primary treatment. Such a treatment may emphasize protection, stabilization, cyclical maintenance, and repair of character-defining landscape features. Changes over time that are part of the landscape's continuum and are significant in their own right may be

Figure 27: The historic birch allee at Stan Hywet Hall, Akron, Ohio was suffering from borer infestation and leaf miner. Dying trees were topped and basal sprout growth encouraged. Next, trees were selectively thinned, and ultimately, when the new growth matured, older trunks were removed. Original rootstock and genetic material were preserved. As illustrated, this preservation treatment took fifteen years to realize. (courtesy Child Associates)

Figure 28: Patterns on the land have been preserved through the continuation of traditional uses such as the grape fields at the Sterling Vineyards in Calistoga, California. (courtesy author)

Figures 29: Rehabilitation was selected as the primary treatment for Columbus Park, Chicago, Illinois. Originally designed and executed between 1917 and 1920 by Jens Jensen, the waterfall, cascades, rocky brook and associated landscape, are well documented and possesses a high level of integrity. (courtesy author)

Figure 30, 31: A 75-mile portion of Skyline Drive at Shenandoah National Park overlooking the Blue Ridge Mountains of Virginia required the rehabilitation of a 22"-high, dry-laid stone wall. The new wall was built to a height of 27" – code normally requires a height of 36". The wall was constructed of percast concrete, clad with split stone and mortar joints. To achieve visual compatibility recessed mortar joints were arranged in a random pattern (courtesy Robert R. Page)

MUSIC PAVILION, TOWER GROVE PARK, ST. LOUIS.

retained, while changes that are not significant, yet do not encroach upon or erode character may also be maintained. Preservation entails the essential operations to safeguard existing resources. (Figures 27-28)

Rehabilitation is often selected in response to a contemporary use or need—ideally such an approach is compatible with the landscape's historic character and historic use. Rehabilitation may preserve existing fabric along with introducing some compatible changes, new additions and alterations. Rehabilitation may be desirable at a private residence in a historic district where the homeowner's goal is to develop an appropriate landscape treatment for a front yard, or in a public park where a support area is needed for its maintenance operations. (Figures 29-31)

When the most important goal is to portray a landscape and its character-defining features at an exact period of time, restoration is selected as the primary treatment. Unlike preservation and rehabilitation, interpreting the landscape's continuum or evolution is not the objective. Restoration may include the removal of features from other periods and/or the construction of missing or lost features and materials from the reconstruction period. In all cases, treatment should be substantiated by the historic research findings and existing conditions documentation. Restoration and reconstruction treatment work should avoid the creation of a landscape whose features did not exist historically. For example, if features from an earlier period did not co-exist with extant features from a later period that are being retained, their restoration would not be appropriate. (Figures 32-34)

In rare cases, when evidence is sufficient to avoid conjecture, and no other property exists that can adequately explain a certain period of history, reconstruction may be utilized to depict a vanished landscape. The accuracy of this work is critical. In cases where topography and the subsurface of soil have not been disturbed, research and existing conditions findings may be confirmed by thorough archeological investigations. Here too, those features that are intact should be repaired as necessary, retaining the original historic features to the greatest extent possible. The greatest danger in reconstruction is creating a false picture of history.

False historicism in every treatment should be avoided. This applies to individual features as well as the entire landscape. Examples of inappropriate work include the introduction of historic-looking benches that are actually a new design, a fanciful gazebo placed in what was once an open meadow, executing an unrealized historic design, or designing a historic-looking landscape for a relocated historic structure within "restoration."

Figure 32-34: Tower Grove Park in St. Louis, Missouri, is a National Historic Landmark. The music pavilion, just north of the main drive is a circular lawn area with radiating walks, white marble busts of eminent composers, walks, and curb. The area was in general decline, especially the marble busts which were suffering from acid rain damage. Based on the excellent documentation in nineteenth century annual reports, postcards and photographic images, this area was recently restored. Illustrated above are a sample historic view, work in progress and the completed restoration project. (courtesy Tower Grove Park)

Figure 35-37: Central Park has developed an in-house historic preservation crew to undertake small projects. A specialized crew has been trained to specifically repair and rebuild rustic furnishings. As illustrated, the restoration of the Dene rustic shelter was achieved by constructing it in the Ramble compound, moving in-place opposite 67th street and completed. (courtesy Central Park Conservancy)

Developing a Preservation Maintenance Plan and Implementation Strategy

Throughout the preservation planning process, it is important to ensure that existing landscape features are retained. Preservation maintenance is the practice of monitoring and controlling change in the landscape to ensure that its historic integrity is not altered and features are not lost. This is particularly important during the research and long-term treatment planning process. To be effective, the maintenance program must have a guiding philosophy, approach or strategy; an understanding of preservation maintenance techniques; and a system for documenting changes in the landscape.

The philosophical approach to maintenance should coincide with the landscape's current stage in the preservation planning process. A Cultural Landscape Report and Treatment Plan can take several years to complete, yet during this time managers and property owners will likely need to address immediate issues related to the decline, wear, decay, or damage of landscape features. Therefore, initial maintenance operations may focus on the stabilization and protection of all landscape features to provide temporary, often emergency measures to prevent deterioration, failure, or loss, without altering the site's existing character.

After a Treatment Plan is implemented, the approach to preservation maintenance may be modified to reflect the objectives defined by this plan. The detailed specifications prepared in the Treatment Plan relating to the retention, repair, removal, or replacement of features in the landscape should guide and inform a comprehensive preservation maintenance program. This would include schedules for monitoring and routine maintenance, appropriate preservation maintenance procedures, as well as ongoing record keeping of work performed. For vegetation, the preservation maintenance program would also include thresholds for growth or change in character, appropriate pruning methods, propagation and replacement procedures.

To facilitate operations, a property may be divided into discrete management zones (Figure 41). These zones are sometimes defined during the Cultural Landscape Report process and are typically based on historically defined areas. Alternatively, zones created for maintenance practices and priorities could be used. Examples of maintenance zones would include woodlands, lawns, meadow, specimen trees, and hedges.

Training of maintenance staff in preservation maintenance skills is essential. Preservation maintenance practices differ from standard maintenance practices because of the focus on perpetuating the historic character or use of the landscape rather than beautification. For example, introducing new varieties of turf, roses or trees is likely to be inappropriate. Substantial earth moving (or movement of soil) may be inappropriate where there are potential archeological resources. An old hedge or shrub should be rejuvenated, or propagated, rather than removed and replaced. A mature specimen tree may require cabling and careful monitoring to ensure that it is not a threat to visitor safety. Through training programs and with the assistance of preservation maintenance specialists, each property could develop maintenance specifications for the care of landscape features.

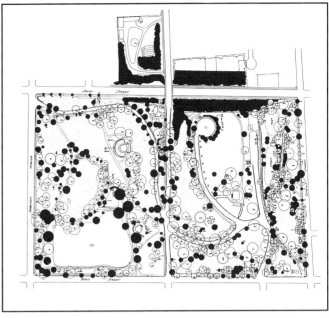

Figure 38 and 39 (above, left and right): The importance of landscape analysis and its ability to inform treatment and maintenance decisions is reflected in these two plans for Downing Park, Newburgh, New York. The plan, rendered in black, top left, illustrates all extant historic plants, while the plan, top right, depicts plantings which are non-historic or invasive for removal or relocation outside of the historic park. (courtesy LANDSCAPES)

Figure 41 (below): A small property of under an acre may only have a few management zones including lawn, trees over lawn, shrub and herbaceous borders. Larger, more complex landscapes such as Jamaica Pond Park, Boston and Brookline, Massachusetts, contains a broader range of management zones including: forests, trees over grass—broad areas, trees over grass—narrow areas, meadows, and mown grass for active recreation amenities or passive use. (courtesy Walmsley/Pressley Joint Venture)

Figure 40: A management decision was made to place a fence around a sentinel tree in Balboa Park, San Diego, California. The fence protects the specimen from root damage—impact from excessive pedestrian compaction or lawn mower damage. (courtesy author).

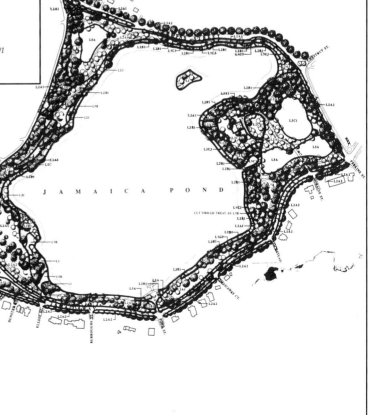

SHRUBS
L3A   NATURALIZED SHRUBS
L3B   ORNAMENTAL SHRUBS
L3C   HEDGES FORMAL
L3D   HEDGES INFORMAL
L3E   ROSEBEDS

GROUND COVERS
L4   GROUND COVER

GRASS
L5A   MEADOW
L5B   LOW MAINTENANCE GRASS
L5C1 HIGH MAINTENANCE GRASS,
      WIDE, FOR SPORTS
L5C2 HIGH MAINTENANCE GRASS,
      WIDE, FOR AMENITY
L5C3 HIGH MAINTENANCE GRASS,
      SMALL

DEVELOPING A PRESERVATION MAINTENANCE GUIDE

In the past, there was rarely adequate record-keeping to fully understand the ways a landscape was maintained. This creates gaps in our research findings. Today, we recognize that planning for ongoing maintenance and on-site applications should be documented—both routinely and comprehensively. An annual work program or calendar records the frequency of maintenance work on built or natural landscape features. It can also monitor the age, health and vigor of vegetation. For example, on-site assessments may document the presence of weeds, pests, dead leaves, pale color, wilting, soil compaction—all of which signal particular maintenance needs. For built elements, the deterioration of paving or drainage systems may be noted and the need for repair or replacement indicated before hazards develop. An overall maintenance program can assist in routine and cyclic maintenance of the landscape and can also guide long term treatment projects.

To help structure a comprehensive maintenance operation that is responsive to staff, budget, and maintenance priorities, the National Park Service has developed two computer-driven programs for its own landscape resources. A Maintenance Management Program (MM) is designed to assist maintenance managers in their efforts to plan, organize, and direct the park maintenance system. An Inventory and Condition Assessment Program (ICAP) is designed to complement

MM by providing a system for inventorying, assessing conditions, and for providing corrective work recommendations for all site features.

Another approach to documenting maintenance and recording changes over time is to develop a manual or computerized graphic information system. Such a system should have the capability to include plans and photographs that would record a site's living collection of plant materials. (Also see discussion of the use of photography under Preparing Existing Conditions Plans, page 5.) This may be achieved using a computer-aided drafting program along with an integrated database management system.

To guide immediate and ongoing maintenance, a systematic and flexible approach has been developed by the Olmsted Center for Landscape Preservation. Working with National Park Service landscape managers and maintenance specialists, staff assemble information and make recommendations for the care of individual landscape features.

Each landscape feature is inspected in the field to document existing conditions and identify field work needed. Recommendations include maintenance procedures that are sensitive to the integrity of the landscape.

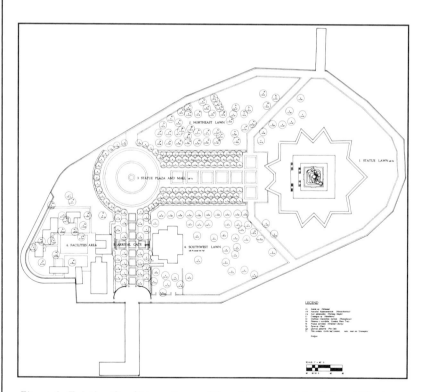

Figure A- Existing Conditions: A map of the existing trees at the Statue of Liberty National Monument is used to indicate necessary preservation maintenance work (Drawn by Margaret Coffin, 1992)

Figure B - Field Inventory, Inspection, and work needed: Within areas of the landscape, each feature is assigned a field identification number. An inspection is conducted to assess the condition, potential problems, such as deadwood or integral decay, and specify work needed. A map (above) is used to locate features that require attention)

Figure C - Feature Data: For each feature that requires special care, a detailed sheet is developed. This contains notes on when to monitor and carry out work, specific procedures, cite potential problems, and perform repair or replacement.

Figure D - Calendar for Monitoring and for Work: All feature-specific monitoring and work recommendations are combined into one seasonal calendar for all areas of the landscape to ensure that important work activities are not overlooked.

Figure E - Record Keeping: A record sheet is created for each type of feature. Maintenance staff may record information relating to changes in condition, major work performed, removal, replacement, propagation and any other events. As records are added too through the years, they become a valuable source of documentation of the landscape's history.

Because landscapes change through the seasons, specifications for ongoing preservation maintenance should be organized in a calendar format. During each season or month, the calendar can be referenced to determine when, where, and how preservation maintenance is needed. For example, for some trees structural pruning is best done in the late winter while other trees are best pruned in the late summer. Serious pests are monitored at specific times of the year, in certain stages of their life cycle. This detailed calendar will in turn identify staff needs and work priorities.

Depending on the level of sophistication desired, one approach to documenting maintenance data and recording change over time is to use a computerized geographical or visual information system.[13] Such a system would have the capability to include plans and photographs that would focus on a site's landscape features.

If a computer is not available, a manual or notebook can be developed to organize and store important information. This approach allows managers to start at any level of detail and to begin to collect and organize information about landscape features (see Box opposite and above). The value of these maintenance records cannot be overstated. These records will be used in the future by historians to understand how the landscape has evolved with the ongoing care of the maintenance staff.

Recording Treatment Work and Future Research Recommendations

The last and ongoing step in the preservation planning process records the treatment work as carried out. It may include a series of as-built drawings, supporting photographic materials, specifications and a summary assessment. New technologies that have been successfully used should be

highlighted. Ideally, this information should be shared with interested national organizations for further dissemination and evaluation.

The need for further research or additional activities should also be documented. This may include site-specific or contextual historical research, archeological investigations, pollen analysis, search for rare or unusual plant materials, or, material testing for future applications.

Finally, in consultation with a conservator or archivist—to maximize the benefit of project work and to minimize the potential of data loss—all primary documents should be organized and preserved as archival materials. This may include field notes, maps, drawings, photographs, material samples, oral histories and other relative information.

Summary

The planning, treatment, and maintenance of cultural landscapes requires a multi-disciplinary approach. In landscapes, such as parks and playgrounds, battlefields, cemeteries, village greens, and agricultural land preserves—more than any other type of historic resource—communities rightly presume a sense of stewardship. It is often this grass roots commitment that has been a catalyst for current research and planning initiatives. Individual residential properties often do not require the same level of public outreach, yet a systematic planning process will assist in making educated treatment, management and maintenance decisions.

Wise stewardship protects the character, and or spirit of a place by recognizing history as change over time. Often, this also involves our own respectful changes through treatment. The potential benefits from the preservation of cultural landscapes are enormous. Landscapes provide scenic, economic, ecological, social, recreational and educational opportunities that help us understand ourselves as individuals, communities and as a nation. Their ongoing preservation can yield an improved quality of life for all, and, above all, a sense of place or identity for future generations.

Selected Reading

Birnbaum, Charles A, guest editor. *Preservation Forum*. "Focus on Landscape Preservation". Washington, D.C.: National Trust for Historic Preservation, Volume 7, No. 3, May/June 1992.

Buggey Susan, guest editor. *APT Bulletin. Special Issue: Conserving Historic Landscapes*. Fredericksburg, VA: Association for Preservation Technology International, Volume XXIV, No. 3-4, 1992.

Burns, John A, and the Staff of HABS/HAER. *Recording Historic Structures*. American Institute of Architects Press, 1989. (Includes chapter on the documentation of Meridian Hill Park, pp. 206-219.)

Diehl, Janet and Thomas S. Barrett, et al. *The Conservation Easement Handbook. Managing Land Conservation and Historic Preservation Easement Programs*, The Land Trust Exchange (now Alliance) and the Trust for Public Land, 1988.

International Committee of Historic Gardens and Sites, ICOMOS-IFLA. *Jardins et Sites Historiques*, Scientific Journal. ICOMOS 1993. Compilation of papers on the subject, in both english and french.

Kelso, William M., and Rachel Most. *Earth Patterns: Essays in Landscape Archaeology*. Charlottesville, VA: University Press of Virginia, 1990.

Stokes, Samuel, N., et al. *Saving America's Countryside: A Guide to Rural Conservation*. Baltimore and London: John Hopkins University Press, 1989.

Tishler, William, editor. American Landscape *Architecture, Designers and Places*. Washington, DC: The Preservation Press, 1989.

Several publications available from the National Park Service deal directly with the preservation of historic landscapes. These include:

America's Landscape Legacy, Brochure, Preservation Assistance Division, 1992.

Guidelines for the Treatment of Historic Landscapes, Preservation Assistance Division, 1992 (Draft).

Case Studies in Landscape Preservation, Preservation Assistance Division in cooperation with the Alliance for Landscape Preservation, 1995.

Cultural Landscapes Bibliography: An Annotated Bibliography of Resources in the National Park System, Park Historic Architecture Division, 1992.

Historic Landscape Directory; A Source Book of Agencies, Organizations, and Institutions Providing Information on Historic Landscape Preservation, Preservation Assistance Division, 1991.

CRM, Cultural Resource Management, Thematic Issues: *The Preservation of Cultural Landscapes*, Volume 14, No.6,

1991; *A Reality Check for Our Nation's Parks*, Volume 16, No. 4, 1993; *Historic Transportation Corridors*, Volume 16, No. 11, 1993; and, *The Interpretation of Cultural Landscapes*, Volume 17, No. 8, 1994.

Pioneers of American Landscape Design: An Annotated Bibliography, Preservation Assistance Division, 1993 (ISBN:0-16-041974-3).

Making Educated Decisions: A Landscape Preservation Bibliography, Preservation Assistance Division, 1994 (ISBN:0-16-045145-0)

National Register Bulletin 18: How to Evaluate and Nominate Designed Historic Landscapes; National Register Bulletin 30: Guidelines for Evaluating and Documenting Rural Historic Landscapes; National Register Bulletin 40: Guidelines for Evaluating and Registering Battlefields; and, National Register Bulletin 41: Guidelines for Evaluating and Registering Cemeteries, Interagency Resources Division.

Endnotes

[1] The cultural landscape definitions are contained in *NPS-28, Cultural Resource Management Guideline*, Release No. 4, 1994, National Park Service.

[2] For an expanded list of offices to contact, see *America's Landscape Legacy* brochure. Free from the National Park Service Preservation Assistance Division.

[3] From Kelso, William, *A Report on the Archeological Excavation at Monticello, Charlottesville, VA, 1979-1981*, Thomas Jefferson Memorial Foundation, 1982.

[4] Lewis, Pierce, "Common Landscapes as Historic Documents," Lubar, Steven and Kingery, W. David (eds.), *Essays on Material Culture*, Smithsonian Institution Press, Washington, DC, 1993, p. 138.

[5] Meinig, D. W. "The Beholding Eye: Ten Versions of the Same Scene," *The Interpretation of Ordinary Landscapes*, Oxford University Press, New York, 1979, pp. 33-48.

[6] See National Park Service *National Register Bulletins* under Selected Reading (opposite).

[7] The Historic American Buildings Survey, HABS, has generated standards for landscape documentation that they now utilize on a number of projects. Specifically, a case study on recording historic landscapes is included in *Recording Historic Structures*, pp. 206-219. See Selected Reading (opposite).

[8] This is being undertaken with technical assistance from the Olmsted Center for Landscape Preservation a partnership between the National Park Service and the Arnold Arboretum of Harvard University that provides cultural landscape technical assistance, technology development and training.

[9] See *National Register Bulletin 16A: How to Complete the National Register Registration Form*. Washington, D.C.: U.S. Department of the Interior, National Park Service, Interagency Resources Division, 1991.

[10] Ibid.

[11] The standards are general principles for the treatment of buildings, structures, sites, objects, districts and landscapes. The treatment standards are one set of standards included in the broader group known as the *Secretary of the Interior's Standards for Archaeology and Historic Preservation*.

[12] The Secretary of the Interior is responsible for establishing professional standards and providing advice on the preservation and protection of all cultural resources listed on or eligible for the National Register of Historic Places. For a copy of the brochure, *The Secretary of the Interior's Standards for the Treatment of Historic Properties*, 1992 contact the National Park Service Preservation Assistance Division (424) Box 37127 Washington, DC 20013-7127.

[13] A visual information system, a computer-aided mapping program with a linked database, has been developed for the historic landscape at the Frederick Olmsted National Historic Site. Data can be accessed directly from a digitized map such as information on each plant including identification, age, location, size, condition, and maintenance history.

Acknowledgements

This publication has been prepared pursuant to the National Historic Preservation Act of 1966, as amended, which directs the Secretary of the Interior to develop and make information concerning historic properties. Comments on the usefulness of this publication may be directed to H. Ward Jandl, Deputy Chief, Preservation Assistance Division, National Park Service, P. O. Box 37127, Washington, D.C. 20013-7127.

The author, Charles A. Birnbaum, Coordinator, Historic Landscape Initiative, Preservation Assistance Division, National Park Service would like to acknowledge the assistance of H. Ward Jandl and Kay Weeks. The Olmsted Center for Landscape Preservation at the Frederick Law Olmsted National Historic Site including Margie Coffin, Lauren Meier, Nora Mitchell, and Charlie Pepper provided invaluable support. In particular, the proposed rewrite on preservation maintenance and historic plant materials was written by Margie Coffin. Significant contributions were also made by Patricia M. O'Donnell, Linda McClelland, Ellen Lipsey, Christine Capella Peters, Robert Page, Ian Firth and Robert Melnick. Useful comments and technical assistance were provided by regional NPS staff (Mary Hughes, Lucy Lawliss, Jill Cowley, Sherda Williams, Michael Crowe, Robbyn Jackson) and staff at the Preservation Assistance Division (Cheryl Wagner, Michael Auer and Anne Grimmer).

37

Appropriate Methods for Reducing Lead-Paint Hazards in Historic Housing

Sharon C. Park, AIA, and Douglas C. Hicks

Lead-based paint, a toxic material, was widely used in North America on both the exteriors and interiors of buildings until well into the second half of the twentieth century. If a "historic" place is broadly defined in terms of time as having attained an age of fifty years, this means that almost every historic house contains some lead-based paint. In its deteriorated form, it produces paint chips and lead-laden dust particles that are a known health hazard to both children and adults. Children are particularly at risk when they ingest lead paint dust through direct hand-to-mouth contact and from toys or pacifiers. They are also at risk when they chew lead-painted surfaces in accessible locations. In addition to its presence in houses, leaded paint

chips, lead dust, or lead-contaminated soil in play areas can elevate a child's blood lead level to a degree that measures to reduce and control the hazard should be undertaken (see Action Level Chart, page 6)

The premise of this Preservation Brief is that historic housing can be made lead-safe for children without removing significant decorative features and finishes, or architectural trimwork that may contribute to the building's historic character (see fig. 1). *Historic housing —* encompassing private dwellings and all types of rental units—is necessarily the focus of this Brief because federal and state laws primarily address the hazards of lead and

Before

After

Figure 1. A large-scale historic rehabilitation project incorporated sensitive lead-hazard reduction measures. Interior walls and woodwork were cleaned, repaired, and repainted and compatible new floor coverings added. The total project was economically sound and undertaken in a careful manner that preserved the building's historic character. Photos: Landmarks Design Associates.

lead-based paint in housing and day-care centers to protect the health of children under six years of age. Rarely are there mandated requirements for the removal of lead-based paint from non-residential buildings.

Ideally, most owners and managers should understand the health hazards created by lead-based paint and voluntarily control these hazards to protect young children. A stricter approach has been taken by some state and federal funding programs which have compliance requirements for identifying the problem, notifying tenants, and, in some cases, remedying lead hazards in housing (see Legislation Sidebar, pg.15). With new rules being written, and new products and approaches being developed, it is often difficult to find systematic and balanced methodologies for dealing with lead-based paint in historic properties.

This Preservation Brief is intended to serve as an introduction to the complex issue of historic lead-based paint and its management. It explains how to plan and implement lead-hazard control measures to strike a balance between preserving a historic building's significant materials and features and protecting human health and safety, as well as the environment. It is not meant to be a "how-to guide" for undertaking the work. Such a short-cut approach could easily result in creating a greater health risk, if proper precautions were not taken. Home renovators and construction workers should be aware that serious health problems can be caused by coming into contact with lead. For this reason, there are also laws to protect workers on the job site (see Worker Safety Sidebar, pg. 4). Controlling the amount of waste containing lead-based paint residue will also reduce the impact on the environment. All of these considerations must be weighed against the goal of providing housing that is safe for children.

Lead in Historic Paints

Lead compounds were an important component of many historic paints. Lead, in the forms of lead carbonate and lead oxides, had excellent adhesion, drying, and covering abilities. White lead, linseed oil, and inorganic pigments were the basic components for paint in the 18th, 19th, and early 20th centuries. Lead-based paint was used extensively on wooden exteriors and interior trimwork, window sash, window frames, baseboards, wainscoting, doors, frames, and high gloss wall surfaces such as those found in kitchens and bathrooms. Almost all painted metals were primed with red lead or painted with lead-based paints. Even milk (casein) and water-based paints (distemper and calcimines) could contain some lead, usually in the form of hiding agents or pigments. Varnishes sometimes contained lead. Lead compounds were also used as driers in paint and window glazing putty.

In 1978, the use of lead-based paint in residential housing was banned by the federal government. Because the hazards have been known for some time, many lead components of paint were replaced by titanium and other less toxic elements earlier in the 20th century. Since houses are periodically repainted, the most recent layer of paint will most likely *not* contain lead, but the older layers underneath probably will. Therefore, the only way to accurately determine the amount of lead present in older paint is to have it analyzed.

It is important that owners of historic properties be aware that layers of older paint can reveal a great deal about the history of a building and that paint chronology is often used to date alterations or to document decorative period colors (see figs. 2, 3). Highly significant decorative finishes, such as graining, marbleizing, stenciling, polychrome decoration, and murals should be evaluated by a painting conservator to develop the appropriate preservation treatment that will stabilize the paint and eliminate the need to remove it. If such finishes must be removed in the process of controlling lead hazards, then research, paint analysis, and documentation are advisable as a record for future research and treatment.

Figure 2. The paint chronology of this mantel, seen in the exposed paint layers in the left corner, proved it had been relocated from another room of the house. To remove a significant feature's paint history and the evidence of its original sequence of color by stripping off all the paint is inappropriate — and unnecessary — as part of a lead hazard reduction project. Careful surface preparation and repainting with lead-free top coats is recommended. Photo: NPS Files.

Figure 3. Significant architectural features and their finishes should not be removed during a project incorporating lead hazard controls. If the decorative stencilling above, or hand grained doors below, or painted murals need repair, then a paint conservator should be consulted. Once loose paint is consolidated or otherwise stabilized, a clear finish or other reversible clear protective surface or coating can be added to areas subject to impact or abrasion. Photos: NPS Files.

Planning for Lead Hazard Reduction in Historic Housing

Typical health department guidelines call for removing as much of the surfaces that contain lead-based paint as possible. *This results in extensive loss or modification of architectural features and finishes and is not appropriate for most historic properties* (see fig. 4). A great number of federally-assisted housing programs are moving away from this approach as too expensive and too dangerous to the immediate work environment. A preferred approach, consistent with *The Secretary of the Interior's Standards for the Treatment of Historic Properties*, calls for removing, controlling, or managing the hazards rather than wholesale—or even partial—removal of the historic features and finishes (fig. 5). This is generally achieved through careful cleaning and treatment of deteriorating paint, friction surfaces, surfaces accessible to young children, and lead in soil (see figs. 6, 7). Lead-based paint that it not causing a hazard is thus permitted to remain, and, in consequence, the amount of historic finishes, features and trimwork removed from a property is minimized.

Because the hazard of lead poisoning is tied to the risk of ingesting lead, careful planning can help to determine how much risk is present and how best to allocate available financial resources. An owner, with professional assistance, can protect a historic resource and make it lead-safe using this three-step planning process:

I.   Identify the historical significance of the building and architectural character of its features and finishes;

II. Undertake a risk assessment of interior and exterior surfaces to determine the hazards from lead and lead-based paint; and,

III. Evaluate the options for lead hazard control in the context of historic preservation standards.

I. Identify the historical significance of the building and architectural character of its features and finishes

The historical significance, integrity, and architectural character of the building always need to be assessed before work is undertaken that might adversely affect them. An owner may need to enlist the help of a preservation architect, building conservator or historian. The State Historic Preservation Office (SHPO) may be able to provide a list of knowledgeable preservation professionals who could assist with this evaluation.

Before

Before

After

After

Figure 4. The typical method for abating lead-based paint through substrate removal is not consistent with the Standards for Rehabilitation. In this project, all the historic trim, base panels, and the transom were removed. While the unit is lead-safe, its character has been severely altered. Figure 5 shows a similar, but successful, balance of historic preservation and lead hazard control work. Photo: NPS Files.

Figure 5. When historic interiors are rehabilitated, it is possible to remove the offending substance, such as deteriorated paint, without removing the features. In this case, the walls were repaired, and the trim and base panels were stripped of paint to a sound substrate, then repainted. Photos: Landmarks Design Associates.

Worker Safety

Current worker safety standards were established by OSHA's 29 CFR Part 1926, Lead Exposure in Construction, Interim Final Rule, which became effective June 3, 1993. These standards base levels of worker protection on exposure to airborne lead dust. They are primarily targeted to persons working within the construction industry, but apply to any workers who are exposed to lead dust for

Low-level heat guns can be used to remove lead-based paint from significant historic windows and trimwork, but a worker exposed to lead dust over an extended period of time must be protected from the hazards created during the process of paint removal. Photo: Williamsport Preservation Training Center.

longer than a specific amount of time and duration. The Interim Final Rule establishes an action level of 30 micrograms of lead dust per cubic meter of air (30 ug/m^3) based on an eight hour, time-weighted average, as the level at which employers must initiate compliance activities; and it also establishes 50 ug/m^3 of lead dust as the permitted exposure level (PEL) for workers.

The standard identifies responsibilities before, during, and after the actual abatement activity necessary to protect the worker. Before the project begins, it requires an exposure assessment, a written compliance plan, initial medical surveillance, and training. The exposure assessment determines whether a worker may be exposed to lead. OSHA has identified a number of work tasks expected to produce dust levels between 50 and 500 ug/m^3 of air, including manual demolition, manual scraping, manual sanding, heat gun applications, general cleanup, and power tool use when the power tool is equipped with a dust collection system. It is an OSHA requirement that, at a minimum, a HEPA filtered half-face respirator with a protection factor of 10 be used for these operations. Initial blood lead level (BLL) base lines are established for each worker. Actual dust levels are monitored by air sampling of representative work activities, generally by an industrial hygienist or an environmental monitoring firm. Protective equipment is determined by the dust level. For all workers exposed at, or above, the action level for over 30 days in a 12-month period, BLLs are tested on a regular basis of every 2 months for the first 6 months and every 6 months thereafter. After completing a project, maintenance, medical surveillance, and recordkeeping responsibilities continue.

HEPA vacuums, HEPA respirators, and HEPA filters, which substantially reduce exposure to lead dust, are available through laboratory safety and supply catalogs and vendors.

Copies of 29 CFR Part 1926, Lead Exposure in Construction: Interim Final Rule, are available from the Department of Labor, Occupational Safety and Health Administration, or may be found in any library with a current edtion of the Code of Federal Regulation (CFR).

Features and finishes of a historic building that exhibit distinctive characteristics of an architectural style; represent work by specialized craftsmen; or possess high artistic value should be identified so they can be protected and preserved during treatment. When it is absolutely necessary to remove a significant architectural feature or finish—as noted in the first two priorities listed below—it should be replaced with a new feature and finish that matches in design, detail, color, texture, and, in most cases, material.

Figure 6. Deteriorating operable windows often contribute to lead dust in a house. Peeling paint and small particles from abraded surfaces collect in window troughs or sills and are then carried inside by air currents, settling on floors. When the lead dust mixes with regular house dust, it can easily be ingested by a child through hand to mouth contact. In homes with small children, floors and other surfaces should be kept as clean as possible to avoid lead contamination.

Figure 7. Chalking exterior paint can cause dangerous lead levels in soil around a house. Lead levels are usually highest in the one foot wide area adjacent to the building foundation. In these cases, the existing soil should be replaced with new soil or sod. This is particularly important if children and small pets play in contaminated areas, then inadvertently track the dirt inside.

Finally, features and finishes that characterize simple, vernacular buildings should be retained and preserved; in the process of removing hazards, there are usually reasonable options for their protection. Wholesale removal of historic trim, and other seemingly less important historic material, undermines a building's overall character and integrity and, thus, is never recommended.

For each historic property, features will vary in significance. As part of a survey of each historic property (see figure 8), a list of priorities should be made, in this order:

- *Highly significant features and finishes that should always be protected and preserved;*

- *Significant features and finishes that should be carefully repaired or, if necessary, replaced in-kind or to match all visual qualities; and*

- *Non-significant or altered areas where removal, rigid enclosure, or replacement could occur.*

This hierarchy gives an owner a working guide for making decisions about appropriate methods of removing lead paint.

Before

After

Figure 8. A survey of the property will help establish priorities for treatment based on its historical significance and physical condition. In this 1878 plank house, the original interlocking planks, corner details, projecting rafter tails, and original windows were considered highly significant features and were carefully stripped of failing paint using chemical poultices and HEPA sanding, then repainted. The less significant, but character-defining, painted porch flooring was replaced in new, but matching material. The non-historic porch screening was removed entirely. Photo before: Bryan Blundell; Photo after: Deborah Birch.

II. Undertake a risk assessment of interior and exterior surfaces to determine hazards from lead and lead-based paint.

While it can be assumed that most historic housing contains lead-based paint, it cannot be assumed that it is causing a health risk and should be removed. The purpose of a risk assessment is to determine, through testing and evaluation, where hazards from lead warrant remedial action (see fig. 9). Testing by a specialist can be done on paint, soil, or lead dust either on-site or in a laboratory using methods such as x-ray fluorescence (XRF) analyzers, chemicals, dust wipe tests, and atomic absorption spectroscopy. Risk assessments can be fairly low cost investigations of the location, condition, and severity of lead hazards found in house dust, soil, water, and deteriorating paint. Risk assessments will also address other sources of lead from hobbies, crockery, water, and the parents' work environment. A public health office should be able to provide names of certified risk assessors, paint

inspectors, and testing laboratories. These services are critical when owners are seeking to implement measures to reduce suspected lead hazards in housing, day-care centers, or when extensive rehabilitations are planned.

The risk assessment should record:

- *the paint's location*
- *the paint's condition*
- *lead content of paint and soil*
- *the type of surface (friction; accessible to children for chewing; impact)*
- *how much lead dust is actively present*
- *how the family uses and cares for the house*
- *the age of the occupants who might come into contact with lead paint.*

a

b

c

Figure 9. A variety of testing methods are used to establish how much lead is in paint and where this paint is located: a home test kit (a) is a good screening device to determine if lead is present, but it should not be relied upon exclusively; an X-ray Fluorescence machine or scanner (b), used by a licensed professional, determines, without disturbing the surface, if lead is present in underlying layers of paint; and a dust wipe test (c), sent to a laboratory for processing, can be used as either a clearance test, once work is completed, or as a monitoring device to determine if lead dust is present on surfaces. Paint chips can also be sent to a laboratory for analysis to determine the exact amount of lead by weight in a sample.

ACTION LEVELS

Readers should become familiar with terminology and basic levels that trigger concern and/or action. Check with the appropriate authorities if you have questions and to verify applicable action levels which may change over time.

Blood lead levels: Generally from drawn blood and not a finger stick test which can be unreliable. Units are measured in micrograms per deciliter (ug/dl) and reflect the 1995 standards from the Centers for Disease Control:

Children: 10 ug/dl; level of concern; find source of lead

15 ug/dl and above; intervention, counseling, medical monitoring.

20 ug/dl and above; medical treatment

Adults: 25 ug/dl; level of concern; find source of lead

50 ug/dl ; OSHA standard for medical removal from the worksite

Lead in paint: Differing methods report results in differing units. Lead is considered a potential hazard if *above the following* levels, but can be a hazard at lower levels, if improperly handled. These are the current numbers as identified by the Department of Housing and Urban Development (1995).

Lab analysis of samples:

5,000 milligram per kilogram (mg/kg) or 5,000 parts per million (ppm), or

0.5% lead by weight.

XRF reading: in milligram per centimeter squared

1 mg/cm^2

lead dust wipe test: in micrograms per square foot

Floors	100 ug/ft^2;
Window sills	500 ug/ft^2;
Window troughs	800 ug/ft^2

Lead in soil: high contact bare play areas, listed as parts per million (ppm):

concern:	400 ppm
interim control	2,000 ppm
hazard abatement	5,000 ppm

It is important from a health standpoint that future tenants, painters, and construction workers know that lead-based paint is present, even under treated surfaces, in order to take precautions when work is undertaken in areas that will generate lead dust. Whenever mitigation work is completed, it is important to have a clearance test using the *dust wipe method* to ensure that lead-laden dust generated during the work does not remain at levels above those established by the Environmental Protection Agency (EPA) and the Department of Housing and Urban Development (HUD) (see Action Levels Chart, above). A building file should be maintained and updated whenever any additional lead hazard control work is completed.

Hazards should be removed, mitigated, or managed in the order of their health threat, as identified in a risk assessment (with 1. the greatest risk and 8. the least dangerous):

1. Peeling, chipping, flaking, and chewed interior lead-based paint and surfaces

2. Lead dust on interior surfaces

3. High lead in soil levels around the house and in play areas (check state requirements)

4. Deteriorated exterior painted surfaces and features

5. Friction surfaces subject to abrasion (windows, doors, painted floors)

6. Accessible, chewable surfaces (sills, rails) if small children are present

7. Impact surfaces (baseboards and door jambs)

8. Other interior surfaces showing age or deterioration (walls and ceilings)

III. Evaluate options for hazard control in the context of historic preservation standards.

The Secretary of the Interior's Standards for the Treatment of Historic Properties—established principles used to evaluate work that may impact the integrity and significance of National Register properties—can help guide suitable health control methods. The *preservation standards* call for the protection of historic materials and historic character of buildings through stabilization, conservation, maintenance, and repair. The *rehabilitation standards* call for the repair of historic materials with replacement of a character-defining feature appropriate only when its deterioration or damage is so extensive that repair is infeasible. From a preservation standpoint, selecting a hazard control method that removes *only* the deteriorating paint, or that involves some degree of repair, is always preferable to the total replacement of a historic feature.

By tying the remedial work to the areas of risk, it is possible to limit the amount of intrusive work on delicate or aging features of a building without jeopardizing the health and safety of the occupants. To make historic housing lead-safe, the gentlest method possible should be used to remove the offending substance—lead-laden dust, visible paint chips, lead in soil, or extensively deteriorated paint. Overly aggressive abatement may damage or destroy much more historic material than is necessary to remove lead paint, such as abrading historic surfaces. Another reason for targeting paint removal is to limit the amount of lead dust on the work site. This, in turn, helps avoid expensive worker protection, cleanup, and disposal of larger amounts of hazardous waste.

Whenever extensive amounts of lead must be removed from a property, or when methods of removing toxic substances will impact the environment, it is extremely important that the owner be aware of the issues surrounding worker safety, environmental controls, and proper disposal (see fig. 10, 11). Appropriate architectural, engineering and environmental professionals should be consulted when lead hazard projects are complex.

Following are brief explanations of the two approaches for controlling lead hazards, once they have been identified as a risk. These controls are recommended by the Department of Housing and Urban Development in *Guidelines for the Evaluation and Control of Lead-Paint Hazards in Housing*, and are summarized here to focus on the special considerations for historic housing:

Interim Controls: Short-term solutions include thorough dust removal; thorough washdown and clean-up of exposed surfaces; paint film stabilization and repainting; covering of lead-contaminated soil; and making tenants aware of lead hazards. Interim controls require ongoing maintenance and evaluation.

Figure 10. The choice of paint removal method will trigger various environmental controls and worker protection. The chemical poultice-type paint remover uses a paper backing that keeps the lead waste contained for proper disposal. The worker is adequately protected by a suit and gloves; for this work a respirator was not required. Local laws required containment and neutralization of any after-wash water run off. Photo: NPS Files.

Figure 11. New methods are being developed or adapted to safely remove lead-based paint from various substrates. On this cast iron building undergoing rehabilitation for apartment units, multiple layers of lead-based paint were removed with pneumatic needle guns with vacuum attachments. Paint chips and waste containing lead-based paint were placed in 55 gallon drums for transport to a special waste site, and the workers were fully protected. The cleaned metal was primed and repainted. Photo: Building Conservation Associates, Inc.

Hazard Abatement: Long-term solutions are defined as having an expected life of 20 years or more, and involve permanent removal of hazardous paint through chemicals, heat guns or controlled sanding/abrasive methods; permanent removal of deteriorated painted features through replacement; the removal or permanent covering of contaminated soil; and the use of enclosures (such as drywall) to isolate painted surfaces. The use of specialized elastomeric encapsulant paints and coatings can be considered as permanent containment of lead-based paint if they receive a 20-year manufacturer's warranty or are approved by a certified risk assessor. One should be aware of their advantages and drawbacks for use in historic housing.

Within the context of the historic preservation standards, the most appropriate method will always be the least invasive. More invasive approaches are considered only under the special circumstances outlined in the three-step

process. An inverted triangle (see fig. 12) shows the greatest number of residential projects fall well within the "interim controls" section. Most housing can be made safe for children using these sensitive treatments, particularly if no renovation work is anticipated. Next, where owners may have less control over the care and upkeep of housing and rental units, more aggressive means of removing hazards may be needed. Finally, large-scale projects to rehabilitate housing or convert non-residential buildings to housing may successfully incorporate "hazard abatement" as a part of the overall work.

Appropriate Methods for Controlling Lead Hazards

In selecting appropriate methods for controlling lead hazards, it is important to refer to Step I. of the survey where architecturally significant features and finishes are identified and need to be preserved. Work activities will vary according to hazard abatement needs; for example, while an interim control would be used to stabilize paint on most trimwork, an accessible window sill might need to be stripped prior to repainting. Since paint on a window sill is usually not a significant finish, such work would be appropriate. Other appropriate methods for controlling lead hazards are summarized in the accompanying chart (see fig. 13).

The method selected for removing or controlling the hazards has a direct bearing on the type of worker protection as well as the type of disposal needed, if waste is determined to be hazardous (see fig. 14). Following are

Figure 12. An inverted triangle makes the point that most of the nation's housing can be made lead-safe using interim control methods, such as dust control, paint stabilization, and good housekeeping. Shaded from light to dark, the lighter interim controls will generally not harm the historic materials. The darker, more aggressive controls, can be implemented with rehabilitation projects where paint removal, selective replacement of deteriorated elements, and encapsulation or enclosure are incorporated into other work.

MANAGING OR REMOVING LEAD-BASED PAINT IN HISTORIC BUILDINGS

Interim solutions, the preferred approach, include a combination of the following:

General maintenance	Dust control	Paint stabilization	Soil treatment	Tenant education
Repair deteriorated materials; Control leaks; Maintain exterior roofs, siding, etc. to keep moisture out of building; Perform emergency repairs quickly if lead-based paint is exposed; Maintain building file with lead test data and reports, receipts or invoices on completed lead mitigation work.	Damp mop floor; wet broom sweep porches and steps; Damp dust window sills and window troughs; Washdown painted surfaces periodically (use tri-sodium phosphate or equivalent, if necessary); Clean or vacuum carpets regularly (use HEPA vacuum if lead dust returns); Undertake periodic inspection with annual dust wipe tests.	Wet-sand loose paint and repaint; Keep topcoats of paint in good condition; Selectively remove paint from friction & chewable surfaces (sills) and repaint; Use good quality latex, latex acrylic or oil/ alkyd paints compatible with existing paint; Consider more durable encapsulating paints and wall lining systems if necessary.	Add bark mulch, sod or topsoil to bare dirt areas with high lead levels; Discourage children from playing in these areas by providing sand box or other safe areas; Do not plant vegetable garden in areas with lead in soil; Be careful that pets do not track contaminated soil inside house.	Notify tenants and workers as to the location of lead-based paint; Instruct tenants to keep property clean; Instruct tenants to notify owner or manager when repairs are necessary; Provide tenants with health department pamphlets on the hazards of lead-based paint.

Hazard abatement removes the <u>hazard</u> - not necessarily all the paint or the feature, and may include:

Paint removal	Paint Encapsulation Enclosure	Replace deteriorated elements	Soil treatment	Compliance
Remove deteriorated paint or paint on friction, chewable, or impact surfaces to sound layer, repaint; Consider using the gentlest means possible to remove paint to avoid damage to substrate: wet sanding, low level heat guns, chemical strippers, or HEPA sanding; Send easily removable items (shutters, doors) off-site for paint stripping, then reinstall and paint.	Consider encapsulating paints with 20 years warranty to seal-in older paint; or use in combination with wall liners to stabilize plaster wall surfaces prior to repainting; Seal lead-based painted surfaces behind rigid enclosures, such as drywall, or use luan or plywood with new coverings over previously painted floors; Use rubber stair treads on painted steps.	Remove, only when necessary, seriously deteriorated painted elements such as windows, doors, and trimwork. Replace with new elements that match the historic in appearance, detailing, and materials, when possible; Replace component element of a friction surface (parting bead or stops of windows) or of impact surfaces (shoe moldings) with new elements.	Remove contaminated soil around foundation to a depth of 3" and replace with new soil and appropriate planting material or paving; If site is highly contaminated from other lead sources (smelter, sandblasted water tank) consult an environmental specialist as well as a landscape architect; Do not alter a significant historic landscape	Be aware of all federal, state and local laws regarding lead-based paint abatement, environmental controls and worker safety; Dispose of all hazardous waste according to applicable laws; Be aware that methods to remove lead-based paint can cause differing amounts of lead dust which can be dangerous to workers and residents.

Figure 13. This chart indicates the wide variety of treatments that can be used to control or eliminate lead-based paint hazards. For historic buildings, the least invasive method should be used to control the hazards identified during a risk assessment and are shown in the lighter shaded portion of the chart. The darker portions show the more invasive hazard control methods which must be carefully implemented to ensure that whenever possible, historic materials are protected. The total abatement of all surfaces is not recommended for historic buildings because it can damage historic materials and destroy the evidence of early paint colors and layering. Prepared by Sharon C. Park, AIA.

IMPACT OF VARIOUS PAINT REMOVAL/ABATEMENT TECHNIQUES

REMOVAL METHOD	IMPACT ON MATERIALS	LEAD DUST GENERATED	IMPACT ON WORKER	IMPACT ON ENVIRONMENT
Wet scraping; wet sanding; repainting	Low: Gentle to substrate; feather edges to obtain smooth paint surface	Low: Misting surfaces reduces lead dust	Low: No special protection for respiration, but wash before eating, drinking, etc.	Low-medium: Debris often general waste; check disposal requirements
Heat gun; paint removal w/ scrapers < 450°F	Low: Gentle to substrate	Medium: Flicking softened paint does create airborne lead dust	Medium: Respirator w/HEPA filters usually required	Medium: Lead-paint sludge is hazardous waste
Chemical stripping on-site; use liquid or poultice; avoid methylene chloride	Low to Medium: Avoid damage to wood texture/grain with long dwell time	Low: Chemicals are moist and reduce lead dust	Low: For lead dust; for volatile chemicals may require solvent filter mask	Medium: Lead residue hazardous; off/rinse must be filtered or contained
Controlled HEPA sanding; primarily for wooden surfaces; sander uses HEPA vacuum shroud	Low to Medium: Avoid gouging wooden surfaces; good for feathering edges	Medium to High: Worker must know how to use equipment	Medium to High: Requires respirator with HEPA filter and possibly containment of area	Medium to High: Paint debris is hazardous and must be contained in drums for disposal
Dry Abrasives on cast iron; CO_2, walnut shells, needle gun removal; can use vacuum shrouds	Low to Medium: Substrate must be durable and in good condition; not for soft or porous materials	Generally High: Large volume of paint chips fall freely unless there is a vacuum shroud	High; Generally requires full suiting, respirators and containment, even if vacuum shroud used	Medium to High: Increased volume of hazardous waste if abrasive is added to lead debris
Chemical stripping off-site; cold tank reduces ungluing caused by hot tank	Medium to High: Elements can be damaged during removal or in tank	Usually low: Take care when removing elements to minimize lead-laden dust	Low: Take care when washing up to remove dust; wash clothes separately	Low to Medium: Stripping contractor responsible for disposal
Feature or substrate removal and replacement	High: Loss of feature is irretrievable; Avoid wholesale removal of significant elements	Usually low: Worker exposure can be high if element hazardous due to high amounts of lead-based paint	Usually low: Varies with lead dust generated; use air monitors and wet mist area	Varies: Must do a TCLP leach test to determine if debris can go to landfill or is hazardous waste

Figure 14. This chart shows how the impact of lead hazard control work can impact a property. The paint or hazard removal methods, shaded from light to dark, are listed from low to medium to high impact on historic materials. Each method will generate varying amounts of lead dust and hazardous materials; the impact on workers and the environment will thus vary accordingly. This information gives a general overview and is not a substitute for careful air monitoring and compliance with worker protection as established by OSHA regulations, and the proper handling/disposal of hazardous waste. Prepared by Sharon C. Park, AIA.

examples of appropriate methods to use to control lead hazards within an historic preservation context.

Historic Interiors (deteriorating paint and chewed surfaces). Whenever lead-based paint (or lead-free paint covering older painted surfaces) begins to peel, chip, craze, or otherwise comes loose, it should be removed to a sound substrate and the surface repainted. If children are present and there is evidence of painted surfaces that have been chewed, such as a window sill, then these surfaces should be stripped to bare wood and repainted. The removal of peeling, flaking, chalking, and deteriorating paint may be of a small scale and undertaken by the owner, or may be extensive enough to require a paint contractor. In either case, care must be taken to avoid spreading lead dust throughout the dwelling unit. If the paint failure is extensive and the dwelling unit requires more permanent hazard removal, then an abatement contractor should be considered. Many states are now requiring that this work be undertaken by specially trained and certified workers.

If an owner undertakes interim controls, it would be advisable to receive specialized training in handling lead-based paint. Such training emphasizes isolating the area, putting plastic sheeting down to catch debris, turning off mechanical systems, taping registers closed, and taking precautions to clean up prior to handling food. Work clothes should be washed separately from regular family laundry. The preferred method for removing flaking paint is the wet sanding of surfaces because it is gentle to the substrate and controls lead dust. The key to reducing lead hazards while stabilizing flaking paint is to keep the surfaces slightly damp to avoid ingesting lead dust. Wet sanding uses special flexible sanding blocks or papers that can be rinsed in water or used along with a bottle mister. This method will generally not create enough debris to constitute hazardous waste (see fig. 15).

Other methods for selectively removing more deteriorated paint in historic housing include controlled sanding, using low-temperature heat guns, or chemical strippers. Standard safety precautions and appropriate worker protection should be used. Methods to *avoid* include uncontrolled dry abrasive methods, high heat removal (lead vaporizes at 1100° F), uncontrolled water blasting, and some chemicals considered carcinogenic (methylene chloride). When possible and practicable, painted elements, such as radiators, doors, shutters, or other easily removable items, can be taken to an off site location for paint removal.

In most cases, when interior surfaces are repainted, good quality interior latex or oil/alkyd paints may be used. The paint and primer system must be compatible with the substrate, as well as any remaining, well-bonded, paint.

Encapsulant paints and coatings, developed to contain lead-based paint, rely on an adhesive bonding of the new paint through the layers of the existing paint. The advantages of these special paint coatings is that they allow the historic substrate to remain in-place; reduce the amount of existing paint removed; can generally be applied without extensive worker protection; and are a durable finish. (They cannot, however, be used on friction surfaces.) The drawbacks include their ability to obscure carved details, unless thinly applied in several applications, and difficulty in future removal. If a specialized paint, such as an elastomeric encapsulant paint, is considered, the manufacturer should be contacted for specific instructions for its application. Unless these specialized paint systems are warranted for 20 years, they are considered as less permanent interim controls.

Lead-dust on interior finishes. Maintaining and washing painted surfaces is one of the most effective measures to prevent lead poisoning. Houses kept in a clean condition, with paint film intact and topcoated with lead-free paint or varnish, may not even pose a health risk. Dust wipe tests, which are sent to a laboratory for processing, can identify the level of lead dust present on floors, window sills, and window troughs. If lead dust is above acceptable levels, then specially modified maintenance procedures can be undertaken to reduce it. All paints deteriorate over time, so maintenance must be ongoing to control fine lead dust. The periodic washing of surfaces with a surfactant, such as tri-sodium phosphate (TSP) or its equivalent, loosens dirt and removes lead dust prior to a water rinse and touch-up painting, if necessary. This interim treatment can be extremely beneficial in controlling lead dust that is posing a hazard (see fig. 16).

Soil/landscape. Soil around building foundations may contain a high level of lead from years of chalking and peeling exterior paint. This dirt can be brought indoors on shoes or by pets and small children if they play outside a house. Lead in the soil is generally found in a narrow band

Figure 15. Wet sanding of interior surfaces will keep dust levels down, reduce the need for workers' protection, and provide a sound surface for repainting. Priming and repainting with oil/alkyd, latex or latex acrylic should be undertaken according to manufacturers' instructions.

Figure 16. Washing windows and cleaning debris from window wells on a periodic basis can substantially reduce lead dust. Using water and tri-sodium phosphate (TSP or equivalent) will remove loose paint, and, after rinsing, the surface can be repainted with latex, oil/alkyd, or latex acrylic paints.

directly adjacent to the foundation. If the bare soil tests high in lead (see Action Levels Chart, pg. 6), it should be replaced to a depth of several inches or covered with new sod or plantings. Care should be taken to protect historic plantings on the building site and, in particular, historic landscapes, while mitigation work is underway (see fig. 17). If an area has become contaminated due to a variety of environmental conditions (for example, a smelter nearby or water tanks that have been sandblasted in the past), then an environmental specialist as well as a landscape preservation architect should be consulted on appropriate site protection and remedial treatments. It is inappropriate to place hard surfaces, such as concrete or macadam, over historically designed landscaped areas, which is often the recommendation of typical abatement guidelines.

Figure 18. *As part of an urban housing grant program, the exterior of this row house was sucessfully made lead-safe and met the Secretary of the Interior's Standards for Rehabilitation. The exterior was washed, then repainted with exterior grade alkyd paint. The decorative roof brackets and cornice were repainted; not removed or covered as is often recommended in typical abatement guidelines. The previously altered, deteriorated window sash were replaced with new sash and jamb liners set within the historic frames. Photos: Deborah Birch.*

Figure 17. *When historic sites are found to contain high levels of lead in bare soil — particularly around foundations — it is important to reduce the hazard without destroying significant landscapes. In many cases, contaminated soil can be removed from the foundation area and appropriate plantings or ground covers replanted in new soil. Photo: Charles A. Birnbaum, ASLA.*

Deteriorating paint on exteriors. Deteriorating exterior paint will settle onto window ledges and be blown into the dwelling, and will also contaminate soil at the foundation, as previously discussed. Painted exteriors may include wall surfaces, porches, roof trim and brackets, cornices, dormers, and window surrounds. Most exteriors need repainting every 5-10 years due to the cumulative effect of sun, wind, and rain or lack of maintenance. Methods of paint removal that do not abrade or damage the exterior materials should be evaluated. Because there is often more than one material (for example, painted brick and galvanized roof ornaments), the types of paint removal or paint stabilization systems need to be compatible with each material (see fig. 18). If paint has failed down to the substrate, it should be removed using either controlled sanding/scraping, controlled light abrasives for cast iron and durable metals, chemicals, or low heat. If chemicals are used, it may be necessary to have the contractor contain, filter, or otherwise treat any residue or rinse water. Environmental regulations must be checked prior to work, particularly if a large amount of lead waste will be generated or public water systems affected.

A cost analysis may show that, in the long run, repair and maintenance of historic materials or in-kind replacement can be cost effective. Due to the physical condition and location of wood siding, together with the cost of paint removal, a decision may be made to remove and replace

these materials on some historic frame buildings. If the repair or replacement of historic cladding on a primary elevation is being undertaken, such replacement materials should match the historic cladding in material, size, configuration, and detail (see fig. 19). The use of an artificial siding or aluminum coil stock panning systems over wooden trimwork or sills and lintels (as recommended in some abatement guidelines) is not appropriate, particularly on principal facades of historic buildings because they change the profile appearance of the exterior trimwork and may damage historic materials and detailing during installation. Unless the siding is too deteriorated to warrant repair and the cost is too prohibitive to use matching replacement materials (i.e., wood for wood), substitute materials are not recommended.

The use of specialized encapsulant paint coatings on exteriors—in particular, moist or humid climates, and, to some extent, cold climates—is discouraged because such coatings may serve to impede the movement of moisture that naturally migrates through other paints or mask leaks that may be causing substrate decay. Thus, a carefully applied exterior paint system (either oil/alkyd or latex) with periodic repainting can be very effective.

Friction Surfaces. Interior features with surfaces that— functionally—rub together such as windows and doors, or are subject to human wear and tear, such as floor and steps, are known as friction surfaces. It is unclear how much lead dust is created when friction surfaces that contain lead-based paint, but are top-coated with lead-free paint, rub together because much of the earlier paint may have worn away. For example, if lead dust levels around windows or on painted floors are consistently above acceptable levels, treating nearby friction surfaces should be considered. If surfaces, such as operable windows, operable doors, painted porch decks, painted floors and painted steps appear to be generating lead dust, they should be controlled through isolating or removing the lead-based paint. Window and door edges can be stripped or planed, or the units stripped on or off site to remove paint prior to repainting. Simple wooden stops and parting beads for windows, which often split upon removal, can be replaced.

Figure 19. In many cases, exterior wood siding can be repaired, selectively replaced, and repainted, as illustrated in this successful residential rehabilitation. Deteriorating wood siding was removed from the foundation to the top of the first floor windows and replaced with matching wood siding. The entire building was repainted. Photos: Crispus Attucks Community Development Corporation.

Figure 20. Operable windows have friction surfaces between the sash and the frames, which can be a source of fine lead dust. In this case, the deteriorated sash was replaced, but the historic frame remains in place, sucessfully isolated from the sash with a simple vinyl jamb liner that is part of the new sash operation.

Figure 21. Painted stairs and floors can cause a problem because lead dust settles between the wooden boards. In this case, the steps were sanded, repainted, and covered with rubber stair treads. The floors could not be effectively cleaned and sealed so they were isolated with a new subflooring, and a washable tile finish installed.

If window sash are severely deteriorated, it is possible to replace them; and vinyl jamb liners can effectively isolate remaining painted window jambs (see fig. 20). When windows are being treated within rehabilitation projects, their repair and upgrading are always recommended. In the event that part or all of a window needs to be replaced, the new work should match in size, configuration, detail, and, whenever possible, material.

Painted floors often present a difficult problem because walking on them abrades the surface, releasing small particles of lead-based paint. It is difficult to remove lead dust between the cracks in previously painted strip flooring even after sanding and vacuuming using special High Efficiency Particulate Air (HEPA) filters to control the lead dust. If painted floors are not highly significant in material, design, or craftsmanship, and they cannot be adequately cleaned and refinished, then replacing or covering them with new flooring may be considered. Stair treads can be easily fitted with rubber or vinyl covers (see fig. 21).

Accessible, projecting, mouthable surfaces. Accessible, chewable surfaces that can be mouthed by small children need not be removed entirely, as some health guidelines recommend. These accessible surfaces are listed as projecting surfaces within a child's reach, including window sills, banister railings, chair rails, and door edges. In many cases, the projecting edges can have all paint removed using wet sanding, a heat gun or chemical strippers, prior to repainting the feature (see fig. 22). If the homeowner feels that there is no evidence of unsupervised mouthing of surfaces, a regular paint may be adequate once painted surfaces have been stabilized. An encapsulant paint that adhesively bonds existing paint layers onto the substrate extends durability. While encapsulant paint systems are difficult to remove from a surface in the future, they permit retention of the historic feature itself. If encapsulant paint is used on molded or decorative woodwork, it should be applied in several thin coats to prevent the architectural detail from being obscured by the heavy paint (see fig 23).

Figure 22. Research has shown that some small children will chew on projecting window sills while teething. As part of a lead hazard control project, the edge of the sill can be stripped to bare wood or an encapsulating paint applied. In this case, a new window sill was installed as part of a window upgrade that retained the historic trim and frame.

Figure 23. Stair banisters and railings are considered mouthable surfaces. In this case, the old paint was wet sanded to a sound layer. Special encapsulant paints were then applied in three thin layers to avoid obscuring the woodwork's fine detailing. It should be noted that many encapsulant paints are now treated with a bitter agent to discourage mouth contact. Photo: Landmarks Design Associates.

Other surfaces showing age or deterioration/ walls and ceilings. Many flat wall surfaces and ceilings were not painted with lead-based paint, so will need to be tested for its presence prior to any treatment. Flat surfaces that contain deteriorating lead-based paint should be repaired following the responsible approach previously cited (i.e., removing loose paint to a sound substrate, then repairing damaged plaster using a skim coat or wet plaster repair (see fig. 25). Drywall is used *only* when deterioration is too great to warrant plaster repair. If walls and ceilings have a high lead content, and extensive paint removal is not feasible, there are systems available that use elastomeric paints with special fabric liners to stabilize older, though intact, wall surfaces.

Figure 24. Historic baseboards are often bumped by brooms and vacuum cleaners, causing lead-based paint chips to fall on the floor. Shoe moldings can be added or replaced to increase protection to the baseboard itself. In this case, because the condition of the interior warranted substantial repair, simple historic board trim was replaced with new matching trim. Note the HEPA filter vacuum in the foreground. Photo: NPS file.

Figure 25. In some cases, skim coating deteriorated plaster and repainting is adequate. If the plaster is seriously damaged or failing, drywall may be considered so long as the molding and window reveal relationships are retained. In this case, plaster between the windows was repaired and repainted and the side wall plaster was replaced with drywall. Photo: Landmarks Design Associates.

Impact Surfaces. Painted surfaces near doorways and along corridors tend to become chipped and scraped simply because of their location. This is particularly true of baseboards, which were designed to protect wall surfaces, and also for doorjambs. Owners should avoid hitting painted impact surfaces with vacuums, brooms, baby carriages, or wheeled toys. Adding new shoe moldings can give greater protection to some baseboards. In most cases, stabilizing loose paint and repainting with a high quality interior paint will provide a durable surface. Clear panels or shields can be installed at narrow doorways, if abrasion continues, or these areas can be stripped of paint and repainted. Features in poor condition may need to be replaced with new, matching materials (see fig. 24).

If a new drywall surface needs to be applied, care should be taken that the historic relationship of wall to trim is not lost. Also, if there are significant features, such as crown moldings or ceiling medallions, they should always be retained and repaired (see fig. 26).

Figure 26. Deteriorated ceiling plaster was removed and a new drywall ceiling installed. The historic ceiling medallion was preserved, and the plaster cornices repaired in place. Photo: Landmarks Design Associates.

Maintenance after Hazard Control Treatment

Following treatment, particularly where interim controls have been used, ongoing maintenance and re-evaluation become critical. In urban areas, even fully lead-safe houses can be re-contaminated within a year from lead or dirt outside the immediate property. Thus, housing interiors must be kept clean, once lead hazard control measures have been implemented. Dust levels should be kept down by wet sweeping porch steps and entrances on a regular basis. Vacuum cleaning and dusting should be repeated inside on a weekly basis or even more often. Vinyl, tile, and wood floor surfaces should be similarly damp mopped. Damp washing of window troughs and sills to remove new dust should be encouraged several times a year, particularly in the spring and fall when windows will be open. Carpets and area rugs should be steam cleaned or washed periodically if they appear to hold outside dirt.

Housing should be inspected frequently for signs of deterioration by both owner and occupant. Tenants need to be made aware of the location of lead-based paint under lead-free top coats and instructed to contact the owners or property managers when the paint film becomes disturbed (see figure 27). Any leaks, peeling paint, or evidence of

Figure 27. Wall leaks can cause historic surfaces to deteriorate, thereby exposing underlayers of lead-based paint. If painted surfaces show signs of deterioration, they should be repaired as soon as possible.

conditions that may generate lead-dust should be identified and corrected immediately. Occupants must be notified prior to any major dust-producing project. Dry sanding, burning, compressed air cleaning or blasting should be not be used. Repairs, repainting, or remodeling activities that have the potential of raising significant amounts of lead dust should be undertaken in ways that isolate the area, reduce lead-laden dust as much as possible, and protect the occupants.

Yearly dust wipe tests are recommended to ensure that dust levels remain below actionable levels. Houses or dwelling units that fail the dust-wipe test should be thoroughly re-cleaned with TSP, or its equivalent, washed down, wet vacuumed and followed by HEPA vacuuming, if necessary, until a clearance dust wipe test shows the area to be under actionable levels (see Action Levels chart). Spaces that are thoroughly cleaned and maintained in good condition are not a health risk (see fig. 28).

Figure 28. This recently completed housing, which is now lead-safe, could become re-contaminated from lead if safe conditions are not maintained. Damp mopping floor surfaces and regular dusting to keep the house clean will ensure its continuing safety.

Conclusion

The three-step planning process outlined in this Brief provides owners and managers of historic housing with responsible methods for protecting historic paint layers and architectural elements, such as windows, trimwork, and decorative finishes. Exposed decorative finishes, such as painted murals or grained doors can be stabilized by a paint conservator without destroying their significance.

Reducing and controlling lead hazards can be successfully accomplished without destroying the character-defining features and finishes of historic buildings. Federal and state laws generally support the reasonable control of lead-based paint hazards through a variety of treatments, ranging from modified maintenance to selective substrate removal. The key to protecting children, workers, and the environment is to be informed about the hazards of lead, to control exposure to lead dust and lead in soil, and to follow existing regulations. In all cases, methods that control lead hazards should be selected that minimize the impact to historic resources while ensuring that housing is lead-safe for children.

LEAD-BASED PAINT LEGISLATION

The following summarizes several important regulations that affect lead-hazard reduction projects. Owner's should be aware that regulations change and they have a responsiblity to check state and local ordinances as well.

Federal Legislation:

Title X (Ten) Residential Lead-Based Paint Hazard Reduction Act of 1992 is part of the Housing and Community Development Act of 1992 (Public Law 102-550). It established that HUD issue "The Guidelines for the Evaluation and Control of Lead-Based Paint Hazards in Housing" (1995) to outline risk assessments, interim controls, and abatement of lead-based paint hazards in *housing*. Title X calls for the reduction of lead in housing that is *federally supported* and outlines the federal responsibility towards its own residential units and the need for disclosure of lead in residences, even private residences, prior to sale.

Interim Final Regulations of Lead in Construction Standards (29CFR 1926.62). Issued by the Department of Labor, Occupational Safety and Health Administration (OSHA), these regulations address worker safety, training, and protective measures. It is based in part on environmental air sampling to determine the amount of lead dust generated by various activities.

Toxic Substance Control Act; Title IV. The Environmental Protective Agency (EPA) has jurisdiction for setting standards for lead abatement. Also, EPA controls the handling and disposal of hazardous waste generated during an abatement project. EPA will develop standards to establish lead hazards, to certify abatement contractors, and to establish work practice standards for abatement activity. EPA Regional Offices can provide guidance on the appropriate regulatory agency for states within their region.

State Laws: States generally have the authority to regulate the removal and transportation of lead based paint and the generated waste generally through the appropriate state environmental and public health agencies. Most requirements are for mitigation in the case of a lead-poisoned child, or for protection of children, or for oversight to ensure the safe handling and disposal of lead waste. When undertaking a lead-based paint reduction program, it is important to determine which laws are in place that may affect your project. Call the appropriate officials.

Local Ordinances: Check with local health departments, Poison Control Centers, and offices of housing and community development to determine if there are laws that require compliance by building owners. Rarely are owners required to remove lead-based paint and most laws are to ensure safety if a project is undertaken as part of a larger rehabilitation. Special use permits may be required when an environmental impact may occur due to a cleaning treatment that could contaminate water or affect water treatment. Determine whether projects are considered abatements and will require special contractors and permits.

Owner's Responsibility: Owners are ultimately responsible for ensuring that hazardous waste is properly disposed of when it is generated on their own sites. Owners should check with their state office to determine if the abatement project requires a certified contractor. (National certification requirements are not yet in place.) Owners should establish that the contractor is responsible for the safety of the crew and that all applicable laws are followed, and that transporters and disposers of hazardous waste have liability insurance as a protection for the owner. If an interim treatment is being used to reduce lead hazards, the owner should notify the contractor that lead-based paint is present and that it is the contractor's responsibility to follow appropriate work practices to protect workers and to complete a thorough clean-up to ensure that lead-laden dust is not present after the work is completed.

Glossary of Terms

Deteriorated Lead-Based Paint: Paint known to contain lead that shows signs of peeling, chipping, chalking, blistering, alligatoring or otherwise separating from its substrate.

Dust Removal: The process of removing dust to avoid creating a greater problem of spreading lead particles; usually through wet or damp collection or through the use of special HEPA vacuums.

Hazard Abatement: Long-term measures to remove the hazards of lead-based paint through selective paint stripping of deteriorated areas; or, in some cases, replacement of deteriorated features.

Hazard Control: Measures to reduce lead hazards to make housing safe for young children. Can be accomplished with interim (short-term) or hazard abatement (long-term) controls.

Interim Control: Short-term methods to remove lead dust, stabilize deteriorating surfaces, and repaint surfaces. Maintenance can ensure that housing remains lead-safe.

Lead-based Paint: Any existing paint, varnish, shellac or other coating that is in excess of 1.0 mg/cm^2 as measured by an XRF detector or greater than 0.5% by weight from laboratory analysis (5,000 ppm, 5,000 *ug/g*, or 5,000 mg/kg). For new products, the Consumer Safety Act notes 0.06% as the maximum amount of lead allowed in paint.

Lead-safe: The act of making a property safe from contamination by lead-based paint, lead-dust, and lead in soil generally through short and long-term methods to remove it, or to isolate it from small children.

Risk Assessment: An on-site investigation to determine the presence and condition of lead-based paint, including limited test samples, and an evaluation of the age, condition, housekeeping practices, and uses of a residence.

Further Reading

Chase, Sara B. *Preservation Brief 28: Painting Historic Interiors.* Washington, DC: US Department of the Interior, National Park Service, 1992.

"Coping with Contamination: A Primer for Preservationist," *Information; Booklet No 70.* Washington, DC: National Trust for Historic Preservation, 1993.

Historic Buildings and the Lead Paint Hazard. Hartford, CT: Connecticut Historical Commission, 1990.

"Health Hazards in National Park Service Buildings", *NPS-76 Housing Design and Rehabilitation.* Washington DC: US Department of the Interior, National Park Service, 1995.

Guidelines for the Evaluation and Control of Lead-Based Paint Hazards in Housing. Washington, DC: US Department of Housing and Urban Development, 1995.

Jandl, H. Ward. *Preservation Brief 18: Rehabilitating Historic Interiors - Identifying and Preserving Character-defining Elements.* Washington, DC: US Department of the Interior, National Park Service, 1988.

MacDonald, Marylee." Getting Rid of Lead." *Old House Journal,* July/Aug 1992.

Myers, John H. *Preservation Briefs 9; Repair of Historic Wooden Windows.* Washington, DC: US Department of the Interior, National Park Service, 1981.

OSHA Lead in Construction Standard (29 CFR 1926.62), Occupational Safety and Health Administration, May 4, 1993 (Federal Register).

Park, Sharon C. and Camille Martone. "Lead-Based Paint in Historic Buildings," *CRM Bulletin.* Washington, DC: US Deparartment of the Interior, National Park Service. Vol. 13, No. 1, 1990.

Park, Sharon C. "Managing Lead in Building Interiors: An Emerging Approach," *Interiors Handbook for Historic Buildings, Vol. II.* Washington DC: Historic Preservation Education Foundation, 1993.

Park, Sharon C ."What to do about Lead-Based Paint," *CRM Bulletin.* Washington, DC: U.S. Department of the Interior, National Park Service. Vol. 17, No. 4, 1994.

The Secretary of the Interior's Standards for the Treatment of Historic Properties. Washington, DC: US Department of the Interior, National Park Service, 1992.

Title X (Residential Lead-Based Paint Hazard Reduction Act of 1992) of Housing and Community Development Act of 1992 (P.L. 102 550), October 28, 1992.

Weeks, Kay D. and David Look, AIA. *Preservation Briefs 10; Exterior Paint Problems on Historic Woodwork.* Washington DC: US Department of the Interior, National Park Service. 1982.

This successfully completed project combined federal low income housing and historic preservation tax credits as part of a substantial rehabilitation that applied lead-hazard reduction methods consistent with the guidance in this Preservation Brief. Photo: Landmarks Design Associates.

Photographs courtesy of the authors unless identified.

Front cover:
Most residences painted prior to 1978 will contain some lead-based paint. It was widely used on exterior woodwork, siding, and windows as well as interior finishes. This apartment stairhall retains its historic character after a successful rehabilitation project that included work to control lead-based paint hazards. Photo: Crispus Attucks Community Development Corporation.

Acknowledgements

Sharon C. Park, AIA, is the Senior Historical Architect for the Preservation Assistance Division of the National Park Service. **Douglas C. Hicks** is the Deputy Chief of the Williamsport Preservation Training Center of the National Park Service. Both authors served on the National Park Service Housing Task Force addressing lead-safe employee housing and on various national panels to discuss combining lead-safe housing, worker safety, and historic preservation concerns.

Kay D. Weeks was technical editor for this publication project. The project was completed under the direction of H. Ward Jandl, Deputy Chief, Preservation Assistance Division. The authors also wish to thank the following individuals for providing technical information or for supplying case study projects: Claudia Kavenagh, Building Conservation Associates, Inc; David E. Jacobs, Armand C. Magnelli, National Center for Lead-Safe Housing; Ellis Goldman, William Wisner, and Catherine Hillard, HUD Office of Lead-Based Paint Abatement; Ellis Schmidlapp, Landmarks Design Associates (Pittsburg, PA); Crispus Attucks Community Development Corporation (York, PA); Charlene Dwin Vaughn and Rebecca Rogers, the Advisory Council on Historic Preservation; George Siekkinen, National Trust for Historic Preservation; Deborah Birch, Einhorn Yaffee Prescott Architects; Baird M. Smith and Quinn Evans Architects; Jack

Waite, Messick Cohen Waite Architects; Jim Caufield, Pennsylvania Historical and Museum Commission; Mike Jackson, Illinois Historic Preservation; Martha Raymond, Ohio Historic Preservation Division; Susan Chandler, Connecticut Historic Commission; Steade Craigo, California Office of Historic Preservation; Christopher Jones, Rocky Mountain Regional Office, NPS; Rebecca Shiffer and Kathleen Catalano Milley, Mid-Atlantic Regional Office, NPS; Peggy Albee, North Atlantic Regional Office, Cultural Resources Center, NPS; Victoria Jacobson, AIA, Mt. Rainier National Park; E. Blaine Cliver, Anne E. Grimmer, Thomas C. Jester, Michael J. Auer, Charles A. Birnbaum, ASLA, and Charles E. Fisher of the Preservation Assistance Division, the National Park Service, and Thomas McGrath, Williamsport Preservation Training Center.

This publication has been prepared pursuant to the National Historic Preservation Act of 1966, as amended, which directs the Secretary of the Interior to develop and make available information concerning historic properties. Comments about this publication should be directed to the Preservation Assistance Division, National Park Service, PO Box 37127, Washington, DC 20013-7127.

38

Removing Graffiti from Historic Masonry

Martin E. Weaver

In Cooperation with the
New York Landmarks Conservancy

Removing graffiti as soon as it appears is the key to its elimination—*and* recurrence. Thus, the intent of this Preservation Brief is to help owners and managers of historic masonry structures find the best way to remove exterior, surface-applied graffiti* quickly, effectively, and safely. The Brief will discuss the variety of materials used to apply graffiti, and offer guidance on how to remove graffiti from all types of historic masonry without harming either the surface or the substrate. Suggestions will also be given regarding the use of physical barriers to protect masonry surfaces from graffiti, and the application of barrier coatings to facilitate graffiti removal. Building managers and owners of historic properties will be advised on the importance of being prepared for rapid graffiti removal by testing different cleaning techniques in advance in order to select the most appropriate and sensitive cleaning technique. Health and safety and environmental concerns are addressed, as well as regulatory matters. Removing graffiti without causing damage to historic masonry is a job for trained maintenance crews, and in some cases, professional conservators, and generally should not be attempted by untrained workers, property owners or building managers. Although the focus of this Preservation Brief is on *historic* masonry, the same guidance may be applied equally to removing graffiti from non-historic masonry.

Identifying the Graffiti and the Masonry

Successful graffiti removal from historic masonry depends on achieving a balance between breaking the bond between the graffiti and the masonry surface without damaging the masonry. This generally requires knowledge both of the materials used to make the graffiti and the masonry on which the graffiti has been executed, as well as knowledge of cleaning methods and materials (Fig. 1). Without this, masonry surfaces can be badly disfigured or damaged during graffiti removal.

Graffiti. Most graffiti is made with spray paints. Although a number of solvents and paint strippers are capable of dissolving or breaking down these paints, some may permanently discolor or stain the masonry surface if not used correctly. As a result, the remaining paint may become

Figure 1. Many stones resemble others, and even concrete can sometimes be mistaken for stone. The stone trim on the Old Merchant's (Seabury Tredwell) House (1832), in Greenwich Village, New York City, is documented as Vermont marble. After establishing the stone type, cleaning methods should be tested in a discrete location in order to determine the most effective means of removing the graffiti without damaging the stone. More than one kind of removal technique may be required when both stone and brick require cleaning. Photo: Mark A. Weber

more difficult, or even impossible, to remove. Poorly thought-out and generally hasty attempts to remove graffiti using harsh chemicals or abrasives can also cause permanent damage to the masonry that may be worse than the graffiti (Fig. 2).

The ability to identify the graffiti material is an important step in successful removal. Numerous kinds of spray paint (polyurethanes, lacquers, and enamels), and brush-applied paints (oils and synthetic resins such as vinyls, acrylics, acetates, methacrylates, or alkyds), as well as permanent felt markers are the materials most often used to make graffiti. But other materials are also used for graffiti, including water-soluble felt markers, ballpoint pens, chalk, graphite and colored pencils, pastels, wax and oil crayons, liquid shoe polish, and lipstick (Fig. 3). The range of materials adopted by graffitists continues to expand.

Paints are composed of pigments that provide color and hiding power; binder that holds the pigments together and to the substrate; and a solvent that allows the pigment/binder mixture to flow. Some spray paints and markers may contain dyes instead of pigments. Paints are applied wet. Generally, as the solvent evaporates, the binder solidifies. The greater the solvent content of the paint, the greater the flow rate, and thus, the greater the ability of the paint to penetrate into masonry pores

The two primary components contained in most graffiti materials—pigment or dye, and binder—may simply remain on the masonry surface, or penetrate into the masonry to varying depths depending on a number of factors, including the surface tension of the substrate and viscosity of the solvent or vehicle. Thus, even the total removal of the pigment or the binder may leave residues of the other component actually in, or below, the surface of the stone. Residual stains, or graffiti "ghosts," such as those from any kind of red paint or the fine black pigments used in spray paints, may be particularly difficult to remove (Fig. 4). With painted graffiti, it is helpful to establish how long it has been on the surface. For most paints that have been on the surface for several weeks or months, hardening processes are likely to be complete or well-advanced; the solubility of the paint is proportionately reduced and it will be more difficult to remove.

Figure 2. Harsh, but ineffective, graffiti removal methods have resulted in permanent damage to granite walls at the General Grant National Memorial in New York City. Photo: Judith M. Jacob

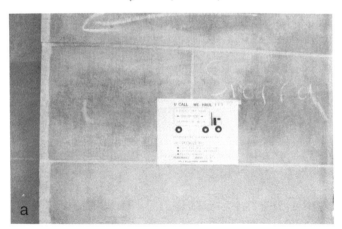

Figure 3 (a-d). A wide variety of materials is used to make surface-applied graffiti on masonry, including (a) chalk, (b) felt-tip marker, (c) felt-tip marker combined with crayon, and (d) felt-tip marker and spray paint on concrete. Photos: (a) Anne Grimmer, (b) Frances Gale, (c) Martin Weaver, (d) Anne Grimmer.

Figure 4 (a-b). After cleaning with an alkaline paint remover, remnants or ghosts of black spray-painted graffiti are still visible and may require poulticing, while the blue paint has been almost completely removed. Photos: Mark A. Weber.

Masonry. The historic masonry substrate must also be identified. As used here, the term *masonry* encompasses all types of natural stones; manufactured clay materials, including brick and terra cotta; and cementitious materials, such as cast stone, concrete and mortar. The common factor among masonry materials is that they are porous, to a greater or lesser extent, and sensitive to abrasion. After identifying the masonry, its condition, including fragility, porosity and permeability, must also be assessed prior to beginning graffiti removal. For example, a smooth, newly-polished granite surface is comparatively easy to clean because it is relatively impermeable and paint vehicles tend to stay on the surface rather than penetrate into microscopic pores. A very smooth, polished surface also has no pits or crevices that will retain particles of pigment or binder. In contrast, weathered marble or limestone may be extremely porous and permeable, with a rough surface on which particles of pigment can easily lodge. The fragility of such a surface can make it impossible to clean the surface even with a bristle brush without risking severe surface loss. A difference in surface texture or finish may also be the reason that a particular cleaning agent will work in one situation but not another.

Some types of masonry may react adversely to contact with the various cleaning agents required to break or dissolve the bond between the graffiti and the masonry surface.

Thus, for purposes of cleaning, masonry types are often categorized according to whether they are acid-sensitive, non-acid sensitive, or alkali-sensitive. *Acid-sensitive* stones consisting of carbonate materials may be damaged or even destroyed by contact with acids. Although, in many instances, acidic cleaning compounds are not effective for graffiti removal and generally should not be used for this purpose, it is useful to know that some acid-sensitive materials include: stones such as limestone, marble, travertine, calcareous sandstones and shales; most polished stones; and glazed architectural terra cotta and glazed brick. *Non-acid sensitive* masonry materials include slate, granite, unglazed architectural terra cotta and unglazed brick. *Alkali-sensitive* stones may contain silicates, or ferrous, soluble iron compounds that can react with alkalis or water to form severe staining. *Alkali-sensitive* stones include some granites, Indiana limestone, and many types of sandstone, especially those that are green or grey in color. Glazed and polished surfaces tend to be damaged by both strong acids and strong alkalis.

Graffiti Removal Methods and Materials

A variety of treatments are available from which to choose the most appropriate method of graffiti removal that will not damage the surface of historic masonry. Removal techniques, which are chosen according to the type of graffiti and the masonry, range from simply erasing pencilled graffiti with soft erasers, or removing chalked graffiti with soft brushes, to poulticing with water (with or without detergents), poulticing with organic solvents or alkali-based paint removers, or applying bleach to remove painted graffiti. In very limited situations, it may mean using very delicate and controlled abrasive means. Successful graffiti removal often requires a combination of cleaning materials and methods.

Poulticing

The most effective method of removing graffiti from masonry usually involves the use of a poultice. A poultice consists of an absorbent material or powder—inert clays such as kaolin or sepiolite, diatomaceous earth (fuller's earth); or cellulose products such as fluff pulp cellulose or shredded paper—mixed with a cleaning solution (a liquid reagent such as water, organic solvent, paint stripper or bleach) to form a paste or slurry. The purpose of a poultice is twofold: it enables a cleaning solution to be kept in contact with the stained area as long as possible, while allowing the cleaning solution to pull the staining material out of the substrate via the poultice without redepositing it in, or restaining, the masonry. A poultice is often covered with a plastic sheet to retard evaporation (Fig. 5). With some extremely porous types of stone, such as marble, although a poultice may remove a stain from one side of the stone, stains can pass completely through the stone and be redeposited on the other side of the masonry slab. Thus, caution should always be exercised in stain and graffiti removal.

Water and Detergent. Graffiti removal from historic masonry should always begin with the gentlest means possible. In some instances, this means low-pressure water washing. Fresh graffiti— one or two days old—made with water-soluble markers may sometimes be removed with water, possibly aided by a neutral or non-ionic detergent.

Figure 5. (a) Here, a commercially-manufactured poultice is being applied to the graffiti ghost that remains on this limestone building after an initial treatment with paint remover; (b) a plastic sheet has been taped over the poultice to slow down the rate of evaporation of the solvents contained in the poultice. Photos: Ken Lustbader.

(Non-ionic detergents which do not ionize in solution, do not deposit a solid, visible residue.) Ammonia can also be effective in removing fresh graffiti. Any detergent should be approached with caution and tested before using because most commercial laundry detergents are not neutral and contain substances which may leave undesirable residues on masonry materials. Usually, the water and detergent should be mixed with an absorbent material and applied in the form of a poultice. Although water washing is often likely to be the gentlest cleaning method for historic masonry, it may not be as effective for removing graffiti because many graffiti materials are not soluble in water.

Organic Solvents and Paint Removers. Most graffiti can be removed without damaging the masonry with proprietary graffiti-removal products and commercial paint strippers containing organic solvents. But, these products should always be tested and used in accordance with manufacturer's instructions included in the product literature. Normally, solvents should be used in a poultice form to prevent them from penetrating into the substrate, and permanently discoloring or staining the masonry. A number of paint-removers are manufactured as thick gels or pastes that cling to the surface, and some commercial paint-removal products include a tough fiber-reinforced paper or cloth backing that retards evaporation and also facilitates neat and clean removal of the used stripper. The advantage of using organic solvents is that they evaporate completely, leaving no residual material in the masonry. However, organic solvents may present a severe health hazard, and workers using them must wear adequate protection. "Off-the-shelf" aerosol graffiti removers generally should not be used because the dissolved paint being removed may run down the wall "staining" a previously clean area; or pigments may also be redistributed by the rinsing and scrubbing recommended by the product manufacturer (Fig. 6).

Alkaline Compounds. Alkaline compounds may be used to remove some oils and greases, and waxes from *non-alkali* sensitive masonry. Like organic solvents, alkaline compounds should generally be used in conjunction with a poultice when removing graffiti. The use of alkaline compounds should always be followed by a weak acid

Figure 6. Although an aerosol graffiti remover has taken off much of the graffiti, it has left new stains where it dripped down the masonry surface. Photo: Ken Lustbader.

wash and a water rinse in order to neutralize—or remove—all the alkaline residues from the masonry. Strong alkalies (pH13-14), such as sodium hydroxide-based paint removers (caustic soda or lye), generally should not be used as they can cause efflorescence and staining on masonry surfaces, if not properly neutralized. Potassium and other hydroxide paint removers may react with iron compounds in some masonry, particularly Indiana limestone, to form dark brown (rust-colored), or black ferric hydroxide stains, which are very difficult to remove.

Bleaches. Alkali-based bleaches such as calcium hypochlorite can sometimes be used very successfully in a poultice to bleach or decolorize certain dyes contained in some paints and inks that cannot readily be removed by other means.

Mechanical or Abrasive Methods. Mechanical treatments include dry or wet blasting, using abrasive grits, such as sand, dolomite powder, aluminum oxide, ground-walnut shells, sodium bicarbonate (baking soda), and others; high-pressure water washing; and mechanical sanding or grinding. All of these abrasive methods will cause damage to masonry and, in most instances, should never be considered as a method of removing graffiti from historic masonry. Abrasive methods used mistakenly by untrained workers to remove graffiti usually result in etching the outline of the graffiti permanently into the masonry (Fig. 7). Some historic masonry materials can be easily damaged by pressure washing even at low or moderate pressures (100-400 psi). Occasionally, however, under very controlled circumstances, a *micro-abrasive* technique may be appropriate for removing graffiti from delicate masonry surfaces, if used at low pressures of 35-40 psi with fine abrasives. This treatment, which must be done very slowly and carefully to avoid damaging the masonry, should be tested first, and undertaken only by a professional conservator. Another exception, even though it is not strictly an abrasive treatment, is using a razor blade as a first step to remove spray paint or felt-tip marker from polished granite. However, this too, should be undertaken only by a *professional conservator*, and only on *polished granite*, which is very hard and generally impervious to scratches.

Laser Cleaning. Although not in general use as a cleaning technique, laser technology offers great promise in the future as a non-damaging method of graffiti removal.

Testing

Before selecting a removal method, all cleaning materials and techniques for removing graffiti from a historic masonry building should be tested on mock-ups or areas of the resource that are not highly visible, but which are representative of typical conditions. Visual observation should be supplemented by the use of a magnifying glass, and spot tests should be carried out with various solvents to help identify the specific graffiti medium, which will aid in its removal. More complex testing using laboratory equipment and more scientific analytical processes may sometimes be necessary in complex situations. Sample areas that represent the desired degree of "cleanliness" should be approved in writing by client, architect, conservator or other appropriate authority. The materials and all the other data necessary to reproduce the desired

Figure 7 (a-b). The first time this spray-painted graffiti appeared it was removed abrasively. As a result, the graffiti was permanently etched into the limestone and cannot be concealed even by the pigmented barrier coating painted over it later. The barrier coating did, however, facilitate non-abrasive removal of graffiti the next time it was applied. Photos: Anne Grimmer.

cleaning results should be meticulously recorded and the accepted sample area preserved for reference until the end of the job. The existence of a "clean" sample for comparison and a signed agreement can avoid unpleasant surprises, misunderstandings, and perhaps legal actions.

When a type of graffiti appears for the first time that was executed with a material not immediately recognizable and for which no countermeasures have been developed, tests may need to be carried out by an architectural conservator to identify the material and to determine effective removal treatments. Agencies with large inventories of graffiti-prone buildings and structures should watch for graffiti made with new materials and experiment with different cleaning methods in order to be prepared when it appears. Such early action can save large sums of money in the long term. (See "Development of a Treatment Plan.")

Development of a Treatment Plan

For managers or owners of historic masonry buildings, or agencies responsible for large inventories of graffiti-prone properties, including parks, highway and railroad bridges and viaducts, bus, train and subway stations, and cemeteries, the development of a treatment plan may be the first step toward an effective graffiti-removal program. It is becoming increasingly common for large or important historic properties to have regular maintenance and disaster plans that include graffiti removal.

When feasible, a separate treatment plan should be prepared for each structure. However, if this is not possible, it is advisable to prepare a variety of treatment plans for specific masonry types. Plans should be prepared to cover all types of masonry that fall under one jurisdiction, management or ownership that are potential targets for graffiti.

Guidance contained in treatment plans should be based on the results of carefully controlled testing to remove a wide variety of common graffiti materials safely, and without damaging the various types of masonry. Individual treatment plans should address all parts of the building or structure that could be disfigured by graffiti, and any features too fragile to be cleaned by anyone other than a conservator should be noted on the plan.

A treatment plan is essentially a cleaning specification, but it should also include information on the following:

- the types and conditions of masonry likely to be targeted by graffiti;

- methods, materials and techniques known to work most successfully in the removal of specific types of graffiti from the surface of each type of masonry;

- sources for materials;

- a list of contractors with expertise in graffiti removal, including names, telephone numbers, information on emergency access to the property, and storage location of materials;

- graffiti-removal methods which may be harmful to the masonry surface;

- contractors or consultants who are **not acceptable** and should not be considered for graffiti removal;

- scaffolding, pumps, or safety equipment that might be required, where it is available, and costs involved; and

- health and safety concerns regarding specific removal treatments, product literature and Material Safety Data Sheets (MSDS).

Health and Safety Considerations

Most of the chemicals used for graffiti removal are dangerous to workers, as well as to others who may be in the vicinity. Organic solvents are toxic by ingestion, inhalation, and skin contact. Material Safety Data Sheets (MSDS), available from the product manufacturer for all paint-removal products, should always be consulted and followed. Identification of hazardous components and checking with chemical reference works will help assure that the least hazardous, but most effective, products are selected.

Generally speaking, it is a sensible policy to carry out all graffiti removal in well-ventilated conditions. Some solvents can be used only outdoors, and sometimes forced ventilation may be necessary even *there*, requiring workers to use air-fed respiratory equipment to avoid wind-blown fumes. Smoking, eating or drinking must not be allowed when cleaning is in progress.

Some materials used for graffiti removal are so corrosive that accidental contact can cause serious, permanent scarring and painful injuries. Wearing appropriate protective clothing must be strictly enforced. Mandatory personal protective equipment (PPE) normally includes face shields or safety glasses; long, chemical-resistant gloves; face masks with respirators for organic solvents; and possibly, full protective clothing with an independent air supply.

All smoking and open flames should be rigorously excluded from work areas; many solvents are flammable or highly explosive in vapor or liquid form when mixed with air. Solvent residue, used swabs, cloths, overalls and all other solvent-contaminated items should be safely and legally disposed of, or properly stored—even overnight—away from potential sources of fire. Electrical equipment may require explosion-proof fittings when used with certain solvents.

When electric pumps and pressure-spraying equipment are used, it is especially important that all necessary precautions be taken to avoid electric shock. Water sprays and puddles on the ground present a potentially dangerous situation, if they come into contact with temporary wiring at worksites where graffiti is being removed. Such hazards must be carefully monitored and controlled.

As with any construction project, attention should always be directed toward the general safety of the workers and passers-by, but also toward possible damage to the resource itself that might result from careless placement of ladders, or scaffolding. Chemicals used for masonry cleaning can also damage adjacent metals, glass, and painted surfaces, as well as vegetation (Fig. 8). Product manufacturers' instructions should always be closely followed to avoid such inadvertent "collateral" damage.

Environmental Considerations

To protect against environmental contamination, including the formation of unwanted ozone at ground level and damage to the ozone layer in the earth's outer atmosphere, legislation has been enacted in some states making it illegal to use even moderate quantities of some solvents — *volatile organic compounds (VOCs)* contained in paint removers. In response to this legislation, many new products are being developed that do not contain VOCs.

After completing graffiti removal, the disposal of chemical products and rinsing effluent must be taken into account. Arrangement for disposal of the cleaning waste should be made *prior* to beginning graffiti removal, especially if it is a project of considerable size. In many places it is illegal to discharge solvents and/or paint residues into sewers or storm drains. The owner or manager of a historic property, or in some cases the individual or firm doing the cleaning or graffiti removal, is responsible for being informed of, and complying with, relevant laws and regulations. Under provisions of the National Historic Preservation Act of 1966, as amended, approval may be required from a state or federal preservation agency before any work can be undertaken on buildings or structures listed in or eligible for listing in the National Register of Historic Places, if such a project involves federal funding or licensing. Many state and local historic district commissions and review boards have their own regulations that require approval for cleaning or graffiti removal work that is undertaken on landmarks or properties in locally designated historic districts.

Barrier Coatings

Anti-graffiti or barrier coatings are intended to facilitate the removal of graffiti from porous as well as non-porous surfaces. These coatings are most commonly transparent, but may also be pigmented. They are available in a variety of formulations designed to serve different needs. The use of barrier coatings to protect graffiti-prone historic masonry surfaces may seem to be an easy preventive solution to a persistent graffiti problem. However, for the most part, these coatings are not the panacea that some advertising might suggest. Some of them simply do not work, and others may cause physical or aesthetic changes or damage to the masonry.

Transparent Coatings. Transparent coatings serve as a barrier between the masonry surface and graffiti, preventing graffiti from penetrating into the masonry. They are also intended to make graffiti removal easier since most graffiti does not adhere well to them. Generally, graffiti applied over transparent barrier coatings can be removed with low-pressure water and a detergent, or with a solvent.

There are basically two kinds of transparent barrier coatings: temporary and permanent. Temporary, or "sacrificial" coatings are removed when graffiti is removed and then must be reapplied. Permanent transparent barrier coatings are more resistant to the water or solvents used to remove graffiti, and remain on the masonry surface when graffiti is removed (although this type of coating also must usually be reapplied after several cleanings). A third type of transparent barrier coating combines temporary and permanent coatings, based on a two-part system. A water-based acrylic sealer is first applied to the masonry surface, after which a sacrificial layer consisting of a polyethylene wax emulsion or dispersion coat is applied over the sealer. When graffiti is removed, the sealer coat remains on the masonry, but the sacrificial coat dissolves and is removed with the graffiti, and thus must be reapplied. (With this two-part system, even the first coat will eventually wear off after multiple cleanings, and must also be reapplied.)

Unfortunately, in application, there are a number of negative aspects of transparent barrier coatings that generally prevent their being recommended for use on historic masonry. First, clear coatings may alter the color of the masonry surface and add a gloss that may be highly visible, or apparent only in certain lighting conditions or when it rains. Second, clear coatings may reduce the water-vapor permeability of the masonry, thereby contributing to possible water-related deterioration. Third, the coating may discolor and change over time. Exposure to ultra-violet light can cause a coating to yellow; dirt build-up may darken the treated surface; and some coatings acquire a sheen when rubbed or brushed against. Such changes are especially noticeable when only a portion of the building has been coated. Furthermore, if coatings are not maintained on a regular basis, usually through periodic removal and reapplication, many coatings tend to fail. What often results is an uneven, "patchy" look to the masonry that can have a very negative impact on the character of the historic building (Fig. 9).

Despite these potential drawbacks, there may be some instances in which the graffiti problem or frequency of occurrence is so severe that application of a transparent barrier coating on historic masonry may be worth considering. Some water-based polysaccharide coatings, and silicone and silicone-based coatings have been used with success on masonry structures. They are essentially

---

Criteria to Consider Before Selecting a Barrier Coating as the Primary Protective Means of Combating Graffiti

What to look for in a Barrier Coating:

- Water-vapor permeable, or "breathable".

- "Invisible" without gloss or sheen, when applied to masonry.

- No change in appearance from uncoated areas when masonry is wet.

- Does not discolor or attract dirt.

- Weathers evenly.

Questions to Ask:

- Will the coating last long enough to offset its cost?

- Will the application and reapplication of the coating be cost effective?

- Will the coating be effective against more than one type of graffiti?

- Can the coating be completely and thoroughly removed, so that, if necessary, paint, or another coating will adhere to the masonry surface?

- Will the building ever need to be repointed or patched? A barrier coating may make this difficult or even impossible.

Before Application:

- Seek advice of an architectural conservator.

- Test coating on an inconspicuous area of masonry, or study the success/failure of the coating in other locations where it has been used.

Figure 8. The cast-iron railing and light fixtures on this stone stoop have been wrapped with plastic sheeting to protect them from damage by chemicals being used to remove the graffiti. Photo: Mark A. Weber.

Figure 9. These photographs illustrate some of the problems inherent in clear barrier coatings. (a) The transparent coating applied to the lower portion of this granite entranceway has darkened it, thus changing the character of the historic masonry. (b) But it is not nearly so obvious or damaging to the building's historic character as the thick and shiny clear coating applied here which resembles a plastic sheathing over the brick. Scratches are highly visible and a surface haze indicates that the coating has begun to deteriorate. (c) This transparent coating is peeling and has failed completely; not only is it an eyesore, but it may also be hard to remove from the brick. Photos: (a-b) Mark A. Weber, (c) Martin E. Weaver.

invisible, and do not change the natural appearance of the masonry. Although less durable than solvent-borne coatings, they are water-vapor permeable (breathable), and may be reapplied to the masonry surface immediately after removing graffiti, while the surface is still damp.

However, extreme caution must be exercised before applying a transparent barrier coating. Experimental test applications should always be tried first on discrete areas that are not highly visible, and the treated areas evaluated over a period of time. Laboratory test results on the performance of coatings applied to samples of like masonry types may be useful to some extent. But because the tests are carried out in a controlled environment, they may not be as accurate or reliable as tests actually carried out on-site where the factors of weather and pollution are the same as those at the location where the coating will be used. If circumstances warrant, and the use of a barrier coating is determined necessary, an architectural conservator should evaluate the test performance of a variety of coatings before selecting one to be applied to historic masonry. Because of the potential for disfigurement, owners of landmark-designated buildings are required by some preservation review boards and landmark commissions to obtain approval before they apply a barrier coating.

Pigmented Coatings. A pigmented barrier coating may be used on masonry as a permanent, preventive barrier coating, or as a *temporary* means of concealing graffiti until it can be removed.

Like a transparent barrier coating, a pigmented barrier coating facilitates the removal of graffiti because graffiti does not adhere well to it. Pigmented barrier coatings that are water-vapor permeable may sometimes be used as a *permanent* barrier coating on non-historic masonry where there is

frequent recurrence of graffiti, and when constant surveillance is not possible (Fig. 10). Although there are some instances in which pigmented barrier coatings may be appropriate on painted historic masonry, they are **not** recommended for unpainted historic masonry because they will change the appearance of the masonry. There is also another kind of pigmented coating that is specially formulated to be used as a *temporary* measure to conceal graffiti that cannot be removed right away. This temporary, vapor-permeable paint is removed when the graffiti is removed.

Pigmented coatings are also not generally recommended as a permanent measure to cover up graffiti. Some graffiti materials, particularly felt markers, bleed through the coating; and repeated applications of the coating or paint can result in a heavy paint build-up on a masonry surface. Another disadvantage of using paint or a pigmented coating to hide graffiti is that it usually appears as an obvious patch on unpainted masonry and tends to attract more graffiti unless the paint can be applied in a discrete, and well-defined area (Fig. 11). If incompatible with either the masonry or the graffiti, such a coating may peel off the masonry surface in an unsightly manner. Like transparent coatings, pigmented coatings may be difficult or impossible to remove completely once their performance or appearance is no longer satisfactory (Fig. 12).

Preventing and Controlling Graffiti

Experience shows that prompt removal of graffiti is one of the most effective measures against its recurrence. Graffiti that is not removed quickly tends to attract more graffiti. Often motivated by a need to have their work seen, graffitists tend to be discouraged from repeating their efforts in a location where their work is quickly removed.

Figure 10 (a) It may be appropriate to consider the application of a barrier coating in order to facilitate removal in some out-of-the-way locations where full-time security is not possible, such as this stairway and bridge underpass next to the C&O Canal. (b) Overpainting graffiti on the stone wall at the left has not been successful; it has resulted in highlighting the defaced stones, thereby attracting more graffiti. Photos: Anne Grimmer.

Figure 11. (a) The first floor of this limestone storefront was painted in an effort to cover graffiti. However, because the paint is poorly matched to the color of the building stone, it is highly visible and now acts as a "magnet" for new graffiti. (b) Similarly, the lowest horizontal band on this stone building, overpainted to cover graffiti, has also attracted more graffiti. Photos: (a) Mark A. Weber, (b) Martin E. Weaver

Apart from removal, effective graffiti-prevention measures can be considered under two headings. The first consists of physical measures involving maintenance, lighting, security and the erection of barriers on or around the property itself. The second focuses on community awareness programs that include neighborhood patrols, community service programs and educational programs in the schools.

Maintenance and Security. Neglect invites vandalism, whereas a well-maintained property encourages civic pride. Thus, careful attention should be given to establishing regular maintenance programs which do not allow properties to reach a point of obvious deterioration or abandonment. Cyclical maintenance also makes good sense economically.

Graffiti is less likely to occur if graffitists can be clearly seen. It is often recommended that accessible, graffiti-prone areas be illuminated with floodlighting or spotlights. Graffiti may also be reduced or prevented by the presence of security guards, park rangers or police officers, or by the visible presence of surveillance cameras. Publicity about arrests and punitive measures against the graffitists, and the general vigilance of the security system may also reduce graffiti.

If they are historically appropriate and compatible with the historic property, soft barriers in the form of low, possibly thorny, shrubs and bushes or other forms of landscaping and planting may be effective deterrents. Such plantings can make it difficult to reach the property by any route other than the approved secure one. Hard barriers provided by fences and transparent screens or shields, such as clear acrylic or other polycarbonate sheets, may also afford some degree of protection. But these can have a negative aesthetic impact on the property's appearance, particularly if the barriers themselves become disfigured by graffiti.

Community Awareness. Community action and education often play an important role in a successful anti-graffiti program. Neighborhood watches can effectively deter graffitists, and can help police and other security agencies in the detection and prevention of graffiti. Intensive public campaigns against graffiti, including presentations in schools, developing programs to foster community pride, and sentencing offenders to remove graffiti in their own community can also be useful. Publicity concerning arrests of graffitists can be a useful preventive tool. (But, on the other hand, frequent newspaper coverage of graffiti outbreaks or even of new community efforts at deterring graffiti can sometimes have the opposite effect by challenging the "creativity" of graffitists.) Community groups trained in proper cleaning techniques can also assist property owners in prompt and non-damaging graffiti removal.

a

Figure 12. (a) Graffiti that was overpainted has been exposed here as a result of the coating's failure. The uneven edges where the overpainting has peeled away will make inconspicuous touch-up difficult. (b) The unsightliness of graffiti bleeding through layers of cracked and peeling paint makes an obvious point that using a pigmented coating was not an appropriate maintenance technique for this stone sculpture base. Photos: (a) Martin E. Weaver, (b) Judith M. Jacob.

Tips for Successful Graffiti Removal

- It is important to pre-wet the masonry surface when using an alkaline paint remover; it is also advisable to pre-wet the masonry surrounding a graffitied area to dilute the effect of any cleaning agents that might be inadvertently splashed or spilled on the unsoiled surface. **Do not wet the area to be cleaned if the cleaning agent is solvent-based or incompatible with water.**

- Always rinse the cleaning agent off the masonry surface starting at the bottom and moving up. This prevents the cleaning agent from running down and staining a lower surface.

- Air temperature can be a factor in graffiti removal. Most paint removers do not work when the air temperature is either very cold or very hot. This may sometimes explain why a method that worked in one instance may not be effective again in another, similar situation.

- Variations within the same type of stone, such as bedding planes, density, finish, or degree of weathering, may explain why some areas of the same stone sometimes clean better that others.

- Even if advance testing has been done and a treatment plan exists, at least some on-the-spot testing will probably be necessary.

- Mortar joints react differently from masonry units, and may require a different cleaning material and/or method to be cleaned effectively.

- Graffiti removal may result in an obviously "clean" spot. Always clean the entire masonry unit that is bounded by mortar joints (but not the joints themselves, unless necessary). The prominence of the clean spot may be minimized by fanning the cleaning out from the spot, and "feathering" it by gradually reducing the strength or thoroughness of the cleaning.

- If it is not possible to completely remove all traces of graffiti without removing some of the masonry surface, it may be preferable to leave the masonry alone. Some graffiti ghosts become less noticeable with time due to fading of the dyes used in paints and markers. Sometimes it may be possible to conceal more obvious graffiti ghosts with carefully-matched paint.

- After graffiti removal, the masonry surface should always be tested with pH strips to make sure all the cleaning materials have been completely removed. Non-staining pH strips, available from chemical supply companies, will indicate whether acids or alkalis remain on the masonry surface.

- Although alkaline paint removers are sometimes ineffective on modern formulations of aerosol paints, they can work well in removing multi-layered graffiti because they last longer.

- What removes graffiti in one instance may not always work again even in what appears to be an identical situation.

- More than one cleaning material and technique may be required to clean a heavily graffitied area if different materials were used to make the graffiti. For example, shapes are often outlined with broad-tip felt markers and then filled in with spray paint.

- Effective graffiti removal often depends on trial-and-error testing, as well as a knowledge of masonry materials, graffiti materials and cleaning techniques.

Suggestions for Removing Graffiti from Historic Masonry

Graffiti	Removal Method	Health and Safety Cautions
Pencil	1. *Erase* with non-abrasive **pencil eraser**. 2. *Wash* with **water and non-ionic detergent**. 3. *Rinse* with **water**.	None.
Chalk/Pastel (not wax or oil-base)	1. *Brush* off with **bristle brush**. 2. *Wash* with **water and non-ionic detergent**. 3. *Rinse* with **water**.	None.

Paint
  Spray (aerosol)
  Non-spray paint
	1. *Poultice* with **paint remover*, organic solvent, or petroleum-based compound****.
	2. *Rinse* with **water, denatured alcohol or mineral spirits**.
	3. *Wash* with **water and non-ionic detergent**.
	4. *Rinse* with **water**.
		+See cautions below for NMP, solvents and petroleum-based compounds.
		
		Wear proper respirator, gloves and eye protection.

Permanent (felt-tip) Marker	1. *Wash* with **water and non-ionic detergent**, if necessary. 2. *Poultice* with **bleach***, paint remover*, organic solvent or petroleum-based compound****. 3. *Wash* with **water and non-ionic detergent**. 4. *Rinse* with **water**.	+See cautions below for NMP, solvents and petroleum-based compounds. Bleach is corrosive, causes chemical burns, and forms toxic gases (chlorine). Wear proper respirator, gloves and eye protection.
Water Soluble (felt-tip) Marker	1. *Wash* with **water and non-ionic detergent**. 2. *Poultice* with **bleach*****. 3. *Wash* with **water and non-ionic detergent**. 4. *Rinse* with **water**.	Bleach is corrosive, causes chemical burns, and forms toxic gases (chlorine). Wear proper respirator, gloves and eye protection.
Ballpoint Pen	1. *Erase* with **non-abrasive pencil eraser**. 2. *Poultice* with **organic solvent or petroleum-based compound****. 3. *Wash* with **water and non-ionic detergent**. 4. *Rinse* with **water**.	+See cautions below for NMP, solvents and petroleum-based compounds. Wear proper respirator, gloves and eye protection.
Crayon Lipstick Shoe Polish	1. *Poultice* with **denatured alcohol, paint remover* or organic solvent****. 2. *Wash* with **water and non-ionic detergent**. 3. *Rinse* with *water*.	+See cautions below for NMP, solvents and petroleum-based compounds. Wear proper respirator, gloves and eye protection.

 * Paint Remover based on N-methyl-2-pyrrolidone (NMP).
 ** Organic Solvent such as acetone, lacquer-thinner, or petroleum-based compound such as dimethyl adipate.
 *** Bleach such as calcium hypochlorite.
 + N-methyl-2-pyrrolidone (NMP) is mildly toxic and may have adverse reproductive effects.
  Solvents and petroleum-based compounds have toxic vapors, are flammable, and require well-ventilated conditions.

These are *suggestions* to assist in graffiti removal. Methods should always be tested first under the supervision and guidance of an architectural conservator.

Summary

Although rapid graffiti removal is the most effective weapon in eliminating graffiti and preventing its recurrence in the same location, hasty, untested removal attempts can disfigure and cause harm to historic masonry. Thus, it is important that the owner or manager of a historic masonry building or structure be prepared with a plan to ensure the prompt removal of graffiti when it occurs. Regularly scheduled maintenance and cleaning programs to eliminate graffiti from historic masonry properties may be assisted by the installation of physical barriers, security systems and lighting, as well as increased community involvement. Successful graffiti removal from historic masonry requires knowledge of a variety of cleaning methods and materials, and an awareness that what works to remove graffiti from one kind of masonry surface may not remove it from another. By testing different cleaning methods in advance, treatment plans will be available, when needed, to provide guidance for safe and sensitive graffiti removal from historic masonry.

Selected Reading

American Geological Institute. *AGI Glossary of Geology and Related Sciences*. Washington, D.C.: American Geological Institute, 1960.

Ashurst, Nicola. *Cleaning Historic Buildings. Vol. I: Substrates, Soiling and Investigations; Vol. II: Cleaning Materials and Processes*. London: Donhead Publishing Ltd., 1994.

"Chemistry Leaves Its Mark on Graffiti." *Chemical Marketing Reporter*. November 14, 1993.

Ehrenkrantz & Eckstut Architects, P.C. *Technical Tips: Removing Graffiti*. New York: New York Landmarks Conservancy, n.d. (1994).

Graffiti Removal Manual. Providence, RI: Keep Providence Beautiful, September 1986.

Grimmer, Anne E. *Keeping it Clean: Removing Exterior Dirt, Paint, Stains and Graffiti from Historic Masonry Buildings*. Washington, D.C.: Preservation Assistance Division, National Park Service, U.S. Department of the Interior, 1988.

Lewis, Richard J. *Hazardous Chemicals Desk Reference*. Second Edition. New York: Van Nostrand Reinhold, 1991.

NIOSH Pocket Guide to Chemical Hazards. Washington, D.C.: National Institute for Occupational Safety and Health, Centers for Disease Control and Prevention, Public Health Service, U.S. Department of Health and Human Services, June 1994.

Reisner, Robert. *Graffiti: Two Thousand Years of Wall Writing*. Chicago: Cowles Book Company, 1971.

Science for Conservators: Conservation Teaching Series. The Conservation Unit of the Museums and Galleries Commission. 3 volumes. New York: Routledge, A Division of Routledge, Chapman and Hall, Inc., 1992.

Torraca, Giorgio. *Porous Building Materials*. Rome: ICCROM, 1988.

Torraca, Giorgio. *Solubility and Solvents for Conservation Problems*. Rome: ICCROM, 1990.

Weaver, Martin E. *Conserving Buildings: A Guide to Techniques and Materials*. New York: John Wiley & Sons, Inc., 1993.

Whitford, Maurice J. *Getting Rid of Graffiti: A practical guide to graffiti removal and anti-graffiti protection*. New York: Van Nostrand Reinhold, Inc., 1992.

Wollbrinck, Thomas. "The Composition of Proprietary Paint Strippers." *Journal of the American Institute for Conservation*. Vol. 32 (1993), pp. 43-57.

Young, Daniel J. *How to Comply with the OSHA Hazard Communication Standard: A Guide to Compliance with OSHA Worker Right-to-Know Regulations*. New York: Van Nostrand Reinhold, 1989.

Acknowledgements

This Preservation Brief was developed under a cooperative agreement between the New York Landmarks Conservancy and the National Park Service. **Mark A. Weber**, Director, Technical Services Center, served as project coordinator for the Conservancy. The author, **Martin E. Weaver**, is the Director of the Center for Preservation Research at Columbia University. He is an internationally recognized expert in the conservation of architectural and cultural resources, a noted lecturer, and author of Conserving Buildings: A Guide to Techniques and Materials, as well as numerous articles on the subject.

Anne E. Grimmer, Senior Architectural Historian, Technical Preservation Services, Preservation Assistance Division, National Park Service, coordinated the development of this Preservation Brief and served as Technical Editor. Technical review of this publication by the following is gratefully acknowledged: Frances Gale, Training Coordinator, National Center for Preservation Technology and Training, National Park Service, Natchitoches, LA; Judith M. Jacob, Architectural Conservator, Building Conservation Branch, Northeast Cultural Resources Center, National Park Service, NY, NY; Andrea Mones-O'Hara, Regional Historic Preservation Officer, National Capital Region, General Services Administration, Washington, DC; Nicolas F. Veloz, Conservator of Outdoor Sculpture and Monuments, National Capital Area Office, National Park Service, Washington, DC; and Michael J. Auer, Timothy Buehner, Charles E. Fisher, and especially Kay D. Weeks, Technical Preservation Services, Preservation Assistance Division, National Park Service, Washington, DC.

This publication has been prepared pursuant to the National Historic Preservation Act of 1966, as amended, which directs the Secretary of the Interior to develop and make available information concerning historic properties. Comments on the usefulness of this publication may be directed to: Technical Preservation Services, Preservation Assistance Division, Center for Cultural Resource Stewardship and Partnerships, National Park Service, P.O. Box 37127, Washington, DC 20013-7127, or Technical Services Center, New York Landmarks Conservancy, 141 Fifth Avenue, NY, NY 10010.

*The word *graffito* (*graffiti*, plural) — is derived from the old Italian diminutive of graffio — to scratch, and the Latin *graphire* — to write. *Graffiti* in contemporary usage has come to mean an inscription, drawings, or markings. Except in very formal or technical applications, *graffiti* is generally considered a "mass" noun and paired with a singular verb.

Cover Photograph: Sandstone gatepost, Springfield Armory National Historic Site, Springfield, Massachusetts. Photo: Judith M. Jacob.

39

Holding the Line: Controlling Unwanted Moisture in Historic Buildings

Sharon C. Park, AIA

Uncontrolled moisture is the most prevalent cause of deterioration in older and historic buildings. It leads to erosion, corrosion, rot, and ultimately the destruction of materials, finishes, and eventually structural components. Ever-present in our environment, moisture can be *controlled* to provide the differing *levels* of moisture necessary for human comfort as well as the longevity of historic building materials, furnishings, and museum collections. The challenge to building owners and preservation professionals alike is to understand the patterns of moisture movement in order to better manage it — not to eliminate it. There is never a single answer to a moisture problem. Diagnosis and treatment will always differ depending on where the building is located, climatic and soil conditions, ground water effects, and local traditions in building construction.

Remedial Actions within an Historic Preservation Context

In this Brief, advice about controlling the sources of unwanted moisture is provided within a preservation context based on philosophical principles contained in the *Secretary of the Interior's Standards for the Treatment of Historic Properties.* Following the Standards means significant materials and features that contribute to the historic character of the building should be preserved, not damaged during remedial treatment (see fig.1). It also means that physical treatments should be reversible, whenever possible. The majority of treatments for moisture management in this Brief stress preservation maintenance for materials, effective drainage of troublesome ground moisture, and improved interior ventilation.

The Brief encourages a systematic approach for evaluating moisture problems which, in some cases, can be undertaken by a building owner. Because the source of moisture can be elusive, it may be necessary to consult with historic preservation professionals prior to starting work that would affect historic materials. Architects, engineers, conservators, preservation contractors, and staff of State Historic Preservation Offices (SHPOs) can provide such advice.

Regardless of who does the work, however, these are the principles that should guide treatment decisions:

- Avoid remedial treatments without prior careful diagnosis.

- Undertake treatments that protect the historical significance of the resource.

- Address issues of ground-related moisture and rain run-off thoroughly.

- Manage existing moisture conditions before introducing humidified/dehumidified mechanical systems.

- Implement a program of ongoing monitoring and maintenance once moisture is controlled or managed.

- Be aware of significant landscape and archeological resources in areas to be excavated.

Finally, mitigating the effects of catastrophic moisture, such as floods, requires a different approach and will not be addressed fully in this Brief.

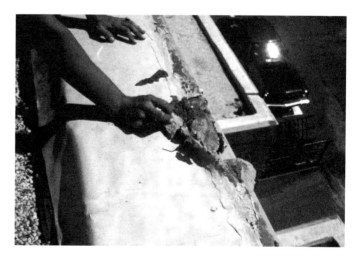

Fig. 1. Moisture problems, if not properly corrected, will increase damage to historic buildings. This waterproof coating trapped moisture from the leaking roof, causing portions of the masonry parapet to fail. Photo: NPS Files.

How and Where to Look for Damaging Moisture

Finding, treating, and managing the sources of damaging moisture requires a systematic approach that takes time, patience, and a thorough examination of all aspects of the problem—including a series of variable conditions (See this page). Moisture problems may be a direct result of one of these factors or may be attributable to a combination of interdependent variables.

Factors Contributing to Moisture Problems

A variety of simultaneously existing conditions contribute to moisture problems in old buildings. For recurring moisture problems, it may be necessary for the owner or preservation professional to address many, if not all, of the following variables:

- Types of building materials and construction systems

- Type and condition of roof and site drainage systems and their rates of discharge

- Type of soil, moisture content, and surface / subsurface water flow adjacent to building

- Building usage and moisture generated by occupancy

- Condition and absorption rates of materials

- Type, operation, and condition of heating, ventilating, cooling, humidification/ dehumidification, and plumbing systems

- Daily and seasonal changes in sun, prevailing winds, rain, temperature, and relative humidity (inside and outside), as well as seasonal or tidal variations in groundwater levels

- Unusual site conditions or irregularities of construction

- Conditions in affected wall cavities, temperature and relative humidity, and dewpoints

- Amount of air infiltration present in a building

- Adjacent landscape and planting materials

Diagnosing and treating the cause of moisture problems requires looking at both the localized decay, as well as understanding the performance of the entire building and site. Moisture is notorious for traveling far from the source, and moisture movement within concealed areas of the building construction make accurate diagnosis of the source and path difficult. Obvious deficiencies, such as broken pipes, clogged gutters, or cracked walls that contribute to moisture damage, should always be corrected promptly.

For more complicated problems, it may take several months or up to four seasons of monitoring and evaluation to complete a full diagnosis. Rushing to a solution without adequate documentation can often result in the unnecessary removal of historic materials—and worse—the creation of long-term problems associated with an increase, rather than a decrease, in the unwanted moisture.

Looking for Signs

Identifying the type of moisture damage and discovering its source or sources usually involves the human senses of sight, smell, hearing, touch, and taste combined with intuition. Some of the more common signs of visible as well as hidden moisture damage (see fig. 2, 3) include:

- Presence of standing water, mold, fungus, or mildew

- Wet stains, eroding surfaces, or efflorescence (salt deposits) on interior and exterior surfaces

- Flaking paint and plaster, peeling wallpaper, or moisture blisters on finished surfaces

- Dank, musty smells in areas of high humidity or poorly ventilated spaces

- Rust and corrosion stains on metal elements, such as anchorage systems and protruding roof nails in the attic

- Cupped, warped, cracked, or rotted wood

- Spalled, cracked masonry or eroded mortar joints

- Faulty roofs and gutters including missing roofing slates, tiles, or shingles and poor condition of flashing or gutters

- Condensation on window and wall surfaces

- Ice dams in gutters, on roofs, or moisture in attics

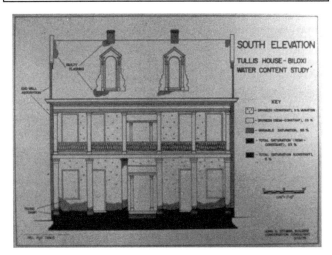

Fig. 2. Historic buildings plagued by dampness problems will benefit from systematic documentation to set a baseline against which moisture changes can be measured. Exterior areas with higher moisture levels may have algae growth or discoloration stains. Drawing: John H. Stubbs.

Fig. 3. The deterioration of this wooden cover was a sign that water was leaking from the fan coil unit behind. Photo: author.

Uncovering and Analyzing Moisture Problems

Moisture comes from a variety of external sources. Most problems begin as a result of the weather in the form of rain or snow, from high ambient relative humidity, or from high water tables. But some of the most troublesome moisture damage in older buildings may be from internal sources, such as leaking plumbing pipes, components of heating, cooling, and climate control systems, as well as sources related to use or occupancy of the building. In some cases, moisture damage may be the result of poorly designed original details, such as projecting outriggers in rustic structures that are vulnerable to rotting, and may require special treatment.

The five most common sources of unwanted moisture include:

- Above grade exterior moisture entering the building
- Below grade ground moisture entering the building
- Leaking plumbing pipes and mechanical equipment
- Interior moisture from household use and climate control systems
- Water used in maintenance and construction materials.

Above grade exterior moisture generally results from weather related moisture entering through deteriorating materials as a result of deferred maintenance, structural settlement cracks, or damage from high winds or storms (see fig. 4). Such sources as faulty roofs, cracks in walls, and open joints around window and door openings can be corrected through either repair or limited replacement. Due to their age, historic buildings are notoriously "drafty," allowing rain, wind, and damp air to enter through missing mortar joints; around cracks in windows, doors, and wood siding; and into uninsulated attics. In some cases, excessively absorbent materials, such as soft sandstone, become saturated from rain or gutter overflows, and can allow moisture to dampen interior surfaces. Vines or other vegetative materials allowed to grow directly on building materials without trellis or other framework can cause damage from roots eroding mortar joints and foundations as well as dampness being held against surfaces. In most cases, keeping vegetation off buildings, repairing damaged materials, replacing flashings, rehanging gutters, repairing downspouts, repointing mortar, caulking perimeter joints around windows and doors, and repainting surfaces can alleviate most sources of unwanted exterior moisture from entering a building above grade.

Below grade ground moisture is a major source of unwanted moisture for historic and older buildings. *Proper handling of surface rain run-off is one of the most important measures of controlling unwanted ground moisture.* Rain water is often referred to as "bulk moisture" in areas that receive significant annual rainfalls or infrequent, but heavy, precipitation. For example, a heavy rain of 2" per hour can produce 200 gallons of water from downspout discharge alone for a house during a one hour period. When soil is saturated at the base of the building, the moisture will wet footings and crawl spaces or find its way through cracks in foundation walls and enter into basements (see fig. 5). Moisture in saturated basement or foundation walls—also exacerbated by high water tables—will generally rise up within a wall and eventually cause deterioration of the masonry and adjacent wooden structural elements.

Builders traditionally left a working area, known as a builder's trench, around the exterior of a foundation wall. These trenches have been known to increase moisture problems if the infill soil is less than fully compacted or includes rubble backfill, which, in some cases, may act as a reservoir holding damp materials against masonry walls. Broken subsurface pipes or downspout drainage can leak into the builder's trench and dampen walls some distance from the source. Any subsurface penetration of the foundation wall for sewer, water, or other piping also can act as a direct conduit of ground moisture unless these holes are well sealed. A frequently unsuspected, but serious, modern source of ground moisture is a landscape irrigation system set too close to the building. Incorrect placement of sprinkler heads can add a tremendous amount of moisture at the foundation level and on wall surfaces.

Fig. 4. Deferred maintenance often leads to blocked gutters and downspouts. This cracked gutter system allowed moisture to penetrate the upper exterior wall, erode mortar joints, and rot fascia boards. Photo: NPS files.

Fig. 5. Excavating this foundation revealed that the downspout pipe had corroded at the " u-trap" and was leaking moisture into the soil. Openings around the horizontal water supply line and cracks in the wall allowed moisture to penetrate the basement in multiple locations. Photo: author.

The ground, and subsequently the building, will stay much drier by 1) re-directing rain water away from the foundation through sloping grades, 2) capturing and disposing downspout water well away from the building, 3) developing a controlled ground gutter or effective drainage for buildings historically without gutters and downspouts, and 4) reducing splash-back of moisture onto foundation walls. The excavation of foundations and the use of dampproof coatings and footing drains should only be used after the measures of reducing ground moisture listed above have been implemented.

Leaking plumbing pipes and mechanical equipment can cause immediate or long-term damage to historic building interiors. Routine maintenance, repair, or, if necessary, replacement of older plumbing and mechanical equipment are common solutions. Older water and sewer pipes are subject to corrosion over time. Slow leaks at plumbing joints hidden within walls and ceilings can ultimately rot floor boards, stain ceiling plaster, and lead to decay of structural members. Frozen pipes that crack can damage interior finishes (see fig. 6). In addition to leaking plumbing pipes, old radiators in some historic buildings have been replaced with water-supplied fan coil units which tend to leak. These heating and cooling units, as well as central air equipment, have overflow and condensation pans that require cyclical maintenance to avoid mold and mildew growth and corrosion blockage of drainage channels. Uninsulated forced-air sheet metal ductwork and cold water pipes in walls and ceilings often allow condensation to form on the cold metal, which then drips and causes bubbling plaster and peeling paint. Careful design and vigilant maintenance, as well as repair and insulating pipes or ductwork, will generally rid the building of these common sources of moisture.

Fig. 6. Uninsulated plumbing pipes close to the exterior wall froze and cracked, wetting this ornamental plaster ceiling before the water supply line could be shut off. As a result, limited portions of the ceiling needed reattaching. Photo: author.

Interior moisture from building use and modern humidified heating and cooling systems can create serious problems. In northern U.S. climates, heated buildings will have winter-time relative humidity levels ranging from 10%-35% Relative Humidity (RH). A house with four occupants generates between 10 and 16 pounds of water a day (approximately 1 – 2 gallons) from human residents. Moisture from food preparation, showering, or laundry use will produce condensation on windows in winter climates.

When one area or floor of a building is air-conditioned and another area is not, there is the chance for condensation to occur between the two areas. Most periodic condensation does not create a long-term problem.

Humidified climate control systems are generally a major problem in museums housed within historic buildings. They produce between 35%-55% RH on average which, as a vapor, will seek to dissipate and equalize with adjacent spaces Moisture can form on single-glazed windows in winter with exterior temperatures below 30 F and interior temperatures at 70 F with as little as 35% RH. Frequent condensation on interior window surfaces is an indication that moisture is migrating into exterior walls, which can cause long-term damage to historic materials. Materials and wall systems around climate controlled areas may need to be made of moisture resistant finishes in order to handle the additional moisture in the air. Moist interior conditions in hot and humid climates will generate mold and fungal growth. Unvented mechanical equipment, such as gas stoves, driers, and kerosene heaters, generate large quantities of moisture. It is important to provide adequate ventilation and find a balance between interior temperature, relative humidity, and airflow to avoid interior moisture that can damage historic buildings.

Moisture from maintenance and construction materials can cause damage to adjacent historic materials. Careless use of liquids to wash floors can lead to water seepage through cracks and dislodge adhesives or cup and curl materials. High-pressure power washing of exterior walls and roofing materials can force water into construction joints where it can dislodge mortar, lift roofing tiles, and saturate frame walls and masonry. Replastered or newly plastered interior walls or the construction of new additions attached to historic buildings may hold moisture for months; new plaster, mortar, or concrete should be fully cured before they are painted or finished. The use of materials in projects that have been damaged by moisture prior to installation or have too high a moisture content may cause concealed damage (see fig. 8).

Fig. 8. Damaging moisture conditions can occur during construction. Peeling paint on this newly rehabilitated frame wall was attributed to wall insulation that had become wet during the project and was not discovered. Photo: NPS Files.

Transport or Movement of Moisture

Knowing the five most common sources of moisture that cause damage to building materials is the first step in diagnosing moisture problems. But it is also important to understand the basic mechanisms that affect moisture movement in buildings. Moisture transport, or movement, occurs in two states: liquid and vapor. It is directly related to pressure differentials. For example, water in a gaseous or vapor state, as warm moist air, will move from its high pressure area to a lower pressure area where the air is cooler and drier. Liquid water will move as a result of differences in hydrostatic pressure or wind pressure. *It is the pressure differentials that drive the rate of moisture migration in either state.* Because the building materials themselves resist this moisture movement, the rate of movement will depend on two factors: the permeability of the materials when affected by vapor and the absorption rates of materials in contact with liquid.

The mechanics, or physics, of moisture movement is complex, but if the driving force is difference in pressure, then an approach to reducing moisture movement and its damage is to reduce the difference in pressure, not to increase it. That is why the treatments discussed in this Brief will look at *managing moisture by draining bulk moisture and ventilating vapor moisture* before setting up new barriers with impermeable coatings or over-pressurized new climate control systems that threaten aging building materials and archaic construction systems.

Three forms of moisture transport are particularly important to understand in regards to historic buildings — *infiltration, capillary action, and vapor diffusion* —remembering, at the same time, that the subject is infinitely complex and, thus, one of continuing scientific study (see

fig. 9). Buildings were traditionally designed to deal with the movement of air. For example, cupolas and roof lanterns allowed hot air to rise and provided a natural draft to pull air through buildings. Cavity walls in both frame and masonry buildings were constructed to allow moisture to dissipate in the air space between external and internal walls. Radiators were placed in front of windows to keep cold surfaces warm, thereby reducing condensation on these surfaces. Many of these features, however, have been altered over time in an effort to modernize appearances, improve energy efficiency, or accommodate changes in use. The change in use will also affect moisture movement, particularly in commercial and industrial buildings with modern mechanical systems. Therefore, the way a building handles air and moisture today may be different from that intended by the original builder or architect, and poorly conceived changes may be partially responsible for chronic moisture conditions.

Moisture moves into and through materials as both a visible liquid (capillary action) and as a gaseous vapor (infiltration and vapor diffusion). Moisture from leaks, saturation, rising damp, and condensation can lead to the deterioration of materials and cause an unhealthy environment. Moisture in its solid form, ice, can also cause damage from frozen, cracked water pipes, or split gutter seams or spalled masonry from freeze-thaw action. Moisture from melting ice dams, leaks, and condensation often can travel great distances down walls and along construction surfaces, pipes, or conduits. The amount of moisture and how it deteriorates materials is dependent upon complex forces and variables that must be considered for each situation.

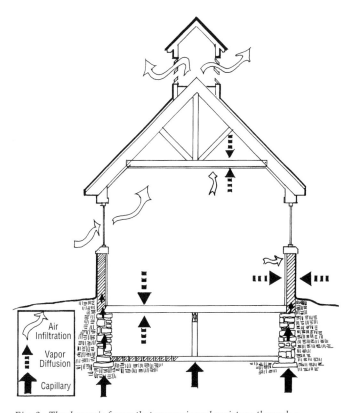

Fig. 9. The dynamic forces that move air and moisture through a building are important to understand particularlly when selecting a treatment to correct a moisture problem. Air infiltration, capillary action, and vapor diffusion all affect the wetting and drying of materials. Drawing; NPS Files.

Determining the way moisture is handled by the building is further complicated because each building and site is unique. Water damage from blocked gutters and downspouts can saturate materials on the outside, and high levels of interior moisture can saturate interior materials. Difficult cases may call for technical evaluation by consultants specializing in moisture monitoring and diagnostic evaluation. In other words, it may take a team to effectively evaluate a situation and determine a proper approach to controlling moisture damage in old buildings.

Infiltration is created by wind, temperature gradients (hot air rising), ventilation fan action, and the stack or chimney effect that draws air up into tall vertical spaces. Infiltration as a dynamic force does not actually move liquid water, but is the vehicle by which dampness, as a component of air, finds its way into building materials. Older buildings have a natural air exchange, generally from 1 to 4 changes per hour, which, in turn, may help control moisture by diluting moisture within a building. The tighter the building construction, however, the lower will be the infiltration rate and the natural circulation of air. In the process of infiltration, however, moisture that has entered the building and saturated materials can be drawn in and out of materials, thereby adding to the dampness in the air (see fig. 10). Inadequate air circulation where there is excessive moisture (i.e., in a damp basement), accelerates the deterioration of historic materials. To reduce the unwanted moisture that accompanies infiltration, it is best to incorporate maintenance and repair treatments to close joints and weatherstrip windows, while providing controlled air exchanges elsewhere. The worst approach is to seal the building so completely, while limiting fresh air intake, that the building cannot breathe.

Fig. 10. Infiltration of damp air can occur around loose-fitting or deteriorated window sash and through cracks or open joints in building exteriors. Photo: Ann Brooks Prueher.

Capillary action occurs when moisture in saturated porous building materials, such as masonry, wicks up or travels vertically as it evaporates to the surface. In capillary attraction, liquid in the material is attracted to the solid surface of the pore structure causing it to rise vertically; thus, it is often called "rising damp," particularly when found in conjunction with ground moisture. It should not, however, be confused with moisture that laterally penetrates a foundation wall through cracks and settles in the basement. Not easily controlled, most rising damp comes from high water tables or a constant source under the footing. In cases of damp masonry walls with capillary action, there is usually a whitish stain or horizontal tide mark of efflorescence that seasonally fluctuates about 1- 3 feet above grade where the excess moisture evaporates from the wall (see fig. 11). This tide mark is full of salt crystals, that have been drawn from the ground and building materials along with the water, making the masonry even more sensitive to additional moisture absorption from the surrounding air. Capillary migration of moisture may occur in any material with a pore structure where there is a constant or recurring source of moisture.

Fig. 11. Capillary rise of moisture in masonry is often accompanied with a horizontal tide-mark line several feet above the grade, as seen here. Removing or redirecting as much ground moisture as possible usually helps reduce moisture within a wall. Photo: NPS Files.

The best approach for dealing with capillary rise in building materials is to reduce the amount of water in contact with historic materials. If that is not possible due to chronically high water tables, it may be necessary to introduce a horizontal damp-proof barrier, such as slate course or a lead or plastic sheet, to stop the vertical rise of moisture. Moisture should not be sealed into the wall with a waterproof coating, such as cement parging or vinyl wall coverings, applied to the inside of damp walls. This will only increase the pressure differential as a vertical barrier and force the capillary action, and its destruction of materials, higher up the wall.

Vapor diffusion is the natural movement of pressurized moisture vapor through porous materials. It is most readily apparent as humidified interior air moves out through walls to a cooler exterior. In a hot and humid climate, the reverse will happen as moist hot air moves into cooler, dryer, air-conditioned, interiors. The movement of the moisture vapor is not a serious problem until the dewpoint temperature is reached and the vapor changes into liquid moisture known as *condensation*. This can occur within a wall or on interior surfaces. Vapor diffusion will be more of a problem for a frame structure with several layers of infill materials within the frame cavity than a dense masonry structure. Condensation as a result of vapor migration usually takes place on a surface or film, such as paint, where there is a change in permeability.

The installation of climate control systems in historic buildings (mostly museums) that have *not* been properly designed or regulated and that force pressurized damp air to diffuse into perimeter walls is an ongoing concern. These newer systems take constant monitoring and back-up warning systems to avoid moisture damage.

Long-term and undetected condensation or high moisture content can cause serious structural damage as well as an unhealthy environment, heavy with mold and mildew spores. Reducing the interior/exterior pressure differential and the difference between interior and exterior temperature and relative humidity helps control unwanted vapor diffusion. This can sometimes be achieved by reducing interior relative humidity. In some instances, using vapor barriers, such as heavy plastic sheeting laid over damp crawl spaces, can have remarkable success in stopping vapor diffusion from damp ground into buildings. Yet, knowledgeable experts in the field differ regarding the appropriateness of vapor barriers and when and where to use them, as well as the best way to handle natural diffusion in insulated walls.

Adding insulation to historic buildings, particularly in walls of wooden frame structures, has been a standard modern weatherization treatment, but it can have a disastrous effect on historic buildings. The process of installing the insulation destroys historic siding or plaster, and it is very difficult to establish a tight vapor barrier. While insulation has the benefit of increasing the efficiency of heating and cooling by containing temperature controlled air, it does not eliminate surfaces on which damaging moisture can condense. For insulated residential frame structures, the most obvious sign of a moisture

diffusion problem is peeling paint on wooden siding, even after careful surface preparation and repainting. Vapor impermeable barriers such as plastic sheeting, or more accurately, *vapor retarders,* in cold and moderate climates generally help slow vapor diffusion where it is not wanted.

In regions where *humidified* climate control systems are installed into insulated frame buildings, it is important to stop *interstitial,* or in-wall, dewpoint condensation. This is very difficult because humidified air can penetrate breaches in the vapor barrier, particularly around electrical outlets (see fig. 12). Improperly or incompletely installed retrofit vapor barriers will cause extensive damage to the building, just in the installation process, and will allow trapped condensation to wet the insulation and sheathing boards, corrode metal elements such as wiring cables and metal anchors, and blister paint finishes. Providing a tight wall vapor barrier, as well as a ventilated cavity behind wooden clapboards or siding appears to help insulated frame walls, if the interior relative humidity can be adjusted or monitored to avoid condensation. Correct placement of vapor retarders within building construction will vary by region, building construction, and type of climate control system.

Surveying and Diagnosing Moisture Damage: Key Questions to Ask

It is important for the building to be surveyed first and the evidence and location of suspected moisture damage systematically recorded before undertaking any major work to correct the problem. This will give a baseline from which relative changes in condition can be noted.

When materials become wet, there are specific physical changes that can be detected and noted in a record book or on survey sheets. Every time there is a heavy rain, snow storm, water in the basement, or mechanical systems failure, the owner or consultant should note and record the way moisture is moving, its appearance, and what variables might contribute to the cause. *Standing outside to observe a building in the rain may answer many questions and help trace the movement of water into the building.* Evidence of deteriorating materials that cover more serious moisture damage should also be noted, even if it is not immediately clear what is causing the damage. (For example, water stains on the ceiling may be from leaking pipes, blocked fan coil drainage pans above, or from moisture which has penetrated around a poorly sloped window sill above.) Don't jump to conclusions, but use a systematic approach to help establish an educated theory — or hypothesis — of what is causing the moisture problem or what areas need further investigation.

Surveying moisture damage must be systematic so that relative changes can be noted. Tools for investigating can be as simple as a notebook, sketch plans, binoculars, camera, aluminum foil, smoke pencil, and flashlight. The systematic approach involves looking at buildings from the top down and from the outside to the inside. Photographs, floor plans, site plan, and exterior elevations — even roughly sketched — should be used to indicate all evidence of damp or damaged materials, with notations for musty or poorly ventilated areas. Information might be needed on the absorption and permeability characteristics of the building materials and soils. Exterior drainage patterns should be noted and these base plans referred to on a regular basis in different seasons and in differing types of weather (see fig. 13).

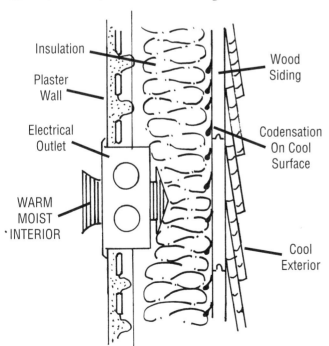

Insulation

Plaster Wall

Electrical Outlet

WARM MOIST INTERIOR

Wood Siding

Codensation On Cool Surface

Cool Exterior

Fig. 12. Vapor diffusion can result in damp air migrating into absorbent materials and condensing on colder surfaces, thereby wetting insulation, damaging electrical conduits, and causing deterioration of the wooden framing. Drawing: NPS Files.

Glossary:

Air flow/ infiltration: The movement that carries moist air into and through materials. Air flow depends on the difference between indoor and outdoor pressures, wind speed and direction as well as the permeability of materials.

Bulk water: The large quantity of moisture from roof and ground run-off that can enter into a building either above grade or below grade.

Capillary action: The force that moves moisture through the pore structure of materials. Generally referred to as rising damp, moisture at or below the foundation level will rise vertically in a wall to a height at which the rate of evaporation balances the rate at which it can be drawn up by capillary forces.

Condensation: The physical process by which water vapor is transformed into a liquid when the relative humidity of the air reaches 100% and the excess water vapor forms, generally as droplets, on the colder adjacent surface.

Convection: Heat transfer through the atmosphere by a difference in force or air pressure is one type of air transport. Sometimes referred to as the "stack effect," hotter less dense air will rise, colder dense air will fall creating movement of air within a building.

Dewpoint: The temperature at which water vapor condenses when the air is cooled at a constant pressure and constant moisture content.

Diffusion: The movement of water vapor through a material. Diffusion depends on vapor pressure, temperature, relative humidity, and the permeability of a material.

Evaporation: The transformation of liquid into a vapor, generally as a result of rise of temperature, is the opposite of condensation. Moisture in damp soil, such as in a crawl space, can evaporate into the air, raise the relative humidity in that space, and enter the building as a vapor.

Ground moisture: The saturated moisture in the ground as a result of surface run-off and naturally occuring water tables. Ground moisture can penetrate through cracks and holes in foundation walls or can migrate up from moisture under the foundation base.

Monitoring instrumentation: These devices are generally used for long term diagnostic analysis of a problem, or to measure the preformance of a treatment, or to measure changes of conditions or environment. In-wall probes or sensors are often attached to data-loggers which can be down-loaded into computers.

Permeability: A characteristic of porosity of a material generally listed as the rate of diffusion of a pressurized gas through a material. The pore structure of some materials allows them to absorb or adsorb more moisture than other materials. Limestones are generally more permeable than granites.

Relative humidity (RH): Dampness in the air is measured as the percent of water vapor in the air at a specific temperature relative to the amount of water vapor that can be held in a vapor form at that specific temperature.

Survey instrumentation: technical instrumentation that is used on-site to provide quick readings of specific physical conditions. Generally these are hand-held survey instruments, such as moisture, temperature and relative humidity readers, dewpoint sensors, and fiber optic boroscopes.

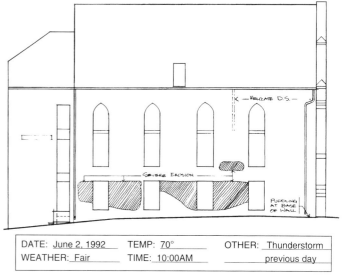

DATE: June 2, 1992	TEMP: 70°	OTHER: Thunderstorm
WEATHER: Fair	TIME: 10:00AM	previous day

Fig. 13. Using sketch plans and elevation drawings to record the moisture damage along with the date, time, and weather conditions will show how moisture is affecting buildings over time. Drawing: Courtesy, Quinn Evans Architects.

It is best to start with one method of periodic documentation and to use this same method each time. Because moisture is affected by gravity, many surveys start with the roof and guttering systems and work down through the exterior walls. Any obvious areas of water penetration, damaged surfaces, or staining should be noted. Any recurring damp or stain patterns, both exterior and interior, should also be noted with a commentary on the temperature, weather, and any other facts that may be relevant (driving rains, saturated soil, high interior humidity, recent washing of the building, presence of a lawn watering system, etc.).

The interior should be recorded as well, beginning with the attic and working down to the basement and crawl space. It may be necessary to remove damaged materials selectively in order to trace the path of moisture or to pinpoint a source, such as a leaking pipe in the ceiling. The use of a basic resistance moisture meter, available in many hardware stores, can identify moisture contents of materials and show, over time, if wall surfaces are drying or becoming damper (see fig. 14). A smoke pencil can chart air infiltration around windows or draft patterns in interior spaces. For a quick test to determine if a damp basement is caused by saturated walls or is a result of condensation, tape a piece of foil onto a masonry surface and check it after a day or two; if moisture has developed behind the foil, then it is coming from the masonry. If condensation is on the surface of the foil, then moisture is from the air.

Comparing current conditions with previous conditions, historic drawings, photographs, or known alterations may also assist in the final diagnosis. A chronological record, showing improvement or deterioration, should be backed up with photographs or notations as to the changing size, condition, or features of the deterioration and how these changes have been affected by variables of temperature and rainfall. If a condition can be related in time to a particular event, such as efflorescence developing on a chimney after the building is no longer heated, it may be possible to isolate a cause, develop a hypothesis, and then test the hypothesis (by adding some temporary heat), before applying a remedial treatment.

If the owner or consultant has access to moisture survey and monitoring equipment such as resistance moisture meters, dewpoint indicators, salt detectors, infrared thermography systems, psychrometer, fiber-optic boroscopes, and miniaturized video cameras, additional quantified data can be incorporated into the survey (see fig. 15). If it is necessary to track the wetting and drying of walls over a period of time, deep probes set into walls and in the soil with connector cables to computerized data loggers or the use of long-term recording of hygrothermographs may require a trained specialist. Miniaturized fiber-optic video cameras can record the condition of subsurface drain lines without excavation (see fig. 16). It should be noted, however, that *instrumentation, while extremely useful, cannot take the place of careful personal observation and analysis.* Relying on instrumentation alone rarely will give the owner the information needed to fully diagnose a moisture problem.

To avoid jumping to a quick—potentially erroneous—conclusion, a series of questions should be asked first. This will help establish a theory or hypothesis that can be tested to increase the chances that a remedial treatment will control or manage existing moisture.

How is water draining around building and site? What is the effectiveness of gutters and downspouts? Are the slopes or grading around foundations adequate? What are the locations of subsurface features such as wells, cisterns, or drainage fields? Are there subsurface drainage pipes (or drainage boots) attached to the downspouts and are they in good working condition? Does the soil retain moisture or allow it to drain freely? Where is the water table? Are there window wells holding rain water? What is the flow rate of area drains around the site (can be tested with a hose for several minutes)? Is the storm piping out to the street sufficient for heavy rains, or does water chronically back up on the site? Has adjacent new construction affected site drainage or water table levels?

How does water/moisture appear to be entering the building? Have all five primary sources of moisture been evaluated? What is the condition of construction materials and are there any obvious areas of deterioration? Did this building have a builder's trench around the foundation that could be holding water against the exterior walls? Are the interior bearing walls as well as the exterior walls showing evidence of rising damp? Is there evidence of hydrostatic pressure under the basement floor such as water percolating up through cracks? Has there been moisture damage from an ice dam in the last several months? Is damage localized, on one side of the building only, or over a large area?

What are the principal moisture dynamics? Is the moisture condition from liquid or vapor sources? Is the attic moisture a result of vapor diffusion as damp air comes up through the cavity walls from the crawl space or is it from a leaking roof? Is the exterior wall moisture from rising damp with a tide mark or are there uneven spots of dampness from foundation splash back, or other ground moisture conditions? Is there adequate air exchange in the building, particularly in damp areas, such as the basement? Has the height of the water table been established by inserting a long pipe into the ground in order to record the water levels?

How is the interior climate handling moisture? Are there areas in the building that do not appear to be ventilating well and where mold is growing? Are there historic features that once helped the building control air and moisture that can be reactivated, such as operable skylights or windows? Could dewpoint condensation be occurring behind surfaces, since there is often condensation on the windows? Does the building feel unusually damp or smell in an unusual way that suggest the need for further study? Is there evidence of termites, carpenter ants, or other pests attracted to moist conditions? Is a dehumidifier keeping the air dry or is it, in fact, creating a cycle where it is actually drawing moisture through the foundation wall?

Does the moisture problem appear to be intermittent, chronic, or tied to specific events? Are damp conditions occuring within two hours of a heavy rain or is there a delayed reaction? Does rust on most nail heads in the attic indicate a condensation problem? What are the wet patterns that appear on a building wall during and after a rain storm? Is it localized or in large areas? Can these rain patterns be tied to gutter over-flows, faulty flashing, or saturation of absorbent materials? Is a repaired area holding up well over time or is there evidence that moisture is returning? Do moisture meter readings of wall cavities indicate they are wet, suggesting leaks or condensation in the wall?

Once a hypothesis of the source or sources of the moisture has been developed from observation and recording of data, it is often useful to prove or disprove this hypothesis with interim treatments, and, if necessary, the additional use of instrumentation to verify conditions. For damp basements, test solutions can help determine the cause. For example, surface moisture in low spots should be redirected away from the foundation wall with regrading to determine if basement dampness improves. If there is still a problem, determine if subsurface downspout collection pipes or cast iron boots are not functioning properly. The above grade downspouts can be disconnected and attached to long, flexible extender pipes and redirected away from the foundation (see fig. 17). If, after a heavy rain or a simulation using a hose, there is no improvement, look for additional ground moisture sources such as high water tables, hidden cisterns, or leaking water service lines as a cause of moisture in the basement. New data will lead to a new hypothesis that should be tested and verified. *The process of elimination can be frustrating, but is required if a systematic method of diagnosis is to be successful.*

Selecting an Appropriate Level of Treatment

The treatments in chart format at the back of this publication are divided into levels based on the degree of moisture problems. Level I covers preservation maintenance; Level II focuses on repair using historically compatible materials and essentially mitigating damaging moisture conditions; and Level III discusses replacement and alteration of materials that permit continued use in a chronically moist environment. It is important to begin

Fig. 17. In testing a theory for the cause of basement wetness, the owner used long black extender pipes to direct roof run-off away from the foundation. This test established that the owner did not need expensive waterproofing of the foundation, but a better drainage system. Photo: Baird M. Smith.

with Level I and work through to a manageable treatment as part of the control of moisture problems. Buildings in serious decay will require treatments in Level II, and difficult or unusual site conditions may require more aggressive treatments in Level III. Caution should always be exercised when selecting a treatment. The treatments listed are a guide and not intended to be recommendations for specific projects as the key is always proper diagnosis.

Start with the repair of any obvious deficiencies using sound preservation maintenance. If moisture cannot be managed by maintenance alone, it is important to reduce it by mitigating problems *before* deteriorated historic materials are replaced (see fig. 18). Treatments should not remove materials that can be preserved; should not involve extensive excavation unless there is a documented need; and should not include coating buildings with waterproof sealers that can exacerbate an existing problem. Some alteration to historic materials, structural systems, mechanical systems, windows, or finishes may be needed when excessive site moisture cannot be controlled by drainage systems, or in areas prone to floods. These changes, however, should, be sensitive to preserving those materials, features, and finishes that convey the historic character of the building and site.

Ongoing Care

Once the building has been repaired and the larger moisture issues addressed, it is important to keep a record of additional evidence of moisture problems and *to protect the historic or old building through proper cyclical maintenance* (see fig. 19) In some cases, particularly in museum environments, it is critical to monitor areas vulnerable to moisture damage. In a number of historic buildings, in-wall moisture monitors are used to ensure that the moisture purposely generated to keep relative humidity at ranges appropriate to a museum collection does not migrate into walls and cause deterioration. The potential problem with all systems is the failure of controls, valves, and panels over time. Back-up systems, warning devices, properly trained staff and an emergency plan will help control damage if there is a system failure.

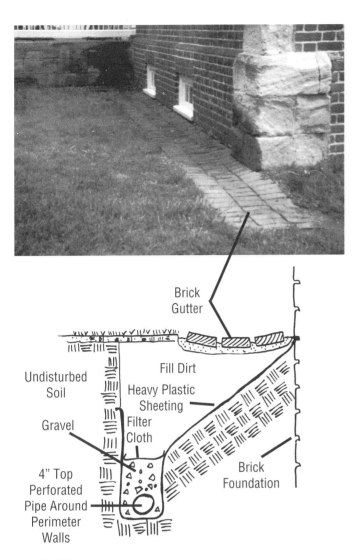

Fig. 18. This detail drawing shows a sub-surface perimeter drain in conjunction with a historic brick ground gutter system to help control roof run-off moisture from entering the historic foundation. Detail: Courtesy, Gunston Hall Plantation. Photo: Elizabeth Sasser.

Brick
Gutter

Undisturbed
Soil

Fill Dirt

Heavy Plastic
Sheeting

Filter
Cloth

Gravel

4" Top
Perforated
Pipe Around
Perimeter
Walls

Brick
Foundation

Fig. 19. Maintaining gutters and downspouts in good operable condition, repairing exteriors to keep water out, redirecting damaging moisture away from foundations and controlling interior moisture and condensation are all important when holding the line on moisture deterioration. Photo: Nebraska State Historical Society.

Ongoing maintenance and vigilance to situations that could potentially cause moisture damage must become a routine part of the everyday life of a building. The owner or staff responsible for the upkeep of the building should inspect the property weekly and note any leaks, mustiness, or blocked drains. Again, observing the building during a rain will test whether ground and gutter drainage are working well.

For some buildings a back-up power system may be necessary to keep sump pumps working during storms when electrical power may be lost. For mechanical equipment rooms, condensation pans, basement floors, and laundry areas where early detection of water is important, there are alarms that sound when their sensors come into contact with moisture.

Conclusion

Moisture in old and historic buildings, though difficult to evaluate, can be systematically studied and the appropriate protective measures taken. Much of the documentation and evaluation is based on common sense combined with an understanding of historic building materials, construction technology, and the basics of moisture and air movement. Variables can be evaluated step by step and situations creating direct or secondary moisture damage can generally be corrected. The majority of moisture problems can be mitigated with maintenance, repair, control of ground and roof moisture, and improved ventilation. For more complex situations, however, a thorough diagnosis and an understanding of how the building handles moisture at present, can lead to a treatment that solves the problem without damaging the historic resource.

It is usually advantageous to eliminate one potential source of moisture at a time. Simultaneous treatments may set up a new dynamic in the building with its own set of moisture problems. Implementing changes sequentially will allow the owner or preservation professional to track the success of each treatment.

Moisture problems can be intimidating to a building owner who has diligently tried to control them. Keeping a record of evidence of moisture damage, results of diagnostic tests, and remedial treatments, is beneficial to a building's long-term care. The more complete a survey and evaluation, the greater the success in controlling unwanted moisture now and in the future.

Holding the line on unwanted moisture in buildings will be successful if 1) there is constant concern for signs of problems and 2) there is ongoing physical care provided by those who understand the building, site, mechanical systems, and the previous efforts to deal with moisture. For properties with major or difficult-to-diagnose problems, a team approach is often most effective. The owner working with properly trained staff, contractors and consultants can monitor, select, and implement treatments within a preservation context in order to manage moisture and to protect the historic resource.

MOISTURE: LEVEL I PRESERVATION MAINTENANCE

Exterior: Apply cyclical maintenance procedures to eliminate rain and moisture infiltration.

Roofing/ guttering: Make weather-tight and operational; inspect and clean gutters as necessary depending on number of nearby trees, but at least twice a year; inspect roofing at least once a year, preferably spring; replace missing or damaged roofing shingles, slates, or tiles; repair flashing; repair or replace cracked downspouts.

Walls: Repair damaged surface materials; repoint masonry with appropriately formulated mortar; prime and repaint wooden, metal, or masonry elements or surfaces; remove efflorescence from masonry with non-metallic bristle brushes.

Window and door openings: Eliminate cracks or open joints; caulk or repoint around openings or steps; repair or reset weatherstripping; check flashing; repaint, as necessary.

A. Inspecting the overall building on at least an annual basis will identify areas needing maintenance. A bucket lift is helpful for large buildings. Photo: author.

Ground: Apply regular maintenance procedures to eliminate standing water and vegetative threats to building/site.

Grade: Eliminate low spots around building foundations; clean out existing downspout boots twice a year or add extension to leaders to carry moisture away from foundation; do a hose test to verify that surface drains are functioning; reduce moisture used to clean steps and walks; eliminate the use of chlorides to melt ice which can increase freeze/thaw spalling of masonry; check operation of irrigation systems, hose bib leaks, and clearance of air conditioning condensate drain outlets.

Crawl space: Check crawl space for animal infestation, termites, ponding moisture, or high moisture content; check foundation grilles for adequate ventilation; seasonally close grilles when appropriate — in winter, if not needed, or in summer if hot humid air is diffusing into air conditioned space.

B. Repair exterior surfaces, paint, and recaulk as needed. Photo: Williamsport Preservation Training Center (WPTC), NPS.

Foliage: Keep foliage and vines off buildings; trim overhanging trees to keep debris from gutters and limbs from rubbing against building; remove moisture retaining elements, such as firewood, from foundations.

Basements and foundations: Increase ventilation and maintain surfaces to avoid moisture.

Equipment: Check dehumidifiers, sump pump, vent fans, and water detection or alarm systems for proper maintenance as required; check battery back-up twice a year.

C. Cleaning out gutters and downspouts should be done at least twice a year. Photo: WPTC, NPS.

Piping/ductwork: Check for condensation on pipes and insulate/seal joints, if necessary.

Interior: Maintain equipment to reduce leaks and interior moisture.

Plumbing pipes: Add insulation to plumbing or radiator pipes located in areas subject to freezing, such as along outside walls, in attics, or in unheated basements.

Mechanical equipment: Check condensation pans and drain lines to keep clear; insulate and seal joints in exposed metal ductwork to avoid drawing in moist air.

Cleaning: Routinely dust and clean surfaces to reduce the amount of water or moist chemicals used to clean building; caulk around tile floor and wall connections; and maintain floor grouts in good condition.

Ventilation: Reduce household-produced moisture, if a problem, by increasing ventilation; vent clothes driers to the outside; install and always use exhaust fans in restrooms, bathrooms, showers, and kitchens, when in use.

MOISTURE: LEVEL II REPAIR AND CORRECTIVE ACTION

Exterior: Repair features that have been damaged. Replace an extensively deteriorated feature with a new feature that matches in design, color, texture, and where possible, materials.

Roofing: Repair roofing, parapets and overhangs that have allowed moisture to enter; add ice and water shield membrane to lower 3-4 feet or roofing in cold climates to limit damage from ice dams; increase attic ventilation, if heat and humidity build-up is a problem. Make gutters slope @ 1/8" to the foot. Use professional handbooks to size gutters and reposition, if necessary and appropriate to historic architecture. Add ventilated chimney caps to unused chimneys that collect rain water.

Walls: Repair spalled masonry, terra cotta, etc. by selectively installing new masonry units to match; replace rotted clapboards too close to grade and adjust grade or clapboards to achieve adequate clearance; protect or cover open window wells.

Ground: Correct serious ground water problems; capture and dispose of downspout water away from foundation; and control vapor diffusion of crawlspace moisture.

Grade: Re-establish positive sloping of grade; try to obtain 6" of fall in the first 10' surrounding building foundation; for buildings without gutter systems, regrade and install a positive subsurface collection system with gravel, or waterproof sheeting and perimeter drains; adjust pitch or slope of eave line grade drains or French drains to reduce splash back onto foundation walls; add subsurface drainage boots or extension pipes to take existing downspout water away from building foundation to the greatest extent feasible.

Crawl space: Add polyethylene vapor barrier (heavy construction grade or Mylar) to exposed dirt in crawlspace if monitoring indicates it is needed and there is no rising damp; add ventilation grilles for additional cross ventilation, if determined advisable.

Foundations and Basements: Correct existing high moisture levels, if other means of controlling ground moisture are inadequate.

Mechanical devices: Add interior perimeter drains and sump pump; add dehumidifiers for seasonal control of humidity in confined, unventilated space (but don't create a problem with pulling dampness out of walls); add ventilator fans to improve air flow, but don't use both the dehumidifier and ventilator fan at the same time.

Walls: Remove commentates coatings, if holding rising damp in walls; coat walls with vapor permeable lime based rendering plaster, if damp walls need a sacrificial coating to protect mortar from erosion; add termite shields, if evidence of termites and dampness cannot be controlled.

Framing: Reinforce existing floor framing weakened by moisture by adding lolly column support and reinforcing joist ends with sistered or parallel supports. Add a vapor impermeable shield, preferably non-ferrous metal, under wood joists coming into contact with moist masonry.

Interior: Eliminate areas where moisture is leaking or causing a problem.

Plumbing: Replace older pipes and fixtures subject to leaking or overflowing; insulate water pipes subject to condensation.

Ventilation: Add exhaust fans and whole house fans to increase air flow through buildings, if areas are damp or need more ventilation to control mold and mildew.

Climate: Adjust temperature and relative humidity to manage interior humidity; Correct areas of improperly balanced pressure for HVAC systems that may be causing a moisture problem.

A. *Mitigate poor drainage with gravel, filter cloth, or the use of subsurface drainage mats under finished paving. Photo: Larry D. Dermody.*

B. *Repair roofs and add ice and water shields at eaves and under valleys in cold climates. Photo: Larry D. Dermody.*

C. *Develop new drainage systems for roof run-off that remove moisture from the base of the building. Photo: WPTC, NPS.*

D. *Install ventilating fans when additional air circulation will improve damp conditions in buildings or reduce cooling loads. Photo: Ernest A. Conrad, P. E.*

A. *This lead sheet was installed at the base of the replacement column to stop rising damp. Photo: Bryan Blundell.*

B. *Wood sills set on grade were replaced with concrete pier foundation and new wooden sill plates. Changes were not visible on the exterior (see C). Photo: WPTC, NPS.*

Exterior: Undertake exterior rehabilitation work that follows professional repair practices —i.e., replace a deteriorated feature with a new feature to match the existing in design, color, texture, and when possible, materials. In some limited situations, non-historic materials may be necessary in unusually wet areas.

Roofs: Add ventilator fans to exhaust roofs but avoid large projecting features whose designs might negatively affect the appearance of the historic roof. When replacing roofs, correct conditions that have caused moisture problems, but keep the overall appearance of the roof; for example, ventilate under wooden shingles, or detail standing seams to avoid buckling and cracking. Be attentive to provide extra protection for internal or built-in gutters by using the best quality materials, flashing, and vapor impermeable connection details.

Walls: If insulation and vapor barriers are added to frame walls, consider maintaining a ventilation channel behind the exterior cladding to avoid peeling and blistering paint occurrences.

Windows: Consider removable exterior storm windows, but allow operation of windows for periodic ventilation of cavity between exterior storm and historic sash. For stained glass windows using protective glazing, use only ventilated storms to avoid condensation as well as heat build-up.

Ground: Control excessive ground moisture. This may require extensive excavations, new drainage systems, and the use of substitute materials. These may include concrete or new sustainable recycled materials for wood in damp areas when they do not impact the historic appearance of the building.

Grade: Excavate and install water collection systems to assist with positive run-off of low lying or difficult areas of moisture drainage; use drainage mats under finished grade to improve run-off control; consider the use of column plinth blocks or bases that are ventilated or constructed of non-absorbent substitute materials in chronically damp areas. Replace improperly sloped walks; repair non-functioning catch basins and site drains; repair settled areas around steps and other features at grade.

C. *The new ground gutter gravel base helps drainage around the concrete foundation (see B above) which is not visible behind the replaced wooden wall shingles. Photo: WPTC, NPS.*

D. *In a flood plain, rotted joists were replaced with a concrete slab and sleepers designed to drain water. Spaced flooring allowed drainage and room for damp wood to swell without buckling. Harper's Ferry Center, NPS.*

E. *Mechanical systems on the lower level were placed on platforms above the flood line. Harper's Ferry Center, NPS.*

— — FOR CHRONICALLY DAMP CONDITIONS

Foundations: Improve performance of foundation walls with damp-proof treatments to stop infiltration or damp course layers to stop rising damp. Some substitute materials may need to be selectively integrated into new features.

> **Walls:** excavate, repoint masonry walls, add footing drains, and waterproof exterior subsurface walls; replace wood sill plates and deteriorated structural foundations with new materials, such as pressure treated wood, to withstand chronic moisture conditions; materials may change, but overall appearance should remain similar. Add dampcourse layer to stop rising damp; avoid chemical injections as these are rarely totally effective, are not reversible, and are often visually intrusive.

Interior: Control the amount of moisture and condensation on the interiors of historic buildings. Most designs for new HVAC systems will be undertaken by mechanical engineers, but systems should be selected that are appropriate to the resource and intended use.

> **Windows, skylights:** Add double and triple glazing, where necessary to control condensation. Avoid new metal sashes or use thermal breaks where prone to heavy condensation.
>
> **Mechanical systems:** Design new systems to reduce stress on building exterior. This might require insulating and tightening up the building exterior, but provisions must be made for adequate air flow. A new zoned system, with appropriate transition insulation, may be effective in areas with differing climatic needs.
>
> **Control devices/Interior spaces:** If new climate control systems are added design back-up controls and monitoring systems to protect from interior moisture damage.
>
> **Walls:** If partition walls sit on floors that periodically flood, consider spacers or isolation membranes behind baseboards to stop moisture from wicking up through absorbent materials.

I. Critically damp foundation walls were protected with a layer of bentonite clay to reduce moisture penetration. This work was in combination with new downspouts that were connected to drainage boots that deposited captures roof run-off away from the foundation.
Photo: Courtesy, Larry D. Dermody and the National Trust for Historic Preservation.

Back Cover: The Diagnosing Moisture in Historic Building Symposium held in Washington, DC, May, 1996, brought together practitioners in the field of historic preservation to discuss the issues contained in this Preservation Brief. Attendees are standing in front of the cascading fountains at Meridian Hill Park, a National Historic Landmark. Photo: Eric Avner.

Reading List

Conrad, Ernest A., P.E. "The Dews and Don'ts of Insulating." *Old House Journal,* May/June, 1996.

Cumberland, Don, Jr. "Museum Collection Storage in an Historic Building Using a Prefabricated Structure." *Preservation Tech Notes.* Washington, DC: National Park Service, issue PTN-14. September, 1985.

Jessup, Wendy Claire, Ed. *Conservation in Context: Finding a Balance for the Historic House Museum.* Washington, DC: National Trust for Historic Preservation (Symposium Proceedings March 7-8, 1994).

Labine, Clem. "Managing Moisture in Historic Buildings" Special Report and Moisture Monitoring Source List. *Traditional Building,* Vol 9, No.2, May-June 1996.

Leeke, John. "Detecting Moisture; Methods and Tools for Evaluating Water in Old Houses." *Old House Journal,* May/June, 1996.

Moisture Control in Buildings. Heinz R. Trechsel, Editor. Philadelphia: American Society for Testing and Materials (ASTM manual series: MNL 18), 1993.

Museums in Historic Buildings (Special Issue). *APT Bulletin.* The Journal of Preservation Technology, Vol 26, No. 3 . Williamsburg, VA: APT, 1996.

Oxley, T.A. and A. E. Gobert. *Dampness in Buildings: Diagnosis, Treatment, Instruments.* London, Boston: Butterworth-Heinemann, 1994.

Park, Sharon C. AIA. *Preservation Brief 24: Heating, Ventilating, and Cooling Historic Buildings: Problems and Recommended Approaches.* Washington, DC: Department of the Interior, Government Printing Office, 1991.

Rose, William. "Effects of Climate Control on the Museum Building Envelope," *Journal of the American Institute for Conservation,* Vol. 33, No. 2. Summer, 1994.

Smith, Baird M. *Moisture Problems in Historic Masonry Walls; Diagnosis and Treatment.* Washington, DC.: Department of the Interior, Government Printing Office, 1984.

Tolpin, Jim. "Builder's Guide to Moisture Meters," Tools of the Trade Vol 2, No. 1 (Quarterly Supplement to *The Journal of Light Construction).* Richmond, Vermont: Builderburg Group Inc. Summer, 1994.

Acknowledgments

Sharon C. Park, AIA is the Senior Historical Architect, Technical Preservation Services, Heritage Preservation Services Program, National Park Service, Washington, D.C. The author wishes to thank the following individuals and organizations for providing technical review and other assistance in developing this publication: The attendees, speakers, and sponsors of the Diagnosing Moisture in Historic Buildings Symposium held in Washington, DC in 1996 and funded by a grant from the National Center for Preservation Technology and Training, National Park Service ; Hugh C. Miller, FAIA; Michael Henry, AIA, PE, PP; Baird M. Smith, AIA; Ernest A. Conrad, P.E.; William B. Rose; Rebecca Stevens. AIA; Wendy Claire Jessup; Elizabeth Sasser, AIA; Bryan Blundell; George Siekkinen, AIA; Larry D. Dermody; Kimberly A. Konrad; Barbara J. Mangum and the Isabella Stewart Gardner Museum, Boston; Gunston Hall Plantation; Friends of Meridian Hill; Friends of Great Falls Tavern; The National Trust for Historic Preservation; Thomas McGrath, Douglas C. Hicks and The Williamsport Preservation Training Center, NPS; the staff at Heritage Preservation Services, NPS, Charles E. Fisher, Brooks Prueher, Anne E. Grimmer, Antoinette Lee, and especially Kay D. Weeks.

This publication has been prepared pursuant to the National Historic Preservation Act, as amended, which directs the Secretary of the Interior to develop and make available information concerning historic properties. Comments about this publication should be directed to de Teel Patterson Tiller, Acting Manager, Heritage Preservation Services Program, National Park Service, P.O. Box 37127, Washington, DC 20013-7127.

Cover Photo: Masonry repointing in a wet environment. Photo: Williamsport Preservation Training Center, NPS.

40

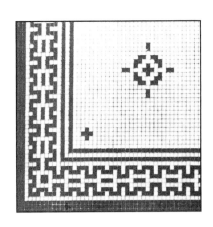

Preserving Historic Ceramic Tile Floors

Anne E. Grimmer and Kimberly A. Konrad

Figure 1. Minton encaustic tile floor, 3rd floor, Patent Office Building (now the National Portrait Gallery), Washington, D.C. Originally constructed between 1836-40 under the supervision of Robert Mills, the upper floors of this portion of the building were restored and redecorated in 1877 in the "Modern Renaissance style" by Cluss & Shulze, Architects, after a disastrous fire. Photo: Jack E. Boucher, HABS Collection.

With a tradition that dates to ancient civilizations, ceramic* tile flooring can be found in a variety of settings in diverse cultures and structures, including residential buildings ranging from large apartment buildings to small private houses, institutional buildings such as government offices and schools, and religious buildings such as cathedrals and mosques. Historically, its widespread use may be attributed to the fact that a readily available natural material—clay—could be converted by a relatively simple manufacturing process—baking or firing—into a very durable, long-lasting and attractive floor tile that is easy to maintain. Ceramic floor tiles exhibit a versatility of colored glazes and decoration, and they range from the plainest terra cotta tiles to highly decorated individual ceramic tiles and elaborately patterned tile floors. Their modularity, as standardized units, make them easy to fit into different sized spaces which also explains much of the popularity of ceramic floor tiles throughout history (Fig. 1).

This Brief begins with an overview of ceramic tiles as a traditional flooring material. It includes an explanation of the various kinds of historic floor tiles used in the United States and how they were made. General guidance is given on preservation treatments, focusing on maintenance, and, when necessary, selective replacement of damaged floor tiles. The Brief is intended to provide owners and managers of historic properties with an understanding of the significance and historical background of ceramic floor tiles, and a basic awareness of maintenance techniques and various deterioration problems to which tile floors are especially prone. In the case of significant historic ceramic tile floors, a professional conservator of ceramics should be consulted to advise in matters of repair, restoration or conservation. Historically, ceramic tiles were used on walls as wainscotting, on fireplace hearths and fireplace surrounds, and even on furniture, as well as for flooring. However, because floor tiles are subject to greater damage and deterioration, they are the primary emphasis of this Brief. Highlights include: a short history of ceramic floor tiles; a description of ceramic tile types; a summary of traditional installation methods; maintenance techniques; and guidance on repair and replacement.

The Tile-Making Process

Clay is an earthen material, moldable or plastic when wet, non-plastic when dry, and permanently hard when baked or fired. It is widely distributed geographically, and often found mixed with sand in soils of a loam type—a mixture of clay, silt and sand. Relatively pure clay is not usually a surface deposit, although, in some cases, it may be exposed by erosion. Clay types vary throughout the world, and even within a region. Each type of clay possesses a unique combination of special properties such as plasticity, hardness and lightness, as well as color and texture, which makes some clays better suited for one kind of ceramic than another. The correct clay mixture needed for a particular purpose can be created by blending clays and adding other materials, but using the wrong type of clay can result in expensive production problems such as crazing (the formation of tiny cracks in a tile glaze) or warping of the tile itself. Traditionally, chalky clays have been preferred for many kinds of ceramic tiles, in part because they produce, when fired, a white body which is desirable for decorating. Other materials can be added, including grog (or ground-up fired clay) that helps aerate the clay and prevents warping, speeds firing and reduces shrinking, or calcined flint, to harden it.

There are several methods used for making ceramic tiles: extrusion; compaction or *dust-pressing*; cutting from a sheet of clay; or molded in a wooden or metal frame. Quarry tiles are extruded, but most ceramic floor tiles, including traditional encaustic, geometric and ceramic "mosaic" tiles are made from refined and blended ceramic powders using the compaction method, known as dust-pressing. Encaustic tiles, which were made by dust-pressing, are unique in that their designs are literally "inlaid" into the tile body, rather than surface-applied. Once formed, tiles are dried slowly and evenly to avoid warpage, then fired in a special kiln that controls high, even heat at temperatures up to 1200°C (or approximately 2500°F) for 30-40 hours. Higher temperatures produce denser tiles with harder glazes. Most ceramic tiles require only one firing to achieve low porosity and become vitrified or glasslike, but some, especially highly decorated tiles, are fired more than once. Non-vitreous and semi-vitreous tiles are fired at lower temperatures and are much more porous.

Historical Background

Historically, the use of ceramic floor tiles goes back to the fourth millennium B.C. in the Near and Far East. The Romans introduced tile-making in Western Europe as they occupied territories. However, that art was eventually forgotten in Europe for centuries until the 12th century when Cistercian monks developed a method of making encaustic floor tiles with inlaid patterns for cathedral and church floors. But, this skill was again lost in the 16th century following the Reformation. Except for finely decorated wall tiles made in Turkey and the Middle East, and Delft tiles made in Holland in the 17th century, ceramic floor tiles were not made again in Europe until almost the mid-19th century.

The modern tile industry was advanced by Herbert Minton in 1843 when he revived the lost art of encaustic tile-making in England. The industry was further revolutionized in the 1840s by the "dust-pressing" method which consisted of compressing nearly dry clay between two metal dies. Dust-pressing replaced tile-making by hand with wet clay, and facilitated mechanization of the tile-making industry. Throughout the rest of the 19th century, dust-pressing enabled faster and cheaper production of better quality floor tiles in a greater range of colors and designs. In the 1850s encaustic tiles were selected for such important structures as the new Palace at Westminster in London, and Queen Victoria's Royal Residence on the Isle of Wight. By the latter part of the 19th century, despite the fact that encaustic tiles were still quite expensive, they had become a common flooring material in many kinds of buildings.

Development of the Tile Industry in America. Although plain, undecorated ceramic tiles were traditionally a common flooring material in many parts of the Americas, especially in Latin and South America, ceramic floor and roof tiles were probably not made in the North American Colonies until the late-16th or early-17th century. It was, however, in the Victorian era that ceramic tile flooring first became so prevalent in the United States. The production of decorative tiles in America began about 1870 and flourished until about 1930.

Like so many architectural fashions of the day, the popularity of ceramic tile floors in America was greatly influenced by the noted architect and critic, Andrew Jackson Downing. In his book *The Architecture of Country Houses*, published in 1850, Downing recommended encaustic floor tiles for residential use because of their practicality, especially in vestibules and entrance halls.

The 1876 Philadelphia Centennial Exposition, with its European and even a few American exhibits of decorative floor tile, was a major factor in popularizing ceramic tile floors in the U.S. Initially, most ceramic tiles—other than purely utilitarian floor tiles—were imported from England, and their relatively high cost meant that only wealthy Americans could afford them. However, when English tile companies realized the potential for profitable export, they soon established agents in major U.S. cities to handle their

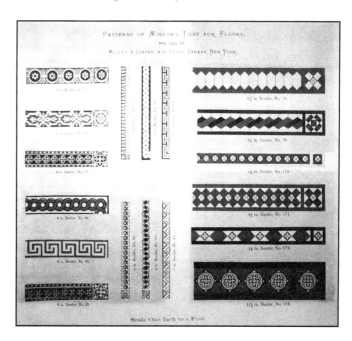

Figure 2. In the 19th century, Minton tiles were sold from this catalogue to American clients—including the Architect of the Capitol—by Miller & Coates, 279 Pearl Street, New York. Photo: David W. Look, AIA.

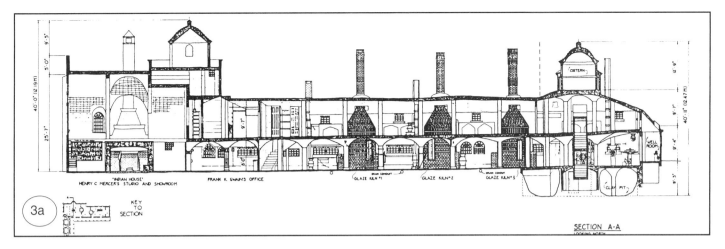

American business (Fig. 2). The English near monopoly actually stimulated the growth of the U.S. tile industry in the 1870s resulting in sharply decreased English imports by 1890.

The location of potteries and ceramic tile factories is dependent upon the ready availability of suitable ball clay (clay that balled or held together), kaolin (a white clay used as a filler or extender), and feldspar (a crystalline mineral), and an accessible market. Since the cost of shipping the manufactured products tended to restrict profitable sales to limited areas, this usually determined whether a factory would succeed. Although the United States Pottery in Bennington, Vermont, is known to have made encaustic tiles as early as 1853, the Pittsburgh Encaustic Tile Company (later the Star Encaustic Tiling Company), was the first successful American tile company, and is generally considered the first to manufacture ceramic tile in the U.S. on a commercial basis beginning in 1876.

At least 25 ceramic tile companies were founded in the United States between 1876 and 1894. In the East, several notable tile firms that were established in this period flourished in the Boston area, such as the Chelsea Keramic Art Works, the Low Art Tile Works, and the Grueby Faience Company. Other East Coast companies organized in the late-19th and early-20th century included the International Tile & Trim Company, in Brooklyn, New York; the Trent Tile Company, Providential Tile Company, Mueller Mosaic Tile Company, and the Maywood Tile Company, all in New Jersey; and the Moravian Pottery and Tile Works in Doylestown, Pennsylvania (Fig. 3).

Many factories were also established in the Midwest—in Indiana, Michigan, and, especially, in Ohio. In the last quarter of the 19th century, the town of Zanesville, Ohio, was the largest center for pottery and tile-making in the world. Some of the factories in Zanesville included: Ohio Encaustic Tile Company; Mosaic Tile Company; Zanesville

Figure 3. (a) The Moravian Pottery and Tile Works, a National Historic Landmark in Doylestown, PA, was designed in the Spanish Mission style and constructed by Henry Chapman Mercer over a period of years from 1911-1917. Tiles were manufactured primarily by hand in keeping with Mercer's Arts and Crafts ideals. (b) Mercer's tiles, seen here in the library, were used throughout his house, Fonthill. (c-e) One of Mercer's most important commissions was the floor of the Pennsylvania State Capitol in Harrisburg. (f) The factory closed in 1930 after Mercer's death, but resumed tile-making in 1974. New tiles are dated and made in the traditional way. (a) Drawing: Leslie S. Claytor, Benita C. Welch, Isabel C. Yang, HAER Collection; (b) Photo: Jack E. Boucher, HABS Collection; (c-e) Photos: Courtesy, Mercer Museum, The Bucks County Historical Society; (f) Photo: Anne Grimmer.

Figure 4. The tiled Presidential Seal in the courtyard of the Pension Building (now the National Building Museum), Washington, D.C., was installed in honor of President William McKinley's second inauguration in 1901. The"heavy Damask design," resembling fabric, that was used to decorate the tiles, indicates they were probably manufactured by The Mosaic Tile Company, Zanesville, Ohio, which first introduced this design. Photo: Kimberly A. Konrad.

Figure 5. Geometric tiles made by the American Encaustic Tiling Company, also in Zanesville, were installed in the corridors of the Pension Building in 1888, several years after the building's completion. Photo: Kimberly A. Konrad.

Figure 6. The Los Angeles Union Passenger Terminal features ceramic tile floors in the Art Deco-style. Photo: HABS Collection.

Majolica Company; and J.B. Owens Pottery, later to become the Empire Floor and Wall Tile Company (Fig. 4). The American Encaustic Tiling Company, established in 1876, was one of the first, and most successful manufacturers in Zanesville (Fig. 5). In the early 1930s it was the largest tile company in the world, producing large quantities of floor tile, plain and ornamental wall tile, and art tile until it closed about 1935, as a result of the Depression. The United States Encaustic Tile Company, Indianapolis, Indiana; Rookwood Pottery, Cincinnati, Ohio; Cambridge Art Tile Works, Covington, Kentucky; and Pewabic Pottery, Detroit, Michigan, were some of the other well-known potteries in the Midwest.

Around the turn of the century, the industry began to expand as tilemakers moved West and established potteries there. Joseph Kirkham started the ceramic tile industry on the West Coast in 1900 when he set up the Pacific Art Tile Company in Tropico, California, after his company in Ohio was destroyed by fire. In 1904 the company became the Western Art Tile Company, surviving for five years until it went out of business in 1909. During the early-20th century, other companies were founded in Southern California, in and around Los Angeles (Fig. 6). Batchelder & Brown, in particular, of Pasadena (later Batchelder-Wilson in Los Angeles), was well-known for its Arts and Crafts-style tiles in the teens and 1920s. By the early 1940s California had become one of the leading producers of tile, especially faience, in the U.S. (Fig. 7) .

Ceramic engineers, potters and artists not only moved frequently from one pottery to another, but often struck out on their own and established new factories when dissatisfied with a former employer. Also, it was not uncommon for one company to reuse a defunct factory or purchase another pottery business, change the name and increase the product line. As a result, many of the companies in existence today are descendants of the early pioneering firms.

Changes in the Tile Industry. The majority of ceramic floor tile made in the U.S. before 1890 was encaustic, but various factories gradually began to develop and produce other kinds of tiles. The Trent Tile Company, among others, started to manufacture both white and colored ceramic mosaic tiles by the mid-1890s (Fig. 8). White vitreous wall tile became available, as well as more decorative tiles with colored glazes, such as the variegated faience glazes intended to give a more hand-crafted appearance that were originated by the Grueby Faience and Tile Company in 1894, and soon adopted by other potteries (Fig. 9).

In the 19th and early-20th century, many ceramic tile firms had their own engraving departments, while some used commercial designs supplied by professional printers. Well-known designers were often commissioned to work on specific product lines for a particular firm. These designers worked for one firm after another which resulted in similar designs being produced by different companies. (Historic ceramic floor tiles were usually identified by a manufacturer's or designer's mark on the back, if they were marked at all.) By the latter part of the 19th century ready-mixed glazes and colors were also available. This was a great advantage for potters who, prior to this, had to mix their own colors and glazes.

During the 20th century, the floor tile industry continued to evolve as much as it had in the previous century. Modern

Figure 7. "Scotty's Castle" in Death Valley, California, was built over a 10-year period, beginning in 1922. Many of the rooms, the salon (a), as well as the kitchen (b), have tile floors. Some are composed of both local, California-made tiles, and Spanish tiles. Photos: Jack E. Boucher, HABS Collection.

Figure 8. The Trent Tile Company advertised its "Ceramic Mosaic Floor" tiles in the 1906 edition of "Sweet's" Indexed Catalogue of Building Construction. Photo: Sharon C. Park, AIA.

Figure 9. Beginning in the late-19th century, a decorative frieze with a relief design, such as this classical egg and dart motif, was often added to highlight plain ceramic wall tile. Photo: Kimberly A. Konrad.

methods of production employed sophisticated machinery, new materials and decorating techniques. In the years following World War II, there were many advances in the industry. Commercially manufactured dust-pressed tiles, which had previously required more than 70 hours just in the kiln, could be made in less than two hours from the raw material stage to finished tiles, boxed and ready to ship. Dried, unglazed tiles were sprayed with colored glaze evenly and automatically as conveyors carried the tiles into the tunnel kilns, and the extrusion process ensured that the tiles were cut to a uniform thickness and size. The changes and developments in the production of floor tile brought forth a wide range of shapes and sizes, along with new colors, glazes and decorating techniques.

After the turn of the century, fewer encaustic floor tiles were used, particularly in residential architecture. The introduction of ceramic mosaic floor tiles was a factor in their decline (Fig. 10). The development of rubber interlocking floor tiles in 1894, along with other, more resilient, flooring materials, was instrumental in the decreased popularity not only of encaustic tiles, but also other ceramic tile flooring. These new materials were not only cheaper, they were not as fragile; they were also lighter and thinner, and easier to install.

Ceramic mosaic tiles remained in common use through the 1930s in part because an innovative development had made laying such small tiles easier. The tiles were pre-mounted in decorative patterns on 12" x 12" sheets of paper, and sold ready to lay in cement. This greatly simplified the tile setter's work, and no doubt was a significant factor in the increased popularity of ceramic mosaic tiles. Sophisticated mosaic floor designs became common in entrance foyers of public and private buildings (Fig. 11). Small, white, unglazed tiles in round, square, octagonal or hexagonal shapes were promoted for their sanitary qualities, particularly for bathroom floors, while larger, rectangular, white, glazed tiles were used for bathroom walls or wainscotting. Colored tiles were also popular, especially

for bathrooms, and even kitchens (Fig. 12). Quarry tile, which was larger and thicker than other ceramic floor tile of this period, was often used in public buildings, as well as for entrance halls, small studies, libraries, dining rooms and even living rooms in private homes. But, by the 1930s, the fashion for art tile had diminished to the point where floor tiles were, for the most part, generally regarded as primarily utilitarian, as opposed to important decorative elements.

Ceramic Floor Tile Types

The **thickness** of historic ceramic floor tiles varied considerably according to their intended use and when they were made. Floor tiles were thicker and harder than wall or ceiling tiles. Stove tiles, meant to retain the heat of the stove, were sometimes as much as several inches thick. Medieval floor tiles were usually one inch thick; encaustic tiles of the Victorian era tended to be slightly thinner. Modern, 20th-century tiles, with the exception of some art pottery tiles, are the thinnest, as a result of modern

Figure 10. Ceramic mosaic tile floors were practical for structures like this Bath House, Hot Springs, Arkansas (1914-1915). Photo: Jack E. Boucher, HABS Collection.

manufacturing methods. The backs of most, but not all, ceramic floor tiles are covered with raised (or sometimes recessed) ridges, circles or squares which help to increase the bonding capability of the tile.

Unglazed and Glazed Tiles

Ceramic floor tiles can generally be divided into two types: **unglazed** and **glazed. Unglazed** tiles include: quarry tiles; encaustic and geometric tiles; and ceramic mosaic tiles, which can be either glazed or unglazed. Most other ceramic floor tiles are **glazed.**

Unglazed Tiles

Quarry tiles are the most basic type of historic ceramic floor tile (Fig. 13). Originally made from quarried stone, they are machine-made using the extrusion process. Quarry tiles are unglazed, semi-vitreous or vitreous, and essentially are square or rectangular slabs of clay baked in a kiln. The colors of quarry tiles are natural earthen shades of gray, red and brown determined by the clay and, to some extent, the temperature and duration of firing. Quarry tiles, which range from 1/4" to 1/2" in thickness, are available in square and rectangular shapes in sizes that include 3", 4-1/4", 6" (one of the most common sizes), 9" and 12" squares; 6" x 12", 6" x 9", 4-1/4" x 9", 3" x 6", and 3" x 9" rectangles; and 4" x 8" hexagon shapes. (Pavers or paver tiles are a simpler, and tend to be somewhat cruder, version of quarry tiles. Like quarry tiles, they are usually unglazed, but slightly thicker. Machine-made pavers are either semi-vitreous or vitreous, and generally formed by dust-pressing, although sometimes are extruded. Hand-made pavers which are common in Mexico and southern Europe are non-vitreous.)

Encaustic tiles are a type of traditional unglazed—yet decorative—floor tile, manufactured by the dust-pressed method. Whereas most ceramic tiles are surface-decorated or decorated with impressed or embossed designs created by a mold, encaustic tiles are unique in that their decorative designs are not on the surface, but are inlaid patterns created as part of the manufacturing process. First, a thin, approximately 1/4" layer of fine, almost powder-dry, clay was pressed into a mold with a relief design at the bottom which formed a depression in the face of the tile. A second, thicker layer of coarser clay was laid over the first layer, then covered with another layer of fine clay. This "sandwich" helped prevent warping and ensured that the body of the tile was strong and had a fine, smooth surface. The layers of clay "dust" were compacted by presses, after which the mold was inverted and the die removed, thus producing a tile with an indented or intaglio pattern on top. After the tile dried, colored slip (liquid white clay colored with dyes), was poured to fill in the intaglio pattern. Each color had to dry before another color of slip was added. The recessed area was overfilled to allow for shrinkage, and after drying for several days, and before firing, the excess slip was scraped off the surface by a rotating cutter that created a flat, although not completely smooth, face. Problems might arise during the firing. Due to the dissimilar rates of contraction of the different clays, the inlaid clay could shrink too much and fall out of the tile recesses; or, the tile could be stained by the different pigments used for the design if impure or unstable (Fig. 14).

By the 1840s, encaustic tiles were made entirely with almost-dry clay using the dust-pressed method. This served to

Figure 11. Ceramic mosaic tiles were used decoratively on the entrance floor of this early-20th century school building. Photo: Kimberly A. Konrad.

eliminate the possibility of staining the body of the tile with other colors and permitted the use of more colors on a single tile. Thus, an encaustic tile can sometimes be dated according to the complexity and the number of colors in its pattern. Red tiles with white figurative patterns were generally the earliest, followed by brown and buff colored tiles. In the 1860s, blue tiles with yellow or buff patterns were popular, succeeded by more subtle color schemes featuring a "chocolate" red with a soft grey. By 1860, up to six colors were used in a single tile to form a pattern. Toward the end of the century, white encaustic tiles with a black or gold design were common, as well as tiles with complicated color patterns of white, black, gold, pink, green and blue. Encaustic tiles were decorated with traditional as well as original designs. Some, particularly intricate, designs were painted on the surface of the tile with opaque colored glazes, instead of being inlaid (Fig. 15). Most major tile manufacturers sold many of the same pre-formed encaustic floor tile patterns through catalogues. Encaustic tiles were produced in a variety of sizes, mostly square or octagonal in shape, and almost any design could be custom-made for a special purpose or to fit a particular space. Historic, 19th-century encaustic tiles were generally slightly less than 1" thick, about 15/16." Cheaper tiles of lesser quality were also made of clay or cement. These designs

Figure 12. These colorful (yellow, black and white), and boldly patterned Art Deco-style ceramic tiles were made in France. Ernest Hemingway's wife, Pauline, brought them back to the U.S. in the 1930s and had them installed in a bathroom in their house in Key West, Florida. Photo: Susan Escherich.

Figure 13. Quarry tiles were used in the corridors on many of the upper floors of the U.S. Department of the Interior Building (1935-1936). They were laid in a pattern identical to the more expensive marble floor tiles that were used in the public spaces. Photo: Brooks Photographers, HABS Collection.

resembled those commonly found on encaustic tiles but applied as a transfer printed pattern, or using a multi-color lithographic or silkscreen process. These are still manufactured and popular in many parts of the world (Fig. 16).

Smaller, single-colored versions of encaustic tiles that, when assembled together form a geometric pattern, are called **geometric tiles** in England. However, in the United States they are generally not differentiated from encaustic tiles. Based on the geometric segments of a six-inch square, they were typically rectangular, square, triangular or hexagonal in shape, and about the same thickness as patterned encaustic tiles (Fig. 17). Geometric tiles were especially well suited for decorative borders, and a wide variety of floor designs could be created with their many shapes, sizes and colors—either alone or combined with patterned encaustic tiles. The cost of producing geometric tiles was much less than of encaustic tiles because each tile involved only one type of clay and one color. By the end of the 19th century, over 60 different shapes and sizes of geometric tiles were available in up to ten colors, including buff, beige or tan, salmon, light grey, dark grey, red, chocolate, blue, white and black.

Ceramic mosaic tiles are essentially smaller versions of geometric tiles (usually no larger than 2-1/4", and no thicker than 1/4") ranging in size from 1/2" to 2 3/16", in square, rectangular or oblong, hexagonal, pentagonal and

trapezoidal shapes. Both vitreous and semi-vitreous mosaic tiles were available, unglazed in solid or variegated colors with a matte finish, or glazed in unlimited colors. Single, one-piece tiles were also fabricated to give the appearance of multiple mosaic pieces. This was achieved with a mold, which gave the appearance of recessed mortar joints separating individual "mosaics" (Fig. 18).

Glazed Tiles

With the exception of quarry tiles, encaustic tiles, and some mosaic tiles, most ceramic floor tiles are decorated with a glaze. While unglazed tiles derive their color solely from the clay, or from oxides, dyes or pigments added to the clay, the color of glazed tiles is provided by the glaze, either shiny or matte. Some potteries specialized in certain kinds of glazes and were famous for them. The earliest and most common method of clay tile decoration made use of tin-glazes which were essentially transparent lead glazes. Tiles were either dipped into the glaze or the glaze was brushed on the tile surface. Glazes were generally made with white lead, flint, or china clays ground up and mixed with finely ground metallic oxides that provided the color. Colored glazes were commonly known as "enamels". Colors included blue derived from cobalt, green from copper, purple from manganese, yellow from antimony and lead, and reds and browns from iron. An opaque glaze was created by adding tin oxide.

Laying Ceramic Tile Floors

19th Century Techniques. Aside from the use of improved tools and modern materials, installation methods have changed little since the mid-19th century. M. Digby Wyatt, an architect for one of the major 19th century encaustic tile manufacturers in Britain, Maw & Co., described this procedure for laying encaustic and geometric tiles in 1857:

First, either an even layer of bricks, a 2-1/2" bed of concrete of quicklime and gravel, or a mixture of Portland cement and clean sharp sand was laid to prepare a solid foundation for the tiles. If the tiles were to be laid over an existing wooden floor, the floor boards had to be pulled up, sawn into short lengths and fitted between the joists. Concrete filled in the spaces and made the base flush with the upper face of the joists, and created a level surface finished within 1" of the finished floor line. A layer of

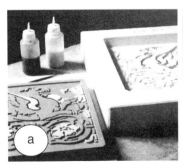 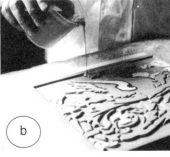 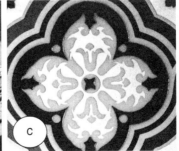 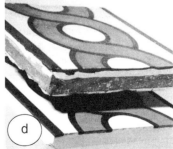

*Figure 14. **Making encaustic tiles.** When finished, a reproduction encaustic tile resembles a historic tile, but the reproduction process is quite different from the traditional method. Designs for reproduction tiles are recreated by a computer from drawings of the original tile. (a) The computer image of the design is transferred to, and machine-cut into, a Plaster of Paris mold. Plastic, buff-colored clay is pressed into the mold to form the main body of the tile, and left to dry for 24 hours. (b) Colored slip, or liquid clay, is poured into the indented portions of the tile to create the pattern. (Each color of slip must dry before another color can be poured.) (c) After drying, and before firing, excess slip is scraped off, leaving the surface of the tile smooth, but the slip-filled areas still slightly recessed. (d) A side view of the 19th-century tile at the top of the photograph clearly shows the 3-layer clay "sandwich," as well as the 2 colors of slip that form the inlaid design. The new tile, below, is slightly thinner and is made from only 1 layer of clay. Photos: (a-b) H&R Johnson Tiles Ltd.; (c-d) Wayne Firth, Office of the Architect of the Capitol.*

Figure 15. The detailed features of the portrait on this round tile in the U.S. Capitol were painted on the surface of the tile rather than inlaid. Photo: David W. Look, AIA.

Figure 16. Historic cement floor tiles in a house at 103 Calle San Jose, Old San Juan, Puerto Rico, feature a design intended to resemble wood parquet. (Note the mismatched repair.) Photo: Jack E. Boucher, HABS Collection.

cement mortar was then laid on top. This allowed the tiles to fit in the same amount of space as the floorboards they replaced.*

Before laying the tiles, skirting boards or shoe moldings were to be removed, and replaced after the tiles were laid. This eliminated having to cut the outer tiles to fit exactly, and resulted in a neater appearance.

Next, the floor design was marked off with mason's string or chalk lines which divided the space into equal quadrants. The first section to be laid out was defined by two parallel strips of wood, or guide pieces, about 4" wide. A level thickness of cement was spread between these strips. The tiles, thoroughly soaked in water, were laid in the cement and leveled with a straight-edge. The foundation had to be kept wet while the tiles were being laid. Small strips of wood temporarily placed at right angles to the guide pieces helped keep elaborate patterns straight.

When the bed was hard, the joints were filled with pure cement mortar—sometimes colored with lamp black, red ochre or other natural pigments—mixed to the consistency of cream. Excess mortar was wiped off the tiles with a piece of flannel or sponge.

---

*The traditional practice of sawing the original floor boards and fitting them between the joists, still used today to maintain a low finished floor profile, has resulted in numerous cracked tiles and other failures. Instead, a better approach is to leave the existing floor boards, if they are in good shape, and install a cementitious backer board (CBU) available in thicknesses ranging from 1/4" to 5/8" as the setting bed for the tiles.

A newly-laid tile floor could not be walked on for 4-6 days until the cement hardened properly. Occasional washing would remove the saline scum that often appeared on the surface right after the tiles were laid.

20th Century Techniques. Almost 50 years later, in 1904, the Tile Manufacturers of the United States of America published *Suggestions for Setting Tile* with the intent of bringing tile-laying up to a uniform standard. This guidance was very similar to that given by Wyatt. But, there were some differences, such as using hollow clay tile as a foundation material and heavy tar paper when laying tile over a wooden floor to protect the floor boards from the moisture of the mortar mix. Emphasis was placed on using the best quality cement, sand, and purest water to obtain a durable tile floor. Soaking the tiles before setting was no longer necessary, but using stiffer mortar was suggested to prevent it from rising up between the tiles.

Tile-laying methods changed somewhat more later in the 20th century, mostly due to the availability of new materials and techniques. By the 1920s small ceramic mosaic tiles were manufactured as 12" square sheets held together by a face-mounted paper "skin." This made it possible to lay the 12" square of tiles as a unit rather than each of the small tiles individually. Mounting the tiles directly in the cement resulted in a very strong bond. But the face-mounted paper obscured the tiles from view making it difficult for the tile-setter to see if the tiles were being laid straight. The fact that the paper was not removed until after the tiles were firmly set in the cement bond coat further complicated

Figure 17. Shown here are typical geometric tile patterns popular in the late-19th century, as illustrated in **Decorative Tile Designs in Full Color.** Selected and arranged by Carol Belanger Grafton. NY: Dover Publications, Inc., 1992, pp. 73, 83.

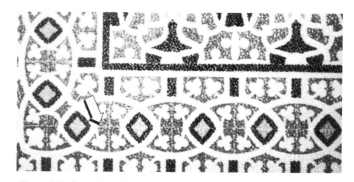

Figure 18. One-piece tiles were made with a mold that created the appearance of mortar joints and individual mosaics, as illustrated in **Decorative Tile Designs in Full Color.** Selected and arranged by Carol Belanger Grafton. NY: Dover Publications, Inc., 1992, p. 87.

Figure 19. Regular maintenance treatments for the historic quarry tile floors in the U.S. Department of the Interior, shown here in a side corridor, include: stripping and waxing once a year; weekly spraying and buffing with a commercial "floor finish revitalizer/cleaner" that is slip resistant; and dust mopping or damp mopping 4 times a week. Photo: Brooks Photographers, HABS Collection.

realignment of crooked tiles. This paper "skin" was eventually replaced with a fabric mesh backing. This permitted the tiles to be aligned as soon as the moisture from the bond coat loosened the mesh from the back of the tile; it also allowed a single tile to be cut away from the mesh and repositioned immediately. Although the fabric mesh made tile setting faster, sometimes it also resulted in a weaker bond by reducing the contact area between the backs of the tiles and the bond coat.

Following World War II, different methods of preparing a foundation for a ceramic tile floor were developed to be more compatible with new materials, such as reinforced concrete, expanded wire mesh, polyethylene and waterproof plywood. New adhesives and grouts also facilitated tile installation, and an increased variety of epoxy and cement mortars allowed for different setting bed thicknesses. But today, after half a century of practical application, some of these "new" materials, such as plywood, particle board, oriented strand boards and other wood panels, are no longer recommended for use with ceramic tile.

Mortar beds are lighter, more flexible, and much thinner than they were previously, having shrunk from several inches to as thin as 3/32". A greater variety of materials are used for setting ceramic floor tiles, including bonding agents and waterproof membranes. Basic installation methods have not changed significantly, but they vary according to the type of subfloor on which the tile is to be laid. While the same concerns for level underlayment and strong adhesion exist, advancement has occurred mostly in the increased speed and ease of laying the tiles.

Historic Ceramic Floor Tile: Preservation and Maintenance

Before undertaking any work more complicated than regular maintenance or a very simple repair on a significant historic ceramic tile floor, or on any historic tile floor where serious damage has occurred, it is recommended that a professional conservator of ceramics, an historical architect, an architectural historian, or a chemist with particular knowledge and experience in this field be consulted. This will ensure that all future work, whether it be regularly-scheduled maintenance or more technical and specialized repair and restoration, is done in accordance with the Secretary of the Interior's *Standards for the Treatment of Historic Properties.*

Cleaning Methods. Ceramic tiles are essentially a practical, low-maintenance flooring material. Yet, even glazed tiles are somewhat porous, and can get dirty and stained, especially in heavy traffic areas or where oil, fat, and grass stains are likely to occur. Although heavily soiled areas may be difficult or impossible to clean completely, in most instances, cleaning ceramic tile floors is relatively easy. Cleaning should always begin with the gentlest means possible, which may be as simple as warm water. Regular maintenance should include sweeping, or preferably dry or damp mopping or vacuuming to reduce grit. Tiles can usually be cleaned with a non-soap-based household floor cleaner, such as one of the commercial products intended for cleaning ceramic tile floors available on the market.

All cleaning and stain-removal products should always be tested on a small, inconspicuous area before using. Abrasive cleaners (including powdered cleansers and even "mildly" abrasive creams) and mechanical equipment can damage and wear away the protective surface, as well as the decorative design on the tiles, and should not be used on ceramic tile floors. Generally, acid-based cleaning solutions should also not be used on ceramic tile floors because they can damage the complex silicates in a glaze. However, there are some acid-based cleaners specially formulated for cleaning and removing coatings from ceramic tile floors that may be acceptable, but even these must be used with caution. Sometimes an acid-based cleaner may, in fact, be needed to remove discoloration or staining caused by lime or cement mortar. But, it should be tested first, used with caution, and applied only to a thoroughly wetted tile floor from which excess water has been removed. Pre-wetting a ceramic tile floor before cleaning is a good policy to observe with all cleaners. The water saturates the porous tile and prevents chemicals or other cleaning agents from penetrating into the tile body. Floor tiles should be always rinsed thoroughly after cleaning.

Figure 20. The surfaces of these late-19th century encaustic tiles have become worn and much of the pattern has been lost after more than 100 years of use. Photo: Anne Grimmer.

Figure 21. These cracked geometric tiles may have been damaged by the repeated passage of heavy equipment over the floor. Photo: Anne Grimmer.

Plastic pot-scrubbers may be effective in loosening and removing superficial dirt without abrading the glazed or vitrified surface of the tiles. Stubborn asphalt or oil stains, scuff marks, or soiling can sometimes be removed with ammonia or one of the household spray products intended for cleaning kitchen or bathroom tiles. If necessary, a solvent may be applied carefully to pre-wetted tiles, but it should not be left on the surface for an extended amount of time as it may cause discoloration. If possible, a stain should always be identified first in order to select the material best-suited to remove it.

Organic growth, such as mold or mildew, can be eliminated with a dilute solution of household bleach and a neutral household detergent, or a dilute (5-10%) solution of tri-sodium phosphate (TSP). After applying either of these solutions, it may be necessary to scrub the floor with a natural bristle or nylon brush, and then rinse with clear water. Even a dilute bleach solution should not be left on a ceramic tile floor for more than a few minutes, since the alkali in the bleach can lead to the formation of a white efflorescent deposit. Efflorescence (a whitish haze of water-soluble salts) may stain and streak the tile, or may even cause minor spalling around the joints.

Regular maintenance of a ceramic tile floor should always begin with vacuuming to remove loose dirt and grit. Then, a mild cleaning solution may be applied and left on the floor for 10-15 minutes, without letting it dry on the tiles. Heavily soiled areas may be scrubbed with a natural bristle or nylon brush to loosen dirt from the tile surface. Finally, the floor should be thoroughly rinsed with clean, clear water, preferably twice, and dried with terry cloth towels, if necessary. Any proprietary cleaning product should always be used in accordance with the manufacturer's directions (Fig. 19).

Protective Coatings. In most instances, traditional ceramic tile floors probably would not have been treated or given a protective coating other than wax. In the 19th century, some encaustic tile floors were treated with linseed oil, but this is not a practice recommended today because linseed oil tends to attract dirt and discolors as it ages. Most historic ceramic tile floors simply acquired a natural "polish" or sheen through use. Because the surface of ceramic tiles is already protected with a fired skin or a glaze, an additional protective coating should generally not be needed.

Opinions differ concerning the use of protective coatings, penetrating sealers, or waxes on ceramic tile floors, and, especially, on historic ceramic tile floors. If properly applied and regularly cleaned, a coating can sometimes be an effective maintenance treatment, but only on interior floors. However, if not adequately or properly maintained, rather than facilitating maintenance of ceramic tile floors in high traffic areas, such coatings may tend to emphasize traffic patterns as they wear away or become scratched. Some coatings may also peel in spots, or cause tile to appear hazy or cloudy if the coating is not applied in accordance with the manufacturer's specifications, or if the tiles are not perfectly clean when the coating is applied. Furthermore, applying such a coating may actually increase maintenance costs, since a coating requires periodic removal and renewal. The frequent removal of a coating can also damage a ceramic tile floor if it is carried out with harsh chemicals or abrasive mechanical equipment. If any coating

Figure 22. Original section drawing of the 2nd and 3rd floors of the House of Representatives Wing of the U.S. Capitol shows how Montgomery C. Meigs ensured the durability of the encaustic tile floors that were laid in the 1850s. He specified that the 3/4" tiles be laid on top of 1/2 to 3/4" mud (or mortar), which, in turn, was to be laid over a coal tar membrane on top of 3" of brick over an air space of 4-6". Photo: Wayne Firth, Office of the Architect of the Capitol.

is considered, a traditional coating, such as floor wax, may be the most suitable. Wax is easy to remove when it becomes worn, and does not impart a high, potentially inappropriate, gloss to the surface.

On the other hand, a penetrating sealer, or *impregnator*, may be worth considering to protect patterned encaustic tiles, or painted or printed tiles featuring a design that might be worn off, particularly in public buildings with a high volume of foot traffic. For example, some manufacturers of new, reproduction encaustic tiles recommend applying a penetrating sealer to the replacement tiles, as well as to the historic tiles. Impregnators do not change the color of the tile surface and, unlike some penetrating sealers, are completely invisible after they have been applied. They can reduce the porosity or water absorption of the tile surface, and provide some protection for the tile (and the grout) against staining. This may be particularly useful on light-colored floors. Whether to apply an impregnator to an historic ceramic tile floor, and what type or product to use, are decisions that should generally made in consultation with a conservator or ceramic tile specialist. *It may also be necessary to comply with certain safety standards and friction requirements of the ADA (Americans with Disabilities Act). The ADA Guidelines recommend "a static coefficient of friction" of 0.6 for level surfaces and 0.8 for ramps. This may require the application of a non-slip sealer or wax to historic ceramic tile floors in some public buildings.*

Despite the non-traditional shiny finish they may impart to a floor surface, two-part, acrylic-based coating systems are commonly used today on historic ceramic tile floors in many public buildings, primarily because they facilitate easy maintenance. If it is decided that a sealer is to be used, a product with a matte or dull finish may be preferable, or more appropriate, for a historic ceramic tile floor than one with a high-gloss.

In some cases, temporary protection may be the best approach until a better solution is found. Non-permanent protection for an historic ceramic tile floor may be as simple as using floor mats at doors or in heavy traffic areas.

Historic Ceramic Floor Tile: Damage and Deterioration Problems

Loss of Tile Surface and Pattern. Ceramic tiles are among the most durable of historic flooring materials, but natural wear and a certain amount of deterioration or damage is inevitable. Some tiles, such as dense, close-textured quarry tiles and ceramic mosaic tiles, resist abrasion and stain absorption very well. But many others, especially patterned encaustic and geometric tiles, are extremely susceptible to abrasion. Heavy traffic can also result in uneven wear, or even cupping, in certain areas of tile floors that get more use than others, such as doorway entrances. The particular clay mix, or the dye or pigment used to color the clay, can also affect the hardness and durability of individual tiles or an entire ceramic tile floor (Fig. 20).

Tile Glaze Failure. Occasionally some glazes can become pitted or powdery as they age. Lead glazes used in the 19th century, which were fired at low temperatures, deteriorated relatively quickly. Glazes have different physical properties from the fired clay tile body itself, and as a result may sometimes crack or craze. Unless the crazing visibly extends into the porous clay of the tile body beneath, this is not generally a serious material failure; however, dirt entering these cracks cannot be removed, and will discolor the tile. If the crazing penetrates through the glaze, it may increase the water absorption of the tile.

Tile Breakage. Ceramic floor tiles are very susceptible to damage and breakage caused when something heavy is dropped. Repeated passage of heavy objects, or carts, over a floor can also crack and break ceramic tiles, as well as heavy vibration from outside traffic (Fig. 21).

Moisture Damage to Tile. Ceramic tile floors have been traditionally viewed as highly waterproof systems that do not require protection from moisture. In reality, however, this is not true. Water-related problems are one of the most common causes for the deterioration and failure of historic tile floors, particularly in bathrooms and other rooms where there is a lot of moisture. Water that is allowed to sit in areas around shower stalls and bathtubs can eventually damage grout and mortar, and loosen tiles. Some of the more porous kinds of tiles that are not as hard-fired may actually begin to powder or spall if subjected to constant moisture.

Loose, Cracked, Broken or Unbonded Tile due to Mortar Failure. The durability of ceramic tile floors depends to a great extent on a sound mortar bed and sound mortar joints. The wrong mortar type or mortar that is inadequately mixed can also spell trouble for a ceramic tile floor. Failure

of a tile floor system laid over a subfloor is often the result of weakened or deteriorated grout or mortar which allows the tiles to become loose. Mortar may also be weakened or loosened by cleaning solutions that are too strong.

Proper tile-laying technique includes the use of a material that will allow for some movement of the tiles. Traditionally, a layer of asphalt (replaced by a layer of plastic or building paper in more modern construction) was inserted to separate the base and the bedding underneath (Fig. 22). This prevents bonding between the base and the bed, and allows for some "relative" movement. It is intended to prevent the ceramic tile floor from arching or ridging, a condition in which single or entire rows of tiles can pop up to relieve tension and separate completely from the bed. When this happens, the condition will probably require taking up and relaying many or all of the tiles.

Tile Damage or Loss caused by Systems Update. The installation of new plumbing, electrical and HVAC systems, or the attachment of new fixtures and furnishings, may be one of the most common sources of damage to an historic ceramic tile floor. Earlier remodeling projects to remove old pipes or to replace "out-dated" bathroom fixtures may have resulted in the loss of floor tiles (Fig. 23). Different shapes and sizes of new fixtures, equipment or pipes may have exposed previously untiled areas that have been inappropriately patched with cement. Careless workers and insensitive installations can also result in damage, breakage or removal of historic floor tiles. All of these conditions will require matching replacement tile.

Historic Ceramic Floor Tile: Repair and Replacement

The Secretary of the Interior's Standards for the Treatment of Historic Properties emphasize the retention and preservation of historic building material. Preservation and repair treatments are always preferable to replacement.

Mortar Joint Repair. Deteriorated mortar joints and loose mortar or grout can generally be repaired. First, the entire floor should be checked for loose tiles that need to be regrouted. Damaged mortar should be carefully removed by hand and the joints wetted or a bonding agent applied in preparation for regrouting. When making mortar repairs, it is important to use grout that matches the old in color and consistency as closely as possible.

Figure 23. These non-matching tiles are inappropriate replacements for original tiles that were damaged during bathroom remodeling. Photo: Anne Grimmer.

(a-b) Above: By the mid-1970s, many of the patterns in the encaustic tile floors had become faint, and some had completely worn off in the most heavily trafficked areas. (c) Below left: Damaged areas of the floor had been patched with salvaged pieces of tile that fit, but did not match. Photos: Wayne Firth, Office of the Architect of the Capitol.

Figure 24. **U.S. Capitol Restoration Project.** Restoration of the historic ceramic tile flooring at the U.S. Capitol is one of the most extensive on-going undertakings of this kind in the U.S. When the Office of the Architect of the Capitol contacted H&R Johnson-Richards, the manufacturer of Minton Hollins tiles, regarding restoration of the tile floors in preparation for the American Bicentennial, the company was unaware of the extent of original Minton encaustic and geometric floor tiles in the U.S. Capitol building. Montgomery C. Meigs, Supervising Engineer, and Architect of the Capitol Extension, Thomas U. Walter, specified Minton encaustic tiles for the floors in the two wings that were added to the Capitol. The tiles were ordered from the factory in England through Miller & Coates, a Minton supplier in New York City, and installed in the 1850s.

When the project was initiated, the intent was to replace only those tiles that were severely damaged or worn. Removing and replacing selected sections of the tile floor in their entirety was determined to be a better approach because of the difficulty of removing one tile without damaging adjacent tiles in good condition, in addition to the difficulty of matching new and old tiles which are slightly different in color, pattern and thickness. This means that sometimes tiles in good condition may have to be removed, but they are salvaged and stored for future reuse.

Before ordering the reproduction tiles, each section of the Capitol floor was drawn and photo-documented. The condition of all the tiles was evaluated based on a rating of one to four (excellent, good, damaged, or, in need of replacement), and color-coded accordingly. Every tile that needed to be replaced was individually numbered and photographed with dimensional, color and grey scales.

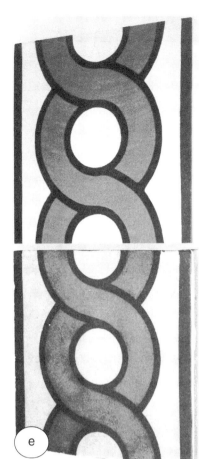

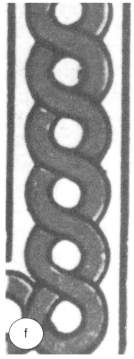

(e) The top tile is a new reproduction of the historic tile below. (f) This design is identified as No. 84 in Miller & Coates' Minton Tile Catalogue (detail Figure 2). (g) What might appear to be an inappropriate repair with non-matching modern tile in the center of the star is, in reality, a neatly executed patch to serve as temporary in-fill for the reproductions that have been ordered. (h) Shown below is a restored section of the Capitol floor. Photos: (e,g,h) Wayne Firth, Office of the Architect of the Capitol; (f) David W. Look, AIA.

(d) Since the early-20th century, making encaustic tiles had, again, become a lost art. Thus, H&R Johnson-Richards not only had to learn how encaustic tiles had been made historically, but, also, how to reproduce them. After studying old records of the early tile manufacturers, the company began reproducing tiles using modern-day computer-assisted technology (CAD/CAM). Drawing: H&R Johnson Tiles Ltd.; Photo: Wayne Firth, Office of the Architect of the Capitol.

513

Figure 25. This comparison of an original, historic encaustic tile (top) with a reproduction encaustic tile (bottom) reveals an obvious difference in thickness, but only a slight difference in the design. Photo: Wayne Firth, Office of the Architect of the Capitol.

Tile Repair. Trying to remove one tile can endanger surrounding tiles. Thus, it may be better to preserve and retain an original historic tile that is only slightly damaged, rather than replace it. Sometimes cracks may be repaired, or a corner or piece of tile that has broken off may be reattached, using an epoxy glue, or grout. If a tile is chipped or a small corner or edge is missing, a carefully executed patch of epoxy—mixed with colored enamel, or mortar tinted to blend with the tile, may be less conspicuous than trying to replace every tile that has even the slightest damage. And, it is a better preservation treatment.

In limited instances, glaze failure or surface powdering of ceramic floor tiles may sometimes be treated successfully by a conservator with a specially formulated, solvent-based, mineral densifying agent (such as silicic acid), followed by a siloxane sub-surface repellent, applied 24 hours later. Under the right circumstances, such a treatment can harden and bind the surface, and lower the absorbency of the tile, and still maintain the vapor transmission. But this is a highly complex undertaking and should only be attempted by a conservator after appropriate testing. Not only are these chemicals highly toxic and dangerous to handle, but if used improperly, they can cause greater damage to the tile!

Tile Replacement. When an individual tile or a larger portion of an historic ceramic tile floor is missing or so severely damaged that it cannot be repaired, or if it has become a safety hazard, then it should be replaced. When a ceramic tile floor has deteriorated as a result of long term wear and abrasion, or from settlement or vibration damage to the setting bed, there are a number of factors that need to be considered before choosing a preservation treatment. If damage to tile's is the result of more than normal wear and tear, the source of the problem needs to be identified, and the problem corrected before replacing the damaged tiles.

Successful replacement not only depends on the availability of matching tiles, but on the condition of the substrate on which the tiles are laid. Before installing the replacement tiles, any problems, such as settlement or vibration, will have to be addressed, and the height of the new setting bed may have to be adjusted for the thickness of the new tiles.

Selective Replacement of Individual Tiles. This cautious approach, typically an attempt to replace only the most seriously damaged tiles, is often taken or considered when only a small number of tiles are involved. Unless old, matching tiles can be found and reused, replacement often requires specially fabricated reproduction tiles. In some instances, individual historic tiles that are damaged may be replaced with matching tiles salvaged from other, less prominent areas of the floor or from other buildings. This is most feasible if the tiles to be replaced are either plain, and easy to match, or decorated with a common historic floor tile pattern.

In order to replace damaged tiles, it can be helpful to identify the manufacturer and the approximate date of the tiles, if possible. However, many mass-produced tiles are not marked and give little or no information as to their origin, although stylistic similarities with other marked tiles may sometimes provide a clue as to the manufacturer. Some decorating firms seldom signed their work, while many firms made bisque tiles (plain, unglazed, once-fired tiles) for other companies, as well as their own use. Identifying marks will generally be found on the back of the tile. A mark impressed or molded into the back of the tile may give the name or initials of the company which made the tile or the bisque; sometimes a printed or painted mark indicates if it was decorated by a different company, or artist. Historic building records and construction documents may provide information about the tile company or supplier. Catalogues of the period may also be useful in identifying the tile manufacturer of unmarked tiles.

Replacing a single damaged tile is based on the ability to remove only the deteriorated tile without harming surrounding tiles. Attempts to remove one or several damaged tiles often fail because a hammer and chisel are used. The shock of the blows to the tile being removed travels through the grout into surrounding tiles and cracks them. To avoid damaging good tiles, all the grout around the tile must be removed. This is best accomplished by an experienced tile installer using a hand tool called a grout saw or, for grout joints wider than 3/8", a dry-cutting diamond blade, mounted in an angle grinder or circular saw.

Other difficulties may be encountered when selectively replacing damaged tiles with reproduction tiles. New tiles, especially encaustic tiles, may be different in thickness and, sometimes, despite the attention to detail of the reproduction process, slightly different in color and design from historic tiles. This can cause both visual and physical problems, especially if the replacements are being laid in a piecemeal fashion.

If the setting bed does not have enough mortar to grip and hold the tile, one new tile laid among the originals will eventually come loose. If the new and old tiles are different thicknesses, the setting bed in which the new tiles are laid must be at a different height to create a level finished surface. In addition, the two levels of setting beds may be of different composition; one may be harder, stronger and less flexible than the other. This may also lead to problems, since the setting bed foundation should act and respond as a unit to the load and stresses placed upon it.

Sectional Replacement of Tiles. In some instances, the best approach may be to remove a complete section of damaged original tiles and replace that section of floor in its entirety with new reproduction tiles. Advantages of this method include the ability to lay a level setting bed, as well as achieving a finished product that is uniform in color and pattern match. Although this approach may involve replacing more original tiles with reproduction tiles than may be absolutely necessary, original tiles that remain in good condition can be saved to be reused in other sections where only a few tiles are damaged. This technique is generally most appropriate either when the section being replaced is the most damaged portion of the floor, or is in a relatively inconspicuous location and the tiles that are removed will supply enough salvaged pieces to permit in-kind repair of a more visually prominent area (Fig. 24).

When laying a section of reproduction tiles, it may be a good idea to use contemporary materials and installation methods such as expansion joints or flexible expansion material. One of the major causes of ceramic floor tile installation failure and cracked, broken or disbonded tiles is the lack of expansion joints. Expansion joints were sometimes used in laying historic ceramic tile floors, and these are frequently the ones that have survived in the best condition. Many preservation contractors hesitate to use conventional expansion joint filler materials because of their limited range of colors. However, there are new flexible sealants in a wide range of colors that are available in either sanded or unsanded textures to match the surrounding grout joints. As a result, the expansion joints are almost invisible. A bonding agent may also be considered—if recommended by the tile manufacturer—and any drawings provided by the manufacturer should be used to guide the installation.

Each preservation technique has advantages and disadvantages that the historic property owner or manger should take into consideration before deciding which one is best suited to the particular flooring problem. For example, slight differences in the shape, size, color and the pattern between the old and the new tiles are frequently encountered. If replacing an entire section, the slightest difference in size and dimension between the original tiles and the reproduction tiles, even if it is as small as 1/8" or 1/16", can mean that the new section of tile will not fit inside an existing border (Fig. 25). Even though drawings and photos are provided to the manufacturer, there may be some variation in the design and pattern size on the new tiles. Thus, they may not align perfectly with the original tiles, and as a result the section of the floor that has been replaced may be quite conspicuous.

Summary

Historic ceramic tiles are a common flooring material in many different kinds of small, as well as large, private and public, structures throughout the United States. Whether plain, or decoratively patterned, traditional ceramic floor tiles are important in defining the character of historic buildings. Although ceramic floor tiles are a practical material, they are also fragile, and can be easily damaged by improper installation techniques, insensitive remodeling, harsh cleaning methods, and even regular daily use. Preserving them requires careful day-to-day maintenance. This should begin with using gentle, non-abrasive methods and materials to clean them, and, in some instances, using an appropriate coating or impregnator to protect them.

Some historic ceramic tile floors, due to their manufacturer, their unique design, or their location in a certain room or within a particular building, may have greater significance than those that are purely utilitarian. Such floors should be

accorded special care, and a ceramics conservator or preservation specialist should always be consulted to prepare responsible maintenance plans and to provide guidance concerning repair treatments and replacement techniques for them.

Unless an historic ceramic tile floor is extensively damaged with many missing and broken tiles and, therefore, potentially hazardous, it may be preferable to leave it alone. An unevenly worn floor surface, worn colors or patterns on the tiles, or slight cracks, chips, or scratches in the tiles themselves does not necessarily mean that the tiles should be replaced. Such relatively minor imperfections seldom detract from the character of an historic ceramic tile floor. They may, in fact, impart character, and be less noticeable or obtrusive than replacement of a single tile or a larger section with new tiles that do not match the originals exactly. Each situation should be evaluated on its own basis before selecting the preservation approach best suited to the project.

Selected Reading

Austwick, Jill. The Decorated Tile: *An Illustrated History of English Tile-making and Design.* New York: Scribners, 1980.

Barnard, Julian. *Victorian Ceramic Tiles.* Greenwich, CT: New York Graphic Society Ltd., 1972.

Bruhn, Thomas P. *American Decorative Tiles, 1870-1930.* Storrs, CT: William Benton Museum of Art, 1979.

Byrne, Michael. *Setting Tile.* Newtown, CT: The Taunton Press, 1995.

Decorative Tile Designs in Full Color. Selected and arranged by Carol Belanger Grafton. New York: Dover Publications, Inc., 1992.

Fidler, John. "Protective Custody: John Fidler examines the options on caring for brick, tile or stone floors." *Traditional Homes.* (August 1989), pp. 112-115.

Furnival, William James. *Leadless Decorative Tiles, Faience & Mosaic.* Stone, Staffordshire: W.J. Furnival, 1904.

Lavenberg, George N. *Ceramic Tile Manual.* Los Angeles: Building News, 1986.

Massey, James C., and Shirley Maxwell. "Decorative Tile: Art for the Victorian and Arts and Crafts Home." *Old-House Journal.* Vol. XIX, No. 2 (March/April 1991), pp. 54-58.

Massey, James C., and Shirley Maxwell. "The Ceramic Circus." *Old-House Journal.* Vol. XXIII, No. 2 (March/April 1995), pp. 46-51.

Riley, Noel. *Tile Art: A History of Decorative Ceramic Tiles.* London: The Apple Press, 1987.

Rosenstiel, Helene Von, and Gail Caskey Winkler. *Floor Coverings for Historic Buildings: A Guide to Selecting Reproductions.* Washington, D.C.: The Preservation Press, 1988.

Taylor, Joseph A. *"Ceramic Tiles in Commerce."* BR Building Renovation. (Fall 1994), pp. 45-48.

The Secretary of the Interior's Standards for the Treatment of Historic Properties with Guidelines for Preserving, Rehabilitating, Restoring and Reconstructing Historic Buildings. Kay D. Weeks and Anne E. Grimmer. Washington, D.C.: U.S. Department of the Interior, National Park Service, Cultural Resource Stewardship and Partnerships, Heritage Preservation Services, 1995.

Tunick, Susan. *American Decorative Tiles.* Sponsored by Assopiastrelle (Association of Italian Ceramic Tile and Refractories Manufacturers), and coordinated by D. Grosser and Associates, Ltd., New York (1991).

Vandenburgh, Jayne M., IBD. "Restoring the Ohio State Senate Building: An American Tile Classic Returns." *Tile Design and Installation.* Vol. 8, No. 1 (January 1995), pp. 32-35.

Wyatt, M. Digby. *Specimens of Geometric Mosaic Manufactured by Maw & Co. of Benthall, near Broseley.* London: M. Digby Wyatt, 1857.

Some Sources for Replacement Tiles

There are a number of companies that offer standard lines of reproduction tiles, while others focus on custom work. Some new lines of reproduction tile attempt to be exact replicas of original tiles from the late-19th and early-20th century, while others are modern interpretations or adaptations of traditional designs, and may not be appropriate as replacement tiles in a preservation or restoration project. For additional sources see: "Traditional Building's Ceramic Tile SourceList," *Traditional Building*, Vol. 9, No. 4 (July/August 1996), pp. 92-93.

Designs in Tile
P.O. Box 358
Mt. Shasta, CA 96067
Custom-made reproduction art tile.

Fulper Tile
P.O. Box 373
Yardley, PA 19067
Reopened factory reproduces historic tiles using original Arts and Crafts-period glazes.

H&R Johnson Tiles Ltd.
Head Office: Highgate Tile Works
           Tunstall, Stoke-on-Trent
           England ST6 4JX
U.S. Office: Johnson USA Inc.
           P.O. Box 2335
           Farmingdale, NJ 07727
Stock and custom reproductions of Minton Hollins encaustic and geometric tiles.

L'Esperance Tile Works
237 Sheridan Avenue
Albany, NY 12210
Custom-made encaustic, geometric, mosaic and other traditional ceramic tiles.

Moravian Pottery and Tile Works
Swamp Road
Doylestown, PA 18901
Reproduction tiles based on Henry Chapman Mercer's original designs.

Motawi Tileworks
33 North Staebler Road, Suite 2
Ann Arbor, MI 48103
Reproduction tiles in Arts and Crafts, Art Nouveau and other styles.

Native Tile and Ceramics
4230 Glencoe Avenue
Marina Del Rey, CA 90292
Reproduction decorative tiles in Southern California tradition of Craftsman, Mission, Art Deco and other styles.

Original Style
Stovax Ltd.
Falcon Road, Sowton Industrial Estate
Exeter, Devon
England EX2 7LF
Reproduction ceramic tiles from 1750-1902.

Pewabic Pottery, Inc.
10125 East Jefferson Avenue
Detroit, MI 48214
Reopened factory reproduces original tile designs and glazes.

Terra Designs Tileworks
241 East Blackwell Street
Dover, NJ 07801
Mosaic tessarae experts, and reproduction of historic ceramic tiles.

Tile Guild
2840 East 11th Street
Los Angeles, CA 90023
Reproduction of traditional Spanish, Portuguese, Dutch, Italian and English tiles.

Tile Restoration Center, Inc.
3511 Interlake N.
Seattle, WA 98103
Reproduction of Arts and Crafts-period tiles.

Helpful Organizations

The American Institute for Conservation of Historic and Artistic Works (AIC)
1717 K Street, N.W., Suite 301
Washington, DC 20006

Ceramic Tile Institute of America, Inc.
12061 Jefferson Boulevard
Culver City, CA 90030-6212

Friends of Terra Cotta, Inc.
771 West End Avenue, 10E
New York, NY 10025

Tile Council of America
P.O. Box 1787
Clemson, SC 29633

Tile Heritage Foundation
P. O. Box 1850
Healdsburg, CA 95448

Acknowledgements

Anne E. Grimmer is Senior Architectural Historian, Technical Preservation Services Branch, Heritage Preservation Services Program, National Park Service, Washington, D.C. **Kimberly A. Konrad** is a Preservation Planner, Boston Landmarks Commission, The Environment Department, City of Boston, MA. The authors wish to thank the following individuals for providing technical review and other assistance in the development of this publication: Marc Tartaro, AIA, and William Allen, Office of the Architect of the Capitol, Washington, DC; Mary Catherine Bluder, Bucks County Historical Society, Doylestown, PA; Michael F. Byrne, Ceramic Tile Education Foundation, Clemson, SC; Milford Wayne Donaldson, FAIA, Los Angeles, CA; Gray LaFortune, CTC, Ceramic Tile Institute of America, Inc., Culver City, CA; Joseph Taylor, Tile Heritage Foundation, Healdsburg, CA; Susan Tunick, Friends of Terra Cotta, Inc., New York, NY; Anne Weber, Ford Forewell Mills and Gatsch, Architects, Princeton, NJ; Glenn Wharton, Wharton & Griswold Associates, Inc., Santa Barbara, CA; Charles E. Fisher, Sharon C. Park, AIA, and, especially, Kay D. Weeks, National Park Service, Washington, DC.

This publication has been prepared pursuant to the National Historic Preservation Act of 1966, as amended, which directs the Secretary of the Interior to develop and make available information concerning historic properties. Comments about this publication should be directed to de Teel Patterson Tiller, Acting Manager, Heritage Preservation Services Program, National Park Service, P. O. Box 37127, Washington, D.C. 20013-7127.

*Ceramic: Any product manufactured from a nonmetallic mineral (such as clay), by firing at high temperatures.

*Cover Logo: "Ceramic Mosaic and Vitreous Floor Tile." American Encaustic Tiling Company, Ltd., Zanesville, Ohio. **"Sweet's" Indexed Catalogue of Building Construction.** NY, NY: The Architectural Record Co., 1906. Photo: Sharon C. Park, AIA.*

41

The Seismic Retrofit of Historic Buildings: Keeping Preservation in the Forefront

David W. Look, AIA, Terry Wong, PE, and Sylvia Rose Augustus

Violent, swift, and unpredictable, earthquakes result from sudden movements of the geological plates that form the earth's crust, generally along cracks or fractures known as "faults." If a building has not been designed and constructed to absorb these swaying ground motions, then major structural damage, or outright collapse, can result, with grave risk to human life. Historic buildings are especially vulnerable in this regard. As a result, more and more communities are beginning to adopt stringent requirements for seismic retrofit of existing buildings. And despite popular misconceptions, the risks of earthquakes are not limited to the West Coast, as the Seismic Zone Map on page 14 illustrates.

Although historic and other older buildings can be retrofitted to survive earthquakes, many retrofit practices damage or destroy the very features that make such buildings significant. Life-safety issues are foremost and, fortunately, there are various approaches which can save historic buildings both from the devastation caused by earthquakes and from the damage inflicted by well-intentioned but insensitive retrofit procedures. Building owners, managers, consultants, and communities need to be actively involved in preparing documents and readying irreplaceable historic resources from these damages (see illus.1).

This Preservation Brief provides essential information on how earthquakes affect historic buildings, how a historic preservation ethic can guide responsible decisions, and how various methods of seismic retrofit can protect human lives *and* historic structures. Because many of the terms used in this Brief are technical, a glossary is provided on page 7. The Brief focuses on unreinforced masonry buildings because these are the most vulnerable of our older resources, but the guidance is appropriate for all historic buildings. Damage to non-structural elements such as furnishings and collections is beyond the scope of this Brief, but consideration should be given to securing and protecting these cultural resources as well.

Planning the retrofit of historic buildings *before* an earthquake strikes is a process that requires teamwork on the part of engineers, architects, code officials, and agency administrators. Accordingly, this Brief also presents guidance on assembling a professional team and ensuring its successful interaction. Project personnel working together can ensure that the architectural, engineering, financial, cultural, and social values of historic buildings are preserved, while rendering them safe for continued use.

1. *Earthquake damage to historic buildings can be repaired in a manner sensitive to their historic character as seen in this ca. 1928 five story apartment building. The owners used a combination of federal rehabilitation tax credits, community development block grants, and post earthquake grants to fund a portion of the rehabilitation and seismic upgrade costs. Photos: Historic Resources Group, Los Angeles.*

Balancing Seismic Retrofit and Preservation

Reinforcing a historic building to meet new construction requirements, as prescribed by many building codes, can destroy much of a historic building's appearance and integrity. This is because the most expedient ways to reinforce a building according to such codes are to impose structural members and to fill irregularities or large openings, regardless of the placement of architectural detail. The results can be quite intrusive (see illus. 2). However, structural reinforcement can be introduced sensitively. In such cases, its design, placement, patterning, and detailing respect the historic character of the building, even when the reinforcement itself is visible.

Three important preservation principles should be kept in mind when undertaking seismic retrofit projects:

- *Historic materials should be preserved and retained to the greatest extent possible and not replaced wholesale in the process of seismic strengthening;*
- *New seismic retrofit systems, whether hidden or exposed, should respect the character and integrity of the historic building and be visually compatible with it in design; and,*
- *Seismic work should be "reversible" to the greatest extent possible to allow removal for future use of improved systems and traditional repair of remaining historic materials.*

It is strongly advised that all owners of historically significant buildings contemplating seismic retrofit become familiar with The Secretary of the Interior's *Standards for the Treatment of Historic Properties,* which are published by the National Park Service and cited in the bibliography of this publication. These standards identify approaches for working with historic buildings, including preservation, rehabilitation, and restoration. Code-required work to make buildings functional and safe is an integral component of each approach identified in the *Standards.* While some seismic upgrading work is more permanent than reversible, care must be taken to preserve historic materials to the greatest extent possible and for new work to have a minimal visual impact on the historic appearance of the building.

2. Standard approaches to seismic retrofit, as seen with the diagonally braced frame crossing in front of the historic windows, are visually intrusive. Solutions, such as using hidden moment frames around the perimeter of the window, will meet the goals of historic preservation and seismic retrofit. Photo: Steade Craigo.

Earthquake Damage to Historic Buildings: Assessing Principal Risk Factors

Typical earthquake damage to most older and historic buildings results from poor ductility—or flexibility—of the building and, specifically, poor structural connections between walls, floors, and foundations combined with the very heavy weight and mass of historic materials that are moved by seismic forces and must be resisted. In buildings that have not been seismically upgraded, particularly unreinforced masonry buildings, parapets, chimneys, and gable ends may dislodge and fall to the ground during a moderate to severe earthquake (see illus. 3). Walls, floors, roofs, skylights, porches, and stairs which rely on tied connections may simply fail. Interior structural supports may partially or totally collapse. Unreinforced masonry walls between openings often exhibit shear (or diagonal) cracking. Upper stories may collapse onto under-reinforced lower floors with large perimeter openings or atriums. Unbraced infill material between structural or rigid frame supports may dislodge. Adjacent buildings with separate foundations may move differently in an earthquake creating damage between them. Poorly anchored wood frame buildings tend to slide off their foundations. Ruptured gas and water lines often cause fire and water damage. Many of these vulnerabilities can be mitigated by understanding how the forces unleashed in an earthquake affect the building, then planning and implementing appropriate remedial treatments.

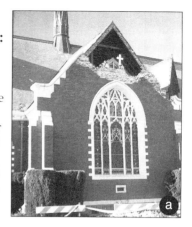

3. Forces from moderate to serious earthquakes caused a) the untied gable to fail, b) the first floor to collapse c) cracks from the pounding effect of adjacent buildings, and d) and diagonal cracks in exterior masonry between windows to form. Photos: David Look.

Six principal factors influence how and why historic buildings are damaged in an earthquake: (1) depth of the earthquake and subsequent strength of earthquake waves reaching the surface; (2) duration of the earthquake, including after-shock tremors; (3) proximity of the building to the earthquake epicenter, although distance is not necessarily a direct relationship; (4) geological and soil conditions; (5) building construction details, including materials, structural systems, and plan configuration; and (6) existing building condition, including maintenance level.

The first three factors—the depth, duration, and proximity to the fault—are beyond human control. Recent earthquakes have shown the fourth factor, geological soil conditions, to be as important as any of the other factors because loose, soft soils tend to amplify ground motion, thereby increasing damage. Further, there is the tendency of soft, unstable soils to "liquefy" as the ground vibrates, causing the building foundations to sink unevenly. This fourth factor, geological and soil conditions, is difficult to address in a retrofit situation, although it can be planned for in new construction. The last two factors—the building's construction type and its existing physical condition—are the two factors over which building owners and managers have control and can ultimately affect how the historic property performs in an earthquake (see illus. 4).

4. The compact size and good condition of the masonry building on the left withstood the earthquake except for the loss of the unsupported chimney at the roof line. The brick building on the right appears to have sustained more damage. Photo: Steade Craigo.

Although historic buildings present problems, the way they were constructed often has intrinsic benefits that should not be overlooked. Diagonal subflooring under tongue-and-groove nailed flooring can provide a diaphragm, or horizontal membrane, that ties the building together. Interior masonry walls employing wire lath with plaster also add strength that binds materials together. The typical construction of older buildings with partition walls that extend from floor to ceiling (instead of just to the underside of a dropped ceiling) also provides additional support and load transfer during an earthquake that keeps shifting floors from collapsing. Moreover, buildings constructed of unreinforced masonry with a wall thickness to height ratio that does not exceed code requirements can often survive shaking without serious damage. The stability of unreinforced masonry walls should not be underestimated; while the masonry may crack, it often does not shift out of plumb enough to collapse.

Type of Building and Construction

A historic building's construction and materials determine its behavior during an earthquake. Some buildings, such as wooden frame structures, are quite ductile and, thus, able to absorb substantial movements. Others, such as unreinforced brick or adobe buildings comprised of heavy individual load-bearing units, are more susceptible to damage from shaking. If an earthquake is strong, or continues for a long time, building elements that are poorly attached or unreinforced may collapse. Most historic buildings still standing in earthquake zones have survived some shaking, but may be structurally weakened.

Buildings of more rigid construction techniques may also have seismic deficiencies. Masonry infill-wall buildings are generally built of steel or concrete structural frames with unreinforced masonry sections or panels set within the frame. While the structural frames may survive an earthquake, the masonry infill can crack and, in some cases, dislodge. The reaction of concrete buildings and concrete frame structures is largely dependent upon the extent and configuration of iron or steel reinforcement. Early buildings constructed of concrete are often inadequately reinforced, inadequately tied, or both, and are thus susceptible to damage during earthquakes.

Recognition of the configuration of the historic structure and inherent areas of weakness are essential to addressing appropriate alternatives for seismic retrofit. For example, the plan and elevation may be as important as building materials and structural systems in determining a historic building's survival in an earthquake. Small round, square, or rectangular buildings generally survive an earthquake because their geometry allows for equal resistance of lateral forces in all directions. The more complex and irregular the plan, however, the more likely the building will be damaged during an earthquake because of its uneven strength and stiffness in different directions. Structures having an "L," "T," "H," "U," or "E" shape have unequal resistance, with the stress concentrated at corners and intersections. This is of particular concern if the buildings have flexible structural systems and/or an irregular layout of shear walls which may cause portions of the building to pull apart.

Similarly, the more complex and irregular a building elevation, the more susceptible it is to damage, especially in tall structures. Large or multiple openings around the building on the ground level, such as storefronts or garage openings, or floors with columns and walls running in only one direction are commonly known as "soft stories" and are prone to structural damage.

Building Condition

Much of the damage that occurs during an earthquake is directly related to the building's existing condition and maintenance history. Well maintained buildings, even without added reinforcement, survive better than buildings weakened by lack of maintenance. The capacity of the structural system to resist earthquakes may be severely reduced if previous alterations or earthquakes have weakened structural connections or if materials have deteriorated from moisture, termite, or other damage. Furthermore, in unreinforced historic masonry buildings, deteriorated mortar joints can weaken entire walls. Cyclical maintenance, which reduces moisture penetration and erosion of materials, is therefore essential. Because damage can be cumulative, it is important to analyze the structural capacity of the building.

Over time, structural members can become loose and pose a major liability. Unreinforced historic masonry buildings typically have a friction-fit connection between horizontal and vertical structural members, and the shaking caused by an earthquake pulls them apart. With insufficient bearing surface for beams, joists, and rafters against the load bearing walls or support columns, they fail. The resulting structural inadequacy may cause a partial or complete building collapse, depending on the severity of the earthquake and the internal wall configuration. Tying the building together by making a positive anchored or braced connection between walls, columns, and framing members, is key to the seismic retrofit of historic buildings.

Putting a Team Together

The two goals of the seismic retrofit in historic buildings are life safety and the protection of older and historic buildings during and after an earthquake. Because rehabilitation should be sensitive to historic materials and the building's historic character, it is important to put together a team experienced in both seismic requirements and historic preservation. Team members should be selected for their experience with similar projects, and may include architects, engineers, code specialists, contractors, and preservation consultants. Because the typical seismic codes are written for new construction, it is important that both the architect and structural engineer be knowledge-able about historic buildings and about meeting building code equivalencies and using alternative solutions. Local and state building officials can identify regulatory requirements, alternative approaches to meeting these requirements, and if the jurisdiction uses a historic preservation or building conservation code. Even on small projects that cannot support a full professional team, consultants should be familiar with historic preservation goals. The State Historic Preservation Office and the local historic preservation office or commission may be able to identify consultants who have been successful in preserving historic buildings during seismic retrofit work. Once the team has been assembled, their tasks include:

Compiling documentation. The team should review all available documentation on the historic building, including any previous documentation assembled to nominate the structure to the National Register of Historic Places, and any previous Historic Structures Reports. Original plans and specifications as well as those showing alterations through time often detail structural connections. Early real estate or insurance plans, such as the *Sanborn Maps,* note changes over time. Historic photographs of the building under construction or before and after previous earthquakes are invaluable. Base maps for geological or seismic studies and utility maps showing the location of water, gas, and electric lines should be also identified. The municipal or state office of emergency preparedness can provide data on earthquake hazard plans for the community.

Evaluating significant features and spaces. The team must also identify areas of a historic building and its site that exhibit design integrity or historical significance which must be preserved. It is critical, and a great challenge, to protect these major features, such as domes, atriums, and vaulted spaces or highly decorative elements, such as mosaics, murals, and frescoes. In some cases, secondary areas of the building can provide spaces for additional reinforcement behind these major features, thus saving them from damage during seismic retrofit work. Both primary and secondary spaces, features, and finishes should, thus, be identified.

Assessing the condition of the building and the risk hazards. The team then assesses the general physical condition of the building's interior and exterior, and identifies areas vulnerable to seismic damage. This often requires a structural engineer or testing firm to determine the strength and durability of materials and connections (see illus. 5). A sliding scale of potential damage is established, based on the probability of hazard by locale and building use. This helps the owner distinguish between areas in which repairable damage, such as cracking, may occur and those in which life-threatening problems may arise. These findings help guide cost-benefit decisions, especially when budgets are limited.

5. A careful program of in-place testing is essential to evaluate the existing seismic capacity of a building. This masonry push-test uses hydraulic jacks to estimate the shear capacity of the wall. Test locations should be in areas that do not destroy significant features and repairs should be carried out carefully. Photo: Architectural Resources Group, San Francisco.

Evaluating local and state codes and requirements. Few codes consider historic buildings, but the California State Historical Code and the Uniform Code for Building Conservation provide excellent models for jurisdictions to adopt. Code officials should always be asked where alternative approaches can be taken to provide life safety if the specified requirements of a code would destroy significant historic materials and features. Some jurisdictions require the removal of parapets, chimneys, or projecting decoration from unreinforced masonry buildings which is not a preservation approach. Professionals on the team should be prepared with alternatives that allow for mitigating potential damage to such features while retaining them through reattachment or strengthening.

Developing a retrofit plan. The final task of the project team is to develop a retrofit plan. The plan may require multiple treatments, each more comprehensive than the last. Treating life-safety issues as well as providing a safe route of exit should be evaluated for all buildings. Developing more comprehensive plans, often combined with future rehabili-tation, is reasonable. Long-term restoration solutions phased in over time as funding is available should also be consid-ered. In every case, owners and their planning teams should consider options that keep preservation goals in mind.

There are significant advantages of completing a seismic survey and analysis even if resources for implementing a retrofit are not yet available. Once the retrofit plan is finished, the project team will have a document by which to assess future damage and proceed with emergency repairs. If construction is phased, its impact to the whole building should be understood. Some partially completed retrofit measures have left buildings more rigid in one area than in others, thereby contributing to more extensive damage during an ensuing earthquake.

Planning for Seismic Retrofit: How Much and Where?

The integrity and significance of the historic building, paired with the cost and benefit of seismic upgrading, need to be weighed by the owner and the consulting team. Buildings in less active seismic areas may need little or no further bracing or tying. Buildings in more active seismic zones, however, may need more extensive intervention. Options for the level of seismic retrofit generally fall into four classifications, depending on the expected seismic activity and the desired level of performance. Realistically, for historic buildings, only the first three categories apply.

1) *Basic Life Safety*. This addresses the most serious life-safety concerns by correcting those deficiencies that could lead to serious human injury or total building collapse. Upgrades may include bracing and tying the most vulnerable elements of the building, such as parapets, chimneys, and projecting ornamentation or reinforcing routes of exit. (see illus. 6). It is expected that if an earthquake were to occur, the building would not collapse but would be seriously damaged requiring major repairs.

2) *Enhanced Life Safety*. In this approach, the building is upgraded using a flexible approach to the building codes for moderate earthquakes. Inherent deficiencies found in older buildings, such as poor floor to wall framing connections and unbraced masonry walls would be corrected (see illus. 7). After a design level earthquake, some structural damage is anticipated, such as masonry cracking, and the building would be temporarily unusable.

7. *More extensive seismic issues can be addressed through structural reinforcement, the most common methods using anchor ties and braces. Shown here is an interior diagonal frame, to be covered, which will dampen and transfer seismic loads in a designed path from foundation to roof. Photo: David Look.*

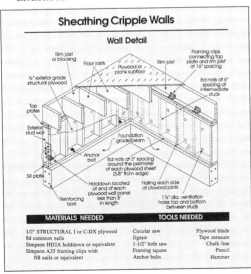

6. *Often simple approaches, such as nailing plywood stiffeners between crawlspace studs and onto floor joist above and bolting sill plates to foundations can make a dramatic difference in protecting a building from seismic damage. Illustration: Reproduced with permission from Home Earthquake Preparedness Guide. EQE Incorporated, San Francisco, CA.*

3) *Enhanced Damage Control*. Historic buildings are substantially rehabilitated to meet, to the extent possible, the prescribed building code provision Some minor repairable damage would be expected after a major earthquake.

4) *Immediate Occupancy*. This approach is intended for designated hospitals and emergency preparedness centers remaining open and operational after a major earthquake. Even most modern buildings do not meet this level of construction, and so for a historic building to meet this requirement, it would have to be almost totally reconstructed of new materials which, philosophically, does not reflect preservation criteria.

Devising the most appropriate approach for a particular historic building will depend on a variety of factors, including the building's use, whether it remains occupied during construction, applicable codes, budgetary constraints, and projected risk of damage. From a design perspective, the vast majority of historic buildings can tolerate a well-planned hidden system of reinforcement. Utilitarian structures, such as warehouses, may be able to receive fairly visible reinforcement systems without undue damage to their historic character. Other more architecturally detailed buildings or those with more finished interior surfaces, however, will benefit from more hidden systems; installation of such systems may even require the temporary removal of significant features to assure their protection. Most buildings, particularly commercial rehabilitations, can incorporate seismic strengthening during other construction work in a way that ensures a high degree of retention of historic materials in place.

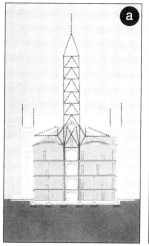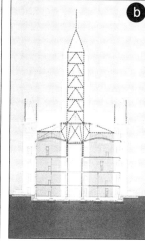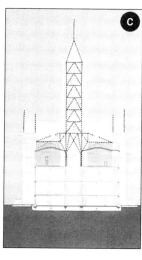

9.These studies for a public building compared, in the shaded areas, the amount of historic material that would be affected by (a) the Uniform Building Code requirements, (b) engineering alternatives that protected significant historic materials, and (c) the use of base isolation systems. The cost for implementing the 3 proposals was similar, and while proposal (c) was selected there were many positive aspects to both (b) and (c). Photos: George Siekkinen, with permission from Ehrenkrantz, Eckstut, & Kuhn Architects.

Assessing the Cost of Seismic Retrofit

Cost plays a critical role in selecting the most appropriate retrofit measure. It is always best to undertake retrofit measures before an earthquake occurs, when options are available for strengthening existing members. Once damage is done, the cost will be substantially higher and finding engineers, architects, and contractors available to do the work on a constricted schedule will be more difficult.

Planned seismic retrofit work may add between $10 and $100 per square foot to the cost of rehabilitation work depending on the level of intervention, the condition of the building, and whether work will be undertaken while the building is occupied. Costs can exceed several hundred dollars a square foot for combined restoration and seismic upgrade costs in major public buildings, in order to provide a level of structural reinforcement that would require only minor repairs after a major earthquake. But maintenance and incremental improvements to eliminate life-safety risks are within the cost realm of responsible upkeep.

Each property owner has to weigh the costs and benefits of undertaking seismic retrofit in a timely manner. Owners may find that an extended engineering study evaluating a wide range of options is worthwhile. Not only can such a study consider the most sensitive historic preservation solution, but the most cost-effective one as well. In many cases, actual retrofit expenses have been lower than anticipated because a careful analysis of the existing building was made that took the durability and performance of existing historic materials into consideration. Most seismic retrofit is done incrementally or incorporated into other rehabilitation work. In large public buildings, seemingly expensive "high-tech" solution such as installing foundation base isolators can turn out to be justified because significant historic materials do not have to be removed, replaced, or replicated (see illus. 9). The cost for a fully retrofitted building can offset the potential loss of income, relocation, and rebuilding after an earthquake. Without careful study, these solutions often are not evaluated.

Some municipalities and states provide low-interest loans, tax relief, municipal bonds, or funding grants targeted to seismic retrofit. Federal tax incentives for the rehabilitation of income-producing historic buildings include seismic strengthening as an allowable expense. Information on these incentives is available from the State Historic Preservation Office. It is also in the best interest of business communities to support the retrofit of buildings in seismically active areas to reduce the loss of sales and property taxes, should an earthquake occur.

Seismic Strengthening Approaches

Seismic strength within buildings is achieved through the reinforcement of structural elements. Such reinforcement can include anchored ties, reinforced mortar joints, braced frames, bond beams, moment-resisting frames, shear walls, and horizontal diaphragms. Most historic buildings can use these standard, traditional methods of strengthening successfully, if properly designed to conform to the historic character of the building. In addition, there are new technologies and better designs for traditional connection devices as well as a greater acceptance of alternative approaches to meeting seismic requirements. While some technologies may still be new for retrofit, the key preservation principles on page 2 should be applied, to ensure that historic buildings will not be damaged by them. For an illustrated design guideline for using some of the more traditional methods on the exteriors of historic unreinforced masonry buildings, see illustration 10 on pages 8-9.

There are varying levels of intervention for seismically retrofitting historic buildings based on the owner's program, the recommendations of the team, applicable codes, and the availability of funds. The approaches to strengthening buildings beginning on page 10 are to show a range of treatments and are not intended to cover all methods. Each building should be evaluated by qualified professionals prior to initiating any work.

Maintenance/Preparedness

Adequate maintenance ensures that existing historic materials remain in good condition and are not weakened by rot, rust, decay or other moisture problems. Without exception, historic buildings should be well maintained and an evacuation plan developed. Expectation that an earthquake will occur sometime in the future should prepare the owner to have emergency information and supplies on hand.

- Check roofs, gutters, and foundations for moisture problems, and for corrosion of metal ties for parapets and chimneys. Make repairs and keep metal painted and in good condition.

- Inspect and keep termite and wood boring insects away from wooden structural members. Check exit steps and porches to ensure that they are tightly connected and will not collapse during an emergency exit.

- Check masonry for deteriorating mortar, and never defer repairs. Repoint, matching the historic mortar in composition and detailing.

- Contact utility companies for information on flexible connectors for gas and water lines, and earthquake activated gas shut-off valves. Strap oil tanks down and anchor water heaters to wall framing.

- Collect local emergency material for reference and implement simple household or office mitigation measures, such as installing latches to keep cabinets from flying open or braces to attach tall bookcases to walls. Keep drinking water, tarpaulins, and other emergency supplies on hand.

Basic/Traditional Measures

This is not an exhaustive list, but illustrates that most measures to reduce life-safety risks rely on using mechanical fasteners to tie a building together. Incorporating these measures can be done incrementally without waiting for extensive rehabilitation (see illus.11-12). An architectural or engineering survey should identify what is needed. Care should be taken to integrate these changes with the visual appearance of the building.

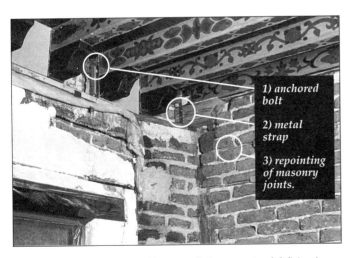

1) anchored bolt

2) metal strap

3) repointing of masonry joints.

11. Limited intervention should correct obvious structural deficiencies, such as tying vulnerable elements together and repointing masonry. Seen here is 1) anchored bolt, 2) metal joist strap, and 3) repointing and reinforcing masonry joints. Upon replastering and painting these reinforcements will not be visible. Photo: Historic Preservation Partners for Earthquake Response.

GLOSSARY:

Anchor Ties or bolts: Generally threaded rods or bolt which connect walls to floor and roof framing. Washers, plates, or rosettes anchor the bolt in place.

Base isolation: the ability to isolate the structures from the damaging effects of earthquakes by providing a flexible layer between the foundations and vertical supports.

Diagonal Braces: the use of diagonal, chevron or other type of bracing (X or K) to provide lateral resistance to adjacent walls.

Core drilling: a type of vertical reinforcement of masonry walls that relies on drilling a continuous vertical core that is filled with steel reinforcing rods and grouting to resist in-plane shear and out-of-plane bending.

Cripple wall: A frame wall between a building's first floor and foundation.

Diaphragm: A floor, roof, or continuous membrane that provides for the transfer of earthquake loading to the exterior or interior shear walls of the structure.

Fiber wrap reinforcement: A synthetic compound of filaments that increase the shear capacity of structural members.

Grouted bolts: anchor bolts set, generally on an angle, in a concrete grout mixture, avoid the problem of using an exposed washer. Requires a greater diameter hole than an anchor bolt with washer.

Lateral forces: Generally the horizontal forces transferred to the building from the dynamic effects of wind or seismic forces.

Life-safety: providing a level of assurance that risk of loss of life is kept to minimal levels. For buildings, this includes strengthening to reduce 1)structural collapse, 2) falling debris, 3)blocking exits or emergency routes, and 4) prevention of consequential fire.

Moment-resisting frame: A steel frame designed to provide in-plane resistance to lateral loads particularly by reinforcing the joint connection between column and beams without adding a diagonal brace. Often used as a perimeter frame around storefronts or large door and window openings.

Seismic retrofit: All measures that improve the earthquake performance of a building especially those that affect structural stability and reduce the potential for heavy structural damage or collapse.

Shear stress: A concept in physics where forces act on a body in opposite directions, but not in the same line. Horizontal forces applied to a wall that is insufficient to move with these forces will crack, often in a diagonal or X pattern. Connections at beams and walls will also crack from shear stress.

Shear wall: A wall deliberately designed to transfer the building's loads from the roof and floors to the foundation thereby preventing a building from collapse from wind or earthquake forces.

Unreinforced Masonry (URM): This designation refers to traditional brick, block, and adobe construction that relies on the weight of the masonry and the bonding capacity of mortar to provide structural stability.

Anchor Bolts:

Typically $\frac{1}{2}$" bolts with flat metal washers (sometimes called plates or rosettes) are probably the most common retrofit procedure. The tie the exterior wall to the floors and roof causing the building to move as a single unit.

The washers are the most noticeable part of the system. Anchor bolt locations are determined by the structural engineer. Decorative washers, such as cast iron stars, carefully placed, can enhance the building. Poorly placed or carelessly aligned washers are very noticeable.

It is important to control rust by painting ferrous metal washers. New washers can be specified as stainless or galvanized steel. In circumstances where washers are visibly intrusive, the preferable solution would be to recess them below the face material. This is particularly applicable to stucco buildings.

Infill Windows:

From an architectural standpoint, infill of openings is not a desirable remedy and should be used only as a last resort. It is often possible to use a braced frames instead of infilling openings, but it may be more expensive.

The purpose of filling the openings is to increase the shear capacity and reduce the stresses on the unreinforced masonry wall. It is not adequate to just infill with the same unreinforced masonry, but generally a reinforced concrete, reinforced block or reinforced brick is specified. If infilling the openings appears to be the only realistic method, the design solution should be sensitive, and if possible, limited to secondary elevations. The opening should be set back and the facing material should be compatible with the surrounding material.

Recommended
• Use decorative washers in areas with high visibility.
• Align washers to create orderly appearance.
• Use stainless or galvanized steel and paint when appropriate, to prevent rust streaks.
• Attempt to conceal the bolts and washers below the exterior finish, when appropriate.

Not Recommended
• The anchor bolts on this building were placed in a haphazard fashion. More care should be taken to align the anchor bolt washers. Also, painting the washers can reduce the unsightly rust streaks that result from weathering.
• Do not place anchor bolts at locations with high relief ornamentation.

Recommended
• Infill of windows should be avoided in all cases. Where absolutely required, however, the appearance of a window opening should be retained to suggest the original visual rhythm of the facade.

Not Recommended
• Infill techniques such as this are not encouraged. Suggestion of a former window opening should have been emphasized by slightly recessing the former opening.

Questions to Ask When Planning Seismic Retrofit:

These questions should be asked with the assistance of the team to determine acceptable alternatives. Since there is never a single right answer, the design team and code officials should work together to determine the appropriate level of seismic retrofit with the lowest visual impact on the significant spaces, features, and finishes of both the interior and exterior of historic buildings.

As with the illustrations above, this guide is not intended to proscribe how seismic retrofit should be done, but rather, to illustrate that every physical change to a building will have some consequence. By asking how impacts can be reduced, the owner will have several options from which to choose.

✦ Can bracing be installed without damaging decorative details or appearance of parapets, chimneys, or balconies?

✦ Are the visible features of the reinforcement, such as anchor washers or exterior buttresses adequately designed to blend with the historic building?

✦ Can hidden or grouted bolts be set on an angle to tie floors and walls together, instead of using traditional bolts and exposed washers or rosettes on ornamental exteriors?

✦ Are diagonal frames, such as X, K, or struts located to have a minimal impact on the primary facade?

✦ Are they set back and painted a receding color if visible through windows or storefronts?

✦ Can moment frames or reinforced bracing be added around historic storefronts in order to avoid unsightly exposed reinforcement, such as X braces, within the immediate viewing range of the public?

Recommended
- All original building ornamentation enhances the architectural value and should be retained and maintained.

Not Recommended
- If it is determined that ornamentation must be secured or removed, effort should be made to secure it. The parapet of this building shows a "scar" where ornamentation was removed.

Securing Exterior Ornamentation:

Ornament is one of the character-defining features of a building. Careful forethought and analysis should always precede alteration of a building's ornament.

Generally methods to secure ornamentation by repair and reinforcing connections should be undertaken. Repairs or reinforcement should blend with the appearance of the ornamentation and should be designed to prevent future failures such as cracking due to thermal and seismic stress or unsightly differential weathering.

If ornamental elements must be removed during the repair process, they should be reinstalled or replaced in-kind. The use of substitute materials may be acceptable if no other options exist.

Exterior Buttresses:

Exterior buttresses, an integral part of Gothic architecture, are not traditionally part of our architecture. In retrofitting an existing building, it is usually better to use an in-wall or interior bracing system rather than a visible exterior system. When used as an exterior bracing system, care must be taken to avoid damage to existing decorative elements. Even if saved, exterior buttresses can obscure decorative elements.

Recommended
- Exterior bracing or buttressing should incorporate the building's natural lines. The exterior steel bracing appears to be an original building element because it runs parallel to the cornice line.

Not Recommended
- The exterior bracing on this building dominates its appearance. Care should be taken to design exterior bracing to blend with or enhance the building's natural lines.

Another problem requiring careful study is the integration of the buttresses with the existing structural system. Their attachment penetrates the building skin making the building more vulnerable to moisture damage. In a few cases where the interior building fabric is highly significant, exterior buttresses may be preferred. Care should be taken to avoid damage or obscuring existing architectural details.

Adapted from "Architectural Design Guide for Exterior Treatments of Unreinforced Masonry Buildings During Seismic Retrofit." Used with permission from the San Francisco Chapter, The American Institute of Architects.

NS TO ASK:

✦ Can shorter sections of reinforcement be "stitched" into the existing building to avoid removal of large sections of historic materials? This is particularly true for the insertion of roof framing supports.

✦ Can shear walls be located in utilitarian interior spaces to reduce the impact on finishes in the primary areas?

✦ Are there situations where thinner applied fiber reinforced coating would adequately strengthen walls or supports without the need for heavier reinforced concrete?

✦ Can diaphragms be added to non-significant floors in order to protect highly decorated ceilings below, or the reverse if the floor is more ornamental than the ceiling?

✦ Are there adequate funds to retain, repair, or reinstall ornamental finishes once structural reinforcements have been installed?

✦ Should base isolation, wall damping systems, or core drilling be considered? Are they protecting significant materials by reducing the amount of intervention?

✦ Are the seismic treatments being considered "reversible" in a way that allows the most amount of historic materials to be retained and allows future repair and restoration?

10. Keeping preservation in the forefront is a critical aspect of seismic retrofit of historic buildings. These key questions will help keep preservation in mind as decisions are made about how best to improve the structural performance of historic buildings.

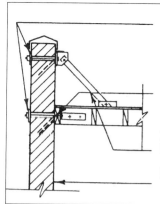

If through-bolts are used, consider exterior appearance in location and detailing of bolt plates

If exterior appearance is sensitive, consider grouted bolts

New steel angle brace attached to existing roof

Masonry wall

12. Bracing parapets, as illustrated here, and supporting chimneys using metal struts or ties, are simple methods to protect these heavy elements from falling. Drawing: Architectural Resources Group.

- Bolt sill plates to foundations and add plywood stiffeners to cripple wall framing around wood frame buildings. Keep reinforcement behind decorative crawlspace lattice or other historic features.
- Reinforce floor and roof framing connections to walls using joist hangers, metal straps, threaded bolts, or other means of mechanical fasteners. Tie columns to beams; reinforce porch and stair connections as well.
- Repair weakened wooden structural systems by adding, pairing, or bracing existing members. Consider adding non-ferrous metal straps in alternating mortar joints if extensive repointing is done in masonry walls.
- Reinforce projecting parapets and tie parapets, chimneys, balconies, and unsecured decorative elements to structural framing. Make the connections as unobtrusive as possible. In some cases, concrete bond beams can be added to reinforce the top of unreinforced masonry or adobe walls.
- Properly install and anchor new diaphragms, such as roof sheathing or subflooring, to the walls of a structure prior to installing finish materials.
- Avoid awkwardly placed exposed metal plates or rosettes when using threaded bolts through masonry walls. When exposed plates will interfere with the decorative elements of the facade, use less visible grouted bolts or plates that can be set underneath exposed finished materials.
- Use sensitively designed metal bracing along building exteriors to tie the unsupported face of long exterior walls to the floor framing. This is often seen along side or party walls in commercial or industrial buildings.

Rehabilitation

When buildings are being rehabilitated, it is generally the most cost effective time to make major upgrades that affect the structural performance of the building (see illus. 13-17). New elements, such as concrete shear walls or fiber reinforcing systems can be added while the structure is exposed for other rehabilitation or code compliance work.

- Inspect and improve all lateral tie connections and diaphragms.

13. Installing diagonal frames, underway in this rehabilitation, are a traditional method of seismic reinforcement. To reduce the impact of the X, K, or diagonal braces, they should be on the inside of the perimeter wall, designed to cross behind solid walls as much as possible, and painted a receding color where visible. Photo: David Look.

steel moment frame

14. The use of a steel moment frame to support the large open storefront during a rehabilitation eliminated the need to place diagonal braces or other intrusive supports in a highly visible area of a historic building. Photo: David Look.

15. The use of fiber composite materials can enhance the shear capacity of existing structural components -beams, columns, and surface elements, such as walls and floors. In this roofing application, the existing roof diaphragm is being strengthened and there is additional benefit to the shear reinforcement of the parapet wall. Photo: The Crosby Group.

17. *The internal grout injection of rubble walls can improve seismic capacity. Care must be taken in formulating the mortar grout and repairing the area where injection occurs. Photo: Architectural Resources Group, San Francisco.*

- Reinforce walls and large openings to improve shear strength in locations of doors, windows, and storefront openings. Carefully locate "X" and "K" bracing to avoid visual intrusion, or use moment frames, which are a hidden perimeter bracing in large openings. From a preservation perspective, the use of a more hidden system in finished spaces is generally preferable.
- Strengthen masonry walls or columns with new concrete reinforcement or fiber wrap systems. Avoid the use of heavy spray concrete or projecting reinforced walls that seriously alter the historic relationship of the wall to windows, trim, and other architectural moldings or details.

- Selectively locate new shear walls constructed to assist the continuous transfer of loads from the foundation to the roof. If these walls cannot be set behind historic finishes, they should be located in secondary spaces in conjunction with other types of reinforcement of the primary spaces or features.
- Consider the internal grouting of rubble masonry walls using an injected grout mixture that is compatible in composition with existing mortar. Ensure that exposed areas are repaired and that the mortar matches all visual qualities of the historic mortar joints in tooling, width, color and texture.
- Evaluate odd-shaped buildings and consider the reinforcement of corners and connections instead of infilling openings with new construction. Altering the basic configuration and appearance of primary facades of buildings is damaging to those qualities that make the building architecturally significant.

Specialized Technologies

New technologies, being developed all the time, may have applicability to historic preservation projects. These specialized technologies include: vertical and center core drilling systems for unreinforced masonry buildings, base isolation at the foundations, superstructure damping systems, bonded resin coatings, and reproducing lost elements in lighter materials (see illus. 18-20). However, many new technologies may also be non-reversible treatments resulting in difficulties of repair after an earthquake. The reinforcement of historic materials with special resins, or the use of core drilling to provide a reinforced vertical connection from foundation to roof may not be as repairable after an earthquake as would more traditional means of wall reinforcement. New technologies should be carefully evaluated by the design team for both their benefits as well as their shortcomings.

Using computer modeling of how historic buildings may act in an earthquake suggests options for seismic upgrade using a combination of traditional methods and new technologies. While most projects involving base isolation and other complex damping

19. *A system of core drilling, shown here, removes internal cored sections of unreinforced masonry from roof to foundations and fills them with grout and reinforcing rods. This may be an option for some unreinforced masonry buildings with significant interiors and exteriors, although it is a less reversible treatment than traditional diagonal frames or shear walls. Photo: David Look.*

citizens of their relative safety. Heavily damaged areas are often secured off-limits and many red tagged, but repairable, buildings have been torn down unnecessarily because owners were unable to evaluate and present a stabilization plan in time (see illus. 21). Owners or members of the preservation community may engage their own engineers with specialized knowledge to challenge a demolition order. Because seismic retrofit is complex and many jurisdictions are involved, the coordination between various regulatory bodies needs to be accomplished *before* an earthquake.

21. *Without a plan in place before an earthquake, buildings that could be repaired are often torn down. The loss of significant numbers of buildings within historic districts can further erode the financial and cultural assets of an area. Photo: David Look.*

During times of emergencies, many communities, banks, and insurance agencies will not be in a position to evaluate alternative approaches to dealing with damaged historic buildings, and so they often require full compliance with codes for new construction for the major rehabilitation work required. Because seismic after-shocks often create more damage to a weakened building, the inability to act quickly—even to shore up the structure on a temporary basis—can result in the building's demolition. Penetrating rain, uneven settlement, vandalism, and continuing after-shocks can easily undermine a building's remaining structural integrity. Moreover, the longer a building is unoccupied and non-income-producing, the sooner it will be torn down in a negotiated settlement with the insurance company. All of these factors work against saving buildings damaged in earthquakes, and make having an action plan essential.

systems constitute only a small percentage of the projects nationwide that are seismically reinforced, they may be appropriate for buildings with significant interior spaces that should not be disturbed or removed during the retrofit. Each building will needs its own survey and evaluation to determine the most appropriate seismic reinforcement.

Post-Earthquake Issues

Should a historic building suffer damage during an earthquake, it is the owner *who has a plan in place* who will be able to play a critical role in determining its ultimate fate. If the owner has previously assembled a team for the purpose of seismic upgrading, there is a greater chance for the building to be evaluated in a timely fashion and for independent emergency stabilization to occur. In most municipalities, a survey, often by trained volunteers, will be conducted as soon as possible after an earthquake, and buildings will be tagged on the front with a posted notice according to their ability to be entered. Typically red, yellow, and green tags are used to indicate varying levels of damage—*no entry, limited entry, and useable*—to warn

Having an emergency plan in place, complete with access to plywood, tarpaulins, bracing timbers, and equipment, will allow quick action to save a building following an earthquake. Knowing how the community evaluates buildings and the steps taken to secure an area will give the owner the ability to be a helpful resource to the community in a time of need.

If the federal government is asked to intervene after a natural disaster, technical assistance programs are available. Often after a disaster, grant funds or low-cost loans from federal, state, and congressional special appropriations are targeted to qualified properties, which can help underwrite the high cost of rehabilitation (see information about FEMA on page 15.)

Conclusion

Recent earthquakes have shown that historic buildings retrofitted to withstand earthquakes survive better than those that have not been upgraded. Even simple efforts, such as bracing parapets, tying buildings to foundations, and anchoring brick walls at the highest, or roof level, have been extremely effective. It has also been proven that well maintained buildings have faired better than those in poor condition during and after an earthquake. Thus, maintenance and seismic retrofit are two critical components for the protection of historic buildings in areas of seismic activity. It makes no sense to retrofit a building, then leave the improvements, such as braced parapets or metal bolts with plates, to deteriorate due to lack of maintenance.

Damage to historic buildings *after* an earthquake can be as great as the initial damage from the earthquake itself. The ability to act quickly to shore up and stabilize a building and to begin its sensitive rehabilitation is imperative. Communities without earthquake hazard reduction plans in place put their historic buildings—as well as the safety and economic well-being of their residents — at risk.

Having the right team in place is important. Seismic strengthening of existing historic buildings and knowledge of community planning for earthquake response makes the professional opinions of the team members that much more important when obtaining permits to do the work. Local code enforcement officials can only implement the provisions of the model or historic preservation codes if the data and calculations work to ensure public safety.

22. When undertaking a substantial rehabilitation to include seismic reinforcement, it is also an opportune time to restore lost or damaged features. The owner of this commercial building, using the Historic Rehabilitation Tax Credits, restored the original bay and parapet gable, and stone detailing that had been removed in an earlier insensitive remodeling. Photo: David Look.

23. Both exteriors and interiors can be severely damaged in an earthquake. This Craftsman Style bungalow was successfully restored and seismically upgraded after the Northridge earthquake in California. Photographs: Historic Preservation Partners in Earthquake Response.

Buildings do not need to be over-retrofitted. A cost-effective balance between protecting the public and the building recognizes that planned for repairable damage can be addressed after an earthquake. Engineers and architects, *who specialize in historic buildings* and who have a working knowledge of alternative options and expected performance for historic structures, are critical to the process.

It is clear that historic and older buildings can be seismically upgraded in a cost-effective manner while retaining or restoring important historic character-defining qualities (see illus. 22, 23). Seismic upgrading measures exist that preserve the historic character and materials of a buildings. However, it takes a multi-disciplined team to plan and to execute sensitive seismic retrofit. It also takes commitment on the part of city, state, and federal leaders to ensure that historic districts are protected from needless demolition after an earthquake so that historic buildings and their communities are preserved for the future.

Seismic Risk Zones

Most local jurisdictions measure seismic risk based on seismic zones established by code, such as the Uniform Building Code with its 4 risk zones [1=low to 4=high]. There are also maps, such as this one, which identify the Effective Peak Acceleration (EPA) which further reflect the light, moderate, and severe shaking risks as a percentage of the acceleration of gravity that can be expected in an area.

In the United States, the greatest activity areas are the western states, Alaska, and some volcanic island areas. However, noted historical earthquakes occurred in Massachusetts (1755), Missouri (1811), South Carolina (1886), and Alaska (1964). The Caribbean Islands and Puerto Rico have been sites of severe earthquakes. The history of earthquakes in the United States has been recorded for over 200 years and new areas of concern include moderate risk areas in southern and mid-western states.

The Richter Magnitude Scale, first published in 1935, records the size of an earthquake at its source, as measured on a seismograph. Magnitudes are expressed in whole numbers and decimals between 1 and 9. An earthquake of a magnitude of 6 or more will cause moderate damage, while one of over 7 will be considered a major earthquake. It is important to remember that an increase of one whole number on the Richter Scale is a tenfold increase in the size of the earthquake.

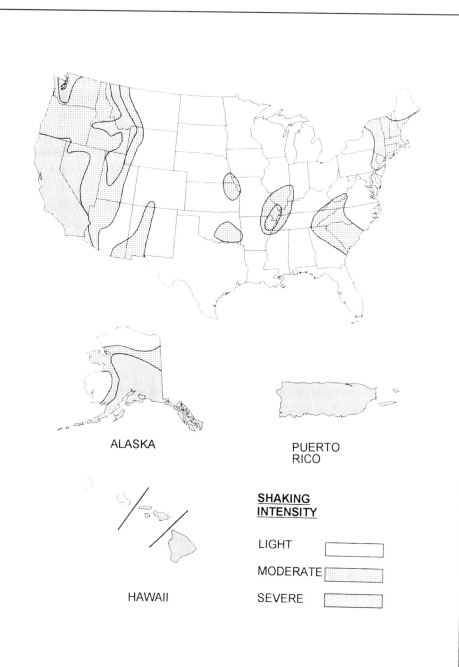

ALASKA

PUERTO RICO

SHAKING INTENSITY

LIGHT

MODERATE

SEVERE

HAWAII

24. *Seismic Map. The shading indicate areas in the United States and Puerto Rico that are affected by the probability of varying shaking intensities. The risk of severe shaking is not limited to the west coast. Map: adapted from Federal Emergency Management Agency, FEMA 74 Guide.*

FURTHER READING

Buildings at Risk: Seismic Design Basics for Practicing Architects. Washington, DC. AIA/ACSA Council on Architectural Research. February, 1992.

Controlling Disaster: Earthquake-Hazard Reduction for Historic Buildings. Washington, DC. National Trust for Historic Preservation. 1992.

Earthquake-Damaged Historic Chimneys: A Guide to the Rehabilitation and Reconstruction of Chimneys. Oakland, CA. Historic Preservation Partners for Earthquake Response. July, 1995.

Eichenfield, Jeffrey. *20 Tools That Protect Historic Resources After an Earthquake; Lessons learned from the Northridge Earthquake.* Oakland, CA. California Preservation Foundation.1996.

History at Risk, Loma Prieta: Seismic Safety & Historic Buildings. Oakland, CA. California Preservation Foundation. 1990.

Kariotis, John C., Roselund, Nels; and Krakower, Michael. *Loma Prieta, An Engineer's Viewpoint.* Oakland, CA; California Preservation Foundation, 1990.

Langenbach, Randolph. "Bricks, Mortar, and Earthquakes; Historic Preservation vs. Earthquake Safety." *Apt Bulletin,* Vol.21, Nos.3/4 (1989), pp.30-43.

Langenbach, Randolph. "Earthquakes: A New Look at Cracked Masonry." *Civil Engineering.* November, 1992. pp. 56-58.

NEHRP Commentary on the Guidelines for the Seismic Rehabilitation of Buildings (second ballot version). Washington, DC. Building Seismic Safety Council (Prepared for Federal Emergency Management Agency) Draft, April, 1997. FEMA 274.

NEHRP Handbook of Techniques for the Seismic Rehabilitation of Existing Buildings. Washington, DC. Building Seismic Safety Council (Prepared for Federal Emergency Management Agency) 1992. FEMA 273.

The Secretary of the Interior's Standards for Rehabilitation with Illustrated Guidelines for Rehabilitating Historic Buildings. Washington, DC. Government Printing Office, 1992.

Seismic Retrofit Alternatives for San Francisco's Unreinforced Masonry Buildings: Estimates of Construction Cost & Seismic Damage. San Francisco, CA. City and County of San Francisco Department of City Planning (prepared by Rutherford & Chekene, Consulting Engineers). 1990.

The Seismic Retrofit of Historic Buildings Conference Workbook. San Francisco, CA. Association for Preservation Technology, Western Chapter. 1991. [contains an excellent bibliography of additional sources].

Schuller, M.P. Atkinson, R.H. and Noland, J.L. "Structural Evaluation of Historic Masonry Buildings."*APT Bulletin,* Vol 26, No. 2/3,pp. 51-61.

State Historical Building Code. Sacramento, CA: State Historical Building Code Board, 1990.

Uniform Code for Building Conservation. Whittier, CA: International Conference of Building Officials, 1991.

The Federal Emergency Management Agency

The Federal Emergency Management Agency (FEMA) — is an independent agency of the federal government, reporting to the President. Since its founding in 1979, FEMA's mission has been to reduce loss of life and property and protect our nation's critical infrastructure from all types of hazards through a comprehensive, risk-based, emergency management program. FEMA works with the state and local governments and the private sector to stimulate increased participation in emergency preparedness, mitigation, response and recovery programs related to natural disasters. To minimize damage-repair-damage cycles, FEMA carries out and encourages preventive activities referred to as hazard mitigation.

The FEMA Hazard Mitigation Program, established in 1988 with the passage of the Robert T. Stafford Disaster Relief and Emergency Assistance Act, offers a framework for protecting historic structures from natural disasters. In the event of a federally declared disaster, state and local governments as well as eligible non-profit applicants may receive financial and technical assistance to identify and carry out cost-effective hazard mitigation activities.

FEMA encourages hazard mitigation projects, including the restoration of buildings, by providing technical assistance and funding through the Hazard Mitigation Grant Program (HMPG), which can underwrite up to 50% of the cost of the project.

FEMA's public-assistance program provides financial and other assistance to rebuild disaster-damaged facilities that serve a public purpose, such as schools, hospitals, government buildings and public utilities.

In terms of technical assistance, FEMA, under a cooperative agreement with the Building Seismic Safety Council has produced two volumes of comprehensive material dealing with the seismic retrofit of existing buildings (see Further Reading). In addition an ongoing project ATC-43 involves earthquake analysis procedures for Unreinforced Masonry Buildings and Reinforced Concrete Buildings. These documents contain nationally applicable technical criteria intended to ensure that buildings will withstand earthquakes better than before. There is a great deal of information that is applicable to historic buildings, although historic buildings are not necessarily identified as a category. Write for FEMA publications at:

FEMA, PO Box 70274, Washington, DC 20024

For current information about emergency activities, federally declared disaster areas, or how to contact regional offices see the

FEMA website: http://www.fema.gov/

For additional information on cultural resource preservation and Historic Rehabilitation Tax Credits see the National Park Service's

NPS website: http://www.cr.nps.gov/

Before	After

25. While it is best to seismically retrofit historic buildings before an earthquake strikes, if earthquake damage is to be repaired, it should be done in a manner respecting the historic character of the building. For this ca. 1925 Mediterranean Revival style building damaged in the Northridge Earthquake in California, financial and planning assistance from the Historic Preservation Partners for Earthquake Response made possible a sensitive rehabilitation. New structural steel and restoration of the historic stucco and decorative tile work and a repaired tile roof reinstated this earthquake damaged building as a major element of the historic district. Photo: Courtesy Historic Preservation Partners for Earthquake Response, M2A Architects.

The Historic Preservation Partners for Earthquake Response was formed after the Northridge Earthquake of 1994 and was comprised of members of the National Park Service, the National Trust for Historic Preservation, The Getty Institute, The California Office of Historic Preservation, the California Preservation Foundation, and the Los Angeles Conservancy. After the earthquake, this organization provided technical assistance and grant funding to various historic buildings. Funding of 10 million dollars from the National Park Service, U.S. Department of the Interior, was made available for the restoration and rehabilitation of cultural resources damaged during this natural disaster. In addition, sub-grants were provided by the National Trust for Historic Preservation and the California Office of Historic Preservation. A number of projects assisted by the Historic Preservation Partners for Earthquake Response are included and used with permission in this *Preservation Brief.*

Acknowledgements

David W. Look, AIA, is the Chief, Cultural Resource Team, Pacific Great Basin Support Office, National Park Service. **Terry Wong, PE,** is the Chief, Structural Engineering, Denver Service Center, National Park Service. **Sylvia Rose Augustus,** is the Historical Architect, Yosemite National Park

The authors wish to thank their collaborator, **Sharon C. Park, FAIA,** Senior Historical Architect, Heritage Preservation Services, NPS, who undertook the technical editing of the publication and took the authors' original manuscript and developed it into the Preservation Brief complete with compiling information from other sources and selecting the photographs. Kay D. Weeks and Michael J. Auer, Heritage Preservation Services, NPS, contributed substantially to the published manuscript by revising the draft with an eye to articulation of policy, organizational structure, and cohesiveness of language.

The authors also wish to thank the following for providing information for the publication and/or reviewing the final draft: Steade R. Craigo, AIA, Senior Restoration Architect, State of California; Randolph Langenbach, Architect, FEMA; Bruce Judd, FAIA, Architectural Resources Group; Melvyn Green & Associates; Cassandra Mettling-Davis and Carey & Co. Inc. Architecture; Curt Ginther, Architect, the University of California, Los Angeles (UCLA) Capital Program; The Crosby Group; American Institute of Architects, San Francisco Chapter; Jeffrey L. Eichenfield, California Preservation Foundation; Michael Jackson, Illinois Historic Preservation Agency; George Siekkinen, the National Trust for Historic Preservation; and colleagues at Heritage Preservation Services, NPS, including: de Teel Patterson Tiller, Chief; Charles E. Fisher, Anne E. Grimmer, John Sandor, and Jason Fenwick.

This publication has been prepared pursuant to the National Historic Preservation Act, as amended, which directs the Secretary of the Interior to develop and make available information concerning historic properties. Comments about this publication should be directed to de Teel Patterson Tiller, Chief, Heritage Preservation Services Program, National Park Service, 1849 C Street, NW, Washington, DC 20240.

Front Cover. Historic buildings damaged by earthquakes can be rehabilitated and seismically retrofitted. The posted tag in the window warns that this building, temporarily, cannot be entered. Photo: David Look.

October, 1997